Property Law

This is an innovative examination of the law's treatment of property. It looks at the nature and function of property rights in resources ranging from land to goods and intangibles, and provides a detailed analytical exposition of the content, function and effect of the property rules which regulate our use of these resources, and the fundamental principles which underpin this structure of rules. It draws on a wide range of materials on property rights in general and the English property law system in particular. The book includes the core legal source materials in property law along with readings from social science literature, legal theory and economics, many of which are not easily accessible to law students. These materials are accompanied by a critical commentary, as well as notes, questions and suggestions for further reading.

ALISON CLARKE is Senior Lecturer in Laws at University College London. She has devised and taught innovative property law courses for undergraduate law students and specialised postgraduate courses in property-related areas in insolvency and maritime law. She spent two years seconded to the Law Commission to work on reform of the law of mortgages and formerly practised as a solicitor in a commercial practice specialising in land transactions. She has written widely on theoretical aspects of property, with particular emphasis on communal land rights and evolving patterns of land usage, whilst continuing to maintain links with law in practice by giving lectures and seminars to professional lawyers on ship mortgages and commercial property.

PAUL KOHLER splits his time between academe and business. A former Sub-Dean at UCL and Head of Best Practice at Nabarro Nathanson, he is currently a law lecturer at New College, Oxford, and is Chairman of LLT (a legal education provider). He works with some of the leading law firms in the UK as a knowledge management and change consultant specializing in the application of new technology to transform working practices. Paul has devised and taught innovative property courses for over a decade and researched and written widely in the field.

The Law in Context Series

Editors: William Twining (University College London) and
Christopher McCrudden (Lincoln College, Oxford)

Since 1970 the Law in Context series has been in the forefront of the movement to broaden the study of law. It has been a vehicle for the publication of innovative scholarly books that treat law and legal phenomena critically in their social, political, and economic contexts from a variety of perspectives. The series particularly aims to publish scholarly legal writing that brings fresh perspectives to bear on new and existing areas of law taught in universities. A contextual approach involves treating legal subjects broadly, using materials from other social sciences, and from any other discipline that helps to explain the operation in practice of the subject under discussion. It is hoped that this orientation is at once more stimulating and more realistic than the bare exposition of legal rules. The series includes original books that have a different emphasis from traditional legal text-books, while maintaining the same high standards of scholarship. They are written primarily for undergraduate and graduate students of law and of other disciplines, but most also appeal to a wider readership. In the past, most books in the series have focused on English law, but recent publications include books on European law, globalisation, transnational legal processes, and comparative law.

Books in the Series

Anderson, Schum and Twining: *Analysis of Evidence*
Ashworth: *Sentencing and Criminal Justice*
Barton & Douglas: *Law and Parenthood*
Bell: *French Legal Cultures*
Bercusson: *European Labour Law*
Birkinshaw: *European Public Law*
Birkinshaw: *Freedom of Information: The Law, the Practice and the Ideal*
Cane: *Atiyah's Accidents, Compensation and the Law*
Clarke & Kohler: *Property Law: Commentary and Materials*
Collins: *The Law of Contract*
Davies: *Perspectives on Labour Law*
de Sousa Santos: *Toward a New Legal Common Sense*
Diduck: *Law's Families*
Elworthy & Holder: *Environmental Protection: Text and Materials*
Fortin: *Children's Rights and the Developing Law*
Glover-Thomas: *Reconstructing Mental Health Law and Policy*
Gobert & Punch: *Rethinking Corporate Crime*
Harlow & Rawlings: *Law and Administration: Text and Materials*
Harris: *An Introduction to Law*
Harris: *Remedies in Contract and Tort*

Harvey: *Seeking Asylum in the UK: Problems and Prospects*
Hervey & McHale: *Health Law and the European Union*
Lacey & Wells: *Reconstructing Criminal Law*
Lewis: *Choice and the Legal Order: Rising above Politics*
Likosky: *Transnational Legal Processes*
Maughan & Webb: *Lawyering Skills and the Legal Process*
Moffat: *Trusts Law: Text and Materials*
Norrie: *Crime, Reason and History*
O'Dair: *Legal Ethics*
Oliver: *Common Values and the Public–Private Divide*
Oliver & Drewry: *The Law and Parliament*
Picciotto: *International Business Taxation*
Reed: *Internet Law: Text and Materials*
Richardson: *Law, Process and Custody*
Roberts & Palmer: *Dispute Processes: ADR and the Primary Forms
    of Decision-Making*
Scott & Black: *Cranston's Consumers and the Law*
Seneviratne: *Ombudsmen: Public Services and Administrative Justice*
Stapleton: *Product Liability*
Turpin: *British Government and the Constitution: Text, Cases and Materials*
Twining & Miers: *How to Do Things with Rules*
Twining: *Globalisation and Legal Theory*
Twining: *Rethinking Evidence*
Ward: *A Critical Introduction to European Law*
Ward: *Shakespeare and Legal Imagination*
Zander: *Cases and Materials on the English Legal System*
Zander: *The Law-Making Process*

Property Law
Commentary and Materials

Alison Clarke and Paul Kohler

CAMBRIDGE UNIVERSITY PRESS
Cambridge, New York, Melbourne, Madrid, Cape Town, Singapore, São Paulo, Delhi

Cambridge University Press
The Edinburgh Building, Cambridge CB2 8RU, UK

Published in the United States of America by Cambridge University Press, New York

www.cambridge.org
Information on this title: www.cambridge.org/9780521614894

First published 2005
Reprinted 2007

A catalogue record for this publication is available from the British Library

ISBN 978-0-521-61489-4 paperback

Transferred to digital printing 2009

Contents

Preface

Property law tends to be regarded by students as both dull and difficult. The main objective of this book is to demonstrate that it is neither. The book is based on the Property Law seminars we devised and taught in the Faculty of Laws at University College London. Like the seminar course, the book looks at the nature and function of property rights in resources ranging from land to goods and intangibles, and provides a detailed analytical exposition of the content, function and effect of the property rules which regulate our use of these resources, and the fundamental principles which underpin their structure.

We draw on a wide range of materials on property rights in general and our property law system in particular, including core legal source materials on selected topics as well as readings from social science literature, legal theory and economics. Inevitably the coverage is not comprehensive, but we have included notes, questions and suggestions for further reading to provide a starting point for anyone wanting to take matters further. As in any other property law book, we draw on a lot of material from decided cases, but to keep the book at a manageable length we have put most of the edited case extracts we use, together with some other materials, on the associated website, www.cambridge.org/propertylaw/ rather than in the book itself. This has enabled us to use much longer extracts than would otherwise have been feasible, and also to introduce a much wider range of materials.

We have both been involved in teaching all the topics covered in this book, but have taken separate responsibility for different parts of the book: Chapters 1–5, 7–8, 10–15 and 17–18 were written by Alison Clarke, and Chapters 6, 9 and 16 by Paul Kohler.

The content of the book has been greatly influenced by the many stimulating contributions made to seminars by students over the years, and by our colleagues who have taught on the seminar course with us at UCL and elsewhere: our thanks go to all of them, and to our respective families and friends for their help and encouragement.

Finally, the book is dedicated by Alison to Leo, and by Paul to his partner, Samantha, and his four daughters, Eloise, Tamara, Bethany and Saskia, whose endless disputes on the ownership and possession of each other's clothes has taught him more about the fundamentals of property than any number of cases in the Court of Chancery.

ALISON CLARKE
PAUL KOHLER
November 2004

Acknowledgments

We would like to thank the following for permission to reproduce the following materials:

- the American Association for the Advancement of Science, Washington, for the extract from Hardin, 'The Tragedy of the Commons' (1968) 162 *Science* 1243;
- Basic Books, for the extracts from Robert Nozick, *Anarchy, State, and Utopia*, reprinted by permission of Basic Books, The Perseus Books Group;
- Bernard Rudden and Oxford University Press, for the extracts from Rudden, 'Things as Thing and Things as Wealth' (1994) 14 *Oxford Journal of Legal Studies* 81, and from Lawson and Rudden, *The Law of Property* (3rd edn, Oxford: Clarendon Press, 2002);
- Carol M. Rose and the *University of Chicago Law Review*, for the extracts from Rose, 'Possession as the Origin of Property' (1985) 52 *University of Chicago Law Review* 73, copyright © 1985 by the University of Chicago;
- the *Columbia Law Review*, for the extract from Lon Fuller, 'Form and Consideration' (1941) 41 *Columbia Law Review* 799, reprinted with the permission of the *Columbia Law Review*;
- the Council of Mortgage Lenders, for the extract from its *Statement of Practice: Handling of Arrears and Possessions* (Council of Mortgage Lenders, 1997);
- David Fox, for the extract from his article, 'Bona Fide Purchase and the Currency of Money' (1996) *Cambridge Law Journal* 547;
- David Haddock and the *Washington University Law Quarterly*, for the extract from Haddock, 'First Possession Versus Optimal Timing: Limiting the Dissipation of Economic Value' (1986) 64 *Washington University Law Quarterly* 775;
- David Sugarman and Kluwer Law International, for the extract from Sugarman and Warrington, 'Telling Stories: Rights and Wrongs of the Equity of Redemption', in J. W. Harris (ed.), *Property Problems: From Genes to Pension Funds* (London: Kluwer, 1997), reprinted with the permission of Kluwer Law International;
- Dhammika Dharmapala, Rohan Pitchford and the *Journal of Law, Economics, and Organization*, for the extract from Dharmapala and Pitchford, 'An Economic Analysis of "Riding to Hounds": Pierson v. Post Revisited' (2002)

18 *Journal of Law, Economics, and Organization* 39, reprinted with permission of Oxford University Press;

- Gregory S. Alexander and the University of Chicago, for the extract from Alexander, *Commodity and Propriety: Competing Visions of Property in American Legal Thought 1776–1970* (Chicago: University of Chicago Press, 1997), copyright © 1997 by the University of Chicago;
- Guido Calabresi, A. Douglas Melamed and the *Harvard Law Review*, for the extract from Calabresi and Melamed, 'Property Rules, Liability Rules and Inalienability: One View of the Cathedral' (1972) 85 *Harvard Law Review* 1089;
- Harold Demsetz and the American Economic Association, for the extract from Demsetz, 'Towards a Theory of Property Rights' (1967) 57 *American Economic Review* 347;
- James Grunebaum and Routledge and Kegan Paul (Taylor & Francis Group), for the extracts from Grunebaum, *Private Ownership* (London and New York: Routledge and Kegan Paul, 1987);
- Jeremy Waldron and Oxford University Press, for the extracts from Waldron, *The Right to Private Property* (Oxford: Clarendon Press, 1988);
- Margaret Jane Radin and the *Washington University Law Quarterly*, for the extracts from Radin, 'Time, Possession, and Alienation' (1986) 64 *Washington University Law Quarterly* 739;
- Matthew Kramer, for the extracts from his book, *John Locke and the Origins of Private Property: Philosophical Explorations of Individualism, Community, and Equality* (Cambridge: Cambridge University Press, 1997);
- New York University Press, for the extracts from J. Roland Pennock and John Chapman (eds.), *Nomos XXII: Property* (New York: New York University Press, 1980);
- Oxford University Press, for the extracts from A. M. Honoré, *Making Law Bind* (Oxford: Clarendon Press, 1987), from Markesinis and Deakin, *Markesinis and Deakin's Tort Law* (5th edn, Oxford: Clarendon Press, 2003), from Alison Clarke, 'Property Law' (1992) 45 *Current Legal Problems* Annual Review, and 'Use, Time and Entitlement' (2004) 57 *Current Legal Problems* 239, from Peter Birks, 'Five Keys to Land Law', in S. Bright and J. Dewar (eds.), *Land Law: Themes and Perspectives* (Oxford: Oxford University Press, 1998), and from A. W. B. Simpson, *A History of the Land Law* (2nd edn, Oxford: Clarendon Press, 1986);
- Paddy Ireland and the *Modern Law Review*, for the extract from Ireland, 'Company Law and the Myth of Shareholder Ownership' (1999) 62 *Modern Law Review* 32;
- Peter Luther, for the extract from his article, 'Williams v. Hensman and the Uses of History' (1995) 15 *Legal Studies* 219;
- Princeton University Press, Terry L. Anderson and Fred McChesney (eds.), *Property Rights: Co-operation, Conflict, and Law* (Princeton: Princeton University Press, 2003), reprinted by permission of Princeton University Press;

- Richard A. Epstein and the *Washington University Law Quarterly*, for the extracts from Epstein, 'Past and Future: The Temporal Dimension in the Law of Property' (1986) 64 *Washington University Law Quarterly* 667;
- Richard Posner and Aspen Publishers, for the extract reprinted from Posner, *Economic Analysis of Law* (6th edn, New York: Aspen Publishers, 2002), with the permission of Aspen Publishers;
- Robert Ellickson and the *Journal of Law, Economics, and Organization*, for the extract from 'A Hypothesis of Wealth-Maximising Norms: Evidence from the Whaling Industry' (1989) 5 *Journal of Law, Economics, and Organization* 83, reprinted with permission of Oxford University Press;
- Roy Goode and Penguin Books, for the extract from R. M. Goode, *Commercial Law* (2nd edn, London: Penguin Books, 1995), reproduced by permission of Penguin Books Ltd;
- Stephen Munzer, for the extract from *A Theory of Property* (Cambridge: Cambridge University Press, 1990);
- Sweet & Maxwell and Tony Weir, for the extract from Weir, *A Casebook on Tort* (10th edn, London: Sweet & Maxwell, 2004);
- Sweet & Maxwell, for the extract from Roper *et al.*, *Ruoff and Roper on the Law and Practice of Registered Conveyancing* (2nd looseleaf edn, London: Sweet & Maxwell, 2003);
- Transaction Publishers, for the extract from Adolf A. Berle and Gardiner C. Means, *The Modern Corporation and Private Property* (New York: Harcourt, Brace & World, 1932), reprinted with the permission of Transaction Publishers;
- the Yale Law Journal Company and William S. Hein Company, for the extract from Hohfeld, 'Fundamental Legal Conceptions as Applied in Judicial Reasoning' (1913) 23 *Yale Law Journal* 16; and
- Yoram Barzel, for the extract from his book, *Economic Analysis of Property Rights* (2nd edn, Cambridge: Cambridge University Press, 1997)

Felix S. Cohen, 'Dialogue on Private Property', was first published in (1954) 9 *Rutgers Law Journal* 357 and is reprinted with permission.

Crown copyright material is reproduced with the permission of the Controller of HMSO and the Queen's Printer for Scotland.

Table of cases

Prudential Assurance Co. Ltd v. Waterloo Real Estate Inc [1999] 17 EG 131,
 CA 269
Public Works Comrs v. Angus & Co., Dalton v. Angus & Co. (1881) LR 6 App Cas
 740, HL 492, 496, 497, 501

Queens Club Garden Estates Ltd v. Bignell [1924] 1 KB 117 617
Quennell v. Maltby [1979] 1 All ER 568, CA 697
Quinn v. Leathem [1901] AC 495, HL 29

R. v. Cavendish [1961] 2 All ER 856, [1961] 1 WLR 1083, CCA 266, 267, 270
R. v. Kelly [1999] QB 621, CA 13, 16, 372
R. v. Oxfordshire County Council, ex p. Sunningwell Parish Council [2000] 1 AC
 335, [1999] 3 All ER 385, [1999] 3 WLR 160, HL 169, 170, 171, 172, 490, 494,
 497, 499–507, 510
R. v. Secretary of State for Transport, ex p. Factortame Ltd: C-48/93 [2001] 1 AC
 524, HL 538
R. v. Suffolk County Council, ex p. Steed and Steed (1996) 75 P&CR 102, CA 502,
 504, 505
R. (Beresford) v. Sunderland County Council [2001] 1 WLR 1327 affd [2001]
 EWCA Civ 1218, CA rvsd [2003] UKHL 60, [2004] 1 AC 889, HL 39, 438, 497,
 510, 511
R. v. Somerset County Council and ARC Southern Ltd, ex p. Dixon [1998] Env LR
 111, (1998) 75 P&CR 175 608
R. v. Tower Hamlets London Borough Council, ex p. Von Goetz [1999] 2 WLR
 582, CA 216
R. v. Warner [1969] 2 AC 256, HL 266, 267, 270
R. v. Westminster City Council and London Electricity Board, ex p. Leicester
 Square Coventry Street Association (1990) 59 P&CR 51 251, 256–8
Radaich v. Smith (1959) 101 CLR 209, Aus HC 274
Rains v. Buxton (1880) 14 Ch D 537 431
Ramnarace v. Lutchman [2001] UKPC 25, [2001] 1 WLR 1651, [2002] 1 PC&R
 28 631, 632
Read v. J Lyons & Co. Ltd [1945] KB 216, CA 219
Recher, Re [1972] Ch 526 604, 605
Regent Oil Co. Ltd v. J. A. Gregory (Hatch End) Ltd [1966] Ch 402, CA 666
Remon v. City of London Real Property Co. [1921] 1 KB 49, CA 619
Rhone v. Stephens [1994] 2 WLR 429, HL 251
Ridley v. Taylor [1965] 1 WLR 611, CA 255
Ropaigealach v. Barclays Bank plc [1999] 3 WLR 17, CA 290, 685, 686, 696
Royal Bank of Scotland v. Etridge (No. 2) and other appeals, Barclays Bank plc v.
 Coleman, Bank of Scotland v. Bennett, Kenyon-Brown v. Desmond Banks & Co.
 (a firm) [2001] 3 WLR 1021, HL 456
Russel v. Russel (1783) 1 Bro CC 269 474

Table of statutes

Australia

Canada

Table of statutory instruments

Table of treaties

Table of EC legislation

Part 1

The concept of property

1

Property law: the issues

1.1. Basic definition

To put it at its simplest, property law is about the legally recognised relationships we have with each other in respect of things. We will want to expand and qualify this statement later – what kinds of relationship, what kinds of thing? – but our starting point is an introduction to the moral, political, social and economic context in which property law operates.

1.2. Illustrative example

Consider the following hypothetical situation, a variation of facts which actually occurred in California in 1976 and which became the subject of a celebrated decision of the Supreme Court of California, *Moore* v. *Regents of the University of California*, 51 Cal 3d 120; 793 P 2d 479 (1990).

John went into hospital to undergo an exploratory operation to aid diagnosis of unexplained stomach pains he had been suffering. During the course of the operation, Dr A removed tissue from John's stomach lining and stored it so that he could carry out further analysis if his initial diagnosis proved to be incorrect. No further analysis proved necessary: Dr A's initial diagnosis was confirmed, John was successfully treated and made a full recovery, and Dr A gave no further thought to the tissue sample.

By chance, however, it became included in material that Dr B was using in research he was carrying out at the hospital. This material included primary cells (i.e. cells taken directly from the body) taken from a number of different patients in the hospital. Dr B was trying to produce a cell line from these primary cells: it is difficult to locate a gene responsible for producing a particular substance or effect using primary cells, because primary cells typically reproduce a few times and then die. One can, however, sometimes continue to use cells for an extended period of time by developing them into a 'cell line', a culture capable of reproducing indefinitely. This is not, however, always an easy task. 'Longterm growth of human cells and tissues is difficult, often an art', and 'the probability of succeeding with any given cell sample is low' (the *Moore* case). Dr B managed to develop from one of John's primary cells a cell line containing genetic material with the potential for development into a cheap, effective and safe cure for AIDS. Dr B sold this cell line to the Columbian Drug Company Ltd for £10 m.

The drugs company, which already owned the patents for a very expensive, not very effective treatment for AIDS, and also for various palliatives for AIDS symptoms, bought the cell line to delay the development of a new drug. It believed, on the advice of its accountants, that it would be in its own financial best interests to continue to market its existing products for as long as possible, and not take steps to develop the new drug until a similarly cheap and effective cure seemed likely to emerge from elsewhere.

What rights and interests might each of these four protagonists plausibly lay claim to in respect of the cell line and its commercial exploitation?

1.2.1.   John

Any legally protected interest that John might have in the cell line must derive from an interest in the cell out of which it was developed, which itself must derive from whatever interest John had in the cell when it was still part of his body. Does John own his body, and, if he does, does it follow that he also owned his body cell?

1.2.1.1.   The unexcised body cell and the question of ownership

At one level, it might seem strange to question whether one owns a part of one's own body, but on closer consideration the issue is rather complex. We need first to take a brief look at what we mean by ownership. We consider the concept in detail in Chapter 6, where we see that, although 'ownership' is often used loosely as a synonym for 'property', it is more accurately used to describe a particular type of property interest – specifically, the most extensive property interest that any individual can have in a mature legal system that recognises the institution of private property. Most Western legal systems recognise the concept of ownership, but characteristically they also recognise lesser property interests as well (such as the right you acquire in a car if you hire it for a fortnight, or the right I acquire over your land if you grant me a right of way over your driveway to reach my garage). For the moment, however, we will concentrate on ownership itself, not on these other types of property interest.

We see in Chapter 6 that, in attempting to formulate a concept of ownership which would be recognisable in any developed Western market economy, Honoré identifies eleven 'standard incidents' of ownership. He sees these incidents as characteristic of a Western conception of ownership (by which he means ownership by an individual, as opposed to ownership by the state or by a corporation or by a group of people). They are not to be applied mechanistically: he is not suggesting that you cannot possibly be said to be an owner of a thing in any mature legal system if the law does not recognise you as having each one of these incidents. What he does say is that, if you do enjoy all these incidents in relation to a particular thing, most mature legal systems would say you owned it – together they are sufficient conditions for ownership, but no one of them is a necessary condition. We look at all eleven of these incidents in Chapter 6, but for present purposes six of them are of particular interest. According to Honoré, in a mature legal system you would typically be said to be the owner of a thing if you have:

1 The right to possess the thing. Possession has a technical meaning and a special significance in English law, which we look at in Chapter 7. For present purposes, you have the right to possess something when the law allocates exclusive physical control of it to you.

2 The right to use the thing. Unlike possession, use is not a technical term. Here Honoré confines use to *personal* use and enjoyment, so he would say that you have the right to use something if you may, at your discretion, make whatever personal use and enjoyment of the thing you wish (leaving aside, for present purposes, use in a way that harms others – this is something we will consider later).

3 The right to manage, which is essentially the right to control the use of the thing, in the sense of being entitled to license others to make personal use of it.

4 The right to the income of the thing. This covers both any naturally accruing profits – the apples produced by your apple tree – and also what Honoré describes as 'a surrogate of use, a benefit derived from forgoing the personal use of a thing and allowing others to use it for reward', for example income produced from capital you invest, or rent received from a flat you let out.

5 The right to the capital. This is the right to deal with the thing itself in any way you choose (although again we must put aside for the moment a dealing which harms others). It includes the right to sell or give it away, or to consume it or damage it or destroy it, or to dictate who should have it when you die.

6 The right of transmissibility. This is quite complex: it concerns the *interest* you have in the thing (i.e. the rights and other claims you have over it) rather than the thing itself. Your interest is transmissible if it is capable of being transferred intact to someone else, in the sense that the consequence of the transfer would be that the transferee would acquire all the rights and claims that you had had in that thing, and you would cease to have them. In other words, a transmissible interest is the antithesis of an interest that is purely personal. My right to legal protection for my reputation is a good example of a right that is not transmissible in English law. If it was transmissible, I would be able to sell it to you, with the result that *you* (and not I) would be entitled to complain and recover damages if a tabloid newspaper published a libellous article about *me*. There are other examples of interests in things that are inherently personal and not transmissible. In Chapter 9 we look at a long-standing controversy (now resolved by Parliament) over the nature of the right that a wife has to occupy her matrimonial home when it is solely owned by her husband (rather than jointly owned, as would now be more usual). It was always accepted that, as long as the couple remain married, she does have such a right, enforceable *personally* against her husband. The issue was whether it was a *property* right that could be enforced against anyone else – specifically, whether her estranged husband could cause her to be evicted from what had been their matrimonial home by selling it to someone else: if her right was a property right, the buyer would have been bound by it and would have had no more right to evict her

than her husband had had; whereas if it was enforceable only personally against her husband it would not affect the buyer and he could evict her. We see later that one of the reasons why the courts were reluctant to recognise that this right was a property right was that it is inherently non-transmissible: my right to occupy the house that my husband and I have been living in as our matrimonial home could not conceivably be held by anyone other than me – if transferred to anyone else, it would necessarily become different in nature. We can also note here why the issue of transmissibility is controversial: if we were to say that transmissibility was a *necessary* condition for an interest to qualify as a property interest, it would exclude a significant category of rights from proprietary status.

Which of these incidents characterise John's relationship to parts of his body while they still form part of his body? As long as we are talking about a small cell in an expendable bit of one's stomach lining, there seems no particular problem with the first five incidents (although some are rather difficult to visualise). However, the sixth does not seem right: we surely would not expect any legal system to treat John's rights in his body parts as transmissible. Whatever rights a legal system recognises we have in our body tissue *while it is still part of our bodies*, they are almost certainly going to be very different from those (if any) it would want to confer on someone who acquires a bit of that tissue after it has been excised: both the moral and the physical context have changed. If this is true, it means that, while we might have a legal system that allows John a right to sell *this bit of body tissue*, his *interest* in it (or at least the interest he has while it is still part of his body) is not transmissible – the buyer will acquire a different set of rights from those that John had when the tissue was still part of his body.

Once we start talking about more important bits of unexcised body tissue, or about live bodies as a whole, the other incidents begin to look inappropriate as well, or at least not acceptable without significant qualifications. The right to possess your body and unexcised parts of it might initially seem unproblematic. In any legal system operating in a society which respects personal autonomy we would expect the law to allocate exclusive physical control over our own bodies and body parts to us. However, even here there may be controversial claims to make exceptions. Can young children (or mentally incapacitated adults) really be given the right to exclusive physical control over their own bodies, and, if not, who should have the ultimate control? Their parents? The state? And what about, for example, hunger strikers, or adult individuals who refuse medical treatment that could benefit them (perhaps blood transfusions) or prevent harm to others (treatment for infectious diseases, or medication to prevent violent behaviour)? And, once we are past this first incident of ownership, everything becomes even more dominated by difficult moral, political and social issues. The second and fifth incidents – the right to use our bodies in any way we want and our right to deal in the capital interest in them – raise fundamental questions about the nature of the society in which we want to live. The first and obvious point is that an absolute right to use our bodies as we want would leave us free to behave in ways that harm, affront or annoy others. A balance must inevitably be struck between our freedom to behave as we want and the rights of others to be free from harm, affront and annoyance, but it is not easy to arrive at a consensus as to where the balance should be struck. Another difficult issue, and if anything even more controversial, is that a right to use our bodies as we choose, and an absolute right to deal in the capital of our bodies, would leave us free to harm ourselves. Is it necessary, or morally or pragmatically justifiable, for the law to curtail our freedom to abuse, harm or destroy ourselves or parts of our bodies?

The right to destroy the thing is only one aspect of the right to the capital interest in a thing. The other aspects – the right to sell it or to give it away – also cause problems when applied to human bodies. Should I be entitled to sell or donate an essential part of my body, without which I cannot function at all, such as my liver, my brain or my heart? Would it make any difference if I was dying anyway, and the donation was for a transplant to someone else which could not succeed if the organ was removed after my death? Rather different, but no less complex, issues arise when we start talking about body parts without which one could function tolerably well, and the removal of which would not be life-threatening – should I be entitled to sell, for example, a limb, an eye, or a kidney? And would it make a difference if it was not a sale but a donation, or if it was prompted by altruism, familial love or duty, or by an inability to withstand family pressure? And what about renewable body parts such as blood, hair, bone marrow, sperm or ova? Should we have an absolute right to sell such body parts to anyone in any circumstances, or should it be absolutely prohibited, or permitted only in some circumstances and subject to certain conditions? It quickly becomes apparent that very different considerations apply depending on the type of body product, and that sale and donation raise quite different issues.

The second and third incidents – the right to manage and the right to income – may also cause us varying degrees of disquiet. Most people would agree that respect for bodily integrity dictates that, if anyone should have the right to permit others to make use of parts of my body, it should be me and no one else. Similarly, if anyone should be entitled to any profits or income accruing from my body or from unexcised body parts, it should be me and no one else. Nevertheless, a formidable range of philosophical, moral, religious and political objections could be made to a legal system that always and in all circumstances allowed me to forgo personal use of parts of my body (or, indeed, the whole) and to license others to make surrogate use of it, whether for my reward or theirs.

So, if we were slavishly to adopt Honoré's incidents here (something he would not himself have advocated), we might be tempted to conclude that you can 'own' some of the small/inessential parts of your body, or at least those not regarded as having any moral, religious or reproductive significance, but not the essential parts. Initially, this may seem a strange conclusion, but it tells us some important things about ownership. First, it tells us that legal systems typically recognise ownership of some things but not of others. Secondly, it demonstrates that, when deciding whether a particular type of thing should or should not be ownable, a legal system is likely to be influenced by a wide range of pragmatic and principled considerations. The same considerations will not necessarily apply in relation to all types of thing, or if they do apply will not carry the same weight – consider, for example, the considerations that would be relevant in deciding whether to recognise ownership of white tigers, water supplies in a desert, sunlight or weapons of mass destruction.

Thirdly, it tells us that ownership is too simple a concept to encompass all the different types and ranges of rights and interests in things that we would expect a mature, efficient and humane legal system to provide. Many of the difficult questions posed above could more appropriately be answered by giving John property rights in his body which fall short of ownership, or by giving him personal rather than property rights. These crucial questions of what amounts to a property right, and the distinction between property and personal rights, are explored in the next four chapters. The specific question of the extent to which English law does in fact recognise property in human bodies and body parts is something we return to in the 'Notes and Questions' section at the end of this chapter.

1.2.1.2. John's interest in the excised body cell

Meanwhile, we have to return to the question of whether John had a property interest in the cell *after* it had been removed from his body. This was the precise issue faced by the Supreme Court of California in the case on which this story is based, *Moore* v. *Regents of the University of California*, 51 Cal 3d 120; 793 P 2d 479 (1990). The *Moore* case, being a decision of the American courts, is not determinative of the issue in this jurisdiction, but it provides a good illustration of the spectrum of moral and philosophical standpoints taken by common law judges on such issues. In the *Moore* case, there was only one doctor involved, not two as in our fictitious example, and the cell was removed from Moore's body in the course of an operation to remove his spleen, as part of his treatment for hairy-cell leukaemia. Moore had consented to the operation and to the removal of his spleen, but he had not been told that the doctor in charge of his treatment had already spotted the potential value of his cells and had already decided to take and use them for a particular research project. The issue was whether Moore had any cause of action against that doctor. It was decided that he had, but the majority held that he had only a personal action for breach of the doctor's disclosure obligations, not an action in conversion, which is the cause of action available to someone who can show an unlawful interference with property rights. The issue that divided the majority from the minority was therefore whether Moore could be said to have property rights in the cells which had been removed from his body. If he had been able to show that he had, this would have given him a basis for a claim to a share in the gigantic profits now being made out of the cell line developed from his body tissue. The majority conclusion was that, for the purposes of conversion law at least, a person cannot be said to have 'property' or 'ownership' in his own body cells once they have been excised from his body (although they were careful to emphasise that 'we do not purport to hold that excised cells can never be property for any purpose whatsoever'). The reasoning which led the majority to this conclusion is important: broadly, they said that to decide otherwise would inhibit socially important medical research, and would give Moore 'a highly theoretical windfall'. The minority, on the other hand, felt strongly that to deny that we have property rights in our own bodies violates the 'profound ethical imperative to respect the human body as the physical and temporal expression of the unique human persona', as Mosk J put it. Also, they were persuaded by the argument that, because the profits to be made from the cell line were a product of both the researcher's skill and Moore's cell, they accordingly ought to be shared proportionately between them (an argument we come across again in Chapter 3). Here, however, we want to note some rather more general points not fully articulated in the *Moore* case, and which we can best appreciate by moving back to our fictitious example, where the question of John's property rights is still open.

1.2.1.3. Continuity of interests and John's interest in the cell line

Assuming for the moment that John does have a property interest in the excised cell, it is worth spelling out why that might give him a proprietary claim in respect of the cell line and the profits made and to be made from it. His claim is essentially a mechanistic one, and it tells us some important (if rather obvious) things about the way property interests behave and the way they are allocated by a legal system. His argument is that, if he had a property interest in his body cell when it was still part of his body, that property interest must necessarily still continue for as long as the cell itself continues to exist, despite changes in form and/or enhancements in value, unless and until something happens to extinguish the interest. Moreover, as long as the *interest* continues to subsist, he must necessarily continue to hold it unless it can be shown to have been passed on to someone else. Property interests do indeed have this mechanistic quality. Leaving aside interests which are specifically limited in time (for example, a ten-year lease of a shop), a presumption of continuance exists, and a person will be presumed to continue to hold an interest which has become vested in him unless there is positive evidence that it has been divested, for example by a sale or gift (we do not lightly find that someone has simply abandoned a property interest). This feature of property interests – essentially, they stay put unless positively ended or moved – is important. Property interests in things carry with them liabilities as well as rights. Also, unlike personal interests, they affect everyone who comes into contact with the thing in question. For both these reasons, it is essential that we know at any given time exactly who has what interests in what thing – consider, for example, the case of contaminated land, or a share in a company on which a dividend has just been declared.

So, if we accept for the purposes of this argument that John did own his cell when it was a part of his body, we need to ask whether anything happened *to the cell* that would have extinguished or modified his interest, or alternatively whether at some stage he disposed of his interest before the cell was developed into a cell line. We know that two things happened to the cell. The first was that it ceased to be part of his body, and we have already said that this event causes such a profound change in John's relationship to it that we might be justified in saying that it changes the nature of his interest, or even extinguishes it altogether. The second thing that happened was that Dr B exercised his skill on it to develop it into a cell line. In other words, as the minority dissent in *Moore* pointed out, even if we assume that John's cell was *an* ingredient in or component of the cell line, it was not the only one: the cell line was the irreversible product of two things – the cell and Dr B's skill and labour. Sophisticated legal systems will necessarily have rules about what happens when things of different ownership become physically and irreversibly mixed. To a certain extent, similar considerations should apply if one of the ingredients is a physical process (such as heat) rather than a tangible thing. The addition of human skill or labour to a thing raises some of the same considerations but also quite different ones. There is an argument that exploitation of resources to the benefit of society as a whole can best be achieved by conferring property interests on those who expend skill and labour on things, regardless of whether in any particular case their contribution has added value to the thing in question. This is the basis of John Locke's arguments justifying property rights that we consider in Chapter 3, and it also forms the basic premise of intellectual property law. In the *Moore* case, it was regarded as axiomatic by the majority. They took the view that the value to society of promoting medical research was so high that it was justifiable – in fact necessary – to allocate the whole of the property interest in the cell line to the doctor: to allow Moore even a proportionate share in the valuable commodity produced when the doctor mixed his skill and labour with Moore's cell would unacceptably lower the incentive for doctors to carry out medical research on human tissue.

There are other things to be said about Dr B's position, and about Dr A, but first there are some other points to be made about John's proprietary claims.

1.2.1.4.   Enforceability of John's interest in the cell line

If John had a property interest in the cell line produced by Dr B which was enforceable against Dr B, does it necessarily follow that it would also be enforceable against the drugs company once the cell line had been sold to the company? We see in Chapter 2 that it is a fundamental characteristic of a property interest in a thing that it is enforceable against everyone who comes into contact with that thing. However, that statement requires some qualification. Common law systems have developed fairly complex sets of rules curtailing the enforceability of interests where, as here, there has been a fragmentation of ownership, as we see in Chapters 14–15 where we look at enforceability in detail. In particular, there are circumstances in which a property interest in a thing will be extinguished by a sale of the thing. The reason for this is that, in a market economy, a legal system that recognises multiple interests in a thing has to reconcile conflicting aims. On the one hand, the full benefits of private property ownership depend on security of interest, and this is best served by a rule that property interests are enforced by law against all the world in all circumstances. On the other hand, the free marketability of resources is hindered by the presence of multiple interest holders whose interests cannot be overridden. For the market to function properly it must be easy for the ownership of resources to pass to those who value them most, but transactions become prohibitively expensive if they require the concurrence of multiple interest holders, especially if their existence is not easily discoverable and identification is difficult. We look more closely at these arguments in Chapter 2. The point we are concerned with here is that most systems balance these competing aims by allowing for some circumstances in which lesser property interests in things can be overridden on a sale of a larger interest in the thing.

In order to understand how this works, it is necessary to appreciate that there are at least two ways of structuring multiple property interests in things, either of which could apply if we conclude that both John and Dr B have property interests in the cell line. One of them is by co-ownership: we could say that John and Dr B co-own the cell line in shares proportionate to the value of their respective contributions. If we adopt Honoré's view of ownership, we would then say that they co-own each of the incidents of ownership. Alternatively, ownership can be fragmented, so that some rights and liabilities become split off and vest in one person while the rest remain vested in or are transferred to someone else. As we see in Chapter 8, only set patterns of fragmentation are permissible, but it would be possible to adopt a pattern of fragmentation which, in effect, gave Dr B all the Honoré incidents of ownership except the right to income, with that right being shared proportionately between John and Dr B. We would then say that Dr B owned the cell line, but his ownership was subject to or encumbered by John's property interest (consisting of a right to a share in the income). However the multiple interests are structured (i.e. whether by co-ownership or by fragmentation) it is the person who holds what Honoré calls the capital interest in the thing who has the capacity and power to sell the thing itself (that, after all, is what the capital interest is). In the case of co-ownership, the capital interest is co-owned, and so there can be no sale or other transfer of ownership without the concurrence of each of the co-owners (although we see later how English law uses the trust to get round the inconvenience this can cause when dealing with co-owned land). If, however, ownership has been fragmented, the capital interest in the thing may well be held by only one of the interest holders. So, for example, if a landowner grants a five-year lease to a tenant, the tenant acquires the right to possess the land for five years (and, in the Honoré classification, the rights to use, income and control for the same period) while the landlord retains the right to capital (and, incidentally, a present right to have possession, use, income and control revert to him in five years' time).

In the interests of marketability, the common law has evolved rules which enable the holder of the capital interest to transfer full ownership of the thing in certain circumstances, so effectively obliterating or overriding any other property interest in the thing held by someone else. In the rules as originally devised by the common law the crucial factors were payment and notice: a *buyer* from the holder of the capital interest in a thing would not be affected by certain types of property interest affecting that thing unless she had notice of them (we consider below why this privilege was, and still is, confined to buyers). This notice rule, which still operates in some areas of property law as we will see later, has the disadvantage of giving such interest holders no reliable means of ensuring that their interests will remain enforceable – at any time their interest might be obliterated by a sale, without the interest holder becoming aware of the fact. A more sophisticated approach is to substitute registration for notice, and make provision for such interest holders to register their interests. It then becomes possible to adopt a rule that registered interests are enforceable against the whole world in all circumstances, whereas unregistered interests are unenforceable against buyers of the capital interest. Such a system has advantages for everyone concerned: property interest holders whose interests are capable of being overridden on a sale are given the means to ensure that their interest will always and in all circumstances be enforced against the whole world. Holders of the capital interest can easily prove their ability to transfer full ownership by pointing to the absence of any registered interests, and buyers need only check the register to find out exactly what they are buying. However, universal registration of all property interests in all things is not feasible, or even desirable, for reasons we look at more closely in Chapter 10, and in most cases of multiple interest holding there is a measure of uncertainty about enforceability of the individual interests, and a corresponding uncertainty for any buyer who wants to acquire full ownership as to whether there do in fact exist lesser interests in the thing that might be enforceable against her. This uncertainty helps to explain why the majority in *Moore* was so convinced that it would inhibit the development of therapeutic medical treatments if the person from whose body the cell was taken (Moore) was treated as having a property interest in the cell line apparently owned by the doctor. There is no registration system in operation for human cells, and so drugs companies would be deterred from buying or investing in cell lines in the possession of researchers because of the difficulty of establishing whether or not researchers in possession of cell lines had the power and capacity to pass on full ownership in any particular case.

1.2.1.5.   Tracing into exchange products: property rights in Dr B's £10 m

To complete the picture on John's property interests, it should be noted that, if he loses his interest in the cell line because it gets overridden on a sale to the drugs company, he may be able to make a proprietary claim against the £10 m the drugs company paid Dr B for the cell line. If this claim succeeds, John's interest will, in effect, shift from the cell line to its proceeds of sale. This results from the doctrine of tracing (largely outside the scope of this book) which allows a claimant whose interest in a thing ceases because the thing itself has passed into the hands of someone against whom his interest is not enforceable, to make an equivalent proprietary claim against any asset received in exchange for the thing. Tracing therefore goes some way towards redressing the imbalance caused by restricting the enforceability of property interests. It prevents a seller, like Dr B, whose ownership interest in a resource was encumbered by a lesser property interest, from being unjustly enriched (the price the drugs company paid Dr B was for the cell line free from John's interest, not the lower price it would have paid for the interest Dr B himself had, i.e. the cell line encumbered by John's interest), and gives John an equivalent property interest to replace the interest he has lost. Exceptions to enforceability generally operate only in favour of purchasers, i.e. those who provide value in exchange for the thing (donees are of no relevance in the marketplace, and so there is no need to give them the same privilege over interest holders). Limiting the privilege to those who provide value in exchange for the resource ensures that the seller will be left holding an asset which can be made available as a compensation for the interest holder whose interest has been overridden. Of course, it may not be much help in any particular case – Dr B might have made a bad bargain and sold the cell line for less than it was worth, or he might have disappeared with the money, or spent it, or gone bankrupt, before John realised what had happened.

1.2.2. Dr A and Dr B and the acquisition and transmission of property interests

We have already seen that Dr B has formidable arguments in support of a claim to have acquired a property interest in the cell line by virtue of having used his skill and labour to develop the cell line from the cell. If the cell itself had been ownerless property when he acquired it, his argument would have been unassailable, both in Lockean theory and in English intellectual property law. The question of whether this is affected by any property interest in the cell that John might have had has already been touched upon. What about Dr A: did he acquire any prior interest in the cell which might affect the question of Dr B's rights in the cell line? Unless we adopt an absolute rule that no one can ever have any property rights in human bodies and excised body parts (and we see in *R. v. Kelly* [1999] QB 621, noted at the end of this chapter, why this would not be a sensible rule), Dr A's claim to have a property interest in the cell looks good, although the precise nature of his interest and the route by which he acquired it will vary depending on the view we take of John's rights. If John had property rights in his cell which (whether or not transformed in nature) survived its excision from his body, Dr A would seem to have a claim to the cell justifiable on the same grounds as those that justify Dr B's claim to the cell line: it was, after all, Dr A's skill and labour that removed the cell from John's body. Alternatively, it might be possible to spell out of John's consent to the operation and to the removal of the cell an implied transfer of his rights in the cell to Dr A (in English law, a gift of a chattel – which is what a cell is – requires an intention to make the gift coupled with physical transfer, both of which could be found here). Even if John's rights in the cell automatically ceased as a matter of law as soon as it was excised from his body (which is what the majority on the *Moore* case would have said), Dr A would have a good case. His case would be based on the argument of first occupancy – i.e. that ownerless property should be allocated to the person who first takes possession of it (notice the difference between this and Locke's labour/desert argument). We see in Chapter 3 and elsewhere that first occupancy has a strong pull in the allocation of property rights, and in particular that it forms the basis of the common law principle that title to things can be derived solely from factual possession. The important point here, however, is that the presumption of continuity of interest which we have already noted will apply here as well. If Dr A has acquired property rights in the cell by any of these routes, they do not appear to have been dislodged by anything that was done by Dr B, unless we can say that the transformation brought about to the cell by Dr B's work is so dramatic as to justify saying that, in the case of this particular irreversible mixture (what is now Dr A's cell with Dr B's skill and labour), property in the mixture should be allocated wholly to the mixer for the policy reasons which persuaded the majority in the *Moore* case. There is no other reason for saying that Dr A's rights have been extinguished: Dr B is not a purchaser. There are certainly no grounds for saying that Dr A has abandoned his interest. Putting something on one side and then forgetting it exists does not constitute abandonment: because property entails obligations and liabilities as well as rights, abandonment has to be made much more difficult than that. Dr A's interest must therefore be presumed to have continued and to have been enforceable against Dr B.

1.2.3.   The drugs company: constraints on the exercise of property rights

We end by looking at the position of the drugs company. We assume that it has acquired ownership of the cell line free from any interest of John, Dr A or Dr B. The issue we want to highlight now is one raised by its proposal to suppress development of the cell line: do property holders have public responsibilities or are they free to exercise property rights taking into account only their own private self-interest? If we think that the public interest should be taken into account, at least where the asset is a unique resource of public importance, as this cell line is, then it may be that it is not appropriate for the asset to be the subject of private ownership at all: it ought instead to be publicly owned. We look at this question of the relative merits of private, public and communal property in the next chapter. However, if we conclude that economic efficiency dictates private ownership, does that necessarily mean that it is desirable or inevitable that the drugs company as private owner must be left free to do whatever it wants with the cell line, even if that means leaving it up to the drugs company to decide whether or not to exploit this potentially valuable public resource for the maximum public benefit?

There are two aspects of this to note here and consider more fully in later chapters. It is certainly not an inevitable feature even of private property that a property owner should be free to do whatever it wants with its assets. It is essential to keep in mind that property rules do not operate in a legal vacuum. There will necessarily be private law constraints to prevent harm to others and to reconcile incompatible uses of resources, for example by neighbouring landowners. In addition, it is possible – perhaps even inevitable – to have some degree of public control over the exercise of private property rights. For example, intellectual property law could impose compulsory licensing on the drugs company, making it a term of any patent it granted to the drugs company (without which it would have no legally protected rights in the cell line) that the scientific details were publicly recorded, and requiring the drugs company to license others to exploit it on payment of a fee to the company. Similarly, competition law might intervene to prevent it abusing its monopoly or dominant position, opening the market in its treatments to competitors. The use it can make of the cell line and of other types of human tissue will also be controlled by various regulatory bodies, who in current English law exercise close control over what can and cannot be done with human tissue. Other types of resource can be expected to attract other types of public regulation. To give an obvious example, planning, environmental and health and safety laws impose controls designed to protect the public interest which will regulate the use we make of a wide range of assets including land, buildings of historic, national or artistic significance, other structures built on land, machinery, natural resources such as minerals, growing crops and animals, and artificial constructs such as rubbish tips.

The second aspect of the freedom of action element in private ownership is the complicating factor of corporate ownership. As we see in Chapter 2, analysis and argument on the nature of property tends to proceed on the assumption that the private interest holder is an individual human being. Do the same considerations apply where, as in our example, the interest holder is a corporation? Ownership of corporate resources is vested in a legal fiction, the corporation, but the corporation can only act by human agents. As a matter of strict law, assets owned by a corporation are managed by one group of people – the directors – solely for another group of people – the shareholders – who, for reasons we look at in Chapter 8, may have no effective control over the actions of the managers. Does this cause corporate owners to behave differently from individual owners? Does it alter the picture if the corporate owner is a global enterprise, economically larger and stronger than many of the nation states in which it operates, and not wholly under the legal or social control of any one legal or social system? The economic effects of the actions of a corporate owner are felt by a constituency which is wider than its shareholders (for example, its employees, its customers and suppliers, and the community in which it operates). In deciding how the corporation uses its assets, are its directors required or even entitled to take the interests of these other constituents into consideration? The actions of individual human owners also of course affect the same wide constituency, but human owners can choose to act altruistically in the use of their assets: if a drugs company was a private individual it could choose to market the drug as cheaply as possible in order to maximise the benefit to the public even if it makes less or no profit for the owner itself. Can a corporate owner do that? Also, human owners routinely acknowledge moral responsibilities in dealing with their assets (for example, towards members of their family, or even to employees or colleagues or customers) and their use of their assets can be motivated by positive desires to confer benefits that they have no legal responsibility to confer (for example, perhaps, to amass as large a fortune as possible to leave to their children when they die), by desires for non-financial rewards such as fame or public esteem, or even vindictive desires to cause harm to others even at a loss to themselves. It is not at all clear how far corporate owners can or should do the same. Should we be making special rules to ensure that, so far as possible, the behaviour of a corporate owner replicates that of an honourable, altruistic human owner, or should we acknowledge the inevitable differences and treat corporate ownership as different in kind from individual private ownership? We return to these questions in Chapter 8, where we look at corporate ownership in the general context of the structures the law uses to enable assets to be held on behalf of and for the benefit of others, and the issues arising out of these varying types of split property holding.

Before doing so, however, we need to refine our notion of property, and this is the subject of the next chapter.

Notes and Questions 1.1

1 Read *Moore* v. *Regents of the University of California*, 51 Cal 3d 120; 793 P 2d 479 (1990) and *R.* v. *Kelly* [1999] QB 621, either in full or as extracted at www.cambridge.org/propertylaw/.

2 Explain the arguments of the majority and the minority in *Moore*. Which do you find more convincing?

3 Why did the Court of Appeal in *Kelly* not feel able to accept that human body parts are always 'property'? On what basis did they nevertheless find that Kelly and Lindsay had been rightly convicted?

4 How does the approach of the English Court of Appeal in *Kelly* differ from the approach of the Supreme Court of California in *Moore*? Do you consider that either court gave proper consideration to the question of whether human body parts ought to be regarded as property?

5 In English law concentration has shifted to the question of the treatment of body parts removed at *post mortem* examination and retained (in particular at how far relatives have any say in the process) and public enquiries have been held into the practice of organ retention at the Bristol Royal Infirmary and the Alder Hey Hospital in Liverpool. For an account of these developments and an analysis of the legal issues they raise see Mason and Laurie, 'Consent or Property?'

2

What we mean by 'property'

2.1. Introduction

In Chapter 1 we provisionally described property law as being about the legal relationships we have with each other in respect of things. We now need to clarify and refine this.

2.1.1. Property as a relationship and as a thing

First, a terminological point. The term 'property' can be used to describe three different aspects of the relationship between people and things. Consider the statement 'I have a right enforceable against you in respect of this car'. 'Property' can be used as an adjective to describe the *nature of the right* I have in the car (as in 'I have a property right in the car, not just a personal right'). Equally, where you and I have a continuing relationship in respect of the car (perhaps I lent it to you, giving rise to the relationship of bailment between us), the term 'property' can be used, again as an adjective but this time to explain the *nature of the relationship* (as in 'bailment is a property relationship'). Finally, 'property' can be used as a noun to denote the thing itself. So, to change the example, if I rent a flat from you, it is terminologically acceptable to say that both you and I have property rights in the flat, and that the lease relationship between us is a property relationship, and that the flat is the property in which each of us has rights.

The use of the term 'property' to denote the thing is sometimes frowned upon. In their introduction to the idea of property in a standard American property textbook, *The Law of Property*, Cunningham, Stoebuck and Whitman dismiss this usage as loose non-lawyerly talk:

> When a layman is asked to define 'property' he is likely to say that 'property' is something tangible 'owned' by a natural person (or persons), a corporation, or a unit of government. But such a response is inaccurate ... [in at least two ways, including that] it confuses 'property' with the various *subjects* of 'property' ... For the lawyer, 'property' is not a 'thing' at all, although 'things' are the subject of property.

However, this is unnecessarily prescriptive. It *is* necessary to be able to distinguish between the thing in respect of which rights are claimed and the rights themselves, but it is not inevitably confusing to describe both as 'property'.

2.1.2. Conceptualising 'things'

Cunningham, Stoebuck and Whitman also ascribe to the unthinking non-lawyer the assumption that property is about tangible things only. As they point out, this is not true. While there must be some 'thing' in respect of which a property right subsists, it need not be a tangible thing. The 'thing' may exist only at the highest level of abstraction. You can have a property right in a song or in shares in a company, and you can have a property right to the flow of water in a stream or to the passage of sunlight through a window or (conceivably) to a pension or to welfare payments, just as much as you can have a property right in a brick, a car or an area of land. We saw in Chapter 1 in relation to property in human bodies and body parts that the law recognises property rights in some things but not in others, and that the decision that a legal system will make as to whether a particular thing can be the subject of property rights is likely to be dictated by pragmatic and principled considerations of varying and fluctuating weights.

If there are good reasons to treat particular rights as property rights, the conceptualisation of the appropriate 'thing' will rarely provide an obstacle. However, perceived practical difficulties in enforcing the rights may be seen as a problem. We see several examples of this in Chapter 9. In *Victoria Park Racing* v. *Taylor* (1937) 58 CLR 479, for example, the High Court of Australia decided that a racecourse owner who organised horse racing at race meetings did not have the exclusive right to view, report or otherwise exploit the race meetings – he had no right to prevent a neighbour from commercially exploiting the event by broadcasting commentaries on the races on the radio. The court had no conceptual difficulty in accepting that a spectacle such as a sporting event might be the subject of a property right, but one of the reasons why it refused to recognise such a right was the practical difficulties it envisaged in enforcing it. They took the view (perhaps misguided, as we see in Chapter 9) that such a right could not be adequately vindicated by the law except by prohibiting everyone else from overlooking the event, even casually from the top of a bus. This they considered to be impractical, and a strong argument against accepting that a property right could exist in a spectacle such as a horse race.

2.1.3. Distinguishing property rights from other rights relating to things

We have just established that there are some *things* in respect of which a legal system will not recognise property rights. But, even if a particular thing can be the subject of property rights, it does not follow that *all rights* in relation to that thing will be property rights. What distinguishes a property right in a thing from other rights in the same thing is the breadth of enforceability of the right. We designate as property rights those rights that the law will uphold against people in general (either the whole world, or everyone except a specified class of exceptions). A right that the law will uphold, but only against a specific person or persons, is not a property right. The simplest of examples is the car hire example given in Chapter 1.

If you own a car but hire it to me for seven days, the rights you have given me in the car (the right to possession of it for seven days) are clearly enforceable against you: if you try to take the car back within the seven-day period, I can call on the law to stop you. In order to be classified as property rights, however, my rights in the car would have to be enforceable not only against you, but against others who come into contact with the car. So, for example, if the police wrongly tow the car away while it is hired to me, I can demand it back from them if my rights in the car are property rights but not if they are not. Similarly, if the day after hiring the car to me you sell it to your uncle, he will be bound by my rights if they are property rights: he will not be entitled to take possession of the car from me until my hire period has expired. If, however, my hire rights are not property rights, your uncle will be entitled to take the car away from me immediately and my only recourse will be against you, for damages for breach of your contractual promise that I could have possession of the car for seven days.

Again, the decision as to whether a particular type of right should be recognised as a property right is dictated by policy reasons. Because property rights have this characteristic of enforceability against the world at large, they are dangerous things, capable of having adverse effects on people not even in contemplation when the rights were created. The justification for allowing enforcement of a right against one particular person is therefore not necessarily sufficient justification for allowing its enforcement against the world at large.

2.1.4.   Rights and other entitlements: Hohfeld's rights analysis

So far we have been talking rather loosely about property 'rights'. However, there is an important distinction to be drawn between being free to use, enjoy or exploit a thing and having a *right* to use, enjoy or exploit it. To make this distinction clear, it is necessary to look more closely at different types of entitlement. Hohfeld's article, 'Fundamental Legal Conceptions' (see Extract 2.1 below) contains a classic analysis of legal entitlements which we can use here. There are interesting and important questions as to the utility and significance of Hohfeld's analysis, in particular as to how far it can be said to be telling us necessary truths about rights, but for present purposes our concern is only to identify different types of entitlement.

Hohfeld was concerned primarily with bilateral legal relationships between people, rather than the unilateral relationship of a person with a thing. He criticised the use of the word 'right' to cover different types of legal entitlement, and the consequent tendency to assume that all legal relationships could be reduced to 'rights' and their correlative 'duties'. He distinguished four different types of entitlement that are commonly subsumed under the general term 'right' – right, privilege, power and immunity – each of which, he says, has its own different opposite (no-right, duty, disability and liability respectively) as well as its own different correlative (duty, no-right, liability and disability). In tabular form this can be shown as represented in Table 2.1.

Table 2.1

Opposites		Correlatives	
Right	No-right	Right	Duty
Privilege	Duty	Privilege	No-right
Power	Disability	Power	Liability
Immunity	Liability	Immunity	Disability

He sees the eight elements appearing in this table of opposites and correlatives as fundamental concepts, best explained by relation to each other rather than by separate definition.

2.1.4.1.   Rights and duties, privileges and no-rights

The difference between the first two pairs of correlatives and opposites can be illustrated by adopting Hohfeld's own example of entitlements to enter land. If a plot of land is owned by me rather than by you, in Hohfeld's terms I have a *right* as against you to exclude you from the land, and you have the *correlative duty* to me not to enter (and of course I have a similar right/duty relationship with all other non-owners). As landowner, I may enter the land myself, in the sense that I am free to do so and you have no entitlement to stop me. Hohfeld categorises my freedom to enter my own land (when viewed in relation to you) as a *privilege* or 'liberty' as against you, and your *correlative* absence of entitlement to stop me as a *no-right* as against me. To put it another way, I owe you no *duty* that I will keep off my own land, and you have no *claim-right* to exclude me from my own land: my *privilege* as against you to enter my own land is the *opposite* of a *duty* to you to keep away, and your *no-right* to exclude me is the *opposite* of a *right* to exclude me. Hohfeld uses the term 'claim' to refer to this kind of right: here we use the term 'claim-right'.

The point of making these distinctions becomes clear from another example used by Hohfeld. He points to an example given by J. C. Gray in *The Nature and Sources of Law* (1909), section 48, which he says demonstrates the inadequacy of a crude rights/duties analysis of property relations. Gray says:

> The eating of shrimp salad is an interest of mine, and, if I can pay for it, the law will protect that interest, and it is therefore a right of mine to eat shrimp salad that I have paid for, although I know it gives me the colic.

Hohfeld points out that there are two distinct groups of relations here, the first of which could exist without the second. The first is that Gray has a *privilege* as against non-owners of the salad (who here we will call X) to eat the salad, and X has the correlative *no-right* that Gray should not eat it (in non-Hohfeldian terms Gray is free to eat his own salad and X is not entitled to object if he does so). The second is that Gray has a *claim-right* against X that X should not prevent him eating the salad, and X has a correlative duty not to interfere (i.e. Gray is entitled to insist that no one prevents him eating it). What Hohfeld means when he says that the first could exist without the second is that it is perfectly possible for Gray to have had a *privilege* to eat the salad even if he did not own it. The example he gives of this is the rather unlikely one of X, now being the owner of the salad, saying to Gray: 'Eat the salad if you can; you have my licence to do so, but I don't agree not to interfere with you.' In such a case, says Hohfeld, Gray has a *privilege* to eat the salad in that, if he manages to do so before X spirits it away, he has not infringed the rights of X or anyone else. He does not, however, have a *right* that X will not interfere with him eating it, in that he would have no ground for complaint if X had thrown it away before Gray got to it.

For our purposes, a more useful example of Gray having a *privilege* but not a *right* to eat the salad would be if shrimp salads grew wild on bushes like black-berries, and he and X came across one: if Gray manages to pick and eat the salad himself he has not infringed the rights of X or anyone else – X has a no-right that Gray should not eat the salad. However, Gray has no *right* to eat the salad, in the sense that he has no right that X will not interfere with his eating it, so if X got there first and either ate it himself or hurled it away, Gray would have no cause for complaint.

It is worth noting that, in the two shrimp salad examples he gives, Hohfeld does not expressly state whether X can eat the salad. It is of course implicit in what he says that, in the first example, Gray may eat it and X may not, whereas, in the second, either of them may do so. Hohfeld does not make this explicit because his focus is not on the positive use of the thing or the allocation of positive use between Gray and X. In Hohfeld's perspective, this is a side issue, peripheral to the central question of the relationship between Gray and X in respect of the shrimp salad, and in particular on the relative precariousness of various different levels of entitlement held by one person – i.e. the extent to which a person can *defend* against outsiders.

However, for our purposes, the allocation of positive use between Gray and X *is* important. There is no difficulty in expressing this in Hohfeldian terms. In the case of our third shrimp salad example (shrimp salads growing wild on bushes), we would say that Gray and X each has a *privilege* to eat the salad, and a *no-right* that the other should not eat it first, which is correlative to the other's *privilege*. This is an important example for our purpose because it describes the situation which occurs where there exists a thing in which no property rights are recognised. In the case of Hohfeld's own first shrimp salad example (where Gray owns the shrimp salad), we would say that Gray has, in addition to his *privilege* to eat the salad, and his *right* that X should not interfere with his eating it (both identified by Hohfeld), a *right* that X should not eat it, the correlative of which is a *duty* on X not to eat it. Strictly speaking, this second *right* of Gray's is subsumed within the first one rather than being additional to it: eating food belonging to someone else is just one way of preventing them from eating it themselves. However, we might want to articulate it as a separate *right* in the hands of Gray if we wanted to have a law whereby X is allowed to interfere with Gray's eating of the salad *by eating it himself first* but not by any other means. We might perhaps want such a law if shrimp salads were scarce and valuable resources (like water in a desert) which the state chose to designate as things that every person has a *privilege* to consume to satisfy their own personal hunger or thirst, plus a *duty* not to despoil.

2.1.4.2.   Privileges and no-rights, and powers and liabilities

The distinction between *right* and *privilege* is therefore a useful tool for property lawyers. Another useful distinction is between *power* and *privilege*. Hohfeld does provide a free-standing explanation of what he means by a 'power'. He defines it as an ability to bring about a change in a given legal relation by one's own volition. An example would be the *power* of A, who is P's agent, to enter on P's behalf into a contract with X. A has the *power* to change P's legal relationship with X by making P contractually bound to X; P has the correlative *liability* to have such contractual duties thrust upon him by A. The *power/privilege* distinction is particularly useful in explaining the property concepts of abandonment and restrictions on alienation.

Abandonment

A, the owner of a gold bracelet (an example we come across in Chapter 11 on acquiring title by possession) has a *power* to change her own legal relation to the bracelet by throwing it away: this extinguishes her interest in the bracelet by the process of abandonment. A component of her ownership interest can therefore be said to be a *power* to abandon it. If she exercises this *power* by throwing the bracelet away, she also and as a consequence changes the relation that the rest of the world has to her in relation to the bracelet. Once the bracelet has been abandoned by A, everyone else in the world acquires a *privilege* as against her to take possession of it for themselves (whereas formerly they had the opposite – a duty owed to A not to take possession from her), plus a *no-right* that anyone else should not do so, plus a *power* to acquire title to it by taking possession of it (although, as we see in Chapter 11, this last element – the power to acquire title by taking possession – is not a new element arising as a result of A's abandonment: it always existed, for reasons explained in Chapter 11).

Effect of restrictions on alienation rights

B, the owner of a watch, has as a constituent of his ownership the *power* to transfer his interest in the watch to X: he has the ability to change the legal relation of both himself and B to the watch, in the sense that by a transfer he can extinguish his own interest and create in X a corresponding interest. It should be noticed that B also has the *privilege* to transfer his interest in the watch to X, in the sense that everyone else in the world has *no-right* that he should not do so.

In both this and the previous example, we describe what the owner can do (abandon the bracelet or transfer the watch) as both a *power* and a *privilege*. Does this mean that these are simply different ways of saying the same thing? The answer is no: an important point for property lawyers is that the two do not necessarily co-exist. This enables us to understand what happens when a restriction is imposed on the inherent 'right' to alienate a property interest. As we noted in Chapter 1, most private property interests are alienable – in fact alienability is such a common feature of private property interests that it is tempting (but wrong, as we see in Chapter 5) to regard it as a necessary criterion for a private property interest. The holder of an alienable property interest can, however, contract *not* to alienate it. If she does so, she loses the *privilege* of alienating the interest as against the person entitled to enforce the contract (in the sense that that person now has the *right* that she should not alienate, and she owes a *duty* to that person not to alienate). Nevertheless, she retains the *power* to do so (in the sense that, if she nevertheless goes ahead and alienates, she will succeed in extinguishing her own interest in the thing and vesting a corresponding interest in the transferee).

This is illustrated by contractual restrictions on a tenant's right to transfer the lease. Suppose L, the owner of a flat, wants to grant a ten-year lease of the flat to T, at a rent of £10,000 per year. The interest that T would acquire in the flat – a ten-year lease – is a property interest and it is inherently alienable. In other words, T would have the *privilege* of transferring it to anyone she wants at any time (no one would have a right that she should not) and she would also have the *power* to do so (she would have the ability, by entering into a deed of transfer, to extinguish her own interest in the flat and vest a corresponding interest in any transferee). However, L will probably not be very happy with that state of affairs. He is willing to give up possession of the flat to T for ten years because (having taken up references etc.) he is reasonably confident that she will pay the rent promptly and not wreck the flat. But he does not want to run the risk that she will transfer it to someone less trustworthy. So, in practice, L may well insist on making it a term of the lease (i.e. L and T will make a binding agreement, as part of the lease agreement) that T will not transfer the lease to anyone without first obtaining L's consent. The effect of this is to remove T's *privilege* to transfer as against L (L now has a *right* that T should not transfer the lease, and T has the correlative *duty* to L not to transfer). However, it has not affected her *power* to do so (because section 52 of the Law of Property Act 1925 says that a deed of transfer of a legal interest in land *will* operate to transfer that interest). If, therefore, notwithstanding this term in the lease, T goes ahead and enters into a deed of transfer with X, the transfer will be effective to pass the lease to X: X will now hold the lease and T will no longer do so. However, T's *duty* not to transfer the lease will have been broken. One of the remedies that a landlord has if a duty imposed on a tenant is broken is to cancel the lease (by the process of forfeiture), and this can be done whether the lease is still held by the tenant who breached the duty or now held by an assignee. The effect of the unauthorised transfer to X will therefore be to give L the *power* to extinguish the lease by forfeiture (i.e. L will have the ability to alter X's relation to the flat by extinguishing the lease interest in the flat now held by X, and also the ability to alter his, L's, own legal relation to the flat by, in effect, taking back that interest).

2.1.4.3.   Powers and liabilities, immunities and disabilities

The nature and significance of this final pair of correlatives appears from an analysis of a fairly common property right – the power of sale held by a non-owner.

A non-owner's power of sale is an exception to the *nemo dat* rule (considered in Chapter 10), which is the basic property principle that, in general, and for obvious reasons, I cannot transfer to you a property interest I do not have. So, if I was now to enter into a deed of transfer with you whereby I purport to transfer to you ownership of Buckingham Palace, the transfer deed will have no effect – you will not thereby acquire ownership of Buckingham Palace. One of the rights, privileges, powers etc. that the Queen has as owner of Buckingham Palace is the *privilege* and *power* to sell it to you, and also an *immunity* from having her ownership divested by anyone else: everyone else has the correlative *disability* (the opposite of a *power*) to alter her legal relationships in respect of Buckingham Palace. As a non-owner I therefore have no *power* to transfer, *unless I acquire the power from some other source* – in which case the Queen as owner of Buckingham Palace will correspondingly lose her *immunity* and acquire instead a *liability* to have her ownership divested by me. I might acquire that power from the Queen: she might have given it to me by power of attorney. Alternatively, I might acquire the power by statute. There are several statutory provisions giving a person power to transfer to a transferee a property interest that the power-holder does not himself have. One example is the power of sale given by section 101 of the Law of Property Act 1925 to a mortgagee, such as a building society, which has taken a mortgage over your house to secure repayment of money it lent you. When you mortgage your house to a building society what happens in legal terms is that you give the building society a property interest (called a mortgage) in the house. You continue to be owner of the house, but the mortgage gives the building society various limited rights/privileges/powers over the house (not as extensive as those of a full owner) which the mortgagee may exercise if you default on repayments of the loan. One of these is a *power* to extinguish both your ownership interest in the house and its own mortgage interest in the house, and to vest the entire ownership in someone else instead. In Hohfeld's terms, by mortgaging your house to the building society you lose your *immunity* from having your ownership divested by someone else. The mortgagee building society has the *power* to sell full ownership of the house to a purchaser, even though it never had full ownership itself. So, if the Queen was to mortgage Buckingham Palace to me to secure repayment of money I had lent her, she would, initially at least, retain ownership of it but would acquire a *liability* to have her ownership divested by me. This of course would have an effect on the value of her interest: we look more closely at this aspect of this example in Notes and Questions 2.1 below.

2.1.5.   Hohfeldian analysis of dynamic property relationships

One of the advantages of using Hohfeld's rights analysis is that it can help to chart the changes that take place in the legal relations between parties at different stages in a dynamic property relationship. We can see how this works by looking at what happens when an option to purchase is first granted and then exercised.

2.1.5.1.   Stage 1: Before the grant of the option

Suppose you own development land worth £2 m. At that point, as we have seen, in Hohfeld's terms you have both a *privilege* and a *power* to sell your ownership.

2.1.5.2.   Stage 2: Grant of the option

You then grant me an option to purchase ownership of the site at any time within the next five years for £2 m. It is tempting to think of this as a simple grant by you to me of a right (but not a duty) to buy the development site for £2 m. But, as Hohfeld points out, something more complex is going on. As soon as you grant me the option, you have lost your *privilege*, as against me, to sell ownership to anyone else. In other words, your *privilege* as against me has been converted into its opposite, a *duty* to me not to sell to anyone else, plus a *liability* that you may be put under a *duty* to sell to me. I have therefore acquired a *right* that you should not sell to anyone else (the correlative of your loss of *privilege* as against me to sell to whoever you want) and a *power* to put you under a *duty* to sell ownership to me for £2 m.

But, just as important, consider what has *not* happened at this stage: I have not yet acquired a *right* that you will sell ownership to me for £2 m, and you have not yet lost your *power* to sell ownership to whoever you want. Your situation is therefore analogous to that of the tenant in the earlier example who contracted with her landlord not to assign her lease. If you do exercise that power by entering into a deed of transfer transferring ownership to P for £3 m (because the value of the site has gone up), P will acquire ownership. The question will then arise whether the amalgam of *right* and *power* that I had against you (which together make up my interest, the option to purchase) is also enforceable against P. As we saw earlier in this chapter, the answer to this will depend on whether the legal system decides to classify an option to purchase as a property interest in the thing over which the option is created (in which case it will, in appropriate circumstances, be enforceable against P) or as a merely personal interest enforceable only against the grantor personally. If it is enforceable against P, that means, in Hohfeldian terms, that P acquires ownership but with a *liability* that I might exercise my *power* to put him under a *duty* to sell ownership to me for £2 m (giving him a loss of £1 m, which he must try to recover from you as damages for breach of your contract promise that you would sell him ownership *immune* from any such *liabilities*). If my option is not enforceable against P, I will sue you for breach of your *duty* not to sell to anyone else (consider what damages I would get).

2.1.5.3.   Stage 3: Exercise of the option

Once I exercise the option, you and I acquire binding obligations to each other: you acquire a *duty* to sell me ownership for £2 m, *and* a *right* that I will buy ownership from you for £2m; I acquire the respective correlatives – a *right* that you will sell to me and a *duty* to buy from you, both at that price. The constituents of my interest are different from what they were at Stage 2 and my interest accordingly is given a different name: I no longer have an option to purchase, I now have an estate contract. But notice that you have still not yet lost your *power* to sell to someone else. You still have the ability to transfer ownership to anyone else in the world. If at this stage you do in fact sell ownership to P for £3 m, the question of whether my estate contract is enforceable against him (i.e. whether his ownership is subject to a *duty* to sell ownership on to me for £2m) will again depend on whether the legal system chooses to classify estate contracts as property interests or purely personal interests. (In our jurisdiction, as we see in Chapter 12, options to purchase and estate contracts *are* property interests, but the legal system imposes a further condition before they become enforceable against someone who has *purchased* ownership: they must have been registered in a public register – for reasons which are obvious.)

2.1.6.   Property rights, property interests and ownership

This brings us on to our final introductory point. It will now be apparent that, in many property relationships each party holds a complex of rights, privileges, duties, liabilities etc. in respect of the thing in question. Despite Hohfeld's strictures, each of the constituent rights, privileges, powers and immunities can loosely but conveniently be called a 'property right' in the relevant thing. The whole complex of rights, duties etc. held by each party is a 'property *interest*' in the thing. Property *interests* are, therefore, complexes of rights, duties etc. held by a person in respect of a thing. In Chapter 1 we noted that the number of different ways in which rights, duties etc. in relation to things can be combined to form property interests is strictly limited. In our jurisdiction there is a relatively short list of recognised property interests, ranging from ownership (which is the most extensive) to such lesser interests as mortgages, easements and charges. The list is exhaustive but expandable: it is always open to Parliament to add a new type of property interest at any time, and on occasions the courts will do so too, either overtly or in the guise of 'discovering' that a claimed type of interest was there on the list all along. We look at this process again in Chapter 9.

Extract 2.1   W. N. Hohfeld, 'Fundamental Legal Conceptions as Applied in Judicial Reasoning' (1913) 23 *Yale Law Journal* 16

FUNDAMENTAL JURAL RELATIONS CONTRASTED WITH ONE ANOTHER

One of the greatest hindrances to the clear understanding, the incisive statement, and the true solution of legal problems frequently arises from the express or tacit assumption that all legal relations may be reduced to 'rights' and 'duties', and that these latter categories are therefore adequate for the purpose of analyzing even the most complex legal interests, such as trusts, options, escrows, 'future' interests, corporate interests, etc. Even if the difficulty related merely to inadequacy and ambiguity of terminology, its seriousness would nevertheless be worthy of definite recognition and persistent effort towards improvement; for in any close reasoned problem, whether legal or non-legal, chameleon-hued words are a peril both to clear thought and to lucid expression. As a matter of fact, however, the above-mentioned inadequacy and ambiguity of terms unfortunately reflect, all too often, corresponding paucity and confusion as regards actual legal conceptions. That this is so may appear in some measure from the discussion to follow.

The strictly fundamental legal relations are, after all, *sui generis*; and thus it is that attempts at formal definition are always unsatisfactory, if not altogether useless. Accordingly, the most promising line of procedure seems to consist in exhibiting all of the various relations in a scheme of 'opposites' and 'correlatives', and then proceedings to exemplify their individual scope and application in concrete cases. An effort will be made to pursue this method:

Opposites		Correlatives	
Right	No-right	Right	Duty
Privilege	Duty	Privilege	No-right
Power	Disability	Power	Liability
Immunity	Liability	Immunity	Disability

RIGHTS AND DUTIES

As already intimated, the term 'rights' tends to be used indiscriminately to cover what in a given case may be a privilege, a power, or an immunity, rather than a right in the strictest sense . . .

Recognizing, as we must, the very broad and indiscriminate use of the term 'right', what clue do we find, in ordinary legal discourse towards limiting the word in question to a definite and appropriate meaning? That clue lies in the correlative 'duty', for it is certain that even those who use the word and the conception 'right' in the broadest possible way are accustomed to thinking of 'duty' as the invariable correlative. As said in *Lake Shore and MSR Co. v. Kurtz*, 10 Ind App 60 (1894):

> A duty or a legal obligation is that which one ought or ought not to do. 'Duty' and 'right' are correlative terms. When a right is invaded, a duty is violated.

In other words, if X has a right against Y that he shall stay off the former's land, the correlative (and equivalent) is that Y is under a duty towards X to stay off the place. If, as seems desirable, we should seek a synonym for the term 'right' in this limited and proper meaning, perhaps the word 'claim' would prove the best . . .

PRIVILEGES AND 'NO-RIGHTS'

As indicated in the above scheme of jural relations, a privilege is the opposite of a duty, and the correlative of a 'no-right'. In the example last put, whereas X has a *right* or *claim* that Y, the other man, should stay off the land, he himself has the *privilege* of entering on the land; or, in equivalent words, X does not have a duty to stay off. The privilege of entering is the negation of a duty to stay off. As indicated by this case, some caution is necessary at this point; for, always, when it is said that a given privilege is the mere negation of a *duty*, what is meant, of course, is a duty having a content or tenor precisely *opposite* to that of the privilege in question. Thus, if, for some special reason, X has contracted with Y to go on the former's own land, it is obvious that X has, as regards Y, both the privilege of entering and the *duty of entering*. The privilege is perfectly consistent with this sort of duty, for the latter is of the *same* content or tenor as the privilege; but it still holds good that, as regards Y, X's privilege of entering is the precise negation of a duty to stay off. Similarly, if A has not contracted with B to perform certain work for the latter, A's privilege of *not* doing so is the very negation of a duty of *doing* so. Here again the duty contrasted is of a content or tenor exactly opposite to that of the privilege.

Passing now to the question of 'correlatives', it will be remembered, of course, that a duty is the invariable correlative of that legal relation which is most properly called a right or claim. That being so, if further evidence be needed as to the fundamental and important difference between a right (or claim) and a privilege, surely it is found in the fact that the correlative of the latter relation is a 'no-right', there being no single term available to express the latter conception. Thus, the correlative of X's right that Y shall not enter on the land is Y's duty not to enter; but the correlative of X's privilege of entering himself is manifestly Y's 'no-right' that X shall not enter.

In view of the considerations thus far emphasized, the importance of keeping the conception of a right (or claim) and the conception of a privilege quite distinct from each other seems evident; and, more than that, it is equally clear that there should be a separate term to represent the latter relation. No doubt, as already indicated, it is very common to use the term 'right' indiscriminately, even when the relation designated is really that of privilege; and only too often this identity of terms has involved for the particular speaker or writer a confusion or blurring of ideas. Thus, Professor Holland, in his work on *Jurisprudence*, referring to a different and well-known sort of ambiguity inherent in the Latin '*Ius*', the German '*Recht*', the Italian '*Diritto*', and the French '*Droit*' – terms to express not only 'a right', but also 'Law' in the abstract – very aptly observes:

> If the expression of widely different ideas by one and the same term resulted only in the necessity for ... clumsy paraphrases, or obviously inaccurate paraphrases, no great harm would be done; but unfortunately the identity of terms seems irresistibly to suggest an identity between the ideas expressed by them.

Curiously enough, however, in the very chapter where this appears – the chapter on 'Rights' – the notions of right, privilege, and power seem to be blended, and that too, although the learned author states that 'the correlative of ... legal right is legal duty', and that 'these pairs of terms express ... in each case the same state of facts viewed from opposite sides'. While the whole chapter must be read in order to appreciate the seriousness of this lack of discrimination, a single passage must suffice by way of example:

> If . . . the power of the State will protect him in so carrying out his wishes, and will compel such acts or forbearances on the part of other people as may be necessary in order that his wishes may be so carried out, then he has a 'legal right' so to carry out his wishes.

The first part of this passage suggests privileges, the middle part rights (or claims), and the last part privileges.

Similar difficulties seem to exist in Professor Gray's able and entertaining work on *The Nature and Sources of Law*. In his chapter on 'Legal Rights and Duties' the distinguished author takes the position that a right always has a duty as its correlative; and he seems to define the former relation substantially according to the more limited meaning of 'claim'. Legal privileges, powers, and immunities are *prima facie* ignored, and the impression conveyed that all legal relations can be comprehended under the conceptions 'right' and 'duty'. But, with the greatest hesitation and deference, the suggestion may be ventured that a number of his examples seem to show the inadequacy of such mode of treatment. Thus, e.g. he says:

> The eating of shrimp salad is an interest of mine, and, if I can pay for it, the law will protect that interest, and it is therefore a right of mine to eat shrimp salad which I have paid for, although I know that shrimp salad always gives me the colic.

This passage seems to suggest primarily two classes of relations: first, the party's respective privileges, as against A, B, C, D and others in relation to eating the salad, or, correlatively, the respective 'no-rights' of A, B, C, D and others that the party should not eat the salad; second, the party's respective rights (or claims) as against A, B, C, D and others that they should not interfere with the physical act of eating the salad, or, correlatively, the respective duties of A, B, C, D and others that they should not interfere.

These two groups of relations seem perfectly distinct; and the privileges could, in a given case, exist even though the rights mentioned did not. A, B, C, and D, being the owners of the salad, might say to X: 'Eat the salad, if you can; you have our license to do so, but we don't agree not to interfere with you.' In such a case, the privileges exist, so that, if X succeeds in eating the salad, he has violated no rights of any of the parties . . . But it is equally clear that, if A had succeeded in holding so fast to the dish that X couldn't eat the contents, no right of X would have been violated.

Perhaps the essential character and importance of the distinction can be shown by a slight variation of the facts. Suppose that X, being already the legal owner of the salad, contracts with Y that he (X) will never eat this particular food. With A, B, C, D and others no such contract has been made. One of the relations now existing between X and Y is, as a consequence, fundamentally different from the relation between X and A. As regards Y, X has no privilege of eating the salad; but as regards A or any of the others, X has such a privilege. It is to be observed incidentally that X's right that Y should not eat the food persists even though X's own privilege of doing so has been extinguished.

On grounds already emphasized, it would seem that the line of reasoning pursued by Lord Lindley in the great case of *Quinn* v. *Leathem* [1901] AC 495 [a trade union case, where a union leader threatened industrial action against one of the customers of a butcher, to persuade the customer to stop doing business with the butcher, because the butcher refused to sack all his non-union employees and employ union members instead; the butcher sued the union leader] is deserving of comment:

> The plaintiff [the butcher] had the ordinary *rights* of the British subject. He was at *liberty* to earn his living in his own way, provided he did not violate some special law prohibiting him from so doing, and provided he did not infringe the rights of other people. This *liberty* involved the *liberty* to deal with other persons who were willing to deal with him. *This liberty is a right* recognized by law; its *correlative* is the general *duty* of every one not to prevent the free exercise of this *liberty* except so far as his own liberty of action may justify him in so doing. But a person's *liberty* or *right* to deal with others is nugatory unless they are at liberty to deal with him if they choose to do so. Any interference with their liberty to deal with him affects him.

A 'liberty' considered as a legal relation (or 'right' in the loose and generic sense of that term) must mean, if it have any definite content at all, precisely the same thing as privilege; and certainly that is the fair connotation of the term as used the first three times in the passage quoted. It is equally clear, as already indicated, that such a privilege or liberty to deal with others at will might very conceivably exist without any peculiar concomitant rights against 'third parties' as regards certain kinds of interference. Whether there should be such concomitant rights (or claims) is ultimately a question of justice and policy; and it should be considered, as such, on its merits. The only correlative logically implied by the privileges or liberties in question are the 'no-rights' of 'third parties'. It would therefore be a *non sequitur* to conclude from the mere existence of such liberties that 'third parties' are under a duty not to interfere, etc. Yet, in the middle of the above passage from Lord Lindley's opinion there is a sudden and question-begging shift in the use of terms. First, the 'liberty' in question is transmuted into a 'right'; and then, possibly under the seductive influence of the latter work, it is assumed that the 'correlative' must be 'the general duty of every one not to prevent', etc.

Another interesting and instructive example may be taken from Lord Bowen's oft-quoted opinion in *Mogul Steamship Co.* v. *McGregor* (1889) 23 QBD 59:

> We are presented in this case with an apparent conflict or antinomy between two rights that are equally regarded by the law – the right of the plaintiffs to be protected in the legitimate exercise of their trade, and the right of the defendants to carry on their business as seems best to them, provided they commit no wrong to others.

As the learned judge states, the conflict or antinomy is only apparent; but this fact seems to be obscured by the very indefinite and rapidly shifting meanings with which the term 'right' is used in the above quoted language. Construing the passage as a whole, it seems plain enough that by 'the right of the plaintiffs' in relation to the defendants a legal right or claim in the strict sense must be meant; whereas by 'the right of the defendants' in relation to the plaintiffs a legal privilege must be intended. That being so, the 'two rights' mentioned in the beginning of the passage, being respectively claim and privilege, could not be in conflict with each other. To the extent that the defendants have privileges the plaintiffs have no rights; and, conversely, to the extent that the plaintiffs have rights the defendants have no privileges ('no privilege' equals duty of opposite tenor).

Thus far, it has been assumed that the term 'privilege' is the most appropriate and satisfactory to designate the mere negation of duty. Is there good warrant for this? ... The closest synonym of legal 'privilege' seems to be legal 'liberty' or legal 'freedom'. This is sufficiently indicated by an unusually discriminating and instructive passage in Mr Justice Cave's opinion in *Allen* v. *Flood* [1898] AC 1 at 29:

> The personal rights with which we are most familiar are: 1. Rights of reputation; 2. Rights of bodily safety and freedom; 3. Rights of property; or, in other words, rights relating to mind, body and estate ... In my subsequent remarks the word 'right' will, as far as possible, always be used in the above sense; and it is the more necessary to insist on this as during the argument at your Lordships' bar it was frequently used in a much wider and more indefinite sense. Thus it was said that a man has a perfect right to fire off a gun, when all that was meant, apparently, was that a man has a freedom or liberty to fire off a gun, so long as he does not violate or infringe any one's rights in doing so, which is a very different thing from a right, the violation or disturbance of which can be remedied or prevented by legal process.

While there are numerous other instances of the apt use of the term 'liberty', both in judicial opinions and in conveyancing documents it is by no means so common or definite a word as 'privilege'. The former term is far more likely to be used in the sense of physical or personal freedom (i.e. absence of physical restraint), as distinguished from a legal relation; and very frequently there is the connotation of *general* political liberty, as distinguished from a particular relation between two definite individuals ...

POWERS AND LIABILITIES

As indicated in the preliminary scheme of jural relations, a legal power (as distinguished, of course, from a mental or physical power) is the opposite of legal disability, and the correlative of legal liability. But what is the intrinsic nature of a legal power as such? Is it possible to analyze the conception represented by this constantly employed and very important term of legal discourse? Too close an analysis might seem metaphysical rather than useful; so that what is here presented is intended only as an approximate explanation, sufficient for all purposes.

A change in a given legal relation may result (1) from some superadded fact or group of facts not under the volitional control of a human being (or human beings); or (2) from some superadded fact or group of facts which are under the volitional control of one or more human beings. As regards the second class of cases, the person (or persons) whose volitional control is paramount may be said to have the (legal) power to effect the particular change of legal relations that is involved in the problem.

This second class of cases – powers in the technical sense – must now be further considered. The nearest synonym for any ordinary case seems to be (legal) 'ability' – the latter being obviously the opposite of 'inability', or 'disability'. The term 'right', so frequently and loosely used in the present connection is an unfortunate term for the purpose – a not unusual result being confusion of thought as well as ambiguity of expression. The term 'capacity' is equally unfortunate; for, as we have already seen, when used with discrimination, this word denotes a particular group of operative facts, and not a legal relation of any kind.

Many examples of legal powers may readily be given. Thus, X, the owner of ordinary personal property 'in a tangible object' has the power to extinguish his own legal interest (rights, powers, immunities, etc.) through that totality of operative facts known as abandonment; and – simultaneously and correlatively – to create in other persons privileges and powers relating to the abandoned object – e.g. the power to acquire title to the latter by appropriating it. Similarly, X has the power to transfer his interest to Y – that is, to extinguish his own interest and concomitantly create in Y a new and corresponding interest. So also X has the power to create contractual obligations of various kinds. Agency cases are likewise instructive … The creation of an agency relation involves, *inter alia*, the grant of legal powers to the so-called agent, and the creation of correlative liabilities in the principal. That is to say, one party, P, has the power to create agency powers in another party, A – for example, the power to convey P's property, the power to impose (so-called) contractual obligations on P, the power to discharge a debt owing to P, the power to 'receive' title to property so that it shall vest in P, and so forth …

Essentially similar to the powers of agents are powers of appointment in relation to property interests. So, too, the powers of public officers are, intrinsically considered, comparable to those of agents – for example, the power of a sheriff to sell property under a writ of execution. The power of a donor, in a gift *causa mortis*, to revoke the gift and divest the title of the donee is another clear example of the legal quantities now being considered; also a pledgee's statutory power of sale.

As regards all the 'legal powers' thus far considered, possibly some caution is necessary. If, for example, we consider the ordinary property owner's power of alienation, it is necessary to distinguish carefully between the legal power, the physical power to do the things necessary for the 'exercise' of the legal power, and, finally, the privilege of doing these things – that is, if such privilege does really exist. It may or may not. Thus, if X, a landowner, has contracted with Y that the former will not alienate to Z, the acts of X necessary to exercise the power of alienating to Z are privileged as between X and every party other than Y; but, obviously, as between X and Y, the former has no privilege of doing the necessary acts; or conversely, he is under a duty to Y not to do what is necessary to exercise the power.

In view of what has already been said, very little may suffice concerning a liability as such. The latter, as we have seen, is the correlative of power, and the opposite of immunity (or exemption). While no doubt the term 'liability' is often loosely used as a synonym for 'duty', or 'obligation', it is believed, from an extensive survey of judicial precedents, that the connotation already adopted as most appropriate to the word in question is fully justified ... Perhaps the nearest synonym of 'liability' is 'subjection' or 'responsibility'. As regards the latter word, a passage from Mr Justice Day's opinion in *McElfresh* v. *Kirkendall*, 36 Iowa 224, 226 (1873) is interesting:

> The words 'debt' and 'liability' are not synonymous, and they are not commonly so understood. As applied to the pecuniary relations of the parties, liability is a term of broader significance than debt ... Liability is responsibility.

...

IMMUNITIES AND DISABILITIES

As already brought out, immunity is the correlative of disability ('no-power'), and the opposite, or negation, of liability. Perhaps it will also be plain, from the preliminary outline and from the discussion down to this point, that a power bears the same general contrast to an immunity that a right does to a privilege. A right is one's affirmative claim against another, and a privilege is one's freedom from the right or claim of another. Similarly, a power is one's affirmative 'control' over a given legal relation as against another; whereas an immunity is one's freedom from the legal power or 'control' of another as regards some legal relation.

A few examples may serve to make this clear. X, a landowner, has, as we have seen, power to alienate to Y or to any other ordinary party. On the other hand, X has also various immunities as against Y, and all other ordinary parties ... For Y is under a disability (i.e. he has no power) so far as shifting the legal interest either to himself or to a third party is concerned; and what is true of Y applies similarly to everyone else who has not by virtue of special operative facts acquired a power to alienate X's property. If, indeed, a sheriff has been duly empowered by a writ of execution to sell X's interest, that is a very different matter: correlative to such sheriff's power would be the liability of X – the very opposite of immunity (or exemption). It is elementary, too, that, as against the sheriff, X might be immune or exempt in relation to certain parcels of property, and be liable as to others. Similarly, if an agent has been duly appointed by X to sell a given piece of property, then, as to the latter, X has, in relation to such agent, a liability rather than an immunity.

... [T]he word 'right' is overworked in the field of immunities as elsewhere ... [T]he best synonym is, of course, the term 'exemption'. It is instructive to note, also, that the word 'impunity' has the same connotation ...

In the latter part of the preceding discussion, eight conceptions of the law have been analyzed and compared in some detail, the purpose having been to exhibit not only their intrinsic meaning and scope, but also their relations to one another and the methods by which they are applied, in judicial reasoning, to the solution of concrete problems of litigation. Before concluding this branch of the discussion a general suggestion may be ventured as to the great practical importance of a clear appreciation of the distinctions and discriminations set forth. If a homely metaphor be permitted, these eight conceptions – rights and duties, privileges and no-rights, powers and liabilities, immunities and disabilities – seem to be what may be called 'the lowest common denominators of the law'. Ten fractions (1/3, 2/5 etc.) may, *superficially*, seem so different from one another as to defy comparison. If, however, they are expressed in terms of their lowest common denominators (5/15, 6/15, etc.), comparison becomes easy, and fundamental similarity may be discovered. The same thing is of course true as regards the lowest generic conceptions to which any and all 'legal quantities' may be reduced.

Notes and Questions 2.1

1   One of the advantages of analysing property relationships in Hohfeld's terms is that it makes it easier to ascertain the value of the constituent elements of the relationship. Consider again the mortgagee's power of sale explained in section 2.1.4.3 above. Suppose the Queen, as owner of Buckingham Palace, mortgages it to me to secure repayment of £10 m I have lent her, at a time when ownership of Buckingham Palace is worth £12 m. The effect of this is that she now holds the ownership interest in Buckingham Palace, but I hold a mortgage interest in it as well, and this gives me (among other things) a power of sale, which includes a *power* to divest her of her ownership in Buckingham Palace. The effect of mortgaging her ownership is therefore to give her a correlative *liability* to have her ownership interest divested if she does not repay me the £10 m on time (providing, and intended to provide, an incentive for her to do so). As soon as she mortgages Buckingham Palace to me, the value of her interest in it therefore falls from £12 m to £2 m (consider why). However, my power of sale gives me a power not only to divest her of her interest in Buckingham Palace but also to divest me of *my* interest in it. In other words, by exercising the power, I will vest in the selected purchaser *her* ownership but with an *immunity* from *my* power – which is worth £12 m. If the Queen does not repay my £10 m on time, I will therefore exercise my power of sale in your favour if you pay me £12 m – and I will take out of that enough to repay my £10 m plus my costs in all this, and pass the balance over to the Queen.

2   In Chapter 1 we consider briefly the legal relations we have with others in respect of our own bodies and body parts. Analyse these in Hohfeld's terms.

3   Some publishers of free newspapers currently distribute them by stacking them in stations and inviting people to help themselves. In Hohfeld's terms, what interests do they and you (as a member of the public) have in a newspaper still in the stack? What changes occur when you take a copy for yourself? At what point in the process do you think this change will occur? (On this last point see further Chapter 10.)

4   Why does the distinction between claim-right and privilege matter? Would it be feasible to have a society in which there were no claim-rights but only privileges? What would such a society be like?

5 Does Hohfeld regard owners as having a claim-right to use the thing they own, or only a privilege? If only a privilege, is this consistent with Honoré's conception of the right to use as one of the core incidents of ownership?

2.2. Private property, communal property, state property and no property

2.2.1. Introduction

If we revert for the moment to using 'property rights' as a loose portmanteau term meaning 'property interests', we can say that so far in this chapter we have been looking at property rights held by individuals (or more accurately legal persons, i.e. adult humans or legal constructs such as companies that have a legal personality separate from that of their human representatives). These are private property rights. However, individuals are not the only entities who can hold property rights. In some circumstances, property rights in things can be held by communities, i.e. groups of individuals identified by reference to a particular locality (for example, the residents of Camden) or by reference to membership of a particular class or ethnic or tribal group (for example, the Murray Islanders in *Mabo* v. *Queensland (No. 2)* (1992) 175 CLR 1, discussed in Chapter 4) or by reference to some other general defining characteristic. We can characterise these property rights as communal property rights. Equally possibly, the state may hold all the property rights in a thing, and allocate the use of the thing to particular citizens by administrative rather than property rules. We would characterise this as public or state property.

Classically, political and economic theory seeks to distinguish private, communal and state property rights, and to establish that a regime recognising only one of the three to the exclusion of the other two is by some measure or other superior.

There are well-recognised difficulties with such analyses. First, there are definitional inconsistencies. There is no consensus over what constitutes communal property and state property or (a separate issue) where the dividing line between the two falls. There is not even a clear line between private property and state property: is a state ruled by an absolute ruler who governs by the principle that all rights in things vest in him for the benefit of himself (in other words, the law enforces no rights in things other than his rights in things) a state property regime or a private property regime which vests all property rights in one person? Secondly, there are intermediate positions between the three absolutes, and it is arguably more accurate to describe the range of interests as a continuum rather than as three self-contained categories. Finally, regimes that recognise only one of the three to the exclusion of the other two exist only in the realm of fantasy.

In this chapter, we are concerned primarily with establishing the distinctions between no-property, communal property, state property and private property. In Chapter 3, we return to these distinctions when we consider the economic justifications made for the institution of property in general, and the related arguments as to the relative efficiency of these different types of property holding.

2.2.2. Distinguishing no-property, communal property, state property and private property

2.2.2.1. No-property: ownerless things

There are some things in respect of which no one has property rights. In Hohfeldian terms, each of us has a *privilege* to use such things (we are free to use them, and the rest of the world has the correlative no-right to object to us doing so), but none of us has the *right* not to have our use interfered with by others, nor the *duty* to abstain from interfering with anyone else's use. To put it in terms of exclusion, none of us has the right to exclude others from such things, nor do we ourselves have the right not to be excluded from use. For example, we cannot complain if careless or profligate use by others spoils or depletes the supply.

Examples are commoner than one might think. One immediately thinks of natural resources which are either not scarce because abundant in supply and not highly valued (like rats in sewers or leaves fallen from trees in autumn) or not scarce because not exhausted by use (like air and sunlight). However, there are also highly industrialised examples which have been created for commercial purposes but to which, for one reason or another, all of us are given free access. These would include free newspapers, radio signals from commercial radio stations, and access to material downloadable from the Internet.

All of these are characterised by the feature that we each have the privilege to use them but no right to complain if our use of them is interfered with by others. *Hunter* v. *Canary Wharf* [1997] AC 655, discussed in Chapter 6, is a case in which the House of Lords decided that terrestrial television signals come within this category. It was held that, although everyone has a *privilege* to receive them, no one has a *right* to do so. Consequently, residents in the Isle of Dogs were held not to be entitled to complain when Canary Wharf Ltd built Canary Wharf Tower which, because of its size and construction, interfered with their television reception by preventing television signals reaching buildings which fell within its 'electro-magnetic shadow'.

It will be apparent from some of the materials discussed in this chapter that these no-property things are sometimes referred to as open access communal property, but for present purposes that term can more usefully be reserved for distinguishing the next category.

2.2.2.2. Open access communal property

Distinction between open access and limited access communal property

The defining characteristic of communal property is that every member of the community has the right not to be excluded from the resource. This is what distinguishes communal property from no-property. An individual who is a member of the community therefore has not only a privilege to use the thing, but also a right not to be excluded from it, and consequently everyone else in the world has a correlative duty not to interfere with their access to it. Communal property may be either open access (everyone in the world is a member of the community), or closed or limited access (membership of the community is limited to those who share a common characteristic such as membership of a club or tribe or residence in a particular locality).

Distinction between open access communal property and no property

Economists tend to regard open access communal property either as the same as no-property or as the same as public property, but in important respects it is distinct from both. It is the right of each member of the community not to be excluded that distinguishes open access communal property from no-property. There are many examples of facilities which are available for public use and to which individual members of the public have a *right* of access, which they would not have if the facilities were, like Internet access, genuinely no-property. We can give as examples of these the right to use public parks and walk along the pavements of public roads. Again, the House of Lords decision in *Hunter* v. *Canary Wharf* [1997] AC 655 points up the distinction. If the claimants had had a right rather than a privilege to receive television signals (i.e. if television reception was open access communal property rather than no-property) they would have had a right not to be subjected to interference with their television reception and they would have succeeded in their claim against the builders of Canary Wharf Tower.

Distinction between open access communal property and state property

Open access communal property differs from state property in two ways. First, in the case of open access communal property, the facility is not necessarily provided by or owned by the state, or indeed by any other public body. So, for example, a public right of way (which is open access communal property) may lie over private land just as it may over the pavement of a road provided by the highways authority. *Hunter* v. *Canary Wharf* is instructive here as well. It would have been open to the House of Lords to find that the residents of the Isle of Dogs had a right not to have their television reception obstructed (that television reception was open access communal property rather than no-property) even if television signals in this country were provided solely by private bodies. The fact that every member of the public is free to use a thing and has a right not to be excluded from it does not make the thing (or the right) into state property.

The second distinction lies in the nature of the relationship between the state and the member of the public in respect of the facility provided by the state. If the user has the right not to be excluded from use by the state (i.e. the state cannot prohibit the use by that individual without changing the law) then we can usefully categorise this as open access communal property rather than as state property. If, on the other hand, the state provides the facility and merely licenses users to use it by permission revocable by administrative action, then we can call this state property.

Adopting this last distinction, library books in public libraries would be categorised as state property, whereas public highways would be open access communal property.

Distinction between allocation and provision of resources

Note that, in two important respects, open access communal property does not provide a guarantee of use for every member of the community. First, the question of *allocation* of available resources – whether everyone in the world should be entitled to use them (open access communal property), or merely be free to use them (no-property) or whether use should be restricted to a limited class (limited access communal property) – is quite distinct from the question of whether anyone should be made responsible for ensuring that the resources are available in the first place. Consequently, a right of every member of the public to unimpeded use of a public park, or the pavement of a public road (the privilege to use and the right not to be excluded), does not connote a correlative duty on the owner of the site to provide the park or pavement in the first place, or to continue to provide existing ones (any more than a right for Isle of Dogs inhabitants to be free from interference by Canary Wharf Tower with their reception of television signals would have imposed a duty on the BBC or anyone else to transmit signals in their direction). There may of course be other reasons why the provider of the facility is not entitled to withdraw or discontinue it. The provision of public parks by local authorities is regulated by statutes which give them no power to divert the land to other uses except in specified circumstances and by following prescribed procedures, but this does not mean that the right of members of the public to use public parks puts local authorities under a duty to provide them. Similarly, private landowners over whose land public rights of way are exercisable have a duty not to obstruct the way, but no duty to maintain it or otherwise ensure that it is available for use.

Secondly, your privilege to use, and your right not to be excluded from, open access property are subject to the like privilege and right of everyone else. In other words, what you have is not an exclusive right to use but a right to use *in common* with everyone else. You may no more interfere with their right than they may with yours. This robs you of any right to complain if someone else is already sitting on the bench in the park where you wanted to sit, or standing on the bit of pavement you wanted to stand on.

Regulation of communal property

This last point reveals an important feature of most types of communal property, whether open access or limited access. Most real-life examples of communal property involve rights to make a *particular* use of a resource, rather than a right to do whatever the users want with the resource, and they tend also to be highly regulated. Sometimes regulation is by formal legal rules (which, for example, tell you quite explicitly what you can and cannot do in public parks or on public rights of way over private farmland) but it may also be by tacitly accepted conventions about behaviour, establishing, for example, that the first person to get to the bench may sit there for as long as she wants.

2.2.2.3. Limited access communal property

Limited access communal property (sometimes referred to as restricted access or closed access communal property) differs from open access communal property in that membership of the community is restricted to a specific class. Each member of the community accordingly has not only a *privilege* to use the resource (everyone else in the world, whether a member of the community or not, has *no-right* to object), and a *right* not to be excluded (giving everyone else a duty not to interfere with her access): she also has a *right* to exclude all non-members of the community.

Distinction between communal property and co-ownership

Limited access communal property is not the same as private co-ownership. Private co-owners are each individually identifiable, and each is entitled to an identifiable share in the resource, even if the share is not yet choate or severable. Members of a family, or a group of friends, or business associates, or members of a club, can hold property as private co-owners. If they do, each individual has a transmissible property interest, i.e. a *power* to assign their share to anyone else, although in practice they may contract with each other not to exercise the power (consider why). Members of a community, on the other hand, are identified by reference to a defining characteristic, and no individual member has a transmissible interest. If the residents of Lambeth have a right to play games on my field (as the inhabitants of Washington were held to have in the playing fields owned by the council in *R. (Beresford)* v. *Sunderland City Council* [2004] 1 AC 889) each resident has a right not to be excluded from the field, a privilege to use the field himself and a right to insist that no non-resident uses it, but he has that interest only because and for so long as he has the defining characteristic of residing in Lambeth. Consequently, he has no power to transfer his interest. If he tries to sell it to his aunt who lives in Wandsworth, the aunt will get nothing because she lacks the necessary characteristic of living in Lambeth; if on the other hand he tries to sell it to a fellow resident of Lambeth, he has nothing to give that the fellow resident does not already have.

However, although this distinction is clear in principle, in practice there are borderline institutions which do not fit easily into either category. We have already said that members of a club can be seen as private co-owners, each of whom has *power* to transmit her share in the club's assets to outsiders but has contracted out of her *privilege* to do so *vis-à-vis* the other members, and indeed this is the conventionally accepted legal analysis as we see in Chapter 16. However, there are difficulties with this analysis, and arguably it is more accurate to describe the club members as communal owners of the club's assets, with each individual member's interest in the assets arising on and by virtue of their acquisition of the defining characteristic of membership, and ceasing automatically when they lose that characteristic (by resigning or dying). Such an interest would by its nature be intransmissible. We look at this particular problem more fully in Chapter 16.

Again, there are types of communal property where each individual user's entitlement *is* tradable, either fully or to a limited extent. Glenn Stevenson records this as one of many variations of communal use currently in use in Swiss alpine grazing (Stevenson, *Common Property Economics*), and as we see in Chapter 5 communal property interests of this type (usually referred to as rights of common) exist in this country as well. Indeed, the recent House of Lords decision in *Bettison* v. *Langton* [2001] UKHL 24, discussed in Chapter 5, has had the effect of converting nearly all communal grazing rights in this country into fully tradable rights (i.e. rights that can be sold separately from the adjoining farms they were originally intended to benefit). Nevertheless, such rights still involve communal resource use and so for most purposes it makes sense to put them in the limited access communal property category rather than the private property category.

Particular use rights rather than general use rights

Like open access communal property, limited access communal property tends to involve particular use rights rather than general use rights (leaving each member of the community free to make a specific use of the resource in common with all the others, rather than allowing each to do exactly as he wishes with it). Also, and again like open access communal property, it tends to be highly regulated, usually, although not necessarily, by self-regulation rather than by regulation by an outside body.

2.2.2.4.   State property

Property interests in things may be vested in the state rather than in individuals or communities. When ownership of a particular resource is vested in the state (or any branch of the state, such as a local authority) individuals may nevertheless be allocated use rights of various types, or even limited management or control rights. However, these rights would not be property rights, in the sense that they would be personal to the holders and not transmissible. So, for example, in the Soviet Union a family which was allocated an apartment might have been granted a tenancy of the apartment that was lifelong and inheritable, but the management and control rights would be held by various government departments, and no one would be able to sell the apartment or grant leases of it. We would therefore say that the apartment was state-owned rather than privately owned. Similarly, state-owned shops in the Soviet Union might have individuals who acted as managers, but they would be managing on behalf of the relevant government departments (for fuller details of both examples, see Michael Heller, 'The Tragedy of the Anticommons', referred to again in the next section).

2.2.2.5.   Anticommons property

If open access communal property denotes a resource which everyone has a privilege to use and a right not to be excluded from, but no right to exclude others from, its mirror image would be a resource which everyone has a right to exclude all others from, but no right or privilege to use for themselves. At first sight, it is difficult to think of a real-life example of such a form of property – usually called anticommons property, as the antithesis of communal property. Its theoretical existence seems to have been first suggested by Frank Michelman in 1982 (in 'Ethics, Economics and the Law of Property', p. 3). However, the usefulness of the concept did not become apparent until it was reformulated by Michael Heller a few years later. In a seminal article, 'The Tragedy of the Anticommons', Heller used the term 'anticommons' to describe a situation in which the ownership rights to a resource are distributed between multiple owners in such a way that each has the right to prevent use by the others, and hence none has the privilege to use for himself (except by consent of all the others, which they are freely entitled to withhold). A simple example (given by Lee Anne Fennell in 'Common Interest Tragedies', discussing Heller's analysis) would be a garden communally owned by ten adjoining houseowners, each of whom has put a separate lock on the gate leading into the garden, so that each houseowner has effectively excluded all the others, but cannot herself use the garden without first persuading all the other houseowners to unlock their locks. However, Heller produced his reformulation in an attempt to explain a phenomenon he (and others) had noted in post-Soviet Moscow. After state ownership of shops was relinquished, shops in Moscow nevertheless remained virtually empty of consumer goods, while at the same time flimsy privately owned metal kiosks, crammed with goods, mushroomed on the pavements outside. Why did the kiosk operators not move into the shops, either by taking leases or by coming to some other arrangement with the shop-owners to operate from there? His diagnosis of the problem was that, because property rights in shops were distributed among a number of different bodies in an attempt to placate or compensate socialist-era stakeholders, shops had become anticommons property: no single individual was given full ownership rights. Instead:

> [i]n a typical Moscow storefront [shop] one owner may be endowed initially with the right to sell, another to receive sale revenue, and still others to lease, receive lease revenue, occupy, and determine use. Each owner can block the others from using the space as a storefront. No one can set up shop without collecting the consent of all of the other owners. (Heller, 'The Tragedy of the Anticommons', p. 623).

This made it prohibitively difficult for the kiosk operators to come to any arrangement with the shop-owners, whereas it was relatively easy for them to operate illegally from the pavement: all they had to do was bribe the local officials responsible for keeping the pavements free from obstruction and pay protection money to the Mafia. As one kiosk operator explained to Heller:

You have to pay bribes to get permission to put your kiosk up on a promising site. And, even after things are all set up, you have to pay bribes to make sure they don't close you down. The mafia is the easiest of all to deal with. They don't charge too much, they tell you exactly what they want up front, and when an agreement is made, they live up to it. They don't come back asking for more ... The hardest part was finding out who was the right [official] to bribe. (Heller, 'The Tragedy of the Anticommons', p. 643)

Unsurprisingly, Heller's conclusion is that anticommons property is inefficient because it tends to cause underuse of the resource, a conclusion that is even more apparent from Fennell's locked garden example. While this articulation of the principle is new, the principle itself is not, and we come across it again in Chapter 8 when we look at the highly complex systems the law has evolved to regulate fragmentation of ownership rights between multiple owners.

2.3.   Economic analysis of property rights

2.3.1.   What economic analysis seeks to achieve

Economics provides a useful tool for the analysis of property rights. As we see later, it has limitations: anyone viewing property solely from an economics perspective would be in danger of forming a distorted view of how societies do and should function. One of the principal criticisms made of economic analysis is that it does not always recognise its own limitations. In general, it aspires to be positive rather than normative, i.e. to describe what *does* happen in the world and predict the consequences of given actions, rather than to prescribe what *ought* to happen and what ought to be done. However, the line between prediction and prescription is easily crossed, and it is easy to confuse (consciously or unconsciously) the *is* with the *ought*, and to present what are essentially normative statements in the guise of statements of inevitable consequences.

Economics was famously defined by Lionel Robbins in 1935 as 'the science which studies human behaviour as a relationship between ends and scarce means which have alternative uses' (*An Essay on the Nature and Significance of Economic Science*). As applied to property rights, the key factors in economics are scarcity of resources and individual choice. As Anderson and McChesney point out (*Property Rights: Co-operation, Conflict and Law*, p. 2), economics emphasises that 'life is a series of choices among alternatives, choices because we face limits. There is only so much time, so much money, so much land, so much oil, and so forth.'

In their introductory explanation of the economic perspective on property rights, Anderson and McChesney start with the basic principle that it is the individual (by which they mean the natural person) which forms the basic unit of analysis. They see economic analysis as being concerned with individual preferences and individual actions rather than with the preferences and actions of abstract entities such as corporations, or communities, societies or governments. Analysis of the preferences and actions of those abstract entities can properly be done only by looking at the preferences and actions of their constituent individuals: 'Not being animate entities, none can act except through the decisions of individuals capable of choosing ... [C]ollective action can only be a manifestation of individual preferences and actions shaped by constraints and conditioned by rules for aggregating individual preferences and actions' (Anderson and McChesney, *Property Rights: Co-operation, Conflict and Law*, p. 3)

In the extract below, Anderson and McChesney give four postulates which they see as guiding the economic analysis of property rights, taking the individual as the basic unit of analysis.

Extract 2.2   T. L. Anderson and F. S. McChesney, *Property Rights: Co-operation, Conflict and Law* (Princeton University Press, Princeton, 2003)

POSTULATE 1: INDIVIDUALS CHOOSE UNDER CONDITIONS OF SCARCITY; NO ONE HAS AS MUCH OF THE WORLD'S RICHES AS HE WOULD LIKE

As already noted, economics begins with the fact that choices are made subject to constraints. Because resources are limited, we must choose which of our unlimited desires to satisfy, meaning we must make tradeoffs. In a world of scarcity, one use of an asset precludes another and, thereby, generates an opportunity cost ... The cost of breathing clean air, building houses, or irrigating crops is measured in terms of the alternative uses that are foregone. Land occupied by a house cannot provide grizzly bear habitat. Water used for irrigation cannot provide a free-flowing stream in which fish can spawn.

POSTULATE 2: INDIVIDUALS ACT RATIONALLY TO PURSUE THEIR SELF-INTEREST BY CONTINUALLY ADJUSTING TO THE INCREMENTAL (MARGINAL) BENEFITS AND INCREMENTAL (MARGINAL) COSTS OF THEIR ACTIONS

Methodological individualism presumes that individuals are rational. By rational we mean that people have well-defined preferences and act systematically to maximize the amount of those things (tangible or intangible) that satisfy those preferences, subject to the cost of achieving satisfaction. An individual's maximization of his satisfaction does not necessarily imply selfishness. Even a person satisfied with what he had for himself would want more for his family, his friends, the members of his church or club, or others. Human desires (including desires to see others better off) are limitless.

But resources are not limitless. Rational maximization therefore requires individuals to weigh the benefits and costs that their choices entail, asking what additional gains there are from additional amounts of a good or service and what must be sacrificed (foregone) to obtain the gains. This does not mean that individuals always measure perfectly and never make mistakes. In fact, making mistakes bears out the assumption of rationality: information is costly to obtain (scarce), so rational actors will never have perfect information when they make their choices ...

POSTULATE 3: SCARCITY AND RATIONAL BEHAVIOR RESULT IN COMPETITION FOR RESOURCES, AND SOCIETAL RULES GOVERN HOW THIS COMPETITION PROCEEDS

Rational maximization of one's satisfaction in the face of resource scarcity means that individuals will compete to own resources conducive to their personal welfare. People will invest time and effort vying with others to determine who gets how much of the resource, and under what conditions. In the case of movie theater seats on opening night, one must arrive early to take first possession ...

The competition for open access resources is costly because the same time and effort spent competing for resources could be expended in other ways. Less obviously, competition for resources may degenerate into violence ... Whatever the type of cost, rational individuals invest in defining rights up to the point where the incremental benefits of competing for resources equal the cost of doing so.

The fact that competition is costly means that individuals may benefit collectively from defining rules to govern competition for resources, choosing those rules that lower the overall costs of resource competition. Individuals might collectively agree, for example, that violence or threats of violence will not be recognized as a way to define property rights. As a way to reduce the costs of violence, rules can be agreed upon privately. For example, there is no statute that requires airline passengers to respect the right of the first passenger who puts his suitcase in the overhead bin to use that space during the flight. Such a rule presumably is preferable to a might-makes-rights system whereby the biggest and strongest passenger takes what he wants, regardless of the desires of others.

Where the number of people competing for a resource is small and the group is homogeneous, there is a greater incentive to minimize wasteful competition for property rights by contracting, rather than warring, over property rights ... Privately contrived and enforced rules may not work best in all situations, however. Increasing group size and heterogeneity at some point may produce the Hobbesian jungle, where life is 'nasty, brutish and short'. Externally imposed rules, embodied in explicit laws or ordinances, then may become preferable to private solutions in minimizing conflict over resources ...

POSTULATE 4: GIVEN INDIVIDUAL RATIONALITY AND SELF-INTEREST, A SYSTEM OF WELL-SPECIFIED AND TRANSFERABLE PROPERTY RIGHTS ENCOURAGES POSITIVE-SUM GAMES WITH MUTUAL GAINS FROM TRADE

Competition for the use of scarce resources can result in conflict or co-operation, depending on the system of property rights. If property rights are not well defined and enforced, the incentive to take by threat or violence increases, with the predictable results that resource owners will invest less in developing their property or even keeping it up ... Likewise, if property rights are not transferable, those who might place a higher value on a scarce resource will have little option to negotiate over it, relative to the incentives to take it by theft or resort to government ... On the other hand, if property rights are well defined, enforced, and transferable, owners can trade their rights with others, making all parties better off.

The potential for gains from trade is revealed by many comparative studies that show economies with greater economic freedom – secure and tradable property rights defended by the rule of law – outperform other economies. For example, in economies with higher levels of economic freedom, per capita gross domestic product grew approximately 2.5 per cent, as compared to a 1.5 per cent decline in economies with less economic freedom between 1980 and 1994 ... Keefer and Knack ... report similarly that the absence of a secure rule of law diminishes rates of economic growth. Norton ... not only finds that growth rates are higher in countries with more secure property rights, but that environmental quality is better. As Norton ... puts it, 'the specification of strong aggregate property rights appears to have an important place in improving human well-being'.

Notes and Questions 2.2

Only private property satisfies the criterion of transferability given in Postulate 4: communal property rights and state property cannot be transferred, but they can be as secure and well defined as private property rights. Does this mean that the benefits mentioned in the final paragraph of the extract can be gained only by private property? Is this what the authors mean by Postulate 4? If so, is Postulate 4 normative (i.e. telling us what sort of property regime ought to be adopted) or positive (i.e. analysing the effect of adopting a particular type of property regime)?

2.3.2. Key concepts in the economic analysis of property rights

The basic economic analysis of the emergence of property rights and the allocation of resources utilises three key concepts – externalities, transaction costs and efficiency.

2.3.2.1. Externalities

When I decide to use a resource of mine in a particular way, some of the effects of that decision will almost invariably fall on others rather than on me. If I do not take those effects into account when deciding whether to adopt that use of that resource, we would say that those effects are *external* to my decision. Effects (good or bad) that are external to a decision are called *externalities*. So, for example, the building of the Canary Wharf Tower had the effect of interfering with television reception for the residents of the Isle of Dogs (see *Hunter* v. *Canary Wharf* [1997] AC 655, discussed in Chapter 6). That effect was an externality as far as the builders of the tower were concerned: they did not take it into account because (as they then thought) they did not need to do so because (as they then thought, and the House of Lords subsequently held) they had no liability in law to refrain from interfering with television signals. Externalities can be good as well as bad. If I own a field and decide to graze sheep on it, it may improve the view of neighbour X (who likes sheep and places a higher value on his land because he can watch them), ruin the garden of neighbour Y (because the sheep stray onto her land through gaps in the fence) and disturb the sleep of neighbour Z (whose bedroom is close to the shed where the sheep are herded at night and in the winter). Each of those effects will be externalities of my decision if I do not take them into account when making my decision.

The problem about externalities, as far as economics is concerned, is that they tend to lead to misuse of resources, because the full costs and benefits of the use are not taken into account. The use of the resource may therefore be *inefficient*, in the sense that a different use or use in a different way might yield a higher aggregate value (i.e. the aggregate benefit to all minus the aggregate costs of all would be higher).

The concept of efficiency in this context requires closer consideration. First, however, it is necessary to consider why it is that the ignoring of externalities tends to lead to misuse of resources.

Suppose that grazing sheep on my field gives an annual benefit of £500 to X (the neighbour who likes sheep), but imposes annual costs of £1,000 each on Y (whose garden is ruined by strays) and Z (whose sleep is disturbed by the noise from the shed). By fencing the field and moving and soundproofing the shed I could eliminate that cost to Y and Z without removing the benefit from X. If the annual costs to me of doing so are £1,500 (or anything less than £2,000) then it would be efficient to do so, because it will increase the *aggregate* of the value (benefit minus cost) for the four of us. Economists, however, would not expect me to choose this value-maximising alternative (i.e. carry out the works) because it would make me personally worse off, despite the net gain it would produce in the aggregate.

A change in the example demonstrates how externalities can lead to an inefficient failure to develop resources as well. Suppose my field is covered in grass which I mow regularly but otherwise do not use, and that this use imposes no costs or benefits on X (the neighbour who likes sheep). If I was to graze sheep on the field it would cost me an extra £100 a year (it would cost me that much more to use sheep to keep the grass cut than to use the mower), but it would confer benefits of £500 a year on X. The value-maximisation solution would be to change from mower to sheep, but again I would not be expected to adopt it because the gain is an externality as far as I am concerned.

Note that, in both examples the existence of externalities does not *necessarily* lead to inefficient use: it would be easy to change the figures so that there would be no net aggregate gain if I carried out the work in the first example or changed from mower to sheep in the second. The problem is that, because all the costs and benefits are not borne by the same person, no one will even make the calculation as to net gain.

Why, though, is the situation in which use *is* inefficient not self-adjusting? Specifically, why don't those who are bearing the externalities offer to pay me an appropriate amount to bear them myself? In the first example, it would seem sensible for Y and Z to offer to pay me anything up to £2,000 a year to carry out the works (if it was exactly £2,000 it would cost them as much as they would gain, so there would be no point, and if it was more they would be paying more than they gain) and sensible for me to accept anything over £1,500 to do so. Similarly, in the second example, X ought to be willing to pay me anything up to £1,000 to graze sheep on the field, and I ought to be willing to accept anything over £100.

Why do people in such situations not make such bargains? Why is the situation not self-adjusting? The answer is *transaction costs*.

2.3.2.2. Transaction costs

The problem about transaction costs becomes apparent if we ask ourselves why the residents of the Isle of Dogs did not bargain with Canary Wharf Ltd either to modify the design of the tower or to install super-aerials for each of their houses, so that the tower did not interfere with their television reception. It may be of course that the cost to Canary Wharf Ltd of doing either of these things would have exceeded the aggregate value of television reception to all residents of the Isle of Dogs. However, let us assume that this was not the case (not inconceivable). Assume that, if the tower is built unmodified, it will block all television signals to 100 residences. Assume also that this will decrease the value of each residence by £50,000, and that the problem could be averted either by a modification of the construction of the tower or by providing each residence with a super-aerial. If either of these solutions would cost less than £5 m in all (i.e. £50,000 × 100), then everyone would be better off if Canary Wharf Ltd adopted one of the two solutions, and charged the home owners as a group an amount greater than its cost of doing so but less than £5 m. It is nevertheless highly unlikely that Canary Wharf Ltd and the residents will ever come to an agreement to do this, and it is worth considering why. Essentially, there are three factors likely to prevent an agreement being reached: imperfect information, the costs of acting in concert, and the additional costs imposed by free-riders and holdouts.

Imperfect information

In order for this bargain to be struck, both Canary Wharf Ltd and the residents need to know (a) that a tower constructed to the proposed specifications will prevent television signals reaching the residents, (b) that the problem could be solved by adopting one of the two solutions (modification of the original design or installation of super-aerials in each residence), (c) what the costs will be to each resident if neither is adopted, and (d) what the costs will be to Canary Wharf Ltd if it adopts either. It will be difficult and expensive for the parties to obtain this information, especially if the problem is not a known problem (consider how a state planning system, on the lines described in Chapter 6, might help if the potential of towers to interrupt neighbours' television reception is known in advance).

Costs of collective action

The difficulties and costs of obtaining all this information will be particularly acute for the residents, private individuals with no pre-existing mechanisms for acting in concert. They must first find some way of organising themselves so that they can seek out this information as a group, avoiding wasteful duplication of cost and effort. They must also set up some sort of organisational structure so that they can raise money to pay agents such as engineers, lawyers and administrators etc. (or find and channel such expertise from among themselves) and make decisions and negotiate as a group rather than as a disparate collection of individuals.

Free-riders and holdouts

Even if the residents do succeed in organising themselves, they will risk wasteful or obstructive action from free-riders and holdouts. Take the problem of free-riders first. Assume the most efficient solution to the problem would be for Canary Wharf Ltd to modify the design of the tower at a cost of £3.5 m, and that the residents are willing to pay them £4 m to do so because otherwise the value of their property will fall by a total of £5 m. A free-rider is a resident who refuses to pay her share of the £4 m because she knows that, if the modification goes ahead, she will get the benefit (uninterrupted television signals) whether she has paid her share or not, and she predicts that the modification will go ahead even if she refuses to pay because the other residents will find some other way of raising the shortfall to avoid frustration of the whole scheme. Free-riding operates in other ways too. All residents who do not participate in the information-gathering/organisational activities are free-riding on the efforts of the activists who do, and the resentment caused by this kind of free-riding is likely to discourage collective action in the first place.

The holdout problem is slightly different. The holdout is the resident who knows that a particular action cannot go ahead without his consent, and therefore refuses to give his consent unless he is paid extra for it. Suppose the most efficient solution would be for Canary Wharf Ltd to install super-aerials in each residence, but that this cannot be done unless they are given access to every residence to lay cables. The holdout will be the resident who refuses access unless paid a large fee, because he knows Canary Wharf Ltd (or the other residents) will have to pay the fee to prevent frustration of the whole scheme.

2.3.2.3.   Efficiency

In general terms, when economists talk about efficiency in relation to resources they mean an allocation of resources in which value is maximised. However, it is necessary to look further at what counts as value-maximisation.

Value

In economics, 'value' is an ambiguous term, as we see later when we look at the distinction between 'use value' and 'exchange value'. For present purposes, however, 'value' can be taken to mean how much someone is prepared to pay for something, or, if they have it already, how much they would demand to part with it (not necessarily the same thing). In assessing value for these purposes, economists do not look at the amount that someone can *afford* to pay for something. What matters is how much they would pay if they had the money. Also, it is necessary to bear in mind that value, when used in this sense, can be dramatically different from utility, or happiness in the utilitarian sense. Posner illustrates the difference with the following example:

> Suppose that pituitary extract is in very scarce supply relative to the demand and is therefore very expensive. A poor family has a child who will be a dwarf if he does not get some of the extract, but the family cannot afford the price and could not even if they could borrow against the child's future earnings as a person of normal height; for the present value of those earnings net of consumption is less than the price of the extract. A rich family has a child who will grow to normal height, but the extract will add a few inches more, and his parents decide to buy it for him. In the sense of value used in this book, the pituitary extract is more valuable to the rich than to the poor family, because value is measured by willingness to pay; but the extract would confer greater happiness in the hands of the poor family than in the hands of the rich one.
>
> As this example shows, the term efficiency, when used ... to denote that allocation of resources in which value is maximized, has limitations as an ethical criterion of social decision-making – although perhaps not serious ones, as such examples are very rare. (Posner, *Economic Analysis of Law*, pp. 11–12)

Pareto efficiency

Strictly speaking, value is maximised when the allocation of resources cannot be bettered, in the sense that it would be impossible to transfer or reallocate the resources in such a way as to make anyone better off without also making at least one other individual worse off. This strict notion of efficiency is called Pareto efficiency (after the nineteenth-century Italian economist and social scientist Vilfredo Pareto), sometimes Pareto superiority or optimality. Pareto efficiency is not a very useful concept, in particular when assessing whether a transaction is efficient, because while voluntary transactions can be expected to make all the *parties* to the transaction better off (if not, they would not have entered into it) they nearly always make someone somewhere worse off to some degree (if only by altering the market price of the resource).

Kaldor-Hicks efficiency

For this reason, economists more usually use a modified concept of efficiency, termed Kaldor-Hicks efficiency. A transaction is efficient in the Kaldor-Hicks sense if it makes someone better off, provided that it does not make someone else worse off *by a greater amount*. Any transaction that produces a net increase in value (lumping all affected persons together and balancing their total losses against their total gains) is therefore Kaldor-Hicks efficient. Again, it is important to appreciate that efficiency in this sense has nothing to do with fairness or justice in distribution. A transaction cannot be Kaldor-Hicks efficient unless it leaves the net gainers with a gain that is great enough to compensate the net losers, but no compensation need actually be made. The outcome will remain efficient even if the gainers pocket all the gain and leave the losers worse off. If the transaction in question *did* involve all losers being fully compensated, and still left the gainers with a net gain, it would be Pareto efficient. Because of this, Kaldor-Hicks efficiency is sometimes called potential Pareto efficiency.

For these two reasons, therefore – because value-maximisation is not the same as happiness or utility-maximisation, and because efficiency requires only that there is a net gain in value or wealth, not that the gain is fairly or justly distributed – most people would not use economic efficiency as the sole criterion for judging the efficacy of property rules. It is, however, *a* criterion, and an important one. An inefficient allocation of resources may be justifiable on the basis that it produces socially or morally desirable ends, but it does require justification.

2.4.   Things as thing and things as wealth

2.4.1.   Functions of things

The final point to note in this chapter is that there are different ways in which an asset might be valued by a person. Specifically, it might be valued for its own intrinsic attributes, or it might be valued for the wealth it represents. In other words, at any one time an asset might serve one of two different functions for its holder: it might be held for its own qualities or it might be held as an investment. In the extract that follows, Bernard Rudden puts this distinction as the difference between things as 'thing' and things as 'wealth'. So, an art gallery that owns a painting by Poussin and a tin of floor polish holds both as thing: it values the Poussin as a painting of the sort that it ought and wants to preserve and display, and it values the tin of floor polish as an aid in polishing the gallery floors. Most assets can be either thing or wealth: if a pension fund held the Poussin as an investment it would be wealth rather than thing, as would a tin of floor polish held by a supermarket as part of its stock.

In the article from which the passage below is extracted, Rudden uses this distinction to mount a sophisticated argument that we are not directly concerned with at this point, although we return to it in Chapter 8 where we look at fragmentation of ownership. For present purposes, it is sufficient to note that, broadly, his thesis is that, when things are treated as thing, modern law uses a fairly uncomplicated set of basic concepts such as ownership and possession, whereas when they are treated as wealth, the law uses concepts and techniques developed for, and more usually regarded as reserved for, feudal landholding. These involve, among other things, dividing entitlements among different people in sequential time slices.

We consider this argument later. Here we are interested only in two preliminary points.

2.4.2.   The idea of a fund

The first is the idea of a fund. When assets are held as an investment, the nature and identity of the assets is usually an irrelevance to the people entitled to the benefit of the investment. They can expect to know the value of the assets held on their behalf, but it is not at all necessary that they know what those assets are. More importantly, one of the functions of the person who holds those investments in their behalf will be to monitor the value of the assets and to sell them and replace them with different types of asset as and when this becomes necessary to preserve or enhance the value of the investment. For all sorts of reasons this will often be done without reference to the beneficiaries. A fund therefore characteristically comprises a fluctuating body of assets, with the discretion as to the composition of the fund (whether, for example, it consists of paintings or shares or money in a bank account) being held by the officer holding the fund rather than by the person entitled to the benefit of the fund.

There are two important aspects of this. One is that the assets comprising the fund at any one time are wealth rather than thing, as far as the beneficiary is concerned. The other is that, when assets are held in a fund to function as wealth rather than as thing, the fund itself becomes an asset (albeit an abstract one), and the law regards the person entitled to the benefit of the fund as having an interest in the abstract entity which is the fund rather than in the specific assets which at any point in time comprise the fund. For further analysis of the idea of property in a fund, see Nolan, 'Property in a Fund', which we look at again in Chapter 18 in the context of floating charges.

2.4.3.   Thing versus wealth

The second preliminary point about the thing/wealth distinction is of socio-economic rather than analytical importance. The law often has to resolve conflicts between persons holding different types of property interest in the same thing. Frequently (though not necessarily), one of these will value the thing as thing and the other will value it as wealth. Should greater weight be given to the former interest than to the latter? Suppose you and your partner jointly own the house you both live in and you go bankrupt. The consequence of going bankrupt is that all your assets must, in effect, be handed over to your creditors and distributed rateably between them. This includes your interest in the house but not of course your partner's interest. So from the moment you go bankrupt your partner holds an interest in the house (as we see later, a 50 per cent share in the whole house) and your creditors, in effect, hold another interest (the other 50 per cent share). Your partner holds his interest as thing (a house to live in), whereas your creditors hold their interest as wealth. They are, necessarily, interested only in the wealth their 50 per cent represents (moving in to live in the house with your partner presumably holds no attractions) but they cannot reach that wealth unless the whole house is sold: realistically, you cannot sell half a house. Should the house be sold? If it is sold, your partner will get 50 per cent of the proceeds, but that will probably not fully compensate him for what he has lost, if he did indeed value his interest in the house as thing rather than wealth. Even assuming he is equally happy living on his own rather than with you, he may well value the amenities provided by your joint house that he has to share with you more highly than he would value those provided by a house costing half the price of which he has the sole use. And of course half the net proceeds of sale of a house is not necessarily enough to finance the purchase of another house, even a much smaller one.

On the other hand, if the house is not sold, your creditors are deprived of the only function of your share in the house which is of any value to them – the right to have it converted into its money equivalent. Which interest should prevail? Is the interest of the person who values the thing as thing more important than the interest of the person who values it as wealth? We return to this point in the Notes and Questions after the extract.

2.4.4. Related conceptions

Finally, parallels can be drawn between this distinction between things as thing and things as wealth and other similarly useful but different conceptions.

2.4.4.1. Fungibles and non-fungibles

Roman law draws a distinction between fungibles and non-fungibles which looks superficially the same as the thing/wealth distinction but is in fact different. A thing is fungible if it is not unique, in the sense that, if lost, it could be replaced by a thing that is to all intents and purposes identical. The archetypal fungible is money: if I drop a £1 coin in the street it is a matter of indifference to me whether I pick up that coin or another £1 coin lying next to it. To revert to the picture gallery example, paintings by Poussin are non-fungible and tins of floor polish are fungible. This explains the difference between the fungible/non-fungible distinction and the wealth/thing distinction. The fungible/non-fungible distinction is not concerned with the different ways in which different people might value the same thing: we can classify a thing as fungible or non-fungible without knowing who holds it and the purpose for which they hold it. A particular tin of floor polish does not become non-fungible just because its holder wants to use it now for polishing floors. It remains fungible because the holder would have no reason to object if you took the tin out of his hand while he was polishing and gave him another tin of the same size and brand instead. The fungible/non-fungible distinction therefore does not enable us to mark the distinctions between the ways different people might value the same thing, which we can mark by using the wealth/thing distinction.

The fungible/non-fungible distinction is complicated by the fact that there are some things that are fungible in some circumstances and non-fungible in other circumstances. For example, a tangible thing that represents value, such as cash or a postage stamp, is fungible when used as currency but can become non-fungible if, for example, a physical abnormality or rarity makes the tangible thing acquire a value in its own right which is greater than its 'face' value. But, even if this does happen, it still does not tell us whether the rare coin or stamp is 'thing' or 'wealth'. This will depend on the purpose for which it is held. A pension fund that holds rare stamps as an investment values them as wealth, whereas a stamp collector (assuming she is of the kind that regards the monetary value of her collection as incidental) values them as thing.

2.4.4.2.   'Use value' and 'exchange value'

Some economists draw a distinction between 'use value' and 'exchange value' which, again, bears some resemblance to the thing/wealth distinction. The use value of a thing depends on the uses to which the thing can be put (or, as it is sometimes put, the human needs or desires it fulfils), whereas its exchange value depends on the value of the thing (usually but not necessarily money) for which it can be exchanged. The point about this distinction is that the use value of a thing is often different from its exchange value. Consumer goods that are not in short supply when new (for example, washing machines, cars and books), and which therefore have a low secondhand value, provide an obvious example. You may buy a new washing machine for £500, even though you know that you will never be able to sell it for more than £300 (the current secondhand price for washing machines of that type in good condition) because its use value for you is higher than its exchange value. For some purposes, it may be necessary to distinguish subjective and exchange value. The value to you of £300 very much depends on its marginal utility to you. If after buying the washing machine you run out of money and have no other means of paying the rent, you may well sell the washing machine for £300: its use value to you remains the same, and so does its objective exchange value (£300), but its exchange value *to you* is now higher than its use value. Alternatively, if you unexpectedly win the lottery, you might decide to buy a new and better washing machine and give the old one to a friend: its exchange value to you is now nil, even though its objective exchange value remains £300.

Historically, this discrepancy between use value and exchange value has been significant in varying schools of economic thought. The distinction between use value and exchange value and the analysis of the relationship between exchange value and labour is fundamental to Karl Marx's argument in *On Capital* and, in a rather different way, to Adam Smith's *Enquiry into the Nature and Causes of the Wealth of Nations* (1776). Adam Smith used the classic water/diamond paradox (water has great use value but no exchange value whereas diamonds have little use value but high exchange value) as an illustration of the way in which, as he argued, labour is the 'real measure' of exchange value:

Every man is rich or poor according to the degree in which he can afford to enjoy the necessaries, conveniencies, and amusements of human life. But after the division of labour has once thoroughly taken place, it is but a very small part of these with which a man's own labour can supply him. The far greater part of them he must derive from the labour of other people, and he must be rich or poor according to the quantity of that labour which he can command, or which he can afford to purchase. The value of any commodity, therefore, to the person who possesses it, and who means not to use or consume it himself, but to exchange it for other commodities, is equal to the quantity of labour which it enables him to purchase or command.

On the other hand, John Law, the Scottish economist and banker who appears to have been the first to articulate the water/diamond paradox (in 1705, in 'Considerations sur le numeraire et le commerce', written in France after he was exiled after a duel) regarded scarcity as the principal creator of exchange value, as would many modern economists.

The use value/exchange value distinction therefore performs a different analytical function from the thing/wealth distinction. The former is primarily concerned with an analysis of the complex concept of value, which is not at issue in the latter. The point about the thing/wealth distinction is that it highlights the different purposes for which the same thing may be held – you can own a diamond because you value its beauty, or as an investment whose nature is a matter of indifference to you. Whichever it is, the diamond still has, for the purposes of the economic arguments where the distinction is relevant, a low use value and a high exchange value.

2.4.4.3.   Property and personhood

In 'Property and Personhood', Mary Jane Radin develops a notion of the relationship between person and things (when valued as thing, although this is not the terminology she uses) which is based on Hegel's concept of persons in *Philosophy of Right*. Her basic thesis is that a special bond arises between a person and certain things that that person treats as his own (in a thing sense rather than a wealth sense) and that it is necessary for the law to recognise this bond in order for that person to achieve proper self-development, or as she puts it 'to be a person'. She terms these things 'personal property'. Not all things valued as thing rather than as wealth come within this personal property category:

Most people possess certain objects they feel are almost part of themselves. These objects are closely bound up with personhood because they are part of the way we constitute ourselves as continuing personal entities in the world. They may be as different as people are different, but some common examples might be a wedding ring, a portrait, an heirloom, or a house.

One may gauge the strength or significance of someone's relationship with an object by the kind of pain that would be occasioned by its loss. On this view, an object is closely related to one's personhood if its loss causes pain that cannot be relieved by the object's replacement. If so, that particular object is bound up with the holder. For instance, if a wedding ring is stolen from a jeweler, insurance proceeds can reimburse the jeweler, but if a wedding ring is stolen from a loving wearer, the price of a replacement will not restore the *status quo* – perhaps no amount of money can do so.

The opposite of holding an object that has become a part of oneself is holding an object that is perfectly replaceable with other goods of equal market value. One holds such an object for purely instrumental reasons.

She makes it clear that things are held purely for instrumental purposes not only when they are held as wealth (i.e. the wedding ring held by the jeweller as part of his stock) but also when they are held as thing but without there being any special bond, so that something else that performed the same function would be regarded as an adequate substitute. She gives as examples things you use in your house like pots and pans, lawn mowers, and light bulbs (Radin, *Reinterpreting Property*, p. 37, n. 2, where the article is reproduced as Chapter 1). These things that do not come within the category of 'personal property' she calls 'fungibles' (i.e. using the term differently from the way in which it is used in section 2.4.4.1 above).

Her analysis provides support for the argument that long use ought in appropriate circumstances to give rise to entitlement, and we look at it again in that context in Chapter 11. For present purposes, however, the important point is that this is a normative as well as a positive analysis: she is arguing not only that such a distinction between things exists, but that, when as a matter of fact there exists such a bond between person and thing, the law ought to recognise it and to give it higher protection than that given to other relations between person and thing.

Extract 2.3   Bernard Rudden, 'Things as Thing and Things as Wealth' (1994) 14 *Oxford Journal of Legal Studies* 81

The traditional concepts of the common law of property were created for and by the ruling classes at a time when the bulk of their capital was land. Nowadays the great wealth lies in stocks, shares, bonds and the like, and is not just moveable but mobile, crossing oceans at the touch of a key-pad in the search for a fiscal utopia. This is not ... meant to denigrate the importance of land as one of the bases of the economic structure, and a factor whose cost enters into the price of everything. In terms of legal theory and technique, however, there has been a profound if little discussed evolution by which the concepts originally devised for real property have been detached from their original object, only to survive and flourish as a means of handling abstract value. The feudal calculus lives and breeds, but its habitat is wealth not land.

The argument can be more precisely stated by distinguishing, not between things as such ... but in terms of their function. A thing may be treated for itself and be possessed, used, and disposed of for its own qualities, however banal they be. In this case, the legal regime applicable treats the object as unique: it is this house we own and live in, this book we sell and no other. On the other hand, every thing may be treated merely as the clothing (in-vestment) worn by a certain amount of wealth. In this case, the relevant law accords it the modest role of a member of a class, perfectly replaceable and subject to an implacable regime of real subrogation.

The distinction between the uniqueness of things considered for themselves and their total convertibility when treated as wealth does not follow the classic lines of fungibility: a pound of flour is unique if its owner wants to make bread with it; a Vermeer in the hands of a pension fund is just another investment. Nor is the distinction necessarily tied to the nature of the object in question: most things can be either possessed for their own sake or held as investments for their income stream or in the hope of capital appreciation. The law of property covers impartially the things we own because we need them – our home, food, and clothing – and those we own but could exist without – the flat we lease and do not live in, the first editions that we dare not read. In other words, in most legal systems things of the same type may be held by some as necessaries and by others as investments, while many persons hold part of their property as both. In defining and protecting entitlements, powers, and so on, the law does not need expressly and initially to distinguish between these purposes.

Nonetheless, such a distinction is attempted in what follows. It is beyond the author's powers to render the difference in simple English. In 1901, Josef Köhler used the terms *Substanzrecht* and *Wertrecht*, but the words do not translate readily. In English, then, and for want of better, the expressions used are 'things as thing' and 'things as wealth'.

THINGS AS THING

The thesis advanced is that, when faced with things treated for themselves, the common law employs a set of concepts familiar to jurists from any country, such as ownership, possession, and publicity. But this approach is masked by certain habits which are bred into the common law systems and have laid down patterns of vocabulary which tend to control perception ...

[He goes on to demonstrate how this is the case in relation to tangible immoveables, tangible moveables, industrial/intellectual intangibles and intangible claims.]

THINGS AS WEALTH

... When treated as wealth, things do not, of course, change their physical form: they are still tangible or intangible, moveable or immoveable. But as each is perceived only as the external form of a value, no member of the class enjoys any privileged status. As an investment each individual object is treated in terms, not of its own inherent qualities, but of its opportunity cost. This last function betokens an important fact: as an item in a portfolio every thing can be changed or converted. Nothing is unique.

When one such object is replaced by another we must turn momentarily to the legal regime applicable to things treated as thing. If, for instance, it is decided – for reasons of investment strategy or tax planning – to sell a mansion house and a racehorse so as to buy some shares and an aeroplane, each of the four transactions will be governed by its particular legal rules, with its own form of transfer, its own register, and so on. But from the point of view of the portfolio, the sales and subsequent purchases effect merely a real subrogation whereby the things sold are transmuted into the sale price which then becomes the things bought. The fund has not changed: the accounts record on one side the disappearance of two assets expressed as sums of money, and on the other the acquisition of the price; the purchase money then leaves the accounts and the shares and patent enter them at asset value. The overall balance is still the same. Maitland said all this first, and put it best: 'The idea of the trust-fund which is dressed up (invested) now as land and now as current coin, now as shares and now as debentures seems to me one of the most remarkable ideas developed by modern English jurisprudence' [Hazeltine *et al.*, *Maitland: Selected Essays*, p. 134] . . .

SOME HESITATIONS AND REFINEMENTS

. . .

Use value/exchange value

A related comment might well be that the scheme put forward is no more than a ponderous restatement of the distinction between use value and exchange value found in some modern English property texts. All that can be said is that neither of these two terms seems quite to express the points made above. Exchange value suggests a momentary monetary assessment at the time of purchase or sale, whereas the notion of a thing functioning as wealth is intended to detach the act of receipt from that of expenditure and to suggest the enduring subjacent value stored in a fund, where any given thing is merely a transient and entirely replaceable investment. Use is not hard to understand, but use value is very problematic, and its relation with exchange value is quite obscure . . .

A functional distinction

After a careful examination of the use of the word [thing], Honoré concludes that 'the investigation of things seems to peter out in a false trail'. This paper's distinction between things as thing and things as wealth is cast in terms, not of the meaning of the word thing, nor of the physical nature of any given object, but of the function attributed to the object in the relation being considered. It may well have no part to play in the situation in which one person is undisputed, absolute, and unlimited owner, for, as there are no competing interests to manage or protect, there is little point in asking why its owner holds it; in fact, the joy of being absolute owner is that one does not have to answer that kind of question. It is clear, of course, that some things by their very nature are more fitted for one function than the other: we would be unwise to invest our life savings in milk, and unlikely to hold government stock for pure enjoyment. It is very difficult, however, to think of anything which could never, for some eccentric in a liberal legal system, serve one or other of the purposes (it is within the author's personal knowledge that at least one shareholder in the New River Company Ltd declined to surrender his share certificates when the company was taken over in 1974. The holder preferred the things themselves, worthless as wealth but rich as symbol, to the expectation of dividends offered by the new shares in London Merchant Securities plc) ...

Notes and Questions 2.3

1   In discussing an example similar to the bankruptcy example in the text (should a house jointly owned by a bankrupt and her partner be sold so that the bankrupt's share can be realised for the benefit of her creditors), Rudden says later on in the article:

> The particular problem could be solved by a policy decision of the legislator. On the one hand, Parliament might agree that a [creditor's] interest is merely in the thing as wealth, whereas [the] family member's interest is in the thing as a dwelling-house, and so be led to lay down a clear if radical rule: that the ... right of the creditor ... is postponed to that of [the family member]. But a quite different policy might also be adopted, which held that the burden of a black sheep should fall on its kin rather than on a stranger dealing for value and in good faith: and this would lead to an equally clear if quite contrary rule. (Rudden, 'Things as Thing and Things as Wealth', p. 96)

Could similar policy considerations be raised in relation to the bankruptcy example? What arguments could be put forward for advocating the adoption of one policy rather than the other?

2   If there is a dispute about entitlement to a thing between A and B and a court decides in favour of A, it can either order B to return the thing to A, or order B to pay damages to A to compensate A for his loss. Would the distinction between things as thing and things as wealth be useful to the court in deciding which of the two it should order? Would it instead be more useful to adopt either the conventional fungible/non-fungible distinction noted in section 2.4.4.1 above, or Radin's personal property/fungible distinction noted in section 2.4.4.3 above?

3

Justifications for property rights

3.1. Introduction: general and specific justifications

In *Property Rights: Philosophic Foundations*, Lawrence Becker draws a distinction between general justification for property rights ('why should there ever be any property rights at all?') and specific justification ('what sorts of people should own what sorts of things and under what conditions?').

In general, we consider general justification in this chapter and specific justification in Chapter 4. However, it is not possible to keep the two wholly separate. If you take an economist's view of property, the question of general justification is viewed as a question of the functions that property rights perform. This, however, quickly develops into arguments about what type of property ownership (private, communal or state ownership) best fulfils these functions. This inevitably dictates, to some extent at least, who should have what sorts of interest in what sorts of thing. We deal with both issues in section 3.2 of this chapter.

John Locke approaches the question of general justification from a different angle. In *Private Ownership*, James Grunebaum points out that property 'rights' necessarily entail exclusion, and in Chapter 2 we see that this is what marks limited access communal property and private property off from no-property and open access communal property. If no-property or open access communal property is reduced either to private ownership or to limited access communal property this necessarily results in a curtailment of everyone else's *privilege* or *liberty* to use that resource. Is it justifiable to rob one person of their *privilege* to make use of a resource in order to confer a *right* to that resource on another? This is the question that concerns Locke, and we consider his response to it in section 3.3 of this chapter.

3.2. Economic justification of property rights

3.2.1. Property and scarcity

Consider the category of resources we looked at in section 2.2.2.1 – what one might call no-property or ownerless things. In the case of such resources, *de facto* use and enjoyment go to the first taker. This causes no problems if the supply of the resource exceeds the demand. If, however, the resource becomes scarce – demand exceeds supply – four consequences are said to follow. First, those who want to make use of the resource will struggle for control of it, leading to friction and costly and dangerous conflict. Secondly, resources that would otherwise be self-replenishing (for example, fisheries or pastureland) will be over-exploited and eventually exhausted. Thirdly, there will tend to be premature exploitation of resources that require time to fulfil their full potential (trees will be felled for timber before they reach the optimum timber-producing age). Fourthly, resources that could be made more valuable by the long-term investment of skill and labour (the prime example is land) will be under-exploited.

Economists (and others) regard the institution of property as a means of solving these problems caused by scarcity of resources. It is generally accepted that any type of property ownership will avert the first consequence. In order to prevent disputes about use, all that is needed is *a* system of rules allocating use and control of the resource. It makes no difference whether the rules provide for state ownership of the resource, or private ownership, or some form of communal ownership, provided the rules are sufficiently observed or enforced.

In the case of the other three consequences, however, views differ. It has been argued that they can be averted only by private ownership of the resource. The classic but now much criticised articulation of this argument is made by the American social biologist Garrett Hardin, in 'The Tragedy of the Commons' (Extract 3.1 below). His basic thesis is that resources that he refers to as 'commons' will inevitably become exhausted once scarce, and that the only way of averting this 'tragedy' (by which he means an inexorable process rather than a story with a sad ending) is by making the resource the subject of private ownership or state ownership. He sees these as least-worse rather than perfect solutions. In the extract we give below, he gives two examples of the 'tragedy of the commons'. The first is a pasture open to all. He argues that each herdsman pasturing animals on the pasture has an incentive to increase the number of animals he puts on the pasture, because he will obtain 100 per cent of the benefit of each additional animal but will bear only a fraction of the cost of the negative effects of doing so (less grazing available for the other animals): these he will share with all the other herdsmen. Since this is true for all herdsmen, he argues, the pasture will inevitably be overgrazed and then exhausted. His second example is pollution, and as he points out the problem is essentially the same as the pasture problem, even though in the case of pollution the problem is putting something (the pollutant) into the commons (i.e. the atmosphere, or a water supply) rather than taking something out. Each individual with the freedom to use the commons – in this case to put, for example, chemical waste into a stream – has the incentive to do so because he will take the full benefit of the cost-saving involved in throwing the waste away rather than processing it but bear only a fraction of the costs imposed on the community by pollution of the stream. In both examples, in other words, the problem is externalities.

Many aspects of Hardin's analysis can be criticised (see Notes and Questions 3.2 below), but for present purposes the important point is that he fails to establish why private ownership provides a better solution in the herdsman example than that which could be provided by limited access communal property. This is partly because he does not make clear the distinctions between no-property, open access communal property and limited access communal property. In Extract 3.2, Harold Demsetz looks more closely at this, both by elaborating the reasons why the individual herdsman and polluter in Hardin's examples would not curb their destructive behaviour, and by subjecting the limited access communal property solution to closer scrutiny.

Two points become clearer from this analysis. The first is that Hardin is wrong to conclude that private property is always the *only* way of averting the tragedy of the commons (if this is indeed what he is saying). It can be averted by a limited access communal property regime, but the society this produces (or, perhaps, the society that chooses this option) will be culturally very different from the one that opts for a predominantly private property holding of the same resource. If the society that adheres predominantly to a communal property regime does so voluntarily (and historically this has not always been the case) it is likely to be a small, highly cohesive and heavily regulated society, and regulation will tend to be by social convention rather than by legal sanctions (consider why). Also, the relative suitability of private property and limited access communal property will vary depending on factors such as the nature of the resource and the prevailing environmental conditions. This was demonstrated most graphically in Glenn G. Stevenson's study of Swiss alpine grazing commons, which have subsisted in some cases for a thousand years, interspersed between both private and government-controlled grazing (Stevenson, *Common Property Economics*). We look at this again in Notes and Questions 3.2 below.

The second point, as James Grunebaum explains in Extract 3.3, is that Demsetz's analysis fails to take sufficient account of state ownership, which, as Hardin himself acknowledged, might well provide solutions to scarcity problems that are both more efficient and more just than those provided by private property. Grunebaum also questions a number of the assumptions Demsetz makes in arguing for the superiority of private property.

The overall conclusion that we might draw from these extracts is that, despite disagreements as to the form property rights might take, there is general agreement on the fundamental point that scarce resources will be best utilised (whether this involves conservation or exploitation) by the imposition of a property rights regime in which rights are clearly demarcated and readily enforceable. We conclude this section with a short example provided by Yoram Barzel in *Economic Analysis of Property Rights* concerning what he describes as the conversion of the North Sea into owned property.

Extract 3.1   Garrett Hardin, 'The Tragedy of the Commons' (1968) 162 *Science* 1243 (reprinted with permission from (1968) 162 *Science* 1243, copyright © 1968 American Association for the Advancement of Science)

THE TRAGEDY OF FREEDOM IN A COMMONS

We may well call it 'the tragedy of the commons', using the word 'tragedy' as the philosopher Whitehead used it: 'The essence of dramatic tragedy is not unhappiness. It resides in the solemnity of the remorseless working of things.' ...

The tragedy of the commons develops in this way. Picture a pasture open to all. It is to be expected that each herdsman will try to keep as many cattle as possible on the commons. Such an arrangement may work reasonably satisfactorily for centuries because tribal wars, poaching, and disease keep the numbers of both man and beast well below the carrying capacity of the land. Finally, however, comes the day of reckoning, that is, the day when the long-desired goal of social stability becomes a reality. At this point, the inherent logic of the commons remorselessly generates tragedy.

As a rational being, each herdsman seeks to maximize his gain. Explicitly or implicitly, more or less consciously, he asks, 'What is the utility to *me* of adding one more animal to my herd?' This utility has one negative and one positive component.

1   The positive component is a function of the increment of one animal. Since the herdsman receives all the proceeds from the sale of the additional animal, the positive utility is nearly +1.

2   The negative component is a function of the additional overgrazing created by one more animal. Since, however, the effects of overgrazing are shared by all the herdsmen, the negative utility for any particular decision-making herdsman is only a fraction of −1.

Adding together the component partial utilities, the rational herdsman concludes that the only sensible course for him to pursue is to add another animal to his herd. And another; and another ... But this is the conclusion reached by each and every rational herdsman sharing a commons. Therein is the tragedy. Each man is locked into a system that compels him to increase his herd without limit – in a world that is limited. Ruin is the destination towards which all men rush, each pursuing his own best interest in a society that believes in the freedom of the commons. Freedom in a commons brings ruin to all.

Some would say that this is a platitude. Would that it were! In a sense, it was learned thousands of years ago, but natural selection favors the forces of psychological denial. The individual benefits as an individual from his ability to deny the truth even though society as a whole, of which he is a part, suffers. Education can counteract the natural tendency to do the wrong thing, but the inexorable succession of generations requires that the basis for this knowledge be constantly refreshed ...

In an approximate way, the logic of the commons has been understood for a long time, perhaps since the discovery of agriculture or the invention of private property in real estate. But it is understood mostly only in special cases which are not sufficiently generalized. Even at this late date, cattlemen leasing national land on the western ranges demonstrate no more than an ambivalent understanding, in constantly pressuring federal authorities to increase the head count to the point where over-grazing produces erosion and weed dominance. Likewise, the oceans of the world continue to suffer from the survival of the philosophy of the commons. Maritime nations still respond automatically to the shibboleth of the 'freedom of the seas'. Professing to believe in the 'inexhaustible resources of the oceans', they bring species after species of fish and whales closer to extinction.

The National Parks present another instance of the working out of the tragedy of the commons. At present, they are open to all, without limit. The parks themselves are limited in extent – there is only one Yosemite Valley – whereas population seems to grow without limit. The values that visitors seek in the parks are steadily eroded. Plainly, we must soon cease to treat the parks as commons or they will be of no value to anyone.

What shall we do? We have several options. We might sell them off as private property. We might keep them as public property, but allocate the right to enter them. The allocation might be on the basis of wealth, by the use of an auction system, It might be on the basis of merit, as defined by some agreed-upon standards. It might be by lottery. Or it might be on a first-come, first-served basis, administered to long queues. These, I think, are all the reasonable possibilities. They are all objectionable. But we must choose – or acquiesce in the destruction of the commons that we call our National Parks.

POLLUTION

In a reverse way, the tragedy of the commons reappears in problems of pollution. Here it is not a question of taking something out of the commons, but of putting something in – sewage, or chemical, radioactive, and heat wastes into water; noxious and dangerous fumes into the air; and distracting and unpleasant advertising signs into the line of sight. The calculations of utility are much the same as before. The rational man finds that his share of the cost of the wastes he discharges into the commons is less than the cost of purifying his wastes before releasing them. Since this is true for everyone, we are locked into a system of 'fouling our own nest', so long as we behave only as independent, rational, free-enterprisers.

The tragedy of the commons as a food basket is averted by private property, or something formally like it. But the air and waters surrounding us cannot readily be fenced, and so the tragedy of the commons as a cesspool must be prevented by different means, by coercive laws or taxing devices that make it cheaper for the polluter to treat his pollutants than to discharge them untreated. We have not progressed as far with the solution of this problem as we have with the first. Indeed, our particular concept of private property, which deters us from exhausting the positive resources of the earth, favors pollution. The owner of a factory on the bank of a stream – whose property extends to the middle of the stream – often has difficulty seeing why it is not his natural right to muddy the waters flowing past his door. The law, always behind the times, requires elaborate stitching and fitting to adapt it to this newly perceived aspect of the commons.

The pollution problem is a consequence of population. It did not much matter how a lonely American frontiersman disposed of his waste. 'Flowing water purifies itself every ten miles', my grandfather used to say, and the myth was near enough to the truth when he was a boy, for there were not too many people. But as population

became denser, the natural chemical and biological recycling processes became over-
loaded, calling for a redefinition of property rights ...

An alternative to the commons need not be perfectly just to be preferable. With real
estate and other material goods, the alternative we have chosen is the institution of
private property coupled with legal inheritance. Is this system perfectly just? As a
genetically trained biologist I deny that it is. It seems to me that, if there are to be
differences in individual inheritance, legal possession should be perfectly correlated
with biological inheritance – that those who are biologically more fit to be the custodians
of property and power should legally inherit more. But genetic recombination continually makes a mockery of the doctrine of 'like father, like son' implicit in our laws of
legal inheritance. An idiot can inherit millions, and a trust fund can keep his estate
intact. We must admit that our legal system of private property plus inheritance is
unjust – but we put up with it because we are not convinced, at the moment, that
anyone has invented a better system. The alternative of the commons is too horrifying
to contemplate. Injustice is preferable to total ruin.

It is one of the peculiarities of the warfare between reform and the *status quo* that it
is thoughtlessly governed by a double standard. Whenever a reform measure is
proposed it is often defeated when its opponents triumphantly discover a flaw in it.

RECOGNITION OF NECESSITY

Perhaps the simplest summary of this analysis of man's population problems is this:
the commons, if justifiable at all, is justifiable only under conditions of low population
density. As the human population has increased, the commons has had to be abandoned in one aspect after another.

First, we abandoned the commons in food gathering, enclosing farm land and
restricting pastures and hunting and fishing areas. These restrictions are still not
complete throughout the world.

Somewhat later we saw that the commons as a place for waste disposal would also
have to be abandoned. Restrictions on the disposal of domestic sewage are widely
accepted in the Western world; we are still struggling to close the commons to
pollution by automobiles, factories, insecticide sprayers, fertilizing operations, and
atomic energy installations.

In a still more embryonic state is our recognition of the evils of the commons in
matters of pleasure. There is almost no restriction on the propagation of sound waves
in the public medium. The shopping public is assaulted with mindless music, without
its consent. Our government is paying out billions of dollars to create supersonic
transport which will disturb 50,000 people for every one person who is whisked from
coast to coast three hours faster. Advertisers muddy the airwaves of radio and television
and pollute the view of travelers. We are a long way from outlawing the commons in
matters of pleasure. Is this because our Puritan inheritance makes us view pleasure as
something of a sin, and pain (that is, the pollution of advertising) as the sign of virtue?

Every new enclosure of the commons involves the infringement of somebody's
personal liberty. Infringements made in the distant past are accepted because no
contemporary complains of a loss. It is the newly proposed infringements that we

vigorously oppose; cries of 'rights' and 'freedom' fill the air. But what does 'freedom' mean? When men mutually agreed to pass laws against robbing, mankind became more free, not less so. Individuals locked into the logic of the commons are free only to bring on universal ruin; once they see the necessity of mutual coercion, they become free to pursue other goals.

Extract 3.2   Harold Demsetz, 'Towards a Theory of Property Rights' (1967) 57 *American Economic Review* 347 at 354–8

THE COALESCENCE AND OWNERSHIP OF PROPERTY RIGHTS

I have argued that property rights arise when it becomes economic for those affected by externalities to internalize benefits and costs. But I have not yet examined the forces which will govern the particular form of right ownership. Several idealized forms of ownership must be distinguished at the outset. These are communal ownership, private ownership, and state ownership.

By communal ownership, I shall mean a right which can be exercised by all members of the community. Frequently, the rights to till and to hunt the land have been communally owned. The right to walk a city sidewalk is communally owned. Communal ownership means that the community denies to the state or to individual citizens the right to interfere with any person's exercise of communally owned rights. Private ownership implies that the community recognizes the right of the owner to exclude others from exercising the owner's private rights. State ownership implies that the state may exclude anyone from the use of a right as long as the state follows accepted political procedures for determining who may not use state-owned property. I shall not examine in detail the alternative of state ownership. The object of the analysis which follows is to discern some broad principles governing the development of property rights in communities oriented to private property.

It will be best to begin by considering a particularly useful example that focuses our attention on the problem of land ownership. Suppose that land is communally owned. Every person has the right to hunt, till, or mine the land. This form of ownership fails to concentrate the cost associated with any person's exercise of his communal right on that person. If a person seeks to maximize the value of his communal rights, he will tend to overhunt and overwork the land because some of the costs of his doing so are borne by others. The stock of game and the richness of the soil will be diminished too quickly. It is conceivable that those who own these rights, i.e. every member of the community, can agree to curtail the rate at which they work the lands if negotiating and policing costs are zero. Each can agree to abridge his rights. It is obvious that the costs of reaching such an agreement will not be zero. What is not obvious is just how large these costs may be.

Negotiating costs will be large because it is difficult for many persons to reach a mutually satisfactory agreement, especially when each holdout has the right to work the land as fast as he pleases. But, even if an agreement among all can be reached, we must yet take account of the costs of policing the agreement, and these may be large, also. After such an agreement is reached, no one will privately own the right to work the land; all can work the land but at an agreed upon shorter workweek. Negotiating costs are increased even further because it is not possible under this system to bring the full expected benefits and expected costs of future generations to bear on current users.

If a single person owns land, he will attempt to maximize its present value by taking into account alternative future time streams of benefits and costs and selecting that one which he believes will maximize the present value of his privately owned land rights. We all know that this means that he will attempt to take into account the supply and demand conditions that he thinks will exist after his death. It is very difficult to see how the existing communal owners can reach an agreement that takes account of these costs.

In effect, an owner of a private right to use land acts as a broker whose wealth depends on how well he takes into account the competing claims of the present and the future. But with communal rights there is no broker, and the claims of the present generation will be given an uneconomically large weight in determining the intensity with which the land is worked. Future generations might desire to pay present generations enough to change the present intensity of land usage. But they have no living agent to place their claims on the market. Under a communal property system, should a living person pay others to reduce the rate at which they work the land, he would not gain anything of value for his efforts. Communal property means that future generations must speak for themselves. No one has yet estimated the costs of carrying on such a conversation.

The land ownership example confronts us immediately with a great disadvantage of communal property. The effects of a person's activities on his neighbors and on subsequent generations will not be taken into account fully. Communal property results in great externalities. The full costs of the activities of an owner of a communal property right are not borne directly by him, nor can they be called to his attention easily by the willingness of others to pay him an appropriate sum. Communal property rules out a 'pay-to-use-the-property' system and high negotiation and policing costs make ineffective a 'pay-him-not-to-use-the-property' system.

The state, the courts, or the leaders of the community could attempt to internalize the external costs resulting from communal property by allowing private parcels owned by small groups of persons with similar interests. The logical groups in terms of similar interests, are, of course, the family and the individual. Continuing with our use of the land ownership example, let us initially distribute private titles to land randomly among existing individuals and, further, let the extent of land included in each title be randomly determined.

The resulting private ownership of land will internalize many of the external costs associated with communal ownership, for now an owner, by virtue of his power to exclude others, can generally count on realizing the rewards associated with husbanding the game and increasing the fertility of his land. This concentration of benefits and costs on owners creates incentives to utilize resources more efficiently.

But we have yet to contend with externalities. Under the communal property system the maximization of the value of communal property rights will take place without regard to many costs, because the owner of a communal right cannot exclude others from enjoying the fruits of his efforts and because negotiation costs are too high for all to agree jointly on optimal behavior. The development of private rights permits the owner to economize on the use of those resources from which he has the right to exclude others. Much internalization is accomplished in this way. But the owner of private rights to one parcel does not himself own the rights to the parcel of another private sector. Since he cannot exclude others from their private rights to land, he has no direct incentive (in the absence of negotiations) to economize in the use of his land in a way that takes into account the effects he produces on the land rights of others. If he constructs a dam on his land, he has no direct incentive to take into account the lower water levels produced on his neighbor's land.

This is exactly the same kind of externality that we encountered with communal property rights, but it is present to a lesser degree. Whereas no one had an incentive to store water on any land under the communal system, private owners now can take into account directly those benefits and costs to their land that accompany water storage. But the effects on the land of others will not be taken into account directly.

The partial concentration of benefits and costs that accompany private ownership is only part of the advantage this system offers. The other part, and perhaps the most important, has escaped our notice. The cost of negotiating over the remaining externalities will be reduced greatly. Communal property rights allow anyone to use the land. Under this system it becomes necessary for all to reach an agreement on land use. But the externalities that accompany private ownership of property do not affect all owners, and, generally speaking, it will be necessary for only a few to reach an agreement that takes these effects into account. The cost of negotiating an internalization of these effects is thereby reduced considerably. The point is important enough to elucidate.

Suppose an owner of a communal land right, in the process of plowing a parcel of land, observes a second communal owner constructing a dam on adjacent land. The farmer prefers to have the stream as it is, and so he asks the engineer to stop his construction. The engineer says, 'Pay me to stop'. The farmer replies, 'I will be happy to pay you, but what can you guarantee in return?' The engineer answers, 'I can guarantee you that I will not continue constructing the dam, but I cannot guarantee that another engineer will not take up the task because this is communal property; I have no right to exclude him.' What would be a simple negotiation between two persons under a private property arrangement turns out to be a rather complex negotiation between the farmer and everyone else. This is the basic explanation, I believe, for the preponderance of single rather than multiple owners of property. Indeed, an increase in the number of owners is an increase in the communality of property and leads, generally, to an increase in the cost of internalizing.

The reduction in negotiating cost that accompanies the private right to exclude others allows most externalities to be internalized at rather low cost. Those that are not are associated with activities that generate external effects impinging upon many people. The soot from smoke affects many homeowners, none of whom is willing to pay enough to the factory to get its owner to reduce smoke output. All homeowners together might be willing to pay enough, but the cost of their getting together may be enough to discourage effective market bargaining. The negotiating problem is compounded even more if the smoke comes not from a single smoke stack but from an industrial district. In such cases, it may be too costly to internalize effects through the marketplace.

Returning to our land ownership paradigm, we recall that land was distributed in randomly sized parcels to randomly selected owners. These owners now negotiate among themselves to internalize any remaining externalities. Two market options are open to the negotiators. The first is simply to try to reach a contractual agreement among owners that directly deals with the external effects at issue. The second option is for some owners to buy out others, thus changing the parcel size owned. Which option is selected will depend on which is cheaper. We have here a standard economic problem of optimal scale. If there exist constant returns to scale in the ownership of different sized parcels, it will be largely a matter of indifference between outright purchase and contractual agreement if only a single, easy-to-police, contractual agreement will internalize the externality. But, if there are several externalities, so that several such contracts will need to be negotiated, or if the contractual agreements should be difficult to police, then outright purchase will be the preferred course of action.

The greater are diseconomies of scale to land ownership the more will contractual arrangement be used by the interacting neighbors to settle these differences. Negotiating and policing costs will be compared to costs that depend on the scale of ownership, and parcels of land will tend to be owned in sizes which minimize the sum of these costs ...

The dual tendencies for ownership to rest with individuals and for the extent of an individual's ownership to accord with the minimization of all costs is clear in the land ownership paradigm ... But it may not be clear yet how widely applicable this paradigm is. Consider the problems of copyright and patents. If a new idea is freely appropriable by all, if there exist communal rights to new ideas, incentives for developing such ideas will be lacking. The benefits derivable from these ideas will not be concentrated on their originators. If we extend some degree of private rights to the originators, these ideas will come forth at a more rapid pace. But the existence of the private rights does not mean that their effects on the property of others will be directly taken into account. A new idea makes an old one obsolete and another old one more valuable. These effects will not be directly taken into account, but they can be called to the attention of the originator of the new idea through market negotiations. All problems of externalities are closely analogous to those which arise in the land ownership example. The relevant variables are identical.

Extract 3.3   James O. Grunebaum, *Private Ownership* (Routledge and Kegan Paul, London and New York, 1987), pp. 158–67

D. PRIVATE OWNERSHIP AND THE ECONOMY

Forms of ownership have different effects upon society's economic organization. Economic organization should be understood as encompassing a society's productive, commercial, and financial activities, i.e. how society materially produces and sustains itself. A form of ownership determines or greatly influences how society's wealth is produced and distributed. This is obvious once ownership is understood as a right constituted relationship between persons with respect to things, and it is the things in life which constitute wealth. Since different specific forms of ownership prescribe different sets of rights over what is owned as well as having different domains of possible own-ables, there are different economic effects upon how well or efficiently what is owned can be used to produce wealth and how justly or equitably wealth is distributed. Some forms of ownership may stimulate economic growth more than others, some may have tendencies towards greater equality of wealth, some may encourage individual effort, some may foster a more rational allocation of the factors of production, and some forms may simplify or reduce the cost of economic decision-making and planning.

The purpose of this section is to examine private ownership and to dispel some of the misconceptions about private ownership's effects upon the economy ...

The private ownership form is claimed to be economically optimific, i.e. as having the best economic consequences. Private ownership is said to give owners rights which permit the economic system to efficiently allocate factors of production including labor, to keep supply and demand near equilibrium, to create sufficient motivation for entrepreneurial activity which is needed to keep economic growth rates near an optimum level, to minimize decision-making or administrative costs, and to provide an efficient distribution of income on the basis of market valued marginal productiv-ity. Other forms of ownership such as communal ownership are supposed to have less economically optimific effects. Inefficiencies in production, market disequilibrium, lack of incentives for growth, incomes which are divorced from marginal productivity, and high administrative decision-making costs are said to plague non-private forms of ownership. From the economic perspective, private ownership is thought to affect society in the best way possible ...

One typical argument for the economic superiority of private ownership is made by Harold Demsetz in the *American Economic Review* [Extract 3.2 above]. He argues that private ownership of land and resources facilitates a more rational use of land and resources, specifically by preventing a too rapid depletion, and that private ownership reduces the costs of internalizing externalities. Demsetz contrasts private ownership with communal ownership. He defines communal ownership as 'a right which can be exercised by all members of the community'; walking a city sidewalk is an example, and 'private ownership implies the community recognizes the right of the owner to exclude others from exercising the owner's private rights'. Demsetz also defines state ownership which he views as implying 'that the state may exclude anyone from the use of a right as long as the state follows accepted political procedures for determining who may not use state-owned property'; but, for some unmentioned reason, state ownership does not enter into his argument. Demsetz argues that, if land and resources are communally owned, i.e. each member having the unlimited right to appropriate for himself, then resources will be depleted too quickly. Each person who tries to max-imize the value of his own right will be able to pass some of the costs on to others. In this situation, the richness of the land and resources will be depleted too quickly to maximize economic return. Communal owners could undertake negotiated agree-ments to slow depletion, but, as Demsetz argues, the costs of negotiation will be high.

Private ownership of land can prevent too quick depletion according to Demsetz's argument:

> If a single person owns land, he will attempt to maximize its present value by taking into account alternative future streams of benefits and costs and selecting that one which he believes will maximize the present value of his privately owned land rights. We all know that this means he will take into account the supply and demand conditions that he thinks will exist after his death. It is very difficult to see how communal owners can reach an agreement that takes account of these costs.

It is not at all clear that this argument proves what it is supposed to prove. That an owner needs to consider the conditions which may occur after his death insofar as they affect the present value of this land makes sense only if the owner intends to sell his land or if he intends to bequeath a valuable piece of land to his heirs. But if the private landowner is only concerned about his own income from the land without any concern about selling it or what he may be able to bequeath, then the private owner might well exploit his land at a rate calculated to maximize his income over his life expectancy. If the owner could know with some precision the date of his death, then, given the assumed values, he rationally should adopt an income maximizing exploitation policy which would have the land depleted at, or just after, the time of his death.

Demsetz's argument is plausible only on the assumption that private owners are also motivated by a concern for the value they can bequeath to their heirs, i.e. they are not exclusively concerned with maximizing their own income from the land but they care about what value the land has for subsequent generations. It should be noted at this point that corporations of one sort or another and extended families can perform the function of considering future value and income if it is assumed that corporations or extended families continue beyond the death of any of their individual members. If members are added to the corporation to replace those who leave, then the corporate management must then consider future income. But unless some assumption is made about care for future generations, there is no superiority in land utilization of private ownership except for possible gain of land value which may last a whole generation instead of only a partial one. Further, if the assumption about motivation which is needed to make Demsetz's private ownership argument plausible is applied in the communal ownership setting, it is not at all obvious that communal owners, who care about what subsequent generations might inherit, would too quickly deplete the land and resources.

The decision-making costs involved in internalizing externalities also depend upon the motivational assumption. Demsetz argues that the decision-making costs for communal owners will be high because of the profitability for the holdout who may extract exorbitant terms. If a concern for the value left to future generations functions as a motive for the holdout also, then it is not clear how high the decision-making costs will be. At this point Demsetz's neglect of state ownership becomes relevant to the argument about decision-making costs since state ownership as an alternative to private ownership is one way of reducing the decision-making costs of communal ownership. A comparison of decision-making costs in private ownership and in state ownership would be the more interesting comparison especially because of the similarities between state ownership and autonomous ownership [a form of ownership Grunebaum discusses in the following chapter]. Joseph Schumpeter points out, in *Capitalism, Socialism and Democracy*, that private owners may have high decision-making costs if they are ignorant of what other private owners are doing, i.e. the information cost component of decision-making costs may be higher in a private ownership competitive economy than in a state ownership economy. Lack of information may also lead to bad decisions which have costs also ...

The second of the supposed economically optimific consequences of private ownership is its role in an economic system which motivates individuals to engage in productive work by the lure of amassing great wealth. Private ownership of labor, land, resources, and the means of production in a free market economy enables some individuals to become wealthy by efficiently producing saleable commodities, on their own or by employing others, thereby strongly motivating individuals who desire wealth to work hard. It is assumed that only the desire for wealth is a powerful enough motive to induce sufficient numbers of individuals to work sufficiently hard so that society as a whole will prosper. It is thought that other forms of ownership in other economic systems either do not provide sufficient motivation for productive work or they must rely upon kinds of motivation which violate the moral requirements of individual autonomy and noncoercion.

The assumption that the desire for wealth is the strongest or primary motive to work has been questioned. While the assumption can be held in extreme forms which are undoubtedly false, a more moderate version of the assumption is surely reasonable, namely, that the desire to be materially well off and secure is a significant motive for engaging in productive work. Some individuals may be motivated by love or benevolence but there is no inconsistency in also believing that the desire for secure material well-being is a strong motive too.

There are forms of ownership which are incompatible with the more moderate assumption about motivation. Specific forms of ownership in which the distribution of wealth or goods is made equally or based upon some principle of need will create disincentives to hard productive work which will vary directly with the strength of the desire for wealth. Forms of communal ownership, in which not only are land and resources communally owned but in which each person's talents and abilities are likewise considered communally owned assets, also may fail to induce sufficient numbers of individuals to work sufficiently hard. If individuals must share their income with others or receive less income than they could in an uncontrolled market for labor because their talents and abilities are considered communally owned assets, then from their perspective they may have disincentives to work since they regard themselves as underpaid. The strength of the disincentive will depend upon the difference between the actual income and the perceived market value of the labor and upon how strong the desire for wealth is in the individuals, i.e. where the desire for wealth is weak the disincentive will be weak and where the desire is strong the disincentive will be strong. It might be possible to find other work incentives than the desire for wealth, well-being or security, such as honor, reputation, or the desire to contribute to the common good. How strong these motives are is a question not yet satisfactorily answered. Other strong motives, such as the desire not to be shot, are both economically and morally undesirable.

Private ownership over the domain of land, resources, the means of production and labor may not be the only form of ownership which is compatible with the assumption about motivation. The salient feature of any economic system which is compatible with the assumption about motivation is a free labor market. In a free labor market each individual has the right to seek the kind of employment he prefers. Any individual has the right to try to become a tax attorney, for example, although market forces and professional standards may restrict the number of individuals so employed to a select few. The root concept behind a free labor market is that each individual has the right to decide how his labor is to be used and that no other members of society, either individually or collectively, may decide for him so long as what he does lies within the bounds of respect for everyone's autonomy. In order, therefore, to attract individuals to labor, jobs must be made sufficiently attractive and, if the assumption about motivation is correct, most of what makes jobs sufficiently attractive are the material rewards which are offered. Potential employers will compete for workers and the purchasers of services will compete for services by offering material incentives. The greater the demand for a kind of labor given its supply or the smaller its supply given the demand, the larger the material rewards will be which are needed to attract sufficient number of individuals to labor. The converse also is true, i.e. less demand or greater supply will lower the size of the needed incentive. Rational wealth seeking individuals will try to choose the kind of employment which maximizes the expected economic return upon their talents, skills, and training. Other non-material non-economic factors such as status or safety might also have a role in guiding choices of employment, but to the extent these factors do have a role the assumption that wealth and security is the primary motive is also weakened.

Private ownership of one's labor is an economic requirement for stimulating hard productive work and for allocating labor to market demand. Private ownership of land, resources, and the means of production is another issue entirely. There appears to be no logical reason why land, resources, and certain factors of the means of production must also be privately owned in order to provide the kinds of incentives required by the motivation assumption. What is essential is that the rewards for labor approximate market valued marginal productivity, but there is no logical impossibility of achieving this even if land, resources, and some of the means of production are not privately owned. For example, economic forces which require managers of communally or collectively owned firms to compete for labor with each other and with self-employment options for workers would create the same free labor market forces as would private owners in similar circumstances. Forms of ownership which do not permit private ownership of land, resources, and all of the means of production are not logically incompatible with the motivation assumption if something resembling private ownership of labor in a free market is part of the economic system. Autonomous ownership in which everyone may participate in decisions concerning land use therefore requires a free labor market because of the right to direct one's own labor. The practical compatibility of a free labor market with autonomous ownership of land, resources and means of production ownership will be discussed later, but it is worth noting here that the practical question seems to center around entrepreneurship and growth rates rather than around the price or rewards for labor.

The last of the alleged economically optimific consequences of private ownership to be discussed is its role in economic growth and technological progress. Technological progress is usually considered a concomitant of economic growth. It is frequently argued that only an economic system based upon private ownership of labor, land, resources, and the means of production will supply sufficient incentives through financial rewards for firms to expand and entrepreneurs to take risks. If neither the manager of the firm nor the entrepreneur is able to share in the profits of expansion or of new technology, then there will be insufficient incentive for adequate growth.

This argument is a corollary of the argument about hard work, centering upon one kind of hard work: that which leads to economic growth as a result of creating new products, new processes, and new services. It is further assumed that the creative initiative required for the discovery and production of new products, processes, and services is inherently individual and cannot be a consequence of bureaucratic administration or a product of special managerial organization. Therefore, specific forms of ownership other than private ownership (i.e. forms of ownership which separate the rights of management and control from the rights to income and equity or which distribute income from the firm and rights to shares in its equity throughout society) will inhibit economic and technical growth because individuals will have insufficient economic reasons for undertaking economically risky activities. Growth rates will therefore be economically inadequate.

The claim that economic and technological growth is inhibited by non-private forms of ownership is not easy to prove empirically since there are so many other variables involved, e.g. the degree of technological and economic development or the scarcity of resources and capital; the data is subject to a variety of plausible alternative interpretations. Not all actual planned or socialist economies have inadequate growth rates in all areas of the economy, nor do all private ownership capitalist economies show adequate growth in all industries and services, e.g. in the United States' steel and automobile production. Since much data is inconclusive, and if the people are motivated as assumed earlier, there appears to be no reason why a society which adopts some form of nonprivate ownership of land, resources, and some of the means of production could not have adequate economic and technological growth. Clauses could be written into managerial contracts with pay incentives to managers who create new goods and services or who expand production and, conversely, extract penalties from managers of firms that decline. Such contracts are already common in private ownership for managers of large firms owned by many shareholders. From the perspective of the manager, there would seem to be little difference whether the stockholders, who ultimately are the source of his incentive contract, are society as a whole or some large sub-set of society. The manager would have the same incentive to expand existing output if needed or to produce new goods. How large or small the manager's incentive would need to be would have to be discovered by trial and error ...

So far it has been tacitly assumed that economic growth is desirable and that the optimum rate of growth is easily calculated. There is, however, no general consensus about what an optimum growth rate should be. Rawls' difficulty in *A Theory of Justice*, in specifying an optimum savings rate, is merely an isomorphism of the growth rate difficulty: how much goods and services ought to be consumed or labor and capital ought to be invested in order to supply future generations with what level of goods, services, and the potential for still further growth. Present sacrifice for future growth may temporarily cause increased unemployment; in fact, Marx believed that economic expansion is profitable only on the condition that an 'army of unemployed' is maintained to keep wages low during the growth-expansion quadrant of the business cycle. How much suffering is justifiable? It is difficult to know with any precision, or with any generality, what an optimum growth rate should be.

The absence of any clear general specification of the growth rate undercuts the objection against planned economies that collective decision procedures will result in too little capital being set aside for future growth. This objection assumes that self-interested individuals will prefer their own present consumption to future consumption by others. Consequently, members of society who are given a voice through collective decision procedures will choose production levels which favor themselves at the expense of future members. Future generations would then inherit capital equipment which is too obsolete and too worn out to adequately satisfy their needs. Thus it is believed only private ownership in which investment decisions are made privately would provide sufficient safeguards for future growth. But this is again Demsetz's argument that private owners concern themselves with economic conditions which go beyond their own life span. It is of course true that some private corporations have such concerns but this may be due to the fact that private corporations are expected to survive their present members. Yet it might be asked why present members of private corporations do not prefer their own present consumption (income from the corporation) to the consumption of future stockholders. Two answers seem to make sense. First (antihypothesi), they do care about the income future stockholders will receive even if it is only their own descendants who inherit the shares of stock. Second, because generations are not discrete, either in society or in the private corporations, stockholders and younger members of society influence the older ones into taking a more long range perspective. In either case, private corporations and planned economies based upon socialist ownership could perform in similar ways.

To summarize briefly this section on the relation of the forms of ownership to economic systems, it is clear that different specific forms of ownership have different effects upon economic systems which need to be explored in any attempt at moral justification for a specific form of ownership such as autonomous ownership. Private ownership may have better economic consequences than some other forms, but private ownership is not uniquely optimific since there are other forms of ownership with equally good economic consequences.

Extract 3.4   Yoram Barzel, *Economic Analysis of Property Rights* (2nd edn, Cambridge University Press, Cambridge, 1997), pp. 101–2

THE CONVERSION OF THE NORTH SEA INTO OWNED PROPERTY

In 1958, the Convention on the Continental Shelf was signed in Geneva … The provisions of the convention divided among the countries bordering the North Sea some of the commonly held attributes of that sea, particularly those related to minerals. Two factors had been working to enhance the value of the North Sea in the years preceding the agreement. First, underwater drilling, which was becoming more widespread, was declining in cost; second, various signs were emerging that the region contained natural gas and crude oil reserves. The countries surrounding the North Sea could conceivably have unilaterally extended their territorial rights towards the middle of the sea. Oil companies, however, were not going to invest resources in searching for oil unless they expected their potential legal ownership and, concurrently, their economic ownership of that oil to be secure. The preceding discussion suggests that the increase in value of the oil resources of the North Sea generated forces to better delineate rights over it.

By reaching an agreement, the countries involved gained ownership of segments of the sea. They could then either exploit their sea rights directly or grant them to private parties and let those private concerns exploit them. Subsequent events proved that the formal agreement and the accurate delineation of borders was ultimately of great value. When the North Sea countries convened to establish rights over the sea, no one knew where oil would be found, so it was easy to arrive at a formula that would give each country the territory nearest to it without generating much dispute regarding the precise setting of borders. The formula actually selected was that any point on the sea (and on the sea bottom) belonged to the country to which the point was closest.

As it turned out, many of the major oil and gas discoveries lay close to the border between the Norwegian and the United Kingdom sectors. Since the border was precisely marked, ownership of these finds was not in dispute. There is little doubt that without the agreement oil companies would not have searched in that area. The value of the clear delineation is further illustrated by the following observation. There is a deep trench in the Norwegian sector of the North Sea. Laying a pipeline across the trench is prohibitively costly. Some of the Norwegian oil deposits are on the United Kingdom side of the trench, which seems to make the United Kingdom a more natural owner of that area than Norway. Consistent with the Coase theorem, however, once rights were delineated, there was little difficulty in developing the area. Indeed, some of the Norwegian oil is shipped by pipeline to the United Kingdom.

Notes and Questions 3.1

1   What does Hardin mean by 'the commons'? Some of the examples he gives (e.g. fish in oceans, air and water into which pollutants are released) are what we describe here as no-property, i.e. an unowned resource which everyone has a

privilege to use but no right not to be excluded from. At least one other (National Parks) is open access communal property, i.e. a resource which everyone has a privilege to use and a right not to be excluded from, and another (grazing land leased by cattlemen on the western ranges) is limited access communal property, where each cattleman-tenant has a privilege to graze cattle, a right not to be excluded from doing so, and a right to exclude non-cattlemen-tenants. Up to a point, Hardin's failure to distinguish these different categories does not matter: his argument (that each individual has a positive and a negative incentive to over-use the resource) applies equally to all three categories. However, the *solution* to the problem of over-use may vary from category to category. In relation to each of the examples given by Hardin, and in the light of what is said in the other materials extracted here, consider whether use regulation might best be achieved:

(a) by making the resource subject to private ownership;

(b) by self-regulation by the users acting in concert;

(c) by state ownership; or

(d) by state regulation by imposition of quotas, or by taxation (most famously advocated by Pigou, *The Economics of Welfare* (consider how this would work)), or by other means.

2   There are many documented cases of (b) above, i.e. cases where users of scarce no-property, or of scarce limited access communal property, have avoided depletion of the resource by self-regulation of their use. See, for example, the elaborate rituals and use patterns associated with use of scarce resources in Australia by aboriginal tribes, documented in *Milirrpum* v. *Nabalco Pty Ltd* (1971) 17 FLR 141 and *Mabo* v. *Queensland (No. 2)* (1992) 175 CLR 1 (both extracted at www.cambridge.org/propertylaw/ and discussed in Chapters 4 and 5), which have been highly successful in *conserving* resources for thousands of years (but not necessarily exploiting them to their full potential). Major studies of similarly long-standing self-regulated communal systems have been produced in response to Hardin's analysis: see, for example, Chakravaty-Kaul, *Common Lands and Customary Law*, Dahlman, *The Open Field System and Beyond* (an analysis of the open field system in medieval England specifically undertaken to demonstrate what Dahlman argued was a highly efficient system of communal land usage, whose eventual disintegration was caused not by Hardin's 'tragedy of the commons' but by other complex social and political factors) and Stevenson, *Common Property Economics* (a study of Swiss alpine grazing commons we refer to again in question 9 below). References to further examples can be found in Ellickson, 'Property in Land'; Fennell, 'Common Interest Tragedies'; and De Alessi, 'Gains from Private Property'.

3   Would the factors that Hardin identifies as leading inexorably to over-exploitation of the pasture be removed if the animals were also communally owned? In other words, has Hardin identified a problem arising only when there is a

mixture of private and communal ownership, which would not arise if all relevant resources were communally owned? At one level, this appears to be the case: if each animal is communally owned, each herdsman shares equally the benefits and detriments of grazing an additional animal. However, this does not alter the argument; it merely converts the problem from one of over-exploitation to one of under-exploitation. If the value of the pasture and the animals grazed there is to be maintained, never mind maximised, it will be necessary for the herdsmen to expend labour on them. But, while each herdsman bears 100 per cent of the burden of the labour he expends, he has to share the benefits accruing from his labour with all the other herdsmen: most of the benefits are external to him. Consequently, so the argument goes, he has no incentive to work harder because he has no means of ensuring that every other herdsman will do the same. In other words, in the case of any type of communal use of resources by human beings, an interface between communal ownership and private ownership is inevitable, for so long as we each own our own labour.

4 Does Demsetz sufficiently distinguish between limited access communal property and no-property? If not, does this affect the force of his arguments?

5 Demsetz assumes that those labouring for the communal good will inevitably work less hard than those labouring exclusively for their own benefit. Examine the arguments he puts forward. Do they, as Grunebaum suggests, oversimplify the issue?

6 Demsetz argues that the interests of future generations must be taken into account if resources are to be put to their optimal use, and that this will only occur if the resource is privately owned. To what extent does Grunebaum disagree with this? Who do you think is right?

7 According to Demsetz, how are externalities internalised by private property? Is he right?

8 Elsewhere in the article, Demsetz applies the same analysis to corporate ownership: see Chapter 8.

9 In his study of Swiss alpine grazing, *Common Property Economics* (referred to above), Glenn Stevenson found a wide variety of patterns of ownership of alpine grazing meadows within a relatively small area of Switzerland, and this appeared to be typical of other parts of Switzerland and also of alpine areas in other countries. Many of the meadows are communally owned (and have been for up to a thousand years); others are privately owned by individuals and either used by the owners personally or let out to other users; others are co-owned by a small number of private co-owners. Communal ownership exists in several different forms. In all cases (private and communal), use is highly regulated, sometimes by state regulation but more usually by elaborate

self-regulation, which also takes a wide variety of forms. Stevenson was unable to establish whether the communally run meadows were more or less efficient than the ones that were privately run. He *was* able to establish (by analysing milk yields) that they were less productive, but it was not possible to tell whether or not this was attributable to other differences: it could have been the case that they would have been even less productive under private ownership. In other words, a possible explanation (perhaps confirmed by the longevity of the mixed pattern of ownership) was that the pattern of ownership which had evolved for each meadow was the one to which it was most suited. As Stevenson concludes (pp. 234–5):

> Whether or not an eventual net revenues analysis [i.e. looking at the productivity relative to the costs input] indicates that commons management is generally poorer than private management, common property will still have its place in specific instances. In Switzerland, natural conditions exist under which only commons will work, regardless of the general incentives inherent in commons management. Particularly the remote areas are unsuitable for private management. Because of the costs of managing the resource privately at these locations, rents under common property may well be higher. Thus, even if generally poorer performance of common property is found in a net revenues analysis, not all commons will be inferior, nor can the conclusion be reached that all commons should be converted to private property. This notion parallels the more general idea that particular resource configurations exist – from fisheries to the atmosphere – for which we are compelled to find common property rather than private property solutions.

10 Barzel refers to the Coase theorem, which is that, in the absence of transaction costs inhibiting the proper working of the market, the efficient allocation of resources will occur wherever the entitlement is first put. We look at this again in Chapter 6.

3.2.2. Viability of single property systems

Even if economic efficiency is the overriding criterion for measuring the success of a particular form of property ownership (and we consider below whether there are other alternative or additional criteria), and even if we are persuaded that in principle private ownership is the most efficient form of ownership, we might nevertheless want to question whether it would be economically efficient to have private ownership of all resources.

As a matter of historical record, in most societies private, communal and state ownership coexist. It is difficult to envisage a society which did not recognise some form of private ownership of some resources, however exiguous. This is probably true even of a wholly Marxist society. As Jeremy Waldron points out (Waldron, *The Right to Private Property*, pp. 425–6) it is an integral part of Karl Marx's argument that private property should be abolished in total. He quotes Marx as responding to bourgeois critics of the socialist programme in the following terms:

> You are horrified at our intending to do away with private property. But in your existing society, private property is already done away with for nine-tenths of the population; its existence for the few is solely due to its nonexistence in the hands of these nine-tenths. You reproach us, therefore, with intending to do away with a form of property the necessary condition for whose existence is the nonexistence of any property for the immense majority of society. In one word, you reproach us for intending to do away with your property. Precisely so; that is just what we intend. (Marx and Engels, *Communist Manifesto*, p. 98)

Waldron comments:

> Throughout his work, Marx is adamant that the indictment against capitalism is not merely the fact that private property happens to be distributed unequally or in a way that leaves millions without any guaranteed access to the means of production; the problem is that private ownership is a form of property that has this characteristic necessarily. No matter how noble your egalitarian intentions, the existence of any distribution of private property rights in the means of production will lead quickly to their concentration in the hands of a few. Thus egalitarian intentions, so far as private property is concerned, are hopelessly utopian, for they underestimate the dynamic tendencies of the system they are interested in. 'For us the issue cannot be the alteration of private property but its annihilation.'

Nevertheless, even Marx had to have some way of recognising something akin to private property in relation to such ownables as one's labour and personal possessions. He refers to such things as 'private possessions', and although he pays little attention to precisely what rights individuals would have in such things they appear to go beyond purely possessory rights, even if not extending to full rights of alienation for reward, bequest and commercial exploitation (see further Grunebaum, *Private Ownership*, pp. 135–40, for a discussion of what these rights might be, consistently with what he terms Marx's free development principle).

At the opposite end of the scale, a society in which all resources are privately owned is probably also not feasible. This is not simply because there are some resources that any society would wish to make available for public use, such as roads and national defence systems. Resources which are to be made available for public use can still be made the subject of a modified type of private ownership which ensures public access, as we know from the privatisation of public utilities that occurred in many Western states in the late twentieth century. Nevertheless, economists recognise a category of resources, usually referred to as public goods, which many argue are most efficiently held by public ownership. As Demsetz has argued elsewhere (Demsetz, 'Ownership and the Externalities Problem', pp. 297–9), in the case of some resources such as the two examples already given, free-rider problems would make private ownership either economically inefficient (as in the case of national defence systems) or too politically contentious to be generally adopted (in the case of privately owned roads). Essentially, the argument is that national defence systems provide benefits which cannot easily be made available only to those willing to pay for the services, and so non-payers can confidently free-ride on payers, knowing they will benefit from enemy attacks being deterred and repulsed just as much as payers will. As far as private ownership of roads is concerned, the free-rider problem is rather different. Private ownership of public roads would be feasible if road owners were entitled to charge for road use, and indeed charging for road use (whether the road is state owned or privately owned) would arguably have the advantage of reducing road use. However, in a situation in which use of roads is free, those who put a low value on their time and therefore do not much mind congestion free-ride on those who put a high value on their time and would therefore pay a toll in order to control the level of traffic (consider why). These free-riders will therefore oppose privatisation of roads, and traditionally there have been enough of them to make their opposition successful. It is worth noting in this connection that the London congestion charge (where the roads remain publicly owned but use is charged for) was made politically acceptable (to the extent it is) only as part of a scheme under which the profits from the charge (i.e. the charges collected, net of costs) are dedicated for use on paying for improvements to public transport, which can be seen as a way of making the internalisation of the externality of congestion politically acceptable.

3.2.3.   Criteria for measuring the success of a particular form of ownership

Economic efficiency is not the only criterion by which we might want to measure the success or the justifiability of a particular form of ownership. Most people would want also to consider the impact that a particular form of ownership regime might have on the organisation of a society that adopted it, and to assess success and justifiability from a moral perspective as well as, or rather than, from an economic perspective. We explore this second point in the next chapter, but it is important to emphasise here that economic efficiency is not something that can be ignored in assessing the moral justifiability of a property regime. As Grunebaum points out (Grunebaum, *Private Ownership*, p. 159):

> The moral perspective takes precedence [over the economic perspective]. But ... [it] should [not] be assumed that economic criteria are wholly irrelevant to a moral justification of a specific form of ownership. Economic inefficiencies can imply a wasteful utilization of resources or labor which from a moral perspective might be unjustified because people might be forced to labor without any productive or beneficial outcome. In a similar way, high administrative costs might consume wealth which morally might be put to better use. Thus an examination of the allegedly

economic optimific effects of private ownership is indeed relevant to the overall moral justification of autonomous ownership as an alternative form of ownership.

There is another difficulty in measuring the justifiability of any particular form of property, also identified by Grunebaum. He makes the point that, while the consequences of practicing a particular form of ownership are clearly relevant in assessing its moral justifiability, in practice it is extremely difficult to discern what those consequences are – a point that could be made with equal force in relation to the assessment of economic efficiency. As he says (Grunebaum, *Private Ownership*, p. 8):

> Specific forms only have tendencies to produce certain consequences 'all else being equal'. In actuality all else is rarely equal and consequences which are elicited in support of conclusions about the practice of a specific form of ownership may be, and sometimes are, explainable by social forces which have little relevance to the society's specific form of ownership. For example, it is claimed that private ownership of the means of production causes increasing concentrations of wealth in the hands of a few. While this may seem plausible it is in fact difficult to prove because counter-vailing forces such as labor unions, progressive income tax measures, and capitaliza-tion by issuing common stock, among other forces, have exerted pressures in the opposite direction. Actual statistics about wealth distribution may by themselves be irrelevant to proving or disproving the claim. This does not mean that moral justifica-tion is impossible. What is implied is that any justification which depends upon predictions about what the consequences will be of practicing a specific form must also discuss other social forces which may affect its tendencies.

3.3.   John Locke's justification for private property

3.3.1.   What Locke was attempting to establish

Jean Jacques Rousseau said in *A Discourse on the Origins of Inequality*:

> The first man who, having enclosed a piece of land, thought of saying 'This is mine' and found people simple enough to believe him, was the true founder of civil society. How many crimes, wars, murders, how much misery and horror the human race would have been spared if someone had pulled up the stakes and filled in the ditch and cried out to his fellow men: 'Beware of listening to this impostor. You are lost if you forget that the fruits of the earth belong to everyone and that the earth itself belongs to no one.'

John Locke's concern is to demonstrate that this is wrong, and to establish that, given the right conditions, it is morally justifiable that those who take resources from their natural state are allowed to keep them for themselves to the exclusion of all others. He is therefore seeking to justify original acquisition of private property rights. He does not deal with transfer of property rights, nor (except incidentally) with questions of redistribution of property rights once resources have already become subject to some form of ownership, whether private or otherwise.

3.3.2. The political context

Locke's argument about original acquisition of property rights was part of a highly charged political debate that was taking place in seventeenth-century England about the legitimacy of private rights as against an absolutist monarchy, and his antagonists in the debate had political views that were very different from those expressed by Rousseau, who was writing some fifty years after Locke's death. What Locke is saying is important to us now irrespective of its historical political context, but it makes it easier to follow what he is saying if we have some idea of the arguments he was trying to meet.

Those who supported absolutist monarchy (most notably, Sir Robert Filmer) disputed the notion, held by Locke and other natural lawyers, that private property rights and other private rights had a legitimacy which was not derived from the state. As far as natural lawyers were concerned, the world was given to people in common by God for their subsistence and preservation (or, as Locke says in paragraph 26, 'God, who hath given the world to men in common, hath also given them reason to make use of it to the best advantage of life and convenience. The earth and all that is therein is given to men for the support and comfort of their being.'). It is from this, they argue, that private property owners derive their rights: private ownership is acquired by individuals taking for themselves things given to 'mankind in common' by God. Consequently, natural lawyers argued (and indeed might still argue), any right that the state has to interfere with private property rights is conferred on the state by the people and can be withdrawn by the people if abused by the state. Such arguments were used to justify the Glorious Revolution in England in 1688 and in support of the French Revolution and the American War of Independence.

Filmer, in common with other supporters of absolutist monarchies and the divine right of kings, rejected this analysis. Filmer traced the derivation of property rights from God to Adam, the first man, and from him by a direct line of descent through his heirs to the monarch, regarded as Adam's only legitimate heir, the inheritor of the dominion over the world and all its resources which God gave to Adam. According to this view, such private property rights as individuals held, they held only by grace of the monarch, who could withdraw them at will. This is the argument Locke is referring to in paragraph 25 when he says that 'if it be difficult to make out "property" upon a supposition that God gave the world to Adam and his posterity in common [i.e. to all people in common], [then] it is impossible that any man but one universal monarch should have any "property" upon a supposition that God gave the world to Adam and his heirs in succession, exclusive of all the rest of his posterity'.

3.3.3.   The problem of consent

Filmer argued that the natural lawyers' analysis of the derivation of property rights was fatally flawed because it failed to explain how private property owners could legitimately have acquired rights from mankind in common. If one person acquires private property rights in a thing that was formerly held by all people in common, this necessarily extinguishes the right or liberty that those people had in the thing. How can this be justified? Earlier natural lawyers, most notably Grotius and Pufendorf, had argued that it was done by the consent of the commoners. Filmer rejected this as an absurdity:

> Certainly, it was a rare felicity, that all men in the world at one instant of time should agree together in one mind to change the natural community of all things into private dominion: for without such a unanimous consent it was not possible for community to be altered: for if but one man in the world had dissented, the alteration had been unjust, because that man by the law of nature had a right to the common use of all things in the world; so that, to have given a propriety of any one thing to any other, had been to have robbed him of his right to the common use of all things. (Filmer, 'Observations', in *Patriarcha*, p. 273)

In Extract 3.5 below, Locke is seeking to defend the natural law position against this attack. He does not do so by defending the consent theory (although, as others have pointed out, it is considerably more sophisticated and plausible than Filmer suggests: see, for example, Stephen Buckle's discussion of Grotius' formulation of the consent theory, and Filmer's misconception of it, in *Natural Law and the Theory of Property*, pp. 161–7). Instead, Locke argues that it is not necessary to look for consent from the commoners, because it is something else that confers legitimacy on the holding of a person who takes resources from the common. His argument is that those who take resources from the common for themselves to the exclusion of all others legitimately acquire rights over the resource if by so doing they mixed their labour with it.

3.3.4.   Locke's justification for original acquisition

This argument of Locke's amounts to more than a 'first come, first served' justification. Awarding property rights to the first taker has considerable attractions, as we see in the next chapter, but this is not what Locke is advocating or defending. He argues that the first taker of a thing from the common legitimately acquires rights not *because* he was first, but *because, and if and only if,* he mixed his labour with the thing he takes. However, he argues, there are two provisos or qualifications to this general principle. The first is that no one is justified in taking more than he needs, so that the surplus spoils (sometimes referred to as 'the spoliation proviso'). The second is that such an appropriation from the commons is justifiable only when 'enough and as good [is] left in common for others' (the 'sufficiency proviso').

The precise scope and significance of these two provisos is unclear (and controversial) but before looking at them more closely we need to clarify Locke's basic premise and then outline the steps in the reasoning by which he arrives at his general principle.

3.3.5. The nature of Locke's commons

Locke talks about the world and its resources being given to mankind 'in common'. Does he mean by this that unallocated natural resources are open access communal property (i.e. resources which everyone has a Hohfeldian claim-right not to be excluded from) or that they are no-property (i.e. resources which everyone has only a Hohfeldian privilege to use, but no right not to be excluded from)? This has always been a highly controversial question, if only because of the political implications of resting Locke's theory in particular and natural law theory in general on an apparent assumption of natural communism. In fact, it is not at all clear what Locke meant: compare the different ways in which Kramer, *John Locke and the Origins of Private Property*, pp. 108–9, Waldron, *The Right to Private Property*, pp. 148–57, Tully, *A Discourse on Property*, pp. 59–64, 95–8 and 124–5, Buckle, *Natural Law and the Theory of Property*, pp. 164–5 and 183–90, Ryan, *Property and Political Theory*, pp. 29–32, and Sreenivasan, *The Limits of Lockean Rights in Property*, pp. 26–9 and 140–5, interpret what Locke actually says on this point. This is not an issue we need to explore here, because the justification problem is essentially the same whether private property robs others of a right not to be excluded from the appropriated resources or just a liberty to use it. As Waldron says, it may be that it requires stronger justification to extinguish a Hohfeldian claim-right in a thing than a Hohfeldian liberty in it, but even this is doubtful if the thing in question provided the basic means of support for the former users. So, for the purposes of the following discussion, we assume that what requires justification is an appropriation of a thing which removes everyone else's right not to be excluded from that thing or their privilege to use and enjoy it for their own self-preservation.

3.3.6. Why mixing labour with a thing should give rise to entitlement

Locke summarises his argument at paragraph 27. His starting point is that we each have 'property' in our own 'person' (the quotation marks are his), in the sense that no one but ourselves has any rights in it. In the same way, he says, the labour of our bodies and the work of our hands is also our own. When we remove something from its natural state by mixing our labour with it, we are joining something of our own to it. By doing this, we make it our own property. He goes on to elaborate the argument, and adds the two provisos (the sufficiency proviso first appearing at the end of paragraph 27 and the spoilation proviso at paragraph 31).

There are obvious problems with this reasoning. We noted in Chapter 1 that the question of whether we own our own bodies is not straightforward, so it may well be necessary to look more closely at the first assumption in Locke's argument, that we each have property in our own bodies. But, even if we accept this first step in the argument, and also accept that our labour is our 'property' in any relevant sense (and there are difficulties with this too), why should the mixing of it with a thing make that thing our property also? Locke gives a number of reasons, which we can take as cumulative or alternative.

His first point (paragraphs 28–30) is that, if we pick an apple from an apple tree growing wild and eat it, everyone must accept that the apple becomes our exclusive property at *some* point in the process, whether when we pick it, or first bite into it, or finish digesting it. There must be some reason for this intuitive acceptance of appropriation from the common that we all have, he says. It cannot be because everyone has consented to the appropriation, because if *everyone's* consent was required to every appropriation we would all starve (this is essentially Filmer's point). However, if it isn't common consent that provides the justification, he says, it must be something else, and the only other thing it can be is the labour expended on the picking of the apple. This is the only thing that adds something to what nature has provided, the only thing that distinguishes this apple from all the other common apples.

This argument does not really take us anywhere on its own. It starts by begging the question, by assuming to be correct ('nobody can deny but' the apple becomes the property of the person who picks and eats it) the very thing that Locke is trying to prove (that unallocated resources properly become the private property of those who appropriate them). It then asserts, rather than demonstrates, that the labour involved in the picking is the only thing that *could* justify allocating the apple to the picker. He does not consider other possibilities: why not say, for example, that it is justifiable to allocate the apple to the picker because apple-picking is the first step towards apple-eating, which represents using the apple for the purpose for which Locke would say God provided it?

However, while this argument does not tell us why mixing our labour with a thing should give us property rights in it, there appears within it a reference to a more substantial argument that Locke develops later on. This is that, until we mix our labour with it, 'the common is of no use' (paragraph 28).

Locke develops this argument more fully in paragraphs 40–4. Locke's point here is that, by mixing our labour with things, we make them more valuable. Natural resources are of little use to us until we have exploited their potential by labouring on them, and if we look at the things that are valuable and useful to us we will find that 90 per cent of their value (later he increases the proportion to 99 per cent) is attributable to the labour that went into producing them. Robert Nozick points out a number of difficulties with this (see Extract 3.6 below). Apart from anything else, we do not always increase the value of things by working on them, and, even if we did, why should this give us exclusive ownership of the whole thing rather than a share in it proportionate to the increase in value? These objections can be met, to some extent at least. If we accept that the full potential use and value of natural resources should be realised, most people would agree that this can only be achieved by individuals labouring on them. Allocating outright ownership to the labourer (regardless of the actual effect on value in each particular case) is an obviously simple and effective incentive and/or reward and/or compensation for the expenditure of the necessary labour. This can be put in religious terms, as Locke does: God provided mankind with natural resources so that people would work to improve them to produce sustenance to preserve their lives, labour being a virtue in itself, and private property being both the reward and the compensation for the expenditure of labour and the means by which God intended natural resources to be developed so that they could sustain humans. Alternatively, we can put it in economic terms: natural resources can be exploited to their fullest extent only by people working on them, and people will choose to undertake the necessary work if they are rewarded by the allocation of private property in whatever is produced by their work. If we rewarded only *successful* work and only to the extent that it was successful – i.e. labour that did in fact end up increasing the value of things, and then only up to the increase in value – we would discourage innovative work and inhibit development. No one would experiment with new ways of preserving or using timber, for example, if they knew that they would be allowed to keep the end product only if and to the extent that the experiment was successful. Also, allocating property rights in this way would require a costly bureaucracy. It would be necessary for the state, or some other official body, to judge who had 'earned' what property rights in what things in every case: someone would have to decide whether you increased the value of the plank by painting it pink (judged by what standard?) and if so whether to a sufficient degree to be allowed to keep it, or just to use it for a limited period of time. This would not just be costly. It would also introduce a degree of day-to-day bureaucratic intervention into the allocation of private property rights that most libertarians would find repugnant. A clear simple rule that labouring on a thing always and automatically allows you to take the thing laboured on avoids these difficulties, and arguably this outweighs the disadvantage that this will result in occasionally rewarding disimprovers.

However, this argument works least well in relation to Locke's prime example of land. To reward labour that increases the productivity of the land (the crops, timber, minerals etc. that Locke refers to in paragraph 43) with *perpetual ownership of the land* seems disproportionate in principle. Why not just ownership of the produce, plus guaranteed use of the land for a period sufficient to enable the produce to be harvested, or alternatively for so long as the land continues to be put to productive use? This does not seem a particularly difficult rule to apply, and it would have the significant advantage of leaving future generations with the opportunity to gain land rights by original acquisition. As John Stuart Mill says (in the course of an argument that land ownership ought to continue only for so long as the owner of the land is its 'improver'):

It is no hardship to any one, to be excluded from what others have produced: they were not bound to produce it for his use, and he loses nothing by not sharing in what otherwise would not have existed at all. But it is some hardship to be born into the world and to find all nature's gifts previously engrossed, and no place left for the newcomer.

('Property in Land', in Mill, *Principles of Political Economy*, Book II, Chapter 2, § 6)

It may be that Locke did not intend that the 'property' justifiably acquired by mixing one's labour with a thing is always necessarily absolute perpetual ownership (although this seems unlikely given the nature of the private property rights he was seeking to defend: for the contrary view see Tully, *A Discourse on Property*). Alternatively, it can be argued (as Sreenivasan has in *The Limits of Lockean Rights in Property*, see in particular Chapter 4) that, regardless of what Locke actually meant, what his argument supports is the acquisition of only limited rights in perpetual resources such as land. Or it may simply be that Locke could face with equanimity the prospect that all land would justifiably have become taken into private ownership (or public or limited access ownership) over time, leaving nothing in the commons for general use, because non-owners would have other means of self-preservation through labour.

3.3.7.   The sufficiency proviso

This brings us to the sufficiency proviso. How are we to understand the qualification that Locke introduces in paragraph 27 when he says that ownership of a natural resource not limitless in supply should go to the person who first labours on the resource 'at least where there is enough, and as good left in common for others'?

Commentators have put forward a variety of ways of interpreting this apparent limitation. It can be read as meaning that it is justifiable to confer ownership of a thing on the person who first mixes her labour with it, but only if this leaves enough like things remaining in the common for others *to appropriate*. As Robert Nozick points out, this interpretation (what he calls the 'stringent' version of the proviso) if applied literally would rule out all acquisition of finite resources, however plentiful the supply (consider why), and as we see in Notes and Questions 3.2 after the extracts, there are other reasons as well for rejecting this interpretation. Arguably, the same objection applies to the second possible interpretation, which is that the appropriation by the person who mixes labour with a thing is justifiable if it leaves enough like things in the common for others to continue to make use of, i.e. if it does not worsen anyone's *liberty to use* that kind of resource. Nevertheless, Nozick takes the view that such a version of the proviso would be contained in 'any adequate theory of justice in acquisition', except that an appropriation that would otherwise be illegitimate because it violated such a proviso could be legitimated by the appropriator compensating the others for their loss. This version of the proviso (Nozick's 'weaker' version) comes close to saying that appropriations are justifiable provided that they do not leave anyone worse off *in general terms*. Interpreted in such a way, there is a danger of robbing the proviso of all effect. As Kramer points out, Locke himself expressed the view that appropriation from the common not only makes society as a whole better off but also provides a positive benefit to all non-owners:

> Locke, of course, not merely believed that all-encompassing swarms of acquisitions would pose no threat to anyone's basic rights; he assumed as well that the all-embracing sweep of ownership would in fact redound to the benefit of nonowners. Since the spread of human dominion over the entirety of the earth would involve the spread of a benign exploitation of the earth's riches, the outcome of that spread would enhance the fortunes of everybody. Somewhat like the Deity's filling of the earth with the glorious knowledge of Himself as envisaged by Isaiah and Habakkuk, the filling of the world with the enterprise and talents of human owners was a situation that blessed all people. Locke often made this point by contrasting the impecuniousness of the American Indians with the comforts of the highly developed land of the English. 'For I aske whether in the wild woods and uncultivated wast of America left to Nature, without any improvement, tillage or husbandry, a thousand acres will yield the needy and wretched inhabitants as many conveniencies of life as ten acres of equally fertile land doe in Devonshire where they are well cultivated?' [Locke, *Two Treatises of Government* (ed. P. Laslett, 2nd edn, Cambridge: Cambridge University Press, 1967), § 37]. In a much-discussed passage, Locke asserted even more explicitly that the spread of labor and ownership throughout a country was a boon to all people, to nonowners as well as owners. Having declared firmly that ''tis *Labour* indeed that *puts the difference of value* on every thing' [Locke, *Two Treatises of Government*, edited by P. Laslett (2nd edn, Cambridge: Cambridge University Press, 1967), § 40, emphasis in original], he proceeded to the following observation:

> > There cannot be a clearer demonstration of any thing, than several Nations of the Americans are of this, who are rich in Land, and poor in all the Comforts of Life; whom Nature having furnished as liberally as any other people, with the materials of Plenty, i.e. a fruitful Soil, apt to produce in abundance, what might serve for food, rayment, and delight; yet, for want of improving it by labour, have not one hundredth part of the Conveniencies we enjoy: And a King of a large and fruitful Territory there feeds, lodges, and is clad worse than a day Labourer in England.
> > [Locke, *Two Treatises of Government*, edited by P. Laslett (2nd edn, Cambridge: Cambridge University Press, 1967), § 41]

In short, far from serving to undermine the ability of people to obtain sustenance, the extending of proprietary dominion to every usable plot of land was the surest means of strengthening that ability – for those who remained landless as well as for the landowners. Once all the earth and the earth's bounty had been appropriated and parceled out, a typical laborer might indeed have very few opportunities to become an owner of land, at least in the short term; still, he would enjoy ready access to a greater supply of comforts and conveniences than was ever within the reach of any landowner during the presocietal stage of humankind. (Kramer, *John Locke and the Origins of Private Property*, pp. 219–20, although note that earlier, at p. 127, Kramer denies that Locke here intends to say that *all* are better off – 'even out-and-out vagabonds').

If this is correct, the proviso would be satisfied automatically in all cases: it could never operate to limit the justifiability of any particular original acquisition.

A more promising line of interpretation involves returning to Locke's starting point, that natural resources were given to mankind in general for their subsistence and the preservation of their lives. If this is the case, then the proviso might be taken to mean that an appropriation of a thing by a person who mixes her labour in a thing is justifiable as long as it leaves others with sufficient opportunity to provide for their own subsistence and preservation by labour – even if this involves labouring for money to acquire property by exchange rather than labouring to appropriate property from the common. Waldron takes this further to link it with what he describes as Locke's doctrine of charity, that property rights also must never stand in the way of human sustenance for those unable to work. This, he suggests, could lead to a proviso to the effect that 'no appropriation is legitimate if (taking everything into account) it makes the survival of any other person less rather than more likely'. (Waldron, *The Right to Private Property*, p. 216).

These widely diverging interpretations of the proviso are attributable not so much to a lack of clarity in Locke's wording, as to the importance of the point for any theory of allocation of property rights. While some of the interpretations are put forward as interpretations of what Locke 'really' meant, for most commentators the primary concern is to establish what would constitute a coherent and appropriate limitation on a labour theory of just acquisition. This involves a closer analysis of Locke's theory than we need here, so for present purposes the important point is to note the range of possible interpretations of the proviso rather than to come to any firm conclusion as to what it 'really' means.

3.3.8. The spoilation proviso

The spoilation proviso as sketched out by Locke in paragraph 31 is easier, particularly if we keep in mind the general thrust of Locke's argument. If, as Locke believed, the world and its resources are provided by God to enable people to sustain and preserve their lives, any appropriation which leads to a waste of resources is illegitimate, regardless of whether it diminishes the supply or the prospects available for others. In Locke's view, God gave people resources to use not to waste, and so even the consent of all the commoners or limitless supply would not justify an appropriation of more than you can use for yourself or pass on to others by exchange. The argument can work just as well if God is removed from the analysis. Environmental concerns might lead us to a similar principle that exploitation of natural resources is unjustifiable if it involves taking more than can be used and wasting the surplus. The spoilation proviso is therefore not made redundant by the invention of money (taking more than you need is legitimate if you can sell the surplus, but not if you are going to have to let it go to waste), nor is it made superfluous by the sufficiency proviso (as Nozick suggests in Extract 3.6 below).

The final points to make about Locke's labour theory of acquisition concern its present scope and relevance.

3.3.9.   The theological dimension to Locke's theory

It was common ground between all sides of the debate in which Locke was engaged that God exists, and that God was the creator of the world and all its resources and the origin of legitimacy for all rights in resources. The issue that divided Locke from his opponents was whether property was then conferred by God on people in general for their common good, as Locke believed, or on the monarchy as the institution entrusted by God to rule the kingdom, as Filmer believed. The essence of the debate was therefore whether rights of the individual derive from the state or arise independently of it. This a question which is relevant beyond the specific theological context in which the debate took place. Also, as we have already noted, Locke's argument mostly works as well whether we believe that natural resources were provided by God for the benefit of humankind, or whether concern for the environment and the proper relationship between people and the world leads us to adopt a similar position on the uses to which natural resources may legitimately be put.

In other words, although Locke believed in a Christian God, his argument need not be confined to property rights arising in a Western Christian society. It is equally applicable to any society that accepts that everyone has a liberty to make use of unappropriated natural resources and an obligation not to waste them, whatever the origin of that liberty and obligation is thought to be.

3.3.10.   Present relevance of Locke's theory

Locke is seeking to justify the original acquisition of private property rights in unallocated resources. Is there any scope for such a theory in modern society? Most of the examples Locke gives concern land or the natural products of land or the resources which it can be made to produce. In Locke's time, vast tracts of what appeared to be unallocated land were being opened up by colonial exploration of the Americas and other continents. There is no unallocated land in this country now, and most resources of any value are already owned by individuals, or companies, or the state, and the same is true of most developed countries. Why then do we need concern ourselves with the question of whether and how original acquisition of property rights can be justified?

This is a point that Kramer discusses at length (Kramer, *John Locke and the Origins of Private Property*, pp. 140–3 and 213–37), but for present purposes three short reasons will do. The first is that original acquisition of land in this country was no more possible in Locke's time than it is today, as he himself points out in paragraph 35. He did not see this as limiting the general application of his analysis.

The second reason why Locke's theory still matters is that original acquisition is not so very rare as to be of only marginal importance. As we noted in Chapter 2, new categories of no-property constantly emerge, and at the point when a new resource comes into being or a pre-existing no-property resource becomes scarce, it becomes necessary to consider whether and how it should be reduced to ownership. Locke's theory attempts to provide an answer to this. It explains, for example, why we might be justified in allocating ownership of a cake to the person who makes it rather than to the owner of the ingredients, and why a doctor who uses a patient's body cells in research might acquire ownership of drugs deriving from those body cells, as we saw in Chapter 1. It also forms the basis for intellectual property rights, not only in the sense that it provides a justification for giving property rights in newly created things to the creator rather than to anyone else, but also in the sense that it might provide the justification for treating the newly created thing as property at all. This point comes up again when we look at recognition of new property interests in Chapter 9.

In short, every society that recognises exclusionary property rights must have a rule allocating ownership of new things, or of previously non-allocated things that someone now wants to exclude others from. Locke tells us what he thinks that rule should be, and we need to consider whether we agree with him.

The third reason why Locke's theory still matters is because a theory of original acquisition is an integral part of any comprehensive justification of property rights. Any theory that attempts to justify, for example, why the state should confer property rights on one person rather than on another, or the confiscation or redistribution of private property by the state, or the colonial acquisition of property rights or (conversely) the survival of indigenous property rights following colonisation, or the recognition of titles derived by inheritance or gift or theft, tells us only part of the story unless it also tells us what legitimised the original property holdings in the first place, and allows us to distinguish legitimate from illegitimate holdings. This is as true now as it was when Locke was writing.

Extract 3.5   John Locke, 'On Property' in *Second Treatise of Government* (1690)

25. Whether we consider natural reason, which tells us that men, being once born, have a right to their preservation, and consequently to meat and drink and such other things as Nature affords for their subsistence, or 'revelation', which gives us an account of those grants God made of the world to Adam, and to Noah and his sons, it is very clear that God, as King David says (Psalm cxv, 16), 'has given the earth to the children of men', given it to mankind in common. But, this being supposed, it seems to some a very great difficulty how any one should ever come to have a property in anything, I will not content myself to answer, that, if it be difficult to make out 'property' upon a supposition that God gave the world to Adam and his posterity in common, it is impossible that any man but one universal monarch should have any 'property' upon a supposition that God gave the world to Adam and his heirs in succession, exclusive of

all the rest of his posterity; but I shall endeavour to show how men might come to have a property in several parts of that which God gave to mankind in common, and that, without any express compact of all the commoners.

26. God, who hath given the world to men in common, hath also given them reason to make use of it to the best advantage of life and convenience. The earth and all that is therein is given to men for the support and comfort of their being. And, though all the fruits it naturally produces, and beasts it feeds, belong to mankind in common, as they are produced by the spontaneous hand of Nature, and nobody has originally a private dominion exclusive of the rest of mankind in any of them, as they are thus in their natural state, yet being given for the use of men, there must of necessity be a means to appropriate them some way or other before they can be of any use, or at all beneficial, to any particular men. The fruit or venison which nourishes the wild Indian, who knows no enclosure, and is still a tenant in common must be his, and so his – i.e. a part of him, that another can no longer have any right to it before it can do him any good for the support of his life.

27. Though the earth and all inferior creatures be common to all men, yet every man has a 'property' in his own 'person'. This nobody has any right to but himself. The 'labour' of his body and the 'work' of his hands, we may say, are properly his. Whatsoever, then, he removes out of the state that Nature hath provided and left it in, he hath mixed his labour with it, and joined to it something that is his own, and thereby makes it his property. It being by him removed from the common state Nature placed it in, it hath by this labour something annexed to it that excludes the common right of other men. For this 'labour' being the unquestionable property of the labourer, no man but he can have a right to what that is once joined to, at least where there is enough, and as good left in common for others.

28. He that is nourished by the acorns he picked up under an oak, or the apples he gathered from the trees in the wood, has certainly appropriated them to himself. Nobody can deny but the nourishment is his. I ask, then, when did they begin to be his? when he digested? or when he ate? or when he boiled? or when he brought them home? or when he picked them up? And it is plain, if the first gathering made them not his, nothing else could. That labour put a distinction between them and common. That added something to them more than Nature, the common mother of all, had done, and so they became his private right. And will any one say he had no right to those acorns or apples he thus appropriated because he had not the consent of all mankind to make them his? Was it a robbery thus to assume to himself what belonged to all in common? If such a consent as that was necessary, man had starved, notwithstanding the plenty God had given him. We see in commons, which remain so by compact, that it is the taking any part of what is common, and removing it out of the state Nature leaves it in, which begins the property, without which the common is of no use. And the taking of this or that part does not depend on the express consent of all the commoners. Thus, the grass my horse has bit, the turfs my servant has cut, and the ore I have digged in any place, where I have a right to them in common with others, become my property without the assignation or consent of anybody. The labour that was mine, removing them out of that common state they were in, hath fixed my property in them.

29. By making an explicit consent of every commoner necessary to any one's appropriating to himself any part of what is given in common, children or servants could not cut the meat which their father or master had provided for them in common without assigning to every one his peculiar part. Though the water running in the fountain be everyone's, yet who can doubt but that in the pitcher is his only who drew it out? His labour hath taken it out of the hands of Nature where it was common, and belonged equally to all her children, and hath thereby appropriated into himself.

30. Thus this law of reason makes the deer that Indian's who hath killed it; it is allowed to be his goods who hath bestowed his labour upon it, though, before, it was the common right of every one. And among those who are counted the civilised part of mankind, who have made and multiplied positive laws to determine property, this original law of Nature for the beginning of property, in what was before common, still takes place, and by virtue thereof, what fish any one catches in the ocean, that great and still remaining common of mankind; or what ambergris any one takes up here is by the labour that removes it out of that common state Nature left it in, made his property who takes that pains about it. And, even among us, the hare that anyone is hunting is thought his who pursues her during the chase. For being a beast that is still looked upon as common, and no man's private possession, whoever has employed so much labour about any of that kind as to find and pursue her has thereby removed her from the state of Nature wherein she was common, and hath begun a property.

31. It will, perhaps, be objected to this, that, if gathering the acorns or other fruits of the earth, etc. makes a right to them, then any one may engross as much as he will. To which I answer, Not so. The same law of Nature that does by this means give us property, does also bound that property too. 'God has given us all things richly.' Is the voice of reason confirmed by inspiration? But how far has He given it to us – 'To enjoy'? As much as any one can make use of to any advantage of life before it spoils, so much he may by his labour fix a property in. Whatever is beyond this is more than his share, and belongs to others. Nothing was made by God for man to spoil or destroy. And thus considering the plenty of natural provisions there was a long time in the world, and the few spenders, and to how small a part of that provision the industry of one man could extend itself and engross it to the prejudice of others, especially keeping within the bounds set by reason of what serve for his use, there could be then little room for quarrels or contentions about property so established.

32. But the chief matter of property being now not the fruits of the earth and the beasts that subsist on it, but the earth itself, as that which takes in and carries with it all the rest, I think it is plain that property in that too is acquired as the former. As much land as a man tills, plants, improves, cultivates, and can use the product of, so much is his property. He by his labour does, as it were, enclose it from the common. Nor will it invalidate his right to say everybody else has an equal title to it, and therefore he cannot appropriate, he cannot enclose without the consent of all his fellow-commoners all mankind. God, when He gave the world in common to all mankind, commanded man also to labour and the penury of his condition required it of him. God and his reason commanded him to subdue the earth – i.e. improve it for the benefit of life and therein

lay out something upon it that was his own, his labour. He that, in obedience to this command of God, subdued, tilled, and sowed any part of it, thereby annexed to it something that was his property, which another had no title to, nor could without injury take from him.

33. Nor was this appropriation of any parcel of land, by improving it, any prejudice to any other man, since there was still enough and as good left, and more than the yet unprovided could use. So that, in effect, there was never the less left for others because of his enclosure for himself. For he that leaves as much as another can make use of does as good as take nothing at all. Nobody could think himself injured by the drinking of another man, though he took a good draught, who had a whole river of the same water left him to quench his thirst. And the case of land and water, where there is enough of both, is perfectly the same.

34. God gave the world to men in common but since He gave it them for their benefit and the greatest conveniencies of life they were capable to draw from it, it cannot be supposed He meant it should always remain common and uncultivated. He gave it to the use of the industrious and rational (and labour was to be his title to it); not to the fancy or covetousness of the quarrelsome and contentious. He that had as good left for his improvement as was already taken up needed not complain, ought not to meddle with what was already improved by another's labour; if he did it is plain he desired the benefit of another's pains which he had no right to, and not the ground which God had given him, in common with others, to labour on, and whereof there was as good left as that already possessed, and more than he knew what to do with, or his industry could reach to.

35. It is true, in land that is common in England or any other country, where there are plenty of people under government who have money and commerce, no one can enclose or appropriate any part without the consent of all his fellow-commoners; because this is left common by compact – i.e. by the law of the land, which is not to be violated. And, though it be common in respect of some men, it is not so to all mankind, but is the joint propriety of this country, or this parish. Besides, the remainder, after such enclosure, would not be as good to the rest of the commoners as the whole was, when they could all make use of the whole; whereas in the beginning and first peopling of the great common of the world it was quite otherwise. The law man was under was rather for appropriating. God commanded, and his wants forced him to labour. That was his property, which could not be taken from him wherever he had fixed it. And hence subduing or cultivating the earth and having dominion, we see, are joined together. The one gave title to the other. So that God, by commanding to subdue, gave authority so far to appropriate. And the condition of human life, which requires labour and materials to work on, necessarily introduce private possessions.

36. The measure of property Nature well set, by the extent of men's labour and the conveniency of life. No man's labour could subdue or appropriate all, nor could his enjoyment consume more than a small part; so that it was impossible for any man, this way, to entrench upon the right of another or acquire to himself a property to the prejudice of his neighbour, who would still have room for as good and as large a

possession (after the other had taken out his) as before it was appropriated. Which measure did confine every man's possession to a very moderate proportion, and such as he might appropriate to himself without injury to anybody in the first ages of the world when men were more in danger to be lost, by wandering from their company, in the then vast wilderness of the earth than to be straitened for want of room to plant in. And the same measure may be allowed still, without prejudice to anybody, full as the world seems. For, supposing a man or family, in the state they were at first, peopling of the world by the children of Adam or Noah, let him plant in some inland vacant places of America. We shall find that the possessions he could make himself, upon the measures we have given, would not be very large, nor, even to this day, prejudice the rest of mankind or give them reason to complain or think themselves injured by this man's encroachment, though the race of men have now spread themselves to all the corners of the world, and do infinitely exceed the small number was at the beginning. Nay, the extent of ground is of so little value without labour that I have heard it affirmed that, in Spain itself a man may be permitted to plough, sow, and reap, without being disturbed upon land he has no other title to, but only his making use of it. But, on the contrary, the inhabitants think themselves beholden to him who, by his industry on neglected, and consequently waste land, has increased the stock of corn, which they wanted. But be this as it will, which I lay no stress on, this I dare boldly affirm, that the same rule of propriety – namely that every man should have as much as he could make use of, would hold still in the world, without straitening anybody, since there is land enough in the world to suffice double the inhabitants, had not the invention of money, and the tacit agreement of men to put a value on it, introduced (by consent) larger possession and a right to them; which, how it has done, I shall by and by show more at large.

37. This is certain, that, in the beginning, before the desire of having more than men needed had altered the intrinsic value of things, which depends only on their usefulness to the life of man, or had agreed that a little piece of yellow metal, which would keep without wasting or decay, should be worth a great piece of flesh or a whole heap of corn, though men had a right to appropriate by their labour, each one to himself, as much of the things of Nature as he could use, yet this could not be much, nor to the prejudice of others, where the same plenty was still left, to those who would use the same industry. Before the appropriation of land, he who gathered as much of the wild fruit, killed, caught, or tamed as many of the beasts as he could – he that so employed his pains about any of the spontaneous products of Nature as any way to alter them from the state Nature put them in, by placing any of his labour on them, did thereby acquire a propriety in them; but if they perished in his possession without their due use – if the fruits rotted or the venison putrefied before he could spend it, he offended against the common law of Nature, and was liable to be punished: he invaded his neighbour's share, for he had no right farther than his use called for any of them, and they might serve to afford him conveniencies of life.

38. The same measures governed the possession of land, too. Whatsoever he tilled and reaped, laid up and made use of before it spoiled, that was his peculiar right; whatsoever he enclosed, and could feed and make use of, the cattle and product was also his. But if either the grass of his enclosure rotted on the ground, or the fruit of his

planting perished without gathering and laying up, this part of the earth, notwith-standing his enclosure, was still to be looked on as waste, and might be the possession of any other. Thus, at the beginning, Cain might take as much ground as he could till and make it his own land, and yet leave enough to Abel's sheep to feed on: a few acres would serve for both their possessions. But as families increased and industry enlarged their stocks, their possessions enlarged with the need of them; but yet it was commonly without any fixed property in the ground they made use of till they incorporated, settled themselves together, and built cities, and then, by consent, they came in time to set out the bounds of their distinct territories and agree on limits between them and their neighbours, and by laws within themselves settled the properties of those of the same society. For we see that, in that part of the world which was first inhabited, and therefore likely to be best peopled, even as low down as Abraham's time, they wandered with their flocks and their herds, which was their substance, freely up and down – and this Abraham did in a country where he was a stranger; whence it is plain that, at least, a great part of the land lay in common, that the inhabitants valued it not, nor claimed property in any more than they made use of; but when there was not room enough in the same place for their herds to feed together, they, by consent, as Abraham and Lot did, separated and enlarged their pasture where it best liked them. And, for the same reason, Esau went from his father and his brother, and planted in Mount Seir.

39. And thus, without supposing any private dominion and property in Adam over all the world, exclusive of all other men, which can no way be proved, nor any one's property be made out from it, but supposing the world, given as it was to the children of men in common, we see how labour could make men distinct titles to several parcels of it for their private uses, wherein there could be no doubt of right, no room for quarrel.

40. Nor is it so strange as, perhaps, before consideration it may appear, that the property of labour should be able to overbalance the community of land, for it is labour indeed that puts the difference of value on everything; and let any one consider what the difference is between an acre of land planted with tobacco or sugar, sown with wheat or barley, and an acre of the same land lying in common without any husbandry upon it, and he will find that the improvement of labour makes the far greater part of the value. I think it will be but a very modest computation to say, that of the products of the earth useful to the life of man, nine tenths are the effects of labour. Nay, if we will rightly estimate things as they come to our use, and cast up the several expenses about them – what in them is purely owing to Nature and what to labour – we shall find that, in most of them ninety-nine hundredths are wholly to be put on the account of labour.

41. There cannot be a clearer demonstration of anything than several nations of the Americans are of this, who are rich in land and poor in all the comforts of life; whom Nature, having furnished as liberally as any other people with the materials of plenty – i.e. a fruitful soil, apt to produce in abundance what might serve for food, raiment, and delight; yet, for want of improving it by labour, have not one hundredth part of the conveniencies we enjoy, and a king of a large and fruitful territory there feeds, lodges, and is clad worse than a day labourer in England.

42. To make this a little clearer, let us but trace some of the ordinary provisions of life, through their several progresses, before they come to our use, and see how much

they receive of their value from human industry. Bread, wine, and cloth are things of daily use and great plenty; yet, notwithstanding acorns, water, and leaves, or skins must be our bread, drink and clothing, did not labour furnish us with these more useful commodities. For whatever bread is more worth than acorns, wine than water, and cloth or silk than leaves, skins or moss, that is wholly owing to labour and industry. The one of these being the food and raiment which unassisted Nature furnishes us with; the other provisions which our industry and pains prepare for us, which how much they exceed the other in value, when any one hath computed, he will then see how much labour makes the far greatest part of the value of things we enjoy in this world; and the ground which produces the materials is scarce to be reckoned in as any, or at most, but a very small part of it; so little, that, even among us, land that is left wholly to nature, that hath no improvement of pasturage, tillage, or planting, is called, as indeed it is, waste; and we shall find the benefit of it amount to little more than nothing.

43. An acre of land that bears here twenty bushels of wheat, and another in America, which, with the same husbandry, would do the like, are, without doubt, of the same natural, intrinsic value. But yet the benefit mankind receives from one in a year is worth five pounds, and the other possibly not worth a penny; if all the profit an Indian received from it were to be valued and sold here, at least I may truly say, not one thousandth. It is labour, then, which puts the greatest part of value upon land, without which it would scarcely be worth anything; it is to that we owe the greatest part of all its useful products; for all that the straw, bran, bread of that acre of wheat is more worth than the product of an acre of as good land which lies waste is all the effect of labour. For it is not barely the ploughman's pains, the reaper's and thresher's toil, and the baker's sweat is to be counted into the bread we eat; the labour of those who broke the oxen, who digged and wrought the iron and stones, who felled and framed the timber employed about the plough, mill, oven, or any other utensils, which are a vast number, requisite to this corn, from its sowing to its being made bread, must all be charged on the account of labour, and received as an effect of that; Nature and the earth furnished only the almost worthless materials as in themselves. It would be a strange catalogue of things that industry provided and made use of about every loaf of bread before it came to our use if we could trace them; iron, wood, leather, bark, timber, stone, bricks, coals, lime, cloth, dyeing-drugs, pitch, tar, masts, ropes, and all the materials made use of in the ship that brought any of the commodities made use of by any of the workmen, to any part of the work, all which it would be almost impossible, or at least too long, to reckon up.

44. From all which it is evident that, though the things of Nature are given in common, man (by being master of himself, and proprietor of his own person, and the actions or labour of it) had still in himself the great foundation of property; and that which made up the great part of what he applied to the support or comfort of his being, when invention and arts had improved the conveniencies of life, was perfectly his own, and did not belong in common to others.

45. Thus labour, in the beginning, gave a right of property, wherever any one was pleased to employ it, upon what was common, which remained a long while, the far greater part, and is yet more than mankind makes use of. Men at first, for the most

part, contented themselves with what unassisted Nature offered to their necessities; and though afterwards, in some parts of the world, where the increase of people and stock, with the use of money, had made land scarce, and so of some value, the several communities settled the bounds of their distinct territories, and, by laws, within themselves, regulated the properties of the private men of their society, and so, by compact and agreement, settled the property which labour and industry began. And the leagues that have been made between several states and kingdoms, either expressly or tacitly disowning all claim and right to the land in the other's possession, have, by common consent, given up their pretences to their natural common right, which originally they had to those countries; and so have, by positive agreement, settled a property among themselves, in distinct parts of the world; yet there are still great tracts of ground to be found, which the inhabitants thereof, not having joined with the rest of mankind in the consent of the use of their common money, lie waste, and are more than the people who dwell on it do, or can make use of, and so still lie in common; though this can scarce happen among that part of mankind that have consented to the use of money.

46. The greatest part of things really useful to the life of man, and such as the necessity of subsisting made the first commoners of the world look after – as it doth the Americans now – are generally things of short duration, such as – if they are not consumed by use – will decay and perish of themselves. Gold, silver, and diamonds are things that fancy or agreement hath put the value on, more than real use and the necessary support of life. Now of those good things which Nature hath provided in common, every one hath a right (as hath been said) to as much as he could use, and had a property in all he could effect with his labour; all that his industry could extend to, to alter from the state Nature had put it in, was his. He that gathered a hundred bushels of acorns or apples had thereby a property in them; they were his goods as soon as gathered. He was only to look that he used them before they spoiled, else he took more than his share, and robbed others. And indeed, it was a foolish thing, as well as dishonest, to hoard up more than he could make use of. If he gave away a part to anybody else, so that it perished not uselessly in his possession, these he also made use of. And, if he also bartered away plums that would have rotted in a week, for nuts that would last good for his eating a whole year, he did no injury; he wasted not the common stock; destroyed no part of the portion of goods that belonged to others, so long as nothing perished uselessly in his hands. Again, if he would give his nuts for a piece of metal, pleased with its colour, or exchange his sheep for shells, or wool for a sparkling pebble or a diamond, and keep those by him all his life, he invaded not the right of others; he might heap up as much of these durable things as he pleased; the exceeding of the bounds of his just property not lying in the largeness of his possession, but the perishing of anything uselessly in it.

47. And thus came in the use of money; some lasting thing that men might keep without spoiling, and that, by mutual consent, men would take in exchange for the truly useful but perishable supports of life.

48. And, as different degrees of industry were apt to give men possessions in different proportions, so this invention of money gave them the opportunity to continue and enlarge them. For supposing an island, separate from all possible commerce with the rest

of the world, wherein there were but a hundred families, but there were sheep, horses, and cows, with other useful animals, wholesome fruits and land enough for corn for a hundred thousand times, as many, but nothing in the island, either because of its commonness or perishableness, fit to supply the place of money. What reason could any one have there to enlarge his possessions beyond the use of his family, and a plentiful supply to its consumption, either in what their own industry produced, or they could barter for like perishable, useful commodities with others? Where there is not something both lasting and scarce, and so valuable to be hoarded up, there men will not be apt to enlarge their possessions of land, were it never so rich, never so free for them to take. For I ask, what would a man value ten thousand or an hundred thousand acres of excellent land, ready cultivated and well stocked too, with cattle, in the middle of the inland parts of America, where he had no hopes of commerce with other parts of the world, to draw money to him by the sale of the product? It would not be worth the enclosing, and we should see him give up again to the wild common of Nature whatever was more than would supply the conveniencies of life, to be had there for him and his family.

49. Thus, in the beginning, all the world was America, and more so than that is now; for no such thing as money was anywhere known. Find out something that hath the use and value of money among his neighbours, you shall see the same man will begin presently to enlarge his possessions.

50. But since gold and silver, being little useful to the life of man in proportion to food, raiment, and carriage, has its value only from the consent of men – whereof labour yet makes in great part the measure – it is plain that the consent of men have agreed to a disproportionate and unequal possession of the earth – I mean out of the bounds of society and compact; for in governments the laws regulate it; they having, by consent, found out and agreed in a way how a man may, rightfully and without injury, possess more than he himself can make use of by receiving gold and silver, which may continue long in a man's possession without decaying for the overplus, and agreeing those metals should have a value.

51. And thus, I think, it is very easy to conceive, without any difficulty, how labour could at first begin a title of property in the common things of Nature, and how the spending it upon our uses bounded it; so that there could then be no reason of quarrelling about title, nor any doubt about the largeness of possession it gave. Right and conveniency went together. For as a man had a right to all he could employ his labour upon, so he had no temptation to labour for more than he could make use of. This left no room for controversy about the title, nor for encroachment on the right of others. What portion a man carved to himself was easily seen; and it was useless, as well as dishonest, to carve himself too much, or take more than he needed.

Extract 3.6   Robert Nozick, *Anarchy, State, and Utopia* (Oxford, Basil Blackwell, 1974), pp. 174–82

LOCKE'S THEORY OF ACQUISITION

... Locke views property rights in an unowned object as originating through someone's mixing his labor with it. This gives rise to many questions. What are the boundaries of what labor is mixed with? If a private astronaut clears a place on Mars, has he mixed his labor with (so that he comes to own) the whole planet, the whole uninhabited universe, or just a particular plot? Which plot does an act bring under ownership? The minimal (possibly disconnected) area such that an act decreases entropy in that area, and not elsewhere? Can virgin land (for the purposes of ecological investigation by high-flying airplane) come under ownership by a Lockean process? Building a fence around a territory presumably would make one the owner of only the fence (and the land immediately underneath it).

Why does mixing one's labor with something make one the owner of it? Perhaps because one owns one's labor, and so one comes to own a previously unowned thing that becomes permeated with what one owns. Ownership seeps over into the rest. But why isn't mixing what I own with what I don't own a way of losing what I own rather than a way of gaining what I don't? If I own a can of tomato juice and spill it in the sea so that its molecules (made radioactive, so I can check this) mingle evenly throughout the sea, do I thereby come to own the sea, or have I foolishly dissipated my tomato juice? Perhaps the idea, instead, is that laboring on something improves it and makes it more valuable; and anyone is entitled to own a thing whose value he has created. (Reinforcing this, perhaps, is the view that laboring is unpleasant. If some people made things effortlessly, as the cartoon characters in *The Yellow Submarine* trail flowers in their wake, would they have lesser claim to their own products whose making didn't cost them anything?) Ignore the fact that laboring on something may make it less valuable (spraying pink enamel paint on a piece of driftwood that you have found). Why should one's entitlement extend to the whole object rather than just to the added value one's labor has produced? (Such reference to value might also serve to delimit the extent of ownership; for example, substitute 'increases the value of' for 'decreases entropy in' in the above entropy criterion.) No workable or coherent value-added property scheme has yet been devised …

It will be implausible to view improving an object as giving full ownership to it, if the stock of unowned objects that might be improved is limited. For an object's coming under one person's ownership changes the situation of all others. Whereas previously they were at liberty (in Hohfeld's sense) to use the object, they now no longer are. This change in the situation of others (by removing their liberty to act on a previously unowned object) need not worsen their situation. If I appropriate a grain of sand from Coney Island, no one else may now do as they will with that grain of sand. But there are plenty of other grains of sand left for them to do the same with. Or if not grains of sand, then other things. Alternatively, the things I do with the grain of sand I appropriate might improve the position of others, counterbalancing their loss of the liberty to use that grain. The crucial point is whether appropriation of an unowned object worsens the situation of others.

Locke's proviso that there be 'enough and as good left in common for others' [paragraph 27] is meant to ensure that the situation of others is not worsened. (If this proviso is met is there any motivation for his further condition of nonwaste?) It is often said that this proviso once held but now no longer does. But there appears to be an argument for the conclusion that, if the proviso no longer holds, then it cannot ever have held so as to yield permanent and inheritable property rights. Consider the first person Z for whom there is not enough and as good left to appropriate. The last person Y to appropriate left Z without his previous liberty to act on an object, and so worsened Z's situation. So Y's appropriation is not allowed under Locke's proviso. Therefore, the next to last person X to appropriate left Y in a worse position, for X's act ended permissible appropriation. Therefore, X's appropriation wasn't permissible. But then the appropriator two from last, W, ended permissible appropriation and so, since it worsened X's position, W's appropriation wasn't permissible. And so on back to the first person A to appropriate a permanent property right.

This argument, however, proceeds too quickly. Someone may be made worse off by another's appropriation in two ways: first, by losing the opportunity to improve his situation by a particular appropriation or any one; and second, by no longer being able to use freely (without appropriation) what he previously could. A stringent requirement that another not be made worse off by an appropriation would exclude the first way if nothing else counterbalances the diminution in opportunity, as well as the second. A weaker requirement would exclude the second way, though not the first. With the weaker requirement, we cannot zip back so quickly from Z to A, as in the above argument; for though person Z can no longer appropriate, there may remain some for him to use as before. In this case, Y's appropriation would not violate the weaker Lockean condition. (With less remaining that people are at liberty to use, users might face more inconvenience, crowding, and so on; in that way the situation of others might be worsened, unless appropriation stopped far short of such a point.) It is arguable that no one legitimately can complain if the weaker provision is satisfied. However, since this is less clear than in the case of the more stringent proviso, Locke may have intended this stringent proviso by 'enough and as good' remaining, and perhaps he meant the nonwaste condition to delay the end point from which the argument zips back.

Is the situation of persons who are unable to appropriate (there being no more accessible and useful unowned objects) worsened by a system allowing appropriation and permanent property? Here enter the various familiar social considerations favoring private property: it increases the social product by putting means of production in the hands of those who can use them most efficiently (profitably); experimentation is encouraged, because with separate persons controlling resources, there is no one person or small group whom someone with a new idea must convince to try it out; private property enables people to decide on the pattern and types of risks they wish to bear, leading to specialized types of risk bearing; private property protects future persons by leading some to hold back resources from current consumption for future markets; it provides alternate sources of employment for unpopular persons who don't have to convince any one person or small group to hire them, and so on. These considerations enter a Lockean theory to support the claim that appropriation of private property satisfies the intent behind the 'enough and as good left over' proviso, not as a utilitarian justification of property. They enter to rebut the claim that because the proviso is violated no natural right to private property can arise by a Lockean process. The difficulty in working such an argument to show that the proviso is satisfied is in fixing the appropriate base line for comparison. Lockean appropriation makes people no worse off than they would be how? This question of fixing the baseline needs more detailed investigation than we are able to give it here. It would be desirable to have an estimate of the general economic importance of original appropriation in order to see how much leeway there is for differing theories of appropriation and of the location of the baseline. Perhaps this importance can be measured by the percentage of all income that is based upon untransformed raw materials and given resources (rather than upon human actions), mainly rental income representing the unimproved value of land, and the price of raw material *in situ*, and by the percentage of current wealth which represents such income in the past.

We should note that it is not only persons favouring private property who need a theory of how property rights legitimately originate. Those believing in collective property, for example those believing that a group of persons living in an area jointly own the territory, or its mineral resources, also must provide a theory of how such property rights arise; they must show why the persons living there have rights to determine what is done with the land and resources there that persons living elsewhere don't have (with regard to the same land and resources).

THE PROVISO

Whether or not Locke's particular theory of appropriation can be spelled out so as to handle various difficulties, I assume that any adequate theory of justice in acquisition will contain a proviso similar to the weaker of the ones we have attributed to Locke. A process normally giving rise to a permanent bequeathable property right in a previously unowned thing will not do so if the position of others no longer at liberty to use the thing is thereby worsened. It is important to specify this particular mode of worsening the situation of others, for the proviso does not encompass other modes. It does not include the worsening due to more limited opportunities to appropriate (the first way above, corresponding to the more stringent condition), and it does not include how I 'worsen' a seller's position if I appropriate materials to make some of what he is selling, and then enter into competition with him. Someone whose appropriation otherwise would violate the proviso still may appropriate provided he compensates the others so that their situation is not thereby worsened; unless he does compensate these others, his appropriation will violate the proviso of the principle of justice in acquisition and will be an illegitimate one. A theory of appropriation incorporating this Lockean proviso will handle correctly the cases (objections to the theory lacking the proviso) where someone appropriates the total supply of something necessary for life.

A theory which includes this proviso in its principle of justice in acquisition must also contain a more complex principle of justice in transfer. Some reflection of the proviso about appropriation constrains later actions. If my appropriating all of a certain substance violates the Lockean proviso, then so does my appropriating some and purchasing all the rest from others who obtained it without otherwise violating the Lockean proviso. If the proviso excludes someone's appropriating all the drinkable water in the world, it also excludes his purchasing it all. (More weakly, and messily, it may exclude his charging certain prices for some of his supply.) This proviso (almost?) never will come into effect; the more someone acquires of a scarce substance which others want, the higher the price of the rest will go, and the more difficult it will become for him to acquire it all. But still, we can imagine, at least, that something like this occurs: someone makes simultaneous secret bids to the separate owners of a substance, each of whom sells assuming he can easily purchase more from the other owners; or some natural catastrophe destroys all the supply of something except that in one person's possession. The total supply could not be permissibly appropriated by one person at the beginning. His later acquisition of it all does not show that the original appropriation violated the proviso (even by a reverse argument similar to the one above that tried to zip back from Z to A). Rather, it is the combination of the original appropriation plus all the later transfers and actions that violates the Lockean proviso.

Each owner's title to his holding includes the historical shadow of the Lockean proviso on appropriation. This excludes his transferring it into an agglomeration that does violate the Lockean proviso and excludes his using it in a way, in co-ordination with others or independently of them, so as to violate the proviso by making the situation of others worse than their baseline situation. Once it is known that some-one's ownership runs afoul of the Lockean proviso, there are stringent limits on what he may do with (what it is difficult any longer unreservedly to call) 'his property'. Thus a person may not appropriate the only water hole in a desert and charge what he will. Nor may he charge what he will if he possesses one, and unfortunately it happens that all the water holes in the desert dry up, except for his. This unfortunate circumstance, admittedly no fault of his, brings into operation the Lockean proviso and limits his property rights. Similarly, an owner's property right in the only island in an area does not allow him to order a castaway from a shipwreck off his island as a trespasser, for this would violate the Lockean proviso.

Notice that the theory does not say that owners do have these rights, but that the rights are overridden to avoid some catastrophe. (Overridden rights do not disappear; they leave a trace of a sort absent in the cases under discussion.) There is no such external (and *ad hoc*?) overriding. Considerations internal to the theory of property itself, to its theory of acquisition and appropriation provide the means for handling such cases. The results, however, may be coextensive with some condition about catastrophe, since the baseline for comparison is so low as compared to productiveness of a society with private appropriation that the question of the Lockean proviso being violated arises only in the case of catastrophe (or a desert-island situation).

The fact that someone owns the total supply of something necessary for others to stay alive does not entail that his (or anyone's) appropriation of anything left some people (immediately or later) in a situation worse than the baseline one. A medical researcher who synthesizes a new substance that effectively treats a certain disease and who refuses to sell except on his terms does not worsen the situation of others by depriving them of whatever he has appropriated. The others easily can possess the same materials he appropriated; the researcher's appropriation or purchase of che-micals didn't make those chemicals scarce in a way so as to violate the Lockean proviso. Nor would someone else's purchasing the total supply of the synthesized substance from the medical researcher. The fact that the medical researcher uses easily available chemicals to synthesize the drug no more violates the Lockean proviso than does the fact that the only surgeon able to perform a particular operation eats easily obtainable food in order to stay alive and to have the energy to work. This shows that the Lockean proviso is not an 'end-state principle'; it focuses on a particular way that appropriative actions affect others, and not on the structure of the situation that results.

Intermediate between someone who takes all of the public supply and someone who makes the total supply out of easily obtainable substances is someone who appropriates the total supply of something, in a way that does not deprive the others of it. For example, someone finds a new substance in an out-of-the-way place. He discovers that it effectively treats a certain disease and appropriates the total supply. He does not worsen the situation of others; if he did not stumble upon the substance no one else would have, and the others would remain without it. However, as time passes, the likelihood increases that others would have come across the substance; upon this fact might be based a limit to his property right in the substance so that others are not below their baseline position; for example, its bequest might be limited. The theme of someone worsening another's situation by depriving him of something he otherwise would possess may also illuminate the example of patents. An inventor's patent does not deprive others of an object which would not exist if not for the inventor. Yet patents would have this effect on others who independently invent the object. Therefore, these independent inventors, upon whom the burden of proving independent discovery may rest, should not be excluded from utilizing their own invention as they wish (including selling it to others). Furthermore, a known inventor drastically lessens the chances of actual independent invention. For persons who know of an invention usually will not try to reinvent it, and the notion of independent discovery here would be murky at best. Yet we may assume that, in the absence of the original invention, sometime later someone else would have come up with it. This suggests placing a time limit on patents, as a rough rule of thumb to approximate how long it would have taken, in the absence of knowledge of the invention, for independent discovery . . .

Notes and Questions 3.2

1 Grunebaum says of Locke:

> the process of grounding ownership upon first appropriation of what is unowned by labour or some other act of appropriation is a question begging presumption in favour of private ownership.
>
> (Grunebaum, *Private Ownership*, p. 155)

Explain what he means, and consider how far he is right.

2 Consider what Locke means when he says that we have 'property' in our own 'person'. Does he mean that we have full ownership of our bodies, or that no person other than ourselves has any rights in our person (here meaning something more than our physical bodies)? Does this affect the validity of his argument? Kramer considers this, and like objections as to whether one can say

that 'the labour of our bodies and the work of our hands is ours' (Kramer, *John Locke and the Origins of Private Property*, pp. 135–40).

3 According to Locke, children and servants do not acquire property in unallocated things by mixing their labour with them. Does he provide a satisfactory explanation for this? If not, can a satisfactory explanation be provided?

4 How would Locke answer Nozick's questions about the precise boundaries of what you acquire when you mix your labour with something? Would this meet the objections implied by Nozick?

5 How would Locke answer Nozick's point about the tomato juice? Would this meet Nozick's objections?

6 Other commentators have objected that there are all kinds of labour that can be undertaken in relation to natural resources which may well increase their value or usefulness but could not be said to amount to 'mixing' or 'annexing' and 'joining' the labour to the resource. Kramer gives the following example:

> Suppose that a person built his hut in proximity to a massive oak, which would furnish ample shade and which would also lend some protection from the wind and from storms. Thitherto, the oak and all the constituents of the hut had gone unpossessed by anyone. While the erection of the hut certainly would count as labor that engendered proprietary rights in the hut itself, it might well count also as an instance of labor that engendered proprietary rights in the oak. Surely, however, no one will profess that the untouched tree was mixed with the hut-builder's labor, in any usual senses of the word 'mixing'.
>
> (Kramer, *John Locke and the Origins of Private Property*, p. 145)

Kramer, however, dismisses these criticisms: he says that Locke's words should be read as 'acceptable shorthand for the deliberate incorporation of useful items into the projects of human beings who were questing for their own survival and comfort' (Kramer, *John Locke and the Origins of Private Property*, p. 145). Is this an acceptable interpretation of what Locke is saying?

7 Explain Nozick's argument that a stringent version of the sufficiency proviso would make all appropriations illegitimate. Is he right? Would the same apply if the proviso was that, as much and as good must be left for others to *use* rather than to *appropriate*? Is this a plausible reading of the sufficiency proviso?

8 Waldron gives other reasons for rejecting the stringent version of the sufficiency proviso, which, as he points out, involves an acceptance of a natural right to private property:

> [T]here is nothing in Locke's argument to indicate that he thought it morally necessary for people to mix their labour with virgin resources. There is nothing remotely corresponding to Hegel's view that a person must embody his freedom in

an external object and so become an owner in order to develop ethically as an individual. On Locke's account, some people get to mix their labour with unowned resources while others do not ... There is nothing in Locke's discussion to indicate that he believed private appropriation satisfied any deep need in man apart from the physical needs that were satisfied by the appropriated resources. Since it is possible for those needs to be satisfied without appropriation, there is no basis for attributing to Locke the [stringent version of the sufficiency proviso] or the general right to private property that would go along with it.

(Waldron, *The Right to Private Property*, pp. 217–18)

9   What does Nozick mean when he says that 'Some reflection of the proviso about appropriation constrains later actions'? To what extent does he think the sufficiency proviso should influence what happens to property holdings after an original acquisition? Is this what Locke is saying?

10   As Nozick says, an inventor's patent does not deprive others of anything because the object invented would not have existed were it not for the inventor. Why, according to Nozick, should the period of protection given by the patent to the inventor nevertheless be limited in time?

4

Allocating property rights

4.1. Introduction

In Chapter 3 we dealt with the question of whether it is justifiable to have exclusionary property rights at all. If we accept that the answer is yes, it then becomes necessary to consider who should have such rights, which amounts to Lawrence Becker's question of specific justification outlined in section 3.2 above: 'What sorts of people should own what sorts of things and under what sorts of conditions?' This is the subject of this chapter.

Just as when considering the general justification for property rights, it is helpful to start with original acquisition. Most legal systems adopt the first occupancy or first taker rule, i.e. that the law will protect the first taker of a thing. In the case of tangible things, this usually means taking physical control of the thing (technically, possession). Intangible things can also be allocated by a first taking rule, however. For example, an inventor of a process gets exclusive rights to exploit it for a limited period by being the first person to patent it. The patent system is essentially a notice filing system, and such systems can also be used to allocate property to the first taker of tangible assets, where the taking of physical control is not feasible, or disproportionately expensive or exclusionary. Mining rights in the developing American West, for example, were sometimes allocated to the first person to file a claim rather than to the first person to enclose the land containing the mine.

We consider the justifications for this first occupancy rule as it operates in the context of original acquisition of things in section 2. However, it is important to appreciate that the spread of the rule goes beyond original acquisition. One of the justifications of the first occupancy rule is that it is simply an aspect of the way in which the law protects holdings generally against strangers, even when unlawfully acquired. In other words, our legal system, in common with others, confers property rights on those who take control of things not only when the thing was previously unowned, but also when there is a pre-existing owner. In the latter case the protection the law gives is more precarious: the taker acquires rights enforceable against everyone *except* the pre-existing owner (or another person who has a prior claim to possession, such as a tenant), whereas in the former case (where the thing was previously unowned) the rights acquired by first taking are enforceable against the whole world. The effect of this wider rule (that all takings give rise to property rights enforceable against strangers) is that, if I lose my necklace and you find it and take possession of it, you acquire ownership of it enforceable against everyone except me. But the rule goes further than this. If you *steal* the necklace from me, you acquire precisely the same rights in it, so that, if your friend snatches it away from you, you will be entitled to recover it from her. In section 4.2 below, we concentrate on the first occupancy rule as it applies to unowned things, and then return to look at the wider rule in Chapter 7. However, it is important to appreciate that many of the factors that justify the first occupancy rule as it applies to unowned things also justify the conferring of property rights on finders and thieves, as we see in Chapter 7.

In sections 4.3 and 4.4 below, we look in more detail at two particular ways in which original acquisition might occur, in both of which pragmatic considerations have had a significant effect on the development of allocation rules. The first is where things are newly created. We deal with this in section 4.3, concentrating on the problem of the allocation of new things that are the income or product of pre-existing things. The second is through capture of resources. This is considered in section 4.4.

The problem of the allocation of resources arises in a different and acute form when one property system becomes superimposed upon another, characteristically when one state assumes control over another through colonisation. Do all inhabitants become subject to the coloniser's property system? If so, this is likely to involve the obliteration of the indigenous population's pre-existing property entitlements (which may well not take the same form as property rights recognisable in the coloniser's system), leaving them with nothing but the right to 'buy into' the new system. Alternatively, if pre-existing property entitlements are to be respected, how are the indigenous entitlements to be assimilated into the coloniser's property system? These are the problems that had to be considered by the courts and then by the legislature in Australia when indigenous Australians sought to reassert their traditional land rights. We look at these issues in section 4.5 below.

4.2. The first occupancy rule

In our legal system, as in many others, the primary rule is that property rights in a previously unowned resource will be allocated to the first person to take that thing into his control, or, as explained in the Introduction, to the first person to stake a claim in an authorised way, for example by filing for a patent. Why do we use this principle for allocating property rights in unowned resources?

4.2.1. Intuitive ordering

One explanation is that it accords with our intuitive ordering of things. We queue at bus stops and for cinema seats. Lueck points out that this is a characteristic way of sharing out temporary use of open access or limited access communal resources:

The use of customary first possession rules in businesses, families, and social settings is universal. In business, first possession is used to establish rights to customer service and to claim merchandise for later purchase. Thus, people claim service by standing in line, putting coats over chairs, depositing earnest money, making reservations, and putting holds on goods. In families, first possession is used to allocate household goods such as books, chairs, and tools. In schools, children claim first dibs on books, seats, and tasks. First possession is well known in labor contracts where it manifests itself as seniority privileges for layoffs, overtime, and other perquisites. At ski resorts, fresh powder is allocated among paying customers by first possession.

. . . Nearly all of these cases have a clear asset owner (e.g. cafe tables, ski hill), so first possession does not grant the victorious claimant perpetual ownership. Instead, the claimant gets a temporary right under the rule of capture . . . Within families, first possession can be viewed as an internal rule of capture associated with common property ownership of family resources and is simply a cheap way to allocate temporary use of an asset. In many cases, the assets are durable (e.g. chairs, parking spaces) . . . [and] the temporary rights of the claimants are not transferable.

(Lueck, 'First Possession as the Basis of Property', p. 218)

Is there, however, a rational basis for this intuitive ordering, and are there disadvantages in adopting it as a basis for legal allocation of unowned resources?

4.2.2. Preservation of public order

Once you have taken physical control of a thing, the law is faced with the choice of either protecting your possession against strangers or standing by while it is snatched away from you. One of the reasons why the law confers rights on the first taker is to prevent a disorderly free-for-all: generally speaking, it is easier and cheaper to preserve the peace by protecting those in possession from intruders than by allowing them to fight it out between themselves. John Stuart Mill goes so far as to say that the jurisdiction of tribunals to protect possessors against intruders may well have pre-dated their jurisdiction to determine rights:

Private property, as an institution, did not owe its origin to any of those considerations of utility, which plead for the maintenance of it when established. Enough is known of rude ages, both from history and from analogous states of society in our own time, to show that tribunals (which always precede laws) were originally established, not to determine rights, but to repress violence and terminate quarrels. With this object chiefly in view, they naturally enough gave legal effect to first occupancy, by treating as the aggressor the person who first commenced violence, by turning, or attempting to turn, another out of possession. The preservation of the peace, which was the original object of civil government, was thus attained; while by confirming, to those who already possessed it, even what was not the fruit of personal exertion, a guarantee was incidentally given to them and others that they would be protected in what was so.

(Mill, *Principles of Political Economy*, Book II, Chapter I, section 2)

There is also the question of proof. Law enforcers seeking to avert public disorder between rival claimants to land or goods need to be able to identify quickly the person to be protected. Physical control is relatively easy to identify on the ground, and so a general direction to law enforcers to protect possessors against intruders will be workable in practice – infinitely more so than, for example, a direction that they should ascertain who is the more deserving, or who first mixed their labour with the thing, or who is capable of using the thing more productively.

4.2.3. Simplicity

The simplicity and certainty of the first occupancy rule is one of its main attractions for Richard Epstein, as he explains in Extract 4.1 below. The first occupancy rule enables property rights to be allocated by a single, simple rule understandable by all without recourse to litigation and according to most people's intuitive feeling of fairness. In order to assess the validity of rival claims to a previously unowned resource, all one need do is ask the simple question: who got there first? As Epstein says, except in the improbable case of a tie, all can be made to depend on the single variable of time, and 'getting a lot of results out of a little bit of information surely enhances the overall efficiency of the system'. However, as David Haddock says in Extract 4.2 in response to Epstein, first occupancy is not the only allocation rule that has the virtue of simplicity. Equally simple would be what he calls a 'mightiest possession' rule, which allocates the whole stock of the resource in question to the strongest (usually the state), who then parcels it out either by auction or in any other way it considers appropriate. As he points out, this is the way modern societies have actually allocated property rights in previously unowned resources such as radio frequencies and oil fields, and will no doubt allocate property rights in the surface of the moon at some stage. Also, in the case of some resources, the advantages of simplicity are outweighed by the economic inefficiencies in allocation to the first taker. Intellectual property rights, for example, do indeed go to the first taker in one sense, but what the first taker gets is property rights strictly limited in time, for reasons Haddock explains. And, in the case of other resources such as uncultivated land, societies have thought it advisable to require settlers to demonstrate not only enclosure but also cultivation or substantial use as a condition of allocation of property rights (see Notes and Questions 4.1 after the extracts).

4.2.4. Signalling

There are other pragmatic justifications put forward for the first occupancy rule. If those who have taken physical control of a thing automatically acquire property rights in it simply by virtue of being there, occupancy can operate as a useful signalling device, allowing outsiders to assume that occupancy more or less guarantees entitlement. Robert Merrill has suggested this:

> Not everyone can do a title search before they act towards apparent property owners as if they, in fact, own the property. For example, all sorts of contractors do work on

property on the assumption that the person living there actually owns it, and it would be very burdensome to force them to do a title search before they extend those types of services. You have people who lend money on the strength of apparent ownership. You have renters that rent from people whom they think are landlords, and so forth. Adverse possession gives some substance to those kinds of third-party reliance interests by suggesting that the appearance of ownership asserted over a period of time is, in fact, going to be actual ownership.

(Merrill, 'Time, Property Rights and the Common Law', p. 681)

Merrill is talking here about wrongful takers (adverse possessors), but much the same point can be made in relation to first occupiers. If entitlement does not go to the first occupier, outsiders have no quick, easy way of ascertaining whether the present occupier has yet done whatever is required to gain entitlement.

4.2.5.   The bond between person and possessions

However, there is clearly more to it than pragmatism. It has often been argued that an emotional bond grows between people and the things they regard as theirs, and that this is a tie that ought to be respected by the law. This is essentially the reason David Hume gives in Extract 4.3 for saying that, in an initial allocation of property rights, it would be 'the most natural expedient' to allocate property in things to those already in possession of them. Similar points about the bond between person and thing possessed have been made by others. So, for example, Jeremy Bentham said:

Everything which I possess, or to which I have a title, I consider in my own mind as destined always to belong to me. I make it the basis of my expectations, and of the hopes of those dependent upon me; and I form my plan of life accordingly. Every part of my property may have, in my estimation, besides its intrinsic value, a value of affection … Everything about it represents to my eye that part of myself which I have put into it – those cares, that industry, that economy which denied itself pleasures to make provision for the future. Thus our property becomes a part of our being, and cannot be torn from us without rending us to the quick.

(Bentham, The Theory of Legislation, Part 1, Chapter 10)

The point is made even more strongly in defence of the adverse possession rule we look at in Chapter 11, where it is argued that over time this bond grows so strong that it justifies allowing the claim of the occupier to defeat even that of the pre-existing owner (see in particular Extract 11.2 below).

4.2.6.   The libertarian justification

For Epstein, however, the central principled (as opposed to pragmatic) justification for the first occupancy rule is that it means that the state can be excluded from decisions about property allocation. For Epstein, and for other libertarians, this is a matter of fundamental political importance: 'The rule thus allows one to organise a system of rights that is not dependent on the will of a sovereign, and makes it possible to oppose on normative grounds the all too frequent historical truth that ownership rights rest upon successful conquest' (Epstein, 'Past and Future', p. 669; also reproduced in Extract 4.1 below). The corresponding disadvantage, of course, is that, if the whole stock of an unowned resource is allocated by the first occupancy rule, important decisions about distribution of the resource, and the best way and pace of using it and exploiting it, will never consciously be made: all of this will have to be settled by the market. As Haddock points out in Extract 4.2, this is not necessarily what a society might want.

4.2.7.   The communitarian objection

One strong political objection to the first occupancy rule is that it favours private ownership of resources over the more complex relationships that can evolve under communal use and ownership. Carol Rose makes this point in Extract 4.4. Nomadic land use and other forms of hunter-gatherer resource use do not involve any one person taking exclusive physical control of the resource as a whole. First occupancy might well dictate which individual person within the community takes each individual item, but the resource as a whole (the land itself, or a species of animal being hunted, or a well providing water) might be used by a number of different individuals and communities, often with a highly formalised but unwritten pattern of usage. If this is not recognised as a 'taking' or 'occupancy' of the resources, and rights are treated as originating only through the first occupancy rule, then people living in this kind of way never acquire rights enforceable against intruders in the land and natural resources they live on. Carol Rose explains the consequences of this for American Indians, and in section 4.5 we look more closely at the similar problems that arose in Australia. Elsewhere in Extract 4.1 below, Epstein argues that it is not the first occupancy rule itself that is causing the problem here, but the failure to recognise the native population's resource use as occupation. Indeed, as he points out, the native population's own claim is firmly based on having got there first. However, as we see in section 4.5, ordering the priority of claims by time is not quite so straightforward where the rival patterns of resource usage are so very different from each other.

4.2.8.   Economic efficiency

This brings us to the difficult question of whether the first occupancy rule is economically efficient. The efficiency advantages that Locke claims for his labour theory of original acquisition can be claimed with more or less equal force for the first occupancy rule. If takers are awarded property rights, this provides an incentive for seeking out, working on and developing resources and making them more productive. However, this does not always work efficiently with all kinds of resource. In some cases, it can lead to premature capture of resources. This is a complex argument which we cannot do full justice to here, but Robert Cooter provides a simple illustration of the problem:

> Suppose there is a piece of land, and in order to establish title to it you have to fence it.
> Suppose the only reason to fence it would be to keep cows on it. Suppose also that it
> wouldn't pay to keep cows on it unless there were a railroad to get them out to market.

Suppose the year is 1820, and you have reason to believe that the railroad is going to arrive in 1830. What do you do? You may have to fence the land now to get title and let the fences rot for a decade until the railroad arrives. In this example the main effect of the investment is redistributive rather than productive. The investment is made solely to establish your title against others. We all know that investments motivated by redistribution rather than production are inefficient. So I think that using the principle of first possession as a judicial principle rather than a metaphysical tale is quite inefficient. When you go outside the land area and look at something like fishing rights, this is even clearer. There is just a great deal of pre-emptive investment.

(Cooter, 'Time, Property Rights, and the Common Law')

Also, as David Haddock points out in Extract 4.2, the first occupancy rule does not necessarily rule out costly competition. It is worth noting, however, that his conclusion that the rule has little to recommend it, is not shared by all economists: see in particular Lueck, who gives a detailed analysis of the economic effects of the rule in varying contexts, and concludes that 'people have tenaciously adopted and retained rules of first possession because they work to establish property rights necessary for wealth creation' (Lueck, 'First Possession as the Basis of Property', p. 222).

Extract 4.1   Richard A. Epstein, 'Past and Future: The Temporal Dimension in the Law of Property' (1986) 65 *Washington University Law Quarterly* 667

Everyone knows and follows the rule of ordinary life that applies to such prosaic matters as waiting in line for theatre tickets or in a cafeteria: 'first come, first served.' The rule of first possession at common law converts that intuition into the analytical foundation for the entire system of private property: the party who takes first possession of a thing is entitled to exclude the rest of the world from it, forever. The element of time is part of the priority rule and of the definition of the property interest acquired.

The rationales for this rule are many and complex. Often the rule has been regarded as something akin to a self-evident truth. But the rule also has clear political and utilitarian virtues that account for its lofty status. These deserve to be mentioned briefly. The first possession rule promotes a system of decentralized ownership: private actions by private parties shape the individual entitlements in ways that do not involve the active role of the state, whose job, as umpire, is neatly restricted to protecting entitlements previously acquired by private means. The rule thus allows one to organize a system of rights that is not dependent upon the whim of the sovereign, and makes it possible to oppose on normative grounds the all too frequent historical truth that ownership rights rest upon successful conquest, nothing more and nothing less. It is not surprising therefore that a variant of the first possession rule exerted so large an influence in the writing of John Locke, whose political mission was to defend a theory of representative government against the power of the Crown.

The first possession rule also has more direct economic virtues for it yields a consistent and exhaustive set of property rights, whereby everything has in principle one, and only one, owner. Vesting ownership in the first possessor makes it highly likely that a person who owns the land will use it efficiently and protect it diligently. At every stage the rule reduces transaction costs. There is no need for a routine lawsuit for the true owner, however identified, to pry property away from the party in wrongful possession. The uniqueness of owners means that development and sale can take place at relatively low cost. The first possession rule does give rise to serious problems in the case of common-pool assets, such as oil, gas and fish. Yet, even here it furnishes a baseline of entitlements which permits the state to organize forced exchanges that, on average work to the long-term advantage of persons with interests in the pool.

. . . The first possession rule represents an ingenious, if intuitive, recognition that time provides the best one-dimensional ruler for making the needed mapping. Time offers a unique measuring rod, sufficient in principle to resolve two or two thousand competing claims for priority. Whoever got there first, wins. Except in the improbable case of ties, an enormous decision-making capability is contained in a single variable. Getting a lot of results out of a little bit of information surely enhances the overall efficiency of the system.

Consider an alternative rule that requires someone to map from n different dimensions to a single answer. The balancing of factors requires tradeoffs among incommensurates that breed uncertainty and, with it, litigation: there is no way to map a plane into a line, while preserving a one-to-one correspondence between the points in the plan and those in the line. Yet making a clear decision one way or the other is of enormous importance. The relatively automatic quality of the first possession rule helps private parties organize their affairs without resorting to litigation. The point should not be overstated, for the first possession rule will not eliminate every factual dispute over who took possession of the land first. Land has a large physical dimension. One person may enter land first, while (with or without knowledge of this entry) another stakes out a claim to the same parcel or part thereof. The problem can be especially acute with mining claims. No legal rule can solve all borderline cases where individuals act in ignorance or disregard of what others have done. As the enormous nineteenth-century debates on possession indicate, once 'possession' becomes the source of rights and duties, it becomes subject to heavy verbal stress.

But so what? The mark of a good legal rule is not whether it resolves all doubtful cases at the margin. No rule can fully capture the distinction between the occasional use of unowned land and its occupation, between the acquisition of full ownership and the claim of limited (e.g. hunting) rights. Yet all of these complications are manageable if the rule generates enough clear cases in routine situations . . . [The first possession rule] provides a marked degree of decisional stability, which is all that can be asked. Any more complicated rule would doubtless have a temporal component to it: for example, a rule that awards ownership to the party who, after enclosure, first makes substantial use of unowned land, unless the prior party in possession had been there a long time.

Who needs it? How much of a temporal priority is needed to offset a substantial use? The rule could only survive because the two features of original acquisition and substantial use are positively correlated, which is itself an argument for making the earlier fact decisive on the question of ownership. The demands for 'substantial use' could only induce a proliferation of borderline cases that place ownership (and hence the right to use and dispose) in limbo until the question of substantial use is resolved. Delay has its costs. A sound system of rights resolves the claims of ownership early in the process to reduce the legal uncertainty in subsequent decisions on investment and consumption. Any system of ownership (including state grants) requires that some positive costs be incurred to establish claims. These costs should be minimized in order to reserve the bulk of resources for the productive use of assets. The first possession rule itself can encourage the premature acquisition of interests, but that cost is tolerable in light of the alternatives. Any system of state grants transfers the cost of land acquisition from the open field to the legislature; while any alternative rule of private acquisition, such as first substantial use, only increases the fraction of resources that must be devoted to the acquisition of claims.

Extract 4.2   David Haddock, 'First Possession Versus Optimal Timing: Limiting the Dissipation of Economic Value' (1986) 64 *Washington University Law Quarterly* 775

As Epstein remarks, priority appears to have the appealing property of uni-dimensionality; it anoints a unique owner for each entitlement according to who got to it first, setting aside the relatively rare tied races. But any uni-dimensional rule will facilitate uniquely defined ownership, and as a positive, predictive matter other candidates seem stronger than the doctrine of first possession. For example, a rule of mightiest possession is uni-dimensional; empirically it is much more important than first possession, considering all regions and epochs of this world. When the Normans invaded England they knew but did not care that the Saxons were there first. Nor did the Saxons care that the Britons had been there even earlier, and so on into the mists of prehistory. True, naked might requires resources to threaten, if not actually to assault, competitors. But first possession also requires coercion to prevent violations; it is in effect a civilized form of mightiest possession.

Moreover, first possession is flawed even as a normative (efficiency) construct when the assumptions of the model are relaxed a bit. Even if violence is suppressed, costly competition will occur in more subtle ways whenever first possession yields economic rents. Consider patent and copyright, where profitable first possession encourages encroachment; or successful new medications followed closely by other medications, 'innovated' at some cost, that differ in arguably trivial ways from the original; or successful new themes in film, literature, or music that raise a plethora of imitators. In a model that I discuss below, the cost of the these other forms of competition will match the cost of the competitive threats of violence that has been replaced.

Occasionally, the simplest versions of either first possession or mightiest possession will be appropriate for a society interested in its own welfare. In the vast majority of instances, however, some other model will be preferable. The interesting issues as they relate to Epstein's paper involve sorting out the instances when a doctrine of first possession makes sense, and when it does not, asking what modifications may be appropriate. Barzel [Barzel, 'Optimal Timing'] has discussed very plausible instances in which first possession not only fails to be the best, but will, in fact, lead to the total dissipation of the value of newly useful resources. Mortensen [Mortensen, 'Property Rights and Efficiency'] and Dasgupta and Stiglitz [Dasgupta and Stiglitz, 'Uncertainty'] have furnished more general models, but in their models first possession also seems rarely to be best, even in the face of the information and transactions costs with which the real world must cope.

I rely heavily on the Barzel model in rejecting Epstein's strong presumption in favor of first possession. I do not try to outline a fully general argument, but instead offer what I believe is sufficient evidence to cause one to doubt Epstein's position. I also mention one particularly important complication of the real world, partial information, that does support the modified version of first possession implicit in patents, copyrights, and related branches of law. But, even here, the doctrine is severely, and appropriately, constrained by time limits during which rights can be enforced ...

I. THE PROBLEM OF PREMATURE OCCUPATION

Securing possession of an entitlement is costly, and the resources expended in this process have alternative uses, so premature possession is undesirable. Awarding entitlements by first possession leads to just such premature expenditures. It does not matter whether the entitlement is a 'free' student ticket to a college football game, which (if the team is popular) induces wasteful pre-dawn occupation of places in line at the ticket office; a patent or copyright; a 'free' farm on the frontier; a legal monopoly over the provision of cable television services; or lobsters taken from the sea. The anticipation of capturing property of future value induces abandonment of alternative pursuits of positive current productivity.

There are policies that curtail premature occupation, although it is not obvious how often they are used with such a purpose explicitly in mind. For example, the sovereign can claim title to all unoccupied lands (mightiest possession), and then sell plots to 'speculators'. Neglecting the international competition for the sovereign's title, such a policy assures that the plots reach their highest valued uses. This policy was in fact utilized in the United States to distribute much of its interior land, although 'squatters' sometimes were able to obtain *ex post* political awards based on first possession. Legally, the interior was unowned simply because earlier first possessors, the American Indians, were not recognized as legal owners. First possession presupposes standing to call on the enforcement powers of the law, so again, as a practical matter, an effective coercive legal authority (mightiest possession) is a prerequisite for a rule of first possession. The Indians did not have mightiest possession, so *ipso facto* they could not support their claims by first possession either. Because we must have coercive legal authority, the issue is when do we also want to rely on a doctrine of first possession. There is a choice of doctrine available once mightiest possession is established.

A benevolent legal authority that was powerful enough to police its assignments of entitlements, and one that also knew everything that ultimately would have positive value, could today assign title to each asset and later avoid the resource drain that comes from individuals trying to establish title. But comprehensive benevolence, power and knowledge do not characterize human institutions. Unowned and formerly worthless items (the deep-sea floor) or previously unknown ones (the electromagnetic spectrum) later become attractive assets. If there are no restraints, a rent-seeking race to establish title ensues. At the margin, expenditures to capture title will equal the value of the asset whose title is sought, so marginal rents are completely dissipated. Those rules of the race that lead to marginal rent exhaustion with the smallest total expenditure on the race itself are the rules that will maximize the inframarginal rents.

Epstein does not ignore such problems, but rather underestimates them. The first possession rule does give rise to serious problems in the case of common-pool assets, such as oil, gas and fish. Yet, even here it furnishes a baseline of entitlements which permits the state to organize forced exchanges that on average work to the long-term advantage of persons with interests in the pool. But whenever any asset is (1) valuable, (2) unclaimed, and (3) available to the first possessor, then it is a common-pool asset – that is the definition. The more narrowly defined subset Epstein seems to have in mind, so-called 'migratory resources', is only one part of a larger and more general common-pool problem.

The lynchpin is a measurement problem – the definability of a resource before it is ready to be exploited. Some resources have insufficient value today to tempt anyone to bear the present costs of establishing and enforcing title, but are recognized to be of increasing value in a growing economy. At the end of World War II nobody owned the floor of the North Sea, but today it is one of the world's most active oil fields. No one owns the Moon's surface today, but it will not surprise me if commercial mining occurs there within my lifetime. Such resources are definable, and for them first possession is a particularly wasteful means of establishing title when compared to alternatives. Not surprisingly, title by first possession is rarely recognized in such instances.

However, other resources cannot even be described at present, for example, many of the next decade's most significant patentable inventions, and as to these resources some of the alternatives to first possession may be unworkable. But two points are crucial: First, before first possession is judged to be an appropriate rule, the sort of informational failing that I have described must be present. Second, even when first possession is an appropriate rule, it will generally be constrained, often by legal limitations on the life of the entitlement ...

... First possession, in the guise of the law of capture, can damage the source of migratory assets and reduce its present value. For example, fractionated ownership of a geological dome containing petroleum creates private incentives to drill wells too closely and to pump too rapidly, for only capture establishes title to the petroleum itself. Drilling fewer wells would increase the discounted stream of gross recovery from the field, as would operating each well more leisurely.

Overly avid fishing or trapping also reduces the long-run value of the pool, both by disrupting breeding patterns and by prematurely interrupting the growth of individual animals. Such losses sometimes induce societies that we consider primitive to establish fairly sophisticated property-rights systems that override a tradition of first possession ...

... I have argued that a prospective rule of first possession has little to recommend it, at least as a rule providing that new entitlements henceforth run in perpetuity to the first party to occupy a property, broadly defined. There are two distinct circumstances in which valuable assets are unowned. First, items previously known, but of no value, acquire value when the economy changes. A rule of first possession in this context induces premature occupation, with returns foregone elsewhere that equal the discounted present value of the returns from the newly acquired asset. In effect, the rule of first possession dissipates the asset's entire net worth.

This accords with the circumstances during the period of occupation of the American continents by European immigrants. Alternatives superior to first possession existed and were used. Commonly, the sovereign claimed title prior to settlement, then sold or bartered the land to settlers or intermediaries.* That technique had long been used to expand the European homelands whenever the sovereign was strong enough to enforce such claims. Abuses can arise when such authority is seized by a sovereign, but usually that dissipates only part of an asset's value – legislators and kings have a private incentive to maximize the net value of the realm they govern; it is their tax base.

A second circumstance where one finds valuable unowned assets concerns innovation, which compounds the difficulty of efficiently establishing entitlements. The asset cannot be well-defined soon enough to avoid all capture costs while still retaining individual incentives to finance research. In these circumstances, a modified rule of first possession is sometimes adopted because alternatives are unworkable. Although such circumstances occasionally apply to unoccupied land, this is the exception rather than the rule.

Finally, regardless of any efficiency aspects it may or may not have, a rule of first possession is an inadequate positive basis for a theory of law. Mightiest possession explains more that has happened and more that has become law than does first possession. Mightiest possession may well be efficient (though not necessarily equitable) due to the sovereign's incentive to maximize the value of his realm and thus his tax base. In contrast, an unconstrained rule of first possession is a rule of stagnation.

Now that mankind is contemplating mining Antarctica and the deepsea floor, the prospective aspects of a doctrine of first possession are very modern issues.

Extract 4.3   David Hume, *A Treatise of Human Nature*, Book III, Part II, pp. 503–5

The general rule, that possession must be stable, is not applied by particular judgments, but by other general rules, which must extend to the whole society, and be inflexible

---

* For example, the United States government bartered a great deal of western land to railroad companies in exchange for new rail construction. The new trackage would not have been profitable without the land grants, and much of the land was worthless without a source of transportation. Due to the new construction, both the railroad companies and the government were able to sell off land that otherwise would have lain idle for some time. There were occasional aberrations, but little of the land was given away through a rule of first possession. Although the prices charged for the government land may strike modern scholars as a ridiculously low token fee, deflating those prices by a price index or contrasting them with other land prices of the day makes them seem more reasonable.

either by spite or favour. To illustrate this, I propose the following instance. I first consider men in their savage and solitary condition; and suppose, that being sensible of the misery of that state, and foreseeing the advantages that would result from society, they seek each other's company, and make an offer of mutual protection and assistance. I also suppose, that they are endowed with such sagacity as immediately to perceive, that the chief impediment to this project of society and partnership lies in the avidity and selfishness of their natural temper; to remedy which, they enter into a convention for the stability of possession, and for mutual restraint and forbearance ...

It is evident, then, that their first difficulty, in this situation, after the general convention for the establishment of society, and for the constancy of possession, is, how to separate their possessions, and assign to each his particular portion, which he must for the future inalterably enjoy. This difficulty will not detain them long; but it must immediately occur to them, as the most natural expedient, that every one continue to enjoy what he is at present master of, and that property or constant possession be conjoined to the immediate possession. Such is the effect of custom, that it not only reconciles us to any thing we have long enjoyed, but even gives us an affection for it, and makes us prefer it to other objects, which may be more valuable, but are less known to us. What has long lain under our eye, and has often been employed to our advantage, that we are always the most unwilling to part with; but can easily live without possessions, which we never have enjoyed, and are not accustomed to. It is evident, therefore, that men would easily acquiesce in this expedient, that every one continue to enjoy what he is at present possessed of; and this is the reason, why they would so naturally agree in preferring it.

[He then adds the following as a footnote]

... It is a quality, which I have already observed in human nature, that, when two objects appear in a close relation to each other, the mind is apt to ascribe to them any additional relation, in order to complete the union; and this inclination is so strong, as often to make us run into errors (such as that of the conjunction of thought and matter) if we find that they can serve to that purpose ... Since, therefore, we can feign a new relation, and even an absurd one, in order to complete any union it will easily be imagined, that, if there be any relations, which depend on the mind, it will readily conjoin them to any preceding relation, and unite, by a new bond, such objects as have already a union in the fancy ... the same love of order and uniformity, which arranges the books in a library, and the chairs in a parlour, contribute to the formation of society, and to the well-being of mankind, by modifying the general rule concerning the stability of possession. And, as property forms a relation betwixt a person and an object, it is natural to found it on some preceding relation; and as property is nothing but a constant possession, secured by the laws of society, it is natural to add it to the present possession, which is a relation that resembles it.

Extract 4.4   Carol M. Rose, 'Possession as the Origin of Property' (1985) 52 *University of Chicago Law Review* 73 at 84

There is a ... subtext to the 'text' of first possession: the tacit supposition that there is such a thing as a 'clear act', unequivocally proclaiming to the universe one's appropriation – that there are in fact unequivocal acts of possession, which any relevant audience will naturally and easily interpret as property claims. Literary theorists have recently written a great deal about the relativity of texts. They have written too much for us to accept uncritically the idea that a 'text' about property has a natural meaning independent of some audience constituting an 'interpretive community' or independent of a range of other 'texts' and cultural artifacts that together form a symbolic system in which a given text must be read. It is not enough, then, for the property claimant to say simply, 'It's mine' through some act or gesture; in order for the 'statement' to have any force, some relevant world must understand the claim it makes and take that claim seriously.

Thus, in defining the acts of possession that make up a claim to property, the law not only rewards the author of the 'text'; it also puts an imprimatur on a particular symbolic system and on the audience that uses this system. Audiences that do not understand or accept the symbols are out of luck ...

In the history of American territorial expansion, a pointed example of the choice among audiences made by the common law occurred when one group did not play the approved language game and refused to get into the business of publishing or reading the accepted texts about property. The result was one of the most arresting decisions of the early American republic: *Johnson* v. *McIntosh* (1823) 21 US (8 Wheat.) 543, a John Marshall opinion concerning the validity of opposing claims to land in what is now a large part of Illinois and Indiana. The plaintiffs in this case claimed through Indian tribes, on the basis of deeds made out in the 1770s; the defendants claimed under titles that came from the United States. The Court found for the defendants, holding that the claims through the Indians were invalid, for reasons derived largely from international law rather than from the law of first possession. But tucked away in the case was a first-possession argument that Marshall passed over. The Indians, according to an argument of the claimants from the United States, could not have passed title to the opposing side's predecessors because, '[b]y the law of nature', the Indians themselves had never done acts on the land sufficient to establish property in it. That is to say, the Indians had never really undertaken those acts of possession that give rise to a property right.

Although Marshall based his decision on other grounds, there was indeed something to the argument from the point of view of the common law of first possession. Insofar as the Indian tribes moved from place to place, they left few traces to indicate that they claimed the land (if indeed they did make such claims). From an eighteenth-century political economist's point of view, the results were horrifying. What seemed to be the absence of distinct claims to land among the Indians merely invited disputes, which in turn meant constant disruption of productive activity and dissipation of energy in warfare. Uncertainty as to claims also meant that no one would make any productive use of the land because there is little incentive to plant when there is no reasonable assurance that one will be in possession of the land at harvest time. From this classical economic perspective, the Indians' alleged indifference to well-defined property lines in land was part and parcel of what seemed to be their relatively unproductive use of the earth.

Now it may well be that North American Indian tribes were not so indifferent to marking out landed property as eighteenth-century European commentators supposed. Or it may be that at least some tribes found landed property less important to their security than other forms of property and thus felt no need to assert claims to property in land. But, however anachronistic the *Johnson* parties' (ultimately mooted) argument may now seem, it is a particularly striking example of the relativity of the 'text' of possession to the interpretative community for that text. It is doubtful whether the claims of any nomadic population could ever meet the common law requirements for establishing property in land. Thus, the audience presupposed by the common law of first possession is an agrarian or a commercial people – a people whose activities with respect to the objects around them require an unequivocal delineation of lasting control so that those objects can be managed and traded.

But perhaps the deepest aspect of the common law text of possession lies in the attitude that this text strikes with respect to the relationship between human beings and nature. At least some Indians professed bewilderment at the concept of owning the land. Indeed, they prided themselves on not marking the land but rather on moving lightly through it, living with the land and with its creatures as members of the same family rather than as strangers who visited only to conquer the objects of nature. The doctrine of first possession, quite to the contrary, reflects the attitude that human beings are outsiders to nature. It gives the earth and its creatures over to those who mark them so clearly as to transform them, so that no one else will mistake them for unsubdued nature.

We may admire nature and enjoy wildness, but those sentiments find little resonance in the doctrine of first possession. Its texts are those of cultivation, manufacture, and development. We cannot have our fish both loose and fast, as Melville might have said [Herman Melville, *Moby-Dick*, Chapter 89] and the common law of first possession makes a choice. The common law gives preference to those who convince the world that they have caught the fish and hold it fast. This may be a reward to useful labor, but it is more precisely the articulation of a specific vocabulary within a structure of symbols approved and understood by a commercial people. It is this commonly understood and shared set of symbols that gives significance and form to what might seem the quintessentially individualistic act: the claim that one has, by 'possession', separated for oneself property from the great commons of unopened things.

Notes and Questions 4.1

1 How does the first occupancy rule differ from Locke's theory of original acquisition? See Waldron, *The Right to Private Property*, pp. 173–4.

2 Epstein later argues that for intangible assets first possession can operate through a 'filing office system' (i.e. property rights assigned to the first to register a claim) and that the same can be done for things like mining claims, where there are difficulties in deciding what in fact constitutes an assumption of possession (compare the similar problem noted by Nozick in Extract 3.6, in

deciding how much Locke's labour-desert theory would award to a private astronaut who clears a place on Mars). However, in response to this, Zerbe relates what actually happened to mining claims in the California gold rush. He referred to a classic study by Umbeck, 'A Theory of Contract Choice and the California Gold Rush', which revealed that mining rights were not assigned wholly according to who first filed claims, because original claims were too large to be enforced: 'What governed the size of claim was a sort of group meeting in which a majority of people were wearing guns, and the majority decided [how the rights should be allocated].' According to Umbeck, the size of claims allocated was the size that an individual person could efficiently control, but Zerbe treats this with some scepticism: 'it is unclear that the efficient size from the individual's point of view would also be the efficient size from the group's point of view' (Zerbe, 'Time, Property Rights, and the Common Law', pp. 804–5).

4.3.   New things

New things can come into existence in a variety of ways. For example, they may come into being through an irreversible mixture of pre-existing things, or as the product of the labour of one or more people (a question we look at in more detail in Chapter 9). The situation we concentrate on here is where the new thing can be regarded as the income or product of a pre-existing thing. Pre-existing things can produce income or natural products in essentially two different ways. In the case of some types of thing, it is inherent in their nature that they will or may produce income or natural products: apple trees produce apples, cultivated fields produce crops, dividends are paid on shares, lottery tickets sometimes produce prizes. But an owner of a thing can also make a thing produce an income by forgoing beneficial use of it and instead granting the right to beneficial use of the thing to someone else for a period of time in exchange for a rent. So, for example, you might agree to lend your money to the bank if the bank pays interest on the loan until it is repaid, or you might agree to grant a lease of your house to students for a year if they pay you £500 a month rent. Whichever way the income or natural product arises, the basic rule is the obvious one: ownership of the income or product automatically accrues to the owner of the thing that produced it, the principal. In most cases, this seems too obvious to mention: of course you own the prize if your lottery ticket bears the winning number, just as you own the apples from your apple tree and the rent accruing if your house is let. Indeed, as we saw in Chapter 1, the right to the income and the natural product of a thing are usually both regarded as standard incidents of ownership of the thing itself.

Again, however, more complex situations may require more elaborate rules. Consider the case of animal progeny. Animals are the natural product of two parents, not of one. Felix Cohen points out in *Dialogue on Private Property*, extracted below, that a legal system considering how to allocate ownership of animal offspring can choose between three possible rules: it can allocate ownership of the offspring to the owner of the mother, or it can allocate it to the owner of the father, or it can adopt a rule that, when an animal is born, it automatically falls within the same category as wild animals, i.e. it is unowned until captured. What factors would lead a system to adopt one rule rather than another?

To appreciate what he says, it is useful to return to the rationale for the obvious simple rule: *why* in the usual case does the owner of the principal automatically also own its income or product? The answer depends to some extent on the nature of the principal. There are some things whose value resides solely in the income or product they will or may produce. The lottery ticket is the obvious example, but the same would be true of the apple tree if owned by a commercial fruit grower. In both cases, there is no point in owning the principal unless you are also guaranteed ownership of its product. In the case of other things, the principal thing can only be made to yield income or natural products, or to produce a higher quality or higher value yield, by the expenditure of skill and labour and/or the addition of improving agents. So, for example, land can be made to yield crops by cultivation and by the investment of fertilisers and fencing. Ownership of the crop provides the incentive for the owner of the land to incur these expenditures, and since all the profit of increased production accrues to the landowner, he has the incentive to increase the productivity of the land whenever increased productivity is cost-effective in terms of the increased investment required to produce it. Further, a blanket rule that ownership of income and natural products automatically accrues to the owner of the principal (however the income or natural products accrue) will leave the owner of the principal free to put the principal to its most productive use – for example to stop growing crops on his land and instead hire it out for pop festivals. There are other reasons for adopting the simple basic rule. Allowing owners to swap beneficial use for rent ensures that beneficial use is put in the hands of those who value it most for the time being.

Cohen's third solution – allocating the ownership of income and natural products to no one – presents problems, both where the product has a negative value and where it has a positive value. To take the first, we need owners to take responsibility for the products yielded by the things they own if those products are harmful in themselves, or capable of causing harm or nuisance to others. This applies to leaves falling from trees as much as to polluting chemicals produced by a manufacturing process. The rule that ownership of the income or product automatically accrues to the owner of the principal provides a basis for the environmental law principle that the polluter pays. On the other hand, where the income or natural product has a positive value, the problem arises because of the first occupancy rule. If income and natural products are ownerless (for example, apples are owned by those who pick them, regardless of who owns the tree), the owner of the principal will have to incur costs excluding others to ensure that he is the first taker, and those who want to engage in trading in the product will have to incur costs in ensuring that they are the first taker. An apple wholesaler would not, therefore, own an orchard but would employ a gang of pickers to lie in wait outside apple trees waiting for them to ripen and meanwhile repelling rival pickers. Allocating ownership of the apples to the owner of the tree therefore eliminates these costs and makes apples cheaper. This is not to say that it is *never* the answer to allocate ownership of natural products to the first taker. There are some natural products that are of value to some people but not to others, and in these cases it may make sense to allot ownership to the first taker. Most societies making extensive use of horses have evolved such a rule about horse dung: the owner of the horse is in the best position to collect it to use as manure, but, if he does not want to do so, the first person to take it may keep it, and indeed anyone who wants horse manure may choose to follow the horse to ensure that he gets there first (see *Haslem* v. *Lockwood* (1871) 37 Conn 500, discussed by Lueck in 'First Possession as the Basis of Property').

Felix Cohen draws on a number of these factors to explain why most legal systems have chosen the rule that ownership of animal offspring accrues to the owner of the mother. However, even in the case of animal progeny, there may be differences in circumstances which justify a different rule. So, for example, as Lord Denning points out in *Tucker* v. *Farm and General Investment Trust Ltd* (extracted at www.cambridge.org/propertylaw/), this rule is replaced by a co-ownership rule in the case of swans, and even in the case of other animals, the right rule for allocating ownership as between the owner of the mother and the owner of the father will not necessarily be the right rule for allocating ownership as between the owner of the mother and the person in possession of the mother. In *Tucker*, the owner of ewes (a hire purchase company) had leased them to a farmer under a hire purchase agreement. Consistently with the reasoning of Felix Cohen, the Court of Appeal held that lambs born to the ewes during the hire period belonged to the farmer, not to the hire purchase company.

Extract 4.5   Felix S. Cohen, 'Dialogue on Private Property' (1954) 9 *Rutgers Law Journal* 357 at 359

THE CASE OF THE MONTANA MULE

C: Mr F, there's a big cottonwood tree at the southeast corner of Wright Hagerty's ranch, about 30 miles north of Browning, Montana, and under that tree this morning a mule was born. Who owns the mule?

F: I don't know.

C: Do you own the mule?

F: No.

C: How do you know you don't own the mule? You just said you didn't know who owns the mule. Might it not be you?

F: Well, I suppose that it is possible that I might own a mule I never saw, but I don't think I do.

C: You don't plan to declare this mule on your personal property tax returns?

F: No.

C: Why not, if you really don't know whether you own it? Or do you know?

F: Well, I never had any relation to any mules in Montana.

C: Suppose you did have a relation to this mule. Suppose it turns out that the mule's father was your jackass. Would that make you the owner of the mule?

F: I don't think it would.

C: Suppose you owned the land on which the mule was born. Would that make you the owner of the mule?

F: No.

C: Suppose you owned a piece of unfenced prairie in Montana and the mule's mother during her pregnancy ate some of your grass. Would that make you the owner of the mule?

F: No, I don't think it would.

C: Well, then you seem to know more about the ownership of this Montana mule than you admitted a few moments ago. Now tell us who really owns the mule.

F: I suppose the owner of the mare owns the mule.

C: Exactly. But tell us how you come to that conclusion.

F: Well, I think that is the law of Montana.

C: Yes, and of all other states and countries, as far as I know. For example, the Laws of Manu, which are supposed to be the oldest legal code in the world, declare:

> 50. Should a bull beget a hundred calves on cows not owned by his master, those calves belong solely to the proprietors of the cows; and the strength of the bull was wasted.
>
> (*Institutes of Hindu Law or the Ordinances of Manu*
> [translated and edited by S. G. Grady, Chapter 10])

Now how does it happen, do you suppose, that the law of Montana in the twentieth century AD corresponds to the law of India of 4,000 years or so ago? Is this an example of what Aristotle calls 'natural justice', which is everywhere the same, as distinguished from conventional justice which varies from place to place and from time to time?

F: Well, it does seem to be in accordance with the laws of nature that the progeny of the mother belong to the owner of the mother.

C: Wouldn't it be just as much in accordance with the laws of nature to say that the progeny of the father belong to the owner of the father?

F: I suppose that might be so, as a matter of simple biology, but as a practical matter it might be pretty hard to determine just which jackass was the mule's father.

C: Then, as a practical matter we are dealing with something more than biology. We are dealing with the human need for certainty in property distribution. If you plant seed in your neighbor's field the biological connection between your seed and the resulting plants is perfectly natural, but under the laws of Montana and all other states the crop belongs to the landowner. And the Laws of Manu say the same thing:

49. They, who have no property in the field, but having grain in their possession, sow it in soil owned by another, can receive no advantage whatever from the corn, which may be produced.

(Institutes of Hindu Law or the Ordinances of Manu
[translated and edited by S. G. Grady, Chapter 10])

Would you say here that, as a matter of certainty it is generally easier to say who owns a field than to say who owned the seeds that were planted in it?

F: Yes, as a general rule I think that would be the case.

C: Then whether we call our rule of property in livestock an example of natural law or not, its naturalness has some relation to the social need for certainty, which seems to exist in 48 different states and 48 different centuries. Do you think that property law reflects some such human demand for certainty?

F: I think it does in the cases we have been discussing.

C: Couldn't we have some other equally certain and definite rule, say that the mule belongs to the owner of the land where it was born.

F: It might be a hard thing to do to locate the mule's birth-place, but the young mule will show us its own mother when it's hungry.

C: Suppose we decided that the mule should belong to the first roper. Wouldn't that be a simple and definite rule?

F: Yes, but it wouldn't be fair to the owner of the mare who was responsible for its care during pregnancy if a perfect stranger could come along and pick up the offspring.

C: Now, you are assuming that something more than certainty is involved in rules of property law, and that somehow such rules have something to do with ideas of fairness, and you could make out a good case for that proposition in this case. But suppose you are trying to explain this to a cowboy who has just roped this mule and doesn't see the fairness of this rule that makes it the property of the mare's owner. Are there any more objective standards that you could point to in support of this rule? What would be the economic consequences of a rule that made the mule the property of the first roper instead of the mare's owner?

F: I think that livestock owners wouldn't be so likely to breed their mares or cows if anybody else could come along and take title to the offspring.

C: You think then that the rule that the owner of the mare owns the mule contributes to economic productivity?

F: Yes.

C: But tell me, is there any reason to suppose that the owner of the mare will be able to raise the mule more economically than, say, the first roper or the owner of the ground on which the mule was born?

F: Well, so long as the mule depends upon its mother's milk, it will be less expensive to raise it if the owner of the mother owns the offspring. And presumably the owner of the mother has physical control over his animals, and no extra effort is involved in his controlling the offspring as long as they are dependent upon their mother.

C: So, in effect, the rule we are talking about takes advantage of the natural dependency of the offspring on the mother animal. By enlisting the force of habit or inertia, this rule economizes on the human efforts that might otherwise be expended in establishing control over the new animal. The owner of the mare has achieved the object of all military strategy – he has gotten there 'fustest with the mostest'. We don't need to pay a troop of Texas Rangers to seize the mule and deliver it to the owner of the jackass father who may be many miles away. But why should we have a simple definite rule in all these cases? Wouldn't it be better to have a more flexible standard so that we might consider in each case what the owner of the mare contributed, what the owner of the jackass contributed, what was contributed by the grass owner who paid for the mare's dinners, and then on the basis of all the facts we might reach a result that would do justice to all the circumstances of each individual case?

F: The trouble with that is that the expense of holding such investigations might exceed the value of the mule.

C: And would it be easier or harder to borrow from the bank to run a livestock business if the owner of a mare or a cow didn't know in advance that it would own the offspring?

F: If I were a banker I'd certainly hesitate to make a livestock loan to a herd owner without such a simple definite rule.

C: Could we sum up this situation, then, by saying that this particular rule of property law that the owner of the mare owns the offspring has appealed to many different societies across hundreds of generations because this rule contributes to the economy by attaching a reward to planned production; is simple, certain, and economical to administer; fits in with existing human and animal habits and forces; and appeals to the sense of fairness of human beings in many places and generations?

F: I think that summarizes the relevant factors.

C: And would you expect that similar social considerations might lead to the development of other rules of property law, and that, where these various considerations of productivity, certainty, enforceability, and fairness point in divergent directions instead of converging on a single solution, we might find more controversial problems of private ownership?

F: That would seem to be a reasonable reference.

Notes and Questions 4.2

1   Examine the reasons Cohen gives for the progeny rule he says applies to the mule. How convincing are they?

2   Read *Tucker* v. *Farm and General Investment Trust Ltd* [1966] 2 QB 421, CA, either in full or as extracted at www.cambridge.org/propertylaw/. Cohen does not consider the issue raised in *Tucker*. If he had done so, do you think he would have come to the same conclusion as the Court of Appeal?

3   What was the purpose of the hiring in *Tucker*? Suppose I own a valuable and rare female giant panda, and I agree to lend it to London Zoo for two years.

While there, it unexpectedly gives birth to a baby panda. Who owns the baby panda?

4   Why did Tucker get no title to the *ewes*? (See Chapter 10 on the *nemo dat* rule.)

4.4.   Capture

Historically, the first occupancy rule has generally been used to establish ownership in what David Haddock described above as 'migratory resources', (sometimes referred to as 'fugitive resources'), although for reasons he touches on increasingly less so in modern societies. We concentrate here on capture of wild animals, which illustrates the basic problem about applying the first occupancy rule to fugitive resources: at what point in the pursuit and capture of the resource will the hunter be taken to have acquired a sufficient hold over the resource to be awarded ownership of it? The first occupancy rule traditionally demands that the claimant gains full control of the resource before he becomes entitled to property rights in it. There are at least three problems with this. The first two we have already noted above: such a rule encourages premature capture of the resource, and also it is not appropriate for some types of resource use such as nomadic land use. The third is that there are some fugitive resources, wild animals being a prime example, where the hunter must make a considerable investment of money and labour in the pursuit before gaining full control of the capture. If an interloper is free to come in and snatch the prey from him before he has gained full control, that investment will be wasted. The social and economic implications of this become apparent in the following extracts.

In the English case of *Young* v. *Hitchens* (1844) 6 QB 606, 115 ER 228 (extracted at www.cambridge.org/propertylaw/), the Court of Queen's Bench treated it as a simple matter of physical control, and refused to give redress to a Cornish pilchard fisherman whose rivals rowed up to his partially closed pilchard nets and drove out the fish already caught in but not yet fully enclosed by the nets. In the classic American fox-hunting case, *Pierson* v. *Post*, 3 Cai R 175, 2 Am Dec 264 (1805), also extracted at www.cambridge.org/propertylaw/, the majority came to the same conclusion (the fox-hunter was held not to have acquired property in the fox before it was taken by the interloper) but not for the same reasons, while in a strong minority judgment Livingston J advocated either awarding the fox to the first hunter or, better still, submitting the matter 'to the arbitration of sportsmen'.

As Robert Ellickson points out in Extract 4.6 below, this is, in effect, what was done in the whaling industry. The whaling community (and he establishes that such a thing did indeed exist in the eighteenth and nineteenth centuries, despite the different nationalities and geographical dispersal of its members) established different norms for different types of whale hunted in different types of environment, and on the whole the courts were prepared to accept these norms on the relatively rare occasions when disputes were brought to court, rejecting the strict control test which the court in *Young* v. *Hitchens* treated as inviolable.

Ellickson also points out that, both in the *Pierson* case and within the whaling trade at the time when the whaling rules evolved, it was axiomatic that efficiency in hunting consisted in achieving the maximum number of kills at the least cost. If this is the proper test for efficiency, then, as he says, it is probably correct that the hunting community can be left to identify the most efficient point of capture, as Livingston J suggested in *Pierson*. However, the norms they develop may not give sufficient weight to wider concerns about overall stock management and conservation.

Notes and Questions 4.3

1 Read *Young* v. *Hitchens* (1844) 6 QB 606, 115 ER 228 and *Pierson* v. *Post*, 3 Cai R 175, 2 Am Dec 264 (1805), either in full or as abstracted at www.cambridge.org/propertylaw/. How does the approach of the courts in the two cases differ?

2 Compare the reason given by the majority for coming to their decision in *Pierson* v. *Post* with the reasons given by Livingston J in the minority. Which do you find more persuasive? If Livingston J was correct, at what point in the hunt would the fox become the huntsman's?

3 In his dissenting judgment in *Pierson* v. *Post*, Livingston J said that 'the decision should have in view the greatest possible encouragement to the destruction of an animal so cunning and ruthless in his career'. If we assume for these purposes that this is correct, and that the aim should be to kill as many foxes as possible, which rule of capture is more likely to achieve this aim – the majority rule (the huntsman acquires no property in the fox until he has captured or killed it, and so the interloper who comes in just before the end of the hunt and kills the fox is entitled to keep it) or Livingston's minority rule (the huntsman had already acquired ownership in the fox before the interloper cut in)? In 'An Economic Analysis of "Riding to Hounds"', Dharmapala and Pitchford attempt to provide an answer to this question. Other commentators have assumed or argued that the majority rule is most likely to have that effect. In particular, as Dharmapala and Pitchford note, Cooter and Ulen argue that the encouragement that the majority rule gives to the killing of foxes in the stealthy manner used by Pierson, counterbalances the discouragement it gives to killing them by the more elaborate means of hunting:

> The majority's rule might lessen the fun of riding to hounds, but it does not necessarily lessen the incentive to kill foxes in less sporting ways. In fact, the rules seem equally efficient at contributing to the objective of killing foxes in order to reduce the damage they do to farms.
>
> (Cooter and Ulen, *Law and Economics*, p. 451)

However, Dharmapala and Pitchford point out that the investment of the two is unequal, and that, to some extent at least, the stealthy killing is parasitic on the huntsman's investment:

The central contention of Justice Livingston's dissent is that assigning property rights to the person who kills the fox would encourage opportunistic behaviour by individuals not participating in the chase. Implicit in his argument is that an initial investment in hounds is an essential pre-condition for flushing out ('starting') foxes; however, once this investment has been made, non-participants may reap the benefits of the investment by killing and capturing the foxes thus discovered. Not only does such behaviour deprive the huntsman who undertook the investment of the value of the fox pelt; more importantly, it also greatly diminishes the participants' enjoyment of the hunt. The prospect of such opportunism thus discourages investment in hounds, and thereby reduces the number of foxes killed … [Livingston also assumes] a fundamental asymmetry between the activities of the huntsman and the 'saucy intruder' … It is assumed that an individual who merely wanders around the countryside, with no assistance from foxhounds, has virtually no chance of encountering and pursuing a fox. Thus the productivity (in terms of the number of foxes killed) of both the huntsman and the intruder depends on the former's prior investment in hounds. If such an assumption accurately reflects the practical realities of fox hunting, then it would appear that the two kinds of activities cannot properly be regarded as substitutes: any disincentive effects of the majority's rule on investment in hounds not only lowers the number of foxes killed by huntsmen while riding to hounds, but also reduces the productivity of the intruders.

(Dharmapala and Pitchford, 'An Economic Analysis of "Riding to Hounds"', pp. 42–3)

They then construct a model of the interaction between a person in Post's position (the huntsman) and a person in Pierson's position (the interloper) to test the implications of this. They conclude that, if all foxes flushed out by huntsmen would have been killed by the huntsmen anyway if the interloper had not intervened, then the minority rule will lead to the greater number of foxes killed. If, on the other hand, the interloper increases the total number of foxes killed (he kills some that would have escaped the huntsmen) then there is something to be said for the majority rule.

4 Dharmapala and Pitchford then apply this analysis to what they argue is an analogous problem that arose over Internet domain names when commercial organisations first started to develop online operations – the problem of cybersquatting. As they explain:

The central problem in this area is that the registration of domain names is undertaken 'on a first-come, first-served basis, irrespective of intellectual property rights in the name' [Golinveaux, 'What's in a Domain Name', p. 641]. This registration process has allowed 'cybersquatters' to register the names of prominent companies as domain names in the hope of selling the rights to these names to the companies when the latter wish to undertake online operations. This basic scenario is closely analogous to the *Pierson* situation analyzed in this article. In stylized form, there are two players, a company A and a cybersquatter B. In the first period, A undertakes an investment (for instance, in product development) that determines the value of its domain name. Simultaneously, B chooses whether or not to register (at a small cost) A's name as a domain name. In the second period (presuming that B's property rights in the domain name are recognized), A and B negotiate over the transfer of rights to the domain name. If the size of the payment from A to B is determined by the relative bargaining power of the two parties, then it will act as a tax on A's return from the investment. Thus A will face a disincentive to invest at the margin, as a fraction of the value created by its investment is appropriated by B. (Dharmapala and Pitchford, 'An Economic Analysis of "Riding to Hounds"', p. 58)

More precisely, the analogy can be stated in the following terms. A's investment is analogous to h, and the resulting value of A's name resembles $f(h)$ (the number of foxes flushed out). The shares of $f(h)$ received by A and B, respectively, in the bargaining outcome are then akin to a and b, where (abstracting from the transaction costs of bargaining) $f(h) = a + b$. Clearly, this situation is analogous to the 'no escape' case analyzed above (in the sense that A would capture the entire value of the investment in the absence of B's activity). It was concluded earlier that, in these circumstances, rule L (assigning property rights to the investor) is optimal. It follows straightforwardly that, in line with this analysis, property rights in the domain name should be assigned to A.

When deciding legal disputes concerning domain names, courts have relied on a 'trademark dilution' theory [see Golinveaux, 'What's in a Domain Name' for a discussion].

However, in a range of cases involving what might be termed 'pure cybersquatting', the outcomes have been consistent with the analysis above. For example, in *Panavision* v. *Toeppen* [945 F Supp 1296 (CD Cal 1996)], the defendant had registered the trademarks of a large number of well-known companies (including Panavision) as domain names, purely for the purpose of subsequently selling the names to these companies. The court granted summary judgment for Panavision, in effect granting property rights in the domain name to the company.

However, there is another category of situations in which the ownership of domain names comes into dispute. These involve a small company or individual conducting a *bona fide* business registering its name as a domain name, where this name is identical to, or closely resembles, the trademark of a large, well-known company. In such instances, the use to which B would put the domain name in the absence of a bargaining solution has some social value (e.g. B could use the site to advertise its products). This situation closely resembles the case analyzed above where the foxes can escape after being flushed out. Essentially, if B registers A's name, then the level of A's investment helps determine the value of the name to B; if B uses the site to advertise products, then the number of people who type in A's name and are inadvertently exposed to B's advertising will depend on the extent of A's reputation, and thus on A's investment in product development. However, as B's activities have some social value, it may not always be optimal to assign property rights in the name to A.

An example of such a scenario is provided by the recent case of *Hasbro* v. *Clue Computing* [66 F Supp 2d 117 (D Mass 1999)]. Hasbro is the company that owns the trademark corresponding to the game 'Clue', while Clue Computing is a less well-known computer consulting firm based in Colorado. Hasbro alleged that Clue Computing's use of the address 'clue.com' diluted the former's trademark. The court, however, held that Clue Computing's behavior did not constitute trademark dilution, and granted rights in the name to Clue Computing. The court argued that:

> while use of a trademark as a domain name to extort money from the mark-holder ... may be *per se* dilution, a legitimate competing use of the domain name is not. Holders of a famous mark are not automatically entitled to use that mark as their domain name ... If another Internet user has an innocent and legitimate reason for using the famous mark as a domain name and is the first to register it, that user should be able to use the domain name.
> [*Hasbro* v. *Clue Computing*, 66 F Supp 2d 117 at 133 (D Mass 1999)]

There are also intermediate cases, in which the legitimacy or value of B's commercial activity may be subject to question.

Extract 4.6   Robert Ellickson, 'A Hypothesis of Wealth-Maximising Norms: Evidence from the Whaling Industry' (1989) 5 *Journal of Law, Economics, and Organization* 83

1. THE PROBLEM OF CONTESTED WHALES

Especially during the period from 1750 to 1870, whales were an extraordinarily valuable source of oil, bone, and other products. Whalers therefore had powerful incentives to develop rules for peaceably resolving rival claims to the ownership of a whale. In *Moby-Dick*, Melville explained why these norms were needed:

> It frequently happens that, when several ships are cruising in company, a whale may be struck by one vessel, then escape, and be finally killed and captured by another vessel ... [Or] after a weary and perilous chase and capture of a whale, the body may get loose from the ship by reason of a violent storm; and drifting far away to leeward, be retaken by a second whaler, who, in a calm, snugly tows it alongside, without risk of life or line. Thus the most vexatious and violent disputes would often arise between the fishermen, were there not some written, universal, undisputed law applicable to all cases ... The American fishermen have been their own legislators and lawyers in this matter.

Melville's last sentence might prompt the inference that whalers had some sort of formal trade association that established rules governing the ownership of contested whales. There is no evidence, however, that this was so. Anglo-American whaling norms seem to have emerged spontaneously, not from decrees handed down by either organizational or governmental authorities. In fact, whalers' norms not only did not mimic law, they created law. In the dozen reported Anglo-American cases in which ownership of a whale carcass was contested, judges invariably held proven whalers' usages to be reasonable and deferred to those rules.

2. THE WHALING INDUSTRY

At first blush it might be thought that whalers would be too dispersed to constitute the membership of a close-knit social group. During the industry's peak in the nineteenth century, for example, whaling ships from ports in several nations were hunting their prey in remote seas of every ocean. In fact, however, the entire international whaling community was a tight one, primarily because whaling ships commonly encountered one another at sea, and because whalers' home and layover ports were few, intimate, and socially interlinked. The scant evidence available suggests that whalers' norms of capture were internationally binding ...

3. THE CALCULUS OF WEALTH MAXIMIZATION

Wealth-maximizing norms are those that minimize the sum of transaction costs and deadweight losses that the members of a group objectively incur. By hypothesis, whalers would implicitly follow this calculus when developing norms to resolve the ownership of contested whales. As a first cut, this calculus would call for a whaling ship's fraction of ownership to equal its fractional contribution to a capture. For example, a ship that had objectively contributed one-half the total value of work would be entitled to a one-half share. In the absence of this rule, opportunistic ships might decline to contribute cost-justified but underrewarded work, leading to deadweight losses.

This first cut is too simple, however, because utilitarian whalers would be concerned with the transaction costs associated with their rules. They would tend to prefer, for example, bright-line rules that would eliminate arguments to fuzzy rules that would prolong disputes. Finding a cost-minimizing solution to whaling disputes is vexing because there is no ready measure of the relative value of separate contributions to a joint harvest. Any fine-tuning of incentives aimed at reducing deadweight losses is therefore certain to increase transaction costs.

4. HYPOTHETICAL WHALING NORMS

In no fishery did whalers adopt as norms any of a variety of rules that are transparently poor candidates for minimizing the sum of deadweight losses and transaction costs. An easily administered rule would be one that made the possession of a whale carcass normatively decisive. According to this rule, if ship A had a wounded or dead whale on a line, ship B would be entitled to attach a stronger line and pull the whale away. A possession-decides rule of this sort would threaten severe deadweight losses, however, because it would encourage a ship to sit back like a vulture and free-load on others' efforts in the early stages of a hunt. Whalers never used this norm.

Equally perverse would be a rule that a whale should belong entirely to the ship whose crew had killed it. Besides risking ambiguities about the cause of a whale's demise, this rule would create inadequate incentives for whalers both to inflict nonmortal wounds and to harvest dead whales that had been lost or abandoned by the ships that had slain them.

To reward early participation in a hunt, whalers might have developed a norm that the first ship to lower a boat to pursue a whale had an exclusive right to capture so long as it remained in fresh pursuit. This particular rule would create numerous other difficulties, however. Besides being ambiguous in some contexts, it would create strong incentives for the premature launch of boats and might work to bestow an exclusive opportunity to capture on a party less able than others to exploit that opportunity.

Somewhat more responsive to incentive issues would be a rule that a whale belonged to a ship whose crew had first obtained a 'reasonable prospect' of capturing it and thereafter remained in fresh pursuit. This rule would reward good performance during the early stages of a hunt and would also free up lost or abandoned whales to later takers. A reasonable-prospect standard, however, is by far the most ambiguous of those yet mentioned, invites transaction costs, and, like the other rules so far discussed, was not employed by whalers.

5. ACTUAL WHALING NORMS

Whalers developed an array of norms more utilitarian than any of these hypothetical ones … Whaling norms were not tidy, certainly less tidy than Melville asserted in *Moby-Dick*. Whalers developed three basic norms, each of which was adapted to its particular context. As will be evident, each of the three norms was sensitive to the need to avoid deadweight losses because each not only rewarded the ship that had sunk the first harpoon, but also enabled others to harvest dead or wounded whales that had seemingly been abandoned by their prior assailants. All three norms were also sensitive to the problem of transaction costs. In particular, norms that bestowed an exclusive temporary right to capture on a whaling ship tended to be shaped so as to provide relatively clear starting and ending points for the time period of that entitlement.

5.1.   Fast-fish, loose-fish

Prior to 1800, the British whalers operating in the Greenland fishery established the usage that a claimant owned a whale, dead or alive, so long as the whale was fastened by line or otherwise to the claimant's boat or ship. This fast-fish rule was well suited to this fishery. The prey hunted off Greenland was the right whale. Right whales, compared to the sperm whales that later became American whalers' preferred prey, are both slow swimmers and mild antagonists. The British hunted them from heavy and sturdy whaling boats. Upon nearing one, a harpooner would throw a harpoon with line attached; the trailing end of the line was tied to the boat. So long as the harpoon held fast to the whale and remained connected by the line to the boat, the fast-fish norm entitled the harpooning boat to an exclusive claim of ownership as against subsequent harpooners. If the whale happened to break free, either dead or alive, it was then regarded as a loose-fish and was again up for grabs. Although whalers might occasionally dispute whether a whale had indeed been fast, the fast-fish rule usually provided sharp beginning and ending points for a whaler's exclusive entitlement to capture and thus promised to limit the transaction costs involved in dispute resolution.

The fast-fish rule created incentives well adapted to the Britishers' situation in Greenland. Because right whales are relatively slow and docile, a whale on a line was not likely to capsize the harpooning boat, break the line, or sound to such a depth that the boatsmen had to relinquish the line. Thus the fast-fish rule was in practice likely to reward the first harpooner, who had performed the hardest part of the hunt, as opposed to free-riders waiting in the wings. Not uncommonly, however, a right whale sinks shortly after death, an event that requires the boatsmen to cut their lines. After a few days a sunken whale bloats and resurfaces. At that point the fast-fish rule entitled a subsequent finder to seize the carcass as a loose-fish, a utilitarian result because the ship that had killed the whale might then be far distant. In sum, the fast-fish rule was a bright-line rule that created incentives for both first pursuers of live whales and final takers of lost dead whales.

5.2.   Iron-holds-the-whale

Especially in fisheries where the more vigorous sperm whales predominated, whalers tended to shift away from the fast-fish rule ... The fast-fish rule's main alternative – the rule that iron-holds-the-whale – also provided incentives to perform the hardest part of the hunt. Stated in its broadest form, this norm conferred an exclusive right to capture upon the whaler who had first affixed a harpoon or other whaling craft to the body of the whale. The iron-holds-the-whale rule differed from the fast-fish rule in that the iron did not have to be connected by a line or otherwise to the claimant. The normmakers had to create a termination point for the exclusive right to capture, however, because it would be foolish for a Moby-Dick to belong to an Ahab who had sunk an ineffectual harpoon days or years before. Whalers therefore allowed an iron to hold a whale for only so long as the claimant remained in fresh pursuit of the iron-bearing animal. In some contexts, the iron-affixing claimant also had to assert the claim before a subsequent taker had begun to 'cut in' (strip the blubber from) the carcass.

American whalers tended to adopt the iron-holds-the-whale rule wherever it was a utilitarian response to how and what they hunted. Following Native American practices, some early New England seamen employed devices called drogues to catch whales. A drogue was a float, perhaps two feet square, to which the trailing end of a harpoon line was attached. The drogue was thrown overboard from a whaling boat after the harpoon had been cast into the whale. This device served both to tire the animal and also to mark its location, thus setting up the final kill. Because a whale towing a drogue was not connected to the harpooning boat, the fast-fish rule provided no protection to the crew that had attached the drogue. By contrast, the iron-holds-the-whale rule, coupled with a fresh-pursuit requirement, created incentives suitable for drogue fishing.

This rule had particular advantages to whalers hunting sperm whales. Because sperm whales swim faster, dive deeper, and fight more viciously than right whales do, they were more suitable targets for drogue-fishing. New Englanders eventually did learn how to hunt sperm whales with harpoons attached by lines to boats … The vigor of the sperm whale compared to the right whale, however, increased the chance that a line would not hold or would have to be cut to save the boat. A 'fastness' requirement would thus materially reduce the incentives of competing boatsmen to make the first strike. The iron-holds-the-whale rule, in contrast, was a relatively bright-line way of rewarding whoever won the race to accomplish the major feat of sinking the first harpoon into a sperm whale. It also rewarded only the persistent and skillful because it conferred its benefits only so long as fresh pursuit was being maintained.

Most important, unlike right whales, sperm whales are social animals that tend to swim in schools … To maximize the total catch, when whalers discovered a school their norms had to encourage boatsmen to kill or mortally wound as many animals as quickly as possible, without pausing to secure the stricken whales to the mother ship. Fettering whales with drogues was an adaptive technology in these situations. The haste that the schooling of whales prompted among hunters also encouraged the related usage that a waif holds a whale. A waif is a pole with a small flag atop. Planting a waif into a dead whale came to signify that the whaler who had planted the waif claimed the whale, was nearby, and intended soon to return. When those conditions were met, the usages of American whalers in the Pacific allowed a waif to hold a whale.

Because a ship might lose track of a whale it had harpooned or waifed, whaling norms could not allow a whaling iron to hold a whale forever. When a mere harpoon (or lance) had been attached, and thus it was not certain that the harpooning party had ever fully controlled the whale, the harpooning party had to be in fresh pursuit and also had to assert the claim before a subsequent taker had begun to cut in. On the other hand, when a waif, anchor, or other evidence of certain prior control had been planted, the planting party had to be given a reasonable period of time to retake the whale and hence might prevail even after the subsequent taker had completed cutting in.

Because the iron-holds-the-whale usage required determinations of the freshness of pursuit and sometimes of the reasonableness of the elapsed time period, it was inherently more ambiguous than the fast-fish norm was. By hypothesis, this is why the whalers who pursued right whales off Greenland preferred the fast-fish rule. The rule that iron-holds-the-whale, however, provided better-tailored incentives in situations where drogues were the best whaling technology and where whales tended to swim in schools. In these contexts, according to the theory, whalers switched to iron-holds-the-whale because they saw that its potential for reducing deadweight losses outweighed its transaction-cost disadvantages.

5.3.   Split ownership

In a few contexts whaling usages called for the value of the carcass to be split between the first harpooner and the ultimate seizer. According to an English decision, in the fishery around the Galapagos Islands a whaler who had fettered a sperm whale with a drogue shared the carcass fifty–fifty with the ultimate taker. The court offered no explanation for why a different norm had emerged in this context, although it seemed aware that sperm whales were often found in large schools in that fishery. The utilitarian division of labor in harvesting a school of whales is different than for a single whale. The first whaling ship to come upon a large school should fetter as many animals as possible with drogues and relegate to later-arriving ships the task of capturing and killing the encumbered animals. The Galapagos norm enabled this division of labor. It also showed sensitivity to transaction costs because it adopted the simplest focal point for a split: fifty–fifty.

Better documented is the New England coastal tradition of splitting a beached or floating dead whale between its killer and the person who finally found it. The best known of the American judicial decisions on whales, *Ghen* v. *Rich*, involved a dispute over the ownership of a dead finback whale beached in eastern Cape Cod. Because finback whales are exceptionally fast swimmers, whalers of the late nineteenth century slew them from afar with bomb-lances. A finback whale killed in this way immediately sank to the bottom and typically washed up on shore some days later. The plaintiff in *Ghen* had killed a finback whale with a bomb-lance. When the whale later washed up on the beach, a stranger found it and sold it to the defendant tryworks. The trial judge held a hearing that convinced him that there existed a usage on the far reaches of Cape Cod that entitled the bomb-lancer to have the carcass of the dead animal, provided in the usual case that the lancer pay a small amount (a 'reasonable salvage') to the stranger who had found the carcass on the beach ...

The norm enforced in *Ghen* divided ownership of a beached finback whale roughly according to the opportunity costs of the labor that the whaler and finder had expended. It thus ingeniously enabled distant and unsupervised specialized laborers with complementary skills to co-ordinate with one another by implicit social contract.

6. CONCLUDING REMARKS

... [A] critic could assert that the whalers' norms described were too short-sighted to be wealth-maximizing. By abetting co-operation among small clusters of competing hunters, the norms aggravated the risk of overwhaling.

The nineteenth-century whalers in fact depleted their fisheries so rapidly that they were impelled to seek whales in ever more remote seas. Had they developed norms that set quotas on catches, or that protected young or female whales, they might have been able to keep whaling stocks at levels that would support sustainable yields.

The arguments that respond to this ... criticism point up some shortcomings of the informal system of social control, as compared to other methods of human co-ordination. Establishment of an accurate quota system for whale fishing requires both a sophisticated scientific understanding of whale breeding and an international system for monitoring worldwide catches. For a technically difficult and administratively complicated task such as this, a hierarchical organization, such as a formal trade association or a legal system, would likely outperform the diffuse social forces that make norms. Whalers who recognized the risk of overfishing thus could rationally ignore that risk when making norms on the ground that normmakers could make no cost-justified contribution to its solution.

Whalers might rationally have risked overwhaling for another reason. Even if overwhaling was not wealth-maximizing from a global perspective, the rapid depletion of whaling stocks may well have been in the interests of the club of whalers centered in southern New England. From their parochial perspective, grabbing as many of the world's whales as quickly as possible was a plausibly wealth-maximizing strategy. These New Englanders might have feared entry into whaling by mariners based in the southern United States, Japan, or other ports that could prove to be beyond their control. Given this risk of hostile entry, even if the New Englanders could have created norms to stem their own depletion of world whaling stocks, they might have concluded that a quick kill was more to their advantage. The whaling saga is thus a reminder that norms that enrich one group's members may impoverish, to a greater extent, those outside the group.

4.5.   Colonisation and property rights

4.5.1.   Introduction

When Britain colonised Australia in the eighteenth and nineteenth centuries, the continent was already inhabited by native Australians, and had been for thousands of years. The effect of British colonisation was that English law, including English property law, became the law of Australia (subsequently modified first by the Crown to meet the special requirements of colonial administration and then by the Australian Government). Up until that time native Australians had of course had relationships between themselves in respect of their personal possessions, the land on which they lived, the natural resources of the land that they used, and the tangible and intangible things they manufactured. What happened to these pre-existing relationships when English property law became the law of Australia? To take a simple (if not wholly typical) example, consider the position of a native Australian living in his own house at the time when that part of Australia was annexed by the Crown. Was he treated under the new Australian law imposed by the Crown as having the same rights and other entitlements in the house (both as against fellow native Australians and as against the new settlers and the new government) as he would have had if he had had full ownership of the house under English law? Or did the law treat his occupation of his house as subject to the same rules, and giving rise to the same entitlements, as existed before colonisation (so that if, for example, there was a pre-existing native Australian rule that all rights in houses automatically pass to the eldest son on the death of the 'owner', this rule would continue to apply here, though not of course to settlers who later built and occupied houses)? Or was he treated under the new law as having no entitlements at all in his own house, or at least none enforceable against new settlers and the new government?

This example concerns a use of resources that would have been very familiar to eighteenth- and nineteenth-century British settlers, as indeed it is to us. However, the issues raised are made more complicated by the fact that this was not always the case. The pattern of relationships that Aboriginal Australians had developed with each other in respect of things was in many respects quite different from that which had developed in England by that time, giving rise to entitlements and obligations that had no counterpart in English law. Also, there were (and are) wide regional differences: quite different patterns had developed in different parts of the country. For example, many native Australian tribes were nomadic, a pattern of land use that does not fall within any recognised category of English property right, and the entitlements and obligations that this entailed differed from tribe to tribe. This complicates the question of the effect of the reception of English law. At the time when English property law became the law of Australia, did the new law recognise these 'alien' use patterns as new species of property rights which would then become an integral part of Australian law? If so, would these new property rights be available to all Australians (new settlers who wanted to live nomadically – perhaps a sensible option in many parts of Australia – or native Australians from a different tribe) or would they be restricted to those who had previously enjoyed them (and what about their descendants)? Or were these varying use patterns simply regarded as giving rise to no entitlements or obligations enforceable by Australian law?

These questions are of course not special to the British colonisation of Australia. They would also have arisen when the Normans colonised Britain in 1066, when Western European countries colonised parts of Africa, the Americas, the Indian sub-continent and other parts of Australasia in the eighteenth, nineteenth and twentieth centuries, and on all colonisations that have taken place before and since.

Historically, such questions have sometimes been settled at the time of colonisation by treaties made between the settlers and the native inhabitants, or by explicit formal expropriation by the colonising state acting within its own legal powers, or simply by the settlers wiping out the native population. In many other cases, however, the settlers neither formally recognised nor expressly abrogated indigenous rights. This is essentially what happened in Australia. On the whole, as a matter of fact rather than law (the legal position is what was in issue in the cases we consider below), native Australian patterns of usage of resources appear to have been tolerated and even recognised to a certain extent. For example, the colonial administration probably regarded the Aboriginal population as having rights and obligations as against each other, and sometimes may even have created or given support to local tribunals or other mechanisms for settling disputes in accordance with local rules (some instances are recounted in Brennan J's judgment in *Mabo (No. 2)*). Also, there is some suggestion that the administration regarded itself as responsible for protecting the Aboriginal population's property against intruders (settlers not authorised by the Crown, or marauders from outside the indigenous group: again, instances are recorded in *Mabo (No. 2)* of the colonial administration expelling 'trespassers and intruders' from the Murray Islands so that 'the Murray Islanders will have Murray Island to themselves' (§§ 13 and 14 of Brennan J's judgment)). However, as a matter of historical fact, the colonial government did not appear to regard native Australians as having patterns of usage of resources that gave rise to legal entitlements as against the state. In other words, the colonial administration did not appear to regard itself as under a legal obligation to respect the occupation and resource usage of the Aboriginals, or to compensate them for any deprivation or infringement of it.

This of course gives rise to immensely important political and ethical questions, both as to the legitimacy of what was done in the past and as to what, if anything, should and could now be done to redress past wrongs. In the cases we consider below, the Australian courts had to consider the *legal* question – was the colonial government legally entitled to treat native resource use patterns in the way that it did, and do surviving or recently extinguished native patterns of resource use now give rise to entitlements enforceable in modern Australian law? This legal question is notionally separate from the political and ethical questions, but as is apparent from the judgments given in the cases extracted here, it is not easily separable from the political and moral context.

In this section, we look at two pivotal Australian decisions. In *Milirrpum v. Nabalco Pty Ltd* (1971) 17 FLR 141, a decision of Blackburn J in the Supreme Court of the Northern Territory, the Aboriginal people who brought the case lost, and it was held that, although their tribes had lived in parts of the Northern Territory for generations before it was annexed in 1863, they had no rights in the land they inhabited, or at least none that had survived annexation. In *Mabo v. Queensland (No. 2)* (1992) 175 CLR 1, however, the tide was turned. The High Court of Australia reversed the effect of *Milirrpum* and established for the first time that Aboriginal Australian people did have rights in the land they inhabited before annexation of Australia by the Crown, that these rights did survive annexation, and that they continue to be enforceable in modern Australian law except in so far as they have been abandoned or extinguished by the Australian government since annexation.

These two cases mark the end of one era and the beginning of another. The *Mabo (No. 2)* decision laid the foundations for a process of recognition of Aboriginal rights in resources that has proved to be fast-moving, complex and politically highly controversial. We sketch out very briefly at the end of this section the developments that have taken place since *Mabo (No. 2)*, but our main concern here is in the basic principles it established. We come back to both *Milirrpum* and *Mabo (No. 2)* later on in the book, in particular in Chapter 5 in the context of a consideration of the nature of property rights, where we look in more detail at the nature of the aboriginal rights and interests now recognised in Australia and Canada, and contrast them with common law private property and communal property rights and interests.

4.5.2. The *Milirrpum* decision and the doctrine of *terra nullius*

In 1968, the Government of Australia granted Nabalco Pty Ltd a forty-two-year mineral lease of land in the Gove Peninsula in the Northern Territory of Australia to enable it to mine the rich fields of bauxite that had been discovered in the area, and to establish a township there. Representatives from several different Aboriginal clans brought this action against Nabalco and the government, claiming that they had property rights in the land in question that would be infringed by Nabalco's activities. They argued that these rights had been in existence before the land became vested in the Crown in 1788, that they were property rights that survived that event and continued in existence unless and until validly terminated by the Crown, that they never had been terminated, and that, consequently, they were still in existence and enforceable against Nabalco.

In order for this argument to succeed, the Aboriginals had to establish two things. First, they had to establish that, as a matter of law, when territory in Australia was acquired by the Crown, property rights of the native inhabitants were legally binding on the Crown unless and until validly terminated by the Crown. If they succeeded in establishing that principle, they then had to establish that, at the time when the territory was acquired by the Crown, their ancestors had indeed had a relationship with the land they inhabited which would be recognisable as a property relationship by English common law.

The action was heard by Blackburn J in the Supreme Court of the Northern Territory. He held that, as a matter of law, any rights of native inhabitants were automatically extinguished when land in Australia was acquired by the Crown. Consequently, the second question – whether these particular clans had had property rights in the land at that time – did not arise. He did nevertheless go on to give that second question detailed consideration (he decided they did not have property rights), and we look at what he said in Chapter 5, but the question we are interested in here is the first question.

The issues and the arguments Blackburn J had to consider in relation to the first question were complex, and so, necessarily, was the reasoning which led him to the conclusion that aboriginal land rights had not survived annexation, but two important strands in his reasoning can be highlighted here.

The first was his view that the question of the effect of colonisation of this part of Australia (New South Wales) had already been established as a matter of law, and that he was bound by authority to accept that conclusion. There had long been a principle of international law that the law in force in a newly acquired territory depended on the circumstances of its acquisition. If it was acquired by *conquest* or *cession* (i.e. the inhabitants of the territory had either been conquered by or had ceded sovereignty to the invading state) then the inhabitants continued to be governed by their own private laws unless and until these laws were positively abrogated by the invading sovereign. However, a sovereign state could acquire new territory by *occupation* (sometimes called *settlement*) if the territory was *terra nullius* – a territory belonging to no one. In a territory acquired by occupation or settlement, the law of the settler became the law of the newly acquired territory and all property vested in the occupying state. Moreover, it had become accepted by the nineteenth century that *terra nullius* extended beyond territory that was genuinely uninhabited to territory that was 'practically uninhabited, without settled inhabitants or settled law' (Lord Watson in *Cooper* v. *Stuart* (1889) LR 14 App Cas 286 at 291). In other words, if a territory was occupied only by 'backward' people who could not be regarded as settled inhabitants or having a settled law, then their territory was regarded as *terra nullius* and so capable of being acquired by settlement or occupation rather than by conquest or cession. When a sovereign state, such as the British Crown or another European colonial nation, acquired territory which was in this condition (i.e. occupied only by people who were taken to be 'backward' or 'barbarian') this was treated in international law as an occupation or settlement of the territory, with the consequence that all indigenous inhabitants were not only treated as subject to the sovereignty of the acquiring state but also became governed solely by its laws – they were treated as having no pre-existing rights arising out of their own system of law.

The justification for this was put by Lord Sumner in the Privy Council in *Re Southern Rhodesia* [1919] AC 211 at 233–4:

> The estimation of the rights of aboriginal tribes is always inherently difficult. Some tribes are so low in the scale of social organisation that their usages and conceptions of rights and duties are not to be reconciled with the institutions or legal ideas of civilised society. Such a gulf cannot be bridged. It would be idle to impute to such people some shadow of the rights known to our law and then to transmute it into the substance of transferable rights of property as we know them.

The difficulty faced by Blackburn J in *Milirrpum* was that, although he heard overwhelming evidence that, as a matter of fact, aboriginal tribes in the Gove Peninsula had always lived in highly sophisticated and stable communities, it had been widely accepted, in particular by the Privy Council in *Cooper* v. *Stuart*, that this part of Australia (New South Wales) was at the time of annexation 'without settled inhabitants or settled law', and that, consequently, it came within the category of a settled or occupied colony in which all resources had vested in the Crown, leaving the Aboriginals with no rights to occupy their ancestral lands. Blackburn J took the view that this categorisation of New South Wales as a settled or occupied colony, whether based on ignorance or on what Brennan J was later to describe in *Mabo (No. 2)* as 'a discriminatory denigration of indigenous inhabitants, their social organisation and customs' (at paragraph 39) was nevertheless a matter of law which he was bound to accept:

> The evidence shows a subtle and elaborate system highly adapted to the country in which the people led their lives, which provided a stable order of society and was remarkably free from the vagaries of personal whim or influence. If ever a system could be called 'a government of laws, and not of men', it is that shown in the evidence before me ... [Nevertheless] ... [w]hether or not the Australian Aboriginals living in any part of New South Wales had in 1788 a system of law which was beyond the powers of the settlers at that time to perceive or comprehend, it is beyond the power of this Court

to decide otherwise than that New South Wales came into the category of a settled or occupied colony. (*Milirrpum*, pp. 267 and 244)

Consequently, he thought he had no alternative but to dismiss the claimants' case.

A second factor which influenced Blackburn J in coming to this conclusion was something that also troubled Dawson J in his dissenting judgment in *Mabo (No. 2)*. It is generally accepted that it is within the power of a sovereign state to extinguish pre-existing property rights, provided that, in doing so, it is acting lawfully according to the rules of its own system (or according to the rules of international law if it is taking over new territory). It is also generally (although not so universally) accepted that, when colonising a new territory, whether inhabited or not, the Crown could lawfully extinguish pre-existing rights without specific legislation provided it made its intentions plain. It seems clear that this is what the Crown thought it had done in Australia. From the outset, the Crown assumed that the land was its own, to use or dispose of absolutely as it saw fit, with no legal constraints imposed by any pre-existing rights of indigenous inhabitants, and it acted on this basis. If the law *as it was perceived to be at the time* was that the Crown was legally entitled to absolute beneficial ownership of Australia, and that any claims of Aboriginal tribes had been extinguished by colonisation, is it now open to the courts to say that this was wrong in law? As Dawson J says in *Mabo (No. 2)*:

> There may not be a great deal to be proud of in this history of events. But a dispassionate appraisal of what occurred is essential to the determination of the legal consequences, notwithstanding the degree of condemnation which is nowadays apt to accompany any account ... The policy which lay behind the legal regime was determined politically and, however insensitive the politics may now seem to have been, a change in view does not of itself mean a change in the law. It requires the implementation of a new policy to do that and that is a matter for government rather than the courts. In the meantime, it would be wrong to attempt to revise history or to fail to recognize its legal impact, however unpalatable it may now seem. To do so would be to impugn the foundations of the very legal system under which this case must be decided. (*Mabo (No. 2)*, paragraph 48)

4.5.3.   Mabo (No. 2)

4.5.3.1.   Terra nullius

The Aboriginals who brought the claims in *Mabo (No. 2)*, the Meriam Indians who inhabited the Murray Islands, used their land in a very different way from the Gove Peninsula Indians. They lived mostly in settled villages rather than nomadically, and lived primarily by cultivating gardens rather than by hunting and gathering. Also, they inhabited a part of Australia that had been annexed to the Crown at a different time and by a different process. The High Court of Australia could therefore technically have allowed the Aboriginals' claim in *Mabo (No. 2)* without overruling *Milirrpum*, confining the effect of *Milirrpum* to the claims of Aboriginal tribes of a culturally similar type who inhabited that locality. As Brennan J said:

> This Court can either apply the existing authorities and proceed to inquire whether the Meriam people are higher 'in the scale of social organization' than the Australian Aborigines whose claims were 'utterly disregarded' by the existing authorities or the Court can overrule the existing authorities, discarding the distinction between inhabited colonies that were *terra nullius* and those which were not.
>
> (*Mabo (No. 2)*, paragraph 39)

The court decided by a majority of six to one (Dawson J dissenting) to follow the latter course. Brennan J described the extended doctrine of *terra nullius* (i.e. treating inhabited territories as if they were uninhabited if the inhabitants were 'so low in the scale of social organisation' that it would be 'idle to impute to such people some shadow of the rights known to our law') as 'an unjust and discriminatory doctrine of the kind that can no longer be accepted':

> 37. It is one thing for our contemporary law to accept that the laws of England, so far as applicable, became the laws of New South Wales and of the other Australian colonies. It is another thing for our contemporary law to accept that, when the common law of England became the common law of the several colonies, the theory which was advanced to support the introduction of the common law of England accords with our present knowledge and appreciation of the facts. When it was sought to apply Lord Watson's assumption in *Cooper* v. *Stuart* that the colony of New South Wales was 'without settled inhabitants or settled law' to Aboriginal society in the Northern Territory [in *Milirrpum*] the assumption proved false . . .
>
> 38. The facts as we know them today do not fit the 'absence of law' or 'barbarian' theory underpinning the colonial reception of the common law of England. That being so, there is no warrant for applying in these times rules of the English common law which were the product of that theory. It would be a curious doctrine to propound today that, when the benefit of the common law was first extended to Her Majesty's indigenous subjects in the Antipodes, its first fruits were to strip them of their right to occupy their ancestral lands . . .
>
> 39. . . . The theory that the indigenous inhabitants of a 'settled' colony had no proprietary interest in the land thus depended on a discriminatory denigration of indigenous inhabitants, their social organization and customs. [T]he basis of the theory is false in fact and unacceptable in our society . . .
>
> 41. If the international law notion that inhabited land may be classified as *terra nullius* no longer commands general support, the doctrines of the common law which depend on the notion that native peoples may be 'so low in the scale of social organization' that it is 'idle to impute to such people some shadow of the rights known to our law' (*Re Southern Rhodesia* [1919] AC at pp. 233–4) can hardly be retained. If it were permissible in past centuries to keep the common law in step with international law, it is imperative in today's world that the common law should neither be nor be seen to be frozen in an age of racial discrimination.

42. The fiction by which the rights and interests of indigenous inhabitants in land were treated as non-existent was justified by a policy which has no place in the contemporary law of this country ... Whatever the justification advanced in earlier days for refusing to recognize the rights and interests in land of the indigenous inhabitants of settled colonies, an unjust and discriminatory doctrine of that kind can no longer be accepted. The expectations of the international community accord in this respect with the contemporary values of the Australian people ... The common law does not necessarily conform with international law, but international law is a legitimate and important influence on the development of the common law, especially when international law declares the existence of universal human rights. A common law doctrine founded on unjust discrimination in the enjoyment of civil and political rights demands reconsideration. It is contrary both to international standards and to the fundamental values of our common law to entrench a discriminatory rule which, because of the supposed position on the scale of social organization of the indigenous inhabitants of a settled colony, denies them a right to occupy their traditional lands.

Consequently, the Court held that, as a matter of law, the rights of Aboriginal Australians survived colonisation and continue to survive unless, and except to the extent that, they have since been extinguished.

This raises two questions that have proved to be crucially important. What counts as a right for these purposes? And precisely what can extinguish Aboriginal rights? We look at the first question in the next chapter. In order to appreciate the importance of the second question, on extinguishment, we need to say something more about what the court decided was the effect of transporting English common law to Australia.

4.5.3.2.   Property, sovereignty and the doctrine of radical title

When a sovereign state acquires new territory (inhabited or uninhabited), it acquires sovereignty over the new territory, which includes the power to create and extinguish property rights. However, as Brennan J explains in paragraphs 44–6, sovereignty is not the same as ownership: in general the fact that a state acquires sovereignty over new territory does not mean that it automatically acquires ownership of all resources in it, even previously unowned ones. All it acquires by assuming sovereignty is power to make the laws to give ownership to itself or to others. In a passage cited with approval by Toohey J (in paragraph 15 of his judgment in *Mabo (No. 2)*), McNeil explains the difference between sovereignty and title to land:

> The former is mainly a matter of jurisdiction involving questions of jurisdiction and constitutional law, whereas the latter is a matter of proprietary rights, which depend for the most part on the municipal law of property. Moreover, acquisition of one by the Crown does not necessarily involve acquisition of the other.

(McNeil, *Common Law Aboriginal Title*, p. 108)

However, when a state acquires new territory, it also brings its own system of law to the new territory, so if, for example, it is an established principle of law in the colonising state that all swans belong to the state, all swans in the new territory will also automatically belong to the state (unless already subject to rights of indigenous people which are binding on the state). In English common law, as a matter of law, all land in this country is ultimately 'owned' by the Crown. This is a principle of law that has been taken to apply in Australia and other colonised territories as well as in England, and in *Mabo (No. 2)* it was used as an argument in support of the Government of Queensland's contention that the annexation of Australia to the Crown vested ownership of all land in Australia.

However, this 'ownership' of land by the Crown is a peculiar vestigial type of ownership, a relic of the feudal system of land ownership that used to operate in this country (as Brennan J explains in paragraphs 48–52 in *Mabo (No. 2)*, and Deane and Gaudron JJ in paragraphs 7 and 8). It is still integral to the technical structure of land ownership in this country, as we see later in Chapter 6, but it has long ceased to have any practical significance here. All that it means is that it is the Crown that has the residual power to grant perpetual private holdings of land (called fee simple or freehold estates, but corresponding in all respects to ownership as described by Honoré), and that, when a fee simple estate is extinguished, the land reverts to the Crown – there can never be any unowned land in England. The extinction of a fee simple estate is a very rare event, and even when it does occur the Crown probably has no power to do anything with the reversionary interest apart from grant a new fee simple estate out of it to someone else. In England, therefore, the Crown's ownership of land has very little content.

In the case of colonised territories, however, it had been argued that the effect of the doctrine of Crown ownership of land was that the Crown automatically became full beneficial owner of all land in the colonised territory, whether previously owned or unowned. This argument was rejected by the majority in *Mabo (No. 2)*. They accepted that the technical feudal common law structure of land ownership was imported into Australia, but they took the view that all this meant was that the Crown acquired what they called 'radical title' to the land, not full ownership. This radical title gave the Crown title to grant beneficial property interests, like fee simple estates and leases, over tracts of land to itself and to others, but it did not of itself give the Crown any rights that overrode pre-existing Aboriginal rights. In other words, the Crown's radical title to the land was held by the Crown subject to Aboriginal rights.

What actually happened in Australia was that the government kept control over the development of resources by granting what were called pastoral leases to settlers to enable them to farm land, and mining and other leases to those, like Nabalco Pty Ltd, who were engaged in extracting and exploiting natural resources. Land taken by settlers under these leases was almost invariably inhabited to some extent by Aboriginal tribes. Sometimes this led to the displacement of the tribes concerned and the disintegration of their way of life, other times not. One of the most important questions faced by the court in *Mabo (No. 2)* was whether these events had had the effect of extinguishing Aboriginal rights.

4.5.3.3.   Extinguishment

The court was divided on this issue. They all agreed that those rights that survived annexation continued to be enforceable unless and until extinguished by one of four events.

Express extinguishment

They all agreed that the rights could have been taken away by the state on or just after annexation by the state expressly declaring them to be extinguished, but equally all agreed that this had not happened.

Implied extinguishment by inconsistent grant

They also all (apart from Toohey J) agreed that Aboriginal rights were extinguished by the Crown either granting inconsistent property rights to others, or taking inconsistent property rights for itself. However, while a bare majority took the view that this was a lawful (if not morally justifiable) extinguishment of Aboriginal rights (Brennan J at paragraphs 81–2; Mason CJ and McHugh J agreeing at paragraph 2; and Dawson J, who dissented on the main point but agreed that, if he was wrong and Aboriginal rights had survived annexation, they would have been extinguished by inconsistent grant), the minority disagreed (Deane and Gaudron JJ at paragraphs 23–4, 29–30 and 60). They took the view that, although the government had the *power* to extinguish Aboriginal rights in this way, they did not have the *right* to do so. In other words, Aboriginal rights were effectively extinguished by the government making inconsistent grants, but the government committed a legal wrong in doing so, and consequently any such extinguishments gave rise to a claim in compensation. This consequence flowed from the view taken by these judges that Aboriginal rights are personal rights only and not property rights (this is a point we return to in the next chapter). Toohey J agreed that extinguishment by the government was unlawful unless proper compensation was paid, but also considered that it was ineffective – so that past inconsistent grants made without compensation did not extinguish the rights, and gave rise to an entitlement to compensation in so far as they interfered with the exercise of the rights (Toohey J at paragraphs 121–7 and his conclusion at paragraph 128(3)).

Abandonment

In Brennan J's view, the nature and content of each Aboriginal tribe's rights in the land they used was to be determined 'according to the laws and customs of the indigenous people who, by those laws and customs, have a connection with the land' (paragraph 83(6)) (we consider further what this might mean in

Chapter 5). It followed from this, in his view, that those rights would be extinguished 'if the clan or group, by ceasing to acknowledge those laws, and (so far as practicable) observe those customs, loses its connection with the land or on the death of the last of the members of the group or clan' (paragraph 83(7); and see also paragraph 66). Mason CJ and McHugh J can be taken to agree with this (paragraph 1), but Deane and Gaudron JJ had reservations. While they agreed that the rights would be extinguished if the tribe abandoned its connection with the land, or if the tribe itself or the relevant group became extinct, they did not think the rights would be lost by an abandonment of traditional customs and ways 'at least where the relevant tribe or group continues to occupy or use the land' (paragraph 59).

Surrender but not alienation

However, they did all agree that, while Aboriginal rights could be surrendered back to the government, they could not be alienated to anyone outside the relevant tribe or group who did not treat themselves as bound by the relevant laws and customs, except by an alienation that was authorised by those laws and customs (Brennan J at paragraph 83(8), and see also 65 and 67; and Deane and Gaudron JJ at paragraphs 21 and 59). So, the Aboriginal tribes could not realise the exchange value of their rights, except in what appear to be the rare cases where some form of alienation of land and/or rights in it was traditionally authorised.

The result of all this, as far as the case of *Mabo (No. 2)* itself was concerned, was that the Meriam Indians were held to have still-subsisting rights in the Murray Islands. It was held as a matter of fact that their rights had not been extinguished by any of the methods that the majority considered to be effective. However, as the majority acknowledged, their conclusion that Aboriginal rights had been extinguished by the government granting inconsistent property rights to others or taking inconsistent property rights for itself could make the judgment of only limited help to other Aboriginal groups. Unsurprisingly, therefore, this particular point proved to be the focus of subsequent case law and legislative developments, briefly noted in section 4.5.4 below.

Notes and Questions 4.4

Read *Milirrpum* v. *Nabalco Pty Ltd* (1971) 17 FLR 141 and *Mabo* v. *Queensland (No. 2)* (1992) 175 CLR 1, either in full or as extracted at www.cambridge.org/propertylaw/, and then consider the following:

1 What are the justifications for recognising Australian Aboriginal rights and treating them as fully enforceable property rights within the present Australian property law system? Consider the following possible justifications:

(1) *First occupancy*. The Aboriginals got there first. What difficulties would the Aboriginals face if relying only on first occupation arguments? Consider the following possible objections:

    (a) their resource use could not be said to amount to occupancy (for a convincing response see Toohey J at paragraphs 18 and 117–18);

    (b) resource use such as theirs that does not permit the right holders (or anyone else) to exploit natural resources, or to alienate their rights so that others can do so, is economically inefficient and will inhibit development of the national economy;

    (c) any first occupancy entitlement that they may have acquired has long been extinguished by adverse possession of European settlers (see further Chapter 11 on extinguishing rights by adverse possession); and

    (d) why should an individual alive now be entitled to rights in resources solely because an ancestor of his exercised such rights in the eighteenth century?

(2) *A Lockean labour theory of acquisition of property rights*. Can the Aboriginal resource use described in *Milirrpum* be categorised as mixing labour in any sense that Locke would have accepted?

(3) *Preservation of indigenous cultures*. Such cultures would otherwise be wiped out by the enforced superimposition of the alien culture of more powerful and more numerous colonisers. It is consistent with this rationale for protecting Aboriginal land rights that the rights should be inalienable and should continue only for so long as their traditional way of life continues (see the points made about extinguishment above), but this must necessarily prevent or inhibit Aboriginal communities from adapting their way of life to suit changing conditions and aspirations. How far is this justifiable?

For an analysis of these and other justifications, see Lokan, 'From Recognition to Reconciliation'.

2 The Native Title Act 1993, which gave legislative form to the *Mabo (No. 2)* decision, provides for Aboriginal rights to be extinguished by surrender to the government but not by alienation, confirming the majority view of the position at common law. Surrender can be on any terms (including in exchange for common law rights in any land). The *Independent* reported on 23 October 1998 that an Aboriginal group from the Northern Territory, the Jawoyn, had given up their claim to about 2,500 acres of horticultural land in the Katherine region in exchange for a renal dialysis facility from the Northern Territory Health Services and an alcohol rehabilitation centre to be provided by the Department of Lands. A Jawoyn spokesman explained that they did this when they discovered that there were no government plans to provide a dialysis unit in the region in the next five years. The report continues:

    At present, Aborigines in the Katherine region have to travel more than 100 miles to Darwin for dialysis. Mr Lee [the Jawoyn spokesman] says this is taking a high toll on family life and removing people from their traditional lands.

On average, life expectancy for Aborigines is 15–20 years below that of other Australians, with alcohol and drug abuse playing a significant role in poor health. The problem is particularly acute in the Northern Territory where the level of renal disease is 50 times higher than the national average . . .

Proving Native Title [under a procedure provided by the Native Titles Act] is an expensive and lengthy process which has angered rural communities, farmers and mineowners who feel their livelihoods are threatened by the claims.

Farmers operating in the Katherine region have already expressed relief that the Jawoyn claim has been settled in exchange for health services. However, Mr Lee says he hopes this agreement will not become a blueprint for further land-rights settlements: 'I think it would be a tragedy if this were repeated. I think it is a moral reminder to the government that they shouldn't be waiting for Aboriginal people to trade their country. They should be providing services as of right for all citizens', he said.

Consider whether arguments that might justify allowing Aboriginal groups to surrender their land rights in such circumstances might also justify allowing them to alienate their rights, for example by sale in the open market.

3 Examine the reasons Dawson J gives in *Mabo (No. 2)* for dissenting from the majority decision that Aboriginal rights were not extinguished by colonisation. Are they convincing?

4 Read the preamble to the Native Title Act 1993, and also sections 3, 10, 11, 223 and 225, either in full or as extracted at www.cambridge.org/propertylaw/. To what extent does it enact the principles established by the High Court of Australia in *Mabo (No. 2)*?

4.5.4.   Developments since *Mabo (No. 2)*

The decision in *Mabo (No. 2)* was confirmed and put on a legislative footing by the federal Native Title Act 1993 but this was not the end of the story. The Act expressly stated its objective of providing for the recognition and preservation of native title (adopting what it referred to as 'the common law definition of native title' and defining it in the words used by Brennan J in *Mabo (No. 2)*), and it set up machinery for settling native title claims. This machinery proved to be slow and cumbersome. There were problems settling appropriate and workable rules of evidence to ensure that Aboriginal groups with oral rather than written traditions were not disadvantaged. Evidence to establish criteria set out in *Mabo (No. 2)* and enacted in the 1993 Act proved difficult and costly to provide. For example, immense research, time and financial resources were needed to establish whether a particular group had, and had maintained, a continuing connection with the land in question in accordance with its law and custom, as was required in order to establish that a group had originally had native title and that it had not subsequently been extinguished. There were provisions for mediation, which again proved difficult to operate for a variety of reasons, including the number of different interested parties involved. The history of the Yorta Yorta claim illustrates the difficulties. There were reported to be 470 parties involved at the mediation stage. The claim was the first to reach trial stage (in 1996) after the 1993 Act came into force, and it was finally disposed of in the High Court of Australia in December 2002. The trial at first instance involved oral evidence from 201 witnesses plus 48 written witness statements, the hearing took 114 days and the transcript of the proceedings ran to 11,600 pages. The claimants lost. By a majority of five to two, the court upheld the trial judge's decision that the Yorta Yorta Aboriginal community had failed to establish the necessary continuing connection in accordance with its law and custom (*Yorta Yorta Aboriginal Community* v. *Victoria* [2002] HCA 58).

The first post-*Mabo (No. 2)* decisions of the High Court of Australia took an expansive view of the scope of native title. In particular, in *Wik Peoples* v. *Queensland* (1996) 187 CLR 1, it was held by a bare majority that the grant by the Crown of pastoral leases in Queensland in the decades leading up to *Mabo (No. 2)* had *not* wholly extinguished native title rights and interests in the areas of land they covered, and that, to the extent that the specific rights of the lessees and the native title holders did not conflict, they co-existed. This decision was highly controversial, its critics claiming that it put in doubt the extent and legitimacy of the land rights of farmers across the whole of Australia. It proved to be the high point for native title. The Native Title Amendment Act was passed in 1998 restricting the effect of *Wik* and making significant changes to the procedures for settling claims, and also cutting back the right to be consulted on future developments which had been given to Aboriginal groups by the 1993 Act. Subsequent High Court of Australia decisions (in particular, *Western Australia* v. *Ward* [2002] HCA 28, *Wilson* v. *Anderson* [2002] HCA and *Yorta Yorta Aboriginal Community* v. *Victoria* [2002] HCA 58) also revealed a more restrictive approach, interpreting the statutory provisions strictly and so as to require detailed proof of the precise traditions and customs of the group claiming title and the way in which they were connected with the land claimed, and putting the burden of proof of continuing connection on the claimants. Commentators have criticised this approach as inconsistent with the broad approach that the majority in *Mabo (No. 2)* appeared to envisage. Toohey J, for example, at paragraph 187 of his judgment in *Mabo (No. 2)*, had said that '[I]t is inconceivable that indigenous inhabitants in occupation of land did not have a system by which land was utilised in a way determined by that society'; and similar views are expressed or implicit in the other majority judgments. The present position, however, is that claimants are required to prove what Toohey J thought could be assumed. In the words of one commentator, this 'renders proof of native title inappropriately difficult' (Bartlett,

'Humpies Not Houses', comparing developments in Australia with those in the United States and Canada).

For fuller details, see also Sackville, 'The Emerging Australian Law of Native Title'; Brennan, *The Wik Debate* (Brennan was one of the judges in the majority in *Mabo (No. 2)* and in the minority in *Wik*); and Tehan, 'A Hope Disillusioned'.

Part 2

The nature of proprietary interests

5

Personal and proprietary interests

5.1. Characteristics of proprietary interests

In this chapter, we outline the distinctive features of property interests and how they differ from non-proprietary interests in things. Most of these points come up again in other chapters (some of them in more detail): the object of this chapter is to draw together some recurrent themes.

5.1.1. General enforceability

We saw in Chapter 2 that the essential characteristic that distinguishes proprietary interests in things from non-proprietary interests is their range of enforceability. A non-proprietary interest is essentially bilateral: generally only one other person is under a duty correlative to the right held by the right holder. A proprietary interest, on the other hand, is generally enforceable: if I hold a property right, everyone in the world (or, in the case of some types of right, everyone in the world except a privileged class) has a correlative duty. The classic illustration of the general enforceability principle is provided by the decision in *Hill* v. *Tupper*, extracted below, where the court held that, where a canal company which had (among its other rights in the canal) an exclusive right to put pleasure boats for hire on the canal, transferred that right to Hill, Hill became entitled to prevent the canal company from also putting boats on the canal for hire, but was not entitled to prevent Tupper, a stranger, from doing so. One of the ingredients of the canal company's proprietary interest in the canal was a proprietary right to put pleasure boats for hire on the canal, but it could not break that right off from its proprietary bundle in such a way that the right remained proprietary when transferred to Hill. As against the canal company, Hill had the exclusive right to put pleasure boats on the canal (so, for example, he could require the canal company to prevent anyone else doing so) but it was enforceable only against the canal company, not against Tupper. It was a personal right, not a property right.

The principle that a proprietary interest is generally enforceable is as near absolute as any principle in English property law. Its obverse – that non-property interests in things are enforceable only bilaterally – requires some qualification, however. First, contract and constructive trust rules may allow a non-proprietary interest to become enforceable against third persons: see, for example, the Contracts (Rights of Third Parties) Act 1999, and *Ashburn Anstalt* v. *Arnold* [1989] Ch 1 for an analysis of the circumstances in which a non-proprietary interest might become binding via a constructive trust. Secondly, economic torts can be said to put everyone in the world under a duty not to interfere with the performance of a particular contract. If I enter into a contract with a hotel that they will provide me with a particular room for ten days, I can sue in tort anyone who induces the hotel to break that contract (assuming I can establish the other necessary elements of the tort). In that sense, therefore, I can be said to have a right to the hotel room for those ten days enforceable against the whole world. However, this does not mean that I have a property right – I have a right *to* the hotel room, not a right *in* it.

General enforceability is therefore a necessary but not so obviously a sufficient condition for an interest to be a property interest.

5.1.2. Identifiability of subject-matter

5.1.2.1.   The basic principle

It follows from the principle of general enforceability that, if my right in a thing is to be a property right, it must be possible to identify the thing in question. Because a property right in a thing is enforceable against everyone who comes into contact with the thing, it must be possible to identify whether or not any particular thing has become burdened in this way. There are two aspects of this. The marketability of things is hindered if it is difficult or impossible for potential buyers to find out whether or not the thing they are proposing to buy is burdened by a property interest held by a third person. This is essentially a labelling problem, and we look at it in Chapters 14 and 15. The other aspect is that a property right cannot attach to a thing in any meaningful way until the thing has been identified. If I own 100 sheep in a field and I sell you five of them but we never separate off your sheep from my sheep, what are we to do if one of the sheep dies, or gives birth to a lamb? We need to know whether it was one of my sheep or one of yours. Similarly, if your university provides you with a room in a hall of residence for you to live in for a year, but on the basis that it can move you from room to room whenever it wants, you may have a personal right as against the university to be provided with *a* room in the hall, but it is difficult to see how you can have a property right in any particular room, because we cannot identify which room it is. We look at these identification problems again in Chapter 12.

5.1.2.2.   Fluctuating assets

There is, however, one important qualification to the identifiability principle to be noted here. It is possible for a fluctuating body of assets to be viewed as a whole, as an abstract thing which continues to exist in an identifiable form even though the component assets making up the whole may change over time. The property interest then attaches to the abstract whole, rather than to the fluctuating component assets. We see in Chapter 2 that this is essentially what a trust fund is. Trustees hold a portfolio of assets for the benefit of beneficiaries, but with the power and the duty to sell any of the assets at any time and replace them with others as and when necessary to maintain or increase the value of the fund as a whole. In such circumstances, it is useful to regard the abstract thing – the fund – as a thing in its own right, and to treat the beneficiaries as having a property interest in the fund rather than in any of the individual assets making up the fund at any one time.

There are other examples of property interests that can exist in an abstract thing which consists of a fluctuating body of assets. Commercially, the most important is the floating charge, which we look at in Chapter 18. By using a floating charge, a business can give a charge to a lender over all its assets of a particular type, rather than over the specific assets it happens to own at any one time. So, for example, a car manufacturer can grant to its lender a floating charge over all its stock of completed cars, without giving a lender a specific charge over any one of the cars. A specific charge (usually called a fixed charge to distinguish it from a floating charge) over a car is a property interest in the car, potentially enforceable against anyone who buys the car. So, if the lender was to have a fixed charge over each of the company's completed cars, this could be highly inconvenient: every time the company wanted to sell a car to a buyer, it would have to ask the lender to give up its charge over that car (and prove to the buyer that it had done so). The advantage of a floating charge over *the stock of cars* is that it does not give the lender a property interest in any specific car, so the company is free to carry on its business of making and selling cars without having to ask the lender every time it wants to sell one. The charge floats over the body of assets, without attaching to any particular one at any particular time. Admittedly, this is not of itself very much use to the lender. The reason a lender takes a charge over a car is so that, if the company fails to repay the loan that the charge secures, the lender has a property interest in the car that enables it to sell the car for itself and take the proceeds of sale to pay off the debt. If it has a floating charge over a stock of cars it has no sufficient property interest in any specific car to enable it do this. However, this problem is avoided by the device of 'crystallisation': on the happening of a specified event (for example, the business goes into liquidation, or fails to make a loan repayment to the lender) the floating charge over the fluctuating stock of cars crystallises and is transformed automatically into a fixed charge over each car then owned by the business at that point in time. The lender can then go ahead and sell each car as chargee if it wants, or exercise any of the remedies available to a chargee.

5.1.3. Significance of alienability

A right or interest is alienable if it is capable of being transferred from its current holder to someone else, so that the transferee steps into the shoes of the transferor. In this sense, then, an alienable right or interest is not personal to the holder. Alienation might take the form of deliberate transfer, or transfer by operation of law, or the automatic passing of the property interest on the death of the holder. Economists and others who regard the creation of a free market in resources as the central rationale for the existence of property rights, regard alienability as the central feature of an efficient property system, as we saw in Chapters 2 and 3.

Indeed, it is often said that alienability is an essential characteristic of a property interest (see, for example, Lord Wilberforce in *National Provincial Bank* v. *Ainsworth* [1965] AC 1175, discussed in Chapter 9, and Blackburn J in *Milirrpum* v. *Nabalco Pty Ltd* (1971) 17 FLR 141 below). However, this is inaccurate in a number of respects.

5.1.3.1.   Inalienability of communal property

First, some communal property rights and interests are not alienable. If the community consists of a fluctuating body of individuals, no one individual can alienate her own interest, and generally the community as a whole cannot alienate its communal interest either. We look at this point again in section 5.2 below.

5.1.3.2.   Status rights

Secondly, inalienable private property rights can be, and frequently have been, created by legislation. These are all essentially status rights – i.e. rights that the holder holds personally, by virtue of a unique status he has, and which cannot be transmitted to anyone else because the status is personal to him. For example, under various statutes some types of residential, business or agricultural tenant remain in possession as tenant after the end of their tenancies either under new statutory tenancies or under their old tenancies, which the statute extends. Such statutory tenancies are undeniably property interests – the tenant is in possession, with an interest enforceable against the whole world – but they are inherently inalienable: the tenant holds the statutory tenancy only by virtue of his status as the former tenant.

5.1.3.3.   Appurtenant rights

Thirdly, some property interests can only be held as appurtenant to other property interests: they cannot be transferred separately from the property interests to which they are appurtenant. This mostly applies only to land interests. For example, an easement, which is a right to make a particular use of land owned by someone else, such as a right to use a path crossing someone else's land, can only be held by someone who also owns neighbouring land which benefits from the easement. Suppose, for example, it would be convenient for me to take a shortcut across your land to get to the University library from my office in the Law Faculty. You can grant me a right of way over your land for this purpose, but it cannot be a property right, because it does not benefit (is not appurtenant to) any land I own. Similarly, if you have granted me a right of way over a path crossing your land to get from my house to the road, this is a property right, but it is appurtenant to the ownership of my house. I cannot sell it to a neighbour unless I also sell the neighbour my house, and, if I do sell my house to anyone, I cannot retain the right of way – if it is not transferred to the person who buys my house, it will simply cease to exist.

Subject to these qualifications, however, alienability is an inherent characteristic of *private* property interests, so firmly embedded that the holder of an alienable property cannot shed the power to alienate her interest. As we saw in Chapter 2 where we looked at this point more closely, even a contractually binding agreement *not* to alienate the interest is ineffective. If, having entered into such an agreement, the right holder nevertheless goes ahead and transfers her interest to a transferee, the transfer is fully effective to move the interest from transferor to transferee. The transferor will, however, be in breach of contract, and the remedies available to the other party to the contract will include damages and even (in the case of some property interests and in some circumstances) the right to terminate the property interests by the process of forfeiture (see below).

5.1.4. Requirement for certainty

We have already said that the subject-matter of a property interest must be certain in the sense that it must be identifiable. The same applies – and for the same reasons – to the identity of the interest holder, to the duration of the interest (if it is of a limited duration, such as a lease, rather than of perpetual duration, such as ownership), and to the precise time when it begins and when it ends. It must be possible to say at any point in time whether or not *at that time* that particular interest is attached to that particular thing, and who it is who holds it. This dictates the degree of certainty required. Leaving aside an anomalously stringent certainty requirement applicable to the duration of leases (which we look at in Chapter 17), it is not necessary that the identity of the interest holder, or the duration of the interest or the beginning and end date should be ascertainable in advance. All that is required is that we can identify the start date when it happens, and that we can identify the interest holder by the start date, and that we can identify the end date when it happens. So, for example, if I die leaving a will in which I leave 'the residue of my estate to my eldest living relative for his or her lifetime, and then to be divided equally between my children then alive', then the certainty requirements are satisfied. The precise content and extent of the subject-matter ('the residue of my estate') will not be known immediately, but it will be known by the time the executors have to vest the interest in the eldest relative, and while no one knows in advance precisely when that will be, everyone will be able to recognise the event when it happens. Similarly, by that date the identity of my eldest living relative will be known, and while at that time no one will know how long he or she will live, or which of my children will still be alive by then, all of these things will be ascertainable at the relevant time.

5.1.5. The *numerus clausus* of property interests

There is an almost infinite variety of non-property rights that can be created in relation to a thing, bounded only by human ingenuity. This is not true of property rights. Only a small range of types of property interest is known to the law. It would be possible to list them all, and it would be a short list. If you own a bicycle, you can give me whatever personal rights in it or to it that you want (a right to ride it every third Wednesday, or scrape paint off the handlebars, or anything else you can think of) and, provided I give consideration so that you become contractually bound by what you promised, I will be able to enforce these rights against you fully as personal rights. However, the *only* property rights you can give me in the bicycle are full ownership of it (you can sell or give it to me), or a mortgage or charge over it (as security for you repaying money you owe me), or a beneficial interest under a trust (you can declare you hold the bicycle on trust for me, so that you hold the legal ownership on trust for me as beneficiary), or you can bail it to me (bailment is a grant of possession of goods for a limited duration and sometimes a limited purpose – and even bailment's place on the property list is controversial, as we see in Chapter 17). Different types of property interest are recognisable in relation to different types of thing – for example, the list of property interests in land is quite different from (and considerably longer than) the list applicable to bicycles and other goods.

This characteristic of property interests seems to apply in most jurisdictions (which perhaps explains why it is still generally referred to by the Latin term *numerus clausus*, meaning literally finite in number), and in this jurisdiction at least it makes the courts extremely reluctant to recognise new types of property interest, as we see in *Hill* v. *Tupper* below. We consider why this should be the case in Chapter 9, where we look at this point in more detail.

5.1.6. Vindication of property rights

It is sometimes said that what distinguishes a property right from a personal right is the availability of specific performance: the courts will order specific perform-ance of an enforceable promise to transfer or grant a property interest in a thing but not a personal right in the thing. Again, this is only partially true. It is more true in the case of land than it is in the case of goods or intangible things. Each piece of land is regarded as unique, and so the court will generally order specific perform-ance of a contractually binding promise to transfer or grant a property interest in land. They would do the same in the case of a property interest in any other unique thing, where damages would not be an adequate remedy, but not many things other than land are regarded as unique in this way.

The converse is more generally true. The courts are very unlikely to order specific performance of a promise to transfer or grant a *personal* right in a thing, even if the personal right relates to land. This remains an important consequence of a decision to categorise a right to occupy land as a lease (a property interest) or a licence (a purely personal right), as we see in Chapter 7. However, even here there are exceptions. For example, in *Verrall* v. *Great Yarmouth Borough Council* [1980] 1 All ER 839 (extracted at www.cambridge.org/propertylaw/), the Court of Appeal granted the National Front specific performance of a two-day licence of a hall that the Conservative-controlled council had granted to them for their annual conference, and which the now Labour-controlled council wanted to revoke. The court rejected an argument that specific performance of a licence can never be ordered, and it is clear from the reasons they gave for ordering it in this case that the courts will take each case on its own merits, and grant specific performance where, for one reason or another, damages would not be an appropriate remedy, whether the interest in question is personal or proprietary.

5.1.7. Termination

We see in Chapter 8 that some property interests continue indefinitely whereas others are limited in duration, to continue either until a particular date or until the happening of a particular event. Those of a limited duration automatically continue for that duration. It is possible to limit a property interest to last only during a person's life-time, and of course this would necessarily be the maximum duration of a status right of the kind we noted above. Subject to this, however, a property interest is not personal to its holder and so nothing happens to the interest when its holder dies or ceases to exist: the property interest simply passes on to the next person entitled.

There are, however, three ways in which property interests can end prematurely.

5.1.7.1. Abandonment

The first, *abandonment*, applies to all types of property interest. It is, however, surprisingly difficult to abandon a property interest: non-use, for example, is not sufficient of itself. We see this in section 5.2 below in relation to communal property interests, and the same is true of private property (for fuller consideration, see Hudson, 'Abandonment', particularly in relation to shipwrecks, which is explored in further detail in Dromgoole and Gaskell, 'Interests in Wrecks').

5.1.7.2. Disclaimer

Any type of property interest can also be given up by a formal procedure known as *disclaimer*, but this is available only to a company in liquidation or a bankrupt individual's trustee in bankruptcy, or to a person who has become entitled to a property interest on the intestacy or under the will of someone else who has died. It is not wholly clear what actually happens to a disclaimed property interest: difficult and complex issues can arise, particularly where the disclaimed interest is a derivative interest like a lease of land (what, for example, is to happen to the landlord's interest, and to any subleases that had been granted: for an exploration, if not a resolution, of these difficulties, see *Hindcastle Ltd* v. *Barbara Attenborough Associates Ltd* [1997] AC 70).

5.1.7.3. Forfeiture

The third way of ending a property interest prematurely if by *forfeiture*. Forfeiture can be described in general terms as a right reserved by the grantor of a property interest to take the property interest back from the grantee on breach by the grantee of one of the terms of the grant. In principle, any property interest may be made forfeitable by the reservation or grant of such a right. In practice nowadays, a right of forfeiture is most likely to be made exercisable over a lease of land, or (less often) over a fee simple interest in land, or over a possessory interests in goods or (increasingly) over intellectual property rights. When the forfeitable interest is a lease of land or a possessory interest in goods (i.e. a bailment), the right to forfeit is exercised by the right holder either physically re-entering/retaking possession of the land or goods, or applying to the court for an order that will have the effect of terminating the forfeitable interest and/or ordering its return to the right holder. In other cases, for example the forfeiture of intellectual property rights, the holder of the right to forfeit will usually have to apply to the court for an order of specific performance of the contractual term requiring the forfeitable interest to be transferred back.

There are two important features of forfeiture to be noted here. The first is that the right to forfeit another property interest is itself a property interest (usually called a right of re-entry). This is incontrovertible where the right is to forfeit an interest in land, but probably also true in other cases (see *Shiloh Spinners Ltd* v. *Harding* [1973] AC 691 for a judicial analysis of the nature of the right of re-entry). Like most other private property rights, a right of re-entry is inherently assignable. When it is exercisable over a lease of land, the right of re-entry is appurtenant to the landlord's interest in the land (i.e. only the landlord for the time being under the lease can forfeit it and the right of re-entry cannot be traded separately from the landlord's interest: see section 5.1.3.3 above). Other types of right of re-entry are usually not appurtenant to any other property interest.

The second distinctive feature of forfeiture is its potentially Draconian effect. Rights of re-entry are usually exercisable only where the holder of the forfeitable interest has committed some breach, and the holder of the right of re-entry will usually exercise it only where the breach has caused or is likely to cause her harm. However, there is no necessary connection between that harm and the gain that will accrue to her by forfeiting the other person's interest, nor between that harm and the loss the other person will suffer if his interest is forfeited. In practice, it is very likely that forfeiture will over-compensate the forfeiter and penalise the interest holder too severely. Take the example of a lease of office premises granted for twenty-five years at a rent of £12,000 a year, which contains a right for the landlord to forfeit the lease if the tenant misses a monthly payment of rent. If after ten years of the lease the tenant fails to pay a month's rent, the landlord can either just sue for recovery of the rent or forfeit the lease. If by that time the rent of £12,000 a year is higher than the market rent for that kind of premises, the landlord will just sue for recovery of the rent: there will be no point in ending the lease and taking the premises back because she is not likely to be able to let them to anyone else at the same rent. If, on the other hand, the £12,000 a year rent is now lower than the market rent, the landlord has every incentive to forfeit the lease at the earliest and most minor breach: she will gain, and the tenant will lose, much more by forfeiting the lease than the £1,000 unpaid rent (which will anyway still be recoverable as due for the period up until forfeiture).

The potential for unfairness is intensified in the case of forfeiture of possessory interests in land and goods by the fact that traditionally the holder of the right to forfeit can choose to exercise it by self-help instead of by judicial process.

For these two reasons, both equity and statute have long intervened in the exercise of rights of re-entry. There is a long-established general equitable jurisdiction to grant relief against forfeiture, now supplemented by specific statutory provisions applicable to different types of property interest, and there is also now some (but by no means complete) statutory regulation of the use of forfeiture without judicial process. In general, relief against forfeiture will almost always be granted if the holder of the forfeitable interest remedies the breach (for example, by paying up all arrears of rent), and, even if that is not possible, relief is still likely to be granted if the gain to one party and/or the loss to the other is disproportionate to the harm caused by the breach.

Just as the right of re-entry is a property interest in its own right, so too is the right to apply to court for relief against forfeiture, at least where the forfeited interest is an interest in land. This is a consequence of the rule in *Walsh* v. *Lonsdale* which we look at in Chapter 12.

5.1.8. Property rights and insolvency

Probably the most important difference in practice between proprietary rights and non-proprietary rights is the difference in the way they are treated on insolvency. When an individual goes bankrupt or a company goes into insolvent liquidation (the process equivalent to bankruptcy for a company), all their property is taken from them (subject to a few exceptions for individuals not relevant here). This property is then sold, and the proceeds of sale are divided between the creditors of the bankrupt or liquidated company, proportionately to the amount of the creditor's claims. Since a debtor who has gone bankrupt or gone into insolvent liquidation is, by definition, insolvent, the total amount of claims against the debtor will exceed the total proceeds of sale of all the assets of the debtor. Consequently, each person who has only a personal claim against the debtor will inevitably receive less than full repayment of their claims on insolvency (see further Chapter 8).

If, however, a creditor has a proprietary right or claim enforceable against the debtor, the position is dramatically different. If a creditor can show that he has a property interest in any asset apparently held by the insolvent debtor, that property interest never forms part of the debtor's property in the first place, so it is never made available to be distributed between the debtor's general creditors. The effect is that the creditor with a proprietary claim is always paid in full. Suppose, for example, that the debtor owns her business premises, worth £1 m, but has granted her bank a mortgage over the premises to secure repayment of a loan of £900,000.

The property of the debtor available to her general creditors will include her property interest in the business premises, which is worth £100,000 (the value of her ownership subject to the bank's mortgage). This can be realised only by selling the premises to a third person subject to the mortgage (in which case the bank will obtain full repayment of the loan from the buyer, who will have to pay that amount to the bank to clear the mortgage off the title) or by paying the bank its full £900,000 to discharge the mortgage, so that ownership of the premises can be sold at its full value. Either way, the bank is repaid in full, and only £100,000 (less the costs of all this) is available to be distributed between the creditors with other claims.

A different example illustrates another difference between proprietary and non-proprietary interests. Consider what your position would be if you took a lease of a house for ten years at a rent of £5,000 a year, or instead took a licence to occupy the same house for the same period at the same price, £5,000 a year. Assume your landlord/licensor goes bankrupt after the first year. If you have a lease, a property interest, the landlord's property interest in the house consists only of his landlord's interest, i.e. his ownership subject to your lease. This is all that can be sold to satisfy his creditors. So the only effect on you of his bankruptcy is that his interest in the house will be sold to an outside person, and you will have a new landlord. If, on the other hand, you had only a licence, this is only a personal interest enforceable against the landlord but not against anyone else. His ownership interest in the house can therefore be sold free from your licence, and the buyer will be entitled to evict you. The proceeds of sale will be paid over to be divided between all creditors with personal claims against your licensor. This will include you: you will have a personal claim against the licensor for breach of the licence, and this will entitle you to damages (consider what damages you will get). However, like all the other creditors with personal claims, in practice you will get only a small proportion of the value of your claim. So, if you have a property interest in the house, you are not affected at all by your landlord's bankruptcy, whereas if you have only the equivalent personal right to occupy the house you will lose your right, and will not be adequately compensated.

Extract 5.1 *Hill v. Tupper* (1863) 2 H&C 121; 159 ER 51

[An incorporated canal company granted to the plaintiff the sole and exclusive right or liberty of putting or using pleasure boats for hire on their canal. Held, that the grant did not create such an estate or interest in the plaintiff as to enable him to maintain an action in his own name against a person who disturbed his right by putting and using pleasure boats for hire on the canal.]

The Company of Proprietors of the Basingstoke Canal Navigation were incorporated ... for the purpose of making and maintaining a navigable canal from the town of Basingstoke, in the county of Southampton, to communicate with the River Wey in the parish of Chertsey, in the county of Surrey. The lands purchased by the company of proprietors, under their parliamentary powers, were by the Act vested in the company. The defendant was the landlord of an inn at Aldershot adjoining the canal, and his premises abutted on the canal bank. The plaintiff, who was a boat proprietor, also occupied premises at Aldershot on the bank of the canal, which he held under a lease from the company of proprietors, and by virtue of the lease claimed the exclusive right of letting out pleasure boats for hire upon the canal, which was the right the defendant was alleged to have disturbed.

The lease under which the plaintiff claimed this right was dated 29 December 1860, and by it ... the said company of proprietors demised to the plaintiff ... for the term of seven years from 24 June 1860, at the yearly rent of £25:

> All that piece or parcel of land containing 19 poles or thereabouts, adjoining Aldershot wharf, situate in the parish of Aldershot aforesaid, and the wooden cottage or tenement, boathouse, and all other erections now or hereinafter being or standing thereon [describing the premises by boundaries, and by reference to a plan], together with the appurtenances to the same premises belonging; and also the sole and exclusive right or liberty to put or use boats on the said canal, and let the same for hire for the purpose of pleasure only.

The lease contained various covenants framed with the object of preventing any interference by the plaintiff's pleasure boats with the navigation of the canal ...

The plaintiff says that, while he was so entitled ... the defendant, well knowing the premises, wrongfully and unjustly disturbed the plaintiff in the possession, use and enjoyment of his said right or liberty, by wrongfully and unjustly putting and using ... boats on the canal for the purposes of pleasure, and by letting boats on the said canal for hire, and otherwise for the purposes of pleasure. By means of which said premises the plaintiff was not only greatly disturbed in the use, enjoyment and possession of his said right and liberty, but has also lost great gains and profits which he ought and otherwise would have acquired from the sole and exclusive possession, use and enjoyment of his said right or liberty, and was otherwise greatly aggrieved and prejudiced. The evidence of the defendant was at variance with that adduced on behalf of the plaintiff upon the question whether the defendant had ever let out boats upon the canal for hire, in the sense of a direct money payment. The defendant did not deny that he kept pleasure boats, and used them upon the canal, but stated that he kept them for the use of his family; he admitted, however, that gentlemen had come from time to time to his inn and used these boats for fishing and bathing. But the defendant also pleaded that ... the plaintiff was not entitled to ... the sole and exclusive right or liberty to put or use boats on the said canal for the purposes of pleasure, nor to let the said boats for hire on the said canal for the purposes of pleasure as alleged.

[Counsel for the plaintiff argued that] [t]he plaintiff's right having been infringed, an action lies for the infringement. The action is not without analogy. The grantee or lessee of a several fishery, or of a right of turbary, or other profit à prendre [an established form of property right] may sue for a disturbance of his right. Here, too, the right claimed is a profit à prendre ...

[Martin B interjected:] The plaintiff is setting up a right of a perfectly novel character. In *Keppell v. Bailey* (2 Myl & K 535) Lord Brougham said:

There are certain known incidents to property and its enjoyment; among others certain burthens wherewith it may be affected, or rights which may be created and enjoyed over it by parties other than the owner; all which incidents are recognized by the law ... But it must not, therefore, be supposed that incidents of a novel kind can be devised and attached to property at the fancy or caprice of any owner ... [G]reat detriment would arise, and much confusion of rights, if parties were allowed to invent new modes of holding and enjoying real property, and to impress upon their lands and tenements a peculiar character.

... [Pollock CB interjected:] If the plaintiff's contention were correct, the number and variety of rights which might thus be created over land for a particular purpose would be infinite. The whole question depends on whether a new species of property can be created, or whether the alleged right merely exists in covenant ...

The Court gave judgment for the defendant:

POLLOCK CB: We are all of opinion that the rule must be absolute to enter the verdict for the defendant on the second plea. After the very full argument which has taken place, I do not think it necessary to assign any other reason for our decision, than that the case of *Ackroyd* v. *Smith* (10 CB 164) expressly decided that it is not competent to create rights unconnected with the use and enjoyment of land, and annex them to it so as to constitute a property in the grantee. This grant merely operates as a licence or covenant on the part of the grantors, and is binding on them as between themselves and the grantee, but gives him no right of action in his own name for any infringement of the supposed exclusive right. It is argued that, as the owner of an estate may grant a right to cut turves, or to fish or hunt, there is no reason why he may not grant such a right as that now claimed by the plaintiff. The answer is, that the law will not allow it. So the law will not permit the owner of an estate to grant it alternately to his heirs male and heirs female. A new species of incorporeal hereditament cannot be created at the will and pleasure of the owner of property; but he must be content to accept the estate and the right to dispose of it subject to the law as settled by decisions or controlled by act of parliament. A grantor may bind himself by covenant to allow any right he pleases over his property, but he cannot annex to it a new incident, so as to enable the grantee to sue in his own name for an infringement of such a limited right as that now claimed.

MARTIN B: I am of the same opinion. This grant is perfectly valid as between the plaintiff and the canal company – but in order to support this action, the plaintiff must establish that such an estate or interest vested in him that the act of the defendant amounted to an eviction. None of the cases cited are at all analogous to this, and some authority must be produced before we can hold that such a right can be created. To admit the right would lead to the creation of an infinite variety of interests in land, and an indefinite increase of possible estates. The only consequence is that, as between the plaintiff and the canal company, he has a perfect right to enjoy the advantage of the covenant or contract; and, if he has been disturbed in the enjoyment of it, he must obtain the permission of the canal company to sue in their name ...

BRAMWELL B: I am of the same opinion.

5.2. Special features of communal property rights

5.2.1. Present scope of communal property

Communal property rights share most of the characteristics of private property rights, but there are some important differences.

In this country, limited access communal property rights generally exist only in relation to land and other natural resources, and they are now all particular use rights. English law does not recognise communal *ownership*, whether of land or of any other resource, nor does it provide mechanisms for communities to hold fee simple estates in land (the equivalent of land ownership in this country, as we see in Chapters 6 and 8). This means that, whenever communal property rights are exercisable over a particular piece of land, there will either be a private fee simple owner of the land or the underlying ownership will be vested in the state (usually the Crown or a local authority). Approximately 1.5 million acres of land in England and Wales are subject to limited access communal property rights, as Lord Nicholls noted in *Bettison* v. *Langton*, extracted at www.cambridge.org/propertylaw/.

5.2.1.1. Rights of common

There are essentially two different types of limited access communal property right surviving in this country. In the first type, sometimes referred to as 'rights of common', the community entitled to make communal use of the resource (perhaps grazing land, or game birds bred or breeding wild in a particular area) consists of ascertainable individuals who hold the right either by virtue of their ownership of adjoining land, or (if the right has become severed from the benefited land, as can sometimes happen) by transfer from someone who owned adjoining land or who could trace their title back to such an owner. This type of communal property is very like the model Hardin had in mind in 'The Tragedy of the Commons', discussed in Chapters 3 and 6, and its present nature and function was recently reviewed by the House of Lords in *Bettison* v. *Langton* [2001] UKHL 24, extracted at www.cambridge.org/propertylaw/.

This type of communal property most closely resembles private property. For present purposes, the important feature of rights of common is that the members of the right-holding community can always be identified at any particular time, and each of them has a distinct right which he can deal with without reference to the others. Some rights of common are appurtenant to the ownership of other land: grazing rights over a particular pasture, for example, will usually be held by the owners of adjoining farms. If the right is appurtenant to other land in this way and is not severable from it, the right cannot be dealt with separately from the land to which it is appurtenant, so in this sense the right is not alienable. It can, however, be surrendered back to the owner of the land over which the right is exercisable, and if this happens the right is extinguished. If the right is not appurtenant to other land (the technical term is 'in gross') or if it is appurtenant but severable, it can be freely alienated in much the same way as a private property right.

Rights of common are therefore communal property only in the sense that they involve communal use of a resource. Regulation of the communal use to avoid Hardin's tragedy of the commons is relatively straightforward. Typically, use will be regulated either by the underlying owner of the land over which the rights are exercisable, or by the users themselves. Self-regulation by the users themselves is made easier by the fact that they are all readily ascertainable at any one time. If the rights are all appurtenant to local neighbouring landholdings this is likely to make self-regulation even more effective, because the right holders will then tend to be bound by social pressures and common interest, with clear lines of communication with each other. They will form a close-knit social group of the kind that Epstein describes in Chapter 4 as capable of developing and maintaining effective self-regulation. The majority decision of the House of Lords in *Bettison* v. *Langton* that all appurtenant grazing rights of common are now severable is therefore likely to have significant effects on self-regulated grazing commons, as we see below (see Notes and Questions 5.1 below).

5.2.1.2. Customary rights

The other type of limited access communal property found in this country consists of what are usually referred to as customary property rights. They are called this because, as we see in Chapter 13, they can be acquired only by long use or custom: they cannot be expressly granted. This is because the community in this type of communal property right consists of a fluctuating body of individuals (defined by reference to a general characteristic, usually residence in a particular locality), and English common law has no mechanism for granting rights to fluctuating bodies of individuals.

The fact that the community consists of a fluctuating body of individuals defined by status has other implications. First, as already noted, neither the rights of the individuals nor the rights of the community as a whole can be alienated. An individual member of the community has no power to transfer his share because he has no power to transfer the status to someone who does not have it. If the community consists of inhabitants of Lambeth, the status of Lambeth-inhabiting can be acquired only by moving there, not by transfer, and once you have moved there you acquire the communal property right automatically and have no need for a transfer from a fellow-inhabitant.

The fact that the community itself *prima facie* cannot alienate its interest is of more practical significance. The problem is that the present members of the community have no power to extinguish the rights of future members of the community. This means that, once customary property rights have come into existence there is no way in which they can be terminated or varied. Unless the law provides some mechanism for freeing the resource from the use, for example by adopting a rule that the rights can be lost by abandonment, or extinguished by a surrender or transfer agreed by the majority of present members, the resource will be perpetually tied to its present use. If conservation of the resource in its present state is an overriding objective, this form of communal property therefore has distinct advantages. As we see in *Milirrpum* v. *Nabalco Pty Ltd* in section 5.3 below, the present members of the Gove Peninsula Aboriginal tribes did not consider themselves to have a collective right to alienate or alter their tribe's pattern of land use, and this has almost certainly been a major factor in the conservation of scarce resources in those areas.

We noted in Chapter 4 that this aspect of Australian native title was changed by the Native Title Act 1993. It is now possible for native title to be extinguished by abandonment, and the present members of a community can extinguish the community's rights for ever by surrendering them to the state in exchange for money or private property rights, or anything else they choose.

This can be contrasted with the present position in relation to English customary rights. As both Lord Denning in *New Windsor Corp.* v. *Mellor* and Lord Hoffmann in *R.* v. *Oxfordshire County Council, ex parte Sunningwell Parish Council* point out, customary rights cannot be extinguished by abandonment, and there is no suggestion in either case that present inhabitants have any power to vary the rights or extinguish them, for example by freeing some of the land affected by the rights in consideration of a payment of money to finance improvement or conservation of the remainder. As noted in both decisions, the Commons Registration Act 1965 makes provision for registering all rights of common and all customary rights, and allows for new customary rights to arise by twenty years' user, but it contains no provisions equivalent to those in the Australian Native Title Act for abandoning, varying, transferring or surrendering customary rights, whether pre-existing or newly arising.

The final point to make about rights held by a fluctuating body of individuals is that there is no mechanism for capping the numbers of those entitled to use the resource. If the number of users can increase without limit, this increases the danger that the resource will be exhausted. This is why customary rights that allow users to take finite resources from the land (for example, to pasture animals or take away timber or dredge for oysters) are rare. Such rights to take resources from other people's land (technically still referred to by the law-French term 'profits a prendre', or just profits) are much more likely to exist as private property rights, or as rights of common, where the number of communal users is fixed. Indeed, English law maintains a general rule that profits *cannot* be held by a fluctuating body of individuals, but it has developed devices to circumvent the rule in order to legitimise long-established customary uses. This has been done by attributing the customary use to a presumed (i.e. fictitious) ancient Crown grant to a corporation, either a real corporation such as a local authority which is then deemed to hold the profit on trust for the benefit of the local users, or to a fictitious corporation comprising the local users. It was on this basis that, for example, local inhabitants were held entitled to continue their long-established custom of dredging for oysters in the River Tamar during a specified period in each year in *Goodman*

v. *Saltash Corp.* (1881–2) LR 7 App Cas 633 (for further reference, see Burn, *Cheshire and Burn's Modern Law of Real Property*, pp. 628–33).

Notes and Questions 5.1

1 Read *Bettison* v. *Langton* [2001] UKHL 24, *New Windsor Corp.* v. *Mellor* [1975] 1 Ch 380, CA, and *R.* v. *Oxfordshire County Council, ex parte Sunningwell Parish Council* [2000] 1 AC 335; [1999] 3 WLR 160; [1999] 3 All ER 385, either in full or as extracted at www.cambridge.org/propertylaw/, and consider the following:

2 Examine the following arguments for and against making profits severable from the land they were originally intended to benefit:
   (a) Robert Walker LJ in the Court of Appeal in *Bettison* v. *Langton* said that, once profits were freely alienable, this would prevent them falling into disuse. This, he said, is because, if they remained tied to the farm, and the farm then became something other than a livestock farm, those rights would not be exercisable by anyone. In other words, profits will not survive unless they are freely marketable, because it is only through exchanges in the open market that profits will end up being held by the person who values them most. This is the classic economic argument in favour of alienability.
   (b) He also said that, once the extent of the profit is limited by some objective fact (such as a specific number of animals) rather than by the nature of the benefiting land, it makes no difference to the burden on the burdened land who owns the right, so there is no need to keep the right tied to a specific piece of land.
   (c) Lord Nicholls in the minority in the House of Lords in *Bettison* v. *Langton* answered (b) by saying 'But in the 1950s the Royal Commission was concerned with wider issues than the position of the owner of the common' (paragraph 19), referring here to what he said was the overriding conclusion of the Royal Commission, i.e. that common land ought to be preserved in the public interest (not in the interests of the rights holders).
   (d) Lord Nicholls also said it would make it more difficult for the various profit holders to co-operate in managing the resource if they were not the neighbouring farm-owners. What was Robert Walker LJ's response to this?
   (e) Lord Nicholls also pointed out that the Department of the Environment, Transport and the Regions, *Good Practice Guide on Managing the Use of Common Land* (June 1998) had expressed the view that 'severance of grazing rights from the associated holdings off the common can reduce the long-term viability of these holdings'. Consider why this should be the case.

   Who is right, on each of these arguments?

3 In *Bettison* v. *Langton*, both Lord Nicholls and Lord Scott agreed that neither the Royal Commission nor Parliament had intended to make all grazing rights severable, and that indeed the policy behind the Royal Commission's report had been to keep the class of severable rights as small as possible. What justification

does Lord Scott give for nevertheless concluding that this is the effect that section 15 of the Commons Registration Act 1965 has had? How do you view this approach to statutory interpretation?

4 If Lord Nicholls' minority view in *Bettison* v. *Langton* was accepted, it would mean that grazing rights which had always consisted of a right to graze a fixed number of animals would be severable and could be freely traded, whereas those that were originally limited by reference to *levancy* and *couchancy* but were converted by the 1965 Act into rights to graze a fixed number of animals were not severable, and could only be sold with the appurtenant land. This would mean treating rights that are now identical but had different historical origins in different ways. Would this be satisfactory? Is this an argument for leaving the issue for Parliament to resolve, so that it can be decided as a matter of policy whether profits ought to be severable, and then make them all or none of them so?

5 If the Royal Commission did not want grazing rights to be severable from the benefited land, why then did it recommend that grazing rights limited by *levancy* and *couchancy* (i.e. which gave such a close and principled link between the extent of the right and the nature of the appurtenant land) should be converted into rights to graze a specific number of animals? This number was not arrived at by looking at the optimum number of animals the burdened land could take while still preserving the public amenity value of the burdened land: it was done by accepting the number claimed by each rights holder, subject to objections made by other commoners and the holder of the burdened land. However, Lord Nicholls seems to have accepted that there was a pre-existing over-grazing problem before 1965: 'it was small wonder if each commoner shifted for himself and crowded as many sheep as he dared on the upland sheepwalk. As a result, the sward was becoming increasingly impoverished through overgrazing.' If that was the problem, was it a good solution to translate the inexact quantifier into a permanently fixed specific number of animals? What other solutions could you suggest?

6 Are there any restrictions on the nature and type of user that will give rise to customary rights? Should there be?

7 Section 22 of the 1965 Act, discussed in *Sunningwell*, was subsequently amended by section 98 of the Countryside and Rights of Way Act 2000 to make it clearer that the 'inhabitants of a locality' for the purposes of class (c) need not be definable with any great precision: these words are now replaced by 'a significant number of the inhabitants of any locality, or of any neighbourhood within a locality'. Consider the effect this will have.

8 In *Mabo (No. 2)*, it was held that Australian native title could be extinguished by Parliament, not only by express legislation but also by inference, by providing

for the grant of inconsistent rights to others or to itself (this was subsequently changed for the future by the Native Title Act 1993). Can English customary rights be extinguished in this way?

9   What are the justifications for treating these recreational customary rights as property rights, and giving them this high level of protection? Compare the justifications given in Chapter 4 for the recognition of Aboriginal native title: which of these apply to these English customary rights?

10 In the light of the conclusion you reach on the previous question, consider the justification for the English rule, confirmed by these cases, that customary rights cannot be lost by non-user.

11 In general, private property rights cannot be lost by non-user either. However, they are subject to the principle of limitation of actions, as we see in Chapter 11. In other words, if I have a private property right or interest, such as fee simple ownership of a plot of land, or a right of way over a path across your adjoining plot of land, the enforceability of my rights is not affected if I never set foot on my land or (with some exceptions) your path. If, however, you do something which is an actionable interference with my interests, such as encroaching on to my plot of land or building a fence across your path, I will lose my right to object (and hence lose the interest itself) if I do not take action to stop you within twelve years (under the Limitation Act 1980 as it stands at present, shortly to be changed to ten years). It appears that limitation of actions does not apply to English customary rights: consider why.

12 The provisions requiring registration of 'new' customary rights under Class c in the 1965 Act are complex and possibly not comprehensive (see Lightman J in *Oxfordshire County Council* v. *Oxford City Council* [2005] EWHC 175 although arguably no longer tenable following the decision of the Court of Appeal in the same case: [2005] EWCA Civ. 175). If this is the case, it is possible for a 'new' Class c right not to appear on the register at all. Consider what practical problems this might cause, bearing in mind the rule that such rights cannot be extinguished by non-user or limitation of action rules.

13 Land can be a town or village green even if it not in a town or a village – it might be a beach forming part of the foreshore, or a river bank, or a patch of land in an urban area, such as a landscaped area left open by a developer. Also, it is clear from Lord Hoffmann's judgment in *Sunningwell* that a broad range of activities is covered by Class c (would it include, for example, picnicking or skateboarding?). Is this likely to discourage owners from keeping such areas open to the public? See further Chapter 13, where we look more closely at how rights can be acquired by long use.

14 At the end of his judgment in *New Windsor*, Lord Denning points out that the 1965 Act provides no mechanism for varying or extinguishing customary rights. Consider what problems this does or could cause.

5.3. Aboriginal land rights

5.3.1. Nature of native title

In Chapter 4, we looked at the justifications for recognising that Aboriginal land use gave rise to rights enforceable against a colonising state and against subsequent settlers, and at how in Australia this proposition was finally accepted by the courts in *Mabo (No. 2)* and then confirmed by the Australian Parliament in the Native Title Act 1993. Similar developments have taken place in the United States (much earlier than in Australia), in Canada, in New Zealand and in other former British colonies. The precise nature and extent of the rights recognised, and the form recognition has taken, has varied from country to country. Here we concentrate on Australia and look more closely at the nature of the rights now recognised there, and how they differ from English property rights.

The term used in Australian law to describe traditional Aboriginal land rights is 'native title'. This term encompasses the very different resource uses of different tribes with differing customs and traditions, occupying a wide variety of geographic environments. In *Mabo (No. 2)*, Brennan J had this to say about the content of native title (at paragraph 64):

> Native title has its origins in and is given its content by the traditional laws acknowledged by and the traditional customs observed by the indigenous inhabitants of a territory. The nature and incidents of native title must be ascertained as a matter of fact by reference to those laws and customs.

As we saw in Chapter 4, the statutory definition given in the Native Title Act 1993 closely follows this formulation.

This means that the term 'native title' tells us nothing about the substance and content of the rights that any particular tribe might have in any particular territory, it only tells us how we can find out what they are. However, in the following paragraphs (see paragraphs 65–72 of his judgment extracted at www.cambridge.org/propertylaw/), Brennan J went on to give general propositions that he said followed from his definition of native title, and, again, these have been largely confirmed by the Native Title Act 1993.

5.3.2. Alienability

First, Brennan J said that only inhabitants indigenous at the time of colonisation and their descendants can hold native title, and the only form of native title they can hold is that which reflects the connection they have with the land under their particular laws and customs. In other words, each tribe has its own form of native title, the substance and content of which is dictated by the laws and customs by which they consider themselves to be bound, and there can be no question of transfer of any of those rights outside the tribe, either to a member of another tribe or to anyone else. Native title is, therefore, wholly inalienable. The only form of alienation that he envisaged was surrender to the Crown, which would result in the extinguishment of the title.

5.3.3. Abandonment

Secondly, he said, if native title is defined by reference to the connection which a community has with a territory under the laws and customs by which it feels itself to be bound, it must follow that it will be lost if the community loses that connection to their territory. It will have lost that connection, in his view, if the community has ceased to acknowledge the relevant laws and (except in so far as impracticable) ceased to observe the relevant customs. Equally, the connection will be lost if the community itself has ceased to exist because the last of the members has died. Although Deane J and Gaudron J expressed reservations about this principle that native title is necessarily lost when the community's traditional way of life is lost, it represents the majority view of the court in *Mabo (No. 2)* and again it has been confirmed by the Native Title Act 1993.

We have seen that this principle does not exist in English common law. English customary rights cannot be lost by non-user, nor (on the whole) can private property rights. It has proved to be controversial in Australia. First, there is the political problem of how to view a disintegration of a community, or an abandonment of its traditional way of life and its connection with its territory, where this was forced on it by the settlers. In the United States native title is not considered to be abandoned if the abandonment resulted from failure to resist white encroachment or from being forced onto a reservation (see Bartlett, 'Humpies Not Houses', p. 27). Secondly, there is an evidential problem. In Australia (unlike in Canada and in the United States, as Bartlett notes in the same article) the onus is put on claimants to *prove* that there has been no abandonment. This can be done only by proving continuity of the community and of its traditional way of life, and continued observance of its laws and customs. This perhaps explains the length and complexity of the proceedings now reaching the courts in Australia.

5.3.4. Variation

However, it seems that, in some respects at least, native title is more flexible than English customary rights. Brennan J envisages that it might change in content if the community adapts its way of life to meet changing conditions, although he appears to have in mind gradual evolutionary change rather than radical change: see paragraph 68 of his judgment. However, even this does not appear to be possible for English customary rights, as we saw in section 5.2 above. Probably of more practical significance is the confirmation in the Native Title Act 1993 that native title can be surrendered to the state in exchange for other rights, even private property rights. Again, there is no such mechanism in English law for exchanging customary rights for rights more appropriate to changed circumstances.

5.3.5.   Extent of native title

This is an issue that was left unresolved in *Mabo (No. 2)* and has proved to be contentious in later cases. Once a tribe has established native title over an area, does this automatically mean that it has general use rights over that area, akin to ownership? If so, the tribe will be treated as having control of that area and entitled to resist all incursions, not just those infringing specific rights, and it will also become entitled to all resources found there (such as oil and minerals) just as a private common law owner would. However, it might also mean that any past government grant of property rights in that geographic area would be treated as inconsistent with the native title and therefore as having extinguished it. If, on the other hand, a successful claim to native title merely confirms the right to use the territory in the way it has always been used, the claimant gets no rights of control over the area or rights to natural resources unless it can prove that it has always had them. It does, however, open up greater possibilities for the co-existence of native title and private property rights. This was the significant step forward made in *Wik Peoples* v. *Queensland* (1996) 187 CLR 1 referred to in Chapter 4, where it was established that both pastoral leases and the native title claimed by the tribes in that case conferred only specific use rights rather than general use rights, so that, to the extent that they were not specifically incompatible, the one would not have extinguished the other. While the consequences of this decision have been largely reversed by the Native Title Amendment Act 1998, this 'bundle of rights' approach has been followed in subsequent cases, and severely criticised by commentators who see it as an unjustifiable limitation on the scope of native title (see, for example, the articles by Bartlett, 'Humpies Not Houses' and Tehan, 'A Hope Disillusioned').

As we can see from *Delgamuukw* v. *British Columbia* [1997] 3 SCR 1010 (extracted at www.cambridge.org/propertylaw/), the Supreme Court of Canada has drawn clearer distinctions between ownership-type rights and specific use rights, and has developed a more sophisticated approach under which land held under aboriginal title can be used in any way, not just in ways it has always been used, but subject to the limitation that it 'cannot be used in any manner that is irreconcilable with the nature of the claimants' attachment to the land' (paragraph 125). Further, it recognises that there is a distinction between this general aboriginal title and aboriginal *rights*, which are essentially specific use rights (paragraphs 137–42).

5.3.6.   Is native title proprietary?

5.3.6.1.   Blackburn J's view in *Milirrpum*

For Blackburn J in *Milirrpum* v. *Nabalco Pty Ltd*, this was an important question. The issues he was asked to decide were argued on the basis that, even if colonisation had not extinguished *all* rights of the indigenous population, the only rights that could have survived were those that were recognisable as proprietary rights by the common law. As we saw in Chapter 4, his firm conclusion was that, whatever the nature of the aboriginal relationship with the lands they inhabited, it was not proprietary.

However, it is important to appreciate that he rejected most of the arguments that the government put forward in support of its contention that the claimants' relationship with their land could not be categorised as proprietary. He refused to accept the government's argument that there was nothing in the aboriginal world that was recognisable as law at all because there was no discernible law-maker or law-enforcer. He rejected this Austinian assumption of what it takes to have a legal system, preferring the more inclusive view that law is no more than 'a system of rules of conduct which is felt as obligatory upon them by the members of a definable group of people' (p. 266). This amounts to an acknowledgment that, whenever people live in a definable community, they can be taken to have a recognisable system of law, and indeed he suggested that any conclusions reached in the past that particular indigenous groups in colonial territories had 'no ordered manner of community life' so as to give rise to a system of law, were based on inadequate anthropological knowledge.

He also rejected the government's argument that the claimants did not form a definable community. It was not necessary, he said, for the community to be defined with any great precision or specificity. It was sufficient to say that there *was* a system of laws recognised as obligatory upon them by those 'who made ritual and economic use of the subject land' (p. 267) – a somewhat circular definition which removes considerable potential obstacles to the recognition of communal property rights.

Finally, he rejected a contention that there was insufficient certainty about which clans were entitled to use precisely which areas. The government argued that the physical boundaries of their use were not sufficiently precise for there to be certainty as to the subject-matter of their rights, nor was there sufficient certainty as to the identity of the holders of the rights in any particular area. We noted above in section 5.1.4 that it is generally necessary that the subject-matter of a right and the identity of the right holder should be certain if the right is to be categorised as a property right. Blackburn J did not disagree with this, but he did not accept that the same degree of precision was required for native title as might be required for common law private property rights. As far as physical boundaries were concerned, he considered that it was sufficient if they were defined 'with ... such precision as the users of the land require for the uses to which the land is put even though this might be less precisely definable than those to which we are accustomed' (p. 271). As to certainty of the right holder, he rejected the contention that 'if there is property in land, there must be either a written or pictorial means of discovering who is the owner of any particular piece of land ... or if that is not possible among primitive people, there must be a sufficient number of witnesses who can produce a register of title out of their memories ... In my opinion, the fallacy in this argument is the assumption that there cannot be rights of property without records or registers of title' (p. 272).

So, he was willing to accept that the Aboriginal peoples inhabited their lands under a system of laws, and that a sufficiently defined community made ritual and economic use of sufficiently defined areas of land. Why then was he not prepared to accept that they had rights to use the land in the way that they did?

In his view, there were three characteristics that property rights tended to have: they involved a right 'to use and enjoy' the subject-matter, a right to exclude others from it, and a right to alienate the rights. These were not present in the relationship the claimants had with their land, he said, and therefore it could not be a proprietary relationship.

It is not clear why any of these three should be thought to be necessary criteria for proprietary status, and in the case of the first two it is equally unclear as to why the claimants in this case could be said to fail to meet the criteria, even if they were necessary. To take the last one first, we have already seen that alienability is not a characteristic of communal property rights (or even of private property rights) where the right holders are defined by reference to a status. Similarly, the right to exclude others is admittedly characteristic of limited access communal property but it does not arise in the case of open access communal property. What marks property off from non-property is the right not to be excluded, not the right to exclude. Here, as far as one can gather from the evidence given in the judgment, the aboriginal population of the territory regarded particular clans as having the right to exclude others from religious sites, and the population as a whole regarded themselves as having a right not to be excluded from the resources whose use they shared, and certainly regarded the proposed activities of Nabalco as an invasion of those rights.

The question of the right to use and enjoy is more complex. It is quite wrong to say that *all* property rights in things give the right holder the right to use and enjoy the thing. Your landlord has a property interest in the house you rent from him, as does your neighbour who has the benefit of a restrictive covenant over it, but this does not give either of them the right to use and enjoy it. The right to use and enjoy is a characteristic incident of *ownership*, not a necessary incident of all property interests. But, even if the right to use and enjoy the land was a necessary ingredient of the kind of interest the Aboriginals claimed to have, it is difficult to see why Blackburn J thought they had failed to establish it.

The problem as he saw it was that the definable communities – the clans – had only a spiritual relationship with the land: they regarded themselves as under a duty to care for the land as a whole, with specific clans having particular responsibility towards specific sites, which they 'used' only in the sense that they performed religious ceremonies there. He accepted that the Aboriginals did of course make economic use of the land – they lived there and were entirely dependent on its natural resources. However, they did so in transient *ad hoc* food-gathering and communal-living groupings – the bands – which appeared to have no particular connection with any particular tribe. Membership of a band was not restricted to any particular tribe, nor did any band feel itself bound to confine its activities to territory associated with one tribe rather than another, and there appeared to be no other defining characteristic that could allow bands to be viewed as right-holding communities. So, he concluded, the only potential right holders were the clans, but they did not appear to regard themselves as having any 'rights' to use and enjoy the land, only duties towards it.

This is a surprisingly narrow conception of ownership to adopt, given the very different cultural context, even if we were to accept that what the claimants had to establish was something resembling ownership. It is not difficult to conceive of a community that regards itself as 'owning' a site while simultaneously regarding itself as bound not to enter it, or bound not to use it for any purpose other than religious observances. European religious organisations own churches and have sacred objects too. It is true that their position might best be described as having a legal right to use and enjoy in any way they choose (perhaps subject to obtaining planning permission) but a moral or spiritual obligation to use for religious purposes only, but who is to say that the same is not true of Aboriginal Australian sacred sites? And, even a legal ban on use and enjoyment is not inconceivable. The common law would have no difficulty with the concept of ownership of an area of land which no one, not even the owner, was entitled to enter or use in any way – perhaps a nature reserve, or an area of contaminated land.

So, the reasons that Blackburn J gave for concluding that native title – if it existed at all, which he doubted – was not proprietary are hardly convincing.

5.3.6.2. The view of the High Court in *Mabo (No. 2)*

In a sense, the question of whether native title is or is not proprietary has become a side issue after the decision of the High Court in *Mabo (No. 2)*. Once it has become established that, whatever native title is, it has survived annexation and has to be recognised by the state, it becomes less significant whether this is because it is proprietary or for some other reason.

In fact, only a minority of the judges in the High Court were prepared to accept that native title is proprietary. Brennan J (with whom Mason CJ and McHugh J agreed) expressed the firm view that it is (paragraph 53 of his judgment), but Deane J and Gaudron J disagreed. In their view, the indigenous peoples had personal but not proprietary rights, and it was for this reason that their rights were effectively extinguished by the government granting inconsistent property rights to others (paragraphs 23–4, 29–30 and 60 of their judgment): if they had had property rights they could not have been extinguished in this way. Neither of the other two judges expressed a concluded view. Dawson J, in the minority, said that, if there was such a thing as native title that survived annexation – which he rejected – it was 'probably not' proprietary in nature but it was unnecessary for him to decide the question (paragraph 80 of his judgment).

5.3.6.3. The Canadian view

The process of recognition of aboriginal land rights began earlier in Canada and developed along different lines, as can be seen from *Delgamuukw* v. *British Columbia* [1997] 3 SCR 1010, extracted at www.cambridge.org/propertylaw/. In particular, the legislative background is different, and, as the Supreme Court of Canada decision in *Delgamuukw* demonstrates, Canadian law is happier with the notion of aboriginal title and aboriginal rights being regarded as proprietary, although again it is not viewed as a determinative factor. Once it is accepted that these are rights that are enforceable against the state and against all others, it makes little sense to argue whether they can in any other sense be called proprietary. However, it is notable that Canadian jurisprudence demonstrates a more sophisticated approach in distinguishing aboriginal title (the right to the land itself) from other aboriginal rights, and recognising that the rights the law recognises – essentially as proprietary – 'fall along a spectrum with regard to their degree of connection with the land' (see paragraph 138), all of which receive constitutional protection.

Notes and Questions 5.2

1 Read *Delgamuukw* v. *British Columbia* [1997] 3 SCR 1010, either in full or as extracted at www.cambridge.org/propertylaw/.

2 According to Lamer CJ in *Delgamuukw*, what is 'aboriginal title'? (See paragraphs 111–32 of his judgment.) How does it differ from Honoré's conception of ownership? How does it differ from 'native title' as defined in section 223(1) and (2) of the Australian Native Title Act 1993, read in the light of section 225(a) and (b) of that Act (see Chapter 4 above)?

3 What does Lamer CJ mean when he says that 'lands subject to aboriginal title cannot be put to such uses as may be irreconcilable with the nature of the occupation of that land and the relationship that the particular group has had with the land which together have given rise to aboriginal title in the first place' (paragraph 128)? Give examples. What reasons does he give for these restrictions? Compare these reasons with the reasons given by Brennan J in *Mabo (No. 2)* for concluding that the uses to which land held by native title may be put must be restricted. Are the Australian restrictions the same as the Canadian ones? Is there any significance in the differences?

4 According to Lamer CJ, what are 'aboriginal rights'? How do aboriginal rights differ from 'aboriginal title'? (See paragraphs 137–41 of his judgment.) What does he mean by a 'site-specific right to engage in a particular activity'? Give examples.

6

Ownership

6.1. The nature of ownership

6.1.1. The basis of ownership

As a working definition we may regard ownership as the ultimate property interest and the means by which we signify the person or persons with primary (but not necessarily exclusive) control of a thing. Such a definition requires us to separate the notions of ownership and property while acknowledging that the terms are often used, somewhat loosely, as synonyms. Property is a broad term which encompasses any interest in a thing whereby the interest holder acquires rights enforceable beyond the original parties to the transaction (or other means) by which the interest was acquired. Thus the term property extends to a range of diverse interests such as easements (such as a right of way over land) and choses in action (such as the benefit of a contract which is normally assignable and may thus be enforced by someone other than a party to the original contract). In contrast, ownership is a particular type of property interest in which the person designated as owner is deemed, in some sense at least, to have the greatest possible interest in the thing. As a subset of property it is consequently concerned with two quite separate sets of relations. The first is the owner's relationship with other people (whether they be non-interest holders or subsidiary interest holders in the thing owned) and the second is the owner's relationship to the thing itself.

6.1.1.1. Ownership and people

The concept of ownership is built upon the right to possess which, as we saw in Chapter 2, in both the private and communal property setting, can be seen as two individual rights which together enable the owner to protect and maintain his possession and hence his ownership. Against non-owners the owner has a primary right to exclude them from the thing owned and, as against fellow owners a primary right not to be so excluded. In private ownership the right to exclude is the most important of these two rights of possession because there will be many more non-owners than owners of the thing (although the right not to be excluded is still important where the thing is jointly owned – see Chapter 16). In contrast, in communal ownership the right not to be excluded is, for comparable reasons, of more significance (although likewise the right to exclude is still important where someone outside the community becomes involved; but cf. Blackburn J's view in *Milirrpum* in section 5.3.6.1 above).

As you will see, neither of these rights are absolute, nor of much significance absent any other entitlements in the thing. They are, however, the rights that underscore ownership, for without them no other rights can be exercised. What, for example, is the point in owning this book if you have no means of excluding non-owners intent on excluding you. Similarly, what benefit arises from a resource being communally owned unless this gives individual members the right not to be excluded from its use.

6.1.1.2. Ownership and things

Ownership provides a bond between the individual and the inanimate. As Hegel argued, private ownership is an assertion of personality whereby the person 'has as his substantive end the right of putting his will into any and every thing and thereby making it his' (Hegel, *Philosophy of Right*, section 44). As Stillman has noted:

[P]roperty for Hegel is essential for men if they are to lead a full life of reason. In owning property, men act in the external world. They dominate Nature. They create social institutions. In shaping the natural and the social orders according to their intentions and goals, men develop and express their own capabilities; in reflecting on the results of their actions, they educate themselves about the world of actuality and about themselves and thereby prepare themselves for further action in the natural and social worlds. At the same time, men claim themselves, their minds and their bodies, as their own properties; from the right to property derive the rights to life and liberty, so that they are permanent subjects and actors, continuously shaping the natural and social worlds and themselves.

Property for Hegel is to be seen not merely as an economic category or the result of utilitarian calculus; not only as a result of labor or convention; not solely as a requisite for social stability or diversity. It is more. For Hegel property is a political and philosophical necessity, essential for the development.

(Stillman, 'Property, Freedom and Individuality', pp. 132–3)

A similar point is made, somewhat more caustically, by Kevin Gray:

Not so long ago I was talking with a couple of Martians at one of those seminars in Oxford organised by Professor Peter Birks. The visitors explained that they were engaged in a piece of joint research on the terrestrial concept of property – a mode of thinking which apparently finds no parallel within their own jurisdiction. The present paper is prompted in some measure by the conversations which I had with the Martian lawyers, for I was stimulated to look afresh, from perhaps a wider perspective, at the strange way in which we humans make claims of 'property' or 'ownership' in respect of the resources of the world ...

My Martian interlocutors reminded me of the highly anomalous nature, unparalleled within our own galaxy, of the terrestrial impulse to view external resources as belonging properly or exclusively to particular members of the human race. Social psychologists like Earnest Beaglehole used to speak of the 'hidden nerve of irrational animism that binds the individual to the object he appropriates as his own'. [Beaglehole, *Property: A Study in Social Psychology*, p. 23] My Martian colleagues were especially intrigued by the fact that, in one of the earliest phrases articulated by almost every human child, there lies the strongest affirmation of this internalised concern to appropriate. The phrase, 'It's mine!', is, of course, literally untranslatable into any of the Martian languages. Yet, as my friends pointed out, even our judges and legislators seem obsessed with the need to formulate human perceptions of the external world in the intangible terms of individualised ownership and 'private property'. Our lives are in every respect dominated by an intuitive sense of property and belonging. (Gray, 'Equitable Property', pp. 157–8)

Gray's cynicism is aimed at the relatively modern tendency, demonstrated for example in Hegel's analysis, of regarding ownership solely in terms of private property. However, as Grunebaum demonstrates in Extract 3.3, it is quite possible to argue that communal ownership engenders a comparable bond between the community and the thing which provides a similar means by which the individual might develop.

6.1.2.   An outline of the difficulties encountered in any consideration of ownership

'What', you might ask, 'is so difficult about *ownership?*' It is, after all, a word in common usage which, unlike many terms in property law, is readily understood by most people from an early age. As Kevin Gray noted above, and any parent will confirm, the cry 'It's mine' (or its equivalent) is one of the first phrases learnt by the emerging infant as they begin to assert rights of (or at least claims to) ownership of various things in their new found world. Thereby displaying, in all its vulgar assertiveness, a certainty about ownership which enables us, in later life, to make decisions and enter into bargains confident in the knowledge as to the rights we are acquiring or forsaking when ownership changes hands. 'Indeed', notes the American jurist Bruce Ackerman (in *Private Property and the Constitution*, p. 116), 'most of the time Layman negotiates his way through the complex web of property relationships that structures his social universe without even perceiving the need for expert guidance.' Yet, despite such seeming certainty, the concept of ownership is more problematic than it would first appear for a number of quite distinct reasons.

6.1.2.1.   The different meanings of ownership

Ownership is a difficult term because its meaning varies according to its context. As you will see repeatedly in this chapter (particularly in section 6.3), the use of ownership in one setting is often not relevant to how it is to be understood in a different setting.

It is consequently important to bear in mind the limitations of the working definition we provided in section 6.1.1, for the reality is somewhat more complex.

6.1.2.2.   Disagreements about ownership

Given this complexity, it is perhaps not surprising that the concept is a source of debate and disagreement. In his writings on property, William Blackstone defined ownership as 'that sole and despotic *dominium* which one man claims and exercises over the external things of the world, in total exclusion of the right of any other individual in the universe' (Blackstone, *Commentaries*, Book II, Chapter 1, p. 2). This appears at variance with the modern habit (see Honoré below) of conceiving of ownership in terms of a bundle of separate (but related) rights including the rights to use, possess and destroy. But this latter-day trend has in turn led Thomas Grey, among others, to argue (see Extract 6.1 below), that the 'bundle of rights' approach 'tends ... to dissolve the notion of ownership' so that we 'no longer need [such] a notion' (Grey, 'The Disintegration of Property', p. 69). While others would argue that, for technical reasons, at least in the context of land law, we never have done (see the quote from Hargreaves at section 6.3.1.1 below). Waldron, on the other hand, suggests that ownership 'expresses the abstract idea of an object being correlated with the name of an individual' (Waldron, *The Right to Private Property*, p. 47) and in formulating his argument (see Extract 6.2 below) rejects the approaches of both Blackstone and Grey by noting that the liberties conferred by ownership are not unlimited (as Blackstone would *appear* to suggest) and by explicitly rejecting Grey's submission (that the concept has no useful role to play).

Despite their seeming incompatibility, the divide between such views is less extreme than it at first appears. The quotation from Blackstone is an oft-cited favourite, much beloved of commentators. However, as Whelan has noted, '[s]ince this seems to be Blackstone's clearest single statement on property, it is often quoted out of context' (Whelan, 'Property as Artifice', p. 118) – with predictable consequences – for an entirely different picture emerges when one reads the paragraph from which the passage was extracted:

> There is nothing which so generally strikes the imagination and engages the affections of mankind, as the right of property; or that sole and despotic dominion which one man claims and exercises over the external things of the world, in total exclusion of the right of any other individual in the universe. And yet there are very few, but will give themselves the trouble to consider the original and foundation of this right ... We think it enough that our title is derived by the grant of the former proprietor, by descent from our ancestors, or by the last will and testament of the dying owner; not caring to reflect that (accurately and strictly speaking) there is no foundation in nature or in natural law, why a set of words upon parchment should convey the dominion of land; why the son should have a right to exclude his fellow-creatures from a determin-ate spot of ground, because his father had done so before him; or why the occupier of a particular field or of a jewel, when lying on his deathbed, and no longer able to

maintain possession, should be entitled to tell the rest of the world which of them should enjoy it after him. (Blackstone, *Commentaries*, Book II, Chapter 1, p. 2)

From this perspective, it is clear that Blackstone did not regard ownership as a single all-embracing right but, as Whelan again notes, rather 'a complex of different rights not accounted for by the simple notion of "sole and despotic dominion"' (Whelan, 'Property as Artifice', p. 119).

If we turn to the views of Grey, we will see a surprising degree of affinity with this position. Central to Grey's thesis is the notion that the modern conception of property 'fragments the unitary conception of ownership into a mere shadowy "bundle of rights"' (Grey, 'The Disintegration of Property', p. 69). Waldron likewise bases his analysis (but not his conclusion) explicitly on such a bundle. Thus, despite their obvious disagreements, all three appear to agree on the basics, conceiving of ownership in terms of a number of separate rights. As you will see in section 6.2 below, the 'bundle of rights' analysis (coupled with associated limitations) is the one constant to which most commentators subscribe (but cf. Penner, 'The "Bundle of Rights"').

Before leaving this point, we should note that much of this chapter is devoted to materials drawn from the liberal tradition of ownership which regards the term as solely a private property concept. However, the ambit of ownership extends further and is equally applicable to common, communal and state property as Honoré acknowledges when he admits the possibility of other formulations of the concept, be they 'either primitive or sophisticated', which do not correspond with his analysis of the 'liberal notion of ownership'.

6.1.2.3. Contradictions within ownership

While property lawyers are, as we saw in Chapter 2, all too ready to disabuse novices concerning their lay notions as to the meaning of property, the same rigour is rarely applied to ownership. However, strictures regarding the fallacy of talking about 'property as things' are equally applicable to our habit of referring to the 'thing's owner'. Bentham's observation that 'in common speech in the phrase *the object of a man's property*, the words *the object of* are commonly left out' again provides an explanation as to how this arises. By conflating the 'object' with the 'property that exists in the object' ownership of property has come to be seen as simply 'ownership of the object' rather than 'ownership of property in the object'. But as the essence of property is rights in respect of things, so ownership of property must be concerned with ownership of rights in respect of things. Thus, when we speak of the owner of a thing, the phrase is meaningless unless we mean by that the owner of rights in the thing. From this perspective, therefore, when we speak of ownership we are simply identifying in whom the property rights reside. This, after all, is what we are doing when we speak about the thing's 'owner'. We are using the term 'owner' to link the property rights that exist in the thing to the person (or persons) in whom those rights currently vest. It is, in other words, a useful shorthand by which we signify the location of certain rights but, as the following extract underlines, all talk of 'owning things' is liable to lead to confusion:

> In everyday conversation we usually speak of 'property' rather than 'property rights' but the contraction is misleading if it tends to make us think of property as things rather than as rights, or of ownership as outright rather than as circumscribed. The concepts of property and ownership are created by, defined by, and therefore limited by, a society's system of law. When you own a car, you own a set of legally defined rights to use the vehicle in certain ways and not in others ... [for] the only things that are owned are property rights. (Dales, *Pollution Property and Prices*, p. 58)

To multiply ownership in this way breaks the single bond that links ownership to things and, while this might appeal to the logician, fails to accord with human nature and sentiment. As we noted in section 6.1.2.2, the identification of ownership with things, rather than rights, is deeply imbedded within our common psyche.

In the face of such difficulties, English law adopts a pragmatic stance:

> Since it seems a pity to have to jettison excellent words like ownership, owner, and own, the last of which, as a verb, has no real equivalent in many other languages, and since English law is not at all committed to any particular usage, there are two alternatives open to us. We can say that the owner of a thing, whether land or a chattel, is the person who can convey the full interest in it to another person ... or on the contrary that what a person owns is an ... interest ... In the former case we attach ownership to the physical object at the cost of reducing the number of owners; in the latter we enlarge the number of owners but attach ownership in every case to an abstract entity. At present the usage [under English law] ... is ambiguous.
> (Lawson and Rudden, *The Law of Property* (2nd edn), p. 116; see also (3rd edn), pp. 81–2)

6.1.2.4.   The division of ownership

Finally, we should note ownership's ability to hive off its various attributes both between different types of owner and between owners and non-owners.

Between different types of owner

Even if one rejects the full rigour of the multiplication of ownerships argument, suggested by Dales and Grey, there is no doubt English law recognises that, to a limited extent at least, different types of ownership interest might exist in the same thing. The classic manifestation of this is the trust, a fundamentally important mechanism under English property law which we will consider in detail in Chapter 8. For present purposes, all you need to know is that, under it, ownership of a thing is split between the trustee and the beneficiary with the various attributes of ownership divided up between them. In broad terms, the trustee is given the right to manage the property on behalf of the beneficiary who has the right to enjoy it. As you will see later, the determination of ownership then becomes dependent upon perspective. More controversially, again as we see in Chapter 8, the ownership of companies has in recent years also been described in terms of split ownership with the classical view of the shareholder as sole owner coming under sustained pressure from new models of corporate governance which seek to reflect the ownership-type interests of a variety of other stakeholders including employees, directors, local communities and the general public (e.g. Ireland, *Company Law and the Myth of Shareholder Ownership*).

Between owners and non-owners

The attributes of ownership might also be divided among a host of non-owners (some of whom, at least, would thereby acquire a property interest in the thing but not its ownership). Take this book for example, which the owner has the right to read, decorate his bookshelf with or sell on to some unsuspecting first year. This list of specific activities might be distilled into three separate entitlements: namely, the right to use the book (by reading it or using it as a door stop etc.); the right to possess the book (by placing it on one's bookshelf or putting it in one's briefcase etc.); and the right to the capital (by selling it to someone else or shredding it etc.). This is by no means a complete list of the attributes of ownership but will suffice for present purposes (see further section 6.2 below).

Now, while such rights clearly come within our lay notion of ownership, it is obvious that, in any particular instance, they are not necessarily a reliable indicator as to where ownership resides. For example, you might have the right to possess the book because you have borrowed it from the library. More controversially, you might possess the book because you have stolen it from the library: see Chapter 7. The library borrower will similarly, of course, enjoy the right to use the book for the period of the loan. More surprisingly perhaps, even the right to the capital might be enjoyed by someone other than the owner as when a pornographic book is destroyed in accordance with a court order which achieves its purpose without requiring ownership of the book to pass to the party entrusted with its disposal.

The aim of the forgoing discussion was to begin to illustrate why the concept of ownership is so difficult to define. No sooner had we grasped hold of the term, by singling out three of its most fundamental incidents, than it slipped from our fingers, as we acknowledged that each of those rights could be exercised by someone other than the owner. As you will see later in this chapter, the same is true of any aspect of ownership that we care to single out. For, in any specific instance, any particular incident of ownership may be held by someone other than the person we would normally identify as the owner of the thing in question.

> **Extract 6.1   Thomas C. Grey, 'The Disintegration of Property', in *Nomos XII: Property* (New York: New York University Press, 1980), Chapter 3, pp. 69–71 and 72–3**
>
> In the English-speaking countries today, the conception of property held by the specialist (the lawyer or economist) is quite different from that held by the ordinary person. Most people, including most specialists in their unprofessional moments,

conceive of property as *things* that are owned by *persons*. To own property is to have exclusive control of something – to be able to use it as one wishes, to sell it, give it away, leave it idle, or destroy it. Legal restraints on the free use of one's property are conceived as departures from an ideal conception of full ownership.

By contrast, the theory of property rights held by the modern specialist tends both to dissolve the notion of ownership and to eliminate any necessary connection between property rights and things. Consider ownership first. The specialist fragments the robust unitary conception of ownership into a mere shadowy 'bundle of rights'. Thus, a thing can be owned by more than one person, in which case it becomes necessary to focus on the particular limited rights each of the co-owners has with respect to the thing. Further, the notion that full ownership includes rights to do as you wish with what you own suggests that you might sell off *particular aspects* of your control – rights to certain uses, to profits from the thing, and so on. Finally, rights of use, profit, and the like can be parceled out along a temporal dimension as well – you might sell your control over your property for tomorrow to one person, for the next day to another, and so on.

Not only can ownership rights be subdivided, they can even be made to disappear as if by magic, if we postulate full freedom of disposition in the owner. Consider the convenient legal institution of the trust. Yesterday A owned Blackacre; among his rights of ownership was the legal power to leave the land idle, even though developing it would bring a good income. Today A puts Blackacre in trust, conveying it to B (the trustee) for the benefit of C (the beneficiary). Now no one any longer has the legal power to use the land uneconomically or to leave it idle – that part of the rights of ownership is neither in A nor B nor C, but has disappeared. As between B and C, who owns Blackacre? Lawyers say B has the legal and C the equitable ownership, but upon reflection the question seems meaningless: what is important is that we be able to specify what B and C can legally do with respect to the land.

The same point can be made with respect to fragmentation of ownership generally. When a full owner of a thing begins to sell off various of his rights over it – the right to use it for this purpose tomorrow, for that purpose next year, and so on – at what point does he cease to be the owner, and who then owns the thing? You can say that each one of many right holders owns it to the extent of the right, or you can say that no one owns it. Or you can say, as we still tend to do, in vestigial deference to the lay conception of property, that some conventionally designated rights constitute 'ownership'. The issue is seen as one of terminology; nothing significant turns on it.

What, then, of the idea that property rights must be rights in things? Perhaps we no longer need a notion of ownership, but surely property rights are a distinct category from other legal rights, in that they pertain to things. But this suggestion cannot withstand analysis either; most property in a modern capitalist economy is intangible. Consider the common forms of wealth: shares of stock in corporations, bonds, various kinds of commercial paper, bank accounts, insurance policies – not to mention more arcane intangibles such as trademarks, patents, copyrights, franchises, and business goodwill.

In our everyday language, we tend to speak of these rights as if they attached to things. Thus we 'deposit our money in the bank', as if we were putting a thing in a place; but really we are creating a complex set of abstract claims against an abstract legal institution. We are told that, as insurance policy holders we 'own a piece of the rock'; but we really have other abstract claims against another abstract institution. We think of our share of stock in Megabucks Corporation as part ownership in the Megabucks factory outside town; but really the Megabucks board of directors could sell the factory and go into another line of business and we would still have the same claims on the same abstract corporation.

Property rights cannot any longer be characterized as 'rights of ownership' or as 'rights in things' by specialists in property. What, then, *is* their special characteristic? How do property rights differ from rights generally from human rights or personal rights or rights to life or liberty, say? Our specialists and theoreticians have no answer; or rather, they have a multiplicity of widely differing answers, related only in that they bear some association or analogy, more or less remote, to the common notion of property as ownership of things ... The conclusion of all this is that discourse about property has fragmented into a set of discontinuous usages. The more fruitful and useful of these usages are those stipulated by theorists; but these depart drastically from each other and from common speech. Conversely, meanings of 'property' in law that cling to their origin in the thing-ownership conception are integrated least successfully into the general doctrinal framework of law, legal theory, and economics. It seems fair to conclude from a glance at the range of current usages that the specialists who design and manipulate the legal structures of the advanced capitalist economies could easily do without using the term 'property' at all.

Notes and Questions 6.1

1 Do you agree that the bundle of rights thesis (which we examine in detail in section 6.3 below) necessarily 'dissolve[s] the notion of ownership'?

2 If you dissect a frog for the purposes of scientific analysis, does that dissolve the notion of frogs or simply help explain how frogs function? Admittedly, ownership is an intangible construct but that surely makes it, if anything, easier to subject to analytical scrutiny (and a lot less messy!).

3 Should it matter whether the thing you own is tangible or intangible especially when the rights you own in the thing are always, by definition, intangible? While property law's unexpected pre-occupation with abstractions confounds our initial expectations, it does not follow from this that ownership is thereby undermined.

4 Does Grey's analysis prove anything except that ownership is more complex than one might initially imagine?

5 How would Grey distinguish 'ownership' from 'property'? Do you agree with his distinction?

Extract 6.2   Jeremy Waldron, *The Right to Private Property* (Oxford: Clarendon Press, 1988), Chapter 2

1. SCEPTICISM ABOUT PRIVATE PROPERTY

Although private property has found its way again to the forefront of attention in jurisprudence and political philosophy, serious discussion is hampered by the lack of a generally accepted account of what private property is and how it is to be contrasted with alternative systems of property rules. As Tawney pointed out:

> It is idle … to present a case for or against private property without specifying the particular forms of property to which reference is made, and the journalist who says that 'private property is the foundation of civilisation' agrees with Proudhon, who said it was theft, in this respect at least that, without further definition, the words of both are meaningless. (Tawney, 'Property and Creative Work', p. 136)

Many writers have argued that it is, in fact, impossible to define private property – that the concept itself defies definition. If those arguments can be sustained, then a work like this is misconceived. If private property is indefinable, it cannot serve as a useful concept in political and economic thought: nor can it be a point of interesting debate in political philosophy. Instead of talking about property systems, we should focus perhaps on the detailed rights that particular people have to do certain things with certain objects, rights which vary considerably from case to case, from object to object, and from legal system to legal system. But, if these sceptical arguments hold, we should abandon the enterprise of arguing about private property as such – of saying that it is, or is not, conducive to liberty, prosperity, or rights – because the term does not pick out any determinate institution for consideration.

Why has private property been thought indefinable? Consider the relation between a person (call her Susan) and an object (say, a motor car) generally taken to be her private property. The layman thinks of this as a two-place relation of ownership between a person and a thing: Susan owns that Porsche. But the lawyer tells us that legal relations cannot exist between people and Porsches, because Porsches cannot have rights or duties or be bound by or recognise the rule. The legal relation involved must be a relation between persons – between Susan and her neighbours, say, or Susan and the police, or Susan and everyone else. But when we ask what this relation is, we find that the answer is not at all simple. With regard to Susan's Porsche, there are all sorts of legal relations between Susan and other people. Susan has a legal liberty to use it in certain ways; for example, she owes no duty to anyone to refrain from putting her houseplants in it. But that is true only of some of the ways that the car could (physically) be used. She is not at liberty to drive it on the footpath or to drive it anywhere at a speed faster than 70 mph. Indeed, she is not at liberty to drive it at all without a licence from the authorities. As well as her liberties, Susan also has certain rights. She has what Hohfeld called a 'claim-right' against everyone else (her neighbours, her friends, the local car thief, everyone in the community) that they should not use her Porsche without her permission. But Susan also owes certain duties to other people in relation to the vehicle. She must keep it in good order and see that it does not become a nuisance to her neighbours. She is liable to pay damages if it rolls into her neighbour's fence. These rights, liberties, and duties are the basic stuff of ownership. But legal relations can be changed, and, if Susan owns the Porsche, then *she* is in a position to change them. She has the power to sell it or give it to somebody else, in which case all the legal relations change: Susan takes on the duties (and limited rights) of a non-owner of the Porsche and someone else takes on the rights, liberties, duties, and powers of ownership. Or perhaps Susan lends or hires the car; that involves a temporary and less extensive change in legal relations. She can bequeath the car in her will so that someone else will take over her property rights when she dies. These are her powers to change her legal situation and that of others. She may also, in certain circumstances, have her own legal position altered in relation to the Porsche: for instance, she is liable to have the car seized in execution of a judgment summons for debt. All these legal relations are involved in what we might think of as a clear case, indeed a paradigm, of ownership. Private property, then, is not only a simple relation between a person and a thing, it is not a simple relationship at all. It involves a complex bundle of relations, which differ considerably in their character and effect.

If that were all, there would be no problem of definition: private property would be a bundle of rights, but if it remained constant for all or most of the cases that we want to describe as private property, the bundle as a whole could be defined in terms of its contents. But, of course, it does not remain constant, and that is where the difficulties begin.

Each of the legal relations involved in Susan's ownership of the Porsche is not only distinct, but in principle separable, from each of the others. It is possible, for example, that someone has a liberty to use an automobile without having any of the other rights or powers which Susan has. Because they are distinct and separable, the component relations may be taken apart and reconstituted in different combinations, so that we may get smaller bundles of the rights that were involved originally in this large bundle we called ownership. But when an original bundle is taken apart like this and the component rights redistributed among other bundles, we are still inclined, in our ordinary use of these concepts, to say that one particular person – the holder of one of the newly constituted bundles – is the *owner* of the resource. If Susan leases the car to her friend Blair so that he has exclusive use of the Porsche in return for a cash payment, we may still say that Susan is really the car's owner even though she does not have many of the rights, liberties, and powers outlined in the previous paragraph. We say the same about landlords, mortgagors, and people who have conceded various encumbrances, like rights of way, over their real estate: they are still the owners of the pieces of land in question. But the legal position of a landlord is different from that of a mortgagor, different again from that of someone who has yielded a right of way, and different too from that of a person who has not redistributed any of the rights in his original bundle: depending on the particular transactions that have taken place, each has a different bundle of rights. If lay usage still dignifies them all with the title 'owner' of the land in question, we are likely to doubt whether the concept of ownership, and the concept of private property that goes with it, are doing very much work at all. The lawyer, certainly, who is concerned with the day-to-day affairs of all these people, will not be interested in finding out which of them really counts as an owner. His only concern is with the detailed contents of the various different bundles of legal relations (for a particularly strong statement of this view, see Grey, 'Disintegration of Property' [Extract 6.1 above]).

As if that were not enough, there are other indeterminacies in the concept of ownership. In America, an owner can leave his goods in his will to more or less anyone he pleases. But an owner's liberty in this respect is not so great in England; it is even more heavily curtailed by statute law in, say, New Zealand: and in France the operation of the doctrine of *legitima portio* casts a different complexion on wills, bequest, and inheritance altogether. What does this show? Does it show that the French have a different concept of ownership from the Americans and the English, so that it is a linguistic error to translate '*propriété*' as 'ownership'? Or does it show that the power of transmissibility by will is not part of the definition of ownership, but only contingently connected with it? If we take the former alternative, we are left with the analytically untidy situation in which we have as many ambiguities in the term 'ownership' as there are distinct legal systems (and indeed distinct momentary legal systems – for each may change in this respect over time). But if we take the latter option, we run the risk of leaving the concept of ownership without any essential content at all. It will become rather like *substance* in Locke's epistemology: a mere substratum, a hook on which to hang various combinations of legal relations.

In fact, I think many legal scholars now do take this latter option. In their view, the term 'ownership' serves only as an indication that some legal relations, some rights, liberties, powers, etc., are in question. On their view, the term does not convey any determinate idea of what these legal relations are. In every case, we have to push the words 'ownership' and 'private property' aside and look to the detail of the real legal relations involved in the given situation (cf. Grey, 'Disintegration of Property' [Extract 6.1 above]; also Ackerman, *Private Property and the Constitution*, pp. 26 *et seq.*).

For completeness, I should mention a third source of indeterminacy. The objects of property – the things which in lay usage are capable of being owned – differ so radically in legal theory, that it seems unlikely that the same concept of ownership could be applied to them all, even within a single legal system. In England, the ownership of a Porsche is quite a different thing from the ownership of a piece of agricultural land. There are different liberties, duties, and liabilities in the two cases. Private property in these comparatively concrete objects is a different matter again from the ownership of intangible things like ideas, copyrights, corporate stock, reputations, and so on. Once again, the common word 'ownership' – 'X owns the car', 'Y owns the land', 'Z owns the copyright' – may be unhelpful and misleading, for it cannot convey any common content for these quite different bundles of legal relations. There is also a similar, though perhaps less spectacular, variation in ownership with different types of *owner*: the ownership of a given resource by a natural person may be a different matter from its ownership by a corporation and different again from its being the property of the Crown. Variations in 'subject' as well as variations in 'object' can make a difference to the nature of the relation.

2. CONCEPTUAL DEFINITION

We owe to H. L. A. Hart the point that, in jurisprudence, as in all philosophy, it is a mistake to think that particulars can be classified under general terms only on the basis of their possession of specified common features. But when jurists express doubts about the usefulness of general terms such as 'private property' or 'ownership', it is usually this sort of definition that they have in mind. They imply that, if we are unable to specify necessary and jointly sufficient conditions which an institution must satisfy in order to be regarded as a system of private property, or which a legal relation must satisfy in order to be regarded as a relation of ownership, then those terms are to be regarded as ambiguous or confused and certainly as analytically unhelpful.

If Hart's point is accepted, however, this scepticism begins to seem a little premature. Conceptual definition is a complicated business and the idea that it always involves the precise specification of necessary and sufficient conditions must be regarded as naive and outdated. A term which cannot be given a watertight definition in analytic jurisprudence may nevertheless be useful and important for social and political theory; we must not assume in advance that the imprecision or indeterminacy which frustrates the legal technician is fatal to the concept in every context in which it is deployed ... Briefly, what I want to say ... is that private property is a *concept* of which many different *conceptions* are possible, and that in each society the detailed incidents of ownership amount to a particular concrete conception of this abstract concept.

Notes and Questions 6.2

1 Why is the bundle of rights which constitutes ownership not constant?

2 What, respectively, do Waldron and Grey each think of the view of 'many legal scholars ... [that] the term *ownership* serves only as an indication that some legal relations, some rights, liberties, powers, etc., are in question'?

3 Why should the concept vary according to both the object and the subject of the relationship?

4 What is the difference between a concept and a conception?

6.2.   The contents of ownership

In this section, we will examine the substantive rights and limitations that, together, constitute ownership. In so doing, we will concentrate on Honoré's article, 'Ownership', which, as has often been noted, is 'a constant point of reference for those seeking to grapple with this highly elusive concept' (Harris, 'Ownership of Land in English Law', p. 143).

6.2.1.   An introduction to Honoré's analysis

It was not until comparatively recently, when Honoré published his essay on the topic in 1961, that the concept of ownership was subjected to rigorous analytical scrutiny. The process had been set in motion by Hohfeld some forty years earlier with the analysis of rights which we considered in Chapter 2. Yet, while that provided the skeleton of an analytical framework, it was Honoré who gave it form by offering a substantive analysis of the interests which, in his view, constitute ownership.

As you will see in Extract 6.3 at the end of this section, Honoré identified eleven, what he termed, 'standard incidents of ownership'. Before considering these, it is important to understand exactly what Honoré was attempting to achieve in this essay. At the outset he makes the following comment:

> [T]he standard incidents of ownership ... may be regarded as necessary elements in the notion of ownership, in the following sense. If a system did not admit them, and did not provide for them to be united in a single person, we would conclude that it did not know the liberal concept of ownership, though it might have a modified version of ownership, either primitive or sophisticated. But the listed incidents, though they may be together sufficient, are not individually necessary conditions for the person of inherence to be designated owner of a particular thing ... [for] ... the use of 'owner' will extend to cases in which not all the listed incidents are present.

Now what is meant by stating that the standard incidents are 'necessary elements' although not 'individually necessary'? Honoré is explicitly *not* attempting to provide a litmus test of ownership whereby any particular link between a person and a thing can be analyzed to see if such-and-such a person is the owner. For his interest lies not with particular person–thing relationships but in the system where such relationships exist. Honoré is, in effect, providing a template in which he lists those incidents with which any system claiming to embrace a liberal notion of ownership must correspond. For example, if one acknowledges that possession is one of the fundamental incidents of ownership, the fact that you are allowed to take possession of a book (by borrowing it from the library) does not imply that you have become the book's owner. However, a society that did not allow anyone to possess anything could not be said to recognise the liberal notion of ownership.

In addition to clarifying Honoré's aims, the quotation also identifies the ambit of the essay with the explicit acknowledgment that it is only concerned with the 'liberal notion of ownership' (i.e. private ownership). As Honoré expressly states, he does not preclude the possibility of other forms of ownership, be they 'either primitive or sophisticated', which do not correspond to the template. Taken on its own terms, therefore, the essay is not attempting to offer a universal jurisprudence of property as applicable to this society as it is, for example, to Chinese communist or pre–colonial aboriginal society. On the contrary, Honoré in his stated aims, is only concerned with what is loosely termed Western society where private property is the norm although (as we saw in Chapter 2) by no means the only form of recognised property interest.

Extract 6.3   A. M. Honoré, 'Ownership', in *Making Laws Bind* (Oxford: Clarendon Press, 1987), pp. 165–79

I now list the standard incidents of ownership. They may be regarded as necessary elements in the notion of ownership, in the following sense. If a system did not admit them, and did not provide for them to be united in a single person, we would conclude that it did not know the liberal concept of ownership, though it might have a modified version of ownership, either primitive or sophisticated. But the listed incidents, though they may be together sufficient, are not individually necessary conditions for the person of inherence to be designated owner of a particular thing. As we have seen, the use of 'owner' will extend to cases in which not all the listed incidents are present.

Ownership comprises the right to possess, the right to use, the right to manage, the right to the income of the thing, the right to the capital, the right to security, the rights or incidents of transmissibility and absence of term, the duty to prevent harm, liability to execution, and the incident of residuarity. This makes eleven leading incidents. Obviously, there are alternative ways of classifying the incidents. Moreover, if we adopted the fashion of speaking of ownership as if it were just a bundle of rights, at least two items in the list would have to be omitted ...

... The present analysis, by emphasising that the owner is subject to characteristic duties and limitations, and that ownership comprises at least one important incident independent of the owner's choice, redresses the balance.

1. THE RIGHT TO POSSESS

The right to possess, namely, to have exclusive physical control of a thing, or to have such control as the nature of the thing admits, is the foundation on which the whole superstructure of ownership rests. It may be divided into two aspects, the right (claim) to be put in exclusive control of a thing and the right to remain in control, namely, the claim that others should not without permission interfere. Unless a legal system provides some rules and procedures for attaining these ends it cannot be said to protect ownership.

It is of the essence of the right to possess that it is *in rem* in the sense of availing against persons generally. This does not, of course, mean that an owner is necessarily entitled to exclude everyone from his property. We happily speak of the ownership of land, yet a largish number of officials have the right of entering on private land without the owner's consent for some limited period and purpose. On the other hand, a general licence so to enter on the property of others would put an end to the institution of landowning.

The protection of the right to possess (still using 'possess' in the convenient though over-simple sense of 'have exclusive physical control') should be sharply marked off from the protection of mere present possession. To exclude others from what one presently holds is an instinct found in babies and even, as Holmes points out (*The Common Law*, p. 213), in animals, of which the seal gives a striking example. To sustain this instinct by legal rules is to protect possession but not, as such, to protect the right to possess, and so not to protect ownership. If dispossession without the possessor's consent is, in general, forbidden, the possessor is given a right *in rem*, valid against persons generally, to remain undisturbed. But he has no right to possess *in rem* unless he is entitled to recover from persons generally what he has lost or had taken from him, and to obtain from them what is due to him but not yet handed over. Admittedly, there may be borderline cases in which the right to possess is partially recognised, as when a thief is entitled to recover from those who oust him and all claiming under them, but not from others.

The protection of the right to possess, and so of one element in ownership, is achieved only when there are rules allotting exclusive physical control to one person rather than another, and that not merely on the basis that the person who has such control at the moment is entitled to continue in control. When children understand that Christmas presents go not to the finder but to the child whose name is written on the parcel, when villagers have a rule that a dead man's things go not to the first taker but to his son or his sister's son, we know that they have at least an embryonic idea of ownership.

To have worked out the notion of 'having a right to' as opposed to mere having or, if that is too subjective a way of putting it, of rules allocating things to people as opposed to rules which forbid forcible taking, was an intellectual achievement. Without it a stable society would have been impossible. Yet the distinction is apt to be overlooked by English lawyers, accustomed as they are to the rule that against a defendant having no title to the land the occupier's possession is itself a title (Pollock and Wright, *Possession in the Common Law* (1888), pp. 91, 95; R. Megarry and H. W. R. Wade, *The Law of Real Property* (5th edn, 1984), p. 104) ...

... The owner, then, has characteristically a battery of remedies in order to obtain, keep, and if necessary get back the thing owned. Remedies such as the action for ejectment, the claim for specific restitution of goods, and the *vindicato* are designed to enable the plaintiff either to obtain or get back a thing, or at least to put pressure on the defendant to hand it over. Others, such as the actions for trespass to land and goods, the Roman possessory interdicts and their modern counterparts, are primarily directed towards enabling a present possessor to keep possession. Few of the remedies mentioned are confined to the owner. Most of them are available also to persons with a right to possess falling short of ownership, and some to mere possessors. Conversely, there will be cases in which they are not available to the owner, for instance because he has voluntarily parted with possession for a temporary purpose, as by hiring the thing out. The availability of such remedies is clearly not a necessary and sufficient condition of owning a thing. What is necessary, in order that there may be ownership of things at all, is that such remedies shall be available to the owner in the usual case in which no other person has a right to exclude him from the thing.

2. THE RIGHT TO USE

The present incident and the next two overlap. On a wide interpretation of 'use', management and entitlement to income fall within use. On a narrow interpretation, 'use' refers to the owner's personal use and enjoyment of the thing owned, and so excludes management and entitlement to income.

The right (liberty) to use the thing at one's discretion has rightly been recognised as a cardinal feature of ownership, and the fact that, as we shall see, certain limitations on use also fall within the standard incidents of ownership does not detract from its importance. The standard limitations on use are, in general, rather precisely defined, while the permissible types of use constitute an open list.

3. THE RIGHT TO MANAGE

The right to manage is the right to decide how and by whom the thing owned shall be used. This right depends, legally, on a cluster of powers, chiefly powers to license acts which would otherwise be unlawful and powers to make contracts: the power to admit others to one's land, to permit others to use one's things, to define the limit of such permission, to contract effectively in regard to the use and exploitation of the thing owned. An owner may not merely sit in his own deck-chair but may validly license others to sit in it, lend it, impose conditions on the borrower, direct how it is to be painted or cleaned, contract for it to be mended in a particular way. This is the sphere of management in relation to a simple object like a deck-chair. When we consider more complex cases, like the ownership of a business, the complex of powers which make up the right to manage is still more prominent. The power to direct how resources are to be used and exploited is one of the cardinal types of economic and political power. The owner's legal powers of management are one, but only one, possible basis for it. Many observers have drawn attention to the growth of managerial power divorced from legal ownership. In such cases, it may be that we should speak of split ownership or redefine our notion of the thing owned. This does not affect the fact that the right to manage is an important element in the notion of ownership. Indeed, the fact that in these cases we feel doubts whether the legal owner really owns is a testimony to its importance ...

4. THE RIGHT TO THE INCOME

To use or occupy a thing may be regarded as the simplest way of deriving an income from it, of enjoying it. It was, for instance, expressly contemplated by the English income tax legislation at the time this was written that the rent-free use or occupation of a house is a form of income. Though it would be even more inconvenient and unpopular to assess and collect such a tax, the same principle must extend to moveables.

Income in the more ordinary sense (fruits, rents, profits) may be thought of as a surrogate of use, a benefit derived from forgoing the personal use of a thing and allowing others to use it for reward; as a reward for work done in exploiting the thing; or as the brute product of a thing, made by nature or by others. Obviously, the line between the earned and unearned income from a thing cannot be firmly drawn.

The owner's right to the income, which has always, under one name or another, bulked large in an analysis of his rights, bulks still larger with the increased importance of income relative to capital. Legally, it takes the form of a claim to the income, sometimes *in rem*, sometimes *in personam*. When the latter is in the form of money, the claim before receipt of the money is *in personam*; and since the income from many sorts of property, such as share and trust funds, is in this form, here is another opportunity for introducing the apophthegm that *obligatio* has swallowed up *res*.

5. THE RIGHT TO THE CAPITAL

The right to the capital consists in the power to alienate the thing and the liberty to consume, waste, or destroy the whole or part of it. Clearly, it has an important economic aspect. The liberty to destroy need not be unrestricted. But a general provision requiring things so far as they are not consumed by use to be conserved in the public interest would be inconsistent with the liberal idea of ownership.

Most people do not, in any case, wilfully destroy permanent assets. Hence, the power of alienation is the more important aspect of the owner's right to the capital of the thing owned. This comprises the power to alienate during life or on death, by way of sale, mortgage, gift, or other mode, to alienate a part of the thing, and partially to alienate it. The power to alienate may be subdivided into the power to make a valid disposition of the thing and the power to transfer the holder's title (or occasionally a better title) to it. 'Title' is an important notion in the analysis of ownership. It denotes the power of the owner (or someone with a lesser interest) to alienate the thing and thereby to transfer the power to alienate and exercise the other rights of an owner or person with a lesser interest. An owner who exercises this power is said to give a good title to the thing in question.

The power to make a valid disposition and the power to transfer title usually concur but are sometimes separate, as when A has a power of appointment over property held in trust by B. Here A has the power to make a valid disposition of the thing, and B the power to transfer the legal title to it. (This example turns on the English distinction between the legal title, which is in B, *and* the equitable ownership, which A has the power to dispose of. But there are also examples in systems which do not admit this distinction.) Again, in some systems a sale or mortgage may be regarded as valid though the seller or mortgagor cannot give a good title at the time of the agreement to sell or mortgage.

An owner normally has both the power of disposition and the power of transferring title. In many early societies disposition on death is permitted but it seems to form an essential element in the mature notion of ownership. The tenacity of the right of testation once it has been recognised is shown by the Soviet experience. The earliest Soviet writers were hostile to inheritance, but gradually Soviet law has come to admit that citizens may dispose freely of their 'personal property' on death, subject to limits not unlike those known elsewhere.

6. THE RIGHT TO SECURITY

An important aspect of the owner's position is that he should be able to look forward to remaining owner indefinitely if he so chooses and if he remains solvent. His right to do so may be called the right to security. Legally, this is in effect an immunity from expropriation, based on rules which provide that, apart from bankruptcy and execution for debt, the transmission of ownership is consensual.

However, a general right to security, availing against others, is consistent with the existence of a power in the state to expropriate or divest. From the point of view of security of property, it is important that when expropriation takes place adequate compensation should be paid. But a general power to expropriate, subject to paying compensation, would be fatal to the institution of ownership as we know it. Holmes' paradox, that where specific restitution of goods is not a normal remedy ... expropriation and wrongful conversion are equivalent, obscures the vital distinction between acts which a legal system permits as rightful and those which it reprobates as wrongful. If wrongful conversion were general and went unchecked, though damages were regularly paid, ownership as we know it would disappear.

In some systems such as English law, a private individual may destroy another's property without compensation when this is necessary in order to protect his own person or property from a greater danger (*Cope* v. *Sharpe* [1912] 1 KB 496; *Cresswell* v. *Sirl* [1948] 1 KB 241). Such a rule is consistent with security of property only because of its exceptional character. Again, the state's or local authority's power of expropriation is usually limited to certain classes of thing and certain limited purposes. A general power to expropriate any property for any purpose would be inconsistent with the institution of ownership. If, under such a system, compensation were regularly paid, we might say either that ownership was not recognised in that system, or that money alone could be owned, 'money' here meaning a strictly fungible claim on the resources of the community. As we shall see, 'ownership' of such claims is not identical with the ownership of material objects and simple claims.

7. THE INCIDENT OF TRANSMISSIBILITY

It is often said that one of the main characteristics of the owner's interest is its duration . . .

. . . What is called unlimited duration comprises at least two elements: (i) that the interest can be transmitted to the holder's successors, and so on *ad infinitum*, and (ii) that it is not certain to determine at a future date. Thus, the fact that in English medieval land law all interests were considered temporary (Hargreaves, *Introduction to the Principles of Land Law* (1952), p. 47) is one reason why the terminology of ownership failed to take root, with consequences which have endured long after the cause has disappeared. These two elements may be called transmissibility and absence of term respectively. We are here concerned with the former.

No one, as Austin points out (Austin, *Jurisprudence* (4th edn, 1873), p. 817), can enjoy a thing after he is dead, except vicariously, so that, in a sense no interest can outlast death. But an interest which is transmissible to the holder's successors (persons designated by or closely related to the holder, who obtain the property after him) is more valuable than one which stops when he dies. This is so because on alienation the alienee or, if transmissibility is generally recognised, the alienee's successors, are thereby enabled to enjoy the thing after the alienor's death so that a better price can be obtained for the thing. In addition, even if alienation were not recognised, the present holder would by the very fact of transmissibility be dispensed *pro tanto* from making provision for his intestate heirs. Hence, for example, the moment when the tenant in fee acquired a heritable, though not yet fully alienable, right was a crucial moment in the evolution of the fee simple. Heritability by the state would not, of course, amount to transmissibility in the present sense. It is assumed that the transmission is in some sense advantageous to the transmitter.

Transmissibility can, of course, be admitted in principle, yet stop short at the first, second, or third generation of transmittees. The owner's interest is, however, characterised by indefinite transmissibility, no limit being placed on the possible number of transmissions, though the nature of the thing may well limit the actual number.

In deference to the view that the exercise of a right must depend on the choice of the holder ... I have refrained from calling transmissibility a right. It is, however, clearly something in which the holder has an economic interest. To revise the notion of right in order to take account of incidents not depending on the holder's choice which are nevertheless of value to him would, however, be a radical step. Thus, if transmissibility were a right, it would be one which neither the holder nor anyone on his behalf could exercise.

8. THE INCIDENT OF ABSENCE OF TERM

This is the second part of what is called 'duration'. The rules of a legal system usually provide for determinate, indeterminate, and determinable interests. The first are certain to determine at a future date or on the occurrence of a future event which is itself certain to occur. In this class come leases for however long a term, copyrights, etc. Indeterminate interests are those, such as ownership and easements, to which no term is set. Should the holder live for ever, he would, barring insolvency, etc., be able to continue in the enjoyment of them for ever. Since human beings are mortal, he will in practice only enjoy them for a limited period, after which the fate of his interest depends on its transmissibility. Again, given human mortality, interests for life, whether of the holder or another, are indeterminate. The notion of an indeterminate interest in the full sense, therefore, requires the notion of transmissibility, but if the latter were not recognised, there would still be value to the holder in the fact that his interest was not due to determine on a fixed date or on the occurrence of some contingency, like a general election, which is certain to occur sooner or later.

On reflection, it will be found that what I have called indeterminate interests are really determinable. The rules of legal systems always provide for some contingencies such as bankruptcy, sale in execution, or state expropriation on which the holder of an interest may lose it. It is true that in most of these cases the interest is technically said to be transmitted to a successor (e.g. a trustee in bankruptcy), whereas in the case of determinable interests the interest is not so transmitted. Yet the substance of the matter is that the present holder may lose his interest in certain events. It is therefore never certain that, if the present holder and his successors so choose, the interest will not determine so long as the thing remains in existence. The notion of indeterminate interests can only be saved by regarding the purchaser in insolvency or execution, or the state, as continuing the interest of the previous owner. This is an implausible way of looking at the matter, because the expropriability and executability of a thing is not an incident of value to the owner, but a restriction on the owner's rights imposed in the social interest. It seems better, therefore, to deny the existence of indeterminate interests, and to classify those which are not determinate according to the number and character of the contingencies on which they will determine. This justifies our speaking of a determinable fee, of fiduciary ownership, etc. These do not differ essentially from full ownership, determinable on bankruptcy or expropriation.

9. THE DUTY TO PREVENT HARM

An owner's liberty to use and manage the thing owned as he chooses is subject to the condition that not only may he not use it to harm others, but he must prevent others using the thing to harm other members of society. There may, indeed, be much dispute over what is to count as harm, and to what extent give and take demands that minor inconvenience between neighbours shall be tolerated. Nevertheless, at least for material objects, one can always point to abuses which a legal system will not allow.

I may use my car freely, but not in order to run my neighbour down, or to demolish his gate, or even to go on his land if he protests; nor may I drive uninsured. These restrictions are of course not confined to owners. Anyone who drives a car has similar duties. The owner's position is special in that he must not allow others to use his car in these harmful or potentially harmful ways. I may build on my land as I choose, but not in such a way that my building collapses on my neighbour's land; nor must I allow anyone else for example, a contractor, to build on my land in such a way. These and similar limitations on the use of things and on permission to use them are so familiar and so clearly essential to the existence of an orderly community that they are often not thought of as incidents of ownership. Some of them are imposed on all who use a thing, whether owners or non-owners. Others are confined to owners, or to those, such as the occupiers of land, who are in most cases also owners. No one may use things in a way which harms others, but owners have a special responsibility to see to it that their property is not used in a harmful way by others.

10. LIABILITY TO EXECUTION

Of a somewhat similar character is the liability of the owner's interest to be taken away from him for debt, either by execution for a judgment debt or on insolvency. Without such a general liability the growth of credit would be impeded and ownership would be an instrument by which the owner could freely defraud his creditors. This incident, therefore, which may be called *executability*, constitutes one of the standard ingredients of the liberal idea of ownership.

It is a question whether any other limitations on ownership imposed in the social interest should be regarded as among its standard incidents. A good case can certainly be made for listing *liability to tax* and *expropriability* by the state. Although it is often convenient to contrast taxes on property with taxes on persons, all tax must ultimately be taken from something owned, whether a material object, a fund, or a chose in action. A general rule exempting the owners of things from paying tax from those things would therefore make taxation impracticable. But it may be thought that, to state the matter in this way is to obliterate the useful contrast between taxes on what is owned and on what is earned. Although, therefore, a society could not continue to exist without taxation, and although the amount of tax is commonly dependent on what the taxpayer owns or earns, and must be paid from his assets, I should not wish to press the case for the inclusion of liability to tax as a standard incident of ownership.

Much the same holds good of expropriability. Although some state or public expropriation takes place in every mature society, and though it is not easy to see how administration could continue without it, expropriation tends to be restricted to special classes of property. We are left with the thought that it is, perhaps, a characteristic of ownership that the owner's claims are ultimately postponed to those of the public authority, even if indirectly, in that the thing owned may within defined limits be taken from the owners to pay the expenses of running the state or to provide it with essential facilities.

11. OWNERSHIP AND LESSER INTERESTS: RESIDUARY CHARACTER

I described the interest of which the standard incidents have been depicted as the greatest interest in a thing recognised by the law, and contrasted it with lesser interests (easements, short leases, licences, special property, mere detention). It is worth looking more closely at this distinction, for it depends partly on a point that the foregoing analysis has not brought out.

I must emphasise that we are not now concerned with the topic of split ownership cases where the standard incidents are so divided as to raise a doubt which of two or more persons interested should be called owner. We are dealing with those simpler cases in which the existence of B's interest in a thing, though it restricts A's rights, does not call in question A's ownership of the thing.

The first point to be noted is that each of the standard incidents of ownership can apply to the holder of a lesser interest in property. The bailee has possession of, and often the right to possess, the goods bailed. The managing director of a company has the right to manage it. The life tenant or usufructuary of a house is entitled to the income from it. The donee of a power of appointment is entitled to dispose of the capital subject to the power. The holder of an easement has a transmissible and non-determinable interest in the land subject to the easement. Yet, without more, we feel no temptation to say that the bailee owns the thing, the managing director the company, the life tenant the house, the donee the capital, or the easement holder the land. What criteria do we use in designating these as lesser interests?

One suggested view is that the rights of the holder of a lesser interest can be enumerated while the owner's cannot (J. von Gierke, *Sachenrecht* (3rd edn, 1948), p. 67; cf. W. Markby, *Elements of Law* (6th edn, 1905), pp. 157–8). This rests on a fallacy about enumeration. The rights, for instance, exercisable over a thing by way of liberty (what may be done with or to the thing) do not together constitute a finite number of permissible actions. The owner and the lessee alike may do an indefinite number and variety of actions, namely, any action not forbidden by a rule of the legal system.

A second view is that the criterion used is the fact that, at least as regards some incidents, the holder of the lesser interest has more restricted rights than the owner. The lessee's interest is determinate, the owner's merely determinable. But, conversely, the lessee has the right to possess and manage the property and take its income. In these respects the owner's interest is, for the time being, more restricted than his own. Nor will it help to say that the owner's rights are more extensive than those of the holder of a lesser interest as regards most of the incidents listed. In the case of a lease, for example, this would lead to the conclusion that the lessee has as much claim to be called owner as the reversioner.

A third suggestion is that some one incident is to be taken as decisive. In the case of all the listed rights, however, it is possible to put examples which would lead to the opposite result from that sanctioned by usage. If A lets B a car on hire, B possesses it but A owns it. The holder of a life interest or usufruct manages and takes the income of the thing, but the *dominus* or reversioner owns it. When trust property is subject to a power of appointment, the donee of the power can dispose of it, but the trustee owns it . . .

. . . Besides these examples, where any of the suggested criteria would give a result at variance with positive law and legal usage, there are many others where the rights in question apply to both or neither of the persons holding an interest in the thing. For instance, some writers appear to treat duration (J. C. W. Turner, 'Some Reflections on Ownership in English Law', (1941) 19 *Canadian Bar Review* 342) as the criterion for distinguishing between ownership and lesser interests. Yet the holder of an easement, like the owner of land, has a transmissible and indeterminate right over it, while, conversely, neither the owner nor the licensee of a copyright has an indeterminate right.

It would be tedious to list examples for the other rights. Clearly, if a criterion is to be found, it must be sought elsewhere. At first sight, a hopeful avenue of inquiry is to ask what happens on the determination of the various interests in the thing under consideration. This brings us to a further standard incident of ownership, namely, its residuary character.

A legal system might recognise interests in things less than ownership and might have a rule that, on the determination of such interests, the rights in question lapsed and could be exercised by no one. Or it could allot them to the first person to exercise them after their lapse. There might be leases and easements: yet, on their expiry, no one would be entitled to exercise rights similar to those of the former lessee or holder of the easement. This would be unlike any system known to us, and I think we should be driven to say that in such a system the institution of ownership did not extend to any thing in which limited interests existed. There would, paradoxically, be interests less than ownership in such things but no ownership of them.

This fantasy is meant to bring out the point that it is characteristic of ownership that an owner has a residuary right in the thing owned. In practice, legal systems have rules which provide that, on the lapse of an interest, rights, including liberties, analogous to the rights formerly vested in the holder of the interest, vest in or are exercisable by someone else. That person may be said to acquire the corresponding rights. Of course, the corresponding rights are not identical with, but correspond to, the former.

It is true that corresponding rights do not always arise when an interest is determined. Sometimes, when ownership is abandoned, no corresponding right vests in another. The thing is simply an ownerless *res derelicta*. It seems, however, a safe generalisation that, when an interest less than ownership terminates, legal systems provide for corresponding rights to vest in another. When easements terminate, the owner can exercise the corresponding rights. When bailments terminate, the same is true. At first sight, it looks as if we have found a simple explanation of the use of the term 'owner', but this turns out to be but another deceptive shortcut. For it is not a sufficient condition of A's being the owner of a thing that, on the determination of B's interest in it, corresponding rights vest in or are exercisable by A. On the determination of a sublease, the rights in question become exercisable by the lessee, not by the owner of the property.

Can we then say that the owner is the ultimate residuary? When the sublessee's interest determines, the lessee acquires the corresponding rights; but when the lessee's right determines, the owner acquires these rights. Hence the owner appears to be identified as the ultimate residuary. The difficulty is that the series may be continued, for on the determination of the owner's interest, the state may acquire the corresponding rights. Is the state's interest ownership or a mere expectancy?

A warning is here necessary. We are approaching the troubled waters of split ownership. Puzzles about the location of ownership are often generated by the fact that an ultimate residuary right is not coupled with present alienability or with the other standard incidents we have listed ...

... We are, of course, here concerned not with the puzzles of split ownership but with simple cases in which the existence of B's lesser interest in a thing is clearly consistent with A owning it. To explain the usage in such cases it is helpful to point out that it is a necessary but not sufficient condition of A's being owner that, either immediately or ultimately, the extinction of other interests would inure to his benefit. In the end, it turns out that residuarity is merely one of the standard incidents of ownership, important no doubt, but not entitled to any pre-eminent status.

Notes and Questions 6.3

1   It is important to note that Honoré adopted the phrase *incidents of ownership* because his analysis is more than simply a list of rights which together constitute the 'ownership' bundle. While the first seven incidents might be accurately described as rights of some kind, the final four are less concerned with rights than with the limitations (or lack of limitation) under which the previously listed rights operate.

2   Do you agree that the *right to use* can be distinguished from both the *right to manage* and the *right to the income*?

3   When considering the *incidence of absence of term* Honoré suggests that 'indeterminate interests are really determinable' because the rules of a legal system always allow for some contingencies (such as bankruptcy) by which the holder of an indeterminate interest might lose it. Consequently, such interests are, 'in ... substance', the equivalent of determinable interests as they have the potential to end if an event which is not certain to happen, such as bankruptcy, does actually occur. Do you agree with this argument? As Honoré explicitly concedes, there is, after all, a difference. When an indeterminate interest is lost in this way, 'the interest is technically said to be transmitted to a successor (e.g. a trustee in bankruptcy), whereas in the case of determinable interests the interest is not so transmitted'. But is this not crucial? As we see in section 8.2, with

determinable interests the interest ends (automatically) on the occurrence of the determining event, while an indeterminate interest is, at least potentially, of infinite duration. The fact that the latter might be taken from its current holder against his will does not equate it with the former. If you, as owner of this book, are adjudged bankrupt, it will vest in the trustee in bankruptcy. The title would, by this mechanism, have changed hands but this is no more than would occur if you sold the book to another or (somewhat curiously) gave it to him for Christmas. In none of these situations has the interest determined and to equate indeterminate interests with determinable ones on the basis of such an argument appears problematic.

4 Would it be more plausible to draw a parallel between indeterminate and determinable interests when the thing, and as a consequence the indeterminate interest held in it, are capable of being destroyed?

5 The duty to prevent harm makes the significant point that ownership of a thing does not give you the freedom to do what you want with the thing owned. As owner of this book, you may read it but you cannot throw it with intent to harm another nor (more subtly) copy it in a way which infringes our copyright (see Chapter 9). The duty to prevent harm consequently extends beyond the physical to the economic and extends to all those limitations on use which apply to things in the interest of others. This is, without doubt, an important point to make, challenging as it does the caricature of ownership as, in the (quoted out of context) words of Blackstone, 'sole and despotic *dominium*' which we introduced earlier. It is, of course, inconceivable to regard ownership in such absolute terms, as Blackstone was at pains to point out when he noted earlier in the *Commentaries* that the Englishman's 'absolute right' to property 'consists in the free use, enjoyment and disposal of all his acquisitions, without any control or diminution, *save only by the law of the land*' (Blackstone, *Commentaries*, Book I, p. 138, emphasis added). However, a number of commentators (such as Waldron) have suggested that, because the duty to prevent harm is not limited to owners, it is misguided to regard this as an incident of ownership. For example, everyone is under a duty not to throw this book at another with intent to harm irrespective of who actually owns the book. Does it follow from this, however, that the duty to prevent harm is not an incident of ownership? As you will see in section 6.5 below, the duty to prevent harm is a fundamentally important limitation on the right to use and (to a lesser degree) the right to possess. To argue that it is not an incident of ownership because non-owners are under a similar duty simply misunderstands Honoré's thesis. He is not concerned with identifying rights that are unique to ownership but rather with describing those rights which any system embracing private ownership must recognise. On occasion, those rights will be exercised by non-owners as, likewise, will any limitation on those rights. However, just because a non-owner might have the right to use this book (if, for example, he borrowed it from you), does not mean

that the right to use is not an incident of ownership and the same argument applies to any limitation on that right (such as the duty to prevent harm).

6 Why do you imagine Honoré changed the title of this ninth incidence of ownership from the *prohibition of harmful use* in the first edition of his article to the *duty to prevent harm* in later editions? Is it legitimate to raise this particular incident to the level of a duty?

7 Why is the essentially negative *liability to execution* essential to the workings of a modern economy?

8 In his final category, Honoré contrasts ownership with lesser interests, by which he means rights vested in others which restrict the owner's rights in the thing without bringing his actual ownership into question. Thus, if you lend this book to a friend, he will, under the informal terms of the loan, acquire the right to possess and use this book for a limited period of time without, at any point, becoming the book's owner. As Honoré illustrates, any of the previously listed rights of ownership can be split off in this way, and this prompts the question how do we still identify one party as the owner and the rest as simply holders of lesser interests in the thing. Do you agree with Honoré that none of the solutions he considers provides a complete answer? What bearing does this have on the issues raised above (sections 6.1.3.3 and 6.1.3.4)?

9 In 'The "Bundle of Rights" Picture of Property', p. 737, is Penner correct when he describes Honoré's purpose to be the provision of 'criteria for the correct application of the term *owner* in English Law'? Why might it more plausibly be argued that that is explicitly what Honoré was not attempting to do?

10 Although this was not his intention, which of Honoré's rights of ownership could be applied to communal ownership? Do some rights need to be modified and are others simply inappropriate outside the field of private ownership?

11 Honoré's purpose in detailing his eleven incidents of ownership was to describe the liberal concept of ownership and, in so doing, he specifically excluded from his endeavours any attempt to provide a universal definition of ownership. It has, however, become commonplace to apply his template to other legal systems quite alien to the liberal tradition, which prompts an inquiry into how far the analysis surpasses its stated aim. In the opinion of some, such as Lawrence Becker, it goes much further:

> Honoré has given an analysis of the concept of full ownership that ... provides a clear overview of the varieties of property rights. I have found his analysis ... to be an adequate tool for describing every description of ownership I have come across, from tribal life through feudal society to modern industrial states. The definition of the elements of ownership that he identifies will vary from society to society, as will the varieties of ownership that are recognized. But ownership is always, as far as I

can tell, analyzable in the terms he proposes ... [from] *primitive* and archaic
societies ... to modern ones. (Becker, 'The Moral Basis of Property Rights', p. 190)

Rather than a description of the liberal concept of ownership, Becker views
Honoré's analysis (which according to his calculations provides 4,080 possible
varieties of ownership model (p. 192)) as a means to describe any system of
ownership both within and beyond the liberal tradition. As we saw in Chapter 2,
every society includes a mixture of private, communal and state ownership
although the particular proportions will differ markedly. Yet, as Munzer indicates
in Extract 6.4 at the end of this section, they may all be analysed by reference to
Honoré's template. For example, in Australian aboriginal society, which we
considered in Chapter 4, equivalents to many of Honoré's incidents can be found
vested not in an individual but in the various groupings within aboriginal society.
In the system described in *Milirrpum* v. *Nabalco Pty Ltd* (1971) 17 FLR 141, the
clans had the right to possess (in the sense necessary to perform their duties in
respect of the sacred sites) while the bands had the right to use (in an economic
sense as hunter-gatherers foraging across the various sites). In contrast, the
society described in *Mabo* v. *Queensland (No. 2)* (1992) 175 CLR 1 invested both
such rights not in clans or bands but in families. Space permitting, one could go
on to analyse in detail each of these systems of ownership by applying Honoré's
list of incidents even though neither system, in any respect, purports to embrace a
liberal conception of ownership. Some would take issue with the basic idea that
every society needs to grapple with the notion of ownership (see Extract 6.5 at the
end of this section from Flathman). We would suggest, however, that any society
which did, could profitably be analyzed from the perspectives offered us by
Honoré. In other words, while we do not possess a universal concept of ownership, Honoré's incidents do provide us with a tool with which to assess differing
approaches to the ownership issues that arise in differing societies.

Extract 6.4   S. Munzer, 'Understanding Property', in S. Munzer, *A Theory of Property* (Cambridge: Cambridge University Press, 1990), Chapter 2, pp. 23–7

The idea of *property* – or, if you prefer, the sophisticated or legal conception of property –
involves a constellation of Hohfeldian elements, correlatives, and opposites; a specification of standard incidents of ownership and other related but less powerful interests;
and a catalogue of 'things' (tangible and intangible) that are the subjects of these
incidents. Hohfeld's conceptions are normative modalities. In the more specific form
of Honoré's incidents, these are the relations that constitute property. Metaphorically,
they are the 'sticks' in the bundle called property. Notice, however, that property also
includes less powerful collections of incidents that do not rise to the level of ownership.
For example, an easement involves primarily a claim-right and a privilege to use the land
of another and secondarily a power to compel enforcement of that claim-right and
privilege. It would be usual to classify an easement as property or a property interest,
even though it does not amount to ownership. Easements, bailments, franchises, and

some licences are examples of *limited property*. Notice, too, that the idea of property will remain open-ended until one lists the kinds of 'things' open to ownership. In a legal system, it will be mainly a descriptive task to compile the list. In political theory, it will be a normative problem to show what things should be open to ownership. The reference to ownable things is a link between the sophisticated and popular conceptions of property. Notice, finally, that, even with a list of ownable things, the idea of property is indeterminate at the margin. No litmus test can separate rights of Property from, say, those of contract in all cases. Nor do lawyers' language and reasoning manifest, or require, such a line. It suffices to be able to describe a person's legal position.

The idea of *property rights* is narrower than that of property. Property rights involve only advantageous incidents. Property involves disadvantageous incidents as well. Meant here is advantage or disadvantage to the right holder or owner. Although property obviously involves disadvantages to persons other than the right holder, it is important to see that there can be disadvantages to the right holder as well. Suppose that someone owns a single-family home in a suburban area. Then she has a duty not to use it in ways prohibited by the law of nuisance or by zoning regulations. She may be disabled from transferring it to others with burdensome restrictions – for example, that no one may use it save for unduly limited purposes. If someone wins a court judgment for damages against her, then, subject perhaps to homestead laws, she has a liability that the home be sold to pay the judgment. The duty, disability, and liability are disadvantageous to her. It would be odd to say that they are part of her property rights in the home. But they are part of what is involved in saying that the home is her property. Similarly, easements, bailments, franchises, and some licences involve limited *property rights* …

… The identification of the owners or right holders facilitates additional terminology. If the owners are identifiable entities distinguishable from some larger group, there is *private property*. The most common example is individual private property, where an individual person is the owner – in severalty, as lawyers say. Other sorts of private property exist when the owners or right holders are persons considered together, such as partnerships and cotenancies, or are artificial entities that represent the financial interests of persons, such as corporations. Contrasted with private property are various sorts of *public property*. Here the owners are the state, city, community, or tribe. Some forms of ownership involve a mixture of private and public property rights.

Understanding property along the lines suggested by Hohfeld and Honoré has the salient advantage of cross-cultural application – that is, the idea of property, though perhaps not a moral and political theory of property, applies to all or almost all societies. If instead, the idea of property were cast in terms of particular economic or cultural data, it would not illuminate very well property in societies different from those which gave rise to the original data and idea. Granted, if property is conceived along the lines advocated here, variation can still occur in who may own property, which incidents comprise ownership or other property interests, and which things can be owned. But the Hohfeld–Honoré analysis starts from the central truth that property involves relations among persons and with respect to things. It enables one to clarify these relations in widely different social settings. Though the analysis is especially well suited to complicated legal systems in developed societies, it also assists social scientists in analysing much simpler situations.

A well-known article by the anthropologist Hoebel brings out the point (E. Adamson Hoebel, 'Fundamental Legal Concepts as Applied in the Study of Primitive Law' (1942) 51 *Yale Law Journal* 951–66). Hoebel argues, first, that Hohfeld's vocabulary sharpens perception of the undeveloped legal and social systems. Hoebel's illustration is Yurok Indian society in northern California prior to the impact of Western civilisation. The Yurok had no formal government but did have an informal arrangement for enforcing legal standards by damages. Yurok law permitted something resembling ownership of fishing sites but with qualifications that Hohfeld's conceptions illuminate. The title holder of a fishing site has an exclusive liberty to fish there. He also has a power to grant a temporary liberty to another person to fish in that spot. Should he exercise the power, however, he comes under a duty to prevent his guest from being injured. Thus, if his guest were to slip and hurt herself while fishing, she would have a claim-right against her host for damages.

Second, Hoebel suggests that Hohfeld's vocabulary can avoid some unnecessary wrangles among anthropologists stemming from the use of overly broad or inapplicable labels. An example is the controversy over the type of ownership of canoes in Melanesia. Some anthropologists held that canoes were 'private property'. Others maintained that they involved 'communal ownership'. Hohfeld's conceptions, Hoebel points out, enable observers to describe accurately what is going on without getting embroiled in a larger dispute over private property and communism. The observers might find that the 'owner' of a canoe has a claim-right that others not damage it, a liberty superior to that of others to use it, a power to sell or give it away, and an immunity from being forced to sell. They might also find that the 'owner' is under a duty to ferry certain travellers, and that failure to discharge the duty would give a traveller a claim-right for damages. Such findings involve a mixture of 'private' and 'communal' elements. They would not be accurately described by prefixing either label, without qualification, to canoe ownership in that society.

Extract 6.5   Richard E. Flathman, 'Impossibility of an Unqualified Disjustificatory Theory' in *Nomos XII: Property* (New York: New York University Press, 1980), Chapter 3, pp. 69–71 and 72–3

PROPERTY RIGHTS AS A UNIVERSAL AND NECESSARY FEATURE OF HUMAN SOCIETIES

'Property right', 'ownership' and related concepts, Becker argues, following A. M. Honoré are family resemblance terms under the rubric of which a considerable variety of elements ... have been brought together in what is indeed a 'prodigious diversity' of combinations (no less than 4,080 by Becker's computations). Realizing this allows us to dispose of the discredited view that some 'primitive' societies were without the concept and the practice of property rights. If we operate with a suitably capacious conception of ownership, Becker argues, 'it is easy to show that private property rights of some sort exist everywhere'. In short, Wittgensteinian premises about language, mediated by A. M. Honoré's application thereof to 'ownership', plus a conceptually sophisticated anthropology, yields the conclusion that rights to private property are a universal phenomenon.

This by no means modest finding is much less than the entire yield of Becker's potent combination of authorities. The finding of universality would support the 'Burkean' argument noted above. But it could not exclude the possibility of a morrow that witnessed the abolition of all 4,080 members of this (truly extended) family. More to the present point, it could not exclude the possibility of a conclusive argument that all 4,080 variants are moral abominations that ought to be abolished. The possibility of such an argument is excluded, however, by Becker's further contention. '[I]t is possible to argue', he goes on to say, 'that they [property rights] are a necessary feature of social organization.' Now, as Hobbes somewhere says, that which is necessary arises not for deliberation. If property rights are not only universal but necessary, any philosopher attempting a general justification or disjustification of them would be pretending to a kind of intellectual purchase that is simply not available.

Becker hastens to caution against a familiar type of misinterpretation of the evidence to which he is responding. Early economic and legal anthropologists, operating with an overly restricted concept of ownership, mistakenly concluded that numerous societies were devoid of property rights. The analogous error in respect to the improved (perfected?) anthropological accounts would be the contention that some specific system of property rights is necessary for social organization. The evidence does not support such a thesis. What the data indicate is that, while property rights exist everywhere, 'what is necessary about them *is just that some exist*'. This leaves abundant room for philosophizing about the 'specific' questions of just which type, form, or variant of property rights would be best suited to this or that social organization and about the 'particular' question of how those rights ought to be distributed. The metatheoretical point that matters here, of course, is just that these are the only questions left open to question. Despite the remarks quoted earlier, it is the clear implication of Becker's necessity thesis that what have passed for general theories of property is one of three things: confused or disguised theories of specific and/or particular justification; metatheoretical remarks that are either demonstrably mistaken or that demonstrate the incoherence of putative general justifications; absurdities. And the practical upshot (one could hardly say the moral upshot) of the argument, one may suppose, is that we might as well resign ourselves to life with some form or other of property rights.

Let us take up the argument by considering the three elements of which it consists, namely: (a) Honoré's Wittgensteinian explication of 'property' and 'ownership'; (b) the claim that property rights are 'found everywhere'; and (c) the inference that they are necessary to social organization.

The present commentator has no quarrel with the 'Wittgensteinian' approach to the definition of ownership. Nor is he competent to question the substance of Honoré's analysis of the standard 'incidents' of ownership. But does this analysis support the conclusion that property rights exist 'everywhere' (whatever, exactly, is meant by that conveniently vague term)? Honoré says that his analysis is of 'mature legal systems', and he leaves open the question whether it holds for societies, organizations, or whatever that do not fall into that category. On the basis of extensive reading in legal and economic anthropology, Becker finds that Honoré's analysis, in only slightly modified form, does work for all of the societies discussed in those materials. Hence his claim that property rights are universal.

Our first objection to this argument concerns the conceptual verisimilitude and perspicuity of the accounts on which it is based. As noted, Becker himself stresses the distortions introduced by the inappropriate conceptualizations employed by nineteenth- and early twentieth-century anthropologists. Those conceptualizations were inadequate, according to Becker, because they were based on an overly narrow understanding of ownership in *their own* (i.e. the anthropologists' own) societies. But what reason does Becker have for thinking that the latterly improved understandings of ownership in mature legal systems (simply granting that the anthropologists in question did employ something like Honoré's conceptualization) itself better prepares scholars to analyze societies that manifestly differ from their own in important ways? Does he have independent evidence against the possibility that one conceptual distortion has been succeeded by another?

The skepticism we are expressing is grounded in that very Wittgensteinian understanding of language from which Becker seems to be proceeding. For Wittgenstein, most concepts take their meaning from the uses to which speakers put them in the course of the activities, practices, and forms of life in which those speakers are engaged. We are not in a position to prove that concepts such as 'possession', 'management', 'alienation', and 'transmission' (which in varying forms and combinations, are among the incidents of ownership in mature legal systems) have no equivalents or close analogues among the Azande, the Zulus, the Hopi, and so forth. But a minimum of knowledge about other differences between those societies and those from which Honoré's analysis is built up is enough to generate our skepticism.

Let us nevertheless assume that analogues to these concepts are indeed to be found, albeit in a great diversity of forms and combinations, 'everywhere'. It is not yet clear that it follows from this assumption, especially if one is working from recognizably Wittgensteinian premises, that it is helpful or enlightening to insist that property rights are a universal phenomenon. Can we imagine Wittgenstein concluding his analysis of such concepts as 'game' and 'understanding' by trumpeting the generalization that games and understanding are universal phenomena? The answer is pretty clearly negative. And the reason it is negative is just that such generalizations, even if in some sense true, deflect us from the point that Wittgenstein is most anxious to establish. '[I]t is our *acting*, which lies at the bottom of the language-game [italics mine].' Where the acting differs, generalizations based on linguistic or grammatical similarities are seriously misleading. Is there a universal pattern of *acting* in respect to ownership? Perhaps. But the least that must be said is that this remains to be shown.

These doubts about the universality thesis, of course, are anything but irrelevant to the necessity thesis. If property rights are not universal, then neither are they necessary. Equally, if the sense in which property rights are universal is insignificant or unenlightening, then the same will be true of the sense in which they are necessary. Because we have only suggested, not established, our objections to the universality thesis, we cannot claim that those objections prove Becker's necessity thesis false or insignificant. But then neither has Becker proved the universality thesis. Until he does so, he too is debarred from simple reliance upon it in arguing for the necessity thesis.

There is, however, at least one objection to the necessity thesis that is independent of the discussion thus far. Unless Becker has some heretofore unappreciated solution to the Humean principle of induction, he can hardly claim that 'the data' themselves are sufficient to 'indicate' that property rights are necessary to all social organizations. Even if we grant universality, necessity remains to be established.

The most extended argument Becker presents for the necessity thesis is made via a passage he quotes from the sociologist Irving Hallowell. 'Since [sic] valuable objects in all human societies must include, at the minimum, some objects of material culture that are employed to transform ... raw materials ... into consumable goods, there must be socially recognized provisions for handling the control of such elementary capital goods as well as the distribution and consumption of the goods that are produced.' Thus far, we have an assertion of a kind familiar to readers of structural-functional sociological theory. Certain functions, it is alleged, must be performed if a society is to maintain itself; therefore certain structures or arrangements, which perform those functions, are necessary. Even if we waive the well-rehearsed objections to this mode of reasoning, Becker's endorsement of the inference Hallowell draws from it is a truly arresting example of begging the question at issue. 'Consequently', Hallowell continues, 'property rights are ... an integral part of the economic organization of any society.'

No doubt property rights are one familiar device for 'handling the control of elementary capital goods' and for regulating the distribution of consumables. Equally, in societies for which the hypotheticals Hallowell had earlier enunciated are true, property rights are 'extremely fundamental'. But what in this argument demonstrates that property rights are the only possible device for doing these things?

Strictly speaking, of course, the answer to this question is 'nothing whatsoever'. Judging from the passage Becker quotes, Hallowell had found that property rights performed this function in numerous societies and, drawing on a deeply controversial general theory, illicitly transformed an empirical generalization into a necessary truth. Whatever Hallowell may have been doing, the most likely explanation for Becker's use of the passage seems to be along the following lines. Becker is operating with a highly latitudinarian concept of ownership, one that gives plausibility – although perhaps an illicit plausibility – to the claim that property rights are universal. This concept of ownership was derived from an analysis of societies in which property rights arguably do 'perform the functions' that Hallowell discusses. Thus when Becker has satisfied himself that the same concept is at work in all societies, he implies that the property rights denoted by the concept do the same job in all societies.

Notes and Questions 6.4

1 Are Flathman's criticism's based upon a private property notion of ownership?

2 Can you, or for that matter Flathman, offer a picture of a society (either existing, past or as a theoretical construct) in which property rights do not exist?

3 How are the terms *ownership* and *property rights* used in the above passage? Do Flathman and Becker treat them as synonyms?

6.3.   The roles played by ownership

6.3.1.   As a legal term of art

Traditionally, English law has been more concerned with establishing possession rather than determining ownership. This is, at least in part, a product of the adversarial system in which our courts are required to choose the better of two competing claims rather than undertake an investigation to discover who, among all the possible claimants in the world, has the best claim to the thing. As a result, the court is freed from the onerous obligation of determining ownership and can concentrate on the simpler task of establishing which of the two parties before it has the better right to possess the thing in question (which can normally be accomplished without deciding who is its owner – see chapter 10). When viewed from this perspective, one can perhaps appreciate why it is often said that English law has little use for the term ownership, in contrast to Roman law where it is traditionally viewed as being of fundamental importance. As Rudden has noted, all the civil-law systems have modelled their treatment of ownership on the Roman law concept of *dominium* which, at least theoretically, gives the owner an almost absolute interest.

> Now one of the most striking institutions of Roman Law was *dominium* ... which ... was ... as near to being absolute as any private law institution can be. The owner had an absolute title, he had an absolute right to dispose of the thing he owned, and his right to use it was limited by so few restrictions of a public law character that it, too, could almost be called absolute. The kinds of incumbrances with which it could be burdened were kept down to the lowest possible number, and where they existed they were carefully distinguished from the *dominium* over the thing, which was regarded as retaining its character of a general undifferentiated right over the thing capable of resuming its original plenitude by the mere disappearance of the incumbrance.
>
>   Now, the concurrence of these various absolutes in a single institution was really a very remarkable peculiarity of Roman law. Doubtless it was and still is very convenient for a person to be able to say: 'This thing is mine; my title to it is absolute; I can do what I like with it subject to certain very obvious restrictions that have to be put on the use of everything of the kind; and, if I wish, I can vest all these rights in another person, by transferring the thing to him.'
>
>   (Lawson and Rudden, *The Law of Property* (2nd edn), p. 115; this passage does not appear to have been repeated in the third edition)

Whether this was of any practical consequence is perhaps harder to assess. Rudden continues by noting that '[i]n actual practice the Roman position cannot have been very different' from the approach under the common law. 'If', for example, 'a plaintiff was protecting his possession or seeking to recover it from a defendant who had dispossessed him directly, he merely proved his possession' in a similar fashion to the means adopted under English law. As Rudden concedes, '[t]here is little that looks absolute' in all of this but what cannot be denied is the prominence given to the notion of ownership as a near-absolute interest under the civil law (through the vehicle of *dominium*) even though at a practical level this is of less significance than it might at first appear.

While the common law failed to accord ownership a similar degree of prominence, it would be a mistake to conclude that the term has no role to play under English law. On the contrary, the lack of a central all-embracing notion of ownership enables the concept to play a number of different roles, and we consequently need to distinguish the various situations in which it is employed.

6.3.1.1.   Ownership's role in land

It is often suggested that, in the particular context of land, the term ownership is simply redundant due to what is known as the doctrine of estates. As we see in section 8.2 below, the doctrine is simply a land-holding mechanism. The estate is an artificial construct, an abstraction, which combines the three dimensions of spatial existence (length x breadth x height) with the fourth dimension (time). The two most important estates are the *fee simple absolute in possession* and the *term of years absolute*. The fee simple is the greatest estate that exists under English law and vests the holder with an interest in the land of potentially infinite duration (cf. the other freehold estates, namely, the life estate which is limited to the lifetime of the original grantee, and the fee tail which normally endures until the death of the last male descendant of the original grantee). In contrast, the term of years is a leasehold estate which has been carved out of the freehold estate of another (normally referred to as the landlord). It is of strictly finite duration, and vests certain rights in the leaseholder for the duration of the lease.

We must now consider what relevance all of this has for the notion that, under English land law, there is no concept of ownership. As noted by Hargreaves, in the following quote, the argument is, in essence, a simple one in which land ownership is contrasted with estate holding:

> By distinguishing the land from the estate, English land law has shown conclusively that, even within a society as individualistic and as legalistic as England in the nineteenth century, ownership is not a necessary legal concept. The problem of ownership remains, but it is not a legal problem: it is the concern of the politician, the economist, the sociologist, the moralist, the psychologist – of any and every specialist who can contribute his grain to the common heap. Ultimately, the philosopher will try to unify this shifting mass into a coherent whole. That he has failed in the past to achieve an acceptable synthesis is not to be wondered at, for the mass is constantly changing from age to age, perhaps even from year to year. The lawyer naturally has his contribution to make, but as the problem is not even fundamentally a legal problem, the final solution does not lie with him. He is concerned with ownership only insofar as it produces consequences within the sphere of his own special technique, roughly indicated by the ideas of legal rights and legal duties. The sum total of those legal rights and duties which inhere at any one time in any one possessor – or tenant – of land is his estate, but whether the possessor is also the

owner, in the wider field of philosophy, cannot be determined by the lawyer or by the art which he practises, for the estate, even the fee simple, does not give the complete data necessary for the formulation, let alone the solution, of the ultimate problem.

(Hargreaves, 'Review of Modern Real Property', p. 17)

There are clear parallels here with the ideas already considered when we briefly discussed the views of Grey and Dales (Extract 6.1 and section 6.1.2.3 above). Hargreaves' point is simply a reiteration of the idea that, as lawyers, we are, in any given situation, only interested in the specific rights which may or may not exist in relation to a thing. In deciding whether A or B can rightfully possess Blackacre, we do not ask 'Who owns the land?' but rather 'Who has the right to possess the land?'. A might have the fee simple which would normally carry with it the right to possess but not if B had an unexpired term of years absolute which would give her the right.

So what implications does this have for the notion of ownership? In essence, there are three possible responses. Grey took the view that focusing on specific rights tended towards the very disintegration of the concept of ownership. In contrast, Dales implicitly argued, not that ownership disintegrated, but that it multiplied with each particular rights holder in the thing being viewed as an owner of the thing in respect of the right (or rights) held. Hargreaves' position is more subtle than either of these approaches. As the above quotation makes clear, he does not suggest that the concept of ownership has disintegrated, for he clearly regards the notion of ownership as an important (although non-legal) concept. Later in the same article, he similarly rejects the multiplication of ownerships approach, calling it a 'venial misuse of words ... to speak of "ownership" of an estate, of an "estate owner" and the like ... [for] ... [o]ne can no more "own" an estate than one can "own" a right'. Compelling as this argument is, it is perhaps worth noting, if only in passing, that it is a misuse of words to which the Law of Property Act 1925 itself subscribes, repeatedly using the phrase 'estate owner' which it defines, not surprisingly, as 'the owner of a legal estate' (section 205(1)(v)).

Such caveats aside, Hargreaves' thesis clearly disentangles the concept of ownership from the property rights that exist in a parcel of land. Ownership of land is, in his view, a non-legal relationship conceptually distinct from the property rights that might exist in respect of it, many of which *may* be vested in the person described as 'owner' but all of which *must* arise in respect of some estate held in the land the most extensive of which is the fee simple estate. Such a view is contentious and not without its critics, including Lawson, who took a quite contrary view:

The estate which has the longest duration is the fee simple, which is now in almost every case perpetual and is equivalent to full ownership.

(Lawson, *The Rational Strength of English Law*, p. 88)

A similar view was taken by Rudden (Lawson and Rudden, *The Law of Property* (2nd edn), p. 115) and is based on the idea that the rights that vest in the holder of the fee simple estate are so great that it is akin to owning the land itself free from all but the most minor of limitations. A rather more subtle approach is adopted by Harris (*Ownership of Land in English Law*, pp. 148–58), who suggests that the term plays an essential role in English land law even though it is not utilised as a term of art, because, as he demonstrates, the concept is used variously to underpin the institutions of land law, within the doctrinal reasoning of the courts and, on occasion, as a legal term in its own right.

6.3.1.2.   Ownership's role in chattels

There is no direct equivalent to the doctrine of estates under the law of personal property. As a consequence, the term 'ownership' is more freely employed in this context in a form which, in many respects, accords with lay perceptions as to its meaning. Technically, the term is used to signify the ultimate property interest in the thing.

6.3.1.3.   Ownership's role in legislation

While the concept of ownership lacks the pivotal role accorded to the term *dominium* under the civil law, terms such as 'ownership' and 'owner' are still encountered in statutes where they play a technical role limited to the context in which they appear. We have already considered one example of this in the Law of Property Act 1925 and it is by no means unique. It will probably not come as a surprise that, given the lack of an all-embracing definition of ownership, the term when it is encountered is defined with regard to the legal consequences that arise. Thus, despite being viewed by some as a 'venial misuse of words', the use of the term 'estate owner' in the Law of Property Act 1925 is unproblematic and uncontentious. Likewise, in *Lloyds Bank* v. *Bank of America* [1938] 2 KB 147, it was said that the term 'owner' which appears in section 2 of the Factors Act 1889 included all those with specific property rights in a thing (including a person whose rights were limited to having taken the thing as security for a loan under a pledge – see Chapter 18).

Such approaches accord with the notion of ownership of rights rather than ownership of things. Under both the Law of Property Act 1925 and the Factors Act 1889, there is likely to be more than one owner of the same thing each with differing rights in it. Thus, under the former, both the holder of the fee simple and the holder of the term of years in the same parcel of land are, under the Act, rightly described as 'estate owners', while, under the latter, both the pledgor and the pledgee are 'owners' for the purposes, at least, of section 2.

It would be a mistake, however, to cite such disparate examples as evidence that, under English law, ownership is always to be equated with rights rather than things. *Hanlon* v. *Law Society* [1980] 2 All ER 763, CA; [1980] 2 All ER 199, HL, for example, involved a trust which we would normally conceive as involving two owners of the trust property (the trustee who owns the legal title and the beneficiary who owns the equitable title – see Chapter 8). However, in this case, both Arnold P in the Court of Appeal and Lord Lowry in the House of Lords stated that, for the purposes of the Legal Aid Act 1974, the ownership of the trustee could be discounted and the beneficiary would be regarded as the sole owner of the property in question. In contrast, in *R. v. Tower Hamlets London Borough Council, ex parte Von Goetz* [1999] 2 WLR 582, the Court of Appeal held that, for the purposes of section 104 of the Local Government and Housing Act 1989, the term 'owner's interest' could include the interest of both trustees and beneficiaries. It is, perhaps, worth emphasising at this point that it is not our purpose to consider the merits of these various decisions. Each is a product of its own particular context, decided under a system in which no all-embracing definition of ownership exists and in which there is, consequently, a degree of flexibility that simply does not exist under the civil law. Such a contextual approach means that great care needs to be taken when considering the term from a technical standpoint. This can be seen in the Sale of Goods Act 1893, for instance, where the term 'owner' is frequently used absent any statutory definition because, even within the limited confines of this particular enactment, it has a meaning which 'assumes significance only in relation to a particular issue with a particular person' (see Battersby and Preston, 'The Concepts of "Property", "Title" and "Owner"', p. 269).

6.3.2.   As an amorphous notion

6.3.2.1.   Ownership as an organising idea

The problem with our discussion so far is that, in concentrating on a number of separate roles played by the concept of ownership, we have over-rationalised the notion and in so doing produced a distorted image which obscures its primary role. For in reality the term is often used with no such specificity as simply an idea which, while by no means vague, is essentially amorphous. In essence, the term is often used simply to signify the bond that exists between 'you' (or 'us') and 'it' with no attempt to define its nature or extent. In this conception of ownership, the owner is the one (or many) whose decision as to what should or should not be done with a thing is regarded as, in the words of Waldron, 'socially conclusive'.

It is in this sense that the term fulfils its primary role by providing a simple, readily understood notion of what it means to be the owner of a thing which, as we noted in section 6.1 above, the non-specialist can employ each time he is con-fronted by what would otherwise be an unfathomable conundrum. On occasion, this will produce the wrong result, as when the owner of a house expresses surprise that he is required to obtain planning permission and cannot do as he pleases with 'his land'. Normally, however, the amorphous concept of ownership provides a simple test that invariably provides non-lawyers with a means of establishing what they can and cannot do with a particular thing, no matter how complex the actual property relationships involved. As you will see in later chapters, the property relationships that arise when, for example, a house is bought with the aid of a mortgage or a car purchased via a lease-back arrangement, are indeed complex but that does not prevent the 'owner', his friends (who might be visiting the house or borrowing the car for the afternoon) and, for that matter, total strangers normally knowing exactly what they can and cannot lawfully do in respect of the property in question.

6.3.2.2.   Ownership as a contested concept

While providing an appreciation of its complexity, dividing ownership, as we have done, into a number of separate roles is also liable to distort the concept by presenting an overly compartmentalised view which underplays its dynamism. As you will have begun to appreciate when we considered the difficulties of ownership in section 6.1 above, there is no general agreement on this issue, and this final role focuses on the contest that ensues. For, as Waldron suggests, quoting the political philosopher W. B. Gallie, it is possible to view ownership as one of those 'concepts whose proper use inevitably involves endless disputes about their proper uses on the part of their users' (Gallie, 'Essentially Contested Concepts'). Such debate is inextricably linked to the concept of ownership. Whenever we speak of it, we are to an extent engaging in a contest as to its true meaning, and this discourse is as crucial to the concept as each of the previous roles we have identified.

6.4.   The limitations of ownership

Ownership in practice never invests the owner with complete control over the thing owned. All ownership of things is subject to limitations which differ in accordance with the practical, social and historical circumstances surrounding the particular object of property in question. Thus the limitations which arise in respect of the ownership of a piece of land are different from the limitations which apply to the ownership of this book or, for that matter, its copyright. However, no matter how diverse the types of property or the limitations that arise in respect of them, it remains true that ownership of anything is subject to some kind of limitation. These essentially negative restrictions are, as Honoré argued, as much an aspect of ownership as the positive rights normally associated with the term, and it is for this reason we have entitled this section the 'limitations *of* ownership', rather than the more usual 'limitations *on* ownership'.

Limitations as to the use of property exist both in the public law and the private law fields, and are normally imposed as a matter of public policy but can on occasion arise by agreement. To examine how these various types of limitation dovetail and interact, we will consider land use restrictions (with the exception of planning law) which provide a particularly graphic illustration of the reasons why limitations on property are an essential aspect of ownership.

6.4.1.   Nuisance

Historically, the use of land has been regulated by means of the law of nuisance. Today, while still the principal common law mechanism in this field, its significance has been much diminished by developments in both the private and public law spheres, such as restrictive covenants and planning and environmental controls. Whilst the law of planning is beyond the remit of this volume, we will concentrate first on the law of nuisance, which provides us with a vivid picture of the symbiotic relationships which characterise all forms of ownership, before going on to consider the relatively recent innovation of the restrictive covenant.

6.4.1.1.   A brief introduction to nuisance

Nuisance is divided into two distinct branches, namely, public and private nuisance, although it is quite possible for the same conduct to amount to an actionable wrong under both categories.

Public nuisance

Public nuisance is defined by Jolowicz as something 'which materially affects the life of a class of Her Majesty's subjects who come within the sphere or neighbourhood of its operation'. Historically, it was, in effect, the common law's response to problems arising out of land use where the effects were too diverse and indiscriminate to expect any individual to take action on his own. In consequence, the law of public nuisance is something of a rag-bag of public wrongs which, in the words of Lord Denning, 'covers a multitude of sins, great and small' (*Southport Corp.* v. *Esso Petroleum Co.* [1954] 2 QB 182 at 196) including, for example, keeping a disorderly house, selling food unfit for human consumption, throwing fireworks in the street and even (in other jurisdictions at least) running a badly organised pop festival (see *Attorney-General for Ontario* v. *Orange Productions Ltd* (1971) 21 DLR (3d) 257).

The law of public nuisance developed against the backdrop of a legislature far less interventionist than we are accustomed to today, and its significance correspondingly declined as Parliament became more accustomed to dealing with specific public hazards by individual legislative action. It does not follow from this that public nuisance is now irrelevant (nor that this area of the law is incapable of further development) but simply that both existing and new public hazards are, these days, more likely to be dealt with specifically by parliamentary enactment rather than by the ingenuity of the common law.

In accordance with its underlying rationale in protecting the interests of the community, public nuisance is a crime for which the perpetrator may be prosecuted. If the criminal sanction proves inadequate, a civil action (to obtain an injunction requiring that the unlawful activity be terminated) may be brought by the Attorney-General or the local authority. However, in the absence of particular damage, individuals are not permitted to bring a civil claim in respect of such a nuisance, as that would open the door to a multiplicity of actions where, by definition, the harm caused has been suffered by the public in general.

Private nuisance

In contrast, private nuisance is a civil wrong (a tort) invariably enforced by individuals bringing a private action in the civil courts. Unlike its public law counterpart, private nuisance is not primarily concerned with promoting the wider interests of the community (cf. *Miller* v. *Jackson*, discussed below) but in balancing the rights of adjoining occupiers of land (although it might plausibly be argued that, in any society which recognises private rights in land, these two aims are not as dissimilar as they might at first appear). As Lord Wright noted in *Sedleigh-Denfield* v. *O'Callahan* [1940] AC 880 at 903: 'A balance has to be maintained between the right of the occupier to do what he likes with his own and the right of the neighbour not to be interfered with', for otherwise modern life would be impossible. If we simply banned all interference with neighbouring land, there would be little one could do with your own lest some extraneous noise or smell happened to waft from it. Similarly, to allow unlimited interference with neighbouring land would give you the right to make surrounding land effectively unusable because of the unlimited amount of disruption you would be at liberty to inflict. Balancing the rights of adjoining occupiers of land is capable of promoting the interests of the wider community by allowing all land within that society to be used effectively. It is then a matter of debate as to how this is to be achieved and as to which criteria are to be used in judging what is an effective use of the land, as we see below.

6.4.1.2.   The requirements of private nuisance

Private nuisance has been described as 'unlawful interference with a person's use or enjoyment of land, or some right over or in connection with it' (Scott LJ in *Read* v. *Lyons & Co. Ltd* [1945] KB 216 at 236). The interference normally comprises a continuous or recurrent activity or condition which may take one of three forms (cf. Gearty, 'The Place of Private Nuisance in a Modern Law of Torts'). You may interfere with your neighbour's land by causing or permitting something to encroach onto his land from your own, such as overhanging branches, tree roots or children repeatedly trespassing. Direct physical injury to the neighbouring land may also amount to a nuisance where it is continuous or repeated, for example when building works on your land cause subsidence to neighbouring properties or where the windows and tiles of a house are repeatedly broken by cricket balls emanating from the village cricket green. Finally, nuisance will also arise as a result of interference with the use or enjoyment of land (often referred to as the amenity of land), for example when noise or smoke emanating from a factory continuously or repeatedly wafts over a neighbouring property. This final variety of nuisance has been described recently by Lord Goff in *Hunter* v. *Canary Wharf* [1997] AC 655 at 692, as the 'typical' form and will be the one on which we concentrate below.

The point to note at the outset is that, while interference with land might constitute a nuisance, it does not in fact follow from this that an actionable nuisance exists in law. As we stated in the previous section, private nuisance is concerned with balancing the rights of adjoining occupiers of land, and, in attempting to achieve such equilibrium, the common law's primary guide is a test of reasonableness. The question to be determined is whether or not the interference in fact is one which it is unreasonable for either the perpetrator to create or the sufferer to bear. If it is unreasonable from *either* (or of course both) these perspectives, the interference will amount to an actionable nuisance and, conversely, only if the interference is reasonable when considered from *both* standpoints will no actionable nuisance arise, as demonstrated in *Christie* v. *Davey* (extracted at www.cambridge.org/propertylaw/).

6.4.1.3.   Private nuisance and private property

The function of private nuisance is to prevent unreasonable interference with private property rights in land. This is unproblematic when the nuisance complained of involves the conceptually clear categories of encroachment on or damage to the land. However, the position is potentially more complicated in respect of interference with use or enjoyment of land. This is because there is a wider class of persons who might legitimately claim to use and enjoy land; and, secondly, because 'use and enjoyment' is necessarily more amorphous than the physical aspects of land which underpin any claim involving encroachment or damage. We will deal with each complication in turn.

Who can sue?

Prior to the decision of the House of Lords in *Hunter* v. *Canary Wharf* [1997] AC 655, there was a groundswell of academic opinion suggesting that the right to sue in private nuisance should be extended beyond those with a proprietary interest in the land. A number of commentators had suggested that gratuitous and contractual licensees such as family members and lodgers (who might legitimately claim to use or enjoy the land although they have no proprietary interest in it) should have *locus standi* to sue in respect of interference to the land they occupy. (See, for example, J. Fleming, *The Law of Torts* (6th edn, 1983), who condemns the 'senseless discrimination' whereby non-interest holders in land are prevented from suing; and *Winfield and Jolowicz on Tort* (14th edn, 1994), pp. 419–20, and Markesinis and Deakin, *Tort Law* (3rd edn, 1994), pp. 434–5, both of whom suggested the right to sue should be extended to long-term lodgers.)

Such proposals have a fine pedigree with Jeremy Bentham, among others, having made similar pleas in the nineteenth century. Notwithstanding the eminence of many of its proponents, the argument is, in all its forms, fundamentally misconceived from both a theoretical and a practical perspective. A property right is, at its most fundamental, a right against the world in respect of some resource (in this case, land) and the tort of nuisance is one of the means by which interest holders in land are able to protect their interest. By definition, someone without an interest in the land does not have rights against the world in respect of that land (but cf. *Manchester Airport plc* v. *Dutton* [2001] 1 QB 133 considered in Notes and Questions 17.3 below). Giving them the right to sue in nuisance would, in effect, grant them such an interest for they would now have rights against the world (i.e. their right to sue anyone who committed an actionable nuisance in respect of the land) in respect of land in which they supposedly had no interest. This is plainly illogical. One either has an interest in the land or one does not. If you belong to the former category, the law provides a number of mechanisms by which you can protect your interest, while, if you are in the latter, you have, as far as the land is concerned, nothing to protect.

Those who have suggested otherwise have, in effect, been implicitly arguing that there are special classes of occupiers (such as spouses, children and long-term lodgers) who should be granted some form of property interest in the land they occupy. However, as the history of reform in this area will confirm (see section 9.2.2 below) the only sensible way of achieving such a goal is by specific legislative enactment creating new property interests in land focused on specific classes of occupier. To do otherwise risks creating an uncertain interest vested in an uncertain class of interest holders which, as we will see in Chapter 9, is the very antithesis of a property right.

Such criticisms are of more than purely theoretical significance. As we saw in Chapter 5, property rights are dangerous things because of their potential to bind the world. If I have a property right in a thing this has significance for everyone else. It is consequently crucial that the number of different interests in a thing be limited and that the existence of potential interest holders should be easily ascertainable. Widening the class of persons capable of suing in private nuisance would have had the effect of increasing the number of interest holders in land many of whom would have been difficult to locate in practice. The point is made graphically in the following extract from the judgment of Lord Goff in *Hunter* v. *Canary Wharf* [1997] AC 655, when, by a four-to-one majority, the House of Lords rejected the Court of Appeal's attempt to widen the class of persons capable of suing in private nuisance to include individuals who resided in a locality yet who had no proprietary interest in the land they occupied:

> For private nuisances of this kind, the primary remedy is in most cases an injunction, which is sought to bring the nuisance to an end, and in most cases should swiftly achieve that objective. The right to bring such proceedings is, as the law stands, ordinarily vested in the person who has exclusive possession of the land [i.e. some form of property interest in it]. He or she is the person who will sue, if it is necessary to do so. Moreover, he or she can, if thought appropriate, reach an agreement with the person creating the nuisance, either that it may continue for a certain period of time, possibly on the payment of a sum of money, or that it shall cease, again perhaps on certain terms ... If anybody who lived in the relevant property as a home had a right to sue, sensible arrangements such as these might in some cases no longer be practicable. Moreover, any such departure from the established law on this subject, such as that adopted by the Court of Appeal in the present case, faces the problem of defining the category of persons who would have the right to sue. The Court of Appeal adopted the not easily identifiable category of those who have a 'substantial link' with the land, regarding a person who occupied the premises 'as a home' as having a sufficient link for this purpose. But who is to be included in this category? It was plainly intended to

include husbands and wives, or partners, and their children, and even other relatives living with them. But is the category also to include the lodger upstairs, or the *au pair* girl or the resident nurse caring for an invalid who makes her home in the house while she works there? If the latter, it seems strange that the category should not extend to include places where people work as well as places where they live, where nuisances such as noise can be just as unpleasant or distracting ... This is, in my opinion, not an acceptable way in which to develop the law.

Given the weight of academic opinion ranged against such an approach, the decision in *Hunter* v. *Canary Wharf* has not met with universal acclaim (see, for example, Extract 6.6 below, from a later edition of Markesinis and Deakin, *Tort Law*). The environmental lobby in particular has criticised the decision as a conservative and regressive one which, in the words of Whiteman, 'Nuisance – The Environmental Tort?', p. 885, fails to 'reflect ... the changing nature of interests in relation to land ... [and] still reflects a world of proprietors whose pursuit of self-interest is regulated by public bodies (e.g. planning authorities) acting in the public interest'. Such criticism is misplaced. The anomalies and uncertainty that would be caused by expanding private nuisance in this way make such a development untenable. If the concerns of the environmental lobby are accepted, the best way forward lies either in reform of the law of public nuisance or in specific legislative enactments rather than in providing an indeterminate group of non-interest holders with an indeterminate interest.

What is protected?

In addition to settling the question as to who was entitled to sue in private nuisance, the House of Lords, in *Hunter* v. *Canary Wharf*, also considered the nature of 'use and enjoyment'. The case concerned the building of the Canary Wharf Tower in London's Docklands the unintended effect of which was to interfere with the television reception of a large number of residential homes in the vicinity of the newly constructed building. The residents consequently sought an injunction claiming that this constituted an interference with the 'use and enjoyment' of their land. Although capable of changing over time and determined to an extent by location, 'use and enjoyment' is primarily a question of law established by precedent. As we will consider in greater detail in Chapter 9, there is no general right to a view under English law. This might seem somewhat surprising, given how often people are influenced in their choice of home by its prospect. However, land use would be severely curtailed if neighbours had the right to complain about loss of view in respect of a planned building (or for that matter an existing one as it is no defence to a claim in nuisance that the interference was there first) and emphasises the point made earlier that establishing an actionable nuisance is a question of law and not fact.

In *Hunter* v. *Canary Wharf*, the House of Lords drew on this line of authority and, in reaffirming that the right to use and enjoy land does not include the right to an unobstructed view, applied it by analogy to interference to television reception. Put simply, the complainants had no property in the reflected light travelling towards their land (which is after all what is constituted by a view) and, by analogy, no property in similarly directed television signals. As a consequence, the court was not required to establish whether the interference was reasonable as it occurred in respect of something to which the residents had no right. However, towards the end of his judgment, Lord Cooke confused the issue by adding the following aside.

> In the light of the versatility of human malevolence and ingenuity, it is well to add [that] ... [t]he malicious erection of a structure for the purpose of interfering with television reception should be actionable in nuisance on the principle of such well known cases as *Christie* v. *Davey* and *Hollywood Silver Fox Farm* v. *Emmett*.

Christie v. *Davey* involved a dispute between two neighbours over noise in which both parties held an estate in the land with a corresponding right of use and enjoyment. The alleged nuisance thus occurred in respect of existing rights vested in both parties. The court's task was to establish whether or not the noise each neighbour generated was a reasonable or unreasonable interference with the use and enjoyment of the other's land and the motive of each side was consequently relevant. A similar point arose in *Hollywood Silver Fox Farm* v. *Emmet*, where there was a dispute between two landowners, one of whom bred silver foxes on his land. During the breeding season, the vixen is very sensitive to noise which can cause it to refuse to breed, miscarry or even eat its young. In the course of their dispute, the adjoining landowner caused a gun to be discharged on his farmland close to where the silver foxes were breeding for the sole purpose of causing such disruption. Again, both parties held estates in the land with a consequent right to use and enjoyment. As this was farmland, this would normally include the right to use the land for purposes associated with farming, including the breeding of animals and the use of shotguns. So, as in *Christie* v. *Davey*, the alleged nuisance occurred in respect of existing rights vested in the parties to the dispute and motive was again clearly relevant to the court's decision that the malicious discharge of the shotgun was an actionable nuisance.

While the neighbours in *Christie* v. *Davey*, *Hollywood Silver Fox Farm* v. *Emmett* and *Hunter* v. *Canary Wharf* all had the right to use and enjoy the land they possessed, use and enjoyment of land does not, in the opinion of the House of Lords at least, include the right to the unobstructed reception of television signals. Thus, *Hunter* v. *Canary Wharf* is substantively different from the two former cases, as the alleged nuisance was in respect of something to which the residents had no right and to which the motives of the person causing the interference would consequently be irrelevant. Contrary to the views of Lord Cooke, the case therefore has little in common with *Christie* v. *Davey* and *Hollywood Silver Fox Farm* v. *Emmett*, both of which involved interference with something in which the residents did have a right and to which the motives of the parties were clearly relevant in establishing whether or not the interference was reasonable.

As these were *obiter* comments, much removed from the facts of the case, it is perhaps not surprising that counsel in the case did not think it appropriate to cite the more apposite *Bradford Corp.* v. *Pickles* [1895] AC 587 either to their Lordships or in the lower courts. Such deficiencies are, of course, a product of the adversarial system where the judge is only expected to utilise the materials placed before him and where counsel are under pressure (both from their clients and, increasingly, from the courts) not to waste time (and therefore money) with arguments that do not directly address the issues in the case. *Obiter* comments consequently need to be viewed with caution as they may well have been made in ignorance of the relevant authorities. As you will see in Notes and Questions 6.8 below, *Bradford Corp.* v. *Pickles*, like *Hunter* v. *Canary Wharf*, involved a nuisance action in respect of something to which the claimant had no rights and, in consequence, the House of Lords unanimously rejected the claim.

6.4.1.4.   The allocation of entitlements

The conventional definition of private nuisance regards the tort as a passive mechanism used to protect private property rights in land. Such an approach, while superficially accurate, ignores the creative role played by nuisance in mapping out the extent of any particular interest in land. In *Christie* v. *Davey*, for example, before an injunction could be issued, the court was required to determine the extent of each party's right to make noise in the privacy of their own home. Similarly, the decision of the House of Lords in *Hunter* v. *Canary Wharf* is based upon a particular conception of the right to use and enjoy residential land which did not extend to granting landowners an interest in television signals yet to be received. The role of nuisance is consequently extremely important in fashioning particular interests in land and in articulating the extent of the particular rights that arise in any given situation. So how does the law allocate such entitlements?

The traditional criteria

As *Christie* v. *Davey* illustrates, the traditional way in which the law deals with nuisances concerning the use and enjoyment of land takes into account various criteria. Factors such as the motives of the parties, the purpose of the activity, its utility, its necessity, the locality in which it takes place, the extent of the disturbance (both in duration and in intensity) and its timing would all be generally relevant but not individually crucial to assessing whether an actionable nuisance of this kind exists (the position is different in respect of the other forms of nuisance: see *St Helen's Smelting Co.* v. *Tipping* (1865) 11 HL Cas 642). The law's primary guide in all of this is a test of reasonableness in which the courts seek to balance the rights of competing landowners. This involves an examination of the (supposed) cause of the interference and its degree and extent, coupled with an assessment of the fairness of the proposed solutions. Over time, this approach has built into a doctrine of precedent which develops incrementally, often by analogy as we saw in *Hunter* v. *Canary Wharf*.

The role of the market

Yet, as Ronald Coase asked some forty years ago (and Posner considers in Extract 6.7 below), is the traditional approach really necessary? Consider two neighbouring landowners, a farmer who grows crops and a rancher who rears cattle on two unfenced plots of land. As cattle are no respecters of legal boundaries, let us assume that, in the course of a year, they trample down £1,500 worth of crops in their frequent forays onto the neighbouring land. Let us further assume that the cost to the farmer of fencing his plot would be £500, while the cost to the rancher of doing so to his larger acreage would be £1,000. On whom should the law place the burden? If one approaches the problem from the traditional lawyer's position, it would seem to be the rancher. His cattle are the cause of the nuisance, and it would seem just that he should bear the cost of alleviating the nuisance by either compensating his neighbour for the £1,500 worth of trampled crops or for building a £1,000 fence. Faced with such a choice, one would expect the rancher to build the fence as it is the cheaper option. But there is another possibility, for the problem of the wandering cattle can equally be solved (as far as these two neighbours are concerned) by the farmer fencing his land. Yet this will cost him £500, and as long as the rancher is liable for the damage caused by the cattle the farmer has no incentive to do so. In contrast, the rancher has every incentive to persuade the farmer because he can alleviate the problem more cheaply than the rancher. The rancher will consequently offer the farmer an amount between £500 and £1,000 (say £750) to build a fence which will both save him money (£250) and reward the farmer (£250) for his efforts. Thus, despite the law placing the burden on the rancher, it is the farmer who, in this example, builds the fence.

What would have happened if the law had placed the burden on the farmer (rather than on the rancher) at the outset by not making the rancher liable for the damage caused by his cattle? In this case, faced with £1,500 worth of potential damage, the farmer would have built the fence for £500, so saving himself £1,000. There would be no opportunity to persuade the rancher to build the fence because it is cheaper for the farmer to do so. Thus, as Coase demonstrated, the farmer builds the fence irrespective of where the law places the initial burden. In the first instance, this is because the rancher pays him to do so, and, in the second, because it is cheaper than bearing the cost of damage to his crops.

Despite its simplicity, the analysis has profound implications for the law, as it appears to suggest that the initial allocation of rights is an irrelevance because the party who values the right the most will, as efficiency dictates, get it in the end; either because he had it from the outset or because he bought it from the person who did. If this is indeed the case, it prompts the question why do we as lawyers go to such trouble balancing out the rights of competing users of land when, no matter what we decide, the market will sort it out in the end. However, as Coase would be the first to point out, the reality is somewhat more complex due (at least in part) to what he described as 'transaction costs'. This is a term which Coase uses to describe all the possible impediments to bargaining (such as communication costs, absence of perfect knowledge, holdout, free-riders etc.) which combine to hinder the efficient allocation of the right (see further Chapter 2 above).

Transaction costs are an inevitable component of any bargaining process, and this has implications for how we initially allocate the right. In their absence, the market will, by definition (because we have defined transaction costs as all impediments to bargaining), assert itself and it would not matter in whom the right was initially vested. But in their presence the market is distorted, making the efficient allocation of the right more difficult and often impossible. From the standpoint of efficiency therefore, rather than toying with notions such as cause, degree and fairness, the court should allocate the right to the party who values it most, for in a perfect market (absent all transaction costs) he is the one who would eventually acquire it.

The role of public policy

The problem with the Coase analysis is that it only concerns itself with economic efficiency (by which the right is given to the person who values it most). However, as we noted in Chapter 2, and as Calabresi and Melamed argue in Extract 6.8 below, this is not the only criterion by which entitlements are set (would Coase agree?). There are also, what they term, *distributional preferences* and *other justice considerations* which need to be considered. By *distributional preferences*, they mean the decisions taken by a society in which resources are reallocated to achieve certain goals. These are infinite and varied but might, for example, include a progressive tax system to redistribute wealth, the provision of subsidised sporting facilities to promote a healthy lifestyle and planning controls to protect the environment. In each case, a perceived good is achieved by manipulating the rewards available. Under a progressive tax system, wealth is passed from richer to poorer, while subsidising sporting facilities transfers resources to those who engage in sport, and environmentally focused planning controls impose costs on those who engage in environmentally hazardous activities. Finally, by *other justice considerations*, Calabresi and Melamed are referring to criteria that have neither an economic or distributional rational but are based on notions of fairness and morality such as making those who cause the nuisance liable even where this achieves no distributional preference and is not economically efficient. To consider how these various criteria are reconciled requires an examination of the means by which entitlements are protected, and this is what we shall turn to next.

6.4.1.5.   The protection of entitlements

Our discussion has thus far concentrated on the substantive rights which might be allocated without considering how those rights, once assigned, should be protected. Yet, while this is an essentially second-order question, it is extremely important as the range of mechanisms by which an entitlement might be protected provides the law with the flexibility to reconcile a number of (often contradictory) aims. In their article, Calabresi and Melamed identified three basic means by which a right might be protected: property rules, liability rules and rules of inalienability.

Property rules

Under this analysis, an entitlement is protected by a *property rule* whenever A (the person with the right) has a free choice as to whether or not he will surrender his entitlement, as when I decide to sell you my car.

Liability rules

An entitlement is protected by a *liability rule* when A stands to lose it for an objectively determined amount, as when the court awards me damages for your negligence in damaging my car.

Rules of inalienability

Finally, an entitlement is protected by a *rule of inalienability* whenever A has a right which he cannot surrender, as when the law intervenes to strike down a purported sale of my car while I am incapacitated through drink or mental illness.

As Munzer has noted, while these rules are, in effect, an alternative to the Hohfeld–Honoré analysis considered in section 6.2 above, they can still be described by adopting Hohfeldian terminology:

> Statements in Calabresi and Melamed's terminology can be paraphrased in Hohfeld's language. If A's entitlement is protected by a property rule, then others have a disability (a no-power) in regard to obtaining the entitlement except at a price agreed to by A. If A's entitlement is protected by a liability rule, then others have a disability in regard to obtaining or reducing the value of the entitlement unless they discharge a duty to compensate A *ex post* by a collectively determined amount. If A's entitlement is protected by a rule of inalienability, A has a disability in regard to transferring the entitlement to others. (Munzer, 'Understanding Property', p. 27)

For philosophical discussion of the work of Calabresi and Melamed, see Coleman and Kraus, 'Rethinking the Theory of Legal Rights', pp. 1340–7.

The combination of rules

From the previous examples involving the car, it will be obvious that entitlements to most things are normally protected by a mixture of all three rules and this is equally true in the context of land use. Let us return to the example of the farmer and the rancher we discussed in section 6.4.1.4 above and the traditional lawyer's approach which fixed the rancher with liability for the damage done to the farmer's crops by the wandering cattle. The farmer's right not to have his crops trampled in the future is protected by a property rule. He can, if he wishes, give up the right, usually on payment of a suitable fee (as when the rancher paid him £750 to fence off his land). In the absence of such an agreement, the farmer can assert his right by suing the rancher and obtaining an injunction requiring the rancher to restrain his cattle from trespassing onto the farmer's land and doing further damage. As for the already trampled crops, the farmer's entitlement is protected by a liability rule in which the court must objectively determine the price to be paid for damage already done to the crops by fixing the level of damages payable to the farmer.

The law of nuisance consequently protects entitlements by a combination of property rules and liability rules. It achieves the former in the guise of injunctions designed to prevent future infringements and the latter by means of awarding damages usually in respect of past transgressions. If we develop the example further, we can also appreciate how a rule of inalienability may be used to protect entitlements in the land use context. Let us assume that, in the wake of concerns involving genetically modified crops, the local planning authority imposes restrictions under which the farmer is prevented from growing such crops within one mile of any neighbouring land. In such a set of circumstances, the rancher would have an entitlement not to have genetically modified crops grown within one mile of his land which he could neither sell (at a subjectively determined price) nor lose (at an objectively determined level) and which would therefore be protected by a rule of inalienability.

The reason we employ these three means of protection is because the setting of entitlements represents a compromise and trade-off between economic efficiency, distributional preferences and other justice considerations. As you will recall, despite it being the less efficient solution, a property rule was adopted which gave the farmer an entitlement not to have crops trampled in the interests of justice because it seemed fair that the rancher should pay for damage caused by his cattle. However, in respect of past damage, a liability rule was adopted as the most efficient means of allowing the rancher to carry on his trade. Otherwise, it would be virtually impossible to engage in any form of human activity because, in a system in which everyone's entitlement not to suffer tortious damage was protected by a property rule, anyone engaged in a potentially tortious act would first have to negotiate to buy the entitlement from every potential victim. Finally, the distributional preference of protecting the environment is achieved by our fictional rule of inalienability which restrains the growing of genetically modified crops within one mile of neighbouring land and imposes the additional costs that arise from such a rule on the party engaged in what is deemed to be the environmentally hazardous activity.

A vivid example of how a variety of preferences might be achieved by using the various rules identified by Calabresi and Melamed is provided by *Miller* v. *Jackson* [1977] QB 966 (extracted at www.cambridge.org/propertylaw/). The case involved a dispute between the users of a village cricket green, and the Millers, who owned a neighbouring house and who, in response to the regular intrusion of cricket balls into their garden, issued a writ alleging nuisance. In the Court of Appeal, three judgments were delivered, each of which reveal very different approaches to the problem. Lane LJ, while regretting his decision, held that the regular intrusion of cricket balls did constitute a nuisance against which an injunction preventing future occurrence should be ordered. In contrast, Lord Denning, placing great emphasis on the importance of cricket to the English way of life and the fact that the cricket green was established before the house was built, stated that no actionable nuisance arose. Finally, Cumming-Bruce LJ, in a pivotal judgment, agreed with Lane LJ that an actionable nuisance arose but held that, rather than an injunction, damages to the order of £400 for past and future nuisances should be payable. Faced with a majority who held that a nuisance had arisen, Lord Denning reluctantly (audaciously?) joined forces with Cumming-Bruce LJ in ordering an award of damages for past and future occurrences as the best means of allowing the cricket to continue.

It might, at this stage, be helpful to consider the three judgments in *Miller* v. *Jackson* by reference to the Calabresi and Melamed analysis. In holding that an injunction should be granted, Lane LJ was protecting the Miller's right not to be disturbed by cricket balls with a property rule. According to his judgment, they had an entitlement which it was up to them to enforce and which they were at liberty to surrender at a price determined only by them. In contrast, Lord Denning, in holding that no actionable nuisance arose, was seeking to protect the cricketers' entitlement to play cricket by means of a property rule which only they could surrender at a price determined by them. The judgment of Cumming-Bruce LJ, in accordance with that of Lane LJ, held that an actionable nuisance arose. However, in deciding that an injunction was not appropriate and that damages should be paid in respect of past and future nuisance, he sought to protect the Miller's entitlement by means of a liability rule in which the right was lost for an objectively determined sum. Finally, in his *obiter* comments expressing surprise that the planning authorities allowed the house to be built so close to the cricket ground, Lord Denning was suggesting that the cricketers' entitlement to play cricket should have been protected by a rule of inalienability. This would have given them the right not to have residential accommodation (which would interfere with their cricket) built within a certain distance of the cricket green which they had no power to surrender (as they play no direct role in the granting of planning permission which might still be refused if they stopped playing cricket). This analysis can be reduced to the tabular representation shown in Table 6.1.

You will notice that there are two empty categories in the table, labelled 'X' and 'Rule 4'. X is unproblematic and would have arisen if legislation had, for example, been passed banning the playing of cricket within a certain distance of land designated as suitable for residential accommodation. In such circumstances, the Millers' would have had an entitlement to be free from cricket balls which they would have had no power to surrender. In contrast, Rule 4, as it is labelled in the article by Calabresi and Melamed, is a remedy not provided for under English law which they submit has the potential to play a useful role in the allocation of entitlements (cf. the American case of *Spur Industries* v. *Webb*, 404 P 2d 700 (1972)).

Under Rule 4, the party causing the disturbance has an entitlement to do so protected by a liability rule whereby the right might be lost for an objectively determined amount. In their article, Calabresi and Melamed argue that, in certain circumstances, this might be the most appropriate remedy and that the law of

Table 6.1

	Millers' entitled to be free from cricket balls	Cricketers' entitled to play cricket
Property rule	Rule 1 Lane LJ's judgment	Rule 3 Lord Denning's judgment
Liability rule	Rule 2 Cuming-Bruce LJ's judgment	Rule 4
Rule of inalienability	X	Lord Denning's *obiter* comments in respect of planning permission

nuisance suffers because there is no cause of action by which this can be achieved. For example, let us assume that in distributing entitlements we are seeking to reconcile economic efficiency in the allocation of land with the distributional goal of promoting cricket within the community. Let us consider how successful each of the four nuisance rules identified by Calabresi and Melamed are in the peculiar circumstances of *Miller* v. *Jackson* on the assumption that:

1 land used for housing is more valuable than land used for cricket greens;
2 property developers are richer than village cricketers;
3 village cricketers would charge far more to give up a right to play cricket than they could afford to pay to acquire such an entitlement in the first place (see note 6 of Notes and Questions 6.5); and
4 residential accommodation and cricket on adjoining land is incompatible because of the level of disturbance caused by the cricket.

The results are set out in Table 6.2. It is perhaps helpful to offer a number of explanations and caveats at this point. You will have noticed that damages are payable under Rules 2 and 4; however, the difference is that, under Rule 2, damages are to be paid by the cricketers rather than the property developer and consequently no transfer of resources occurs, as in Rule 4, which might encourage the cricketers to relocate. Under Rule 3, where the entitlement to disturb is protected by a property rule, the property developers might pay a sufficiently high sum to persuade the cricketers to do this but, because of factors such as tradition and the assumption we made at point 3 above, the cricketers might set an unrealistically high price to surrender their entitlement or refuse to do so at any cost. Only under Rule 4 is there the potential to use the land efficiently by forcing the cricketers to accept a sum from the property developers adequate to allow them to relocate which consequently achieves the twin aims of promoting the efficient use of land while encouraging the playing of cricket.

Finally, it is important to note the limits of the above example. It is not, in any sense seeking to prove that Rule 4 is always the best solution, nor even that it usually

Table 6.2

	Economic efficiency (housing more valuable than cricket)	Distributional preference (promoting cricket)
Rule 1 Property rule used to protect right of residential occupiers not to be disturbed by cricket	Land can be used for residential purposes	Adjoining land cannot be used for cricket
Rule 2 Liability rule used to protect right of residential occupiers not to be disturbed by cricket such that damages payable are: a. low b. high	a. Land cannot be used for residential purposes b. Land can be used for residential purposes	a. Adjoining land can be used for cricket b. Adjoining land cannot be used for cricket
Rule 3 Property rule used to protect right of cricketers to cause disturbance	Land cannot be used for residential purposes	Adjoining land can be used for cricket
Rule 4 Liability rule used to protect right of cricketers to cause disturbance	Provided damages are set at the appropriate level, land can be used for residential purposes	Cricketers paid a suitable amount to relocate and continue playing cricket somewhere else

is, but simply that there might be a set of circumstances where it offers the most appropriate means of allocating entitlements. In the absence of Rule 4 therefore, the law of nuisance arguably provides an incomplete means of allocating entitlements.

Notes and Questions 6.5

Consider the following notes and questions both before and after reading *Christie* v. *Davey* [1893] 1 Ch 316 at 326–9 and the materials highlighted below (either in full or as extracted at www.cambridge.org/propertylaw/).

1 Would an injunction have been issued against Davey if, rather than being motivated by malice, he was simply a performance artist rehearsing his act?

2 What would have been the court's attitude if Davey had been a somewhat more timorous person whose only malicious act consisted of him occasionally drumming his fingers on the wall?

3 Is it relevant that the case took place in the nineteenth century when, in the absence of radio and television, musical evenings at home were an established part of suburban life? Would a court today be more or less tolerant of the degree of noise created by the Christies?

4 Were both sides in the case entitled to play instruments continuously from 9.00 am to 11.00 pm every day?

5 How would the court have decided the case if the Christies had chosen to practise by repeatedly playing a score which they knew Davey disliked?

6 Can you think of an example of a nuisance which it would not be unreasonable for the victim to bear made actionable by the unreasonableness of the perpetrator? (See *Hollywood Silver Fox Farm* v. *Emmett* [1936] 2 KB 468.)

7 What issues did the court consider in assessing whether either party had acted unreasonably? Was any single issue critical?

Extract 6.6   Markesinis and Deakin, *Tort Law* (5th edn, Oxford: Clarendon Press, 2003), pp. 472–3

By reconfirming the validity of the ... restrictive interpretation of the list of possible claimants, the majority decision of the House of Lords in *Hunter* v. *Canary Wharf Ltd* has gone against a number of Commonwealth judgments as well as a bold attempt by a majority of our own Court of Appeal to liberate our law from its past. None the less, the majority decisions embody a rigorous analysis of the existing case law (as well as the history of the tort) and in this sense provide interesting (for students if not for practitioner) insights into how differing judicial philosophies and techniques can affect a dispute.

The examination – necessarily brief – of this aspect of this case must start by quoting an interesting observation by Lord Cooke. The learned Lord thus stressed, it is submitted correctly, that:

[I]n logic more than one answer can be given [to this problem]. Logically, it is possible to say that the right to sue for interference with the amenities of a home should be confined to those with proprietary interests ... No less logically the right can be accorded to all who live in the home. *Which test should be adopted ... is a question of the policy of the law. It is a question not capable of being answered by analysis alone. All that analysis can do is to explore the alternatives ...* The reasons why I prefer the alternative [to the position adopted by the majority] ... is that it gives better effect to widespread conceptions concerning the house and family. ([1997] 2 WLR 684 at 719 (emphasis added))

Lord Cooke would thus have been willing to respond to the appeal of textbook writers to attempt 'a degree of modernisation' in the law 'while freeing it from undue reliance upon the technicalities of land law'. One suspects that such an approach to case law development would have appealed to judges such as Lord Denning or pioneering jurists such as Professor John Fleming of the Berkeley Law School. But it was doomed to failure in the current climate that prevails in our highest court where, for instance, Lord Hoffmann boldly stated that 'the development of the common law should be rational and coherent. It should not distort its principles and create anomalies merely as an expedient to fill a gap.' Once this is accepted as the cornerstone of the philosophy of the majority, the resolution of the dispute acquires a certain legalistic tone. Thus the question implicitly becomes what technical arguments can be found in favour of the *status quo*. Between them, the majority had little difficulty finding three; and one cannot deny their force (once one accepts the basic premise that one is not free to break free from the existing technicalities of land law). Thus, Lord Goff argued that the current state of the law could claim 'certainty' and 'efficiency' on its side. To these two points one must add Lord Hoffmann's analysis of Lord Westbury's views ... [f]or once one accepts the view that in his *St Helen's* judgment Lord Westbury did not intend to create two separate torts (one dealing with material interference and one with interference with enjoyment), it follows logically and inexorably that only those with an interest in land can sue. The decision in *Hunter* thus does more than tackle, for the time being at least, a particular problem area of the law in nuisance: it gives us some revealing insights into the views our judges have about the interplay of interpretation and development of the law.

Notes and Questions 6.6

1 Is it correct to describe arguments based on 'efficiency' or 'certainty' as technical?

2 Reread the quote from Lord Goff (section 6.4.1.3 above). Does it have 'a certain legalistic tone' or is it based on a practical assessment of the issues?

3 Should the 'development of the common law ... be rational and coherent' or is it right to 'create anomalies ... to fill a gap'?

4 Was the decision of the majority based upon 'the existing technicalities of land law' or an appreciation of the practical difficulties that would otherwise ensue?

5 Would the approach of Lord Cooke have turned nuisance into a tort against persons rather than land? Would such a reclassification confront the problems identified by Lord Goff?

6 Does the reaction to the decision also 'give us some revealing insights into the views' of academics about the importance of both principle and practicalities?

Notes and Questions 6.7

Consider the following notes and questions both before and after reading *Hunter* v. *Canary Wharf* [1997] AC 655 (either in full or as extracted at www.cambridge.org/propertylaw/).

1 What difference, if any, would it have made if the interference to television reception was made by something emanating from Canary Wharf?

2 Why might the residents have had rights in respect of television signals which had reached their land if they did not have rights in respect of signals on the way to their land?

3 Should the courts have paid any regard to the motive for building Canary Wharf?

4 Do you agree with Lord Lloyd's view that *Bank of New Zealand* v. *Greenwood* [1984] 1 NZLR 525 is 'not ... easy to reconcile with' the requirement that there can be 'no legal redress in nuisance' where 'there is nothing emanating from the defendant's land'?

5 In the context of a modern city, what interests should the law of nuisance seek to reconcile?

6 Are the interests of the community of any relevance in determining whether an actionable nuisance has arisen?

Notes and Questions 6.8

Consider the following notes and questions both before and after reading *Bradford Corp.* v. *Pickles* [1895] AC 587 (either in full or as extracted at www.cambridge.org/propertylaw/).

1 Why do you think water running in defined channels was treated differently from percolating water?

2 Why did the status of percolating water change once it was appropriated?

3 Would Bradford Corporation have succeeded if Pickles' extraction of the percolating water had caused physical damage to their land such as subsidence? (See *Stephens* v. *Anglian Water Authority* [1987] 1 WLR 1381.)

4 Why, do you think, are all water supplies, whether percolating or channelled, now generally subject to a statutory-based licensing system (see question 1 in Notes and Questions 3.1 above)?

5 Can you think of any other forms of unowned property which might enter onto your land (see section 2.2.2.1 above)? What rules should or do apply to it before and after appropriation (see the discussion of wild animals in section 4.4 above)?

6 Does your neighbour have any claim against you if you appropriate such property when it is on (i) your land (ii) his land (iii) someone else's land and (iv) common land?

7 How might Locke have justified the decision in the case, and would such an analysis confirm the answers you reached in the above question?

Extract 6.7   Richard A. Posner, *Economic Analysis of Law* (6th edn, New York, Aspen Publishers, 2002), pp. 42–8

[P]roperty rights aren't really exclusive, in the sense of giving the owner of a resource the absolute right to do with it what he will and exclude the whole world from any participation or say in the use of the resource. Absolute rights would conflict. If a railroad is to enjoy the exclusive use of its right of way, it must be permitted to emit engine sparks without legal limitation. The value of its property will be impaired otherwise. But if it is permitted to do that, the value of adjacent farmland will be reduced because of the fire hazard from the sparks. Is the emission of sparks an incident of the railroad's property right (i.e. part of his bundle of rights) or an invasion of the farmer's property right (or bundle)?

Before answering this question, we must ask whether anything turns on the answer, which in turn will require us to consider . . . the Coase Theorem . . . Suppose that the right to emit sparks, by enabling the railroad to dispense with costly spark-arresting equipment, would increase the value of the railroad's right of way by $100 but reduce the value of the farm by $50, by preventing the farmer from growing crops close to the tracks. If the farmer has a legal right to be free from engine sparks, the railroad will offer to pay, and the farmer will accept, compensation for the surrender of his right; since the right to prevent spark emissions is worth only $50 to the farmer but imposes costs of $100 on the railroad, a sale of the farmer's right at any price between $50 and $100 will make both parties better off. If instead of the farmer's having a right to be free from sparks the railroad has a right to emit sparks, no transaction will occur. The farmer will not pay more than $50 for the railroad's right and the railroad will not accept less than $100. Thus, whichever way the legal right is assigned initially, the result is the same: the railroad emits sparks and the farmer moves his crops.

The principle is not affected by reversing the numbers. Assume that the right to emit sparks would increase the value of the railroad's property by only $50 but would reduce the value of the farmer's property by $100. If the railroad has a right to emit sparks, the farmer will offer to pay and the railroad will accept some price between $50 and $100 for the surrender of the railroad's right. If instead the farmer has a right to be free from emissions, there will be no transaction, since the farmer will insist on a minimum payment of $100 while the railroad will pay no more than $50. So, as Coase showed, whatever the relative values of the competing uses, the initial assignment of legal rights will not determine which use ultimately prevails . . .

. . . It does not follow, however, that the initial assignment of rights is completely immaterial from an efficiency standpoint. Since transactions are not costless, efficiency is promoted by assigning the legal right to the party who would buy it – the railroad in our first hypothetical situation and the farmer in the second – if it were assigned initially to the other party. Moreover, as we shall see, the cost of transacting is sometimes so high relative to the value of the transaction as to make transacting uneconomical. In such a case, the initial assignment of rights is final.

Unfortunately, assigning the property right to the party to whom it is more valuable is incomplete as an economic solution. It ignores the costs of administering the property rights system, which might be lower under a simpler criterion for assigning rights; and it is difficult to apply in practice. The engine spark example was grossly oversimplified in that it permitted only two property right assignments, a right to emit sparks and a right to be free from sparks. If administrative (mainly information) costs are disregarded, the combined value of the farmer's and the railroad's property might be maximized by a more complex definition of property rights, such as one that permitted the farmer to grow one kind of crop but not another, to plant nothing within 200 feet of the tracks, and to have no wooden buildings within 250 feet of the tracks, while permitting the railroad to emit sparks only up to a specified level. The possible combinations are endless, and it is unrealistic to expect courts to discover the optimum one – and uneconomical to make them search too hard for it! But in most cases, and without excessive cost, they may be able to approximate the optimum definition of property rights, and these approximations may guide resource use more efficiently than would an economically random assignment of property rights.

Some examples may help to clarify this fundamental point. Under English common law, a landowner who built in such a way as to so block his neighbor's window that the neighbor would need artificial light to be able to read in the half of the room nearest the window was considered to have infringed the neighbor's property rights, provided that the neighbor had had unobstructed access to light for 20 years (why this qualification?). Consider the consequences if the property right had instead been given to the building party. Ordinarily, the cost to the person whose windows were blocked would exceed the cost to the other person of setting back his wall slightly (all that would be necessary, given how limited the right was), so the former would buy the right. The assignment of the right to him in the first instance avoids the transaction and its attendant costs. But the courts did not extend the rule to protect distant views. If A had a house on a hill with a beautiful prospect, and B built a house that ruined the prospect, A could not claim an invasion of his property rights even if the value of his property had fallen. Here the presumption of relative values is reversed. A house with a view commands a large land area. The values that would be created by developing such an area are likely to exceed the loss of value to the one landowner whose view is impaired ...

... The economic theory of property rights implies that rights will be redefined from time to time as the relative values of different uses of land change. The fencing of cattle again provides an illustration. Suppose cattle wander off the land where they are grazing and onto a neighbor's land, where they damage his crops. Should the cost be borne by the neighbor on the theory that he should have fenced the cattle out, or by the owner of the cattle on the theory that he should have fenced them in? The answer would seem to depend (and a comparison of rules over time and between different common law jurisdictions suggests it does depend) on the ratio of cattle to crops. If there are more cattle than crops (more precisely, if more land is devoted to grazing than to crop growing), it will be cheaper for the farmers to fence their land than for the ranchers to fence theirs, and the law will place the burden of fencing on the farmers; but the burden will be reversed when the ratio of land uses reverses.

Are you concerned that continually redefining property rights to secure efficiency under changing conditions might create instability and discourage investment? X buys a farm long before there is a railroad in his area. The price he pays is not discounted to reflect future crop damage from sparks, because the construction of a railroad line is not foreseen. But eventually a line is built and is near enough to X's farm to inflict spark damage on his crops. He sues the railroad but the court holds that the level of spark emission is reasonable because it would be more costly for the railroad than for the farmer to prevent the crop loss. With property values thus exposed to uncompensated depreciation by unforeseen changes in neighboring land uses, the incentive to invest in farming will be reduced. But ... a reduced level of investment in farming may be an efficient adjustment to the possibility that some day the highest value of the farmer's land may be as a dumping ground for railroad sparks.

A more serious problem when property rights are subject to being redefined as values change is that, for people who are averse to risk, uncertainty is a source of disutility. Whether any of the methods of eliminating the risks created by uncertainty would be feasible in the situation under discussion may be doubted. However, the amount and consequences of the uncertainty are easily exaggerated. If a harmful neighboring land use is foreseen at the time of sale, the price of land will be reduced, accordingly, and the buyer will have no disappointed expectations. If the use is unforeseen chances are that it lies well in the future, and a cost to be incurred in the far future will (unless astronomical) have little impact on present decisions ... The alternative – always to assign the property right to the prior of two conflicting land uses – would be highly inefficient, for the latter use will often be the more valuable.

Notes and Questions 6.9

1   From the standpoint of efficiency who should bear the cost of damage to the crops: the farmer or the rancher?

2   Why might it be argued that the answer to question 1 is counter-intuitive? What does that tell you about your intuition?

3   Should the court only concern itself with the efficient allocation of the right?

4   Why, in reality, is it impossible to expect the court to be able to determine the most efficient solution?

5   What effect, if any, will the initial allocation of the right have on the relative wealth of the farmer and the rancher? What are the efficiency implications of your answer?

6 Studies have shown that people often demand more to give up a right than they would be willing to pay to acquire the same right. What implications does this have for the Coase analysis?

7 Do social norms and customs have any bearing on (i) transaction costs and (ii) the Coase analysis?

Extract 6.8   Guido Calabresi and A. Douglas Melamed, 'Property Rules, Liability Rules and Inalienability: One View of the Cathedral' (1972) 85 *Harvard Law Review* 1089

The first issue which must be faced by any legal system is one we call the problem of 'entitlement'. Whenever a state is presented with the conflicting interests of two or more people, or two or more groups of people, it must decide which side to favor. Absent such a decision, access to goods, services, and life itself will be decided on the basis of 'might makes right' – whoever is stronger or shrewder will win. Hence the fundamental thing that law does is to decide which of the conflicting parties will be entitled to prevail. The entitlement to make noise versus the entitlement to have silence, the entitlement to pollute versus the entitlement to breathe clean air, the entitlement to have children versus the entitlement to forbid them – these are the first order of legal decisions.

Having made its initial choice, society must enforce that choice. Simply setting the entitlement does not avoid the problem of 'might makes right'; a minimum of state intervention is always necessary. Our conventional notions make this easy to comprehend with respect to private property. If Taney owns a cabbage patch and Marshall, who is bigger, wants a cabbage, he will get it unless the state intervenes. But it is not so obvious that the state must also intervene if it chooses the opposite entitlement, communal property. If large Marshall has grown some communal cabbages and chooses to deny them to small Taney, it will take state action to enforce Taney's entitlement to the communal cabbages. The same symmetry applies with respect to bodily integrity. Consider the plight of the unwilling ninety-eight-pound weakling in a state which nominally entitles him to bodily integrity but will not intervene to enforce the entitlement against a lustful Juno. Consider then the plight – absent state intervention – of the ninety-eight-pounder who desires an unwilling Juno in a state which nominally entitles everyone to use everyone else's body. The need for intervention applies in a slightly more complicated way to injuries. When a loss is left where it falls in an auto accident, it is not because God so ordained it. Rather it is because the state has granted the injurer an entitlement to be free of liability and will intervene to prevent the victim's friends, if they are stronger, from taking compensation from the injurer. The loss is shifted in other cases because the state has granted an entitlement to compensation and will intervene to prevent the stronger injurer from rebuffing the victim's requests for compensation.

The state not only has to decide whom to entitle, but it must also simultaneously make a series of equally difficult second order decisions. These decisions go to the manner in which entitlements are protected and to whether an individual is allowed to sell or trade the entitlement. In any given dispute, for example, the state must decide not only which side wins but also the kind of protection to grant. It is with the latter decisions, decisions which shape the subsequent relationship between the winner and the loser, that this article is primarily concerned. We shall consider three types of entitlements – entitlements protected by property rules, entitlements protected by liability rules, and inalienable entitlements. The categories are not, of course, absolutely distinct; but the categorization is useful since it reveals some of the reasons which lead us to protect certain entitlements in certain ways.

An entitlement is protected by a property rule to the extent that someone who wishes to remove the entitlement from its holder must buy it from him in a voluntary transaction in which the value of the entitlement is agreed upon by the seller. It is the form of entitlement which gives rise to the least amount of state intervention: once the original entitlement is decided upon, the state does not try to decide its value. It lets each of the parties say how much the entitlement is worth to him, and gives the seller a veto if the buyer does not offer enough. Property rules involve a collective decision as to who is to be given an initial entitlement but not as to the value of the entitlement.

Whenever someone may destroy the initial entitlement if he is willing to pay an objectively determined value for it, an entitlement is protected by a liability rule. This value may be what it is thought the original holder of the entitlement would have sold it for. But the holder's complaint that he would have demanded more will not avail him once the objectively determined value is set. Obviously, liability rules involve an additional stage of state intervention: not only are entitlements protected, but their transfer or destruction is allowed on the basis of a value determined by some organ of the state rather than by the parties themselves.

An entitlement is inalienable to the extent that its transfer is not permitted between a willing buyer and a willing seller. The state intervenes not only to determine who is initially entitled and to determine the compensation that must be paid if the entitlement is taken or destroyed, but also to forbid its sale under some or all circumstances. Inalienability rules are thus quite different from property and liability rules. Unlike those rules, rules of inalienability not only 'protect' the entitlement; they may also be viewed as limited or regulating the grant of the entitlement itself.

It should be clear that most entitlements to most goods are mixed. Taney's house may be protected by a property rule in situations where Marshall wishes to purchase it, by a liability rule where the government decides to take it by [compulsory purchase], and by a rule of inalienability in situations where Taney is drunk or incompetent. This article will explore two primary questions: (1) In what circumstances should we grant a particular entitlement? and (2) In what circumstances should we decide to protect that entitlement by using a property, liability, or inalienability rule?

I. THE SETTING OF ENTITLEMENTS

What are the reasons for deciding to entitle people to pollute or to entitle people to forbid pollution, to have children freely or to limit procreation, to own property or to share property? They can be grouped under three headings: economic efficiency, distributional preferences, and other justice considerations ...

II. RULES FOR PROTECTING AND REGULATING ENTITLEMENTS

Whenever society chooses an initial entitlement it must also determine whether to protect the entitlement by property rules, by liability rules, or by rules of inalienability. In our framework, much of what is generally called private property can be viewed as an entitlement which is protected by a property rule. No one can take the entitlement to private property from the holder unless the holder sells it willingly and at the price at which he subjectively values the property. Yet a nuisance with sufficient public utility to avoid injunction has, in effect, the right to take property with compensation. In such a circumstance the entitlement to the property is protected only by what we call a liability rule: an external, objective standard of value is used to facilitate the transfer of the entitlement from the holder to the nuisance. Finally, in some instances we will not allow the sale of the property at all, that is, we will occasionally make the entitlement inalienable.

This section will consider the circumstances in which society will employ these three rules to solve situations of conflict. Because the property rule and the liability rule are closely related and depend for their application on the shortcomings of each other, we treat them together. We discuss inalienability separately.

A. Property and liability rules

Why cannot a society simply decide on the basis of the already mentioned criteria who should receive any given entitlement, and then let its transfer occur only through a voluntary negotiation? Why, in other words, cannot society limit itself to the property rule? To do this it would need only to protect and enforce the initial entitlements from all attacks, perhaps through criminal sanctions, and to enforce voluntary contracts for their transfer. Why do we need liability rules at all?

In terms of economic efficiency the reason is easy enough to see. Often the cost of establishing the value of an initial entitlement by negotiation is so great that, even though a transfer of the entitlement would benefit all concerned, such a transfer will not occur. If a collective determination of the value were available instead, the beneficial transfer would quickly come about.

[Compulsory purchase] is a good example. A park where Guidacres, a tract of land owned by 1,000 owners in 1,000 parcels, now sits would, let us assume, benefit a neighboring town enough so that the 100,000 citizens of the town would each be willing to pay an average of $100 to have it. The park is Pareto-desirable if the owners of the tracts of land in Guidacres actually value their entitlements at less than $10,000,000 or an average of $10,000 a tract. Let us assume that in fact the parcels are all the same and all the owners value them at $8,000. On this assumption, the park is, in economic efficiency terms, desirable – in values foregone it costs $8,000,000 and is worth $10,000,000 to the buyers. And yet it may well not be established. If enough of the owners hold out for more than $10,000 in order to get a share of the $2,000,000 that they guess the buyers are willing to pay over the value which the sellers in actuality attach, the price demanded will be more than $10,000,000 and no park will result. The sellers have an incentive to hide their true valuation and the market will not succeed in establishing it.

An equally valid example could be made on the buying side. Suppose the sellers of Guidacres have agreed to a sales price of $8,000,000 (they are all relatives and at a family banquet decided that trying to hold out would leave them all losers). It does not follow that the buyers can raise that much even though each of 100,000 citizens *in fact* values the park at $100. Some citizens may try to free-load and say the park is only worth $50 or even nothing to them, hoping that enough others will admit to a higher desire and make up the $8,000,000 price. Again, there is no reason to believe that a market, a decentralized system of valuing, will cause people to express their true valuations and hence yield results which all would *in fact* agree are desirable.

Whenever this is the case an argument can readily be made for moving from a property rule to a liability rule. If society can remove from the market the valuation of each tract of land, decide the value collectively, and impose it, then the holdout problem is gone. Similarly, if society can value collectively each individual citizen's desire to have a park and charge him a 'benefits' tax based upon it, the free-loader problem is gone. If the sum of the taxes is greater than the sum of the compensation awards, the park will result.

Of course, one can conceive of situations where it might be cheap to exclude all the free-loaders from the park, or to ration the park's use in accordance with original willingness to pay. In such cases, the incentive to free-load might be eliminated. But such exclusions, even if possible, are usually not cheap. And the same may be the case for the market methods which might avoid the holdout problem on the seller side.

Moreover, even if holdout and free-loader problems can be met feasibly by the market, an argument may remain for employing a liability rule. Assume that, in our hypothetical, free-loaders can be excluded at the cost of $1,000,000 and that all owners of tracts in Guidacres can be convinced, by the use of $500,000 worth of advertising and cocktail parties, that a sale will only occur if they reveal their true land valuations. Since $8,000,000 plus $1,500,000 is less than $10,000,000, the park will be established. But if collective valuation of the tracts and of the benefits of the prospective park would have cost less than $1,500,000, it would have been inefficient to establish the park through the market – a market which was not worth having would have been paid for.

Of course, the problems with liability rules are equally real. We cannot be at all sure that landowner Taney is lying or holding out when he says his land is worth $12,000 to him. The fact that several neighbors sold identical tracts for $10,000 does not help us very much; Taney may be sentimentally attached to his land. As a result, [compulsory purchase] may grossly undervalue what Taney would actually sell for, even if it sought to give him his true valuation of his tract. In practice, it is so hard to determine Taney's true valuation that [compulsory purchase] simply gives him what the land is worth 'objectively', in the full knowledge that this may result in over or under compensation. The same is true on the buyer side. 'Benefits' taxes rarely attempt, let alone succeed, in gauging the individual citizen's relative desire for the alleged benefit. They are justified because, even if they do not accurately measure each individual's desire for the benefit, the market alternative seems worse. For example, fifty different households may place different values on a new sidewalk that is to abut all the properties. Nevertheless, because it is too difficult, even if possible, to gauge each household's valuation, we usually tax each household an equal amount.

The example of [compulsory purchase] is simply one of numerous instances in which society uses liability rules. Accidents is another. If we were to give victims a property entitlement not to be accidentally injured we would have to require all who engage in activities that may injure individuals to negotiate with them before an accident, and to buy the right to knock off an arm or a leg. Such pre-accident negotiations would be extremely expensive, often prohibitively so. To require them would thus preclude many activities that might, in fact, be worth having. And, after an accident, the loser of the arm or leg can always very plausibly deny that he would have sold it at the price the buyer would have offered. Indeed, where negotiations after an accident do occur – for instance pretrial settlements – it is largely because the alternative is the collective valuation of the damages.

It is not our object here to outline all the theoretical, let alone the practical, situations where markets may be too expensive or fail and where collective valuations seem more desirable. Economic literature has many times surrounded the issue if it has not always zeroed in on it in ways intelligible to lawyers. It is enough for our purposes to note that a very common reason, perhaps the most common one, for employing a liability rule rather than a property rule to protect an entitlement is that market valuation of the entitlement is deemed inefficient, that is, it is either unavailable or too expensive compared to a collective valuation.

We should also recognize that efficiency is not the sole ground for employing liability rules rather than property rules. Just as the initial entitlement is often decided upon for distributional reasons, so too the choice of a liability rule is often made because it facilitates a combination of efficiency and distributive results which would be difficult to achieve under a property rule. As we shall see in the pollution context, use of a liability rule may allow us to accomplish a measure of redistribution that could only be attained at a prohibitive sacrifice of efficiency if we employed a corresponding property rule.

More often, once a liability rule is decided upon, perhaps for efficiency reasons, it is then employed to favor distributive goals as well. Again, accidents and [compulsory purchase] are good examples. In both of these areas the compensation given has clearly varied with society's distributive goals, and cannot be readily explained in terms of giving the victim, as nearly as possible, an objectively determined equivalent of the price at which he would have sold what was taken from him.

It should not be surprising that this is often so, even if the original reason for a liability rule is an efficiency one. For distributional goals are expensive and difficult to achieve, and the collective valuation involved in liability rules readily lends itself to promoting distributional goals. This does not mean that distributional goals are always well served in this way. Ad hoc decision-making is always troublesome, and the difficulties are especially acute when the settlement of conflicts between parties is used as a vehicle for the solution of more widespread distributional problems. Nevertheless, distributional objectives may be better attained in this way than otherwise.

B. Inalienable entitlements

Thus far, we have focused on the questions of when society should protect an entitlement by property or liability rules. However, there remain many entitlements which involve a still greater degree of societal intervention: the law not only decides who is to own something and what price is to be paid for it if it is taken or destroyed, but also regulates its sale – by, for example, prescribing pre-conditions for a valid sale or forbidding a sale altogether. Although these rules of inalienability are substantially different from the property and liability rules, their use can be analyzed in terms of the same efficiency and distributional goals that underlie the use of the other two rules.

While at first glance efficiency objectives may seem undermined by limitations on the ability to engage in transactions, closer analysis suggests that there are instances, perhaps many, in which economic efficiency is more closely approximated by such limitations. This might occur when a transaction would create significant externalities – costs to third parties.

For instance, if Taney were allowed to sell his land to Chase, a polluter, he would injure his neighbor Marshall by lowering the value of Marshall's land. Conceivably, Marshall could pay Taney not to sell his land; but, because there are many injured Marshalls, free-loader and information costs make such transactions practically impossible. The state could protect the Marshalls and yet facilitate the sale of the land by giving the Marshalls an entitlement to prevent Taney's sale to Chase but only protecting the entitlement by a liability rule. It might, for instance, charge an excise tax on all sales of land to polluters equal to its estimate of the external cost to the Marshalls of the sale. But where there are so many injured Marshalls that the price required under the liability rule is likely to be high enough so that no one would be willing to pay it, then setting up the machinery for collective valuation will be wasteful. Barring the sale to polluters will be the most efficient result because it is clear that avoiding pollution is cheaper than paying its costs – including its costs to the Marshalls.

Another instance in which external costs may justify inalienability occurs when external costs do not lend themselves to collective measurement which is acceptably objective and nonarbitrary. This nonmonetizability is characteristic of one category of external costs which, as a practical matter, seems frequently to lead us to rules of inalienability. Such external costs are often called moralisms.

If Taney is allowed to sell himself into slavery, or to take undue risks of becoming penniless, or to sell a kidney, Marshall may be harmed, simply because Marshall is a sensitive man who is made unhappy by seeing slaves, paupers, or persons who die because they have sold a kidney. Again, Marshall could pay Taney not to sell his freedom to Chase the slaveowner; but again, because Marshall is not one but many individuals, free-loader and information costs make such transactions practically impossible. Again, it might seem that the state could intervene by objectively valuing the external cost to Marshall and requiring Chase to pay that cost. But since the external cost to Marshall does not lend itself to an acceptable objective measurement, such liability rules are not appropriate.

In the case of Taney selling land to Chase, the polluter, they were inappropriate because we *knew* that the costs to Taney and the Marshalls exceeded the benefits to

Chase. Here, though we are not certain of how a cost–benefit analysis would come out, liability rules are inappropriate because any monetization is, by hypothesis, out of the question. The state must, therefore, either ignore the external costs to Marshall, or if it judges them great enough, forbid the transaction that gave rise to them by making Taney's freedom inalienable.

Obviously, we will not always value the external harm of a moralism enough to prohibit the sale. And obviously also, external costs other than moralisms may be sufficiently hard to value to make rules of inalienability appropriate in certain circumstances; this reason for rules of inalienability, however, does seem most often germane in situations where moralisms are involved . . .

. . . Finally, just as efficiency goals sometimes dictate the use of rules of inalienability, so, of course, do distributional goals. Whether an entitlement may be sold or not often affects directly who is richer and who is poorer. Prohibiting the sale of babies makes poorer those who can cheaply produce babies and richer those who through some nonmarket device get free an 'unwanted' baby. Prohibiting exculpatory clauses in product sales makes richer those who were injured by a product defect and poorer those who were not injured and who paid more for the product because the exculpatory clause was forbidden. Favoring the specific group that has benefited may or may not have been the reason for the prohibition on bargaining. What is important is that, regardless of the reason for barring a contract, a group did gain from the prohibition.

This should suffice to put us on guard, for it suggests that direct distributional motives may lie behind asserted nondistributional grounds for inalienability, whether they be paternalism, self-paternalism, or externalities. This does not mean that giving weight to distributional goals is undesirable. It clearly is desirable where on efficiency grounds society is indifferent between an alienable and an inalienable entitlement and distributional goals favor one approach or the other. It may well be desirable even when distributional goals are achieved at some efficiency costs. The danger may be, however, that what is justified on, for example, paternalism grounds is really a hidden way of accruing distributional benefits for a group whom we would not otherwise wish to benefit. For example, we may use certain types of zoning to preserve open spaces on the grounds that the poor will be happier, though they do not know it now. And open spaces may indeed make the poor happier in the long run. But the zoning that preserves open space also makes housing in the suburbs more expensive and it may be that the whole plan is aimed at securing distributional benefits to the suburban dweller regardless of the poor's happiness.

III. THE FRAMEWORK AND POLLUTION CONTROL RULES

Nuisance or pollution is one of the most interesting areas where the question of who will be given an entitlement, and how it will be protected, is in frequent issue. Traditionally, and very ably in the recent article by Professor Michelman, the nuisance-pollution problem is viewed in terms of three rules. First, Taney may not pollute unless his neighbor (his only neighbor let us assume), Marshall, allows it (Marshall may enjoin Taney's nuisance). Second, Taney may pollute but must compensate Marshall for damages caused (nuisance is found but the remedy is limited to damages). Third,

Taney may pollute at will and can only be stopped by Marshall if Marshall pays him off (Taney's pollution is not held to be a nuisance to Marshall). In our terminology rules one and two (nuisance with injunction, and with damages only) are entitlements to Marshall. The first is an entitlement to be free from pollution and is protected by a property rule; the second is also an entitlement to be free from pollution but is protected only by a liability rule. Rule three (no nuisance) is instead an entitlement to Taney protected by a property rule, for only by buying Taney out at Taney's price can Marshall end the pollution.

The very statement of these rules in the context of our framework suggests that something is missing. Missing is a fourth rule representing an entitlement in Taney to pollute, but an entitlement which is protected only by a liability rule. The fourth rule, really a kind of partial [compulsory purchase] coupled with a benefits tax, can be stated as follows: Marshal may stop Taney from polluting, but if he does he must compensate Taney.

As a practical matter it will be easy to see why even legal writers as astute as Professor Michelman have ignored this rule. Unlike the first three it does not often lend itself to judicial imposition for a number of good legal process reasons. For example, even if Taney's injuries could practicably be measured, apportionment of the duty of compensation among many Marshalls would present problems for which courts are not well suited. If only those Marshalls who voluntarily asserted the right to enjoin Taney's pollution were required to pay the compensation, there would be insuperable free-loader problems. If, on the other hand, the liability rule entitled one of the Marshalls alone to enjoin the pollution and required all the benefited Marshalls to pay their share of the compensation, the courts would be faced with the immensely difficult task of determining who was benefited how much and imposing a benefits tax accordingly, all the while observing procedural limits within which courts are expected to function.

The fourth rule is thus not part of the cases legal scholars read when they study nuisance law, and is therefore easily ignored by them. But it is available, and may sometimes make more sense than any of the three competing approaches. Indeed, in one form or another, it may well be the most frequent device employed. To appreciate the utility of the fourth rule and to compare it with the other three rules, we will examine why we might choose any of the given rules.

We would employ rule one (entitlement to be free from pollution protected by a property rule) from an economic efficiency point of view if we believed that the polluter, Taney, could avoid or reduce the costs of pollution more cheaply than the pollutee, Marshall. Or to put it another way, Taney would be enjoinable if he were in a better position to balance the costs of polluting against the costs of not polluting. We would employ rule three (entitlement to pollute protected by a property rule) again solely from an economic efficiency standpoint, if we made the converse judgment on who could best balance the harm of pollution against its avoidance costs. If we were wrong in our judgments and if transactions between Marshall and Taney were costless or even very cheap, the entitlement under rules one or three would be traded and an economically efficient result would occur in either case. If we entitled Taney to pollute and Marshall valued clean air more than Taney valued the pollution, Marshall would pay Taney to stop polluting even though no nuisance was found. If we entitled Marshall to enjoin the pollution and the right to pollute was worth more to Taney than freedom from pollution was to Marshall, Taney would pay Marshall not to seek an injunction or would buy Marshall's land and sell it to someone who would agree not to seek an injunction. As we have assumed no one else was hurt by the pollution, Taney could now pollute even though the initial entitlement, based on a wrong guess of who was the cheapest avoider of the costs involved allowed the pollution to be enjoined. Wherever transactions between Taney and Marshall are easy, and wherever economic efficiency is our goal, we could employ entitlements protected by property rules even though we would not be sure that the entitlement chosen was the right one. Transactions as described above would cure the error. While the entitlement might have important distributional effects, it would not substantially undercut economic efficiency.

The moment we assume, however, that transactions are not cheap, the situation changes dramatically. Assume we enjoin Taney and there are 10,000 injured Marshalls. Now *even if* the right to pollute is worth more to Taney than the right to be free from pollution is to the sum of the Marshalls, the injunction will probably stand. The cost of buying out all the Marshalls, given holdout problems, is likely to be too great, and an equivalent of [compulsory purchase] in Taney would be needed to alter the initial injunction. Conversely, if we denied a nuisance remedy, the 10,000 Marshalls could only with enormous difficulty, given free-loader problems, get together to buy out even one Taney and prevent the pollution. This would be so even if the pollution harm was greater than the value to Taney of the right to pollute.

If, however, transaction costs are not symmetrical, we may still be able to use the property rule. Assume that Taney can buy the Marshalls' entitlements easily because holdouts are for some reason absent, but that the Marshalls have great free-loader problems in buying out Taney. In this situation the entitlement should be granted to the Marshalls unless we are sure the Marshalls are the cheapest avoiders of pollution costs. Where we do not know the identity of the cheapest cost avoider it is better to entitle the Marshalls to be free of pollution because, even if we are wrong in our initial placement of the entitlement, that is, even if the Marshalls are the cheapest cost avoiders, Taney will buy out the Marshalls and economic efficiency will be achieved. Had we chosen the converse entitlement and been wrong, the Marshalls could not have bought out Taney. Unfortunately, transaction costs are often high on both sides and an initial entitlement, though incorrect in terms of economic efficiency, will not be altered in the marketplace ...

[W]e are likely to turn to liability rules whenever we are uncertain whether the polluter or the pollutees can most cheaply avoid the cost of pollution. We are only likely to use liability rules where we are uncertain because, if we are certain, the costs of liability rules – essentially the costs of collectively valuing the damages to all concerned plus the cost in coercion to those who would not sell at the collectively determined figure – are unnecessary. They are unnecessary because transaction costs and bargaining barriers become irrelevant when we are certain who is the cheapest cost avoider;

economic efficiency will be attained without transactions by making the correct initial entitlement.

As a practical matter we often are uncertain who the cheapest cost avoider is. In such cases, traditional legal doctrine tends to find a nuisance but imposes only damages on Taney payable to the Marshalls. This way, if the amount of damages Taney is made to pay is close to the injury caused, economic efficiency will have had its due; if he cannot make a go of it, the nuisance was not worth its costs. The entitlement to the Marshalls to be free from pollution unless compensated, however, will have been given *not* because it was thought that polluting was probably worth less to Taney than freedom from pollution was worth to the Marshalls, nor even because on some distributional basis we preferred to charge the cost to Taney rather than to the Marshalls. It was so placed *simply because we did not know* whether Taney desired to pollute more than the Marshalls desired to be free from pollution, and the only way we thought we could test out the value of the pollution was by the only liability rule we thought we had. This was rule two, the imposition of nuisance damages on Taney. At least this would be the position of a court concerned with economic efficiency which believed itself limited to rules one, two, and three.

Rule four gives at least the possibility that the opposite entitlement may also lead to economic efficiency in a situation of uncertainty. Suppose for the moment that a mechanism exists for collectively assessing the damage resulting to Taney from being stopped from polluting by the Marshalls, and a mechanism also exists for collectively assessing the benefit to each of the Marshalls from such cessation. Thus – assuming the same degree of accuracy in collective valuation as exists in rule two (the nuisance damage rule) – the Marshalls would stop the pollution if it harmed them more than it benefited Taney. If this is possible, then even if we thought it necessary to use a liability rule, we would still be free to give the entitlement to Taney or Marshall for whatever reasons, efficiency or distributional, we desired.

Actually, the issue is still somewhat more complicated. For just as transaction costs are not necessarily symmetrical under the two converse property rule entitlements, so also the liability rule equivalents of transaction costs – the cost of valuing collectively and of coercing compliance with that valuation – may not be symmetrical under the two converse liability rules. Nuisance damages may be very hard to value, and the costs of informing all the injured of their rights and getting them into court may be prohibitive. Instead, the assessment of the object damage to Taney from foregoing his pollution may be cheap and so might the assessment of the relative benefits to all Marshalls of such freedom from pollution. But the opposite may also be the case. As a result, just as the choice of which property entitlement may be based on the asymmetry of transaction costs and hence on the greater amenability of one property entitlement to market corrections, so might the choice between liability entitlements be based on the asymmetry of the costs of collective determination.

The introduction of distributional considerations makes the existence of the fourth possibility even more significant. One does not need to go into all the permutations of the possible tradeoffs between efficiency and distributional goals under the four rules to show this. A simple example should suffice. Assume a factory which, by using cheap coal, pollutes a very wealthy section of town and employs many low income workers to produce a product purchased primarily by the poor; assume also a distributional goal that favors equality of wealth. Rule one – enjoin the nuisance – would possibly have desirable economic efficiency results (if the pollution hurt the homeowners more than it saved the factory in coal costs), but it would have disastrous distribution effects. It would also have undesirable efficiency effects if the initial judgment on costs of avoidance had been wrong and transaction costs were high. Rule two – nuisance damages – would allow a testing of the economic efficiency of eliminating the pollution, even in the presence of high transaction costs, but would quite possibly put the factory out of business or diminish output and thus have the same income distribution effects as rule one. Rule three – no nuisance – would have favorable distributional effects since it might protect the income of the workers. But if the pollution harm was greater to the homeowners than the cost of avoiding it by using a better coal, and if transaction costs – holdout problems – were such that homeowners could not unite to pay the factory to use better coal, rule three would have unsatisfactory efficiency effects. Rule four – payment of damages to the factory after allowing the homeowners to compel it to use better coal, and assessment of the cost of these damages to the homeowners – would be the only one which would accomplish both the distributional and efficiency goals.

An equally good hypothetical for any of the rules can be constructed. Moreover, the problems of coercion may as a practical matter be extremely severe under rule four. How do the homeowners decide to stop the factory's use of low grade coal? How do we assess the damages and their proportional allocation in terms of benefits to the homeowner? But equivalent problems may often be as great for rule two. How do we value the damages to each of the many homeowners? How do we inform the homeowners of their rights to damages? How do we evaluate and limit the administrative expenses of the court actions this solution implies?

The seriousness of the problem depends under each of the liability rules on the number of people whose 'benefits' or 'damages' one is assessing and the expense and likelihood of error in such assessment. A judgment on these questions is necessary to an evaluation of the possible economic efficiency benefits of employing one rule rather than another. The relative ease of making such assessments through different institutions may explain why we often employ the courts for rule two and get to rule four – when we do get there – only through political bodies which may, for example, prohibit pollution, or 'take' the entitlement to build a supersonic plane by a kind of [compulsory purchase], paying compensation to those injured by these decisions. But all this does not, in any sense, diminish the importance of the fact that an awareness of the possibility of an entitlement to pollute, but one protected only by a liability rule, may in some instances allow us best to combine our distributional and efficiency goals.

We have said that we would say little about justice, and so we shall. But it should be clear that, if rule four might enable us best to combine efficiency goals with distributional goals, it might also enable us best to combine those same efficiency goals with other goals that are often described in justice language. For example, assume that the factory in our hypothetical was using cheap coal *before* any of the wealthy houses were built. In these circumstances, rule four will not only achieve the desirable efficiency and distributional results mentioned above, but it will also accord with any 'justice' significance which is attached to being there first. And this is so whether we view this justice significance as part of a distributional goal, as part of a long run efficiency goal based on protecting expectancies, or as part of an independent concept of justice.

Thus far, in this section we have ignored the possibility of employing rules of inalienability to solve pollution problems. A general policy of barring pollution does seem unrealistic. But rules of inalienability can appropriately be used to limit the levels of pollution and to control the levels of activities which cause pollution.

One argument for inalienability may be the widespread existence of moralisms against pollution. Thus it may hurt the Marshalls – gentlemen farmers – to see Taney, a smoke-choked city dweller, sell his entitlement to be free of pollution. A different kind of externality or moralism may be even more important. The Marshalls may be hurt by the expectation that, while the present generation might withstand present pollution levels with no serious health dangers, future generations may well face a despoiled, hazardous environmental condition which they are powerless to reverse. And this ground for inalienability might be strengthened if a similar conclusion were reached on grounds of selfpaternalism. Finally, society might restrict alienability on paternalistic grounds. The Marshalls might feel that, although Taney himself does not know it, Taney will be better off if he really can see the stars at night, or if he can breathe smogless air.

Whatever the grounds for inalienability, we should reemphasize that distributional effects should be carefully evaluated in making the choice for or against inalienability. Thus the citizens of a town may be granted an entitlement to be free of water pollution caused by the waste discharges of a chemical factory; and the entitlement might be made inalienable on the grounds that the town's citizens really would be better off in the long run to have access to clean beaches. But the entitlement might also be made inalienable to assure the maintenance of a beautiful resort area for the very wealthy, at the same time putting the town's citizens out of work.

Notes and Questions 6.10

Consider the following notes and questions both before and after reading *Miller* v. *Jackson* [1977] 3 All ER 338 (either in full or as extracted at www.cambridge.org/propertylaw/).

1 Is it legitimate for Lord Denning to place emphasis on the fact that the cricket green was there first? Why under English law are such considerations normally irrelevant?

2 Do damages payable for future nuisance amount to a licence to commit wrong?

3 Should a judge, who held that no nuisance arose, play a role in determining the appropriate remedy in respect of an activity which the majority found to be an actionable nuisance?

4 Do you agree with the majority opinion that an injunction should not be granted because the interests of the public at large in the provision of cricket facilities outweigh the rights of an individual who must have known there was a likelihood of this type of disturbance when the house was purchased? Is private nuisance an appropriate mechanism for achieving a balance between the rights of the individual and the public at large?

6.5. Restrictive covenants

A restrictive covenant is a private law mechanism whereby land use is restricted. Initially, the device was no more than a contractual undertaking in which the purchaser of a portion of land agreed with the vendor to certain restrictions on how the purchased land would be used. As a contractual right the restrictive covenant was, however, of no avail once a subsequent title holder, who was not a party to the original contract, entered the frame. In an agrarian and static society where there was a technological limit on what you could do with your land so as to affect your neighbour (and little if any demographic pressure) this did no great harm and there was consequently no need (and thus no pressure) to extend it beyond its contractual limitations (especially before the onset of widespread free-hold ownership loosened the restrictions which the great landowners imposed by means of the tenurial relationship). But come the Industrial Revolution and with it demographic upheaval, the spread of freehold ownership and the technology to blight neighbouring land, one can see why the law, after a suitable period, was compelled to respond. The ability to build 'dark satanic mills ... in England's green and pleasant land' (William Blake, *Jerusalem*), particularly the green and pleasant land bordering your own, had the potential to inhibit the alienation of land for there was now a very real disincentive in selling a portion of your land. The vendor had no means of protecting the land he retained from being affected by such developments on the land parted with, and every incentive to retain rather than sell any portion of his land.

The recognition of the proprietary status of restrictive covenants thus became an economic imperative freeing up the market in land (see generally Simpson, *A History of the Land Law*). A series of cases culminating in *Tulk* v. *Moxhay* (1848) 2 Ph 774 (Extract 6.9 below) established the restrictive covenant as a species of property right and thus provided a mechanism whereby it was possible to sell a portion of land safe in the knowledge that subsequent owners of the plot sold could not do something that would spoil the enjoyment (economic worth) of the plot retained.

Specifically, the principle established by these cases is that, once two plot owners enter into an agreement restricting the use of one plot of land for the benefit of the other, then, provided certain conditions are satisfied, that agreement will be enforceable between all subsequent owners of the two plots. In many respects *Tulk* v. *Moxhay* proved to be the high water mark in the development of this principle, and in later cases the courts took care to confine it so that now fairly detailed requirements must be satisfied before a restrictive covenant can be enforced between successors in title (see *R. v. Westminster City Council and the London Electricity Board, ex parte Leicester Square Coventry Street Association* (1990) 59 P&CR 51 (Extract 6.10 below). For full details of the rules governing the passing of the benefit and the burden of covenants, see Gray and Gray, *Elements of Land Law* (4th edn), paragraphs 13.21–13.116).

By far the most important of the limitations subsequently imposed on the *Tulk v. Moxhay* doctrine is that it applies only to negative obligations – promises *not* to do something. For to enforce positive covenants against subsequent owners would place too great a burden on the land, making potential buyers liable for difficult to quantify expense, and thereby undermining the marketability of land and the basis for recognition of covenants as proprietary interests in the first place. Although the covenant in *Tulk v. Moxhay* itself was couched in positive terms (a promise by the purchaser of Leicester Square positively to maintain it in its then state as an ornamental garden square), the seller in that case sought only to enforce its negative element – i.e. to prevent the purchaser's successors from using it for anything else. He did not try to enforce the positive obligations undertaken (to keep the iron railings in repair, maintain the gardens etc.). It soon became established (and was reaffirmed by the House of Lords as recently as 1994 in *Rhone v. Stephens* [1994] 2 WLR 429) that no matter how the covenant is worded, a positive obligation is never enforceable between anyone other than the original contracting parties. So Mr Tulk and his successors could not make subsequent owners of Leicester Square use it as a garden square, they could only stop them taking positive steps to use it for any other purpose.

By way of contrast, in one important respect the scope of the restrictive covenant has been extended by the courts so that it can now provide a local regulatory law enforceable by and between all neighbours in an area. This extension involves a relaxation of the basic rule evolved from *Tulk v. Moxhay* that the only people who can enforce a restrictive covenant are those who can prove that they now own at least part of the land which was (a) owned by the promisee at the time when the promisor made the promise, and (b) intended to be benefited by the restriction. As demonstrated by *R. v. Westminster City Council and the London Electricity Board, ex parte Leicester Square Coventry Street Association* (1990) 59 P&CR 51 (Extract 6.10 below), this can be difficult to prove. More importantly, it threatened to impose an arbitrary restriction on enforceability in cases where the original seller sold off more than one plot, and wanted to subject each of them to similar restrictive covenants. Supposing, for example, a seller wanted to divide his land into three plots and sell them all off for residential development. He could require the buyer of each plot to covenant with him not to use the plot for anything other than residential purposes, but if the basic rule was applied strictly the enforceability of these covenants would then depend entirely on the order in which he sold the plots.

The seller would cease to have any interest in enforcing the covenants once the last plot was sold but who else could enforce the covenant? Admittedly, the covenant given by the buyer of the first plot to be sold could always be enforced by buyers and all subsequent owners of the second and third plots. But the covenant given by the buyer of the second plot could not be enforced by the buyer and subsequent owners of the first plot, and neither he nor the owner of the second plot would be able to enforce the covenant given by the buyer of the third plot. To avoid this unsatisfactory result the courts developed the idea of a 'building scheme' or 'scheme of development': provided there is an intention to impose a scheme of mutually enforceable restrictions on all land within a clearly defined area, the entire development is subject to the scheme from the moment the vendor sells the first plot. From then on, each owner is entitled to enforce the restrictions against every other owner within the designated area. The essential element here is reciprocity: the courts must be satisfied not only that the seller intended to set up such a mutually enforceable scheme, but also that the original buyers bought on the understanding that the restrictions would be mutually enforceable between themselves (*Elliston* v. *Reacher* [1908] 2 Ch 374; *Re Dolphin's Conveyance* [1970] 1 Ch 654; and *Emile Elias & Co. Ltd* v. *Pine Groves Ltd* [1993] 1 WLR 305, PC). For this reason, even the seller becomes bound by the scheme once it has crystallised on the first sale: thereafter even he can be restrained from using any as yet unsold land within the area in breach of the restrictions, and all subsequent sales he makes must be subject to similar restrictions (*Brunner* v. *Greenslade* [1971] Ch 993). Building schemes appear to be highly effective with developers routinely imposing them in new housing and industrial estates, presumably because their existence enhances the value of the individual units.

Nevertheless, there is an obvious potential for restrictive covenants to inhibit the development of the restricted land and reduce its marketability, whether or not they form part of a building scheme. To a certain extent this is checked by two factors. The first is that a restrictive covenant will not be enforceable against a subsequent buyer of the burdened land unless he had notice of it when he bought the land (a requirement central to the reasoning in *Tulk* v. *Moxhay*, but now taken care of by registration, which constitutes notice for these purposes). This removes the danger that the fear of hidden restrictive covenants might limit marketability of land generally (see further Chapter 15).

The second is that statutory machinery now exists to eliminate or modify restrictive covenants that have outlived their usefulness. The fairly elaborate jurisdiction set up by section 84 of the Law of Property Act 1925 and greatly expanded by amendments made in 1969 (see Notes and Questions 6.12 below) allow anyone interested in land affected by a restrictive covenant to apply to the Lands Tribunal, which has power to discharge or modify the covenant if satisfied that one of four grounds specified in section 84(1) exists – broadly, that the covenant is either obsolete or impedes some reasonable use of the burdened land for public or private purposes, or that the proposed change will not injure the person entitled to the benefit. A successful applicant can be ordered to pay compensation to anyone suffering loss because of the discharge or modification of the covenant.

Extract 6.9   *Tulk v. Moxhay* (1848) 2 Ph 774

Tulk held the freehold interest in 'Leicester Square Garden or Pleasure Ground, with the equestrian statue then standing in the centre thereof and the iron railings and stone work round the same', and also several houses surrounding the Square. In 1808, he sold the Square to Elms. In the conveyance Elms covenanted with Tulk:

> that Elms, his heirs, and assigns should ... at all times thereafter at his and their own costs and charges, keep and maintain the said piece of ground and square garden and the iron railings round the same in its then form, and in sufficient and proper repair as a square garden and pleasure ground, in an open state, uncovered with any buildings, in neat and ornamental order ...

Elms later sold the Square to someone else, and eventually it was sold on to Moxhay, who admitted that he knew all about the covenant at the time when he bought it. Moxhay wanted to build on the Square. Tulk, who remained owner of the houses surrounding the Square, sought an injunction to prevent him from doing so. The Master of the Rolls granted an injunction to restrain Moxhay from using the Square for any purpose other than as 'a square garden and pleasure ground in an open state, and uncovered with buildings'. Moxhay appealed.

LORD COTTENHAM LC: That this court has jurisdiction to enforce a contract between the owner of land and his neighbour purchasing a part of it that the purchaser shall either use or abstain from using the land purchased in a particular way is what I never knew disputed. Here there is no question about the contract. The owner of certain houses in the square sells the land adjoining, with a covenant from the purchaser not to use it for any other purpose than as a square garden. It is now contended, not that the vendee could violate that contract, but that he might sell the piece of land, and that the purchaser from him may violate it without this court having any power to interfere. If that were so, it would be impossible for an owner of land to sell part of it without incurring the risk of rendering what he retains worthless. It is said that, the covenant being one which does not run with the land, this court cannot enforce it, but the question is not whether the covenant runs with the land, but whether a party shall be permitted to use the land in a manner inconsistent with the contract entered into by his vendor, with notice of which he purchased. Of course, the price would be affected by the covenant, and nothing could be more inequitable than that the original purchaser should be able to sell the property the next day for a greater price, in consideration of the assignee being allowed to escape from the liability which he had himself undertaken.

... I think this decision of the Master of the Rolls perfectly right, and, therefore, that this motion must be refused with costs.

Appeal dismissed.

Notes and Questions 6.11

1   It was said above that the impetus for the development of the restrictive
covenant was that an inability to regulate the use of sold-off portions of land
inhibited the alienability of land. But this is not the reason given by Lord
Cottenham. What reason does he give, and how convincing is it? If the seller
knows that his buyer can immediately resell the land free from the covenant,
what will be the difference in the price at which he will sell (a) with the covenant
and (b) without it?

2   Do the arguments put forward by Lord Cottenham apply with equal force to
positive covenants (for example, to keep the sold-off land fenced off, or to
maintain buildings on it in good repair)? What are the reasons for refusing to
allow positive covenants to be enforced against successors of the original
covenantor? What are the consequences? (See further Law Commission,
Transfer of Land: The Law of Positive and Restrictive Covenants (Law
Commission Report No. 127, 1984).)

Notes and Questions 6.12

Consider the following notes and questions both before and after reading Extract
6.10 below and section 84 of the Law of Property Act 1925:

1   Why should enforcement of restrictive covenants be confined to those who now
hold an interest in the land that was owned by the original covenantee and was
intended to be benefited by it? Compare the equivalent rule applicable to
easements, i.e. that the easement must accommodate a dominant tenement (see
further section 8.6 below on the distinction between those property interests
that can exist 'in gross' and those that can only exist as appurtenant to another
property interest).

2   Consider what the outcome would have been if the association had been able to
prove that it was the present owner of some of John Augustus Tulk's land, and
the LEB had then applied to the Lands Tribunal to have the covenant discharged
under section 84 of the Law of Property Act 1925. How satisfactory would this
outcome be?

3   The Lands Tribunal has a very broad discretion under section 84. It can refuse
an application even if it is unopposed, and even if one or more of the statutory
grounds for discharge or modification are established (consider why this should
be so: see *Re University of Westminster* [1998] 3 All ER 1014, CA). Conversely, it
can order the discharge or modification of a covenant which has only just been
entered into, even if the applicant is the original covenantor so that the
discharge or modification enables the covenantor to escape a contractual

obligation freely entered into (see *Cresswell* v. *Proctor* [1968] 1 WLR 906; and
Ridley v. *Taylor* [1965] 1 WLR 611). Also, it can, and quite often does, discharge
or modify covenants within a building scheme: consider whether this is likely to
make building schemes more or less useful (see *Re Kennet Properties'*
Application (1996) 72 P&CR 353, LT).

4   The section 84 jurisdiction is quite widely used: in the six years from 1998 to
    2003, between 40 and 55 applications were made to the Lands Tribunal each
    year (see *Judicial Statistics*, published by the Department of Constitutional
    Affairs, available at www.dca.gov.uk/jsarlist.htm). Despite this, it is thought
    that large numbers of obsolete restrictive covenants still exist, and that this
    impedes the development of land (see Law Commission, *Transfer of Land:*
    Obsolete Restrictive Covenants (Law Commission Report No. 201, 1991)). What,
    if anything, does this tell us about the effectiveness of the jurisdiction?

5   Restrictive covenants provide a means of private land use regulation – essen-
    tially regulation by neighbours in their own selfish private interest – whereas the
    planning system is the means by which land use is regulated in the public
    interest. To what extent may/must the Lands Tribunal take the public interest
    into account when deciding whether a restrictive covenant should be discharged
    or modified? (see section 84(1B) of the Law of Property Act 1925; *Gilbert* v.
    Spoor [1983] Ch 27; and *Re Martin's Application* (1989) 57 P&CR 119 at 125).

6   How might restrictive covenants and the section 84 jurisdiction of the Lands
    Tribunal be analysed from the perspective of property rules and liability rules
    (see Calabresi and Melamed in Extract 6.8 above)? Does this provide a clue as to
    why the legislature has vested such a jurisdiction in the Lands Tribunal?

7   In addition to the statutory jurisdiction under section 84, the court has a general
    equitable jurisdiction to refuse to enforce a restrictive covenant. It will do so if it
    considers that the person seeking to enforce the covenant has lost the right
    either because of his conduct (for example, acquiescence in past breaches) or
    because of some radical change in circumstances. But this jurisdiction is very
    much narrower than the statutory jurisdiction, and it now appears confined to
    cases where it would be unconscionable for the applicant to seek to enforce the
    covenant in view of what has happened: see further *Chatsworth Estates Co.* v.
    Fewell [1931] 1 Ch 224 (on change in the character of the neighbourhood);
    Shaw v. *Applegate* [1977] 1 WLR 970, CA; and *Gafford* v. *Graham* (1998) 77
    P&CR 73, CA (acquiescence).

Extract 6.10   *R. v. Westminster City Council and the London Electricity Board, ex*
***parte Leicester Square Coventry Street Association* (1990) 59 P&CR 51**

The subsequent history of Leicester Square, begun in *Tulk* v. *Moxhay*, shows the
strengths and limitations of the restrictive covenant as a means of regulating land

use. By 1851, Moxhay had died, and his widow sold the Square to James Wyld, a geographer, who wanted to build in the Square a 60-foot high plaster scale model of the Earth. Wyld sought the permission of the Tulk family (who still owned Tulk's adjoining houses and so held the benefit of the restrictive covenant): permission was granted in exchange for Wyld granting the Tulk family an option to buy back half the Square in ten years' time. The model (named 'Wyld's Monster Globe') was duly built, but ten years later it was demolished, and John Augustus Tulk (who had inherited the Tulk houses from his grandfather, the original Tulk) exercised the option to buy back half the Square. John Augustus Tulk planned to build on the Square, just as Moxhay had planned. This caused a public outcry, but at that time there was no way in which such development could be prevented: there was no public regulation of land use (the planning system had yet to be invented) and Grandfather Tulk's restrictive covenant was of no use since the only person entitled to enforce it was John Augustus Tulk himself. Eventually, in 1874, a local MP, Albert Grant, bought out John Augustus Tulk (entering into a restrictive covenant in the same terms as the original covenant given by Moxhay to Grandfather Tulk) and also bought up all other interests in various parts of the Square which had been sold off, and presented the whole of the Square to the local authority to be used as a public park. Then in the 1980s the local authority, Westminster City Council, decided to grant the London Electricity Board (LEB) a 999-year lease of the subsoil of the Square for £2.5 million, to enable the LEB to build a large electricity substation underneath the Square. The £2.5 million was to be used towards the £4 million that Westminster City Council planned to spend on 'improving and revitalising' the Square. The whole scheme was strongly opposed by the local traders' and residents' association (comprised mainly of the owners of the cinemas and restaurants surrounding Leicester Square) because they feared their trade would be disrupted by the building works. Despite opposition from the association, Westminster City Council granted the LEB planning permission to build the substation. The association then tried to use the restrictive covenant to prevent the substation being built. Specifically, they argued that the grant of the lease by Westminster City Council to the LEB was invalidated by section 131(1) of the Local Government Act 1972, which gave local authorities power to dispose of land held by them but then provided that 'nothing ... shall authorise the disposal of any land by a local authority in breach of any ... covenant which is binding upon them'. The association ultimately lost on this point as well: it was held that, although the restrictive covenant was still enforceable, the disposal of the subsoil to the LEB was not a breach of it – the breach would occur later, when the LEB started to carry out the building works. So why not sue the LEB for breach of the covenant? The problem was that no one could discover who was now entitled to enforce the covenant. As Simon Brown J explained, the covenant could only be enforced against Westminster City Council (or the LEB) if they held land originally intended to be burdened by the covenant when it was reimposed by Albert Grant in 1874, and it could only be enforced by whoever now held land which John Augustus Tulk then held and which was intended to be benefited by the covenant:

SIMON BROWN J: ... Is the covenant binding upon Westminster [and therefore on the LEB when it acquired the lease]? To establish this the association have to satisfy me on the balance of probabilities: (a) that the burden of the covenant ran with the land; (b) that the benefit of the covenant was annexed to the covenantee's land; and (c) that nothing has happened subsequent to the giving of the covenant to render it inoperative – such, for instance, as the merging of title in the burdened and dominant lands ...

The burden of a covenant runs with the covenantor's land provided first that it is negative – as plainly this one was; secondly, that it was intended to run with that land – an intention here manifest from the reference to Albert Grant's 'heirs or assigns'; and, thirdly, that the covenantee at the date of the covenant owned other land which would benefit from it. It is this last element of the association's case that Westminster contend is wanting. Mr Colyer [counsel for Westminster City Council] submits that there is simply no evidence before me to establish on the balance of probabilities that the covenantee, John Augustus Tulk, did at the date of his conveyance to Albert Grant on April 20, 1874 retain other land in or sufficiently near to Leicester Square to benefit from the covenant. I disagree. In the absence of any contrary evidence I regard as sufficient proof of this requirement the reference in the covenant itself to:

> JAT his heirs and assigns owners for the time being of freehold property in Leicester Square aforesaid.

It seems to me inconceivable that this could be a reference to the property actually being sold and one would hardly suppose that Mr Tulk and his advisers (even 25 years after the family's celebrated case) were unaware of the long-established legal require-ment that for the covenant to run with the burdened land the covenantee must retain land capable of benefiting from it.

Was the benefit of the covenant annexed to the covenantees' land? The principles were usefully set out in Megarry and Wade on the *Law of Real Property*:

> The benefit will be effectively annexed to the land so as to run with it if in the instrument the land is sufficiently indicated and the covenant is either stated to be made for the benefit of the land, or stated to be made with the covenantee in his capacity of owner of the land; for then in either case it is obvious that future owners of that land are intended to benefit ...

... Adopting this approach the answer is surely plain. The same words in the covenant which I hold to have established that John Augustus Tulk retained land capable of benefiting indicate also that he was taking the covenant for the benefit of that retained land and with the intention that its future owners should reap that benefit.

Has anything occurred since this covenant was given on April 20, 1874 to render it inoperative?

The factual position is simply this: since the covenant was first imposed it ran, always with the purchaser's notice, with the several dispositions of the burdened land. Nothing, however, is known about the subsequent disposition of the dominant land, that retained by Mr Tulk. In particular, despite apparently strenuous efforts by the association, no one has discovered who now enjoys the benefit of the covenant. Does that matter? Mr Jones for the LEB argues that it does. He contends that it constitutes a fatal flaw in the association's case; without identification of the retained land the covenant is extinguished upon the first subsequent assignment of the burdened land. That at least is how I finally understood the submission. It is advanced candidly without authority and expressly recognising that it goes further and wider than Mr Colyer for Westminster felt able to go. I reject it. Indeed, it seems to me to fly in the face of accepted principle. As Megarry and Wade put it:

> Once the benefit of the covenant is annexed to land, it passes with the land to each successive owner, tenant or occupier, even if he knew nothing of it when he acquired the land.

The same view is expressed in the seventh edition of Preston and Newsome on *Restrictive Covenants Affecting Freehold Land* in a passage at paragraph 19 citing Simonds J in *Lawrence v. South County Freeholds Ltd* [1939] Ch 656:

> Such a benefit may pass with the land to which it has been annexed, even though the purchaser is unaware of it ... a hidden treasure which may be discovered in the hour of need ...

In short, I conclude that this covenant remains binding on Westminster, its benefit a 'hidden treasure' in the hands of the present owner (whoever he may be) of Tulk's retained land. Whether, of course, that owner will discover it, or indeed regard the present time as his hour of need, remains to be seen.

7

Possession

7.1. The nature of possession

7.1.1. Introduction

'Possession' can be described as the intentional exclusive physical control of a thing. A person who takes physical control of land or goods, with the intention of excluding all others from it or them, acquires possession of it or them as a matter of law. This is the case even if the taking of control was unlawful. So, if a thief steals your book or a squatter moves into your house, possession passes from you to her as a matter of fact and as a matter of law (although it has to be said that the courts have not always been happy to accept this: see section 7.4.1 below). Of course, this unlawful removal of possession from you does not affect your *right* to possession – you remain entitled to take possession back for yourself (subject to the public order safeguards considered in section 7.4 below) or to ask the court to put you back in possession and/or order appropriate compensation. The fact remains, however, that until you take such a step the taker/squatter is in law in possession.

In Chapter 2, we considered why a legal system might want to adopt such a rule. In this chapter, we look more closely at what amounts to possession, how it fits into the legal taxonomy of property interests, and how it can be acquired, transmitted, lost and regained, as well as at the broader implications of the basic rule that possession confers entitlement.

7.1.2. Possession, ownership and proprietary interests

In his essay 'Ownership', extracted in Chapter 6 above, Honoré put the right to possession as the first of his necessary ingredients in the notion of ownership, and indeed described it as 'the foundation on which the whole superstructure of ownership rests'.

In one sense, possession is simply an ingredient of ownership, as Honoré suggests. It is inherent in our idea of ownership that an owner of a thing has the right to take and keep physical control of it, to the exclusion of all others. However, the interrelationship between the two is more complex than this suggests.

The first point to make is that, procedurally, English law is more concerned with possession than with ownership. The law protects possession, in the sense that anyone who is in possession is entitled to redress from the courts if that possession is unlawfully threatened or invaded. The law regards any person who is in fact in possession of land or goods as lawfully in possession, and any invasion of that possession as unlawful *unless made by someone with a better right to possession*. In other words, once a person has acquired possession, by any means whether lawful or unlawful, they thereby become *entitled* to possession as against everyone except a person with a better right to possession. Consider again the example just given of a thief or squatter who takes possession of your book or land. We said there that, by taking possession in fact, the taker acquires possession in law. What this comes down to is that simply by taking possession from you, the taker *thereby* acquires a better right to possession than everyone except you. Two aspects of this must be emphasised here. First, if you as the owner go to court to obtain redress from the taker you will win, but not because you are the owner: you will win because, as owner, you have a better right to possession than her, the taker. For reasons we look at in Chapter 10, the courts resolve questions of disputed entitlement by looking at relative rights to possession rather than at ownership. Secondly, the law is happy to protect the possession of thieves and other unlawful takers – not, admittedly, against true owners (although, as we see in Chapters 10 and 11, it may in time come to this, through the operation of limitation of action rules), but certainly as against all other comers. Why this should be the case is considered in detail in Chapter 11, but we will also have something to say about it here, because it gives the context to pragmatic decisions made by the courts on questions of what degree of use/control amounts to the physical control required for possession.

The next, and connected, point about the relationship between ownership and possession is that possession plays a key role in the process of proving entitlement to a thing. Again, this is something that is looked at in more detail in Chapter 10, but for present purposes it is sufficient to note that it is much easier to prove possession than it is to prove ownership. Ownership is in fact rather difficult to prove. Most things – even tangible things – are not authoritatively labelled with the name of their owner, and there is no gigantic universal register on which all ownership of all things is recorded, so there is no obvious way of proving conclusively that that you do in fact own the thing (the book, the picture, the land) you say you own. Possession, on the other hand, is relatively easy to demonstrate: you can prove that you are in possession of a thing simply by demonstrating that you are in fact in exclusive physical control of the thing, with the intention of excluding all others from it. And possession is not only easier to prove than ownership, it is also a reasonably good indicator of ownership, because, as a matter of observable fact, in the vast majority of cases possession coincides with ownership. Consequently, in our system at least, the basic principle that has evolved is that possession is *prima facie* proof of title: if you can show that you are in possession of a thing you will be assumed by law to be the owner of it, in the absence of evidence to the contrary.

The final point to make about the relationship between ownership and possession is this. To say that the law protects possession against strangers is just another way of saying that possession of a thing is a right in relation to the thing enforceable against third parties. In this sense, therefore, possession is by definition proprietary. It is also proprietary in the sense that the right acquired by taking possession is transmissible, as Pollock and Wright point out in their classic nineteenth-century treatise on possession:

> We have seen that possession confers more than a personal right to be protected against wrongdoers; it confers a qualified right to possess, a right in the nature of property which is valid against every one who cannot show a prior and better right. Having reached this point, the law cannot stop at protecting and assisting the possessor himself. It must protect those who stand in his place by succession or purchase; the general reasons of policy are at least as strong in their favour as in his, their case at least as meritorious. And the merits of a purchaser for value, who perhaps had no means of knowing the imperfection of his vendor's title, are clearly greater than those of the vendor himself. The qualified right of property which arises from possession must therefore be a transmissible right, and whatever acts and events are capable of operating to confirm the first possessor in his tenure must be capable of the same operation for the benefit of those who claim through him by such a course of transfer as would be appropriate and adequate, if true ownership were present in the first instance, to pass the estate or interest which is claimed. Hence the rule that Possession is a root of Title is not only an actual but a necessary part of our system.
>
> (Pollock and Wright, *Possession in the Common Law*)

However, although possession is in this sense proprietary, in the common law taxonomy of property interests, possession is an ingredient of property interests rather than an interest in its own right. We have already said that possession is an ingredient of ownership, but one of the ways in which an owner can subdivide his ownership in a thing is by granting to someone else the right to possession of the thing, retaining to himself ownership-minus-possession. Depending on the terms on which possession is granted, the grantee will then herself hold a derivative property interest in the thing (for example, a lease, or a beneficial interest under a trust, or a bailee's interest) of which possession is the primary ingredient. So, possession is not of itself a property interest, but it is a necessary ingredient in a variety of different property interests. We return to this point in Chapter 17 below.

7.1.3. What is possession?

It is not always easy to decide whether the control over, or the use to which a person puts, a thing is such that that person can be said to be in possession of the thing. Essentially, the law looks at two aspects of the relationship between the person and the thing: first, the nature and degree of physical control exerted by the person over the thing, and, secondly, the intention with which that control is exerted (traditionally, the *animus possidendi*). What is required is that the person should have effective control of the thing, with the intention of excluding the rest of the world from it. These two factors – factual control and intention – will initially be considered separately, although as will soon become apparent, they are to a large extent interdependent.

7.1.3.1. Factual control

The nature and degree of factual control required to constitute possession varies depending on a number of factors. It is often said that the control must be exclusive – i.e. such as to exclude all others from the use of the thing – but even this requirement varies in stringency depending on the circumstances. In the cases considered under the heading 'The nature of the thing possessed' below, where there are practical difficulties in excluding all others, the exclusivity requirement is very relaxed. On the other hand, it is probably at its strictest when assessing when, if at all, possession has passed from a person in possession to an intruder claiming to have dispossessed him. In the latter case, it is not possible for both rival claimants to be in possession at the same time – possession must be in one or the other of them, or in neither, but it cannot be in both. As Pollock and Wright said:

> Physical possession is exclusive, or it is nothing. If two men have laid hands on the same horse or the same sheep, each meaning to use it for his own purpose and exclude the other, there is not any *de facto* possession until either of them has gotten the mastery. (Pollock and Wright, *Possession in the Common Law*, p. 21)

It is in deciding which of them has 'gotten the mastery', and at what point, that their respective entitlements become relevant.

The relevance of title

First, the person with the better title will find it easier to prove factual control than the person with a weaker title or no title at all. If there is any doubt as to which of two people is in possession, the one with the better title will be assumed to be in possession unless the other can prove substantial, unequivocal factual control. The classic statement of this comes from the judgment of Maule J in *Jones* v. *Maynard* (1849) 2 Ex 804 at 821:

> [I]t seems to me, that, as soon as a person is entitled to possession, and enters in the assertion of that possession, or, which is exactly the same thing, any other person enters by command of that lawful owner, so entitled to possession, the law immediately vests the actual possession in the person who has so entered. If there are two persons in a field, each asserting that the field is his, and each doing some act in the assertion of the right of possession, and if the question is, which of those two is in actual possession, I answer, the person who has the title is in actual possession, and the other person is a trespasser. They differ in no other respects. You cannot say that it is joint possession; you cannot say that it is a possession as tenants in common. It cannot be denied that one is in possession, and the other is a trespasser. Then that is to be determined, as it seems to me, by the fact of the title, each having the same apparent actual possession – the question as to which of

the two really is in possession, is determined by the fact of the possession following the title, that is, by the law, which makes it follow the title.

It follows that different degrees of factual control are required of different parties, depending on the circumstances – actions which are sufficient to demonstrate factual control on the part of the person with the right to possession might well be insufficient if performed by a trespasser claiming to have taken control or by some other person. In *Lows* v. *Telford* (1875–6) LR 1 App Cas 414 (Extract 7.1 below), for example, where the House of Lords held that possession had passed from Telford to Lows at the point when Lows, having broken into the premises in Telford's absence, was in the process of changing the locks (the crucial point at which Telford climbed in through a window and threw Lows out), the decisive factor was that Lows had a better right to possession of the premises than Telford. Had Lows been a trespasser, the result might have been different.

Powell v. *McFarlane* (1979) 38 P&CR 452 (extracted at www.cambridge.org/ propertylaw/) provides another and more extreme example: compare the respective uses of the field made by Powell the trespasser (who was held not to have acquired possession) and McFarlane the paper owner (held not to have lost possession despite not having used or even visited the field for several years). This case also demonstrates how difficult it is to divorce the question of control from the question of intention: in deciding whether Powell had acquired possession, the court assessed the significance of what he had done on the field by reference to the intention with which he had done it. As we will see below, this is not a particularly easy task for the court to perform – a point equally evident from *Fowley Marine (Emsworth) Ltd* v. *Gafford* [1968] 2 QB 618, CA (extracted at www.cambridge.org/propertylaw/).

This point, that it is easier for a rightful taker to prove she is in possession than it is for a wrongful taker, has occasionally been misunderstood by the courts and taken to mean that possession does not shift from a person rightfully in possession to a wrongful taker unless and until the owner has 'acquiesced' in the taking, and that, consequently, a wrongful taker never acquires possession at all if no such 'acquiescence' takes place. So, for example, in *McPhail* v. *Persons Unknown* [1973] Ch 447 at 456, CA, Lord Denning said of squatters who had broken into, and were now living in, empty local authority houses:

> They were trespassers when they entered, and they continued to be trespassers as long as they remained there. The owner never acquiesced in their presence there. So the trespassers never gained possession ... As Sir Frederick Pollock put it [in *Pollock on Torts* (15th edn, 1951), p. 292]: 'A trespasser may in any case be turned off land before he has gained possession, and he does not gain possession until there has been something like acquiescence in the physical fact of his occupation on the part of the rightful owner.'

If 'acquiescence' means just that the owner has stopped trying to exert physical control himself, this is uncontroversial: as *Powell* v. *McFarlane* demonstrates, it is difficult for any taker to prove sufficient acts of intentional exclusive control for so long as the rightful possessor is still trying to exert *some* degree of control, however slight. Lord Denning, however, seems to be going much further than this, and attempting to introduce a requirement that no wrongful taker can acquire possession without a positive act of acceptance (if not permission) on the part of the person entitled to possession. Such a requirement would be inconsistent with the fundamental principles of relativity of title considered in Chapter 10. It would also be quite inconsistent with the many cases where a trespasser or wrongful taker has been held to be in possession of land or goods in circumstances where the person entitled to possession was either unaware of the trespass or taking or was aware of it and opposed to it but made only ineffectual attempts to regain possession: see, for example, *Mount Carmel Investments Ltd* v. *Peter Thurloe Ltd* [1988] 1 WLR 1078, CA.

The nature of the thing possessed

Secondly, the nature and degree of control required varies depending on the nature of the thing said to be possessed. Some things are more susceptible to exclusive physical control than others. It is relatively easy to maintain total exclusionary control of some things – small chattels, lockable vehicles, self-contained buildings, for example – and in such cases a person claiming to be in possession is likely to have to demonstrate total physical control by showing that they can prevent all others from using or intruding on the thing. In the case of other things, however, it may be impossible, pointless or unnecessarily expensive to ensure that all outsiders are excluded. In such cases, very attenuated physical control may suffice. *Fowley Marine (Emsworth) Ltd* v. *Gafford* [1968] 2 QB 618, CA (extracted at www.cambridge.org/propertylaw/) is a good illustration. There, the plaintiff was held to be in possession of the bed and foreshore of a channel of tidal water over which there were public rights of navigation. Since there was no question of the plaintiff being able to exclude anyone from the channel, the court accepted that the fact that the plaintiff had laid (and licensed others to lay) permanent moorings in the bed was sufficient to establish possession. It had been suggested for the defendant that the plaintiff could have done more to demonstrate possession, such as setting up permanent and visible markers to delineate the area, but Willmer LJ rejected this as 'quite unrealistic' (and a possible obstruction to navigation: the channel was in Chichester harbour). It may be similarly unrealistic to expect a possessor to take all steps necessary to prevent infringements of their own rights: see Lord Watson in *Lord Advocate* v. *Young* (1887) LR 12 App Cas 544 at 553, to the effect that, in the case of property like foreshore, it is 'practically impossible' to prevent occasional infringements of the possessor's rights 'because the cost of preventive measures would be altogether disproportionate to the value of the subject'. The same point can be seen in *The Wik Peoples* v. *State of Queensland* (1996) 187 CLR 1 (extracted at www.cambridge.org/propertylaw/), where one of the issues was whether 'pastoral leases' granted to cattle ranchers over vast tracts of desert land in Australia conferred possession on the grantees. The minority took the view that it was not incompatible with the grantees having possession that any drover or traveller was entitled to ride or drive stock across the land on traditional stock routes and to depasture the stock 'on any part of the land which [was] within a distance of half a mile from the road and [was] not part of an enclosed garden or paddock under cultivation, and which [was] not within a distance of one mile from the principal homestead or head station' (Brennan CJ at 2–3; compare Toohey J at 8–9 and Gaudron at 14–15; and see also *Goldsworthy Mining Ltd* v. *Federal Commissioner of Taxation* (1973) 128 CLR 199, where a dredging lease of an area of sea-bed was held to confer possession even though the Crown as landlord reserved rights of access for navigation and all minerals and petroleum).

The purpose for which the thing is used

This is closely allied to the previous point. If the use to which you put a thing does not require you to exclude all others from its use, can you nevertheless be said to be in possession of it? This question arises in an acute form in the native land use cases. Can those who make nomadic use of a tract of land be said to be in possession of the land, or even of the sites which they periodically visit? It may be that the answer is yes, if, even though they do not wholly exclude others all the time, they can nevertheless demonstrate an ability and intention to prevent others making any use of the land or sites in question which interferes with their own use. So, for example, one might say that nomadic users manifest an intention to be in exclusive control of 'their' land if they take steps to prevent others exhausting or polluting the resources of a site which they customarily visit, or prevent others using 'their' sites at the time when they customarily use it, or prevent others impeding the routes over which they customarily travel from site to site. On the other hand, it may be that possession is simply an inappropriate concept in the context of such use of things, and that a more simple and fruitful way forward would be to recognise that, in such cases, possession is not an appropriate prerequisite for title. These points are considered in more detail in section 7.2.2 below in the context of particular and general use rights.

Control through agents and control of contents

Finally, there are two rather obvious points that are worth making at this point. The first is that you can be in possession of a thing without personally having any physical control over it if someone else has physical control on your behalf, for example in her capacity as your employee or agent. This is demonstrated by the decision in *Sullivan* v. *Earl of Caithness* [1976] 2 WLR 361 (extracted at www.cambridge.org/propertylaw/), although, as will be seen there, this may perhaps leave us with some awkward questions about precisely where the principal has possession. Secondly, the person in possession of a thing is also *prima facie* in possession of all its contents. This is explicable on the basis that, if you are in physical control of a container, you must also be in physical control of its contents. However, complications can arise where the possessor of the container (which might be a box, or a locked room, or an area of land) is unaware of either the existence of its contents or their precise nature: see *R. v. Cavendish* [1961] 2 All ER 856, CA, and *R. v. Warner* [1969] 2 AC 256 (both extracted at www.cambridge.org/propertylaw/). Also, there can be difficulties where others have access to the 'container'. We look at this point again in Chapter 11 in the context of the 'finding' cases, where we consider the relative claims to lost and abandoned goods that can be made by those who find and take possession of them, and those with freehold and leasehold interests in the land on (or in) which the goods are found. As will be seen in Chapter 11, the law has become considerably confused by a failure to appreciate that it is possession that forms the basis of any claim by finders and landowners.

7.1.3.2. Intention required

Intention to exclude

The difficulty of divorcing the acts said to constitute possession from the intention with which those acts were performed has already been noted. What then precisely is the intention required? It has been said that there must be an intention 'in one's own name and on one's own behalf, to exclude the world at large, including the owner with the paper title if he be not himself the possessor, so far as is reasonably practicable and so far as the processes of the law will allow' (Slade J in *Powell* v. *McFarlane*, extracted at www.cambridge.org/propertylaw/). It is important to clarify what is *not* required. First, it does not matter that the acts of possession were performed in the mistaken belief that the actor was owner. *Ex hypothesi*, such a person can have no intention to exclude the true owner. He does, however, have the intention to exclude the whole world, and that is all that is required. Those who take possession in the mistaken belief that they are entitled to do so are as much in possession as those who consciously take as trespassers (*Lodge* v. *Wakefield Metropolitan Borough Council* [1995] 38 EG 136, CA). Secondly, it is not necessary that the person assumed control with the intention of acquiring or assuming ownership: what is at issue here is possession (i.e. exclusive physical control).

However, this still leaves us with difficulties. Must the possessor's intention be to exclude the whole world for ever, or is it sufficient that he intends to do so only for a limited time or until some future event occurs? Suppose, for example, a person enters into possession mistakenly believing that the paper owner has granted him a lease of the land in question. Is his possession adverse as against the paper owner? Or take the position of a person who consciously takes over land as a trespasser, knowing that the true owner will not be using the land until some future event occurs (the true owner might be serving a long prison sentence, or have bought the land for road widening purposes and have no use for it until the road is to be built). Assume also that the trespasser knows that she is likely to be evicted by the true owner when that future event occurs. Is the trespasser in possession? It would be odd if the answer was to depend on whether her present intention is to resist the true owner's attempts at eviction if and when they happen, rather than to go quietly when asked to leave. Is there any sensible dividing line that can be drawn between on the one hand those who have no intention of excluding the true owner but know there is no likelihood of the true owner taking steps to evict them for the time being and intend to stay for as long as that state of affairs continues, and on the other hand those who want to exclude the whole world but are aware that, if the true owner ever does take serious steps to evict them, they will probably bow to the inevitable and leave? To draw a distinction between the two is hard to justify in principle and, one suspects, not easy to do in practice. Nevertheless, applying the above formulation of Slade J in *Powell* v. *McFarlane*, those with the former state of mind are not in possession, whereas those with the latter are: see further *Buckinghamshire County Council* v. *Moran* [1990] Ch 623, where the Court of Appeal appeared to find no difficulty with the point.

Effect of ignorance

This problem has already been touched on above: can you be in possession – i.e. in intentional physical control – of something if you are unaware of its existence? At first sight, the necessary element of intention might appear to be wholly lacking in such a case. However, as already suggested, the answer probably lies in seeing this as a container/contents problem. In other words, in most cases, if you are in intentional control of a container – whether land, a building, or a box – you can safely be assumed to intend to be, and to in fact be, in control of its contents. In these cases, difficulties arise only when the contents prove to be different from those you thought were there (Class A drugs and not scent: see *R.* v. *Warner*, extracted at www.cambridge.org/propertylaw/) or wholly unexpected (stolen goods dumped in your yard, as the defendant claimed in *R.* v. *Cavendish* [1961] 1 WLR 1083, extracted at www.cambridge.org/propertylaw/). On the other hand, there are circumstances where it would not be appropriate to assume that the person in control of the container also has, or intends to exert, control over the contents. For example, it might not be appropriate to make this assumption about goods dropped or abandoned in the public part of a shop, or in an airport lounge open to the public (see *Bridges* v. *Hawkesworth* (1851) 21 LJ QB 75 and *Parker* v. *British Airways Board* [1982] QB 1004, in Chapter 11), or perhaps about the contents of parcels entrusted to the Post Office for delivery.

Extract 7.1   *Lows* v. *Telford* (1875–6) LR 1 App Cas 414

Telford and Westray were lawfully in possession of warehouse premises in Carlisle as tenants. Their landlord had, however, mortgaged the premises to a Mr Lows, and in his capacity as mortgagee Mr Lows was entitled to take possession of the premises at any time (see further Chapter 18). One morning, just before 6.00 am, when no one was there and without any warning, Lows broke into the premises with a carpenter and another man. They got in by taking off the old lock, and they were just in the process of putting on a new one when Telford and Westray arrived. Telford and Westray got a ladder, climbed in by a side window and threw Lows and his men out. Lows brought what was in effect a private prosecution against them for forcible entry (see now section 6 of the Criminal Law Act 1977). Unsurprisingly, they were acquitted by the jury, and they in turn brought this action against Lows for malicious prosecution. The issue turned on whether, at the time when Telford and Westray re-entered through the side window and attacked Lows, they were still technically in possession of the premises and therefore merely defending their own possession, or whether Lows had already acquired possession by then. The court concluded that possession, 'although obtained in a very rough and uncourteous way', had already passed to Lows.

LORD SELBORNE: [Lows] had the legal title; he had (when no one was present to oppose him) effected an actual entry into the premises, beyond all doubt for the purposes of taking possession, and he by himself and his servants had already acquired such a dominion and control over the property, when Westray first came upon the ground, that [Telford and Westray] could not enter it without putting a ladder against the house and getting in through the window. I cannot doubt that in these circumstances and upon this evidence his possession was legally complete and exclusive; and that it was forcibly disturbed by the respondents.

[Lord Hatherley took the same view, and accordingly it was held that Lows had reasonable cause for bringing the prosecution, which therefore was not malicious.]

Notes and Questions 7.1

1 Consider whether the North American Indian land use described by Rose in Extract 4.4 in Chapter 4 above can and should be described as possessory (see further section 7.2.2 below)

2 Read *Powell* v. *McFarlane* (1979) 38 P&CR 452, either in full or as extracted at www.cambridge.org/propertylaw/ (if reading in full, note that parts of the judgment not included in the extract must now be read subject to the House of Lords decision in *J. A. Pye (Oxford) Ltd* v. *Graham* [2002] UKHL 30: see Notes and Questions 11.4 below), and consider the following questions:
    (1) It is clear from what Slade J says that the crucial element for the adverse possessor to prove is that he had the requisite intention – the *animus possidendi*. How, then, is the court to discover what that intention was? Slade J says that this must be inferred from what the intruder actually did on the land, and that statements of intention are of little probative value. What are the justifications for ignoring statements of intention? Do you agree with Slade J's reasons for disregarding contemporaneous statements of intention as well as those made after the event? How interested are the courts in discovering what the adverse possessor *actually* intended?
    (2) Why should it be more difficult for intruders to prove that they are in possession than it is for owners to do so? Examine the reasons given by Slade J.

(3) In both *Powell* v. *McFarlane* and *Tecbild Ltd* v. *Chamberlain* (1969) 20 P&CR 633 (referred to by Slade J in *Powell* v. *McFarlane*), the intruders failed on the ground that their activities were as consistent with an intention to derive some benefit/ enjoyment from the land as they were with an intention to take possession of it to the exclusion of the paper owner. What more would Mr Powell and Mrs Chamberlain have had to do to manifest unequivocally an intention to take possession, given the character of the land in question?

(4) Consider the statement made by Slade J towards the end of this extract that a dispossessor must make his intentions clear before he can be said to be in possession. What does he mean? Is he right? See further *Prudential Assurance Co. Ltd* v. *Waterloo Real Estate Inc.* [1999] 17 EG 131, CA.

3   Read *Fowley Marine (Emsworth) Ltd* v. *Gafford* [1968] 1 All ER 979, CA, either in full or as extracted at www.cambridge.org/propertylaw/, and consider the following questions:

(1) Compare the intentions of those who laid permanent moorings in the Rythe in the mistaken belief that they were entitled to do so by virtue of a customary right, or by virtue of a right incidental to the public right of navigation, and the intentions of Fowley Marine, who laid them in the (possibly) mistaken belief that they owned the Rythe. Why is the second a possessory intent whereas the first is not?

(2) If Gafford had laid his permanent mooring in the mistaken belief that he owned that part of the bed of the Rythe, would Fowley Marine have succeeded in its trespass action against him?

(3) Was Fowley Marine able and/or entitled to exclude anyone from the Rythe? What use could it make of the Rythe for itself? See further section 7.2.2 below on particular and general use rights.

(4) Is it possible for different users to be in 'concurrent' possession of land, as suggested by the judge at first instance? Consider why the Court of Appeal rejected this analysis, and compare Pollock and Wright quoted at section 7.1.2 above.

4   Read *Wik Peoples* v. *Queensland* (1996) 187 CLR 1, either in full or as extracted at www.cambridge.org/propertylaw/. In view of the nature of the land, what additional rights would the pastoral lessees have had to have been given before they could be said to have had exclusive possession? If they had been granted exclusive possession, would this have been inconsistent with the continuation of any native land rights? (Compare *Fowley Marine* v. *Gafford* above, and see also section 7.2.1 below.)

5   Read *Sullivan* v. *Earl of Caithness* [1976] 2 WLR 361, CA, either in full or as extracted at www.cambridge.org/propertylaw/, and answer the following questions:

(1) Explain the distinction that May J makes between 'possession' and 'custody'. Is the distinction valid?

(2) If Caithness' mother kept the guns in a locked cupboard to which she had the only key, who would have been in possession of the guns – Caithness or his mother?

(3) If the government bans private possession of all guns, and requires local authorities to pay compensation to every person formerly in possession of guns in their area, will Caithness be entitled to receive compensation from both Oxfordshire and Surrey?

(4) Suppose Oxfordshire County Council decided to pass a bye-law banning all private ownership of firearms, so that it became an offence to be in possession of a firearm in Oxfordshire. Assuming Surrey County Council had no such bye-law, so possession of guns was legal in Surrey, would Caithness be committing an offence under the Oxfordshire bye-law?

6 Read *R. v. Cavendish* [1961] 1 WLR 1083, CA, either in full as or extracted at www.cambridge.org/propertylaw/, and consider the following:

(1) Assume Cavendish did not know Lisle and knew nothing at all about the stolen oil, and that there was no prior arrangement between them. Suppose then that Lisle, knowing Cavendish had previous convictions for offences of dishonesty (which he did), had left the drums in Cavendish's yard in the belief that Cavendish would accept them and pay him for them as soon as Cavendish returned and discovered them. Would Cavendish then be in possession of the drums? If yes, at what point would he acquire possession?

(2) Assume the same facts, but suppose also that Lisle told the fitter who helped him unload the drums that they were stolen. At that point, would Cavendish have acquired possession of the drums? Would it make any difference if the fitter then accepted the drums on Cavendish's behalf because he too believed that Cavendish was the sort of person who would buy stolen goods? If this belief was genuinely held by the fitter, but in fact wholly ungrounded and totally mistaken, who would have been in possession of the drums once they had been unloaded into the yard and Lisle had driven away?

(3) A distinction is sometimes (as here) drawn between 'actual' and 'constructive' possession. The former is meant to cover cases where the possessor has actual, personal, physical control of something and actually knows it, whereas the latter covers cases where either or both of these elements are deemed. Both, however, constitute possession in law.

7 Read *R. v. Warner* [1969] 2 AC 256, either in full or as extracted at www.cambridge.org/propertylaw/, and consider the following:

(1) In your bedroom there is a cardboard box, put there by a friend, which contains a substance which is a controlled drug. Consider whether, in each of the following circumstances, you are in possession of the drug:

(a) The box was left there by your friend without your knowledge. You have just discovered the existence of the box and the nature of its contents, and have decided to hand it in to the police, but have not yet had an opportunity to do so. Would it make any difference if (i) you decide to keep it instead, or (ii) you have not yet decided what to do with it?

(b) You know the box is there, but the box is sealed and you do not know what it contains.

(c) You know the box is there, and it is sealed, but you believe it contains cabbages. Would it make any difference if you thought it contained (i) prescription drugs lawfully acquired by your friend or (ii) jewellery stolen by your friend?

(d) You believe the box contains the controlled drug, but in fact it contains only cabbages.

(2) Is the distinction drawn between differences in kind and differences in quality satisfactory in this context? Can you suggest a better test to apply in deciding whether a person in possession of a container is in possession of its contents?

(3) Is the Post Office in possession of the contents of parcels entrusted to it for delivery?

7.2. Possession of land

7.2.1. Leases and licences

We have seen that possession means intentional exclusive physical control. However, it is possible to be in intentional exclusive physical control of land without being in possession of it. Here the essential distinction to be drawn is between possession (in this context usually referred to as 'exclusive' possession, although the 'exclusive' is redundant – as we saw earlier, possession is necessarily exclusive) and occupation. A person granted the right to possession of land acquires a property interest, whereas a person granted a right to occupy it – even if it is exclusive occupation – acquires only a personal right. Specifically, if L, the fee simple owner of land, grants T the right to possession of the land for a limited period of time, then T acquires a lease of the land. One of the rights that T enjoys by virtue of having possession as a tenant is the right to exclusive occupation of the land during the lease – i.e. the right to occupy it to the exclusion of L and of any third party. In this context, then, 'possession' includes, but means something more than, exclusive occupation.

The fee simple owner can of course grant someone a personal right to occupy the land for a limited period without granting him possession of the land. Such a right – a 'licence' – might be exclusive in the sense that it gives the grantee a personal right to exclude the owner for the duration of the permission. Nevertheless, the right will be purely personal and not proprietary, and it will not be enforceable against anyone other than the grantor. So, for example, the grantee will have no right to bring an action against a stranger who evicts him – only the owner will be able to do this (see *Hill* v. *Tupper* (1863) 2 H&C 121; 159 ER 51, Extract 5.1 above).

7.2.1.1. Why the distinction matters

For a number of reasons, it is important to be able to distinguish between a lease and a licence to occupy. The first is that a lease, characteristically of private property interests, is in principle assignable and enforceable against third parties, whereas a licence is not. In a lease, the landlord and tenant may have agreed to a contractual restriction on the tenant's right to assign the lease, but this will be effective in contract only. In other words, a transfer of the lease by the tenant to a third party will always be effective to pass the title to the lease to the transferee, even if the transfer is in breach of contract. If the assignment does amount to a breach of contract, the landlord's primary remedy will be to take action against the transferee, who has now become the tenant. As for enforceability against third parties, this means not only that the tenant can defend his possession against intruders, as we saw above, but also that, if the landlord sells its interest in the land, the lease will be fully effective and enforceable against the landlord's buyer (assuming any land registration requirements are satisfied: see further Chapter 15 for the circumstances in which leases require registration). By contrast, because a licence to occupy is personal to the grantee, it is neither assignable by the licensee nor enforceable against third parties such as buyers of the licensor's interest, except through the very limited mechanisms applicable to any other contractual right.

The second reason why it is necessary to distinguish leases and licences is that statutory protection for occupiers (whether residential, business or agricultural) has traditionally been available only for tenants, not licensees. In the case of residential premises in particular, landowners have sought to disguise leases as licences in order to avoid giving occupiers the rent control, security of tenure and protection against unlawful eviction conferred on tenants by the Rent Acts. This reason is less pressing than it once was. This is partly because a dramatic decrease in statutory protection for residential occupiers has made the issue less important from the landlord's point of view, and partly because some of the more recent statutory protection has been drafted so as to cover those who occupy residential premises as licensees as well as tenants. However, there continue to be important statutory rights which are available only to tenants and not to licensees – see, for example, the enfranchisement rights conferred on tenants by statutes from the Leasehold Reform Act 1967 to the Leasehold Reform, Housing and Urban Development Act 1993, and the statutory covenants for structural and exterior repair implied into residential tenancies by the Landlord and Tenant Act 1985 as amended (the source of the problem in *Bruton* v. *London & Quadrant Housing Trust* [1999] 3 WLR 150, HL, discussed in Notes and Questions 17.5 below).

Thirdly, it is sometimes said that licences, unlike leases, are revocable by the grantor. However, this is misleading. The truth is that, in the case of leases, there are strict formal rules governing the permissible duration of the lease and the mechanisms by which it can be terminated. These are considered in detail in Chapter 17, but broadly the position is that there are two main categories of lease, the fixed-term tenancy where the lease is for a single fixed period stated in advance – for example, ten years – which automatically expires at the end of the period, and the periodic tenancy where the lease continues for recurring periods – for example, weekly, monthly or yearly – until terminated by a notice to quit of a prescribed length. There are two additional categories: the tenancy at will (where the tenant is allowed to remain in possession until required by the landlord to leave) and the tenancy at sufferance (where the tenant is in possession without the permission of the landlord but on sufferance) and as we see in Chapter 17 these are both terminable at will by either landlord or tenant. In the case of licences, on the other hand, the duration of the permission to occupy, and the question of whether (and if so how) it can be withdrawn, depend entirely on the contract agreed between the parties: see *Winter Garden Theatre (London) Ltd* v. *Millennium Productions Ltd* [1948] AC 173, HL. Whether or not the right is legally enforceable depends on ordinary contract rules, so, for example, a grant of a right to occupy land for a fixed period in exchange for a lump-sum payment or licence fee is no more revocable that a grant of a lease for an equivalent period. The remedies available to the grantee for a wrongful revocation may be different: a lessee has a wide range of property remedies available as well as contractual remedies such as damages, whereas a licensee can rely only on contractual remedies. However, even using only contractual remedies, a licensee may nevertheless still be able to restrain a threatened revocation of the licence in breach of contract (see the *Winter Garden* case and *Verrall* v. *Great Yarmouth Borough Council* [1981] QB 202 noted in Chapter 5 and extracted at www.cambridge.org/propertylaw/).

The final distinction between leases and licences to be noted here is that the *caveat emptor* principle generally applies to leases but not to licences. One important consequence of this is that, subject to limited exceptions, a landlord gives no warranties about the state and condition of the land or that it is fit for the purposes for which it is let. This is not true in relation to licences (see *Wettern Electric* v. *Welsh Development Agency* [1983] 2 WLR 897), so in this respect at least licensees of land can be in a stronger position than lessees.

7.2.1.2.   Distinguishing leases from licences

If these are the reasons why it is important to be able to distinguish a lease from a licence, how easy is it to draw the distinction in practice? The first point to make is that 'licence' is a broad term covering any permission to make any kind of use of any thing. When used in relation to land as opposed to other things, it covers not only the grant of a personal right to occupy the land but also the grant of any right to make use of the land in any other way which is purely personal and not proprietary. The difficulty in distinguishing leases and licences of course arises only where the licence amounts to the grant of a full right to occupy land.

There have been many judicial attempts at identifying the essential difference between a personal right to occupy land and a right to possession of it. In *Marchant* v. *Charters* [1977] 3 All ER 918, CA (extracted at www.cambridge.org/propertylaw/), Lord Denning described the difference as one of 'the nature and quality of the occupancy. Was it intended that the occupier should have a stake in the room or did he have only permission for himself personally to occupy the room?' However, in later cases, the courts have preferred to rely on the exclusive possession test propounded by Windeyer J in the High Court of Australia in *Radaich* v. *Smith* (1959) 101 CLR 209 at 222:

> What then is the fundamental right which a tenant has that distinguishes his position from that of a licensee? It is an interest in land as distinct from a personal permission to enter the land and use it for some stipulated purpose or purposes. And how is it to be ascertained whether such an interest in land has been given? By seeing whether the grantee was given a *legal right of exclusive possession* of the land for a term or from year to year or for a life or lives. If he was, he is a tenant. And he cannot be other than a tenant, because a legal right of exclusive possession is a tenancy and the creation of such a right is a demise. To say that a man who has, by agreement with a landlord, a right of exclusive possession of land for a term is not a tenant is simply to contradict the first proposition by the second. A right of exclusive possession is secured by the right of a lessee to maintain ejectment and, after his entry, trespass. A reservation to the landlord, either by contract or statute, of a limited right of entry, as for example to view or repair, is, of course, not inconsistent with the grant of exclusive possession. Subject to such reservations, a tenant for a term or from year to year or for a life or lives can exclude his landlord as well as strangers from the demised premises. All this is long-established law: see *Cole on Ejectment* (1857), pp. 72–3, 287, 458.

It is now taken as established by the House of Lords in *Street* v. *Mountford* [1985] AC 809 (extracted at www.cambridge.org/propertylaw/), that this exclusive possession test is conclusive: an occupier cannot be a tenant if he does not have exclusive possession. However, this test is not as straightforward as it might seem, and it has not always proved easy to apply.

There are a number of difficulties. First, can we take it that the converse is true – i.e. that any person granted exclusive possession must have a lease (or some other proprietary interest entitling the holder to possession) rather than a licence? In principle the answer ought to be yes, but, as we see in Chapter 17, the courts have not always been willing to accept this.

Secondly, there is a persistent tendency to confuse possession with exclusive occupation (see, for example, how often in the judgment of Lord Templeman in *Street* v. *Mountford* 'possession' is used when what is meant is 'exclusive occupation' and *vice versa*). It is certainly true that, if a grant does not confer on the grantee the right to exclude all others – if, for example, it requires the grantee to share occupation with the grantor or with others granted rights by the grantor – then the grantee cannot be said to be in possession and so cannot be a tenant (see the joined cases *A. G. Securities* v. *Vaughan* and *Antoniades* v. *Villiers* [1990] 1 AC 417, extracted at www.cambridge.org/propertylaw/). However, it does not follow that someone who *is* given exclusive occupation rights by a grantor necessarily has possession (or any other proprietary rather than personal right). His exclusive occupation rights may be simply personal (i.e. enforceable against the grantor only), in the same way as the exclusive right to put pleasure boats on Basingstoke Canal was enforceable only against the grantor in *Hill* v. *Tupper* (1863) 2 H&C 121;

159 ER 51 (Extract 5.1 above) in which case he can only have a licence and not a lease. So we come back to the 'nature and quality' question posed by Lord Denning – when do exclusive occupation rights amount to possession and when are they merely personal rights to occupy? The courts have had particular difficulty with cases where the grantor is a social provider of housing (for example, a charity, as in *Gray* v. *Taylor* [1998] 1 WLR 1093, CA, extracted at www.cambridge.org/proper-tylaw/) or a local authority or housing association providing hostel accommodation or temporary housing for homeless persons. The courts have often expressed doubts as to whether the occupiers of such housing ought to have the full range of statutory rights conferred on tenants, but are faced with the difficulty that Parliament has not given social landlords wholesale exemption from the relevant statutory provisions.

Once it became established that exclusive possession is the conclusive determinant of a lease, landlords who wanted to disguise leases as licences adopted devices designed to ensure that their grantees did not have exclusive possession. Three such devices have received the attention of the House of Lords. The first two, considered by the House of Lords in the joined cases of *A. G. Securities* v. *Vaughan* and *Antoniades* v. *Villiers* [1990] 1 AC 417 (extracted at www.cambridge.org/propertylaw/) depend on the notion that exclusive occupation is an essential ingredient of possession. They involve granting the occupant a right to occupy that is not exclusive, either by the landlord reserving to itself the right to move in and share occupation with the grantee at any time, or by the landlord reserving a right to grant third parties rights to come and share occupation with the grantee. The courts have found it relatively easy to deal with such cases. If such rights are genuinely reserved, then the grantee does not have a right to exclude and therefore does not have possession and therefore cannot be a tenant, but if the provision reserving such rights is merely a sham, not reflecting the intentions of the parties, it will be disregarded and the reality of the situation will be recognised (see *Somma* v. *Hazelhurst* [1978] 1 WLR 1014, discussed by Lord Templeman in *Street* v. *Mountford*, and also *Antoniades* v. *Villiers*).

The second way of avoiding a grant of exclusive occupation depends on there being more than one intended occupier of the premises. Instead of granting all the intended occupiers a joint right to occupy the whole (which would have the effect of making them joint holders of an exclusive right to occupy the whole) the landlord grants each of them a separate right to occupy the premises, sharing occupation with the others. The courts have found this more difficult: there is no pretence here, in that each of the sharers is indeed sharing with the others. The sham – if there is one – lies only in treating the sharers as having separate interests in cases where in truth the intention was that they should jointly hold a single interest and be entitled as a group to exclusive occupation as against the landlord. The conclusion the courts have reached is that they will read the separate agreements as conferring a single joint interest when this is what the parties intended, but only where all the technical requirements for the creation of a joint interest are satisfied – i.e. only where the intention is that each sharer should have an identical interest, starting and ending simultaneously: see *A. G. Securities* v. *Vaughan* (extracted at www.cambridge.org/propertylaw/), where the limitations of this approach are apparent.

The third device designed to ensure that occupants are licensees and not tenants is more sophisticated, depending on the *nemo dat* principle considered in Chapter 10 (i.e. that no one can grant another person a greater interest in a thing than she herself already has). This device involves ensuring that the occupants are granted their rights to occupy by someone who has contractual rights to manage the land but no interest in the land itself. Typically, the owner of the land grants exclusive rights to manage the land to a management company without granting it any proprietary interest in the land. The management company then grants occupation rights to the intended occupier. Since the grantor of the right to occupy has no property interest in the land, it is unable to confer a property interest on the grantee, so the occupation right granted can only be a licence and not a tenancy. However, despite the logic of this conclusion, the courts have been reluctant to accept it in cases where the parties clearly intend the occupier to have precisely the same rights and obligations in relation to the land as he would have if he was in possession. In *Bruton* v. *London & Quadrant Housing Trust* [1999] 3 WLR 150 (discussed in Notes and Questions 17.5 below), the House of Lords concluded that in such a case the occupier does indeed have a lease (at least for the purposes of imposing statutory repairing liability on the landlord) although, as we see in Chapter 17, there are considerable difficulties in seeing how this fits in with established property principles.

Notes and Questions 7.2

1 Read *Marchant* v. *Charters* [1977] 3 All ER 918, CA, either in full or as extracted at www.cambridge.org/propertylaw/, and consider the following:
   (1) Lord Denning stated in this case:
   [Whether an occupant is a tenant or a licensee] does not depend on whether he or she has exclusive possession or not. It does not depend on whether the room is furnished or not. It does not depend on whether the occupation is permanent or temporary. It does not depend on the label which the parties put on it. All these are factors which may influence the decision but none of them is conclusive.

   To what extent is Lord Denning still correct, in the light of subsequent cases?
   (2) What did Lord Denning mean by 'a stake in the room'? What facts led him to conclude that Mr Charters did not have one, and therefore was a licensee?
   (3) Did Mrs Marchant grant Mr Charters the exclusive right to occupy the room?

2 Read *Street* v. *Mountford* [1985] AC 809, either in full or as extracted at www.cambridge.org/propertylaw/, and consider the following:

(1)   Does it follow from what Lord Templeman says that it is possible (a) to be
      granted the right to possession of land, and yet still have only a licence (i.e. a non-
      proprietary right), or (b) for possession to be a free-standing proprietary status,
      not just an ingredient of an acknowledged proprietary interest such as ownership,
      lease etc.? See further section 17.3.1.6 below on this point.

(2)   Lord Templeman said that, if an occupier is granted exclusive occupation,
      the *prima facie* intention to create a tenancy will nevertheless be negatived
      'where the owner, a requisitioning authority, had no power to grant a tenancy'.
      Consider why this should be the case (see *Bruton* v. *London & Quadrant
      Housing Association* [1999] 3 WLR 150, HL, discussed in Notes and Questions
      17.5 below)

3   Read *Gray* v. *Taylor* [1998] 1 WLR 1093, CA, either in full or as extracted at
    www.cambridge.org/propertylaw/, and consider the following:
(1)   The first example Sir John Vinelott gives (of a beneficiary properly being required
      to pay for occupation of land held on trust for him) concerns a private trust. But
      the trust in this case is not a private trust but a public charitable trust. In a
      charitable trust, unlike a private trust, the trustees do not hold the trust property
      on trust for individual beneficiaries. Instead, they hold it on trust for the abstract
      charitable purpose for which the trust was created. So, for example, Oxfam holds
      its assets on trust for the relief of poverty, not on trust for the people on whom it
      spends its money. Those people who do happen to benefit from the charitable
      purpose being carried out are therefore not 'beneficiaries' of the trust in the
      technical sense: they have no *locus standi* to enforce the trust (this can be done
      only by the Attorney-General) and they have no interest in the trust property.
      Mrs Taylor's occupation of the flat could not therefore have been attributable
      to any trustee–beneficiary relationship.
(2)   Compare the outcome and reasoning in this case with that in *Family Housing
      Association* v. *Jones* [1990] 1 WLR 779, CA, where occupants of housing
      provided by a housing trust pursuant to its purpose of providing short-term
      accommodation for the homeless were held to be tenants and not licensees
      (they had exclusive occupation: the opposite conclusion was reached by the
      House of Lords in *Westminster City Council* v. *Clarke* [1992] 2 AC 288, where the
      terms imposed on residents of a homeless persons' hostel resulted in them not
      having exclusive occupation of any one room). Slade LJ expressed misgivings
      about the effect of the court's decision:
      [W]hatever their wishes or intentions, it may at least be difficult for bodies charged
      with responsibilities for the housing of the homeless to enter into any arrange-
      ment pursuant to section 65(2) of the Housing Act 1985 under which the person
      housed is to enjoy exclusive occupation of premises, however temporarily,
      without conferring on that person security of tenure by virtue of the Act ... The
      result must be substantially to reduce the choice of methods available to bodies
      such as the housing association for dealing with their always limited supplies

of housing stock. I am not sure that this result will necessarily inure to the benefit of the class of homeless persons in this country viewed as a whole. (*Family Association* v. *Jones* [1990] 1 WLR 779 at 793)

See further *Bruton* v. *London & Quadrant Housing Association* [1999] 3 WLR 150, HL, discussed in Notes and Questions 17.5 below.

4   Read the joined cases of *A. G. Securities* v. *Vaughan* and *Antoniades* v. *Villiers* [1990] 1 AC 417, either in full or as extracted at www.cambridge.org/propertylaw/, and consider the following:
   (1)   Lord Templeman gives two alternative reasons why clause 16 of the *Antoniades* licence should be ignored. Underlying the first is the proposition that, if the Rent Acts were not applicable (as they probably would now not be), the effect of clause 16 would be that Mr Villiers and Ms Bridger would initially jointly have a tenancy of the flat, but that this tenancy would automatically be converted into a licence if Mr Antoniades ever chose to exercise his power to share possession. Is this consistent with what Lord Oliver says? If not, which of them is correct?
   (2)   His second reason is that it was a sham, not reflecting the genuine intention of the parties. What factors does the court take into consideration in deciding whether to treat an expressly agreed term as a sham? What is the relevance of the subsequent actions of the grantor?
   (3)   In *Antoniades* v. *Villiers*, consider what the status of each of the parties would be if, soon after moving in, the couple split up and one of them left. Who would be liable for the payment of what rent? What if a third person then moved in with the one who remained, and signed a separate licence document with Mr Antoniades?
   (4)   Explain why the occupants in *A. G. Securities* v. *Vaughan* could not together hold a tenancy of the flat as joint tenants. Could they have held such a tenancy as tenants in common?

7.2.2. Possession and particular use rights

7.2.2.1.   General and particular use rights

A person entitled to possession of land is entitled to make whatever use of it she wants (subject only to any restrictions of the type considered in Chapter 6 such as nuisance, planning law, restrictive covenants etc.). A right to use land only for a particular, specified purpose, as opposed to general unrestricted use, cannot amount to possession but it may nevertheless constitute a property interest of some kind. The same is as true of communal and public property rights as it is of private property rights. So, for example, the communal use rights enjoyed by the inhabitants of New Windsor over Bachelors' Acre (to use it 'for lawful sports and pastimes': *New Windsor Corp.* v. *Mellor* [1975] 1 Ch 380, discussed in Notes and Questions 5.1 above) are particular use rights which do not give the inhabitants possession of Bachelors' Acre but nevertheless do give them property rights over it.

The use rights of the Murray Islanders in *Mabo* v. *Queensland (No. 2)* (1992) 175 CLR 1, discussed in Chapter 4, may at first sight look more like possessory rights, especially when contrasted with the particular use rights of the aboriginal clans in *Milirrpum* v. *Nabalco Pty Ltd* (1971) 17 FLR 141 (also Chapter 4), but the result of the Australian High Court's decision in *Mabo (No. 2)* and of the Australian Native Titles Act 1993 is that the holders' rights will continue only for so long as they are exercised in the same way. In this sense, their authorised use is particular not general: they cannot use the land for any purpose other than that for which they have always used it, so that a Murray Islander whose family has always used a particular tract of land as a house and garden has a property right to use it for that particular purpose, but no right whatsoever to use it for any other purpose, and even that particular use right will expire if it is not exercised (compare common law rights of common). Public rights and customary rights in England and Wales also tend to be particular rather than general use rights: consider, for example, a public right of way, or a right to use a public park, or the public navigational rights in *Fowley Marine (Emsworth) Ltd* v. *Gafford* [1968] 1 All ER 979, CA, discussed in Notes and Questions 7.1 above.

7.2.2.2. Compatibility of particular and general use rights

Two aspects of particular use rights, considered in detail in Chapter 8, should be noted here. The first is this. In a common law system like ours, a particular use right is necessarily exercisable over land in which someone else has a general use right (there is always at least a residual title somewhere). What happens when the particular use authorised by the right is so extensive that it makes the other person's general use right nugatory? This does not appear to be viewed as a problem in relation to communal or public particular use rights. In *Fowley Marine (Emsworth) Ltd* v. *Gafford* [1968] 1 All ER 979, CA, discussed in Notes and Questions 7.1 above, for example, the fact that there were public navigation rights over the Rythe was held not to be inconsistent with Fowley Marine being in possession of the Rythe, even though it meant that Fowley Marine could not actually make much use of the Rythe. Similarly, in *New Windsor Corp.* v. *Mellor* [1975] 1 Ch 380, discussed in Notes and Questions 5.1 above, Lord Denning said that, while a customary use must be reasonable to amount to a communal property right, it was not an objection that it prevented the servient owner from making any use of the land.

However, as we see in Chapter 8, incompatibility with possessory rights is seen as a problem in relation to private particular use rights. The only significant categories of private particular use rights recognised as proprietary in our system are easements (a right to do a specified thing on someone else's land, or run a specified service over it) and profits (a right to take something from someone else's land). Any particular use right which fails to fall within the confines of these two categories cannot be proprietary and will take effect in contract only (see, for example, the right to run pleasure boats over someone else's canal in *Hill* v. *Tupper*

(1863) 2 H&C 121; 159 ER 51, Extract 5.1 above). As will be seen from *Re Ellenborough Park* [1956] Ch 131, discussed in Notes and Questions 8.3 below, the scope of easements is strictly confined, and a major constraint is that the use authorised must not exclude the servient owner from using the land himself. This objection has led the courts to refuse to accept a right to roam over someone else's land as an easement, although this is not perhaps easy to reconcile with other court decisions accepting as easements rights of a more obvious commercial value: see, for example, *Re Ellenborough Park* itself, discussed in Notes and Questions 8.3 below, where residents' rights to use a communal garden laid out as part of a residential estate were held to be easements.

The second point arises in the aboriginal land rights contexts. As we see in Chapter 9, one of the reasons for the reluctance to recognise aboriginal land usage as proprietary has been a tendency to regard property and ownership as synonymous. A failure to appreciate that particular use rights are historically and analytically firmly established as property interests in the common law system can mislead the courts and others into measuring aboriginal land claims solely against a general use yardstick, and categorising any user right not amounting to possession as non-proprietary. The Australian Native Titles Act 1993 now recognises the diversity of land use rights requiring protection, and section 35(1) of the Canadian Constitution Act 1982 also distinguishes between aboriginal title and aboriginal particular use rights (including 'site-specific' rights: see *Delgamuukw* v. *British Columbia* [1997] 3 SCR 1010, discussed in Notes and Questions 5.2 above). Nevertheless, the reluctance to equate native non-general land user with traditional common law particular use rights still persists: see, for example, the assumption made in *Mabo (No. 2)*, *Delgamuukw* and *Wik Peoples* that a government grant of a fee simple or lease would extinguish native title rights. This appears to be on the basis that subjection to particular use rights is incompatible with a holding of a common law possessory interest, something that is demonstrably not the case.

7.3. Possession of goods: bailment

7.3.1. Nature of bailment

We have seen that, in the case of land, if a person has a proprietary interest in the land which carries with it the right to possession of the land, he can grant the right to possession away to another person for a limited period. The grantee then has a lease of the land, and 'lease' denotes both the interest held by the grantee and the ensuing relationship between grantor and grantee which subsists for the duration of that interest. Similarly, in the case of goods, the person with the proprietary interest in the goods which carries with it the right to possession (typically, the owner) can grant away that right to possession to another person for a limited period. This creates not a lease but a bailment, and again 'bailment' denotes both the interest held by the grantee and the ensuing relationship between grantor and grantee.

However, while there are similarities between lease and bailment, there are also significant differences. Most importantly, leases are exclusively consensual – they can only come into existence by a positive, deliberate grant of an interest by one person to another (which is not to say that it cannot be done inadvertently: see Chapter 17 as to the circumstances in which a grant will be implied by law). Consequently, there is always a contractual relationship between the grantor and the grantee which co-exists with the property relationship between them. Bailment, on the other hand, has a much wider ambit – although *precisely* how much wider is controversial. It clearly covers all consensual grants of possession, but it also covers at least some (and arguably all) cases where a person takes possession without the knowledge and consent of the owner. Thus, a relationship of bailment exists between a finder of goods and the owner, and also between a thief and the owner. We consider the precise ambit of bailment in detail in Chapter 17, but for present purposes we will assume that the relationship of bailment arises whenever goods are in the possession of a non-owner who realises that she is not the owner. Because, as we saw earlier, possession requires intentional physical control, this excludes from the bailment category those cases where a person inadvertently or unconsciously acquires control of someone else's goods (at least until the point where they realise the true position). So, for example, if someone slips a stolen wallet into my pocket without my knowledge, I am not the owner's bailee of the wallet unless and until I find it and realise that it is not mine. But, even after excluding these cases, this still leaves bailment covering a very wide and disparate range of situations. Not surprisingly, therefore, bailments are usually categorised according to the purpose of the bailment and/or the circumstances in which it arose, and the incidents of the relationship – the rights, duties and obligations of bailor and bailee – vary enormously from one category to another.

7.3.2. Rights, duties and obligations of bailor and bailee

Since bailments are not necessarily consensual, it follows that there is not always a contractual relationship between bailor and bailee. Whereas in leases the content of the relationship is determined by looking at the contractually agreed terms as well as by those terms implied by law, in bailments we often have to look elsewhere to discover the rights and obligations of the parties to the relationship.

We noted earlier that property law has traditionally taken surprisingly little notice of goods. Consequently, contract and tort lawyers have been allowed to make the running in the development of the law, and in the case of bailment in particular it is now hard to tease the proprietary elements out from the interstices of contract and tort. We shall see later in this chapter that one of the consequences of this is that the law has been very slow to develop proprietary remedies for the recovery of goods. Another consequence, and the one of more immediate relevance here, is that bailment has been seen as part of the law of obligations rather than the law of property. The attention of lawyers has therefore been concentrated not so much on the rights of the parties arising out of the bailment relationship but on their obligations. Indeed, as we see in Chapter 17, the whole debate on the proper ambit of bailments is conducted in terms of obligations. This is one reason why, whereas in the case of leases such classification as there is depends on the duration of the rights conferred on the tenant, bailments are classified by reference to the purpose of the bailment or the circumstances in which it arose: it is this that tends to dictate the level of obligation imposed on the bailee by the bailment by both tort and (where there is one) contract. So, for example, the airline which takes custody of your luggage when you book into a flight has a greater obligation to take care of it for you than a person who finds it in the street if you have lost it.

As far as the rights of the parties are concerned, the obvious and important point to make is that, since bailments are not necessarily consensual, it follows that the bailee does not necessarily have a right to possession *as against the bailor* – whenever the bailment is not authorised by the bailor (for example, bailments arising out of finding, or theft, or unauthorised sub-bailment) the bailor has a better right to possession than the bailee *even during the currency of the bailment relationship*. This is to be contrasted with leases of land, where the lessee necessarily has a better right to possession than the lessor for so long as the lease lasts.

However, it must be emphasised that all bailees, even those with no right to possession as against their bailor, necessarily have a better right to possession than the rest of the world. In this respect, they are in a wholly different category from licensees. Whereas licensees, whether of land or of goods, have purely personal rights enforceable only against those who granted them the rights, bailees necessarily by virtue of the fact that they have possession, have rights in relation to the goods enforceable against the whole world in the sense that they can restrain all outsiders from interfering with their rights. We return to this point in Chapter 17, when we consider how far bailments can be said to be proprietary.

7.4. Protection of possession

7.4.1. Protection of property rights by protection of possession

To a large extent, English law protects property rights by protecting possession rather than by protecting ownership. If you want to bring an action for the recovery of land or goods you must prove that the thing is yours in the sense that you have a right to possession of it rather than yours in the sense that you own it. Similarly, if you are seeking redress for interference with or damage to property, your action will be framed as a complaint of interference with your possessory rights, rather than interference or damage to the thing itself or to your ownership rights.

7.4.2. Tort and the protection of property rights

7.4.2.1. **The role of tort in the protection of property rights**

Apart from this focus on possession rather than ownership, there are two other peculiarities about English law's protection of property rights. The first is that, particularly in the case of goods, the main mechanism for dealing with complaints about infringements of property rights is the law of tort. So, for example, although property law provides a direct action for the recovery of possession of land, there is no equivalent action for the recovery of goods. Instead, if your complaint is that someone has wrongfully deprived you of your goods, you will have to rely on the specialised tort of conversion (considered further below). Similarly, a complaint about damage to goods or an interference with their use and enjoyment will have to be dealt with by the tort of trespass to goods (or possibly negligence). Even in relation to land, tort law has a significant role to play in the protection of property rights. As we have said, a complaint that someone is wrongfully in possession of your land will be dealt with by a straightforward property action for the recovery of possession. If, however, your complaint is of damage to land, or any other inter-ference with the exercise of property rights over it or your use and enjoyment of it, again you will usually have to rely on tort law – this time on nuisance (considered in Chapter 6) or trespass to land – although there may be other avenues to pursue if you can demonstrate a proprietary relationship between yourself and the defen-dant, such as a leasehold relationship.

In Extract 7.2 below, Weir considers the problems caused by this reliance on tort law for the protection of property rights. As he explains, some of the practical difficulties have now been removed, or at least ameliorated, by the Torts (Interference with Goods) Act 1977. In particular, the Act gives the court a general jurisdiction to make an order for the delivery of goods in any action for wrongful interference with goods (the generic term used in the 1977 Act for all the torts protecting property rights in goods). This removes a significant failing in the previous law. As we see below, a person complaining of wrongfully withheld goods usually has to rely on the tort of conversion, and the only remedy for conversion used to be damages: the court had no power to order the return of the goods themselves. This was unobjectionable in the case of most fungible goods where the complainant was likely to be interested only in the financial loss suffered, but was obviously inadequate where, for whatever reason, the complainant valued the thing as thing rather than as wealth, to adopt the terminology Bernard Rudden uses in 'Things as Thing and Things as Wealth' (Extract 2.3 above). Section 2(2) of the 1977 Act now gives the court power to make such an order instead of or as well as ordering damages.

However, as Weir points out, despite the changes made by the 1977 Act, the basic problem remains that tort law is in many respects an inappropriate mechanism for dealing with protection of property rights. In particular, in tort law the emphasis is on the commission of a wrong by the defendant, and this gives rise to significant complications in many areas of the law relating to goods, and to unnecessary differences between rules applicable to land and those applicable to goods. So, for example, the rules applicable in deciding when, if at all, the owner of lost goods loses his title to them (noted briefly in Chapter 10) are not only complex in themselves but wholly different from those applicable where a person has lost possession of land.

7.4.2.2. Scope of the property torts

The role of the tort of nuisance is considered in some detail in Chapter 6. Detailed consideration of the other property torts is beyond the scope of this book, but for present purposes it is helpful to have a broad understanding of the way in which the most important ones – conversion and trespass – work.

Conversion

What amounts to a conversion of goods?

It is not easy to provide a definition of conversion which is both short and accurate. Very broadly, it involves a wilful interference with someone else's goods by dealing with them in a way that is inconsistent with that person's title and possession of them – Weir describes it as '[treating] goods as if they were [yours] when they are not' (Weir, *A Casebook on Tort*, p. 476; and see also the judicial analyses in *Kuwait Airways Corp.* v. *Iraqi Airways Co.* [2002] UKHL 19 at paragraphs 37–44 and *Marcq* v. *Christie Manson & Woods Ltd* [2003] EWCA Civ 731). It covers such actions as wrongfully taking goods (either by taking possession for yourself, even temporarily, or by depriving the person entitled to possession by wrongfully delivering the goods to someone else), wrongfully detaining them (for example, by failing or refusing to return bailed goods to the owner when he becomes entitled to them and demands their return), wrongfully disposing of or receiving them (so that, on an unauthorised sale of goods, both the seller and the buyer are liable in conversion), and wrongful destruction of goods (damage falling short of destruction would be trespass, not conversion). Whatever it is that constitutes the interference must be done intentionally, but the wrongdoer need not realise that what is being done is wrongful. So, for example, an auctioneer innocently selling stolen goods may be liable in conversion, because he is intentionally and wrongfully depriving the owner of possession even though he does not realise it, and so too is an innocent purchaser of wrongfully sold goods. Finders, however, are not liable in conversion unless and until they do anything adverse to the rights of the true owner, such as refusing to return the found goods to the owner, nor are bailees holding over after the bailment has ended.

There used to be a separate tort of detinue, partially overlapping conversion, but this has now been subsumed into the tort of conversion by section 2 of the Torts (Interference with Goods) Act 1977.

Who can sue

Although conversion is traditionally described as an action for the protection of ownership of goods (for example, in the Law Reform Committee's *Eighteenth Report on Conversion and Detinue* (Cmnd 4774, 1971), paragraph 13), this is misleading, in that it is only the possessor of goods, or the person with an immediate right to possession, who can sue in conversion. Ownership is neither a necessary nor a sufficient condition. So, if you the owner of goods have parted with possession of them (for example, by a bailment for a fixed period, or by mortgaging them), you cannot sue a third party wrongdoer in conversion, but your bailee or mortgagee can do so. Your bailee or mortgagee will, however, be liable in conversion to you if they do anything in breach of or outside the terms of the bailment or mortgage which gives you an immediate right to the return of the goods and which is adverse to your possessory rights (for example, by wrongfully selling or refusing to return the goods).

Remedies

It will be apparent from the above that the tort of conversion has the potential for over-compensating the claimant and unfairly penalising the defendant. As Weir points out in Extract 7.2 below, there is a problem about multiplicity of defendants since the events causing the loss of the claimant's goods may have involved a series of conversions by different people, each of whom is *prima facie* liable to compensate the claimant for the full value of the lost goods. This is so even if the claimant is only a bailee, with a limited interest in the goods. Also, in assessing damages, the conduct of the defendant is irrelevant (the liability of the thief who steals the goods is the same as that of the innocent purchaser who buys the stolen goods from him), as is the amount (if any) of the defendant's gain. All these problems were considered by the Law Reform Committee's *Eighteenth Report on Conversion and Detinue* (Cmnd 4774, 1971) and as a result substantial changes in the law were made by the Torts (Interference with Goods) Act 1977.

Trespass

What amounts to trespass

Both trespass to goods and trespass to land involve an unlawful direct physical interference with someone else's possession. No damage to the land or goods is necessary – any direct physical interference is actionable. Unlike conversion, trespass is not a strict liability tort: the interference must probably be intentional or negligent. There is a defence of necessity to an action in trespass (for example, that the defendant was acting in the public interest to avert danger) but it is of very limited scope, and has been held not to justify homeless people taking over vacant local authority housing (*Southwark London Borough Council* v. *Williams* [1971] 1 Ch 734, CA) nor protesters against GM food digging up GM crops (*Monsanto* v. *Tilly* [2000] Env LR 313, CA).

Who can sue

Trespass is an injury to possession, and the only claimant is the person who was actually in possession of the land or goods at the time of the trespass (although see Palmer, *Bailment*, pp. 204–6, for some exceptional cases when a bailor can also sue and also *Monsanto* v. *Tilly* [2000] Env LR 313, CA). The claimant need not also be the owner – in the case of goods, finders, and even thieves, can sue in trespass, since it is accepted that both are in possession, as we see in *Costello* v. *Chief Constable of Derbyshire Constabulary* [2001] 3 All ER 150 discussed in Chapter 11. Indeed, a non-possessing owner may well be the defendant: it is a trespass for a bailor to interfere with or remove the goods during and contrary to the terms of the bailment, as it is for a landlord to interfere with or take back possession of the premises during the lease, except when authorised to do so by the lease.

Remedies
The usual tort remedies of damages (assessed by reference to the harm caused to the claimant) and injunction are available, and in addition, where the trespass involved removal of goods, the claimant is entitled to their return under section 3 of the Torts (Interference with Goods) Act 1977.

7.4.3. Self-help remedies

7.4.3.1. Survival of self-help remedies
The second peculiarity of the legal protection of property rights in this jurisdiction is the survival of self-help remedies. In general (subject to some partial and relatively recent statutory restrictions relating to residential premises considered below), those claiming a right to possession of land or goods in the hands of others are free to take possession of them for themselves without having recourse to the courts, provided they do so peaceably (as to which see below). This applies not only to owners seeking to recover possession from wrongful takers, but also to those seeking to recover possession from those who were once lawfully in possession but whose possessory rights have now expired (for example, former bailees and former tenants). It also applies where a person is in possession by permission of the claimant, which the claimant now unilaterally withdraws. So, mortgagees of land or goods who have retained the right to take possession of the mortgaged property at any time during the mortgage (a not uncommon situation: see Chapter 18) may exercise that right simply by physically seizing possession, and the same applies to landlords of non-residential premises and bailors where the lease or bailment is at will or terminable by notice by the grantor (Chapter 17). It even applies where the claimant's right to possession consists only of a right to forfeit the otherwise superior possessory right of the person in possession because of some breach of obligation. So, for example, landlords whose tenants are in breach of one of the terms of the lease can seize their tenants' goods by levying distress and, if the premises are non-residential, prematurely terminate the lease by retaking possession on a breach of the terms of the lease. Court procedures are available for both of these processes, but the landlord does not always have to use them: in most cases it can instead opt for self-help and physically seize possession for itself.

Nineteenth-century legal historians saw this tolerance towards self-help remedies as an indication of the sophistication of our legal system and our respect for the rule of law:

Had we to write legal history out of our own heads, we might plausibly suppose that, in the beginning law expects men to help themselves when they have been wronged, and that, by slow degrees, it substitutes a litigatory procedure for the rude justice of revenge. There would be substantial truth in this theory. For a long time law was very weak, and as a matter of fact it could not prevent self-help of the most violent kind. Nevertheless, at a fairly early stage in its history, it begins to prohibit any and every attempt to substitute force for judgment. Perhaps we may say that, in its strife against violence it keeps up its courage by bold words. It will prohibit utterly what it cannot regulate.

This at all events was true of our English law in the thirteenth century. So fierce is it against self-help that it can hardly be induced to find a place even for self-defence ... [The thought is] that self-help is an enemy of law, a contempt of the king and of his court ... [However] it would be a great mistake were we to suppose that during the later middle ages the law became stricter about this matter; it became laxer ... In our own day our law allows an amount of quiet self-help that would have shocked Bracton. It can safely allow this, for it has mastered the sort of self-help that is lawless.

(Pollock and Maitland, *The History of English Law*, vol. 2, p. 572)

Holdsworth took the same view:

The aim of early bodies of law is to induce men to submit to the decision of the court instead of helping themselves to what they deem to be their rights, or instead of prosecuting the feud against those who have injured them. Early law endeavours, therefore, to limit rigidly the conditions under which the individual may have recourse to self-help. It attempts, not so much to arbitrate between the parties, as to secure the observance of rules which will prevent the individual helping himself without the sanction of the court ...

But although early law can thus set conditions for the exercise of the right of self-help, no body of law can altogether repress it – nor, if it was able, would it be desirable to do so. If the individual can be allowed to help himself quietly to his rights without disturbing the general public, if as a rule the individual does not try to help himself unless he has right on his side, it will save time and trouble if the individual is allowed to act. But these conditions are not complied with till the rule of law has become second nature. In primitive times the individual, whenever he has the power or the opportunity, will help himself; and it is such self-help on all occasions that it is desirable to repress. Therefore, we find that early law limits, or rather attempts to limit, far more narrowly than later law the sphere of private action.

(Holdsworth, *A History of English Law*, vol. II, pp. 99–100)

See also Holdsworth, *A History of English Law*, vol. III, pp. 278 *et seq.*, and the similar views expressed by Maitland, 'The Beatitude of Seisin', p. 26; compare the rather different historical analysis provided by Lawson, *Remedies of English Law*, p. 25, who ascribes the English tolerance of self-help to the fact that 'the main lines of private law had already been laid down by the early years of the nineteenth century, before the belated establishment of organised professional police forces, and hence at a time when the ordinary citizen had frequently no public authority to look to for help in redressing his wrongs'.

However, this nineteenth-century confidence did not survive long into the twentieth century, and in the latter half of the twentieth century Parliament enacted quite extensive statutory restrictions on taking possession of residential property without judicial process (see below). During the same period there has also been significant judicial condemnation of self-help remedies. In *Billson* v. *Residential Apartments Ltd* [1992] 1 AC 494 at 536, Lord Templeman described forfeiture of leases by physical re-entry as a 'dubious and dangerous method' of determining the lease, and in *McPhail* v. *Persons Unknown* [1973] Ch 447 at 456–7, CA, Lord Denning emphasised the obvious point about disturbance of the peace:

> The owner [seeking to recover possession of land from squatters who had broken into the premises] is not obliged to go to the courts to obtain possession. He is entitled, if he so desires, to take the remedy into his own hands. He can go in himself and turn them out without the aid of the courts of law [see now Part II of the Criminal Law Act 1977]. This is not a course to be recommended because of the disturbance which might follow … In a civilised society, the courts should themselves provide a remedy which is speedy and effective, and thus make self-help unnecessary.

In line with this, the Law Commission has been recommending curtailment of self-help since 1985, with some back-tracking in 1998. In 1985, it made a firm recommendation that the ban on forfeiting leases by physical entry should be extended to all leases (Law Commission, *Codification of the Law of Landlord and Tenant: Forfeiture of Tenancies* (Law Commission Report No. 142, 1985): 'the loss of his tenancy is usually a serious matter for a tenant whether he is in occupation or not, and we do not think it should ever occur except by consent or with the authority of the court': paragraph 3.8) and by abolishing the physical taking of goods as distress for rent (Law Commission, *Distress for Rent* (Law Commission Report No. 194, 1991): see further Extract 7.3 below). In 1998, it appeared to have a change of heart, and published a consultative document retreating from its earlier position and provisionally concluding that forfeiture of tenancies by physical re-entry is 'nowadays frequently used by landlords as an effective management tool' and should therefore be preserved after all (Law Commission, *Landlord and Tenant Law: Termination of Tenancies by Physical Re-entry: A Consultative Document* (Law Commission Consultative Document, January 1998)). However, there are signs that it is now moving back to its former position, and its most recent consultation paper, *Termination of Tenancies for Tenant Default* (Law Commission Consultation Paper No. 174, 2004) puts forward proposals for a complete overhaul of forfeiture which would leave little room for self-help.

The main obstacle in the way of parliamentary reform is the perceived inadequacy of court procedures for landlords and mortgagees seeking possession in response to default. In *Kataria* v. *Safeland plc* (1998) 05 EG 155, CA, where a landlord had forfeited the lease of 'a modest walk-in kiosk' by physical re-entry (behaviour described as 'monstrous' in the circumstances by the judge at first instance), Brooke LJ complained in the Court of Appeal:

> Twelve years ago, the Law Commission recommended the introduction of a statutory scheme whereby business landlords too [i.e. like residential landlords] would be required to obtain a court order before proceeding to re-enter, see [Law Commission, *Codification of the Law of Landlord and Tenant: Forfeiture of Tenancies* (Law Commission Report No. 142, 1985)]. Nearly four years ago the Commission published a draft Bill to give effect to that recommendation: see [Law Commission, *Landlord and Tenant Law: Termination of Tenancies Bill* (Law Commission Report No. 221, 1994)]. Nothing has been done and nothing will be done to implement these recommendations unless and until fast track procedures are put in place to help landlords to obtain possession orders speedily in clear and obvious cases. In the meantime, landlords are, in my judgment, at liberty as a matter of law to go on behaving as [the landlord] did in this case if they consider it proper to do so.
>
> (*Kataria* v. *Safeland plc* [1998] 05 EG 155 at 157)

Whatever view one takes of the merits of self-help remedies in general, there are obvious dangers in allowing a claimant to achieve by self-help a result that could not be achieved by invoking judicial process. This has caused considerable problems in English law. In many cases, where a claimant can choose whether to proceed by physical action or by judicial process, the court has power, if application is made to it, to postpone the order of possession, or grant it subject to conditions, or even refuse possession altogether and order damages instead. Indeed, as we saw above, until 1977, the court had no power at all to make a possession order in favour of a claimant seeking to recover his goods in an action for conversion (and even now has only a discretion as to whether to do so or not), and yet at all times such a claimant has been entitled to bypass the courts and retake those goods for himself. In a dissenting judgment in the Court of Appeal decision in *Billson* v. *Residential Apartments Ltd* [1991] 3 WLR 264, where the majority accepted an interpretation of section 146 of the Law of Property Act 1925 which resulted in tenants losing their right to apply to the court for relief against forfeiture if the landlord re-entered peacefully, but not if the landlord proceeded by judicial process, Nicholls LJ pointed out the dangers:

> [I]f the landlord chooses to effect the forfeiture by forcing his way into the premises, he is in a better position than if he had applied to the court for an order for possession ... [I]f he takes the law into his own hands, and without further warning to the tenant retakes possession of the leased property, no application for relief from forfeiture can then be made. The court is powerless ... That cannot be right. Such a conclusion would be an incitement to all landlords to re-enter forcibly whenever they can do so ... Nor can it be right to encourage law-abiding citizens to embark on a course

which is a sure recipe for violence … The policy of the law is to discourage self-help when confrontation and breach of the peace are likely to follow. If a tenant, who is in breach of covenant, will not quit but persists in carrying on his business despite the landlord's right of re-entry, the proper course for a responsible landlord is to invoke the due process of the law and seek an order for possession from the court. But a landlord can hardly be expected to do so if, in terms of his legal rights, he will be severely prejudiced thereby. Nor can he be expected to respect, or even understand, a law which tells him that he should not resort to violence or force in such circumstances but tells him at the same time that, if he does forcibly re-enter, his position in law will be better than if he invokes the court's process.

In that case, Nicholls LJ's minority view was subsequently upheld by the House of Lords, reversing the Court of Appeal decision. However, the Court of Appeal has recently confirmed that essentially the same inconsistency still exists in the case of mortgagees seeking possession of dwelling-houses (see further *Ropaigealach* v. *Barclays Bank plc* [1999] 3 WLR 17, CA, and for an analysis of the law relating to retaking of goods without a court order, where the same problems can arise, see the Law Reform Committee's *Eighteenth Report on Conversion and Detinue* (Cmnd 4774, 1971) paragraphs 116–26, 'Recaption of Chattels').

7.4.3.2.   Restrictions and deterrents

There are express statutory provisions which prohibit the use of self-help in some circumstances. Where they apply, they restrict the circumstances in which residential occupiers can be evicted without a court order. In particular, if you are a landlord of premises let as a dwelling, you cannot enforce any right to forfeit the lease except by judicial process if any person is lawfully residing there because of section 2 of the Protection from Eviction Act 1977. Also, if the premises were 'let' as a dwelling ('let' here, but not in section 2, covering the grant of a licence as well as a tenancy) and the tenancy or licence has now expired, you cannot recover possession from the former tenant or licensee except by judicial process (section 3 of the 1977 Act). However, section 3 does not apply to all residential tenancies and licences: if the tenancy or licence is 'excluded' (as to which see section 3A), former tenants and licensees can still be evicted by physical re-entry.

In all other cases, if you are entitled to possession, you are entitled to take it for yourself by physical action. However, there are reasons why you might prefer not to do so, but rely on the court instead. The first is that the consequences of getting it wrong can be severe. If it turns out that you were not after all entitled to possession at that time, or were not entitled to take it for yourself without judicial process, you will be liable at common law for damages for trespass. In addition, in the case of land, if the person you evicted or tried to evict was a 'residential occupier', you will be committing both the statutory tort of unlawful eviction (sections 27–32 of the Housing Act 1988) and the criminal offence of unlawful eviction (section 1 of the Protection from Eviction Act 1977). For the purposes of both the tort and the crime, 'residential occupier' covers not only a tenant or licensee of residential property but also anyone else occupying premises as a residence 'whether under a contract or by virtue of any enactment or rule of law giving him the right to remain in occupation or restricting the right of any other person to recover possession of the premises'. This includes most, but not all, lawful residential occupiers – mortgagors, for example, are not included, for reasons apparent from Chapter 18. Damages for the tort of unlawful eviction are measured primarily by reference to the gain accruing tó the taker rather than the loss suffered by the victim.

The other good reason for not taking possession of land by physical entry is the danger of committing a criminal offence under section 6 of the Criminal Law Act 1977, which applies even to lawful takers. Unsurprisingly, the criminal law has always taken steps to regulate physical taking of possession of land. This area of law used to be governed by a network of ancient statutes, the Forcible Entry Acts, whose obscurity and uncertainty of ambit was of itself sufficient to deter most people from resorting to self-help remedies. However, all these ancient offences were swept away by the Criminal Law Act 1977 and replaced by the section 6 offence of using or threatening violence to secure entry to premises. Section 6 provides that:

(1)   ... any person who, without lawful authority, uses or threatens violence for the purpose of securing entry into any premises for himself or for any other person is guilty of an offence, provided that –
  (a) there is someone present on those premises at the time who is opposed to the entry which the violence is intended to secure; and
  (b) the person using or threatening the violence knows that that is the case.

It is expressly provided that the offence is committed whether the violence is directed against the person or against property, and that the fact that a person has any interest in or right to possession of premises does not mean that they have 'lawful authority' for these purposes. This offence is probably less extensive and certainly more clearly defined than the old Forcible Entry Acts. Nevertheless, the danger of incurring criminal liability (and the attendant bad publicity) remains a powerful deterrent.

7.4.4. Unlawful eviction and harassment

The common law has not evolved satisfactory remedies to protect residential occupiers of land from harassment by their landlords. The torts of nuisance and trespass, and the property actions for non-derogation from grant or breach of covenant for quiet enjoyment, have not proved to be adequate either in deterring landlords from harassing or unlawfully evicting their tenants or in compensating tenants who have suffered such treatment. They are now supplemented by the statutory tort of unlawful eviction already referred to, together with the additional tort of unlawful harassment (sections 27–32 of the Housing Act 1988), and the criminal offence equivalents in sections 2–4 of the Protection from Eviction Act 1977.

7.4.5. Trespassing and the criminal law

Those who take possession of land unlawfully have always been exposed to criminal liability if their entry involved violence directed at people or property. Since 1977, however, it has also become possible in some circumstances to incur criminal liability simply by being in possession of land as a trespasser. Section 7 of the Criminal Law Act 1977 makes it a criminal offence to fail to leave residential premises having been required to do so by either a 'displaced residential occupier' or a 'protected intending occupier', if you are on the premises as a trespasser after having entered as such. The 1977 Act also makes it an offence to enter on or to be in possession of a foreign mission (as defined) as a trespasser, and to trespass with an offensive weapon (sections 8 and 9 respectively). These offences are now augmented by the public order offences set out in Part V of the Criminal Justice and Public Order Act 1994, which cover miscellaneous examples of 'collective trespass or nuisance on land'. For the scope of these new public order offences, see further *Winder* v. *DPP*, *The Times*, 14 August 1996 and *DPP* v. *Barnard*, *The Times*, 9 November 1999.

Extract 7.2   Tony Weir, *A Casebook on Tort* (7th edn, London: Sweet & Maxwell, 1992), pp. 473–8

If England had a rational system of law there would be no need for a special section on torts to chattels ... It is quite true that goods get lost or stolen as well as damaged, and that commercial wrongdoing is not exactly like dangerous behaviour, but the tort of negligence can perfectly well embrace cases where a person has been indirectly deprived of a physical asset and the tort of trespass can cope with cases of forthright snatching. In a rational system this would be quite adequate, for a plaintiff who had lost goods would obtain tort damages from a defendant only if he was to blame for their loss.

Two conditions would have to be fulfilled before the role of tort could be so sensibly restricted: first, the law of property must provide a means whereby the owner of goods can get them back from whoever is in possession of them without any right to retain them; secondly, the law of contract, rather than the law of tort, must regulate the right of contractors to the property they contract about. Neither condition is satisfied in England.

PROPERTY

The common law has no special remedy for the owner of a thing who wishes to claim it back from the person in possession of it. This gap has therefore to be filled by a remedy in tort. Unfortunate consequences ensue. The first is to introduce into tort law an area of liability without fault: this is unavoidable, because however innocent a person may be in acquiring possession of a thing he must deliver it up to the true owner unless he has some special right to retain it. The second consequence is to raise problems about who may sue: in a property remedy we would naturally define the plaintiff in terms of his *ownership* or other property right, but when the remedy is in tort one tends to regard the plaintiff's loss as a necessary and sufficient criterion of eligibility to sue. This may, thirdly, give rise to multiple plaintiffs when different people have concurrent interests in the thing. Tort has its own problems, as we have seen, when several people suffer loss as a result of injury to person or property, but these problems will be greatly extended if we make tort perform a property role as well. Fourthly, what of the plaintiff's behaviour? In tort cases his contributory negligence has a role to play in reducing the damages he obtains. This can hardly happen in a property remedy: the owner either gets his thing back or he doesn't. Fifthly, what of the defendant? In a property remedy we would insist that the defendant be in actual possession of the thing: after all, an owner who wants his thing back must sue the person who actually has it. In a tort suit we would be more interested in the defendant's past behaviour – what did he do with the thing? – than in his present position or possession. Sixthly, if the owner, not being bound to sue the present possessor, can sue all those through whose hands the goods have passed, there will be grave problems of multiple defendants. We have seen what happens in proper tort cases – the victim may sue any or all of the tortfeasors until he has been paid off, and then those who have paid more than their fair share can claim contribution from those who have paid less ... but one cannot simply apply this solution to litigation about lost property. Finally, what order is the judge to make? In tort cases he orders the defendant to pay monetary compensation, but in a property remedy he may have to order specific restitution, and if that is impossible he will be tempted to order the defendant to pay the value of the thing even if that differs from the sum which he would award as compensation. These are the problems which arise when tort takes on the role of property law.

Extract 7.3   Alison Clarke, 'Property Law' (1996) 49 *Current Legal Problems* 97 at 111–15

DISTRESS FOR RENT

In a Report issued this year [Law Commission, *Distress for Rent* (Law Commission Report No. 194, 1991)] [the Law Commission] condemns distress as wrong in principle and recommends its abolition, but only when promised improvements to court procedures for recovery of rent are made.

The right for landlords to distrain for overdue rent arises automatically from the obligation to pay rent. It allows the landlord to enter the let premises as soon as rent is due and seize goods found there (not necessarily belonging to the tenant), and then either retain them until the rent is paid, or sell them and recover the rent from the proceeds. Leave of the court is required for distraint in the case of some but not all residential tenancies. Significantly, it is used in practice by landlords only when leave of the court is not required. The law relating to distress is ancient and of labyrinthine complexity.

The recent increase in the use of self-help remedies has been particularly marked in the case of distress for rent. The Commission explains that when it first looked at distress in 1966 [Law Commission, *Interim Report on Distress for Rent* (Law Commission Report No. 5, 1966)] it found that its use was extremely limited. The subsequent Working Paper published in 1986 [Law Commission, *Distress for Rent* (Law Commission Consultative Document No. 97, 1986)], which expressed the provisional view that it should be abolished, was written on that assumption.

Responses to the Working Paper, however, revealed a different picture. It was clear that the use of distress had increased considerably (although the evidence was insufficient to permit an accurate estimate of the extent of the increase). While most (not all) people can face the abolition of an obsolescent remedy with reasonable equanimity, it takes some fortitude to persist with the plan to abolish at a time when it has re-emerged as a useful remedy, particularly when the reason for its re-emergence appears to be a breakdown in the machinery for exercise of the alternative remedies.

Nevertheless, the decision by the Commission to recommend that abolition should be delayed until the alternatives are improved comes as a disappointment. As the Report itself explains, the Civil Justice Review Body set up in 1985 has already made detailed recommendations for the introduction of a new rent action, precisely in order to remedy the defects in rent collection by judicial process which have driven landlords back to self-help. The Commission explains the considerable progress that has been made in expanding and implementing the recommendations for reform ...

[However], after cataloguing the enormous problems of landlords faced with the 'expense, delay, ineffectiveness and uncertainty of court proceedings' which were revealed in the course of the Commission's consultation process, it concludes:

> It is clear that landlords do have a genuine grievance about the court system and that it is failing to provide them with an adequate means of recovering rent arrears. The Civil Justice Review gives hope for improvement, but it cannot yet be said whether or when this aim will be achieved.

Neither the proposed new rent action nor the Lord Chancellor's programme has received universal acclaim, and of course it is by no means a foregone conclusion that any promised reform will work even if it is carried out. Nevertheless, it takes a certain degree of timidity and pessimism, unexpected qualities to find in a law reform agency, to assume that it will not until the contrary has been proved.

Whatever view is taken of the Law Commission's recommendation to delay abolition, it could hardly be accused of timidity in relation to the primary recommendation itself. Although reporting that 'a large majority' of those who responded to the working paper were opposed to total abolition of distress, the Commission reported that 'No response to our consultation suggested any justification for its retention which met the fundamental objections to it.' It gives the fundamental objections as these:

> 3.2 We see distress for rent as wrong in principle because it offers an extra-judicial debt enforcement remedy in circumstances which are, because of its intrinsic nature, the way in which it arises and the manner of its exercise, unjust to the debtors, to other creditors and to third parties. The characteristics of distress for rent which contribute to this are:
>
> (a) priority given to landlords over other creditors;
> (b) vulnerability of third parties' goods;
> (c) harshness which is caused by the limited opportunity for the tenant to challenge the landlord's claim, the scope for the rules of distress to be abused, the

unexpected intrusion into the tenant's property and the possibility of the sale of the goods at an undervalue;

(d) disregard of the tenants' circumstances which demonstrates its general lack of recognition of a modern approach to debt enforcement.

These criticisms are devastating, and fully justified by the detail that follows [see Part III of the Report]. The best that can be said for distress is that it is so awful that the mere threat of its use is enough to make most people pay up – the argument that kept wholesale imprisonment for debt alive in this country until 1971. The Commission notes that such statistics as there are appear to suggest that, when threatened but not used, distress is a highly effective remedy [*ibid.*, paragraph 3.10]. When used, it is dismally inefficient: goods normally taken tend to be such that the cost to the tenant of losing them far exceeds the price they will fetch when sold [*ibid.*, paragraphs 3.16 and 3.17]. It is difficult to accept that such a remedy should be allowed to continue to exist, and a matter for regret that the Law Commission drew back from recommending its immediate abolition.

Notes and Questions 7.3

1 Other common law jurisdictions have abolished distress for rent without the qualms expressed by the Law Commission, although, as the Commission pointed out, in many cases this may have been because it was little used, or because 'the other available methods for recovering rent arrears were able to absorb the additional work without difficulty'. However, events succeeding the North Carolina Court of Appeals decision in *Spinks* v. *Taylor*, 266 SE 2d 857 (NC App 1980) (concerning the legality of the landlord's practice of padlocking a tenant's front door as soon as any rent was overdue) reveal that at least one state in the United States has done so in the face of procedural problems as bad as, if not worse than, ours. The brief for the appellee, the landlord Mr Taylor, is said to have revealed that, because Mr Taylor's local magistrate's court was unable to hear all ejectment actions filed each day, the clerk's office imposed a limit of ten ejectment actions per landlord per day, with an overall limit of twenty-five ejectment actions a day (so, presumably, not all landlords were allowed their full allowance of ten every day). Since Mr Taylor had 825 tenants and approximately 400 of them were in default by the seventh of each month, and since he preferred to take action when tenants were not more than one month in arrears, it must have been virtually impossible for him to have all his actions heard. Nevertheless, the immediate legislative response to the court's decision that his padlocking procedure was valid was to pass the Landlord Eviction Remedies Act in 1981 prohibiting all self-help remedies forthwith (distress as well as forfeiture by actual re-entry) for landlords of residential premises.

2   A footnote to Extract 7.3 suggests that the numerical majority in favour of retention may not be altogether surprising: 'It is a fact of life for law reformers that lenders, landlords, and sellers (repeat players) tend to be over-represented in responses to consultation, whereas borrowers, tenants and consumers (single shot players) are under-represented. Equally, those who respond tend to come from the reputable end of the market, not given to perpetrating the abuses that unsatisfactory law makes available to the less scrupulous. Consequently, their experience tends to be of the system working at its best.'

3   Consider the 'fundamental objections' to distress for rent expressed by the Law Commission noted above. To what extent do they apply to self-help remedies in general?

8

Fragmentation of ownership

8.1. Introduction

One of the distinctive features of English property law is that it can accommodate a wide range of property interests subsisting in the same thing at the same time, each held by a different person. As we pointed out in Chapter 6, in our system property is not synonymous with ownership. The rights and obligations which Honoré described as the attributes of 'the full liberal concept of ownership' need not all be held by the same person at the same time. They may be shared between and distributed among any number of different people in a number of different ways.

However, this fragmentation of ownership is highly systematised. While an owner can by contract give any person a personal right to exercise any of his ownership-type rights and obligations in any way, for any purpose and for any length of time, there are only strictly limited ways in which ownership-type rights can be subdivided and redistributed so as to leave each right holder or group of holders with a distinct property interest, as opposed to merely personal rights against the grantor. This results in a formalised structure of interdependent property interests, which is what we will be examining in this chapter. In Chapter 9, we then look at the gateways to this structure by considering why it is regulated in the way that it is – i.e. why we limit the range of property interests recognised in our system in the way that we do – and when and how the structure can be modified so as to give proprietary status to novel rights, or to novel regroupings of established rights.

8.2. Present and future interests

The first distinction to be made is between present interests (i.e. a present right to have enjoyment of a thing now) and future interests (i.e. a present right to have enjoyment of it at some point in the future). In our system it is not only possible to limit the length of time for which a property interest will last, but also to create a property interest where the enjoyment of the thing is deferred, so that enjoyment will not commence until a future date. By combining the two, the enjoyment of a thing can be divided up into time slices. Take the following example: you and I have an aunt, a composer, who dies leaving the copyright in her music to me for the first ten years after her death and thereafter to you for the remainder of the copyright period. When she dies we will both acquire property interests in her music: I will have a present right to have the royalties paid to me for the next ten years, and simultaneously you will hold a present right to have the royalties paid to you from a date ten years on.

In this example, both my right and your right are property interests, but, as you might expect, this is not true of all the ways in which one might divide enjoyment of a thing into time slices. We consider here the basic technical rules which determine how enjoyment of a thing can be split up in this way so as to give rise to separate, simultaneous property rights to successive enjoyment of a thing. These rules are not particularly difficult, but they are of ancient origin, mostly vestigial remains of long-abandoned social and legal constructs, and consequently their rationale can be obscure and the terminology unfriendly.

8.2.1. Interests in possession, in reversion and in remainder

The first point starts as essentially a matter of vocabulary. Present rights to present enjoyment are said to be 'in possession', whereas present rights to future enjoyment are either 'reversionary' (or 'in reversion') or 'in remainder'. There is no qualitative difference between a reversionary interest and a remainder interest: the distinction lies in the identity of the person who first acquires the interest. Specifically, reversionary interests involve enjoyment reverting back to the holder of the larger interest out of which the reversionary interest was carved, whereas remainder interests involve a movement of enjoyment forward to someone else. This distinction is significant because, while reversionary interests can, like remainder interests, be created deliberately, they will also arise by operation of law to fill any gap in a chain of time-sliced property interests. The general principle (not always to be applied too mechanistically, as we see later) is that, whenever rights to enjoyment of a thing are split up into time slices, the proprietary right to each slice must be vested in somebody, and unless it has been effectively allocated elsewhere by the grantor, it will automatically vest in the grantor. This is what Honoré describes as the 'residuarity' element in ownership.

An example will make this clearer. Going back to our composer aunt, assume that, while alive, she held a ninety-nine-year lease of her studio and also owned a piano. As owner of the piano, she would be entitled to its use and enjoyment for a period unlimited in time. Consider three possible situations:

1   When still alive, she gives both the piano and the lease of the studio to me for my lifetime, and then to you absolutely. As soon as the gift is made I acquire an interest in possession in both the piano and the lease (I will be entitled to the exclusive use of the piano and the studio during my lifetime – or, in the case of the studio, until the lease ends, if earlier), and you acquire an interest in remainder in them (i.e. you acquire a

present right that, when I die, you will become absolute owner of the piano and holder of the lease for the rest of its term).

2 When still alive, she makes a gift of both piano and lease to me for my life, but states that, after my death, they are to revert to her. Again, that gives me an interest in possession in the piano and the lease, but this time it gives her an interest in reversion in them.

3 When still alive, she makes a gift of both piano and lease to me for my life, but this time says nothing about what is to happen to them after I die. In general, the result will be the same as in (2) above: I acquire an interest in possession and she acquires an interest in reversion. Her interest arises under a resulting trust because the law requires someone to hold the future interest, and the only possible contenders are the grantor who failed to dispose of it elsewhere, or the Crown as the repository of ownerless property (*bona vacantia*). In general, the law prefers to make the interest revert back to the grantor under a resulting trust, although it will go to the Crown as *bona vacantia* in some circumstances, as Lord Browne-Wilkinson explains in his judgment in *Westdeutsche Landesbank* v. *Islington London Borough Council* [1996] AC 669 (Extract 8.1 below).

There are a few other things to say about present rights to future enjoyment. The first is that your remainder interest (in example (1) above) and the aunt's reversionary interest (in (2) and (3) above) are property interests, not personal to you or her. Consequently, they can be sold or given away, and if you or she die before me still holding your respective interests, the interest will simply pass to whoever it is who becomes entitled to your property on your death (as to which see below). So, in example (1), it makes no difference if I am aged three when our aunt makes the gift and you are aged ninety (leaving aside complications about how minors hold property interests). We both still acquire property interests in the studio and the piano, even though you are unlikely to survive long enough to enjoy yours personally.

Secondly, when reversionary and remainder interests are sold or inherited, the terminology remains the same: a person who buys or inherits an interest in the piano or the copyright from you gets a remainder interest, and the person who buys or inherits the interest from the aunt gets a reversionary interest.

8.2.2. Absolute entitlements, contingent entitlements and mere expectancies

When rights to enjoyment are divided up into time slices, the ending of one person's right to present enjoyment and the beginning of the next one's are made to depend on the happening of a future event. Some future events are certain to happen – for example, the death of a human person, or the arrival of a specified date. Other future events may or may not happen, depending on various factors.

8.2.2.1. Absolute entitlements

If the commencement of the right to present enjoyment is dependent on the happening of a future event that is certain to happen, then the interest is said to be absolute (here meaning unconditional: 'absolute' can also mean unlimited in time, as in example (1) above). The interest is absolute even if we do not know in advance *when* the future event is going to happen, provided it is certain that it *will* happen. Suppose when our aunt died she also left a sum of money (say £10,000) to me for life and then to you absolutely (here meaning unlimited in time). During my lifetime you have an absolute (i.e. unconditional) interest in the £10,000, because it is certain that enjoyment of the £10,000 will eventually pass to you (or the person who has bought or inherited the interest from you), even though no one knows when that might happen.

8.2.2.2. Contingent interests and expectancies

On the other hand, the commencement of enjoyment may be made dependent on the happening of a future event which is not certain to happen, but which may or may not happen. In that case, the interest is said to be contingent – future enjoyment is not certain, but contingent on that thing happening. Different kinds of contingency must be distinguished, because not all types of contingent interest are capable of being proprietary. Take the following examples:

1   You and I agree that I will sell you my land in six months' time for £100,000 if by then I have received planning permission to develop it in accordance with the application I made last month. Here, your right to have the land in six months' time for £100,000 is contingent (a) on you paying me £100,000 on the due date (an event within your control) and (b) on planning permission being granted by the planning authority (an event outside the control of either of us).

2   I give £10,000 to trustees to pay the income for the next twenty-one years to my niece for so long as she remains unmarried but if and when she marries to pay the income to you. Your right to receive any income from the £10,000 is contingent on my niece marrying within the next twenty-one years. Again, this is an event outside the control of either of us, but it is within the control of a prior-interest holder (my niece).

3   You and I agree that I will sell you my land in six months' time for £100,000 if by then you serve notice on me that you want to buy at that price. Your right to buy the land is an 'option to purchase'. It consists of a right to acquire the land in six months' time, contingent (a) on your serving notice and (b) on your paying the money on the due date. Both these events are within your control.

4   You and I agree that, if I decide to sell my land within the next six months, I will sell it to you for £100,000 if you serve notice on me that you want to buy it at that price. Your right here is a 'right of pre-emption'. It consists of a right to acquire the land, which, as in the previous example, is contingent on two factors within your control (your serving notice on me and paying the price when due) but it is also contingent on a factor wholly within my control: my decision to sell in the first place.

5   I make a will leaving you £10,000. As long as I am still alive, your right to get the £10,000 is contingent (a) on my actually having £10,000 when I die (more or less within my control, and certainly not within yours) and (b) on my not changing my will (wholly within my control).

In all five examples, you have a contingent right to future enjoyment, but not all of the five give you property interests. In examples (1), (2) and (3), you have an immediate property interest, as we see in Chapter 12, and the same is mostly now true of example (4) (after earlier uncertainties) whereas in example (5) you definitely do not. The distinction that the law seeks to draw here is between contingent *rights* and 'rights' that are not, properly speaking, rights at all, but mere hopes or expectancies. The law is clear that contingent *rights* are capable of giving rise to property interests, however remote the contingency, whereas mere expectancies are not, however likely it is that the contingency will occur. So, to add a variation to an earlier example, suppose our aunt dies leaving £10,000 to me (then aged three) for my lifetime, and then to you (then aged ninety) absolutely (i.e. unlimited in time), but this time your interest is made contingent on you surviving me. As long as you and I are both alive, you have a property interest in the £10,000 (a contingent remainder interest), unlikely though it is that you or anyone else will ever get to enjoy it (consider what would happen if you sold the interest to someone during your lifetime). Compare this with what would happen if I, a ninety-year-old millionaire, make a will leaving everything to you, my only relative and friend. Until I actually die, you will have no property interest whatsoever in any of my assets, regardless of how likely it is that you will get all of it very soon.

What then is the critical distinction between a contingent right and no right at all, if it is not the likelihood of receiving benefit? The question arises in a broad range of different contexts, so it is not possible to provide a definitive answer. Nevertheless, a common thread appears to be dependency on the will of the benefit-conferrer. In *Pritchard* v. *Briggs* [1980] Ch 338, which we look at in Chapter 12, the Court of Appeal held that a right of pre-emption (example 4 above) was not a property interest because the holder's right is dependent on the volition of the seller. It was not made clear why this factor should be conclusive, nor whether the same applies to any other contingency which is in the seller's control in the sense that he can decide whether or not to bring it about. In the case of rights of pre-emption which relate to land, the effect of *Pritchard* v. *Briggs* has been reversed, at least in registered land, by section 115 of the Land Registration Act 2002, without, however, throwing any light on this particular issue.

In the context in which rights of pre-emption arise, a more promising test to apply in deciding whether a contingent right is proprietary or not might be to ask whether outsiders can easily tell whether or not the contingency has occurred. In *Pritchard* v. *Briggs*, the key issue was whether the interest was to have the quintessentially proprietary attribute of enforceability against third parties. As we saw in Chapter 5, there are good reasons for demanding that no interest should be enforceable against third parties unless third parties can easily ascertain the interest. For present purposes, this means being able to find out not only that the interest exists, but also whether or not any contingencies have been satisfied. A registration requirement (which now exists for rights of pre-emption in registered land by virtue of section 115 of the Land Registration Act 2002) will alert outsiders that I hold a right of pre-emption over your land, but it cannot help them find out whether you have taken the decision that will trigger off my right to insist that you sell to me. This is something that is inherently difficult both for me and for outsiders to ascertain, except perhaps retrospectively (when you demonstrate by selling to someone else that you made a prior decision to sell). However, it is perfectly possible to have a right of pre-emption where the contingency is not the seller arriving at a state of mind about selling but the seller providing some external manifestation of that state of mind: 'if the seller decides to sell' is necessarily difficult to ascertain, but 'if the seller serves notice on the buyer that he has decided to sell' is not. Nevertheless, this distinction was not drawn either in the Court of Appeal decision in *Pritchard* v. *Briggs* or in section 115 of the 2002 Act: before the 2002 Act, both types of right of pre-emption were incapable of binding third parties, whereas now both are fully enforceable against third parties.

8.2.2.3.   Alternative contingencies

If a person has a contingent interest – i.e. an interest where the commencement of enjoyment is contingent on the happening of an event which may never happen – then it must follow that someone else will simultaneously hold the mirror-image contingent interest – an interest where enjoyment is dependent on that event not happening. For the reason given in section 8.2.1 above, if no one is specified as the holder of this mirror-image contingent interest, it will belong to the grantor. So, in the example given at the end of section 8.2.2.2 above (our aunt dies leaving £10,000 to me, then aged three, for life, with remainder to you, then aged ninety, provided you survive me), the aunt's estate will include a reversionary right to the £10,000 on my death, contingent on you not surviving me.

8.2.3.   When interests vest

To state the obvious, only a person who exists and is identifiable can hold a present *right* to future enjoyment of a thing. Suppose my aunt dies leaving £10,000 to me for my life, and then to my husband for life, and then to my eldest child absolutely ('absolutely' here meaning unlimited in time). If when she dies I am unmarried and have no children, it would be a nonsense to say that, at that point my husband and eldest child have property interests in the £10,000. Their interests can only vest in them when they come into existence. So, when my aunt dies, I acquire a life interest in possession in the £10,000. If and when I marry thereafter, my husband will acquire a contingent remainder interest in the £10,000 (contingent because he may not still be my husband when I die), and, if and when I first have a child, that child will also acquire a contingent remainder interest (consider why contingent, and consider also why, given the circumstances, a contingent reversionary interest in the £10,000 will form part of my aunt's estate when she dies).

Our legal system has never been very happy about allowing people to create these inchoate interests which will not vest in a person until some time in the future. We consider why this is so in section 8.2.8 below.

8.2.4. Alienation, management and control

When there are successive property interests in a thing, only the person with the absolute (i.e. unlimited in time) interest is entitled to the *capital* in the thing: the holder of an interest which is limited in time is entitled only to income/enjoyment type benefits. What these income/enjoyment type benefits are of course varies depending on the nature of the thing in question, whether it is a symphony, a piano, a sum of money or a piece of land. Whatever the nature of the thing, however, this immediately leads us into problems about alienation, management and control. Take alienation first. Each interest holder can of course deal independently with her own property interest in the thing (for example, sell or mortgage it or give it away), but none of them individually has the capacity to make an effective disposition of any greater interest in the thing (because of the *nemo dat* rule: see Chapter 10). If they do all want the whole thing sold (i.e. so that the buyer acquires absolute ownership) they are all going to have to act in concert – they must all get together, all agree the terms of the transaction, and all co-operate in the mechanics of carrying it out. This will be difficult enough when all interests in the thing are vested in people who exist (think of the holdout problems, and what you do if some of them are minors). When some interests are not yet vested, it will be impossible.

· But alienation is not the only problem. What is to happen about management and control of the thing in which all these interests subsist? There would be advantages in giving practical charge of the thing to the person with the interest in possession, who has the present right of enjoyment, but there would be disadvantages too – it can put her in a very difficult position with serious conflicts of interest. Who is to ensure that she does indeed take only the income-type benefit and not consume any capital? And who is to ensure that the thing will continue to provide long-term income benefits for future interest holders, and that its capital value is preserved?

One way out of these difficulties is to use a trust. We look at this more closely below, but in essence it involves taking management and control out of the hands of the successive interest holders and giving them, together with absolute title to the thing, to a trustee (in practice, usually two trustees, for reasons considered below). The trustee then has the capacity to deal with the property as absolute owner, and also the power to manage and control it, but in all these matters he will be required to act in the interests of the successive interest holders, balancing their respective interests where they conflict. The use of a trust is in fact mandatory whenever an interest in land is divided into successive time slices (as for example when my aunt's lease of her studio was given to me for my lifetime in the example above) and it is also usual where there are successive interests in money or in other things which are either fungible (consider why) or non-commercial (consider why), or where there are inchoate future interests, or interest holders who are minors (again, consider why). So, in the studio and piano examples above, when my aunt made the gift she would have had to transfer the lease to a trustee to hold on trust for me for my lifetime then for you or her, and for convenience she probably would have done the same thing with the piano, although it would not have been essential.

An alternative way of dividing ownership of land and goods is to use leasehold durations. The owner grants the lessee possession of the land or the object for either a fixed period (say ninety-nine years, as in the studio example) or a periodic duration (as for example when a landlord grants you a monthly tenancy of a flat, which either you or the landlord can terminate at any time by giving the other one month's notice to quit). When land-holding is divided up into leasehold durations no trust is necessary.

8.2.5. Interests of contingent duration

So far we have been considering only those contingent interests where the happening of the contingency triggers off the commencement of enjoyment. However, contingencies may mark the end of an interest as well as its beginning. An interest of contingent duration (a right to something until the happening of an event which may never happen, or subject to forfeiture if it happens) can be carved out of a fixed duration interest as well as out of an interest of indefinite duration.

In either case, the principle of residuarity applies, in just the same way as when an interest of a fixed duration is carved out of a longer interest or one of indefinite duration. So, whenever an interest of a contingent duration arises, an alternate interest automatically vests in someone else – if you give me your car until I marry, you automatically (unless you specify another destination for it) acquire a reversionary right to have the car back if and when I do marry. For every interest of contingent duration, there exists in the wings another interest where the commencement of enjoyment depends on the happening of the contingency which will end the contingent duration interest. It may of course happen that there comes a point when it is certain that the contingency can never occur (I die unmarried, for example). If and when that happens, the alternate interest lapses, and the contingent duration interest (my right to the car until I marry) loses its limitation – in this case there will be nothing to now stop it continuing indefinitely, so that I will die owning the car absolutely.

There are two ways in which an interest can have a contingent length like this, and although superficially they look similar they are significantly different in effect. The first is where the duration of the interest is from the outset measured by reference to the happening of the future contingent event: the example just given comes within this category. This is a determinable interest. The second is where the interest is made *terminable* on the happening of the contingency (you give me your car, but reserve the right to take it back if I marry). This is an interest subject to a condition subsequent.

8.2.5.1. Determinable interests

The distinguishing feature of a determinable interest is that, on the happening of the future contingency, the determinable interest itself automatically expires, and the alternate reversionary/remainder interest waiting in the wings (here called a 'possibility of reverter') is automatically converted into an absolute, unconditional entitlement. This automatic transmission of title from one person to another is potentially dangerous: there is nothing to alert outsiders to the change in entitlement, and even the parties themselves may be unaware that it has happened. For this reason, such interests are nearly always now created under a trust, so that the title is vested in a trustee, who is required to hold the property on trust first for the determinable interest holder until the contingency occurs, and then on trust for the reversioner. Outsiders therefore deal only with the trustee and are not concerned with whether the beneficial interest has shifted from the determinable interest holder to the reversioner, and the duty of ensuring that the benefit goes to the reversioner once the contingency has occurred is placed on the trustee. This use of a trust is compulsory if the determinable interest is in freehold (as opposed to leasehold) land: the Law of Property Act 1925, Schedule 1, Part I, converted all legal determinable fee simple and determinable life interests into equitable interests under a trust.

8.2.5.2. Interests subject to a condition subsequent

An interest subject to a condition subsequent is quite different. It is essentially an interest of a specified duration (it could be perpetual, or limited to a life time, or to a period of years) which will become terminable prematurely if and when a future event occurs. The conceptual difference from a determinable interest is that, whereas in the latter the contingency measures the duration of the interest, in the former it defeats or forfeits an interest prematurely. However, the practical difference is that, in the case of an interest subject to a condition subsequent, none of this happens automatically. Instead of automatically terminating the interest, the contingency merely gives the alternate interest holder the right to elect to forfeit the interest. The terminology is that the creation of an interest subject to a condition subsequent automatically confers on someone else a right of entry ('alternatively called a right to forfeit), and the happening of the contingency makes that right of entry or forfeiture exercisable. Unless and until it is exercised, the original interest continues.

This leads to two important further differences from determinable interests. First, because the shift in title requires a positive, provable act on the part of the holder of the right of entry or forfeiture, there is no great difficulty in ascertaining whether it has occurred or not. Consequently, there is no particular reason to hide these interests behind a trust, and in practice a trust would not normally be used here, even if the interest is in freehold land. The provisions of the Law of Property Act 1925 which impose a trust whenever there are successive interests in freehold land do not apply to a fee simple interest subject to a condition subsequent, and section 7 of the 1925 Act specifically provides that a fee simple subject to a right of entry is to be treated as a fee simple absolute (i.e. not subject to a contingency) and is therefore capable of being legal rather than merely equitable (a distinction we consider further in section 8.3 below).

The second difference is in the attitude of the law. A determinable contingency is regarded more or less neutrally, as an event marking the passing of benefit from one person to another. Rights of entry or forfeiture, on the other hand, are regarded as essentially punitive. The contingency making them exercisable tends to be a breach of an obligation, or the happening of an event which the grantor of the interest wanted to discourage (classically in family settlements, inappropriately marrying or not marrying). This has led to two consequences. The first is that the courts have tended to construe conditions subsequent much more strictly than determinable conditions. The second is that equity has evolved an extensive jurisdiction to grant relief against forfeiture of an interest by the exercise of a right of entry or forfeiture, on the basis that the right was conferred only as security for performance of the obligation, and if that can be secured in some other way, the interest ought to be allowed to continue.

8.2.5.3. Distinguishing determinable and forfeitable interests

Despite this real distinction between determinable and forfeitable interests, and the very real difference in their consequences and effects, the courts have traditionally regarded it as a matter of form rather than substance, allowing it to depend on the wording used rather than the intention of the grantor. So, a grant of a right to enjoyment 'during' a state of affairs, or 'while' it continues or even 'until' it stops, will usually be taken to create a determinable interest, automatically ending when the contingency arises, while a right of enjoyment 'provided that' or 'on condition that' a future event does not happen, or 'but [terminable] if' it does happen, will create an interest subject to a condition subsequent.

8.2.6. Requirement of certainty

Whether a contingency triggers off enjoyment, measures the duration of an interest, or confers on someone a right to terminate it prematurely, the contingency must be certain. If it is not certain, it will be void, the consequences of which are considered in section 8.2.7 below.

However, 'certainty' is a notoriously slippery concept. The basic rule in this context is that a contingency must be certain in the sense of being objectively ascertainable as a matter of fact, even if difficult to prove in practice. So, if I give you an option to buy my land next Wednesday 'if the weather is bad on the immediately preceding Tuesday', your option is void because the contingency is uncertain: bad weather is a matter of opinion not a matter of fact ('if more than one inch of rain falls in my garden on Tuesday' would do). Another way of putting it, and one that makes sense of the rule, is that the contingency must be such that, *at the time when the parties need to know*, it will be objectively ascertainable whether or not the contingency has occurred. So, I can direct my trustees to pay the income of a £10,000 trust fund to the Royal Shakespeare Company 'while it continues its present policy of regularly staging plays by Shakespeare' but not 'for so long as the present high standard of verse-speaking in its Shakespeare productions is maintained'. In such a gift, where income is to be paid indefinitely unless and until a contingency occurs, the trustees need to be able to ascertain the point at which to stop paying. In the first case the trustees should have no difficulty in spotting an official change in policy (which presumably would require some formal process or public announcement) whereas in the second it would be a matter of subjective judgment whether, at any particular point in time, standards of verse-speaking could be said to be no longer what they were.

However, the line between subjective judgment and objective ascertainment is not always tightly drawn, and the courts are more flexible in some cases than in others. For example, forfeiting contingencies tend to be construed more strictly than those measuring duration (another real distinction between interests subject to a condition precedent and determinable interests), whereas those that trigger off entitlement are construed less strictly than either.

Further, in some cases, the courts are not satisfied with objective ascertainability at the point when the parties need to know, and require in addition that the parties should be able to predict in advance when, if at all, the contingency will occur. This very narrow concept of certainty has recently been reaffirmed as the one appropriate to the long-established rule that the duration of a lease must be certain. When measuring the permissible duration of leases, the lease will not be valid unless each party knows from the outset the maximum duration of its liability under the lease. This means that, although I can create a valid trust of my land for my daughter 'until the highways authority certifies that the land is required by the local authority for road-widening purposes' (because although we do not know when, if ever, this will happen, we do know that we will know that it has happened when it does happen), I cannot lease the same land to her for a duration described as 'until the highways authority certifies the land is required by the local authority for road-widening purposes': see *Prudential Assurance* v. *London Residuary Body* [1992] 2 AC 386, in which the House of Lords reaffirmed the strict rules for certainty of duration of leases, considered in Chapter 17 where the effect of such a grant, and the rationale of the rule, are considered in more detail.

8.2.7. Successive interests in land and the doctrine of tenures and estates

As we saw in Chapter 6, the primary method of classifying interests in land is by duration. This is true of interests carrying general rights of enjoyment to land, and also of some rights of particular user such as easements and profits, but for the moment we will focus on general use rights. There are two distinct systems in operation here. One is the ancient system of tenures and estates, and the other is the rather more recent leasehold system which has been grafted onto the tenure and estates system.

8.2.7.1. Tenures and estates

This classification by duration of enjoyment is derived from the ancient feudal doctrines of tenures and estates, although very little of the elaborate feudal structure now remains, apart from the terminology. As explained in Chapter 6, the feudal theory was that land was 'owned' by the Crown, and let out to subjects on various types of holding ('tenures') which required the holder to perform services for the Crown in exchange for enjoyment of the land, each type of tenure requiring a different type of service. A holder of a tenure from the Crown could then 'subinfeudate' (in effect, sublet, although modern lease terminology is best avoided here). This would mean that the right to enjoy the land would be sub-contracted to someone else, for a different (or even the same) type of tenure, in return for services to be performed by the sub-holder to the original holder, and the sub-holder could then himself sub-subinfeudate to someone else. Consequently, a pyramid of tenures could build up, so that, in respect of any given piece of land, there would be one person who held directly from the Crown, delivering the appropriate services, and then a chain of sub- and sub-sub-holders, each sub-contracting rights of enjoyment in exchange for services, down to the person who actually had physical use of the land.

Each of these tenures could last for various permissible durations ('estates'). So, in feudal theory, 'tenure' described the nature of the land-holding – what you had to do in order to be permitted to enjoy the land – and 'estate' described the duration of the holding – how long this enjoyment would be permitted to last.

Detailed knowledge of the different types of tenure and estate that could exist is no longer necessary for an understanding of our present system. However, it does help to appreciate the underlying principles of sovereignty and power, the inherently personal nature of the system, and the way it was engrafted onto the pre-existing land-holding and land-using systems. This assumed contemporary significance in Australia when the courts had to consider the legal effect of imposing the common law tenures and estates systems on aboriginal land use patterns, and reference should be made here to the analyses of the concepts of tenures and estates given in the judgments in *Mabo (No. 2)* extracted in Chapter 4, and also to Simpson, *A History of the Land Law*. Three other general points might be made here. First, it is probably more accurate to regard feudal theory as an *ex post facto* rationalisation of the Norman conquest rather than as a factual description of how interests in land were in fact created and allocated following the Norman conquest. Secondly, whether literally true or not, the feudal structure almost certainly did not wholly supplant pre-existing property interests, nor was it spread uniformly over the whole country: customary rights and public rights (fishing, navigation, rights of way etc.) are probably pre-feudal in nature.

Thirdly, later developments were pragmatic rather than principled, with legislators showing no interest in preserving the coherence of the feudal structure, so that, even if feudal theory did once give an accurate picture of land-holding, it very soon ceased to do so.

We have never formally abolished this system of classifying land interests according to tenure and estate. However, it has become rationalised and simplified to such an extent that it now does little more than explain the terminology we use when describing land interests, and gives some coherence to what would otherwise seem to be puzzlingly arbitrary rules about what we can and cannot do with land interests in our system.

The most dramatic simplification has been in relation to tenure. Only one of these feudal tenures now survives – freehold tenure – and there are no longer any incidents or services attached to it. Also, it has long been impossible for a holder of land by any tenure to subinfeudate. Since there had always been a natural process of elimination of tenures by forfeiture to the Crown (for example, on dying without an heir) the inevitable result was the eventual collapse of the tenurial pyramid. The consequence of these changes is that all land in this country is now held by freehold tenure (with some relatively trivial Crown land exceptions): a landowner does not own her piece of land, she holds it of the Crown by freehold tenure. But holding land by freehold tenure is identical in effect to owning it: the tenure holder does not have to make any payments or perform any services to the Crown, and is fully entitled to full ownership-type rights in the land, except in so far as she has passed some or all of them on to someone else by using one of the modern fragmentation devices described in this chapter.

As far as estates are concerned, the present system bears less resemblance to its feudal origins. There are now only two types of estate deriving from the feudal system. The first is the fee simple estate (sometimes called the freehold estate), a genuine relic of the feudal system, which denotes indefinite, or perpetual, duration. The second is the life estate, which measures duration by reference to a specific person's life. This also is a genuine relic of the feudal system, but it is now of little significance because it is confined to equitable interests under a trust of land – the only way in which land can be held for a duration measured by reference to a life is for it to be held on trust for a person whose interest has that duration.

So, a person who we would regard as owner of a piece of land technically does not own the land but holds it by freehold tenure for an estate in fee simple. Section 1 of the Law of Property Act 1925 then refines this further by providing that the property interest that such a person has will not be a legal interest (more properly termed a legal estate) unless the fee simple estate is absolute (in the sense of being unconditional) and in possession (as opposed to in reversion or in remainder). Putting all this together, it means that the person who appears to the outside world to be the full owner of land holds the land by freehold tenure for a legal estate in fee simple which is absolute and in possession.

8.2.7.2. Estates in particular use rights

Estates are also used to measure the duration of particular use rights, most notably easements and profits. Easements and profits are usually granted for a fee simple duration (i.e. to last perpetually) and the same applies to those that arise by long use through prescription (logically, since prescription is based on a presumed original grant, as we see in Chapter 13). They can also be granted for a leasehold duration (see below). Again, section 1 of the Law of Property Act 1925 has refined this further, and provides that easements and profits will only take effect as legal interests if for a duration equivalent to an estate in fee simple which is absolute (i.e. unconditional) and in possession (as opposed to in remainder or in reversion), or if for a leasehold duration which is absolute. The permissible leasehold durations are outlined below.

8.2.7.3. Leases

The leasehold system developed separately from the tenures and estates system, but was grafted onto it so that the two are now fully integrated. Confusingly, terminology borrowed from the tenurial system is sometimes used in relation to leases, so one occasionally sees a reference to a leasehold estate or leasehold tenure, but this has nothing to do with the feudal-based tenures and estates system. 'Leasehold estate' or 'leasehold tenure' simply denotes an interest in land which lasts for a leasehold duration or to an entitlement to possession of land for a leasehold duration. Also, the term 'tenant', which would once have been used to describe someone who holds a feudal tenure, is now generally used to describe the person who holds a lease.

A lease is an entitlement to possession of land for a prescribed duration. The four permissible types of duration are explained below. A lease can only come into existence by being carved out of a fee simple interest or out of a lease for a longer duration. In other words, a fee simple owner (i.e. a person who holds land by freehold tenure for an estate in fee simple absolute in possession) creates a lease of the land by granting to the lessee the right to possession of the land for one of the four permissible durations, and a person who already holds a lease can grant someone else a sublease by granting him possession for a lesser duration.

Leases are categorised according to their duration. The only permissible categories are a fixed-term lease (where possession is granted for a fixed length of time), a periodic lease (which continues indefinitely for successive periods, usually of a week, a month, a year or two years, until terminated by either party serving notice to quit on the other), a tenancy at will (which can be terminated by either party at any time) and a tenancy at sufferance (where the tenant is present only at the sufferance of the landlord, and can be made to leave at any time). We look at all this in more detail in Chapter 17.

For all practical purposes, 'lease' means the same as 'tenancy'. The former tends to be used for longer fixed-term interests and the latter for shorter and periodic interests, and for interests at will and at sufferance.

8.2.8.   Restrictions on the power to create future interests

If I am the holder of a property interest in a resource and the property interest is in possession and is of unlimited duration, then I am free to exploit or preserve the resource as I like (subject to rules about not harming others etc.). I can consume, preserve or alienate the capital, and use or save or otherwise exploit as much of the income value as I like. In classic economic theory, this promotes the most efficient use of the resource in which I have the interest: if someone values it more highly than I do because he could use it more efficiently, there are no obstacles to prevent its transfer from me to him at a price advantageous to each of us.

However, if I exercise my freedom to do as I like with the resource by creating successive limited interests in it, then I am limiting the freedom of action of my successors to make use of the resource in the way they consider most appropriate. Unsurprisingly, therefore, there have always been limitations on the power of an owner to fragment ownership by dividing it up into successive interests of limited duration. These rules – the most important of which is the rule against perpetuities – are outside the scope of this book, but essentially they involve restricting the owner's right to create unlimited successive future interests by invalidating the offending future interests. For an analysis of these rules, their present effect and utility, and recommendations for their reform, reference should be made to Law Commission, *The Rule Against Perpetuities and Excessive Accumulations* (Law Commission Report No. 251, 1998).

8.3.   Legal and equitable interests

In this jurisdiction, all property interests can be categorised as either legal or equitable. There are three questions to be considered here. First, what does the distinction between legal and equitable mean? Secondly, which interests are legal and which are equitable? And, thirdly, what are the consequences of categorising an interest as legal rather than equitable?

8.3.1.   Origin of the legal/equitable distinction

Equitable interests were originally those property interests that were recognised by the Chancery courts but not by the common law courts. There were several circumstances in which the Chancery courts would regard someone other than the legal title holder as having a proprietary interest in a thing. These can be divided into two main types – the 'failed formality' type of interest, and the 'novel' type of interest.

8.3.1.1.   Failed formality interests

This is essentially a matter of title and is dealt with in detail in Chapters 10 and 12, but for present purposes the important point is that the common law would (and still does) require various specific formalities to be complied with before it would recognise that a property interest had been transferred or granted by one person to another. For example, if I want to grant you a ten-year lease of my house, I must do so by executing a deed: if I do not use a deed, you will not get a legal lease even if you move in and pay the agreed rent and we both act throughout the ten years as if you had the lease which I have purported to grant you. However, the Chancery courts were more flexible, and in certain circumstances they would regard you as having a lease even though all the requirements for creating a valid legal lease had not been observed. You would then have an equitable lease rather than a legal lease. This still applies today, and it applies to any type of property interest: all property interests that can be legal (fee simple interests in land, leases, mortgages, easements, choses in action such as the right to sue on a debt) can also be equitable, and the way to tell whether the interest is legal or equitable is to look at the way in which it was created or transferred to the present holder.

8.3.1.2. Novel interests

In addition, the Chancery courts created or recognised some proprietary interests which had no legal equivalent. As Neave *et al.*, in *Sackville and Neave* explain, these were interests 'developed by equity to mitigate the harshness of rigid common law rules and to satisfy a commercial need which the common law left unfulfilled'. The most obvious example is the one that arose out of equity's creation of the institution of the trust, which split entitlement to benefit from a thing from management and control of it. This was done by requiring the legal owner of a thing to use it not for his own benefit but for the benefit of someone else. The proprietary interest of the beneficiary is equitable, and there is no legal counterpart. The equitable interest of a beneficiary under a trust is not the only novel property interest created by equity and which has no legal equivalent. Others include the restrictive covenant (considered in Chapter 6), estate contracts and options to purchase (considered in Chapter 12), and both the charge and the mortgagor's equity of redemption (Chapter 18). Consequently, although there are equitable equivalents of all interests that can exist as legal interests, the reverse is not true: some equitable interests have no legal equivalent.

8.3.2. Legal and equitable interests now

Once the jurisdictions of the common law and Chancery courts were merged, all courts recognised both legal and equitable property interests, but continued to categorise them as legal or equitable, depending on the jurisdiction in which they originated and the way in which they were created or transferred. This distinction between legal and equitable status has been perpetuated, for reasons which will become apparent below, but some significant changes in the content of each category have been made by statute. First, there have been some additions: whenever a new property interest is now created by statute, it will be expressly stated whether the interest is to be legal or equitable. So, for example, the spouse's statutory right of occupation in the matrimonial home created by the Matrimonial

Homes Act 1967 (now in the Family Law Act 1996) and considered in Chapter 9 is stated to take effect 'as if' it were an equitable interest.

Secondly, some long-established property interests have been recategorised. This has been particularly significant in relation to interests in land.

8.3.2.1.   Interests in land

In the case of land, the most significant recategorisation was made by the Law of Property Act 1925, which aimed to limit the number of legal interests that could co-exist in any one piece of land. As part of this process, it recategorised some legal interests as equitable and produced a short, definitive and closed list of interests which could be legal. As a result, some types of interest such as a life estate in land, which before 1925 could be either legal or equitable depending on how it was created, can now only be equitable. This definitive list of legal interests appears as section 1 of the Law of Property Act 1925. Any interest that appears on this list can be either legal or equitable: which it is, in any particular case, will depend on how it was created or transferred to the present holder. Any interest not on the list can only be equitable, unless it is a novel interest subsequently created by statute and expressly stated to take effect as if it was legal.

8.3.2.2.   Interests in goods

The structure of legal and equitable interests in goods is much less complex. Legal (as opposed to equitable) ownership of goods is often said to be indivisible: the only legal interests recognised are ownership, mortgage (although since in goods this involves transfer of ownership it is not really a separate category) and bailment. Since, as we see in Chapter 17, the proprietary status of bailment is not beyond dispute, this leaves a very short list indeed. Apart from these, all other interests in goods are equitable.

8.3.3.   The significance of the legal/equitable distinction

The major differences between legal and equitable interests are that the formalities necessary for their creation and transfer are different, and, in general, legal interests are enforceable against a wider range of third parties than equitable interests. Both these points are dealt with in detail in Chapters 12–14.

8.3.4.   Three common fallacies

At the risk of introducing confusion where none was felt before, it is worth mentioning here three common fallacies about the distinction between equitable and beneficial interests and trusts and beneficial interests, and the interrelation of legal and equitable interests. They are all considered further by Lord Browne-Wilkinson in *Westdeutsche Landesbank* v. *Islington London Borough Council* [1996] AC 669 (Extract 8.1 below).

8.3.4.1.   Equitable interests and beneficial interests

Because the interest of a beneficiary under a trust is such a well-known equitable interest, the terms 'beneficial interest' and 'equitable interest' are often confused and used interchangeably, as if they mean the same thing. They do not. The interest of a beneficiary under a trust is a beneficial interest, and a legal owner of a thing who is entitled to it for his own benefit is sometimes referred to as the legal and beneficial owner. The beneficial interest of a beneficiary under a trust in necessarily an equitable interest, but, as we have seen, it is just one of many different types of equitable interest – an equitable interest is not necessarily a beneficial interest.

8.3.4.2.   Over-identification of equitable interests with trusts

The second fallacy follows on from the first. It is often assumed that a trust arises whenever ownership is fragmented between legal and equitable interest holders, and whenever a legal title holder has no right to beneficial use. Neither is true. The first is self-evident: if I grant you a restrictive covenant or an equitable charge over my legal fee simple interest in land, no trust arises. The second is apparent from the next section in this chapter: there are many other ways of fragmenting management, control and benefit apart from by using a trust.

8.3.4.3.   Absolute ownership does not include equitable beneficial ownership

The third fallacy is the assumption that an absolute owner has both legal ownership and the (or an) equitable beneficial interest in the thing. This arises out of a fundamental misunderstanding of the way fragmentation of property interests works. The equitable interests of beneficiaries under a trust are beneficial interests, in the sense that they are interests that carry with them a right to the benefit of the property. However, not all interests that include the right to take the benefit of the property are equitable interests (consider, for example, legal leases). Most importantly for present purposes, absolute owners (in the Honoré sense) are entitled to the benefit of the thing owned, but it would be wrong to say that they have an equitable interest in the thing: it is their legal interest in the thing that entitles them to beneficial enjoyment, and will continue to do so unless and until either they transfer it to someone else by a legal disposition, or equity steps in and allocates it elsewhere, by recognising someone other than a legal interest holder as the person entitled to beneficial enjoyment.

Extract 8.1   *Westdeutsche Landesbank Girozentrale* v. *Islington London Borough Council* [1996] AC 669

[In the *Westdeutsche* case, the bank had paid money over to the local authority pursuant to a contract which was subsequently held to be void (because it was held to be *ultra vires* for a local authority to enter into a finance agreement of that type). When the local authority received the money, it paid it into a bank account also containing money from other sources: at that point, neither the local authority nor the bank knew that there was anything wrong with the transaction. Once it was established that the transaction was *ultra vires*, it was accepted that the local authority had to repay the money, but the bank argued that, because the money was paid under a void contract, the local authority held it on resulting trust for the bank. The House of Lords rejected the bank's argument. During the course of his judgment, Lord Browne-Wilkinson said this:]

The bank submitted that, since the contract was void, title did not pass at the date of payment either at law or in equity. The legal title of the bank was extinguished as soon as the money was paid into the mixed account, whereupon the legal title became vested in the local authority. But, it was argued, this did not affect the *equitable* interest, which remained vested in the bank (the retention of title point). It was submitted that, whenever the legal interest in property is vested in one person and the equitable interest in another, the owner of the legal interest holds it on trust for the owner of the equitable title: 'the separation of the legal from the equitable interest necessarily imports a trust.' . . .

THE BREADTH OF THE SUBMISSION

Although the actual question in issue on the appeal is a narrow one, on the arguments presented it is necessary to consider fundamental principles of trust law. Does the recipient of money under a contract subsequently found to be void for mistake or as being *ultra vires* hold the moneys received on trust even where he had no knowledge at any relevant time that the contract was void? If he does hold on trust, such trust must arise at the date of receipt or, at the latest, at the date the legal title of the payer is extinguished by mixing moneys in a bank account: in the present case it does not matter at which of those dates the legal title was extinguished. If there is a trust two consequences follow: (a) the recipient will be personally liable, regardless of fault, for any subsequent payment away of the moneys to third parties even though, at the date of such payment, the 'trustee' was still ignorant of the existence of any trust (see [Burrows, 'Swaps and the Friction Between Common Law and Equity' (1995) 3 *Restitution Law Review* 15]); (b) as from the date of the establishment of the trust (i.e. receipt or mixing of the moneys by the 'trustee') the original payer will have an equitable proprietary interest in the moneys so long as they are traceable into whomsoever's hands they come other than a purchaser for value of the legal interest without notice. Therefore, although in the present case the only question directly in issue is the personal liability of the local authority as a trustee, it is not possible to hold the local authority liable without imposing a trust which, in other cases, will create property rights affecting third parties because moneys received under a void contract are 'trust property'.

THE PRACTICAL CONSEQUENCES OF THE BANK'S ARGUMENT

Before considering the legal merits of the submission, it is important to appreciate the practical consequences which ensue if the bank's arguments are correct. Those who suggest that a resulting trust should arise in these circumstances accept that the creation of an equitable proprietary interest under the trust can have unfortunate, and adverse, effects if the original recipient of the moneys becomes insolvent: the moneys, if traceable in the hands of the recipient, are trust moneys and not available for the creditors of the recipient. However, the creation of an equitable proprietary interest in moneys received under a void contract is capable of having adverse effects quite apart from insolvency. The proprietary interest under the unknown trust will, quite apart from insolvency, be enforceable against any recipient of the property other than the purchaser for value of a legal interest without notice . . .

THE RELEVANT PRINCIPLES OF TRUST LAW

(i) Equity operates on the conscience of the owner of the legal interest. In the case of a trust, the conscience of the legal owner requires him to carry out the purposes for which the property was vested in him (express or implied trust) or which the law imposes on him by reason of his unconscionable conduct (constructive trust).

(ii) Since the equitable jurisdiction to enforce trusts depends upon the conscience of the holder of the legal interest being affected, he cannot be a trustee of the property if and so long as he is ignorant of the facts alleged to affect his conscience, i.e. until he is aware that he is intended to hold the property for the benefit of others in the case of an express or implied trust, or, in the case of a constructive trust, of the factors which are alleged to affect his conscience.

(iii) In order to establish a trust there must be identifiable trust property. The only apparent exception to this rule is a constructive trust imposed on a person who dishonestly assists in a breach of trust who may come under fiduciary duties even if he does not receive identifiable trust property.

(iv) Once a trust is established, as from the date of its establishment the beneficiary has, in equity, a proprietary interest in the trust property, which proprietary interest will be enforceable in equity against any subsequent holder of the property (whether the original property or substituted property into which it can be traced) other than a purchaser for value of the legal interest without notice.

These propositions are fundamental to the law of trusts and I would have thought uncontroversial. However, proposition (ii) may call for some expansion. There are cases where property has been put into the name of X without X's knowledge but in circumstances where no gift to X was intended . . . These cases are explicable on the ground that, by the time action was brought, X or his successors in title have become aware of the facts which gave rise to a resulting trust; his conscience was affected as from the time of such discovery and *thereafter* he held on a resulting trust under which the property was recovered from him. There is, so far as I am aware, no authority which decides that X was a trustee, and therefore accountable for his deeds, at any time before he was aware of the circumstances which gave rise to a resulting trust.

Those basic principles are inconsistent with the case being advanced by the bank. The latest time at which there was any possibility of identifying the 'trust property' was the date on which the moneys in the mixed bank account of the local authority ceased to be traceable when the local authority's account went into overdraft in June 1987. At that date, the local authority had no knowledge of the invalidity of the contract but regarded the moneys as its own to spend as it thought fit. There was therefore never a time at which both (a) there was defined trust property and (b) the conscience of the local authority in relation to such defined trust property was affected. The basic requirements of a trust were never satisfied ...

THE RETENTION OF TITLE POINT

It is said that, since the bank only intended to part with its beneficial ownership of the moneys in performance of a *valid* contract, neither the legal nor the equitable title passed to the local authority at the date of payment. The legal title vested in the local authority by operation of law when the moneys became mixed in the bank account but, it is said, the bank 'retained' its equitable title.

I think this argument is fallacious. A person solely entitled to the full beneficial ownership of money or property, both at law and in equity, does not enjoy an equitable interest in that property. The legal title carries with it all rights. Unless and until there is a separation of the legal and equitable estates, there is no separate equitable title. Therefore, to talk about the bank 'retaining' its equitable interest is meaningless. The only question is whether the circumstances under which the money was paid were such as, in equity, to impose a trust on the local authority. If so, an equitable interest arose for the first time under that trust.

This proposition is supported by ... *Vandervell* v. *Inland Revenue Commissioners* [1967] 2 AC 291 at 311, 317 *per* Lord Upjohn and Lord Donovan, *Commissioner of Stamp Duties* v. *Livingston* [1965] AC 694 at 712 [see Notes and Questions 8.2 below] and Underhill and Hayton, *Law of Trusts and Trustees* (15th edn, 1995), p. 866.

THE SEPARATION OF TITLE POINT

The bank's submission, at its widest, is that, if the legal title is in A but the equitable interest in B, A holds as trustee for B.

Again, I think this argument is fallacious. There are many cases where B enjoys rights which, in equity, are enforceable against the legal owner, A, without A being a trustee, for example an equitable right to redeem a mortgage, equitable easements, restrictive covenants, the right to rectification ... Even in cases where the whole beneficial interest is vested in B and the bare legal interest is in A, A is not necessarily a trustee, for example where title to land is acquired by estoppel as against the legal owner; a mortgagee who has fully discharged his indebtedness enforces his right to recover the mortgaged property in a redemption action, not an action for breach of trust.

The bank contended that where, *under a pre-existing trust*, B is entitled to an equitable interest in trust property, if the trust property comes into the hands of a third party, X (not being a purchaser for value of the legal interest without notice), B is entitled to enforce his equitable interest against the property in the hands of X because X is a trustee for B. In my view the third party, X, is not necessarily a trustee for B: B's equitable right is enforceable against the property in just the same way as any other specifically enforceable equitable right can be enforced against a third party. Even if the third party, X, is not aware that what he has received is trust property B is entitled to assert his title in that property. If X has the necessary degree of knowledge, X may himself become a constructive trustee for B on the basis of knowing receipt. But unless he has the requisite degree of knowledge he is not personally liable to account as trustee: *Re Diplock's Estate* [[1951] AC 251] and *Re Montagu's Settlement Trusts* [1987] Ch 264. Therefore, innocent receipt of property by X subject to an existing equitable interest does not by itself make X a trustee despite the severance of the legal and equitable titles. Underhill and Hayton, *Law of Trusts and Trustees*, pp. 369–70, while accepting that X is under no personal liability to account unless and until he becomes aware of B's rights, does describe X as being a constructive trustee. This may only be a question of semantics: on either footing, in the present case the local authority could not have become accountable for profits until it knew that the contract was void.

RESULTING TRUST

This is not a case in which the bank had any equitable interest which pre-dated receipt by the local authority of the upfront payment. Therefore, in order to show that the local authority became a trustee, the bank must demonstrate circumstances which raised a trust for the first time either at the date on which the local authority received the money or at the date on which payment into the mixed account was made. Counsel for the bank specifically disavowed any claim based on a constructive trust. This was plainly right because the local authority had no relevant knowledge sufficient to raise a constructive trust at any time before the moneys, upon the bank account going into overdraft, became untraceable. Once there ceased to be an identifiable trust fund, the local authority could not become a trustee: *Re Goldcorp Exchange Ltd (in receivership)* [1995] 1 AC 74 [see further Chapter 12]. Therefore, as the argument for the bank recognised, the only possible trust which could be established was a resulting trust arising from the circumstances in which the local authority received the upfront payment.

Under existing law a resulting trust arises in two sets of circumstances:

(A) Where A makes a voluntary payment to B or pays (wholly or in part) for the purchase of property which is vested either in B alone or in the joint names of A and B, there is a presumption that A did not intend to make a gift to B: the money or property is held on trust for A (if he is the sole provider of the money) or in the case of a joint purchase by A and B in shares proportionate to their contributions. It is important to stress that this is only a *presumption*, which presumption is easily rebutted either by the counter-presumption of advancement or by direct evidence of A's intention to make an outright transfer: see *Underhill and Hayton*, pp. 317 *et seq.*, *Vandervell* v. *Inland Revenue Commissioners* [1967] 2 AC 291 at 312 *et seq.* and *Re Vandervell's Trusts (No. 2)* [1974] Ch 269 at 288 *et seq.*

(B) Where A transfers property to B *on express trusts*, but the trusts declared do not exhaust the whole beneficial interest: *ibid.* and *Barclays Bank Ltd* v. *Quistclose Investments Ltd* [1970] AC 567.

Both types of resulting trust are traditionally regarded as examples of trusts giving effect to the common intention of the parties. A resulting trust is not imposed by law against the intentions of the trustee (as is a constructive trust) but gives effect to his presumed intention. Megarry J in *Re Vandervell's Trusts (No. 2)* suggests that a resulting trust of type (B) does not depend on intention but operates automatically. I am not convinced that this is right. If the settlor has expressly, or by necessary implication, abandoned any beneficial interest in the trust property, there is in my view no resulting trust: the undisposed-of equitable interest vests in the Crown as *bona vacantia*: see *Re West Sussex Constabulary's Widows, Children and Benevolent (1930) Fund Trusts* [1971] Ch 1.

Applying these conventional principles of resulting trust to the present case, the bank's claim must fail. There was no transfer of money to the local authority on express trusts: therefore a resulting trust of type (B) above could not arise. As to type (A) above, any presumption of resulting trust is rebutted since it is demonstrated that the bank paid, and the local authority received, the upfront payment with the intention that the moneys so paid should become the absolute property of the local authority. It is true that the parties were under a misapprehension that the payment was made in pursuance of a valid contract. But that does not alter the actual intentions of the parties at the date the payment was made or the moneys were mixed in the bank account. As the article by William Swadling, 'A New Role for Resulting Trusts?' (1996) 16 *Legal Studies* 110 at 133 demonstrates, the presumption of resulting trust is rebutted by evidence of any intention inconsistent with such a trust, not only by evidence of an intention to make a gift.

Professor Birks, 'Restitution and Resulting Trusts', in *Equity and Contemporary Legal Developments*, p. 335 at p. 360, while accepting that the principles I have stated represent 'a very conservative form' of definition of a resulting trust, argues from restitutionary principles that the definition should be extended so as to cover a perceived gap in the law of 'subtractive unjust enrichment' (p. 368) so as to give a plaintiff a proprietary remedy when he has transferred value under a mistake or under a contract the consideration for which wholly fails. He suggests that a resulting trust should arise wherever the money is paid under a mistake (because such mistake vitiates the actual intention) or when money is paid on a condition which is not subsequently satisfied.

As one would expect, the argument is tightly reasoned but I am not persuaded. The search for a perceived need to strengthen the remedies of a plaintiff claiming in restitution involves, to my mind, a distortion of trust principles. First, the argument elides rights in property (which is the only proper subject-matter of a trust) into rights in 'the value transferred' (see p. 361). A trust can only arise where there is defined trust property: it is therefore not consistent with trust principles to say that a person is a trustee of property which cannot be defined. Second, Professor Birks' approach appears to assume (e.g. in the case of a transfer of value made under a contract the consideration for which subsequently fails) that the recipient will be deemed to have been a trustee from the date of his original receipt of money, i.e. the trust arises at a time when the 'trustee' does not, and cannot, know that there is going to be a total failure of consideration. This result is incompatible with the basic premise on which all trust law is built, namely, that the conscience of the trustee is affected. Unless and until the trustee is aware of the factors which give rise to the supposed trust, there is nothing which can affect his conscience. Thus neither in the case of a subsequent failure of consideration nor in the case of a payment under a contract subsequently found to be void for mistake or failure of condition will there be circumstances, at the date of receipt, which can impinge on the conscience of the recipient, thereby making him a trustee.

Notes and Questions 8.1

Explain why, according to Lord Browne-Wilkinson, the consequences he notes under the headings 'The breadth of the submission' and 'The practical consequences of the bank's argument' must follow if the local authority holds the money on trust for the bank (see further section 14.2 below on the enforceability and priority of property interests).

8.4.   Fragmentation of management, control and benefit

In this section, we consider mechanisms for fragmenting the management, control and benefit aspects of ownership. These mechanisms can be put into three categories. The first is corporate property holding, where property is held by an artificial legal person such as a company. The second is managerial property holding, where property is held by a non-beneficial owner – in other words, held or controlled by one person for the benefit of another. Examples falling within this second category are where property is held by trustees, or by administrators of the estates of people who have died or gone bankrupt. The third category is group property holding, where property is held not by a single person but by a group of people for their own benefit, whether as co-owners or as communal owners (a distinction we will look at more closely later on).

These three categories are not exclusive: artificial persons can be co-owners and can also hold property on behalf of others as managerial owners. So, for example, it is quite common to have a trust where the trust property is jointly held by two companies on trust for (say) their employees. However, for the present we will consider each category in isolation.

8.4.1.   Corporate property holding

A corporation is, in law, a person in its own right and as such it has many of the attributes of a real person – it can hold property, enter into contracts, commit torts and crimes, and sue and be sued in the courts. But of course it cannot itself make decisions to do any of these things, or take any action to implement those decisions – all this has to be done by human persons acting on its behalf. So, while it makes perfect sense to say that a corporation holds property for its own benefit, it is not quite the same thing as saying that a human person holds property for her own benefit. A human person who owns a book can be left to decide for herself what to do with it, whether to read it, sell it at a profit or a loss, give it away, or destroy it. If a corporation owns the book, none of these things can happen unless some human person decides that they shall happen. Who makes these decisions, and for whose benefit, and who controls the decision-maker?

There are different types of corporation, but by far the most important (numerically and economically) in this jurisdiction is the limited liability company. In a limited liability company, as Harold Demsetz explains in Extract 8.2 below, the company itself owns its assets and its shareholders own shares in the company. The company's assets consist initially of money supplied by the shareholders in exchange for shares in the company issued to them. The shareholders' liability is limited in that they cannot be called on to provide any more money to meet the liabilities of the company: once the company has been formed and the shareholders have paid the full price of their shares over to the company, the only assets available to meet claims by creditors of the company are those owned by the company. In other words, by joining in the formation of a company or buying shares subsequently issued by it, a shareholder chooses how much of his personal wealth to risk in the enterprise to be carried out by the company.

In traditional theory, ownership of the company's assets is fragmented in the following way. Title to the assets is held by the company, but the assets themselves are managed by the board of directors, who are required to use the assets to carry out the purposes for which the company was formed, in order to provide a profit for the shareholders. This profit is distributed to the shareholders by way of dividends on their shares from time to time declared by the board. The board's management of the assets is controlled by the shareholders, who have the power to appoint and dismiss the directors, and whose consent (given by voting at company meetings) is required for the exercise of various powers.

If this model provided an accurate description of the way in which companies operate in practice, then, according to classical economic theory, they ought not to work at all in a market economy. Indeed, Adam Smith (writing before the rise of the limited liability company) thought it was impossible for a company to function efficiently:

> The directors of such companies ... being the managers rather of other people's money than of their own, it cannot well be expected that they should watch over it with the same anxious vigilance with which the partners in a private copartnery frequently watch over their own ... Negligence and profusion ... must always prevail, more or less, in the management of such a company. It is upon this account that joint stock companies [the precursor of the modern limited liability company] ... have seldom been able to maintain the competition against private adventurers. They have, accordingly, very seldom succeeded without an exclusive privilege, and frequently have not succeeded with one. Without an exclusive privilege they have commonly mismanaged the trade. With an exclusive privilege they have both mismanaged and confined it. (Smith, *The Wealth of Nations*, vol. II, p. 229)

This objection to corporate ownership is more fundamental than might at first sight appear. The problem is not simply inadequate control over management: as we see below, there are many different ways in which controls can and have been built into the basic corporate mechanism. The real objection, as Berle and Means first pointed out in their classic analysis of corporate property holding in 1932, *The Modern Corporation and Private Property* (Extract 8.3 below), is that corporate ownership subverts the profit function which Adam Smith considered integral to the efficiency and social utility of private property.

However, the fact is that most business enterprises do in practice choose to operate through the medium of a limited liability company, and, contrary to Adam Smith's experience, there is no modern evidence that they do so less efficiently than individually owned businesses. How then can this apparent gap between theory and practice be explained?

One possible answer lies in the fact that the strict division between management, control and benefit described in the traditional analysis of corporate ownership rarely occurs in practice. This is particularly true of the smallest and the largest companies.

Take first the case of small companies, which numerically form the vast proportion of all companies. Most small companies are 'closely held' – i.e. the directors and shareholders are the same people: a study published in 1985 revealed that, in about 80 per cent of British small companies, the directors of the company held 90 per cent or more of the shares (Carsberg *et al.*, *Small Company Financial Reporting*, p. 79). In these companies, the individual shareholder/directors have management and control of the assets and keep all the benefit for themselves, so the division of management, control and benefit is purely notional. Corporate ownership in these cases is therefore practically indistinguishable from individual ownership. Even limited liability is likely to be illusory: individuals trading through close companies will almost certainly be required to mortgage their personal assets and give personal guarantees to secure lending to the company.

In relation to very large companies, the traditional model of corporate ownership is a better match, but it is misleadingly simplistic. For these purposes, largeness can be equated with listing on a stock exchange. These companies of course vary enormously, but there are some typical characteristics that make them radically different from closely held companies. First, in many large companies the board of directors does not manage, but hires and fires others to manage for them. This transforms its function from management to control over management – the function performed in the traditional model by the shareholders. Secondly, control by the board is only part of a complex network of control over management of large companies. In particular, there is massive regulatory control exerted by the listing authorities, partly to protect the interests of the shareholders but mainly to preserve the integrity of the market.

Thirdly, the shareholders have only an attenuated connection with the assets of the company. They have no day-to-day control over management, except in those comparatively rare cases where a single individual or group of individuals controls a significant proportion of the shares. Leaving aside those exceptional cases, many of the shareholders have never and will never contribute towards the capital of the company. Most of them are not the original suppliers of capital to the enterprise, and although some of them subsequently supplied capital by buying new issues of shares from the company, many of them bought their shares on the stock market, paying the purchase price not to the company but to the shareholder seller. Indeed, many of them have no direct interest in the profitability of the enterprise. While some shareholders buy shares with the long-term aim of earning income in the form of dividends declared on those shares, others do so primarily in order to make a profit on resale of the shares in the market. Consequently, the correlation between the movement of share prices on the stock market and the profitability of the companies in question is not straightforward (see further Hadden, *Company Law and Capitalism*, pp. 71–5, and the review of current theories of correlation between the two by Cheffins, *Company Law: Theory, Structure and Operation*, pp. 54–8).

The allocation of management, control and benefit in these large companies is radically different from that which occurs in the traditional model. Nevertheless, Berle and Means argue that this merely exacerbates the problems of corporate property holding, and that the constraints that make private property efficient and socially beneficial are even less effective in this kind of company than they are in the traditional model.

The Berle and Means thesis was highly influential in its time, as Gregory S. Alexander explains in *Commodity and Propriety* (Extract 8.4 below), although mainstream modern economists concerned with corporate governance now largely reject its assumptions as to the nature of a corporation. On this modern view – the 'nexus of contracts' theory of the company – the artificial legal person, the corporation, is an irrelevance, and the company is more aptly viewed as a network of explicit and implicit bargains entered into voluntarily by individuals who interact on the basis of reciprocal expectations and behaviour. The classic exposition of the nexus of contracts theory is found in 0-Easterbrook and Fischel, *The Economic Structure of Corporate Law*, and see also Cheffins, *Company Law: Theory, Structure and Operation*, pp. 31–47. For a critical analysis rejecting the nexus of contracts approach, see Ireland, 'Company Law and the Myth of Shareholder Ownership': he describes it as 'the company law equivalent of Mrs Thatcher's "there is no such thing as society"'.

Regardless of which theory of the corporation provides the most fruitful approach to questions of corporate governance, for property theorists the Berle and Means thesis remains a useful analysis of the fragmentation of ownership that occurs in corporate property holding and the nature of corporate property holding (see, for example, Jeremy Waldron, *The Right to Private Property*, pp. 57–9, who describes the Berle and Means account as still the best discussion, while taking the view that corporate property is best seen as 'a mutation of private property rather than as a distinct form of property in its own right').

Extract 8.2   Harold Demsetz, 'Towards a Theory of Property Rights' (1967) 57 *American Economic Review* 347

The interplay of scale economies, negotiating cost, externalities, and the modification of property rights can be seen in the most notable 'exception' to the assertion that ownership tends to be an individual affair: the publicly held corporation. I assume that significant economies of scale in the operation of large corporations is a fact and, also, that large requirements for equity capital can be satisfied more cheaply by acquiring the capital from many purchasers of equity shares. While economies of scale in operating these enterprises exist, economies of scale in the provision of capital do not. Hence, it becomes desirable for many 'owners' to form a joint-stock company.

But if all owners participate in each decision that needs to be made by such a company, the scale economies of operating the company will be overcome quickly by high negotiating cost. Hence a delegation of authority for most decisions takes place and, for most of these, a small management group becomes the *de facto* owners. Effective ownership, i.e. effective control of property, is thus legally concentrated in management's hands. This is the first legal modification, and it takes place in recognition of the high negotiating costs that would otherwise obtain.

The structure of ownership, however, creates some externality difficulties under the law of partnership. If the corporation should fail, partnership law commits each shareholder to meet the debts of the corporation up to the limits of his financial ability. Thus, managerial *de facto* ownership can have considerable external effects on shareholders. Should property rights remain unmodified, this externality would make it exceedingly difficult for entrepreneurs to acquire equity capital from wealthy individuals. (Although these individuals have recourse to reimbursements from other shareholders, litigation costs will be high.) A second legal modification, limited liability, has taken place to reduce the effect of this externality. *De facto* management ownership and limited liability combine to minimize the overall cost of operating large enterprises. Shareholders are essentially lenders of equity capital and not owners, although they do participate in such infrequent decisions as those involving mergers. What shareholders really own are their shares and not the corporation. Ownership in the sense of control again becomes a largely individual affair. The shareholders own their shares, and the president of the corporation and possibly a few other top executives control the corporation.

To further ease the impact of management decisions on shareholders, that is, to minimize the impact of externalities under this ownership form, a further legal modification of rights is required. Unlike partnership law, a shareholder may sell his interest without first obtaining the permission of fellow shareholders or without dissolving the corporation. It thus becomes easy for him to get out if his preferences and those of the management are no longer in harmony. This 'escape hatch' is extremely important and has given rise to the organized trading of securities. The increase in harmony between managers and shareholders brought about by exchange and by competing managerial groups helps to minimize the external effects associated with the corporate ownership structure. Finally, limited liability considerably reduces the cost of exchanging shares by making it unnecessary for a purchaser of shares to examine in great detail the liabilities of the corporation and the assets of other shareholders; these liabilities can adversely affect a purchaser only up to the extent of the price per share.

Extract 8.3   Adolf A. Berle and Gardiner C. Means, *The Modern Corporation and Private Property* (New York: Harcourt, Brace & World, 1932), pp. 299–301

[In this classic (and now hotly disputed) analysis of property holding by limited liability companies first published in 1932, Adolf A. Berle and Gardiner C. Means estimated that approximately 300,000 companies then registered in the United States controlled at least 78 per cent of business wealth in the country. This was not spread evenly between all companies: the 200 largest companies were estimated to control between 45 per cent and 53 per cent of all corporate wealth, between 35 per cent and 45 per cent of all business wealth, and between 15 per cent and 25 per cent of national wealth.]

The socially beneficent results to be derived from the protection of property are supposed to arise, not from the wealth itself, but from the efforts to acquire wealth. A long line of economists have developed what might be called the traditional logic of profits. They have held that, in striving to acquire wealth, that is, in seeking profits, the individual would, perhaps unconsciously, satisfy the wants of others. By carrying on enterprise he would employ his energy and wealth in such a way as to obtain more wealth. In this effort, he would tend to make for profit those things which were in most demand. Competition among countless producers could be relied upon in general to maintain profits within reasonable limits while temporarily excessive profits in any one line of production would induce an increase of activity in that line with a consequent drop of profits to more reasonable levels. At the same time, it was supposed that the business man's effort to increase his profits would, in general, result in more economical use of the factors of production, each enterprise having to compete with others for the available economic resources. Therefore, it has been argued that, by protecting each man in the possession of his wealth and in the possession of any profits he could make from its use, society would encourage enterprise and thereby facilitate the production and distribution of goods desired by the community at reasonable prices with economic use of labor, capital, and business enterprise. By protecting property rights in the instruments of production, the acquisitive interests of man could thus be more effectively harnessed to the benefit of the community.

It must be seen that, under the condition just described, profits act as a return for the performance of two separate functions. First, they act as an inducement to the individual to risk his wealth in enterprise, and, second, they act as a spur, driving him to exercise his utmost skill in making his enterprise profitable. In the case of a private enterprise the distinction between these two functions does not assume importance. The owner of a private business receives any profits made and performs the functions not only of risk-taking but of ultimate management as well. It may be that in the past when industry was in the main carried on by a multitude of small private enterprises the community, through protecting property, has induced a large volume of risk-taking and a vigorous conduct of industry in exchange for the profits derived therefrom.

In the modern corporation, with its separation of ownership and control, these two functions of risk and control are, in the main, performed by two different groups of people. Where such a separation is complete one group of individuals, the security holders [here meaning the shareholders and those who provide loan finance for the company] ... perform the function of risk-takers and suppliers of capital, while a separate group exercises control and ultimate management. In such a case, if profits are to be received only by the security holders, as the traditional logic of property would require, how can they perform both of their traditional economic roles? Are no profits to go to those who exercise control and in whose hands the efficient operation of enterprise ultimately rests?

It is clear that the function of capital supplying and risk-taking must be performed and that the security holder must be compensated if an enterprise is to raise new capital and expand its activity just as the workers must be paid enough to insure the continued supplying of labor and the taking of the risks involved in that labor and in the life based on it. But what if profits can be made more than sufficient to keep the security holders satisfied, more than sufficient to induce new capital to come into the enterprise? Where is the social advantage in setting aside for the security holder, profits in an amount greater than is sufficient to insure the continued supplying of capital and taking of risk? The prospect of additional profits cannot act as a spur on the security holder to make him *operate* the enterprise with more vigour in a way to serve the wants of the community, since he is no longer in control. Such extra profits if given to the security holders would seem to perform no useful economic function.

Furthermore, if all profits are earmarked for the security holder, where is the inducement for those in control to manage the enterprise efficiently? When none of the profits are to be received by them, why should they exert themselves beyond the amount necessary to maintain a reasonably satisfied group of stockholders? *If* the profit motive is the powerful incentive to action which it is supposed to be, and *if* the community is best served when each enterprise is operated with the aim of making the maximum profit, would there not be great social advantage in encouraging the control to seize for themselves any profits over and above the amount necessary as a satisfactory return to capital?

Extract 8.4   Gregory S. Alexander, *Commodity and Propriety: Competing Visions of Property in American Legal Thought 1776–1970* (Chicago: University of Chicago Press, 1997), pp. 342–50

BERLE AND MEANS AND THE PROBLEM OF CORPORATE PROPERTY

By the time of the Great Crash of 1929, it was abundantly clear to anyone who cared to look that the shift to the large corporation as the dominant mode of doing business and with it, corporate equity and debt instruments as the dominant form of property, was now completed and irreversible. Attacks on the modern industrial corporation by critics like Edward Bellamy and Thorstein Veblen had utterly failed to slow the rapid growth of the business corporation or to weaken its enormous economic power.

The phenomenal growth of corporate power, together with the stock market's crash and the ensuing economic depression, engendered in the 1930s an intellectual milieu of skepticism about the validity of the classical theory of economic behavior. That theory posited that the natural forces of market competition by themselves would force firms to supply the best products that consumers wanted at the lowest possible prices. Those that did not would decline and eventually shut down through a process of natural economic selection. The upshot of this theory was that, since market equilibrium was self-maintaining, government intervention in the workings of the market was unjustified.

A central assumption of this theory was that the same person or group of persons would both supply and manage capital for a business venture. Since they would reap the gains or suffer the losses of their own decisions, self-interest would lead these persons to operate the firm as efficiently as they could. The emergence of the modern industrial corporation undermined that assumption and with it, at least in the view of critics, the coherence of the classical theory itself. Among all of the critiques of that theory and of corporate capitalism generally that appeared between 1890 and 1930, no work was more influential than A. A. Berle and G. C. Means's famous book, *The Modern Corporation and Private Property*.

Berle initiated the project under a grant to Columbia University from the Social Science Research Council and was the book's principal author. Means, who was a member of Columbia's economics faculty, contributed to the study primarily by collecting a substantial body of statistical data documenting the concentration of corporate ownership and the diffused distribution of stockholdings. Berle had joined the Columbia law faculty shortly after a split on that faculty had led several prominent Realists to leave. Despite the departure of important figures like William O. Douglas, Herman Oliphant, and Underhill Moore, however, Legal Realism still exerted considerable influence at Columbia, largely through the presence of Karl Llewellyn and Edwin Patterson. Institutional economics, championed by Robert L. Hale, also remained an important intellectual force at Columbia during the time of the Berle study. The book reflected the influence of both strands of thought.

Berle and Means developed two related claims: first, the central characteristic of the modern corporation is the separation of the control of property from its beneficial ownership; second, corporate managers and beneficial owners (i.e. shareholders) do not share the same incentives, undermining the key assumption of the classical model of the market. Berle and Means connected the two claims together in this central passage:

It has been assumed that, if the individual is protected in the right both to use his property as he sees fit and to receive the full fruits of its use, his desire for personal gain, for profits, can be relied on as an effective incentive to his efficient use of any industrial property he may possess.

In the quasi-public corporation, such an assumption no longer holds. [I]t is no longer the individual himself who uses his wealth. Those in control of that wealth, and therefore in a position to secure industrial efficiency and produce profits, are no longer, as owners, entitled to the bulk of such profits. Those who control the destinies of the typical modern corporation own so insignificant a fraction of the company's stock that the returns from running the corporation profitably accrue to them in only a very minor degree. The stockholders, on the other hand, to whom the profits of the corporation go, cannot be motivated by those profits to a more efficient use of the property, since they have surrendered all disposition of it to those in control of the enterprise.

The implication of these claims for the economic function of property was, they thought, profound. At least in the industrial context, the role of property had fundamentally changed. Property no longer performed the economic function that classical economic theory traditionally ascribed to it. 'Must we not', they asked rhetorically, 'recognize that we are no longer dealing with property in the old sense? Does the traditional logic of property still apply? Because an owner who also exercises control over his wealth is protected in the full receipt of the advantages derived from it, must it necessarily follow that an owner who has surrendered control of his wealth should likewise be protected to the full?'

For Berle and Means, the upshot of these changes in the nature of the business corporation and its concomitant effect on the function of property in the business sector was clear: 'The explosion of the atom of property destroys the basis of the old assumption that the quest for profits will spur the owner of industrial property to its effective [i.e. efficient] use.' Large corporations could not be counted on to serve either the interests of shareholders, as the corporation's owners, or of the public generally. Since self-interest alone was inadequate, the only alternative mechanism for assuring that corporations were governed in the public interest was government regulation. Government had 'to strip itself of the illusion that it might recreate the classical society of small competitors and proceed with the structural reforms needed to stabilize the economy'.

What made *The Modern Corporation and Private Property* so influential was not originality: virtually nothing in the book, certainly none of its major arguments, was completely new. Well-known books by Harvard economists Thomas Nixon Carver and William Z. Ripley had earlier argued that shareholders of large corporations had little, if any, meaningful power over corporate policy. Before them, Thorstein Veblen had developed a similar theory of the evolution of corporate structure. Still earlier, the great English economist Alfred Marshall had pointed out in 1890 that large corporations were 'hampered by ... conflicts of interest between shareholders and ... the directors'.

Three factors explain the book's phenomenal success. First, unlike Veblen, Carver and other critics of the corporation, Berle and Means (primarily Means) backed up their criticisms with a substantial body of statistical data. These data were intended to prove two points: that corporate wealth was concentrated in a few corporations and that ownership of corporate stock was broadly dispersed. The data effectively created the impression that a relatively small group of managers now dominated the nation's economy.

The second factor was the book's timing. The date of its first publication (1933) was ideal. After the stock market crash, the general public was quite receptive to a critical treatment of corporate power. As George Stigler and Claire Friedland have pointed out, '[t]he 1930s was a period of accelerating movement away from a competitive, unregulated market. Reasons for distrusting such a system . . . were in demand for the new rhetoric of public policy, and Berle and Means nicely met that need.' Policy-oriented lawyers and social scientists were no less ready than John Q. American to hear an analysis of corporate governance that emphasized the need for external control. The crash had seemed to validate Carver's and Ripley's earlier predictions of the disastrous consequences of leaving the modern corporation unregulated. The time could not have been more ripe for a study of the modern corporation that focused on its enormous power.

The third factor was the book's functional and institutionalist approach to the study of corporations. Between 1920 and 1930 a debate raged among legal scholars over the 'true' nature of the corporation. The law reviews were filled with articles, most of which were aridly conceptualist, debating whether the corporation is a 'real entity' or merely an aggregation of contractual relationships. By 1930, this debate had run out of intellectual steam. The philosopher John Dewey, who had considerable contact with both the law school and the economics faculties at Columbia and whose work both influenced and was influenced by them, wrote in 1926 that legal writers and courts should disconnect specific issues concerning corporations from disputes over the appropriate conceptual theory of the corporation: how law and society treat the corporation, and what powers the corporation was given, depended on political and economic choices, not on formal analysis.

Heeding Dewey's advice, Berle and Means simply ignored the whole 'real entity' debate. Instead, they focused on how the modern business corporation actually functioned in American society. The functional approach was perfectly suited to Berle and Means's intended audience, for the book was not directed at professional economists, or at least not the academic economic establishment. Its real target was lawyers, especially those academic lawyers who were most interested in and involved with the making of public policy – Legal Realists and their economic allies. Berle and Means's methodology effectively synthesized the institutional perspective of institutional economics and the functionalist outlook of the Legal Realists. Substantively, their analysis echoed the two dominant themes of Progressive and Realist legal-economic writers that the market was a realm of power and that economic institutions were not wholly private in character. In particular, Berle and Means's argument that large corporations were not really private institutions but were actually 'quasi-public' strongly reiterated and bolstered earlier arguments by Hohfeld, Hale, Ely, Commons, and others that there was no categorical distinction between the public and private in market transactions. While the economic profession was not especially interested in this line of criticism, the academic legal profession, especially its elite stratum, certainly was.

PUBLICLY CONTROLLING THE PRIVATE CORPORATION

Berle and Means's most significant contribution was to sketch a theory that would provide an alternative to the affectation doctrine of *Munn* v. *Illinois* as the theoretical foundation for government regulation of corporate activities. As we have already seen, that doctrine provided that there was no constitutional obstacle to legislative regulation of, for example, the rates that businesses charged their customers when the corporation was of the type that was 'affected with a public interest'. In effect, the affectation doctrine denied that such corporations were solely private. While the US Supreme Court did not formally abandon that doctrine until the 1934 decision in *Nebbia* v. *New York*, it lost virtually all intellectual credibility among lawyers well before then. It was, as the Yale Legal Realist Walton Hamilton put it, the product of the view of a generation for whom the then-new fourteenth amendment was part of 'the old constitution'. To a different generation, it sounded (if one was inclined to value liberty of contract above all) suspiciously hostile to property rights or (if one had taken the Realist turn) meaningless, since all businesses were in some sense affected with a public interest. By 1930, its demise as a justification for legal control of corporate activities in general to insure that corporations act for the common welfare was a foregone conclusion.

Berle and Means attempted to fill the gap by advancing a novel theory. They argued that the 'traditional logic of property' did not apply to the modern large corporation. Corporate power should not be exercised for the exclusive benefit of the shareholders but for the benefit of society as a whole. Shareholders are, they argued, passive property owners who have 'released the community from the obligation to protect them to the full extent implied in the doctrine of strict property rights'. This leaves the community in a position to demand that the relationship between corporate property and the community be reconfigured in a way that recognizes that in the context of the modern industrial corporation the public/private distinction had lost much of its credibility:

> Neither the claims of ownership nor those of control can stand against the paramount interests of the community ... Rigid enforcement of property rights as a temporary protection against plundering by control would not stand in the way of modification of these rights in the interest of other groups. When a convincing system of community obligations is worked out and is generally accepted, in that moment the passive property right of today must yield before the larger interests of society ... It is conceivable – indeed it seems almost essential if the corporate system is to survive – that the 'control' of the great corporations should develop into a purely neutral technocracy, balancing a variety of claims by various groups in the community and assigning to each a portion of the income stream on the basis of public policy rather than private cupidity.

The precise content of the obligation that the corporation owes to the community remained obscure. Berle and Means never explained what the specific features of that obligation were or which constituencies are included in the notion of the 'community'. Rather, they vaguely called for something resembling what late twentieth-century corporate lawyers call 'corporate social responsibility'. But it is not entirely clear just how the Berle and Means analysis relates to the modern discourse of corporate social responsibility.

The phrase 'corporate social responsibility' today may mean either of two different ideas. The first is that the officers of large, publicly held corporations should focus exclusively on the shareholders' dominant preference, which is presumed to be profit-maximization, rather than serving their own personal interests. The second meaning grows out of a quite different concern. It advocates what is sometimes called 'corporate voluntarism', that is, corporate actions that sacrifice profit-maximization to pursue other social objectives.

These two ideas have inconsistent implications for legal control over corporate managers. The first idea requires tighter legal control over corporate officers and directors. Corporate voluntarism, on the other hand, requires relaxing legal controls over managers, giving them greater discretion so that they can fulfill their responsibilities to the community.

These two meanings were the subject of a famous debate between Berle and the noted Harvard professor of corporate law, E. Merrick Dodd. Dodd supported the idea of corporate voluntarism, and he was unconcerned that corporate managers would exercise greater discretion in their own interests rather than the interests of social groups in addition to shareholders. He based his confidence on the theory that

> [p]ower over the lives of others tends to create on the part of those most worthy to exercise it a sense of responsibility. The managers, who along with the subordinate employees are part of the group which is contributing to the success of the enterprise by day-to-day efforts, may easily come to feel as strong a community of interest with their fellow workers as with a group of investors whose only connection with the enterprise is that they or their predecessors in interest invested money in it.

Berle regarded this view as wildly naive. He simply did not think that corporate managers could be trusted to act in the interest of anyone other than themselves if they were given discretion to do so. Because of the separation of control from ownership, private property no longer performed, in the industrial setting, its disciplining role. Therefore, management powers had to be subjected to some form of legal control. One possible form is the requirement that managers act exclusively in the interest of shareholders. That approach, which Berle analogized to the controls that equity places on trustees, adopted the profit-maximization version of corporate responsibility.

Berle considered strict, trustee-like controls over corporate managers to be clearly preferable to open-ended managerial discretion, if those two were the only available options. His reluctance to abandon profit-maximization as the sole objective of corporate officers and directors was rooted in social welfare considerations.

Doubtless reflecting anxiety about the economic insecurity that millions of Americans were then facing during the Great Depression, he wrote, 'When [corporate property] and the income stream upon which [corporate stockholders] rely are irresponsibly dealt with, a large portion of the group merely devolves upon the community; and there is presented a staggering bill for relief, old age pensions, sickness-aid, and the like.' Removing from shareholders their economic security so that corporate property could be used to serve the interests of other groups was simply robbing Peter to pay Paul unless the government simultaneously adopts 'a system ... by which responsibility for control of national wealth and income is so apportioned and enforced that the community as a whole, or at least the great bulk of it, is properly taken care of'.

Berle presented his obligation-to-the-community theory as a third way, an alternative to the 'managerial discretion' theory and the 'strict property rights of shareholders' theory. He recognized that this theory had to be clearly developed, but he warned that 'you cannot abandon emphasis on "the view that business corporations exist for the sole purpose of making profits for their stockholders" until such time as you are prepared to offer a clear and reasonably enforceable scheme of responsibilities to someone else'. Once the shareholders' interests were adequately taken care of, though, the community had a legitimate claim to have other groups' interests protected as well. These included 'fair wages, security to employees, reasonable service to their public, and stabilization of business'. A program along those lines might well shift some corporate profits from shareholders to employees and other groups to whom corporations conventionally do not owe fiduciary duties, but so long as the shareholders' basic welfare needs were served, they had no legitimate basis for demanding that their profits be maximized. The corporation was, after all, a quasi-public institution, and its legal obligations had to be defined consistently with its character.

Subsequent to writing *The Modern Corporation and Private Property*, Berle's views became more obscure still. In 1954, he conceded that his dispute with Dodd 'has been settled (at least for the time being)' squarely in favor of Professor Dodd's contention. He now considered corporate management to be free to practice social responsibility. Still later, however, he asserted that his concession was only that things had changed in fact, not that they had changed for the better. 'Things being as they are', he wrote, 'I am unabashed in endeavoring to seek the best use of a social and legal situation whose existence can neither be denied nor changed.'

Berle never got around to describing an alternative 'scheme of responsibilities' for corporations. Oddly enough, he did not support proposals to reconstitute boards of directors to include representatives of employees or consumers or calls formally to redefine the goals of management.

8.4.2. Managerial property holding

There are a number of other property holding mechanisms which involve the separation of title and benefit, in the sense that the property holder is not only precluded from taking a personal benefit from the property but is also put under positive duties to administer it for the benefit of others. The most well known of these mechanisms is the trust, evolved by equity precisely for this purpose, but there are other analogous situations where the law cannot or will not allow a property holder to continue to enjoy the benefit of the property. The most obvious circumstances in which such situations arise is where a property holder dies or is made bankrupt. However, although these situations are analogous to each other and to the trust, there are important differences between them. There has been a tendency to overlook these differences and assume that all such managerial property holding mechanisms must conform analytically to the trust model – in particular, to assume that, since the property holder is no longer entitled to benefit from the property, there must be someone else who is entitled to the benefit in precisely the same way as a beneficiary under a trust is entitled to benefit. However, as we see below, the courts have rejected such attempts to force all types of managerial property holding into the trusts straitjacket, and now accept that different allocations of management, control and benefit are appropriate in these very different circumstances.

8.4.2.1.   Trust

In a trust, title to property is held by one or more trustees who are required to use it not for their own benefit but for the specific purpose of the trust. This might be to carry out a specified, usually charitable, purpose, or it might be to administer the property for the benefit of specified people – the beneficiaries. For example, I might transfer £10,000 to you on terms that you will hold it on trust for my two children until they have reached the age of eighteen. This would usually (subject to the precise terms I impose) mean that you will have to invest the £10,000 so that it produces an income, and then you will have to make sure that that income is spent on the children while they are under eighteen, and then hand over half the capital representing the original £10,000 to each child on her eighteenth birthday.

This is not the only way in which a trust can come into existence. Instead of transferring the £10,000 to you to hold on trust for my children, I might have made myself trustee of it, by declaring that I hold it on trust for them. These are both examples of an express creation of a trust. But a trust might also be imposed on me by the law (historically, by equity) whether I intend it to happen or not, either via a resulting trust in the circumstances Lord Browne-Wilkinson describes in the extract from *Westdeutsche Landesbank* v. *Islington London Borough Council* given above, or via a constructive trust. A constructive trust is imposed in circumstances where the court regards it as unconscionable for the legal title holder to use the property for his own benefit. So, for example, if you and I buy a house together in my name, but on the common understanding that it is to be ours jointly, and on the strength of this you pay half the mortgage payments, equity will impose a constructive trust on me so that I am required to hold the title to the house on trust for us jointly (*Lloyds Bank plc* v. *Rosset* [1990] 1 AC 107).

Here we are not concerned with how a trust comes into existence. What we are interested in is how ownership is fragmented once property is subjected to a trust, however that came about. So, to go back to the first example, if I give you £10,000 to hold on trust for my children, what is the position of each of us – you the trustee, me the creator of the trust or settlor, and the children as beneficiaries?

The trustee

It is clear that you as trustee hold the title to the £10,000 and to the investments you buy with the money. In this sense, you can be said to be the owner, but this ownership is of no value to you because you are not allowed to take any benefit from these assets for yourself. In fact, one can go further and say that this owner-ship has a negative value in your hands. I would not expect you to take it on except as a favour to me, or for payment, because it will involve you taking on positive duties to take care of the assets and to ensure they produce a good return for my children and are used exclusively for their benefit. You can therefore be said to have title to the £10,000 and any investments from time to time representing it, and the right, power and duty to manage them, but no benefit from them.

The settlor

It is equally well established, although perhaps not so obvious, that I as the person who created the trust, the settlor, cease to have any role once the trust is set up. I have transferred my title to you, and unless I specifically reserved a right to benefit for myself in some way, or reserved rights or powers to direct you what to do (both unlikely in practice) I no longer have any say in what happens to anything, not even a right to object if you commit any breach of the duties I have imposed on you. The fact that trust law has evolved in such a way that the settlor is left with no function is less surprising when you consider how often trusts have to operate without a settlor: many expressly created trusts are made by will (so the settlor has died by the time the trust comes into operation) or because the settlor knows she will be unable to manage the assets personally and those not expressly created but imposed by law never had a settlor.

The beneficiaries

The position of the beneficiaries is more complex. In general terms, they clearly have the benefit of the trust property, in that you as trustee are under a duty to manage it on their behalf, but how is that duty enforced, and can the beneficiaries be said to have any interest in the property held on trust for them, as opposed to in any payments you might eventually make to them out of the trust?

The answer to the first question is that it is the courts who invented the trust in the first place, and they retain a supervisory jurisdiction over them. In practice, this means that they enforce the duties of the trustees, on application made to them by the beneficiaries.

A crucial element in the interest of a beneficiary is therefore the right to apply to the court for redress if the trustees fail in carrying out any of their duties. This is a chose in action, and is in itself a valuable property interest. Is it, however, possible to go further and say that the beneficiary has a property interest in the trust property itself? Could one say, for example (and ignoring for the moment the question of whether minors can hold property interests), that my children have any interest in the £10,000 you hold on trust for them, or in any investments you buy with it to hold on their behalf?

One immediate apparent difficulty can be cleared out of the way to start with, and this is the precise identity of the assets in which they might be said to have an interest. There are two reasons why we might hesitate to say that they have an interest in the original £10,000, or in any of the specific investments you buy with it. The first is that expenses will be incurred in the administration of the trust, and taxes will be payable in respect of the assets you are holding on trust. You as trustee are not of course expected to pay these out of your own pocket: you will pay them out of the trust assets. The beneficiaries can therefore never assume that any particular asset will be given to them or even used for their direct benefit: you might instead decide to sell it to raise the money to pay taxes and expenses. The second is that, because you as trustee have the duty to invest the money, you must be free to buy and sell specific assets at your discretion without asking or even telling the children, and you must also have the power to sell any given asset freed from any obligation that it should be used for the benefit of the children. For these reasons, it is difficult to see how the children can be said to have any interest in any particular assets, except in the very general sense that they have the right to insist that they are used only for purposes authorised by the trust. This was the conclusion reached by the minority in the House of Lords in the classic case, *Baker* v. *Archer-Shee* [1927] AC 844. The majority view – that the beneficiary did have an interest in each investment – is understandable in the taxation context they were considering, but would be an inaccurate analysis of the beneficiary's position if taken outside that context.

However, there is a more convincing analysis not canvassed in the *Archer-Shee* case. If viewed more abstractly, it can be seen that what you as trustee are holding is a *fund*, a fluctuating body of assets from time to time representing the original £10,000, out of which you as trustee deduct the proper expenses of the fund, and the balance of which must ultimately go to the children and to no one else. Viewed in this light, it is perfectly intelligible to say that, while the children have no property interest in any specific asset vested in you as trustee, they do have an interest in the abstract fund represented by the assets you hold from time to time on their behalf. This is the analysis implicitly accepted by both the Court of Appeal and the House of Lords in another taxation case, *Gartside* v. *Inland Revenue Commissioners* [1968] AC 553, although they differed over the question of when a beneficiary can be said to have an interest, in the sense of an entitlement to benefit, as opposed to an expectancy of benefiting. For further analysis of the idea of property in a fund see Nolan, 'Property in a Fund'.

8.4.2.2. Administration of property on death

Since property interests are, by definition, not personal to the interest holder, it follows that, when a person dies holding a property interest, that property interest continues to exist. This does not of course apply to interests whose duration is fixed by reference to the holder's lifetime. Take, for example, the case of an option to purchase an interest in land, which is itself an interest in land for the reasons given in section 12.3.4 below. If I was to grant you an option to purchase the freehold interest in my house at any time during your lifetime for £100,000, the option will automatically expire when you die, whereas if we had agreed that the option was exercisable at any time over the next fifty years, the option will continue for the full fifty-year period despite your death before then.

So what actually happens to that option if you die before the fifty-year period is up? Ultimately, all your property (the option included) will go to whichever of your relatives becomes qualified to take under sections 45 and 46 of the Administration of Estates Act 1925 as amended, unless you left a will directing that it should go elsewhere. However, this cannot happen instantaneously when you die. Someone has to carry out the bureaucratic task of sorting out what property you had, paying all your debts out of it (which may involve selling some or all of it), and identifying who is now entitled to what out of what is left. You, the testator, can choose who is to carry out that task by appointing that person as executor in your will, and, if you do that, then the title to all your property will automatically vest in that person when you die (sections 1 and 3 of the Administration of Estates Act 1925). If you do not appoint an executor, anyone claiming an interest in your property can apply to the court to be appointed as an administrator to carry out the same functions. This will necessarily take some time, and so pending the appointment of an administrator the title to all your property vests in a public official, the Public Trustee, who has no function other than to hold the nominal title until it can be passed on to an administrator (section 9 of the 1925 Act, as substituted by section 14 of the Law of Property (Miscellaneous Provisions) Act 1994).

Your executor or administrator (collectively called 'personal representatives') will not only have title to your property but will also have extensive powers to deal with it while carrying out the administration of your affairs. The Administration of Estates Act 1925 as amended gives personal representatives powers equivalent to those held by trustees over trust property and clearly, since their function is to get your property together, pay off your debts and their expenses and then pass the balance on to your beneficiaries, they can be said to be under a duty to exercise these powers over your property for the benefit of these prospective beneficiaries. They are certainly not entitled to exercise them for their own benefit. Does this mean that the people who will ultimately take the net assets left after administration of your estate have a beneficial interest in your property during the course of the administration, just as a beneficiary under a trust would have? This question has caused some confusion in the past. It had been argued that, when you die holding property beneficially, the beneficial interest must be somewhere pending its ultimate transfer to your beneficiaries. It cannot be in abeyance. It cannot be held by your personal representatives because, like trustees, although they are nominally the owners they are not allowed to use the property for their own benefit. Therefore, the argument goes, they must be holding it for the benefit of the prospective beneficiaries, and therefore those beneficiaries must be taken to have the beneficial interest in your assets from the moment you die. This, however, is a very mechanistic view of property interests. Just because it is possible to split the nominal title and the beneficial interest in property between two people through the mechanism of a trust, it does not necessarily follow that, whenever someone holds only the nominal title to property (i.e. they hold property that they are not allowed to use for their own benefit), there must be someone else somewhere who holds the beneficial interest. The title holder may be holding the property for some abstract purpose (consider, for example, the trustees of a charitable trust) or with the duty to administer it for the benefit of some as yet unascertained persons. Provided there is in place some mechanism for ensuring that the title holders do indeed use the property for the requisite purposes and not for their own benefit, there is no practical reason why anyone else should have to have property rights either in the specific assets themselves or (as in a trust) in the fund comprising those assets and their net proceeds. In *Commissioner of Stamp Duties (Queensland)* v. *Livingston* [1965] AC 694 (extracted at www.cambridge.org/propertylaw/), it was finally established that this is the correct analysis of how the property of a deceased person is held pending its transfer by the personal representatives to those who are ultimately identified as the appropriate beneficiaries. One might say that the beneficial interest is in abeyance from the date of death until the net estate is distributed, or, perhaps more accurately, one might say that there simply is no beneficial property interest during that period. Ownership has been fragmented in such a way that management has been allocated to one person and control to another (or others: see below) but no one has a proprietary right to benefit.

8.4.2.3. Bankruptcy and liquidation

A similar situation arises when a property holder becomes insolvent, but there are some significant differences. In the case of company liquidations (but not individual bankruptcy) the split between title, management and control is more complex. Given the already existing fragmentation of control, management and benefit existing in a solvent company, this is unsurprising. What happens on liquidation is that title to the company's assets remains in the company, but the directors lose all their management powers. From that point onwards, the company can act only through the liquidator, who takes on all the directors' powers and also enjoys additional statutory powers to enable him to get in all the company's assets, ascertain all its liabilities and then distribute the assets among the creditors. Once this process has been completed, the company is wound up and formally ceases to exist. Although this may look superficially similar to the task carried out by the administrator of the assets of someone who has died, the important difference is that the liquidator is an officer of the court with powers and duties to scrutinise both the behaviour of the company's directors in the period leading up to insolvency, and transactions entered into by the company during that period.

In the bankruptcy of an individual, the trustee in bankruptcy performs very similar functions, but also takes on title to all the bankrupt's assets. Title to the property of a bankrupt automatically transfers from the bankrupt to her trustee in bankruptcy as soon as the bankruptcy order is made, and the trustee then has statutory powers and duties essentially the same to those enjoyed by a liquidator.

An additional complicating factor in both liquidation and bankruptcy is that there is a significant process to be gone through before it can be established who will receive what payments from the estate. Anyone who thinks they may be entitled must first put in a proof of their claim, and it is for the liquidator or trustee in bankruptcy to determine the admissibility and value of each claim. Contingent claims, claims for future debts and claims for as yet unascertained amounts are all allowable (for example, a claim for damages for personal injury where neither liability nor quantum has yet been settled) and the liquidator or trustee in bankruptcy must put a value on each of these (subject to a right of appeal to the court). At the outset, the question of precisely who is a prospective beneficiary, and precisely what their interest might be, is therefore much less clear than it is in the case of an estate of a deceased person.

Given these factors, it is not surprising that the courts have had no difficulty in concluding that neither the creditors nor anyone else has a beneficial interest in the insolvent's assets pending completion of the liquidation or bankruptcy, as we see from *Ayerst* v. *C&K (Construction) Ltd* [1976] AC 167, extracted at www.cambridge.org/propertylaw/.

Notes and Questions 8.2

1   Read *Commissioner of Stamp Duties* v. *Livingston* [1965] AC 694, either in full or as extracted at www.cambridge.org/propertylaw/, and consider the following:

(1)   The court acknowledged that someone in Mrs Coulsdon's position has a 'transmissible interest' in the unadministered estate, in the sense that, if she dies, the right to receive the benefit under the testator's will will pass to whoever becomes entitled to *her* property on *her* death. Similarly, if instead of dying she had become bankrupt when the testator's estate was still in the course of administration, her right to receive the benefit under the testator's will would have passed automatically to her trustee in bankruptcy. According to Viscount Radcliffe, what is the nature of this transmissible right that she holds at this point? Is it a property right? If yes, why was it not a 'beneficial interest in real property in Queensland or ... beneficial personal property [interest] locally situate in Queensland'?

(2)   According to Viscount Radcliffe, why is an unadministered estate incapable of forming a trust fund? Do you agree? See section 8.4.2.1 (under the heading 'The beneficiaries') above on the idea of property in a fund.

(3) If by his will Mr Livingston had left his widow a specific item he owned – perhaps the house where they lived, or his wedding ring – should Mrs Coulsdon be taken to have any property interest in that item pending completion of the administration by the executors?

(4) Compare the position of executors with that of (a) company directors (b) trustees and (c) liquidators. In each case, who has title to the assets? Who the right/power to manage them? For whose benefit must they exercise those rights/powers? What is the mechanism for ensuring (i) that they do not exercise them for their own benefit and (ii) that they do exercise them to realise the maximum benefit for those intended to benefit?

2 Read *Ayerst* v. *C&K (Construction) Ltd* [1976] AC 167, either in full or as extracted at www.cambridge.org/propertylaw/. In argument, counsel for the taxpayer argued that the mere fact that restrictions are imposed by law or contract on an owner's right to use his property does not deprive him of the beneficial ownership of it:

> In the case of a tree preservation order one is deprived of the right to cut it down but not of the beneficial ownership. A company in liquidation, though it must pay its creditors, holds its property for its own benefit. Its assets remain its assets though they must be dealt with in a particular way [by the liquidator, acting as a 'superior director' of the company] ... The liquidator has fiduciary duties imposed by statute but is not really a trustee. The beneficial ownership is not in the creditors ... A company only ceases to be the beneficial owner of its assets if the beneficial ownership passes to someone else. A man remains the beneficial owner of his property, however much the law may restrain the use of it.

Do you agree that an owner of a tree subject to a tree preservation order remains beneficial owner of it? Do you agree with the final sentence? Is there a valid distinction to be drawn between a person who is prohibited from using her property, and a person who is required to use it wholly for the benefit of someone else?

8.5. Group ownership

Only legal entities can hold private property interests. Human beings, corporations and partnerships come within the category of legal entity, but many other socially recognised groupings (for example, married couples, families, parent and subsidiary companies, and unincorporated associations) do not, even though there may be a legally recognised relationship between the members of the group. However, it is possible for two or more legal entities to hold the same private property interest simultaneously, through private co-ownership.

Private co-ownership must be distinguished from public ownership and communal ownership. We considered the differences between private ownership, public ownership and communal ownership in Chapter 2. As we saw there, in the case of communal property rights, as a member of the community you cannot be excluded from use and benefit by any other member of the community but you do not have any separate or separable property right that can be sold or bequeathed to anyone else: the only way in which any person can become or cease to be entitled to use and benefit is by joining or leaving the community. Private co-ownership resembles communal ownership in that no co-owner can be excluded from use and benefit by any other co-owner, and no co-owner has a separate interest during the co-ownership. However, it differs from communal ownership in that, in general (subject to exceptions explained below), in private co-ownership each co-owner has a *separable share* in the co-owned property, and, once it has been notionally separated off, that share can be sold or bequeathed to someone else, who thereby becomes a new member of the co-ownership group. By the same token, every private co-owner continues to have a proprietary entitlement unless and until it is positively transferred to someone else (or, in the case of a joint holder who dies before severing his interest, until he dies: see below).

It will be apparent from the above that, in this jurisdiction we do not recognise private co-ownership where the right to participate is defined by reference to status. In other words, the co-owners must comprise a fixed (as opposed to a fluctuating) group of ascertained legal entities. In fact, the *only* types of co-ownership that we now recognise are ownership in common and joint ownership (usually called tenancy in common and joint tenancy where the co-owned interest is an interest in land).

In ownership in common, each co-ownership has a defined but not yet separated off (and not necessarily equal) share in the co-owned interest. For example, you and I might own a car in common, with me having a one-fifth and you having a four-fifths share. We are each equally entitled to the use and benefit of the car, in the sense that neither of us can exclude the other from any part of it (although see below as to what happens if we fail to agree on a *modus vivendi*). Neither of us can sell or otherwise deal with the car except with the co-operation of the other. If, however, the car is hired out or sold, I will be entitled to a one-fifth share in the hire fee or sale price and you will take the other four-fifths. Although I cannot sell the car itself without your co-operation, I can at any time sell or give my one-fifth *share* in it to anyone else (in which case of course I will take the whole of any sale proceeds of my share) and you can do the same with your four-fifths. And, if either of us dies, our respective share will go to our personal representatives, to be passed on to whoever becomes entitled to inherit our property.

Joint ownership differs from ownership in common in one crucial respect. Instead of each co-owner having a defined but not yet separated off share, as in ownership in common, each joint owner is fully entitled to the whole of the co-owned interest, subject only to the exactly similar entitlement of each of the other joint owners. Furthermore, no individual joint owner can sell or give away his joint ownership interest. However, what he can *always* do (subject to the exceptions below) is to convert his joint ownership interest into an interest in common, which he can then either keep as a separable but as yet unseparated share in the co-ownership, or sell or give away, as he chooses. He can do this unilaterally at any time provided (if he is an individual) it is done before he dies. If he dies without having converted his joint interest into an interest in common (and an attempt to do so by will is too late) then on his death his interest expires, and the other joint interests are correspondingly enlarged. If during his lifetime he attempts to deal separately with his own interest under the joint ownership (for example, by purporting to sell or mortgage it) this will *automatically of itself* sever his interest from the joint ownership – i.e. convert his joint interest into an interest in common – and the purported sale or mortgage or whatever will take effect over what is now his interest in common.

In practical terms, therefore, joint owners can separate off their interests as easily as can tenants in common, except in the cases considered below where the joint tenancy is made unseverable by statute. This leaves only two differences between joint ownership and ownership in common which are of any importance in practice. First, in any joint ownership, the entitlements of each joint owner are necessarily equal, so if there are five joint owners and one severs (i.e. converts her joint interest into an interest in common) she will now hold a one-fifth share and the other four will jointly hold a four-fifths share (her action has no effect on the relationship between the other four – they remain joint owners of their share). Secondly, as already explained, when a joint owner dies, her interest expires and the entitlement of the survivors is correspondingly enlarged, whereas, when an owner in common dies, he dies owning a share which is passed on to whoever inherits his property and the entitlements of the other owners in common are not affected in any way. In technical terms, joint owners have a right of survivorship (as each dies, the survivors' entitlements enlarge, until the last survivor takes everything) whereas owners in common do not.

In all other respects, however, joint ownership and ownership in common are identical in effect. Like owners in common, joint owners can only dispose of or deal with the jointly owned asset by acting in unison, and any proceeds of any dealing or disposition are divisible rateably between them (in the case of joint ownership, necessarily in equal shares). Meanwhile, however, just as in the case of ownership in common, no joint owner can be excluded from the use and benefit of the jointly owned asset or any part of it by any other joint owner.

It will be apparent from the above that, in practice, private co-ownership, whether by ownership in common or by joint ownership, would often be unworkable without mechanisms for resolving disputes and enforcing co-operation between the owners. We consider these mechanisms in Chapter 16, but one of them, applicable only to co-owned interests in land, must be briefly mentioned here. This is the automatic imposition of a trust on all co-owned interests in land. Specifically, when co-owners acquire an interest in land, it automatically vests in them (or in whoever they nominate, or, if they fail to nominate anyone and there are more than four of them, in the first four of them named as co-owners in the vesting document) as trustees, to hold on a special statutory trust – the trust of land – now regulated by the Trusts of Land and Appointment of Trustees Act 1996. Under this trust, the trustees hold the interest in question on trust for all the co-owners as beneficiaries. Both the trustees' nominal title and the beneficial interest are co-owned. However, the trustees *must* hold the nominal title as joint owners (and any attempt to sever and convert a trustee's interest into an interest in common will be ineffective), whereas the beneficial interest can be held by the beneficiaries either in common or jointly, and, if jointly, then any beneficiary is free to sever and convert her joint entitlement into an interest in common at any time. The advantages of using the trust mechanism as a means of regulating the relationships between the co-owners themselves, and between them as a group and outsiders, is considered in detail in Chapter 16. However, for present purposes the relevant point is that it enables management to be separated from benefit, and confers management either on a single person (the co-owners can, if they want, decide to have only one trustee although for reasons which are considered in section 14.4 below this is rare and inadvisable) or on a limited group who are subject to the court's supervisory jurisdiction over trustees, and who can only act effectively in concert (because of the compulsory joint tenancy) and none of whom has a separable share (again because of the compulsory joint tenancy). This has advantages even when each co-owner is both a trustee and a beneficiary. This occurs very frequently – for example, if husband and wife decide to co-own their matrimonial home, they will nowadays probably decide to both hold the legal title to the fee simple, which must then be held by them jointly on trust for themselves either as beneficial tenants in common or as beneficial joint tenants. The advantage of imposing a trust even in such simple cases as this is that it then brings into operation statutory machinery (now contained in the 1996 Act) which gives the court effective powers to adjudicate between the co-owners when disputes arise. See further Chapter 16.

8.6.   General and particular use rights

Some property interests allow the holder to make general use of the resource in question, whether for a limited or unlimited periods of time, and whether solely or in conjunction with others. Others, however, allow the holder to make only a limited, specific use of a resource over which some other person has general use rights. As we see in Chapter 9, the courts are particularly reluctant to expand the range of specific, or particular, use rights which are recognised as property rights.

Particular use rights encompass private, communal and public property rights. They fall within two general categories: rights to *use* someone else's land in a particular way (to walk across it, or have your drainage pipes run through it, or use it for recreational purposes) and rights to take a specific resource from someone else's land (to extract gravel from it, or cut down and take away trees or crops growing on it). We look at most of these rights – communal and public rights to make a particular use of someone else's land, and rights to take resources from someone else's land – in Chapters 5 and 13. Here we concentrate on easements – i.e. private proprietary rights to make a particular use of someone else's land.

The modern statement of the requirements to be satisfied before a right can be classified as an easement appears in the judgment of Evershed MR in *Re Ellenborough Park* [1956] Ch 131, extracted at www.cambridge.org/propertylaw/. One of the points that is clear from his judgment is that, unlike a profit, an easement cannot exist in gross: it must be appurtenant to the land it benefits, and cannot be severed from that land and traded separately as a free-standing property right. Why is this? There are (at least) two possible answers. One of them is that the law will not give proprietary status to a right to make use of (and therefore diminish the value of) someone else's land unless that right enhances the value/utility of another piece of land: because land is in limited supply, no piece of land should be permanently diminished in value by the imposition of a proprietary burden (which will hinder development and change of use and restrict the uses that can be made of the land, and therefore make it less easy to sell, and increase the complexity and therefore the cost of the sale process) unless it will produce a corresponding permanent enhancement of the value of some other piece of land – the production of an increase in wealth generally is not sufficient. This would explain why I can have a proprietary right to use part of your land as a car park to serve my adjoining office and shop development (as in *London & Blenheim Estates Ltd* v. *Ladbroke Retail Parks Ltd* [1992] 1 WLR 1278), but cannot have a proprietary right to use it as a car park to enhance my business of running car parks.

The second possible answer is that the link between the use of one piece of land and the enhancement of the value of another piece of land provides a reasonably precise but flexible measure for quantifying the measure of the burden on the burdened land. If we know that a right of way over a pathway in a garden is for the benefit of the adjoining house and garden, this tells us the type and quantity of the traffic the path can expect to have to bear over the years. This explanation is consistent with the allied rule that a change in the character of the benefited land which has the effect of increasing or altering the nature of the burden on the burdened land extinguishes the easement (see *Atwood* v. *Bovis Homes Ltd* [2000] 3 WLR 1842).

Notes and Questions 8.3

1 Read *Re Ellenborough Park* [1956] Ch 131, either in full or as extracted at www.cambridge.org/propertylaw/, and consider the following:
   (1) Explain what is meant by the following:
        (a) an easement cannot exist in gross;
        (b) an easement must accommodate the dominant tenement;
        (c) a right cannot be an easement unless it is capable of forming the subject-matter of a grant.

(2) How do you distinguish a right that accommodates the dominant land from a right that provides a benefit to the owners/occupiers of the dominant land? Is it relevant to consider whether the dominant land would fetch a higher price if sold with the benefit of the right?

2 What, if any, are the objections to categorising the following as easements:
  (a) car-parking rights (see the first instance decision in *London & Blenheim Estates Ltd* v. *Ladbroke Retail Parks Ltd* [1992] 1 WLR 1278);
  (b) rights to wander at will over the servient land; and
  (c) a right to a 'prospect' (i.e. a view over neighbouring land) or a right to the passage of radio/television signals across neighbouring land (see *Hunter* v. *Canary Wharf*, discussed in Chapter 6 above).

3 If the owner of the dominant land benefiting from an easement acquires additional adjoining land, should she be entitled to exercise the easement for the benefit of the additional land as well as for the benefit of the original dominant land? Compare *Harris* v. *Flower* (1904) 74 LJ Ch 127, CA, laying down the basic rule that the dominant land cannot be unilaterally extended in this way (applied and confirmed by the Court of Appeal in *Peacock* v. *Custins* [2001] 13 EG 152, at least partly on the basis that the original grantor could have extracted a higher price for the right if it was then known that it would, in effect, provide a greater benefit for the grantee) with *National Trust* v. *White* [1987] 1 WLR 907, where the Court of Appeal held that the benefit of the right of way extended to additional land acquired by the National Trust to make a car park for visitors to the archaeological site on the original dominant land.

4 The burden imposed on the servient land by an easement is a purely negative one. Consequently (unless the grantor and grantee agree otherwise), the servient owner is under no duty to carry out work to facilitate the exercise of the right: for example, she is not liable to maintain or carry out repairs to a path over which the dominant owner has a right of way. The dominant owner may himself carry out maintenance and repair work to a track over which he has a right of way, but may not improve it (*Mills* v. *Silver* [1991] 2 WLR 324). Sometimes the grant of an easement is expressly made subject to the dominant owner contributing towards repair and maintenance costs: on what basis is such an obligation enforceable against successors in title of the original dominant owner? (See *Hallsall* v. *Brizell* [1957] Ch 169.)

9

Recognition of new property interests

In this chapter, we will consider the essentially dynamic quality of property. While it is important that the categories of property are clear and certain, it does not follow from this that the list should be eternally fixed and incapable of development. As you will see, there is constant pressure to recognise new property interests, although, for reasons we shall examine, it is not easy for an interest to cross the threshold into property. However, the history of property bears witness to the constant expansion of the range of property interests in response to society's changing needs and increasing complexity.

In section 9.1 we will consider the reasons why the property label is (and is not) attached to certain interests. While in section 9.2, we shall illustrate the dynamic nature of property by examining examples of interests that have (at least intermittently!) been accorded proprietary status. We will contrast this, in section 9.3 where we consider the law's general reluctance to embrace new property interests, with an example that did not even fleetingly cross the property threshold. This will enable us to examine the principles which under-score the recognition of new property interests before subjecting them to a critical evaluation, in section 9.4, when we consider a comparative and economic study which casts doubt on much that has gone before. Finally, in section 9.5 we will turn to speculate on possible new directions in which the law of property might develop.

9.1. Why are certain interests regarded as property?

In order to consider why the property label is attached to certain interests we need briefly to consider the abstract function of property, the reason why it is only adopted as a measure of last resort and finally the requirements that must first be satisfied before any interest can be accorded proprietary status.

9.1.1. The function of property

The property label basically performs three related functions which we will briefly consider here although they are covered in much greater detail in Part I.

9.1.1.1.   As a means of allocating scarce resources

There would be no need to have property rights in a world of infinite resources. For what would be the point in distinguishing yours from mine (or theirs from ours) if there were no limitations on what was available. For it would not matter how much your neighbour took as there would always be more than enough left for you to take (and as much as you wanted without, in turn, causing any problems for those who came along afterwards). Property rights are in effect a response to scarcity where it becomes important to demarcate rules governing the use of finite resources, for otherwise there will be endless disputes and conflicts in respect of how the particular resource should be exploited.

9.1.1.2.   As an incentive to promote their management

The property label also provides an incentive that tends to promote the more productive management of such resources. There is little point in your (or our) cultivating a field if its harvest can be reaped by another. Similarly (although not the same – can you say why?), what would the point be in the Sony Corporation, for example, expending time and effort (and therefore money) in developing a new invention if there was no means of preventing others usurping their design or process (but not simply the idea – see section 9.5.2 below)? The institution of property enables rules to be established that prevent such takings and so provide an economic incentive towards better husbandry of both existing and new resources.

9.1.1.3.   As a moral, philosophical or political statement

Property is one of the means by which moral, philosophical and political perceptions are given tangible expression. It does not (for these purposes at least) much matter what general justification we offer as to why the farmer in the field should (or for that matter should not) reap the benefits of the harvest. For whether your argument is founded on Marxism or libertarianism, utilitarianism or natural justice, attaching the property label is the first stage in the process. Yet this is more problematic than it at first appears when it comes to specific justifications concerning what sort of things should be considered property. While disagreements over who should reap the harvest will probably all proceed on the assumption that the harvest is a suitable object in which property rights (of some kind) might vest, the same would not be true, for example, of a human kidney. For the debate there would centre not on who should own but about whether anyone should be capable of owning such a thing.

9.1.2.   The danger of property

Property rights are dangerous things. For, unlike contractual rights, they have the power to bind third parties who are not party to the legitimate processes by which interest holders acquire their interest. Thus if you purchase a stolen car from a thief, you will normally be bound by the interest of the person from whom the car was stolen. For as long as they remain owner their claim will bind third parties such as you despite your lack of knowledge concerning the car's provenance. You would consequently have no defence to an action in conversion brought by the legitimate owner and would have to make do with a personal claim against the (often disappeared) thief. Similarly, if you as the owner of an estate in land grant a legal easement (see Chapter 8) to me, my interest will attach to the land and bind whosoever purchases the estate from you irrespective of whether they knew about this interest burdening their estate (subject to the rules about registration we consider in Chapter 15). This might have very serious consequences for the purchaser if my easement is incompatible with the purpose for which he bought the estate in the first place.

We will consider elsewhere the various means by which these potential difficulties might be surmounted (see Chapters 14 and 15 below). However, it is necessary here to note that the traditional approach of property law to the problem (both in this jurisdiction and beyond – see Extract 9.2 below) has been to limit the number of different types of property interest that might exist. This is often referred to by the shorthand term *numerus clausus* which, literally translated, means 'finite number', in recognition of the limited list of property interests known to the law. Third parties are, in this way, protected from being surprised by novel interests that they could not possibly have foreseen. We will consider the legitimacy of this approach in section 9.4 below, but must now content ourselves with noting that the courts and legislature have, in the face of these concerns, taken an extremely cautious approach to the recognition of new property interests.

Thus a right holder's interest will not be accorded the status of a property right if the interest can be adequately protected without making the interest binding on third parties. For example, in *Hill* v. *Tupper* (1863) 2 H&C 121; 159 ER 51 (see Extract 5.1 above), the owners of a canal entered into a contract with Hill granting him the 'exclusive right' to hire out boats on the canal. However, Tupper, a local publican, was allegedly hiring out boats on the same stretch of canal, and Hill consequently sued him for infringing his 'exclusive right' to do so. The court unanimously held that Hill's exclusive right to hire was simply a contractual right between him and the owner of the canal which consequently gave him no rights against third parties such as Tupper. In contrast, the owner of the canal (who by definition did have a property interest in it) could prevent third parties such as Tupper trespassing onto the canal and in failing to do so breached his contract with Hill, who could sue him accordingly. Thus Hill's interest could be adequately protected without the need to turn the 'right to ply for hire' into a new property interest in land.

9.1.3.   The requirements of property

Before an interest can be accorded proprietary status, it must fulfil certain conditions. If it lacks certainty, potential transferees of the interest will be reluctant to assume it, as they will not know what they are getting. More importantly, potential transferees of a *different* property interest in the *same* thing will be put off acquiring that different interest because they will not know how the interest they are acquiring will be affected by the uncertain interest. Similarly, it is often said that a property interest in a thing must have a degree of stability and predictability, for otherwise it will again put off potential transferees of that and any other property interest in the thing. (See the discussion on *National Provincial Bank* v. *Ainsworth* [1965] AC 1175 in Extract 9.1 below where we consider the argument that these criteria are circular and self-fulfilling – can you see why?)

We have so far concentrated on problems which would affect future dealings with a specific thing which was subject to an uncertain, unstable or unpredictable property interest. However, a much more fundamental problem would arise if the interest, while not necessarily suffering from any of these vices, was simply difficult for third parties to identify. For then potential transferees would not only be put off acquiring a specific thing but would have a very real disincentive in acquiring anything which might have such an interest attached (whether or not it in fact did) because there would be no easy means of finding out. This, in part, explains the law's historic reluctance (considered briefly above) to welcome novel property interests into the fold. Arguably, if the system was too willing to do so, purchasers would be more reluctant to acquire interests in things generally as they might latterly be subjected to other (possibly conflicting) interests that no one knew existed at the time of acquisition but which the courts were subsequently willing to hold were subsisting at that time.

9.2.   The dynamic nature of property

It is time to redress the balance. The preceding discussion has described a system which one might be forgiven for assuming was static and rigid with little prospect of change or development. But this is simply not the case for, despite the law's reluctance to embrace new property interests, the pace of human development is such as to make the recognition of new interests an economic and/or social necessity. Prior to the invention of the printing press, for example, there was little incentive in recognising a general property right to copy books. Yet, in the wake of Guttenberg's invention coupled with (and linked to) the emergence of a sufficiently large literate audience, it is hardly surprising that a law of copyright (literally the right to copy) should soon follow. Nor that the pressure to recognise a legally enforceable right to copy came not from authors struggling with their muses but from those with the technological expertise to benefit from such a right, namely, the publishers and printers (see Feather, 'Authors, Publishers and Politicians').

The history of the common law is littered with such instances. As society changes, the notion of what is and what is not a useable resource capable of being the subject of property also changes. For example, up until the sixteenth century, there is little evidence of the term property being applied to land under the English common law

(Seipp, 'The Concept of Property in the Early Common Law'). In 1828, when C. J. Swan, the Secretary to the Real Property Commissioners, invited Bentham to help the Commission in its deliberations, one of his first tasks was to list those things which were not regarded as property and which had not been included in Blackstone's work on the subject, such as company shares and copyright (Sokol, 'Bentham and Blackstone on Incorporeal Hereditaments').

We will consider two examples, one primarily economic and the other broadly social, in which the courts have grappled with the difficulties inherent in such an endeavour. We will begin with the restrictive covenant before turning to the wife's (or is it the spouse's?) right of occupation.

9.2.1.   The recognition and limits of the covenant as a proprietary interest

The recognition, in *Tulk* v. *Moxhay* (1848) 2 Ph 774, of the restrictive covenant (whereby the owner of land is restricted from using it in certain ways) as a property interest in land similarly evolved in response to economic pressures stemming from the industrial revolution and social change in respect of demographic upheaval and the breakdown of the feudal structures which had previously controlled land use (see Chapter 6 for a more detailed account). Despite the generality of some of the language employed in the case, subsequent decisions did much to limit the principle, including a requirement drawn from the law of easements that there must be both a dominant and a servient tenement (*London County Council* v. *Allen* [1914] 3 KB 642). In other words, the benefit of a restrictive covenant must attach to some land (referred to as the *dominant tenement*) and cannot exist in gross (i.e. unattached to land).

In spite of the somewhat arcane nature of the language employed, the restriction can be readily understood if one adopts a practical perspective. A restrictive covenant limits what can be done on a piece of land (referred to as the *servient tenement*) and while there were compelling social and economic reasons for recognising the proprietary status of such a restriction these held only in so far as the restriction benefited other land. The restrictive covenant enabled owners of land to sell the freehold interest in a portion of their land safe in the knowledge that they could impose restrictions on the land disposed of that would survive subsequent changes of ownership and ensure that things were not done with it which would devalue the land retained. This had the effect of freeing up the market in land and promoting alienability even though taken in isolation the burdened land is arguably made less attractive by subjecting it to restrictions in this way.

However, the balance only tilts towards alienability provided there is a dominant tenement able to benefit from the restriction. If there was no such requirement a restrictive covenant might have an entirely negative effect on alienability for it would then continue to make the servient tenement less attractive to potential purchasers without necessarily promoting the alienability of other land. For without the dominant tenement requirement there would be no need for the seller to retain any land with an aspect that needed preserving. Consequently, as such a vendor has no economic interest in how the sold land is subsequently utilised, the courts at the turn of the last century chose to provide him with no proprietary means of restricting its use. (There are, of course, strong environmental arguments to the contrary but it would be anachronistic to criticise judges from another era for failing to take account of issues which are, in any case, today catered for by other mechanisms – see Chapter 6.)

It would seem to follow from such an analysis that the principle of *Tulk* v. *Moxhay* would be inapplicable to chattels because as moveables they can always be removed from a source of interference. But before the principle of a dominant and servient tenement had been fully established, by cases subsequent to *Tulk* v. *Moxhay*, Knight Bruce LJ in *De Mattos* v. *Gibson* (1859) 4 De G&J 276 at 282 made the following observation:

> Reason and justice seem to prescribe that, at least as a general rule, where a man by gift or purchase, acquires property from another with knowledge of a previous contract, lawfully and for valuable consideration made by him with a third person, to use and employ the property for a particular purpose in a specified manner, the acquirer shall not, to the material damage of the third person, in opposition to the contract and inconsistently with it, use and employ the property in a manner not allowable to the giver or the seller. This rule, applicable alike in general as I conceive to moveable and immoveable property, and recognised and adopted, as I apprehend, by the English law, may, like other general rules, be liable to exceptions arising from special circumstances, but I see at present no room for any exception in the instance before us.

The case concerned an interlocutory application by the hirer of a ship seeking an injunction to prevent both the owner and the ship's mortgagee (who, at the time he acquired his interest, knew of the charterparty under which the terms of hire were fixed) acting in a way which was inconsistent with the charterparty. It is clear, from the above extract, that in holding that the mortgagee would be bound Knight Bruce LJ was drawing on the comparatively recent case of *Tulk* v. *Moxhay* decided little more than a decade before. In contrast, the other judge in the case, Turner LJ, seems much less persuaded, leaving the matter open because in his view it deserved greater consideration than could be devoted to it at an interlocutory hearing. This would not appear to have taken place for when it came to the full hearing it was held, on appeal by Lord Chelmsford LC, that the charterparty was 'far too uncertain and indefinite' to enforce. Thus the position of the third party mortgagee ceased to be an issue with the Lord Chancellor offering no more than the *obiter* aside that the mortgagee should 'abstain from any act which would have the immediate effect of preventing [the charterparty's] performance'.

Lord Chelmsford cited no authorities in support of his proposition and, in light of the introduction of the dominant tenement requirement, many judges took the view that (even had it once been so) the principle could no longer be said to apply to chattels. Thus, in *Barker* v. *Stickney* [1919] 1 KB 121 at 132, Scrutton LJ stated that 'a purchaser of chattels is not to be bound by mere notice of stipulations made by his vendor unless he was himself a party to the contract in which the stipulations were made'. Such dissent was neither new nor confined to the higher courts. In *Taddy* v. *Sterious* [1904] 1 Ch 354 at 356, for example, Swinfen Eady J had already stated at first instance that '[c]onditions of this kind do not run with goods and cannot be imposed upon them' even though *De Mattos* v. *Gibson* was seemingly to the point and had been cited to him.

Despite the less than auspicious reception, Knight Bruce LJ's *dictum* was resurrected by the Privy Council in *Lord Strathcona Steamship Co.* v. *Dominion Coal Co.* [1926] AC 108 (see Notes and Questions 9.1 below). The case again concerned a charterparty (can you begin to speculate why this might be significant?) whereby the Dominion Coal Company chartered a ship for ten years. During that time, the ownership of the ship changed hands on a number of occasions eventually being bought by the Lord Strathcona Steamship Company who obtained the ship on the following terms:

> The steamer is chartered to the Dominion Coal Company … [and] the buyers undertake to perform and accept all responsibilities thereunder as from date of delivery in consideration of which the buyers shall receive from date of delivery all benefits arising from said charter.

Despite agreeing to these terms, the Lord Strathcona Steamship Company refused to honour the charterparty. In response, the Dominion Coal Company sought a declaration that they were obliged so to do and an injunction restraining the ship from being used in a way that was inconsistent with the charterparty. The judgment of the board was given by Lord Shaw who, in granting the charterer the relief sought, stated that the *dicta* of Knight Bruce LJ in *De Mattos* v. *Gibson*, 'notwithstanding many observations and much criticism of it in subsequent cases, is of outstanding authority … [for] equity would grant an injunction to compel one who obtains a conveyance or grant *sub conditione* from violating the condition of his purchase to the prejudice of the original contractor'.

The case received much adverse comment, particularly from Diplock J in *Port Line* v. *Ben Line Steamers* [1958] 2 KB 146, which we will deal with below after you have had a chance to examine the primary materials yourself. This will also afford us an opportunity to examine Lord Shaw's reasoning in the case and a possible alternative rationale offered by Browne-Wilkinson J in *Swiss Bank Corp.* v. *Lloyds Bank Ltd* [1979] Ch 548. However, before embarking on this task, and without seeking to prejudge the issues, we suggest you consider what relevance the following words of Lawson and Rudden (*The Law of Property*, p. 30) might have in resolving the apparent inconsistencies evidenced by the case law:

> Ships are indeed governed by special rules of law and are for some purposes treated almost as though they were floating plots of land.

Can you also suggest how such an approach might be consistent with the general thesis of this chapter that, despite its reluctance to do so, the law is willing (and able) to recognise new proprietary interests when there are compelling economic or social reasons so to do?

Notes and Questions 9.1

Consider the following notes and questions both before and after reading *Lord Strathcona Steamship Co.* v. *Dominion Coal Co.* [1926] AC 108 and the materials highlighted below (either in full or as extracted at www.cambridge.org/propertylaw/).

1 Why do you think the Privy Council resurrected the principle of *De Mattos* v. *Gibson* (1859) 4 De G&J 276, after more than half a century in which the *ratio* had often held to be inapplicable in respect of other forms of personalty (e.g. *McGruther* v. *Pitcher* [1904] 2 Ch 206; *Barker* v. *Stickney* [1919] 1 KB 121)? Were the facts of the case, the particular type of property involved or the make-up of the court important factors in the decision?

2 Can you identify what interest (if any) the covenantees had in the chartered vessel other than their contractual rights under the charter? Do you think the charterers had any interest that might sensibly be described as proprietary (see *Port Line* v. *Ben Line Steamers* [1958] 2 KB 146)?

3 Does Lord Shaw's reference to constructive trusteeship clarify or obscure the issues? Does the use of such language require one to identify what property is subject to the trust and why it would be nonsensical to describe the ship itself in such terms (see *Saunders* v. *Vautier* (1841) Cr & Ph 240)? Why would it be equally unsatisfactory to describe the benefit of the charter as the trust property, and what obstacles lie in the way of identifying the benefit of the covenant in the conveyance of the trust as the subject-matter of the trust (see Moffat, *Trusts Law*, pp. 140–1)?

4 Could it be argued that the *De Mattos* v. *Gibson* principle applied by Lord Shaw is the equitable counterpart of the tort of knowing interference with contractual rights? (See *Swiss Bank Corp.* v. *Lloyds Bank Ltd* [1979] Ch 548; cf. 'Covenants, Privity of Contract and the Purchaser of Personal Property', pp. 82–3).

5 Section 34 of the Merchant Shipping Act 1894 provides:

> Except so far as may be necessary for making a mortgaged ship or share available as security for the mortgaged debt, the mortgagee shall not by reason of the mortgage be deemed the owner of the ship or share, nor shall the mortgagor be deemed to have ceased to be owner thereof.

Are there any clues in this provision to suggest that the decision in *Lord Strathcona Steamship Co.* v. *Dominion Coal Co.* is correct in the limited context of maritime law?

6 What solutions to the practical issues raised by the case, beyond the confines of shipping, are provided under the Contracts (Rights of Third Parties) Act 1999?

9.2.2.   The recognition of a proprietary right to occupy the matrimonial home

Under the common law a wife has long had a right to occupy the 'matrimonial home' (*Gurasz* v. *Gurasz* [1970] P 11). This is based upon the marriage contract and the now anachronistic view that a husband is under a non-reciprocal duty to maintain his wife, although it is arguable (but by no means established) that, to the extent that any such duty still exists under the common law, it should now be borne equally by both parties to the marriage (see the comments of Ewbank J in *Harman* v. *Glencross* [1985] Fam 49 at 58B–C).

The common law right was clearly a personal one owed by the husband to his wife and having no bearing on third parties. Thus a third party who acquired an interest from the husband did not need to concern him or herself with any right of occupation owed by the vendor to his wife. However, in a series of cases in the 1950s and 1960s, the Court of Appeal, under the Master of the Rolls, Lord Denning (in response to new social pressures stemming from the increasing incidence of marriage breakdown), engaged in a process which sought to elevate the personal right into a proprietary one by means of what became known as the 'deserted wife's equity'. Under this approach the wife's personal right against her husband was transformed into an *equity* binding on most categories of third party from the moment he deserted her. As an *equity* the right, in broad terms, bound everyone with the exception of purchasers without notice (including constructive notice – see section 14.3.1 below) of the *equity*. As Gray has noted, the consequences of this common law development were simply ludicrous:

> The deserted wife's equity became a nightmare for conveyancers ... impos[ing] an embarrassing onus of enquiry on any third party entering into any transaction (e.g. sale, lease or mortgage) with a man whose household included a resident adult female. In order to be safe from adverse claims to occupy, the purchaser had to inquire, first, whether that woman was the wife of the vendor/lessor/mortgagor and, second, whether the marriage (if there was one) was happy and stable. (Gray, *Elements of Land Law* (2nd edn), p. 159)

According proprietary status to the deserted wife's right to occupy lacked the certainty and ease of identification necessary to enable the conveyancing system to work efficiently. While it is not uncommon for more than one party to have a right to occupy land (by reason of their contributions to the purchase price or arising under such doctrines as constructive trust and proprietary estoppel) interests arising in such a manner are not as susceptible to the same criticisms (although they are hardly immune – see Moffat, *Trusts Law*). The deserted wife's equity, however, stretched the boundaries of property too far, and, in *National Provincial Bank* v. *Ainsworth* [1965] AC 1175, the House of Lords heralded a return to orthodoxy by roundly rejecting Lord Denning's heresy.

Although justified, the conservative nature of their Lordships' approach clearly failed to address the social issues which had caused the Court of Appeal to adopt such a radical stance in the first place. Lord Wilberforce, however, was adamant that (while some of the problems might be alleviated) it was ultimately not the role of the courts to solve society's ills in this way:

> The deserted wife therefore, in my opinion, cannot resist a claim from a 'purchaser' from her husband whether the 'purchase' takes place after or before the desertion. As regards transactions subsequent to the desertion this disability is somewhat mitigated by three factors. First, if it appears that the husband is threatening to dispose of the house in such a manner as to defeat her rights, she may be able to obtain an injunction to restrain him from doing so ... Secondly, the courts have ample powers to detect, and to refuse to give effect to, sham or fraudulent transactions ... Thirdly, there are some extensive powers conferred by statute (Matrimonial Causes (Property and Maintenance) Act 1958 [see now section 37 of the Matrimonial Causes Act 1973]) to set aside dispositions aimed at defeating the wife's right to maintenance ... *As regards those cases (and I recognise that they may exist) which fall outside, the deserted wife may be left unprotected – she may lose her home. As to them, it was said by Roxburgh J in Churcher v. Street [1959] Ch 251, 258: 'It would have been an advantage, in my view, if Parliament, rather than a higher court, had intervened, because in order to prevent certain cases of injustice to deserted wives, a position has been brought about which may produce considerable injustice to other people ...' I respectfully agree with this statement.* (*National Provincial Bank* v. *Ainsworth* [1965] AC 1175 at 1258–9, emphasis added)

Within two years Parliament had responded to this call by introducing a statutory scheme now contained in sections 30–31 of the Family Law Act 1996. Under the scheme both spouses have a personal right to occupy the family home which they might turn into a property right binding on third parties by registering that right in the land register (specifically, by entry of a notice: see section 15.2.4.3 below). We will deal with how the scheme works in Notes and Questions 9.2 below when we consider why statute, rather than the common law, was better able to deal with this particular issue. Ultimately, however, the spouse's statutory right to occupy the matrimonial home should be seen as a new type of property interest created by the legislature in response to social change and pressure.

Notes and Questions 9.2

Consider the following notes and questions both before and after reading the extract from *National Provincial Bank* v. *Ainsworth* [1965] AC 1175 below (a longer version, along with further materials, is also available at www.cambridge.org/propertylaw/).

1 What type of property interest was the deserted wife's equity and what were the consequences of this categorisation?

2 If Mrs Ainsworth had won the case in the House of Lords, and it had been held that all wives did have such a right of occupation, and that it was a property interest:

(a) Would husbands have had the same right as wives? Would unmarried couples living together as husband and wife have been in the same position as married couples?

(b) When would a wife's right have arisen as against her husband, and when would it have arisen as against third parties? Why was this distinction made?

(c) When would the wife's right end?

(d) If a purchaser wanted to buy a house from a man who appeared to be the sole holder of the fee simple absolute in possession of the land, how could the purchaser find out whether or not the man had a wife who claimed this right of occupation? What would have happened if, after completing the purchase, he discovered for the first time that there *was* a wife and she *did* have such a right?

3 Why was Lord Wilberforce convinced that the deserted wife's equity should not be a property right and what were the weaknesses he identifies in Lord Denning's short-lived creation?

4 Is there a degree of circularity in Lord Wilberforce's analysis?

5 What was the solution of the legislature under sections 30–31 of the Family Law Act 1996? Is the right granted under the Act a personal or a proprietary right, and why is that an unfair question? What is the effect of section 31(10), and why is there an alternative mechanism under section 31(12)?

6 Which was the better solution – the one developed by Denning's Court of Appeal or the one created by the legislature in the wake of *National Provincial Bank* v. *Ainsworth*?

7 Is the history of the deserted wife's equity a cautionary tale demonstrating the folly of judicial law-making or an example of how important it is to have a proactive Court of Appeal willing and able to challenge orthodoxy and the prevailing legal consensus?

Extract 9.1   *National Provincial Bank* v. *Ainsworth* [1965] AC 1175 at 1247–8

The position, then, at the present time, is this. The wife has no specific right against her husband to be provided with any particular house, nor to remain in any particular house. She has a right to cohabitation and support; but, in considering whether the husband should be given possession of property of his, the court will have regard to the duty of the spouses to each other, and the decision it reaches will be based on a consideration of what may be called the matrimonial circumstances. These include such matters as whether the husband can provide alternative accommodation and, if so, whether such accommodation is suitable having regard to the estate and condition of the spouses; whether the husband's conduct amounts to desertion, whether the conduct of the wife has been such as to deprive her of any of her rights against the husband. The order to be made must be fashioned accordingly; it may be that the wife should leave immediately or after a certain period; it may be subject to revision on a change of circumstances.

The conclusion emerges to my mind very clearly from this that the wife's rights, as regards the occupation of her husband's property, are essentially of a personal kind: personal in the sense that a decision can only be reached on the basis of considerations essentially dependent on the mutual claims of husband and wife as spouses and as the result of a broad weighing of circumstances and merit. Moreover, these rights are at no time definitive, they are provisional and subject to review at any time according as changes take place in the material circumstances and conduct of the parties.

On any division, then, which is to be made between property rights on the one hand, and personal rights on the other hand, however broad or penumbral the separating band between these two kinds of rights may be, there can be little doubt where the wife's rights fall. Before a right or an interest can be admitted into the category of property, or of a right affecting property, it must be definable, identifiable by third parties, capable in its nature of assumption by third parties, and have some degree of permanence or stability. The wife's right has none of these qualities, it is characterised by the reverse of them.

9.3.   The general reluctance to recognise new property rights

In deference to the dangers inherent in recognising new interests in property, both the restrictive covenant and the spousal right to occupy, considered in the previous section, have, in respect of their proprietary quality, both been heavily circumscribed in an attempt to overcome such difficulties. The restrictive covenant is limited to land (and possibly ships) and bound by stringent rules relating to the transmission of both its benefit and burden; while the spousal right to occupy the matrimonial home only acquires a proprietary status once notice is given to the world via statutory registration procedures.

Despite the excesses of Lord Denning's Court of Appeal during the history of the short-lived 'deserted wife's equity', the law's usual approach in this area is rather more cautious displaying a deep-seated reluctance to embrace too readily new property interests. We have already seen, in *Hill* v. *Tupper* (Extract 5.1 above), one example of the court's refusal to recognise a novel property right. In this section, we will concentrate on another case, *Victoria Park Racing* v. *Taylor* (1937) 58 CLR 479 (Extract 9.2 below) in which, despite compelling arguments to the contrary, the Australian High Court declined an invitation to recognise what would in effect have been (from some perspectives at least) a proprietary right to a view.

9.3.1.   The facts of *Victoria Park Racing* v. *Taylor*

The case involved a dispute between two neighbours. Victoria Park Racing owned a racecourse known as Victoria Park at which they held regular horse race meetings to which the public were charged an admission fee to attend. Taylor owned a plot of land adjoining the racecourse on which he built a platform overlooking the racecourse and from where he allowed a commentator called Angles to broadcast live commentaries on the races. According to Latham CJ, Angles 'describe[d] the races in a particularly vivid manner', and the racecourse owners sought an injunction preventing him from broadcasting from his vantage point as, in their view, the live commentaries were having a deleterious effect on the number of people paying to attend the race meetings. But the High Court of Australia, by a majority of three to two, confirmed the decision of the judge at first instance, Nicholas J, and refused the injunction sought.

9.3.2. The views of the majority

The approach of the majority in *Victoria Park Racing* v. *Taylor* is characterised by extreme judicial caution, even conservatism, in which much is made of the lack of judicial authority for the arguments raised by the racecourse owners. The court, in the words of Latham CJ, was 'not ... referred to any authority in English law which supports the general contention that, if a person chooses to organise an entertainment ... he has a right to obtain from court an order that [a third party] shall not describe ... what they see'. And similarly that '[n]o authority has been cited to support ... [the] proposition' that 'such description is wrongful'. In a similar fashion, Dixon J stated that the interest Victoria Park Racing sought to protect was 'not an interest falling within any category which is protected at law or in equity'. While McTiernan J went even further down this route in (arguably incorrectly) stating that 'there are no legal principles [as opposed to authorities] which the court can apply to protect the [racecourse owners]'.

Such statements should be contrasted with the approach evident in *Tulk* v. *Moxhay* and *Hill* v. *Tupper*, where the judgments all proceed on the basis that the court can and will recognise new rights where there are compelling reasons so to do. In contrast, the majority in *Victoria Park Racing* v. *Taylor* seem to base their decision on the simple fact that the right claimed would be a novel one and must therefore fail, irrespective of the economic or social grounds for recognising it. There are, we would suggest, powerful reasons for agreeing with the majority decision in the case, which we will canvass below. However, in choosing to concentrate on a (self-perpetuating) lack of previous authority, such arguments are left unheard.

9.3.3. The views of the minority

Rather than arguing directly for the proposition that it is possible to own a spectacle, the minority in the case approached the matter more obliquely, primarily from the perspective of nuisance. While suggesting, in the words of Evatt J, that the broadcasters were acting in an 'unreasonable', 'grotesque' and 'dishonest' way and endeavouring to 'reap where they had not sown', the judgments concentrate on the issue of the nuisance caused to the racecourse owners by the activities of Taylor and Angles. Thus, according to Rich J, because '[a] man has no absolute right "within the ambit of his own land" to act as he pleases', the court was quite justified in issuing an injunction to prevent the unreasonable activities undertaken by Taylor on the adjoining land from interfering with the 'usual, reasonable and profitable' use that the racecourse owners were making of their land.

It is understandable that, in holding Taylor liable for his actions, the minority should concentrate on the specific cause of action under which that liability arose. However, implicit in their reasoning is an assumption about the rights that should be protected under the law of nuisance which would have represented a marked departure for the law (see section 9.5.2 below). Traditionally, the courts have refused to recognise a general property right to a view (see *Hunter* v. *Canary Wharf* discussed in section 6.4.1.2 above), yet neither Rich J nor Evatt J acknowledged how radical was the departure they were in effect advocating. That is, of course, not to say that such a development would necessarily have been wrong, but rather that it was necessary to explicitly consider the underlying issues prior to embarking upon such a path.

9.3.4.   The significance of the case

Why, you might ask, have we given such prominence to an Australian case of no more than persuasive authority in the English courts? Despite its relative obscurity, the case is, as Gray has noted (Gray, 'Property in Thin Air', pp. 266–7), a 'pivotal' one which 'reverberates with a significance which has outlived its particular facts' because 'the conflict between the majority and minority views in this case throws up critical clues to the identification of the *propertiness* of property'.

The case is, like *Tulk* v. *Moxhay*, a product of its time. As Evatt J noted '[t]he fact that there is no previous English decision which is comparable to the present does not tell against the plaintiff because … simultaneous broadcasting … [and] television [are] quite new' (*Victoria Park Racing* v. *Taylor* (1937) 58 CLR 479 at 519) It was consequently necessary to map out the limits of property in the face of such technological advances, and it is important to assess how well the case resolves these issues. For, despite Evatt J's observation, it is arguable that the judgments in general fail to rise to the challenge.

Thus in their various ways the three majority judgments all lay emphasis on the lack of previous authority for the propositions advocated on behalf of the racecourse owners. But this is inappropriate when the court is asked to address how the common law should respond to technological advances which pose challenges not confronted in the past. Thus, rather than concentrate on the absence of authority, the judgments would have better achieved their purpose by considering the potential problems from recognising what was in effect, property in a view. For the law's historic reluctance to do so is based upon the very real difficulties that would necessarily arise in practice. The recognition of a general property right to a view would place undue restrictions on the development of land which are simply not sustainable in a modern society and which can more efficiently be performed by public rather than private mechanisms such as planning law (see *Hunter* v. *Canary Wharf* discussed in section 6.4.1.2 above).

In spite of their apparent radicalism, the two minority judgments may be similarly criticised. Rather than confront the practical difficulties that would arise in extending the law of nuisance in the way that they envisage, both judgments place their greatest emphasis on the justice of the racecourse owners' case. Yet this was not in dispute, and to elevate it in this way simply falls into the 'hard cases making bad law' trap that judges, above all others, should know to avoid. Thus the language of misappropriation used by both Evatt J (who as we have seen castigated the defendant for seeking 'to reap where it had not sown': *Victoria Park Racing* v. *Taylor* (1937) 58 CLR 479 at 514) and Rich J (who spoke of the defendant 'appropriating . . . part of the profitable enjoyment of the plaintiff's land to his own commercial ends': *ibid.*, p. 501) simply misses the point of the endeavour. For while no one sought to argue that what Taylor and Angles did was morally correct that did not make it necessarily unlawful.

The value of the case consequently lies more in what it does not say than in what it actually does. This is what Gray was referring to when he talked about the 'clues' the case offers. But we should avoid being too critical at this juncture. In *Tulk* v. *Moxhay*, for example, despite our earlier plaudits, it would be an exaggeration to suggest that the court directly confronted the issues when welcoming another interest into the property fold. By concentrating on the conscience of the new owner of the burdened land, the court in many respects did much to obscure the proprietary quality of the interest they had thereby recognised. That only emerged gradually in subsequent cases. This is the reason why it was at that stage, rather than at the outset, that the restrictions noted earlier were introduced to limit the dangers that might otherwise arise from this upstart new property right. Occasionally, of course, the issues are confronted directly, as in *Hill* v. *Tupper* and *National Provincial Bank* v. *Ainsworth*, but often the matter adopts the role of Banquo's ghost: present but unseen by all but the audience watching from afar.

Notes and Questions 9.3

Consider the following notes and questions both before and after reading the extracts from *Victoria Park Racing* v. *Taylor* (1937) 58 CLR 479 below (a longer version, along with further materials, is also available at www.cambridge.org/propertylaw/).

1 What consequences would a contrary decision in *Victoria Park Racing* v. *Taylor* have produced? No matter what the cause of action, would a contrary finding have in effect established property in a spectacle?

2 How unfair were the actions of Angles and Taylor? Was the court swayed by the form of competition provided by Angles? How would Locke have viewed the dispute?

3 Is a microphone more akin to a quill than a camera? Would it have been different if the defendant had shot a video rather than broadcast a voice?

4 Would an analysis rooted in public policy rather than legal precedent provide a different outcome? To what extent do the judgments embrace notions of public policy and what does this say about the role of case law? Stripped of the rhetoric

of law, is legal discourse on property ever anything more than a debate on different perceptions of the general good?

5   What is the significance of the conflict between the majority and minority views in the case (See Gray, 'Property in Thin Air'.)

6   Is there a difference in the judicial techniques used by Latham CJ and Dixon J as compared to those of Rich and Evatt JJ? Are there any parallels to the contrasting approaches of the Court of Appeal and House of Lords in *National Provincial Bank* v. *Ainsworth*?

7   In Libling, 'The Concept of Property', David Libling argued that English law ought to adopt the following principle:

> Any expenditure of mental or physical effort, as the result of which there is created an entity, whether tangible or intangible, vests in the person who brought the entity into being, a proprietary right to the commercial exploitation of that entity, which right is separate and independent from the ownership of that entity.

Do you agree? Would it cause any practical problems? If the judges in *Victoria Park Racing* v. *Taylor* had adopted this as a correct statement of law, would the decision of the court have been different?

Extract 9.2   *Victoria Park Racing* v. *Taylor* (1937) 58 CLR 479

LATHAM CJ: This is an appeal from a judgment for the defendants given by Nicholas J in an action by the Victoria Park Racing and Recreation Grounds Co. Ltd against Taylor and others ...

The plaintiff company carries on the business of racing upon a racecourse known as Victoria Park. The defendant Taylor is the owner of the land near the racecourse. He has placed an elevated platform on his land from which it is possible to see what takes place on the racecourse and to read the information which appears on notice boards on the course as to the starters, scratchings, etc., and the winners of the races. The defendant Angles stands on the platform and through a telephone comments upon and describes the races in a particularly vivid manner and announces the names of the winning horse. The defendant, the Commonwealth Broadcasting Corporation, holds a broadcasting licence under the regulations made under the Wireless Telegraphy Act 1905–1936 and carries on the business of broadcasting from station 2UW. This station broadcasts the commentaries and descriptions given by Angles. The plaintiff wants to have the broadcasting stopped because it prevents people from going to the races and paying for admission. The evidence shows that some people prefer hearing about the races as seen by Angles to seeing the races for themselves. The plaintiff contends that the damage which it thus suffers gives, in all the circumstances, a cause of action ...

I am unable to see that any right of the plaintiff has been violated or any wrong done to him. Any person is entitled to look over the plaintiff's fences and to see what goes on in the plaintiff's land. If the plaintiff desires to prevent this, the plaintiff can erect a higher fence. Further, if the plaintiff desires to prevent its notice boards being seen by people from outside the enclosure, it can place them in such a position that they are not visible to such people. At sports grounds and other places of entertainment it is the lawful, natural and common practice to put up fences and other structures to prevent people who are not prepared to pay for admission from getting the benefit of the entertainment. In my opinion, the law cannot by an injunction in effect erect fences which the plaintiff is not prepared to provide. The defendant does no wrong to the plaintiff by looking at what takes place on the plaintiff's land. Further, he does no wrong to the plaintiff by describing to other persons, to as wide an audience as he can obtain, what takes place on the plaintiff's ground. The court has not been referred to any principle of law which prevents any man from describing anything which he sees anywhere if he does not make defamatory statements, infringe the law as to offensive language etc., break a contract, or wrongfully reveal confidential information. The defendants did not infringe the law in any of these respects ...

It has been argued that by the expenditure of money the plaintiff has created a spectacle and that it therefore has what is described as a quasi-property in the spectacle which the law will protect. The vagueness of this proposition is apparent upon its face. What it really means is that there is some principle (apart from contract or confidential relationship) which prevents people in some circumstances from opening their eyes and seeing something and then describing what they see. The Court has not been referred to any authority in English law which supports the general contention that, if a person chooses to organize an entertainment or to do anything else which other persons are able to see, he has a right to obtain from a court an order that they shall not describe to anybody what they see. If the claim depends upon interference with a proprietary right it is difficult to see how it can be material to consider whether the interference is large or small – whether the description is communicated to many persons by broadcasting or by a newspaper report, or only to a few persons in conversation or correspondence. Further, as I have already said, the mere fact that damage results to a plaintiff from such description cannot be relied upon as a cause of action.

I find difficulty in attaching any precise meaning to the phrase 'property in a spectacle'. A 'spectacle' cannot be 'owned' in any ordinary sense of that word. Even if there were any legal principle which prevented one person from gaining an advantage for himself or causing damage to another by describing a spectacle produced by that other person, the rights of the latter person could be described as property only in a metaphorical sense. Any appropriateness in the metaphor would depend upon the existence of the legal principle. The principle cannot itself be based upon such a metaphor.

Even if, on the other hand, a spectacle could be said to exist as a subject-matter of property, it would still be necessary, in order to provide the plaintiff in this case with a remedy, to show that the description of such property is wrongful or that such description is wrongful when it is widely disseminated. No authority has been cited to support such a proposition ...

RICH J [dissenting]: ... A man has no absolute right 'within the ambit of his own land' to act as he pleases. His right is qualified and such of his acts as invade his neighbour's property are lawful only in so far as they are reasonable having regard to his own circumstances and those of his neighbour. The plaintiff's case must, I am prepared to concede, rest on what is called nuisance. But it must not be overlooked that this means no more than that he must complain of some impairment of the rights flowing from occupation and ownership of land. One of the prime purposes of occupation of land is the pursuit of profitable enterprises for which the exclusion of others is necessary either totally or except upon conditions which may include payment. In the present case in virtue of its occupation and ownership, the plaintiff carries on the business of admitting to the land for payment patrons of racing. There it entertains them by a spectacle, by a competition in the comparative merits of race-horses, and it attempts by all reasonable means to give to those whom it admits the exclusive right of witnessing the spectacle, the competition, and of using the collated information in betting while that is possible on its various events. This use of its rights as occupier is usual, reasonable and profitable. So much no one can dispute. If it be true that an adjacent owner has an unqualified and absolute right to overlook an occupier whatever may be the enterprise he is carrying on and to make any profitable use to which what he sees can be put, whether in his capacity of adjacent owner or otherwise, then to that extent the right of the occupier carrying on the enterprise must be modified and treated in law as less extensive and ample than perhaps is usually understood. But can the adjacent owner, by virtue of his occupation and ownership, use his land in such an unusual way as the erection of a platform involves, bring mechanical appliances into connection with that use, i.e. the microphone and land line to the studio, and then by combining regularity of observation with dissemination for gain of the information so obtained give the potential patrons a mental picture of the spectacle, an account of the competition between the horses and of the collated information needed for betting, for all of which they would otherwise have recourse to the racecourse and pay? To admit that the adjacent owner may overlook does not answer this question affirmatively ...

There can be no right to extend the normal use of his land by the adjoining owner indefinitely. He may within limits make fires, create smoke and use vibratory machinery. He may consume all the water he finds on his land, but he has no absolute right to dirty it. Defendants' rights are related to plaintiffs' rights and each owner's rights may be limited by the rights of the other ... What appears to me to be the real point in this case is that the right of view or observation from adjacent land has never been held to be an absolute and complete right of property incident to the occupation of that land and exercisable at all hazards notwithstanding its destructive effect upon the enjoyment of the land overlooked. In the absence of any authority to the contrary I hold that there is a limit to this right of overlooking and that the limit must be found in an attempt to reconcile the right of free prospect from one piece of land with the right of profitable enjoyment of another ... Indeed, the prospects of television make our present decision a very important one, and I venture to think that the advance of that art may force the courts to recognize that protection against the complete exposure of the doings of the individual may be a right indispensable to the enjoyment of life. For these reasons I am of opinion that the plaintiff's grievance, although of an unprecedented character, falls within the settled principles upon which the action for nuisance depends. Holding this opinion it is unnecessary for me to discuss the question of copyright raised in the case.

I think that the appeal should be allowed.

DIXON J: The foundation of the plaintiff company's case is no doubt the fact that persons who otherwise would attend race meetings stay away because they listen to the broadcast made by the defendant Angles from the tower overlooking the course. Beginning with the damage thus suffered and with the repetition that may be expected, the plaintiff company says that, unless a justification for causing it exists, the defendants or some of them must be liable, in as much as it is their unauthorized acts that inflict the loss. It is said that, to look for a definite category or form of action into which to fit the plaintiff's complaint, is to reverse the proper order of thought in the present stage of the law's development. In such a case, it is for the defendants to point to the ground upon which the law allows them so to interfere with the normal course of the plaintiff's business as to cause damage.

There is in my opinion little to be gained by inquiring whether in English law the foundation of a delictual liability is unjustifiable damage or breach of specific duty. The law of tort has fallen into great confusion, but, in the main, what acts and omissions result in responsibility and what do not are matters defined by long-established rules of law from which judges ought not wittingly to depart and no light is shed upon a given case by large generalizations about them. We know that, if upon such facts as the present the plaintiff could recover at common law, his cause of action must have its source in an action upon the case and that, in such an action, speaking generally, damage was the gist of the action. There is perhaps nothing wrong either historically or analytically in regarding an action for damage suffered by words, by deceit or by negligence as founded upon the damage and treating the unjustifiable conduct of the defendant who caused it as [a] matter of inducement. But, whether his conduct be so described or be called more simply a wrongful act or omission, it remains true that it must answer a known description, or, in other words, respond to the tests of criteria laid down by establishing principle.

The plaintiff's counsel relied in the first instance upon an action on the case in the nature of nuisance. The premises of the plaintiff are occupied by it for the purpose of a racecourse. They have the natural advantage of not being overlooked by any surrounding heights or raised ground ... They have been furnished with all the equipment of a racecourse and so enclosed as to prevent any unauthorized ingress or, unless by some such exceptional devices as the defendants have adopted, any unauthorized view of the spectacle. The plaintiff can thus exclude the public who do not pay and can exclude them not only from the presence at, but also from knowledge of, the proceedings upon the course. It is upon the ability to do this that the profitable character of the enterprise ultimately depends. The position of and the improvements to the land thus fit it for a racecourse and give its occupation a particular value. The defendants, then proceed by an unusual use of their premises to deprive the plaintiff's land of this value, to strip it of its exclusiveness. By the tower placed where the race will be fully visible, and equipped with microphone and line, they enable Angles to see the spectacle and convey its substance by broadcast. The effect is, the plaintiff says, just as if they supplied the plaintiff's customers with elevated vantage points round the course from which they could witness all that otherwise would attract them and induce them to pay the price of admission to the course. The feature in which the plaintiff finds the wrong of nuisance is the impairment or deprivation of the advantages possessed by the plaintiff's land as a racecourse by means of a non-natural and unusual use of the defendant's land.

This treatment of the case will not I think hold water. It may be conceded that interferences of a physical nature, as by fumes, smell and noise, are not the only means of committing a private nuisance. But the essence of the wrong is the detraction from the occupier's enjoyment of the natural rights belonging to, or in the case of easements of the acquired rights annexed to, the occupation of land. The law fixes those rights. Diversion of custom from a business carried on upon the land may be brought about by noise, fumes, obstruction of the frontage or any other interference with the enjoyment of recognized rights arising from the occupation of property and, if so, it forms a legitimate head of damage recoverable for the wrong; but it is not the wrong itself. The existence or the use of a microphone upon neighbouring land is, of course, no nuisance. If one who could not see the spectacle took upon himself to broadcast a fictitious account of the races he might conceivably render himself liable in a form of action in which his falsehood played a part, but he would commit no nuisance. It is the obtaining a view of the premises which is the foundation of the allegation. But English law is, rightly or wrongly, clear that the natural rights of an occupier do not include freedom from the view and inspection of neighbouring occupiers and of other persons who enable themselves to overlook the premises. An occupier of land is at liberty to exclude his neighbour's view by any physical means he can adopt. But, while it is no wrongful act on his part to block the prospect from adjacent land, it is no wrongful act on the part of any person on such land to avail himself of what prospect exists or can be obtained. Not only is it lawful on the part of those occupying premises in the vicinity to overlook the land from any natural vantage point, but artificial erections may be made which destroy the privacy existing under natural conditions. In *Chandler* v. *Thompson* (1811) 3 Camp 80 at 82; 170 ER 1312 at 1313, Le Blanc J said that, although an action for opening a window to disturb the plaintiff's privacy was to be read of in the books, he had never known such an action maintained, and when he was in the common pleas he had heard it laid down by Eyre LCJ that such an action did not lie and that the only remedy was to build on the adjoining land opposite to the offensive window. After that date, there is, I think, no trace in the authorities of any doctrine to the contrary.

In *Johnson* v. *Wyatt* (1863) 2 De GJ&S 18 at 27; 46 ER 281 at 284, Turner LJ said: 'That the windows of the house may be overlooked, and its comparative privacy destroyed, and its value thus diminished by the proposed erection ... are matters with which, as I apprehend, we have nothing to do', that is, they afford no ground for an injunction. This principle formed one of the subsidiary reasons upon which the decision of the House of Lords was based in *Tapling* v. *Jones* (1865) 11 HLC 290 at 317; 11 ER 1344 at 1355. Lord Chelmsford said:

> ... the owner of a house has a right at all times ... to open as many windows in his own house as he pleases. By the exercise of the right, he may materially interfere

with the comfort and enjoyment of his neighbour; but of this species of injury the law takes no cognizance. It leaves everyone to his self-defence against an annoyance of the description and the only remedy in the power of adjoining owner is to build on his own ground and so to shut out the offensive windows.

When this principle is applied to the plaintiff's case it means, I think, that the essential element upon which it depends is lacking. So far as freedom from view or inspection is a natural or acquired physical characteristic of the site, giving it value for the purpose of the business or pursuit which the plaintiff conducts, it is a characteristic which is not a legally protected interest. It is not a natural right, for breach of which a legal remedy is given, either by an action in the nature of nuisance or otherwise. The fact is that the substance of the plaintiff's complaint goes not to interference with its enjoyment of the land, but with the profitable conduct of its business. If English law had followed the course of development that has recently taken place in the United States, the broadcasting rights in respect of the races might have been protected as part of the quasi-property created by the enterprise, organisation and labour of the plaintiff in establishing and equipping a racecourse and doing all that is necessary to conduct race meetings. But courts of equity have not in British jurisdictions thrown the protection of an injunction around all the intangible elements of value, that is value in exchange, which may flow from the exercise by an individual of his powers or resources whether in the organization of a business or undertaking or the use of ingenuity, knowledge, skill or labour. This is sufficiently evidenced by the history of the law of copyright, and the fact that exclusive rights to invention, trade marks, designs, trade name and reputation are dealt with in English law as special heads of protected interests and not under a wider generalization ...

In dissenting from a judgment of the Supreme Court of the United States, by which the organized collection of news by a news service was held to give it in equity a quasi-property protected against appropriation by rival news agencies, Brandeis J gave reasons which substantially represent the English view and he supported his opinion by a citation of much English authority: *International News Service* v. *Associated Press*, 248 US 215 (1918). His judgment appears to me to contain an adequate answer both upon principle and authority to the suggestion that the defendants are misappropriating or abstracting something which the plaintiff has created and alone is entitled to turn to value. Briefly, the answer is that it is not because the individual has by his efforts put himself in a position to obtain value for what he can give that this right to give it becomes protected by law and so assumes the exclusiveness of property, but because the intangible or incorporeal right he claims falls within a recognized category to which legal or equitable protection attaches ...

In my opinion the right to exclude the defendants from broadcasting a description of the occurrences they can see upon the plaintiff's land is not given by law. It is not an interest falling within any category which is protected at law or in equity. I have had the advantage of reading the judgment of Rich J but I am unable to regard the considerations which are there set out as justifying what I consider amounts not simply to a new application of settled principle but to the introduction into the law of new doctrine ...

EVATT J [dissenting]: ... Here the plaintiff contends that the defendants are guilty of the tort of nuisance. It cannot point at once to a decisive precedent in its favour, but the statements of general principle in *Donoghue* v. *Stevenson* are equally applicable to the tort of nuisance. A definition of the tort of nuisance was attempted by Sir Frederick Pollock (Indian Civil Wrongs Bill, c. VII, section 55), who said:

> Private nuisance is the using or authorizing the use of one's property, or of anything under one's control, so as to injuriously affect an owner or occupier of property
>
> (a) by diminishing the value of that property;
> (b) by continuously interfering with his power of control or enjoyment of that property;
> (c) by causing material disturbance or annoyance to him in his use or occupation of that property.
>
> What amounts to material disturbance or annoyance is a question of fact to be decided with regard to the character of the neighbourhood, the ordinary habits of life and reasonable expectations of persons there dwelling, and other relevant circumstances ...

At an earlier date, Pollock CB had indicated the danger of too rigid a definition of nuisance. He said (*Bamford* v. *Turnley* (1862) 3 B&S 66 at 79; 122 ER 27 at 31; [1861–73] All ER Rep 706 at 710):

> I do not think that the nuisance for which an action will lie is capable of any legal definition which will be applicable to all cases and useful in deciding them. The question so entirely depends on the surrounding circumstances – the place where, the time when, the alleged nuisance, what, the mode of committing it, how, and the duration of it, whether temporary or permanent ...

In the present case, the plaintiff relies upon all the surrounding circumstances. Its use and occupation of land is interfered with, its business profits are lessened, and the value of the land is diminished or jeopardized by the conduct of the defendants. The defendants' operations are conducted to the plaintiff's detriment, not casually but systematically, not temporarily but indefinitely; they use a suburban bungalow in an unreasonable and grotesque manner, and do so in the course of a gainful pursuit which strikes at the plaintiff's profitable use of its land, precisely at the point where the profit must be earned, namely, the entrance gates. Many analogies to the defendants' operations have been suggested, but few of them are applicable. The newspaper which is published a considerable time after a race has been run competes only with other newspapers, and can have little or no effect upon the profitable employment of the plaintiff's land. A photographer overlooking the course and subsequently publishing a photograph in a newspaper or elsewhere does not injure the plaintiff. Individuals who observe the racing from their own homes or those of their friends could not interfere with the plaintiff's beneficial use of its course. On the other hand, the defendants' operations are fairly comparable with those who, by the employment of moving picture films, television and broadcasting, would convey to the public generally

(i) from a point of vantage specially constructed; (ii) simultaneously with the actual running of the races; (iii) visual, verbal or audible representations of each and every portion of the races. If such a plan of campaign were pursued, it would result in what has been proved here, namely, actual pecuniary loss to the occupier of the racecourse and a depreciation in the value of his land, at least so long as the conduct is continued. In principle, such a plan may be regarded as equivalent to the erection by a landowner of a special stand outside a cricket ground for the sole purpose of enabling the public to witness the cricket match at an admission price which is lower than that charged to the public bodies who own the ground, and at great expense organize the game.

In concluding that, in such cases, no actionable nuisance would be created, the defendants insist that the law of England does not recognize any general right of privacy. That is true, but it carries the defendants no further, because it is not merely an interference with privacy which is here relied upon, and it is not the law that every interference with private property must be lawful. The defendants also say that the law of England does not forbid one person to overlook the property of another. That also is true in the sense that the fact that one individual possesses the means of watching, and sometimes watches, what goes on in his neighbour's land, does not make the former's action unlawful. But it is equally erroneous to assume that under no circumstances can systematic watching amount to a civil wrong, for an analysis of the cases of *J. Lyons & Sons* v. *Wilkins* [1899] 1 Ch 255, and *Ward Lock & Co. Ltd* v. *Operative Printers Assistants Society* (1906) 22 TLR 327, indicates that, under some circumstances, the common law regards 'watching and besetting' as a private nuisance, although no trespass to land has been committed ...

In the United States, in the case of *International News Service* v. *Associated Press* 248 US 215 at 255 (1918), Brandeis J regarded the *Our Dogs* case (*Sports and General Press Agency Ltd* v. *Our Dogs Publishing Co. Ltd* [1916] 2 KB 880) as illustrating a principle that 'news' is not property in the strict sense, and that a person who creates an event or spectacle does not thereby entitle himself to the exclusive right of first publishing the 'news' or photograph of the event or spectacle. But it is an extreme application of the English cases to say that, because some overlooking is permissible, all overlooking is necessarily lawful. In my opinion, the decision in the *International News Service* case evidences an appreciation of the function of law under modern conditions, and I believe that the judgments of the majority and of Holmes J commend themselves as expositions of principles which are not alien to English law ...

If I may borrow some phrases from the majority decision, I would say that in the present case it is indisputable that the defendant broadcasting company had 'endeavoured to reap where it has not sown', and that it has enabled all its listeners to appropriate to themselves 'the harvest of those who have not sown'. Here, too, the interference with the plaintiff's profitable use of its land takes place 'precisely at the point where the profit is to be reaped, in order to divert a material portion of the profit from those who have earned it to those who have not': 248 US 215 at 240 (1918). For here, not only does the broadcasting company make its own business profits from its broadcasts of the plaintiff's races, it does so, in part at least, by conveying to its patrons and listeners the benefit of being present at the racecourse without payment. Indeed, its expert announcer seems to be incapable of remembering the fact that he is not on the plaintiff's course nor broadcasting with its permission, for, over and over again, he suggests that his broadcast is coming from within the course. The fact that here, as in the *International News Service* case, the conduct of the defendants cannot be regarded as honest should not be overlooked if the statement of Lord Esher is still true that 'any proposition the result of which would be to show that the common law of England is wholly unreasonable and unjust, cannot be part of the common law of England' (quoted in *Donoghue* v. *Stevenson* [1932] AC 562 at 608–9; [1932] All ER Rep 1 at 25).

The fact that there is no previous English decision which is comparable to the present does not tell against the plaintiff because not only is simultaneous broadcasting or television quite new, but, so far as I know, no one has, as yet, constructed high grandstands outside recognized sports grounds for the purpose of viewing the sports and of enriching themselves at the expense of the occupier.

9.4.   A comparative confirmation and an economic critique

This chapter has proceeded on the basis of assumptions canvassed in section 9.1.2 above that there is a general reluctance to recognise new property interests. This, briefly, is because of their capacity to bind third parties and the (supposed) deleterious effects on alienation that would arise by too ready an acceptance of novel property rights. Such assumptions would appear to be borne out by comparative experience. As Rudden has noted:

> In all non-feudal systems with which I am familiar (whether earlier, as at Rome, or later), the pattern is (in very general terms) similar: there are less than a dozen sorts of property entitlement. Three confer possession, either now or later, good against strangers: fee (ownership, full or bare), life estate (usufruct) and lease ... [then there are the] non-possessory and non-security rights [which I] will ... give ... the name servitudes ... [such as] easements, profits, restrictive covenants, equitable servitudes, real covenants, land obligations ... [and finally] ... security interests. (Rudden, 'Economic Theory v. Property Law', pp. 241–2)

Rudden's purpose is to question whether this universal approach to property is correct, and he proceeds by considering the legal justifications said to support it. He begins by refuting the argument that there is no demand for a more extensive list of property interests by pointing to the pressures that do (and will continue to) exist. Next he considers the claim that third parties will then be bound by interests of which they had no notice. While acknowledging the importance of this issue, Rudden notes it is manifestly possible to create registers by which third parties might be given notice and that, in any case, the presence of notice has never been either a necessary or a sufficient ground for granting proprietary status in the past. He then moves on to consider the objection that it is wrong to bind third parties by obligations (particularly positive ones) to which they have not personally consented but refutes this, ultimately, by the example of the lease which already does this within the proprietary field. Rudden's final substantive argument is raised against the charge of *pyramiding* (by which it is claimed that land titles will become unduly complicated by the multiplying tiers of proprietary interests) that he suggests might be dealt with by providing a version of the section 84 procedure under which the Lands Tribunal is empowered to discharge or modify obsolete restrictive covenants (see Notes and Questions 6.12 above).

Rudden takes an equally robust view of the economic arguments typically used to buttress the legal ones. First, he refutes the marketability argument by suggesting that burdening land with novel interests would not affect its marketability but simply its price. He then considers the standardisation argument in which someone who sells a non-standard product is said to impose costs on others because, from then on, everyone has to investigate what they are buying to see whether it is bound by such an interest. Rudden refutes this with the following aside:

> First, nowhere does there exist an active wholesale market in immoveables; second, every buyer may know today that, as a matter of property law, he could be bound only by certain stereotyped obligations, but he does not know what fancies any particular seller will seek to exact as a matter of contract.

Rudden continues by wondering why, if it is obvious that in a market economy contractual obligations will multiply, the opposite seems to occur in respect of property interests. After all, he argues, while the information costs in finding out about land would increase if there were a greater number of potential property interests capable of existing in it, this 'may be outweighed when it comes to acquiring' the land by the negotiation costs which would otherwise be required by the seller seeking to impose such obligations as a matter of contract (do you agree?). Rudden is equally dismissive of the land utilisation argument which suggests it is important not to sterilise land by imposing positive obligations upon it. On the contrary, he rightly contends, positive obligations might actually augment the value of both the dominant and servient tenements. The difficulty is, of course, that it is hard to quantify costs which might well extend well beyond the lifetime of the (otherwise contracting) original parties. While he does not address that point when dealing with the land utilisation issue, he does do so in his final comments on the durability of property interests. 'Contracts are born to die', he states, while by contrast 'the relations of property are built to endure' (Rudden, 'Economic Theory v. Property Law', p. 259) thus it is consequently more difficult to free your land from a property burden rather than a contractual one. But Rudden is unconvinced, noting Epstein's point ('Notice and Freedom of Contract in the Law of Servitudes', p. 1361) that making an interest proprietary rather than contractual 'only changes the identity of the party who must initiate the transaction' (but is not the point that with contractual burdens there is often no need for such a terminating transaction because the burden will die of its own accord) while acknowledging that, in situations where the 'property entitlements and correlative burdens are widely dispersed, there will be holdout and free-rider difficulties' (Rudden, 'Economic Theory v. Property Law', p. 259).

Notes and Questions 9.4

Consider the following notes and questions both before and after reading B. Rudden, 'Economic Theory v. Property Law: The "Numerus Clausus" Problem', in Eekelaar and Bell (eds.), *Oxford Essays in Jurisprudence: Third Series* (Oxford: Oxford University Press, 1987), p. 239.

1 How, if at all, is Rudden's argument weakened by (despite the title of the essay) basing all his examples on land and at no stage considering the applicability or otherwise of much of what he says to non-land such as moveables?

2 Does the normative view of property rights we discuss below in the next section expose Rudden's legal arguments as little more than puff? While there might be no conceptual reason why we cannot embrace an ever-increasing list of property interests, along with complicated registration and removal schemes, why on earth would the market want to saddle itself with such burdens? Would the market, rather than academics insulated in their ivory towers, be willing to absorb the inevitable increase in both transaction and regulation costs for no apparent gain or advantage just so as to pander to the whims of the insane, simple, eccentric and idealistic?

3 Do you agree with Rudden's assertion that burdening land with novel interests would not affect its marketability but simply its price? Would lenders be willing to lend on property where the effect of novel encumbrances was not established and which as a consequence held little prospect of ever becoming so?

4 Is Rudden correct to assert that 'nowhere does there exist an active wholesale market in immoveables'? Do not developments within the realms of commercial property such as PISCES (where a common data standard is being established to allow for the easy transmission of real estate data between purchasers, vendors and their advisers – see www.pisces.co.uk) and REITs (Real Estate Investment Trusts, in which investors will be able to invest in a tranche of commercial property with similar flexibility to the way in which they can already invest in portfolios of shares, options and bonds) show that that is exactly where the market is heading? Contrary to Rudden's assertion, REITs are in fact already popular in overseas markets including the US, France, Japan and Australia, and are likely to be introduced into the UK following a consultation launched by the Chancellor of the Exchequer in March 2004.

5 Is there any substance in Rudden's assertion that uncertainty already exists within the market as no purchaser knows 'what fancies any particular seller will seek to exact as a matter of contract'? What would the attitude of the market and third party advisers such as agents and lawyers be to a seller who repeatedly tried to impose novel contractual liabilities on prospective purchasers?

9.5. The future of property

In the film *Total Recall*, Arnold Schwarzenegger inhabits a planet on which there is a shortage of oxygen and where, as a consequence, property in air is a valuable and alienable commodity. In contrast, the earth's atmosphere has until recently been conceived of in terms of an infinite resource. This is why Cohen, in the Socratic dialogue considered in Extract 4.5 above, uses air as an example of something to which the property label is simply inapplicable:

C: Would you agree that air is extremely valuable to all of us?
E: Yes, of course.
C: Why then is there no property in air?
E: I suppose because there is no scarcity.
C: Suppose there was no scarcity of any material object.
E: I suppose then there would be no property in material objects.

But this extract is based upon lectures given more than half a century ago, and Cohen's example has, arguably, not survived environmental developments to the contrary. There are now EC directives on air quality the effect of which appears to give individual citizens property rights in air (see Case C-361/88, *Commission of the European Communities* v. *Federal Republic of Germany* [1991] ECR I-2567 and Case C-59/89, *Commission of the European Communities* v. *Federal Republic of Germany* [1991] ECR I-2607). Similarly, in the wake of developments such as the Kyoto Summit on global warming, a market in pollution permits has been established on the Chicago Board of Trade, the effect of which is to turn air quality into a tradable resource. As United States government spokesmen Melinda Kimble noted, while discussing the emerging market in sulphur and carbon dioxide permits, 'we can trade anything' (*Newsnight*, BBC2, 28 May 1998), by which she means not that everything is property but that anything is capable of being made the subject of property. For, as we saw above, property is, from one perspective at least, simply a shorthand means of allocating scarce resources.

Now you might, at this juncture, accuse us of begging the question. What, after all, is meant by a resource? Definitions do, of course, exist, and tend to focus on the subject-matter to which property rights might attach: but this misses the point. For example, in what today seems little more than a parody of the words of Melinda Kimble, the future Liberal Prime Minister (generally recognised as the most socially liberal and radical mainstream politician of his age), W. E. Gladstone, some 200 years earlier made his debut in Parliament speaking in support of slavery, the abhorrent and inherently racist notion of individuals owning property rights in their fellow human beings. While it is now completely unacceptable to commodify human beings in this way, technological advances are (almost paradoxically) causing us to re-examine moral arguments against commodification of the human body. Thus, in the face of the shortage of organs available for transplantation, judicial and academic voices can now be heard advocating the recognition of limited rights of property in non-renewable body parts (*R.* v. *Kelly* [1999] QB 621 and see also the Bristol Royal Infirmary Inquiry, *Interim Report: Removal and Retention of Human Material* (2001) available at www.bristol-inquiry.org.uk), and, as we briefly noted in Chapter 1, no less complex issues have to be faced about the way in which we treat other types of body part, whether attached or unattached to the living or the dead (see *Moore* v. *Regents of the University of California*, 51 Cal 3d 120; 793 P 2d 479 (1990), discussed in Chapter 1).

Faced with such a pragmatic approach to property, there seems little point offering a characterisation which seeks to transcend that reality. From this perspective, property is no more than a normative set of relationships which might be attached to whatever subject-matter society deems it necessary or beneficial to make the subject of property. We are sorry if that destroys the mystique but that really is all it is. Those who seek to offer a definition that goes beyond this are simply attempting to make property support a philosophical, moral or political burden that it cannot bear. Now we might well, of course, have views as to whether or not human body parts should be regarded as property but that is not because we have a definition of property to which they do or do not correspond but because we have certain views on the efficacy (be that in practical, moral, ethical or whatever terms) of making them subject to such a regime. In other words, it is not towards the definition of the subject-matter, but the consequences of the categorisation, that we look, when we debate whether something should or should not be regarded as property. Thus society might in the near future recognise some form of property in *in situ* kidneys, and whether or not it does has nothing to do with any definition of property to which it might subscribe but with the moral and practical consequences of adopting such a stance. That is not, of course, to deny the legitimacy of asking such questions, but simply to note they are matters to which property alone cannot provide an answer. For property is, in short, an essential mechanism for the workings of any society but is separate from the values that determine the parameters of what is and is not recognised as property within that particular setting.

Looking to the future we can but speculate. For example, in both cyberspace and outer space, the pressure to recognise new property rights is growing. The Internet has the potential to stretch the current boundaries of intellectual property to breaking point. In the face of the contemptuous disregard of the rules of copyright (and the inability to effectively counter such infringements), it is at least arguable that this will have profound long-term implications for the development of intellectual property rights in both virtual and perhaps even non-virtual reality. In the realm of outer space, speculation concerning water deposits on the Moon has renewed interest in the once purely academic question of ownership rights in space. There are, it is true, two international treaties on the subject, namely, the Outer Space Treaty and the Moon Treaty, the latter of which outlaws property rights in celestial bodies. However, it is surely indicative that in the light of technological advance the Moon Treaty has been signed by fewer than ten countries of which only Australia has any pretensions in respect of space exploration.

In the face of such flux we will end this chapter by considering two broad developments in this area, the new property thesis and the emergence of what is often referred to as quasi-property.

9.5.1. The new property thesis

In his article, 'The New Property', Reich argued that the new forms of wealth (such as welfare benefits) which had arisen in the wake of the increased role of government demand the same legal protection as that accorded to private property. The reason for adopting such a strategy was, basically, twofold. Tactically, Reich appeared to be trying to entrench welfare payments by bringing them within the ambit of the constitutional safeguard preventing the deprivation of 'property without due process of law', while, as a polemic, the article was attempting to utilise the rhetorical power of private property.

This has led some to question how 'property rights differ from rights generally – from human rights or personal rights or rights to life or liberty, say' (Grey, 'The Disintegration of Property', p. 71). In his view, the term has become so broad as to play no useful role in, so to speak, its own right. A similar point was made by Ronald Sackville who, in rejecting Macpherson's attempt in 'Capitalism and the Changing Concept of Property' to redefine the 'concept and institution of property', noted that '[b]y expanding the concept of property to the point where it is all-encompassing, Macpherson removes its value as an analytical tool' (Sackville, 'Property Rights and Social Security', p. 250). Rather than blame Macpherson, however, Grey points to modern developments in the field (or should we, in deference to him, say *estate*) of property for bringing this about.

The charge is a serious one and the answer so pragmatic that it might disappoint. For, while there are obvious dangers in defining a term so broadly that it ceases to be of any value absent words of limitation, it is simply wrong to assert that we have, as yet, reached that point in respect of *property*. At times, admittedly, some commentators have fallen into this trap. While (for reasons we will touch on below) we would not lay this charge at Macpherson's door, it is, for example, possible to argue that Reich's *New Property* thesis suffers from just such excess. As we have seen, his argument that new forms of wealth (such as welfare payments) require the same legal protection as that accorded to private property is, from one perspective at least, simply opportunistic. Yet, as a polemic seeking to harness the rhetorical power of private property, the baby appears to have become submerged beneath the bathwater. The property parallel performs no analytical function and is simply weakened by the association. In contrast, as we saw above, used properly (which is, after all, at the heart of the term's ontological root) the term *property* is simply a means of signposting what is (and what is not) regarded as a resource. (See Ackerman, *Private Property and the Constitution*; Etheleriadis, 'The Analysis of Property Rights'; and Waldron, *The Right to Private Property*.)

There is indeed a danger in defining *property* so broadly that it ceases to retain any real analytical force: but we must be careful. Sackville, for example, specifically exempted Reich from this charge when criticising Macpherson's approach on the surprising ground that 'the phrase "the new property" is not intended to … be regarded analytically as identical to a claim … to ownership of goods or an interest in land'. In his view, it was possible to use the term outside its normal confines provided one did not go as far as Macpherson who 'suggests that the concept must be broadened to embrace the right not to be excluded from the use or benefit of the community's accumulated productive resources'.

But the latitude Sackville extends to Reich is arguably as ill-deserved as the criticism he directs towards Macpherson. As Sackville himself admits, Reich's use of the term takes it outside its analytical frame of reference: he is simply attempting to harness the rhetorical power of private property without engaging in any serious attempt to analyse the *new property* in such terms. But this is exactly what we should avoid because it devalues the *property* label by turning it into little more than a political clarion call. In contrast, Macpherson was concerned not with hyperbole but with the far more profound task of re-evaluating the analytical definition of property by returning it to its historical roots. In his view, 'from Aristotle down to the seventeenth century, property was seen to include … both an individual right to exclude others from some use or enjoyment of some thing, and an individual right not to be excluded from the use or enjoyment of things that society had declared to be for common use – common lands, parks, roads, waters'. Thus, in describing pensions and the subsidised services of a modern welfare state in terms of property, Macpherson was attempting to re-establish an analytical concept of property that extended beyond the private to embrace once more the commons.

Notes and Questions 9.5

Consider the following notes and questions both before and after reading Reich, 'The New Property', and the materials highlighted below.

1 Does Reich's use of the property epithet strengthen or weaken his analysis?

2 Is the concept of property strengthened or weakened by its use in such a context?

3 Despite its fame (as the most heavily cited article ever published by the *Yale Law Journal*), Reich's thesis has not, as he has himself admitted, had a radical effect on the legal definition of property (Reich, 'Beyond the New Property: An Ecological View of Due Process') possibly because it was not ultimately

necessary. It is after all perhaps not without significance that Reich was able to make the same arguments a few years later in Reich, 'Individual Rights and Social Welfare' without at any point using the term 'property'.

4   In what way is Macpherson's use of the term 'property' in 'Human Rights as Property Rights' different to Reich's approach? Is it a distinction of degree or substance?

5   Macpherson considered that the difference between private and common property was rooted in the concept of exclusion, and contrasted the *right to exclude* that is generally regarded as the hallmark of a private property right with the *right not to be excluded* which he regarded as the key component in communal property. Does such an analysis suggest Macpherson is more or less justified than Reich in the way in which he employs the term 'property' (cf. Sackville, 'Property Rights and Social Security')?

6   Under the Human Rights Act 1998, the European Convention on Human Rights was incorporated into English law. Under Article 1 of the First Protocol to the Convention, property is protected in the context of possession, while under Article 8 the right to privacy extends to one's home and correspondence. Does such an approach equate more with Reich's or Macpherson's analysis of property rights, and would either of them draw comfort from the property rights jurisprudence that has emerged since the Act came into force on 2 October 2000? (See Rook, 'Property Law and the Human Rights Act 1998' and Halstead, 'Human Property Rights'.)

7   Do you agree with Grey, 'The Disintegration of Property', p. 69, when he asserts that property rights are often in effect transitory, and liable 'to disappear as if by magic':

> Yesterday A owned Blackacre; among his rights of ownership was the legal power to leave the land idle, even though developing it would bring in a good income. Today A puts Blackacre in trust, conveying it to B (the trustee) for the benefit of C (the beneficiary). Now no one any longer has the legal power to use the land uneconomically or to leave it idle – that part of the rights of ownership is neither in A nor B nor C, but has disappeared.

Is this really a disappearing rabbit or simply a *trompe-l'oeil*? Has the right disappeared or just become more difficult to see? Before Blackacre was settled on trust there was no difficulty because as sole owner A would necessarily bear the loss arising from leaving the land idle. But introducing a trust into the equation necessarily complicates matters for now ownership of Blackacre is divided between B and C and it consequently becomes necessary to determine on whose shoulders the loss should fall if the land is again left idle. As trustee, B has the right to manage the land and if he chooses not to do so it seems sensible for the loss to fall on his shoulders in the form of his liability to C in breach of trust which, despite the somewhat pejorative tone, is a compensatory remedy which does not seek to punish the trustee (see Hanbury and Martin, *Modern Equity*, p. 650).

8   In 'Property in Thin Air', Kevin Gray states that '[p]roperty is not theft – it is fraud … a vacant concept oddly enough like thin air'. The argument is characteristically provocative and appears to be a staging post en route to his latter, more ambitious attempt to 'reconceive the law of property' as part of a process 'creating a new commonwealth of dignity and equality' (Gray, 'Equitable Property'). Gray's argument is, of course, much more complex than these various snapshots can do justice to, but is there, at its core, an irresoluble paradox? Can an argument with foundations built upon the essential vacuity of property reach a conclusion that proclaims its central importance? Does Gray manage to square the circle in the following extract, and is it appropriate to quote Bentham at this point in the argument?

> In the exercise of this dual role the notion of property serves both to concretise individual material needs and aspirations and to protect a shared base for constructive human interactions. Indeed, in a subtle mimicry of our thoughts and emotions, the language of *property* catches in a peculiarly acute form many of our reactions to the experience of living. The present paper has sought, however, to articulate a deep scepticism about the meaning and terminology of property. *Property* is a term of curiously limited content; as a phrase it is consistently the subject of naïve and unthinking use. *Property* comprises, in large part, a category of illusory reference: it forms a conceptual mirage which slips elusively from sight just when it seems most attainably three-dimensional. Perhaps more accurately than any other legal notion it was *property* which deserved the Benthamite epithet, 'rhetorical nonsense – nonsense upon stilts'. (Gray, 'Property in Thin Air', p. 305)

9   Could a *laissez faire* utilitarian such as Bentham really hold such views or has he been quoted out of context? Is it significant that, when he wrote these words, Bentham was not ridiculing property but the supposed natural right to things such as property?

9.5.2.   The emergence of quasi-property

In recent years there has emerged what is commonly termed quasi-property which, although not property in the absolute meaning of the term, displays (from certain perspectives at least) enough of a proprietary aspect to make the property parallel a useful tool of analysis. Much of what we now regard as intellectual property began life as a form of quasi-property right which has slowly developed into fully fledged property interests that can be traded in the marketplace. And this is a still developing process with newly established rights such as moral rights (which preserves among other things the artist's right to be identified as the creator of the work of art) occupying a similar hinterland. Thus, while an artist now has a right, exercisable against third parties, to be identified as author of a work, which endures long after he has sold the piece, one cannot simply use the property right parallel as a premise from which to argue that he must similarly retain a right to be paid on subsequent dispositions of the work (although as testament to property's constant state of flux there are occasional suggestions, much to the chagrin of the London auction houses, that just such a right to a levy on future sales should be introduced: *PM*, Radio 4, 16 February 2000).

The views of the minority in *Victoria Park Racing* v. *Taylor* may similarly be seen in this light as can the arguments of those commentators and judges who have sought to broaden the ambit of nuisance by advocating that persons without a property interest in the land (such as licensees and relatives) should have *locus standi* to sue (Chapter 6). The category has also been explicitly recognised in the United States where the Supreme Court, in *International News Service* v. *Associated Press*, 248 US 215 (1918), held that an injunction would issue to prevent one news service unfairly competing with another by copying news stories published on the East Coast of America for sale to customers on the West Coast. Pitney J delivering the majority view held that a 'quasi-property' in news existed to the extent necessary to issue an injunction, even though there was no need to consider 'the general question of property in news'. However, the case is also note-worthy for the powerful dissent of Brandeis J:

> [T]he fact that a product of the mind has cost its producer money and labor, and has a value for which others are willing to pay, is not sufficient to insure to it this legal attribute of property. The general rule of law is that the noblest of human productions – knowledge, truths ascertained, conceptions and ideas – become after voluntary communication to others free as the air [note our earlier comments] to common use ... Such takings and gainful use of a product of another which, for reasons of public policy, the law has refused to endow with the attributes of property, does not become unlawful because the product happens to have been taken from a rival and is used in competition with him. The unfairness in competition which hitherto has been recognised by the law as a basis for relief ... involves fraud or force or the doing of acts otherwise prohibited by law. In the 'passing-off' cases (the typical and most common case of unfair competition) the wrong consists in fraudulently representing by word or act that defendant's goods are those of the plaintiff.

Yet, although this is correct, it would be a mistake to assume that the proprietary parallel therefore has no role to play. The law of 'passing off' does protect property rights (in at least some senses of the word) as noted, somewhat hesitantly, by Lord Parker in *A. G. Spalding Bros.* v. *Gamage Ltd* (1915) 84 LJ Ch 449 at 450:

> There appears to be considerable diversity of opinion as to the nature of the right, the invasion of which is the subject of what are known as passing-off actions. The more general opinion appears to be that the right is a right of property. This view naturally demands an answer to the question – property in what? Some authorities say, property in the mark, name or get-up improperly used by the defendant. Others say property in the business or goodwill likely to be injured by the misrepresentation ... [I]f the right

invaded is a right of property at all there are, I think, strong reasons for preferring the latter view ... [for] cases of misrepresentation by the use of a mark, name or get-up do not exhaust all possible cases of misrepresentation.

The point is accepted less equivocally by Danckwerts J in *J. Bollinger* v. *Costa Brava Wines Co. Ltd* [1960] Ch 262, where he simply states that, in passing-off actions, the law 'is interfering to protect rights of property'. In recent years, the law of passing off has arguably gone even further to, in effect, substantively create new rights of property, as witnessed in *British Telecom* v. *One in a Million Communications Ltd* [1999] 1 WLR 903, where a number of large companies including BT, Virgin and Marks and Spencer successfully obtained an injunction against a company which had registered Internet domain names for these and other well-known companies in circumstances where it is extremely doubtful whether there was any real likelihood of passing off actually occurring.

This seems a questionable development. Yet the difficulty is not caused by the quasi-property label we have attached to the right but rather the Court of Appeal's reluctance to confront the real issues in the case. Aldous LJ, who gave the only judgment in the case, proceeds on the basis that British Telecom owned the name (rather than the trade mark) 'British Telecom' and had a right to exploit that name in any medium. Yet, while in the context of an act of passing off the law adopts a proprietary approach in recognising the company's right not to suffer damage to their good name, that does not provide a premise from which to assert a property right to their name even where there is no likelihood of such damage.

The quasi-property category thus provides a means by which the subtleties of the property label can be appreciated and kept within acceptable bounds as can be seen in the context of confidential information where, for example, the property label provides, from some perspectives, a useful means of analysis while in other respects it would be deeply misleading. As Gummow J stated, when considering the proprietary quality of confidential information in *Breen* v. *Williams* (1995–6) 186 CLR 71 at 129, 'it [is not] acceptable to argue that, because in some circumstances, the restraint of an apprehended or continued breach of confidence may involve enjoining third parties ... it follows that the plaintiff who asserts an obligation of confidence therefore has proprietary rights in the information in question which, in turn found a new species of legal right'.

Notes and Questions 9.6

Consider the following notes and questions both before and after reading *British Telecom* v. *One in a Million* [1999] 1 WLR 903 and the materials highlighted below (either in full or as extracted at www.cambridge.org/propertylaw/)

1 Is the decision consistent with Lord Diplock's judgment in *Erven Warnink Besolten Vennootschap* v. *Townend & Sons (Hull) Ltd* [1979] AC 731 at 742?

2 Should you be able to own your name in the same way in which you own your identity or a trade mark?

3 Does a high-tech company such as BT that was intimately involved in the emerging Internet sector have anyone but itself to blame for not registering a domain name before someone else did? What would Locke make of the defendant's actions in the case?

4 Why is it both correct and incorrect to describe confidential information as property, and why does such an approach aid, rather than obscure, understanding (see Kohler and Palmer', Information as Property')?

Part 3

The acquisition and disposition of property interests

10

Title

10.1. What we mean by 'title'

Like many property law terms, the word 'title' is used in a number of different senses. It is often used loosely to refer to someone's right or interest in a thing, but it also has a number of technical meanings. For example, it can be used to refer not to a person's proprietary interest in a thing, but to their *entitlement* to that interest as against another person. As Professor Goode explains in *Commercial Law* at pp. 52–4:

> A person's interest in an asset denotes the quantum of rights over it which he enjoys against other persons, though not necessarily against *all* other persons. His title measures the strength of the interest he enjoys in relation to others.

This is the sense in which the word 'title' will be used here. In this jurisdiction it is particularly important to be able to distinguish a person's entitlement to an interest from the interest itself because our system is primarily concerned with relativity of title rather than with absolute title. In other words, when a person claims to be entitled to a particular interest in a thing, it is usually sufficient for him to prove that his entitlement, or title, to the interest is better than that of the person disputing his claim: it is rarely necessary for him to prove absolute entitlement.

For reasons which will become apparent, it is possible for two or more people to have titles to the same interest in a thing. These rival titles will each be recognised by law, but they will be of different relative strengths, and in a dispute about entitlement to the thing (or more accurately, entitlement to ownership or to some other interest in the thing) between any two of them the court is interested only in the relative strengths of their titles. In other words, in order to win, one of them only has to show that he has a better title than the other party to the dispute, not that he has an absolute title (i.e. a better title than anyone else in the world). And the person with the inferior title (or with no title at all) will not usually be able to defeat the claim of the other by demonstrating that there is a third party, not a party to this dispute, who has the best title of all.

Before looking more closely at these issues concerning relativity of title, it is useful to consider how titles arise.

10.2.   Acquiring title: derivative and original acquisition of title

The possibility of rival titles arises because titles can be acquired not only by *derivative acquisition* but also by *original acquisition*.

10.2.1.   Derivative acquisition: disposition or grant

Derivative acquisition covers those cases where your title is derived from that of the previous title holder. This can be done by way of a disposition – in other words, the whole of your predecessor's interest is disposed of to you by, for example, his selling or giving it to you, or by your inheriting it from him when he dies. Alternatively, your interest might derive from that of your predecessor by grant – in other words, by his retaining his interest but granting you a lesser interest carved out of it. The obvious example of a grant is where the holder of a fee simple interest in land grants you a lease of that land. To translate this into title/interest terms, you derive your title to the lease from his fee simple, to which he still has a good title, except that his fee simple interest is now reversionary on your lease. If you were then to mortgage your lease to the bank, the bank would acquire a title to its mortgage derived from your title to the lease.

10.2.2.   Original acquisition

By way of contrast, a title can be *original*, in the sense of not being derived from anyone else's title. *Original acquisition* occurs in at least three types of situation. The first is where someone becomes the first ever (hence original) interest holder in the thing. We have already looked at some of the cases which fall within this category: as we saw in Part I, there are circumstances in which the law treats a person as having an interest in a thing by virtue of having created it or mixed her labour with it in a Lockean sense, or by having taken an unowned thing and reduced it into private ownership by taking possession of it (for example, by capturing a wild animal, or drawing percolating water, or taking possession of an unowned thing).

Original acquisition of title is not, however, confined to these situations where what is acquired is the first ever interest in a newly created or previously unowned thing. In addition, a new title to a thing can arise notwithstanding the fact that someone else already has a title to that thing. This new title does not derive from, but is independent of, the pre-existing title. For present purposes, the most significant way of acquiring a new title to a thing to which someone else is already entitled is the same as the way of acquiring a title to an unowned thing – i.e. by taking possession of it. It is central to our property law system that possession is itself a root of title, and this applies not only to previously unowned things but also to things to which someone else already has title. The basic principle is that, by taking possession of a thing, you become *entitled* to possession of it against every-one except a person with a better right to possession. We will look at the rationale of this rule later, but for present purposes the important point is that the title you acquire is a new one: it is not derived from that of any previous or current interest holder. It is not effective against a pre-existing title holder but it *is* effective against everyone else. So, you have a title to the thing you have taken, but so too does the pre-existing title holder. Your title is weaker than hers but stronger than that of a person who has no title. The pre-existing title holder does not have to put up with this situation: she has a better right to possession than you, and can have you evicted or require you to give up possession to her. Unless and until she does so, however, you and she have rival titles to the same interest.

It is important to appreciate that a title acquired by taking possession can be defeated only by someone with a better *right to possession* of the thing in question; it cannot be defeated by someone who has a pre-existing interest in the thing which does not carry with it the right to possession. Take, for example, the case of a person who has granted a lease of land or bailed goods to another person. The essence of a lease and of a bailment is that possession of the land or goods is transferred to someone else for a specified period. If therefore *during that period* an outsider takes possession, it is the tenant/bailee, and not the landlord/bailor, who can take action against the outsider. The landlord/bailor will, however, become entitled to take action against the outsider as and when the lease/bailment ends and the right to possession consequently reverts to them.

Before taking this further, it is worth noting two points here. The first is that, as will be apparent from what has just been said, a person who is in possession of a thing may have become entitled to possession by acquiring an interest in the thing which carries with it a right to possession – in other words, he has possession by virtue of having the interest. Alternatively, he may be entitled to an interest in the thing (and hence entitled to possession) simply by virtue of being in possession of it. Possession and title are, therefore, closely interrelated in our system. The second point is that it may not matter much to outsiders which of the two explanations is the correct one in any particular case – the very fact of possession is sufficient guarantee that the possessor has *some* title even if it is not immediately clear whether it is an absolute title that will defeat all rivals, or one that is liable to be defeated by the 'true' owner.

For the sake of completeness, it is also worth mentioning here one other way in which a new title can arise independently of a pre-existing title. This is where someone with no title at all to a thing nevertheless purports to transfer title to an innocent purchaser. The general rule in English law is *nemo dat quod non habet* – no one can give a better title than he himself has or has the authority to confer. So, for example, you acquire no title from a con-man who 'sells' you the Royal Albert Hall (unless you manage to take possession of it, in which case you acquire *a* title by virtue of your possession, but not a title that will be effective against the 'true' owner). However, there are exceptions to the *nemo dat* rule, and when they apply the purchaser acquires a title which is not only good against the rest of the world but will also defeat the pre-existing title. The *nemo dat* rule and the exceptions to it will be considered in more detail in section 10.7 at the end of this chapter.

10.3. Relativity of title

The idea of relativity of title, which is a key point in our notion of title, now requires some elaboration. We have seen that, in property disputes, the question at issue tends to be whether one party has a better claim to a property interest than another, not whether either of them is the absolute or 'true' owner of it. What each party has to prove is that he has a better title than the other, not that he has a better title than anyone else in the whole world. And, as a general rule (to which there are exceptions, as we see below in the note on the *ius tertii*), the holder of the better title will win as against the holder of the lesser title, even if the lesser title holder can prove that someone else who is a not a party to the litigation is the 'true' owner of the interest.

So, to take the simplest example, if you are walking across a field and see and pick up a gold bracelet, you acquire possession of it and by doing so you acquire a title to it. This title is better than that of any person who has *no* right to possession of the bracelet. So, if your companion snatches the bracelet from you, you can successfully sue her for its return (or damages): she will not be able to defeat your claim by showing that the bracelet 'really' belongs to someone else. On the other hand, the person who dropped the bracelet in the first place *prima facie* has a better right to possession of it than you (unless he can be shown to have lost his title by, for example, having abandoned the bracelet, or to have temporarily transferred the right to possession to someone else by a bailment), and therefore a stronger title than you have. And – in circumstances we will look at later – the same might be true of the owner or occupier of the field or of the Crown.

Essentially, the same applies in relation to land, although the broader range of interests that can exist in land brings added complications. So, as we saw in Chapter 7, a squatter who takes possession of land by taking intentional physical control of it thereby acquires a title to an interest in it. He can be dispossessed by anyone with a better right to possession – by, for example, the holder of the fee simple absolute in possession if the land had not been let, or by the leaseholder if it had. But by taking possession the squatter has acquired a *right* to possession, and consequently the court will protect his possession against strangers. So, if the situation is that O was dispossessed by S1, who in turn was then dispossessed by S2, O has a better title than S1 and S2, but S1 has a better title than S2, who in turn has a better title than X (representing the rest of the world). If S1 applies to the court to regain possession from S2 he will win, and if S2 applies to the court for an injunction to restrain a trespass by X *she* will win: in neither case will the court be concerned that there are others in existence who are entitled to evict the applicant, nor will it be relevant in either case that the applicant seized possession for himself or herself entirely without justification.

This focus on relativity of title rather than absolute title requires some explanation. The nature of our civil justice system clearly has something to do with it, whether as a matter of cause or effect. Our civil courts have evolved as forums for settling disputes between the individuals who come before the courts, rather than as truth-finding tribunals, and consequently they are ill-equipped to enquire into the rights and interests of people who are not present before the court. This is conspicuously true in relation to property disputes. To be sure of producing a definitive answer to the question 'Who owns this book?' or 'Who is entitled to possession of this land?' you need an inquisitorial rather than an adversarial system. In a system such as ours where the only information the court has is that provided by the opposing parties, it is perhaps safer for the courts to confine themselves to relative rather than to absolute entitlement.

However, it would be misleading to think of property law solely in terms of litigation. In a private property law system one of the main functions of the law is to regulate the buying and selling of property interests. At first sight, a system geared towards assessing relative strengths of titles rather than discovering the true owner might appear rather inappropriate for dealing with such straightforward commercial transactions. If you are proposing to spend a large sum of money buying a picture or a house or a car, you want to know that you will get an absolute title, not just one that will stand up against some but not all comers. And, by the same token, if you want to mortgage your interest in your house to a building society, you might expect the building society to insist that you demonstrate absolute entitlement to the land, not merely *an* entitlement which may or may not be vulnerable to other as yet unspecified claimants.

However, on closer examination, the distinction between absolute title and relative title is less great than at first appears. The truth is that absolute title is in practice somewhat elusive. Property interests are, after all, abstract things, even though the subject-matter of the interest (the picture or the car or the house) may be concrete enough. How do you prove entitlement to an abstraction? In fact, we rely principally on three things – possession, provenance, and registration – but, as we shall now see, none of these can be guaranteed to locate absolute entitlement in all cases.

10.4. Proving title

As we have already seen, you might be entitled to a property interest because it originated in your hands or because it was transferred or granted to you from the previous holder by an authorised transmission. *Proving* your entitlement in either of these cases is a different matter. In fact, modern legal systems have had to evolve fairly elaborate rules and conventions about proving title. Without such special provision the difficulties in proving title would be formidable: to be *completely* certain of obtaining an absolute title, any prospective purchaser of your property interest would need to be satisfied, if you claim to be the original title holder, that the facts which in law give rise to title by original acquisition did indeed occur *and* that you have not since then transferred your interest to someone else, or granted away any subsidiary interest. And, if you are claiming to be entitled as a successor of the original title holder, your prospective purchaser would in addition need proof that you acquired your interest from someone who was then entitled to it, who in turn acquired it from the legitimate holder, and so on right back to the original title holder.

In most cases, therefore, conclusive proof of entitlement would be prohibitively expensive, if not impossible, to provide. A legal system that wants to encourage a market in property interests must therefore adopt mechanisms and rules that make it safe for purchasers to assume that apparent owners *are* absolute owners, or at the very least lessen the risks of a successful challenge to a purchaser's title. In our system we rely largely on registration and possession, buttressed by conventions about proving provenance and by limitation of action rules. Each of these will be considered in turn.

10.4.1. Role of registration

At first glance it might seem that registration could provide a complete answer to the problem of proving title. If we had a universal and unchallengeable register of all property interests in all things, then in theory all problems about title and relativity of title could be made to disappear. Registration itself could be made the unique title-conferrer, so that, if you were named in the register as holder of a particular interest, you would *be* the legitimate holder of it, and if you were not, you would not. However, this is simply not feasible, nor would it be desirable in practice even if it could be achieved. There are a number of reasons for this. The first is that registration is appropriate for surprisingly few types of property interest. One problem is that any register must be updated every time a dealing with the property occurs, and every update takes time and costs money. This makes it pointless to require registration of interests in things which are worth less than the cost of making an application for registration, or in things which are so ephemeral that they will have ceased to exist before the process of registering transfers in title is completed, or in things so frequently exchanged that they change hands faster than the registry can record changes in title. Another problem is that, in the case of tangible things, registration cannot work unless each individual thing is easily distinguishable from every other like thing. This means that registration is ruled out for all types of tangible property except those where each individual item is unique (such as pieces of land, or works of art, or racehorses) or can be made so by fixing on an identification mark or name plate (so, for example, it would be feasible to set up a system for registration of car ownership, although we have not yet done so in this country).

Even where registration is feasible and otherwise desirable, there is a fundamental problem about making the register unchallengeable. This is that any registration system is necessarily parasitic on some other title-proving system:

the registrar must know whom to enter on the register. In any system, if I wanted to be registered as entitled to all hitherto wild rabbits in the country, or to the fee simple interest in my neighbour's house, then presumably I would have to produce to the registrar something like the captured rabbits, or some evidence that my neighbour had duly transferred his fee simple to me. It follows that, even in the case of fully registrable property interests, it is impossible to achieve a total identification between the 'true' owner and the registered owner. At any one time there will always be some people *entitled* to be registered (because they can produce the necessary proof to the registrar) but not yet registered, and others who *are* registered but are no longer, or were never, entitled to be (because they have since sold their interest, or gone bankrupt, or were entered on the register by mistake or by dishonesty or fraud). One of the most difficult questions that any registration system has to resolve is the extent to which it will disregard the claims of the 'true' owner as against those of the registered owner. There is little point in having a registration system at all if a registered owner can always be defeated by a 'true' owner. On the other hand, few people would find acceptable a system whereby the register is *always* conclusive evidence of title (so that, for example, you and your neighbour have to swap houses because the registrar inadvertently confused the numbering of the houses). Compensation from the state or the registrar for any loss caused by a 'mistake' in the register can of course increase the acceptability of such a system, but it reintroduces the need to be able to prove entitlement to an interest (and hence entitlement to compensation for its loss) by some means other than entry on the register.

For these reasons it is not feasible in practice to register all property interests, nor would it be desirable to do so even if it was feasible, and even in the case of property interests which are subject to registration, other methods of proving title will still be relevant to varying degrees. We look at registration in some detail in Chapter 15, but here it is sufficient to note that at present in this jurisdiction we have relatively little registration compared to other jurisdictions. We have fairly sophisticated registration systems in operation in relation to some intellectual property rights, an as yet uncompleted registration system for land (which even when completed will provide for registration of some but not all interests in land), and virtually no registration at all for any kind of interest in chattels other than aircraft and ships. And, in most if not all of our registration systems, the correctness of the register can be challenged on the grounds that it does not reflect the 'true' ownership of the property interests recorded there, as we see in Chapter 15.

Registration, then, necessarily has only a limited role in proving titles. What English law has traditionally relied on instead is possession, backed up by conventions about proving provenance and by limitation of action rules.

10.4.2. Possession as a root of title

We have already seen that possession of a thing gives a good title to an interest in that thing, which can be defeated only by someone who can prove that they have a better right to possession of that thing. In other words, simply by virtue of being in possession of a thing, a person acquires not only a right to possession but also a good title to an interest in the thing, effective against all except those who have a better title. This rule that possession confers title is central to our title proving system. Whatever the rationale of the rule (and we shall be looking at that more closely in the next chapter) its effect is that the outside world can, for the most part, safely assume that apparent owners are actual owners. And, for present purposes, the important point is that someone offering to sell an interest in a thing can prove *an* entitlement to the interest simply by demonstrating that she is in possession of the thing. Of course, the *value* of her entitlement (i.e. the price a buyer would be willing to pay her for the interest) will vary depending on the likelihood of there existing someone with a better title who is able and willing to challenge her title. The role of provenance and of limitation of actions is to diminish the risk of a successful challenge.

10.4.3. Provenance

In practice, the prospective seller who is in possession of a thing can best show that there is *unlikely* to be anyone anywhere with a better title to it if she can show its provenance – in other words, if she can explain the origin and subsequent history of the thing, tracing the devolution of her title down from that of the original interest holder. So, for example, you can prove *almost* conclusively to a potential buyer that no one has a better title than you to a cake in your possession if you can prove that it was sold to you by a baker and that the baker baked it out of his own materials using his own labour which he had not contracted out to anyone else. The difficulty of eliminating *all* possibility of the existence of a better title is apparent even from this simple example, if only because of the regressive nature of the enquiry, and the problem of proving the negative (for example, that the baker had not already sold the cake to someone else before he took your money for it, that you did not buy it as agent for someone else, that you did not sell it to your companion when you left the shop and then offer to carry it home for her, etc.). However, as is equally apparent, it is fairly easy to achieve an acceptably high degree of probability that no one has a better title in such a case: in fact, in the real world, few prospective cake buyers would bother even to ask you where you got the cake from, never mind enquire into the ownership of the baker's labour and materials.

As a general rule, the more valuable the thing, the more likely it is that a purchaser will want to investigate the seller's title to the thing, going beyond the fact of possession and enquiring into the provenance of the seller's interest. In the case of goods not subject to registration whose value does not warrant the cost of elaborate investigation, most buyers are happy to take a risk and rely on possession, particularly where there is nothing in the surrounding circumstances to arouse suspicion (compare, for example, the enquiries you would make before buying a car radio in a pub – assuming you were anxious to obtain an unchallengeable title – with those you would make if buying the same radio from a shop).

Works of art and archaeological finds are good examples at the opposite extreme. At present, there is no register covering these items in this jurisdiction, and buyers rely on a combination of possession and provenance, tracing the history of the work from its creation, or the time and place of its finding, up to and including how it came into the seller's hands, with provenance performing the additional function of authenticating the thing itself. If a seller is in possession of a work of art but is unable to produce all the evidence necessary to prove its provenance, this gap in the evidence will affect the price obtainable for his interest precisely to the extent that it (a) increases the possibility of there existing someone who has, and is likely to assert, a better title to the work, and (b) throws doubt on the authenticity of the work.

Historically, provenance has also been of prime importance in proving titles to interests in land (and it continues to be of some significance even though we now have a land registration system covering the whole country, since the process of putting all land titles on the register has not yet been completed). For obvious reasons, it is rarely if ever possible for a seller of an interest in land in this country to trace his title back to that of the first ever interest holder. Nevertheless, the further back a seller can trace his title, the smaller the risk that someone with a better title will appear to challenge it. Consequently, for centuries the accepted method of proving titles to land in this country has been for the seller to demonstrate that he is in possession of the land (or can put the buyer in possession on completion of the sale), *and* show an unbroken chain of title going back for a specified number of years (currently fifteen years, progressively reduced from sixty over a period from 1874). This system is still in operation in relation to land where the title has not yet been put on the land register. So, if you now want to buy a house and you discover that the seller's title (to be precise, his title to the fee simple absolute in possession of the land) is not registered, you will require him to produce the document by which *he* acquired his title (usually a deed by which his predecessor sold the fee simple to him); in addition, if this occurred less than fifteen years ago, you will also require him to give you proof (by producing the original documents of transfer) of how *his* seller, and his seller's seller, acquired their titles, and so on going back to a transfer of the title which happened not less than fifteen years ago. If he can do this, it will not *guarantee* that he has (and hence can transfer to you) an absolute title, but it will lessen the risk that there is someone around able and likely to make a successful challenge to his title. The degree of risk is then reduced still further by the operation of limitation of action rules, as we shall now see.

10.4.4. Extinguishing title by limitation of action rules

In relation to both goods and land, limitation of action rules (of ancient origin, but now contained in the Limitation Act 1980) lessen the risk of old titles resurfacing. They do this by eliminating dormant claims. Precisely how this operates in relation to property interests will be considered in the next chapter, but for present purposes it is sufficient to note that all claims relating to property (and indeed to anything else) are extinguished without compensation if the claim is not brought before the court within a specified number of years after the cause of action first arose – generally twelve years in the case of actions to recover land and six years in other cases. The position has been modified somewhat in relation to registered land by the Land Registration Act 2002, but leaving aside these changes (which we look at in Chapter 11) if someone in possession of land is dispossessed, or goods are taken from their owner, the possessor/owner's claim to recover the land or goods will be lost if not brought before the court within the limitation period. And, once the claim is lost, so too is the possessor/owner's title. So, to take again the example of the squatter, if Squatter A takes possession of O's land on 1 January 1990, O immediately becomes entitled to recover possession from Squatter A. Mechanistically, this means that O becomes entitled either to retake possession by physically evicting Squatter A (subject to the safeguards considered in Chapter 7) or to apply to the court for a possession order against Squatter A. Ignoring for the moment the changes made by the Land Registration Act 2002, if O has done neither of these things by 31 December 2001, he loses his right to do either, *and in addition* his title to the land is irrevocably extinguished. If between 1 January 1990 and 31 December 2001 Squatter A is evicted by Squatter B, this does not affect O's position: O will have to bring his possession action against Squatter B rather than Squatter A, but his right to does so will still expire on 31 December 2001.

This is of tremendous importance in relation to proving titles to interests in land. In cases not covered by the Land Registration Act 2002, if your seller can prove that his title can be traced back through an unbroken chain to a transfer which took place at least fifteen years ago, he is effectively demonstrating that, even if his title *does* derive directly or indirectly from someone who dispossessed the 'true' owner, that dispossession cannot have taken place within the last fifteen years. Since in most cases the limitation period runs from the date of dispossession and expires after twelve years, any title that was better than his will therefore almost certainly have been extinguished. The risk that someone can assert a better title is, therefore, negligible. It is not *completely* eliminated, because there are various exceptions to the limitation of action rules which either delay the start of the twelve-year period or postpone or extend its effect. For example, if at the time when a squatter takes possession, the land is let to a tenant, the limitation period for the tenant expires twelve years later but the limitation period *for his landlord* (i.e. the person who then holds the fee simple in reversion on the tenancy) does not start until the date the tenancy ends (because it is only then that the landlord becomes entitled to possession), and it will continue to run for another twelve years from then. So, even if, when you bought your house, you satisfied yourself that your seller's title can be traced back to a legitimate purchase at least fifteen years ago, you still will not have eliminated the possibility that someone may turn up in the future who is able to prove that she is now entitled to the reversion on a lease of your land, and that your title is derived from that of a squatter who dispossessed her tenant some time before the start of the fifteen-year period you investigated. However, the chances of this happening are so small as to be hardly worth considering, and the same applies to the other events which can postpone or extend the limitation period. So, for all practical purposes, the combination of the conventions for proving the provenance of titles and the limitation of action rules make unregistered titles to land as fully marketable as registered titles.

In relation to goods, the limitation of action rules are less effective in extinguishing dormant claims. This is for technical reasons which will be considered in the next chapter, but essentially the problem is that time does not run in favour of thieves (and goods, unlike land, can be stolen), nor does it start to run in favour of innocent takers (such as finders) unless and until they commit the tort of conversion. The role that limitation of actions plays in proving title is therefore more restricted. Nevertheless, even in relation to goods, the combination of provenance and limitation of actions is enough to make most goods fully marketable most of the time.

10.4.5.   Relativity of title and the *ius tertii*

One final point to note about relativity of title is that there are some exceptional cases where a defendant in a title dispute can successfully defend the action by pleading a *ius tertii* – i.e. by showing that a third party has a better title than the plaintiff has. It has already been seen that the basic principle is that, in any dispute about title, the law is concerned only with the relative strengths of the titles of the rival claimants: it is not concerned to establish the 'true' ownership of the thing in question, and a court will order the return of the thing to the claimant who can prove he holds the stronger title, even if it can be proved that there exists someone else whose title is stronger still. This was recently reaffirmed in the High Court by His Honour Judge Rich in *Ezekial* v. *Fraser* [2002] EWHC 2066 (a case concerning disputed possession of a house), where he reviewed all the authorities and confirmed the basic principle that the *ius tertii* of the 'true' owner is no defence in a possession action brought by the first wrongful takers of the house against those who subsequently dispossessed them.

However, a statutory exception to this general principle, applicable only to goods, was created by section 8 of the Torts (Interference with Goods) Act 1977 partially implementing recommendations made in 1971 by the Law Reform Committee in its *Eighteenth Report on Conversion and Detinue* (Cmnd 4774, 1971). The most important effect of this is that it ensures that a defendant does not have to pay damages for wrongful interference with goods to a claimant who is not the owner. This applies only if the 'true' owner can be found and is willing to be joined as a party, and then only at the price of having to pay damages to the true owner instead. This is of immense practical importance to a defendant faced with the threat of multiple liability for damages in tort arising out of the wrongful interference with goods: as a consequence of this provision and section 7, the threat of double liability is removed.

10.5.   The *nemo dat* rule

The *nemo dat* rule is that no one can give to another a greater interest in a thing than he himself has. However, the application of the rule is determined by policy not logic, and when policy reasons demand, English law sees no conceptual difficulty in making exceptions to the rule. The classic statement of the policy considerations at work here was made by Lord Denning in *Bishopsgate Motor Finance Corp. Ltd* v. *Transport Brakes Ltd* [1949] 1 KB 322 at 336–7:

> In the development of our law, two principles have striven for mastery. The first is for the protection of property: no one can give a better title than he himself possesses. The second is for the protection of commercial transactions: the person who takes in good faith and for value without notice should get a good title. The first principle has held sway for a long time, but it has been modified by the common law itself and by statute so as to meet the needs of our times.

Decisions as to whether, in any particular circumstance, an exception should be made to the *nemo dat* rule have tended to be made on an *ad hoc* basis, and consequently the detailed picture is complicated and technical. However, the following broad principles can be abstracted.

10.5.1. Scope of the *nemo dat* rule

First, it is helpful to distinguish the situations in which the *nemo dat* rule is relevant from essentially similar situations which English law views as involving issues of priority and enforceability rather than the *nemo dat* rule. There are at least four different ways in which you can try to give someone more than you yourself have, and the *nemo dat* rule affects only two of them. In order to distinguish between them it is necessary to revert to the distinction made at the beginning of this chapter between title and interest. In general, the *nemo dat* rule is concerned with title, not with quantum of interest. To make this clearer, consider the following four situations:

1   You purport to transfer something in respect of which you have no interest or title whatsoever. It might be that you never had any interest in the thing: for example, you might purport to sell to T a car you have just stolen, or to mortgage the Royal Albert Hall to M. Alternatively, you might once have had an interest in the thing but have since lost it: for example, you purport to sell to T a car you once owned but have already sold to X.

2   *Nemo dat* and section 62 of the Law of Property Act 1925. You do have an interest in the thing, but the interest you actually hold is not as extensive as the one you purport to transfer. For example, you purport to sell the fee simple in land to P when all you have is a monthly tenancy of the land, or you hire a car from O and then purport to sell it to P.

3   Priority of derivative interests. You have an interest in the thing and you then grant lesser interests in the thing to a series of grantees, each lesser interest being actually or potentially incompatible with the others. For example, you hold the legal fee simple in your house and you first grant a seven-year lease of the house to T, then you mortgage the legal fee simple to M1 and then you mortgage it again to M2. Or you charter your ship to C for twenty-one years, then allow it to become subject to a lien to secure S's charges for rescuing the ship, and then mortgage the ship to M.

4 Enforceability of derivative interests. You have an interest in a thing but having already granted lesser interests to third parties (as in 3 above), you now purport to transfer your interest to P free from any lesser interests. So, taking the examples given in 3, you now purport to sell to P the fee simple in your house free from T's lease and the mortgages to M1 and M2, and to sell the ship to P free from C's charterparty, S's lien, and M's mortgage.

In Case 1, the issue is whether you can give a better *title* to the interest you are purporting to transfer or create than the title you yourself have: in resolving this issue, the only relevant principle is the *nemo dat* rule.

Case 2 is slightly more complicated. In determining whether you can give a good title *to the interest you are purporting to transfer or create*, the relevant principle is again the *nemo dat* rule, as in Case 1, but there is also a separate and subsidiary issue: if because of the *nemo dat* rule you fail to confer a good title to *that interest*, might you nevertheless succeed in conferring a good title to the lesser interest you do in fact have? The answer is usually yes, because of the basic property principle that a disposition of a greater interest than you have will be effective to dispose of whatever interest you do have in the same thing. This is enshrined in section 62 of the Law of Property Act 1925 (not confined to land) and the same result can be achieved via the doctrine of partial performance, as demonstrated in *Thames Guaranty Ltd v. Campbell* [1985] QB 210 (i.e. if this is what the buyer wants, the court will order you to perform your contract up to the extent you can do so, and pay damages to compensate for the shortfall).

Cases 3 and 4, on the other hand, have nothing to do with the *nemo dat* rule at all. In Case 3, each grantee will get a good title to the interest you purport to grant to him, but the issue is whether that interest will be postponed to or take priority over the interests of the other grantees. English law treats that issue as a question of *priorities* between the competing lesser interests, and ranks them between themselves in an order arrived at by applying special priority rules.

Similarly, in Case 4, there is no difficulty about title: there is no reason why P should not get a good title to the fee simple – the only issue is whether she will take the interest subject to or free from the encumbrances you have carved out of that interest. English law treats that issue as a question of the *enforceability* of each of the lesser interests as against P, governed by special enforceability rules. While priority rules and enforceability rules have close affinities with the *nemo dat* rule (and with the common law *bona fide* purchaser rule Lord Denning contrasted with it in the above quotation from *Bishopsgate Motor Finance Corp. Ltd* v. *Transport Brakes Ltd* [1949] 1 KB 322), they are not explicitly based on them and it avoids confusion in this context if they are kept distinct. Priority and enforceability of interests are therefore considered separately in Chapter 14.

In cases where the *nemo dat* rule is relevant – Cases 1 and 2 – the balance drawn between the *nemo dat* rule and the *bona fide* purchaser rule varies depending on the nature of the property in question. In the following sections we consider first some general principles applicable to all types of property and then the specific principles applicable to goods, money and land respectively.

10.5.2. General principles applicable to all property

10.5.2.1. Registration and the *nemo dat* rule

Where registration of title systems apply, it is registration itself which confers title. So, even a purchaser from someone with an unimpeachable title will not himself acquire a good title unless and until he becomes registered as title holder. And conversely anyone who becomes registered as title holder thereby acquires a better title than anyone else in the world, even if the registration was simply a mistake, or was procured by forgery or a trick. This is essentially what happens in our system of registration of title to land under the Land Registration Act 2002, and also in our system for registering interests in ships under the Merchant Shipping Act 1995.

In such a system, the *nemo dat* rule has no application. If T is registered as title holder, but X, who has no title whatsoever, executes a transfer deed in favour of P and P manages to become registered as title holder instead of T, then P acquires a good title and T's title is extinguished. This is a purely mechanical process. The court (or the Registrar) might have a power to order rectification of the register so as to divest P of his title and reinstate T, but rectification is neither as of right nor retrospective, and it is unlikely to be ordered to the detriment of any innocent purchaser who acts on the faith of P's registration.

10.5.2.2. Dispositions to volunteers

It is a basic principle of English law that a donee can never be in a better position than his donor. In accordance with this principle, a volunteer (i.e. a transferee who gave no consideration for the transfer) can never obtain a better title or a greater interest than his transferor, whatever the nature of the property. There are only two qualifications to be made to this. The first is the point already made about registration – once a volunteer's interest is registered, his title is as good as anyone else's (although some registration systems treat registered volunteers less favourably than registered purchasers when it comes to issues of enforceability, as we see in Chapter 15 below). The second qualification to be made is that the donee might have some sort of general law defence, such as estoppel, which will effectively prevent the true owner asserting his title.

This basic principle that a volunteer can never obtain a better title than his transferor is entirely consistent with the policy enunciated by Lord Denning in *Bishopsgate Motor Finance Corp. Ltd* v. *Transport Brakes Ltd* [1949] 1 KB 322, quoted above, that exceptions to *nemo dat* arise out of the need to protect commercial transactions: in the absence of some added factor such as estoppel, gifts are not regarded as requiring the same protection.

10.5.2.3. Powers of sale

There are some circumstances in which the holder of an interest in a thing is invested with a special power to confer on a purchaser a greater interest in the thing than she herself possesses. The interest held by the seller is nearly always a security interest, such as a mortgage or charge or lien. For example, a mortgagee whose mortgage was made by deed has a statutory power of sale (conferred by section 101(1)(i) of the Law of Property Act 1925), and this enables the mortgagee to confer on a purchaser the *mortgagor's* interest in the thing in question, free from the mortgage and from any other derivative interest to which the mortgage takes priority (section 104 of the Law of Property Act 1925). So, suppose you hold the fee simple in your house and first mortgage it to the Building Society, and then (without the Building Society's authority) grant a seven-year lease of it to T. If you then fail to make the agreed payments under the mortgage, the Building Society (which holds no interest in your house other than the mortgage) is nevertheless able to confer on P, a purchaser, the fee simple interest in the house, free from the mortgage and free from T's lease.

Most of these special powers of sale are statutory, but a few (mainly of ancient origin, such as the power of a pledgee of goods to sell them on default by the pledgor) are common law.

10.5.3.   The application of the *nemo dat* rule to goods

In transactions relating to goods *nemo dat* is the basic rule, but there are several common law and statutory exceptions to it. The rule is now set out in section 21(1) of the Sale of Goods Act 1979 and the statutory exceptions appear in sections 23–26.

Superficially, these exceptions to the *nemo dat* rule are rational enough. They all arise where the good faith purchaser has bought from someone who has *apparent* authority to sell, either as owner or as agent, even if he has no actual title or authority, and in most cases this misleading appearance will have been produced by the true owner. So, for example, the exceptions in section 25 depend on the true owner having transferred possession of the goods or their documents of title to the seller, even though the true owner has not yet parted with all his interest in the goods. Similarly, the exceptions in section 24 can only arise where a buyer of goods has allowed his seller to remain in possession of them or their title deeds, so allowing his seller to continue to pass himself off as true owner. Even the exception in section 23 depends on the true owner not yet having taken steps to have the voidable title of the seller set aside. So, at first glance it looks as if the good faith purchaser is preferred over the true owner only where the true owner has in some way contributed towards the purchaser's mistaken belief that he is dealing with someone with power or authority to sell.

Until recently, there was an additional common law exception (later embodied in statute) which did not conform to this pattern. By this exception, abolished by section 1 of the Sale of Goods (Amendment) Act 1994, a good faith purchaser would acquire a good title to any goods sold in market overt. 'Market overt' meant a market legally constituted by statute, charter or custom (covering, under this last heading, all shops in the City of London) and sales had to be open and made between sunrise and sunset. Now that this exception of sales in market overt has been abolished, it is impossible for a thief to pass on a good title to goods (i.e. a better title than that of the true owner: even a thief will acquire, and can transmit, a possessory title good against everyone except the true owner: see further Chapter 11) except in the rare cases where the circumstances outlined in the previous paragraph also happen to exist.

However, although when seen in outline the exceptions to the *nemo dat* rule seem rational, the appearance is misleading. In reality the superficially clear statutory rules are riddled with inconsistencies and enmeshed in a mass of over-technical and not always coherent case law rules. For a detailed analysis reference should be made to Goode, *Commercial Law*, Chapter 16, which Professor Goode concludes with the following comment:

> The present patchwork of legislative provisions detailing the exceptions to the *nemo dat* rule can hardly be described as satisfactory. The legislation has generated a vast amount of case law and has given rise to grave problems of interpretation, often resolved at a highly technical level. In 1989, in a review on behalf of the government directed primarily at security interests in personal property [Diamond, *A Review of Security Interests in Property*] Professor Aubrey Diamond recommended that the existing statutory provisions be replaced with a broad principle that, where the owner of goods has entrusted them to, or acquiesced in their possession by, another person, then an innocent purchaser of those goods should acquire good title. In January 1994, the Department of Trade and Industry issued a Consultation Paper inviting comments on this proposal and on particular exceptions to the *nemo dat* rule. The ensuing abolition of the market overt principle appears to have owed nothing to this Consultation Paper, and it is unclear what provoked its publication. It is to be hoped that no government department will ever in the future seek to deal with such a complex set of issues in such an ill-conceived document, a mere eight pages long, containing no analysis, no reasoning, no discussion of the policy issues and no detailed proposals. (Goode, *Commercial Law*, p. 485)

10.5.4.   The application of the *nemo dat* rule to money

'Money' can mean at least three different things. First, it can refer to physical coins or notes, valued not as currency but rather for the intrinsic value of the paper or metal out of which they are made, or as curios. It is characteristic of coins and notes valued in this way that their market value bears little resemblance to their face value. Viewed in this way, coins and notes behave just like any other goods – the *nemo dat* rule prevents title passing on a transfer by a non-owner unless any of the statutory or common law exceptions apply.

Secondly, money can mean physical coins or notes valued as currency rather than for the intrinsic value of the paper or metal out of which they are made, and fungible in the sense that any unit is interchangeable with any other unit or combination of units of the same denomination: this is what Goode calls physical money (Goode, *Commercial Law*, pp. 490–1). In the case of physical money there is a blanket exception to the *nemo dat* rule in favour of a good faith purchaser. Even a thief can pass title to physical money to a good faith purchaser – indeed, it is the essence of currency that recipients for value and in good faith acquire a good title.

Thirdly, there is what Professor Goode calls intangible money – for example, money in a bank account. Money in an intangible form is analytically quite different from physical money, and different considerations arise when it comes to resolving competing claims to it. When you pay physical money into your bank account you cease to own it. Instead, the bank owes you an equivalent amount, and you acquire a chose in action against the bank – a right to sue the bank for payment of the amount it owes you. *Nemo dat* problems therefore do not arise in the same form.

The classic statement of the principle that the *nemo dat* rule has no application to physical money or intangible money comes from *Miller* v. *Race* (1758) 1 Burr 452:

> William Finney sent by post to Bernard Odenbury a bank note for the payment of £21 10s to himself or bearer on demand. Odenbury never received it: there was a mail robbery and the note was taken by the robbers. The following day the bank note was paid over to Miller, an innkeeper, who received it in the ordinary course of his business and gave valuable consideration for it, not knowing that it had been stolen. However, by the time Miller presented the note to the bank for payment, Finney had told the bank about the robbery and instructed them to stop payment. The bank therefore refused either to pay Miller or to return the note to him.
>
> Miller brought this action against Race (the bank clerk concerned). The action was in trover, and in order to succeed in the action it was necessary for Miller to prove that he had a good title to the note.
>
> It was accepted by all the parties that at that time such bank notes were treated as cash, passing from one person to another as cash, by delivery only and without any further enquiry or evidence of title.
>
> It was held by the court that the plaintiff, Miller, having acquired the note in good faith and for value, had acquired a good title to it even as against Finney, the true owner. The bank note was to be treated as currency and consequently the *nemo dat* rule did not apply. The judgment of the court was given by Lord Mansfield.
>
> LORD MANSFIELD: ... [I have] no sort of doubt, but that this action was well brought, and would lie against the defendant in the present case; upon the general course of business, and from the consequences to trade and commerce, which would be much incommoded by a contrary determination.
>
> It has been very ingeniously argued ... for the defendant. But the whole fallacy of the argument turns upon comparing bank notes to what they do not resemble, and what they ought not to be compared to, namely, to goods, or to securities, or documents for debts.
>
> Now they are not goods, nor securities, nor documents for debts, nor are they so esteemed: but they are treated as money, as cash, in the ordinary course and transaction of business, by the general consent of mankind, which gives them the credit and currency of money to all intents and purposes. They are as much money as guineas themselves are, or any other current coin that is used in common payments as money or cash ...

... It has been quaintly said 'that the reason why money cannot be followed is because it has no earmark', but that is not true. The true reason is, upon account of the currency of it: it cannot be recovered after it has passed in currency. So, in case of money stolen, the true owner cannot recover it after it has been paid away fairly and honestly upon a valuable and *bona fide* consideration, but before money has passed in currency, an action may be brought for the money itself ...

Apply this to the case of a banknote. [If a person finds a dropped bank note] an action may lie against the finder, it is true (and it is not at all denied), but not after it has been paid away in currency ...

Here, an inn-keeper took it, *bona fide*, in his business from a person who made an appearance of a gentleman. Here is no pretence or suspicion of collusion with the robber ... Indeed, if there had been any collusion, or any circumstances of unfair dealing, the case had been much otherwise. If it had been a note for £1,000 it might have been suspicious, but this was a small note for £21 10s only, and money given in exchange for it.

... The case of *Ford* v. *Hopkins* Hil 12 W 33, in Lord Chief Justice Holt's court, was also cited and was an action of trover for million lottery tickets. But this must be a very inaccurate report of that case: it is impossible that it can be a true representation of what Lord Chief Justice Holt said. It represents him as speaking of bank notes, exchequer notes and million lottery tickets as like to each other. Now no two things can be more unlike to each other than a lottery ticket and a bank note. Lottery tickets are identical and specific: specific actions lie for them. They may prove extremely unequal in value; one may be a prize, another a blank. Land is not more specific than lottery tickets are. It is there said 'that the delivery of the plaintiff's ticket to the defendant, as that case was, was no change of property' And most clearly it was no change of the property ...

[But] a bank note is constantly and universally, both at home and abroad, treated as money, as cash, and paid and received as cash; and it is necessary for the purposes of commerce that their currency should be established and secured.

In 'Bona Fide Purchase and the Currency of Money', David Fox considers the historical background to Lord Mansfield's explanation of currency. He argues that, although the old common law rationale for currency was that 'money has no earmark', it was supplanted by the *bona fide* purchaser rule. He locates the origin of the *bona fide* purchase rule as the modern rationale of currency in the practices of bankers and commercial people who wished to promote the free circulation of bills of exchange and promissory notes. The courts of common law and equity gradually absorbed these commercial practices and gave legal force to the rights of *bona fide* purchasers of bills and notes. When Lord Mansfield explained the currency of money in terms of *bona fide* purchase he was therefore not declaring a new rule, but expressing in a refined and principled way a rule which had been evolving in the common law during the previous sixty years. Fox concludes:

As was true of his contributions in other areas of the commercial law, Lord Mansfield's skill lay in the clear formulation of existing principles and in his grasp of the practical reasons on which they were founded. It is apparent from the tone of Lord Mansfield's judgment that the rule of *bona fide* purchase was already well established. He thought that any suggestion that banknotes were governed by the *nemo dat* rule because they were earmarked was hopelessly outdated. He dismissively referred to the 'no earmark' maxim as 'quaint'. He delivered a fully reasoned judgment, not because he was declaring new law, but because he wanted to avoid any doubts in the commercial community about the rights of *bona fide* purchasers.

Two points stand out in Lord Mansfield's judgment. First, he gave priority to the commercial functions of money as a medium of exchange, not to its attributes as a chattel. '[Banknotes] are not goods, not securities, nor documents for debts ... but are treated as money, as cash, in the ordinary course and transaction of business, by the general consent of mankind; which gives them the credit and currency of money.' Because banknotes were functionally identical to coins they too should have the attribute of currency. He rejected the 'no earmark' maxim as the real reason why money could not be followed. If money was no longer to be considered as a kind of chattel, the rules for passing of property should not depend on its physical appearance and the possibility of the owner recovering possession of it. In consequence he made *bona fide* purchase the reason for the currency of coins as well as banknotes. Traditionally, coins passed as currency because they had no earmark. The result of *Miller* v. *Race* was to extend *bona fide* purchase from its origins in the special rules governing negotiable instruments, so that it explained the currency of all kinds of property that circulated as money.

The other important point was the commercial justification for the *bona fide* purchase rule. He was concerned, as usual, that the common law should not hamper trade and commerce. The 'general course of business', said Lord Mansfield, 'would be much incommoded' if the recipient of a lost note did not have a valid claim against the issuing bank, or if he were liable to the original owner. He did not elaborate. He was perhaps alluding to the inconvenience that would be caused if transactions which appeared to be closed had to be reopened because a creditor later found that he was liable to return a banknote which had been stolen from its original owner. The assurance of getting title by *bona fide* purchase would mean that the creditor would not have to investigate whether the payer actually had title to the money that he tendered in payment ...

Bona fide purchase now underlies the currency of all forms of money – coins, banknotes and purely abstract sums represented as bank balances. It is a common law rule, historically distinct from the much wider equitable defence of *bona fide* purchase for value without notice. The common law rule only applies to money. A person who acquires the legal title to any kind of property in good faith for valuable consideration and without notice takes it clear of any equitable rights. The rationale of the defence is that a *bona fide* purchaser has an untainted conscience so he ought not to be bound by equities affecting the property he received ...

Currency is a special legal attribute which allows a recipient of money to take a fresh legal title which is good against the whole world. Money passes into currency in this way when it is received by a *bona fide* purchaser for valuable consideration. At this point the title of any previous owner of the money from whom it may have been stolen is extinguished. It helps money to circulate readily in the economy in that it reduces the need for recipients to make detailed inquiries into the title of people who tender money in payment of debts or to buy goods.

The rule of *bona fide* purchase originated in the practices of merchants and bankers in the late seventeenth and eighteenth centuries. The common law progressively absorbed these practices, refined them and gave them the status of legal rules. Lord Mansfield's decision in *Miller* v. *Race* was the final point in this process. It confirmed that *bona fide* purchase was the rationale for the currency of all kinds of money. The decision put an end to the old common law rule that coins had the attribute of currency because they had 'no earmark' by which their original owner could specifically identify them.

10.5.5.   The application of the *nemo dat* rule to land

10.5.5.1.   The general principle

Except where title is registered, the *nemo dat* rule is absolute in relation to land dealings – there are no exceptions whatsoever. Except in cases where registration itself confers title, it is impossible for anyone, even a purchaser for value in good faith, to acquire any title whatsoever to an interest in land by virtue of a purported disposition by someone who himself has no title.

However, although there are no true exceptions to this rule, there are two important reservations to make.

10.5.5.2.   After-acquired property

The first is that, if someone who tried to sell something to which they had no title *does* later acquire title to it, equity will treat the purported sale as retrospectively effective. So, if I purport to sell Buckingham Palace to you for £1,000, then clearly you can acquire no interest in Buckingham Palace if I had no interest to start with. If, however, I subsequently do acquire title to Buckingham Palace, equity will require me to transfer that title to you, and until I do so will treat you as already entitled in equity (see further below).

10.5.5.3.   Interests by estoppel

The second reservation is more important in relation to the grant of derivative interests. If I purport to grant you, say, a lease or a mortgage of land to which I have no title, then again clearly I cannot confer on you any interest in the land which is effective against the true owner, or indeed against anyone else. However, as between ourselves, I will not be allowed to deny that the interest I purported to create does exist. To take again the Buckingham Palace example, I cannot by granting you a lease of Buckingham Palace give you any rights in Buckingham Palace which are enforceable against the Queen or against anyone else. I will, however, have created in you an interest which is enforceable against me – as against me, you have a tenancy by estoppel in Buckingham Palace. There are two reasons why this may be worth having. The first is the one given above: if the Queen does later transfer Buckingham Palace to me, your lease will automatically and retrospectively be validated (the estoppel will be 'fed'). The second, however, is that, even if that never happens, I will not be allowed to act as if you had no lease. This will be important if I have lesser rights in relation to Buckingham Palace, which are not sufficient to enable me to grant you a lease, but nevertheless are sufficient to enable me to give you some *de facto* use of it. This was the point which the court had to consider in *Bruton* v. *London & Quadrant Housing Trust* (discussed in Notes and Questions 17.5 below).

10.6. Legal and equitable title

A final general point to make about title is that not all titles to property interests are legal. There are some circumstances in which equity will treat a person as entitled to an interest even though in law he has no entitlement. In these circumstances, the interest that the person has is equitable, and so, necessarily, is his title.

Equitable titles, for the most part, can only be acquired by derivative acquisition. This is because the methods of acquiring title by original acquisition that we now recognise in this jurisdiction all evolved long before the emergence of equity, and, for one reason or another, equity has never intervened in this area to any significant extent. Consequently, titles acquired by taking possession of a thing, or by becoming the first-ever interest holder in a thing, have historically always been legal and, subject to one exception, this remains the case in all circumstances. The exception is where, as in our system of registration of title to interests in land, statute has made *legal* entitlement to an interest dependent on registration. When this applies even the title acquired by taking possession of a thing will be equitable unless and until the possessor registers it.

In the case of acquisition of titles by derivative acquisition, however, equity has had a significant effect on the basic common law rules. In the following extract from *Commercial Law*, Professor Goode explains how equitable entitlement arises:

> Equity, although not directly overriding the common law, effectively modified the strict rules of transfer, originally by acting on the conscience of the obligor and ordering him to perfect at law the transfer that he had undertaken to carry out, or the trust he had undertaken to observe, and later by treating as done that which ought to have been done. An agreement to transfer ownership, provided that it was of such a kind as to be enforceable by specific performance, was given effect in equity as if the transfer had already been executed, so that, while legal title remained in the intended transferor, beneficial ownership was held to vest immediately in the intended transferee. Similarly, equity gave effect to the trust by insisting that the transferee honour the condition upon which the property was transferred to him. Initially, this too was a purely personal obligation binding only on the trustee, but over time it was extended to cover purchasers with notice of the trust, donees (with or without notice) and also the trustee's heirs, personal representatives and creditors. Ultimately, it became established that a trust would bind anyone into whose hands the property passed other than a *bona fide* purchaser of the legal title for value without notice. Hence the

interest of the beneficiary under a trust, like that of a party to whom another had contracted to sell or mortgage property, started as a purely personal right against the trustee and later became converted into a full-blooded property interest; and when the object of the trust was ownership itself, as opposed to a limited interest, the beneficiary had now to be recognised as the beneficial owner.

Equitable title to property (whether land or goods) thus involves divided ownership, legal title being in A and beneficial ownership in B. When A holds the legal title primarily for the benefit of B, the relationship is that of trustee and beneficiary. But division of ownership may also occur without a trust relationship, namely, when A holds the legal title primarily for his own interest, as in the case of a mortgage. Divided ownership in one form or another is the essence of equitable title. If both legal and beneficial ownership are vested in the same person, there is no scope for equity to operate on the asset, and no separate equitable interest can be said to exist. One consequence of this is that the legal and beneficial owner cannot transfer a bare legal title while reserving to himself equitable ownership. If he wishes to produce this result, he must do it by way of transfer of his entire interest, followed by a charge or declaration of trust in his favour by the transferee. In other words, the equitable interest must be created by way of grant, not by way of exception or reservation. Another consequence is that equitable tracing rights are not available to the legal and beneficial owner. His claim rests on his legal ownership.

Though an equitable interest can be carved out of the legal title, the converse is not true. The holder of an equitable interest can transfer only an equitable interest. Hence equitable ownership can be acquired in any of the following ways:

(a) by an agreement to transfer a legal or equitable title;
(b) by a present transfer which is defective at law, e.g. for want of compliance with some legally requisite formality, such as an instrument by deed;
(c) by creation of a trust, either

    (i) by the intended transferor declaring himself to be a trustee for the intending transferee, or
    (ii) by transfer of the asset to a third party to hold as trustee for the intending transferee;

(a) by a purported present transfer of an after-acquired asset;
(b) by a transfer made by one whose title is purely equitable . . .

As in the case of legal ownership, it is necessary, when discussing ownership in equity, to distinguish interest and title, interest denoting the quantum of the right to the asset, title the strength of that right as against others. The range of interests that can exist in equity is considerably greater than the range of legal interests; for whereas almost every interest capable of subsisting as a legal estate or interest can equally subsist in equity, there are many interests which (through a combination of common law rules and statutory restrictions) can exist only in equity. These include future interests, life interests, remainders and executory interests, charges on goods and any mortgage of goods granted after and during the currency of a legal mortgage given by the same mortgagor.

Though the principle of relativity of title applies to equitable interests, it operates somewhat differently than in relation to legal interests. In the first place, an equitable right or interest can be acquired only by charge or assignment [except, of course where it arises by statute or operation of law], not by possession, though the delivery of possession may evidence an intention to make a transfer. Secondly, possession is itself a purely legal concept. Whereas there can be equitable ownership, there is no such thing as equitable possession ... Thirdly, an equitable interest is not as marketable as a defeasible legal interest, for it is on its face subject to a legal interest outstanding in another, and is liable to be overridden by a transfer of the legal interest to a *bona fide* purchaser for value without notice. Fourthly, whereas there can be only two concurrent legal interests in goods, there is no limit to the number of concurrent equitable interests that can subsist in goods.

In this passage, Professor Goode draws a distinction between those interests that can exist only as equitable interests and those that can be either legal or equitable. In this latter group, typically the equitable interest arises where a legal title holder intends to transfer or grant a legal estate or interest to the grantee but for one reason or another (essentially, examples (a) (b) and (d) given by Professor Goode) has not yet completed the process necessary to carry out that intention. When this happens, the intended transaction is effective in equity although not (or not yet) effective in law. It would therefore be logical to say that what the grantee has at this stage is an equitable title to the legal interest he is intended to get. However, legal terminology telescopes title and interest at this point, and what we say instead is that the grantee has at this stage an equitable *interest*. The fact that the entitlement is equitable makes the interest itself equitable (or means the same as saying that the interest itself is equitable). So, for example, if you hold a legal lease of land and you enter into a binding agreement to sell it to your cousin (Professor Goode's example (a)) or you purport to transfer it to her outright but by mistake use a transfer document which is not a deed (his example (b)), the legal title to the legal lease remains with you but your cousin is said to acquire an equitable lease (her title to it being necessarily equitable) rather than an equitable title to your legal lease. This is because of the operation of the rule in *Walsh* v. *Lonsdale*, which we consider further in Chapter 12.

As far as title is concerned, though, what it comes down to is that by legal title we mean the entitlement to a legal interest, whereas by equitable title we mean the entitlement to an equitable interest. Consequently, an enquiry into how equitable entitlement arises is essentially an enquiry into how equitable interests arise.

11

Acquiring title by possession

11.1. Introduction

When a person takes or retains possession of land or goods without the consent of the person entitled to them, three consequences follow. The first is that the person taking possession thereby acquires a title to an interest in the land or goods that is immediately effective against the whole world except those with a better right to possession. The second (modified but not removed altogether for registered land by the Land Registration Act 2002) is that the person who is dispossessed thereby acquires a right to recover possession (or, in the case of goods, a right to sue for damages and/or the return of the goods) which will be lost if not exercised within a limitation period. The third is that a title lost because not exercised within the limitation period is extinguished. It is not transferred to the usurper – the title the usurper acquired by taking possession in the first place simply becomes no longer subject to challenge from the person whose title is extinguished.

There are two distinct principles requiring justification here. We considered the justifications for the first principle – that possession, even if wrongfully taken, confers an entitlement protectable by law – in Chapter 7. In this chapter, we concentrate on the second principle – that those entitled to possession will be deprived of all entitlement without compensation merely as a result of neglecting to take action against usurpers in time. The justifications for this second principle deserve separate attention: what justifies the protection of possession against strangers may also, but need not necessarily, justify its protection against those with a better right. Before considering these justifications, however, it is necessary to appreciate how the system operates in this jurisdiction.

11.2. The operation of adverse possession rules

In both registered and unregistered land, the adverse possessor acquires title by taking possession. The process by which the paper owner's title is extinguished, however, now differs depending on whether the land is registered or unregistered.

11.2.1. Unregistered land

In *unregistered land* the paper owner's title is extinguished through the operation of the Limitation Act 1980. If the paper owner has taken no action to dispossess the adverse possessor within twelve years of the adverse possessor taking possession of the land, it loses its right to bring proceedings to evict the adverse possessor (section 15 of the Limitation Act 1980). The only action that will suffice is either evicting the adverse possessor or commencing proceeding against her. The twelve-year period runs from the moment that the adverse possessor takes possession, not from any earlier date (if any) when the paper owner moves out of possession (paragraph 1 of Schedule 1 to the Limitation Act 1980). Once the twelve year period has elapsed, the title of the paper owner is automatically extinguished (section 17 of the Limitation Act 1980). The twelve-year deadline is postponed if the paper owner can prove fraud, concealment or mistake, so that the twelve years do not start to run until the paper owner has discovered, or could with reasonable diligence have discovered, the fraud, concealment or mistake (section 32 of the Limitation Act 1980).

11.2.2. Registered land

In registered land the Limitation Act 1980 does not operate to extinguish either the paper owner's right to recover possession from the adverse possessor or the paper owner's title. Instead, the Land Registration Act 2002 has introduced a procedure whereby, after ten years of adverse possession, the adverse possessor may apply to become registered owner in place of the paper owner (paragraph 1 of Schedule 6 to the 2002 Act). The period of ten years was chosen in preference to twelve in anticipation of a general change in limitation periods recommended by the Law Commission in its report on limitation of actions (Law Commission, *Limitation of Actions* (Law Commission Report No. 270, 2001)). If the Land Registry is satisfied that the applicant does indeed have a *prima facie* case (paragraph 2 of Schedule 6) it must then notify the registered owner, who has sixty-five business days in which to object. If no objection is received by the end of that period, then the adverse possessor will be registered as owner and the paper owner will lose his title. If, however, the paper owner *does* object, he then has a further two years within which he can bring proceedings for possession to evict the adverse possessor. If he fails to do so within the two-year period, then the Land Registry will register the adverse possessor as owner and the paper owner will lose his title. Fuller details of the procedure, and an assessment of its likely effect, are given in Clarke, 'Use, Time and Entitlement' (Extract 11.4 below).

11.2.3. What counts as 'adverse' possession

In both registered and unregistered land, a claimant can only succeed if she can demonstrate that she has indeed been in possession for the requisite period. In the leading modern case on adverse possession, *J. A. Pye (Oxford) Ltd* v. *Graham* [2003] UKHL 30 (extracted at www.cambridge.org/propertylaw/), the House of Lords made it clear that the adjective 'adverse' does not impose any additional requirement on a person who claims to have been in adverse possession for these purposes. In earlier cases, it had been said that the claimant had to prove not only that she had taken, and continued to be in, possession, but that the possession was in some sense 'adverse' to that of the paper owner. This involved questioning the intentions of both the adverse possessor (Had she intended to acquire ownership?) and the paper owner (Had the adverse possessor's actions interfered with his use of and intentions towards the land?). Slade J examined this approach in *Powell* v. *McFarlane*, discussed in Chapter 7, where an additional difficulty facing Mr Powell was that, however extensive his use of the field, it never interfered with McFarlane's present use of the property (because he had no present use for it) nor did it interfere with McFarlane's future plans for it. Slade J concluded that this prevented Mr Powell's possession from being 'adverse'. The effect of this decision on this particular point was reversed by paragraph 8(4) of Schedule 1, Part I, to the Limitation Act 1980, but nevertheless the argument resurfaced in a modified form. In this modified form attention was focused on the requirement of intention on the part of the intruder, and it was said that the intruder could not establish the requisite *animus possidendi* unless he could prove an intention to exclude the true owner *for all time*: it was not sufficient merely to show a continuing intention to exclude the paper owner for the time being. In practice, such a requirement is as insurmountable a hurdle for an adverse possessor as the implied licence doctrine. This is because of the court's insistence (emphasised by Slade J in *Powell* v. *McFarlane*) first that the intruder's intention must be inferred solely from what he did rather than from what he said, and, secondly, that the intention must be unequivocally manifested. If you look only at what the intruder does, even the most absolute assumption of physical control of land (such as locking it up and keeping the only key) is equally compatible with an intention to exclude the owner unless and until his future plans come to fruition as it is with an intention to exclude him for all time. The Court of Appeal faced up to this argument in *Buckinghamshire County Council* v. *Moran* [1990] Ch 623, and decisively rejected it, but not, however, without raising some other problems.

However, in *J. A. Pye (Oxford) Ltd* v. *Graham*, the House of Lords rejected all these arguments. Lord Browne-Wilkinson emphasised that the only question is whether the squatter has been in possession in the ordinary sense (paragraph 35). As he said:

> To be pedantic the problem [of definition] could be avoided by saying there are two elements necessary for legal possession:
>
> 1. A sufficient degree of physical custody and control ('factual possession');
> 2. An intention to exercise such custody and control on one's own behalf and for one's own benefit ('intention to possess').
>
> What is crucial to understand is that, without the requisite intention, in law there can be no possession (paragraph 40).

He also emphasised (at paragraph 45) that the intention of the owner is irrelevant, and, while Lord Hope and Lord Hutton disagreed with this, both Lord Bingham and Lord Mackay expressed agreement with Lord Browne-Wilkinson, so this can be taken to be the decisive majority view.

It was also confirmed that the intention necessary on the part of the adverse possessor is the intention to *possess* not the intention to *own*: as Lord Browne-Wilkinson said, to suggest otherwise is 'heretical and wrong' (paragraph 45).

Consistently with this, it has been held that the paper owner's knowledge of the adverse possession is irrelevant – time begins to run as soon as adverse possession is taken, whether or not the paper owner is aware of it and even if he does not realise that he is entitled to object. So, for example, in the Court of Appeal decision in *Palfrey* v. *Palfrey* (1974) 229 EG 1593, the paper owner's title was extinguished even though he did not realise until long after the expiry of the limitation period that he had any interest whatsoever in the property (many years earlier, without telling him or anyone else, his grandfather had executed a deed transferring title to him). The position would, however, be different if fraud, concealment or mistake led to the paper owner being unaware of the adverse possession, as noted above.

It also follows that you can be in adverse possession even if you mistakenly believe you are the true owner. It had been accepted by the first-instance judge in *Hughes* v. *Cork* that in such a case you would never be in adverse possession because you never had an intention to exclude the paper owner, but this was firmly rejected by the Court of Appeal ([1994] EGCS 25) where Saville LJ exposed the fallacy in the argument:

> The learned Judge appears to have held that it is impossible for someone who believes himself to be the true owner to acquire title by adverse possession since such a person cannot, ex-hypothesi, have an intention to exclude or oust the true owner. If this were the law then only those who knew they were trespassing, that is to say doing something illegal, could acquire such a title, while those who did not realise that they were doing anything wrong would acquire no rights at all. I can see no reason why, as a matter of justice or common sense, the former but not the latter should be able to acquire title in this way. What the law requires is factual possession i.e. an exclusive dealing with the land as an occupying owner might be expected to deal with it, together with a manifested intention to treat the land as belonging to the possessor to the exclusion of everyone else.
>
> Obviously, if the possessor knows or believes someone else has the paper title to the land he must intend to exclude that person along with everyone else. But in the absence of such knowledge or belief it is in my judgment sufficient ... simply to establish a manifest intention to exclude everyone.

11.2.4.   Effect on third party interests

When someone takes possession of land the interest they acquire title to is a fee simple estate in the land. At first sight, it might seem that, since the paper owner's title is never transferred to the adverse possessor, there is no reason why derivative interests carved out of the paper owner's interest (for example, easements, covenants and mortgages) should be enforceable against the adverse possessor. However, this pushes the metaphor of property interests as bundles of rights too far. While in one sense third party rights in land are rights taken out of the grantor's bundle of rights, they are nevertheless rights in the *land* enforceable against the whole world (subject to rules about registration or *bona fide* purchasers). It therefore follows that, while an adverse possessor does not take over the paper owner's interest, nevertheless rights in the land enforceable against the paper owner will also be enforceable against the adverse possessor, just as they would be against anyone else who acquires an interest in the land without paying for it (i.e. other volunteers): see the decision of the Court of Appeal in *Re Nisbet and Potts' Contract* [1906] 1 Ch 386, and also, for a modern application of the principle, *Carroll* v. *Manek* (2000) 79 P&CR 173 (person acquiring title to a hotel in Harrow-on-the Hill by adverse possession held to take subject to the mortgage over it granted to a bank by the paper owner before the paper owner's title was extinguished).

11.3.   Why established possession should defeat the paper owner

Having sketched out how the system works, we can now return to the question of justification. In Chapter 4, we considered why possession should give rise to entitlement by looking at why the law protects the first person to take possession of a thing against all intruders. As we saw there, a variety of moral, social and economic arguments can be put in support of this basic principle that the law protects possessors against intruders. As long as we are considering only the rival claims of possessors and intruders, these arguments apply with equal force whether the possessor took possession lawfully or unlawfully. In this chapter, however, we want to consider how far these arguments take us when we are faced with the rival claims of the unlawful possessor and the 'true' owner who has failed to assert his entitlement over a long period of time.

In Extract 11.1 below, Richard Epstein sees the reconciliation of these rival claims as a balancing exercise, with the scales tipping over in favour of the possessor largely because of the practical problems of proof in adjudicating stale claims. He makes the point that it is not just that stale claims are difficult to adjudicate: if adjudicated, they are likely to be decided wrongly because poor evidence creates a bias in favour of the party with the weaker case, in much the same way as the weaker tennis player is favoured by a poor quality tennis court. John Stuart Mill points out another problem with stale claims: if long-dispossessed rightful owners can bring them, so too can spurious claimants, and their chances of succeeding or at least putting the rightful possessor to considerable trouble increase as the evidence grows scantier with time:

> According to the fundamental idea of property, indeed, nothing ought to be treated as such, which has been acquired by force or fraud, or appropriated in ignorance of a

prior title vested in some other person; but it is necessary to the security of rightful possessors, that they should not be molested by charges of wrongful acquisition, when by the lapse of time witnesses must have perished or been lost sight of, and the real character of the transaction can no longer be cleared up. Possession which has not been legally questioned within a moderate number of years, ought to be, as by the laws of all nations it is, a complete title. Even when the acquisition was wrongful, the dispossession, after a generation has elapsed, of the probably *bona fide* possessors, by the revival of a claim which had been long dormant, would generally be a greater injustice, and almost always a greater private and public mischief, than leaving the original wrong without atonement. It may seem hard that a claim, originally just, should be defeated by mere lapse of time; but there is a time after which (even looking at the individual case, and without regard to the general effect on the security of possessors), the balance of hardship turns the other way. With the injustices of men, as with the convulsions and disasters of nature, the longer they remain unrepaired, the greater become the obstacles to repairing them, arising from the aftergrowths which would have to be torn up or broken through. In no human transactions, not even in the simplest and clearest, does it follow that a thing is fit to be done now, because it was fit to be done sixty years ago. It is scarcely needful to remark, that these reasons for not disturbing acts of injustice of old date, cannot apply to unjust systems or institutions; since a bad law or usage is not one bad act, in the remote past, but a perpetual repetition of bad acts, as long as the law or usage lasts. (John Stuart Mill, *Principles of Political Economy*, Book II, Chapter II, section 2)

However, as Mill says, this is not just a question of practicalities. He and others argue that there comes a point when possession has been established for such a long period that it would be unjust to interfere with it, even in favour of someone who can prove that it was wrongly taken from them or their predecessors in the first place. For some commentators such as Radin, this is because of the importance of the bond between persons and possession that we looked at in Chapter 4. In her article, 'Time, Possession, and Alienation' (Extract 11.2 below), she argues that this justifies not only rewarding the first taker, but also protecting her against even the 'true' owner once the bond between true owner and possessions has been slackened by time to the point where it is now weaker than the bond that has been built up between the wrongful taker and the possessions. She also expresses doubts about the coherence of Epstein's stance, and tests Epstein's arguments, and the general justification for allowing acquisition of title by adverse possession, by viewing them from first Lockean, then utilitarian, and then Hegelian standpoints.

Radin points out the Lockean arguments (not necessarily put by or even acceptable to Locke himself) for favouring those who have made use of a thing for a long period over those who have allowed it to stand idle, and economic efficiency arguments can point the same way as well. In Extract 11.3 below, Carol Rose notes these arguments but suggests that the law might alternatively be interpreted as one that penalises those who fail to maintain clear communications of their entitlements, favouring instead those who are allowed, through the true owner's neglect, to put out signals of ownership to the rest of the world.

11.4. Adverse possession and registration

If titles to property interests are registered, is adverse possession still justifiable? As we see in Chapter 15, the process of registering all titles to land is now nearing completion in this country. Does this make adverse possession law redundant? As Rose points out, registration takes over the communication role from possession, and does so more clearly and unequivocally. It also takes over possession's role as title prover, and, as Dockray has demonstrated in his article, 'Why Do We Need Adverse Possession?', the early development of adverse possession in this jurisdiction was strongly influenced by its importance in the pre-registration conveyancing system.

However, this does not touch the other rationales for adverse possession put forward above, and, even in relation to its functions of proving title and communicating claims, it may be that possession can never be wholly replaced by registration: see the comment made by Merrill below in response to Epstein, and also the article by Clarke, 'Use, Time and Entitlement' (Extract 11.4 below). A joint Law Commission and Land Registry report on the reform of land registration, *Land Registration for the Twenty-First Century: A Conveyancing Revolution* (Law Commission Report No. 271, 2001) expressed the strong view that it was wrong in principle that an owner should ever lose title to an adverse possessor, and that this was a necessary evil in an unregistered land system because it facilitated unregistered conveyancing, but was no longer justifiable in registered land. As a consequence of the recommendations made in the report, the Land Registration Act 2002 has made significant changes to the way adverse possession law operates in relation to registered land in this country, as we see below.

The arguments put forward in the Law Commission's report are set out in Clarke's article (Extract 11.4 below). In outline, it is asserted in the report that allowing the true owner's title to be extinguished as against an adverse possessor is 'at least in some cases, tantamount to theft' and has given rise to 'growing public disquiet'. The report gives as principal support for both assertions the *dictum* of Neuberger J in *J. A. Pye (Oxford) Ltd* v. *Graham* [2002] Ch 676, 710 quoted by Clarke, without, however, making any reference to the very different views expressed by the Court of Appeal in the same case. In the Court of Appeal it had been argued on behalf of the true owner that the English law which allows the title of the true owner to be extinguished in favour of an adverse possessor contravenes Article 1 of the First Protocol to the European Convention on Human Rights, by depriving the owner of his possessions or interfering with his peaceful enjoyment of them. This was rejected decisively by the Court of Appeal: as Mummery LJ said ([2001] EWCA Civ 117):

> [The provisions of the Limitation Act 1980 extinguishing the title of the paper owner] do not deprive a person of his possessions or interfere with his peaceful enjoyment of them. They deprive a person of his right of access to the courts for the purpose of

recovering property if he has delayed the institution of his legal proceedings for 12 years or more after he has been dispossessed of his land by another person who has been in adverse possession of it for at least that period. The extinction of the title of the claimant in those circumstances is not a deprivation of possessions or a confiscatory measure for which the payment of compensation would be appropriate: it is simply a logical and pragmatic consequence of the barring of his right to bring an action after the expiration of the limitation period.

Even if, contrary to my view, that Convention right potentially impinges on the relevant provisions of the 1980 Act, those provisions are conditions provided for by law and are 'in the public interest' within the meaning of article 1. Such conditions are reasonably required to avoid the real risk of injustice in the adjudication of stale claims, to ensure certainty of title and to promote social stability by the protection of the established and peaceable possession of property from the resurrection of old claims. The conditions provided in the 1980 Act are not disproportionate; the period allowed for the bringing of proceedings is reasonable; the conditions are not discriminatory; and they are not impossible or so excessively difficult to comply with as to render ineffective the exercise of the legal right of a person who is entitled to the peaceful enjoyment of his possessions to recover them from another person who is alleged to have wrongfully deprived him of them.'

The joint Law Commission and Land Registry report, however, demonstrates a fundamentally different approach. It categorises the typical adverse possessor as a 'landowner with an eye to the main chance who encroaches on his or her neighbour's land'. As pointed out by Clarke in Extract 11.4 below, this is not an accurate description of the adverse possessors we see in English reported decisions: as one might expect, they fall very much within the three categories that Radin identifies (see Extract 11.2 below concerning the role of good faith). However, the main thrust of the report is, first, that the stale claims justification is not applicable in registered land, and, secondly, that allowing adverse possessors to acquire registered title is incompatible with the principle of indefeasibility of title. For the reasons given by Clarke in Extract 11.4 below, neither of these arguments is wholly convincing.

11.5.   Good faith and the adverse possessor

One of the innovations introduced by the Land Registration Act 2002 is an attempt to differentiate between 'good faith' and 'bad faith' adverse possessors. The way in which this is done, and the likely effect of the provisions, is considered by Clarke in Extract 11.4 below, but it should be noted that otherwise, as a matter of law, it is settled that 'bad faith' is not a bar to an adverse possession claim in English law. Whether 'bad faith' on the part of the adverse possessor *should* be relevant is a matter of controversy. Many of the justifications for adverse possession we look at below apply with equal force whether possession was taken in good faith or in bad faith, and it has been strongly argued that the adverse possessor's state of mind *ought* to be irrelevant in this context: see in particular Goodman, 'Adverse Possession of Land – Morality and Motive'. However, as Radin points out in 'Time, Possession, and Alienation', pp. 746–50, it does rather depend on which rationale for adverse possession you consider predominant. After distinguishing three different paradigms of adverse possession case – the 'squatters' case, where aggressive trespassers take something they know does not belong to them, the 'color of title' case, where the possessor mistakenly believed she was entitled, and the 'boundaries' case, where the boundary line observed in practice by neighbours does not correspond with what their documents say, and eventually one of them litigates to correct the discrepancy – Radin considers the utilitarian, personhood and Lockean stances on the required state of mind of the adverse possessor:

1. UTILITARIANISM

The utilitarian argument is often stated as requiring simply that titles must be cleared to facilitate transactions now (i.e. for the immediate future). In this form, at least, the utilitarian argument seems to favor the objective standard making state of mind evidence irrelevant. State of mind evidence is one more cost of litigation, and presumably will result in fewer titles being cleared.

Utilitarianism can countenance all three paradigms, and does not privilege the 'color of title' case over the case of the aggressive, productive trespasser. But the 'boundary' case seems unclear. Once the discrepancy between the record books and the lived boundaries is discovered, does it maximize the gain for the system as a whole to change the records to reflect the lived boundaries or to change the lived boundaries to correspond with the records? . . .

2. PERSONHOOD

. . . Personality theory might seem to favor an explicit 'good faith' standard on the issue of the adverse possessor's state of mind, because it is unclear how one's personhood can become bound up with ownership of something unless she thinks she owns it. This may be its salient applicable intuition to modern law. If one of the things adverse possession does is protect developed expectations, in the sense of bonds between persons and things, it is hard to see how these bonds can be as strong in the case of people who know the object is not theirs. On the other hand, it seems Hegel contemplated that binding yourself to an object you know is not yours will ultimately make it yours. Still, it seems personality theory is more comfortable with the 'color of title' case than with 'squatters'. In the 'boundary' case, it would recommend, more clearly than would utilitarianism, that the boundaries as they are lived should after a while supersede the boundaries on paper . . .

3. LOCKEAN ENTITLEMENT

As already discussed, the pure Lockean theory does not countenance adverse possession. But perhaps it colors the theory of adverse possession anyway by lending some sympathy to 'squatters'. After all, if property is acquired from the common by a nonowner simply by taking it and using it, can we not sympathize with someone who does likewise with owned but unused property, especially if she does not know it is owned?

If 'bad faith' is to be taken into account, it might be desirable to do so in some way other than by making it an absolute bar to a claim. For example, Epstein, 'Past and Future: The Temporal Dimension in the Law of Property', pp. 685–9, has suggested that there could be a longer limitation period for bad faith takers. This, he argues, would both respect what he sees as the basic intuition that bad faith takers ought to be penalised, and promote finality, and it would remain justifiable on utilitarian grounds:

> Persons who engage in deliberate wrongs constitute a greater threat than those who make innocent errors or are simply negligent: there is a greater danger that intentional wrongdoers will do it all again. They are both bad people in the individual cases and a menace in the future, so in this context deterrence and retribution move hand in hand.

However, Radin has questioned the utilitarian good sense of this:

> But if the 'wrongdoers' are productive and the title holders are passive, are the 'wrongdoers' so wrong in the utilitarian sense? And, to carve out a subset of 'bad faith' cases makes evidence of 'bad faith' relevant in every case. This is a cost to the system and will fail to clear some titles where an accusation of 'bad faith' is wrongly made to stick. (Radin, 'Time, Possession, and Alienation', p. 747, n. 21)

Rather more promisingly, it has been suggested that those who lose their titles through a bad faith dispossession should be entitled to damages from the dispossessor, a suggestion that utilises Calabresi and Melamed's distinction (discussed in Chapter 6 above) between property rules and liability rules (Calabresi and Melamed, 'Property Rules, Liability Rules and Inalienability', Extract 6.8 above). This suggestion was made by Merrill in 'Property Rules, Liability Rules, and Adverse Possession', and summarised as follows:

> Helmholz's study totally convinced me that courts give extraordinary significance to their intuitions about whether or not the act of original entry was taken in good faith or bad faith. The legal doctrine, with the exception of a few states . . . does not take this fact into account. What you have is a very unfortunate phenomenon of courts manipulating a doctrine that does not explicitly take good faith and bad faith into account to reach results that very much follow a pattern that the good faith possessor obtains title by adverse possession and the bad faith possessor does not. This situation creates immense amounts of tension and uncertainty because the doctrine says one thing and the courts come up with a different set of outcomes and results.
>
> What I would like to suggest . . . is that you bifurcate the question of title and the question of treatment of the good faith and bad faith possessor. I suggest that we ignore the question of good faith and bad faith for adverse possession purposes – we would continue to transfer title to the bad faith possessor after the statute of limitations has run – but then grant an independent action for indemnification to the true

owner. If the true owner could show that the original entry was taken in bad faith, the true owner would obtain damages from the bad faith possessor equal to the fair market value of the property at the time of the original entry. Essentially, you would have a system of liability rules for bad faith possessors, and a system of property rules to adjudicate the question of title. Given my views about the important role adverse possession plays in facilitating real property transactions, I would not, absent this problem, advocate using liability rules here. But since we do have the problem of the bad faith possessor, and we see that the courts are overwhelmingly inclined to give that significance, it would be better as kind of a second best solution to let courts do justice at the stage of remedy by awarding damages against the bad faith possessor than struggling to ignore the issue for purposes of determining title.'

Extract 11.1   Richard A. Epstein, 'Past and Future: The Temporal Dimension in the Law of Property' (1986) 64 *Washington University Law Quarterly* 667

The major cost associated with the passage of time is uncertainty. For risk-averse individuals, that uncertainty creates a cost that greater certainty could reduce. In addition, any increase of uncertainty increases the scope of the discretion lodged in both public and private hands. That discretion spurs private litigation that generates high administrative costs and high error rates. The passage of time therefore creates pressures, both public and private, to take steps to ensure that legal rights and duties do not depend on events that are remote from the present, either past or future. These practical demands often clash with the strict principles of corrective justice, where the passage of time is of no particular consequence in determining the relative rights and duties of all persons. As an abstract principle each violation of individual rights appears to require full redress on a case-by-case basis. The ungainly structure of legal doctrine is sometimes explained by the difficult task of reconciling these two inconsistent tendencies in a wide range of specific contexts . . .

A. FIRST POSSESSION: PRIOR IN TIME IS HIGHER IN RIGHT

Temporal issues arise with evident urgency in the law of real property. Land itself lasts forever, and the improvements upon it can last for a very long time. The durability of the asset means that no one person can consume it in a lifetime, so that any legal relations with respect to land will of necessity involve a large number of persons over a long period of time. How then are these relationships to be sorted out?

[He then considers the reasons why the law protects first possessors: see Extract 4.1 above.]

At a normative level, the first possession rule precludes totally the acquisition of title by adverse possession. If no person is able to profit by his own wrong, then acts of adverse possession are by definition out of bounds, are flatly illegal, whether done by private parties or by the state.

Original acquisition starts the process by creating rights against the world. Within a framework of corrective justice, the passage of time, without more, has no influence upon the rights or duties of the parties to any dispute. Time is a wholly neutral factor, as the system operates upon the assumption that individual rights and duties are a function solely of individual actions, to which personal credit or responsibility can be assigned. Thereafter, only voluntary acts of transfer (including transfer at death) can change the status of the legal title, while only acts of aggression (or deceit) by outsiders can give owners tort remedies against strangers.

In *Anarchy, State and Utopia*, Robert Nozick offers a historical account of justice, which is consistent with his theoretical perspective, but which is in no way sensitive to questions of temporal degree: rights are strictly determined by temporal priority. The older the title, the better the title – period. Sequence is everything; the magnitude of the interval is nothing.

Nozick's view of the first possession rule, like his view of entitlements generally, closely follows the pattern of common law rules of entitlements. Yet his analysis, as a species of ideal theory, fails to recognize that no system of justice works without frictions. These frictions generate a set of counterprinciples that are as important as the basic entitlements they limit. As a matter of high principle, what comes first is best; as a matter of evidence and proof, however, what comes last is more reliable and certain. As a result, any operating legal system responds to a powerful pressure to make everything turn on events that lie in or close to the present. Time dims recollections and allows people to forget or to suppress unpleasant evidence. It does not take a profound knowledge of human cognition or motivation to conclude that all evidence decays with time. One could quarrel over rate of decay. The decay function may or may not be linear, but it surely increases monotonically with time, and for many types of evidence it is probably steep. What should be done to counter the problem?

B. ADVERSE POSSESSION

1. Tension between principle and proof

The conflict between principle and proof manifests itself in the law of adverse possession. That body of law could scarcely arise in a world of zero transaction costs, for the true owner could always put the adverse possessor out instantly and regain possession of the land. When transaction costs are zero the wrongdoer will always be identified, and litigation will be error free. But practical frictions can dominate the system and shape its legal rules. Wrongs are not always instantly uncovered; it takes money to identify a wrongdoer, and more money to bring a suit, which could be erroneously decided. As time passes, it is more likely that the original or subsequent title will be split (by deed, and especially by will) among a large number of individuals, making management of a suit clumsy and awkward. With time, memories fade and witnesses die: no one can recall who did what to whom. Time forces a greater reliance upon documentary evidence, and even that may be forged, lost, altered or destroyed ...

What about the claim of the original owner against the adverse possessor? Here the pragmatic questions of proof are in systematic tension with the remorseless doctrines of original acquisition. In this situation, it is quite possible that the benefit of making the right determination decreases with time, given the way in which it disrupts present expectations of an adverse possessor who may well have improved or developed the land. Yet, even if the benefits of restoring the original owner remain roughly constant over time, the basic point remains unchanged. The costs of making that determination continue to mount over time, so that at some point the lines cross, so that it ceases to be worthwhile to determine the facts on which an original and remote claim of right rests.

To be sure, one could try to compromise the difference by imposing new or heavier burdens of proof upon the plaintiff, or by making certain types of evidence (e.g. a purported deed to the property) necessary to establish the claim. Yet these inter-mediate solutions, taken by themselves, are defective. The passage of time does not work to the equal disadvantage of both sides. Indeed, to say that the change of time-frame has no effect at all on the outcome is a contradiction in terms. To the contrary, the passage of time, like any other reduction in the quality of evidence, produces a systematic bias for the weaker side.

To see the point, one can think of a tennis match between two professionals. Normally, one expects the better player to win. Yet, if the game is played on a rough surface, an element of randomness is introduced into the contest, shifting the odds back towards even, which thus works systematically in favor of the inferior player. In the extreme case (for instance, where the game is played in a junkyard or on the side of a cliff), the random elements completely dominate the skill elements; and the results of the game have little correlation to the players' skills. Litigation is like that. The passage of time tends to help the party with the weaker case by giving greater prominence to the random elements of the case. The moving party sues because there is some scrap of evidence that supports the claim, while all evidence on the other side is lost or misinterpreted. To avoid these situations, at some point it becomes necessary to end litigation, not to redefine its parameters. Hence the case for the statutes of limitations that lie at the core of the modern judicial doctrines of adverse possession.

The statute of limitations should be evaluated from the same institutional perspec-tive that is brought to the first possession rule. The key value of the rule does not derive from the way it handles doubtful cases at the margin. It stems from the way in which the well-crafted statute of limitations shapes the primary conduct of private parties, thus preventing certain kinds of cases from being litigated at all. The point is not novel and was well brought out over sixty-five years ago by Ballantine [in his article, 'Title by Adverse Possession'] who in two brief paragraphs was able to articulate the tension between the search for perfect justice in a world of imperfect institutions:

> Title by adverse possession sounds, at first blush, like title by theft or robbery, a primitive method of acquiring land without paying for it. When the novice is told that by the weight of authority not even good faith is a requisite, the doctrine apparently affords an anomalous instance of maturing a wrong into a right con-trary to one of the most fundamental axioms of the law. 'For true it is, that neither fraud nor might can make a title where there wanteth right.'
>
> The policy of statutes of limitation is something not always clearly appreciated. Dean Ames, in contrasting prescription in the civil law with adverse possession in our law, remarks: 'English lawyers regard not the merit of the possessor, but the demerit of the one out of possession.' It has been suggested, on the other hand, that the policy is to reward those using the land in a way beneficial to the community. This takes too much account of the individual case. The statute has not for its object

to reward the diligent trespasser for his wrong nor yet to penalize the negligent and dormant owner for sleeping upon his rights; the great purpose is automatically to quiet all titles which are openly and consistently asserted, to provide proof of meritorious titles, and correct errors in conveyancing.

Ballantine is right to regard the choice between merit and demerit theories as a second order problem. He is also right on the institutional significance of statutes of limitations. The statute spares the rightful owner the costs of litigation that might otherwise be needed to establish title. The statute protects against claims that are most potent in principle, but most dubious in fact. It thus enhances the marketability of title by shortening the period during which prospective purchasers and lenders (both noted for their squeamishness) need examine the state of the title. That squeamishness arises from the enormous practical difference between a perfect title and a flawed one, however small the flaw. There is a real discontinuity at the origin, which is not replicated elsewhere in the distribution. *Any* doubt about the status of the title requires that everyone must shift from the deterministic to the probabilistic mode. Someone must estimate the extent of the risk, which is itself no trivial problem. Small risks are hard to measure, and they may provide telltale evidence of major weakness in the title. The minimum loss to uncertainty therefore is not the expected value of the defect in the title, but some threshold level of the legal and business expenses necessary to estimate it. These costs are greatest where the clouds on the title are oldest.

The statute of limitations generally avoids these title-clearing costs. Most critically it avoids them where title is in fact impeccable. The statute induces individuals to bring suit early, when it is more likely to be manageable, and the outcome correct. So viewed, protection of the guilty is not an end in itself, but the inevitable and necessary price paid in discharging the primary function of protecting those with proper title. [As Ballantine said, probably quoting Frederick Pollock]: 'It is better to favor some unjust than to vex many just occupiers.' What drives the statute is the need to control high administrative error and transactions costs. The statute's effectiveness would be wholly undermined if it were used to bar only invalid claims, for then the statute would bar claims only after they are litigated, when it is too late. The doctrine of adverse possession accepts the principle, prior in time is higher in right; but it marries this principle to a procedural system that makes it unnecessary to run the full course in order to establish the needed temporal priority. The contradiction between corrective justice and statutes of limitations is overcome because the error rate, when measured against the ideal of a rule of first possession, is lower with the statute of limitations than it is without it.

The theoretical justification for the general statute can, I think, be neatly explained by an analogy to the general principles of forced exchanges that dominate the law of eminent domain. The system of corrective justice provides all individuals with a framework of rights based upon the rules of first possession and voluntary subsequent transfer. The question is whether the removal of some of these rights through general rule can be justified on the ground that the shift in entitlement increases the overall utility of each individual, roughly in proportion to his original holdings. With statutes of limitations generally, it is difficult to think of any important component of subjective value that would require distinguishing between wealth and utility in estimating the value in prior entitlements. While there are subjective values in the ownership of land, they can be fully protected by bringing timely suit. The question with statutes of limitations, as with other general rules, reduces therefore to this question: is the protection that each party is afforded *ex ante* by a statute of limitations worth more than the right of action that he might otherwise possess?

The argument in favor of statutes of limitations in the abstract is very simple. The reduction in error, administrative and transaction costs brings about a gain that can be shared by all parties to the system. In a world where everyone has an equal probability of being plaintiff or defendant, the shift in the laws should work to universal advantage. In a world in which some persons have a systematic bias to take the property of others, the question is less clear cut, for scoundrels may get (net) benefit from the limitations period. But, even here the overall gains from the statute seem so large that a substantial portion must inure to everyone subject to the rules in question. Everyone shares, for example, in the reduction in the administrative costs of operating the system; and they retain their full rights of suit where these have their greatest value. Those individuals who break the rules most frequently can be subject to additional sanctions, whether criminal penalties or punitive damages, within the limitation period to equalize the overall gains.

The real questions are not whether a statute of limitations in the round works some Pareto superior move. Instead, the harder question is one of fine tuning. What is the best way to structure the rules of adverse possession in order to maximize the general gain? Here in principle the usual caveats apply. One wants to consider this question, *ex ante*, both for the individual and for the aggregate. But as all players operate pretty much behind the veil of ignorance, with adverse possession it is possible to indulge a useful simplification not possible in many other contexts. The distributional question is not key. Any gain to the whole will maximize the gain to each of the parts.

Notes and Questions 11.1

1. Epstein seems to have land mainly in mind when he talks about the utilitarian benefits of adverse possession. Do his arguments apply with equal force to title to goods?

2. There are other utilitarian arguments for adverse possession, in addition to those given by Epstein. In response to Epstein's paper, Merrill (in 'Symposium', p. 813) lists some of them. In particular, he points out the importance of reliance, on the part of both the adverse possessor and third parties. In the case of the former, he says: 'We want at some point in time to be able to encourage people to invest and make improvements on their property even if they have questionable title to it. Adverse possession strengthens those expectation interests or gives some substance to them.' In the case of third party reliance, he makes the important point that we noted in Chapter 4: even when

there is a system of registration of titles to property interests in operation some third parties still have to rely on apparent ownership.

3. Ellickson, like Radin in the extract below, points out the incongruity of a libertarian – someone who believes that the law should allow individuals to pursue their own ends, as they individually define them, with a minimum of state interference – supporting adverse possession, which requires that the interest of the original owner should be sacrificed for the greater good of others: 'Libertarian principles make the expropriation of property without compensation highly suspect. Moreover, adverse possession in effect makes a landowner police against intruders. Libertarians usually bridle at the legal creation of affirmative obligations to act' (Ellickson, 'Adverse Possession and Perpetuities Law', p. 725). Would this criticism be met by a requirement that the adverse possessor (or perhaps the state?) should pay compensation to the owner whose title had been extinguished?

Extract 11.2   Margaret Jane Radin, 'Time, Possession, and Alienation' (1986) 64 *Washington University Law Quarterly* 739

I. TIME AND PROPERTY THEORY

A. Lockean entitlement

. . . [T]he temporal dimension is irrelevant to the Lockean theory of property [in that], at least in its classic form, it is only a theory of just acquisition, concerning itself only with the moment in which entitlements come into being. Entitlements come into being through mixing one's labor with an unowned object, or, in Epstein's version, through occupancy or first possession of an unowned object, and thereby are fixed forever. Thus, one moment in time is relevant to entitlement, the moment when non-property becomes property; but the temporal dimension of human affairs, our situation in an ongoing stream of time, is irrelevant.

The term 'just acquisition' belongs to the prominent neo-Lockean, Robert Nozick, who theorizes that justice in holdings ideally consists of whatever results from just acquisition and sequences of just transfers. This corresponds to saying that a holding is just if a valid chain of title and a valid root of title (in original acquisition out of the common) can both be shown. Here a temporal element enters in; the chain of title extends in time from original acquisition to today. Thus, in neo-Lockean theory, there is a temporal element connected with just transfer, but not with initial entitlement itself.

In a non-ideal world, there are sometimes rip-offs and frauds instead of just transfers. This makes necessary a third kind of theory in addition to a theory of just acquisition and a theory of just transfer; namely, a corrective justice theory, which Nozick calls a theory of rectification. Because Nozick is engaged mainly in ideal theory, he does not develop a theory of rectification. Whether a neo-Lockean theory of corrective justice would contain temporal elements is therefore unclear, but it seems, at least, that a Nozickian theory of corrective justice would not allow time to diminish the force of old harms. In Neo-Lockean ideal libertarian justice there seems to be no statute of repose [i.e. statute of limitations]. Once the chain is tainted somewhere between original acquisition and today, corrective justice seems to require that titles be redistributed to undo the effect of the oppression or fraud, no matter how long ago. To say less than this would undermine the absolute nature of the Lockean rights of property acquisition and free contract.

B. Utilitarianism

Utilitarian theory is more directly time-bound. In act-utilitarianism the preferred or justified course of action is to maximize welfare (or utility, or whatever is the maximand) right now. But human interactions and our environment are dynamic, so as time moves on the preferred or justified course of action changes. Furthermore, in determining the preferred course of action the future is what governs. To judge an act by its consequences for utility is, from the standpoint of the time of making the decision, to rest rightness on prediction.

In rule-utilitarianism, the preferred or justified course of action is to maximize welfare (or whatever) in 'the long run' in contradistinction to right now. Hence, the dynamic nature of human affairs is more directly implicated in the preferred course of action. One consequence of this is that in rule-utilitarianism we are always cognizant of systemic concerns: How will any given choice affect the entire system of entitlements and expectations as it produces and maintains welfare over time? Thus, time is embedded at the heart of rule-utilitarianism. Indeed, its temporal heart harbors its deepest puzzles. How long is the long run? Does it include future generations? If so, how do we attribute utility (or whatever) to them, and how do we compare it with the utility of people alive today? Is the utility of people who are not alive today but were alive yesterday of any relevance? If so, at what point does the utility of the dead cease to count? In order to maximize utility, should we (in light of the principle of decreasing marginal utility) maximize population until everyone is at a bare subsistence level? And so forth.

C. Property and personhood

Time is also at the heart of the personality theory, but in a different way. In the Hegelian theory, ownership is accomplished by placing one's will into an object. A modern extrapolation of this idea suggests that the claim to an owned object grows stronger as, over time, the holder becomes bound up with the object. Conversely, the claim to an object grows weaker as the will (or personhood) is withdrawn. In other words, in personality theory the strength of property claims is itself dynamic because over time the bond between persons and objects can wax and wane.

Because personality theory concerns individual rights and not general welfare, it does not harbor the same temporal puzzles as rule-utilitarianism. Since it places entitlement in the present state of the relationship between person and object and not in some aboriginal appropriation, it also avoids the major problem of the Lockean individual rights theory. Personality theory must struggle instead with how to construe the notion of personhood and the notion of relationships between persons and objects. In coherence and contextualist philosophical views, these central notions themselves are developing through history; that is, they have a temporal dimension.

II. ADVERSE POSSESSION

In this section, I shall comment on two aspects of Epstein's treatment of adverse possession, suggesting that his lack of clear focus on the varying role of the temporal element in the different theories of property results in some distortions. First, Epstein sees a tension between Lockean entitlement theory, which he refers to as 'principle', and what appears to be a form of rule-utilitarianism, which he refers to as 'pragmatic'. With respect to this opposition of principle and pragmatics, I suggest that Epstein himself is in tension with regard to the extent of his commitment to Lockean entitlement or rule-utilitarianism as his primary normative theory. Second, Epstein ignores personality theory. This might mean that he finds it wholly implausible as an explanatory/justificatory theory, and if so I differ with him. I think it sheds interesting light on some aspects of the problem of adverse possession.

A. Entitlement and utilitarianism: principle versus pragmatics?

First, let us consider the tension between Lockeanism and rule-utilitarianism with regard to adverse possession; that is, with regard to awarding title to present possession of sufficient length rather than seeking first possession. 'As a matter of high principle', Epstein says, 'what comes first is best; as a matter of evidence and proof, however, what comes last is more reliable and certain.' But why is it important to be reliable and certain, rather than simply pursuing what is best, letting the chips fall where they may? If entitlement is a matter of natural right, superior to all manipulations of the state in the interest of social welfare, why isn't this a matter of *Fiat justicia, ruat caelum*? For Epstein, at least, it is important to be reliable and certain because that will maximize the general gain. This is implicitly a species of rule-utilitarianism known as transactions-costs economics.

But now we are prompted to ask, if rule-utilitarianism governs entitlements now, why doesn't it govern entitlements then? That is, why doesn't Epstein simply argue that it is efficiency, suitably construed as 'long-run' or dynamic, that governs entitlements? If efficiency governs entitlements, then there is no tension between 'high principle' and the merely 'pragmatic', there is just the problem of what really is efficient, given the dynamic nature of the system. Certainly, the principle of first possession could be reconstrued in rule-utilitarian terms: It makes utilitarian sense to get things out of the common and into the control of a single decision-maker, and the principle of first possession is (the argument would run) cheaper to agree upon than others that might present themselves. The problem for a utilitarian who is trying to be a libertarian at the same time is rather that the thoroughgoing rule-utilitarian approach to entitlement seems not to be absolute; it seems, in fact, to require redistribution of entitlements under certain circumstances.

In other words, under thoroughgoing rule-utilitarianism, rearrangement of entitlements over time through means other than transfer by contract between individuals cannot be confined to adverse possession. Whatever assumptions we choose about the long run and the role of the utility of future generations, etc., it is hard to construct a utilitarian argument concluding that an entitlement gained through first possession is fixed for all time. Utilitarianism is too empirical for such absolutes. For utilitarianism, 'pragmatics' *is* 'high principle'. All we have is some giant balance weighing the welfare gain from certainty of planning and transacting, and from not disturbing the 'subjective' value of developed expectations of continued control over resources, against the welfare losses from holdouts against land reform, or implementation of new technology, or the demoralization of the have-nots *vis-à-vis* the haves, etc. The advantage of Lockean (and Nozickian) natural rights theory is that it seems proof against non-contractual redistribution. The disadvantage is that it cannot account for adverse possession, which it appears the functioning legal system – the enforcer of those 'absolute' entitlements – cannot do without. Hence Epstein's tension. Does he intend to defend a pluralist meta-ethic? (Are absolute natural rights somehow involved in a paradoxical coexistence with utility maximization as the sole good?) Or does he intend to abandon natural rights theory and face the difficulties of utilitarian ethics? Epstein has not yet squarely faced this problem.

B. Property theory and adverse possession

Now let me complicate the question by throwing another 'ethic' into the hopper. For personality theory, adverse possession is easy, at least if one is envisioning possession by natural persons who successively occupy land. The title follows the will, or investment of personhood. If the old title holder has withdrawn her will, and the new possessor has entered, a new title follows. Title is temporal because the state of relations between wills and objects changes.

[She gives Hegel's own formulation of this in a footnote:]

'The form given to a possession and its mark are themselves externalities but for the subjective presence of the will which alone constitutes the meaning and value of externalities. This presence, however, which is use, employment, or some other mode in which the will expresses itself, is an event in time, and what is objective in time is the continuance of this expression of the will. Without this the thing becomes a *res nullius*, because it has been deprived of the actuality of the will and possession. Therefore, I gain or lose possession of property through prescription' (Hegel, *Philosophy of Right*, § 64 (T. Knox trans., 1952)). The result of this theory is to attach normative force, and not merely practical significance, to the bond developing between adverse possessor and object over time; and to attach normative force, as well, to the 'laches' of the title holder who allows this to happen.

Notes and Questions 11.2

1. Do you agree with Radin's argument that Epstein's utilitarian justification for adverse possession is incompatible with his general natural rights theory of property?

2. Compare Radin's personality theory argument for protecting adverse possessors with the arguments put forward by Hume and Bentham quoted in Chapter 4 above. Does the point made by Bentham argue for or against removing and conferring title by adverse possession?

3. Commenting on Radin's paper, Ellickson (in Merrill (ed.), 'Symposium', p. 814) points out that there is a utilitarian advantage in acknowledging the strength of the link between a person and a thing they have come to regard as their own, in relation to land at least:

> A utilitarian should see value in protecting people's territorial roots. The notion of territoriality is extremely important in biology. The sociobiologists who have ventured to apply biological theory to humans have understandably created controversy. Yet it is plausible that humans are to some degree territorial, and that this tendency has helped shape adverse possession law. Someone who resides or works on a particular piece of land has, in Peggy Radin's terms, invested his personhood in it, or, in my terms, is vulnerable to suffering demoralization costs upon being dispossessed from the property ... [In this paper] I therefore treat damage from uprooting as a demoralization cost. During the early stages of adverse possession, I assume demoralization considerations favor the original owners, but as time passes the adverse possessor can lay claim to deeper roots.

See further below, where he argues that this, together with other factors, can be utilised as a means of calculating an optimal length for limitation periods.

Extract 11.3   Carol M. Rose, 'Possession as the Origin of Property' (1985) 52 *University of Chicago Law Review* 73

[In adverse possession] we seem to have an example of a reward to the useful laborer at the expense of the sluggard. But the doctrine is susceptible to another interpretation as well; it might be designed, not to reward the useful laborer, but to require the owner to assert her right publicly. It requires her to make it clear that she, and not the trespasser, is the person to deal with if anyone should wish to buy the property or use some portion of it.

Courts have devoted much attention to the elements of a successful claim of adverse possession. [She then gives a number of examples from American cases.] No matter how much the doctrine of adverse possession seems to reward the one who performs useful labor on land at the expense of the lazy owner who does nothing, the crucial element in all these situations is, once again, communication ...

In Illinois, for example, an adverse possessor may establish his claim merely by paying taxes on the property, at least against an owner who is familiar with real estate practice and records. Why is this? Naturally, the community likes to have taxes paid and is favorably disposed towards one who pays them. But more important, payment of taxes is a matter of public record, and the owner whose taxes are paid by someone else should be aware that something peculiar is happening. Just as important, the *public* is very likely to view the taxpayer as the owner. If someone is paying taxes on my

vacant lot or empty house, any third person who wants to buy the house is very likely
to think that the taxpayer is the owner because people do not ordinarily pay taxes on
land they do not own. If I want to keep my land, the burden is upon me to correct the
misimpression. The possibility of transferring titles through adverse possession once
again serves to ensure that members of the public can rely upon their own reasonable
perceptions, and an owner who fails to correct misleading appearances may find his
title lost to one who speaks loudly and clearly, though erroneously . . .

[She then considers why it is that property owners should make and keep their
communications clear (see Extract 4.4 below) and argues that the communication
must be in language that is understood. She illustrates this by reference to the
American case, *Pierson v. Post*, 3 Cai R 175, 2 Am Dec 264 (1805), discussed in
Chapter 4 above.]

The dissenting judge in *Pierson v. Post* may well have thought that fox hunters were
the only relevant audience for a claim to the fox; they are the only ones who have
regular contact with the subject-matter. By the same token, the mid-nineteenth-
century California courts gave much deference to the mining-camp customs in
adjudicating various Gold Rush claims; the Forty-Niners themselves, as those most
closely involved with the subject, could best communicate and interpret the signs of
property claims and would be particularly well served by a stable system of symbols
that would enable them to avoid disputes.

The point, then, is that 'acts of possession' are, in the now fashionable term, a 'text',
and that the common law rewards the author of that text. But, as students of
hermeneutics know, the clearest text may have ambiguous subtexts. In connection
with the text of first possession, there are several subtexts that are especially worthy of
note. One is the implication that the text will be 'read' by the relevant audience at the
appropriate time. It is not always easy to establish a symbolic structure in which the
text of first possession can be 'published' at such a time as to be useful to anyone. Once
again, *Pierson v. Post* illustrates the problem that occurs when a clear sign (killing the
fox) comes only relatively late in the game, after the relevant parties may have already
expended overlapping efforts and embroiled themselves in a dispute. Very similar
problems occurred in the whaling industry in the nineteenth century: the courts
expended a considerable amount of mental energy in finding signs of 'possession'
that were comprehensible to whalers from their own customs and that at the same time
came early enough in the chase to allow the parties to avoid wasted efforts and the
ensuing mutual recriminations.

Some objects of property claims do seem inherently incapable of clear demarcation –
ideas, for example. In order to establish ownership of such disembodied items we find
it necessary to translate the property claims into sets of secondary symbols that our
culture understands. In patent and copyright law, for example, one establishes an
entitlement to the expression of an idea by translating it into a written document and
going through a registration process – though the unending litigation over ownership
of these expressions, and over which expressions can even be subject to patent or
copyright, might lead us to conclude that these particular secondary symbolic systems
do not always yield widely understood markings. We also make up secondary symbols

for physical objects that would seem to be much easier to mark out than ideas; even property claims in land, that most tangible of things, are now at their most authoritative in the form of written records.

It is expensive to establish and maintain these elaborate structures of secondary symbols, as indeed it may be expensive to establish a structure of primary symbols of possession. The economists have once again performed a useful service in pointing out that there are costs entailed in establishing any property system. These costs might prevent the development of any system at all for some objects, where our need for secure investment and trade is not as great as the cost of creating the necessary symbols of possession.

Notes and Questions 11.3

In Rose's rationale, adverse possession is justified by reference to acts of the owner, rather than by reference to what is done by the adverse possessor. In relation to land, does modern English law show a tendency to concentrate on what the owner did or on what the adverse possessor did? See section 11.4 below. Is the same balance apparent in the way English law treats goods? See section 11.5 below.

Extract 11.4   Alison Clarke, 'Use, Time and Entitlement' (2004) 57 *Current Legal Problems* 239

ADVERSE POSSESSION

In English law, title derives from possession. A person who takes *de facto* exclusionary physical control of land thereby acquires a right to possession of the land which the law protects against everyone except the true owner. The only right that a squatter ever acquires at common law is a title to the land based on its possession of the land, and it acquires this right immediately, simply *by* taking exclusionary physical control and at the point *when* exclusive physical control is taken. At common law lapse of time does nothing to mature or perfect this right – all it does is to eliminate the rival title of the true owner. Adverse possession is simply part of the law of limitation of actions, eliminating the right of the true owner to bring an action for possession if the right is not exercised within 12 years of it accruing. More importantly for present purposes, not only is the squatter not required to prove that she has positively used and enjoyed the land over a period of time, it is irrelevant whether or not she has *ever* made positive use of it. All she has to demonstrate is that she has excluded all others.[1] This is what robs a Lockean justification of adverse possession of much of its force in our legal

---

1 T. L. Anderson and P. J. Hill, 'The Evolution of Property Rights', in T. L. Anderson and F. S. McChesney (eds.), *Property Rights: Co-operation, Conflict, and Law* (Princeton, 2003), pp. 135–6, note that, in the nineteenth-century American West under various homesteading laws ownership of frontier land was allocated to those who took first possession *and* took up occupancy (typically the acreage to which title could be claimed was limited) *and* made some specified use of (amounting to an investment in) the land, such as by building cabins, digging irrigation ditches, planting trees etc. Use does therefore appear to have been necessary for the claim to mature into a legal title. The adverse economic effects of this (premature settlement decisions, optimistically

system: the law does not award the land to the squatter rather than the 'true' owner because the former has demonstrated that she has made productive use of an unused or underused resource. The most one can say is that a 'true' owner who did not notice, or object to, being deprived of use of a resource for 12 years was making less productive use of it (in the short term, at any rate) than the squatter who at least bothered to take and keep control over it for a sustained period.

In other words, adverse possession simply rewards long *possession* by eliminating rival titles. If it also rewards long use and enjoyment, it does so only incidentally.

This absence of identity between possession and use is even more marked in the personal property equivalent of adverse possession. Although such questions are, oddly, located in personal property law under the heading of 'finding', it is now accepted that even a wrongful taker of possession of goods immediately acquires a title based on possession which is instantly enforceable against everyone but the person with a better right to possession, such as the true owner. It is the taking of physical control that does this, not long (or indeed any) use. The elimination of the title of the 'true' owner is a question of the disentangling of the complex limitation rules applicable to the tort of conversion, where the only relevant factor is the nature of the taker's act of taking. The question of what use was made of the thing since then is irrelevant.

ADVERSE POSSESSION AND THE LAND REGISTRATION ACT 2002

In the case of adverse possession, the Land Registration Act 2002 has made it dramatically more difficult for long use to ripen into unchallengeable title over time. Why has this been done? The 2002 Act implements recommendations made by the Land Registry and the Law Commission in their joint report, *Land Registration for the Twenty-First Century: A Conveyancing Revolution* (Law Commission Report No. 271, 2001, 'the 2001 Report') following publication of a joint consultation paper, *Land Registration for the Twenty-First Century: A Consultative Document* (Law Commission Consultation Paper No. 252, 1998, 'the 1998 Consultative Document'). In the 1998 Consultative Document and the 2001 Report two justifications for the changes can be discerned, although they are not always clearly distinguished from each other.

The first is, in essence, that the law of adverse possession is a bad thing *per se*, capable of operating harshly and disproportionately in practice, justifiable in unregistered land because it facilitates unregistered conveyancing, but no longer justifiable when that rationale is removed by registration of title (the 'necessary evil' argument). The second is that the law of adverse possession is incompatible with the principle of indefeasibility underlying registration of title (the 'incompatibility' argument). Each of these is considered below.

---

mis-estimating the productivity of the land, resulting in up to 80 per cent relinquishment of claims in some areas) are also noted: *ibid*. See also D. Lueck in 'First Possession as the Basis of Property' in *Property Rights: Co-operation, Conflict, and Law, ibid.*, 210, and also G. D. Libecap in 'Contracting for Property Rights' in the same volume at 150 and 156, noting similar respect given (by law and custom) to 'beneficial use' over and above physical control in Brazilian law.

THE NECESSARY EVIL ARGUMENT

As far as the first justification is concerned the basic premise – and for present purposes the most significant point – is that it is wrong in principle that a title should be defeated by a long-standing failure to take action to evict a squatter. Here, if anywhere, is the point at which one might expect a discussion of the fundamental question of whether long use should give rise to entitlement, and, if it should, whether the entitlement should trump that of the pre-existing title holder. However, the question is given no serious consideration in either the 1998 Consultative Document or the 2001 Report. Instead, the focus is on what is seen as the unfairness to the title holder of losing title through inaction.

So, for example, in paragraph 10.5 of the 1998 Consultative Document the law of adverse possession is described as 'at least in some cases, tantamount to sanctioning a theft of land'. This essentially hostile view appears again in the 2001 Report, most notably in paragraphs 2.70 and 2.71, the introductory explanation of why the drastic curtailment of the right of adverse possessors to acquire an unchallengeable title is being recommended.[2] These passages deserve detailed attention here.

Paragraph 2.70 starts by pointing to a perceived problem of public antagonism:

> . . . at the practical level, there is growing public disquiet about the present law. It is perceived to be too easy for squatters to acquire title . . .

Evidence given to substantiate this amounts to no more than a single *Daily Mail* headline:[3] 'Swat the squatters: Owners to be protected from home hijackers',[4] plus a *dictum* of Neuberger J, speaking at first instance in *J. A. Pye (Oxford) Ltd* v. *Graham* [2002] Ch 676, 710. Neuberger J's comments, as hostile to the institution of adverse possession as those of the Land Registry and the Law Commission, do not, however, purport to represent the views of anyone other than himself:

> A frequent justification for limitation periods generally is that people should not be able to sit on their rights indefinitely, and that is a proposition to which at least in general nobody could take exception. However, if as in the present case the owner of land has no immediate use for it and is content to let another person trespass on the land for the time being, it is hard to see what principle of justice entitles the trespasser to acquire the land for nothing from the owner simply because he has been permitted to remain there for 12 years. To say that in such circumstances the owner who has sat on his rights should therefore be deprived of his land appears to me to be illogical and disproportionate. Illogical because the only reason that the owner can be said to have sat on his rights is because of the existence of the 12-year limitation period in the first place; if no limitation period existed he would be

---

2 A fuller explanation appears in Part XIV of the 2001 Report, further reference to which is made below.
3 To be precise, the evidence provided is a reference forward to paras. 14.1 and 14.2 of the Report: these paras. refer to the *Daily Mail* headline and the Neuberger J *dictum* quoted here in this para., plus some paras. in Part X of the 1998 Consultative Document which are not in point here.
4 Appearing in the *Daily Mail* of 2 September 1988. Even this, however, turns out to be self-referential: the article concerned the Law Commission and Land Registry's own 1998 Consultative Document.

entitled to claim possession whenever he actually wanted the land … I believe that the result is disproportionate because, particularly in a climate of increasing awareness of human rights including the right to enjoy one's own property, it does seem draconian to the owner and a windfall for the squatter that, just because the owner has taken no steps to evict a squatter for 12 years, the owner should lose 25 hectares of land to the squatter with no compensation whatsoever.

Reliance on this *dictum* is all the more surprising because although it is quoted in full (not at this point in the 2001 Report but later on, at the opening of Part XIV which sets out the detailed recommendations on adverse possession, where it is said to 'encapsulate the concerns' that prompted the recommendations), at no point in the Report is it made clear that the Court of Appeal expressed the opposite view in the same case (at [2001] EWCA Civ 117, paragraph 52) reversing the decision of Neuberger J and also rejecting a submission that the law of adverse possession contravenes Article 1 of the First Protocol of the European Convention on Human Rights. In this context, Mummery LJ in the Court of Appeal said:

> 52. …. (2) [The provisions of the Limitation Act 1980 extinguishing the title of the paper owner] do not deprive a person of his possessions or interfere with his peaceful enjoyment of them. They deprive a person of his right of access to the courts for the purpose of recovering property if he has delayed the institution of his legal proceedings for 12 years or more after he has been dispossessed of his land by another person who has been in adverse possession of it for at least that period. The extinction of the title of the claimant in those circumstances is not a deprivation of possessions or a confiscatory measure for which the payment of compensation would be appropriate: it is simply a logical and pragmatic consequence of the barring of his right to bring an action after the expiration of the limitation period.
>
> (3) Even if, contrary to my view, that Convention right potentially impinges on the relevant provisions of the 1980 Act, those provisions are conditions provided for by law and are 'in the public interest' within the meaning of article 1. Such conditions are reasonably required to avoid the real risk of injustice in the adjudication of stale claims, to ensure certainty of title and to promote social stability by the protection of the established and peaceable possession of property from the resurrection of old claims. The conditions provided in the 1980 Act are not disproportionate; the period allowed for the bringing of proceedings is reasonable; the conditions are not discriminatory; and they are not impossible or so excessively difficult to comply with as to render ineffective the exercise of the legal right of a person who is entitled to the peaceful enjoyment of his possessions to recover them from another person who is alleged to have wrongfully deprived him of them.

This recognition by the Court of Appeal that there is a positive value in protecting 'established and peaceable possession of property from the resurrection of old claims' finds no echo in the Land Registry and Law Commission argument. Instead, the 2001 Report piles on the opprobrium by adding (still at paragraph 2.70):

Precisely because it is so easy, adverse possession is also very common. Although the popular conception of a squatter is that of a homeless person who takes over an empty house (for whom there is understandable sympathy) the much more typical case in practice is the landowner with an eye to the main chance who encroaches on his or her neighbour's land.

Again, no statistical or even anecdotal evidence is provided to substantiate any of these assertions – i.e. that adverse possession is easy and very common, and that the typical squatter is a 'landowner with an eye to the main chance'. In fact, an acquaintance with recent case law – a poor substitute for empirical research – would suggest that, if anything, the popular conception of the typical squatter is probably nearer the mark than that of the Land Registry/Law Commission. An electronic database search (in Westlaw) reveals 44 adverse possession cases decided in the years 2000 and onwards. On a very rough categorisation, 6 of these concerned a 'landowner with an eye to the main chance' who encroached on to his neighbour's land. One could perhaps add to this group another two cases which appeared to involve casual trespass by strangers (as opposed to neighbours), taking over derelict land for their own use. 10 cases, on the other hand, concerned a 'homeless person taking over an empty house', and another 17 concerned occupiers whose possession either was or had been authorised at some stage (former tenants, prospective purchasers, relatives living in houses owned by a deceased whose estate had never been administered, directors or their relatives living in company owned property, a co-owner, and a former owner whose title had been divested by compulsory purchase). Four more appeared to arise out of genuine disagreement over boundaries, and another four arose where a parcel of land had been wrongly included in or excluded from a conveyance.[5] All of this of course proves nothing, in the absence of evidence of how often adverse possession in each category results in litigation (we know, for example that many local authorities have procedures for regularising squatting in empty residential property by granting licences or tenancies to established squatters), and evidence that this sample is representative. It does, however, perhaps leave the onus on the Land Registry and the Law Commission to explain how they arrived at their model of the typical squatter as the neighbouring landowner 'with an eye to the main chance'.

However, resting on this assumption, in paragraph 2.71 of the 2001 Report the Law Commission and Land Registry then question the soundness of the policy against allowing stale claims and allowing owners to sleep on their rights:

> . . . it is possible for a squatter to acquire title by adverse possession without the owner realising it. This may be because the adverse possession is either clandestine or not readily apparent.[6] It may be because the owner has more land than he or she can realistically police. Many public bodies fall into this category. A local authority, for example, cannot in practice keep an eye on every single piece of land that it owns to ensure that no one is encroaching on it.

---

5 Another two arose out of reverter of titles under the School Sites Act 1841.
6 Here, a case *is* given to substantiate the proposition, albeit one reported 123 years ago: *Rains* v. *Buxton* (1880) 14 ChD 537, concerning adverse possession of a cellar.

Now one might think that, in popular opinion, this is precisely what local authorities should be doing. Even while keeping the focus wholly on the paper owner and ignoring the merits, if any, of the person who has meanwhile been making use of the land, land management practices that allow a public landowner not to notice that it has an adverse possessor for 12 years are difficult to justify, however great its unused land stock. The Law Commission and the Land Registry, however, take a different view. They cite in support of this proposition – i.e. as a case in which a local authority did not realise that a squatter was acquiring title to a piece of land because it could not in practice keep an eye on it – a well-known case, *Buckinghamshire County Council* v. *Moran* [1990] Ch 623 which they describe as involving 'a wealthy businessman who enclosed a piece of land that was owned by a County Council and was being kept by them as a "land bank" for future road-widening purposes'.

Leaving aside the trivial detail that the land appears to have been acquired in connection with a proposed bypass rather than for road-widening,[7] a reading of the reported Court of Appeal decision in *Buckinghamshire County Council* v. *Moran* [1990] Ch 623 reveals that what the case actually involved was a plot of land bought by the Council *thirty years* before they finally got round to bringing possession proceedings against Moran. The Council had done nothing to the land since acquiring it. They had not even fenced it off from Moran's adjoining garden. This was despite repeated requests from Moran's predecessor complaining about children trespassing on the land who were annoying him. So to call it a 'land bank' is perhaps slightly over-dignifying it. Moreover, far from failing to notice that someone was encroaching on the land, the Council had been in sporadic correspondence with Moran himself about it for more than 10 years before finally starting proceedings, and had known for at least five years before that that the land was being maintained by Moran's predecessor as part of his garden. Also, Moran did not enclose the land himself. This was done by the couple who sold him the house. It appears that Moran bought their possessory title to the land when he bought the house, which is not quite the same thing as clandestine land-stealing. The only thing the law report fails to reveal is whether or not he was a wealthy businessman.[8]

For present purposes, however, the significant point is that the Land Registry and Law Commission did not think it worth even considering whether those who had been making use of the land for thirty years thereby acquired any moral claim to it that might outweigh the claims of the title holder who had no use for it.

Instead, the Land Registry and Law Commission conclude paragraph 2.71 of the 2001 Report by giving other examples of what they perceive to be inappropriate losses of title through the doctrine of adverse possession, not justified by the principle that defendants should be protected from stale claims and claimants should not sleep on

---

7 The 1998 Consultative Document is more accurate: see fn 50 to para. 10.19 of the 1998 Consultative Document.

8 It *does* reveal that he originally moved into the house with his mother but later moved out (so presumably could afford to live separately from his mother), and that Conservative Party functions were held in the garden (so presumably one or both were Conservative Party members) – perhaps not conclusive evidence of wealth.

their rights. Again, the focus is entirely on the hazards of the title owner, rather than on any merits of the user of the land:

> ... the owner may not even realise that a person is encroaching on his or her land. He or she may think that someone is there with permission and it may take an expensive journey to the Court of Appeal to discover whether or not this is so. (For a striking recent illustration, see *J. A. Pye (Oxford) Ltd* v. *Graham* [2001] EWCA Civ 117; [2001] 2 WLR 1293, below, paragraph 14.1, where the issue was whether what had initially been possession under licence (in that case a grazing licence) had ceased to be so.) In none of these examples is a person in any true sense sleeping on his or her rights. Furthermore, even if a landowner does realise that someone – typically a neighbour – is encroaching on his or her land, he or she may be reluctant to take issue over the incursion, particularly if it is comparatively slight. He or she may not wish to sour relations with the neighbour and is, perhaps, afraid of the consequences of so doing. It may not only affect relations with the neighbour but may also bring opprobrium upon him or her in the neighbourhood. In any event, even if the policy against allowing stale claims is sound, the consequences of it under the present law – the loss for ever of a person's land – can be extremely harsh and have been judicially described as disproportionate.

It is difficult to see how the facts in the *J. A. Pye (Oxford)* case can be said to justify any of these observations, and again surprising to find the Court of Appeal's conclusion, in the same case, that the operation of the law is *not* harsh and disproportionate, passed over in silence in favour of Neuberger J's view that it is.

Stale claims in registered land

However, the kernel of the Law Commission and Land Registry necessary evil argument is that, even if – contrary to their apparent view – adverse possession is justifiable in relation to unregistered land because it furthers the policy of dis-allowing stale claims, the justification is removed in registered land. The implica-tion is that claims never stale in registered land because we always know who the landowner is.

This claim is frequently made[9] but it is not immediately obvious why it should be true. In unregistered land, disputes about the identity of the paper title holder have not been particularly common, at least over the last century when unregistered conveyanc-ing has been relatively efficient, if not swift. It is not usual for adverse possessors to claim that title was in fact transferred to them by deeds now lost, or that for some other reason they actually do hold the paper title. In most reported adverse possession cases the identity of the paper owner is not in issue. Registration of title ensures that a person who relies on her paper title as entitling her to evict a possessor, can never be defeated by a claim that at some time in the past title was transferred to the possessor or a predecessor by deeds that are now lost. However, it settles no questions of significance

---

9 See, for example, Martin Dockray, 'Why Do We Need Adverse Possession'? (1985) *Conveyancer* 272, where, however, the issue is fully explored.

in the common case of the opportunistic taker of vacant land, nor in cases where the adverse possession originated in possession which was or was thought to be lawful, nor even (since in our registration system boundaries are not guaranteed) in boundary dispute cases. In a perfect registration system it might be possible to eliminate cases arising because of parcels of land wrongly included or excluded from conveyances, but in the real registration world gaps and overlaps between adjoining registered titles do occur,[10] and will continue to do so unless we move to a system where all titles are surveyed. In all these typical adverse possession cases the decision turns not on the identity of the paper title holder but on what people might have done or intended, either at the time when possession first moved from paper owner to possessor, and/or at some subsequent time. Evidence of such matters stales quickly, and it is for this reason that there should be some limitation period during which displaced paper owners must bring their claims to recover possession. The stale claims problem, properly understood, is therefore not significantly ameliorated by registration of title.

Stale claims under the 2002 Act

Ironically, the changes made to adverse possession law by the LRA 2002 seem likely to make the stale claims problem worse, in at least two ways. Under the 2002 Act an adverse possessor may apply to become the registered owner of the land in place of the 'true' owner after 10 years of adverse possession (LRA 2002 paragraph 1 Schedule 6). Since this is two years less than the 12 years prescribed under the old law it looks superficially like a step in the right direction of bringing matters to court quicker. However, this is misleading. On receipt of such an application the Land Registry must notify the registered proprietor,[11] and may not register the applicant's title if the registered owner objects within 65 business days.[12] All stops will be pulled out to find the registered owner: the Land Registry must also notify any registered lessor, mortgagee or chargee[13] and any other person who can satisfy them that they could be adversely affected[14] so that the Land Registry can chase up the registered owner and spur him into action, and the Land Registry has itself said that it will usually arrange for its surveyor to inspect the land (at the squatter's cost) when the original application is made and then notify any other person 'known or suspected from other available information or our local knowledge to have become entitled to the estate affected'.[15] If after all this the registered proprietor is rounded up and objects, the registered proprietor is given a further two years in which to bring possession proceedings to evict the squatter. It is only if he fails to do so within

---

10 See, for example, *Johnson* v. *Shaw* [2003] EWCA Civ 894, *Prestige Properties Ltd* v. *Scottish Provident Institution* [2002] EWHC 330 (purchaser's search certificate wrongly showed strip between titles, believed to belong to vendor, as unregistered when it fact it was registered, partly under one of the vendor's titles but the rest under a neighbour's title), *Epps* v. *Esso Petroleum Co.* [1973] 1 WLR 1071, ChD, and *Chowood Ltd* v. *Lyall* [1930] 2 Ch 156.

11 LRA 2002 para. 2(1)(a) Sched. 6. There is a preliminary hurdle for the applicant – she must first satisfy the Land Registry that she has a *prima facie* case.

12 Land Registration Rules 2003, r. 189.

13 LRA 2002 para. 2(1)(b)–(e).   14 Land Registration Rules 2003, r. 194.

15 Land Registry Practice Guide 4 (March 2003) paras. 5.1 and 5.3.

the two year period that the squatter becomes entitled to be registered as proprietor in his place. There is therefore every incentive for the squatter to delay making an application for as long as possible – the longer she leaves it, the more likely it will be that the registered proprietor will prove to be untraceable. Equally, if the squatter does not make the first move to regularise her position, there is no incentive for the registered proprietor to bring matters to a head by bringing possession proceedings against her: however long the registered proprietor delays, he will never jeopardise his certainty of success.

Distinguishing the 'good' squatter from the 'bad' squatter

The second way in which the 2002 Act may well make the stale claims problems worse is by embarking on the brave but perhaps foolhardy enterprise of trying to distinguish the good squatter from the bad squatter. It has done this by providing exceptions to the general rule: in these exceptional cases the applicant will be entitled to become registered as proprietor after ten years notwithstanding objections by the paper owner. This will occur whenever one of the three 'conditions' set out in paragraph 5(2)–(4) of Schedule 6 to the 2002 Act applies:

(2) The first condition is that –
  (a) it would be unconscionable because of an equity by estoppel for the registered proprietor to seek to dispossess the applicant, and
  (b) the circumstances are such that the applicant ought to be registered as the proprietor.
(3) The second condition is that the applicant is for some other reason entitled to be registered as the proprietor of the estate.
(4) The third condition is that –
  (a) the land to which the application relates is adjacent to land belonging to the applicant,
  (b) the exact line of the boundary between the two has not been determined under rules under section 60,
  (c) for at least ten years of the period of adverse possession ending on the date of the application, the applicant (or any predecessor in title) reasonably believed that the land to which the application relates belonged to him, and
  (d) the estate to which the application relates was registered more than one year prior to the date of the application.

It is at this point only that consideration of the merits of the squatter appears, but even at this point the issue of worth arising out of long user does not arise. Instead, the criterion is, essentially, reasonable belief in authenticity of title, which is quite a different matter. Distinguishing the good squatter from the bad squatter by reference to this criterion may or may not be a good idea in principle, and indeed we know that it can be done in practice. In 1983, Richard Helmholz reviewed the 850 appellate decisions on adverse possession in the United States reported since 1966 and demonstrated that, despite a law which made good faith on the part of the squatter irrelevant, 'good guy' squatters consistently won and 'bad guy' ones consistently lost[16] – which could be described as the courts making the distinction for themselves without any help from the law. There are certainly some English cases which illustrate a similar tendency.[17] More orthodoxly, other legal systems appear to achieve the same objective by having a specific good faith requirement, deriving from Roman law.[18]

However, there are two major objections to the way in which it has been done by the 2002 Act provisions. The first, not strictly relevant here, is that this is not a very good way of distinguishing the 'good guys' from the 'bad guys' even accepting the authenticity of title criterion. The first two conditions appear otiose (any applicant satisfying either of these conditions ought to be entitled to rectification of the register without having to rely on having been in adverse possession for a prolonged period) whereas the third is very narrowly confined, covering only the genuine boundary dispute and not extending to any other case in which the applicant acted in good faith in the sense of believing herself to be entitled to be there for reasons other than the mere fact of having actually been there for a prolonged period.

Problems of proof

However, the more important objection is that these conditions entitling long users to become registered owners – the first and third in particular – are almost certainly going to require proof of events and intentions of both parties going back much longer than the ten years specified, since the genuineness of a belief held for the last ten years will almost certainly require explanation of intentions and events occurring earlier, probably at the time when the applicant's possession first became adverse. For reasons already given, it seems likely that adverse possession cases will not come before the courts until very many years after the squatter first took possession – far more than ten. Are we really expecting the courts to be able to ascertain whether, decades ago, a person acquired a mistaken belief and then sustained it over the decade preceding the application?

It is no help to say that the burden of proof is on the squatter, and so only in the clearest and most meritorious of cases will a squatter be able to take advantage of these 'good faith' exceptions. We would do well to remember the tennis match analogy provided by Richard Epstein in support of his argument that lapse of time favours the person with the *least* meritorious case:

> To be sure, one could try to compromise the difference by imposing new or heavier burdens of proof upon the plaintiff ... Yet these intermediate solutions, taken by themselves, are defective. The passage of time does not work to the equal

---

16 R. Helmholz, 'Adverse Possession and Subjective Intent' (1983) 61 *Washington University Law Quarterly* 331, although see also R. A. Cunningham, 'More on Adverse Possession: A Rejoinder to Professor Helmholz' (1986) 64 *Washington University Law Quarterly* 1167.

17 For an example of articulated bias against the bad faith squatter see *Tecbild Ltd* v. *Chamberlain* (1969) 20 P&CR 633, 643, CA, where Sachs LJ described Mrs Chamberlain's claim to the field as an 'impudent attempt to gain £1,000-worth of property without having any right to it in law' and said that it 'rightly failed'.

18 See further Helmholz, 'Adverse Possession'.

disadvantage of both sides. Indeed, to say that the change of time-frame has no effect at all on the outcome is a contradiction in terms. To the contrary, the passage of time, like any other reduction in the quality of evidence, produces a systematic bias for the weaker side.

To see the point, one can think of a tennis match between two professionals. Normally, one expects the better player to win. Yet, if the game is played on a rough surface, an element of randomness is introduced into the contest, shifting the odds back towards even, which thus works systematically in favor of the inferior player. In the extreme case (for instance, where the game is played in a junkyard or on the side of a cliff), the random elements completely dominate the skill elements; and the results of the game have little correlation to the players' skills. Litigation is like that. The passage of time tends to help the party with the weaker case by giving greater prominence to the random elements of the case. The moving party sues because there is some scrap of evidence that supports the claim, while all evidence on the other side is lost or misinterpreted. To avoid these situations, at some point it becomes necessary to end litigation, not to redefine its parameters. Hence the case for the statutes of limitations that lie at the core of the modern judicial doctrines of adverse possession.[19]

Problems of proof of distant events in this context are exacerbated where corporate owners are involved, a significant factor given the steady increase in incorporation.[20] For a variety of reasons, corporate owners can make poor witnesses of events that happened in the past, and even worse witnesses of their own past intentions. Because corporations almost necessarily intend and act by individuals acting in concert and therefore presumably in communication with each other, they probably produce more contemporaneous written and oral evidence of their intentions and actions than most individuals acting in their personal capacity. However, there is a tendency for little of this to survive long, perhaps because efficient corporations have less pressing motives to bear the expense of archiving material than individuals have, or because most companies have much shorter lives than most individuals,[21] or because their lives

---

19 R. A. Epstein, 'Past and Future: The Temporal Dimension in the Law of Property' (1986) 64 *Washington University Law Quarterly* 667.
20 The number of companies in England and Wales registered on the Companies Register increased from 1,250,300 at the start of 1998–9 (itself an increase of 7 per cent/8 per cent on the previous year) to 1,569,400 at the start of 2002–3: DTI Report for the year ended 31 March 2003, *Companies in 2002–2003* (July 2003) ('the 2003 DTI Report'), Table A1. Table A4 charts the steady rise in the annual number of new incorporations from 1862 (5,000) to 2003 (293,200).
21 The 2003 DTI Report gives the average age of companies on the register at 31 March 2003 as 9.5 years, with 90 per cent of all registered companies having been registered in the last 24.3 years: *ibid.*, Table A5. Listed companies (perhaps more likely to be significant property holders than small companies) show a similar age profile: of the 1,543 companies listed on the London Stock Exchange as at 27 February 2004 only 3 had attained the biblical life span for humans of three score and ten; the vast majority were under the age of 50 (1,414 out of 1,543), nearly two-thirds were under 14 years old (957 out of 1543) and 283 were under the age of 4: website of the London Stock Exchange.

are liable to be ended in dormancy or by liquidation or takeover[22] – events which are likely to lead to the destruction or dissipation of most records.[23]

If long use was *of itself* sufficient to confer entitlement these difficulties in proof would not much matter. Use tends to be an observable fact. But our adverse possession system depends on establishing possession, not use, and intention is an essential component of possession. Consequently, most adverse possessions are in some way or another dependent on establishing not only who did what, but also who intended what, at or since the inception of the requisite period.

Effect of the 2002 Act changes on the incidence of adverse possession

Those who do *not* agree that long use should give rise to entitlement – i.e. those who accept the necessary evil argument – may well consider that all these problems are a price worth paying if the consequence of the changes made by the 2002 Act is a decrease in the incidence of adverse possession. However, while it seems a fairly safe bet that the 2002 Act will result in a decrease in the number of adverse possessors who succeed in becoming registered proprietors, it seems unlikely that it will have any effect on the *incidence* of adverse possession. Indeed, there is every reason to think that there will be a significant *increase* in the number of long-term adverse possessors, i.e. in the incidence of 'established and peaceable possession of property' by people unauthorised by the registered proprietors.[24] Despite what the Law Commission and Land Registry say about landowners with an eye to the main chance, reported cases at least tend to suggest that many if not most adverse possessors take possession either mistakenly[25] or because they want the benefit of immediate use, rather than with an eye on the possibility of ultimately acquiring unchallengeable ownership ten or twelve years later.[26] They are therefore unlikely to be deterred by the prospect of their possession remaining technically challengeable for an indefinite period. The most likely effect of the new provisions is that adverse possessors will simply cease to

---

22 In 2002–3 15,756 companies in England and Wales went into insolvent liquidation, and another 2,738 were in some other form of insolvency procedure (Table C2 of the DTI 2003 Report). A survey carried out by Paul Dunne and Alan Hughes suggests that the proportion of company 'deaths' attributable to takeover by another company varies from about 41 per cent for small companies (assets under £1m) to about 72 per cent for the largest companies (assets over £64m): 'Age, Size, Growth and Survival: UK Companies in the 1980s' (1994) 42 *Journal of Industrial Economics* 115.

23 For recent examples of the critical importance of lost documentary evidence of the actions and intentions of corporate owners in this context see *R. (Beresford)* v. *Sunderland City Council* [2003] UKHL 60 (the problem is brought out most clearly in the first instance judgment reported at [2001] 1 WLR 1327 at para. 47) and *Johnson* v. *Shaw* [2003] EWCA Civ 894.

24 Mummery LJ in the Court of Appeal decision in *J. A. Pye (Oxford) Ltd* v. *Graham* [2001] EWCA Civ 117, in the passage quoted above.

25 I.e. because of a mistake over boundaries, or some other mistaken belief about entitlement or capacity.

26 In a number of reported decisions the squatter describes his state of mind as intending to stay until the paper owner takes steps to throw him out – a state of mind that the courts have sometimes found difficult to reconcile with the necessary intention to be in exclusive physical control, to the exclusion of the owner as well as the rest of the world: see, for example, *Powell* v. *McFarlane* (1979) 38 P&CR 452, *Buckinghamshire* v. *Moran* [1990] Ch 623 and *J. A. Pye (Oxford) Ltd* v. *Graham* [2001] EWCA Civ 117.

attempt to register their titles. Even those who dislike adverse possession cannot think this is a good thing. A land registrar's worst nightmare must be a land-holding system in which titles are regularly traded off the register, so that, eventually the register's record of property holding ceases to bear any relation to reality.[27] This is reported to have happened (in very different circumstances) in New Zealand earlier on in the twentieth century, when adverse possession was not permitted in relation to registered titles. In 1965, the New Zealand Land Registrar, D. J. Whalan, wrote:

> One of the claims of the supporters of the Torrens [registration] system is that it makes for certainty of title. However, paradoxically, in New Zealand, because Statutes of Limitation do not apply to land under the Land Transfer Act [i.e. land to which title is registered] a large number of titles are uncertain which would be quite secure, or would become secure with the passage of time, if they were not subject to the Act.
>
> In many cases, and in particular, in some of the mining areas, land has been purchased, title taken and then the purchaser either has abandoned the property or in some cases disposed of it by the simple process of handing over the certificate of title (sometimes with a crude form of transfer endorsed on it) on payment of the purchase money.
>
> In the latter case the chain of title can sometimes be established and the title cleared, but this is often a difficult and expensive matter. The expense often deters the current holder from clearing his title, which he hands on to his purchaser by means of an 'off the register' dealing. In the former case a person who takes possession of abandoned lands has a better title to it than anyone except the registered proprietor or his personal representatives, but his rights must always be postponed to his or theirs. Thus these titles are less than certain than those not under the Act [i.e. than those outside the registration system] because if they were not under the Act they would be subject to the Statute of Limitation and the defects would be cured when the limitation period had elapsed ...
>
> Unless there is a change in the law the number of defective Land Transfer titles must tend to increase, as it is submitted that there is at present no satisfactory way of clearing the defects.[28]

That, of course, is not remotely like the situation we are in here in this country now. But we could arrive at something like it over the next few decades if long-undisturbed adverse possession titles prove to be marketable. Would you buy a house, or a farm, or office premises if someone other than the seller was registered as owner of it but the seller and her predecessors in title indisputably had been in undisturbed

---

27 This is recognised in the joint Law Commission and Land Registry Consultation Paper and Report, where it is acknowledged that one of the justifications for adverse possession that does apply to registered land is that 'if possession and ownership become wholly out of kilter, it renders land unmarketable': para. 10.7 of Law Commission 254 and paras. 14.54–14.55 of Law Commission 27.
28 D. J. Whalan, 'Title by Possession and the Land Transfer Act' (1963) 48 *New Zealand Law Journal* 524. He concludes that 'Strict adherence to the principle of excluding [the operation of the Limitation Acts] is not an essential feature of the Torrens system [i.e. of registration of title, based on indefeasibility of title]. Indeed, it [i.e. the exclusion of the Limitation Acts] has been described [by Harvey J in *Turner* v. *Myerson* (1918) 18 STR (NSW) 133, 136] as "one of the great flaws in the system"': *ibid.*, at 528.

possession for decades? Until the LRA 2002 came into force the answer would probably have been no. Any well advised buyer would insist on the seller applying to the Land Registry to be registered as proprietor, because buyer and seller would know that if what the seller said was true – i.e. if she had indeed been in undisturbed possession – she would obtain registration with no difficulty. But now that both buyer and seller know that an application will be self-defeating because it will simply provoke an objection that otherwise might never be made, it is fairly certain that no one is going to go near the Land Registry. No doubt few buyers will pay the same price they would have paid for a perfect title, but it is equally likely that few buyers will simply walk away, particularly if (as will often be the case) the problem affects only part of the seller's title. If this is correct it means there will be a market for second rate titles, and if enough of them are traded often enough then title insurers may conceivably decide it is worth their while to step in. Once this happens, the market will be secured.

The incompatibility argument

The second justification given by the Law Commission and Land Registry for curtailing the entitlement of possessors to gain registered title is that it is incompatible with the principle of indefeasibility of title underlying land registration. This, however, is based on a misconception (no less so for being widely held).[29] This justification appears in (among other places in the Consultative Document and 2001 Report) paragraph 14.6(1) of the 2001 Report:

> Registration of title should of itself provide a means of protection against adverse possession ... Title to registered land is not possession-based as is title to unregistered land. It is registration that vests the legal estate in the owner and that person's ownership is apparent from the register.[30]

And, again, in paragraph 2 of the Land Registry Practice Guide 4 published after the 2002 Act came into force:

> [Under the pre-2002 Act law] the doctrine of adverse possession did not fit easily with the fundamental concept of indefeasibility of title which underlies the system of land registration. It is registration, not possession, that vests the legal estate in the owner and that person's ownership is apparent from the register.

But this is a false antithesis. In registered land, as in unregistered land, a person acquires a legal estate by taking adverse possession, and in any common law registration system it would be a very strange registration system that provided otherwise. In unregistered land there are three avenues through which a legal estate can become

---

29 Despite what was said by Whalan, quoted in the previous footnote, the conception is shared by some Law Commissions in some (but not all) other Commonwealth countries: a survey appears in the Law Commission Consultation Paper 'Limitation of Actions' Law Commission 151 (1998) paras. 10.59–10.123.
30 The omitted words make it clear that the intention is, however, to restrict the protection, not eliminate it altogether, for the reasons given in paras. 14.1–14.4. For further discussion of this justification see also paras. 10.5–10.17 Law Commission 254 and 2.73 in Law Commission 271.

vested in someone. The first is by it being conveyed or granted to him by a deed,[31] the second is by operation of law,[32] and the third is by him taking adverse possession. In registered land the first of these avenues is replaced by registration[33] but the other two remain precisely the same.[34]

The truth is that titles are no less relative in registered land than they are in unregistered land. Even in registered land a squatter acquires a title to the fee simple good against the whole world except a person with a better right to possession simply by taking adverse possession. The person who has a better right to possession might include not only the registered proprietor but also any prior squatter dispossessed by this squatter. In the situation in which registered owner O is dispossessed by squatter A, who is in turn dispossessed by squatter B, there are three titles here which the law will vindicate, and the outcome of a title dispute between any claimant and any defendant will depend not on who the registered owner is, but on the relative strengths of their respective titles (if any). This is true in registered land as well as in unregistered land, and as true under the 2002 Act scheme as it was under the 1925 Act scheme. Adverse possession gives rise to *a* legal title, in registered land as in unregistered land. The principle of indefeasibility of title simply ensures that the *best* title is always the registered title. A registered title system based on indefeasibility of title will then have to work out some system whereby the person who *should* have the best title becomes entitled to *become* registered title holder in place of the present registered title holder. For example, it might want to adopt a rule that a personal representative or trustee in bankruptcy is entitled to become registered in place of a deceased or bankrupt title holder, or that a person registered as title holder by mistake (a neighbour is registered as title holder of your house through an administrative slip) is removed. It may or may not want also to have a rule that persons who have held possessory titles for a certain period can become entitled to become the registered title holder, but it is hard to see how the adoption of such a rule could be said to undermine the principle of indefeasibility of title.

A registration system *could* – in theory at least – abolish *all* titles except registered titles. It could provide that title could never be acquired except by registration. But that would mean abolishing the basic common law principle that the law protects *de facto* possessors against strangers, and it is surely inconceivable that any mature legal system would want to do that.

It is certainly not done by the 2002 Act. Indeed, it is as a direct consequence of the continued existence of relativity of title that the 2002 Act introduced the new rule that the period of adverse possession on which a claimant can rely includes time during which a predecessor in title was in adverse possession but not time during which a prior squatter, dispossessed by this squatter, was in possession.[35]

---

31 LPA 1925 s. 52.   32 E.g. on death or bankruptcy or the dissolution of a company.
33 s 27(1) of the 2002 Act, replacing the similar provision of the 1925 Act.
34 The legal effect of a disposition by operation of law is preserved by s. 27(5) of the 2002 Act.
35 Para. 11 of Schedule 6 to the 2002 Act and para. 14.21 of Law Commission 271. It is clear from the Explanatory Notes published with the Land Registration Bill that para. 11 was intended to implement the recommendation to this effect made in para. 14.21 of Law Commission 271, but not so clear that it achieves it. Para. 1(1) of Sched. 6 restricts the right to apply to be registered as

So, neither the necessary evil argument nor the incompatibility argument take us far in a consideration of why long use should *not* give rise to entitlement in the case of adverse possession of registered land.

Notes and Questions 11.4

Read *J. A. Pye (Oxford) Ltd* v. *Graham* [2002] UKHL 30, either in full or as extracted at www.cambridge.org/propertylaw/, and consider the following:

1. It is argued above that the good faith/bad faith distinction drawn in the Land Registration Act 2002 does not draw a satisfactory line between the morally reprehensible taker, the morally neutral taker, and the morally praiseworthy taker. Do you agree? Where on these two spectrums would you put the adverse possessors in *J. A. Pye (Oxford) Ltd* v. *Graham*?

2. If we were to introduce a more general good faith/bad faith distinction into our law, how would we deal with successive squatters? Would we consider only whether the original taker was in good faith, or would we want to look also (or instead) at the 'innocence' or 'guilt' of successor squatters?

3. As Radin pointed out, enquiries into states of mind are costly, and particularly unsatisfactory when they concern someone's state of mind more than twelve years ago. If we are to penalise those who know they are taking what does not belong to them, where should the burden of proof lie? Should we concern ourselves only with what they actually knew (actual notice) or should we also consider what they ought to have known (constructive notice)? If we were to adopt either Epstein's or Merrill's suggestions for dealing with bad faith takers, which would be the more costly?

4. If allocating blame by taking into account the good faith or bad faith of the taker, should we not also take into account the degrees of sympathy we feel for

proprietor to 'a person ... [who] has been in adverse possession ... for a period of ten years ... ', and para. 11(1) then provides that a person is in adverse possession for these purposes if, but for s. 96 of the 2002 Act (which excludes the operation of s. 15 of the LA 1980), 'a period of limitation ... [under s. 15 of the 1980 Act] would run in his favour in relation to the estate'. Section 15 of the 1980 Act is neutral as to the person *in whose favour* a limitation period runs, but its effect is to make the limitation period run from the date of first dispossession (even if that dispossessor was dispossessed by the current squatter). The limitation period therefore 'runs in favour' of the current squatter under s. 15 of the 1980 Act during the period when the prior squatter was in adverse possession, as well as when she herself is. It could therefore be said that the current squatter is 'in adverse possession' within the meaning of para. 11 even before she got there – i.e. also during the period of adverse possession of the prior squatter she dispossessed. The express provision in para. 11(2) of two other situations where the claimant is 'to be regarded' as having been in adverse possession during periods when someone other than she herself is, is an indication that the prior possession of the dispossessed predecessor is not intended to count, but then para. 11(3) reintroduces the notion that, except where expressly provided to the contrary by the 2002 Act, it is the 1980 Act provisions which are to be used to determine when a person is or is not to be treated as being in adverse possession.

the paper owner? Consider how, if at all, the following factors relating to the paper owner could and should be taken into account:

(a) The paper owner is the middle-aged son of the adverse possessor. She is now aged 85, she was widowed during the First World War, and the property in question is the cottage where she has lived since 1915, and where she brought up her son and other children (*Palfrey* v. *Palfrey* (1974) 229 EG 1593, CA: inauspiciously for the son, the case was heard in the Court of Appeal by Lord Denning MR, and Cairns and Stephenson LJJ; he lost).

(b) The paper owner paid no consideration for the title, and did not realise he had it (*Palfrey* v. *Palfrey* again).

(c) The paper owner allowed potentially useful land to lie sterile, without making any attempt to let it to someone who could use it, or to prevent or licence the adverse possessor's use (*Buckinghamshire County Council* v. *Moran* [1990] Ch 623 and *Tecbild Ltd* v. *Chamberlain* (1969) 20 P&CR 633).

(d) The paper owner neglected the property, which would have deteriorated unless someone had moved in and taken over maintenance (any case in which there are buildings on the land).

(e) The paper owner abandoned the property (*Mount Carmel Investments Ltd* v. *Peter Thurloe Ltd* [1988] 1 WLR 1078).

(f) The building on the disputed land had always been accessible only from the adverse possessor's own land, the paper title holder had made no attempt to assert the title for nearly forty years, and the first action of the present holder of the paper title (a property developer) was to remove the tiles from the roof (*Fairweather* v. *St Marylebone Property Co. Ltd* [1963] AC 510).

(g) The paper owner's non-use of the land was more environmentally advantageous than the use made of it by the adverse possessor (for example, a squatter using as a rubbish dump land that the paper title holder is trying to preserve as a wilderness).

5. Compare the views expressed above as to the justifications for extinguishing the paper owner's title with those expressed by Lord Bingham and Lord Hope in *J. A. Pye (Oxford) Ltd* v. *Graham*. Do you agree with Lord Hope that the 'old regime' was unfair, first in not requiring compensation to be paid, and secondly 'in the lack of safeguards against oversight or inadvertence on the part of the registered proprietor'?

11.6. Goods

All the arguments about allowing possessors to acquire titles by taking possession, and extinguishing paper titles after long adverse possession apply with more or less equal force in relation to goods. However, there are three differences between land and goods which are highly significant here, and which explain why the law operates in a rather different way in relation to goods.

11.6.1.   Taking and theft

The first difference is that the law of theft applies to goods (and all other property) but not to land. 'Bad faith' takers of goods are therefore treated significantly differently from bad faith takers of land. First, they invariably commit a criminal offence, whereas, as we saw in Chapter 7 above, the same is not necessarily true of bad faith takers of land. Secondly, as we shall see in the following paragraphs, time will not run in their favour under the Limitation Act 1980.

11.6.2.   Protection of title by tort

The second significant difference between goods and land in this context is that legal title to goods is protected by the law of tort rather than the law of property. The only actions available to owners seeking to recover goods from takers are tort actions: there is no property action equivalent to the action to recover land. As Bell explains:

> If I am in possession of your car without your permission, the law might logically allow you to bring an action to recover it simply on the basis of your ownership, without having to assert some species of wrongdoing on my part. Nevertheless, at least in relation to personal property, and essentially for historical reasons, the common law has no such action for vindicating property rights. To recover your property, you must allege the commission of a tort: conversion by a wrongful assumption of rights inconsistent with yours ... or trespass by wrongfully taking possession in the first place. (Bell, *Modern Law of Personal Property in England and Ireland*, p. 17)

We considered these torts and the way they operate in relation to possession of goods in Chapter 7. The important point here is that the relevant action which an owner must bring to vindicate his title against a taker is a tort action, not a property action, and therefore the relevant provisions of the Limitation Act 1980 are sections 2–4, which are significantly different from the provisions which relate to land.

11.6.3.   The Limitation Act 1980 and title to goods

The most important difference between the tort provisions and the property provisions of the 1980 Act is that whereas in actions to recover land time in effect runs from the time when the taker takes possession, in the case of the equivalent actions in relation to goods time does not start to run unless and until the tort of conversion is committed. As we saw in section 7.4.1 above, this does not necessarily coincide with taking possession. So, for example, if I pick up someone else's bracelet from the floor, mistakenly believing it to be mine, I commit the tort of conversion (consider why) and time starts to run against the true owner of the bracelet. If, on the other hand, I pick it up realising it is not mine and, like Mr Parker in *Parker v. British Airways Board* [1982] QB 1004 (discussed in Notes and Questions 11.5 below), I hand it in to the lost property office, I do not commit conversion and time does not start to run (although consider what the position would be if the lost property office cannot find the owner and returns the bracelet to me and I decide to keep it for myself).

A further complication is that time never runs in favour of a thief (although it will run in favour of a good faith purchaser from the thief: section 4). I will be guilty of theft of the bracelet if I take it with the intention of permanently depriving the owner of it, for example if I pick it up from the floor knowing it is not mine and take steps to ensure that the owner will not find it (perhaps by slipping it into my pocket and telling no one about it).

The combined effect of sections 3 and 4 is therefore that the question of whether time starts to run when, for example, I pick up a lost bracelet, depends on my state of mind then and on what I do next. This is a matter of public policy, enshrined in section 4. See *Gotha City* v. *Sotheby's (No. 2)*, *The Times*, 8 October 1998 (a case concerning a picture taken from Germany to Russia in 1946 and later reclaimed by the Federal Republic of Germany); and see also Byrne-Sutton, 'The Goldberg Case: A Confirmation of the Difficulty in Acquiring Good Title to Valuable Stolen Cultural Objects'.

It should also be noted that the special provisions about theft discussed above are *additional* to the provision postponing the limitation period in cases of fraud, deliberate concealment on the part of the defendant and mistake (i.e. section 32 of the 1980 Act, already noted above in relation to land).

Once time has run against the owner of goods, he is in the same position as the owner of unregistered land – his title is extinguished (by virtue of section 3(2)) and therefore he will be unable to resist an action in conversion by the taker even if he manages to retake possession without the aid of the court.

11.6.4. Finders

Another important difference between takers of land and takers of goods is that the factual context tends to be different. Questions about possessory title to goods tend to arise when the true owner has lost the goods – something that cannot happen in the case of land. This gives rise to a particular kind of title dispute that cannot arise in the case of land: when goods have escaped from the custody of their owners, they will necessarily be in or on the land of someone (usually someone other than the owner). The law then has to decide who has a better possessory title – the finder of the goods or the person in or on whose land they were found. This was considered by the Court of Appeal in *Parker* v. *British Airways Board* [1982] QB 1004 (extracted at www.cambridge.org/propertylaw/).

Two different analyses of 'finding' are revealed in this case. That put forward by Eveleigh and Cairns LJJ is firmly centred on the basic principle that possession provides a root of title which will defeat all other titles other than that of the owner and that of a person with a better right of possession. Thus, a finder acquires title to goods by taking possession of them, and the occupier of the land (or chattel) on which the goods were found can assert a better title only if he can show that he himself was in possession of the goods when the finder took them. On this analysis (although Eveleigh and Cairns LJJ are non-committal on these points) it is irrelevant whether the goods were lost, abandoned, hidden, or simply left in their right place, and it is equally irrelevant whether the 'finder' took possession by genuinely 'finding', or by stealing, or by absent-mindedly walking off with something he thought was his own. *A fortiori*, it is irrelevant whether the finder was a trespasser or lawfully on the occupier's land. All of this must follow from the Court of Appeal decision in *Costello* v. *Chief Constable of Derbyshire Constabulary* [2001] 3 All ER 150 (extracted at www.cambridge.org/propertylaw/). By the same token, attachment of the goods to the land is only relevant if the degree of attachment is sufficient to make them part of the realty – if it is, ownership (even as against the true owner) shifts to the owner of the land (subject to some refinements as between landowner and tenant of the land if they constitute tenant's fixtures).

The second analysis – that put forward by Donaldson LJ – assumes that finders are a special category of taker. This involves making three distinctions. The first, between innocent takers on the one hand and thieves and trespassers on the other, is clearly at odds with the basic principle that possession itself founds title, and that possession is acquired by a combination of intention and physical control, irrespective of whether it is acquired wrongfully or unlawfully. The second, between lost and abandoned goods on the one hand and those cached or in their right place on the other, is objectionable on the same ground. If I take your book with the intention of assuming possession of it, I acquire possession of it regardless of whether, at the time I took it, the book was lying in the street where you had lost it or thrown it away, or hidden by you under a cushion in a friend's house, or in its proper place on your bookshelf. The third distinction assumed by Donaldson LJ involves adopting detailed and illogical rules on attachment of goods to the land which are special to finding cases, seemingly with no justification for departing from established rules on annexation and fixtures.

Notes and Questions 11.5

Read *Parker* v. *British Airways Board* [1982] QB 1004, CA, and *Costello* v. *Chief Constable of Derbyshire Constabulary* [2001] 3 All ER 150, either in full or as extracted at www.cambridge.org/propertylaw/, and consider the following:

1. In *Waverley Borough Council* v. *Fletcher* [1996] QB 334, the Court of Appeal had to consider the claims of Mr Fletcher, who found a medieval brooch in a public park, using his metal detector. The brooch was buried about nine inches below the surface of the ground. Mr Fletcher was lawfully in the park but, unknown to him, use of metal detectors in the park was forbidden. The council, owners of the park, brought an action against him claiming they were entitled to the brooch. The Court of Appeal found in the council's favour, on the basis that where, as here, an object is found *in, under or attached to* the land (as

opposed to lying on top of it), the owner of the land has a better title than a finder. The reasons given by the Court of Appeal were:

(a) intention to be in possession of the land can usually be taken to encompass also an intention to be in possession of everything in, under or attached to the land;

(b) an object in, under or attached to the land has become part of the land, as a fixture; and

(c) in removing the object, the finder will have damaged the land and committed trespass.

How convincing are these reasons? In particular, in the light of the decision in *Costello*, is (c) a relevant consideration?

2. If the object is found on (or in, under or attached to) land which is let by the owner to a lessee, who has a better title to the object: the owner or the lessee? See Köhler, 'Kentucky Fried Chicken'.

3. Explain what Lightman J means in *Costello* when he says that the title of a thief is fragile. In what ways, if at all, is it different from a title acquired by a good faith finder?

4. Examine the rights and duties of finders and occupiers that Donaldson LJ lists in *Parker* v. *British Airways Board*. To what extent are they simply a result of the liabilities you acquire as bailee when you knowingly take goods into your possession (see Chapter 17), and a restatement of what has to be done in order to avoid committing the tort of conversion and the criminal offence of theft?

5. If an item of historic or artistic or cultural importance is found and the owner is untraceable, other considerations come into play: see the Treasure Act 1996 (as amended by the Treasure (Designation) Order 2002, SI 2002 No. 2666) which replaces the old law of treasure trove.

6. For the difficult and interesting questions arising where the object is a shipwreck, see Dromgoole and Gaskell, 'Interests in Wrecks'.

12

Transfer and grant

12.1. Derivative acquisition

In Chapter 11, we looked at the way property interests are acquired by original acquisition, in particular by taking possession of things. In this chapter, we look at the derivative acquisition of property interests, through transfer of interests and through the grant of subsidiary property interests. In most cases, a property interest passes from one person to another, or is carved out of a larger property interest, because the parties intend this to happen and deliberately take steps to achieve it. The transaction may be a gift from one to the other or it may be part of a bargain, with value provided in exchange. We are mostly concerned in this chapter with straightforward intentional dispositions like these.

There are two principal issues is this chapter. The first concerns the way in which property interests pass from one person to another. This is essentially a matter of formalities – the formal requirements that the law imposes for a property interest to pass from one person to another. We look at this in sections 12.2 and 12.3 below. Section 12.2 covers general principles about formalities rules, why we have such rules and what the rules are. Section 12.3 highlights one particular and complex area, which is how and when equitable property rights arise out of contracts to acquire property rights in the future, and out of attempted legal transactions which fail because of a failure to comply with formalities rules.

The second issue considered in this chapter is the point in time at which a property interest passes from one person to another. For reasons outlined in Chapter 5, it is essential that property passes at a fixed and ascertainable point so that everyone knows whether or not, at any point in time, a thing is or is not affected by the interest. This causes problems when people want to deal in things before they have become precisely identified. We look at some of these problems in section 12.4.

12.2. Formalities

12.2.1. Nature and content of formalities rules

If you have a property interest in a thing and you want to transfer that property interest to me, or you want to grant me a derivative interest, the disposition will not be effective unless it is made in the way required by law for a transaction of that nature. There are formalities prescribed for most property transactions. These formalities may differ depending on the nature of the property (whether it is land, goods, money etc.), whether your title is legal or equitable, whether you are giving this interest to me or selling it to me, and, if it is a gift, whether you are making it during your lifetime or by will so that it will take effect on your death. Mostly (but not necessarily) they involve some kind of writing or other record-making. As Peter Birks says, '[f]ormal requirements require people to do things in particular ways, usually ways which put them to some extra trouble' (Birks, 'Five Keys to Land Law', Extract 12.1 below).

Pollock and Maitland describe a wide variety of symbolic acts that have been necessary over the ages, in this country and across Europe, to achieve a transfer of land from one person to another. It might have involved the physical presence of the parties, either on the land in question or in a church or a court, and the presence of witnesses. In addition to physical presence, some ceremonial acts might have been required signifying delivery of possession of the land from one person to another, such as a perambulation of the boundaries in the presence of witnesses, or a symbolic renunciation of possession by the transferor 'leaping over the encircling hedge', or passing or throwing a ceremonial rod to the transferee, or an elaborate transfer of symbolic totems:

> A knife is produced, a sod of turf is cut, the twig of a tree is broken off; the turf and twig are handed by the donor to the donee; they are the land in miniature, and thus the land passes from hand to hand. Along with them the knife may also be delivered, and it may be kept by the donee as material evidence of the transaction; perhaps its point will be broken off or its blade twisted in order that it may differ from other knives. But before this the donor has taken off from his hand the war glove, gauntlet or thong, which would protect the hand in battle. The donee has assumed it; his hand is vested or invested; it is the vestita manus that will fight in defence of this land against all comers; with that hand he grasps the turf and twig. ('Ownership and Possession', in Pollock and Maitland, *The History of English Law*, Book II, Chapter IV, § 3, p. 85)

As they say, 'One could not be too careful; one could not have too many ceremonies' (*ibid.*, p. 90).

The formalities now required in this country are less elaborate, although not much less diverse. In this chapter, we look only at those relating to goods and land, but even these are formidably complex.

The first thing to say is that there are generally two occasions in a property interest's life when formal requirements must be observed. The first is when the property interest is first created, if it is created by grant of a derivative interest. The second is whenever the interest is subsequently transferred from one person to another. The first source of complexity is that the formalities required at these two stages are not always the same. So, for example, as we see in section 54(2) of the Law of Property Act 1925, a lease of land for a term not exceeding three years can be created orally (subject to the limitations provided in section 54(2)) but once it has come into existence it cannot be transferred except by deed (confirmed by the Court of Appeal in *Crago* v. *Julian* [1992] 1 WLR 372).

As to the content of the formalities rules for goods and land, in order to make a gift of goods – perhaps you want to give your car to me – you must either use a deed or deliver the goods with the intention of transferring title to them, as we see in *Re Cole* [1964] 1 Ch 175 (extracted at www.cambridge.org/propertylaw/) and in *Glaister-Carlisle* v. *Glaister-Carlisle, The Times*, 22 February 1968 (Extract 12.3 below). If, on the other hand, you want to sell the car to me, no formalities are required: legal title to goods passes as and when the parties intend it to pass (sections 17 and 18 of the Sale of Goods Act 1979, as amended) and there is no need for a deed, or writing, or even for you to deliver the car to me. Similarly, no formalities are required to create an equitable interest in goods, but once the equitable interest comes into existence it can only be transferred by signed writing satisfying section 53(1)(c) of the Law of Property Act 1925, whether the transfer is a gift or a sale. So, you can declare that you hold your car on trust for your uncle (so, in effect, granting him an equitable interest in the car) orally and without using any formalities, but if he then wants to sell or give his trust interest to me he can only do so by signed writing.

In the case of land, the grant of a legal interest in land, and outright gifts and sales of legal interests, must be made by deed (section 52(1) of the Law of Property Act 1925: the relatively few exceptions are listed in section 52(2), amplified by section 54(2), and the other exceptional cases discussed in section 12.2.5 below should also be noted). Declarations of trust relating to land do not have to be *made* in writing, but there does have to be written and signed *evidence* of the declaration, as required by section 53(1)(b) of the 1925 Act. Signed writing is, however, required to create any other type of equitable interest in land and also to dispose of any equitable interest, but in some cases the writing must satisfy the require-ments of section 53(1)(a) or (c) of the 1925 Act, while in others it must satisfy the rather different requirements of section 2 of the Law of Property (Miscellaneous Provisions) Act 1989 (a confusion we look at more closely in section 12.3 below). Also, special provision is made for *agreements* to make a future disposition of an interest in land: they too must satisfy the requirements laid down by section 2 of the 1989 Act. This is more significant than might appear at first sight. Sales of fee simple interests in land and also grants and sales of long leases tend to be preceded by protracted negotiations, and it is usual practice for the buyer and seller to enter into a formal contract some days or weeks before the transaction itself takes place. This contract will be entered into as soon as the terms of the transaction are agreed, and once that is done and the parties know that they are now committed to the transaction they can go ahead and make the necessary practical and legal arrange-ments for the transaction itself to be completed. So, the parties will first enter into a contract complying with section 2 of the 1989 Act and then some time later the transfer or grant itself will be made by deed as required by section 52 of the 1925 Act.

12.2.2. Registration and electronic transactions

There are two additional complicating factors. The first, registration, is not new. Registration of property interests in ships dates back to 1601, and registration of titles to land to the nineteenth century. Registration may operate as a formalities requirement, in the sense that there are registration systems under which the sanction for non-registration is either invalidity or unenforceability of the interest (a distinction we consider further below). However, this is not the only way to run a registration system. As we see in Chapter 15, it is possible to have a registration system where registration is entirely voluntary, as in the British Shipping Registry. In such cases, the incentive to register is not provided by fear of the consequences of non-registration but by the desire to obtain the benefits that registration will provide. In such systems, registration is therefore not a matter of formalities.

Electronic transactions, on the other hand, do pose new questions about the form and function of formalities rules. In order to transfer shares in a company, the traditional procedure is for the transferor to execute a stock transfer form and deliver it and the share certificates to the transferee, who then produces them to the company, which effects the transfer by making the appropriate entry in its register of shares and then sends the stock transfer form to the transferee. However, dealers can now elect to carry out share transactions on the London Stock Exchange using the CREST centralised settlement system, a paperless stock transfer system, instead of following the traditional paper document procedure, and the same is due to happen to land transactions requiring registration at the Land Registry. As far as land is concerned, provision is made for this by Part 8 of the Land Registration Act 2002, and it is currently anticipated that the electronic transfer scheme will be piloted in 2006 and then introduced incrementally from 2007 (Land Registry, *Defining the Service: E-conveyancing* (July 2004), available at www.landreg.gov.uk/ assets/library/documents/defining_the_servicev1.pdf). This raises two questions about formalities. The first is whether and if so how to replicate traditional formal acts such as signing, witnessing and reciting agreed terms when the document is in electronic rather than paper form, a question already considered by the Law Commission in *Electronic Commerce: Formal Requirements in Commercial Transactions* (December 2001). The second is whether to shift formal requirements to an earlier stage in the transaction, by formalising the way in which agents can prove that they entered into transactions with the authority of their client. Under the land registration system it is presently envisaged that a registrable property interest will be granted and transferred electronically and not by a document (section 91 of the 2002 Act), and that this will be carried out not by the parties themselves but by their agents. The same applies in the CREST share settlement system: ordinary sharedealers must buy and sell their shares through brokers under this system. But agents, whether brokers acting for sharedealers or solicitors acting for clients buying and selling land, are professionals who need to be able to prove that they are or were indeed authorised by their clients to do what they did. In a pre-electronic system the client signifies to the other party that he intends to be bound by some face-to-face communication, such as delivery or speech, or more sophisticatedly by signing and handing over the document which effects the transaction, which both records the terms agreed and signifies the intention to be bound by them. In an electronic system where the transaction is carried out physically by the party's agent, other systems of authentication must evolve.

Formalities rules are therefore in a somewhat fluid state at the moment, and consequently it is particularly important that we have a clear idea of why we have formalities rules, and the functions they are intended to perform. Before looking at these questions, however, there are some general points to be made.

12.2.3.   Validity and enforceability against third parties

There are two principal ways in which a legal system can 'punish' non-compliance with formality requirements. The strictest punishment is invalidity: the transaction (whether the creation or grant of the interest) does not take effect at all unless and until the formalities are completed. The most lenient is non-enforceability against third parties: the transaction is fully effective between those who were parties to it, but does not confer on the transferee/grantee an interest enforceable against the rest of the world. In between these two extremes there are two sub-species. In some cases, in a variation of the invalidity sanction, compliance with the formal requirement is necessary to make the transaction take effect *in law*, but failure to comply will not of itself prevent the transaction taking effect *in equity*. So, for example, in registered land the grant or transfer of a registrable property interest will not result in the grantee or transferee acquiring a legal interest unless and until it is completed by registration, but up until registration the grantee/transferee will have the equivalent equitable interest, provided all the other formal requirements for granting or transferring that kind of interest have been complied with. Similarly, a legal mortgage of land must be made by deed (because of section 52 of the Law of Property Act 1925) but if the mortgage is *not* made by deed it will still take effect as an *equitable* mortgage, but in this case provided it satisfies the appropriate formalities for equitable mortgages (which, because of the rule in *Walsh* v. *Lonsdale*, are those set out in section 2 of the Law of Property (Miscellaneous Provisions) Act 1989, as we see in section 12.3 below).

In other cases, now deservedly rare, a variation of the enforceability sanction applies and the effect of failure to comply with the formalities rule is that the transaction is valid but not enforceable at all, not even as between the parties. This used to apply to contracts for the disposition of an interest in land. By section 40 of the Law of Property Act 1925 no formalities were necessary for the formation of a valid contract for the disposition of an interest in land, but such a contract was not enforceable unless evidenced either by writing signed by the person against whom enforcement was sought, or by part performance of the contract by the party seeking to enforce it. This problematic concept of a valid but non-enforceable contract could cause problems. In *Morris* v. *Baron* [1918] AC 1, where the contract was governed by statutory provisions identical to section 40 (section 4 of the Sale of Goods Act 1893), the parties entered into a contract which complied with the statutory provisions but they then superseded that contract with another one, which did not. It was held that neither contract was enforceable: the first because it had been rescinded by the valid second contract, and the second because it did not comply with the statutory provisions and so was not enforceable even though valid. For this and other reasons, section 40 was repealed and replaced by section 2 of the Law of Property (Miscellaneous Provisions) Act 1989 in which the sanction for non-compliance is invalidity, not unenforceability.

12.2.4.   Effect of compliance on passing of title

The common law usually takes an entirely mechanistic view of the passing of legal title. The general principle is that, if the necessary formalities are used, the legal title passes automatically, even if the transaction is one that can be corrected by the operation of some common law or equitable principle such as fraud or misrepresentation or mistake. Leaving aside those cases where formalities affect enforceability only, as far as legal title is concerned compliance with formalities is a necessary and a sufficient condition for validity. If the formalities are not completed legal title does not pass, however much the parties want it to or think it has. As Megarry J said in *Re Vandervell (No. 2)* [1974] Ch 269 at 294: 'To yearn is not to transfer.' If, on the other hand, the formalities *are* completed, legal title will pass, however unintended, or unnoticed, or unjust the result may be. The clearest illustration is provided by the difference in effect of fraud and forgery, as we see in Chapter 16 in the context of registered land. If I trick you into signing a deed transferring your fee simple interest in your house to me, I become the legal owner of the fee simple and will remain so unless and until you can persuade a court to order me to transfer it back to you. If, on the other hand, I forge your signature on the transfer deed, the legal fee simple stays with you. It never passes to me because there has been no deed as required by section 52 of the Law of Property Act 1925, because by section 1 of the Law of Property (Miscellaneous Provisions) Act 1989 a valid deed must be signed by the person making the deed, and you did not sign it.

12.2.5.   Transactions excepted from formalities rules

Sometimes interests come into existence in such a way that it would be inappropriate to require formalities to be observed. In these circumstances, formalities are not required. They can be put into three categories:

12.2.5.1.   Equitable modification of legal rules

Equity may intervene and require a legal title holder to hold on trust for someone else. This may be because it would be unconscionable for the legal title holder to keep it for herself (in which case a constructive trust would be imposed), or because equity infers an intention that the legal title holder should not benefit (in which case a resulting trust arises). Again, formalities rules would be self-defeating, and indeed they are expressly excluded by section 53(2) of the Law of Property Act 1925.

12.2.5.2.   Implied rights

In certain circumstances, a grant of an interest is implied by law, again without the need for compliance with formalities. Implied easements come within this category, including those implied by necessity, such as a right of way implied over retained land when an area which would otherwise be landlocked is sold off. Such an easement takes effect as a legal easement even though, necessarily, not made by deed and so not complying with section 52 of the Law of Property Act 1925.

12.2.5.3.   Rights acquired by possession or prescription

The title to goods and land which is acquired by taking possession of them is a legal title, and again it is acquired without the need to comply with formalities, as we saw in Chapter 11. Similarly, the question of formalities does not arise where rights in land are acquired by long user giving rise to customary rights or by operation of the prescription rules we look at in Chapter 13.

In all three of these categories, however, once the interest has come into existence formalities rules come back into operation, in the sense that they must be complied with on any subsequent dealings with the interest. As far as transfer of interests is concerned, exception from formalities rules is, unsurprisingly and inevitably, given for transfers by operation of law. These include the automatic transfer of title from debtor to trustee in bankruptcy that we considered in Chapter 8.

12.2.6.   Deeds and prescribed forms

Two types of formal requirement require some explanation. At the higher end of the formalities scale is a requirement that an action must be done by deed. A deed is now just any piece of signed writing that satisfies the not very stringent requirements of subsections (2) and (3) of section 1 of the Law of Property (Miscellaneous Provisions) Act 1989. The 1989 Act simplified and rationalised the old law about deeds, implementing the recommendations of the Law Commission report, *Deeds and Escrows* (Law Commission Report No. 163, 1987). The most significant change was the abolition of the need for individuals to seal deeds. Sealing originally involved the imprint of a real seal on real wax, but as far as individuals were concerned this had long degenerated into fixing an anonymous mass-produced self-adhesive red sticker on to the document. The sealing requirement was therefore removed by section 1 of the 1989 Act for individuals. Similar provisions were made for companies by the Companies Act 1989 which introduced a new section 36A into the Companies Act 1985 abolishing the former requirement that each company must keep a common seal and permitting companies to execute deeds by the signature of their officers only. However, the new regime for companies has proved less successful than the provisions for individuals, and the Law Commission has recommended further changes (Law Commission, *The Execution of Deeds and Documents by or on Behalf of Bodies Corporate* (Law Commission Report No. 253, 1998)).

Section 1 of the 1989 Act also removed the restriction that a deed had to be made on paper or parchment. The requirement that it must be signed suggests that it must still be made on some tangible substance, and consequently section 91(4) and (5) of the Land Registration Act 2002 has had to make special provision for documents in the prescribed electronic form 'to be regarded for the purposes of any enactment' as a deed, once electronic transfer of registered land interests comes into operation.

As a result of the changes made in 1989, deeds now require very little formality. Only the party making the deed need sign it, whereas in contracts for the disposition of land, governed by section 2 of the 1989 Act, all parties must sign. So, if I want to sell my fee simple interest in my house to you, only I need sign the transfer deed, whereas you and I would both have to sign a contract that I would sell it to you next week (consider why). The signature must be witnessed by someone who must also sign, if it is to be a deed. There are no requirements about what the deed must actually say, except that it must either describe itself as a deed or state that it is signed as a deed. Again, this is in contrast to section 2 of the 1989 Act which provides that the contract will not be valid at all unless it contains all the terms agreed between the parties.

A much higher level of formality is, however, sometimes required by statute for some particular types of transaction. For example, the document may be required to be in a prescribed form and to contain specified information. Prescribed forms such as those required for pre-computerised land registry and shipping registry transactions were originally required for bureaucratic convenience. Now, however, prescribed forms are most likely to be required for consumer protection reasons. So, for example, there are detailed regulations governing the form and content of agreements covered by the Consumer Credit Act 1974, as we see in *Wilson v. First County Trust (No. 2)* [2003] UKHL 40 below, requiring among other things the inclusion of 'health warnings' and prescribing print size and the positioning and prominence given to certain classes of information.

12.2.7. Why have formalities rules

With this proliferation and variety of forms of formality it is easy to lose sight of what it is that formalities rules are seeking to achieve, both in general terms and in relation to any particular type of property transaction.

Like all rights, property rights are invisible, but they differ from most other rights in that they are also generally transferable and inheritable. The fundamental point about formalities, as Peter Birks points out in the extract from 'Five Keys to Land Law' (Extract 12.1) below, is that they are the medium through which these invisible rights are made apparent. He is concerned specifically with grants and transfers of property rights in land – as he says, you cannot see a fee simple, or an easement or a restrictive covenant – but the same applies to all property rights. It is intangible rights to things that are traded and made the subject of gifts or inheritance, not the things themselves, and even tangible things are not usually able to carry labels telling us whom they belong to. This is something that has to be recorded elsewhere, either on a register, or on a paper record of a transaction, or in people's memories.

Formalities rules are therefore there to tell the world who owns what, but there is more to it than that. The classic analysis of the functions of formalities was provided by Lon Fuller in Extract 12.2 below. He said that formalities could perform three functions: evidentiary, cautionary and 'channelling'.

12.2.7.1. The evidentiary function

Fuller means by this no more than that a formal requirement such as writing or attestation by a witness provides evidence of the happening and meaning of the event (the formation of a contract, or the transfer of an interest in land). This is for the benefit of the parties themselves and their successors, should they later disagree, and also in the interests of justice generally, because it means there will be adequate evidence on which courts can adjudicate disputes. However, as other commentators have pointed out, it goes further than that. Formalities such as witness and signatures can also provide evidence of the identities of the parties (that they were who they said they were, and not impersonators) and that they knew what they were doing and did it intentionally rather than inadvertently. Rules prescribing form and content such as section 2 of the Law of Property (Miscellaneous Provisions) Act 1989, requiring all the terms agreed to be reduced to writing, also ensure that there will be reliable evidence of precisely *what* it was that was agreed.

12.2.7.2. The cautionary function

Again, this is straightforward, though no less important. Many formalities are designed to put people to extra trouble, as Birks says, so that they are made aware of the significance of what it is that they are doing. This will force them to stop and think, and guard against 'rash and ill-considered decisions that they may regret later', as Patricia Critchley puts it in 'Taking Formalities Seriously'. This might explain why it is more difficult to give goods away than it is to sell them, as we see from *Re Cole* below. The unfamiliar formality might also, so Critchley argues, prompt people to seek legal help in completing the documentation, and the lawyer might then be able to give them general advice about the implications of the proposed transaction and 'should be able to detect and prevent the application of external pressure'. This argument, however, should be treated with some caution. It is unrealistic to expect a lawyer paid simply to steer a client through the formalities for completing a transaction to also volunteer advice about the desirability of entering into the transaction, as countless undue influence cases have demonstrated. In *Royal Bank of Scotland plc* v. *Etridge (No. 2)* [2001] 3 WLR 1021, the House of Lords set down guidelines for solicitors retained by banks to advise wives and others about the implications of mortgaging their homes to secure their husband's business debts. Lord Nicholls emphasised the difference between instructing a lawyer to obtain the wife's execution of the mortgage, and instructing him to advise on the nature and effect of the transaction and ensuring that she is entering into it free from improper pressure or influence. In order to perform the latter function properly, he said, the solicitor would need to be provided by the bank with details of the financial situation of the parties and the proposed arrangements, and then 'as a core minimum' explain and discuss the detailed points he outlined in paragraph 65 of his judgment. The Conveyancing and Land Law Committee of the Law Society, in a guidance note it subsequently issued to solicitors, warned that 'to comply properly' with Lord Nicholls' guidelines 'is likely to take several chargeable hours' (*Undue Influence – Solicitors' Duties Post 'Etridge'* (May 2002)), and in *Greene King plc* v. *Stanley* [2001] EWCA Civ 1966, the court noted that the solicitor who charged £50 for obtaining the wife's execution of the mortgage documentation had a charge-out rate of £80 an hour, 'tending to confirm' the trial judge's findings that he had done just that, and not given her any advice about the desirability of entering into the transaction.

In 'The Statute of Frauds in the Light of the Functions and Dysfunctions of Form', Joseph Perillo also argues that, so far as the warning function is concerned, formalism can sometimes be self-defeating if it requires the provision of too much information. This is a particular problem with take-it-or-leave-it non-negotiable standard form agreements which are rarely read before signature, and if read not easily understood. The government-prescribed form requirements we noted above, which specify not only the information that must be contained in certain agreements, but also the form in which it is presented, are an attempt to address this problem.

12.2.7.3. The channelling function

Fuller sees this as one of the most important functions of formalities. As he puts it, rules stating that transactions will not take legal effect unless put in a legal form offer 'channels for the legally effective expressions of intention'. They tell those who do *not* want transactions to have a particular legal effect how to avoid that happening, and they tell those who *do* want them to have a particular effect how to achieve that end. This message can then be read both by courts who have to adjudicate disputes between them and, most importantly in the case of property rights, by third parties potentially affected by the interest. We see an excellent illustration of the importance of this in the rules that govern the enforceability of equitable interests that we consider in Chapter 14. The general rule is that, in the absence of a registration system, the enforceability of equitable property interests in things is governed by the good faith purchaser rule: they are enforceable against the whole world except a good faith purchaser of a legal interest in the thing who does not have actual, constructive or imputed notice of the interest. The disadvantage of this rule from the point of view of the equitable interest holder is that it does not give her any channel through which to make known the existence of her interest. The best channel for her would of course be registration. If there is a requirement that her interest is not enforceable against third parties unless registered, this might lead to unfortunate results if she neglects to register the interest and the property is then bought by someone who was well aware of her interest all along, as happened in *Midland Bank Trust Co. Ltd* v. *Green* [1981] AC 513, as we see in Chapter 14. However, it does at least mean that she has some means of ensuring in advance that her interest will be enforceable against all comers: she does not have to worry about how she is going to ensure that prospective purchasers of the property find out about her.

Perillo makes essentially the same point when he says that formalities can have the advantage of 'earmarking' the point at which promise or negotiation changes into obligation:

> When the law provides that clothing a promise with a particular formality will transform the promise into an obligation, the formality has at least two functional consequences. First, the judicial task of determining the parties' intentions is facilitated. Secondly, and of equal importance, it enables the parties to search out and find the appropriate device to accomplish their intent to create an obligation. (Perillo, 'The Statute of Frauds in the Light of the Functions and Dysfunctions of Form', p. 49)

This too provides a justification for the comparatively strict formalities rules for making gifts. As Perillo says:

> [Such transactions] are normally made to, or on behalf of, a close friend, a relative, or a prospective spouse or in-law. In this context, the earmarking function of form requirements is quite important. It is very easy, often years later, to construe words expressing high hopes and favorable omens as words of promise or *vice versa*. Form requirements can serve to sort out promises from expressions of sanguine expectations. (Perillo, 'The Statute of Frauds in the Light of the Functions and Dysfunctions of Form', p. 54)

12.2.7.4.   Other functions

Critchley identifies two other advantages that can flow from requiring land transactions to comply with formal requirements, and again these apply with equal force to most types of property transaction.

Clarifying terms

A requirement such as that contained in section 2 of the Law of Property (Miscellaneous Provisions) Act 1989, that all the terms of the transaction must be in writing and signed by the parties, has the advantage of forcing the parties to sort out and come to an agreement on all the detailed terms of the transaction before committing themselves. As Critchley says, the rule helps to clarify the terms of the transaction because 'the very act of reducing the agreement to writing will help to highlight gaps or uncertainties in its terms' (Critchley, 'Taking Formalities

Seriously', p. 515). This not only benefits the parties, it also ensures that a clear record of the terms is available for third parties such as purchasers proposing to buy subject to the interest created. The benefit to the parties may, however, not be so obvious in all legal cultures, as Perillo notes:

> A leading Japanese industrialist has written of the discomfort and apprehension felt by Japanese businessmen when faced with the 'American insistence on spelling out the smallest details in writing' (referring to C. Fujino, 'Get to Know the Japanese Market', *New York Times*, July 8, 1973; Mr Fujino was then president of the Mitsubishi Corporation). His attitude is reflected in the lack of either writing requirements or of a parol evidence rule in the Japanese legal system. There is a genuine possibility, then, that a legal system may not wish to induce parties to thrash out the potential difficulties in advance, but to induce ongoing informal dispute resolution in the course of the contractual relationship. (Perillo, 'The Statute of Frauds in the Light of the Functions and Dysfunctions of Form', p. 54)

Publicity

Some property interests such as mortgages and charges pose such threats to prospective purchasers that it is justifiable to insist that they should be put in such a form that the existence and terms of the interest are made apparent to the whole world. Registration is the ideal solution, but there are other possibilities. Under the Land Charges Act 1972 (now applicable only to the relatively few unregistered land titles in this country) mortgages and charges of land are not enforceable against third parties unless *either* the mortgage or charge is registered *or* the mortgagee holds the borrower's title deeds. This works because in unregistered land the owner is unable to deal with the property without the title deeds, so there is no danger of third parties being misled. The Law Commission nevertheless took the view that even this was insufficient, and recommended that no mortgage or charge over land should be enforceable against third parties unless made in writing (Law Commission, *Transfer of Land – Land Mortgages* (Law Commission Report No. 204, 1991)) and while this was never implemented by Parliament, the courts achieved the same result by a different route in *United Bank of Kuwait* v. *Sahib* [1997] Ch 107, as we see in section 12.3 below.

State functions

Requirements of writing and registration can provide both a paper record of transactions on which tax can be levied, and also data from which statistical evidence can be gathered. The best example in this country of the fiscal role of formalities used to be stamp duty, which until very recently was levied not on property transactions but on the documents by which the transactions were effected. This was changed by the Finance Act 2003, partly because large-scale land developers were increasingly using conveyancing devices to avoid passing value by documents liable to stamp duty, but also because the scheme was clearly not going to be viable once transactions could be effected electronically.

The data collection role, however, continues to be important. National property registers provide the best possible repository of information about the social, economic and demographic distribution and movement of property holdings, and it is significant that current plans for electronic conveyancing envisage links between the Land Registry system and government departments such as the Inland Revenue Stamp Office and Valuation Office Agency (paragraph 1.2 of Land Registry, *Defining the Service: E-conveyancing* (July 2004)).

12.2.8.   Disadvantages

12.2.8.1.   Hard cases

All these advantages of formalities rules require careful scrutiny because the disadvantages are so unpalatable. The main problem is that strict implementation of formalities rules can lead to unjust outcomes in individual cases. As Lord Nicholls said in *Wilson* v. *First County Trust (No. 2)* [2003] UKHL 40 below, 'The unattractive feature of this approach is that it will sometimes involve punishing the blameless *pour encourager les autres.*' Individuals are made to suffer undeservedly, or are allowed to break promises, defeat legitimate expectations or keep undeserved benefits, solely in order to preserve the integrity of the system. The rule in *Walsh* v. *Lonsdale*, considered in section 12.3 below, and equitable doctrines of estoppel and resulting and constructive trusts can help to avert the unjust consequences of a failure to comply with formalities in some cases, but, as we see in *Lloyds Bank plc* v. *Carrick* [1996] 4 All ER 630 below, there are limits to their effectiveness.

In *Wilson* v. *First County Trust (No. 2)*, the House of Lords had to consider whether this was compatible with the rights guaranteed by the European Convention on Human Rights. The case concerned section 127 of the Consumer Credit Act 1974, which provides, in effect, that, if a loan agreement covered by the 1974 Act does not contain prescribed information, it will be enforceable only on an order of the court. The section also provides that, in most cases, if the lender fails to comply with the formalities requirements by omitting prescribed information, the court has a broad discretion to make whatever order it considers just, having regard to the prejudice caused by the contravention and the degree of culpability for it. However, section 127(3) provides that, in the case of some specified failures, this does not apply, and the court has no discretion: it must refuse to make an enforcement order. The effect of this is that both the credit agreement and any mortgage or charge securing it will be unenforceable, so the lender will be unable to recover the loan at all. In the *Wilson* case, Mrs Wilson had borrowed £5,000 from a pawnbroker for six months, pawning her car to secure repayment of the loan. She was charged a 'document fee' of £250 which was added on to the loan, so that the total amount of credit was specified in the loan agreement as £5,250. One of the terms that has to be included in any loan agreement covered by the 1974 Act is the total amount of credit, and if the lender fails to comply with this, section 127(3) applies and the loan is wholly unenforceable. The House of Lords held that, by making the honest mistake of specifying £5,250 as the total amount of credit, the lenders mis-stated the total amount of credit and therefore the loan was unenforceable, even though the mistake had not in any way misled or disadvantaged Mrs Wilson. She was therefore entitled to keep both the £5,000 and the car. The House of Lords concluded that this Draconian outcome was not an infringement of the lender's rights guaranteed by Article 6(1) of, and Article 1 of the First Protocol to, the European Convention on Human Rights (guaranteeing rights to a fair hearing and to peaceful enjoyment of possessions), because section 127(3) pursued a legitimate aim of protecting consumer debtors and the statutory bar on enforcement was not disproportionate to this aim.

In other types of transaction, however, the policy aim of formalities rules is not so obviously compelling, although it is doubtful whether the courts would come to any different conclusion, given the longevity and ubiquity of formalities rules in most European legal systems.

12.2.8.2. Costs

The other disadvantage of formalities rules is that they add to the costs of transactions, not so much because they involve direct expenditure but because, as Peter Birks says, they are designed to put people to extra trouble. In high-value transactions this may be easily outweighed by the advantages gained by imposing the formalities, but this will rarely be the case for low-value frequently traded items. This provides some explanation for the lack of formal requirements for the sale of goods.

Extract 12.1   Peter Birks, 'Five Keys to Land Law', in S. Bright and J. Dewar (eds.), *Land Law: Themes and Perspectives* (Oxford: Oxford University Press, 1998), Chapter 18

Formal requirements oblige people to do things in particular ways, usually ways which put them to some slight extra trouble. It might be, for example, that the law would treat a promise as binding only if you made it meekly kneeling upon your knees. In practice, writing and registration are the formalities usually insisted upon. There can be lighter and heavier versions of both.

Land law insists on formality above all at two crucial points in the acquisition of real rights, contract and conveyance. If a landowner decides to make a gift, there will be no contract. Suppose she wants to give her daughter the fee simple in a strip of woodland. She will move straight to the conveyance, for centuries done by deed. The conveyance confers the real right. The sacrosanct formal requirement of a deed is now being made to give way to public registration and, more precisely, to computerized entries on the register. Direct gifts of land, other than by will, are not all that common. Another kind of gratuitous transfer is a conveyance to trustees upon trusts declared by the settlor. The declaration of a trust of land, which accompanies the conveyance, has to be evidenced in writing.

Generally speaking, a conveyance follows a contract, usually a contract of sale. Contracts to convey interests in land are void unless they are made in writing. The usual sequence is, first, an informal agreement 'subject to contract'; secondly, the formal contract made in writing, by which the parties for the first time become bound to make, and take, the conveyance; thirdly, the conveyance, which confers the right. In England there is usually a deplorable delay between the first and second stages, though in Scotland the lawyers manage to move from stage one to stage two in two or three days.

This delay means that parties are forced to rely on each other long before there is any legal tie. The unscrupulous can then exploit the fact that there is no sanction for withdrawal during this long first stage. The result is gazumping and gazundering. A gazumper is a seller who suddenly says that he will withdraw unless the buyer pays more. A gazunderer is a buyer who threatens to pull out unless the seller will take less. These practices are unknown in Scotland. They are not a by-product of formality. They are a by-product of the practice of the professionals who run the housing market and in particular of their practice in not executing the formal contract at the point at which all contracts are normally finalized – namely, the moment from which the parties need to be able to rely on one another.

What does formality facilitate? What ends does it serve? Even though it lies outside the land law, it is convenient to answer by reference to the best-known formality of all. Everyone knows that a last will has to be made in writing and signed before witnesses. It is no use just scribbling it on the back of an envelope or whispering it to one's best friend. There are huge advantages in this formal requirement. It helps the person making the will think hard about the job to be done. Later, it goes a long way towards eliminating doubt and argument at a juncture in human affairs at which strife is all too near the surface. All hell would break out if a deceased's last will were a matter of proving by general evidence, and in the absence of the only person who could really know, what the last wishes really were. The formal will settles the matter.

It is much the same in land law. There is an extra reason too. It derives from the invisibility of real rights. Just as one cannot see a fee simple, so one cannot see an easement or a restrictive covenant. A neighbour's right to pass over a field does not reveal itself in a pink line, nor will even an infra-red camera disclose his right to restrict or forbid building. If one is buying a fee simple from a company, and a firm of solicitors is in daily occupation of the premises doing the business of soliciting, one might reasonably infer that the firm holds a lease. But still a lease is not visible, nor a pyramid of subleases. Real rights have to be made apparent through documents. Acquiring land would otherwise be a nightmare unless the law made really massive erosions of the principle of *nemo dat*. In relation to land, massive erosions of that principle are wholly unacceptable. Some such erosion does indeed have to be tolerated. We have already seen that the price of equity's recognition of real rights created without formality is just such an erosion, the defence of *bona fide* purchase for value without notice. Moreover, the protection of the system of registration involves some inevitable sacrifice of unregistered interests.

There is an inescapable tension. Formality breeds hard cases. What of the person who did not know or was badly advised? She did the job but not in the precise way in which the law required it to be done. In such cases, there is a terrific clash between two simple principles. One is that you cannot have your cake and eat it. You cannot take the advantages of formality and at the same time let off all those who do things in their own informal way.

The other is that pain should not be inflicted except in case of pressing necessity. It is not so easy to send someone away empty-handed who would have taken a fortune if only the right piece of paper had been used. Wherever there are formal requirements, there will be litigation in which these two principles meet head to head.

Whether the rigour of the one will yield ground to the merciful other will depend on several factors, most obviously on the value attached to the formality in question, also on the scale of the exception likely to be created by a concession. If the formality is thought to be really valuable (like the formal requirements of wills), concessions are unlikely to be made, unless perhaps it can be shown that the facts in question will recur infrequently or for some other reason pose no substantial threat to the policy of certainty through formality. One crucially important factor is whether the interests of any third party are involved, in such a way as to be threatened if effect is given to the informal transaction. And has that third party given value? The defence of *bona fide* purchaser for value without notice, which we have already met, illustrates the respect due to the interests of a stranger who has given value. And, where the sanctity and efficacy of a register are at stake, that stranger is likely to prevail even without proof of good faith.

Suppose that you have dealt informally with me, in circumstances in which a decent argument can be made that, but for failure to satisfy formal requirements, you would have an interest in my house. If it is just a matter between you and me, with no stranger involved, it may be possible for you to make some headway. It will be more difficult if I have already sold my legal fee simple in the house to some stranger. You will have a much harder time against that stranger who has given value. Suppose the law untouched by the requirement of registration. Your informally created equitable interest, even if you succeed in establishing that you acquired one, will be vulnerable to the defence of *bona fide* purchase without notice. If we add back the requirement of registration, that still fiercer hurdle stands in your way. It is highly unlikely that you will have registered your interest, which in the absence of special circumstances will be void against the buyer from me.

Some interests override the register. They bind even without registration. This represents the attempt of the legislator to anticipate the most obvious instances of the problem endemic in formality. One category of overriding interest is the interest of a person in actual occupation [see Chapter 15 below]. In *Hodgson* v. *Marks* [1971] Ch 892 an elderly lady conveyed her house to her lodger in a thoroughly ill-advised attempt to protect him from her nephew. The nephew was hostile to the lodger's influence. She had no real intent that the lodger should have the substance of ownership of the house. But, so far as the formal requirements of the law were concerned, she had reserved no interest for herself. The lodger sold and conveyed the land to a third party. The old lady found herself in danger of losing her house. It was not so very difficult to find that on these facts she had obtained an equitable interest under a non-express trust. But she had, of course, not registered that equitable interest. The purchaser from the lodger maintained that he was not bound by it. She was saved by the fact that she had been in actual occupation at the time of the sale. The underlying idea is that a buyer can see to his own protection from adverse interests held by those in occupation. Questions can be put. However, the interest of a person in occupation overrides the register simply because its owner is in occupation. It is not necessary to prove that the buyer was at fault in failing to make reasonable enquiries: 'If there is actual occupation, and the occupier has rights, the purchaser takes subject to them. If not, he does not. No further element is material' (Lord Wilberforce in *Williams & Glyn's Bank Ltd* v. *Boland* [1981] AC 487 at 504) . . .

The value of legal certainty, which the equitable jurisdiction seems on occasion to undermine, is in general reinforced by insistence on the rigour of formality, especially as against strangers who have given value. Formality has meant writing in one form or another, but nowadays it means above all the public registration of real rights in land. The legislator, in providing that some interests override the register, has attempted to foresee the cases in which, even against strangers, the destruction of unregistered interests would give rise to screams of pain.

Notes and Questions 12.1

1   Overriding interests are interests that, in registered land, are enforceable against third parties even if not mentioned anywhere on the register. We come back to this justification for overriding interests in Chapter 15.

2   Peter Birks says that prospective sellers and buyers should become contractually bound to proceed at the point at which they 'need to be able to rely on each other'. Is that the same point as the point at which they wish to be put under a binding obligation to proceed?

3   Compare the formalities requirements imposed by section 52 of the Law of Property Act 1925 and those imposed by section 2 of the Law of Property (Miscellaneous Provisions) Act 1989. Which are the more onerous? How far are the differences between the two justifiable?

4   Which of the provisions of section 53 apply to land only, and which apply to other kinds of property as well? In the light of the justifications given in this chapter for formalities rules, should it be possible for declarations of trust to be made orally?

Extract 12.2   Lon Fuller, 'Form and Consideration' (1941) 41 *Columbia Law Review* **799**

§ 2. THE EVIDENTIARY FUNCTION

The most obvious function of a legal formality is, to use Austin's words, that of providing 'evidence of the existence and purport of the contract, in case of controversy'. The need for evidentiary security may be satisfied in a variety of ways: by requiring a writing, or attestation, or the certification of a notary. It may even be satisfied, to some extent, by such a device as the Roman stipulatio, which compelled an oral spelling out of the promise in a manner sufficiently ceremonious to impress its terms on participants and possible bystanders.

§ 3. THE CAUTIONARY FUNCTION

A formality may also perform a cautionary or deterrent function by acting as a check against inconsiderate action. The seal in its original form fulfilled this purpose remarkably well. The affixing and impressing of a wax wafer – symbol in the popular mind of legalism and weightiness – was an excellent device for inducing the circumspective frame of mind appropriate in one pledging his future. To a lesser extent any requirement of a writing, of course, serves the same purpose, as do requirements of attestation, notarization, etc.

§ 4. THE CHANNELING FUNCTION

Though most discussions of the purposes served by formalities go no further than the analysis just presented, this analysis stops short of recognizing one of the most important functions of form. That a legal formality may perform a function not yet described can be shown by the seal. The seal not only insures a satisfactory memorial of the promise and induces deliberation in the making of it. It serves also to mark or signalize the enforceable promise; it furnishes a simple and external test of enforceability. This function of form Ihering described as 'the facilitation of judicial diagnosis', and he employed the analogy of coinage in explaining it.

> Form is for a legal transaction what the stamp is for a coin: just as the stamp of the coin relieves us from the necessity of testing the metallic content and weight in short, the value of the coin (a test which we could not avoid if uncoined metal were offered to us in payment), in the same way legal formalities relieve the judge of an inquiry whether a legal transaction was intended, and – in case different forms are fixed for different legal transactions – which was intended.

In this passage it is apparent that Ihering has placed an undue emphasis on the utility of form for the judge, to the neglect of its significance for those transacting business out of court. If we look at the matter purely from the standpoint of the convenience of the judge, there is nothing to distinguish the forms used in legal transactions from the 'formal' element which to some degree permeates all legal thinking. Even in the field of criminal law 'judicial diagnosis' is 'facilitated' by formal definitions, presumptions, and artificial constructions of fact. The thing which characterizes the law of contracts and conveyances is that in this field forms are deliberately used, and are intended to be so used, by the parties whose acts are to be judged by the law. To the business man who wishes to make his own or another's promise binding, the seal was at common law available as a device for the accomplishment of his objective. In this aspect form offers a legal framework into which the party may fit his actions, or, to change the figure, it offers channels for the legally effective expression of intention. It is with this aspect of form in mind that I have described the third function of legal formalities as 'the channeling function'.

In seeking to understand this channeling function of form, perhaps the most useful analogy is that of language, which illustrates both the advantages and dangers of form in the aspect we are now considering. One who wishes to communicate his thoughts to others must force the raw material of meaning into defined and recognizable channels; he must reduce the fleeting entities of wordless thought to the patterns of conventional speech. One planning to enter a legal transaction faces a similar problem. His mind first conceives an economic or sentimental objective, or, more usually, a set of overlapping objectives. He must then, with or without the aid of a lawyer, cast about for the legal transaction (written memorandum, sealed contract, lease, conveyance of the fee, etc.) which will most nearly accomplish these objectives. Just as the use of language contains dangers for the uninitiated, so legal forms are safe only in the hands of those who are familiar with their effects. Ihering explains that the extreme formalism of Roman law was supportable in practice only because of the constant availability of legal advice, gratis.

The ideal of language would be the word whose significance remained constant and unaffected by the context in which it was used. Actually, there are few words, even in scientific language, which are not capable of taking on a nuance of meaning because of the context in which they occur. So in the law, the ideal type of formal transaction would be the transaction described on the Continent as 'abstract', that is, the transaction which is abstracted from the causes which gave rise to it and which has the same legal effect no matter what the context of motives and lay practices in which it occurs. The seal in its original form represented an approach to this ideal, for it will be recalled that extra-formal factors, including even fraud and mistake, were originally without effect on the sealed promise. Most of the formal transactions familiar to modern law, however, fall short of the 'abstract' transaction; the channels they cut are not sharply and simply defined ...

§5. INTERRELATIONS OF THE THREE FUNCTIONS

Though I have stated the three functions of legal form separately, it is obvious that there is an intimate connection between them. Generally speaking, whatever tends to accomplish one of these purposes will also tend to accomplish the other two. He who is compelled to do something which will furnish a satisfactory memorial of his intention will be induced to deliberate. Conversely, devices which induce deliberation will usually have an evidentiary value. Devices which insure evidence or prevent inconsiderateness will normally advance the *desideratum* of channeling, in two different ways. In the first place, he who is compelled to formulate his intention carefully will tend to fit it into legal and business categories. In this way the party is induced to canalize his own intention. In the second place, wherever the requirement of a formality is backed by the sanction of the invalidity of the informal transaction (and this is the means by which requirements of form are normally made effective), a degree of channeling results automatically. Whatever may be its legislative motive, the formality in such a case tends to effect a categorization of transactions into legal and non-legal.

Just as channeling may result unintentionally from formalities directed towards other ends, so these other ends tend to be satisfied by any device which accomplishes a channeling of expression. There is an evidentiary value in the clarity and definiteness of contour which such a device accomplishes. Anything which effects a neat division between the legal and the non-legal, or between different kinds of legal transactions, will tend also to make apparent to the party the consequences of his action and will suggest deliberation where deliberation is needed. Indeed, we may go further and say that some minimum satisfaction of the *desideratum* of channeling is necessary before measures designed to prevent inconsiderateness can be effective. This may be illustrated in the holographic will. The necessity of reducing the testator's intention to his own handwriting would seem superficially to offer, not only evidentiary safeguards, but excellent protection against inconsiderateness as well. Where the holographic will fails, however, is as a device for separating the legal wheat from the legally irrelevant chaff. The courts are frequently faced with the difficulty of determining whether a particular document – it may be an informal family letter which happens to be entirely in the handwriting of the sender – reveals the requisite 'testamentary intention'. This difficulty can only be eliminated by a formality which performs adequately the channeling function, by some external mark which will signalize the testament and distinguish it from non-testamentary expressions of intention. It is obvious that by a kind of reflex action the deficiency of the holographic will from the standpoint of channeling operates to impair its efficacy as a device for inducing deliberation.

Despite the close interrelationship of the three functions of form, it is necessary to keep the distinctions between them in mind since the disposition of borderline cases of compliance may turn on our assumptions as to the end primarily sought by a particular formality. Much of the discussion about the parol evidence rule, for example, hinges on the question whether its primary objective is channeling or evidentiary . . .

§ 6. WHEN ARE FORMALITIES NEEDED? THE EFFECT OF AN INFORMAL SATISFACTION OF THE *DESIDERATA* UNDERLYING THE USE OF FORMALITIES

The analysis of the functions of legal form which has just been presented is useful in answering a question which will assume importance in the later portion of this discussion when a detailed treatment of consideration is undertaken. That question is: In what situations does good legislative policy demand the use of a legal formality? One part of the answer to the question is clear at the outset. Forms must be reserved for relatively important transactions. We must preserve a proportion between means and end; it will scarcely do to require a sealed and witnessed document for the effective sale of a loaf of bread.

But assuming that the transaction in question is of sufficient importance to support the use of a form if a form is needed, how is the existence of this need to be determined? A general answer would run somewhat as follows: The need for investing a particular transaction with some legal formality will depend upon the extent to which the guaranties that the formality would afford are rendered superfluous by forces native to the situation out of which the transaction arises – including in these 'forces' the habits and conceptions of the transacting parties.

Whether there is any need, for example, to set up a formality designed to induce deliberation will depend upon the degree to which the factual situation, innocent of any legal remolding, tends to bring about the desired circumspective frame of mind. An example from the law of gifts will make this point clear. To accomplish an effective gift of a chattel without resort to the use of documents, delivery of the chattel is ordinarily required and mere donative words are ineffective. It is thought, among other things, that mere words do not sufficiently impress on the donor the significance and seriousness of his act. In an Oregon case, however, the donor declared his intention to give a sum of money to the donee and at the same time disclosed to the donee the secret hiding place where he had placed the money. Though the whole donative act consisted merely of words, the court held the gift to be effective. The words which gave access to the money which the donor had so carefully concealed would presumably be accompanied by the same sense of present deprivation which the act of handing over the money would have produced. The situation contained its own guaranty against inconsiderateness.

So far as the channeling function of a formality is concerned it has no place where men's activities are already divided into definite, clear-cut business categories. Where life has already organized itself effectively, there is no need for the law to intervene. It is for this reason that important transactions on the stock and produce markets can safely be carried on in the most 'informal' manner. At the other extreme we may cite the negotiations between a house-to-house book salesman and the housewife. Here the situation may be such that the housewife is not certain whether she is being presented with a set of books as a gift, whether she is being asked to trade her letter of recommendation for the books, whether the books are being offered to her on approval, or whether – what is, alas, the fact – a simple sale of the books is being proposed. The ambiguity of the situation is, of course, carefully cultivated and exploited by the canvasser. Some 'channeling' here would be highly desirable, though whether a legal form is the most practicable means of bringing it about is, of course, another question.

Extract 12.3   *Glaister-Carlisle* v. *Glaister-Carlisle, The Times,* 22 February 1968, CA

When a husband, vexed with his wife because he believed she had carelessly allowed his white miniature poodle bitch to mate with her black poodle, threw the bitch at her, saying 'She is your responsibility now', the conduct and words were so equivocal that English law would not regard it as a perfected gift of the poodle by him to her.

The Court of Appeal (the Master of the Rolls, Edmund Davies LJ and Cairns J) so held in allowing an appeal by Mr Thomas Glaister-Carlisle from the decision of Judge Glanville-Smith declaring in proceedings under section 17 Married Women's Property Act 1882 that the poodle was the property of his wife, Mrs Phyllis Mary Glaister-Carlisle. The Court of Appeal declared that the bitch was the husband's property and ordered that it be handed over to him within seven days.

The Master of the Rolls said that the bitch had lived up to her name, Springtime Ballyhoo. She had had an illicit love affair with a black pedigree poodle, Alexis, who lived in the same house. One expected consequence of this was that she had puppies. Other unexpected consequences were that on one occasion the police were called in; lawyers had been consulted; the magistrates had heard about it; the county court judge had decided it; and now the Court of Appeal had to consider it.

Her dam was owned by the husband and she was born in 1960. The husband registered her in his name with the Kennel Club. He was clearly her owner. He wanted her to have puppies and took her by arrangement to a Miss Evans, who owned Alexis. The dogs mated; the bitch had puppies; and in 1962 her owner married Miss Evans. They set up house and had the dog and bitch with them.

In September 1964, the wife had a broken leg. As they did not want the bitch to have puppies again, the wife had apparently asked the husband to take her to a Mrs Boon to get her out of the way, but it was not done in time. One afternoon when the wife was in a room unable to get out of her chair she heard skirmishing in the next room and a little squeak. She thought the dogs had probably mated and told her husband. There seemed to have been a row, each blaming the other.

Much of the case depended on what then happened. There were two versions. The husband's version was that he said: 'I say they have mated. This time you can bear the responsibility and expense . . . If there is a litter you win; if no litter you lose', and that the wife seemed to agree. The wife said that the husband had picked up the bitch, had thrown it at her, and had said that 'She is your responsibility now', that he had wanted to put the bitch down but instead had given it to her.

After the row the husband took the bitch to Mrs Boon for three weeks and paid the bill. Later, when it was plain she was going to have puppies, they both took her to Mrs Boon and the wife paid. The wife took the puppies. During that time the parties had been at arm's length and in February 1965 the husband left the house.

About May there was an uproar when he tried to claim the bitch, and he was bound over. From that time he said he kept watch, trying to see the bitch. Lawyers' letters were exchanged; and eventually the husband began proceedings under section 17 of the Married Women's Property Act 1882 to determine to whom the animal belonged. On Christmas Day 1966 he kidnapped the bitch and again there were proceedings. Eventually, the matter came before the county court judge on the one question: Did the bitch belong to wife or husband?

The judge found there had been a gift by the husband to the wife. The husband now appealed, saying there was no evidence on which he could so find and that he made the wrong inference from the facts he found. Accepting that the appeal from the county court in regard to property under £200 in value, like the bitch, was only on points of law, was the judge justified in the inference he drew?

Under the common law, in order that there should be a gift, there must be a delivery of possession by the one to the other, an acceptance, and above all a manifest intention by words or conduct to transfer the property absolutely from one to the other.

As between husband and wife it was often very difficult, because, as was said in *Bashall* v. *Bashall* (1894) 11 TLR 152, a husband might often deliver a thing to his wife not so that it should be her property but so that she should have its use and enjoyment. There it was a pony and trap, a saddle, and a dog; and the court held that she must show that the husband had done that which amounted to delivery and that, if the facts proved were equivocal, she must fail. And, in *Re Cole* [1964] 1 Ch 175 at 192 Lord Justice Harman said that if the act in itself was equivocal it did not constitute delivery.

The same must apply to the conduct or words which manifested intention. They must be clear and unequivocal; if they were not, the gift was not established.

In the present case there was no suggestion that it was an ordinary kind of gift made out of natural love and affection. The conduct was equivocal. Therefore, the property remained where it started, in the husband. The appeal should be allowed.

Lord Edmund Davies, concurring, said that the case sprang from the passions aroused by pedigree poodles. Why dogs should inspire strong emotions was not far to seek. Aldous Huxley said that 'To his dog, every man is a Napoleon – hence the popularity of dogs.' Despite her amorous activities, so popular was Springtime Ballyhoo that the rival claimants had, doubtless at considerable expense, brought the dispute about her ownership right up to the Court [of Appeal].

The present case was the direct converse of *Re Cole* in which Lord Justice Harman had observed that the English law had always been chary of the recognition of gifts. Here there had been a clear act of delivery of his poodle by the husband to the wife. The question was: What intention accompanied the act? In his Lordship's view, on the proved facts, no gift was intended or effected. It was most improbable that in the autumn of 1964 the husband would be animated by any sort of generous impulse towards his wife. The dispute was symptomatic of deeper and graver issues; but the wife had not established the gift.

Mr Justice Cairns concurred in allowing the appeal.

Notes and Questions 12.2

1   Read *Re Cole* [1964] 1 Ch 675, either in full or as extracted at www.cambridge.org/propertylaw/. What is the difference between constructive delivery and symbolic delivery? What sort of things may be delivered in these ways, and how?

2   If you share a house with a friend and you own all the furniture in the house, and you want to give it to her, how would you do it? Why is it so difficult?

3   In *Re Cole*, Pearson LJ appears to suggest that a gift of goods is not validly made unless and until it is accepted. Is this correct? See Hill, 'The Role of the Donee's Consent'.

4   Read *Lloyds Bank plc* v. *Carrick* [1996] 2 All ER 630, CA, and *Wilson* v. *First County Trust (No. 2)* [2003] UKHL 40, either in full or as extracted at www.cambridge.org/propertylaw/, and consider the following:
    (a)   Explain why there was a contract between Mrs Carrick and her brother in law.

(b) What does *Carrick* tell us about the proprietary interests acquired when a prospective purchaser enters into a contract to purchase an interest in land? (See further section 12.3 below.)

(c) Is it accurate to describe a person who has an estate contract in land as a beneficiary under a trust? How does the relationship between seller and estate contract holder differ from the trustee–beneficiary relationship?

(d) What does a claimant have to prove to demonstrate that she is entitled to an interest in land under a constructive trust? Was Mrs Carrick able to prove the necessary elements? Why did her claim based on constructive trust fail?

(e) What does a claimant have to prove to demonstrate that she is entitled to an interest in land by virtue of proprietary estoppel? Was Mrs Carrick able to prove the necessary elements? Why did her claim based on proprietary estoppel fail?

(f) Would the outcome have been different if the events had taken place after section 2 of the Law of Property (Miscellaneous Provisions) Act 1989 had come into force?

(g) After you have read Chapter 15 below, consider whether the outcome would have been different if Mr Carrick's title had been registered at the Land Registry.

(h) Write a letter to Mrs Carrick explaining the policy considerations which justified the Court of Appeal in coming to its decision, and why the Human Rights Act will not help her.

12.3.   Contractual rights to property interests

12.3.1.   Estate contracts and the rule in *Walsh* v. *Lonsdale*

If you and I enter into an agreement today that I will sell my fee simple interest in my land to you on 1 January next year for £100,000, this has two proprietary consequences. The first is that the right you acquire today (i.e. the legally enforceable right to acquire the fee simple on 1 January) is itself an equitable proprietary interest, usually called an estate contract. We can call this the 'estate contract rule'. The second is that from the moment when you have performed your part of the contract (suppose for example you pay me the money as agreed on 1 January but I refuse to transfer the fee simple to you) you acquire in equity the interest you have contracted to buy: from that point you hold the equitable fee simple in my land, and I have only the bare legal title. We can call this the 'rule in *Walsh* v. *Lonsdale*', this being the case which established the rule.

Both of these rules result from the operation of the equitable principle that 'equity treats as done that which ought to be done'. As far as the estate contract rule is concerned, the point is that, as a result of entering into a contract to buy an interest in land, you acquire a contract right that equity will enforce by an order of specific performance. You have a present right to a property interest in the future, contingent only on matters within your own control (i.e. your paying over the money), and if the contingency is satisfied equity will order completion of the transaction by ordering me to transfer the legal title to you. As we saw in Chapter 8, in these circumstances equity treats that present right to acquire a property interest in the future as a present property right. It is a *sui generis* right, consisting only of a right to call for the future property interest when the time comes, but it is proprietary in the sense that it is enforceable against third parties.

As far as the rule in *Walsh* v. *Lonsdale* is concerned, it comes into operation at the later stage when you satisfy the contingency by performing your part of the bargain. At this point you are entitled to specific performance of the agreement: equity will now order it as soon as you ask for it. Equity treats as done that which you are entitled to ask it to do – it treats you as already having what it will order me to give you. Hence you have the equitable fee simple from that point.

This was the principle established in the case of *Walsh* v. *Lonsdale* (1882) 21 ChD 9 (Extract 12.4 below). A mill owner agreed to let a weaving shed to a tenant for seven years at a fixed rent payable annually in advance, to be calculated according to the number of looms run by the tenant. The lease was never actually granted, but the tenant did go into possession of the weaving shed and started paying a rent at the agreed level, but he paid it in arrears rather than in advance. This continued for about three years until disagreements arose and the mill owner started proceedings for distress for rent. The issue was whether the rent was payable in advance or in arrears. It was (and is) a general principle of landlord and tenant law that, if a landowner allows someone into possession of her land and accepts rent without formally granting a lease, a legal periodic tenancy arises by implication of law, the terms of which are dictated by the way in which the rent is in fact paid. So, if as in *Walsh* v. *Lonsdale* itself the rent was actually paid annually in arrears, the tenancy implied will be a yearly tenancy at a rent paid annually in arrears. We see this rule in operation in *Prudential Assurance Co. Ltd* v. *London Residuary Body* [1992] 2 AC 386, discussed in Chapter 17. The question the court had to decide in *Walsh* v. *Lonsdale* was therefore whether the tenant was in possession under this rule (in which case the rent was payable in arrears) or whether he was in possession under the terms of the lease he had agreed to take but never in fact had taken (where the rent was payable in advance). The court said it was the latter, because in equity the tenant acquired the lease he contracted to take as soon as he performed his part of the contract by taking possession and paying rent. In other words, he had an equitable lease on the agreed terms as soon as he moved in, so there was no question of a legal yearly tenancy arising by implication of law.

12.3.2.   Application to property other than land

Neither the estate contract rule nor the rule in *Walsh* v. *Lonsdale* appears to apply to interests in goods. This has never been established as a matter of decision by the courts, but it was strongly stated by Atkin J in *Re Wait* [1927] 1 Ch 606, and endorsed (but again not as a matter of decision) by Lord Brandon in the House of Lords in *The Aliakmon* [1986] 2 WLR 902 at 910–11 (see Extract 12.5 below). The reason given for the exception is important and perhaps surprising. Since the estate contract rule and the rule in *Walsh* v. *Lonsdale* depend on the availability of specific performance, and specific performance is not generally available as a remedy to enforce contracts for the sale of goods, it might be thought that this would be given as the reason for excluding such contracts from these rules, but it is not. Instead, it is said that these rules should not apply because it is contrary to the policy of the Sale of Goods Act 1893 (and its successors) to allow equitable interests in goods to arise out of sale contracts.

This justification does not of course apply to interests in property other than goods, which suggests that the exception to these two rules should be limited to goods and not extend to other property such as shares and other intangibles.

12.3.3. The failed formalities rule

12.3.3.1. The general rule

If the contract to which the estate contract rule and the rule in *Walsh* v. *Lonsdale* apply is an agreement for the future disposition of an interest in land (as it is in the example given above), then section 2 of the Law of Property (Miscellaneous Provisions) Act 1989 applies, and the contract must be made in writing signed by the parties and containing all the agreed terms. Suppose, however, there is no preliminary contract stage. What is to happen if I just sell you my fee simple interest in my land for £100,000 without our first having entered into a contract to do so, but I fail to use the correct formality (perhaps I confuse sections 52 and 53 of the Law of Property Act 1925 and sign a statement written on the back of an envelope that I transfer the fee simple to you, but do not make it into a deed by adding that I sign it as a deed and getting someone to sign as a witness). The result will be that I will have your £100,000 but you will not have the legal fee simple – the legal title will not have been passed to you by deed, so I still have it. Can the rule in *Walsh* v. *Lonsdale* help you here and give you the equitable fee simple?

Before the Court of Appeal decision in *United Bank of Kuwait plc* v. *Sahib* [1997] Ch 107, the answer was unequivocally yes. Failed transactions that fail only because of a failure to use the correct formalities take effect in equity provided value has been given. Equity treats your payment of the money as performance of your part of an agreement it deemed us to have made for the sale and purchase of my fee simple for £100,000, and therefore as entitling you to specific performance of the obligation to transfer the fee simple that such an agreement would have imposed on me. Since you have an equitable right to call for the fee simple now, equity treats you as already having it, on the principle of treating as done that which ought to be done. In other words, you have the equitable fee simple and I have only a bare legal title. So, the general rule is that, whenever a transfer or grant of a property interest fails because of a failure to use the correct formalities, equity treats the transfer or grant as effective in equity provided the transferee/grantee has paid consideration. Even if there has been no prior contract to enter into the transaction, equity acts on the basis that there had been, provided the transferee/grantee has done what he would have been obliged to do if there had been such a contract.

12.3.3.2.   The failed formalities rule as it applies to land

As a result of the decision in *United Bank of Kuwait plc* v. *Sahib* [1997] Ch 107, CA, however, this general rule is modified in relation to interests in land. This, the court said, is a consequence of section 2 of the Law of Property (Miscellaneous Provisions) Act 1989.

The *Sahib* case concerned an attempt by Mr Sahib to mortgage the house he owned jointly with his wife to a bank to secure various business borrowings. He made it clear to the bank that he was offering them the legal fee simple interest in the house as security, but he did not succeed in executing the deed that would have been required to create a legal mortgage (not least because his wife did not appear to know anything about it). He did, however, arrange for the title deeds to be held on behalf of the bank as security. It had long been established that a deposit of title documents with the intention of granting security over the property to which the title documents relate creates an equitable mortgage or charge over that property. This is taken to have been established or at least confirmed by the decision in *Russel* v. *Russel* (1783) 1 Bro CC 269 in relation to land and by *Harrold* v. *Plenty* [1901] 2 Ch 314 in relation to shares in a company. However, it was not clear whether this was a *sui generis* mortgage rule, or just an application of the failed formalities rule. There are problems with both analyses which need not concern us here, but the significant point for present purposes is that in *Sahib* the Court of Appeal held, first, that the principle that an equitable mortgage arises when title documents are deposited with intent to create security was an application of the failed formalities rule, but secondly that the failed formalities rule could no longer apply to land transactions unless the failed transaction satisfied the requirements of section 2 of the Law of Property (Miscellaneous Provisions) Act 1989. Consequently, it was held, a deposit of title deeds could no longer create an equitable mortgage.

This is not particularly important as far as mortgage law is concerned. The Law Commission had already recommended that it should no longer be possible to create any kind of security interest without signed writing, for the reasons we discussed earlier in this chapter. However, the reasoning adopted by the Court of Appeal is equally applicable to all failed formality land transactions, and consequently the decision has had the effect of modifying the failed formality rule for land transactions.

The modified rule is that an attempted transfer or grant of an interest in land which fails because of a failure to comply with the required formalities will take effect in equity but only if it satisfies section 2 of the 1989 Act, that is if it is made in writing signed by all the parties and containing all the agreed terms. This is an unsatisfactory outcome. It is, to say the least, unlikely that someone who out of ignorance or carelessness fails to use the correct formalities will nevertheless happen to adopt these section 2 formalities. The failed formality rule has therefore been robbed of most of its effectiveness in land transactions. Secondly, the section 2 formalities were intended to apply to the very specific circumstance of a prior contract to enter into a land transaction in the future: they were never intended to act as a minimum level of formality that had to be observed before a failed legal transaction could be allowed to take effect in equity. Not surprisingly, they are wholly inappropriate for this purpose.

As we see in Notes and Questions 12.3 below, the reasoning adopted by the Court of Appeal in coming to this decision is as unsatisfactory as the outcome. Nevertheless, it must be taken to represent the state of the law as it now is, and as the law stands the modified rule applies to land transactions.

12.3.3.3. Failed formalities rule as it applies to other property

The reasoning that led Atkin J to conclude in *Re Wait* that contracts for the sale of goods do not confer property rights on the buyer, would also exclude the failed formalities rule from application to outright sales of goods. However, since no formalities are required for the sale of goods, the question does not arise. It does, however, arise in the case of other types of property where there are formal requirements for a transfer or grant of a legal interest. In such cases, there is no reason why the failed formalities rule should not apply in the general form described in section 12.3.3.1 above, so that, if the correct formalities for transferring or granting a legal title are not used, the transaction will nevertheless take effect in equity provided the buyer has given value or otherwise started to perform its part of the bargain. Section 2 of the 1989 Act is of course not relevant, and the goods exception should not apply since its rationale appears firmly grounded in the policy of the Sale of Goods Acts, as noted above.

Extract 12.4   *Walsh v. Lonsdale* (1882) 21 ChD 9

By an agreement dated 29 May 1879, between the Plaintiff and Defendant it was agreed that the Defendant should grant and the Plaintiff accept a lease of a weaving-shed known as Providence Mill with the engine-house and other buildings belonging thereto (except cottages) and the steam-engine and other machinery thereon for a term of seven years from the time when the shed should be put in working order by the Defendant; the lessee at his own expense to find sufficient steam power for driving the looms and other machinery. The rent was to be £2 10s per loom per annum for so many looms as the lessee shall run. The lessee shall not run less than 300 looms during the said first year, and he shall in every year afterwards run not less than 540 looms ...
The rent was to be payable in advance. The lease was never granted but the Plaintiff was let into possession on 1 July 1879 and continued to operate the looms there until 1882, paying rent in arrears. The Defendant issued a distress for rent which he claimed was due on the basis that the rent was payable in advance. The Plaintiff brought this action for damages for improper distress.

JESSEL MR: It is not necessary on the present occasion to decide finally what the rights of the parties are. If the Court sees that there is a fair question to be decided it will take security so that the party who ultimately succeeds may be in the right position. The question is one of some nicety. There is an agreement for a lease under which possession has been given. Now since the Judicature Act the possession is held under the agreement. There are not two estates as there were formerly, one estate at common law by reason of the payment of the rent from year to year, and an estate in equity under the agreement. There is only one Court, and the equity rules prevail in it. The tenant holds under an agreement for a lease. He holds, therefore, under the same terms in equity as if a lease had been granted, it being a case in which both parties admit that relief is capable of being given by specific performance. That being so, he cannot complain of the exercise by the landlord of the same rights as the landlord would have had if a lease had been granted. On the other hand, he is protected in the same way as if a lease had been granted; he cannot be turned out by six months' notice as a tenant from year to year. He has a right to say, 'I have a lease in equity, and you can only re-enter if I have committed such a breach of covenant as would if a lease had been granted have entitled you to re-enter according to the terms of a proper proviso for re-entry.' That being so, it appears to me that being a lessee in equity he cannot complain of the exercise of the right of distress merely because the actual parchment has not been signed and sealed.

Notes and Questions 12.3

Read *United Bank of Kuwait plc* v. *Sahib* [1997] Ch 107, either in full or as extracted at www.cambridge.org/propertylaw/, and consider the following questions.

1 Section 2 of the Law of Property (Miscellaneous Provisions) Act 1989 is intended to apply to contracts to transfer or grant an interest in land *at a future date*. When Mr Sahib deposited the title deeds of the house with the bank as security for the various loans they had made to his business, did he and the bank intend that he *would* mortgage the house to them at some future date, or that he *was thereby* mortgaging it to them?

2 Why might the formalities appropriate for entering into an agreement with your bank to mortgage your house to them at a future date be different from those appropriate for mortgaging it to them now to secure repayment of money they have already lent you?

3 In the failed formality cases up until *Sahib*, it was assumed that the failed formality rule depended on equity *deeming* there to have been a prior contract to enter into the transaction, in circumstances when in fact there had been no such contract. In cases where there *was in fact* a prior contract, there was no need to have a failed formality rule. The contract itself (made enforceable by the grantee/transferee's acts of, for example, paying over the money in the case of a failed transfer on sale, or moving into possession and paying rent in the case of a failed lease, which were sufficient under section 40 of the Law of Property Act 1925) would have given the grantee/transferee the appropriate equitable interest anyway

under the rules discussed in section 12.3.1 above. In other words, the failed formality rule depended on equity assuming the existence of a contract that they knew either did not exist or could not be proved to have existed. In *Sahib*, the Court of Appeal accepted this to the extent that they said that, before 1989, the action of depositing the title deeds with intention to create security was *presumed* to have been done in part performance of a prior contract. In other words, they accepted that, before 1989, courts were not concerned to enquire whether there actually had been such a contract – when and where it was made, and what it said – once they were satisfied that the title deeds were deposited with the intention of granting security, nor would they have refused to accept that the deposit of title deeds created an equitable mortgage if presented with positive proof that there had been no prior contract, as Peter Gibson LJ accepted in response to the fourth of counsel for the bank's seven numbered points. The difficulty felt by the Court of Appeal in *Sahib* was that, under section 40 of the Law of Property Act 1925, a valid contract could have been made in any form, but would not have been enforceable unless recorded in a written memorandum or evidenced by part performance, so there was no great difficulty in equity assuming the *existence* of the prior contract. Under section 2 of the 1989 Act, on the other hand, there is no contract at all unless a piece of writing satisfying the requirements of section 2 is brought into existence. The Court of Appeal appeared to take the view that, if there is no such writing in existence, equity cannot presume that a prior contract existed because they know it did not. Are they right? If you do not regard yourself as bound to enquire whether there actually was a prior contract or not, is it any more difficult to presume the existence of a written contract than it is to presume the existence of an oral contract? Does it make any sense to say that you will presume that a contract existed, but only if there is evidence that it did exist? After the 1989 Act, as before it, if there is a valid prior contract to enter into a transaction, followed by a botched attempt to carry out the transaction, we have no need of a failed formality rule to rescue the prospective transferee: she already has the appropriate equitable interest by virtue of the contract. It is only in cases where there was no prior contract that we need the failed formality rule.

4   Neither the Law Commission nor Parliament intended section 2 of the 1989 Act to affect *immediate* dispositions of interests in land, such as the creation of a mortgage having immediate effect by depositing title documents. This is the second of the seven numbered points made by counsel for the bank. What was the Court of Appeal's response? Is it convincing?

Extract 12.5   *Leigh and Sillivan Ltd* v. *Aliakmon Shipping Co. Ltd (The Aliakmon)* [1986] 2 WLR 902 at 910–11

[Buyers of steel coils sought to recover damages in tort in respect of damage caused to the goods during shipment at a time when (under the terms of that particular sale contract) risk had passed from the sellers to the buyers but property in the goods had not. The House of Lords confirmed the long-established principle that a plaintiff has no claim in negligence for loss suffered by him by reason of damage caused to goods, unless he had either legal ownership or a possessory title to the goods at the time when the loss or damage occurred; the House of Lords approved a long line of cases concerning claims by contractors, insurers, tug owners and time charterers which established that contractual rights in relation to the goods were not sufficient to found a claim in negligence, and also approved the decision of Roskill J in *The Wear Breeze* [1969] 1 QB 219 to the effect that the same applied where the contractual right the plaintiff had was a contractual right to purchase the goods.

The buyers argued, *inter alia*, that (a) equitable ownership was sufficient to found a claim in negligence and (b) a contractual right to purchase confers equitable owner-ship on a buyer once ascertained goods have been appropriated to the contract. The House of Lords rejected (a) as contrary to principle and authority, as follows:]

[Where a person] is the equitable owner of goods and no more, then he must join the legal owner as a party to the action [in tort for negligence], either as co-plaintiff if he is willing or as co-defendant if he is not. This has always been the law in the field of equitable ownership of land and I see no reason why it should not also be so in the field of equitable ownership of goods.

[It was therefore unnecessary to deal with (b). Lord Brandon nevertheless said:]

With regard to the second proposition, I do not doubt that it is possible, in accordance with established equitable principles, for equitable interests in goods to be created and to exist. It seems to me, however, extremely doubtful whether equitable interests in goods can be created or exist within the confines of an ordinary contract of sale. The Sale of Goods Act 1893 ... is a complete code of law in respect of contracts for the sale of goods. The passing of the property in goods the subject-matter of such a contract is fully dealt with in sections 16 to 19 of the Act. Those sections draw no distinction between the legal and the equitable property in goods, but appear to have been framed on the basis that the expression 'property', as used in them, is intended to comprise both the legal and the equitable title. In this connection I consider that there is much force in the observations of Atkin J in *Re Wait* [1927] 1 Ch 606, 635–6, from which I quote only this short passage:

It would have been futile in a code intended for commercial men to have created an elaborate structure of rules dealing with rights at law, if at the same time it was intended to leave, subsisting with the legal rights, equitable rights inconsistent with, more extensive, and coming into existence earlier than the rights so carefully set out in the various sections of the code.

These observations of Atkin J were not necessary to the decision of the case before him and represented a minority view not shared by the other two members of the Court of Appeal. Moreover, Atkin J expressly stated that he was not deciding the point. If my view on the first proposition of law [i.e. (a) above] is correct, it is again unnecessary to decide the point on this appeal. I shall, therefore, say no more than that my provisional view accords with that expressed by Atkin J in *Re Wait*.

Notes and Questions 12.4

1   What did Atkin J mean when he said it would have been *futile* to create an elaborate structure of rules to govern the transfer of legal property interests on sale, if it was intended also to allow equitable interests to arise out of a sale contract? Is he right?

2   What are the disadvantages of not allowing equitable property interests to arise out of contracts for the sale of goods? Do different considerations apply to fungible and non-fungible goods (see section 2.4.4.1 above for the distinction between the two)?

12.3.4.   Options to purchase, rights of pre-emption and rights of first refusal

In Chapter 8, we saw how present entitlements to acquire a property interest in the future can range from more or less absolute rights to 'rights' that are subject to so many contingencies that they amount to no more than mere hopes or expectancies. The law is not prepared to treat 'rights' at this latter end of the scale as property rights, but inevitably there are difficulties in deciding precisely where to draw the line. This problem is particularly acute in the case of contractual rights to acquire property interests. In the preceding paragraphs we have been concentrating on rights arising out of unconditional contracts, but not all contracts are unconditional, and indeed a contract to acquire a property interest may be asymmetrical, giving the purchaser an option but not an obligation to purchase, or conversely only a right of pre-emption or a right of first refusal rather than an absolute right to purchase.

Two problems arise here. The first is whether all these rights are property rights. After considerable uncertainty the Court of Appeal in *Pritchard* v. *Briggs* [1980] Ch 338 (extracted at www.cambridge.org/propertylaw/) decided that rights of pre-emption fell on the wrong side of the line and were not property interests. However, this decision was made entirely on doctrinal rather than on policy grounds and it has been greatly criticised. The Law Commission and Land Registry recommended that it should be reversed in so far as it affected registered land (Law Commission and HM Land Registry, *Land Registration for the Twenty-First Century: A Conveyancing Revolution* (Law Commission Report No. 271, 2001), paragraphs 5.26–5.28 (Extract 12.6 below)), and section 115 of the Land Registration Act 2002 was enacted with the intention of implementing this, although how far it has been successful is debatable, as we see below. Meanwhile, in any event, the Court of Appeal in *Dear* v. *Reeves* [2001] EWCA Civ 277 (extracted at www.cambridge.org/propertylaw/), declined to follow *Pritchard* v. *Briggs* and held that a right of pre-emption is a property interest within the Insolvency Act 1986, and therefore a right of pre-emption held by a bankrupt will pass to his trustee in bankruptcy to be sold for the benefit of his creditors. Almost simultaneously, in *Bircham & Co. Nominees (No. 2) Ltd* v. *Worrell Holdings Ltd* [2001] EWCA Civ 775 (extracted at www.cambridge.org/propertylaw/), a different division of the Court of Appeal, proceeding on the basis that *Pritchard* v. *Briggs* was correctly decided, pointed out that there were at least three different things that could loosely be referred to as rights of pre-emption. First, a distinction has to be drawn between what is usually referred to as a right of first refusal (where, if the grantor decides to sell, the grantee has the first right to refuse an offer to purchase at the price at which the grantor is willing to sell) and a right of pre-emption (where, if the grantor decides to sell, the grantee has a right to purchase at a fixed price, or a price not chosen by the grantor). Secondly, some rights of pre-emption and rights of first refusal become options to purchase as soon as the grantor offers to sell to the grantee: these are those where the grantee has a fixed period within which it may accept the offer, and the grantor cannot withdraw the offer during that period. The right of pre-emption in *Pritchard* v. *Briggs* fell within this category. On the other hand, other rights of pre-emption and rights of first refusal do not become options to purchase until the grantee accepts the offer: these are the ones where the grantor is still given a fixed period within which it may accept the offer, but the offer may be withdrawn at any time before acceptance. This was the position in *Bircham & Co. Nominees (No. 2) Ltd* v. *Worrell Holdings Ltd*.

This brings us to the second problem. At what point must an option to purchase and a right of pre-emption satisfy section 2 of the Law of Property (Miscellaneous Provisions) Act 1989? If it is at the time when the interest is first created, this should cause no difficulties, because most options to purchase and rights of pre-emption are made in writing and signed by both parties. If, however, it is at the stage in the procedure when *both parties would (apart from section 2) have become contractually bound to the sale*, this is likely to mean that no contract will ever come into existence, because that stage is usually triggered by writing signed by only one of the parties. In *Spiro* v. *Glencrown Properties Ltd* [1991] Ch 537 (extracted at www.cambridge.org/propertylaw/), Hoffmann J decided that, in the case of options to purchase, it is the document that creates the option to purchase that must satisfy section 2 of the 1989 Act. In *Bircham & Co. Nominees (No. 2) Ltd* v. *Worrell Holdings Ltd*, however, the Court of Appeal expressed agreement with this but then held that the position was different in the case of rights of pre-emption (hence the importance of pinpointing exactly the point at which both parties became bound to proceed with the sale). The effect on this of the subsequent enactment of section 115 of the Land Registration Act 2002 is not at all clear, as we see below.

What is apparent from all these cases is that the differences between the rights that inhabit the spectrum from unconditional right to mere expectancy are analytically differences of degree rather than differences of kind. This does not mean that it is wrong to treat some as property rights and others not, but it does mean that if a line is to be drawn somewhere policy reasons ought to dictate where the line falls. As the following extracts demonstrate, however, this is not the approach that the courts (or indeed Parliament) have always adopted.

Notes and Questions 12.5

1 Read *Pritchard* v. *Briggs* [1980] Ch 338, either in full or as extracted at
   www.cambridge.org/propertylaw/, and consider the following:
   (a) According to the Court of Appeal, how does a right of pre-emption differ
       analytically from (i) a right to purchase under an unconditional contract and
       (ii) an option to purchase? What reasons do they give for concluding that these
       differences justify their conclusion that a right of pre-emption is not a property
       interest, whereas the other two are? How convincing are these reasons?
   (b) How does a right of pre-emption differ from a right to purchase under a *conditional*
       contract for sale? Does it make any difference whether the fulfilment of the
       condition in the conditional sale contract is dependent on the volition of the seller,
       or the volition of the buyer, or outside the control of both of them? Should it?
   (c) According to each of the members of the Court of Appeal in *Pritchard* v. *Briggs*
       at what stage, if any, does a right of pre-emption become a property interest?
       Consider what problems are caused by each of their analyses.
   (d) Is the Court of Appeal right to equate a right of pre-emption with the hope of
       a person who is a beneficiary in the will of a living testator? Consider what
       Mummery LJ says about this in *Dear* v. *Reeves* below.

2 Read *Dear* v. *Reeves* [2001] EWCA Civ 277, either in full or as extracted at
   www.cambridge.org/propertylaw/, and consider the following:
   (a) What would Mr Reeves' trustee in bankruptcy gain by exercising the right of
       pre-emption? What was the likelihood of his being given the opportunity to do so?
   (b) Is the reason given in paragraph 31 for distinguishing *Pritchard* v. *Briggs* com-
       pelling? *Pritchard* v. *Briggs* concerned *enforceability* of the interest, whereas *Dear* v.
       Reeves concerned the *alienability* of it: does this throw any light on whether it
       might be justifiable to treat a right of pre-emption as a purely contract right for
       the purposes of registering interests in land, but as a property interest for bank-
       ruptcy purposes, so as to ensure that it passes to the trustee in bankruptcy and
       does not remain in the bankrupt's own hands? See in particular what Mummery
       LJ says at paragraph 40: would these factors be relevant to the issues that arose in
       Pritchard v. *Briggs*?

3 Read *Spiro* v. *Glencrown Properties Ltd* [1991] Ch 537 and *Bircham & Co.
   Nominees (No. 2) Ltd* v. *Worrell Holdings Ltd* [2001] EWCA Civ 775, either in
   full or as extracted at www.cambridge.org/propertylaw/, and consider the
   following:
   (a) Is the Court of Appeal decision in *Bircham* consistent with the reasoning of
       Hoffmann J in *Spiro*? Is it consistent with the objectives of section 2 of the 1989
       Act?
   (b) Consider the practical effects of the decision in *Bircham*: is it likely that writing
       satisfying section 2 will ever come into existence when a right of pre-emption is
       exercised? If not, does this matter?

(c) What is the effect of section 115 of the Land Registration Act 2002 on this decision? (see above).

(d) Examine the reasons Hoffmann J gave in *Spiro* for regarding himself as justified in departing from the 'irrevocable offer' analysis of options to purchase. Are they valid reasons?

Extract 12.6   Law Commission and HM Land Registry, *Land Registration for the Twenty-First Century: A Conveyancing Revolution* (Law Commission Report No. 271, 2001)

RIGHTS OF PRE-EMPTION

5.26. In the Consultative Document we gave the following critical explanation of the present legal position of rights of pre-emption:

> A right of pre-emption is a right of first refusal. The grantor undertakes that he or she will not sell the land without first offering it to the grantee. It is similar to but not the same as an option, because the grantee can purchase the property only if the grantor decides that he or she wants to sell it.
>
> The precise status of a right of pre-emption was uncertain until the decision of the Court of Appeal in *Pritchard* v. *Briggs*, an uncertainty that that decision has not wholly dispelled. In some cases, it had been held that it was merely a contractual right and could never be an equitable proprietary interest. In others, the right was held to create an equitable interest in land from its inception. There are also a number of statutory provisions which were enacted on the assumption that rights of pre-emption created interests in land.
>
> In *Pritchard* v. *Briggs* a majority of the Court of Appeal expressed the view that a right of pre-emption did not confer on the grantee any interest in land. However, when the grantor chose to sell the property, the right of pre-emption became an option and, as such, an equitable interest in land. It should be noted that the remarks of the Court of Appeal were only *obiter* and have been recognised as such. They have been much criticised, and this criticism has not escaped judicial attention. Not only was there no previous authority for 'this strange doctrine of delayed effectiveness', but if it is correct its effects can be unfortunate:
>
> (1) It can lead to something 'which a sound system of property law ought to strive at all costs to avoid: the defeat of a prior interest by a later purchaser taking with notice of the conflicting interest', as indeed happened in *Pritchard* v. *Briggs* itself. For example, if A grants B a right of pre-emption which B immediately registers, and A then mortgages the land to C, it seems likely that C will not be bound by the right of pre-emption because the execution of the mortgage probably does not cause the pre-emption to crystallise into an equitable interest. C could therefore, in exercise of his paramount powers as mortgagee, sell the land free from B's right of pre-emption.
>
> (2) Although the person having the benefit of a right of pre-emption may register it at the time it is created . . . the right is effective for the purposes of priority

only from the moment when the grantor demonstrates an animus to sell the land, not from the date of registration.

5.27. In the Consultative Document, we recommended that a right of pre-emption in registered land should take effect from the time when it was created and not, as *Pritchard* v. *Briggs* suggested, only from the time when the grantor decided to sell. This recommendation was supported by 96 per cent of those who responded to the point. It was clear from the tenor of the responses that the result in *Pritchard* v. *Briggs* was not well regarded because of the practical difficulties to which it gave rise.

5.28. The Bill provides that a right of pre-emption in relation to registered land has effect from the time of creation as an interest capable of binding successors in title . . . In other words, it takes its priority from the date of its creation. If the *dicta* in *Pritchard* v. *Briggs* do represent the present law, then the Bill changes the law in its application to registered land. The change is therefore prospective only. It applies to rights of pre-emption created on or after the Bill comes into force.

Notes and Questions 12.6

1 What precisely was *obiter dicta* in *Pritchard* v. *Briggs*: the unanimous conclusion that the right of pre-emption was not a property interest, or the majority conclusion that it becomes a property interest at the time when the grantor decides to sell?

2 The Law Commission and Land Registry report gives, in effect, two grounds for criticising the decision in *Pritchard* v. *Briggs* (i.e. the two numbered points in paragraph 5.26). The first is question-begging: it is only contrary to property law principles for a right of pre-emption to be defeated by a subsequent property interest if a right of pre-emption is itself a property interest. This is the question at issue here, not something that can be assumed in an argument seeking to convince us that it *should be* a property interest. The second requires closer scrutiny: consider what practical ill-effects would follow if an interest is registered before it becomes a property interest, and will only become a property interest on the happening of a future event.

3 A better test for deciding whether rights of pre-emption ought to be classified as property interests might be to consider whether people might have good commercial and/or social reasons for wanting them to be enforceable not only against the original parties but also against anyone who subsequently acquires an interest in the land. If we apply this test, should rights of pre-emption be classified as property interests?

4 The wording of section 115(1) of the Land Registration Act 2002 which implements this recommendation closely follows the wording of the recommendation itself:

> A right of pre-emption in relation to registered land has effect from the time of creation as an interest capable of binding successors in title ...

It is not clear whether the courts are going to be prepared to read this as meaning that for all purposes a right of pre-emption affecting a registered title is to be treated as a property interest. If they are not, section 115 will not necessarily help to resolve questions such as those raised (before it came into force) in *Dear* v. *Reeves* and in *Bircham & Co. Nominees (No. 2) Ltd* v. *Worrell Holdings Ltd*.

5 Section 115 does not define 'right of pre-emption'. Does it cover rights of first refusal?

12.4. Unascertained property

12.4.1. The problem of identification

We said in Chapter 5 that a property right cannot attach to a thing until the thing has been identified, and the same applies if the thing has not yet come into existence. As we saw in Chapter 5, this does not prevent the law recognising property rights in fluctuating bodies of assets, such as trust funds and the assets covered by a floating charge. In this section, we look at the other ways in which the law deals with the difficulties arising when people want to deal with not yet ascertained or not yet existing assets.

12.4.2. Unascertained goods

When it comes to buying and selling unascertained goods, there are statutory rules to regulate the position. The basic rule in sale of goods is that property in the goods passes when the parties intend it to pass – usually when the goods are paid for or delivered (section 17 of the Sale of Goods Act 1979). However, this basic rule is modified in the case of unascertained goods: by section 16 of the 1979 Act the *earliest* point at which property in unascertained goods can pass is the point when the goods are ascertained. This means that, when unascertained goods are sold, property passes at the time they are ascertained or at the time when the parties intend it to pass, whichever is the later. So, if you go into a book shop and order a book which is not yet published, paying for it in advance, and a copy is subsequently sent to you, the *earliest* point at which you can become owner of the book is the point when a specific copy has been earmarked for your order – perhaps when the bookseller picks a copy out of the pile and puts your order form in it, or, if they are sending out several copies to different people, when they address one of the packages to you. You may of course have agreed with the bookseller that it will not become yours until a later date – perhaps when they post it to you, or until you receive it – but no matter what you and the bookseller agree, you could not have acquired property rights in any book at the point when you paid for it, because at that stage no one had identified which copy was yours.

In practice, however, people do sometimes pay for goods before they have been ascertained, and sometimes even deal in unascertained goods. The Law Commission considered some of the problems that can arise when this happens in its report, *Sale of Goods Forming Part of a Bulk* (Law Commission Report No. 215, 1993), including the situation that arose in *Re London Wine Co. (Shippers) Ltd* [1986] PCC 121. There a company sold wine to customers on terms that the wine would be paid for immediately but left in storage with the company, for which the customers also paid storage charges. The company issued customers with 'certificates of title' but never actually earmarked any particular bottles for any specific customer. When the company went insolvent, it was held that none of the customers had any property rights in any of the bottles in the company's warehouse. The court followed the majority Court of Appeal decision in *Re Wait* [1927] 1 Ch 606, where a similar conclusion was reached when sub-purchasers bought and paid for 500 tons of wheat out of a cargo of '1,000 tons . . . ex *Challenger*' and their seller then went bankrupt before the wheat could be delivered to them. Both decisions were approved by the Privy Council in *Re Goldcorp Exchange Ltd* [1995] AC 74, where mail order customers who thought they had bought gold bullion from a bullion dealer were held to have no proprietary rights in the bullion left in stock when the dealer went into liquidation. In *Re Stapylton Fletcher* [1994] 1 WLR 1181, on facts very similar to those in *Re London Wine Co. (Shippers)*, the court was able to find that cases of wine which had been separately stored and all of which had been sold to identified customers in identified amounts, had become the property of all those customers as co-owners, but the conditions necessary for this co-ownership solution to apply at common law did not often arise. Accordingly, the Law Commission recommended that the Sale of Goods Act 1979 should be amended to provide a similar solution whenever there were sales of unascertained goods, provided they formed part of an ascertained bulk. This recommendation was implemented by the Sale of Goods (Amendment) Act 1995, which added new sections 20A and 20B to the 1979 Act. Under these new provisions, when there is such a sale the buyer becomes co-owner of the bulk as soon as she has paid any part of the purchase price, and then becomes full owner of her own items as soon as they are earmarked as hers.

12.4.3.   Other unascertained property

A more difficult question is whether the general rule about dispositions of unascertained property applies to property other than land and goods. The reasons for not allowing property to pass by a sale or gift of 'five of my sheep in that field' or 'one of the flats in my apartment block' are not so compelling where the property is intangible. In *Hunter* v. *Moss* [1993] 1 WLR 934 (extracted at www.cambridge.org/propertylaw/), the Court of Appeal had to consider whether Mr Moss' declaration that he held 5 per cent of the shares in his company on trust for his employee Mr Hunter gave Mr Hunter an equitable interest in the appropriate number of shares. It was decided that it did, even though there was no identification of the shares to be held on trust, because the shares were all identical and, as Dillon LJ said, the case was 'a long way' from cases such as *Re London Wine Co. (Shippers) Ltd* which were 'concerned with the appropriation of chattels and when the property in chattels passes'.

This decision has been heavily criticised, as Neuberger J notes in *Re Harvard Securities Ltd* [1998] BCC 567, extracted at www.cambridge.org/propertylaw/. However, the House of Lords refused leave to appeal from the decision ([1994] 1 WLR 614) and Neuberger J himself felt bound to follow it in *Re Harvard Securities Ltd*. He accordingly decided that under English law where a broker's nominee company held a large shareholding on behalf of an identified list of customers who had each paid for a specific number of shares, each customer was entitled in equity to the appropriate number of shares, even though the broker had not earmarked which shares were held for which customer. In the case of identical intangible property such as shares or a debt or a fund, it therefore appears established that a transfer or grant of a property interest in a specified portion or specified number of items out of a bulk is effective in equity even though the part of the bulk affected has not been identified.

As can be seen from Neuberger J's judgment in *Re Harvard Securities*, academic critics of this position have argued that the reasoning in *Hunter* v. *Moss* is not supportable. The conclusion itself has also been attacked, but perhaps with less justification. There are at least two grounds on which it can be supported. The first is that the risk of identification problems arising is greater for goods than it is for intangibles. There are practical reasons why, if I hold 100 sheep, 100 £1 coins and 100 grains of sand, and either sell ten of each to you or declare I hold ten of each on trust for you, we need to know which are mine and which are yours. A sheep might die or have lambs, a coin might be lost, and a few grains of sand might blow away: were these mine or yours? This is not such a problem with shares and other intangibles. Most of the things that can happen to some but not all of a collection of identical chattels cannot happen to some but not all of a collection of identical intangibles. As a matter of company law, all shares of the same class must be treated in the same way by the company: it is not possible to declare dividends or make rights issues on some but not others. And shares and other intangibles cannot die or be destroyed or get lost.

The only real problem that can arise is if the holder of the as yet undivided up collection of intangibles creates inconsistent rights in part of it in favour of a third party, but even here the scope for ambiguity is small. In the simple situation in which I own 100 shares of the same class and either sell 50 to you or declare I hold 50 of them on trust for you, but remain registered owner of all of them, there can be no doubt as to whose shares are affected if I make any disposition of them as if still beneficially entitled to them. As a matter of general principle any purported disposition of a property interest will operate to pass whatever interest the disponor actually has (via either section 63 of the Law of Property Act 1925, not confined to land, or the doctrine of partial performance confirmed by the Court of

Appeal in *Thames Guaranty* v. *Campbell* [1985] QB 210). So, any sale or mortgage of shares by me will automatically bite on my shares first: if I sell or mortgage 50 or fewer of them, it will be mine that are sold or mortgaged, and, if more than 50, the first 50 will be mine and the remainder will be yours. It is only in more complex cases that prior identification could matter. For example, if a thief manages to acquire legal title to some of the shares (for example, by stealing some of the share certificates and forging my signature on a share transfer form) and so succeeds in selling them to an innocent purchaser, it would become necessary to know whether he had stolen my shares or yours. Similarly, if, after I had sold you 50 shares or declared I held them on trust for you, I then sold the rest to your brother or declared I held them on trust for him, still keeping all the shares in my name and unallocated to either of you, there would be an identification problem if I sold ten of them to an innocent purchaser and disappeared with the money. There would be no way of telling whether the innocent purchaser had acquired 'your' shares or your brother's.

However, in both these cases co-ownership in equity is clearly the best solution, and there seems no reason why the courts should not adopt it, as they did in *Re Stapylton Fletcher* [1994] 1 WLR 1181. In other words, both the lost shares and the remaining ones are treated as co-owned so that, in effect, losses are shared proportionately. This is what is done in the analogous situation in which identical goods belonging to different people become mixed (as in *Spence* v. *Union Marine Insurance Co. Ltd* (1868) LR 3 CP 427) and where funds of different beneficiaries are used to acquire a single asset (as in *Foskett* v. *McKeown* [2001] 1 AC 102), and there seems no reason in principle why it should not be done here. It certainly produces a better and fairer outcome for the innocent participants than the goods rule, which says that, because we cannot identify which of two possible claimants owns which item, neither of them can have it. Also, it causes no hardship to innocent third parties: since the co-ownership interest is equitable only, it will not be enforceable against a good faith purchaser without notice of the interest, as we see in Chapter 14.

In other words, the other principled reason for supporting the conclusion in *Hunter* v. *Moss* is that it produces a fairer outcome than the goods rule. This is of course an argument against the goods rule rather than an argument for distinguishing between goods and intangibles, but there is something to be said for putting a limit on the scope of a bad rule, even if the limit is logically not entirely sustainable.

Notes and Questions 12.7

Read *Hunter* v. *Moss* [1994] 1 WLR 452 and *Re Harvard Securities Ltd* [1998] BCC 567, either in full or as extracted at www.cambridge.org/propertylaw/, and consider the following:

1 What criticisms have textbook writers made of the reasoning in *Hunter* v. *Moss*, according to Neuberger J in *Re Harvard Securities*? Are they convincing?

2 What reasons does Neuberger J give for distinguishing shares from chattels? He describes himself as 'not particularly convinced' by the distinction. Are you?

3 If shareholding and sharedealing become wholly electronic, so that shares are no longer numbered and share certificates are no longer issued, would this give added support to the Court of Appeal decision in *Hunter* v. *Moss*?

4 Write the leading judgment in the House of Lords on appeal from the Court of Appeal decision in *Hunter* v. *Moss* (heard after *Re Harvard Securities*).

13

Acquiring interests by other methods

13.1. Introduction

There are a number of ways in which titles to, and interests in, things can be acquired and lost, apart from by express grant or transfer. Titles and interests can arise by implication of law, for example by estoppel or via a resulting or constructive trust or through the presumed intentions of the parties, as briefly noted in Chapter 8. Also, titles and interests can automatically pass from one person to another by operation of law, for example on death or bankruptcy, again as we saw in Chapter 8. In this chapter, we concentrate on another way in which interests can arise without an express grant, namely, by long user.

An interest in someone else's property can be acquired by prescription, a process which involves using someone else's property in a particular way for a sufficiently long period. The process applies not just to private property rights (notably easements and profits) but also to communal property rights, and public rights such as (but not confined to) public rights of way.

The process of acquiring a right like this by long use has obvious similarities with the process of eliminating a rival title by adverse possession but, as we see below, there are important differences between the two.

13.2. The difference between adverse possession and prescription

Unlike Roman-law-based systems, English law has never treated long enjoyment as a means of acquiring title. As we saw in Chapter 11, in English law non-owners instantly acquire titles to land and other tangibles by the mere act of taking factual possession, and the only function of lapse of time is to bar the true owner from his right to object and extinguish his better rival title. The adverse possessor's title is choate and complete from the outset: it is not acquired by long user. However, while ownership cannot be acquired by long user, particular use rights can. If a particular use is made of someone else's land for a sufficiently long time, and the use is of a type, falling short of possession or occupation, that could have constituted a property right if expressly granted, then the use will ultimately become legitimised. So, while in adverse possession law long use merely operates to eliminate rival titles, prescription is a means by which proprietary rights are acquired over a period of time, the right in question remaining inchoate until the appropriate time has elapsed.

However, these significant analytical differences between the two doctrines should not blind us to their essential similarities: they are both processes by which a property right is acquired by one person at the expense of another, and without payment, and in both cases the effect of the process is to legitimise long user.

13.3.   Why long use should give rise to entitlement

Having said that, English law displays an unfortunate ambivalence towards the rationale for prescription. In *R. v. Oxfordshire County Council, ex parte Sunningwell Parish Council* [1999] 3 WLR 160, HL (extracted at www.cambridge.org/propertylaw/), Lord Hoffmann treats it as axiomatic that '[a]ny legal system must have rules of prescription which prevent the disturbance of long-established *de facto* enjoyment'. However, as we see from the extract below, this is not a view that is universally held. In 1966, the Law Reform Committee published a report on *The Acquisition of Easements and Profits by Prescription* (Law Reform Committee, Fourteenth Report, Cmnd 3100), concluding by a majority that it ought to be abolished, at least as far as easements were concerned. As far as the majority was concerned, '[t]here is no reason why a person who wishes to acquire an easement over someone else's land should not adopt the straightforward course of asking for it'.

Nevertheless, there are economic arguments for legitimising long-term particular use, but they are perhaps not quite as straightforward as those justifying the extinguishment of title by adverse possession. The law of adverse possession requires an owner who has made no use of his resource for twelve years to give up ownership altogether, leaving unchallengeable ownership with the person who arguably values it more, and to that extent increasing total utility. Over a period of years ownership is (in effect although not in law) transferred from one person to another. The establishment of particular use rights by long usage, however, does not involve a shift in ownership from the owner but a dilution or qualification of it. This will almost invariably involve a consequent diminution in value of the owner's interest, whoever holds it. The question of whether there will nevertheless be an overall increase in total utility will therefore depend on whether this diminution in value is compensated by the value acquired by the particular use holder. Legitimising the recreational use made by people in a particular locality of a site with development potential may, for example, diminish the value of the site to the owner by more than the value of the right to the right holders. However, this is not necessarily so. The user may have managed to capture for himself an economic benefit from a resource controlled by someone else, without reducing the economic value of the resource to the resource holder, or by reducing it by less than the value of the benefit acquired by the user (thus increasing total utility). The fact that the owner has failed to object over a long period may perhaps be a good indication that this is what has happened. The likelihood that this is the explanation for the owner's inaction is increased by the imposition of a requirement (absent in adverse possession law) that the owner should genuinely have acquiesced in the user (embodied in the rule, considered below, that the user must have been as of right). And the strict regulation of the type of, and circumstances in which, particular use rights that can have proprietary status – as we saw in Chapter 9, only a very narrow range of interests qualifies, and they must be appurtenant to land which is positively benefited, or if in gross and/or enjoyed by a fluctuating class, the benefit extracted from the land must be rigidly specified – also serves to restrict the ways in which, and the extent to which, an enforced dilution of ownership can occur. This might also explain and justify the rule that profits in gross can rarely arise by prescription.

However, even if the acquisition of rights by prescription is efficient, it does not necessarily follow that the user should acquire the rights without payment. A system whereby long use entitles the user to buy the right is feasible, in theory at least. Under such a system, the effect of long user would be to entitle the user to require the servient owner to *sell* the right to him at a price fixed by law. In other words, the servient owner's right to restrain the prescriber's use by an action in nuisance or trespass would be converted from an entitlement protected by a property rule to an entitlement protected by a liability rule, to adopt the analysis discussed in Chapter 6 (Calabresi and Melamed, 'Property Rules, Liability Rules and Inalienability').

Such a scheme was actually brought into operation by the Vehicular Access Across Common and Other Land (England) Regulations 2002 (SI 2002 No. 1711, made under section 68 of the Countryside and Rights of Way Act 2000) allowing those who had long used vehicular access ways over common land to buy the right to do so from the owner of the common land. However, the scheme was brought in after a series of Court of Appeal decisions made it impossible to acquire such a right by prescription, and it became redundant when those decisions were reversed by the House of Lords in *Bakewell Management Ltd* v. *Brandwood* [2004] UKHL 14 (see Clarke, 'Use, Time and Entitlement').

Despite the superficial attractions, there are difficulties with such a scheme. First, in the case of those uses which did have a lawful origin, the user will already have 'paid' for the right: why should she have to pay again? The leading case of *Tehidy Minerals* v. *Norman* [1971] 2 QB 528, CA, for example, concerned land that clearly was ancient grazing land, on which the predecessors of the current grazers had grazed animals as of right back to a date at which our legal system provided no system of formal grant. It is difficult to see why they should now have to buy that right. Also, as a practical matter, in many cases the servient owner will have bought the land with knowledge of the user, and at an appropriately discounted price (this was certainly true in *Tehidy Minerals* v. *Norman*, where the mining company bought the land from the lord of the manor expressly subject to the grazing rights). Any payment to him will therefore be a windfall, and not easy to justify. It is true that there is a danger of circularity in the argument here: if we changed the law so that long use gave rise to a right to buy the right, arguably the market value of land would not be affected by the existence of inchoate adverse rights. However, this presupposes a perfect market, and the reality might be more complex.

Finally, the basis on which the price would be fixed is not clear. Should it be based on increase in value to the dominant land, or decrease in value to the servient land? In the Vehicular Access Across Common and Other Land (England) Regulations 2002, the price is based on the value of the dominant land and the longevity of the *premises* (i.e. the buildings) benefited by the right of way. If the buildings were in existence on 31 December 1905 the price is 0.25 per cent of the open market value of the dominant land (valued with the benefit of the easement), rising to 0.5 per cent for buildings in existence on 30 November 1930 and 2 per cent in all other cases (regulation 11(1), (2) and (4) of the Regulations). Residential premises replacing other premises on the same site which were also in residential use are treated as in existence on the date when the former premises were in existence (regulation 11(3)). The rationale for this is not obvious: why should the price be cheaper the longer the use has lasted? And why should the diminution in value of the servient land not be a factor?

13.4.   Rationale

Even among those who do agree with Lord Hoffmann that long use should indeed give rise to entitlement, there is an unfortunate ambivalence over the rationale for the rule. Do we allow property rights to be acquired by prescription because we consider that it is socially and economically desirable that long-established use of resources should be legitimised, whatever its origin, or because we take long-established use as evidence of original legitimacy? This question has divided judges and commentators for centuries. Since the end of the nineteenth century the courts have insisted that the latter is the fundamental principle on which prescription is based in this jurisdiction, and while there is a high level of artificiality about this, nevertheless it has had a profound effect on the development of the law.

13.4.1.   Ascendancy of the presumed grant rationale

The *locus classicus* for the debate about the rationale of prescription is the House of Lords decision in *Dalton* v. *Angus* (1881) LR 6 App Cas 740. The question at issue was the nature of the acknowledged right of a landowner to have the buildings on her land supported by adjoining land. It was common ground that such a right could arise in certain circumstances. The issue was what those circumstances were, and this in turn depended on the nature of the right itself. The facts were that the claimant bought one of two adjoining houses and converted it into a coach factory, which involved increasing the weight thrown onto a stack of brickwork within the building. Twenty-seven years later, the stack collapsed, bringing the whole factory down with it, when the adjoining owner demolished his house and excavated the land under it to a depth of several feet. The claimant was held entitled to damages from the adjoining owner and his contractor. By the time the case reached the House of Lords it was common ground that ownership of land automatically carries with it a 'natural' right for the land itself (as opposed to any buildings on it) to be supported by adjoining land, so that any action on adjoining land that causes *the land* to collapse will be wrongful. The rationale for this rule is reasonably clear: the physical stuff of land is interdependent, each piece of soil dependent for support on all adjoining pieces of soil. However (and again this was common ground), there is a further rule that a landowner has a similar right of support for 'ancient' buildings on the land (for these purposes, buildings more than twenty years old). In other words, it was accepted that any action on adjoining land that causes the collapse of an 'ancient' building is similarly wrongful. What was at issue was the rationale for this second rule. Three possible analyses were canvassed by the twelve judges who heard the appeal (five members of the House of Lords, and seven additional judges whose opinions they sought). The first was that this right of support for buildings which have been there for more than twenty years is a 'natural' right, just like the natural right of support for the soil and similarly automatically accruing, except that the accrual does not take place until the building has been there for twenty years. The second possible analysis was that this right of support for buildings was an easement acquired by prescription, and that this happened *automatically* by virtue of the twenty-year *de facto* enjoyment of support, regardless of the intentions of the neighbouring owner providing the support. The third analysis – ultimately preferred by the majority of the House of Lords judges – was that it was indeed an easement arising by prescription, but that this *and all other prescriptive rights* were founded on presumed grant by the neighbouring owner whose land provided the support.

The acceptance by the House of Lords of this third analysis thus firmly bases prescription on the 'revolting fiction' of a presumed but now lost grant (the epithet was conferred by Lush J at first instance). There is little doubt that in the case itself it was indeed a fiction – there was no evidence to suggest that the claimants had sought any promises from the defendant when it carried out the works twenty-seven years earlier, and none of the judges expressed the slightest interest in finding out what had actually occurred at that time.

13.4.2. Effect of the 'revolting fiction'

The danger of basing a rule on a fiction is the temptation to treat it as grounded in fact. In particular, there is a strong temptation for the courts to find that no right has been acquired in a particular case because the circumstances are such that no such right could conceivably have been expressly granted. Also, there is a danger that the fiction will cloud the issue of what is to be done about prescriptive rights in a registration system. If we think that there are policy reasons for allowing long use to become legitimised, there is no reason why prescription should not operate in a registered land system (as indeed it does in some states of Australia, despite the indefeasibility principle underpinning Torrens registration). If, however, prescription is essentially just a rule of evidence, in the sense that long user merely provides evidence from which one may or must infer an initial grant, it is redundant in a registration system where the only admissible evidence of a grant is an entry on the register.

13.5.   When long use gives rise to a prescriptive right

If I habitually park my car in your yard I will ultimately acquire a proprietary right to do so, provided that certain conditions are satisfied. The first and obvious point to make is that prescription does not enlarge the category of particular use rights which have proprietary status. It can only legitimise my use of your land if the *right* to make that use of your land could have existed as a proprietary right if you had expressly granted it to me. Aside from this, the acquisition of rights by prescription is governed by an unjustifiably elaborate body of rules, founded in artificiality and never successfully rationalised – an example of common law development of rules by accretion at its very worst.

At present, rights can be acquired by prescription through a variety of common law and statutory routes. These routes developed cumulatively over a period of centuries, each new route providing an alternative to, rather than a replacement of, its precursor, as Lord Hoffmann explains in *Sunningwell*, where he gives a detailed account of the routes currently extant. As he demonstrates, for present purposes the most important point is that, in very broad terms, it is still possible to acquire a private right (i.e. an easement or profit) or a customary right (now governed by the Commons Registration Act 1965) or a public right of way by use for more than twenty years *as of right*.

At the heart of each of these routes is the fiction already noted, that long use is attributable to a lawful origin. The basis of the fiction is the superficially rational inference that, if a pattern of behaviour has persisted over a sufficiently long period (a stranger uses someone else's land as if entitled to do so, and the landowner acquiesces in the use), it must be because the use was authorised in the first place. However, in at least two respects, this is highly artificial.

13.5.1.   The problem of negative uses

First, the inference of prior, positive authorisation may be appropriate in the case of what are called 'positive' particular use rights, but it is entirely inappropriate in the case of 'negative' ones. A positive particular use right is one that allows me to do something on your land which would otherwise be actionable by you as a trespass or a nuisance. A right of way over your land or a right to pick the apples from your tree are good examples. The very first time I cross your land or take your apple I commit a trespass unless you authorise me to do so. If I have done so uninterruptedly for twenty years, it is reasonable to draw the inference that you authorised me to do it at the outset: it seems a more likely explanation than that you, having had the legal right to object for more than twenty years, have nevertheless chosen not to exercise it. In other words, prescription in the case of positive particular use rights has many similarities with the elimination of titles by limitation: in both cases, the defendant's right has been infringed for a long period and the defendant has chosen not to vindicate his rights: in the case of acquisition of titles by long user we say that the consequence of failing to complain about breach of your rights is that you lose them, whereas in the case of prescription we say that, if you fail to complain about infringement of your rights for a sufficiently long period we will infer from that that you authorised the infringement in the first place.

In the case of a negative particular use right, however, the position is quite different. A negative particular use right is one that allows me to prevent you from interfering with natural or man-made forces that would otherwise reach my land. These forces might include light and air, flowing water, the physical support provided by your land for whatever is on my land, and terrestrial television signals. There are two important points about these negative rights. First, in the absence of an easement, I do not have a *right* to receive these forces, but only a *liberty* to make use of them. Secondly, when I exercise my liberty to enjoy these forces, I do not infringe any *right* of yours. As long as your land is in a physical state that does not, as a matter of fact, cause any interruption to these forces, I will receive all these forces as a matter of course and you will have no cause of action. If you do not want me to receive any of these forces, it is always open to you to physically interrupt, obstruct or divert them from me (and we know from *Bradford Corp.* v. *Pickles* (discussed in Notes and Questions 6.8 above) that I cannot complain even if you do so with the sole purpose of injuring or annoying me). In other words, from the outset I had a liberty to receive the forces and you had a liberty to obstruct them. So, from the outset I had no need of your authorisation to 'use' the light, or air, or support etc. for twenty years: I would automatically receive them unless and until you exercised your liberty to interrupt them. It is of course possible that at some point I might decide that the receipt of these forces is so important to me that I want to convert my liberty to receive them over your land into a right – in other words I might want to buy from you a *promise* not to interrupt these forces. This can be done in English law: it would amount to a restrictive covenant entered into by you, restricting the user of your land so as not to interfere with a particular enjoyment of my land (consider how this could have been done in the case of *Bradford* v. *Pickles*). However, it would be odd to infer from the fact that I have enjoyed uninterrupted receipt of these forces for twenty years that you positively *promised* not to interrupt them: this is a promise I had no need for, and you had no reason to give. A much more likely explanation is that you did nothing because you had no selfish reason to develop your land in a way that would interrupt my receipt of these forces, and no desire to do so for the sole purpose of injuring or annoying me. This point was made forcefully by the judges in the minority in *Dalton* v. *Angus* (1880–1) LR 6 App Cas 740, who argued that a right to support for buildings from neighbouring land automatically accrued after twenty years' use as a matter of law, not as a matter of inference of prior grant. Nevertheless, the majority disagreed and reaffirmed the basic principle that a right to support for buildings is not an inherent right, and as such it can originate only in express grant or prescription, which in itself can only arise out of a presumed prior grant.

13.5.2.   Rights that can be granted but not acquired by prescription

Secondly, there are some particular use rights – and again these are on the whole negative particular use rights rather than positive ones – that can arise by express agreement but cannot be acquired by prescription. If all that prescription does is to provide a rule of evidence that long use is proof of an original grant, this is rather odd. If a particular type of property right can arise out of an express agreement between the parties, what logical reason is there for saying that we cannot presume the existence of such an express agreement from the fact that it has been long enjoyed? The answer lies in expediency rather than logic, and again it reveals the artificiality of the implied grant principle. Rights that cannot be acquired by prescription include some, but not all, negative particular use rights. Negative particular use rights that *can* be acquired by prescription include a right of support for buildings on my land from your land (as we know from *Dalton* v. *Angus*), and rights to the passage of light and air through specific windows and defined channels. Negative rights that *cannot* be acquired by prescription include a right of prospect (i.e. a right not to have my view over your land spoilt or interrupted by anything done on your land), a right to receive light or air over your land other than through defined windows or defined channels, and (as we know from *Hunter* v. *Canary Wharf*) a right to receive television or radio signals over your land. All of these rights can, however, be expressly conferred on me, as a land-owner, in the same way as any other negative particular use right can be conferred on me, i.e. by the indirect means of your entering into a restrictive covenant with me promising that nothing will be done on your land to interrupt my receipt of these forces. Why will the law of prescription not operate to presume from the fact that I have long enjoyed such a view, or such light and air, that, at some time in the past, you covenanted not to interrupt them, when it will presume such a covenant in the case of long enjoyment of uninterrupted light and air through windows and defined channels, or a right of support for specific buildings? Lord Blackburn in *Dalton* v. *Angus* gives compelling reasons why, as a matter of policy, such rights should not arise by long enjoyment, but no reasons at all as to why it is justifiable, as a matter of evidence, to infer a prior valid authorisation from long user in the one case but not in the other. In distinguishing between a right to light through a specific window and a right to a view, he said:

[In *Aldred's Case* 9 Co Rep 57b, Lord Coke remarked that damages could be recovered for obstructing an ancient window because] '[I]t may be that, before time of memory, the owner of the said piece of land has granted to the owner of the said house to have the said windows without any stopping of them, and so the prescription may have a lawful beginning; and Wray CJ then said that, for stopping as well of the wholesome air as of light, an action lies, and damages shall be recovered for them, for both are necessary ... But he said that, for prospect, which is a matter only of delight and not of necessity, no action lies for stopping thereof, and yet it is a great commendation of a house if it has a long and large prospect, *unde dicitur, laudaturque domus longos quae prospicit agros*. But the law does not give an action for such things of delight.'

... The distinction between a right to light and a right of prospect, on the ground that one is matter of necessity and the other of delight, is to my mind more quaint than satisfactory. A much better reason is given by Lord Hardwicke in *Attorney-General* v. *Doughty* 2 Ves Sen 453, where he observes that if that was the case there could be no great towns. I think this decision, that a right of prospect is not acquired by prescription, shows that, while on the balance of convenience and inconvenience, it was held expedient that the right to light, which could only impose a burthen upon land very near the house, should be protected when it had been long enjoyed, on the same ground it was held expedient that the right of prospect, which would impose a burthen on a very large and indefinite area, should not be allowed to be created, except by actual agreement. And this seems to me the real ground on which *Webb* v. *Bird* 10 CB (NS) 268, 13 CB (NS) 841 [no right to the passage of air to a windmill could be acquired by prescription] and *Chasemore* v. *Richards* 7 HLC 349 [no right to percolating water] are to be supported. The rights there claimed were analogous to prospect in this, that they were vague and undefined, and very extensive. Whether that is or is not the reason for the distinction, the law has always ... been that there is a distinction; that the right of a window to have light and air is acquired by prescription, and that a right to have a prospect can only be acquired by actual agreement.

13.6. User as of right and the problem of acquiescence

As Lord Hoffmann points out in *R.* v. *Oxfordshire County Council, ex parte Sunningwell Parish Council*, as a consequence of the fiction that long use is attributable to lawful origin, it is necessary to prove that the user was 'as of right', and this in turn involves a requirement that the servient owner has acquiesced in the use. This is inherently unsatisfactory. There is no necessary connection between a failure to object and an acknowledgment that, having granted the right in the first place, one is not entitled to object. Also, there are considerable difficulties in establishing what amounts to acquiescence for these purposes, as demonstrated in *R. (Beresford)* v. *Sunderland City Council* [2003] UKHL 60 (extracted at www.cambridge.org/propertylaw/), where the House of Lords reached a radically different conclusion from that reached by the Court of Appeal and the judge at first instance. Permission and acquiescence can sometimes look very similar, as can restraint and acquiescence: when does neighbourly tolerance (raising no objection when your neighbour parks in your yard) merge into acquiescence?

13.7. The future of prescription

The Law Commission is currently undertaking another review of the law of prescription, but it is difficult to see how any significant progress can be made without jettisoning the presumed grant fiction. It is causing particular difficulties at the moment in the case of negative easements, where it is tending to disguise the fundamental underlying problem that some 'negative' rights presently categorised as easements ought perhaps to be recategorised as 'natural rights' automatically appurtenant to land unless expressly bargained away. The problem is particularly acute in relation to rights of support and drainage rights, where often neither dominant nor servient owner is aware that one is impinging on the other. In determining whether the impingement should be a matter of right, the length of time for which the state of affairs has continued appears of doubtful relevance.

The real question is whether the servient owner should be given the initial entitlement to be free from the burden (so that the dominant owner has to buy it off him) or whether the initial entitlement should go to the dominant owner, so that, for example, anyone who wanted to develop his land would have to 'buy' the right to interfere with support for and drainage from the land of his neighbours. Tang Hang Wu explains the problem:

> The objections in extending the natural right of support to lateral support of buildings are two-fold. First, it is said that such a right favours the first person who builds. Second, to grant a right of lateral support would deprive the owner of the adjoining land of the corresponding right to excavate and dig on his own land ...
>
>   The criticism that the existence of an automatic right of lateral support of buildings favours the first to build has some force. Two English Law Commissions grappled with this problem. The earlier Law Reform Committee (14th report of the Law Reform Committee, Cmnd 3100, 1966) had proposed a system whereby a person who proposed to build would be able to acquire a right of support before he commenced building. First, the builder serves his neighbour with a notice of his intention to build. If his neighbour took no action, the builder acquires a right of support immediately. If the neighbour serves a counter notice, the matter would be referred to the Land Tribunal who would adjudicate over the case. The Land Tribunal could award either a right of support on payment of compensation or deny such a right as it thought fit. If the procedure was not invoked the builder acquires no right of support.
>
>   The Law Commission in considering this issue in 1971 took a different view (Law Commission Working Paper No. 36, *Appurtenant Rights*, 1971, pp. 30–1). Their reasoning was as follows:

It is appreciated that the 'automatic right' [of lateral support] approach gives an advantage to the owner who builds first. Nevertheless, it seems preferable to put the burden of support on the second builder when he comes to excavate rather than to encourage disputes in anticipation of a situation which may never become an issue between the two owners. It must be remembered that this approach has operated for many years under the London Buildings Act. We are not aware of any hardship caused by its operations. Moreover, in modern conditions it is thought to be reasonable to regard building as a normal use of land which can be undertaken freely provided it conforms to planning control and does not infringe a neighbour's existing rights.

On balance, this author is of the view that the Law Commission's stand in 1971 is preferable. The Law Commission has correctly pointed out that, in light of modern planning and zoning requirements by the relevant authorities, a landowner should be free to utilise his land so long as it conforms to such control. Further, the earlier Law Reform Committee's suggestion is untenable. If adopted, it is foreseeable that a builder would be involved in a messy, protracted and expensive dispute even before he starts construction. This is clearly not desirable. There is also the very real practical problem on how a tribunal would award compensation for the right of lateral support. Is it to be premised on the estimated increase in the costs of a hypothetical construction of a building to the neighbour in future? Would inflation be one of the factors to be taken into account? The earlier proposal by the Law Reform Committee involves too much uncertainty and hence should be rejected. (Tang Hang Wu, 'The Right of Lateral Support of Buildings from the Adjoining Land')

Extract 13.1   R. v. *Oxfordshire County Council, ex parte Sunningwell Parish Council* [2000] 1 AC 335; [1999] 3 WLR 160; [1999] 3 All ER 385

[The facts and the opening part of Lord Hoffmann's judgment were discussed in Notes and Questions 5.2 above. Briefly, the inhabitants of Sunningwell claimed that they had used the glebe land in Sunningwell for sports and pastimes as of right for not less than twenty years, and that, therefore, Oxfordshire County Council was obliged to register the glebe land as a village green under the Commons Registration Act 1965. As Lord Hoffmann explained, the principle issue was whether their user had been 'as of right'.]

LORD HOFFMANN: . . . The principal issue before your Lordships thus turns on the meaning of the words 'as of right' in the definition of a green in section 22(1) of the 1965 Act. The language is plainly derived from judicial pronouncements and earlier legislation on the acquisition of rights by prescription. To put the words in their context, it is therefore necessary to say something about the historical background.

Any legal system must have rules of prescription which prevent the disturbance of long-established *de facto* enjoyment. But the principles upon which they achieve this result may be very different. In systems based on Roman law, prescription is regarded as one of the methods by which ownership can be acquired. The ancient *Twelve Tables* called it *usucapio*, meaning literally a taking by use. A logical consequence was that, in laying down the conditions for a valid *usucapio*, the law concerned itself with the nature of the property and the method by which the acquirer had obtained possession. Thus *usucapio* of a *res sacra* or *res furtiva* was not allowed and the acquirer had to have taken possession in good faith. The law was not concerned with the acts or state of mind of the previous owner, who was assumed to have played no part in the transaction. The periods of prescription were originally one year for moveables and two years for immoveables, but even when the periods were substantially lengthened by Justinian and some of the conditions changed, it remained in principle a method of acquiring ownership. This remains the position in civilian systems today.

English law, on the other hand, has never had a consistent theory of prescription. It did not treat long enjoyment as being a method of acquiring title. Instead, it approached the question from the other end by treating the lapse of time as either barring the remedy of the former owner or giving rise to a presumption that he had done some act which conferred a lawful title upon the person in *de facto* possession or enjoyment.

[Lord Hoffmann explained that, in the case of squatters and finders, rightful owners would lose their right to get their property back if they failed to bring a court action within a specified period, which in medieval times was calculated by reference to various past events, most famously the accession of Richard I in 1189.]

The judges used this date by analogy to fix the period of prescription for [customary rights and other private and public rights such as rights of way]. In such cases, however, the period was being used for a different purpose. It was not to bar the remedy but to presume that enjoyment was pursuant to a right having a lawful origin. In the case of easements, this meant a presumption that there had been a grant before 1189 by the freehold owner.

As time went on, however, proof of lawful origin in this way became for practical purposes impossible. The evidence was not available. The judges filled the gap with another presumption. They instructed juries that, if there was evidence of enjoyment for the period of living memory, they could presume that the right had existed since 1189. After the Limitation Act 1623 ... the judges treated 20 years' enjoyment as ... giving rise to the presumption of enjoyment since 1189. But these presumptions arising from enjoyment for the period of living memory or for 20 years, though strong, were not conclusive. They could be rebutted by evidence that the right could not have existed in 1189; for example, because it was appurtenant to a building which had been erected since that date. In the case of easements, the resourcefulness of the judges overcame this obstacle by another presumption, this time of a lost modern grant. As Cockburn CJ said in the course of an acerbic account of the history of the English law of prescription in *Bryant v. Foot* (1867) LR 2 QB 161 at 181:

> Juries were first told that from user, during living memory, or even during twenty years, they might presume a lost grant or deed; next they were recommended to make such presumption; and lastly, as the final consummation of judicial legislation, it was held that a jury should be told, not only that they might, but also that they were bound to presume the existence of such a lost grant, although neither judge nor jury, nor any one else, had the shadow of a belief that any such instrument had ever really existed.

The result of these developments was that, leaving aside the cases in which it was possible to show that (a) the right could not have existed in 1189 and (b) the doctrine of lost modern grant could not be invoked, the period of 20 years' user was in practice sufficient to establish a prescriptive or customary right. It was not an answer simply to rely upon the improbability of immemorial user or lost modern grant. As Cockburn CJ observed, the jury were instructed that, if there was no evidence absolutely inconsistent with there having been immemorial user or a lost modern grant, they not merely could but should find the prescriptive right established. The emphasis was therefore shifted from the brute fact of the right or custom having existed in 1189 or there having been a lost grant (both of which were acknowledged to be fictions) to the quality of the 20-year user which would justify recognition of a prescriptive right ... It became established that such user had to be, in the Latin phrase, *nec vi, nec clam, nec precario*: not by force, nor stealth, nor the licence of the owner ... The unifying element in these three vitiating circumstances was that each constituted a reason why it would not have been reasonable to expect the owner to resist the exercise of the right – in the first case, because rights should not be acquired by the use of force, in the second, because the owner would not have known of the user and in the third, because he had consented to the user, but for a limited period. So in *Dalton v. Henry Angus & Co., Comrs of HM Works and Public Buildings v. Henry Angus & Co.* (1881) LR 6 App Cas 740 at 773, Fry J (advising the House of Lords) was able to rationalise the law of prescription as follows:

> ... the whole law of prescription and the whole law which governs the presumption or inference of a grant or covenant rest upon acquiescence. The Courts and the Judges have had recourse to various expedients for quieting the possession of persons in the exercise of rights which have not been resisted by the persons against whom they are exercised, but in all cases it appears to me that acquiescence and nothing else is the principle upon which these expedients rest.

In the case of easements, the legislature intervened to save the consciences of judges and juries by the Prescription Act 1832 [which, in effect, provided an additional method of statutory prescription for easements, so that, in the cases where the Act applied, if the claimant could prove twenty years' uninterrupted use 'as of right', his claim could not be defeated by proof that the right could not have existed for time immemorial or that it could not be attributed to a lost modern grant].

Thus in a claim under the Act, what mattered was the quality of enjoyment during the 20-year period. It had to be by a person [claiming 'as of right', which was subsequently held] to have the same meaning as the older expression *nec vi nec clam nec precario* ...

My Lords, I pass now from the law concerning the acquisition of private rights of way and other easements to the law of public rights of way. Just as the theory was that a lawful origin of private rights of way could be found only in a grant by the freehold owner, so the theory was that a lawful origin of public rights of way could be found only in a dedication to public use. As in the case of private rights, such dedication would be presumed from user since time immemorial, that is from 1189. But the common law did not supplement this rule by fictitious grants or user which the jury were instructed to presume ... user for any length of time since 1189 was merely evidence from which a dedication could be inferred. The quality of the user from which dedication could be inferred was stated in the same terms as that required for private rights of way, that is to say *nec vi nec clam nec precario*. But dedication did not have to be inferred; there was no presumption of law ... This made the outcome of cases on public rights of way very unpredictable and was one of the reasons for the passing of the Rights of Way Act 1932, of which section 1(1) provided:

> Where a way, not being of such a character that user thereof by the public could not give rise at common law to any presumption of dedication, upon or over any land has been actually enjoyed by the public as of right and without interruption for a full period of twenty years, such way shall be deemed to have been dedicated as a highway unless there is sufficient evidence that there was no intention during that period to dedicate such way ...

The words 'actually enjoyed by the public as of right and without interruption for a full period of 20 years' are clearly an echo of the [equivalent words in the Prescription Act 1832] ... Introducing the Bill into the House of Lords (HL Debates, 7 June 1932, col. 737), Lord Buckmaster said that the purpose was to assimilate the law on public rights of way to that of private rights of way (84 HL Debates (1931–2), col. 637). It therefore seems safe to assume that 'as of right' in the 1932 Act was intended to have the same meaning as [the equivalent words in the 1832 Act].

My Lords, this was the background to the definition of a 'town or village green' in section 22(1) of the 1965 Act. At that time, there had been no legislation for customary rights equivalent to the 1832 Act for easements or the 1932 Act for public rights of way. Proof of a custom to use a green for lawful sports and pastimes still required an inference of fact that such a custom had existed in 1189. Judges and juries were generous in making the required inference on the basis of evidence of long user. If there was upwards of 20 years' user, it would be presumed in the absence of evidence to show that it commenced after 1189. But the claim could still be defeated by showing that the custom could not have existed in 1189. Thus in *Bryant* v. *Foot* (1867) LR 2 QB 161 a claim to a custom by which the rector of a parish was entitled to charge 13s for performing a marriage service, although proved to have been in existence since 1808, was rejected on the ground that, having regard to inflation it could not possibly have existed in the reign of Richard I. It seems to me clear that class 'c' in the definition of a village green must have been based upon the earlier Acts and intended to exclude this kind of defence. The only difference was that it allowed for no rebuttal or exceptions. If the inhabitants of the locality had indulged in lawful sports and pastimes as of right for not less than 20 years, the land was a town or village green. But there is no reason to believe that 'as of right' was intended to mean anything different from what those words meant in the 1832 and 1932 Acts.

In *R.* v. *Suffolk County Council, ex parte Steed* (1996) 75 P&CR 102 at 111–12 Pill LJ also said that 'as of right' in the 1965 Act had the same meaning as in the 1932 Act. In holding that it required 'an honest belief in a legal right to use ... as an inhabitant ... and not merely a member of the public' he followed *dicta* in three cases on the 1932 Act and its successor legislation, section 31(1) of the Highways Act 1980, which I must now examine.

The first was *Hue* v. *Whiteley* [1929] 1 Ch 440, a decision of Tomlin J before the 1932 Act. The dispute was over the existence of a public footpath on Box Hill and the judge (at 444) found that for 60 years people had 'used the track to get to the highway and to the public bridle road as of right, on the footing that they were using a public way'. Counsel for the landowner, in reliance on *A-G* v. *Antrobus* [1905] 2 Ch 188 (which concerned the tracks around Stonehenge), argued that the user should be disregarded because people used the path merely for recreation in walking on Box Hill. The judge said (at 445) that this made no difference:

> A man passes from one point to another believing himself to be using a public road, and the state of his mind as to his motive in passing is irrelevant. If there is evidence, as there is here, of continuous user by persons as of right (i.e. believing themselves to be exercising a public right to pass from one highway to another), there is no question such as that which arose in *Attorney-General* v. *Antrobus*.

The decision in the case was that the reasons why people used the road were irrelevant. It was sufficient that they used it as of right. I rather doubt whether, in explaining this term parenthetically as involving a belief that they were exercising a public right, Tomlin J meant to say more than Lord Blackburn had said in *Mann* v. *Brodie* (1884–5) LR 10 App Cas 378 at 386, namely, that they must have used it in a way which would suggest to a reasonable landowner that they believed they were exercising a public right. To require an inquiry into the subjective state of mind of the users of the road would be contrary to the whole English theory of prescription, which, as I hope I have demonstrated, depends upon evidence of acquiescence by the landowner giving rise to an inference or presumption of a prior grant or dedication. For this purpose, the actual state of mind of the road user is plainly irrelevant.

Tomlin J's parenthesis was picked up by the Court of Appeal in *Jones* v. *Bates* [1938] 2 All ER 237. The defendant asserting a right of footpath adduced overwhelming evidence of user for many years, including evidence of the plaintiff landowner's predecessors in title that they had never stopped people from using the path because they thought it was a public right of way. The judge in the Hastings County Court nevertheless rejected this evidence as insufficient to satisfy section 1(1) of the 1932 Act. The Court of Appeal by a majority held that he must have misdirected himself on the law (there was no right of appeal on fact from a county court) and ordered a new trial. But the case contains some observations on the law, including a valuable exposition by Scott LJ of the background to the 1932 Act. The two majority judgments of Slesser and Scott LJJ both cite Tomlin J's parenthesis with approval. But the question of whether it is necessary to prove the subjective state of mind of users of the road in addition to the outward appearance of user did not arise and was not discussed.

Slesser LJ (at 241), after citing Tomlin J's parenthesis, went on to say that 'as of right' in the 1932 Act had the meaning which Cotton LJ had given to those words in the 1832 Act in *Earl De la Warr* v. *Miles* (1881) 17 ChD 535 at 596: ' ... not secretly, not as acts of violence, not under permission from time to time given by the person on whose soil the acts were done'. This makes one doubt whether he was concerned with the subjective minds of the users.

Scott LJ ([1938] 2 All ER 237 at 245) also quoted Tomlin J with approval but went on to say: 'It is doubtless correct to say that negatively [the words 'as of right'] import the absence of any of the three characteristics of compulsion, secrecy or licence – *nec vi, nec clam, nec precario*, phraseology borrowed from the law of easements – but the statute does not put on the party asserting the public right the onus of proving those negatives ...'

Scott LJ was concerned that the county court judge had placed too high a burden upon the person asserting the public right. If he proved that the right had been used so as to demonstrate belief in the existence of a public right of way, that was enough. The headnote to *Jones* v. *Bates* summarises the holding on this point in entirely orthodox terms: 'The words in the Rights of Way Act, 1932, section 1(1), "actually enjoyed by the public as of right and without interruption", mean that the way has been used without compulsion, secrecy or licence, *nec vi, nec clam, nec precario*.'

Finally, in *R.* v. *Suffolk County Council, ex parte Steed* (1996) 75 P&CR 102 at 112 Pill LJ referred to his own discussion of the subject at first instance in *O'Keefe* v. *Secretary of State for the Environment* [1996] JPL 42. On the basis of passages from *Jones* v. *Bates* he had there expressed the view that 'as of right' meant user 'which was not only *nec vi, nec clam, nec precario* but was in the honest belief in a legal right to use' (see [1996] JPL 42 at 52) ...

My Lords, in my opinion the casual and, in its context, perfectly understandable aside of Tomlin J in *Hue* v. *Whiteley* [1929] 1 Ch 440, has led the courts into imposing upon the time-honoured expression 'as of right' a new and additional requirement of subjective belief for which there is no previous authority and which I consider to be contrary to the principles of English prescription. There is in my view an unbroken line of descent from the common law concept of *nec vi, nec clam, nec precario* to the term 'as of right' in the 1832, 1932 and 1965 Acts. It is perhaps worth observing that, when the 1832 Act was passed, the parties to an action were not even competent witnesses and I think that Parke B would have been startled by the proposition that a plaintiff asserting a private right of way on the basis of his user had to prove his subjective state of mind. In the case of public rights, evidence of reputation of the existence of the right was always admissible and formed the subject of a special exception to the hearsay rule. But that is not at all the same thing as evidence of the individual states of mind of people who used the way. In the normal case, of course, outward appearance and inward belief will coincide. A person who believes he has the right to use a footpath will use it in the way in which a person having such a right would use it. But user which is apparently as of right cannot be discounted merely because, as will often be the case, many of the users over a long period were subjectively indifferent as to whether a right existed, or even had private knowledge that it did not. Where Parliament has provided for the creation of rights by 20 years' user, it is almost inevitable that user in the earlier years will have been without any very confident belief in the existence of a legal right. But that does not mean that it must be ignored. Still less can it be ignored in a case like *R. v. Suffolk County Council, ex parte Steed* when the users believe in the existence of a right but do not know its precise metes and bounds. In coming to this conclusion, I have been greatly assisted by Mr J. G. Riddall's article 'A False Trail' (1997) 61 Conv 199.

I therefore consider that *Ex p. Steed* was wrongly decided and that the county council should not have refused to register the glebe as a village green merely because the witnesses did not depose to their belief that the right to games and pastimes attached to them as inhabitants of the village. That was the only ground upon which [the Inspector] advised the council to reject the application. But Miss Cameron, who appeared for the board, submitted that it should have been rejected for other reasons as well. Although these grounds did not form the basis of any cross-appeal, your Lordships considered that, rather than put the parties to the expense of further consideration by the county council followed by further appeals, it would be convenient to consider their merits now [he went on to consider these points, in the passage from his judgment discussed in Notes and Questions 5.2 above] ...

Miss Cameron's third and final point was that the use of the glebe was not as of right because it was attributable to neighbourly toleration by successive rectors and the board. She relied upon the following passage in [the Inspector's] report:

> It appears to me that recreational use of the glebe is based on three factors. First, the glebe is crossed by an unfenced footpath so that there is general public access to the land and nothing to prevent members of the public straying from the public footpath. Second, the glebe has been owned not by a private owner but by the rector and then the Board, who have been tolerant of harmless public use of the land for informal recreation. Third, the land has been used throughout for rough grazing so that informal public recreation on the land has not conflicted with its agricultural use and has been tolerated by the tenant or grazier.

I should say that I do not think that the reference to people 'straying' from the footpath was intended to mean that recreational user was confined to people who set out to use the footpath but casually or accidentally strayed elsewhere. That would be quite inconsistent with the findings of user which must have involved a deliberate intention to go upon other parts of the land. I think [the Inspector] meant only that the existence of the footpath made it easy for people to get there. But Miss Cameron's substantial point was based upon the finding of toleration. That, she said, was inconsistent with the user having been as of right. In my view, that proposition is fallacious. As one can see from the law of public rights of way before 1932, toleration is not inconsistent with user as of right. (See also *Mills* v. *Silver* [1991] Ch 271 at 281 *per* Dillon LJ.) When proof of a public right of way required a finding of actual dedication, the jury were entitled to find that such user was referable to toleration rather than dedication: *Folkestone Corp.* v. *Brockman* [1914] AC 338. But this did not mean that the user had not been as of right. It was a finding that there had been no dedication despite the user having been as of right. The purpose of the 1932 Act was to make it unnecessary to infer an actual dedication and, in the absence of specific rebutting evidence, to treat user as of right as sufficient to establish the public right. *Alfred F.*

Beckett Ltd v. *Lyons* [1967] Ch 449, in which the court was invited to infer an ancient grant to the Prince Bishop of Durham, in trust for the inhabitants of the county, of the right to gather coal on the sea shore, was another case in which the question was whether an actual grant could be inferred. One of the reasons given by the Court of Appeal for rejecting the claim was that the coal gathering which had taken place could be referable to tolerance on the part of the Crown as owner of the sea shore. But the establishment of a class 'c' village green does not require the inference of any grant or dedication. As in the case of public rights of way or private easements, user as of right is sufficient. [The Inspector's] remarks about toleration are therefore, as he himself recognised, not inconsistent with the quality of the user being such as to satisfy the class 'c' definition.

Miss Cameron cautioned your Lordships against being too ready to allow tolerated trespasses to ripen into rights. As Bowen LJ said in *Blount* v. *Layard* [1891] 2 Ch 681 at 691:

> ... nothing worse can happen in a free country than to force people to be churlish about their rights for fear that their indulgence may be abused, and to drive them to prevent the enjoyment of things which, although they are matters of private property, naturally give pleasure to many others besides the owners, under the fear that their good nature may be misunderstood.

On the other hand, this consideration, if carried too far, would destroy the principle of prescription. A balance must be struck. In passing the 1932 Act, Parliament clearly thought that the previous law gave too much weight to the interests of the landowner and too little to the preservation of rights of way which had been for many years in *de facto* use. As Scott LJ pointed out in *Jones* v. *Bates* [1938] 2 All ER 237 at 249, there was a strong public interest in facilitating the preservation of footpaths for access to the countryside. And, in defining class 'c' town or village greens by reference to similar criteria in 1965, Parliament recognised a similar public interest in the preservation of open spaces which had for many years been used for recreational purposes. It may be that such user is attributable to the tolerance of past rectors of Sunningwell, but, as Evershed J said of the origins of a public right of way in *A-G* v. *Dyer* [1947] Ch 67 at 85–6:

> It is no doubt true, particularly in a relatively small community ... that, in the early stages at least, the toleration and neighbourliness of the early tenants contributed substantially to the extent and manner of the use of the lane. But many public footpaths must be no less indebted in their origin to similar circumstances, and if there is any truth in the view (as stated by Chief Justice Cardozo) that property like other social institutions has a social function to fulfil, it may be no bad thing that the good nature of earlier generations should have a permanent memorial.

I would allow the appeal and direct the Oxfordshire County Council to register the glebe as a village green.

[The other members of the court all expressed agreement with Lord Hoffmann's speech, and the appeal was allowed.]

Extract 13.2   Law Reform Committee, *The Acquisition of Easements and Profits by Prescription* (Law Reform Committee Fourteenth Report, Cmnd 3100, 1966)

ABOLITION OR IMPROVEMENT?

30. It is clear from the foregoing statement of the existing position that the law of prescription is unsatisfactory, uncertain and out of date, and that it needs extensive reform. The first and most important question for consideration, then, is whether any system of prescription should be preserved, or whether, subject to suitable transitional arrangements, prescription should be abolished and easements should in the future be capable of being created only by grant. If abolition is desirable, the only further question is what transitional provisions are necessary. If, on the other hand, prescription is to be preserved in some form, we must consider how far the law should be reformed.

31. Of the professional bodies whom we consulted three (the Chartered Land Agents' Society, the Law Society and the Society of Labour Lawyers) favoured abolition. So also did Professor Crane. The rest of those whom we consulted, including the Bar Council and the Conveyancers' Institute, favoured the retention of some form of statutory prescription so far as easements are concerned.

Recommendation in favour of abolition

32. By a small majority we have decided to recommend that, subject to the necessary transitional arrangements, the prescriptive acquisition of easements should be abolished. We would not replace prescription by any other method of acquisition, except for rights of support which we discuss separately later in this report (paragraphs 84 to 96). The main considerations which have persuaded the majority to favour abolition are, briefly, that there is little, if any, moral justification for the acquisition of easements by prescription, a process which either involves an intention to get something for nothing or, where there is no intention to acquire any right, is purely accidental. Moreover, the user which eventually develops into a full-blown legal right, enjoyable not only by the dominant owner himself but also by his successors in title for ever, may well have originated in the servient owner's neighbourly wish to give a facility to some particular individual, or (perhaps even more commonly) to give a facility on the understanding, unfortunately unexpressed in words or at least unprovable, that it may be withdrawn if a major change of circumstances ever comes about.

33. There is no reason why a person who wishes to acquire an easement over someone else's land should not adopt the straightforward course of asking for it. The tendency of modern legislation over a wide field, albeit not universal, is to expect people's rights and liabilities to be defined in writing (cf. section 5 of the Agricultural Holdings Act 1948, section 4 of the Contracts of Employment Act 1963 and sections 5 to 9 of the Hire Purchase Act 1965) and the same principle should apply to the means by which easements may be acquired. Moreover, if easements could be acquired only

by written grant, many of the doubts about the precise nature and extent of the easement would, we hope, disappear. In the absence of a grant, there does seem to be considerable difficulty in finding a formula which will not do injustice to a servient owner by rendering him liable to have far more extensive rights imposed on him than he could be said to have recognised by acquiescence (see paragraphs 76 to 79 below).

34. There are also arguments in favour of abolition based as much on practical convenience as on any general theory. It will not be very long now – comparatively speaking, at least – before compulsory registration of title to land on sale will become universal throughout the country, and the aim here should be for the register to be, as far as possible, a true mirror of the title. No doubt this ideal can never be absolutely achieved, but easements arising from prescription certainly constitute one of the most troublesome of the 'overriding interests' which bind the land without being registered. (Public rights of way are much more likely to be visible on inspection of the land than are private rights of way or other easements.) So it is not simply a question of balancing the disappointment of someone who is deprived of what he may think is a long-established right against the chagrin of a man who finds that his good nature or carelessness has allowed his neighbour to steal a march on him. The interests of the general public come into the picture as well; and the advantage to the community of being able to rely on the accuracy and completeness of the register ought to be allowed to tip the scales against the continuance of prescription.

35. Moreover, if a servient owner is to be liable to be saddled with easements created by prescription, then the law ought to provide him with some simple and cheap method of protecting himself against what may otherwise be imposed upon him by the passage of time. The only satisfactory way of doing this is by some system of registration and there are considerable doubts as to the feasibility of this (see paragraphs 64 to 75). Even if it is feasible, it seems doubtful whether those exceptional cases where prescription does meet a genuine need (like that in paragraph 38(e)) would justify the elaborate administrative arrangements that a new system of registration would involve.

36. We do not consider that it is necessary or appropriate for the same legal rules to apply to the acquisition of easements by prolonged enjoyment as apply to the acquisition of title to land by adverse possession. Certainty of title to land is a social need and occupation of land which has long been unchallenged should not be disturbed. Moreover, a squatter's occupation of land is sufficiently notorious to invite preventive action. There is no comparable need to establish easements, and user even 'as of right' may be insidious. The creation of easements, which may limit the use or development of the servient land, should not be encouraged. No serious hardship would result if in future, subject to appropriate transitional safeguards, no easement could be acquired by prescription.

Minority view in favour of retention

37. We think it desirable, however, having regard in particular to the smallness of the majority in favour of abolition and the sharp division of opinion in the evidence

submitted to us on this issue, to set out briefly the views of those members of the Committee who favour retaining some form of prescription and to describe in a subsequent part of this Report (paragraphs 39 to 81) the new system of prescription which we would unanimously recommend in the event of retention.

38. The arguments which in the view of the minority can be used against the considerations urged in favour of abolition in the preceding paragraphs of this report are

(a) Many of the unsatisfactory characteristics of the existing law in the field of prescription can be remedied by the simplifications and amendments discussed later in this report and do not call for the abolition of prescription.

(b) There is no less moral justification for the acquisition of easements by prescription than there is for obtaining a title to land by adverse possession: to represent prescription as a process of 'easement stealing' is to ignore the fact that it involves open enjoyment over a long period in the assertion of a right, and that it is a process designed to give legal recognition and validity to a state of affairs of long-standing, in which successive servient owners may have acquiesced.

(c) The dominant owner for the time being is not in most cases a person who wishes to acquire an easement, but a person who believes or assumes that he is entitled to an easement. This may well have played some part in inducing him either to buy the dominant land or to lay out money on it. Moreover, prescription is a process designed to apply not only to cases where there has in fact been no grant, but also to cases in which there may have been a grant which has been mislaid. The well-settled principle of English law that long-continued possession in assertion of a right should, if possible, be presumed to have had a legal origin (*per* Lord Herschell in *Phillips* v. *Halliday* [1891] AC 228, at p. 231) remains as valid as ever. It would be widely accepted by the public as fair and right that a servient owner who has not for many years taken the trouble to protest against the open enjoyment over his property by a neighbour of a benefit of a kind capable of existing as an easement should be debarred from putting an end to such enjoyment.

(d) In spite of the differences between adverse possession and prescription, the same fundamental considerations apply to them. Anyone who has for a sufficient period had undisputed and uninterrupted enjoyment of something capable of subsisting as a property right, notwithstanding the actual or constructive knowledge of him who might otherwise claim to be the true owner, should be allowed to retain the subject-matter (whether corporeal or incorporeal) as his own property and the other party should be barred from disputing his ownership. If it is accepted that a *status quo* of long-standing ought to be given legal recognition, prescription has not outlived its usefulness. Conveyancers are frequently faced with the question whether a prescriptive title cannot be established: in other words, the *de facto* position often does not accord with the known documentary title.

(e) It should not be assumed that the doctrine is only called in aid where there has in fact been no grant. An easement may well be granted by a deed which does not in any other way affect the title to either the servient or the dominant tenement: the servient owner may retain no counterpart and his successors may be ignorant of, or overlook, the existence of the grant. Unless and until the easement is disputed, the dominant owner and his successors may have no occasion to refer to the grant, and a long period may elapse during which the grant becomes lost.

(f) Although there has been much registration of title to land, universal registration is still a long way off. The application of compulsory registration to the whole of England and Wales would not in any event mean that the title to all land would at once become registered. The question whether prescription should be abolished or preserved should not be decided on grounds primarily applicable to registered land.

Notes and Questions 13.1

Read the above extracts and *R. (Beresford)* v. *Sunderland City Council* [2003] UKHL 60, either in full or as extracted at www.cambridge.org/propertylaw/, and consider the following:

1   As a result of the House of Lords' interpretation of the Commons Registration Act 1965 in *R.* v. *Oxfordshire County Council, ex parte Sunningwell Parish Council*, new communal property rights can now come into existence at any time by virtue of use for twenty years. Consider whether such a communal right could be expressly granted: if not, why not?

2   Explain the difference between acquiescence, toleration and permission. If a landowner has tolerated a use of his land by someone else, should the *de facto* use ripen over time into a right enforceable against the landowner? Examine the arguments on this point considered by Lord Hoffmann in *Sunningwell*. Are the remarks of Evershed J in *Attorney-General* v. *Dyer* [1947] Ch 67 at 85–6, quoted by Lord Hoffmann, consistent with the analysis of prescriptive rights accepted by Lord Hoffmann?

3   Is the line drawn by the House of Lords in *Beresford* between acquiescence and permission satisfactory? In what circumstances, according to the House of Lords, can a right arise by prescription notwithstanding 'implied permission'?

4   Consider the arguments of the majority and the minority in the Law Reform Committee on the issue of abolition of prescription. Which do you find more convincing? Registration of title is much further advanced now than it was in 1966, the date of this report: what effect, if any, does this have on the arguments put by both sides?

5   Devise a scheme, applicable to all kinds of private right, whereby all that could be acquired by prescription would be entitlement to buy the right, on the lines of the scheme set out in the Vehicular Access Across Common and Other Land (England) Regulations 2002 (SI 2002 No. 1711) referred to in the text above. Would it be possible to devise a scheme that met the objections put in the text

above to such schemes? On what basis would you determine the price? Could an analogous scheme be devised for communal and public rights acquired over privately owned land?

6   Examine the criticisms made by Lord Walker at the end of his speech in *Beresford*. To what extent are they justified? What steps should the council have taken to prevent the local residents acquiring this right by prescription? Is this satisfactory?

14

Enforceability and priority of interests

14.1. Rationale of enforceability and priority rules

Any legal system that allows multiple property interests to subsist in the same thing at the same time must have rules governing their enforceability and priority. Enforceability questions arise when O, the holder of a property interest (for example, the fee simple interest in a plot of land, or a twenty-one-year lease of a flat, or ownership of a painting), grants a subsidiary interest to someone else, S (for example, O grants S a right of way over the plot of land, or sublets the flat to her for five years, or declares he holds the painting on trust for her), but then transfers his own interest to P. In what circumstances will S's interest in the plot of land, the flat and the painting be enforceable against P, so that P holds it subject to S's interest?

Priority questions arise when two or more subsidiary interests are carved out of O's interest, and we need to know which takes priority over the other. The subsidiary interests might all be of the same nature – for example O might first mortgage his fee simple in the plot of land, his lease of his flat and his picture to his Bank B to secure his overdraft of £1 m, but then have a charging order made under the Charging Orders Act 1979 over all three assets to secure a debt of £500,000 he owes to C. If the total value of the three assets is less than £1.5 m, B and C need to know how their interests rank as between themselves. If O fails to repay the two debts, the three assets will have to be sold so that the debts can be paid out of the proceeds of sale, and the person whose interest ranks first will be paid in full before the other is paid anything at all. However, priority questions can also arise where the subsidiary interests are of a different nature and incompatible with each other, like the right of pre-emption and the option to purchase in *Pritchard* v. *Briggs* discussed in see Chapter 12.

A market in property interests can only work effectively if there are effective enforceability and priority rules. Buyers need to know what they are buying, and holders of subsidiary interests need to know how to protect their interests so that they are discoverable by and enforceable against buyers, and not defeated by other incompatible interests arising in the same asset. This demands clear and simple rules that are rigorously applied. If our goal is to increase the marketability of property interests, we need to have, and to apply strictly, rules that lay down procedures to be followed by those who want to ensure that the assets they buy are not subject to interests they knew nothing about, and by those who want to ensure that their interests are fully protected. Anyone who follows the correct procedure should then be guaranteed that their position will be safeguarded in all circumstances.

However, such a system comes at a heavy price. If the system is to work effectively, an interest holder who does not use the procedure provided to protect his interest should lose the interest, or at least not be able to enforce it against, or take priority over, those who do follow the correct procedures. This may produce a result that is unjust, or disproportionately harsh, on the interest holder. The failure to use the protection machinery might not have been the interest holder's fault: the circumstances might have been such that he could not reasonably have been expected to use it. Alternatively, the consequences of losing his interest might be wholly disproportionate to his fault in not protecting it, and far outweigh the disadvantage the other party would suffer if it had to take subject to the interest. And what about cases where the other party is seeking to rely on the strict letter of the rules in order to take free from an interest it knew about all along? Should the system provide a means of escape for such cases? If not, or if the escape route does not help, should the courts be free to come to a decision that they consider just as between the parties, even at the risk of undermining the integrity of the system?

This is another example of the 'inescapable tension' Birks identifies in Extract 12.1 above. In the context of formalities rules he refers to the clash between two simple principles, one being that that 'you cannot take the advantages of formality and at the same time let off all those who do things in their own informal way', the other being that 'pain should not be inflicted except in case of pressing necessity'. Precisely the same clash occurs in applying the rules we are looking at in this and the next chapter, and as we see in the cases extracted in these two chapters, finding the 'right' balance is just as problematic. Before looking at this in more detail, however, it is necessary to establish what enforceability and priority rules we have in this jurisdiction.

14.2. Enforceability and priority rules

14.2.1. The basic rules

The basic rules are reasonably straightforward. They apply to all property interests, not just interests in land, and the principle underlying them all is that, once a property interest has come into existence, it should not lightly be set aside in favour of a later interest – in other words, the principle 'first in time is first in right' that we identified in Chapters 7 and 11 as underlying the first possession principle.

In the case of any property interest which is not covered by a registration system, the rules differ depending on whether the interest is legal or equitable. As far as enforceability is concerned, the basic rule is that, if the interest is legal, it is enforceable against the whole world. If it is equitable, it is enforceable against the whole world, but with two exceptions. First, an equitable interest is not enforceable against someone who can prove that she is a good faith purchaser for value of a legal interest in the asset without notice of the interest holder's interest (sometimes referred to as 'equity's darling'). This is known as the doctrine of notice. Secondly, equitable interests under a trust (and some other types of property interest) are capable of being 'overreached' when the trustee transfers the trust asset to a third party: if such an interest is overreached, it is not enforceable against the transferee. The elements of good faith and notice in the doctrine of notice, and the concept of overreaching, are all crucial here, and we will need to look at them in some detail (see below).

As to priority, legal interests rank for priority purposes according to the date on which they were created. The basic rule is the same for equitable interests, but with two exceptions. First, priority under the basic rule may be forfeited if the court considers that an interest holder's conduct makes it inequitable for him to take priority over a later interest. Primarily this will occur if he allows evidence of his interest to be suppressed so that anyone who later takes an interest in the asset is deceived into believing that there are no prior encumbrances. This requires more than a simple omission by the prior-interest holder to protect his interest by registration (or by whatever other means are available in the circumstances), as we see in *Freeguard* v. *Royal Bank of Scotland plc* (1998) 79 P&CR 81 (discussed in Notes and Questions 14.1 below). However, it is clear from this case that the prior-interest holder's inequitable conduct does not have to be directed at subsequent encumbrancers, whether actual or potential: the prior-interest holder can lose priority even if his motive was to perpetrate a quite different deception on someone entirely different.

The second exception to the basic rule that equitable interests rank by date of creation is that, if there are two or more mortgages or charges over an equitable interest under a trust, priority between them depends on the date on which each mortgagee gives notice of his mortgage to the trustee, except where the later mortgagee had notice of the earlier mortgage. This is known as the rule in *Dearle* v. *Hall* (1823) 3 Russ 1; 38 ER 475; for further details see De Lacy, 'The Priority Rule of Dearle v. Hall Re-stated'.

14.2.2. Impact of registration

In an ideal world, a registration system could conceivably have just two rules: interests will be enforceable if but only if they are entered on the register; and interests will take priority from the date of entry on the register. But in the real world such a system is probably not achievable, and arguably not desirable either. Compromises have to be made to draw a balance between conflicting goals of certainty and fairness just as they do in unregistered systems, as we see in the next chapter.

Another real world complication, of more immediate relevance to this chapter, is that, while registration systems usually provide rules about enforceability and priority of interests in the assets they cover, they do not necessarily apply to *all* interests in those assets. The most common gap is 'off-register' interests or dealings, in other words those that could not have been registered or protected on the register, or could have been but were not. A registration system could provide that all such interests and dealings are simply void for all purposes, and indeed this appears to be the ultimate goal of the Land Registration Act 2002 for all interests other than a strictly limited 'overriding' class, as we see in Chapter 15. However, more commonly, registration systems merely make such interests and dealings ineffective as against purchasers who acquire registered titles or registered interests. This means that the position as between off-register interests has to be governed by general unregistered rules about enforceability and priority. In the case of land registration, the gap is even wider because, broadly, only fee simples, leases, easements, profits and mortgages can actually be registered on the register. All other interests can be 'protected' by entry on the register, which does ensure enforceability against subsequent registered proprietors but does not confer *priority* as against other unregistered interests, whether or not also 'protected' on the register. This is why, in *Freeguard* v. *Royal Bank of Scotland* (1990) 79 P&CR 81 (discussed in Notes and Questions 14.1 below), priority between the option to purchase and the later equitable charge had to be resolved using general equitable priority rules, even though titles to all the land in question were registered under the Land Registration Acts, and even though the later interest, the charge, was protected by an entry on the register.

Notes and Questions 14.1

Read *Freeguard* v. *Royal Bank of Scotland plc* (1998) 79 P&CR 81, either in full or as extracted at www.cambridge.org/propertylaw/, and consider the following:

1 Whom did the Freeguards intend to deceive or defraud? Who was in fact misled? What does this tell us about the kind of conduct that will cause a prior-interest holder to lose priority to a subsequent encumbrancer?

2 What should the Freeguards have done to protect their interest if they had wanted to ensure that it took priority over all subsequent *equitable* interests? (See section 15.2.4 below.) If the Freeguards had failed to protect their interest simply through ignorance, would it have taken priority over the bank's charge? What could the bank have done to ensure that its charge was not subject to any prior interest it knew nothing about? (See sections 15.2.6 and 15.3 below.)

14.3. The doctrine of notice

The category of good faith purchaser of a legal interest without notice is referred to as equity's darling because those who fall within this category are given special exemption by equity from the fundamental principle that once a property interest comes into existence it should not be set aside in favour of later interests. The doctrine of notice should therefore be seen as a compromise solution, a balance struck between conflicting needs to preserve pre-existing entitlements and to provide the certainty necessary for an efficient market in property interests to operate. This explains the requirement of good faith and the fact that the exemption extends only to purchasers. If the only justification for disturbing pre-existing entitlements is to promote marketability, there is no reason in principle to favour donees (they are not players in the market) nor those who act in bad faith (markets can operate well enough without them). The issue then becomes one of drawing the balance between equitable interest holders and good faith purchasers, often both innocent victims of a fraud or deception perpetrated by a seller who has a pre-existing proprietary relationship with the equitable interest holder.

In *Pilcher* v. *Rawlins* (1871–2) LR 7 Ch App 259 (Extract 14.1 below), the court took the view that, if the good faith purchaser neither knew nor had the means of knowing about the prior equitable interest (i.e. was without notice in the technical sense we consider below), a court of equity had no jurisdiction to interfere with the legal title he had acquired from the seller. The purchaser's conscience was not affected in any way and so equity had no grounds for intervening. But it is worth noting that the court considered that to be the correct outcome not only as a matter of jurisdiction but also as a matter of fairness. If anyone could be said to be at fault here apart from the dishonest trustee, they said, it must be the person who initially chose to enter into an ongoing property relationship with a trustee who turned out to be dishonest, rather than the complete stranger who later comes on the scene.

However, it is clear even from *Pilcher* v. *Rawlins* (and overwhelmingly confirmed by later cases) that the court of equity did not intend the doctrine of notice to be a flexible doctrine, to be applied only after balancing levels of fault on the part of each interest holder in each case. That would largely remove the benefit of certainty of outcome that the rule was indeed to provide. The doctrine of notice is intended to be inflexible, so that purchasers and interest holders know in advance what they need to do in order to safeguard their respective interests. The fairness and effectiveness of the doctrine need to be assessed with this in mind.

14.3.1. Notice

This is central to the doctrine. 'Notice' bears a special meaning here. As pointed out in *Pilcher* v. *Rawlins*, it covers not only what the purchaser actually knows (actual notice) but also what he should have known (constructive notice) and what any agent of his knows or ought to have known (imputed notice). The modern formulation appears in section 199(1)(ii) of the Law of Property Act 1925:

(1) A purchaser shall not be prejudicially affected by notice of –

(i) ...

(ii) any [other] instrument or matter or any fact or thing unless

    (a) it is within his own knowledge, or would have come to his knowledge if such inquiries and inspections had been made as ought reasonably to have been made by him; or

    (b) in the same transaction with respect to which a question of notice to the purchaser arises, it has come to the knowledge of his counsel, as such, or of his solicitor or other agent, as such, or would have come to the knowledge of his solicitor or other agent, as such, if such inquiries and inspections had been made as ought reasonably to have been made by the solicitor or other agent.

There are two important points to be made about constructive notice. The first is that the nature and extent of the 'inquiries and inspections' that 'ought reasonably to have been made' by the purchaser depend on the particular circumstances of the case, as can be seen from *Kingsnorth Trust Ltd* v. *Tizard* [1986] 1 WLR 783 (extracted at www.cambridge.org/propertylaw/). However, the courts will test what it would have been reasonable for that purchaser to have done by reference to what is regarded as good practice in that sort of situation. This means that, in routine transactions such as buying or taking mortgages over houses, farms, factories or offices, prospective buyers and mortgagees (or, rather, their advisers) know what steps they have to take in order to find out what pre-existing interests affect the premises, and are guaranteed to take free from any interests not revealed by taking those steps. Essentially, they know that, if they carry out a routine investigation of the seller/mortgagor's title and make a physical inspection of the property, they should find out, or at least be alerted to, everything that they will be deemed to know under the doctrine of notice.

Secondly, the question of whether the purchaser had notice of the prior interest is largely objective. Because of the existence of the constructive and imputed categories of notice, the question of what the purchaser actually knew is not usually disputed. Instead, the argument concentrates on an objective inquiry as to what inquiries and inspections ought reasonably to have been made in the circumstances, and what would have been discovered if they had been made. In other words, the purchaser does not have to satisfy the court that he took all reasonable steps to enquire whether there were any encumbrances. He will take free from any that do exist even if he took no steps at all, provided he can satisfy the court that reasonable inquiries and investigations would not have revealed the existence of the interest. This is what the finance house failed to do in *Kingsnorth Trust Ltd* v. *Tizard*: it failed to satisfy the judge that the enquiries and inspections that ought reasonably to have been made *bearing in mind that suspicions ought to have been raised* (i.e. by the discrepancies in what Mr Tizard had said about his marital status in application forms and to the surveyor) would not have revealed the existence of Mrs Tizard's interest in the house.

Occupation has a dual role in the concept of constructive notice as it applies to purchasers and mortgagees of land. There is a general rule, sometimes referred to as the rule in *Hunt* v. *Luck*, that purchasers and mortgagees of land have constructive notice of the interests of anyone who is in occupation of the land (assuming the occupation is reasonably discoverable, as we see in *Kingsnorth Trust Ltd* v. *Tizard*). This is because, as noted above, it is not unnaturally assumed that any reasonable person buying or taking a mortgage over land would actually go and look at it (or at least send an agent), and the presence of someone other than the seller in occupation of the land should alert them to the possibility that the occupier might have rights in the land.

However, although the courts have traditionally seen this as the rationale for the rule in *Hunt* v. *Luck*, this favouring of occupiers over purchasers can also serve to mark the distinction between those who value their interest as thing and those who value it as wealth (adopting Rudden's terminology, as discussed in Extract 2.3 above). In other words, people who have an interest in land that they also occupy are those most likely to regard the monetary value of their interest as an inadequate substitute for the interest itself (consider, for example, the case of Mr and Mrs Flegg in *City of London Building Society* v. *Flegg*, extracted at www.cambridge.org/propertylaw/). Purchasers, on the other hand, can usually be compensated in money terms if they have to take subject to a prior interest. In any case, where the issue is whether a particular interest is enforceable against a particular purchaser or mortgagee, the loser will nearly always be entitled to claim damages from the seller in compensation. Since damages would generally be adequate compensation for a purchaser or mortgagee but inadequate compensation for the prior-interest holder who is in occupation, this provides an additional justification (in theory at least) for a general rule that purchasers and mortgagees take subject to the interests of prior-interest holders in occupation. In practice, in unregistered land this argument has an air of unreality about it because such cases tend to arise where the seller/mortgagor has disappeared or is insolvent, so that there is no prospect of anyone recovering anything from her. However, we return to this argument in Chapter 15 in the context of registered land, where the existence of a state indemnity fund opens up the possibility of alternative ways of compensating the loser.

14.3.2. Good faith

In order to take advantage of the doctrine of notice, a purchaser must show not only that he had no notice of the interest but also that he acted in good faith. In *Midland Bank Trust Co. Ltd* v. *Green* [1981] AC 513, Lord Wilberforce confirmed that this requirement is indeed separate from and additional to the requirement that the purchaser must be without notice. In the context in which it was said, it makes sense. Lord Wilberforce was considering whether a requirement of good faith should be imported into the Land Charges Act 1972 so that a purchaser who would otherwise have taken free from a prior interest (i.e. because it was not registered as required by the Act) would take subject to it if she had acted in bad faith. If such a requirement is imported into a registration scheme, it clearly makes sense to say that the court would have to look at factors going beyond the question of whether the purchaser had notice of the interest, given that the presence of notice does not of itself amount to bad faith, as Lord Wilberforce pointed out. However, in the context of the doctrine of notice itself, it is not clear what it adds. If a purchaser or mortgagor does not have notice of a prior interest, it is difficult to envisage the sort of behaviour or motive on his part that would constitute bad faith *in relation to the prior-interest holder*. Bad faith in relation to anyone or anything else (for example, entering into the transaction in order to evade a tax liability, or to cheat or deceive someone else) surely has no bearing on the question of whether the purchaser should take subject to an interest he knows nothing about, and if he really does know nothing about the prior interest it is difficult to see how he can act in bad faith in relation to it.

14.3.3. Effectiveness of the doctrine of notice as an enforceability rule

We saw above that the doctrine of notice is a reasonably fair and effective enforceability rule as far as purchasers are concerned. It performs the channelling function we discussed in section 12.2.7.3 above in relation to formalities rules, in the sense that it provides purchasers with a relatively clear procedure to follow in order to take free from prior interests of which they have no knowledge. Also, if we accept the arguments in *Pilcher* v. *Rawlins* and take into account the incidental effect of the *Hunt* v. *Luck* rule noted above, it draws a reasonably fair balance between the competing interests of prior-interest holder and purchaser.

However, it is marred by a fundamental flaw as far as interest holders are concerned. It provides the interest holder with no sensible means of ensuring that her interest will come to the notice of any subsequent purchaser: if you were Mrs Tizard, what *could* you have done, once you were separated from your husband, to ensure that he did not sell or mortgage the house to a purchaser who would take free from your interest? This is a serious objection. It means that, while the doctrine of notice might provide a reasonably satisfactory way of ordering conflicting interests once a disaster has happened, it gives interest holders no means of ensuring that the disaster never happens in the first place.

Extract 14.1   *Pilcher v. Rawlins* (1871–2) LR 7 Ch App 259

[This case concerned two frauds perpetrated by W. H. Pilcher (a solicitor and originally one of three trustees of the Jeremiah Pilcher Trust) and Robert Rawlins (the report reveals that he had been a solicitor, but not why he was no longer one). The fraud we are concerned with related to land at Whitchurch. In 1851, Rawlins held the legal fee simple absolute in possession in the Whitchurch land, and he mortgaged it to the trustees of the Jeremiah Pilcher Trust, to secure the payment to the Trust of £8,373 lent to him by the trustees out of the trust fund. This mortgage took the form of a transfer of the legal fee simple to the trustees, with a proviso that it would be transferred back to Rawlins when he repaid the money (the form that legal mortgages commonly took before 1926).

By 1856, W. H. Pilcher was the sole surviving trustee of the Jeremiah Pilcher Trust, and thus the sole holder of the legal fee simple in the Whitchurch land. In that year, in order to help Rawlins fraudulently obtain money from Stockwell and Lamb (who were trustees of another trust), W. H. Pilcher transferred the legal fee simple in the Whitchurch land back to Rawlins even though Rawlins had not repaid the £8,373 borrowed from the Jeremiah Pilcher Trust. This enabled Rawlins to pretend to Stockwell and Lamb that he held the full legal and equitable interest in the Whitchurch land, free from any mortgage or equitable interest: he was able to convince them of this by showing them all the title deeds of the Whitchurch land including the conveyance by which the legal fee simple was originally vested in him, but suppressing the 1851 mortgage to the Jeremiah Pilcher Trust and the 1856 transfer back by W. H. Pilcher to Rawlins. As a result, Stockwell and Lamb lent Rawlins £10,000 from their trust fund, and to secure repayment of that loan Rawlins purported to mortgage the Whitchurch land to Stockwell and Lamb by transferring the legal fee simple to them, with a proviso that they would transfer it back to him when he repaid the £10,000. The effect of this was to vest the legal fee simple of the Whitchurch land in Stockwell and Lamb: the issue in the case was whether they held subject to or free from the interests of the beneficiaries under the Jeremiah Pilcher Trust. In other words, did Stockwell and Lamb hold the legal fee simple on trust for the Jeremiah Pilcher beneficiaries, or on trust for the Stockwell and Lamb beneficiaries?

The Pilcher beneficiaries brought this action against Rawlins, W. H. Pilcher (who had taken a half share in the £10,000 paid over by Stockwell and Lamb) and Stockwell and Lamb (who, it was accepted, knew nothing of the fraud) to determine this question. The following judgments were given in the Court of Chancery allowing an appeal from the decision of the Master of the Rolls that Stockwell and Lamb held on trust for the Pilcher beneficiaries.]

LORD HATHERLEY, the Lord Chancellor: The defendant Rawlins could not have transferred the legal estate in the property except through the medium of the reconveyance of 1856, and the Master of the Rolls considered the case to be similar in that respect to the case of *Carter* v. *Carter* 3 K&J 617 ... The case now before us differs in many respects from the case of *Carter* v. *Carter*. An intentional fraud has been committed, and the parties to it have been enabled to effect their purpose owing to the cestuis que trust allowing the trustee, originally one of three, to become the sole trustee. As sole trustee he necessarily had possession of the title deeds to the mortgaged estate; so that, by the reconveyance to the mortgagor, the mortgagor became possessed of the legal estate, and by keeping back the whole mortgage transaction, was enabled to show a complete legal title to the property. Had he disclosed the mortgage, I think that the mortgage deed would have put the parties dealing with him on inquiry; but as matters were conducted, the mortgagee [Stockwell and Lamb] acquired the legal estate and entered into possession of the property without notice of the prior charge, and must, I think, be entitled to hold it.

The plea of purchase without notice states only possession on the part of the professed owner, conveyance of the estate, and absence of notice; and the cases undoubtedly have gone very far ... in showing that, on such a plea, when proved, equity declines all interference with the purchaser, having, as is said, no ground on which it can affect his conscience. I confess that the extent to which this doctrine has been carried was not wholly satisfactory to me when I decided *Carter* v. *Carter* ... [but the] present case is not such a case, and I can therefore concur with the view of the Lord Justices that the decree must be reversed.

SIR W. M. JAMES LJ: I entirely concur in the conclusion to which the Lord Chancellor has arrived ... I propose simply to apply myself to the case of a purchaser for valuable consideration, without notice, obtaining, upon the occasion of his purchase, and by means of his purchase deed, some legal estate, some legal right, some legal advantage; and, according to my view of the established law of this Court, such a purchaser's plea of a purchase for valuable consideration without notice is an absolute, unqualified, unanswerable defence, and an unanswerable plea to the jurisdiction of this Court. Such a purchaser, when he has once put in that plea, may be interrogated and tested to any extent as to the valuable consideration which he has given in order to show the *bona fides* or *mala fides* of his purchase, and also the presence or the absence of notice; but when once he has gone through that ordeal, and has satisfied the terms of the plea of purchase for valuable consideration without notice, then, according to my judgment, this Court has no jurisdiction whatever to do anything more than to let him depart in possession of that legal estate, that legal right, that legal advantage which he has obtained, whatever it may be. In such a case, a purchaser is entitled to hold that which, without any breach of duty, he has had conveyed to him ...

I am therefore of the opinion that, whatever may be the accident by which a purchaser has obtained a good legal title, and in respect of which he has paid his money and is in possession of the property, he is entitled to the benefit of that accident ...

Sir G. MELLISH LJ: I agree in the conclusion to which the Lord Chancellor and the Lord Justice have arrived. I do not think it necessary to give any opinion whether *Carter* v. *Carter* was rightly decided ... But I think that it cannot be supported on the grounds upon which the Master of the Rolls thought it had been decided ... [He], as I understand his judgment, held that a purchaser for valuable consideration, who has obtained a conveyance of the legal estate, is in this Court always to be held to have notice of the contents of the deeds which form a link in the chain by which the legal estate was conveyed to him. And he held that the doctrine of constructive notice ought to be enlarged, and that, although in point of fact the deed in question was never produced to the purchaser – although he had neither knowledge nor the means of knowledge of its contents – although he and his advisers were guilty of no negligence whatever in not obtaining knowledge of its contents – yet, nevertheless, he must in this Court be held to have notice of the contents [of any deed he would need to produce in order to prove his title] ...

The general rule seems to be laid down in the clearest terms by all the great authorities in equity, and has been acted on for a great number of years, namely, that this Court will not take an estate from a purchaser who has bought for valuable consideration without notice; and I find that [Stockwell and Lamb] are very clearly purchasers for valuable consideration without notice. Unless this doctrine of constructive notice, enlarged as it has been by the Master of the Rolls, is to prevail, I am of opinion that [Stockwell and Lamb] have made out their case.

As it is admitted that, with the exception of what is supposed to have been said in *Carter* v. *Carter*, this rule of constructive notice, as laid down by the Master of the Rolls, has never been established, I will proceed to consider it a little upon principle. It happens, curiously enough, that [Stockwell and Lamb] are themselves trustees for other cestuis que trust, and the question then arises which of the two sets of cestuis que trust are to bear the loss. Is the loss to fall upon the cestuis que trust whose trustee has fraudulently conveyed away the estate which was entrusted to him? Or is the loss to fall upon those whose trustees have honestly taken a conveyance of that estate and who have advanced the money of their cestuis que trust on the faith of that estate which they have really got?

It is surely desirable that the rules of this Court should be in accordance with the ordinary feelings of justice of mankind. Now if the first set of cestuis que trust, those who will unfortunately have to bear the loss, were asked how it happened that they suffered this loss, they would answer that their father conveyed the estates to their uncle, and he turned out to be a dishonest man, and parted with the estate. That is an explanation which any ordinary man of intelligence would understand. It might not be satisfactory to the losers, but they must see at once how it came to happen that they lost their estate. If you trust your property to a man who turns out to be a rogue, it stands to reason that you may lose it. But supposing the Master of the Rolls' doctrine to prevail, and supposing the other cestuis que trust were to be asked how they had lost their property, the answer would be: 'Our trustee invested our property on mortgage on the faith of a person who said that he had the legal estate, and who had it, and who conveyed it to our trustee as a security for the sums advanced, our trustee being guilty of no negligence whatsoever, having taken the advice of a perfectly competent conveyancer in order to see that the title was a good one. But the Court of Chancery says that we have lost it because our trustees had notice of the prior mortgage, though they had, in fact, no notice whatever. They had neither knowledge nor means of knowledge, but nevertheless the Court of Chancery says that, according to its doctrine, they had notice.' The only conclusion which any one would come to is that these cestuis que trust had been deprived of their property by the Court of Chancery, for reasons which, to an ordinary mind, were perfectly incomprehensible.

Notes and Questions 14.2

Read the above extract and *Kingsnorth Trust Ltd* v. *Tizard* [1986] 1 WLR 783, either in full or as extracted at www.cambridge.org/propertylaw/, and consider the following:

1   Explain why Stockwell and Lamb did not have constructive notice of the interests of the Pilcher beneficiaries, whereas Kingsnorth Trust Ltd did have

constructive notice of Mrs Tizard's interest. What do these two cases tell us about the inquiries and inspections that purchasers and mortgagees are reasonably expected to make?

2   What justifications did the judges give for preferring the claims of the Stockwell and Lamb beneficiaries to those of the Pilcher beneficiaries? Would the decision, or the justifications given for the decision, have been different if Stockwell and Lamb had not been trustees – if, for example, they were commercial moneylenders lending their own money in the course of business? Should it?

3   If, after discovering the fraud, Stockwell and Lamb had then sold the fee simple (as mortgagees are entitled to do) to Rawlins' sister, and she happened to know about the fraud, would Rawlins' sister take subject to or free from the interests of the Pilcher beneficiaries? See *Wilkes* v. *Spooner* [1911] 2 KB 473.

14.4.   Overreaching

14.4.1.   Nature and scope of overreaching

There are two ways of describing overreaching. One is to say that it is the process by which interests in land are transferred to the proceeds of sale of the land when the legal title is sold to a purchaser, so that the purchaser takes free from the interest and the equitable interest holder acquires instead an equivalent interest in the proceeds of sale now held by the seller. This is essentially the way in which it was described by Sir Benjamin Cherry, the principal draftsman of the Law of Property Act 1925 which reformulated the pre-existing principle of overreaching. Referring to section 2(1) of the 1925 Act, he said:

> This subsection collects and states the various means by which, where a legal estate in land is affected by any one or more equitable interests or powers, that legal estate can be conveyed to a purchaser in such a way that the purchaser is not concerned with the title to the equitable interest or power, or to obtain the concurrence of the owner thereof. On the other hand, the equitable interest is not defeated or destroyed by the disposition, but is shifted so as to become a corresponding interest or power in or over the proceeds. The conveyance to the purchaser is then said to 'overreach' the equitable interest or power. The expression 'overreach' is not defined in the Act, but this is the sense in which it has been used since 1882. An overreaching conveyance must be distinguished from one which wholly destroys some interest or right, e.g. a conveyance of land affected by a restrictive covenant made after 1925 which is not protected by registration as a land charge.

This was also the view of the Law Commission, implicit in both the Working Paper and the Report on Overreaching which we consider below.

However, overreaching has been described in a radically different way. In *State Bank of India* v. *Sood* [1997] Ch 276 (see below), Peter Gibson LJ adopted the definition given by Charles Harpum in 'Overreaching, Trustees' Powers and the Reform of the 1925 Legislation', namely, that overreaching is merely a process by which pre-existing interests are subordinated to later interests created by dispositions made under a trust. In other words, on this view, contrary to what Cherry says, overreaching is just a means of extinguishing pre-existing interests on a disposition to a purchaser.

If the second is adopted in preference to the first, it has a profound effect on the scope of the doctrine, as we see below. In order to appreciate the significance of the difference, however, it is necessary first to outline how the overreaching machinery provided by the Law of Property Act 1925 operates.

14.4.2.   Operation of overreaching

Overreaching is not confined to interests under a trust of land, but this is where it most often occurs. Provision for trustees of land to overreach equitable interests generally is made by section 2(1) of the Law of Property Act 1925 (as amended by paragraph 4 of Schedule 3 to the Trusts of Land and Appointment of Trustees Act 1996):

> (1) A conveyance to a purchaser of a legal estate in land shall overreach any equitable interest … affecting that estate, whether or not he has notice thereof … (ii) if the conveyance is made by trustees of land and the equitable interest … is at the date of the conveyance capable of being overreached by such trustees … and the requirements of section 27 of this Act respecting the payment of capital money arising on such a conveyance are complied with.

A conveyance includes the grant of a mortgage or a lease as well as the transfer of a fee simple (section 205(1)(ii) of the 1925 Act). The requirements of section 27 respecting the payment of capital money which are referred to here are that, notwithstanding anything to the contrary in any instrument creating the trust, 'the proceeds of sale or other capital money' arising out of the conveyance must not be paid to fewer than two persons as trustees of the trust, or to a trust corporation as trustee (section 27(2)).

Section 2(1) refers to equitable interests in general, but section 2(2) and (3) then effectively cut the category of equitable interests that can be overreached down to beneficial interests under trusts, by excluding (among other things) commercial equitable interests such as restrictive covenants, easements, estate contracts and options to purchase (section 2(3)). The significance of this is that overreaching was intended to apply only to interests in land which could properly be represented in money terms, in the sense that an interest in the proceeds of a sale of the land would be an acceptable substitute for an interest in the land itself. This could never be true of commercial interests such as easements or covenants: if an easement or covenant is overreached it is effectively destroyed. At the time of the 1925 legislation, however, it was true of interests under what are now called trusts of land, because they were primarily used as investment devices. If the principal function of the trust fund is to act as an investment for the beneficiaries, it is entirely appropriate that, when the trustees decide to change the composition of the fund from land to money, the interests of the beneficiaries should automatically transfer from the land to the money and not affect the person purchasing the land from the trustees. Now that trusts of land are more often used as a vehicle for home ownership, the application of overreaching is more problematic, as we see below.

The general effect of section 2(1) is therefore that, when trustees of land sell or mortgage trust land, the interests of the beneficiaries will be overreached and not be enforceable against the purchaser or mortgagee, provided the capital money (the sale proceeds in the case of a sale, and the money lent to the trustees in the case of a mortgage securing that loan) is paid to at least two trustees or a trust corporation. On the face of it, this is an elegant and effective enforceability rule which manages to preserve the value of the prior interests without hindering the marketability of the land. Problems have arisen, however, because money is no longer an adequate substitute for some of the interests to which it applies, and because the decision in *State Bank of India* v. *Sood* [1997] Ch 276 (see below) has both eroded the protection of the two-trustees rule (such as it is) to the disadvantage of prior-interest holders, while at the same time narrowing the range of transactions which can have overreaching effect, to the disadvantage of purchasers. We look at the first of these problems first.

14.4.3.   Overreaching the interests of occupying beneficiaries

As the Law Commission pointed out in its 1989 report on overreaching, since 1925 there has been a dramatic change in the proportion of dwellings that are owner-occupied, and in the proportion of owner-occupied dwellings that are jointly owned (see Extract 14.2 below). In the case of all the millions of jointly owned owner-occupied dwellings in this country, the property is held on trust and the interests of the beneficiaries are overreachable, and yet, in the vast majority of these cases, the beneficiaries regard themselves as owner-occupiers and not as people who have a purely financial stake in the property. There are therefore significant numbers of beneficiaries for whom the overreaching machinery set up by the 1925 Act, which protects financial interests only, provides inadequate protection. If all the occupying beneficiaries are also trustees, this is of no consequence, because the property cannot be sold or mortgaged without the concurrence of all of them. Similarly, if there is only one trustee (usually because the beneficiary or beneficiaries acquired their interests under a resulting or constructive trust by paying part of the purchase price of the property), this particular problem should not arise because a sale or mortgage by one trustee cannot overreach beneficial interests (although see below as to the extent to which the decision in *State Bank of India* v. *Sood* has undermined this principle). The real problem arises where there are two trustees but they are not also, or not the only, beneficiaries in occupation of the property. In these cases, although as a matter of trust law they should consult the occupying beneficiaries before selling the property (see below), any disposition they make will overreach the beneficiaries' interests whether they do so or not.

In *City of London Building Society* v. *Flegg* [1988] AC 54 (extracted at www.cambridge.org/propertylaw/), the House of Lords was invited to reverse this position and hold that trustees could not overreach the interests of beneficiaries in occupation without their consent. The *Flegg* case provides a good illustration of the fragility of the protection that overreaching provides for beneficiaries. The non-trustee beneficiaries were Mr and Mrs Flegg, who lived in a house, 'Bleak House', with their daughter and son-in law, Mrs and Mr Maxwell-Brown, who held the legal title on trust for the four of them. The overreaching transaction was a mortgage over Bleak House which the Maxwell-Browns granted to the City of London Building Society to secure repayment of a sum of money the building society had lent to the Maxwell-Browns. The effect of the overreaching mechanism was to require the Maxwell-Browns to hold the loan on trust for themselves and the Fleggs. This of itself did not prejudice the financial position of the Fleggs: the effect of the grant of the mortgage was to deplete the value of the Maxwell-Browns' fee simple (still held on trust for themselves and the Fleggs) by an amount precisely equal to the amount of the loan, so the Fleggs' beneficial interest in the loan money compensated them exactly for what they had lost. What caused the Fleggs' loss was the Maxwell-Browns' breaches of trust: the Maxwell-Browns defaulted on repayment of the loan, so entitling the building society to sell the house free from all the beneficial interests, and dissipated the loan money instead of keeping it safe for the Fleggs. The building society was therefore entitled to evict the Fleggs from their home, leaving them with just a personal claim against the Maxwell-Browns (apparently now insolvent and in prison).

The Fleggs' argument was, essentially, that the Maxwell-Browns should not have been able to put their home at risk in this way by mortgaging the fee simple without their consent. Put more precisely, it was argued on their behalf that beneficiaries in occupation of trust land were protected against overreaching without their consent by section 14 of the Law of Property Act 1925. Section 14 provides:

> This Part of this Act shall not prejudicially affect the interest of any person in possession or in actual occupation of land to which he may be entitled in right of such possession or occupation.

On the face of it, this is an attractive argument. The overreaching machinery provided by the Law of Property Act 1925 appears in sections 2 and 27 of the Act, both in 'this Part' of the Act (i.e. Part I). The interests of beneficiaries in occupation of land are prejudicially affected by an overreaching disposition made without their consent if it will deprive them of the benefit of occupation of the land (although see Lord Oliver's response to this point). The last part of the section is admittedly not apt to cover beneficiaries in occupation of the trust land: they do not have an interest in the land 'in right of' (i.e. by virtue of) their occupation. However, none of those who *do* have an interest in land 'in right of' their possession or occupation could conceivably be covered by section 14 (adverse possessors, for example, are already clearly covered by section 12: see further Notes and Questions 14.3 below). Consequently, so the argument goes, section 14 must be read as *not* limited by these words (i.e. as if the words 'to which he may be entitled in right of such possession or occupation' were omitted) – otherwise section 14 is robbed of all meaning.

However, the House of Lords rejected the argument and held that the Fleggs' interests were overreached by the mortgage to the building society, and consequently the building society was entitled to evict them from their home. They declined the invitation to construe section 14 so as to restrict the overreaching of the interests of beneficiaries in occupation, not so much because of the technical difficulties of construing it in that way, but because of the unlikelihood that it could have been intended, in 1925, to bear such a meaning, and the significant restriction on the operation of the overreaching machinery that would be introduced for the first time if they accepted such a construction.

However, the reaction to the *Flegg* decision prompted the Law Commission, already involved in a reconsideration of the whole of the law relating to trusts of land, to carry out a separate consultation exercise on overreaching. In a Working Paper published in 1988, they canvassed the possibility of reforming the machinery so that either occupying beneficiaries' interests could not be overreached without their consent, or the protection given by the two-trustees rule should be reinforced by requiring at least one of the trustees to be a solicitor or licensed conveyancer. As a result of the consultation exercise, they published a report recommending the former (see Extract 14.2 below).

The trusts of land project was completed and eventually resulted in the enactment of the Trusts of Land and Appointment of Trustees Act 1996, but the recommendations made about overreaching the interests of occupying beneficiaries were never implemented.

14.4.4. Transactions capable of overreaching beneficiaries' interests

If, as suggested above, overreaching is indeed the process by which the interests of beneficiaries transfer from land held on trust for them to its proceeds of sale when it is sold or mortgaged by the trustees, it would seem to follow that their interests will not be overreached by a transaction that does not produce proceeds of sale. If a 'sale' or mortgage of trust land by trustees which involves no immediate capital payment by the purchaser/mortgagee to the trustees nevertheless 'overreaches' the beneficial interests under the trust, overreaching means no more than extinguishing, and affords the beneficiaries no protection whatsoever.

In *State Bank of India* v. *Sood* [1997] Ch 276, the Court of Appeal accepted that this would be the effect of allowing beneficial interests to be overreached by transactions which did not produce capital money, but nevertheless held that section 2(1)(ii) of the Law of Property Act 1925 had to be construed to produce this result. In the case itself, two members of the Sood family jointly held the legal title to the house they lived in with five other members of the family. They mortgaged the house to the bank to secure repayment of money borrowed on overdraft by them and a family company. As usually occurs when a mortgage or charge secures borrowings on overdraft, some of the money had been borrowed before the mortgage was granted and more was borrowed later (i.e. the overdraft increased), but there was no capital sum of money advanced by the bank to the two title holders at the time of the mortgage. The bank called in the overdraft, there was default in repayment and the bank sought possession of the house with a view to enforcing the security. The other five members of the family claimed to have beneficial interests in the house and argued that their interests were not over-reached by the mortgage because no capital money had been paid to two trustees. The issue, therefore, was whether section 2 of the Law of Property Act 1925 requires compliance with section 27 of the Act (i.e. payment of capital money to two trustees) *in the case of all dispositions* by the trustees (which would mean that only dispositions for capital money could overreach beneficial interests) or whether section 27 comes into play only in the case of dispositions that do produce capital money. The Court of Appeal said the latter construction was the correct one: overreaching takes place on any *intra vires* disposition by trustees provided that, if capital money arises under the transaction, it is paid to at least two trustees or a trust corporation.

In coming to this decision, the court was persuaded that any other construction would be contrary to the policy of the 1925 legislation. They accepted that trustees may, acting within their powers, enter into transactions which do not produce capital money (for example, an exchange of land, or the grant of a lease without a premium). It must have been the policy of the Act that the beneficial interests under the trust would be overreached by such *intra vires* transactions, and therefore section 2(1)(ii) cannot be read so as to be restricted to transactions producing capital money.

Peter Gibson LJ acknowledged that the result of adopting such a construction was not 'entirely satisfactory'. This understates the difficulties. From the beneficiaries' point of view, the loss of the protection that the overreaching mechanism was intended to supply is significant. Mortgages to secure borrowings on overdraft are not uncommon. Moreover, the decision in *Sood* would seem to extend to allowing such mortgages to overreach beneficial interests even where there is only one trustee. The two-trustees rule appears only in section 27, and if section 27 comes into play only when capital money arises there is nothing left in section 2 to require two trustees for overreaching to take effect. It is true that 'trustees' appears in the plural in the opening words of section 2(1)(ii) but this hardly seems sufficient, given that the use of singulars and plurals is not conclusive in construing statutes (under section 6(c) of the Interpretation Act 1978, words in the plural include the singular, and *vice versa*).

From the point of view of purchasers, the effect of *Sood* is no more satisfactory. In his article, 'Overreaching, Trustees' Powers and the Reform of the 1925 Legislation', Charles Harpum argued that transactions by trustees could only overreach the beneficiaries' interests if the transaction was *intra vires*, meaning that the trustees had the power and the authority to enter into. This had never been suggested before in any of the cases on overreaching, and there are strong policy reasons why it should not be restricted in this way, as we see below. However, in *Sood*, Peter Gibson LJ assumed it to be correct. This is *obiter*, because it was common ground that the mortgage the Soods granted was within their powers. However, if it is correct, it significantly decreases the protection that overreaching provides for purchasers, because it becomes necessary for purchasers to check the authority of the trustees to enter into the transaction. To make matters worse, it is by no means clear which transactions count as authorised for these purposes. In 'The Impact of the Trusts of Land and Appointment of Trustees Act 1996 on Purchasers of Registered Land', Graham Ferris and Graham Battersby argued that the 1996 Act had curtailed trustees' powers for these purposes, but this view has been criticised (Martin Dixon, 'Overreaching and the Trusts of Land and Appointment of Trustees Act 1996'; and see also Ferris and Battersby, 'Overreaching and the Trusts of Land and Appointment of Trustees Act 1996 – A Reply to Mr Dixon'). Also, Ferris and Battersby have subsequently argued persuasively that the Harpum analysis accepted by Peter Gibson LJ in *Sood* is unconvincing in other respects (Ferris and Battersby, 'The General Principles of Overreaching and the Reforms of 1925').

This uncertainty as to the scope of overreaching of course defeats its object. If it is not immediately clear to purchasers on the face of the transaction whether it is one that will overreach beneficial interests, their only safe course is to enquire into the details of the trust in all cases, which was precisely what the 1925 legislation was seeking to avoid.

14.4.5.   The two-trustees rule

A final word needs to be said about the effectiveness of the two-trustees rule. It was introduced by the 1925 legislation on the basis, as the Law Commission put it, that 'two heads (containing consciences as well as brains) ought to be better than one' (Law Commission, *Trusts of Land: Overreaching* (Law Commission Consultative Document No. 106, 1988), paragraph 3.1). In that working paper, the Law Commission invited views on whether this was the best method of providing protection to beneficiaries, or whether perhaps the safeguard should be strengthened to require one of the trustees to be a solicitor. However, there was little support for change on consultation, and the Law Commission concluded that the added complications in conveyancing that would be caused by such a change outweighed any benefits (see Extract 14.2 below). Consequently, the two-trustees rule remains.

Extract 14.2   Law Commission, *Transfer of Land: Overreaching: Beneficiaries in Occupation* (Law Commission Report No. 188, 1989)

PART II THE PRESENT LAW

Introductory

2.1. It is an established, flexible and convenient feature of English land law that property can be legally owned by trustees, who hold it on behalf of one or more beneficiaries. The nature of the beneficiaries' interests can vary widely, as indeed can the degree of formality with which they are created. The fact that the law can accommodate many different and separate ownership interests in the same property, whether they are concurrent or consecutive, gives owners the chance to deal with their property in almost any way they choose. It can, however, present real problems when the land comes to be disposed of – a purchaser needs to be assured that he is acquiring the whole of the interest for which he contracted. If that interest has been fragmented, proving title can be complicated, costly and time-consuming. 'The central dilemma of land law is how to reconcile security of title with ease of transfer.'[1]

2.2. This dilemma was tackled in the property legislation of 1925, because before 1926 'the purchaser had to examine the lengthy, and, for this purpose, mainly irrelevant, provisions of the settlement in order to discover the principal facts essential to his obtaining a good title ... To discover these facts was often a tedious task, for the settlement was a long document setting out the trusts in full and a purchaser often had to waste time in reading clauses which were of no interest to him in order to ascertain a few simple facts. There were corresponding inconveniences to the beneficiaries and trustees.'[2] The 1925 legislation effected a compromise by making land held in trust freely marketable, while preserving the interests of the beneficiaries under those trusts, by the device of overreaching, which had originally been developed by conveyancing practitioners in connection with express trusts for sale, as a means of keeping the equities off the legal title.

. . .

2.6. In recent years there has been a sharp increase in the number of married couples acquiring their matrimonial homes and other property in joint names.[3][9] Commercial property owned by partnerships is normally also held in this way. In every case, the legal owners are technically trustees, even if they are themselves the beneficiaries for whom they hold the land.

2.7. At the same time, as the incidence of ownership by more than one person has increased, the concept of equitable interests arising informally has been developed. So, where two people contribute to the purchase price of the property which is then conveyed into the name of only one of them, both contributors are equitable tenants in common.[4][10] The contribution which entitles someone to a share of the property in equity may be made after the purchase. In one case, where an agreement to share could be implied and one member of a couple who were living together did a great deal of physical work to a property belonging to the other, she was held to have an equitable interest.[5][11] The claimant has to demonstrate a common intention that, even if he did not contribute to the purchase price, he and the legal owner should both have beneficial interests in the property and that he acted to his detriment on the basis of that intention, believing he would acquire a beneficial interest.[6][12]

1 Megarry and Wade, *The Law of Real Property*, 5th ed. (1984), p. 141.   2 *Ibid.*, p. 327.
3 Fifty-one per cent of all owner-occupied homes bought in 1960–1 were purchased in joint names; in 1970–1, the equivalent figure was 74 per cent (source: Todd and Jones, *Matrimonial Property* (1972). p. 80). Experience suggests that this increasing trend has continued.
4 *Bull* v. *Bull* [1955] 1 QB 234.   5 *Eves* v. *Eves* [1975] 1 WLR 1338.
6 *Grant* v. *Edwards* [1986] Ch 638.

2.8. Although the courts consider these circumstances most frequently in relation to living accommodation, the rules affect all types of property for whatever purpose it is owned ...

Overreaching

2.9. One of the main objectives of the 1925 property legislation was to simplify conveyancing and the proof of title to land, by separating legal and equitable interests. The aim was to permit dealings with legal estates without reference to, or even in ignorance of, the equitable beneficial interests. There was no intention to defeat the interests of trust beneficiaries, but rather to ensure that they become rights against whatever was for the time being subject to the trust, without hampering the ability of trustees to dispose of any property. This was achieved by 'the principle of "overreaching" by which equitable interests such as the interest of the beneficiaries under trusts are kept off the title to the legal estate, and are overreached on the sale of the legal estate to a purchaser who accordingly takes free of them'.[7][16] On a sale, e.g. the beneficiary's claims are transferred to the proceeds of sale, but only if the money is paid to two trustees or a trust corporation.[8][17]

...

Safeguard for beneficiaries

2.18. Clearly, any beneficiary whose interest is overreached needs to be reassured that his position has not been prejudiced. His safeguard is, in the majority of cases, directions as to payment of the consideration for which the legal estate is sold.[9][48] On a sale ... by a trustee for sale, the money must be paid to or applied by the direction of at least two persons as trustees for sale ... or a trust corporation ... If the appropriate requirement for payment is not fulfilled, there is no overreaching.

2.19. The requirement to pay capital money to two trustees or a trust corporation was newly introduced by the 1925 legislation. 'The safeguard against mistake or fraud of having at least two trustees or a trust corporation where capital money falls to be received, is a fairly obvious reform; it became essential when additional powers ... to overreach equitable interests were conferred.'[10][50] That comment, in the early years after the 1925 legislation, may be seen as over-optimistic about the strength of the safeguard for beneficiaries. In a recent case, a couple bought a house to accommodate themselves and the wife's parents and all contributed to the cost of it. A mortgage by the legal owners *pro tanto* overreached the older couple's interest, and on the mortgagors' default the mortgagee's claims took priority.[11][51]

2.20. In the case of a statutory trust for sale, the trustees must so far as practicable consult the beneficiaries of full age before selling. They must give effect to the wishes of

---

7 Parker and Mellows, *Modern Law of Trusts*, 5th ed. (1983), p. 5.
8 Paras. 2.18–2.19 below. A trust corporation means the Public Trustee, a corporation appointed by the court to act as trustee in a particular case, or a corporation entitled to act as a custodian trustee under the rules made pursuant to the Public Trustee Act 1906, section 4; Law of Property Act 1925, section 205(1)(xxviii).
9 Law of Property Act 1925, section 2(1), (2); Settled Land Act 1925, sections 72(1), 94(1).
10 Wolstenholme and Cherry, *Conveyancing Statutes*, 12th ed. (1932), p. 268.
11 *City of London Building Society* v. *Flegg* [1988] AC 54.

the beneficiaries, or of the majority of them, so far as consistent with the general interests of the trust. However, a purchaser is not concerned to see that the trustees have complied, so a sale without the beneficiaries having been consulted, or in defiance of their wishes, is valid[12][52] ...

PART III NEED FOR REFORM

Change of circumstances

3.1. The 1925 legislation compromise between the need to protect beneficiaries under trusts of land and the demand for certainty and simplicity in conveyancing was satisfactory, and perhaps ideal, in the circumstances in which it was intended to operate. A purchaser from trustees could ignore the beneficial interests so long as he was careful to observe simple precautions in paying the price. This successfully hid the terms of the settlement 'behind the curtain'. Buying from trustees became as simple as buying from a single beneficial legal owner which it certainly had not been previously. At the same time, the financial interest of the beneficiary was safeguarded by transferring his claim to the proceeds of sale. So long as the trustees properly conducted the affairs of the settlement, it was not important to the beneficiary by what assets his interest was secured.

3.2. Doubts about these provisions arise now because, over the years, the patterns of land ownership and the use of settlements have changed. Although the rules with which we are concerned affect all types of real property, the changes relating to residential property are most significant. Since 1925, both the number of dwellings in England and Wales and the percentage of them which are owner-occupied have jumped dramatically.[13][3] Couples have increasingly bought owner-occupied housing in their joint names, and this trend was accelerated by the decision in *Williams & Glyn's Bank Ltd* v. *Boland* [1981] AC 487 following which lending institutions encouraged borrowers to buy jointly so that they, the institutions, had the advantage of the statutory overreaching rules. These couples are technically trustees for sale, whether they hold on trust only for themselves, as is often the case, or whether there are others with beneficial interests.

3.3. For this reason, there is now a very large number of cases in which trust beneficiaries occupy trust property as their homes. Sometimes, also, the trust property is where they carry on business. Generally, the trust is a conveyancing technicality, imposed by the Law of Property Act 1925 as part of the scheme to confine normal conveyancing to legal estates. Most individuals in this position would be surprised to hear themselves referred to as trustees or as beneficiaries; they regard themselves

---

12 Law of Property Act 1925, section 26(3).

13 Statistics are not available for 1926 (the year in which the 1925 legislation came into effect). In 1931, there were 9.4 m dwellings in England and Wales (source: Census of England and Wales 1931), compared with 20.35 m in 1988 (source: Housing and Construction Statistics). The proportion of dwellings which were owner-occupied was 11.24 per cent in 1914, 32.46 per cent in 1938 and 67.19 per cent in 1988 (source: Department of the Environment). There are therefore about 6.5 times as many owner-occupied dwellings now as there were when the 1925 legislation came into force.

simply as joint owners. The changes in circumstances have exposed the 1925 rules for the device which they are. 'If the framers of the property legislation in 1925 had been able to foresee the growth in joint ownership of property which, coupled with the vast increase in the breakdown of marriage,[14][6] has exposed the artificiality of the statutory trust for sale, they might have made clearer provision for the protection of beneficial interests without widening the enquiries needed to be made by a purchaser.'[15][7]

Protecting occupation of property

3.4. In our working paper we said, 'we are not in this exercise primarily concerned with protecting beneficiaries' financial interests. It is their prospect of enjoyment of the land itself and its loss where overreaching occurs upon which we wish to focus.'[16][8] Some of those who responded agreed with this view. One correspondent said, 'I do not think it right that people in actual occupation of property should be in peril of losing their home as a result of the overreaching process.' Another pointed out that 'almost all other occupiers [of residential property] have some protection from arbitrary eviction'.

3.5. We remain of the view that reform is required here. There are four main reasons. First, the exclusively financial protection given by the 1925 legislation is no longer appropriate for occupiers of their own homes; their real concern is often with the enjoyment of the property itself which will be lost after overreaching. Secondly, as the general understanding of many of the beneficiaries with whom we are concerned is that they are joint owners, they should have appropriate ownership rights. There is scant justification for the law giving preference to the wishes of one joint owner over those of another, simply because the former was constituted trustee of the legal estate. Thirdly, it is unsatisfactory that the consequences which a sale visits upon a beneficiary in occupation are different depending whether the legal estate happens to have been vested in one, or in more than one, person. Fourthly, it is difficult to defend the situation in which someone not married to the legal owner in actual occupation of their home, and in which they own a share, has less right to remain there than a husband or wife without any such ownership interest.[17][9]

3.6. Accordingly, we reject one possible option which we put forward in the working paper, do nothing.[18][10]

3.7. In seeking a solution, we nevertheless recognise the importance of avoiding unnecessary complications in conveyancing. As we pointed out, 'it is important not to lose sight of the advantages for the public in facilitating reasonably speedy and safe conveyancing'.[19][11] This point was emphasised by many of the respondents to the working paper, who were practical conveyancers. One solicitor wrote, 'it would not be

---

14 Between 1961 and 1986 the divorce rate rose from 2.1 per 1,000 married people to 12.9 per 1,000: see *Facing the Future: A Discussion Paper on the Ground for Divorce* (1988), Law Com. No. 170, Appendix A.

15 Ruoff and Roper, *Law and Practice of Registered Conveyancing*, 5th ed. (1986), p. 822.

16 Working Paper, para. 6.1.

17 The non-owning spouse has occupation rights under Matrimonial Homes Act 1983, s. 1(11).

18 Working Paper, para. 6.14.   19 Working Paper, para. 6.2.

appropriate for anything to be put forward that would have the effect of making conveyancing more difficult and/or expensive'.

3.8. Another reform option would be to require beneficiaries, who wanted to be consulted before the property was disposed of, to register their interests. The corollary to this would be that in the absence of registration overreaching would apply without the beneficiary having any right to withhold consent.[20][12] We commented, 'this proposal can be rejected as being both complex and unrealistic'.[21][13] It did, nevertheless, attract limited support. One firm of solicitors considered 'that requiring an occupying beneficiary to register his interest produces a degree of certainty as to who has such an interest'. However, we agree with the academic lawyer who said, 'The real problem is the case of the casual contributor, who is unaware of the need to protect his or her position.' Several Mothers' Union groups suggested that 'since few beneficiaries would anticipate difficulties later on, they would not themselves take the necessary action'. This is the nub of the difficulty in this approach to reform. The objective must be to confer greater rights on those whom fairness dictates should have them. To do so in such a way that the procedural requirements will defeat the claims of many who are intended to benefit is not a satisfactory way forward. We do not doubt that a lot of people whose ownership interests derive from contributing to the purchase price of a property or from spending money on improvements would fail to register their claims, because they would not know of the need to do so.

3.9. Nevertheless, the need to alert purchasers and others interested in the property remains, and efficient conveyancing demands that beneficiaries' interests can be readily discovered. In our view, the very fact of a beneficiary's occupation of the property will provide a sufficient, although not an infallible, advance warning that he may have an interest, so that appropriate enquiries can be made. This is already the case for registered land,[22][14] and it is what in practice alerts people to the existence of beneficial interests which will not be overreached.[23][15] We therefore consider that there is no need for beneficiaries to be required to take further steps, and our principal recommendation, set out in Part IV,[24][16] is made on that basis.

PART IV REFORM PROPOSALS

Principal recommendation

4.1. We have concluded that the present protection of the interests of equitable owners in occupation of property is, in some circumstances, inadequate. The owner of an equitable interest which carries a right of occupation is entitled to two distinct benefits: a right to the value of the interest and the right to enjoy occupation. When the owner of a legal estate is in a similar position, the law protects each right separately; if the owner opts to remain in possession, he cannot be obliged to rely solely on the alternative financial right. The effect of overreaching is, however, to oblige the equitable owner to surrender his occupation

---

20 Working Paper, para. 6.3.   21 Working Paper, para. 6.4.   22 See para. 2.21 above.
23 By virtue of *Williams & Glyn's Bank Ltd* v. *Boland* [1981] AC 487; para. 2.22 above.
24 Para. 4.3 below.

right in favour of his financial one, without the chance to make a choice. We see no reason why equitable owners should be at a disadvantage in this respect.

4.2. We are, however, conscious of the need to maintain arrangements which will not unduly interfere with conveyancing. This leads us to place our emphasis on protecting the rights of owners of equitable interests who are in actual occupation of the property. That very fact of occupation can be used to alert prospective purchasers and mortgagees to the claims of the equitable owners. It means that the protection of occupation rights does not extend to those who, while they are entitled to occupy, are not currently exercising the right. While that means that equitable owners will sometimes be at a disadvantage, when compared with legal owners, it seems to us to be a reasonable compromise. It offers the right to continue in occupation, to those who are already there, so it is likely to extend the new protection to those who most need it, and of course protection extends to those who enter later.

4.3. Our principal recommendation, to protect the occupation rights of those with an equitable interest in property, can be succinctly stated:

> A conveyance of a legal estate in property should not have the effect of overreaching the interest of anyone of full age and capacity who is entitled to a beneficial interest in the property and who has a right to occupy it and is in actual occupation of it at the date of the conveyance, unless that person consents.

Notes and Questions 14.3

Read the above extract and *City of London Building Society* v. *Flegg* [1988] AC 54 and *State Bank of India* v. *Sood* [1997] Ch 276, either in full or as extracted at www.cambridge.org/propertylaw/, and consider the following:

1 The statutory provisions about trustees' duties to consult beneficiaries and act in accordance with their wishes now appear in the Trusts of Land and Appointment of Trustees Act 1996. For an analysis of the effect of these changes on overreaching powers, see Harpum, 'Overreaching, Trustees' Powers and the Reform of the 1925 Legislation'; Ferris and Battersby, 'The Impact of the Trusts of Land and Appointment of Trustees Act 1996 on Purchasers of Registered Land'; Dixon, 'Overreaching and the Trusts of Land and Appointment of Trustees Act 1996'; Ferris and Battersby, 'Overreaching and the Trusts of Land and Appointment of Trustees Act 1996 – A Reply to Mr Dixon'; Ferris and Battersby, 'The General Principles of Overreaching and the Reforms of 1925'.

2 Explain why the House of Lords in *Flegg* refused to accept the interpretation of section 14 of the Law of Property Act 1925 put forward on behalf of the Fleggs. What does section 14 mean?

3 Why was 'Bleak House' not put in the joint names of the Fleggs and the Maxwell-Browns? Is this a relevant factor in considering whether the Fleggs' interests should be overreachable without their consent?

4   In *Sood*, counsel for the beneficiaries conceded that, even on their construction of section 2(1)(ii) of the 1925 Act, the interests would be overreached if even a tiny proportion of the total sum borrowed had been advanced at the time of the mortgage, and this conclusion appears inescapable on the wording of the section. The truth probably is that the draftsmen did not have in mind transactions where the consideration was to paid at a later date, whether by instalments of rent or staged payments of capital. Consider how, if at all, they could have adapted the overreaching machinery in section 2 to cover such payments.

5   Are beneficiaries better off or worse off as a result of the decision in *Sood*? What about purchasers?

6   Discuss whether the law should be changed so that overreaching could not take place without the consent of beneficiaries in occupation of trust property. Could this operate to the disadvantage of other beneficiaries?

7   Write a paper addressed to the government either putting forward proposals for the reform of the law of overreaching or recommending that no changes should be made.

15

Registration

15.1. What are registration systems for?

In this chapter, as in the previous one, we are looking at registration primarily as a means of protecting private property rights. A property registration system can provide more effective ways of dealing with, or averting, the kind of difficulties over the enforceability and priority of property interests that we considered in the previous chapter, and can also facilitate proof of title, as we noted in Chapter 10. This not only makes the assets the subject of the registration system more freely marketable – assets are more easily traded if title can be proved quickly, cheaply and with certainty – but also helps promote security of title. Infringements of an interest holder's rights are easier to combat (and therefore less likely to occur) when the interest holder's title is beyond dispute.

However, it is important to appreciate that a state might decide to set up a property registration system for purposes other than the protection of private rights. One of our oldest property registers, the Shipping Registry, was set up by the Navigation Act 1660 primarily for the protection of British trade. British-owned ships were required to be registered in their local British port to enable the port authorities to ensure that foreign-owned ships did not trade from British ports, and that various privileges were accorded only to British-owned ships. Protectionism re-emerged as the publicly articulated objective of changes made to the ship registration regime by the Merchant Shipping Act 1988, which required all previously registered fishing vessels to reapply for registration, and introduced a requirement that eligibility for registration was limited to fishing vessels whose owners (and at least 75 per cent of shareholders) were British citizens resident and domiciled in the United Kingdom. In making these changes, the stated intention of the British government was to protect British fishing communities by preventing Spanish nationals buying up British ships in order to take advantage of the United Kingdom's fishing quota under the European Community's common fisheries policy. The common fisheries policy had been adopted by the EC out of concern for overfishing of stocks in the North Sea and Atlantic Ocean, and was intended to ensure equality of access to fishing grounds for Member States (and exclusion of everyone else), having regard to the needs of regions where the local population is dependent on fishing. As it happened, this attempt to use registration to defend the British quota failed. The European Court of Justice held that the registration conditions were contrary to EC law, and the House of Lords ordered the British government to pay compensation to the shipowners who had been unable to re-register (see further *R. v. Secretary of State for Transport, ex parte Factortame Ltd (No. 5)* [2001] 1 AC 524). Nevertheless, ship registration (both in this country and abroad) continues to serve as a mechanism for the international regulation of safety standards and the welfare of crew. International conventions oblige all countries bound by them to impose regulatory regimes on all ships registered in that country, and entry to a port in any particular country may depend on the ship being registered in a country which imposes such regimes and enforces them to an acceptable degree.

Ship registration is also of course intended to facilitate the buying, selling and mortgaging of ships, but unlike land registration (and for obvious reasons) it operates on an international as well as a national level in this respect. In particular, the main function internationally of registration in national shipping registers is to act as an internationally recognised 'badge' of entitlement, which enables foreign courts to assume that the person registered as owner or mortgagee of a ship in the national register on which the ship is registered is indeed entitled under domestic law, without having to enquire into the property rules applicable in that particular jurisdiction. One consequence of this is that unregistered interests are not internationally recognised, a severe disadvantage given that ships tend to sail between jurisdictions. So, for example, English law recognises equitable property interests in British ships and they are fully enforceable in English courts but they are not enforceable in any other jurisdiction because they are not registrable under the British Merchant Shipping Act 1995, the current ship registration statute.

As far as land registration is concerned, our registration of title system differs from most European systems in that the first attempts at a national system were not made until the mid-nineteenth century, when the idea of land as a tradable commodity first started to emerge. The overriding consideration then was (as it was when the present system was introduced by the Land Registration Act in 1925, and as it still was when the 1925 Act was amended and replaced by the Land Registration Act 2002) to make conveyancing simpler and cheaper – in other words, to increase the marketability of land.

This is in marked contrast to the way in which most other European land registration systems evolved. In many European jurisdictions the impetus for cataloguing land came from the state, and the motive was to protect the interests of the state by gathering information to enable the state to levy tax. This was the origin of the cadastre, a systematic record of land-holdings sometimes said to have been devised in the Austrian Empire in the eighteenth century (see, for example, the short history given in *Ruoff and Roper on the Law and Practice of Registered Conveyancing*, Extract 15.1 below) but probably dating back much earlier than that (the Domesday book is an early English example). The cadastre forms the basis of most continental European land registration systems, which consequently are regarded as operating primarily for public purposes (now for land regulation and environmental protection as well as for taxation), whereas our system's primary objective is purely private – to increase the marketability of land.

As Ruoff and Roper point out in Extract 15.1 below, these fundamental differences in purpose between cadastral-based systems and ours have led to significant structural differences between their systems and ours, which we must now look at in more detail.

15.2. Characteristics of the English land registration system

15.2.1. Privacy

A cadastral system necessarily involves revealing details of private ownership to the state, and in modern times, where the cadastre plays a central role in land regulation and environmental protection, to other members of the public as well. In our system, until very recently, privacy was regarded as paramount. The land register was not opened for public inspection until December 1990 when the Land Registration Act 1988 came into force (and then only after a protracted parliamentary struggle) and the Land Registration Rules 2003 (SI 2003 No. 1417) made under the Land Registration Act 2002 still make elaborate provision for applicants to delete 'prejudicial information' in leases and mortgages before they have to be made available for public inspection (rules 136–138). 'Prejudicial information' is defined in rule 131 as any information which, if disclosed to the public generally or to specific persons, would or would be likely to cause 'substantial unwarranted' damage or distress, or 'prejudice the commercial interests' of the applicant. The Registrar must accept an application to treat information as coming within this category if 'satisfied that [it] is not groundless' (rule 136(3)).

Similarly, the Land Registry has been slow to share its information with other government departments, and it is only now that arrangements are being made to do so systematically (see Land Registry, *Annual Report and Accounts 2002–2003*, item 6 of their business objectives for 2002/3, which they report they have achieved).

15.2.2. Comprehensiveness

A fundamental difference between cadastral-based systems and ours is that a cadastre is geographically comprehensive (at least in relation to populated areas of the country surveyed) and is compiled systematically and usually all in one go, whereas in our system individual plots of land are added to the register sporadically, by a process which has not yet been completed and probably never will be.

Under our system, voluntary registration of individual plots of land has been at least theoretically possible ever since the system was brought into operation by the Land Registration Act 1925, but registration does not become compulsory unless and until a triggering event occurs. Because the system has always been geared towards marketability of land, the only triggering event is a dealing with the land – either a transfer on sale, or, since 1997, the grant of a lease for more than twenty-one years (reduced from forty years by the Land Registration Act 1997, and now reduced again down to seven years by section 4 of the Land Registration Act 2002) or a legal mortgage over a fee simple or such a lease (section 4 of the 2002 Act).

This means that land which is not traded simply never gets on the register unless the title holder chooses to put it there. In addition, the process has been prolonged still further because it was decided in 1925 to limit compulsory registration to specified areas of England and Wales, and to progressively add additional areas of compulsory registration only as and when resources permitted. It was only if land was in area of compulsory registration that a plot of land had to be put on the register following a dealing with it: in other areas registration was merely voluntary, and indeed for many years a shortage of resources led to prolonged suspensions or restrictions of voluntary registration. This process of gradually extending compulsory registration to cover the whole of England and Wales was not completed until 1 December 1990: the last areas to be brought in comprised the districts of Babergh, Castle Point, Forest Heath, Leominster, Maldon, Malvern Hills, Mid Suffolk, Rochford, St Edmundsbury, South Herefordshire, Suffolk Coastal, Tendring, Wychavon and Wyre Forest, all under the Registration of Title Order 1989 (SI 1989 No. 1347).

As a consequence of all this, although there are 18.87 million registered titles in England and Wales (as at the end of 2003), the Land Registry estimates that there are about 3–4 million still to go (Land Registry, *Annual Report and Accounts 2002–2003*). The Land Registry reports that it is now taking active steps to encourage voluntary registration. In its *Annual Report and Accounts 2002–2003*, for example, it says that it is working with, among others, the National Playing Fields Association to register playing fields and the Court Service to register 180 court buildings, and also reports that it has managed to complete registration of all its own land (*ibid.*, p. 41). However, the option of completing the process by compulsion was rejected in the joint Law Commission and Land Registry report whose recommendations were implemented by the Land Registration Act 2002 (Law Commission and HM Land Registry, *Land Registration for the Twenty-First Century: A Conveyancing Revolution* (Law Commission Report No. 271, 2001)) – for no very good reason, as we see in Extract 15.2 below. Consequently, despite the report's recommendation that the matter be re-examined in five years' time, it remains a real prospect that we will never have a comprehensive land registration system.

This sporadic, transaction-based approach to putting land on the register has had a profound effect on two aspects of our registration system. The first is the way in which boundaries are treated, and the second is the limited range of interests in land that are eligible for registration. We look at these in the next two sections.

15.2.3.   Boundaries

One of the points of a cadastre is to draw up a map or catalogue of the area settling the boundaries between differently owned lots. However, this is not easy to do in a registration system like ours where individual lots are haphazardly and sporadically put onto the register. In any event, it was decided in 1925 not to do it: boundaries have never been guaranteed under the Land Registration Acts (see now sections 60 and 61 of the 2002 Act; the procedure referred to in section 60(3) for allowing the Land Registry to determine the exact line of the boundary in specified cases dates back to 1925, but is very rarely used). The land register does indeed include a definitive map, and the Land Registry works closely with the Ordnance Survey and has pioneered the development of digital mapping techniques, but nevertheless it takes no responsibility for the accuracy of the boundaries between registered properties. This is perhaps inevitable. When an application is made for the first registration of title to a plot of land which has never before been put on the register, the registry hears only the applicant's side of the story as to where the boundaries lie between her plot and those of her neighbours. Conflicting views are unlikely to come to light until the neighbours make their own applications for registration, if then. Consequently, boundary disputes are as common in registered land as in unregistered land, and the position of the boundaries on the register is of no significance when it comes to resolving such disputes. Also, it seems clear from reported cases on rectification of the register that areas of land do sometimes end up registered under two different titles held by different people, and conversely that landlocked areas between titles can be overlooked and never be registered at all.

15.2.4.   Restricted class of registrable interests

15.2.4.1.   Distinguishing 'substantive' registration and 'protection' on the register

The most striking feature of our land registration system is that only some types of property interest can actually be registered. This is a direct consequence of our system's focus on marketability.

Property interests which cannot be registered are not wholly excluded from the system. There are two other methods (i.e. not involving actual registration of the interest) by which their existence can be made known on the register. These are sometimes referred to as ways of 'protecting' the interest on the register, although as we see below the protection actually offered is not extensive. The term 'substantive registration' is often used (although not in the legislation) to distinguish genuine registration of an interest from this somewhat ambiguous protection provided by 'protection' of it.

15.2.4.2.   Registration

The only interests that can be actually registered are:

1   a legal estate in fee simple absolute in possession;

2 a legal lease for a term of more than seven years (with some exceptions);
3 a legal charge by way of legal mortgage;
4 a profit in gross (with a perpetual duration or for a term of more than seven years);
5 a legal easement or profit which is appurtenant to a registered fee simple or lease;
6 a rentcharge; and
7 a franchise and a manor.

See sections 2–4 of the 2002 Act, and also section 1 of the Law of Property Act 1925 which supplies the definition of the term 'legal estate' as it appears in the 2002 Act.

Only the first five of these are of any significance. Rentcharges were prospectively abolished by the Rentcharges Act 1977: no new ones can be created after 21 August 1977 and most will have ceased to exist by 2037. Franchises and manors are relics of Crown prerogative and the feudal system – interesting, but rarely encountered.

Leaving these aside, the content of the list is dictated by the fact that the primary objective of the system is to facilitate dealings with land. Fee simples, leases and profits in gross are on the list because they can be, and in practice regularly are, separately traded (profits particularly so as a consequence of the decision in *Bettison* v. *Langton* [2001] UKHL 24, as we saw in Chapter 5). For this reason, each of them is given a separate title number and what amounts to (but is not described in the Act as) a separate file. Legal charges by way of legal mortgage (now the only type of legal mortgage or charge that can be granted over a registered fee simple or lease) are on the list of registrable interests because the most important remedy of the mortgagee is to sell the mortgagor's interest (free from the mortgage) if there is a default, and registration of the title to the mortgage facilitates a sale as mortgagee. Registered mortgages are not given a separate title number or a separate file: they are registered against, and in the file of, the fee simple, lease or profit they are charged on.

The appearance on the list of appurtenant easements and profits is anomalous in that, by definition, they cannot be separately traded. If expressly granted they are usually granted in a transfer of either the benefited or the burdened land, in which case they will be registered automatically. If granted by a separate deed, the grantee has to take steps to register the easement as appurtenant to the benefited land (i.e. appearing under the benefited title's title number and in its file) and to have an appropriate entry made in the file of the burdened title. Legal easements arising by prescription, or otherwise arising informally, are registrable in theory, but in practice this is rarely a practical proposition.

We consider the effect of registration below, but as already noted for present purposes the important point is that *no other type of interest in land* can be registered.

15.2.4.3. 'Protection' by notice or restriction

The 2002 Act, like its predecessors, provides two protection mechanisms which can be used either for interests which cannot be registered, or for those which can be registered but are not.

The first is by entry of a 'notice' in the file of the registered title affected by the interest (sections 32–39 of the 2002 Act). This ensures that the interest will be enforceable against subsequent purchasers of that title, as we see below, but it has no other effect. In particular, it provides no guarantee of the validity of the interest. If the interest is ineffective as against that particular purchaser for some other reason, for example because not created using the correct formalities, the entry of a notice will not make it enforceable: section 32(3). Also, it does not have any priority effect: as we see below, interests protected by notice take priority from the date they are created, not the date on which they appear on the register. Finally, only some, but not all, non-registrable interests can be protected by entry of a notice. Important categories of interest are excluded, most notably interests under a trust of land, leases granted for a term of less than three years and interests registrable under the Commons Registration Act 1965 (section 33).

The other – and very different – method of protection is to enter a 'restriction' in the file of the registered title affected by the interest (sections 40–47). A restriction does not make the interest enforceable against anyone, nor does it necessarily even identify the interest. It certainly does not validate the interest, nor give it priority over any other interest. All it does is to alert prospective purchasers of the registered title of any limitations there may be on the registered title holder's powers. If, for example, the title holders are trustees and so unable to overreach interests under the trust except in the circumstances noted in the previous chapter, this limitation on their powers will be stated in a restriction entered in the title holder's file. Similarly, if the registered title holder is unable to sell or grant leases without first notifying or obtaining the consent of a specified person, this too will be stated in a restriction in his file.

It will be apparent from the above that the principle of overreaching applies in registered land. Beneficiaries under a trust of land certainly cannot register their interests, nor are they given any means of protecting them against an unwanted overreaching disposition. All they can do is enter a restriction against the trustees' title pointing out to purchasers what a purchaser has to do to overreach their interests.

15.2.4.4.   The overriding interest class

To complete the picture, it has to be noted here that the fact that a property interest in land in neither registered nor protected on the register does not necessarily mean that it is unenforceable against registered title holders. The Land Registration Acts have always recognised the concept of overriding interests – i.e. interests which are fully enforceable even though not appearing on or apparent from the register. The 2002 Act has restricted the categories of overriding interests, but they still remain highly significant. In particular, they include short leases (which can be neither registered nor protected by notice) and *any* interest in land where the interest holder is in actual occupation of the land, as we see below. One effect of this is that overreachable interests of beneficiaries under a trust who are in occupation of the land will usually nevertheless be fully enforceable, *provided they are not overreached*. In other words, overreaching not only applies to registered land, it operates in registered land in precisely the same way as it operates in unregistered land.

15.2.5. The mirror, curtain and guarantee principles

Commentators on land registration frequently quote the comment made by T. B. F. Ruoff (Chief Land Registrar for many years) in *An Englishman Looks at the Torrens System* (published in Sydney, Melbourne and Brisbane in 1957), that the fundamental features of common law registration systems in general and the Torrens and English land registration systems in particular are the 'mirror principle', the 'curtain principle' and the 'guarantee principle'. Gray and Gray usefully summarise Ruoff's principles in the following way:

THE 'MIRROR PRINCIPLE'

6.11. The register of title is intended to operate as a 'mirror', reflecting accurately and incontrovertibly the totality of estate and interests which may at any time affect the registered land. In this sense, 'the register is everything' [quoting Lord Buckmaster in *Creelman* v. *Hudson Bay Insurance Co.* [1920] AC 194 at 197].

THE 'CURTAIN PRINCIPLE'

6.12. Trusts relating to the registered land are kept off the title, with the result that third parties may transact with registered proprietors safe in the assurance that the interests behind any trust will be overreached.

THE 'INSURANCE PRINCIPLE'

6.13. The state itself guarantees the accuracy of the registered title, in that an indemnity is payable from public funds if a registered proprietor is deprived of his title or is otherwise prejudiced by the correction of any mistake in the register. (Gray and Gray, *Elements of Land Law* (4th edn), paras. 6.11–6.13)

We see below that, despite what Ruoff says, the insurance principle he articulates differs in important respects from the indemnity principle which actually underlies the Land Registration Acts, and that in any event the system we actually have falls far short of the ideal contemplated by either of those principles. As far as Ruoff's other two principles are concerned, the second contradicts the first. How can a system both aspire to provide an accurate mirror of property interests affecting land and at the same time construct a curtain behind which a significant class of interests is required to hide? This is not the only reason for scepticism about the mirror principle. A system that offers genuine registration only to a limited class of property interests can hardly be said to be taking its mirror aspirations seriously, while the existence and content of the overriding interest class raises the whole question of whether a mirror is really what we want in any event. We return to this point when we look at overriding interests in more detail below.

15.2.6.   Consequences of non-registration

Looking at registration systems in general, there are various ways of dealing with a failure to utilise the registration machinery provided. One way is to make registration entirely optional, a privilege that can be acquired by any eligible person who chooses to take advantage of it. This involves providing benefits for those who register which are not available to those who do not. At the other end of the spectrum, registration can be made compulsory and the system can not only withhold benefits from those who default but also impose penalties on them.

Ship registration moved from one extreme to the other within a relatively short period. Under the Merchant Shipping Act 1894, which was the principal registration Act for nearly a century, it was compulsory for a British ship to be registered in the British Shipping Registry, and failure to comply was a criminal offence. However, the Merchant Shipping Act 1988 made registration voluntary, and then, under the Merchant Shipping Act 1995, the effect of registration was limited to five years, so that anyone who wants to enjoy the benefits of registration must reapply every five years. Registration is therefore now a privilege. This works because it is virtually impossible for a ship to operate unless it is registered in some jurisdiction or other, so the only real option facing a ship owner is where, not whether, to register.

As far as land registration is concerned, we have already seen that from the outset the system has relied on both compulsory and voluntary routes for entry into the system, and seems likely to continue to do so. However, once titles are in the system, it has always been compulsory to use the registration machinery whenever the registered title holder makes a 'registrable disposition' (defined in section 27 of the 2002 Act to cover, essentially, any transfer of the interest itself, any grant of a lease for more than seven years, any grant of a legal mortgage, and any grant of a legal easement or profit). Any such disposition must be 'completed by registration', i.e. the person taking the benefit of the disposition must apply to the Land Registry to be registered as title holder. At present, there are two sanctions provided for failure to do so. The first is that the disposition does not have *legal* effect until the person taking the benefit of the disposition has become registered – i.e. until registration, her interest remains equitable only (section 27(1)). The second is that her interest may not be enforceable against anyone else who acquires a registrable interest in the land for valuable consideration and becomes registered title holder of his interest. This is because of section 29 of the 2002 Act, which provides in effect that any purchaser (meaning anyone who acquires his interest for valuable consideration) who becomes a registered title holder takes free from any interest that is neither registered, nor protected on the register by a notice, nor categorised as an overriding interest. A person who acquires an interest under a registrable disposition but does not register, is therefore vulnerable under section 29: her interest will not be enforceable against subsequent registered proprietors who gave valuable consideration unless she decided to protect her interest by notice instead of by registering it (allowable, but not usually advisable) or unless her interest is overriding (because, for example, she happened to be in actual occupation of the land, as we see below). However, this is the only other sanction provided for non-registration. Her interest will not be affected in any other way. It will remain valid as between herself and the person who granted her the interest, and enforceable against anyone other than a registered purchaser (to the same limited extent as any other unregistered equitable interest is).

This sanction of non-enforceability against subsequent purchasers makes sense in a registration system aimed primarily at facilitating marketability. Marketability requires no more than that purchasers will not be affected by interests not on the register: it has no interest in seeing that interests off the register cannot exist at all for any purpose. A sanction of invalidity for all purposes would only be appropriate if there were other reasons why the state wanted the register to provide a complete record of all interests in land (as for example it might if our register also functioned as a cadastre). However, under section 93 of the 2002 Act, the government is given power to make rules (intended to be made when electronic conveyancing is sufficiently advanced) which will change the sanction for non-registration from unenforceability to invalidity. Surprisingly little justification has been provided for this dramatic swing to the far extreme of compulsion. In fact, it appears from paragraphs 2.59–2.68 and 13.74–13.82 of the Law Commission's report (see Extract 15.2 below) that, as far as the Law Commission and Land Registry are concerned, a sufficient justification for moving to an invalidity sanction is that technological developments enable us to do so.

Extract 15.1 R. B. Roper *et al.*, *Ruoff and Roper on the Law and Practice of Registered Conveyancing* (2nd looseleaf edn, London: Sweet & Maxwell, 2003)

REGISTRATION SYSTEMS: CONTINENTAL EUROPE

The prevalence of the cadastre in continental Europe has led to a fundamental difference between, on the one hand, the land registration systems in many European countries which are based on the cadastre and, on the other hand, those focused on the registration of title or registration of deeds as is the case in the British Isles, Germany and countries which have the Torrens system. The cadastre was devised during the eighteenth century, principally in the Austrian Empire. It was then fully developed by Napoleon whose Commission, set up in 1807, contained terms of reference as follows:

> To survey more than 100 million parcels; to classify these parcels by fertility of the soil and to evaluate the productive capacity of each one; to bring together under the name of each owner a list of the separate parcels he owns; to determine, on the basis

of their total productive capacity, their total revenue and to make of this assessment a record which should thereafter serve as the basis of future assessments.

This was clearly instituted to serve the needs of the state for the purpose of the assessment and collection of revenue, whereas the purpose of deeds or title registration is to protect the interests of landowners. A cadastral system has three main points of difference from a system of title registration.

(i)   A cadastre is a systematic record designed to prevent a landowner evading the payment of tax. The compilation of a register of title, in contrast, is usually sporadic when and where transactions occur.
(ii) A cadastre necessitates classification and valuation so that the tax can be assessed, whereas registration of title is not directly concerned with value. Cadastre plans do not admit to any flexibility in the interpretation of boundaries as is found where registration is with general boundaries only.
(iii) A cadastre is primarily concerned with the payment of taxes and not with proof of ownership as is the case with the registration of title nor with the aim of giving publicity to conveyancing transactions as is the case with deeds registers.

Where there has been a marriage between title registration and the cadastre, the cadastre incorporates registration of title and the resulting system consists of the following two basic parts:

(i)   a cartographic part consisting of large-scale maps which are based on surveys including aerial photographs and which indicate the division into parcels of an area together with appropriate parcel identifiers;
(ii) a descriptive part containing registers or files which record 'legal facts' (deeds) or 'legal consequences' (titles) and other physical or abstract attributes concerning the parcels depicted on the map.

From the registration of title point of view there is a potential weakness in a cadastre-based system in that priority may be given to the maintenance and expansion of fiscal information and to items of unchanging character, such as the type of soil, to the prejudice of the effective recording of matters vitally important for property owners for the creation and disposition of interests in land. This was the case in parts of Eastern Europe where the requirements of the state were taking precedence over the needs of landowners, as indeed they had in the original Napoleon concept. Nevertheless, there is great potential for development here as can be seen in the system developed in Sweden where the land records are held on two registers, each operated by a separate government organisation. The first is the 'Property Register' or cadastre which is maintained in cadastral offices spread throughout the country. The second is the 'Land Register', which is maintained in land registries that are adjuncts of the Lower Courts. From the comprehensive information obtained from these registers and from other national and local authorities a Land Data Bank has been developed on a central basis which contains not only data essential to land titles but also information on many other matters relating to the land including values for taxation purposes and planning matters.

Notes and Questions 15.1

1 See also paragraph 3.004 in Ruoff and Roper for a comparison of the English system with Torrens-based systems, which originated in Australia and now apply throughout most of Australasia. Most developing countries and former communist states introducing land registration for the first time have opted to base their systems on the Torrens system rather than on the English Land Registration Act model.

2 The concentration on the interests of the state that Ruoff and Roper see as a potential weakness of cadastral systems is seen by others as a strength. In 1995, the International Federation of Surveyors published a *Statement on the Cadastre*, 'highlight[ing], from an international perspective, the importance of the cadastre as a land information system for social and economic development', and made these claims for the modern role of a cadastre:

> It may be established for fiscal purposes (e.g. valuation and equitable taxation), legal purposes (conveyancing), to assist in the management of land and land use (e.g. for planning and other administrative purposes), and enables sustainable development and environmental protection ... It provides governments at all levels with complete inventories of land-holdings for taxation and regulation. But today, the information is also increasingly used by both private and public sectors in land development, urban and rural planning, land management, and environmental monitoring ... The cadastre plays an important role in the regulation of land use. Land use regulations [permitting development] stipulate [for example] ... the necessary access to water and sewerage, roads etc. [and] the cadastre forms an essential part of the information required by the private developer, landowners, and the public authorities to ensure that benefits are maximised and costs (economic, social, and environmental) are minimised. (www.fig7.org.uk/publications/cadastre/statement_on_cadastre.html)

They also stressed the importance of encouraging developing countries to develop cadastral systems to meet 'the needs and demands in societies with customary and informal land tenure systems' and concluded that the cadastre although 'important in early societies, [is] even more important today from a global perspective due to its role in economic development and environmental management'.

Extract 15.2   Law Commission and HM Land Registry, *Land Registration for the Twenty-First Century: A Conveyancing Revolution* (Law Commission Report No. 271, 2001)

FIRST REGISTRATION

2.9. We consider that, in principle, the remaining unregistered land should be phased out as quickly as possible and that all land in England and Wales should be registered. As we have indicated above (paragraph 2.6) the continuation of two parallel systems of conveyancing, registered and unregistered, has absolutely nothing to commend it. Furthermore, as the result of a change to an open register in 1990, the contents of the register are now public. The register is no longer something of concern only to conveyancers but provides an important source of publicly available information about land, a resource in which there is an increasing interest. However, the Bill [now the Land Registration Act 2002] does not introduce any system to compel the registration of all land that is presently unregistered. This may at first sight appear paradoxical, but there are three particularly compelling reasons for not doing so at this juncture.

2.10. First, we consider that it would be premature to do so. Not only have the changes made by the 1997 Act only recently started to have effect, but the present Bill will offer considerable additional benefits to those whose titles are registered, quite apart from the conveyancing advantages should they wish to sell or deal with their land. We therefore anticipate a very significant rise in voluntary first registration as a result. Compulsion should not be employed in our view until it is clear that existing provisions have been given an opportunity to work.

2.11. Second, compulsory registration is at present triggered by the making of many of the commonest dispositions of unregistered land. It is not at all easy to devise a system of compelling compulsory registration of title other than one that operates on a disposition of the land in question. The mechanisms of compulsion in such situations are not self-evident and there are dangers of devising a system that could be heavy handed. Any such system would obviously have to comply with the European Convention on Human Rights. The means employed would therefore have to be proportionate to the desired ends.

2.12. Third, the implementation of the present Bill, which makes such striking and fundamental changes to the law governing registered land and the methods of conveyancing that apply to it, is likely to stretch the resources of both the conveyancing profession and HM Land Registry for some years after its introduction. We doubt that it would be possible to accommodate a programme for the compulsory registration of all the remaining unregistered land at the same time.

2.13. Nevertheless, we recognise that total registration is a goal that should be sought within the comparatively near future. We therefore recommend that ways in which all remaining land with unregistered title in England and Wales might be brought on to the register should be re-examined five years after the present Bill is brought into force.

Compulsory use of electronic conveyancing

2.59. There is power in the Bill [now section 93 of the Act] to make the use of electronic conveyancing compulsory. The way that the power will operate, if exercised, is that a disposition (or a contract to make a disposition) will only have effect if it is:

1   made by means of an electronic document;
2   communicated in electronic form to the Registry; and
3   simultaneously registered.

2.60. This is a power that will not be exercised lightly. When solicitors and licensed conveyancers enter into network access agreements with the Registry, they will be required to conduct electronic conveyancing in accordance with network transaction rules. Those transaction rules are likely to provide that the dispositions and contracts to make dispositions are made in the manner explained in the previous paragraph. In other words, those rules will ensure that electronic dispositions are simultaneously registered, which is the single most important technical objective of the Bill. However, as we explain in Part XIII of this Report [paragraphs 13.74 *et seq.* below], it may be necessary to exercise the statutory power to secure that technical objective notwithstanding what can be done under the network transaction rules.

2.61. There are, in any event, other reasons why the Bill has to contain a power to make electronic conveyancing compulsory. It is inevitable that the move from a paper-based to an all-electronic system of conveyancing will take some years and that the two systems will necessarily co-exist during this period of transition. However, that period of transition needs to be kept to a minimum for two principal reasons. The first is that it will be very difficult both for practitioners and for the Land Registry to have to operate two distinct systems side by side. Secondly, if electronic conveyancing is to achieve its true potential and deliver the savings and benefits that it promises, it must be the only system. This can be illustrated by the example of a typical chain of domestic sales. As we have indicated above, it will be possible to manage chains in an all-electronic system. However, if just one link in that chain is conducted in the conventional paper-based manner, the advantages of electronic chain management are likely to be lost. A chain moves at the speed of the slowest link. A paper-based link is in its nature likely to be slower than an electronic one and will not be subject to the scrutiny and controls of those links in the chain that are electronic and therefore managed. There must, therefore, be a residual power to require transactions to be conducted in electronic form. It is hoped that the eventual exercise of the power will be merely a formality because solicitors and licensed conveyancers will have chosen to conduct conveyancing electronically in view of the advantages that it offers to them and to their clients. Not only will it make the conduct of conveyancing easier and faster for them, but they will also have to compete with other practitioners who have elected to adopt the electronic system ...

Do-it-yourself conveyancing

13.72. Although the number of persons who conduct their own registered conveyancing is very small – it is understood to be less than 1 per cent of transactions – it is plainly important that they should still be able to do so, even when all registered conveyancing has become paperless. We mentioned the issue of 'do-it-yourself conveyancers' in the Consultative Document. Our provisional view was that such persons would have to lodge the relevant documents with a district land registry, which would, as now, register the transaction. This approach would deny do-it-yourself conveyancers the opportunity to take advantage of electronic conveyancing. It could also have deleterious effects if, say, such a person was involved in a chain of other transactions. We have therefore reconsidered the matter and the Bill adopts a different approach.

13.73. Once there is a land registry network, the registrar is to be under a duty to provide such assistance as he thinks appropriate for the purpose of enabling persons engaged in qualifying transactions who wish to do their own conveyancing by means of the land registry network. The duty does not, however, extend to the provision of legal advice. (It would be wholly inappropriate for the Registry, in effect, to be in competition with conveyancing practitioners. The Registry has neither the wish nor the resources to do so.) It is envisaged that the way in which this will operate is that a person who is undertaking his or her own conveyancing, will be able to go to a district land registry for this service. The registrar will carry out the necessary transactions in electronic form on his or her instructions. Obviously, that person will be required to pay an appropriate fee for the service that will reflect the costs involved to the Registry.

THE POWER TO MAKE ELECTRONIC CONVEYANCING COMPULSORY AND TO REQUIRE THAT ELECTRONIC DISPOSITIONS SHOULD BE SIMULTANEOUSLY REGISTERED

The objective of the power

13.74. We have briefly explained in Part II of this Report why the Bill contains and needs to contain a power by which, in due course, the use of electronic conveyancing could be made compulsory (paragraphs 2.59–2.61). In particular, we explained that it might be necessary to require at least some transactions to be effected electronically because otherwise the benefits of electronic conveyancing could be lost. We also explained that the power of compulsion was linked to the single most important technical aim of the Bill. That is to bring about the situation in which many transactions involving registered land will have no effect unless registered. Much of the thinking underlying this Bill rests on that principle. However, it can only happen if the making of the transaction and its registration are simultaneous and that in turn is possible only if both can be effected electronically.

13.75. The power to make electronic conveyancing compulsory is found in Clause 93 [now section 93 of the Act] and, as the comments in the last paragraph suggest, it has twin objectives. If the power is exercised, it will require, in relation to any disposition or contract to make such a disposition that is specified in rules, that:

(1) the transaction shall only take effect if it is electronically communicated to the registrar; and
(2) the relevant registration requirements are met.

13.76. In other words, it will be possible to require not only that a particular disposition (or contract to make a disposition) should be effected in electronic form, but that it should only have effect when it is entered on the register in the appropriate way. Those two elements will occur simultaneously. This double effect of the power is essential to an understanding of its purpose. The objective is to link inextricably the elements of making a contract or disposition electronically and the registration of that contract or disposition. Although there will be no contract or no disposition at all unless and until registration occurs, an electronic system means that these two steps can be made to coincide. There will no longer be any registration gap because it will no longer be possible to create or dispose of rights and interests off the register (as it is at present). This is the goal that all registration systems have so long sought to attain. Its benefits are considerable.

13.77. The absence of any period of time between the transaction and its registration eliminates any risk of the creation of third party interests in the interim. It also means that there is no risk that the transferor may destroy the interest after its transfer but before its registration, as where X plc assigns its lease to Y Ltd and X plc surrenders the lease to its landlord after assigning it but before the assignment is registered (*Brown & Root Technology Ltd* v. *Sun Alliance and London Assurance Co.* [2000] 2 WLR 566).

13.78. At present, the priority of an interest in registered land, other than a registrable disposition that has been registered, depends upon the date of its creation, not the date on which it is entered on the register. That will remain so under the Bill [see now section 28 of the Act]. However, the exercise of the power under Clause 93 will mean that a transaction and its registration must coincide. In this way, the register will become conclusive as to the priority of many interests in registered land, because the date of registration and the date of disposition or contract will be one and the same.

13.79. Quite apart from the reasons already given why electronic conveyancing might be made compulsory in relation to at least some transactions there is, therefore, also an important legal goal to be achieved by doing so. It is to make an inextricable link as a matter of law between the making of a transaction and its registration. It is true that network transaction rules can achieve the effect that a transaction and its registration coincide. But if by some mischance in a particular case that did not happen, a transaction might still have some effect between the parties (as it would now) if it were not registered. There is a risk that the mere fact that this could happen might undermine one of the goals of ensuring simultaneity of transaction and registration, namely, that a person could rely on the register as being conclusive as to priority. It is therefore necessary to have statutory provision to ensure the linkage between a transaction and its registration.

The application of the power

13.80. The power in Clause 93 will apply to a disposition of:

(1)   a registered estate or charge; or
(2)   an interest which is the subject of a notice in the register;

where the disposition is one specified by rules. The scope of the power will, therefore, be determined by rules. This means that the power can (and doubtless will) be exercised progressively. As the use of electronic conveyancing becomes the norm in relation to particular transactions, the power to require them to be made electronically and simultaneously registered could then be exercised. Given the considerable importance of this power, the Lord Chancellor is required to consult before he makes any rules under it. There are two points that should be noted about the power.

13.81. The first is of some general importance. The power conferred by the Bill would mean that it was possible to require a disposition of an interest protected by a notice to be made electronically and registered. This is something new under the Bill. It is not at present possible to register transfers of such interests. The types of interest to which this power is likely to be applied include:

(1) a profit à prendre in gross that has not been registered with its own title;
(2) a franchise that has not been registered with its own title;
(3) an equitable charge;
(4) the benefit of an option or right of pre-emption.

13.82. The extension of the system of title registration to interests that were protected by notice and not registered with their own titles was canvassed in the Consultative Document [but not recommended in the Report, and therefore not achieved in the Act].

Notes and Questions 15.2

1 Compare the justifications given here for invalidating an interest for non-registration with the arguments put in Extract 12.1 about the principles to be applied in applying sanctions for failure to comply with formalities rules. Does this sanction satisfy Peter Birks' principle that 'pain should not be inflicted except in case of pressing necessity' (Extract 12.1 above)?

2 To what extent could equitable doctrines such as estoppel come to the aid of a person whose interest is invalidated through non-registration? See Dixon, 'The Reform of Property Law and the Land Registration Act 2002: A Risk Assessment'.

3 If the invalidity sanction is to be extended to interests protected by notice, the intention appears to be that the *initial* protection by notice would still not guarantee the validity of the interest protected, nor have any priority effect, but that any subsequent dealing with the interest would be wholly ineffective (even as between the parties) if it was not recorded on the register that the dealing had taken place. Is this a satisfactory substitute for registration, as far as the interest holder is concerned?

15.3.   Enforceability and priority of interests under the Land Registration Act 2002

It follows from what we said in the previous section that the basic enforceability and priority rules in registered land are as follows.

15.3.1.   Registrable interests

Registrable interests do not become legal interests until the holder's title is registered (section 27(1) of the 2002 Act). Once registered, the interest is enforceable against the whole world and takes priority from the date of registration.

15.3.2.   All other interests

As far as all other interests are concerned – i.e. interests that are registrable but not registered, and interests that are not registrable at all – the position is as follows.

15.3.2.1.   Enforceability

One of the two following rules applies:

1   section 29 of the 2002 Act applies, and the interest is not enforceable against someone who takes under a disposition for valuable consideration and becomes a registered title holder, unless the interest is either protected by notice (section 29(2)(a)(i)) or is an overriding interest within Schedule 3 to the Act (section 29(2)(a)(ii)); but
2   an overreachable interest *which is overreached* cannot affect the purchaser/mortgagee whose purchase/mortgage overreached the interest, even if the overreachable interest had been protected by notice (not possible for interests under a trust, but possible for other overreachable interests) or by restriction, and even if the interest would otherwise have been an overriding interest because the interest holder was in actual occupation. This was confirmed by the House of Lords in *City of London Building Society* v. *Flegg* [1988] AC 54 (considered in Notes and Questions 14.3 above).

15.3.2.2.   Priority

The date of any protection on the register (i.e. entry of notice or restriction) is irrelevant for priority purposes. Priority is governed by the unregistered land priority rules considered in Chapter 14, i.e. all interests rank for priority purposes by date of creation (confirmed by section 28 of the 2002 Act) but a prior equitable interest holder can lose priority to a later interest holder by unconscionable conduct of the kind discussed in *Freeguard* v. *Royal Bank of Scotland plc* (1998) 79 P&CR 81 (discussed in Notes and Questions 14.1 above).

15.4.   Overriding interests

15.4.1.   Justifications for overriding interests

The existence of a class of interests that are enforceable against registered title holders even though not appearing anywhere on the register is contentious. Three arguments have been put forward for having such a class, only the last of which is now tenable.

The first is that those interests that are easily discoverable by a purchaser, because they would be obvious on an inspection of the property, should be enforceable against her regardless of whether they are discoverable from the register. This argument, if accepted, would undermine the fundamental principle of registration: purchasers are entitled to assume that they will not be affected by any interest not appearing on the register, whatever their conduct and whatever their knowledge. They should not be expected to look elsewhere. The only inroads that should be allowed into this fundamental principle are those that relate to the nature of a prior-interest holder's interest, or the circumstances in which it arose, or the conduct of the prior-interest holder. In other words, whatever justifies treating an interest as overriding, it ought to be something relating to the interest holder, not something relating to the conduct of the purchaser.

The second argument is that there are some transient interests, too trivial or fleeting or too numerous, that should not be put on the register, either because it would be a waste of resources or because it would impose too heavy an administrative burden on the Land Registry. This made some sense when we had a paper-based registration system, where each registration involved physical processes of entry, filing, storage and eventual deletion. However, it is a strange argument to hear in the context of a wholly computerised system for registering interests in land. Few interests in land are either trivial or transient – the most short-lived are probably short-term residential tenancies, and even these are unlikely to last for less than three or six months, and anyway make up in importance to the interest holder what they lack in length. Recording events of this duration should not be beyond the demands of a modern computerised system, nor should sheer weight of numbers be the obstacle it was in a paper-based system.

The third argument is, however, compelling. Peter Birks, in Extract 12.1, describes the provision of an overriding interest category in the Land Registration Act as 'the attempt of the legislator to anticipate the most obvious instance of the problem endemic in formality'. In other words, there is an inevitable tension between the need to protect prior-interest holders who for one reason or another could not have been expected to use the machinery provided for this purpose, and the need to guarantee to prospective purchasers that the register tells them all they need to know about the property.

15.4.2.   Principles to be applied

In its *Third Report on Land Registration* (Law Commission Report No. 158, 1987, an earlier attempt at reform of land registration), the Law Commission put it in this way:

> We have mentioned the theoretical ideal of the mirror principle. However, it should be appreciated that this is a conveyancer's ideal which can only prevail at the price of restricting someone else's rights. The conflict was plainly put by our predecessors fifteen years ago [in Law Commission Working Paper No. 37 (1971), paragraph 7]:
>
> > From the point of view of purchasers of registered land, it is clearly desirable that as many as possible of the matters which may burden the land should be recorded on the register of the title to the land. We aim at simplifying conveyancing, and a reduction in the number of overriding interests would contribute to that end. A balance must, however, be maintained between, on the one hand, the interests of purchasers of land and, on the other, the legitimate interests of those who have rights in the land which might be prejudiced by a requirement that such rights must be recorded on the register to be binding on a purchaser. Those who advocate eliminating or drastically reducing

the number of overriding interests sometimes, we think, tend to look at the matter solely from the point of view of purchasers of land without paying sufficient regard to the interests of others.

The ideal of a complete register of title is certainly compatible with the policy of the law for over one hundred and fifty years of both simplifying conveyancing and maintaining the security of property interests on the one hand and the marketability of land on the other. But the longevity of a policy hardly guarantees its acceptability today in the light of modern developments affecting land ownership. Plainly, no policy should be followed blindly which works against rather than for 'rights conferred by Parliament, or recognised by judicial decision, as being necessary for the achievement of social justice' (Lord Scarman in *Williams & Glyn's Bank Ltd* v. *Boland* [1981] AC 487 at 510). Put simply, it may be unjust to require that a particular interest be protected by registration on pain of deprivation. Apart from this basic aspect, also militating against the ideal of a complete register are the various matters the nature of which is such that recording them on the register would be 'unnecessary, impracticable or undesirable'. Thus there are self-evident difficulties in reproducing in verbal form on the register rights which are acquired or arise without any express grant or other provision in writing ... These considerations persuade us to adopt two principles, with the first being subject to the second:

(1) in the interests of certainty and of simplifying conveyancing, the class of right which may bind a purchaser otherwise than as the result of an entry in the register should be as narrow as possible, *but*

(2) interests should be overriding where protection against purchasers is needed, yet it is either not reasonable to expect or not sensible to require any entry on the register.

... The considerations and principles just outlined emerged fairly clearly as essentially supported following various consultations.

They went on to recommend, however, that overriding interests should be linked to the payment of indemnity, so that anyone who suffered loss as a result of taking an interest in land subject to an overriding interest should be fully compensated. This has never been implemented, and this means that the question of whether a purchaser or mortgagee must take subject to an overriding interest assumes an importance it does not necessarily have to have. We return to this point later.

In accordance with the principles articulated by the Law Commission, obvious candidates for inclusion in a list of overriding interests would seem to be informally created interests, such as those arising under resulting or constructive trusts or estoppel and those arising out of possession or long use, such as the interests of those with possessory titles or whose interests arise by prescription, and also interests arising by operation of law.

15.4.3. Overriding interests under the 2002 Act

The interests that actually fall within the overriding interest category now are set out in Schedule 3 to the 2002 Act (with different transitional arrangements arising on first registration set out in Schedule 1). They do not marry particularly well with the description just given. The 2002 Act cut down the 1925 Act's list of overriding interests, implementing the recommendations of the joint Law Commission and Land Registry report (*Land Registration for the Twenty-First Century: A Conveyancing Revolution* (Law Commission Report No. 271, 2001)). This report adopted much the same principles as those advocated by the Law Commission in its *Third Report on Land Registration* (Law Commission Report No. 158, 1987), although with considerably less sympathy for the interest holder who neglects to use the machinery provided (see Part VIII of the 2001 report) and without supporting the recommended linkage of overriding interests with the payment of indemnity.

One of the ways is which the 2002 Act has attempted to reduce the category of overriding interests marks a radical change from the 1925 Act. The 1925 Act kept scrupulously away from the idea of notice as a factor governing the enforceability of interests, for the reasons given by the House of Lords in *Williams & Glyn's Bank Ltd* v. *Boland* [1981] AC 487. The 2002 Act has broken away from this, and in two categories has made discoverability of the interest a criterion for overriding status, as we see below.

The most important of the Schedule 3 interests are leases for a term not exceeding seven years (Schedule 3, paragraph 1: see paragraph 1(a) and (b) for the relatively insignificant exceptions), the interests of persons in actual occupation (paragraph 2), legal (but not equitable) easements and profits (paragraph 3, with highly significant exceptions in paragraph 3(1) and (2)), and customary and public rights. The second and the third require further examination.

15.4.4. Easements and profits

As we saw in Chapter 13, easements frequently arise by implication and/or long use. Sometimes they take effect as legal interests, but not always. Following the principles stated by the Law Commission in its *Third Report on Land Registration* (Law Commission Report No. 158, 1987), one would expect them all to qualify for overriding status – there seems no logical reason why equitable easements which are informally created should be treated differently from legal easements. Nevertheless, this is what the Act achieves. More importantly, the Act has tried to cut down the class by limiting it, in effect, to those easements and profits that the purchaser in question either knew about or should have known about. It does this by introducing a kind of 'discoverability' test. Paragraph 3 of Schedule 3 provides that even a legal easement or profit will not be overriding if it 'would not have been obvious on a reasonably careful inspection of the land over which the easement or profit is exercisable' (paragraph 3(1)(a)). There are two exceptions provided to this. The first is that an easement or profit which does not pass the discoverability test will nevertheless be overriding if it is 'within the actual knowledge of the person to whom the disposition is made' (paragraph 3(1)(a)). Secondly, it will not be required to pass the discoverability test if the person entitled to it 'proves that it has been exercised in the period of one year ending with the day of the disposition' (paragraph 3(2)).

There are several difficulties with all this. It not only reintroduces the idea of notice into land registration (so reintroducing the very problems that registration is designed to overcome, as we saw in Chapter 14), it produces it in a form that is quite different from (and not apparently superior to) the traditional concept of actual/constructive/imputed notice we considered in Chapter 14. What, for example, is to be the role of imputed notice here? Can it really be intended that an 'undiscoverable' easement or profit will be enforceable against a purchaser if she actually knows about it, but not if her solicitor and surveyor know about it but omit to tell her? And what is the justification for protecting discoverable but not undiscoverable easements? The latter could include rights over drainage, water and power conduits that are essential for the reasonable use of the benefited land but that even the holder of the easement does not realise she has. It is difficult to see why the burden of such rights should not pass automatically with the burdened land regardless of registration, and it is surely an unnecessary complication to require the easement holder to prove use within the year before the disposition.

But the most important objection to the introduction of this discoverability test is that it is based on the doubtful premise that the two conflicting principles adopted by the Law Commission in its *Third Report on Land Registration* (that purchasers should take free from interests not on the register, but vulnerable interest holders should be protected) can best be resolved by limiting both the immunity of the purchaser and the protection of the prior-interest holder by factors relating to the purchaser rather than factors relating to the prior-interest holder. This seems hard on both. As far as prior-interest holders are concerned, a person who cannot reasonably be expected to protect her interest on the register is no less in that position simply because her interest is undiscoverable. As to purchasers, their claim to take free from interests not appearing on the register is not based on justice but on practicalities – this is the best way of ensuring that trading in interests in land is fast, inexpensive and straightforward. If a purchaser's protection depends in every case on a minute enquiry into what he knew or should have discovered, the object is defeated.

15.4.5.   Interests of persons in actual occupation: the 1925 Act

All these arguments apply, and with even greater force, to this category of overriding interest. The 2002 Act formulation of the category is considerably more complex than its 1925 Act equivalent, but it retains two crucial elements from the 1925 Act formulation, so making it necessary to understand both.

In the Land Registration Act 1925, the equivalent category was set out in section 70(1)(g):

(1) All registered land shall ... be deemed to be subject to such of the following overriding interests as may be for the time being subsisting in reference thereto ... (that is to say) –

...

(g) The rights of every person in actual occupation of the land or in receipt of the rents and profits thereof, save where enquiry is made of such person and the rights are not disclosed.

The House of Lords decision in *Williams and Glyn's Bank* v. *Boland* [1981] AC 487 (see Notes and Questions 15.3 below) established two important points about this, both of which continue to be relevant in the 2002 Act formulation. The first concerns the scope of the rights which will be overriding if the right holder is in occupation. The second is the meaning of 'actual occupation'.

15.4.5.1.   What rights are covered?

It was accepted in *Webb* v. *Pollmount Ltd* [1966] Ch 584 (and never subsequently doubted) that *all* proprietary interests in land are overriding if the right holder is in occupation of the land, not just those where there is some causal connection between the interest and the occupation. A causal connection between the two would exist where it is the interest that entitles the occupier to be in occupation: this would cover for example tenants, or those with interests under a trust, or contractual purchasers allowed into possession even though the purchase was never completed, like Mrs Carrick in *Lloyds Bank* v. *Carrick* [1996] 2 All ER 630 (see Notes and Questions 12.2 above). Equally, a causal connection would exist where it is the occupation – in the form of possession – that gave rise to the right, which would cover those who have acquired title by taking possession. It is consistent with the second principle stated in the Law Commission's *Third Report on Land Registration* that all these people should be protected, because significant numbers of them fall within the category of persons who could not reasonably be expected to register their interest. Their case is made stronger by the fact that they will tend to value their interest as thing rather than wealth (adopting Rudden's terminology, as discussed in Extract 2.3 above). Because the right to occupy the land is associated with their interest in the land, they almost certainly put the value of their interest higher than its monetary value.

None of this applies when there is no causal connection between the occupation and the right. Why should, for example, a mortgage or an easement over land, or an option to purchase it, be enforceable simply because the holder of the interest happens also to occupy the land? These are not interests that usually arise informally, and there seems no reason why they should be put in the overriding interest category.

However, the House of Lords has confirmed that no causal connection is necessary, and there is nothing in the 2002 Act formulation to justify a different conclusion under the 2002 Act.

5.4.5.2.   Actual occupation

It was also confirmed by the House of Lords in *Boland* that 'actual occupation' is not a term of art. It is a question of fact whether or not someone actually occupies somewhere: all that is required is physical presence. In particular, the House of Lords emphasised that it is not appropriate, when considering whether a person is in actual occupation, to look at whether a purchaser could reasonably have been expected to discover, or appreciate the significance of, their occupation. To do that would be to import into the section notions of notice that Parliament intended to exclude. Thus, the argument that a wife could not be in 'actual occupation' of the house she lived in with her husband (the registered title holder) because her occupation was a 'shadow' of his was firmly rejected.

However, subsequent cases have revealed that it is not always so easy to see what amounts to actual occupation.

Physical presence

First, it is clear that it cannot require *constant* physical presence. No one would suggest that you cease to be in occupation of your house when you go off to work every day, or go out shopping. But what if the absences are more prolonged? What if you go into hospital to have a baby, like Mrs Chhokar in *Chhokar* v. *Chhokar* [1984] FLR 313, or occupy your holiday cottage only occasionally because you spend most of your time in your other house, or are absent from your home because you are working abroad, or in prison, or away at university? In all these cases, it must be a question of degree, and the crucial question is what test we should apply in deciding the borderline cases. We could look at how it appears to outsiders, and say that you are in actual occupation if there are outward manifestations of your occupation, such as presence of belongings, publishing that place as your address in a telephone directory or using it as a billing address for credit cards, or perhaps having supermarket shopping delivered there. But this would be quite inconsistent with what the House of Lords said in *Boland*. It would, in effect, import an element of notice.

The alternative approach is to focus on the intentions of the occupier, and ask whether the occupier considered herself to be still in occupation (or, to introduce an objective element, whether a reasonable person in her position would regard herself as still in occupation). This would involve enquiries into, for example, intention to return, or whether the interest holder has left the place in a state such that she can come back whenever she wants, perhaps by leaving her belongings there and not packed away, and by not meanwhile putting the place to some other use or letting someone else occupy it. This is not simple, but it is consistent with the *Boland* principle that the focus should be on the interest holder, and not on whether the purchaser could have discovered the occupation or the interest.

Personal occupation

Difficulties become more acute where the premises are of a type that is usually occupied by things and not by people. In *Kling* v. *Keston Properties Ltd* (1983) 49 P&CR 212, the holder of a right of pre-emption over a garage was held to be in actual occupation of it by parking his car there, and presumably the same would be true of a person who had a property right over, for example, warehouse premises where he stored goods. Taking the matter even further, in *Malory Enterprises Ltd* v. *Cheshire Homes (UK) Ltd* [2002] EWCA Civ 151, the Court of Appeal accepted that a property development company was in actual occupation of derelict land when all it did was to maintain a fence to keep out vandals, board up ground floor windows of a derelict building on the land, and occasionally dump rubbish by the fence.

In cases such as these, the courts appear to be equating use with occupation. Do they mean that if you make *any* physical use of premises you occupy them, even if you use them only for the vestigial purposes permitted by the nature of the premises, as in *Malory*, and even if one might in other circumstances more accurately describe the premises as 'unoccupied' (*Malory* again)? What if your physical use is shared by others? We know that you can be in occupation of premises even if you share personal occupation with others: is the same true where you are merely one of several people making use of premises by putting goods there?

The questions are difficult to answer because it is not clear why those who are not in personal occupation should have the protection afforded by the overriding interest category, if it is not the reason rightly precluded by *Boland*. In other words, these cases make sense if one regards actual occupation as a means of alerting potential purchasers to the fact that there may be a prior-interest holder whose interest does not appear on the register. They are more difficult to justify if it is the fact of actual occupation that makes the interest holder deserving of special protection.

Non-residential premises

In the case of non-residential premises, actual occupation in the *Boland* sense causes no particular difficulty if the interest holder is personally present on the premises and personally carrying on business there on his own behalf. However, 'constructive' presence via an employee may be problematic, as may personal presence *as* an employee: is actual occupation something that one can do on someone else's behalf? These issues were canvassed, if not conclusively settled, by the courts in *Strand Securities Ltd* v. *Caswell* [1965] Ch 958 (where, however, it was not accepted that the interest holder's step-daughter occupied on her step-father's behalf) and *Abbey National Building Society* v. *Cann* [1991] 1 AC 56, and *Stockholm Finance Ltd* v. *Garden Holdings Inc.* [1995] NPC 162 (where there was the added complication that the interest holder was a company). Again, the difficulty with these cases is that the courts are not always clear whether they are looking at occupation as a means of giving notice to potential purchasers, or as a factor justifying the conferment of protection on prior-interest holders.

15.4.6.   Interests of persons in actual occupation: the 2002 Act

The interests of persons in actual occupation are overriding interests under the 2002 Act as well, but the definition is different in several significant respects. The new definition, which appears in paragraph 2 of Schedule 3 to the 2002 Act, is (in so far as relevant here) as follows:

INTERESTS OF PERSONS IN ACTUAL OCCUPATION

2. An interest belonging at the time of the disposition to a person in actual occupation, so far as relating to land of which he is in actual occupation, except for –

. . .

(b) an interest of a person of whom inquiry was made before the disposition and who failed to disclose the right when he could reasonably have been expected to do so;
(c) an interest –

i. which belongs to a person whose occupation would not have been obvious on a reasonably careful inspection of the land at the time of the disposition, and
ii. of which the person to whom the disposition is made does not have actual knowledge at that time; . . .

15.4.6.1.   Causal link between interest and occupation

The first point to make about this is that there is nothing to suggest that 'interest' is intended to mean anything different from what 'right' meant under section 70(1)(g) of the 1925 Act, and so consequently it is still not necessary for there to be any causal link between the interest and the occupation.

15.4.6.2.   Meaning of 'actual occupation'

Equally, there is nothing to suggest that 'actual occupation' is intended to bear a different meaning from that which it bore in section 70(1)(g) of the 1925 Act. If it does indeed mean the same, the old cases on what constitutes actual possession will therefore continue to be relevant. The paragraph is worded in such a way that 'actual occupation' appears to operate as a threshold test. In other words, a person claiming an overriding interest under this heading must first satisfy the court that she is in actual occupation within the meaning adopted in the old cases, before it can be established whether she is disqualified by paragraph 2(b) or (c) of Schedule 3.

15.4.6.3.   The 'notice' element

By far the most important change is the qualification introduced by paragraph 2(c), which makes it explicit that actual occupation confers overriding status on interests only where the occupation would have been 'obvious' on a reasonably careful inspection of the land. The same criticisms can be made of this as are made in section 15.4.4 above in relation to the similar qualification of the easement and profit overriding interest category. By introducing what amounts to a 'notice' qualification, the 2002 Act compounds the conceptual confusion as to the justifications for having an overriding interest class in the first place, and then makes matters worse by adopting an idiosyncratic notion of what constitutes notice, which is not obviously better than the traditional one.

There are other problems with the wording. Under paragraph 2(c)(i), it is the occupation, and not the interest, that has to be obvious. That means that, if a reasonably careful inspection would have thrown up clues as to the existence of the interest, but not as to the occupation (as could be said to have happened in *Kingsnorth Trust Ltd* v. *Tizard*, discussed in section 14.3.1 above), the interest will not be overriding.

Also, the timing of the 'reasonable inspection' is odd. The intention is surely that the purchaser/mortgagee should not be bound by an interest that he would not have discovered if he had made a reasonably careful inspection *at a time when it is reasonable to expect him to make an inspection*. If you are buying or taking security over land, the reasonable time to make an inspection is when there is still time for you to withdraw if there turns out to be something about the land that makes you decide not to proceed, or at least to renegotiate the terms. The 'time of the disposition' (i.e. the time when your purchase or mortgage is completed) is leaving it hopelessly late. Also, on this wording, if the title holder hides all traces of the interest holder's occupation at the sensible time (i.e. the time when you – reasonably – do in fact make your inspection) but puts everything back by the date of the disposition, you will take subject to the interest – which is presumably not what was intended.

15.4.6.4.   Can minors be in actual occupation?

There are other changes worth noting. The unnecessary 'save where enquiry is made' proviso in section 70(1)(g) (unnecessary because only confirming what would anyway be the case under the general law) is retained but qualified so that it applies only to someone who fails to disclose his interest 'when he could reasonably have been expected to do so'. Enquiries of occupying interest holders are so rarely made in practice that this seems hardly worth saying. However, it may serve to provide another ground for challenging the already dubious decision of the Court of Appeal in *Hypo-Mortgage Services Ltd* v. *Robinson* [1997] 2 FLR 71, where it was held that a minor could not be in actual occupation under section 70(1)(g) of the 1925 Act. The reasons given were first, that minor children of a legal title holder 'are only there as shadows of occupation of their parents' (a concept flatly rejected by the House of Lords in *Boland*), and, secondly, that minors could not have been intended to have been included because 'no enquiry can be made' of them 'in the manner contemplated by that provision' (presumably because they would be too young to understand, or to take responsibility for their reply). Since the provision now contemplates that there may be circumstances when an interest holder could be asked but it would not be reasonable to expect him to give an accurate response, this ground for the decision also disappears. However, if the intention of the 2002

Act *was* to allow the interests of minors to be overriding, this is a very oblique way of doing it.

15.4.6.5.   Occupation of part

The opening words of paragraph 2 reverse the effect of the decision of the Court of Appeal in *Ferrishurst Ltd* v. *Wallcite Ltd* [1999] 1 EGLR 85, where it was held that a person has an overriding interest over the whole of the land to which his interest relates, even if he is in actual occupation of only part of it. The decision attracted some criticism, and, as Robert Walker LJ accepted in the case itself, it could lead to anomalous results:

> [Counsel for the purchaser] suggested the example of a tenant of a small flat in the Barbican in the City of London who happened to have an option to purchase the freehold reversion to the entire Barbican estate, neither the lease nor the option being noted against the freehold title. That would, he suggested, mean that so long as he was in actual occupation of his flat, his option would bind a purchaser of the freehold of the entire estate; and also, he suggested, any tenant who subsequently took a lease of another flat in the Barbican.
>
> The example is rather far-fetched but it still merits consideration. A purchaser of the entire Barbican estate would undoubtedly be advised by his solicitors that he should before completion make inquiries of every person who appeared to be in actual occupation of any part of the estate. Whether he would follow that advice to the letter would be up to the purchaser. He might prefer to rely on his rights against the vendor, who would presumably not be impecunious.

However, the reversal of the rule brings its own difficulties. As a result of the 2002 Act, the interest of the person in occupation will be enforceable against a purchaser only in respect of the part of the land the interest holder occupies, not in respect of the rest of it. Ascertaining precisely how much of a title is occupied is easy enough when the occupation is clearly confined to a physically discrete unit, as in the Barbican example, but not so easy when the land in the title is not divided into physically discrete units. Also, an interest over just the occupied part may not be of much use to the interest holder. In *Ferrishurst*, the Court of Appeal had had to distinguish an earlier Court of Appeal decision, *Ashburn Anstalt* v. *Arnold* [1989] Ch 1, where the opposite conclusion had been reached, leading precisely to such a result. The lessee of a shop had given up the lease of his shop in exchange for a right to a new lease of a shop to be built in a new development which was to be built on land including the site of his old shop. The decision that his right to a new lease was confined to the site of the old shop resulted in his having a right to a lease of a shop but only if one was built in a position in the new development where no shop unit was to be, or could possibly be, positioned. Even worse, it may lead to an outcome that is inefficient overall, in that allowing the interest holder's right to be enforceable over part of the purchaser's title may diminish the value of the purchaser's title by an amount that is greater than the value to the interest holder of an interest over only part of the land.

15.4.7. Complexity

On this last point, as in most of the others commented on above, the 2002 Act arguably has made matters worse by over-refinement. In seeking to cut down the number and type of interests that can be overriding, the Act in general refines the pre-existing categories by introducing qualifications. But, even if these qualifications produce a better balance between interest holders and purchasers in individual cases, replacing crude bright line rules with 'fairer' nuanced ones does purchasers few favours. Enforceability rules work best for purchasers when they are simple and produce predictable results, and the introduction of elements such as reasonableness, subjective knowledge, discoverability and uncertainty in boundaries inevitably makes outcomes less certain.

Notes and Questions 15.3

Read *Williams & Glyn's Bank Ltd* v. *Boland* [1981] AC 487, either in full or as extracted at www.cambridge.org/propertylaw/, and consider the following:

1 Compare the view expressed by the House of Lords in *Boland* about the need to protect interest holders in occupation, to that expressed by the Law Commission and Land Registry in their joint report, *Land Registration for the Twenty-First Century: A Conveyancing Revolution* (Law Commission Report No. 271, 2001) (Extract 15.2 above). Which do you think is correct?

2 What steps did the House of Lords consider it reasonable for prospective purchasers and mortgagees to take in order to discover whether there were any overriding interests affecting the property? If all such steps are taken, would it lead to the discovery of all such interests?

3 Despite the House of Lords' strong rejection of the argument that notice was relevant in construing section 70(1)(c), in later Court of Appeal decisions the court tended to drift back to the test of discoverability when trying to decide in marginal cases whether the interest holder could be said to be in actual occupation: see, for example, the Court of Appeal decisions in *Lloyds Bank plc* v. *Rosset* [1989] Ch 350 (interest holder supervising builders carrying out restoration work), *Hypo-Mortgage Services Ltd* v. *Robinson* [1997] 2 FLR 71 (young children in occupation with their parents) and *Malory Enterprises Ltd* v. *Cheshire Homes (UK) Ltd* [2002] 3 WLR 1, CA (derelict land).

4 Since the *Boland* decision, it has become very much more common for husbands and wives (and unmarried couples) to put their family homes in their joint names, a development encouraged by bank and building society mortgagees

because it enables them to overreach any beneficial interests. Also, in the immediate aftermath of the *Boland* decision, it became standard practice for institutional mortgagees to require all occupiers to sign 'consent' forms, confirming they agreed to the mortgage. On what basis would such a consent be binding on an interest holder? (See *Woolwich Building Society* v. *Dickman* [1996] 3 All ER 204.) Can the consent of a prior-interest holder ever be implied? (See *Paddington Building Society* v. *Mendelsohn* (1985) 50 P&CR 244.)

15.5. Indemnity

15.5.1. Function of indemnity

A land registration system provides an opportunity to solve one of the perennial problems of any property law system – how to balance the interests of innocent property holders whose interests conflict through some mistake or fraud, so that neither loses. In an unregistered system, one of the conflicting interest holders must lose, and there will be no prospect of compensation unless recovery can be made from the person responsible for the mistake or fraud. A registration system, however, can be made to generate an insurance fund out of which those who suffer loss can be compensated, via fees charged for dealing with registration applications.

To a certain extent this is what is done in our land registration system. Schedule 8 to the 2002 Act makes provision for the payment of indemnities by the Land Registrar, replacing provisions originally found in section 83 of the 1925 Act and amended by the Land Registration Act 1997. Under Schedule 8, indemnity is payable in essentially two circumstances. The first is to a person who suffers loss by reason of a rectification of the register or a mistake whose correction would involve rectification of the register (paragraph 1(1)(a) and (b): for an analysis of the circumstances in which the register can be rectified, see Farrand and Clarke, *Emmet and Farrand on Title*, paragraphs 9.022–9.029). The second is to a person who suffers loss by reason of a mistake in the registration process (for example, a mistake in a search result, or in a copy document kept at the registry, or a lost document): paragraph 1(1)(c)–(h). It is then provided by paragraph 5 that no indemnity is payable on account of any loss suffered by a claimant wholly or partly as a result of his own fraud, or as a result of his own lack of proper care (with the indemnity to be reduced proportionately if only partly as a result of his own proper care).

15.5.2. Shortfall in the provision of indemnity

The problem with all of this is that, while the indemnity should cover all cases where loss is caused by a malfunctioning of the system, it does not even aspire to cover all cases where the land registration machinery has to resolve the conflicting interests of innocent parties to the loss of one or other of the interest holders.

Three examples illustrate the shortfall. The first and most important is that indemnity has never been payable to those who suffer loss when the register is rectified to give effect to an overriding interest, because, it is said, no loss is suffered *by the rectification* – the title was subject to the overriding interest all along (see *Re Chowood's Registered Land* [1933] Ch 574 and *Re Boyle's Claim* [1961] 1 WLR 339). As noted above, the Law Commission recommended that this should be reversed, as this would 'go some way to enabling an acceptable balance to be achieved between competing innocent interests' (Law Commission, *Third Report on Land Registration* (Law Commission Report No. 158, 1987), paragraph 2.12; the proposal is set out in detail in paragraphs 2.6 to 2.14). The recommendation has never been implemented.

The second is demonstrated by the case of *Norwich and Peterborough Building Society* v. *Steed* [1993] Ch 116, CA. There a couple had tricked the registered proprietor into transferring the title in her house to them, and they had become registered as proprietors in her place and then charged the house to an innocent mortgagee. It was held that the original owner was entitled to have the register rectified against the couple but not against the innocent mortgagee (in other words, she got her title back but subject to the mortgage). Under Schedule 8, she would not be entitled to indemnity to compensate her for having to take subject to the mortgage. The transfer to the couple was voidable but not void at the time the couple mortgaged the house, so the mortgage was valid and so its registration was not a mistake. Since there was no rectification against the mortgagee, and no mistake to be corrected, there would be no entitlement to indemnity.

Finally, the same kind of problem can arise where there is a transfer which is void for some reason other than forgery (indemnity is expressly provided for those taking in good faith under forged disposition by paragraph 1(2)(b)). In *Malory Enterprises Ltd* v. *Cheshire Homes (UK) Ltd* [2003] 3 WLR 1, the innocent purchaser bought a derelict development site from a company which was, in effect, impersonating the actual registered proprietor (a different company with a similar name) and duly registered its title. The register was rectified to restore the real owner, on the doubtful basis that the purchaser never acquired more than the bare title (the transfer to it was void, so the beneficial interest never left the real owner, it was held) and also on the basis (equally doubtful) that the real owner's interest was overriding. The question of indemnity was never settled by the court, but it seems clear that, under Schedule 8, the purchaser would get no indemnity. It suffered no loss by reason of the rectification – its registration had always been subject to the real owner's beneficial interest.

15.5.3.   Cost

Indemnity is payable out of a fund which is fed by profits made by the Land Registry out of the fees it charges for dealing with applications. On present figures, resources are more than adequate to meet an increase in the provision of indemnity.

The number of indemnity claims is insignificant in comparison with the number of applications the Land Registry deals with every year. According to the Land Registry's *Annual Report and Accounts 2002–2003*, they dealt with nearly 27 million applications in the year 2002/3, of which over 3.5 million were applications of registration. During the same period, they received 799 claims for indemnity, and paid out a total of £2,656,998.99 (£1,559,424.87 in respect of loss, minus £5,950.37 recovered under section 83(10) of the Land Registration Act 1925 – the Land Registry can sue any person responsible for causing the loss – plus £1,102,573.49 in costs). The largest payment was approximately £194,000 (including interest) in respect of loss arising from a forged transfer of a registered property. As the *Annual Report and Accounts* explains:

> The title was not rectified to reinstate the true owner, a company incorporated in Gibraltar, because by the time the forgery came to light the property had passed into the hands of innocent third parties who were in possession of it. The true owner was, however, entitled to be indemnified under section 83 of the Land Registration Act 1925. The whereabouts of the persons who committed the fraud are unknown, and the police have been unable to trace them. We have not, therefore, been able to try to recover the money from them under our statutory rights of recourse.

During the same period, the Land Registry's fee income was some £415 million, and towards the end of the accounting year in question they brought out the Land Registration Fee Order 2003 (SI 2003 No. 2092) adjusting fees *downwards* with a view to reducing fee income by 10.5 per cent. After meeting all costs and expenses (including a payment of £2.4 million towards the indemnity fund), they were left with a surplus of £97.9 million, £22.3 million of which was paid to the government via the Consolidated Fund.

Part 4

Proprietary relationships

16

Co-ownership

16.1. Introduction

We have already seen in Chapter 8 how ownership can be fragmented in a variety of ways to form a complex matrix of interlocking interests. It can be sliced across time via the mechanism of present and future interests; split at a qualitative level into its legal and equitable components; or divided via mechanisms that from a functional perspective separate management from enjoyment. The unifying factor in all of this is that in each case ownership has been sliced in such a way as to create two (or more) interests that are conceptually and functionally quite distinct from the other. For example, an interest in possession gives its holder wholly different rights to those belonging to the remainderman despite the fact that both interests are held in respect of the same object of property. Likewise, a legal interest gives those in whom it is vested a very different interest to that enjoyed by equitable interest holders in the same thing. The directors of BP, for example (or any other plc), possess rights which are quite distinct from those held by its shareholders.

In contrast, this chapter deals not with different interests in the same thing but with shared interests. The hallmark of co-ownership is that ownership has only been split (if at all) at a quantitative, and not a qualitative, level. If you and I co-own Blackacre, whether as private co-owners or as members of an association, the unifying notion is that our interests (whether as private co-owners or as members of the association) are (at a conceptual level) identical with all our fellow co-owners or association members. True, in certain circumstances (in the private property context) one person's interest might be bigger than the others' which admittedly, at a procedural level, might offer remedies that are not open to the other co-owner(s). But this should not obscure the fact that the co-owners have interests that are conceptually (if not always practically) identical.

Classically, treatises on English law describe co-ownership as a peculiarly narrow concept concerned only with the vesting of some form of shared title in private co-owners. We in contrast, after examining this aspect of co-ownership in the realms of both personalty and realty, will continue by considering other forms of co-ownership, including (briefly) the statutory form introduced under the Commonhold and Leasehold Reform Act 2002 (also considered in Chapter 17) and other manifestations not normally recognised as such, including membership of unincorporated associations and public trust doctrine.

16.2. The classical approach to co-ownership: joint tenancies and tenancies in common

16.2.1. Basic concepts

Lawson and Rudden give a broad overview of the essentials of co-ownership in the following extract.

Extract 16.1   F. H. Lawson and B. Rudden, *The Law of Property* (3rd edn, Oxford: Clarendon Press, 2002), pp. 92–7

Ownership of the same thing at the same time and in the same way by a number of persons has been general from very early times. Indeed, some students of very early law think that ownership by communities such as families, tribes, or households preceded ownership by individuals. Roman law admitted common ownership and it has survived everywhere in one form or another. Everyday examples in English law are found where domestic partners together own their home, its furnishings, and the 'family car', or where commercial partners run a business. In such situations the law regulates both internal and external relations. It must handle the rights of the co-owners among themselves; and at the same time it needs to facilitate transactions so that third parties can simply and safely acquire, or lend money on the security of, the whole thing, or the rights of one of its co-owners.

In English law today there are two kinds of co-ownership, in accordance with which two or more persons enjoy what are called concurrent interests. They are respectively joint ownership and ownership in common. The reader needs to be warned, however, that for historical reasons they are often called 'joint tenancy' and 'tenancy in common'. In this context, the expression has nothing to do with leases ... [The] word tenancy comes from Latin via French and means 'holding'.

OWNERSHIP IN COMMON

The difference between joint owners and owners in common is that each of the latter owns an individual asset, a separate but not separated share in the asset held in common. Traditionally, it is called an 'undivided' share: this rather puzzling name means that, while the share itself is of course separate from the others, it does not entitle its owner to a particular physical part of the asset. But the 'undivided' share can be alienated (without needing the consent of the other co-owners) and will pass by will or on intestacy. The simplest way to grasp the idea is to think of shares in a company. The shareholders each have a separate thing which they can alienate or leave to pass on death, but none of them can go to the company's head office, point at a particular room and say 'I claim my share' (all the shareholders acting together would have to wind up the company – the legal person – and pay its debts before they could physically divide its assets among themselves). So if there are two owners in common of a house each has a separate, though intangible, asset: it is the house which is not divided into separate shares. There is no need for the co-owners' shares to be equal. Although equality is the default status, other factors – such as agreement, or unequal contribution to the purchase price – may result in their having shares of unequal proportion and value.

JOINT OWNERSHIP

Joint ownership – or joint 'tenancy' to use the common legal name – is distinguished from tenancy in common by the striking rule that 'survivor takes all'. This means that, on death, a joint owner simply drops out: no interest in the asset held jointly descends under the deceased's will or by intestacy. So if something is given as a present to A, B, and C jointly and B dies, A and C between them own the gift. If A then dies, it goes to C who is now the sole owner with, of course, power to dispose of the whole thing while alive or on death. This right of survivorship at first sight gives such unfair results that it is difficult to see why anyone should want to hold property that way. But there are three factors that ensure the survival of the regime.

1 *Severance.* A co-owner can turn the joint entitlement into a separate, though undivided, share, i.e. can become owner in common. This is done most simply by giving notice to the others; and if the joint owner becomes insolvent, the trustee in bankruptcy will certainly take this step. So, in the example above, of a present being given to A, B, and C jointly, if A gives such a notice to B and C, A then holds a one-third separate, though notional, share in the undivided asset. The remainder is held by B and C as joint owners. If B then dies, the rule of survivorship means that C now owns a two-thirds share which will pass on C's death. So by giving notice, A has avoided the risk of losing everything by dying first, but has also forgone the chance of taking by survivorship if one of the others dies first.

2 *Spouses/domestic partners.* English law has no special category of matrimonial or family property: the default status of its property law applies to spouses the same regime that it does to strangers. So if, on getting married, the wife buys the house and the husband the car, the one is hers, the other his. But spouses and other domestic partners often wish that, on the death of one, most or all of the deceased's property will go to the survivor. This can be done, of course, by making a will, but it can also be achieved if they are joint owners of the home and other family assets. As regards the family home and similar property, including bank accounts, it is quite common for spouses or domestic partners to hold the assets jointly. Indeed, if the asset is transferred into both their names without more, the default rule will ensure that they hold jointly.

3 *Trustees.* Trustees are appointed to their office in order to hold and manage assets for the benefit of someone else. While there may be a single trustee (especially if it is a corporate body) it is common, when human beings are trustees, for there to be more than one (and usually two, three, or four). But of course these persons also have their own private assets, family, creditors, and so on. It would be extremely inconvenient if, on the death of one of them, some share of the trust property devolved on the personal

representatives of the deceased and then had to be separated from the private assets. Consequently, they always hold the trust assets jointly. Any attempt to sever and turn their holding into an undivided share would not work, so a trustee who dies simply drops out. If there is only one left, another is commonly appointed so that the trust property never devolves on the death of a trustee. Indeed, by a nineteenth-century statute, a human being can be joint trustee with a company, although it is virtually certain that the latter will outlive the former.

Any property may be held by concurrent owners. Partners, for instance may well be owners in common – that is, have separate shares in – the goodwill of their business, debts due to it, patents, copyrights and the like. Tangible moveables may be held in a similar way – racehorses owned by a syndicate are one example. A commercial example is to be found in the ownership of fungibles held in bulk, such as oil or grain aboard ship. By a fairly recent reform of the law on sale of goods, a buyer of goods which form part of an identified bulk owns a share in the bulk proportionate to the amount bought and paid for: so if that is 10 per cent at the time of purchase and the ship then unloads, for other consignees, half of the bulk, the buyer's share will be 20 per cent of the remainder.

Whether holding jointly or in common, all concurrent owners are entitled to possess and use the property. If it produces an income, say by being leased, they share the rent equally or, if they hold in common, in proportion to their holdings. To alienate the property they must, in principle, all agree, and must all concur in physical division. This is fair treatment among the co-owners, but can give rise to holdout problems and to disputes whose resolution might be very costly in comparison with the value of the thing owned. Consequently, in the case of chattels, the Law of Property Act 1925 (section 188) gives the court power to overcome a deadlock and to override the wishes of a minority interest. For land it laid down a different system, since amended, and explained below.

The two categories of co-ownership outlined above are exhaustive and mutually exclusive. They are exhaustive, in that nowadays they are the only two types which remain, older varieties having been long abolished in England and Wales. They are mutually exclusive, in the sense that the same people cannot at one and the same time have both joint and common entitlements to the enjoyment of property: the rule for joint holding – that the survivors take – is entirely incompatible with the rule for holding in common – that the deceased's estate takes. Because of this, when something is transferred to co-owners, it is important to know whether they are to hold jointly or in common. In most cases, of course, the transfer will make it clear: 'to A and B in equal shares'; or 'to A and B jointly'. But where it is unclear, and the transfer says only 'to A and B', the law needs default rules which, in the absence of any other indication, can be applied to solve the problem. The main ones are as follows:

1   If A and B are trustees, they take jointly.
2   If A and B are business partners, they take in common beneficially, though they will be joint managers of the business and joint holders of its assets.

3 If A and B are buyers who provided the purchase money in unequal shares, they take in common in the same shares.

4 If A and B fall into none of these three categories, they take jointly.

The first three default rules are perfectly sensible. The fourth, residual, rule may produce unexpected disappointments to the heirs of whichever co-owner dies first, and in some common law jurisdictions it has been altered, so that they are presumed to be owners in common. However, it is still the rule of English law; an argument in its favour is that it is relatively easy for a joint owner to become an owner in common by simply writing a letter to the others stating that he is severing his interest from theirs.

CONCURRENT INTERESTS IN FINANCIAL ASSETS

In considering the notion of a share in property, the reader is confronted with an intangible. A share in a horse is not the horse: you cannot ride it, nor can anyone tell by looking at the animal that you own a share in it. To sell the horse you would hand over the animal itself. But some other method – typically documentary – has to be used in selling a share in the horse. Yet such intangibles are often very valuable. The concept proves very useful in the modern world of dematerialized securities. Under this system investors have no separate share certificates or bonds – indeed these do not exist – nor are shares in listed companies numbered. It is thus impossible to say that they own any specific, identified, securities. What each investor has is an account with the custodian of a pool of identical securities, denoting entitlement to a share in the financial asset constituted by the pool. This protects the investment from the custodian's creditors in the event of the custodian's insolvency. Though of course if the financial asset itself becomes worthless (by collapse of the issuer of the securities or squandering by the custodian) the investor's property interest dies and he or she is left to whatever personal unsecured claim may be available.

CONCURRENT INTERESTS IN LAND

A word needs to be said here about the variant of co-ownership which is mandatory in England and Wales for any situation in which two or more persons are concurrently entitled to the possession of land. Above it was said that two (or more) persons cannot at the same time enjoy property jointly and in common. But it is perfectly possible for the same two or more persons to manage property jointly but enjoy it in common. It is not unusual to find two or more people holding joint powers of control and management in trust for themselves as owners in common. This means that, among themselves, each has a separate inheritable share as to the enjoyment of the property (its use, rents, and so on). But to the outside world they are joint owners, so a purchaser from the survivors need not concern herself with the estate of any deceased co-owner. So long as, in good faith, she pays the price to the survivors (and, in the case of land, so long as there are two of them) she takes free from any claim. The survivors hold the purchase price 'on trust' for themselves and for the deceased, whose share is fully protected against their insolvency, and largely protected against their dishonesty. This technique is obligatory if the object is land. When two or more persons are concurrently entitled to freehold or leasehold land (whether jointly or in common) the title is held by them jointly as trustees with power to sell the land.

Notes and Questions 16.1

1   The common law is said to only provide for two different types of co-ownership – joint ownership and ownership in common. Do these two types of ownership adequately cover all types of 'common' ownership? Are they, for example, appropriate vehicles for dealing with:
    (a) family property?
    (b) the interests of flat-sharers (or other sharers of residential property who do not have family or co-habitation links with each other)?
    (c) property held by societies?
    (d) common rights of recreation enjoyed by the residents of New Windsor?

2   Do you agree with the premise with which this extract begins? Has private co-ownership supplanted its communal forebear or only supplemented it?

3   During this chapter consider what other types of co-ownership are recognised under either the common law or statute and what (if any) omissions exist.

4   What rights and obligations should co-owners have as against each other, and what actions will they need if their interests diverge?

5   The right of survivorship is sometimes described colloquially as the 'poor man's will'? To what do you think this refers, and of what relevance is it in light of provisions such as the Inheritance (Provision for Family and Dependants) Act 1975?

6   Is severance essentially a unilateral or multilateral act? Why is a joint owner not permitted to sever secretly and why, in the testamentary context, is severance by will a conceptual impossibility anyway?

7   Do you think the vast majority of joint owners understand the concept of survivorship or know about their rights to sever? Why might it be argued that the poor man's will is more akin to a secret lottery?

16.2.2.   A comparison of joint tenancies and tenancies in common

There are two features that distinguish joint tenancies from tenancies in common, one associated with their creation and the other their determination.

16.2.2.1.   Four unities versus one

A joint tenancy is commonly said to comprise the four unities of possession, interest, title and time, while only the first, possession, is a necessary pre-condition for a tenancy in common. We will briefly consider this aspect of the distinction, but before doing so we should note the comments of Deane J who, in *Corin* v. *Patton* (1990) 169 CLR 540 at 572–3, cautions how the 'traditional ritual' of the four unities 'cloaks some obscurity of precise meaning, some overlapping between the unities and some conceptual difficulties about the essential character of joint tenancy'. Indeed, it is hard to find any case in which the appealing symmetry of the four unities has played any significant role beyond that which arises in the context of shareholdings under unity of interest. In reality, at least when considering the unities of title and time, they are no more than descriptions of the nature of a joint tenancy rather than hallmarks of authenticity – useful as an illustration but too imprecise for much else beyond.

Unity of possession

Unity of possession is critical to co-ownership, not only to joint tenancies and tenancies in common but also to the non-traditional examples of co-ownership we will consider below insofar as possession is a component of that shared right. It expresses the idea that all co-owners have the same right to use the thing as their fellow co-owners. Thus all the joint tenants of the fee simple estate in Blackacre have an equal right to possess the whole; as do all the tenants in common of a racehorse; and all the members of an association in respect of its assets (although they might, of course, collectively agree to limit the individual members' exercise of that right) – for how else can each individual in each group of co-owners enjoy their property rights in the shared thing?

Unity of interest

Unity of interest goes beyond unity of possession, signifying not only that all the co-owners have the same right to use the co-owned thing during the currency of their co-ownership but that the right to use arises from the same interest. In many respects, it is the one unity that, at a practical level, differentiates joint tenancies from tenancies in common. Thus under a joint tenancy of Blackacre all the co-owners own the same shared interest rather than separate shares in the same interest which is the hallmark of a tenancy in common. As Bagnall J noted in *Cowcher* v. *Cowcher* [1972] 1 WLR 425, '[a] joint interest in equal shares is a contradiction in terms' because each joint tenant is joint owner of the whole rather than an individual owner of his share in the whole. True, as we know from the unity of possession requirement, the interests of the tenants in common have not been divided up (hence the use of the term 'undivided share' to refer to the tenant in common's interest) but it is, nonetheless, a share in the whole, rather than a shared whole that they each own. It follows from this that the quantum of each share can (but does not have to) vary under a tenancy in common, although, as Bagnall J noted above, all talk of shares (be they equal or unequal) brings us squarely within the territory of the tenancy in common and breaks the unity of interest required under a joint tenancy.

Unity of title

Unity of title is concerned with how the interest originally arose and requires each joint tenant to derive his interest from the same act or document. Yet, as we shall see in *Antoniades* v. *Villiers* (where two separate but identical leasehold agreements each signed by one of two purported tenants in common were construed as two parts of the same document granting a joint tenancy to the pair), the courts have little difficulty side-stepping the formalistic implications of this unity. Despite such scepticism, however, the practical implications of unity of title are extremely important in the context of land-holding where (for reasons we considered in Chapter 10) the investigation of title is much more complex than it is with chattels. Under section 34(2) of the Law of Property Act 1925, statute has sought to reduce one aspect of this complexity by requiring that the legal title in land can only be held under a joint tenancy (and not a tenancy in common, which can only exist, if at all, behind a trust) so ensuring that (no matter how complex it is) there is only one title to investigate when any dealings take place in respect of the co-owned estate.

Unity of time

Unity of time simply requires the interest of each joint tenant to vest at the same time, which of course follows from their each owning the same interest derived from the same title.

Notes and Questions 16.2

Consider the following notes and questions both before and after reading *Antoniades* v. *Villiers* [1988] 2 WLR 1205, CA; [1990] AC 417, HL, and *A. G. Securities* v. *Vaughan* [1988] 2 All ER 173, CA; [1990] AC 417, HL, and the materials highlighted below, either in full or as extracted at www.cambridge.org/propertylaw/.

1   In what circumstances would it be appropriate for co-owners to choose one rather than the other form of co-ownership? Would it ever be appropriate for two or more companies to hold property as joint tenants?

2   Can you reconcile the approach of the Court if Appeal in *Antoniades* v. *Villiers* with its approach in *A. G. Securities* v. *Vaughan*. What were the grounds of the decision in each case and what would have been the effect if leave to appeal to the House of Lords had not been granted? Can you think of any sensible reason why the Court of Appeal reached two decisions that were so diametrically opposed? Do you agree with the analysis of any of the judges who gave judgment in the Court of Appeal?

3   What implications does the judgment of the House of Lords in *Antoniades* v. *Villiers* hold for unity of title? Is it a sensible decision that elevates substance

above form, or does it show how meaningless the four unities are when it comes to establishing the nature of any particular example of co-ownership? Why would even an affirmative answer to the latter question not undermine the importance of unity of title?

4 In *A. G. Securities* v. *Vaughan*, could it be argued that the four tenants held a single tenancy of the flat as tenants in common? Why was such an argument not pursued on their behalf and what implications does that hold for a system of law founded upon the doctrine of precedent?

5 Why does section 34(2) of the Law of Property Act 1925 prohibit tenancies in common of a legal estate or interest in land, and limit the number of legal co-owners to four? What would be the effect of a transfer purporting to convey a fee simple interest in land to 'all the second-year law students at New College Oxford absolutely as tenants in common'?

6 Why can the legal title to a chose in action be similarly co-owned only under a joint tenancy while the legal title to personalty can be held either under a tenancy in common or jointly? (See *Re McKerrell, McKerrell* v. *Gowans* [1912] 2 Ch 648 at 653.)

16.2.2.2.   The right of survivorship (and how to avoid it)

The single most important factor distinguishing joint tenancies from tenancies in common is, of course, the right of survivorship which flows logically from the joint tenants' unity of interest. Under the right of survivorship, the interest of a joint tenant who predeceases one or more surviving joint tenants simply ends with his death. It does not pass to the remaining joint tenants, nor anyone else for that matter, but is simply determined by his death with a consequent reduction in the number of join tenants until only one remains. At this point, the joint tenancy comes to an end, enabling the sole survivor and owner to do as he wishes with his property including, of course, the right to pass his title by will or on intestacy.

Arguably, the right of survivorship is a throwback to a bygone age where the principle tended to reflect the wishes of co-owners in the context of family assets such as smallholdings and stock-in-trade. Whether or not it should still have a role to play in a modern era – in which co-ownership (even in the limited private property sense considered in this section) arises in a multiplicity of circumstances, often marked by a complexity which tends to undermine the simple rationale of survivorship – is perhaps open to question. Admittedly, equity's distaste for the inequities of survivorship (whereby a beneficial tenancy in common is presumed in all cases of unequal contribution and where the term share – or its equivalent – is used) and the presumption whereby a tenancy in common (either of the legal title in chattels or behind a trust in the context of land) arises in certain types of co-ownership such as business partnerships (see *Malayan Credit* v. *Jack Chia-MPH Ltd* [1986] AC 549) does much to redress the balance. Additionally, in relation to the legal title to land, the requirement under section 34(2) (which permits only a joint tenancy of the legal estate) again aids simplicity and cuts transaction costs by ensuring nothing needs to be done on the death of a legal joint tenant (who simply disappears from the legal title). However, the default position under which co-owners hold as joint tenants except in particular circumstances or where the parties have expressly stated that they hold as tenants in common ensures that survivorship continues to play an important and often inappropriate role in the allocation of property rights on death.

As noted above by Lawson and Rudden, the remorseless and Darwinian logic of a principle in which the spoils go to the fittest (or at least the longest surviving) is often said to be ameliorated in practice by the ease with which a joint tenancy can be severed allowing the joint tenant henceforth to hold his interest under a tenancy in common. On its face, this is indeed true, but, as we shall see, the practical reality of severance, along with the somewhat rigid way in which it has been applied by the judiciary, tend to undermine the utility of a mechanism which, even if subject to a more benign judicial approach, would always be handicapped by the relative ignorance of many joint tenants who have no knowledge that they hold as such let alone the principle of survivorship and their right to sever.

Severance at common law

No discussion of severance at common law can take place without an examination of Page Wood VC's *dictum* in *Williams* v. *Hensman* (1861) 1 J&H 546 at 557–8; 70 ER 862 at 867 which appears to have been elevated, in the century following what was in all probability simply an extempore judgment, into something more akin to a statutory codification:

> A joint-tenancy may be severed in three ways: in the first place, an act of any one of the persons interested operating upon his own share may create a severance as to that share. The right of each joint-tenant is a right by survivorship only in the event of no severance having taken place of the share which is claimed under the *jus accrescendi* [i.e. the right of survivorship]. Each one is at liberty to dispose of his own interest in such manner as to sever it from the joint fund – losing, of course, at the same time, his own right of survivorship. Secondly, a joint-tenancy may be severed by mutual agreement. And, in the third place, there may be a severance by any course of dealing sufficient to intimate that the interests of all were mutually treated as constituting a tenancy in common. When the severance depends on an inference of this kind without any express act of severance it will not suffice to rely on an intention, with respect to the particular share declared only behind the backs of the other persons interested. You must find in this class of cases a course of dealing by which the shares of all the parties to the contest have been effected, as happened in the cases of *Wilson* v. *Bell* and *Jackson* v. *Jackson*.

Applying this *dictum*, it is usually said that there are consequently three ways of severing at common law:

1 acting upon one's share;
2 mutual agreement; and
3 mutual conduct.

But do you think it is sensible to regard this *dictum* as laying down three distinct (and mutually exclusive) means of severance? Note the logical fallacy inherent in the first category – how can one act upon one's share as a joint tenant given that a joint tenant has no share in the co-owned property until a severance has been effected? Furthermore, do you think it is sensible to regard the second and third categories as mutually exclusive requirements or simply as different points on a continuum illustrating when it would be equitable for the court to regard severance as having taken place? In his article, 'William v. Hensman and the Uses of History', Peter Luther notes that it is possible to read Page Wood VC's *dictum* less as an authoritative statement cast in stone than as a staging post en route to a liberal conception of severance based on fairness rather than formality. Luther says:

> The concept of the severance cases from the nineteenth century and earlier – focusing as they do on marriage settlements and bequests to a multiplicity of residuary legatees – appears far removed from that of the twentieth-century cases. To a great extent these concern matrimonial or quasi-matrimonial joint tenancy, which must have been a rare phenomenon in Page Wood's time: property acquired by a couple would normally have been held by the now obsolete tenancy by entireties, in which severance was not possible, while property already owned by a wife when she married would normally have been assigned on marriage to the trustees of her marriage settlement. In many of the modern cases legal action follows the breakdown of the couple's relationship. This change in focus would appear to have made it even more necessary that a liberal attitude to severance should be adopted. Marriage and co-habitation are, after all, states of choice, which can be brought to an end with (in many cases) as few (or fewer) formalities as are required for their commencement. And, if they are brought to an end there is a good chance that they will end in an atmosphere of acrimony. Couples occupied with terminating their emotional relationship will have quite sufficient to keep their minds busy without considering whether they have formed, or communicated, an unequivocal desire to bring another, possibly unappreciated, legal relationship to an end. In addition, to contemplate, discuss or agree severance of a joint tenancy requires contemplation of one's own (or one's partner's) death. For the vast majority of people this must be an activity engaged in as seldom as possible, and its only physical manifestation will be a reluctant and long-deferred visit to a solicitor to make a will. Cases in which the courts must consider both the breakdown of a relationship and the consequences of the death of one of the parties must inevitably be emotionally charged, and the courts' continued emphasis on 'intention' in such circumstances appears at times distinctly unrealistic. To an extent the problems posed by the severance cases mirror those the courts face in other types of dispute arising out of domestic co-ownership: There is an obvious similarity between the modern severance cases and the line of cases involving equitable co-owners who are seeking to claim

priority over a mortgagee who is seeking to take possession of a mortgaged property. In these cases the courts will also look at the parties' actions and their knowledge, and will impute to them an 'intention' on the basis of these factors. Again, as in the severance cases, this can lead to strained reasoning: claimants who had no knowledge, or at any rate no real appreciation, of events that were happening around them are deemed not merely to know about those events, but also to have formed a particular intention as to the (even less appreciated) legal consequences of the events. Similar reasoning can be detected in cases where the central issue is not whether the parties have terminated a joint tenancy (or, as in the mortgage cases, formed an 'intention' as to priority between claimants), but whether they agreed that there should be any form of co-ownership at all. When the courts investigate claims that a constructive trust has been created, very similar problems of 'intention' arise, and for the same reason: the acts of the parties in very different (and, in general, happier) circumstances must be scrutinised in the light of the eventual breakdown of their relationship.

The early nineteenth-century approach appears somewhat more satisfactory. The cases from this period may include formal rhetoric, terms such as 'course of dealing', 'intention' and 'inferred agreement', but it is apparent that much of this language is designed simply to justify (or indeed conceal) the exercise of a broad notion of equity. Where the right of survivorship caused injustice, the courts would attempt to remedy that injustice. Page Wood's judgment in *Williams* v. *Hensman*, adopting and adapting the 'course of dealing' from *Jackson* v. *Jackson* and quietly approving the bold decision in *Wilson* v. *Bell*, was thus not a mere reiteration of long-established principles, but part of an incremental progression towards a more liberal approach. It would be unfortunate if either an over-close study of Page Wood's impromptu words, or an over-zealous search for their antecedents, were to hinder this.

Powerful as this analysis is, that is not how history has judged a *dictum* which today is increasingly regarded, in almost in a formalistic way, as articulating the three means by which a severance at common law might arise.

16.2.2.3. Acting upon one's share

Despite the logical fallacy considered above, this is the most unproblematic aspect of modern-day severance and is simply a different formulation of the rule that destruction of any of the unities of interest, title or time destroys the very basis of the joint tenancy (cf. the loss of unity of possession which terminates the co-ownership itself). For example, if a joint tenant sells his 'share', unity of title is lost, while if he decides to mortgage it that necessarily terminates the unity of interest. It might seem obvious but it is important for what comes next to note that severance under this head only requires a unilateral (but irrevocable) act. Difficult theoretical questions arise as to what happens if a joint tenant secretly mortgages his share in circumstances where the other joint tenants are none the wiser. It would seem there is no objection to concealed acts amounting to severance under this head (see, for example, *First National Securities* v. *Hegerty* [1985] QB 850 and *Ahmed* v. *Kendrick* (1988) 56 P&CR 120 at 126). But would the heirs of the mortgagor be able to point to his unilateral act as evidence of severance where none of the other joint tenants knew that any such act had taken place in circumstances where it was likely that no such evidence would have emerged had the mortgagor been the sole survivor? The courts are clearly alive to the dangers of a joint tenant adopting a 'heads I win, tails you lose' stance and it is likely that estoppel arguments would be used to prevent heirs claiming a share in such a scenario (see *Re Murdoch and Barry* (1976) 64 DLR (3d) 222 at 229).

16.2.2.4. Mutual agreement

If one ignores the somewhat tautologous formulation, this too expresses a simple and, on its face, hard-to-doubt truth that joint tenants can, if they so wish, agree to sever the joint tenancy and henceforth co-own as tenants in common still maintaining unity of possession but no longer subject to the lottery of survivorship. However, in practice this has proved more problematic than it might at first appear due to the fact that the parties are often quite ignorant of the subtleties of survivorship. Thus their discussions, such as they are, are directed not towards effecting a severance but to terminating the co-ownership itself. If during the currency of those negotiations one party dies, the courts are often faced with the difficult task of attempting to locate an agreement to sever in circumstances where it is quite obvious that the parties had no knowledge of how they co-owned and less still the consequences of survivorship or how these might be avoided. In *Nielson-Jones* v. *Fedden* [1975] Ch 222, for example, where on the break-up of their marriage the parties agreed to sell their jointly owned house to enable the husband to buy a new house, Walton J makes the following seemingly logical observation in circumstances where the husband had died suddenly before the parties had decided how to finally divide up the proceeds of sale:

> It appears to me that, when parties are negotiating to reach an agreement, and never do reach any final agreement, it is quite impossible to say they have reached any agreement at all. Certainly, it is not possible to say that they have reached an agreement to sever merely because they have, in the course of those negotiations, reached an interim agreement for the distribution of comparatively small sums of money.

But the argument loses much of its force once one acknowledges that the agreement to which he refers throughout the first sentence is not an agreement to sever but an agreement to divide up the proceeds of sale (i.e. an agreement to end the co-ownership and not just the joint tenancy). In reality, the only way to find an agreement to sever in circumstances where the parties have no knowledge of how they co-own nor its consequences, is to impute one (see the views of Sir John Pennycuick below in *Burgess* v. *Rawnsley*). Now if the courts were tempted to go down this path, surely an interim agreement to distribute at least some of the proceeds would be enough to allow them to impute an agreement to sever as the circumstances would surely indicate that the right of survivorship was no longer an appropriate means of allocating their co-owned (and soon to be separated) interests should either of them die before the co-ownership had ceased?

However, when it comes to dividing up assets in the family home, the House of Lords at least has set its face against imputing agreements (at least in the context of constructive trusts – see *Pettitt* v. *Pettitt* [1970] AC 777 and *Gissing* v. *Gissing* [1971] AC 886 and generally Moffat, *Trusts Law*, pp. 454–8 – but cf. *Midland Bank* v. *Cooke* [1995] 4 All ER 562 and in another context *Bristol & West Building Society* v. *Henning* [1985] 2 All ER 606 and *Equity and Law Home Loans* v. *Prestidge* [1992] 1 All ER 909). It could, of course, be argued that the same arguments do not apply in the context of severance where there is little likelihood that imputing an agreement to sever will have any effect on third party lenders or transferees in the way it can when imputing an agreement to share the proceeds in the constructive trust setting. Nonetheless, against this backdrop, the courts would seem to have little appetite to begin imputing agreements to sever, particularly as a less problematic means of ushering in a more liberal approach to severance already exists in the form of mutual conduct.

16.2.2.5.   Mutual conduct

Mutual conduct releases the courts from the need to find an agreement to sever, by focusing on the course of dealings between co-owners to establish whether they regarded themselves as in effect owning a severed share as co-tenants. Rather than looking backwards to (implicitly) establish the co-owners' knowledge as to the circumstances of their co-ownership, this approach looks forward to take account of the co-owners' mutual assumptions and aspirations in respect of the co-owned property.

Given the relative ignorance of most co-owners, this approach has obvious advantages providing the court with a means of adopting a sensible conclusion as to whether the parties acted in such a way to one another as to make survivorship no longer an appropriate mechanism for allocating their property rights on death. To those who argue that this sounds like the worst excesses of Denning's Court of Appeal and a return to palm tree justice, we would argue that, in the particular circumstances of survivorship (where one is not dealing with interests that might impinge on third party lenders or transferees), there is no downside to adopting a stance that emphasises fairness, and (as Peter Luther argued above) is fully in line with the stance adopted by Page Wood VC in *Williams* v. *Hensman*. It would be wrong, however, to give the impression that the courts have embraced such an approach. On the contrary, they have adopted a somewhat narrower view, as represented by the majority opinion in *Burgess* v. *Rawnsley* which we shall consider in Extract 16.2 below, along with Denning's more radical approach, after first considering the statutory form of severance.

16.2.2.6.   Statutory severance

In addition to the common law forms of severance, a statutory form also exists under section 36(2) of the Law of Property Act 1925, whereby a joint tenant can unilaterally sever his interest by serving a written notice on all the other joint tenants. Unlike the common law forms of severance, which apply to joint tenancies of all types of property, it is arguable that this additional mechanism only applies to land (but cf. the comments of Denning and Pennycuick in *Burgess* v. *Rawnsley* in Extract 16.2 below) and offers a clear and simple means of avoiding the lottery of survivorship. There is no requirement that the notice be signed, nor, under section 196(3) of the Law of Property Act 1925, even read or received provided there is evidence that it has been duly posted to all the other joint tenants. Thus, in *Kinch* v. *Bullard* [1999] 1 WLR 423, where a wife retrieved a written notice from the doormat of her husband's house after he had been hospitalised with a serious heart attack, the court held severance had occurred immediately the process of delivery to the other joint tenant's last-known abode or place of business had begun with her posting of the letter.

Notes and Questions 16.3

Consider the following notes and questions both before and after reading *Burgess* v. *Rawnsley* [1975] Ch 429, Extract 16.2 below.

1 What is meant by the *ius accrescendi* and how fundamental is this right to the distinction between joint tenancy and tenancy in common? Without such a right, would it be a distinction without meaning? Why does such a right exist? What are the drawbacks?

2 Why does the common law 'favour' joint tenancy? What is the attitude of equity? Why then does equity normally follow the law and in what circumstances will it be prepared to presume a tenancy in common even though there is a joint tenancy at law?

3 What is meant by severance? Is it essentially a unilateral or bilateral act? Can severance be hidden, or secret? What do Gray and Gray (*Elements of Land Law* (4th edn), para. 11.76) mean when they say that 'the "act" which operates on the joint tenant's share must have a final and irrevocable character which effectively estops any future claim that longevity has conferred the benefits of survivorship on that co-owner'?

4 Should the oft-quoted *dictum* of Page Wood VC in *Williams* v. *Hensman* (1861) 1 J&H 546 at 557–8; 70 ER 862 at 867 be subjected to detailed textual scrutiny as if it were a legislative enactment? Does the language adopted by Sir John Pennycuick in *Burgess* v. *Rawnsley* when he refers to 'rule 2' and 'rule 3' reveal any underlying assumptions about the status of this *dictum*?

5 Is there any significance in Page Wood VC's expression of regret at the start of the judgment that 'the legislature has not thought fit to interpose by introducing the rule, that express words shall be required to create a joint tenancy, in place of the contrary rule which is established'?

6 Was Page Wood VC's judgment a mere 'reiteration of long-established principles' or 'part of an incremental progression towards a more liberal

approach' or simply a failed attempt to move towards a more liberal regime of severance? How have subsequent courts interpreted *Williams* v. *Hensman*?

7   In situations where there is severance by agreement, can the courts meaningfully talk of an agreement to sever in circumstances where the parties do not know there is anything that needs severing? Can one even infer an agreement in such circumstances? Are the courts really being asked to infer an immediate common intention to sever from which to impute an agreement?

8   Should the formality requirements under section 2 of the Law of Property (Miscellaneous Provisions) Act 1989 apply to severance by mutual agreement?

9   Does Browne LJ in *Burgess* v. *Rawnsley* hold that severance has taken place via mutual agreement or mutual conduct? Does he treat these as separate categories or different points on a continuum? How do Pennycuick's and Denning's approaches differ both from Browne LJ's and from each other's?

10   What is important when there is severance by a course of dealings? Do the courts need to be able to discover (or impute) an immediate common intention to sever (see *McDowell* v. *Hirschfield* [1992] 2 FLR 126; [1992] Fam Law 430) or simply discover (or impute) an immediate unilateral intention to sever which has been communicated to the other joint tenants? What were the views of Denning and Pennycuick on this point in *Burgess* v. *Rawnsley*? How, in the opinion of the Court of Appeal, was the joint tenancy severed?

11   If two parties are discussing the price at which one party will sell their interest to the other, have we not already passed the point at which the rights of survivorship continue to provide a sensible allocation of property rights on death? Why is an offer and counter-offer not sufficient to evidence that that point has been reached?

Extract 16.2   *Burgess* v. *Rawnsley* [1975] Ch 429

[An elderly man and woman purchased a house together under a mutual misunderstanding as to the nature of their relationship. On discovering that the woman did not share his romantic intentions, the man orally agreed to buy out her share. However, she then withdrew from the arrangement and the man subsequently died.]

LORD DENNING MR: ... The important finding is that there was an agreement that she would sell her share to him for £750. Almost immediately afterwards she went back upon it. Is that conduct sufficient to effect a severance?

Mr Levy submitted that it was not. He relied on the recent decision of Walton J in *Nielson-Jones* v. *Fedden* [1975] Ch 222, given subsequently to the judgment of the judge here. Walton J held that no conduct is sufficient to sever a joint tenancy unless it is irrevocable. Mr Levy said that in the present case the agreement was not in writing. It could not be enforced by specific performance. It was revocable and was in fact revoked by Mrs Rawnsley when she went back on it. So there was, he submitted, no severance.

Walton J founded himself on the decision of Stirling J in *Re Wilks, Child* v. *Bulmer* [1891] 3 Ch 59. He criticised *Hawkesley* v. *May* [1956] 1 QB 304 and *Re Draper's Conveyance* [1969] 1 Ch 486, and said that they were clearly contrary to the existing well-established law. He went back to *Coke upon Littleton*, 189a, 299b and to *Blackstone's Commentaries*. Those old writers were dealing with legal joint tenancies. *Blackstone* said, 8th ed. (1778), vol. 11, pp. 180, 185:

> The properties of a joint estate are derived from its unity, which is fourfold. The unity of interest, the unity of title, the unity of time, and the unity of possession ...
> [A]n estate in joint tenancy may be severed and destroyed ... by destroying any of its constituent unities.

[A]nd he gives instances of how this may be done. Now that is all very well when you are considering how a legal joint tenancy can be severed. But it is of no application today when there can be no severance of a legal joint tenancy, and you are only considering how a beneficial joint tenancy can be severed. The thing to remember today is that equity leans against joint tenants and favours tenancies in common.

Nowadays everyone starts with the judgment of Sir William Page Wood VC in *Williams* v. *Hensman* (1861) 1 John & Hem 546 ... Page Wood VC distinguished between severance 'by mutual agreement' and severance by a 'course of dealing'. That shows that a 'course of dealing' need not amount to an agreement, expressed or implied, for severance. It is sufficient if there is a course of dealing in which one party makes clear to the other that he desires that their shares should no longer be held jointly but be held in common. I emphasise that it must be made clear to the other party. That is implicit in the sentence in which Page Wood VC says:

> [I]t will not suffice to rely on an intention, with respect to the particular share, declared only behind the backs of the other persons interested.

Similarly, it is sufficient if both parties enter on a course of dealing which evinces an intention by both of them that their shares shall henceforth be held in common and not jointly. As appears from the two cases to which Page Wood VC referred of *Wilson* v. *Bell*, 5 Ir Eq R 501 and *Jackson* v. *Jackson*, 9 Ves Jun 591.

I come now to the question of notice. Suppose that one party gives a notice in writing to the other saying that he desires to sever the joint tenancy. Is that sufficient to effect a severance? I think it is. It was certainly the view of Sir Benjamin Cherry when he drafted section 36(2) of the Law of Property Act 1925. It says in relation to real estates:

> ... where a legal estate (not being settled land) is vested in joint tenants beneficially, and any tenant desires to sever the joint tenancy in equity, he shall give to the other joint tenants *a notice in writing of such desire or do such other acts or things as would, in the case of personal estate, have been effectual* to sever the tenancy in equity ...

I have [emphasised] the important words. The word 'other' is most illuminating. It shows quite plainly that in the case of personal estate one of the things which is effective in equity to sever a joint tenancy is 'a notice in writing' of a desire to sever. So also in regard to real estate.

Taking this view, I find myself in agreement with Havers J in *Hawkesley* v. *May* [1956] 1 QB 304, 313–14, and of Plowman J in *Re Draper's Conveyance* [1969] 1 Ch 486. I cannot agree with Walton J [1975] Ch 222, 234–5, that those cases were wrongly decided. It would be absurd that there should be a difference between real estate and personal estate in this respect. Suppose real estate is held on a joint tenancy on a trust for sale and is sold and converted into personal property. Before sale, it is severable by notice in writing. It would be ridiculous if it could not be severed afterwards in like manner. I look upon section 36(2) as declaratory of the law as to severance by notice and not as a new provision confined to real estate. A joint tenancy in personal estate can be severed by notice just as a joint tenancy in real estate.

It remains to consider *Nielson-Jones* v. *Fedden* [1975] Ch 222. In my view it was not correctly decided. The husband and wife entered upon a course of dealing sufficient to sever the joint tenancy ... Furthermore, there was disclosed in correspondence a declaration by the husband that he wished to sever the joint tenancy; and this was made clear by the wife. That too was sufficient.

It remains to apply these principles to the present case. I think there was evidence that Mr Honick and Mrs Rawnsley did come to an agreement that he would buy her share for £750. That agreement was not in writing and it was not specifically enforceable. Yet it was sufficient to effect a severance. Even if there was not any firm agreement but only a course of dealing, it clearly evinced an intention by both parties that the property should henceforth be held in common and not jointly.

BROWNE LJ: ... Mr Levy conceded, as is clearly right, that if there had been an enforceable agreement by Mrs Rawnsley to sell her share to Mr Honick, that would produce a severance of the joint tenancy; but he says that an oral agreement, unenforceable because of section 40 of the Law of Property Act 1925, is not enough. Section 40 merely makes a contract for the disposition of an interest in land unenforceable by action in the absence of writing. It does not make it void [but see now section 2 of the Law of Property (Miscellaneous Provisions) Act 1989]. But here the plaintiff is not seeking to enforce by action the agreement by Mrs Rawnsley to sell her share to Mr Honick. She relies upon it as effecting the severance in equity of the joint tenancy. An agreement to sever can be inferred from a course of dealing (see Lefroy B in *Wilson* v. *Bell*, 5 Ir Eq R 501, 507 and Stirling J in *Re Wilks, Child* v. *Bulmer* [1891] 3 Ch 59) and there would in such a case *ex hypothesi* be no express agreement but only an inferred, tacit agreement, in respect of which there would seldom if ever be writing sufficient to satisfy section 40. It seems to me that the point is that the agreement establishes that the parties no longer intend the tenancy to operate as a joint tenancy and that automatically effects a severance ...

This conclusion makes it unnecessary to consider the important and difficult questions of what the effect of negotiations not resulting in an agreement or of a mere declaration would have been and, in particular, the problem raised by the decision of Plowman J in *Re Draper's Conveyance* [1969] 1 Ch 486, and Walton J in *Nielson-Jones* v. *Fedden* [1975] Ch 222. Further, if the evidence and the conclusion that there was an agreement in this case are rejected, I doubt whether there was enough evidence in this particular case as to a course of dealing to raise the question of the application of Page Wood VC's third category, 1 John & Hem 546, 557. I therefore prefer not to express any final opinion on these points. Lord Denning MR has dealt with them in his judgment and I have the advantage of knowing what Sir John Pennycuick is going to say about that aspect of the case. I agree with both of them that Page Wood VC's third category is a separate category from his second category. I agree also that the proviso to section 36(2) of the Law of Property Act 1925 seems to imply that notice in writing would, before 1925, have been effective to sever a joint tenancy in personal property. It is clear that section 36(2), as Sir John Pennycuick is going to point out, made a radical alteration in the previous law by introducing the new method of severance by notice in writing, and that cases before 1925, in particular *Re Wilks, Child* v. *Bulmer* [1891] 3 Ch 59, must now be read in the light of this alteration. I agree that an uncommunicated declaration by one joint tenant cannot operate as a severance.

SIR JOHN PENNYCUICK VC: ... It is not in dispute that an agreement for severance between joint tenants effects a severance. This is the rule 2 propounded by Sir William Page Wood VC in *Williams* v. *Hensman*, 1 John & Hem 546, 557. The words he uses are contained in one sentence: 'Secondly, a joint tenancy may be severed by mutual agreement.' For a clear and full general statement as to severance of a joint tenancy, see *Halsbury's Laws of England*, 3rd edn, vol. 32 (1980), p. 335. In the present case the judge found as a fact that Mr Honick and Mrs Rawnsley at the beginning of July 1968 agreed upon the sale by her to him of her share at the price of £750 ... Once that finding of facts is accepted, the case falls squarely within rule 2 of Page Wood VC. It is not contended that it is material that the parties by mutual consent did not proceed to carry out the agreement. Rule 2 applies equally, I think, whether the agreement between the two joint tenants is expressly to sever or is to deal with the property in a manner which involves severance. Mr Levy contended that in order that rule 2 should apply the agreement must be specifically enforceable. I do not see any sufficient reason for importing this qualification. The significance of an agreement is not that it binds the parties, but that it serves as an indication of a common intention to sever, something which it was indisputably within their power to do. It will be observed that Page Wood VC in his rule 2 makes no mention of specific enforceability. Contrast this position where severance is claimed under his rule 1 by reason of alienation by one joint tenant in favour of a third party ...

Mr Mummery advanced an alternative argument to the effect that, even if there were no agreement by Mr Honick to purchase Mrs Rawnsley's share, nevertheless the mere proposal by Mr Honick to purchase her share would operate as a severance under rule 3 in *Williams* v. *Hensman*, 1 John & Hem 546, 557 ...

I do not doubt myself that, where one tenant negotiates with another for some arrangement of interest, it may be possible to infer from the particular facts a common intention to sever even though the negotiations break down. Whether such an inference can be drawn must I think depend upon the particular facts. In the present case the negotiations between Mr Honick and Mrs Rawnsley, if they can be properly described as negotiations at all, fall, it seems to me, far short of warranting an inference. One could not ascribe to joint tenants an intention to sever merely because one offers to buy out the other for £X and the other makes a counter offer of £Y.

I think it may be helpful to state very shortly certain views which I have formed in the light of the authorities.

(1) I do not think rule 3 in Page Wood VC's statement, 1 John & Hem 546, is a mere sub-heading of rule 2. It covers only acts of the parties, including, it seems to me, negotiations which, although not otherwise resulting in any agreement, indicate a common intention that the joint tenancy should be regarded as severed. I do not overlook the words which I have read from Page Wood VC's judgment, namely, that you must find a course of dealing by which the shares of the parties to the contract have been affected. But I do not think those words are sufficient to import a binding agreement.

(2) Section 36(2) of the Law of Property Act 1925 has radically altered the law in respect of severance by introducing an entirely new method of severance as regards land, namely, notice in writing given by one joint tenant to the other.

(3) Pre-1925 judicial statements, in particular that of Stirling J in *Re Wilks, Child* v. *Bulmer* [1891] 3 Ch 59, must be read in the light of this alteration in the law and, in particular, I do not see why the commencement of legal proceedings by writ or originating summons or the swearing of an affidavit in those proceedings, should not in appropriate circumstances constitute notice in writing within the meaning of section 36(2). The fact that the plaintiff is not obliged to prosecute the proceedings is I think irrelevant in regard to notice.

(4) Perhaps in parenthesis because the point does not arise, the language of section 36(2) appears to contemplate that even under the existing law notice in writing would be effective to sever a joint tenancy in personalty: see the words 'such other act or thing'. The authorities to the contrary are rather meagre and I am not sure how far this point was ever really considered in relation to personalty before 1925. If this anomaly does exist, and I am afraid I am not prepared to say positively that it does not exist, the anomaly is quite indefensible and should be put right as soon as possible.

(5) An uncommunicated declaration by one party to the other or indeed a mere verbal notice by one party to another clearly cannot operate as a severance.

(6) The policy of the law as it stands today, having regard particularly to section 36(2), is to facilitate severance at the instance of either party, and I do not think the court should be over-zealous in drawing a fine distinction from the pre-1925 authorities.

(7) The foregoing statement of principles involves criticism of certain passages in the judgments of Plowman J and Walton J in the two cases cited. Those cases, like all other cases, depend on their own particular facts, and I do not myself wish to go on to apply these *obiter* statements of principle to the actual decisions in these cases.

16.2.3. Use of co-owned property

16.2.3.1. Land

Prior to the enactment of the Trusts of Land and Appointment of Trustees Act 1996, co-ownership of land operated behind what was known as the trust for sale. This was a device adopted by the framers of the Law of Property Act 1925 to provide a mechanism that would facilitate the marketability of land by adopting a trust form whose default position was sale rather than retention of the co-owned land. Under the trust for sale, the land would (at least theoretically) have to be sold unless the trustees unanimously decided to postpone sale. As part of a process freeing up the market in land, the adoption of this mechanism should not be under-estimated although it is clear with hindsight that in over-emphasising marketability the Act went too far and elevated the exchange value of land above its use value (see section 2.4.4.2 above).

Admittedly, an important aspect of land ownership is its exchange value in both the commercial and the residential settings. However, the residential market is primarily concerned with the use value of land. Owner-occupiers do, of course, buy with an eye to their investment but their main purpose in purchasing land is (by definition) to provide themselves and their families with a home. To correct the obvious imbalance inherent in the trust for sale form, the courts in the decades following the 1925 Act slowly developed an approach that sought to supplant the preference for sale by asking what was the *collateral purpose* in buying the land to act as a counterweight to the impetus towards sale.

As we shall see, much of this case law is still relevant, but first we must consider the effect of the Trusts of Land and Appointment of Trustees Act 1996 which sought to restore equilibrium by adopting the trust of land rather than the trust for sale in all cases of co-ownership – replacing the statutory bias towards sale with a form that was neutral as between sale and retention to ensure that neither the exchange value nor the use value of land was elevated above the other. Although trusts for sale can still be expressly created, they are no longer imposed as a matter of course, and under section 4 trusts for sale created both before and after the 1996 Act take effect as trusts of land with the trustees given discretion to postpone sale as they think fit.

In considering use of co-owned land, we will concentrate on section 12 of the 1996 Act, under which beneficiaries in possession behind a trust of land have a conditional right to occupy the land, subject to the exclusions and restrictions detailed in section 13. Sections 12 and 13 provide:

12 THE RIGHT TO OCCUPY

(1) A beneficiary who is beneficially entitled to an interest in possession in land subject to a trust of land is entitled by reason of his interest to occupy the land at any time if at that time –

(a) the purposes of the trust include making the land available for his occupation (or for the occupation of beneficiaries of a class of which he is a member or of beneficiaries in general), or

(b) the land is held by the trustees so as to be so available.

(2) Subsection (1) does not confer on a beneficiary a right to occupy land if it is either unavailable or unsuitable for occupation by him.

(3) This section is subject to section 13.

13 EXCLUSION AND RESTRICTION OF RIGHT TO OCCUPY

(1) Where two or more beneficiaries are (or apart from this subsection would be) entitled under section 12 to occupy land, the trustees of land may exclude or restrict the entitlement of anyone or more (but not all) of them.

(2) Trustees may not under subsection (1) –

(a) unreasonably exclude any beneficiary's entitlement to occupy land, or

(b) restrict any such entitlement to an unreasonable extent.

(3) The trustees of land may from time to time impose reasonable conditions on any beneficiary in relation to his occupation of land by reason of his entitlement under section 12.

(4) The matters to which trustees are to have regard in exercising the powers conferred by this section include –

(a) the intentions of the person or persons (if any) who created the trust,

(b) the purposes for which the land is held, and

(c) the circumstances and wishes of each of the beneficiaries who is (or apart from any previous exercise by the trustees of those powers would be) entitled to occupy the land under section 12.

(5) The conditions which may be imposed on a beneficiary under subsection (3) include, in particular, conditions requiring him –

(a) to pay any outgoings or expenses in respect of the land, or

(b) to assume any other obligation in relation to the land or to any activity which is or is proposed to be conducted there.

(6) Where the entitlement of any beneficiary to occupy land under section 12 has been excluded or restricted, the conditions which may be imposed on any other beneficiary under subsection (3) include, in particular, conditions requiring him to –

(a) make payments by way of compensation to the beneficiary whose entitlement has been excluded or restricted, or

(b) forgo any payment or other benefit to which he would otherwise be entitled under the trust so as to benefit that beneficiary.

(7) The powers conferred on trustees by this section may not be exercised –

    (a) so as prevent any person who is in occupation of land (whether or not by reason of an entitlement under section 12) from continuing to occupy the land, or

    (b) in a manner likely to result in any such person ceasing to occupy the land, unless he consents or the court has given approval.

(8) The matters to which the court is to have regard in determining whether to give approval under subsection (7) include the matters mentioned in subsection (4)(a) to (c).

Notes and Questions 16.4

1 What were the rationale and advantages of the trust for sale?

2 Who has a right to occupy under a trust of land? What are the alternative conditions that must be satisfied under section 12, and what is meant by the second one? Do these conditions have to be satisfied only at the outset or must they continue to be satisfied for the beneficiary to remain in occupation? Does the legal owner have a right of occupation? Do beneficiaries with remainder or reversionary interests have such a right? If land is bought for an investment does any right of occupation arise?

3 What do you think is meant by 'unavailability' and 'unsuitability' in section 12(2)? In *Chun* v. *Ho* [2003] 1 FLR 23, Parker LJ stated that:

> There is no statutory definition or guidance as to what is meant by 'unsuitable' in this context, and it would be rash indeed to attempt an exhaustive definition or explanation of its meaning. In the context of the present case it is, I think, enough to say that 'suitability' for this purpose must involve a consideration not only of the general nature and physical characteristics of the particular property but also a consideration of the personal characteristics, circumstances and requirements of the particular beneficiary. This much is I think, clear from the fact that the statutory expression is not simply 'unsuitable for occupation' but 'unsuitable for occupation by him', that is to say by the particular beneficiary.

4 Is a beneficiary liable to make payments in respect of occupation, and can he claim repayment of expenditure on the land?

5 In what circumstances might the right to occupy be excluded? Is it sufficient that the condition was satisfied at the outset, or must it continue to be the case for the right of occupation to continue? What is the relationship between section 12 and section 13?

6 Why will the trustees' power to determine entitlements under section 13 rarely be helpful in solving disputes between co-owners? Why does section 13 give trustees the power to impose reasonable conditions on the beneficiary in

occupation? Of whose views must the trustees take account when exercising their powers under section 13, and what is the position of beneficiaries already in occupation? What power does the court have to resolve issues relating to the trustees' exercise of their power?

7   What are the implications of the following analysis:

> What the Act seeks to do is to impose a regime that is quite hostile to the very nature of co-ownership as it has existed for centuries. If two people A and B are co-owners they enjoy unity of possession. This is the hallmark of their relationship *inter se*. The fact that they happen to be beneficiaries under a trust of land and that the legal estate is vested in others on trust for them is quite immaterial. Parliament has not abolished unity of possession. Indeed, the Act expressly preserves both forms of beneficial co-ownership [see paragraphs 3 and 4 of Schedule 2 to the 1996 Act]. Unity of possession, therefore, survives, and with it the incidents attaching to it at common law. Parliament readily accepted the [Law] Commission's proposals for the right to occupy [and] sections 12 and 13 passed through the entire legislative process without any comment or discussion. Perhaps these sections will operate successfully for succession trusts of land. What they certainly fail to do is to provide satisfactorily for the occupational rights of co-owners. The statutory rights seriously erode the general law rights to occupy. The Commission's claim to place concurrent interest owners in a comparatively better position is ill-founded. Fortunately, though no doubt unwittingly, the general law rights of co-owners relating to occupation have been preserved. They can be resorted to and enforced in any situation in which it is advantageous to do so. In this vital area of occupation, it is submitted that the [1996] Act may well turn out to be a dead letter. (Barnsley, 'Co-owners' Rights to Occupy Trust Property', pp. 144–5)

8   Under section 30 of the Family Law Act 1996, a spouse with no property rights might still assert a right of occupation in the family home. If a party has a right to occupy (either under section 12 of the Trusts of Land and Appointment of Trustees Act 1996 or under section 30 of the Family Law Act 1996), what power does the court have to vary those occupation rights? What is the position of cohabitants with no property interest in the family home?

16.2.3.2.   Chattels

For obvious reasons (but do you know what these are?), co-ownership of chattels is not subject to the same regime as co-ownership of land. Unity of possession dictates that each co-owner has the right to possess the property and, as against the rest of the world, may exercise full rights of ownership whether or not he is acting with the consent of his fellow co-owners.

In cases of dispute between co-owners, section 188 of the Law of Property Act 1925 provides that a co-tenant with at least a half-share (by value) of the co-owned chattel may make an application to the court for an order of division. However, in Australia at least, according to *Re Gillie, ex parte Cornell* (1996) 70 PCR 254, a co-owner (of any proportion) is lawfully entitled to unilaterally take his share of co-owned personalty providing this can be done without destroying the character or identity of the property which must consequently be physically severable, forming a common bulk of homogeneous quality.

Notes and Questions 16.5

Consider the following notes and questions both before and after reading *Re Gillie, ex parte Cornell* (1996) 70 PCR 254, *Spence* v. *Union Marine Insurance* (1868) LR 3 CP 427 and *Dennis* v. *Dennis* (1971) 45 ALJR 605, either in full or as extracted at www.cambridge.org/propertylaw/.

1   Should the rules governing the resolution of disputes between co-owners of chattels also apply to disputes between co-owners of land?

2   In *Re Gillie*, why was one co-owner held to have excluded the other when she only appropriated half of the herd?

3   What role (if any) would there be for section 188 of the Law of Property Act 1925 if *Re Gillie* was applied in this jurisdiction?

4   Is the judgment a sensible and practical solution or one that will promote self-help and conflict? What should the attitude of the courts be to extra-judicial means of settling co-ownership disputes?

5   Why might it be argued that the approach advocated in *Re Gillie* creates more problems than it solves? Do you think adoption of the judgment in England and Wales would reduce or increase the likelihood of such cases being litigated?

6   In *Dennis* v. *Dennis* (1971) 45 ALJR 605, a dispute arose as to the ownership of a racehorse and whether or not (in an echo of a similar dispute that recently arose between the manager of Manchester United and two shareholders in the club) one party had acquired a proprietary or personal interest. Why are such disputes particularly likely to arise in the context of personal property?

7   What is the difference between owning one-half of a horse and being entitled to one-half of the net winnings and one-half of the sale price?

8   In *Spence*, why did the court decide it was a tenancy in common and not a joint tenancy?

16.2.4.   Sale and other dispositions of co-owned property

16.2.4.1.   Land

As we have seen, prior to the enactment of the Trusts of Land and Appointment of Trustees Act 1996, the courts had developed the 'collateral purpose' doctrine in order to redress the balance and subvert the preference for sale inherent in the trust for sale machinery that arose in all cases of co-ownership (whether or not covered by the Law of Property Act 1925 – see *Bull* v. *Bull* [1955] 1 QB 234). Relying on a broad interpretation of the now repealed section 30 of the Law of Property Act 1925, the courts assumed a wide discretion including a discretion to refuse an order for sale while the collateral (or secondary) purpose of the trust was still capable of being fulfilled. However, in *Jones* v. *Challenger* [1961] 1 QB 176, in reversing the decision of the court of first instance which had refused to order a sale of the matrimonial home following the breakdown of the couple's marriage, Devlin LJ noted:

> The test is not what is reasonable. It is reasonable for the husband to want to go on living in the house, and reasonable for the wife to want her share of the trust property in cash. The true question is whether it is inequitable for the wife, once the matrimonial home has gone, to want to realise her investment. Nothing said in the cases which I have cited can be used to suggest that it is, and, in my judgment, it clearly is not. The conversion of the property into a form in which both parties can enjoy their rights equally is the prime object of the trust; the preservation of the house as a home for one of them singly is not an object at all. If the true object of the trust is made paramount, as it should be, there is only one order that can be made.

Although what amounted to a collateral purpose capable of surviving the breakdown of a relationship, such that a court would be justified in exercising its discretion under section 30 to postpone sale, depended upon the facts of each individual case, the presence of school-age children was normally a deciding factor, as illustrated in *Re Evers* [1980] 1 WLR 1327:

> This approach to the exercise of the discretion given by section 30 has considerable advantages in these 'family' cases. It enables the court to deal with substance, that is, reality, rather than form, that is, convenience of conveyancing; it brings the exercise of the discretion under this section, so far as possible, into line with exercise of the discretion given by section 24 of the Matrimonial Causes Act 1973; and it goes some way to eliminating differences between legitimate and illegitimate children in accordance with present legislative policy: see, for example, Part II of the Family Law Reform Act 1969.
>
> The relevant facts in the present case must now be examined. There is little or no dispute between the parties about them. Both the mother and the father have been married and divorced. The mother had two children of her marriage, both boys, now aged ten and eight. She met the father in May 1974. In August 1974, they began to live

together at the father's former matrimonial home; the two boys remained in the care of their father, the mother visiting them regularly. Early in 1976 the mother became pregnant by the father and gave birth to the child, who is the subject of the wardship proceedings, on December 22, 1976. At about that time, the two older boys joined their mother and from then until the separation in August 1979 all five lived together, at first at the father's former matrimonial home, until in April 1978 [when] the parties jointly acquired the cottage which is the subject of these proceedings. This property was purchased for £13,950, of which £10,000 was raised jointly on mortgage. The balance was provided as to £2,400 by the mother and as to £1,050 plus expenses by the father. The mother's contribution was derived from her share of her former matrimonial home. On April 28, 1978, the property was conveyed into their joint names as trustees upon a bare trust for sale with power to postpone the sale in trust for themselves as joint tenants.

The irresistible inference from these facts is that, as the judge found, they purchased this property as a family home for themselves and the three children. It is difficult to imagine that the mother, then wholly responsible for two children, and partly for the third, would have invested nearly all her capital in the purchase of this property if it was not to be available to her as a home for the children for the indefinite future. It is inconceivable that the father, when he agreed to this joint adventure, could have thought otherwise, or contemplated the possibility of an early sale without the consent of the mother. The underlying purpose of the trust was, therefore, to provide a home for all five of them for the indefinite future. Unfortunately, the relationship between the father and the mother broke down very soon, and the parties separated at the beginning of August 1979 in circumstances of great bitterness ...

It was argued that the father ought to be allowed to 'take his money out' or 'to realise his investment'. In point of fact, his investment amounted to less than one-fifth of the purchase price of the property, and was smaller than the mother's investment. The major part of the purchase price was provided by the mortgagees, and the mother is prepared to accept full responsibility for paying the interest on the mortgage, and keeping up the capital repayments. The father has a secure home with his mother. There is no evidence that he has any need to realise his investment. It is an excellent one, combining complete security with considerable capital appreciation in money terms. His share is now said to be worth about £5,000, i.e. it has more than doubled in value in two years. On the other hand, a sale of the property now would put the mother into a very difficult position because she cannot raise the finance to rehouse herself or meet the cost of borrowing money at present rates. So there is no justification for ordering a sale at the present time.

For these reasons the judge was right not to order an immediate sale but the form of his actual order is not satisfactory. Under section 30, the primary question is whether the court should come to the aid of the applicant at the 'particular moment and in the particular circumstances when the application is made to it ... see *Re Buchanan-Wollaston's Conveyance* [1939] 1 Ch 738, 747. In the present case, at the present moment and in the existing circumstances, it would be wrong to order a sale. But circumstances may change unpredictably. It may not be appropriate to order a sale when the child reaches 16 years – a purely arbitrary date – or it may become appropriate to do so much sooner, for example on the mother's remarriage, or on it becoming financially possible for her to buy the father out. In such circumstances, it will probably be wiser simply to dismiss the application while indicating the sort of circumstances which would, *prima facie*, justify a further application. The ensuing uncertainty is unfortunate but, under this section, the court has no power to adjust property rights or to redraft the terms of the trust. Ideally, the parties should now negotiate a settlement on the basis that neither of them is in a position to dictate terms. We would therefore dismiss the father's appeal, but would vary the order to dismiss the application on the mother's undertaking to discharge the liability under the mortgage, to pay the outgoings and maintain the property, and to indemnify the father so long as she is occupying the property.

These matters are now governed by sections 14–15 of the Trusts of Land and Appointment of Trustees Act 1996, but, as the purposes behind the trust are still relevant to rights of occupation under section 12 and to the exercise of the court's discretion under section 14, it is generally accepted that the jurisprudence of 'collateral purpose' will continue to provide guidance in disputes arising under the 1996 Act (see Law Commission, Transfer of Land: Trusts of Land (Law Commission Report No. 181, 1989) paragraph 12.9).

Notes and Questions 16.6

Consider the following notes and questions both before and after reading *Jones* v. *Challenger* [1961] 1 QB 176, *Re Evers* [1980] 1 WLR 1327, *Re Citro* [1990] 3 WLR 880, *Abbey National plc* v. *Moss* [1994] 1 FLR 307, *Mortgage Corp. Ltd* v. *Shaire* [2001] Ch 743, *Re Holliday* [1981] Ch 405, *White* v. *White* [2003] EWCA Civ 924, section 30 of the Law of Property Act 1925 (now repealed), sections 14–15 of the Trusts of Land and Appointment of Trustees Act 1996, sections 335A–337 of the Insolvency Act 1986 and the cases listed below, either in full or as extracted at www.cambridge.org/propertylaw/.

1   Who was entitled to apply to the court for an order under section 30 of the 1925 Act?

2   By what criteria were the courts guided in exercising this discretion? What was the strength of the *sale* presumption of the trust for sale? Were different criteria applicable to different types of application?

3   What is the extent of the court's jurisdiction under the 1996 Act? What has happened to the preference for sale?

4   What role will the case law on the repealed section 30 have in the interpretation of the 1996 Act? What is the significance of section 15 of the 1996 Act? What is the position of secured creditors?

5 What facts might give rise to exceptional circumstances under section 335A(3) of the Insolvency Act 1986? What was really exceptional in the facts of *Re Holliday* [1981] Ch 405?

6 How do the provisions of sections 14–15 of the Trusts of Land and Appointment of Trustees Act 1996 and sections 335A–337 of the Insolvency Act 1986 dovetail with the provisions concerning the family to be found in section 24 of the Matrimonial Causes Act 1973, section 15 of the Children Act 1989 and Part IV of the Family Law Act 1996 (see *White* v. *White* [2003] EWCA Civ 924)?

7 Does the Human Rights Act 1998 have any role to play in this area?

16.2.4.2. Chattels

A purported sale by a co-owner of the entire interest without the consent of the other co-owners will be subject to the *nemo dat* rule and (unless one of the exceptions applies – see section 10.5 above) the purchaser will only acquire the seller's own interest which he will henceforth hold as tenant in common with the other co-owners. A co-owner who destroys or disposes of his fellow co-owners' interests is liable in conversion under section 10 of the Torts (Interference with Goods) Act 1977. This liability extends to situations where the co-owner purports to dispose of the entire interest even in circumstances where the other co-owners' interests are not lost, although this applies only to situations where he has purported to dispose of the entire interest rather than some lesser interest such as pledge or bailment.

16.3. Other forms of co-ownership

16.3.1. Commonhold

As we shall see in Chapter 17, a new form of statutory co-ownership has been introduced under the Commonhold and Leasehold Reform Act 2002 to help alleviate the problems faced by owners of flats particularly in multi-unit developments where the leasehold model has not generally proved a success in providing effective management of the common areas and resources. Commonhold uses the company structure to provide the freehold owners of individual units with membership of a commonhold association with its own legal personality in which the common parts of the development are vested. Only the unit-holders are permitted to belong to the association which is governed according to rules and regulations agreed by the membership and publicised via a 'Commonhold Community Statement'.

16.3.2. Unincorporated associations

The unincorporated association creates real difficulties for lawyers, for, as the name so crudely asserts, unlike the commonhold associations considered above, they lack a corporate identity and thus have no legal personality. Some commentators have gone so far as to state that they do not therefore exist, and, while this is plainly not so, it is equally clear that they occupy a twilight legal world in which their existence is admitted but not wholly catered for (see Rideout, 'The Limited Liability of Unincorporated Associations'). The difficulties are most acute when property is purportedly given to such an association, for the law is then faced with the seemingly insoluble problem of trying to vest property in something in which title cannot vest. As many of these gifts take the form of testamentary dispositions (where the willing donor thus has no second chance to perfect his gift), the courts are rightly reluctant to declare them void and therefore embark upon often ingenious, but rarely convincing, attempts to solve the conundrum.

There were originally two basic ways in which a donor's gift to an unincorporated association might be construed (in the absence of the gift being construed as a charitable disposition or one of the small category of anomalous purpose trusts). The simplest method was to regard it as an outright gift to the existing members of the association, each of whom had a legal personality in which the interest could vest via either a joint tenancy or a tenancy in common. Despite its simplicity, there were two major drawbacks with this approach. First, with the rare exception of gifts intended to benefit existing members only, it did not perfect the gift in the way the donor intended. For, as a tenant in common (either from the outset or after unilaterally severing the joint tenancy), an individual member had an undivided share which he could do with as he liked without any obligation to use it in accordance with the purposes for which it was made. Secondly (in theory, if not in practice), there were onerous formal requirements to be met every time the membership of the association changed: under section 53(1)(c) of the Law of Property Act 1925, any member who subsequently left retained his interest unless he disposed of it by signed writing; any member who subsequently joined received no interest unless assigned to him in a similar fashion; while (save for joint tenants) even a member who died did not thereby lose his interest which devolved according to his will or intestacy.

The other way in which a gift might be validated was to regard it, not as an outright disposition, but as a gift on trust either for the purposes of the association or for present and future members. This did, indeed, avoid the drawbacks associated with absolute dispositions. Rather than ignoring the donor's wishes, these were now given priority under the terms of the trust. Equally, the formality issues were side-stepped because the gift did not vest in the current membership but was an endowment in which the capital was preserved with only the interest expended upon the present members and/or the current purposes. But the price paid was a high one. As a gift on endowment, there were very real perpetuity problems which meant that, unless limited to the perpetuity period, the trust would be void from the outset (*Leahy* v. *Attorney-General for New South Wales* [1959] AC 457). While, if held to be a gift for the purposes of the association, it was additionally liable to be regarded as a purpose trust which offended the beneficiary principle because the beneficial interest was unowned. Admittedly, the courts did develop haphazard strategies to overcome these problems: occasionally appearing to regard unincorporated associations as exceptions to the beneficiary principle; and at other times avoiding perpetuity problems by regarding the trust as limited to current (and not future) members (*Re Drummond* [1914] 2 Ch 90, in which case it was unclear how it did not take effect as an absolute gift with all the attendant problems considered above). Notwithstanding such devices, the general position remained that a gift on trust for the purposes of the association or for its present and future members was liable to fail.

As a consequence, and despite the weaknesses in the first construction, a presumption developed in its favour, with the courts doing their best to validate gifts to unincorporated associations by, where possible, construing them as absolute dispositions to the current membership. But, while this preserved the gift, it did not take account of the donor's wishes and provided no means by which a disposition could be made in favour of present and future members. In the face of this, Cross J in *Neville Estates* v. *Madden* [1962] Ch 832 at 849 offered a third possible construction. Under this approach, there was still 'a gift to the existing members ... but subject to their respective contractual rights and liabilities towards one another as members of the association'. Thus, while the gift would vest in each member, it would do so subject to contractual obligations preventing them from taking their share and doing with it what they will. This is clearly a better solution, but it does not answer all the difficulties. For a start, the court has to be able to find either express or implied terms which contain such mutual undertakings which is not always possible (there was no contract between the members of the various orders in *Leahy* v. *Attorney-General for New South Wales* [1959] AC 457, for example). And, even if these can be established, we are still confronted by the formality problems that dog the first solution. Admittedly, the *inter vivos* requirements of the Law of Property Act 1925 could conceivably be catered for under a suitably drafted contract which each member might be made to sign upon joining; but the same could not be done in respect of the *post mortem* requirements of the Wills Act 1837. More fundamentally, despite appearances to the contrary, this construction does not (technically at least) take us much further in complying with the donor's intentions. It is not the terms of the gift, after all, but the rules of the association which determine whether or not the gift can be construed in such a way (see Matthews, 'A Problem in the Construction of Gifts to Unincorporated Associations'). Admittedly, in determining the rules, the courts do (by means of the implied term) engage in a degree of artistic licence, but the carrot is here wagging the dog with the gift, in effect dictating the rules. Furthermore, the rules can normally be changed (and according to some must always be capable of so being – *per* Vinelott J in *Re Grant* [1979] 3 All ER 359) which means that a gift which the donor specifically did not intend to pass to the membership will do just that, for instance on dissolution or as the result of a members' ballot.

Despite these and other more questionable criticisms, the 'contract holding theory' (as it soon became known) is the new orthodoxy. Yet it is at best little more than a fudge which relegates the wishes of the donor to the margins. This can ultimately be traced back to the courts' implicit assumption that the problem is essentially a private property matter which can best be solved by private law solutions. Thus gifts to unincorporated associations are made to vest in individual members of the association with scant regard for the formal difficulties of such an approach, nor the essential artificiality of construing a gift to the association as a gift to its members. But why are we so constrained? An unincorporated association is clearly an example of communal ownership in which the members of the association form the community. As Macpherson noted in 'Human Rights as Property Rights', under communal ownership the primary right of each individual is the right not to be excluded from the communal resource and is derived, not from the vesting of a particular interest, but from one's status as a member of a community. Thus we do not need to concern ourselves with the formal requirements of vesting because no vesting takes place. And, as a consequence, there are no legal formalities with which to comply when someone either acquires that status upon joining the association or loses it at the moment they leave (whether at the behest of themselves or their fellow members or after the seductive embrace of the grim reaper).

Now some will argue that all of this is foreign to the common law. But, as we showed in Chapter 2, notions of communal property pre-date what are often regarded as fundamental principles of English law such as the doctrine of tenure. More importantly, they continue to play a fundamental role including in specific areas such as common land, public rights of way, public spaces and highways, rights of navigation, and fishing rights, and more generally by fixing the limits of private property which is always circumscribed (to differing extents depending upon the type and nature of the thing) in deference to the wider interests of the community. And, while many of these issues will be played out beyond the narrow confines of the Chancery lawyer's field of competence, in areas as diverse as the law of obligations (e.g. *Hunter* v. *Canary Wharf* [1997] AC 655), public law (e.g. sections 79–82 of the Environmental Protection Act 1990) and the criminal law (e.g. section 3 of the Road Traffic Act 1972), this is by no means always so, and nor does it, in any sense, weaken the argument (see *New Windsor Corp.* v. *Mellor* [1975] 3 All ER 44; *Attorney-General, ex rel. Yorkshire Derwent Trust* v. *Brotherton* [1991] 3 WLR 1126; and Kohler, 'The Whittling Away of Way').

Even if one accepts the theoretical possibility of a communal property analysis of unincorporated associations, this does not, of itself, provide a means by which a gift to such an association will be perfected. However, developments in the law of trusts have provided an analysis which squares the circle of communal ownership with the necessary vesting of the formal legal title. In *Re Denley* [1969] 1 Ch 393, money was left on trust to provide a sports ground primarily for the use of company employees. Counsel for the residuary legatees argued that this was a void purpose trust which contravened the beneficiary principle (as the beneficial interest was not vested in anyone). However, in an imaginative judgment, Goff J held that the trust was valid, despite the beneficial interest being unowned, because there were indirect beneficiaries (the company employees) who, despite not owning the trust property, still had *locus standi* to enforce the trustees' obligations.

The decision is a highly practical and sensible one and mirrors to some extent the position which pertains in respect of personal representatives who hold the legal title of the deceased's estate subject to the control, but not on behalf of, the beneficiaries under the will who are not, at that stage at least, regarded in law as owning the equitable interest. It also has an obvious application to unincorporated associations, as recognised generally by textbook writers who see in it a means of dealing with some of the difficulties that arise in respect of gifts on endowment. In the light of *Re Denley*, the members for the time being will be the indirect beneficiaries with *locus standi* to enforce the trust whenever a gift is made for the purposes of an association. Thus the only problem with gifts on endowment becomes one of perpetuity, which can always be dealt with by means of a suitably drafted disposition limiting the trust to the perpetuity period, at which point the capital passes either under the terms of the trust or under the principle of resulting trusts. But even this is not certain, for it is possible to argue that *Re Denley*-type purpose trusts are saved by the Perpetuities and Accumulations Act 1964 from invalidity because they are subject to the rule against remoteness of vesting rather than the rule against inalienability and are thus outside the exclusionary terms of section 15(4) (see Hayton and Marshall, *Cases and Commentary on the Law of Trusts* (9th edn), p. 196 – but cf. (10th edn), pp. 200–2). This is, however, of little solace when most gifts to unincorporated associations are not by way of endowment and, even where it is possible to construe a gift in this way, the courts lean heavily towards the 'contract holding' analysis.

Yet there is no reason why the *Re Denley* approach should be restricted to gifts on endowment. It is surely possible to construe any gift to an unincorporated association in this manner so that legal title vests in the officers of the association who are empowered to spend both interest and capital on the purposes of the trust with individual members having *locus standi* to enforce its terms but with no *Saunders* v. *Vautier* (1841) 10 LJ Ch 354 right to vary them or claim the beneficial interest for themselves. Admittedly, this does make the trust more inflexible but it would at least elevate the wishes of the donor above those of the membership who do, after all, retain the option of refusing the proffered gift. Once we had ventured down such a path, there might be room for manoeuvre allowing a degree of variation (not dissimilar to the *cy-près* doctrine encountered in the law of charities) but stopping short of allowing the membership to claim the equitable interest as their own (see Gardner, 'New Angles on Unincorporated Associations').

The point appeared to be accepted in *Re Lipinski* [1977] 1 All ER 33, where (in dealing with a bequest held expressly to be not by way of endowment) Oliver J stated that *Re Denley* 'accord[s] both with authority and common sense'. The case involved a gift to the Hull Judeans (Maccabi) Association to be used solely for the maintenance and construction of a new building where it would have been quite possible to regard the association's members as indirect beneficiaries, with the ability to enforce but no beneficial interest to own. However, while purporting to adopt the reasoning of Goff J in *Re Denley*, Oliver J slips into the language of beneficial ownership in holding that '[t]he *beneficiaries*, as members of the association for the time being, are the persons who could enforce the purpose and they must, as it seems to me, be entitled not to enforce it or, indeed, *to vary it*' (emphasis added). Thus, despite suggestions to the contrary, Oliver J takes an approach which vests title, and the ultimate decision on how it is utilised, in the membership with the donor's wishes yet again being relegated to the margins.

Despite its ultimate failings, *Re Lipinski* does at least offer a tantalising glimpse of a more radical approach to the problems of unincorporated associations. The seeds of a fully fledged communal property analysis of their property holding capacity are at least planted if, ultimately, left unwatered. More obliquely (but perhaps of greater significance), Cross J in *Neville Estates* v. *Madden* [1962] Ch 832 invokes a different type of ownership model when, in adopting the now favoured construction, he appears to contemplate (without going into detail) a new form of co-ownership model distinct from either the traditional joint tenancy or the tenancy in common. Generally, however, the courts have failed to recognise the true significance of unincorporated associations, and this can be traced ultimately to a failure to recognise the true ambit of property law. If one is schooled in a tradition that emphasises only private property, it is hardly surprising that, when faced with difficulties of this nature, the courts adopt a private property analysis. Thus, even though unincorporated associations are self-evidently examples of communal ownership and a trust model exists by which they can be made to dovetail easily into the current law of property, the courts favour an approach which does violence to both principle and formality while relegating the donor's intentions to the margins or beyond.

Notes and Questions 16.7

Consider the following notes and questions both before and after reading *Leahy* v. *Attorney-General for New South Wales* [1959] AC 457, *Neville Estates* v. *Madden* [1962] Ch 832, *Re Denley* [1969] 1 Ch 393, *Re Recher* [1972] Ch 526, *Re Lipinski* [1977] 1 All ER 33 and *Re Grant* [1979] 3 All ER 359, either in full or as extracted at www.cambridge.org/propertylaw/.

1 What is an unincorporated association?

2 In *Leahy*, Viscount Simonds said that a purported gift to an unincorporated association could be analysed in three different ways, the correct analysis in any particular case depending on the intention of the donor. What are these three analyses? Why, according to Viscount Simonds, will the gift be void

unless it can be analysed in the first of these three ways? Why did he refuse to adopt the first analysis in this case?

3   Have the perpetuity problems referred to in *Leahy* been resolved by section 4(4) of the Perpetuities and Accumulations Act 1964?

4   A fourth analysis was pointed out in *Re Recher*. Does it satisfactorily explain how unincorporated associations hold property, and, if so, how can a member lose his vested interest absent compliance with section 53(1)(c)?

5   What was the fifth analysis employed in *Re Lipinski*? Does this offer a more imaginative solution to the conceptual difficulties posed by unincorporated associations? Does the analysis *implicitly* reject a private property solution in favour of communal property?

6   In *Grant*, why was the gift void? Could the Chertsey and Walton Constituency Labour Party secede from the Labour Party? If it did, what would happen to its property?

7   What do you think of Vinelott J's analysis in *Re Grant* of *Re Denley*? Is it convincing?

8   Can an association make a rule that it cannot change its rules without the consent of another body? If so, how (if at all) can it change that rule? Does it make any difference if the other body set up the association in the first place, and drafted its rules (including the rule about changing its rules)?

9   Can someone who gives money to an unincorporated association ensure that it is used for the purposes intended by the donor?

10   Can someone who gives money to the Conservative Party ensure that it is used for the purposes intended by the donor? Is a gift by will of money to the Conservative Party valid?

11   Are unincorporated associations really an example of communal property with members rights determined as a consequence of status rather than vesting?

16.3.3.   Extending the limits of co-ownership: public trusts

If we step back from unincorporated associations for a moment, it does not take much to realise that the *Re Denley*-type purpose trust provides a means by which we might give renewed impetus to the ownership aspirations of communities. Such observations are not new in the context of trusts in general. Across the Atlantic, as Gray ('Equitable Property') has illustrated, the rhetorical and conceptual power of the trust has long been utilised to this end. International lawyers, for example, have invoked trust rhetoric in conceiving of an 'intergenerational equity' whereby each generation, as trustees, is burdened by obligations owed to future generations, as beneficiaries (Weiss, 'The Planetary Trust'). On a more substantive level, the historic public trust doctrine, which initially confirmed state ownership (in the absence of Crown title) of navigable waters and tidelands on behalf of all citizens, seems to be in the process of extending beyond such narrow confines to include more general environmental resources such as the countryside (see *Paepcke* v. *Public Buildings Commissioner of Chicago*, 263 NE 2d 11 (1970)) and wildlife (see *Wade* v. *Kramer*, 459 NE 2d 1025 (1984)). Such developments have been at the behest of academics who have long seen the potential for such advances in both the width (Sax, 'The Public Trust Doctrine in Natural Resources Law') and the jurisdictional ambit (Ausness, 'Water Rights, the Public Trust Doctrine and the Protection of Instream Uses') and have contributed to a general change in the tone of the debate concerning environmental issues. In his seminal article, 'Should Trees Have Standing? – Towards Legal Rights for Natural Objects', for example, Christopher Stone argued that natural objects might be represented or defended by a friend with legal personality; this was echoed within days in the dissenting opinion of Justice William O. Douglas in the United States Supreme Court case of *Sierra Club* v. *Morton*, 405 US 727 (1972).

Interesting as these examples are, they are of little significance to the development of English trust law. In so far as the American public trust doctrine involves notions of trust, it is a specialised mechanism whose origin can be traced to the peculiar circumstances of the American Revolution and the displacing of Crown sovereignty by that of the people (see McCay, 'The Making of an Environmental Doctrine', pp. 85–7). In this jurisdiction, the public trust is limited to its charitable incarnation whereby trusts that fulfil certain requirements bestowing charitable status are exempt from some of the rules applicable to private trusts such as the rule against perpetual trusts and the beneficiary principle (see below). These conditions are not easy to fulfil, and require the trust, *in a way that the law recognises*, to promote the public benefit by relieving poverty, advancing religion or education or otherwise benefiting the community. While charitable trusts clearly have a role to play in the context of environmentalism and the aspirations of communities, they do not provide a complete answer. The law of charities develops incrementally on a case-by-case basis, which means that it tends to lag behind developments in society in general. Thus, in *Re Grove-Grady* [1929] 1 Ch 557, a gift to set up an animal refuge where the animals would be free from molestation by man was, somewhat surprisingly from today's perspective at least, deemed not to be charitable because no public benefit was deemed to arise. One suspects this is a precedent that would not survive a renewed outing in the Court of Appeal, but it underlines the essential conservatism of the law of charities made all the worse by a conception of the public good which requires judges to adopt an approach that necessarily favours the *status quo*. In *National Anti-Vivisection Society* v. *Inland Revenue Commissioners* [1948] AC 31, a trust to promote anti-vivisection was held not to be charitable because (i) on balance the House of Lords was not convinced its aims were in the public interest and (ii) it was deemed to be too political because it advocated a change in the law. (Cf. the American *Restatement on the Law of Trusts*, p. 374, which states that: 'The courts do not take sides or attempt to decide which of two conflicting views of promoting the social interests of the community is the better adapted for the purpose, even though the views are opposed to each other. Thus a trust to promote peace by disarmament, as well as a trust to promote peace by preparedness for war, is charitable.')

It is thus to the law of private trusts, and *Re Denley* in particular, that we must turn for a mechanism that will provide communities and others with an ownership vehicle which will function irrespective of whether or not their aspirations are deemed to be of benefit to the public. Again, such an approach is not new. The case for stewardship is often articulated by reference to the trustee–beneficiary relationship (for example, Lucy and Mitchell, 'Replacing Private Property', p. 584), but this is usually as a simile with little substantive content (see Gray, 'Equitable Property', p. 206). Yet the *Re Denley*-type purpose trust, with its provision of a trustee in whom the legal title vests, does seem to offer communities without legal personality a substantive mechanism whereby they can enjoy open-textured interests such as estates in land.

For the purposes of communal property and common property rights in the environment, this could be an extremely important development. For in *Re Denley* lies the roots of what could become a fully fledged public trust doctrine removed from the constricting embrace of charitable status. In *Re Denley*, Goff J invokes the possibility of a purpose trust in which no one owns the beneficial interest yet which is freed from the threat of invalidity because of the presence of indirect beneficiaries capable of enforcing the trustees' obligations. Because a community is a collection of individuals with no legal personality of its own, a structure that does not require there to be an owner offers obvious possibilities. The trust can be held for the purpose of promoting the community's aims while the individual members of the community will qualify as persons with sufficient interest to enforce the trustees' obligations. There is, in such an analysis, the potential for such a trust to develop further to create a mechanism for promoting environmental goals by regarding the public in general as the indirect beneficiaries of such a trust with the necessary capacity to enforce the trustees' obligations. This, however, would require some conception of the public good which might necessarily collapse back into nothing more than a question regarding charitable status, which, after all, is the mechanism which currently exists in respect of purpose trusts deemed to be in the public interest. The real potential of the *Re Denley*-type purpose trust lies in its capacity to provide communities with a mechanism to promote their aims irrespective of whether or not those aims are regarded as being in the public interest. This has obvious advantages over the current analysis of such communities, which tends to deal with them as nothing more than a gathering of individuals each with a vested and, from a proprietary stance at least, alienable interest.

The question which needs to be addressed is: what does it take to become an indirect beneficiary with power to enforce the trustees' obligations? This is, in effect, a question about *locus standi* and to whom the court will listen in any dispute concerning the exercise of the trustees' duties – a point to which Goff J pays little heed, simply stating that:

> [T]here may be a purpose or object trust, the carrying out of which would benefit an individual or individuals, where that benefit is so indirect or intangible or which is otherwise so framed as not to give those persons any *locus standi* to apply to the court to enforce the trust, in which case the beneficiary principle would, as it seems to me, apply to invalidate the trust. (*Re Denley* [1969] 1 Ch 373 at 382–3)

This, coupled with his insistence that all the indirect beneficiaries need to be capable of being listed, underlines that the decision is not as radical as one might imagine (although he may be excused on this latter point, as *Re Denley* pre-dates *McPhail* v. *Doulton* [1971] AC 424, the case in which the House of Lords eventually removed the shackles from certainty of object). Thus, despite its liberal approach to the beneficiary principle, there is still a strong conservative element in the judgment which acts as a brake on the potential developments we have outlined above. From the tone of his comments, it seems likely that Goff J would not have needed much persuasion that a particular purpose was too abstract. This has necessarily led commentators to downplay its significance. Even Cotterrell ('Some Sociological Aspects'), who can normally be relied upon to offer interesting and illuminating insights in this field, has contented himself with the rather tame (but no doubt accurate) observation that 'the scope and long-term influence of this decision remains unclear'.

It would consequently be over-optimistic to see in *Re Denley* anything more than the potential to give new impetus to the ownership aspirations of communities within our society. However, it stands as a judgment which offers the possibility of such development which, with its reliance on a test of *locus standi*, empowers the community, by making their rules as to membership the litmus test of standing. In the public law arena, of course, the question of *locus standi* is still a matter of debate and argument. Yet, in the context of *Re Denley*, such issues seem less problematic, for here the court is relieved of the task of formulating a test of standing because the community, by reason of its status as a community, must necessarily have provided one (cf., in the public law context, *R.* v. *Somerset County Council, ex parte Dixon* [1998] Env LR 111; (1998) 75 P&CR 175). Of course, the test might not be referred to as such, and in many instances will be implicit rather than explicit. However, some form of test must exist, for otherwise it would be meaningless to talk of a community if there is no method of identifying to whom it applies. Thus, under a liberal interpretation of *Re Denley*, a community possesses a means by which legal title can be held on behalf of its members each of whom holds the common property right not to be excluded from the resource so held, provided they retain their status as members of the community.

17

Leases and bailment

17.1. Introduction

As we saw in Chapter 7, the essential similarity between leases and bailments is that, in both cases, possession becomes vested in a non-owner for a limited period. If the thing in question is land, the interest created is a lease, and if it is a chattel the interest created is a bailment. However, as we see in this chapter, the differences between leases and bailments are much greater than the similarities. Although the common law originally considered each to be part of the law of personal property, they have very different historical roots and have developed along separate lines so that, even now, there is almost no resemblance between the two legal institutions. This causes some difficulty in our legal system. A lease of land is a sophisticated but somewhat inflexible institution, not easily adjustable to meet changing social and commercial expectations (see, for example, *Prudential Assurance* v. *London Residuary Body* [1992] 2 AC 386, discussed below), and this can limit its usefulness. On the other hand, it is a clearly defined property interest which is relatively easy to protect and enforce against third parties, and it would be very useful if a similar interest could be created in goods, particularly commercially tradable ones like aircraft, works of art or computer equipment. However, although bailments of such goods are often called leases, they remain in law bailments, and it is very doubtful whether even the most careful drafting can give a bailee of goods the same rights and protection as a lessee of land.

17.2. Leases and bailments compared

17.2.1. Consensuality

Leases are consensual, in the sense that they can only come into existence as a result of a deliberate grant of rights by one person to another. The grant may be implied by law rather than expressed, and is somewhat attenuated in the case of the anomalous tenancy by sufferance (see section 17.3.1.4 below, under the heading 'Sufferance'), but nevertheless it remains the essential origin of the interest. Further, there is nearly always an enforceable contract between the original lessor and the original lessee, i.e. the lessee almost invariably provides consideration for the grant of possession in the form of rent and/or payment of a capital sum premium. Consensuality is, however, required only for the initial creation of the lease. Once it has come into existence, either party can assign their interest to anyone else (because their interests are proprietary) and their role in the leasehold relationship created by the grant of the lease will then shift to their assignee, whether the assignment was unauthorised by the other or not, and even if it was expressly prohibited.

Bailments, on the other hand, need not be consensual, even in their inception. Some bailments arise by express grant, which necessarily involves consensuality but not necessarily consideration. Others may be authorised by the bailor but not involve consensus between bailor and bailee. For example, when you post a parcel to an overseas address, you impliedly authorise the post office to transfer possession of the parcel, and the duty to transport it to the addressee, to a string of carriers. You will have a direct bailment relationship with each of those carriers, even though you and they may not be specifically aware of each other's existence, and will certainly not have entered into any direct contractual relationship. There are yet other bailments which are more or less wholly unauthorised. The extent of this category of bailment is uncertain, but it appears to encompass all cases where a person consciously takes someone else's goods into their possession. It would therefore include the relation- ship that arises between the owner of lost goods and their finder, and also that between the owner of stolen goods and their thief. In these cases, of course, there is no question of consensus between bailor and bailee.

17.2.2.   Contract

It follows from the above that, while there is nearly always a legally enforceable contract between the original parties to a lease, this is not the case in all bailments. This has important repercussions when considering the rights and duties of the parties. In the case of a lease, the rights and duties of the parties derive both from the nature of the property interest each holds in the land and the consequent ongoing proprietary relationship between them, and from the terms of the contract made between the original parties. The same is true of consensual bailments supported by consideration: the rights and duties of the parties derive from the proprietary relationship that arises out of the fact that the one has possession of goods owned by the other, as well as from the contract in which they agreed the terms on which this should happen. However, in the case of non-consensual bailments, there is no underlying agreement at all between the parties, which means that their rights and duties are dictated solely by the incidents that the law has ascribed to their respective property interests and to that relationship. And, in gratuitous consensual bailments, there is the added complication that any rights and obligations which the parties have expressly or impliedly agreed between themselves are not contractually enforceable.

17.2.3.   Enforcement

The presence or absence of a contract also has important repercussions on the actions and remedies available for breach of any of the terms of the relationship.

Leases are primarily enforced by specialised property actions (actions claiming forfeiture, possession, recovery of rent etc.) but the parties may also bring ordinary contract actions for damages for breach of a term of the lease and, increasingly but controversially, may rely on other contract doctrines such as specific performance, rescission for repudiatory breach, and frustration. The enforcement of bailments is based on wholly different principles. If there is a contract between the parties, it is enforceable in the same way as any other contract relating to chattels. But, as explained in Chapter 7, English law has failed to develop property actions for the enforcement of interests in chattels and, instead, the parties are forced to rely on tort actions. So, whereas the enforcement of leases is governed by property and contract principles, the enforcement of bailments is governed by varying mixtures of contract and tort.

17.2.4.   Duration and purpose

Leases are classified according to the duration of the interest granted, whereas in the case of bailments the classification depends primarily on either the purpose for which possession is granted or (in the case of unauthorised bailments arising for example by mistaken receipt or finding) on the means by which it was acquired. Duration and purpose are treated quite differently in the law of leases and the law of bailments. In the case of land, it is duration which marks the lease off from the fee simple, and, perhaps as a result, the rules governing allowable durations of leases are inflexible and (at present at least) rigidly enforced by the courts (see below). No such rules apply to bailments. The law of leases, on the other hand, is not much interested in the purpose for which possession is granted. A person in possession of land as a lessee may *prima facie* use it for any purpose she wants: any restriction that the lessor wants to impose must be imposed by contract. The same is not necessarily true of bailments, even those where possession is deliberately granted by the bailor. In some bailments, such as consensual hire of goods, the bailee may do more or less whatever she wants with the goods, whereas in others the way in which the bailee may use the goods is strictly confined (consider, for example, what you are entitled and required to do with a coat as a cloakroom attendant, a dry cleaner, or a person who hired it from a clothes-hire shop).

17.2.5.   Beneficial use

This brings us to a difference of fundamental importance between leases and bailments. In both, possession is split off from ownership, but whereas in a lease of land possession connotes beneficial use, in a bailment of goods there is no necessary connection between the two. More specifically, a grant of a right to possession of land for a leasehold term automatically carries with it the full right to make beneficial use of the land, in an income sense (i.e. full rights to make income use, in the Honoré sense). The tenant is entitled to use the land for whatever purposes she wants or for none at all, at all or any times, and to allow any other person use of the land on whatever terms she chooses, and to keep all income benefits from the land (apples from the trees). This inherent right to use can be (and often is) cut down by contract. So, for example, a lease of a shop would normally contain a contractual stipulation that the tenant can use the premises only as a shop, and it might specify the type of shop and the hours in which the shop may stay open, or even positively require the tenant to keep the shop open and trading during normal retail hours. But these are only contractual restrictions, and subject to them the tenant remains entitled to do whatever she likes and to take whatever income benefit accruing from the land that she wants.

The same is not true of bailments. The extent to which a bailee may make beneficial use of the chattel and take income benefits that accrue during her possession varies depending on the type of bailment, and in some cases it may be wholly absent. In other words, bailment can be wholly onerous, and the right to exclude the owner from beneficial use (which exists in all authorised bailments) does not necessarily entitle the bailee to make beneficial use of the goods for herself.

17.2.6. Proprietary status

Leases are traditionally regarded as necessarily proprietary – by granting a lease, the lessor grants an estate in the land which is recognised both by the common law and by statute as a property interest. Recently, the House of Lords has taken the view that there can be such a thing as a non-proprietary lease (see *Bruton* v. *London and Quadrant Housing Trust* [2000] 1 AC 406, discussed in Notes and Questions 17.5 below), but this is at best anomalous and it remains true that, in principle, leases are property interests.

The proprietary status of bailments, on the other hand, has always been a matter of controversy: some would deny proprietary status to all types of bailment; others take the view that bailees always necessarily have a proprietary interest in the goods; while others say that it is not possible to give a clear-cut answer, and that in most types of bailment the interest is proprietary in some senses but not in others. We look at this in detail below.

17.2.7. Inherent obligations of the possessor

The *caveat emptor* principle is more or less firmly established in relation to leases. With some very limited common law and statutory exceptions which neither the courts nor Parliament have shown enthusiasm to extend, the lessor gives no warranties about the state and condition of the land or that it is fit for the purposes for which it is let. This creates a curious lacuna of responsibility in the land-lord–tenant relationship – neither has a *prima facie* responsibility for repair. In the case of bailments, the picture is dramatically different. Even gratuitous bailees can have a liability to take care of the goods in some circumstances, and, in the case of non-gratuitous bailments, it is the bailee's obligation to take care of the goods which forms the defining characteristic of the relationship.

17.3. Leases

With these differences in mind, we now look more closely at the nature of the lease, and at various aspects of the leasehold relationship.

17.3.1. Nature of the lease

We saw in Chapter 7 that a great deal turns on whether a grant of a right to occupy land creates a lease or a mere personal permission to be there. It has been established by the House of Lords in *Street* v. *Mountford* [1985] AC 809, discussed in Chapter 7, that the necessary and sufficient conditions for it to amount to a lease are that possession of the land should be granted for a duration that is certain. In Chapter 7, we dealt with the difficult question of when the grant of a right to occupy land amounts to a grant of possession for these purposes. Here we concentrate on the question of duration, which gives rise to other, equally difficult, problems.

The first problem is this. When we say that possession must be granted for a duration that is certain, what exactly do we mean by 'certain', and what is the effect of a grant of the right to possession for a period which is not certain? The second arises out of the first: is it possible to grant a right to possession of land for a limited period *without* conferring a proprietary leasehold interest on the grantee? And, if it is, is it possible for the thing created to be a proprietary interest which is not a lease, or even a lease which is not a proprietary interest? We consider these questions in the following paragraphs.

17.3.1.1.   Duration: the four basic categories

Since 1925, there have been four categories of lease, classified according to the duration of the tenant's interest:

1 fixed-term tenancy;
2 periodic tenancy;
3 tenancy at will; and
4 tenancy at sufferance.

We look at the distinctive features of each of these before considering the overall requirement that the duration of a lease must be certain.

17.3.1.2.   Fixed-term tenancies

The legal position

A fixed-term lease is a lease for a fixed period which is specified in advance in the lease itself. At the end of the specified period, the lease automatically expires. The period is usually specified by reference to a number of years or a specific date (for example, a lease for ten years, or until 25 December 2010). The question of whether it can be specified by reference to any other future event is one we consider below.

There are no restrictions on the length of the period: it may be for one day or 1,000 years. Also, the period may be discontinuous. In *Smallwood* v. *Sheppards* [1895] 2 QB 627, a lease of a fairground site to a proprietor of swings and roundabouts for three successive bank holidays in a year was held to be valid, and it was accepted in *Cottage Holiday Associates Ltd* v. *Customs and Excise* [1983] QB 735 that this meant that a time-share arrangement whereby the occupant was entitled to possession of a holiday cottage in Cornwall for one week a year for eighty years was a valid lease for a single period comprised of eighty discontinuous weeks.

Length of fixed-term leases in practice

Leases for as short a time as a few days are unusual but not unknown. Very long leases, on the other hand, are commonly used, particularly in two situations. The first is where the tenant is required under the lease to develop the land by erecting buildings on it at its own expense. In such a case, terms of, for example, 99 or 125 years have traditionally been used, as a rough measure of the estimated life of the buildings, on the basis that the tenant ought to be entitled to the full benefit of the buildings it paid for. This continues to be a factor in determining the length of the term in modern commercial development leases where the development is to be financed by the tenant.

The second common situation in which a very long lease will be used is where the parties would like to grant the tenant a fee simple interest in the land but are deterred from doing so because the land in question is physically dependent on other land (typically, a horizontally divided slice of land, such as a maisonette or flat). It is possible to grant a fee simple interest in a horizontally divided slice of land, but until recently it was highly inadvisable to do so, because positive covenants (for example, to keep common structural parts in repair) are not enforceable between adjoining freehold owners except by using not always reliable contract mechanisms. This is a consequence of the courts' decision to confine the effect of *Tulk* v. *Moxhay* to restrictive covenants, as we saw in Chapter 6. This is not a problem in leaseholds because positive obligations can easily be made enforceable between tenants of a common landlord. Consequently, those who wish to acquire an ownership-type interest for an indefinite period in a horizontally divided slice of land until recently had no realistic alternative to the long lease, typically for a symbolic period of 99 or 999 years. This has long been a standard form of tenure for residential flats, and its resemblance to ownership is increased by extensive statutory rights for tenants holding such leases to buy out their landlord's interest or obtain an extended lease when the original lease expires (exercisable by tenants individually under the Leasehold Reform Act 1967 as amended or collectively under Part III of the Landlord and Tenant Act 1987 as amended) or insist that the landlord hands over management to a manager approved by the tenants (see the amendments made by the Commonhold and Leasehold Reform Act 2002). The close approximation to ownership is reflected in the market price of such leases.

A long lease of a residential flat will typically be granted for a premium (an initial lump-sum payment) and a nominal rent, and the amount of the premium, and the capital value of the lease as and when the tenant chooses to sell it, can be expected to be much the same as the market price for an equivalent freehold property, and (assuming full statutory rights apply) is likely to remain stable, subject to market fluctuations, throughout the term of the lease.

Commonhold as an alternative to the long residential lease

However, the Commonhold and Leasehold Reform Act 2002 has introduced, with effect from September 2004, a commonhold system to be used as an alternative to the long lease where there are developments of multiple units. The commonhold regime (very similar to the systems variously known as strata titles, condominium and commonhold which have long operated in the United States, Australia, New Zealand, Canada and many other Commonwealth countries) enables holders of individual units within a residential or commercial development to each hold a fee simple interest in their own unit, and also jointly hold the fee simple in the common parts of the development via a company of which the unit-holders are the sole members.

It remains to be seen whether commonhold will prove popular. While it has the advantage for unit-holders that collectively they will be solely responsible for the management of the development, the rights conferred on unit-holders as against each other (individually and collectively) are less extensive than those that long leaseholders have against landlords under the statutory provisions noted above, and this may prove to be a problem. For further details of the statutory scheme and an assessment of its likely effects, see Farrand and Clarke, *Emmet and Farrand on Title*, Chapter 28A.

Commercial premises

Leases of commercial premises such as offices and shops and industrial premises are usually relatively short. A review carried out by the British Property Federation and the Investment Property Database of new leases granted in 1999–2000 gives an average duration of 15.7 years (BPF/IPD, *Annual Lease Review 2000*). In this country, it is very common for businesses to trade from leasehold rather than freehold premises, and at first sight a lease length of 15–20 years might seem rather strange – not long enough for stable businesses in need of permanent premises, and too long for short-lived or expanding ones. However, there are several factors which introduce flexibility. First, landlords are willing to commit themselves to relatively long leases because it is possible to include rent review provisions in the lease, providing for the rent payable under the lease to be periodically increased (or, exceptionally, decreased) to keep in line with market rents. The House of Lords confirmed the validity of provisions allowing rents in leases to be reviewed in this way in *United Scientific Holdings Ltd* v. *Burnley Borough Council* [1978] AC 904, and such provisions are now routinely included in leases of all types of commercial premises. Tenants, on the other hand, have a variety of mechanisms available to enable them either to stay longer than the originally agreed term or to leave early. There is a statutory security of tenure system for commercial tenants which entitles them to apply for a new lease (on essentially the same terms but at a market rent) when their old lease expires. The new lease must be granted by their landlord unless the landlord can demonstrate that it requires the premises for redevelopment or for its own use. However, the adoption of this scheme is now virtually voluntary, as a result of recent changes made to the governing statute, Part II of the Landlord and Tenant Act 1954 which greatly simplify the procedure for opting out: for further details, see Farrand and Clarke, *Emmet and Farrand on Title*, Chapter 27.

Assignment and premature termination of fixed-term lease

As to leaving prematurely, most leases, whether of residential or commercial premises, are fairly easily traded, so a tenant who wants to move out early should be able to sell the lease, depending on the state of the market and on how onerous the terms of the lease are. We look at this in more detail below where we consider the statutory regulation of rights to alienate and the effect that alienation has on the enforcement of the terms of the lease.

For tenants not willing to rely on the market to provide a buyer when they need one, it is possible (and in commercial leases fairly common) to include in the lease a break clause, i.e. a contractual provision giving the tenant, or indeed the landlord, an option to terminate the lease early, either after a fixed number of years or on the happening of a future event. The courts construe break clauses quite strictly. In particular, if the option to terminate is made exercisable on the happening of a future event, it will be invalid unless the future event is sufficiently certain. This does not require the parties to be able to predict at the outset *when*, if ever, the future event is going to occur. It does, however, require that, if the event does occur, it will be objectively ascertainable that it has done so. So, an option for the tenant to terminate the lease before the end of the term 'if it gives the landlord six months' written notice of its desire to do so' is valid, whereas an option to terminate 'at the end of the first year of the lease if too much rain falls in that year' is void. This becomes relevant in relation to the rules about certainty of duration of leases, as we see below.

17.3.1.3.   Periodic tenancies

Nature

A periodic tenancy continues from period to period (for example, from week to week, month to month, or year to year) until terminated by either party giving notice to quit to the other. A periodic tenancy can therefore last indefinitely, but each party has the option to bring it to an end at any time by serving notice to quit. The periodic tenancy was a comparatively late development, not finally recognised by the courts until 1702, by which time it had become common in practice as a means of giving tenants a marginally less precarious interest than the tenancy at will, as Simpson notes in *A History of the Land Law* (Extract 17.1 below), and analysis of its nature can still cause the courts difficulty, as can be seen from *Hammersmith and Fulham London Borough Council* v. *Monk* [1992] 1 AC 478, discussed below.

In practice, the precariousness of a periodic tenant's interest is lessened by three factors. First, the courts strictly enforce common law and statutory regulations as to the length of notice required to terminate periodic tenancies (as to which see sections 5 and 3 of the Protection from Eviction Act 1977, as amended by the Housing Act 1988, and also *Queens Club Garden Estates Ltd* v. *Bignell* [1924] 1 KB 117). Secondly, statutory regimes applicable to residential, business and agricultural tenants (which are beyond the scope of this book) confer varying degrees of security of tenure on periodic tenants.

Contractual fetters on notice to quit

Thirdly, the parties themselves may decide to include as a term of the tenancy a contractual fetter on the landlord's (or the tenant's) right to terminate by serving notice to quit. This will usually take the form of a postponement of the right to serve notice to quit until a specified future date or the happening of a future event. The courts' approach to these restrictions on the right to terminate by notice to quit is markedly different from their approach to contractual rights to terminate fixed-term tenancies early. They will treat any such restriction as invalid not only if it is uncertain but also if it is repugnant to the nature of a periodic tenancy. A restriction which removes the landlord's right to serve notice to quit altogether comes within this latter category, and is therefore void (*Centaploy Ltd* v. *Matlodge Ltd* [1974] Ch 1) and presumably it would be equally repugnant to the nature of the periodic tenancy to have a provision removing the tenant's right to serve notice to quit. However, it is not clear whether a very long postponement of either party's right to terminate by notice to quit would be void on repugnancy grounds. *Doe d Warner* v. *Browne* (1807) 8 East 165; 103 ER 305, and *Cheshire Lines Committee* v. *Lewis & Co.* (1880) 50 LJ QB 121, discussed in Lord Templeman's speech in *Prudential* (below), would seem to suggest that, but in *Midland Railways Co.'s Agreement, Charles Clay & Sons Ltd* v. *British Railways Board* [1971] Ch 725, the Court of Appeal expressed the view that nothing short of a complete removal of either party's right to terminate would fall foul of the repugnancy rule (Russell LJ at 733, giving the judgment of the Court). The decision in *Midland Railway Co.'s Agreement* was overruled by the House of Lords in *Prudential* (below) on the question of when a postponement of the right to serve notice to quit would be void for uncertainty, but nothing was said about the separate question of when it would be void for repugnancy.

As to the requirement of certainty, this is much stricter than in the case of break provisions. Where the right to serve notice to quit is postponed until the happening of a future event, the future event must be certain in the sense that the parties must be able to predict *at the outset* when it will occur. This matches the test for certainty of duration for fixed-term leases, as we see below.

17.3.1.4. Tenancy at will

A tenancy at will is a tenancy which can be ended at any time by either party. It is of ancient origin (Megarry and Wade, *The Law of Real Property*, p. 655, describe it as 'probably the original type of tenure onto which the doctrines of estates were superimposed'), but, although it appears always to have been accepted as a form of tenancy, it has few, if any, of the hallmarks of a property interest. It is said to terminate automatically if either the landlord or the tenant dies or alienates his interest (*Wheeler* v. *Mercer* [1957] AC 416 at 427 *per* Viscount Simonds, who described it as 'unlike any other tenancy, except a tenancy at sufferance, to which it is next-of-kin. It has been properly described as a personal relation between the landlord and his tenant'; and see also *ibid.*, p. 432 *per* Lord Cohen), and Megarry and Wade suggest it might more properly be regarded as 'a mere relationship of tenure unaccompanied by . . . any estate or interest which can exist as a right *in rem*'.

At one time the tenancy at will was also said to be anomalous in that it did not conform to the rule that the duration of a tenancy must be certain. However, there now seems no great difficulty in accommodating it within the formula for ascertaining certainty of duration laid down by the House of Lords in *Prudential*: see further below.

The precariousness of the relationship created by the tenancy at will might lead one to ask why anyone would ever willingly enter into one, whether as landlord or tenant, especially since the periodic tenancy gives both parties very nearly as much flexibility (either can terminate their obligation whenever they want on giving the appropriate notice) but considerably more security (both know they will be given the requisite period of notice before their right to rent or possession, as the case may be, ends). The main reason is that statutory security of tenure for tenants generally applies to periodic tenancies but not to tenancies at will (see *Wheeler* v. *Mercer* [1957] AC 416 on the protection of business tenants under Part II of the Landlord and Tenant Act 1954). Landlords who want, or are prepared to allow, someone to take possession as a temporary measure, but do not want to create a tenancy attracting security of tenure, might therefore choose a tenancy at will, and in appropriate cases (i.e. where it is clear that the tenant's possession was intended to be temporary but there was no express agreement as to duration) the courts will infer that a tenancy at will was what was intended by them. The classic cases are where a prospective tenant has been let into occupation while the detailed terms of the lease are still being negotiated, or a purchaser let into possession before completion of the purchase, or a tenant holds over after the end of a contractual tenancy and the landlord allows him to remain temporarily, whether for humanitarian reasons, or while negotiating terms for a new lease: see, for example, *Javad* v. *Aquil* [1991] 1 WLR 1007.

In addition, there are other cases where a tenancy at will arises by operation of law, most importantly where a tenant goes into possession under a lease which proves to be void (see *Prudential* below: if no rent was paid the tenant will be taken to have a tenancy at will – his possession has throughout been with permission, but can now be terminated or given up at will – whereas if rent was paid there will be a periodic tenancy, as we see in section 17.3.1.5 below).

Tenancy at sufferance

A tenancy at sufferance arises whenever a person is in possession without either the positive assent or the positive dissent of the landlord. Typically, it arises where a tenant holds over after the end of a tenancy without the landlord's consent but before any active objection has been made by the landlord: *Remon* v. *City of London Real Property Co. Ltd* [1921] 1 KB 49, CA, in which Scrutton LJ described it as a 'tenure … probably invented to prevent [the former tenant] obtaining a title by adverse possession …' (at 59). By its very nature, it can never be deliberately granted by a landlord. It is an *ex post facto* rationalisation of a position which, for strategic reasons, the courts wish to categorise as tenancy rather than trespass. It probably does not extend to cover the position of a former tenant holding over in spite of active objection from the landlord (*Remon*) although the gradations can be quite subtle here: compare the classic description of a tenancy at sufferance as describing the situation that arises when 'that which cannot be changed has to be endured'.

Extract 17.1   A. W. B. *A History of the Land Law* (2nd edn, Oxford: Clarendon Press, 1986), pp. 253–4

[I]n the developed law the periodic tenancy is recognized as a form of lease; the typical example is the yearly tenancy, which will continue until it is determined by six months' notice on either side, and such tenancies are extremely common. Such periodic or 'running' leases obviously pose a problem in legal analysis which is glossed over in modern textbooks, for in a sense they do not conform to the rule which requires a lease to be for a fixed term – they are in effect leases for an uncertain duration, determinable by notice. They are not leases for a fixed term with an option to renew; such an analysis is quite unrealistic. In short they are anomalous, and when they first came before the courts at the end of the fifteenth and the beginning of the sixteenth centuries they provoked a great deal of controversy. In 1506, a lease for one year, and then from year to year as the parties pleased, at a fixed rent, was held to be a lease at will only. A case in 1522 on the same type of lease provoked a long discussion in the Common Pleas, and the judges were divided. Upon grounds of convenience, for such arrangements were common, Brudenell CJ and Pollard J were prepared to hold that by such an arrangement a lease for one year was created at once, followed by successive one-year terms for each year in which the arrangement was continued; if the tenant, with the consent of the landlord, continued in possession for one day of a new year, then a fixed term for the whole of that year was created. Fitzherbert and Brooke JJ were not so sympathetic. Such an arrangement, in their view, created a lease for one year and no more; thereafter the tenant who remained in possession became a tenant at will only. If the arrangement was expressed as a lease for *years* 'at the will of the parties', or 'for as long as the parties pleased', then they would treat it as a lease for a fixed term of two years (to give effect to the plural 'years') followed by a tenancy at will. For two centuries thereafter the dispute as to the nature of periodic tenancies continued its arid course. In 1601, [in *Agard* v. *King* Cro Eliz 775] Gawdy and Fenner JJ adopted the view of Brudenell CJ and Pollard J. Popham CJ introduced another quaint construction, for he held that a lease 'from year to year as the parties pleased' created a term of two years (from year to year = two years) followed by a tenancy at will. Popham's view was adopted in 1606 [in *The Bishop of Bath's Case*, 6 Co Rep 35b] where the court was confronted with a lease 'for a period of one year and so from year to year for as long as both parties should please'; three years are mentioned, and these are added up to confer a term of three years followed by a tenancy at will. This sort of absurd construction would lead one to say that a lease from 'year to year to year to year' would create a term of four years; neither common sense nor logic recommends it. Eventually, the view of Brudenell and Pollard triumphed when the great Holt CJ adopted it in 1702 [in *Leighton* v. *Theed* (1702) 1 Ld Raymond 707] and in the course of the eighteenth century the dispute died out.

Notes and Questions 17.1

Read the above extract and *Hammersmith and Fulham London Borough Council* v. *Monk* [1992] 1 AC 478, either in full or as extracted at www.cambridge.org/propertylaw/, and consider the following:

1 In the light of the decision in *Prudential* (below), can periodic tenancies now be said to 'conform to the rule which requires a lease to be for a fixed term', as Simpson says?

2 The analysis described by Simpson in the above extract as 'quite unrealistic' was subsequently adopted by the House of Lords in *Hammersmith* v. *Monk*. Is Simpson nevertheless right?

3 Would it have been justifiable for the House of Lords in *Monk* to have distinguished *Summersett's Case* on policy grounds, i.e. to have held that, although one of the joint holders of the *landlord's* interest can effectively terminate a periodic tenancy, termination by *tenant's* notice to quit requires the concurrence of *all* holders of the tenancy?

4 As a result of this decision, all joint tenants must concur in exercising a break clause in a fixed-term tenancy, and in surrendering a fixed-term tenancy to the landlord, but any one of them can terminate a periodic tenancy by serving notice to quit without the concurrence of the others. How does the House of Lords justify this distinction in this case? Is it justifiable?

5 Lord Bridge says that the 'third principle strand' which he identifies in the arguments for Mr Monk 'confuse[s] the form with the substance'. Explain what he means. Is he right?

6 Joint holders of a periodic tenancy (as any other tenancy) now hold the tenancy on trust for themselves under a trust of land (see Chapter 16). Does this make any difference to the arguments put in this case? In particular, will service of notice to quit by one without the concurrence of the others now constitute a breach of trust, and if it does (a) will it be effective and (b) can it be restrained by injunction? (See *Notting Hill Housing Trust* v. *Brackley* [2001] EWCA Civ 601, CA, on the position under a trust of land under the Trusts of Land and Appointment of Trustees Act 1996, and *Crawley Borough Council* v. *Ure* [1996] QB 13, CA, on the position under a pre-1996 Act trust for sale)

7 What hardship is caused to joint tenants by the decision in *Hammersmith* v. *Monk*? What hardship would have been caused if the House of Lords had come to the opposite conclusion?

17.3.1.5.   Certainty of duration

One of the defining characteristics of a leasehold, as opposed to a freehold, interest is that it is of a limited duration, and it has long been accepted that the limit of the duration must be certain. But what does 'certain' mean in this context? In *Prudential Assurance Co. Ltd* v. *London Residuary Body* [1992] 2 AC 386 (extracted at www.cambridge.org/propertylaw/), the House of Lords held that it means that both parties must know from the outset the earliest date on which their commitment under the lease can be brought to an end – or, as the House of Lords put it, the maximum duration of their liability under the lease. If the lease is for a fixed duration, this appears to mean that the lease must be for a specific period of time, with a known end date (it is difficult to think of any event other than the happening of a date which would satisfy the test), although it may legitimately be made terminable earlier on the happening of an objectively ascertainable event, either at the option of one or other of the parties, or automatically. If the lease is periodic, it means that either there must be no fetter on the right of each party to terminate by notice to quit, or, if there is a fetter, it must either be for a fixed period of time (i.e. until a specified date), or, if fixed by reference to an objectively ascertainable future event, it must be phrased as an alternative to a specified future date, the right to terminate by serving notice to quit returning on whichever of the alternatives occurs first (see the examples in *Prudential*). Consequently, a fixed-term lease 'until the landlord requires the land for road-widening' was held void, as would be an annual periodic tenancy in which the landlord's right to terminate by notice to quit was postponed 'until the landlord requires the land for road-widening'. This reasserted what the House of Lords took to be the orthodox position as formulated by the Court of Appeal in *Lace* v. *Chantler* [1944] KB 368, where a lease granted during the Second World War 'for the duration of the war' was held to be of uncertain duration and therefore void.

The consequence of a lease being held to be of uncertain duration is that the lease is void. However, if the tenant has already taken possession under the void lease, he will acquire by operation of law either a legal periodic tenancy (if rent was paid) or a tenancy at will. Consequently, the landlord (and the tenant) will be entitled to bring the relationship to an end immediately, by serving the appropriate notice to quit if it is a periodic tenancy, or by merely notifying the other party if it is a tenancy at will.

If, on the other hand, the lease was a periodic tenancy to start with, but there is a fetter on the right to terminate by notice to quit which postpones the right for an uncertain duration, the fetter will be void but the lease itself will be valid. Again, the effect will be that either party can take immediate steps to terminate by giving the appropriate notice to quit.

In both cases, the clearly expressed intentions of the parties will be defeated. Their intentions would in many cases be effectuated if, instead of this rigid, complex certainty rule, we adopted the more general, flexible rule that the duration of a lease must be measured by reference to the happening of an objectively ascertainable future event, so that, when that event occurs, it is clear to both parties that it has done so. Why then have we adopted the rigid, complex rule?

The majority in the House of Lords in *Prudential* expressed distaste for the complex rule and opted for it only in order to avoid upsetting long-established property relationships. The minority gave it more positive support. Part of their motivation appears to have been a desire to produce a formulation of the rule that accommodates not only fixed-term leases but also periodic tenancies, tenancies at will and tenancies at sufferance. The complex rule achieves this, although it is not wholly clear why such uniformity is thought necessary. In addition to this, however, those positively in favour of the rigid, complex rule also clearly considered that the general, flexible rule was inherently objectionable.

In order to evaluate these objections, it is useful to look more closely at the sorts of future events which might be used to measure the duration of a lease:

1   Some future events have the twin characteristics of inevitability and predictability – they must occur, and we know in advance when that will be. However, it is difficult to think of any future event that falls into this category apart from a specified future date (1 July 2015) or the end of a specified period of time (10 years from today). There can be no objection on the grounds of certainty of duration either to a fixed-term lease which is to last until such an event, or to a periodic tenancy in which the right to terminate by notice to quit is postponed until the happening of such an event, and such leases are indeed valid under the *Prudential* test and under any reasonably conceivable alternative test.

2   There are other events which are inevitable but we do not know in advance when they will occur. Most, if not all, of these refer in one way or another to the life of some person or thing – for example, a lease granted to you 'until the death of your aunt', or perhaps 'until your aunt ceases to be employed by' the landlord, or 'for so long as you

remain the registered owner' of some specified chattel, such as a ship, which has a limited lifespan, or a lease to an existing tenant of premises adjoining his existing premises 'for so long as you remain tenant of your existing premises'. Following *Prudential*, a lease for such a duration is void (as is a fetter on the right to terminate a periodic tenancy until the happening of such an event). It is difficult to see why this should be the case. At any given point in time the parties know where they stand, and so do all third parties. There is no possibility of the limitation in the lease operating in any way which is contrary to the intentions or expectations of the parties – the uncertainty as to the end date, and the precise perimeters of the uncertainty, are patent from the outset. It is not at all difficult to think of plausible reasons why the parties might want to link the duration of their relationship to such an event. What possible objections can there be to permitting them to do so?

3   Those first two categories of inevitable event must be distinguished from events which may never happen, which raise additional problems. There are distinguishable sub-categories here as well. There are some future events which are due to happen on a specific date, but which might just end up happening earlier or later, or perhaps even never happening at all. As examples, take a lease of training facilities granted to an athletics team 'until the start of the next Olympic Games', or a flat let to a law student 'until the end of your LLB course'. Such a lease is void under the *Prudential* test (consider why). As in the previous category, there are plausible reasons why the parties might want to link their relationship to such an event, and so if possible they ought to be permitted to do so, especially where, as in the examples given, it is very likely that everything will turn out precisely as anticipated. What are the objections to permitting it? The first is that a change in the predicted date (the Olympic Games might be postponed for four years, or the student might fail exams and take a year out to resit) might make the lease operate in a way that was significantly different from that intended by one or both of the parties. The second is that, if the event never happens at all, the lease will last perpetually. This is not only (probably) contrary to the expectations of the parties: it also converts the lease into a freehold rather than a leasehold estate – the interest loses the essential characteristic of limited duration. Are these two objections sufficient to justify invalidating the lease altogether and substituting instead a periodic tenancy, thus *guaranteeing* that the parties intentions will be frustrated, even if the anticipated event does indeed happen on schedule? Since it is overwhelmingly likely that the event will happen as and when anticipated, a more appropriate approach might be to treat it as a valid lease which does not expressly state what is to happen in the unlikely circumstances of the event not happening on the due date, an omission which can be rectified by an implied term. If you were to ask the parties at the outset what was to happen in that eventuality they could probably tell you, and it should be possible for the court to infer from the other terms of the lease and from the surrounding circumstances what their response would be.

4   Does the same apply where not only is the event not inevitable, but the parties do not know at the outset when it will occur if it occurs at all? The *Prudential* lease ('until the landlord requires the land for road-widening') comes within this category, and so too does the *Lace* v. *Chantler* lease (technically at least, the perpetual continuation of the

Second World War was a logically possible outcome, although perhaps not a realistic possibility). Although this may look superficially like a variation on category 3 above, in fact it is much closer to category 2. The parties are well aware from the outset that the duration of their commitment is uncertain in point of time, and presumably they deliberately elected to choose that so that it could be precisely geared to the happening of the future event. In some of these cases the parties will have intended the lease to mean exactly what it says – in other words, that if the event never happened the lease should last perpetually. Lord Browne-Wilkinson thought this was the parties' original intention in the *Prudential* case. If this is the case, the only possible justification for invalidating the lease is the structural reason given above – a lease of unlimited duration is not a lease at all but rather the grant of an interest for a freehold estate. If this is thought to be a significant objection, the answer might be to let it take effect instead as an assignment of the grantor's freehold interest (in much the same way as a purported subletting for a term longer than the unexpired residue of the lessor's lease automatically takes effect as an assignment of that lease) with a right of re-entry for the grantor exercisable if and when the event occurs. In other cases, the parties will not have intended that, but will have omitted to make express provision for what is to happen if the event is delayed longer than expected, or never happens at all. Like category 3, the obvious remedy here would be an implied term if it is sufficiently clear what the parties intended, resorting to invalidity only if they have left the matter so unclear that any implied term would be imposing on them terms they never would have agreed.

5   Finally, there are those events which are predictable but not inevitable – in other words, we know in advance when, if at all, they will occur but there is just a chance that they may never happen at all. An example (it is difficult to think of many others) would be a lease to you 'until your aunt reaches the age of 45' (she may die before then). Such a lease is probably void under the *Prudential* test, although the problem is not so much one of certainty of duration as the possibility of (almost certainly unintended) perpetual duration. This is really just a simplified version of category 2, and an even more obvious candidate for the implied term solution. In nearly all cases it can be inferred that the parties intended either that the lease should last until the forty-fifth anniversary of the aunt's birth, or that it should end on her death if she dies under 45, and one would not expect it to be particularly difficult to decide which it was.

However, these categories are not distinguished in *Prudential*, and no consideration is given to the alternative methods by which the parties' intentions can be respected without violating the doctrine of estates.

Notes and Questions 17.2

Read *Prudential Assurance Co. Ltd* v. *London Residuary Body* [1992] 2 AC 386, either in full or as extracted at www.cambridge.org/propertylaw/, and consider the following:

1   In a periodic tenancy, is a postponement of the right to serve notice to quit for 99 years void or valid?

2   Would a licence to occupy for the duration of the war be effective? (See *Lace* v. *Chantler* [1944] KB 368.) What about a licence to occupy 'until average temperatures in England have become significantly affected by global warming'?

3   Does preserving the integrity of the system justify defeating the parties' intentions, if those intentions are clear?

4   One of the justifications given by Lord Templeman is that the object of the parties could be achieved by other means – for example, granting the lessee a 99-year lease terminable by the landlord on deciding to use the land for road-widening. Consider the adequacy of this alternative. Would any of the other alternatives suggested by Lord Templeman have effectuated the parties intentions entirely?

5   The House of Lords held that, although the lease was void, the tenant nevertheless held the land under a valid periodic tenancy. Explain why. What would have been the position if no rent had been payable during the period of the tenant's occupation? Consider why the courts adopt this device to avoid making the occupation retrospectively unlawful: see further section 17.3.1.6 below.

17.3.1.6.   Grant of possession not giving rise to fixed-term/periodic tenancy

Supposing I, an owner, grant you a right to possession of my land for a limited period: will you necessarily thereby acquire a lease, even if the certainty of duration rule is not satisfied?

The position in principle is clear. The answer must be yes, unless the transaction is such as to give you another recognised type of possessory property interest (we consider below what these interests might be). This is because, although possession is by its nature proprietary in the sense that it is enforceable against third parties, it is not of itself a free-standing property interest. It is the central ingredient of ownership, but the only way in which I, as owner, can transfer it to you is by granting you a known species of property interest which carries with it a right to possession. I am not free to grant you the right to possession on any terms I choose, but only on terms that give rise to a known species of property interest. Although there are suggestions to the contrary in recent cases (which we look at in detail below) we know from *Hill* v. *Tupper* (Extract 5.1 above) that this is true: property interests can only be subdivided in recognised ways.

There is of course another way in which you, as non-owner, can get possession from me: you can simply take it without my consent, by taking physical control of the land with the intention of excluding the whole world, including me. If you do not have that intention you are not in possession. But, even in that case, what you will acquire is a title to a known species of property interest (i.e. a possessory title to ownership, which will mature into an absolute title to ownership if and when my better title is extinguished by the Limitation Act 1980: see Chapters 7 and 10), not possession as a free-standing interest in itself.

In other words, in principle a person in possession of land must either have a possessory title to ownership (i.e. as an adverse possessor) or have a lease of the land, or have some other proprietary interest in the land which carries with it the right to possess it.

We have said that this is clear in principle, but it has to be said that this is not a view uniformly recognised by the courts. In order to assess the significance of these apparent departures from principle, however, it is first useful to enumerate the recognised ways in which possession can be split off from ownership in the case of land, apart from by the grant of a lease.

The list is not long: if you are in possession of land and you are not the absolute beneficial owner, or a trespasser with a possessory title to ownership, or a tenant, you will fall within one of the following categories:

1 *A legal mortgagee who has exercised his right to possession.* A legal mortgagee has an inherent right to possession of the mortgaged land. As we see in Chapter 18, this is because a legal mortgagee of land either has, or is deemed to have, a lease of the land.

2 *A mortgagor allowed to remain in possession by the mortgagee.* It is established law that an owner who has granted a legal mortgage but has been allowed to remain in occupation pending default is in possession. This is so whether he has been allowed to remain in possession at the will of the mortgagee or on contractually enforceable terms that the mortgagee will not exercise its right to possession until default. After some uncertainty, the courts concluded that, in such circumstances, the mortgagor does not have a merely personal right to occupy as against the mortgagee, nor is he a subtenant of the mortgagee (unless it is clear that this was what the parties intended). Instead, he has a *sui generis* possessory right, enforceable against third parties and enforceable against the mortgagee. See further Chapter 18.

3 *A pledgee.* If it is possible to have a pledge of land (which, as we see in Chapter 18, is not certain), then what the pledgee has is possession of the land and a right to remain in possession until performance of the obligation secured by the pledge. This is because this is what a pledge is – a delivery of possession of a thing as security for the payment of a debt or performance of some other obligation.

4 *A beneficiary under a private trust of land.* In a private trust of land, which necessarily involves ownership being split between trustee and beneficiary, a beneficiary in some circumstances has a right to possession enforceable against the trustee and the rest of the world (although capable of being overreached (and therefore not affect third parties) by certain transactions entered into by the trustee). So, although it is technically possible for a trustee of land to grant a beneficiary a lease of the land (or any other interest in it), it is also possible for a beneficiary to have a right to possession *qua* beneficiary as against the trustee – i.e. the right to possession can be attributable solely to the trustee–beneficiary relationship. As we noted in Chapter 7, this is not true of a public charitable trust (or a private purpose trust, although this is less likely to arise). In a public trust, the 'beneficiary' of the trust is the abstract purpose of the trust (e.g. to provide housing for homeless persons). Any land held by the trustees is held on trust to carry out that purpose, not on trust for those on whom the trustees choose to confer benefit (i.e. the homeless people they house). If therefore those people are given a right

to possession of the land enforceable against the trustees, this cannot be referable to any trustee–beneficiary relationship – it can only arise because the trustees have granted them some property interest such as a lease.

5   *A holder of statutory rights of occupation.* There are some statutory rights of occupation which are purely personal in that they are non-transmissible and automatically cease on death or change of status, but which are nevertheless enforceable against the whole world, including the owner. Examples include the statutory tenancy which arises after the expiry of a contractual tenancy protected by the Rent Acts, and the statutory rights of occupation conferred on spouses which originated in the Matrimonial Homes Act 1967, and is now in the Family Law Act 1996. The 'tolerated trespass' status considered in the next section should probably also be treated as coming within this category. There is no doubt that such occupiers are in possession of the land, and that their possession is solely attributable to their statutory rights (or, in the case of *Stirling* v. *Leadenhall Residential 2 Ltd* [2001] EWCA Civ 1011 to the court order permitting them to remain in possession, paying mesne profits as trespassers, pending execution of a possession warrant). In other words, the statutory or court-sanctioned status entitles them to a right of possession.

6   *Miscellaneous anomalous use rights.* In *Foster* v. *Warblington Urban District Council* [1906] 1 KB 648, CA, Fletcher Moulton LJ considered the juridical nature of an 'oyster laying' – the right to deposit oysters, caught elsewhere, in marked beds on land privately owned by someone else, in a place where oysters are not naturally found (the idea being to fatten the oysters for consumption). He concluded that it is a private property right, and that interference with the enjoyment of the right (in this case, by the local authority polluting the oysters with sewage, an event confirmed by a subsequent outbreak of typhoid fever among the guests at a mayoral banquet in Winchester who had eaten them) was therefore actionable as a nuisance or trespass. However, he and the other members of the Court of Appeal unanimously held that the control that the oyster merchant, the holder of the right, exercised over the oyster beds amounted to *de facto* possession of them, and that that of itself was sufficient to entitle him to bring an action in nuisance, whether or not he could prove he had lawful title to the beds, or had acquired title by adverse possession, or had some other proprietary right in them such as the 'oyster laying' posited by Fletcher Moulton LJ. It is implicit in Fletcher Moulton LJ's judgment that the oyster merchant's possession of the oyster beds could quite properly be attributable to the oyster laying – in other words, that his right to use the oyster beds for the particular purpose of depositing and fattening oysters carried with it a right to take a degree of control over the beds, in order to prevent interference with the oysters, which amounted to exclusive possession of the beds. Such a right to make a particular use of land which entitles the user to exclude all others, including the true owner, is anomalous (consider why it cannot amount to an easement or a profit à prendre), pre-dating the rigid classification of incorporeal hereditaments that we now have. There may well be other similar isolated survivors, but they have no great significance for present purposes.

So, if we leave aside this last anomalous category, what it comes down to is that a person in possession of land may be an absolute owner, a trespasser with a title to ownership good against the whole world except the absolute owner, a tenant, a mortgagee, a mortgagor, a pledgee, a beneficiary under a private trust, or a person with statutory occupation rights.

The position taken here is that this is an exhaustive list, with tenancy as the residual category. In other words, if I as an owner allow you to take or remain in *possession* of my land (which necessarily entails conferring on you a *right* to exclude me as well as the rest of the world) for anything less that a perpetual duration, and in law it does not amount to a grant to you of any of these other types of property interest, you will be a tenant. If the certainty of duration rule (or indeed formalities rules) prevent it from being a fixed-term tenancy, then it will take effect by operation of law as a tenancy at will terminable at will, or (once the concept of periodic tenancy had become accepted in the eighteenth century) a periodic tenancy terminable by due notice to quit, provided the court can infer that from periodic payments of rent. (See Simpson, *A History of the Land Law*, pp. 252–5, citing *Littleton on Tenures*, section 68 on tenancies at will, and quoting Blackstone, *Commentaries*, Book II, Chapter 9, section II.) We see this basic principle in operation in *Prudential* in the previous section: the tenancy until the land was required for road-widening was void because of uncertain duration, but a periodic tenancy was implied because the 'tenant' undoubtedly had been in possession paying a periodic rent.

The contrary view is that the list is not exhaustive, and that it is perfectly possible for you to be in possession of my land without your having any possessory property interest whatsoever. This view, which as we see below has attracted considerable judicial support (if not much by way of direct decision), appears to arise at least partly out of the lingering confusion between possession (the proprietary right to exclude the whole world including the owner) and exclusive occupation (the personal right to use the land and exclude the owner from beneficial use). Although the House of Lords decision in *Street* v. *Mountford* [1985] AC 809 went some way towards reaffirming the distinction between the two concepts (by reaffirming that possession, as opposed to occupation, is a necessary condition for a tenancy), the terminology used by Lord Templeman in his leading speech does not always clearly mark the distinction, and this has proved a fertile source of misunderstanding in subsequent cases.

There are four passages in his speech which have caused particular problems. In each of these he considers the possible interests that an occupier of residential accommodation might have. In three of them at the crucial point he uses the term 'possession' when the context suggests he means 'occupation', and in the fourth, although he uses the term 'occupation', in subsequent cases it has sometimes been assumed that he meant possession. Here are the four passages:

Passage 1

There can be no tenancy unless the occupier enjoys exclusive possession; but an occupier who enjoys exclusive *possession* [emphasis added] is not necessarily a tenant. He may be owner in fee simple, a trespasser, a mortgagee in possession, an object of charity or a service occupier. To constitute a tenancy the occupier must be granted exclusive possession for a fixed or periodic term certain in consideration of a premium or periodical payments. The grant may be express, or may be inferred where the owner accepts weekly or other periodic payments from the occupier.

Here he describes an owner in fee simple, a trespasser, a mortgagee in possession, an object of charity and a service occupier as all being in *possession* and not just in occupation. However, while this is true of the first three categories, as we have seen, it is certainly not true of the last two, and he himself makes this clear in the succeeding paragraphs. In relation to 'object of charity' he goes on to refer to cases in which it was held that there was no tenancy because there was no intention to create legal relations at all – cases involving what Lord Denning described in *Facchini* v. *Bryson* [1952] 1 TLR 1386 as 'a family arrangement, an act of friendship or generosity, or such like'. It goes without saying that, if there is no enforceable agreement between the parties, the occupier can have no *right* to exclude the grantor, just a personal permission to be there. Such a person is by definition not in possession, merely in occupation. As to 'service occupier', he makes it clear in the paragraphs immediately following the one just quoted that he does not regard service occupiers as having possession:

> Occupation by service occupier may be eliminated. A service occupier is a servant who occupies his master's premises in order to perform his duties as a servant. In those circumstances, the possession and occupation of the servant is treated as the possession and occupation of the master and the relationship of landlord and tenant is not created: see *Mayhew* v. *Suttle* (1854) 4 E&B 347; 119 ER 137. The test is whether the servant requires the premises he occupies in order the better to perform his duties as a servant:
>
> > Where the occupation is necessary for the performance of services, and the occupier is required to reside in the house in order to perform those services, the occupation being strictly ancillary to the performance of the duties which the occupier has to perform, the occupation is that of a servant.
>
> See Mellor J in *Smith* v. *Seghill Overseers* (1875) LR 10 QB 422 at 428.

This is clearly inconsistent with possession passing from master to servant, giving the servant a stake in the room entitling him to exclude the master. So, service occupiers are not tenants because they do not have possession. It is not correct to describe them as persons who have possession but are nevertheless not tenants.

Passage 2

Exclusive possession is of first importance in considering whether an occupier is a tenant: exclusive possession is not decisive because an occupier who enjoys exclusive *possession* [emphasis added] is not necessarily a tenant. The occupier may be a lodger or service occupier or fall within the other exceptional categories mentioned by Denning LJ in *Errington* v. *Errington* [i.e. 'the circumstances and conduct of the parties show that all that was intended was that the occupier should be granted a personal privilege with no interest in the land'].

Although all these categories are referred to as having possession not occupation, Lord Templeman has already explained that this is not the case for service occupiers, nor for the categories given by Denning LJ, which were cases where there was no intention to create legal relations at all. As to lodgers, Lord Templeman referred to them earlier as the paradigm residential occupier who does not have possession:

> In the case of residential accommodation there is no difficulty in deciding whether the grant confers exclusive possession. An occupier of residential accommodation at a rent for a term is either a lodger or a tenant. The occupier is a lodger if the landlord provides attendance or services which require the landlord or his servants to exercise unrestricted access to and use of the premises. A lodger is entitled to live in the premises but cannot call the place his own ... If, on the other hand, residential accommodation is granted for a term with exclusive possession, the landlord providing neither attendance nor services, the grant is a tenancy; any express reservation to the landlord of limited rights to enter and view the state of the premises and to repair and maintain the premises only serves to emphasise the fact that the grantee is entitled to exclusive possession and is a tenant.

Passage 3

In the following passage, it is clearest of all from the context that, although he uses the term 'possession', he means occupation:

> Sometimes it may be difficult to discover whether, on the true construction of an agreement, exclusive possession is conferred. Sometimes it may appear from the surrounding circumstances that there was no intention to create legal relationships. Sometimes it may appear from the surrounding circumstances that the right to exclusive possession is referable to a legal relationship other than a tenancy. Legal relationships to which the grant of exclusive *possession* might be referable *and which would or might negative the grant of an estate or interest in the land* [emphasis added] include occupancy under a contract for the sale of the land, occupancy pursuant to a contract of employment or occupancy referable to the holding of an office.

The words in italics confirm that the categories given here are intended to be (as indeed they are) examples of purely personal, non-proprietary rights. This is confirmed by the reference to occupancy under a contract for the sale of land. As we saw in section 17.3.1.1 above, a purchaser allowed into possession before completion and a tenant allowed into possession pending negotiations for a new or renewed lease have traditionally been classified as tenants at will or, sometimes, periodic tenants. It was only once such tenancies came to attract security of tenure that the courts had reason to doubt whether the parties intended to give the occupier proprietary rather than purely personal rights during the interim period. In appropriate cases, therefore, the courts have discerned a difference in the *nature and quality* of the rights granted by the owner, and accepted that, in order to avoid security of tenure, the grantor has elected to grant only the very limited right of personal occupation (so giving rise to a licence), rather than the more extensive rights over the land which would arise out of a grant of possession (and therefore the grant of a lease). There do not appear to be any cases prior to *Street* v. *Mountford* (and there are none cited there) where the courts have held that such an occupier can be in *possession* and yet not have a tenancy. In subsequent cases, however, this passage has been taken to be authority for that proposition.

Passage 4

The impression that the terms 'possession' and 'occupation' are being used indiscriminately in these three passages, as if they mean the same thing, is reinforced by the fourth passage, where a similar list of categories reappears, this time given as examples of a person in *occupation* who has no tenancy:

> In *Errington* v. *Errington* [a no intention to create legal relations case] and in the cases cited by Denning LJ there were exceptional circumstances which negatived the *prima facie* intention to create a tenancy, notwithstanding that the occupier enjoyed exclusive *occupation* [emphasis added]. The intention to create a tenancy was negatived if the parties did not intend to enter into legal relationships at all, or where the relationship between the parties was that of vendor and purchaser, master and service occupier, or where the owner, a requisitioning authority, had no power to grant a tenancy. These exceptional circumstances are not to be found in the present case, where there has been the lawful, independent and voluntary grant of exclusive possession for a term at a rent.

And see also, in the same vein, his criticism of the judge in *Murray, Bull & Co. Ltd* v. *Murray* [1953] 1 QB 211, which he said was wrongly decided, who he said 'failed to distinguish between, first, conduct which negatives an intention to create legal relationships, second, special circumstances which prevent exclusive *occupation* from creating a tenancy and, third, the professed intention of the parties'.

The way in which subsequent courts have tended to interpret these passages is exemplified in the Privy Council decision in *Ramnarace* v. *Lutchman* [2001] UKPC 25, where the issue was whether a person who went into rent-free occupation of land with the permission of the owner, on the understanding that she could live there until she could afford to buy the land, was a tenant at will or a licensee. Relying on *Street* v. *Mountford*, the Privy Council came to the entirely orthodox conclusion that she was a tenant because she had been granted possession, but it is clear from the judgment of Lord Millett that he regards *Street* v. *Mountford* as providing authority for the proposition that possession of land 'may be referable to a legal relationship other than a tenancy or to the absence of any legal relationship at all' (see paragraph 16 of his judgment). We consider the objections to this proposition in Notes and Questions 17.3 below.

There are other cases in which the courts have assumed that *Street* v. *Mountford* is authority for the proposition that a person in possession may be merely a licensee. It is not easy to understand what is meant by this proposition. If it is intended to mean that possession can be, and is here, a free-standing proprietary status, which in this instance happens to be held by someone who also holds a purely personal right to occupy (i.e. the licence), then the licence appears to be otiose: once a person has been granted a right to exclude all others, including the owner, for a period on terms (i.e. possession), what further role does the licence (a personal right to exclude the owner) have to play? So, the proposition that a person may have been granted possession of land as well as a licence to be on the land seems no different in content from the proposition that possession of land may be, and is here, granted as a free-standing proprietary interest – and, as we saw above, there are formidable *numerus clausus* objections to this.

If, on the other hand, the proposition that a person in possession of land may be a licensee is intended to mean that possession is in some sense an *ingredient* of the licence granted – i.e. you are granted a licence, by virtue of which you become entitled to possession of the land – we are left with an irreconcilable contradiction in terms.

By virtue of a licence, a grantee has a personal right to exclude the grantor but no right to be on the land or to exclude others which is enforceable against anyone other than the grantor (cf. the classic definition of a licence as that which 'properly passeth no interest nor alters or transfers property in any thing, but only makes an action lawful, without which it would have been unlawful': Vaughan CJ in *Thomas v. Sorrell* (1673) Vaugh 330 at 351). But possession is by definition an exclusive right to be on the land which *is* enforceable against everyone. If that is what you as a licensee hold, it is difficult to see how anyone could describe you as coming within the *Thomas v. Sorrell* definition of a licensee (and nearly as difficult to see how your position could possibly differ from that of a tenant).

Notes and Questions 17.3

Read *Ramnarace* v. *Lutchman* [2001] UKPC 25; [2001] 1 WLR 1651; [2002] 1 P&CR 28, either in full or as extracted at www.cambridge.org/propertylaw/, and consider the following:

1 At paragraph 16, Lord Millett appears to be saying that possession can be 'attributable' to proprietary interests in land which do not themselves confer a right to possession on the interest holder: 'a purchaser who is allowed into possession before completion and an occupier who remains in possession pending the exercise of an option each has in equity an immediate interest in the land to which his possession is ancillary. They are not tenants at will.' It is not entirely clear what this means. If you have a contractual right to purchase a fee simple, or an option to purchase which, once exercised, will mature into a contractual right to purchase, you *do* have an immediate equitable interest in the land, but it is not an interest which entitles you to take possession of the

land. It does not entitle you to take possession of the land now – your vendor is entitled to possession now, not you, and if you went into possession he would be entitled to mesne profits and an order for possession. Nor does it give you a present right to possession in the future: all it gives you is a present right to have in the future an interest in land which *will* entitle you to possession, and that is not at all the same thing. The position may well change once you have paid over the purchase price and complied with all the terms of the contract, if the date for completion has passed and title has still not been passed over to you. By that stage the vendor will hold the title on a bare trust for you, and you *will* have acquired an equitable interest in the land which entitles you to possession as against your trustee – i.e. the interest of an absolute owner in equity. The authority Lord Millett cites in support of this proposition is *Essex Plan Ltd* v. *Broadminster* (1988) 56 P&CR 353 at 356. In that case, in the passage referred to, Hoffmann J assumes that this novel proposition – possession can be 'ancillary and referable to' an equitable right to call for a legal estate – follows from Passages 3 and 4 of Lord Templeman's speech in *Street* v. *Mountford*. Is he right?

2 How does Mrs Ramnarace's situation differ from the situations Lord Millett was describing in paragraph 16?

3 For other instances where the court has held or suggested that a person may be in possession while remaining just a licensee, see, for example, *Westminster City Council* v. *Clarke* [1992] 2 AC 288, *Hounslow London Borough Council* v. *Twickenham Garden Developments Ltd* [1971] Ch 233 at 257 and *Manchester Airport plc* v. *Dutton* [2000] QB 133. In *Dutton*, the issue was whether the claimant could be said to be in possession for the purposes of bringing an action to evict trespassers, which does not necessarily raise the same considerations. Nevertheless, these cases lead Gray and Gray to conclude that '[i]n [more] recent years it has become established that possession, although one of the badges of a tenancy, is not necessarily denied to all kinds of licensee' (Gray and Gray, *Elements of Land Law* (3rd edn), p. 355).

17.3.1.7. The tolerated trespasser status

As we noted above, the courts have had considerable difficulty in categorising the status of tenants entering into possession during negotiations for a lease, or holding over after the end of their tenancy, particularly in cases where the category chosen would determine whether or not the tenant acquires statutory security of tenure. In order to avoid giving occupiers in such situations statutory protection that the courts considered unintended and inappropriate, the courts have variously categorised such arrangements as giving rise to tenancies at will or at sufferance, or as licences rather than as tenancies. In the case of secure tenancies granted under the Housing Act 1985, none of these avenues of escape is available, for reasons which will become apparent. In *Burrows* v. *Brent London Borough*

Council [1996] 1 WLR 1448 (also extracted at www.cambridge.org/propertylaw/), the House of Lords faced the difficulty that any forbearance by the landlord, allowing the tenant to remain after the landlord had succeeded in obtaining a court order bringing the tenancy to end for just cause (non-payment of rent, annoyance to neighbours etc.), would appear to give rise to a new tenancy or licence attracting security all over again, which in its turn could not be ended without repeating the whole procedure. In order to avoid this inconvenient result, the House of Lords came up with a new status for such occupiers – that of 'tolerated trespasser', described by Clarke LJ in *Pemberton* v. *Southwark London Borough Council* [2000] 1 WLR 1672, CA, as 'a recent, somewhat bizarre, addition to the dramatis personae of the law'. It might perhaps have been better (or at least have less potential to mislead) if they had opted instead for the rather less wide-ranging description used by Lord Jauncey at one point – 'a state of statutory limbo'. This was the approach taken by the courts at the beginning of the twentieth century, when they had to consider the juristic nature of the status of tenants given security of tenure under the emerging Rent Acts. The Acts permitted tenants (and their successors) to remain in possession after their tenancies had ended, under what was called a 'statutory tenancy'. The nature of the statutory tenancy initially caused the courts some difficulty: it was non-assignable, but binding on third parties and not terminable except on grounds specified by statute, and by processes laid down by statute. Eventually, after flirting with analyses drawing on tenancies at will, the court settled for the conclusion that the status was *sui generis* – a status of irremoveability conferred by statute.

In cases subsequent to *Burrows*, however, the courts have shown little inclination to keep the status of 'tolerated trespass' similarly confined. Immediately after *Burrows*, it might have been possible to argue that 'tolerated trespass' was similarly a *sui generis* status that could only arise out of that particular statutory leasehold relationship (see *Pemberton* v. *Southwark London Borough Council* [2000] 1 WLR 1672, CA, and *Lambeth London Borough Council* v. *Rogers* (2000) 32 HLR 361; [2000] 03 EG 127, CA, referred to in *Pemberton*). However, in *Stirling* v. *Leadenhall Residential 2 Ltd* [2001] 3 All ER 645; [2001] EWCA Civ 1011, the court found it to exist in a different context, simply by virtue of a court order permitting the retention of possession pending execution of a possession warrant, on payment of stated regular amounts by way of mesne profits.

What is clear from these subsequent cases is that the 'tolerated trespass' is not necessarily going to be a temporary short-lived state, bridging a short gap until the former tenant breaches the terms of the agreement and leaves, or something else happens which re-establishes him as a tenant. In *Pemberton*, the 'tolerated trespass' lasted for five years, during which all payments to be made by the tenant appeared to have been made promptly. So, during what may be an extended period like this, what precisely is the relationship between former tenant and former landlord? It is now established that the 'tenant' has exclusive possession as against the 'landlord', and is in possession with the landlord's permission (or perhaps acquiescence? – see

Stirling v. *Leadenhall*) rather than adversely, but that none of the terms of the former tenancy apply (*Pemberton*). This means the landlord can take no action against the 'tenant' for any breach of covenant, other than a failure to pay the sums agreed under the agreement, nor can the 'tenant' rely on any of the express or implied obligations of the landlord under the former tenancy, for example as to repair. Whatever rights and obligations they have towards each other therefore appear to arise from the fact that the 'tenant' has possession (and therefore, as it was held in *Pemberton*, can bring actions in nuisance against the 'landlord') and the fact that the premises remain the 'tenant's' home for the purposes of the Human Rights Act (see further *Pemberton*). The situation is further complicated, and the artificiality heightened, by the fact that, in the *Burrows*-type case, the 'tenant' (but not, it would seem, the 'landlord') can at any time apply to have the possession order discharged, and it seems likely that, if it does so at a time when the terms of the agreement have been complied with, the court will agree. Once this is done, the old secure tenancy will revive with retrospective effect, allowing the parties to take advantage of the former tenancy terms in respect of events that took place during the limbo period (see *Rogers*). 'Trespass' is not, therefore, a wholly satisfactory epithet.

Notes and Questions 17.4

Read *Burrows* v. *Brent London Borough Council* [1996] 1 WLR 1448; [1996] 4 All ER 577, either in full or as extracted at www.cambridge.org/propertylaw/, and consider the following:

1 Why, according to Lord Browne-Wilkinson, is a tenant holding over after the end of a secure tenancy in a different position from a tenant holding over after the end of any other type of tenancy?

2 Lord Browne-Wilkinson describes the secure tenancy as *sui generis*, and says decisions on other holding-over situations are not helpful here, and Lord Jauncey refers to the occupation as 'deriving' from the provisions of the 1985 Act, and refers to the Act as giving the court the power 'to create a state of statutory limbo'. Does this mean that the status of tolerated trespasser cannot arise in any circumstances other than following on after a secure tenancy?

3 Explain how the facts of this case differ from those in *Greenwich London Borough Council* v. *Regan* (1996) 28 HLR 469; (1996) 72 P&CR 507. What did the Court of Appeal in *Regan* decide was the status of the tenant in that particular case?

4 Explain how, according to Lord Browne-Wilkinson, a secure tenancy terminated by an immediate unconditional possession order can be revived *after* the date specified in the order as the date on which possession must be given up.

5 Lord Jauncey took the view that the wording of section 85 of the Housing Act 1985 itself supports the contention that a tenant against whom a possession order has been made might remain in possession in a capacity other than that of tenant: explain his argument, and consider its validity.

6 What were the absurdities that persuaded the Court of Appeal that the effect of the agreement was to grant Ms Burrows a new tenancy? Explain how they are avoided by the analysis adopted by the House of Lords, and examine the reasons given by Lord Browne-Wilkinson for his conclusion that Parliament could not have intended such an agreement to give rise to a new tenancy.

7 It was not argued in this case that the effect of the agreement was to create a licence, or a tenancy at will, or a tenancy at sufferance. Why not? If it had been argued, what arguments could have been put by Lord Browne-Wilkinson for saying that it did not fall within each of these categories?

8 Explain what, as a result of this decision, the difference is between a licence, a tenancy at will, a tenancy at sufferance, and the status of tolerated trespasser.

9 If a tolerated trespasser remains in possession as such for ten years, will he be entitled to apply to the Land Registry to be registered as proprietor as an adverse possessor? See section 11.2.2 above.

10 Lord Browne-Wilkinson said: 'the parties plainly did not intend to create a new tenancy or licence, but only to defer the execution of the order so long as Miss Burrows complied with the agreed conditions.' Is this more correctly categorisable as a fixed-term tenancy of uncertain duration?

11 Does a 'tolerated trespasser' have an interest in land? If so, what is it?

17.3.1.8. Non-proprietary leases?

At this point we need to return to a question posed in Chapter 10. Suppose I am in practical control of land but have no property interest in it, and I then purport to grant a lease of it to you. If you move in, take exclusive physical control of the land and pay me rent, do you acquire a lease of the land? In Chapter 10, we concluded that you would be precluded from having a tenancy because of the *nemo dat* rule, but that you would have a tenancy by estoppel. As we noted there, a tenancy by estoppel has two essential features. The first is that, even though there is no tenancy as far as the rest of the world is concerned, the purported grant is effective as between you and me, in the sense that I will be estopped from denying the existence of, or acting in any way inconsistent with the existence of, the tenancy. The second essential feature is that the estoppel can be fed, so that, if I subsequently acquire a sufficient interest in the land, your tenancy by estoppel will automatically be transformed into a real tenancy, enforceable against the whole world.

Now we must consider a variation on this situation. Suppose that the facts are identical, except that I am completely honest with you throughout. I tell you that I have no interest in the land which would enable me to grant you a lease, and when I hand over exclusive physical control to you I tell you that what I am granting to you is necessarily a licence, not a lease. What is your position then? At first sight, it might seem quite straightforward. Because of the *nemo dat* rule, you cannot have a lease. And, because both of us know that I am unable to grant you a lease, and I never pretended that that was what I was doing, there does not seem room for me to be estopped from denying it.

In *Bruton* v. *London & Quadrant Housing Trust* [1998] QB 834, CA, the Court of Appeal held that such a situation could not give rise to a tenancy (nor, for reasons which will be considered below, a tenancy by estoppel). However, the House of Lords ([2001] 1 AC 406) disagreed, and concluded unanimously that, although there was no tenancy by estoppel, there *was* a lease – but one which was not enforceable against third parties.

In order to appreciate the arguments that persuaded the House of Lords, it is necessary to look more closely at the factual context. Local authority landowners do not have the same powers to dispose of their land as absolute owners have. They are given specific statutory powers of disposition, and, if they purport to make a disposition that they have no power to make, the disposition will be void. Local authorities who own residential accommodation do have statutory powers to let it to residential occupiers. As a result of the decision in *Street* v. *Mountford* [1985] AC 809, if they do grant possession to residential occupiers, the grant will almost certainly be construed as a tenancy, even if it is called something else. Consequently, the occupier will be entitled to require the local authority to keep the property in repair under section 11 of the Landlord and Tenant Act 1985, and will also be a secure tenant and as such entitled to security of tenure under the Housing Act 1985 as amended. There are circumstances in which local authorities wish to avoid these consequences, and the *Bruton* case concerned a stratagem designed to enable them to do so.

The stratagem requires two steps to be taken. First, the local authority transfers occupation and control of the residential property to a body to whom it has no statutory power to dispose, in this case a housing trust. Whatever the terms of the transfer, so the argument goes, it cannot confer any proprietary interest on the housing trust because, if it did, that would be an *ultra vires* disposition and therefore void. The transfer will, however, put the housing trust in unchallengeable factual control of the property, and therefore put it in a position to take the second step, which is for it to grant exclusive occupation of the property to a residential occupier. The housing trust is then able to argue that, whatever the terms of the agreement it makes with the residential occupier, it cannot amount to a tenancy because of the *nemo dat* rule.

The policy issue confronting the House of Lords was therefore whether a local authority and a housing trust, each of which had the power and the capacity to grant occupiers tenancies of houses – which, if granted, would have had the inevitable consequence of making the grantor liable for repair – were able to avoid that consequence by structuring the transaction in this way. The House of Lords held that they could not do so, but only by adopting an analysis which involved acceptance of the principle that a lease need not necessarily be proprietary.

Their reasons for doing so, and the reasons which persuaded Millett LJ to come to the opposite conclusion in the Court of Appeal, are given in the following extracts from the judgments. The question of whether there are alternative analyses that might have led to the same conclusion as that reached by the House of Lords, but doing less violence to conventional property law principles, is considered subsequently.

Meanwhile, however, the conclusion appears to be that yes, according to the House of Lords (or, more accurately, as a result of their decision: see *Milmo* v. *Carreras* [1946] KB 306, CA, extracted at www.cambridge.org/propertylaw/) there is such a thing as a non-proprietary lease. It comes into operation whenever the *nemo dat* rule precludes the grant of a proprietary lease, provided that the grantor makes no secret of his lack of capacity (if he did, it would be a tenancy by estoppel) and the intention of both grantor and grantee is that the grantee should have the same rights in the land as he would have if he did have a lease.

Notes and Questions 17.5

Read *Bruton* v. *London & Quadrant Housing Trust* both in the Court of Appeal ([1998] QB 834; [1998] 3 WLR 438; [1997] 4 All ER 970) and in the House of Lords ([2000] 1 AC 406; [1999] 3 WLR 150; [1999] 3 All ER 481), and *Milmo* v. *Carreras* [1946] KB 306, CA, either in full or as extracted at www.cambridge.org/propertylaw/, and consider the following:

1   Why was the fact that 'the trust was a responsible landlord performing socially valuable functions' held not to be 'an exceptional circumstance', rendering Mr Bruton a licensee rather than a tenant? Should it have been?

2   By the time the case reached the House of Lords, how long had Mr Bruton been living in the flat? In the circumstances that had arisen, who should have been responsible for repairing the flat?

3   Is the decision of the House of Lords that Mr Bruton *has* a lease of the flat, or that he is to be treated for the purposes of the Landlord and Tenant Act 1985 as if he has a lease of the flat?

4   According to Lord Hoffmann, is Mr Bruton's 'lease' enforceable against third parties? If not, is it a property interest or is it an interest personal to Mr Bruton?

5   Explain the difference between lack of *capacity* to grant a lease and lack of *title*. Why, according to Millett LJ, does lack of capacity prevent a tenancy by estoppel

from arising, whereas lack of title does not? In this case, the council lacked capacity, whereas the trust lacked title. Why then, according to Millett LJ, did the agreement between the trust and Mr Bruton not give rise to a tenancy by estoppel? (See further section 10.5.5.3 above.)

6   How does this non-proprietary lease differ from a tenancy by estoppel? If, during the course of the 'lease', the grantor acquires a sufficient proprietary interest, will the lease automatically become proprietary?

7   There are other possible analyses of the situation in *Bruton* which would have allowed the House of Lords to avoid the conclusion that Mr Bruton had a non-proprietary lease. Consider the following:

a.   Could it have been argued that, even if Mr Bruton was only a licensee, he still had a 'lease' for the purposes of section 11 of the Landlord and Tenant Act 1985, and therefore the housing trust was bound by the statutory duty to repair? Some public-sector licences come within the definition of 'secure tenancy' under the Housing Act 1985 as amended (see section 19(3)) and consequently the licensee is entitled to the limited degree of security of tenure conferred by that Act. There are some very specific detailed exclusions from the status of secure tenancy, including some (but not all) lettings/licences to homeless persons and students, but it is not clear from the facts whether any of these exceptions would have applied here. Assuming none of them applied, it is at least arguable that Mr Bruton was a secure tenant of the housing trust: the relevant wording of the Housing Act 1985 as amended does not appear to exclude the possibility that the 'landlord' of a secure tenancy may be a public sector body which lacks the capacity and/or title to grant a lease (see sections 79 and 80). Since 'lease' in section 11 of the Landlord and Tenant Act 1985 (defined in section 17 of the Act) clearly applies to tenancies which are 'secure tenancies', should it not apply also to licences which are 'secure tenancies'? There seems no reason in principle why the grantors of one should have different repairing obligations from the grantors of the other.

b.   Alternatively, could it be argued that Mr Bruton had a lease which was granted to him by *the council* (which did have capacity and title to do so), acting by its agent, the housing trust, and that therefore the council had a statutory duty to repair under section 11 of the Landlord and Tenant Act 1985? Whatever the agreement between the council and the housing trust actually said, the council authorised the housing trust to give occupiers of the premises a degree of control over the premises which amounted in law to possession. In other words, even though the agreement purported to prohibit the housing trust from granting leases, its sole purpose was to authorise the trust to grant on the council's behalf rights to residential occupiers which would in law amount to leases.

c.   Another possible analysis is to distinguish possession acquired as a matter of fact, which does not give rise to a lease, from possession granted by a person with capacity to an owner, which does. Mr Bruton can be said to have acquired possession of the house by moving in and establishing the requisite degree of physical control over it, with the intention of excluding all others, with the connivance of the person who had *de facto* physical control of the house, although no title to it. On this analysis, possession is not *granted* to Mr Bruton by anyone, so he does not have a lease and is not entitled to rely on section 11 of the Landlord and Tenant Act 1985. By virtue of being in possession, he has a better right to possession than anyone other than the council, which has not granted away the right to possession that it has by virtue of being fee simple owner. The council has, however, in effect contractually bound itself to the trust, which has in turn contractually bound itself to Mr Bruton, that its better right to possession will not be asserted against a person let into possession by the trust on agreed terms. Whether this is something that could be relied on by Mr Bruton as a defence to a possession action brought by the council is another matter.

8   Consider what effect, if any, the decision of the House of Lords in *Bruton* has on what was said in *Milmo* about the relationship created by the contract made between the tenant and the intended subtenant. Would Milmo have succeeded in obtaining a possession order against Carreras? Would Milmo be liable to Carreras for repairs under section 11 of the Landlord and Tenant Act 1985?

17.3.2. Alienability

17.3.2.1.   Inherent alienability

A lease is a property interest, and for present purposes this has several important consequences.

Alienability of tenant's interest

The first is that the lease itself – i.e. the tenant's interest – is inherently alienable. Subject to any contractually agreed restriction, the tenant is free to assign the lease without obtaining the consent of, or even informing, the landlord. And, if the tenant dies or goes bankrupt, the lease is unaffected – it simply passes by operation of law on to whoever becomes entitled to the tenant's property under the rules considered in Chapter 8. The precise effect that assignment of the lease has on the enforceability of the terms of the lease, which is complicated, is summarised below, but the position in principle is that, as the lease passes from one person to another, whether by assignment or by operation of law, the person for the time being holding the lease steps into the shoes of the original tenant, becoming entitled to possession of the land on the same terms as those originally agreed between the original contracting parties.

Subleases and other derivative interests granted by the tenant

The second consequence of the proprietary status of a lease is that the tenant is free to grant derivative property interests (including, importantly, mortgages, charges and subleases) out of its lease without reference to the landlord, again subject to any contractual agreement to the contrary. A sublease is essentially a sub-contracting of the right to possession to a third person for a period which is less than the tenant's term (if it is the same or longer, it takes effect as an outright assignment of the tenant's lease: *Milmo* v. *Carreras* [1946] KB 306, CA, above). A subletting does not operate in the same way as an assignment: in a subletting the tenant is not disposing of its interest to the subtenant but carving a lesser interest out of it. The subtenant does not therefore step into the tenant's shoes as an assignee does, but takes possession from him on terms agreed between the two of them, which may well be different from the terms contained in the headlease. Consequently, there is no direct relationship between head landlord and subtenant: the intermediate tenant remains liable to the head landlord to observe the terms of the headlease, and simultaneously, while the subtenancy continues, the subtenant is liable to the intermediate tenant to observe the terms of the sublease.

Effect of termination of lease on derivative interests

In principle, since derivative interests such as subleases and mortgages and charges of the lease are carved out of the lease, they will automatically be extinguished when the lease ends. This is not always a just or convenient result, particularly where the tenant ends the tenancy voluntarily and/or prematurely by surrender, disclaimer or serving notice to quit, or loses it by forfeiture. The courts have a variety of statutory and equitable jurisdictions which enable them to grant relief in some form or another to the derivative interest holder in some but not all of these cases: for details reference should be made to standard landlord and tenant textbooks.

Alienability of landlord's interest

Another consequence of the proprietary status of the lease is that it is enforceable against third parties, in particular against any person to whom the landlord assigns her interest. This leaves the landlord free to assign her interest at any time to whomever she wants without reference to the tenant (again, subject to any agreement to the contrary). The assignment will have no effect on the validity or enforceability of the lease (assuming any necessary registration requirements have been satisfied), and, subject to the complications noted below, the assignee will step into the assignor's shoes as landlord under the lease. The same applies on any assignment of the landlord's interest by operation of law.

Concurrent leases and other derivative interests granted by the landlord

The landlord's interest is, necessarily, one that carries with it the right to possession for a period which is longer than that which has been granted to the tenant – usually the freehold interest in the land. This interest is an interest which is reversionary on the lease, i.e. the right to possession will revert to the landlord when the lease ends. There is no reason why the landlord should not grant derivative interests, such as mortgages or charges or easements, out of this reversionary interest (in principle not binding on the tenant, although this may be affected by enforceability rules: see Chapters 14 and 15 above). It may even grant another lease of the same land to another person out of the reversion, with the intention that this second lease, which may be shorter or longer than the first lease, will run concurrently with the first lease. This second lease (called a concurrent lease or lease of the reversion) cannot grant the tenant a better right to possession than that already granted to the first tenant (although there may be exceptional circumstances where registration rules could make this happen: see Chapters 14 and 15 above). What it does do is to, in effect, give rise to a temporary loan of the landlord's reversion to the second tenant for the period when the two leases overlap. The relationship that this creates between the landlord, the first tenant and the second tenant helps explain why anyone would want to do this. If I grant you a lease of my flat for five years from 1 January 2002 at a rent of £10,000 a year, with a covenant by me to carry out repairs to the flat, and then grant my brother another lease of the flat from 1 January 2003 for two years at a rent of £6,000 a year, the effect will be that, for the period of my brother's lease, he will step into my shoes as your landlord under your lease. In other words, he will be entitled to collect and keep for himself your rent of £10,000 a year for those two years, and he will also be liable to you for carrying out whatever repairs are needed during that time. During that two-year period the relationship between you and me will be in abeyance – I have effectively sub-contracted all the rights and liabilities attaching to it to my brother. The relationship between me and my brother during that time will be governed by the terms of the two-year lease I granted him – i.e. he will have to pay me £6,000 a year and comply with whatever other terms we agreed in that lease. If the lease I had granted him was for a period expiring *after* the end of your lease – say from 1 January 2003 until 31 December 2010 – the effect would be the same except that, when your lease ended in 31 December 2006, he would become entitled to possession of the flat, continuing to pay me the £6,000 a year under his lease until it ended in 2010. Concurrent leases are sometimes created deliberately for commercial reasons, but they can also be ordered by the court under the Landlord and Tenant (Covenants) Act 1995 (although in those circumstances they are called overriding leases: see below), and even arise inadvertently (see, for example, *Fuller* v. *Judy Properties Ltd* (1992) 64 P&CR 176, CA).

17.3.2.2. Restrictions on alienability

The original landlord and tenant can, and frequently do, agree contractual restrictions on the tenant's right to assign or sublet. Contractual restrictions on the landlord's right to alienate are equally possible in principle but unusual in practice. Contractual restrictions on the tenant's alienation rights are more common in leases at a full rent, less so in long residential leases granted at a low rent and for a premium (consider why). It is important to appreciate that such restrictions, whether imposed on the landlord or on the tenant, are effective in contract only – they cannot invalidate any assignment or subletting actually made, even if made in breach of contract. The breach of contract will of course be actionable by the other party.

Some statutory security of tenure regimes also impose restrictions on tenants' alienation rights, either directly (see, for example, sections 91–93 of the Housing

Act 1985, applicable to public sector residential tenancies which qualify as secure tenancies) or indirectly, whether by giving holding-over tenants purely personal rights not to be removed (as under the Rent Acts regime which is now being phased out, under which tenants acquired after the expiration of their contractual tenancies a 'protected tenancy', described by the courts as a mere 'status of irremoveability': *Keeves* v. *Dean* [1924] 1 KB 685) or by making the security of tenure depend, in effect, on the tenant's continuing to occupy the premises for its own purposes after the end of the contractual term (e.g. under Part II of the Landlord and Tenant Act 1954, applicable to business tenants).

17.3.2.3.   Statutory control of contractual restrictions

A landlord's freedom to restrict the tenant's right to alienate by imposing contractual restraints has long been restricted both by market forces and by statute. The basic statutory position (which at first sight looks odd) is that *absolute* prohibitions against alienation are valid, whereas *qualified* ones – that the tenant may not alienate without the consent of the landlord – are automatically subject to a proviso that the landlord may not unreasonably withhold consent (section 19(1)(a) of the Landlord and Tenant Act 1927). It leaves the landlord with only three options: he can remove the tenant's right to alienate altogether; he can impose no restraints whatsoever, leaving the tenant to do whatever it wants; or he can allow the tenant to alienate after obtaining his consent, which he may not unreasonably withhold. In most cases, it seems that market forces compel him to choose either the second or third option: absolute prohibitions against alienation are rarely found, either in commercial or in residential leases of any significant duration. This may not explain why section 19(1) omitted to regulate or invalidate them in the first place, but it probably does explain why the anomaly has not subsequently been removed.

This leaves landlords with limited room for manoeuvre. The second option – imposing no restrictions at all on the tenant's inherent alienation rights – may be appropriate in situations where the identity and financial standing of the person holding the lease is relatively unimportant (for example, long residential leases granted at a premium and a nominal rent, where restrictions are rarely imposed), or where the tenant has invested heavily in the premises and demands a fully marketable property interest (as in building leases, where restrictions are actually prohibited by statute except during the last seven years of the term: see section 19(1)(b) of the Landlord and Tenant Act 1927. In other cases, where landlords need or want more control, they are required to accept the statutory limitation that their consent to any application by the tenant to assign or sublet may not be unreasonably withheld (nor, since the Landlord and Tenant Act 1988 came into force, unreasonably delayed). This limitation has been strictly construed by the courts, who have insisted that the reasons on which the landlord's decision is based must be related to that particular lease and that particular landlord–tenant relationship (see Balcombe LJ in *International Drilling Fluids Ltd* v. *Louisville Investments (Uxbridge) Ltd* [1986] Ch 513 at 519, Extract 17.2 below) and that the reasonableness of the decision must be assessed by reference to objective criteria and not by reference to any pre-ordained standards set by the landlord (*Re Smith's Lease* [1951] 1 All ER 346). This insistence that landlords must make objectively justifiable decisions has been further reinforced by section 1(6) of the Landlord and Tenant Act 1988 which has reversed the burden of proof, so that the onus is now on the landlord to prove that its response to a tenant's application to assign or sublet was both reasonable and prompt, although subsequently somewhat eroded for landlords of commercial premises by the Landlord and Tenant (Covenants) Act 1995. As a recompense for losing their right to insist that tenants who have assigned their interests in the lease should nevertheless remain liable for the rent for the rest of the term of the lease, landlords of non-residential leases can now lay down in advance specific criteria for 'reasonableness': section 22 of the Landlord and Tenant (Covenants) Act 1995, adding provisions of extraordinary complexity to section 19 of the Landlord and Tenant Act 1927.

Extract 17.2   *International Drilling Fluids Ltd* v. *Louisville Investments (Uxbridge) Ltd* [1986] Ch 513 at 519

BALCOMBE LJ: . . . From the authorities I deduce the following propositions of law:

1   The purpose of a covenant against assignment without the consent of the landlord, such consent not to be unreasonably withheld, is to protect the lessor from having his premises used or occupied in an undesirable way, or by an undesirable tenant or assignee: *per* A. L. Smith LJ in *Bates* v. *Donaldson* [1896] 2 QB 241, 247, approved by all the members of the Court of Appeal in *Houlder Brothers & Co. Ltd* v. *Gibbs* [1925] Ch 575.
2   As a corollary to the first proposition, a landlord is not entitled to refuse his consent to an assignment on grounds which have nothing whatever to do with the relationship of landlord and tenant in regard to the subject-matter of the lease.
3   The onus of proving that consent has been unreasonably withheld is on the tenant [now reversed by section 1(6) of the Landlord and Tenant Act 1988].
4   It is not necessary for the landlord to prove that the conclusions which led him to refuse consent were justified, if they were conclusions which might be reached by a reasonable man in the circumstances: *Pimms Ltd* v. *Tallow Chandlers Co.* [1964] 2 QB 547, 564.
5   It may be reasonable for the landlord to refuse his consent to an assignment on the ground of the purpose for which the proposed assignee intends to use the premises, even though that purpose is not forbidden by the lease: see *Bates* v. *Donaldson* [1896] 2 QB 241, 244.
6   There is a divergence of authority on the question, in considering whether the landlord's refusal of consent is reasonable, whether it is permissible to have regard to the consequences to the tenant if consent to the proposed assignment is withheld.
7   Subject to the propositions set out above, it is in each case a question of fact, depending upon all the circumstances, whether the landlord's consent to an assignment is being unreasonably withheld.

Notes and Questions 17.6

1 In *Mount Eden Land Ltd* v. *Straudley Investments Ltd* (1996) 74 P&CR 306 at
   310, CA, Phillips LJ approved Balcombe LJ's propositions and said that he
   would add to them that it would normally be reasonable for a landlord to refuse
   consent or impose conditions on a grant of consent in order to prevent his
   rights under the lease being prejudiced, but not in order to improve or enhance
   those rights. Approval of the Balcombe propositions was also given by the
   House of Lords in *Ashworth Frazer Ltd* v. *Gloucester City Council* [2001] 1 WLR
   2180.

2 Despite Balcombe LJ's conclusion that reasonableness is a question of fact in
   every case, the question of the reasonableness of a landlord's decision has
   continued to attract considerable litigation: for examples of what has and has
   not been considered by the courts to be reasonable, see Farrand and Clarke,
   Emmet and Farrand on Title, paragraphs 26.156–26.161.

17.3.3.   Effect of alienation on enforceability

17.3.3.1.   Introduction: the basic principle

We said at the beginning of this chapter that the rights and obligations of the
landlord and tenant under a lease derive partly from the nature of their proprietary
relationship and partly from the terms of the contract made between the original
parties. In this section, we look at how enforcement of the terms of the lease is
affected by either or both of the original parties assigning their interest.

***Automatic transmission of benefit and burden of proprietary terms: the privity of
estate principle***

The basic principle is that which applies to all property interests which involve a
continuing relationship between grantor and grantee: whoever acquires the respective property interests of the grantor and of the grantee automatically becomes
bound by, and entitled to the benefit of, all the terms which bound the original
grantor and grantee, in so far as they relate to that interest. This applies not only to
those terms that arise out of the inherent nature of the proprietary relationship
created, but also to any additional terms contractually agreed between the original
grantor and grantee which relate to that property interest. This is traditionally
termed the privity of estate principle. In the case of a lease, it means that all the
terms of the lease originally enforceable by and against the original tenant and
landlord are *prima facie* enforceable by and against whoever happens to hold
the lease and the landlord's reversionary interest at the relevant time: assignees
of the original landlord and the original tenant simply step into the shoes of
their predecessors. In so far as it relates to leases, this automatic transmission
principle is now enshrined in section 3 of the Landlord and Tenant (Covenants)
Act 1995.

Post-assignment liability: the privity of contract principle

In the case of leases the picture is complicated by an additional factor. This is traditionally termed the 'privity of contract principle'. Where this principle applies (and its scope has been curtailed, although not removed altogether, by the Landlord and Tenant (Covenants) Act 1995), the original contracting parties remain *contractually* liable for compliance with the terms of the lease even after they have parted with their interest under the lease. However, the right to *enforce* this contractual liability does not remain with the other original contracting party but instead passes to whoever acquires *their* property interest. In other words, where this principle applies, even after assigning all interest in the premises, the original landlord can be sued in contract for any breach of any of the landlord's obligations under the lease by whoever happens for the time being to hold the tenant's interest, and the original tenant can be sued post-assignment by whoever happens to hold the landlord's interest.

Combined effect of automatic transmission of benefit and burden and post-assignment liability

Before Parliament intervened to curtail the operation of the privity of contract principle in 1995, the combined effect of these two principles was this:

1 only the current holders of the landlord's and tenant's interests were entitled to the benefit of the terms of the lease, and only they could enforce the terms of the lease; but
2 they could enforce the terms of the lease not only against each other but also against the original parties to the lease.

This remains the picture after the 1995 Act, except that the circumstances in which post-assignment liability can arise are now limited. In the following sections we look at all this in more detail.

17.3.3.2.   Non-proprietary terms

As a matter of general property principle, when one person grants a property interest to another, the terms they agree between themselves only acquire proprietary status (i.e. become enforceable by and against their successors) in so far as they relate to the property interest granted. Suppose you and I are neighbours, and we agree that you can have a right of way over my drive to reach the road from your garden, for a fee simple duration, provided you give me weekly piano lessons. Even if I grant you the easement by deed and record the piano lessons in the deed as the consideration for the grant, the provision about piano lessons will not become a term of the easement. So, if you and I subsequently sell our houses, your buyer will be entitled to the right of way over my drive, but will not be required to give me or my buyer piano lessons. The obligation to provide piano lessons is personal to you and me.

This is just as true of leases as it is of any other property interest. In the past, it has not always been easy to tell whether a particular term in a lease was purely personal, or whether it was intended to have proprietary effect so that it would be enforceable between successors as well as between the original parties. The test used to be whether the term 'had reference to the subject-matter of the lease' (see sections 141 and 142 of the Law of Property Act 1925) which was taken to mean the same as 'touch and concern the land'. This test, which attracted considerable and not easily reconcilable case law, still applies to leases granted before 1 January 1996. However, for leases granted after that date, the position has now been simplified by the Landlord and Tenant (Covenants) Act 1995. Section 3(6) of the 1995 Act makes *all* landlord covenants and tenant covenants enforceable by and against successors *except* those 'which (in whatever terms) [are] expressed to be personal to any person' (section 3(6)(a), reinforced by section 2(1)(a), which expressly provides that the Act applies to all landlord covenants and tenant covenants 'whether or not the covenant has reference to the subject-matter of the tenancy'). It follows that *any* term of a lease can now be made personal to the original parties and not affect successors in title, however closely related to the subject-matter of the lease.

Whether the converse is also true – that any term, however *unrelated* to the lease, can be made to have proprietary effect – is not so clear. On the face of it, this is what the Act seems to say. Section 3 expressly states that the benefit and burden of *all* 'landlord covenants' and 'tenant covenants' pass automatically, unless they are expressed to be personal. 'Landlord covenant' and 'tenant covenant' are given the broadest possible definitions in section 28(1): 'covenant' is defined to include 'term, condition and obligation', and a landlord/tenant covenant is defined as a 'covenant falling to be complied with by' the landlord/tenant. And it is implicit in the wording of section 2(1)(a) just quoted that landlord and tenant covenants may have *no* 'reference to the subject-matter' of the lease. However, this does not sit easily with fundamental property principles, which would not normally allow contracting parties to give proprietary effect to an inherently personal obligation – for example, our piano lesson arrangement – by the simple expedient of including it in a totally unrelated lease agreement (see *BHP Petroleum Great Britain Ltd* v. *Chesterfield Properties Ltd* [2002] 2 WLR 672, CA).

17.3.3.3.   Derivative interest holders

Derivative interest holders – most importantly for present purposes, subtenants – have an interest carved out of the tenant's interest, which is in turn carved out of the lessor's interest. However, they do not themselves become subject to or entitled to the benefit of any of the terms of the lease. In the traditional terminology, they are not privy to the estate created by the grant of the lease. In practical terms, this means that a subtenant has no right to possession as against the landlord (although the landlord is nevertheless not entitled to possession as against the subtenant during the lease: consider why) and the tenant's covenants in the lease to pay rent, carry out repairs etc. are not enforceable by the landlord against the subtenant.

Equally, the tenant's rights and liabilities as against the landlord remain wholly unaffected by any sublease the tenant may have granted. So, if a ten-year lease includes a covenant by the tenant not to cause a nuisance on the premises, and the tenant sublets for most of the term with the knowledge and consent of the landlord to a subtenant who causes a nuisance, the landlord cannot sue the subtenant but can sue the tenant. This applies whether the tenant is the original tenant or an assignee: the tenant for the time being who is liable to the landlord because of the privity of estate principle remains liable despite having sublet.

17.3.3.4.   Statutory restriction of post-assignment liability

As a result of the Landlord and Tenant (Covenants) Act 1995, no tenant can be made liable for breaches of covenant committed after he has assigned the lease, provided the assignment was lawful (i.e. not made in breach of covenant). The only exception is that, in some circumstances, a tenant who assigns the lease can be made to guarantee the liabilities of his immediate successor, by entering into an 'authorised guarantee agreement'. As far as landlords are concerned, they are not automatically released from liability on assignment as tenants are, but they can apply for release (initially to the tenant, and then to the court if the tenant refuses). For details of the operation of the statutory scheme, and an examination of its tortuous genesis and the difficulties it was designed to resolve, see Law Commission, *Landlord and Tenant Law: Privity of Contract and Estate* (Law Commission Report No. 174, 1988) and Clarke, 'Property Law'.

17.4. Bailment

17.4.1. Essential features of bailment

The essential prerequisite for a bailment relationship is that goods should be in the possession of someone who is not their owner, on terms that the owner is entitled to have the goods back (the very same ones, not substitutes or the money equivalent). Bailment applied only to goods, not to land or to intangibles.

When goods are temporarily passed on by their owner to someone else, it is important to establish whether the transferor is transferring *ownership* to the transferee but with the intention that the transferee will hold on trust for the transferor (so creating a trust relationship), or whether the transferor is transferring the full beneficial owner-ship but on the understanding that the transferee will repay to the transferor the value of them (a debt relationship), or whether the transferor is merely transferring *possession* and so creating a bailment relationship. Consider the case of cash taken from a prisoner when she is imprisoned. The cash is handed over to the prison governor and the prisoner is entitled to get it back when she is released. But precisely what she will get back depends on whether the governor acquires ownership of the cash but on terms that he holds it on trust for her (in which case he must invest it for her benefit and account to her for the capital and interest when the trust ends on her release), or acquires absolute ownership but then owes her that amount to be repaid on release (in which case she should be repaid precisely the same amount, with interest if applicable, even if the cash has been lost or was poorly invested), or acquires only possession, in which case he must return the very notes and coins to her (to her disadvantage if the value of the currency has fallen during her sentence). In *Duggan* v. *Governor of Full Sutton Prison* [2004] EWCA Civ 78, it was held that the governor acquired full beneficial ownership of the cash – unsurprisingly, since that meant that his duty to repay was on terms set by the statutory provisions entitling him to take it in the first place, which did not require the payment of interest. The possibility that he might be holding as bailee was not, however, canvassed (consider why).

17.4.2.   Categories of bailment

The classic categorisation of bailments was given by Holt CJ in *Coggs* v. *Bernard* (1703) 2 Ld Ray 909; 91 ER 25. The issue in the case was whether Bernard, the defendant, was liable to Coggs for loss caused when a cask of Coggs' brandy broke open while being transported by Bernard. At Coggs' request, Bernard took several hogsheads of brandy belonging to Coggs from one cellar to another. In the process, one of the casks was 'staved' and several gallons of brandy were spilt. We are not told why Bernard carried out this service for Coggs, except that he was not paid to do so nor was he a common (i.e. professional) porter or carrier, and we are not told how the damage occurred except that Bernard 'managed them so negligently, that for want of care in him' the damage was caused. It was decided that Bernard was liable. In considering why this should be the case, Holt CJ distinguished six types of bailment:

> The first sort of bailment is, a bare naked bailment of goods, delivered by one man to another to keep for the use of the bailor; and this I call a depositum ... The second sort is, when goods or chattels that are useful, are lent to a friend gratis, to be used by him; and this is called commodatum, because the thing is to be restored in specie. The third sort is, when goods are left with the bailee to be used by him for hire; this is called locatio et conductio, and the lender is called locator, and the borrower conductor. The fourth sort is, when goods or chattels are delivered to another as a pawn, to be a security to him for money borrowed of him by the bailor; and this is called in Latin vadium, and in English a pawn or a pledge. The fifth sort is when goods or chattels are delivered to be carried, or something is to be done about them for a reward to be paid by the person who delivers them to the bailee, who is to do the thing about them. The sixth sort is when there is a delivery of goods or chattels to somebody, who is to carry them, or do something about them gratis, without any reward for such his work or carriage, which is this present case.

For more than two centuries after *Coggs* v. *Bernard*, it remained uncertain how far beyond these categories bailment extends. As a consequence of the Privy Council decision in *The Pioneer Container* [1994] 2 AC 324 (discussed in Notes and Questions 17.7 below), however, it can now be taken that a bailment relationship arises whenever a person voluntarily takes the goods of another into his possession. This applies even if the owner was unaware of the fact or objected to possession being taken, as appears from *Mitchell* v. *Ealing London Borough Council* [1979] QB 1 and *Sutcliffe* v. *Chief Constable of West Yorkshire* (discussed below). Consequently, it appears settled that finders and thieves are bailees.

The only other qualification is that a bailment relationship cannot arise between the owner and the possessor of an object if the possessor is unaware of the existence of the owner, either because he mistakenly believes that he himself is the owner, so I am not your bailee if I pick up your pen from the floor believing it to be mine, at least until I realise my mistake, although see *AVX Ltd* v. *EGM Solders Ltd, The Times,* 7 July 1982 (extracted at www.cambridge.org/propertylaw/), or because he mistakenly believes someone else is the owner. This latter point was established by the Court of Appeal in *Marcq* v. *Christie Manson & Woods Ltd* [2003] EWCA Civ 731, where it was said that Christies could not be the bailee of the true owner of a painting which was in their possession because it was handed to them by a thief who had stolen it from the true owner and wanted Christies to auction it for him.

17.4.3.   Characteristics of bailment

We have already (at the beginning of this chapter) noted the significant characteristics of bailment, in particular that possession as a bailee does not necessarily entitle the bailee to make use of the goods for his own benefit (in only two of the six *Coggs* v. *Bernard* categories – loan and hire – is the bailee entitled to use the goods himself). The precise rights conferred on the bailee in other cases depend on the category.

Also, it is possible to have a consensual bailment that is not enforceable in contract. In three of the six *Coggs* v. *Bernard* categories there will usually be no contract because there is no consideration (gratuitous custody, loan, and carriage of or performance of some service on goods). The agreed terms of these relationships are nevertheless enforceable. It is also clear that bailment relationships can give rise to rights and obligations between bailor and bailee even in non-consensual bailments. So, for example, the bailment relationship that was held to exist in *The Pioneer Container*, between the owner of the goods (the bailor) and the shipowner (the sub-bailee) in whose ship the goods were lost, entitled the shipowner to take advantage of the exclusive jurisdiction clause in the contract it had entered into with its immediate bailor (the shipper). In such cases, it is the bailment relationship itself which is the source of the rights and obligations, as was made clear in *The Pioneer Container*.

In other words, bailment is an independent source of obligations, not just a relationship. In order to establish the duties and obligations of the parties, it is permissible (and necessary) to look not only at the terms agreed between them which are contractually enforceable (if any) and at the law of tort, but also at an independent pool of rules which we can call the law of bailment. This might, for example, make a term agreed between owner and possessor give rise to enforceable rights and liabilities even though not supported by consideration and therefore not enforceable through contract rules. It might also have to be called upon to give us answers to questions such as the permissible use the possessor might make of the goods in question. This would seem to establish a sufficient common thread to mark bailment relationships off from other, non-possessory, transactions or relationships involving goods (although this is not universally accepted: see, for example, the arguments to the contrary put by McMeel, 'The Redundancy of Bailment').

17.4.4.   Liabilities of the bailee

Leaving aside specific duties imposed on the bailee by contract or agreement, the bailee's principle duty is to return the goods at the end of the bailment. In some types of bailment, such as those arising out of finding and theft, that might involve a positive duty to seek out the owner, as suggested in *Parker* v. *British Airways Board* [1982] QB 1004 (discussed in Notes and Questions 11.5 above), and in all cases the bailee is expected to return the goods promptly and in the manner contemplated by the terms of the bailment (as demonstrated in *Mitchell*).

While the bailment continues, the bailee is liable to take care of the goods. Much of Holt CJ's judgment in *Coggs* v. *Bernard* is taken up by a consideration of the different standards of care imposed on each of the categories of bailee he identified, and indeed the main object of the categorisation was to differentiate between levels of liability. However, in this respect bailment is heavily dominated by tort, and it is apparent from what is said below in *Mitchell*, *Sutcliffe* and *AVX* that bailees' liabilities have followed the general tort trend in being assimilated into a general duty to take reasonable care of the goods, reasonableness being determined in each case by the particular circumstances of the case.

This applies only for so long as the bailee remains entitled to hold the goods under the terms of the bailment, and only for so long as he is acting in accordance with its terms. Once a bailee steps outside the terms of the bailment, however, the courts seem inclined to treat him as what they term an insurer of the goods – in other words he is strictly liable for any loss or damage, as Ealing London Borough Council was held to be in the *Mitchell* case. It would seem to follow from this that a thief (who is not entitled to hold the goods) and a finder who makes no effort to find the owner, are both strictly liable for any loss or damage to the goods. This would make sense of what Lord Donaldson said about the rights and liabilities of finders in *Parker* v. *British Airways Board* (see section 11.6.4 above).

What is less readily understandable is that the gratuitous custody category of bailee appears to incur duties to look after the goods just as much as (and not very differently from those imposed on) the bailee who takes custody for reward. This was accepted unquestioningly in *Coggs* v. *Bernard* (and indeed Mr Bernard was himself a gratuitous bailee for custody, and duly held liable for the loss of the brandy). At first sight, gratuitous custody looks like an act of simple kindness or altruism, whereas custody for reward looks more like a commercial contract for the provision of services. On closer examination of the circumstances in which custody arises, however, it becomes apparent that many gratuitous custodies are prompted by commercial considerations rather than altruism, as for example when you deposit your coat in the cloakroom in a restaurant. And that, even where this is not the case, custody, whether undertaken altruistically or not, involves an assumption of responsibility for someone else's property, which is something characteristically regulated by law. Whether this is altogether fair on bailees like Mr Bernard and Ealing London Borough Council is another matter.

In any event, the fact that the law has always imposed liabilities on gratuitous bailees demonstrates how far removed the law of bailment is from the law of contract (which as a rule does not enforce promises unless supported by consideration) and from the law of equity (which in principle does not assist donees). Furthermore, it appears that the standard of care expected from the gratuitous bailee will be determined (and may well be increased) by any undertakings he may have expressly or impliedly given as to the type or level of service he will be providing, or the circumstances in which it will be provided: this is apparent from both *Coggs* v. *Bernard* and from *Mitchell*, where the council's liability arose out of its failure to keep to the undertaking that it had given to hand over the furniture where and when it said it would.

A final point to emphasise is the decisive role that possession plays here: a gratuitous *bailee* of goods (i.e. someone who has them in his possession) has a duty to take reasonable care of them during the bailment, but the same is not true of someone who has a degree of control over the goods which falls short of possession: see *Tinsley* v. *Dudley* [1951] 2 KB 18.

Notes and Questions 17.7

Read *The Pioneer Container, KH Enterprise* v. *Pioneer Container* [1994] 2 All ER 250, PC; *Mitchell* v. *Ealing London Borough Council* [1979] QB 1; *Sutcliffe* v. *Chief Constable of West Yorkshire* (1995) 159 JP 770; [1996] RTR 86; *The Times*, 5 June 1995; and *AVX Ltd* v. *EGM Solders Ltd*, *The Times*, 7 July 1982, either in full or as extracted at www.cambridge.org/propertylaw/, and consider the following:

1 According to the Privy Council in *The Pioneer Container*, in what circumstances will a bailment relationship arise? If it was not created consensually, what are the terms of the relationship?

2 Examine the reasons given by the Privy Council in *The Pioneer Container* for concluding that the shipowner could take advantage of the exclusive jurisdiction clause in its contract with the shipper. What does this tell us about the sources of the terms of a bailment relationship? Does it make sense *in the factual context of this case* to say that one of its terms might be (at the option of one of the parties) a term of a contract that that party entered into with a third party? Would it make sense in other factual contexts?

3 If there is no contract between bailor and bailee (either because the bailment did not arise consensually, or because it was consensual but there was no consideration), are its terms enforceable? If so, by what mechanism? In particular, are the agreed terms of a gratuitous bailment (such as in *Mitchell*) enforceable, and, if so, how?

4 Explain the significance of the fact that in *Mitchell* the council could not prove whether the furniture was stolen from the garage before or after it failed to meet Mr Mitchell as arranged. Why was the onus of proof on the council?

5 Consider what the position would have been if, when Mrs Mitchell was evicted, she had left her furniture behind in the flat, the local authority had taken no steps to put it into storage, and it had then been stolen from the flat. Would the local authority have been a gratuitous bailee of the furniture? Would it have been liable to Mrs Mitchell for its loss?

6 What duties are owed by a bailee to a bailor? What standard of care is expected from a bailee? Does it make any difference whether the bailment is for reward or (as in *Mitchell* and *Sullivan*) gratuitous? Should it?

7 It appears from *AVX Ltd* v. *EGM Solders Ltd* that a person in possession of the goods in the mistaken belief that he is the owner has no duty whatsoever – but he *must* take reasonable steps to ascertain that they are indeed his goods. If he fails to do so and the goods are lost or damaged, is he liable as insurer, or is it a lesser standard of care, appropriate to someone who has goods thrust upon them?

17.4.5.   Is bailment proprietary?

In Chapter 5, we identified three possible indicia of a proprietary interest, as opposed to a personal right. These are exclusivity (the interest carries with it a right to exclude others from enjoyment), exigibility/enforceability against non-parties (the interest is attached to the thing, in the sense that those subsequently dealing with that thing will be bound by the interest holder's rights in the thing), and alienability (the interest can be passed from one person to another, so in that sense is not personal to the original holder). As we noted in Chapter 5, the third of these is by no means necessary for an interest to be proprietary, but we probably can say that an interest that *does* have this characteristic is proprietary. Measured by these criteria, does bailment confer a proprietary interest on the bailee?

17.4.5.1.   Possession and exclusivity

The first point to make is that, since a bailee has possession, not only does he necessarily have the right to exclude the whole world, but also his interest is necessarily proprietary because possession is proprietary. It was argued above in relation to leases that a person in possession of land who does not hold any other proprietary interest in the land which carries with it the right to possession must necessarily have a lease of the land. For the same reason, it must follow that the interest of a bailee is a property interest. This is now widely accepted. Sir William Holdsworth, (1933) 49 LQR 576, p. 580, had this to say:

> It is obvious that, if A has let ... his chattel to B, and has transferred its possession to B, and if he then sells to C, C can only take it subject to B's legal rights, whether C has notice of those rights or not.

Similarly, Nigel Furey, in 'Goods Leasing and Insolvency', pp. 788–9, argues that goods-leasing contracts are binding on the trustee in bankruptcy of both owner and lessee *once possession has passed to the lessee*, because the passing of possession confers real rights on the lessee. In coming to this conclusion, he relies on the following from Goode, *Proprietary Rights and Insolvency in Sales Transactions*, p. 7:

> [P]ossession is itself a real right, exercisable against everyone except a person having a better right to possession. A person who, though not the owner, holds possession with the intention of asserting ownership is treated by the law as the owner, and as entitled to legal protection as such, against everyone except the true owner or a person deriving title through or under him or acting with his authority. Since the true owner usually shows up, we can for practical purposes disregard this second best possessory title. This leaves us with the possessory rights of the holder of a limited interest, i.e. a bailee who is in possession not as mere custodian but for an interest of his own, e.g. under a pledge, a lien or a hiring, hire-purchase or conditional sale agreement.
>
> It is important to note that what confers a real right on the bailee in the first instance is not the agreement pursuant to which possession is to be given to him but the delivery of possession itself. For example, an agreement to supply equipment on lease for five years does not of itself give the intended lessee a right *in rem*, and if the lessor were to become bankrupt before delivering possession the lessee's remedy would be restricted to a proof in the bankruptcy.
>
> Once possession has been given to the lessee, thereby conferring on him a real right in the leased goods, the quantum of that right is measured by the terms of the leasing agreement, so that he may hold possession against the trustee for the rest of the five-year period.

McMeel, in 'The Redundancy of Bailment', also concludes that bailment is proprietary, for this and other reasons, and further support is provided by the Court of Appeal in *Bristol Airport* v. *Powdrill* [1990] Ch 744, where it was held that an aircraft lease confers a proprietary interest on the lessee, albeit for the purpose of the Insolvency Act 1986, which, as the Court of Appeal noted, defines property 'in the widest possible terms'.

17.4.5.2. Alienability

The only doubts that can arise surround the questions of alienability and enforceability against third parties. As far as alienability is concerned, an interest can be said to be alienable if the interest can be passed on to someone else in the same form, so that the assignee holds the interest on the same terms as the assignor. It is not necessary that the assignor should cease to be liable after assignment: as noted above, until the Landlord and Tenant (Covenants) Act 1995 lessees of land continued to be liable under the lease after assignment. Since a person assumes the character of a bailee simply by voluntarily assuming possession of a thing, as established by *The Pioneer Container*, it must follow that, when a bailee purports to transfer his interest and delivers possession to his transferee, the transferee will become *a* bailee of the owner – but this does not necessarily mean that the first bailee's interest has been assigned. The decision in *The Pioneer Container* unfortunately is of no direct help here, as it concerned a sub-bailment rather than an assignment of a bailment. However, it is difficult to see why an assignment of the bailment should *not* result in the transferee taking on the same terms as the transferor, since by the act of accepting the transfer he can be said to be assuming possession on the same terms as those that bound his transferor.

17.4.5.3.   Enforceability against third parties

The issue here is whether a person who purchases or takes a mortgage or charge over goods that have been bailed is bound by the interests of a bailee of the goods. There are shipping cases (discussed in Chapter 9 above) concerning purchasers and mortgagees who have been held not entitled to interfere with the performance of charterparties which would seem to support the proposition that bailments are enforceable against third parties, since charterparties which confer possession on the charterer are bailments: see further Clarke, 'Ship Mortgages', pp. 693–5. However, these cases have not escaped criticism by the courts, and it has been argued by William Swadling in 'The Proprietary Effect of a Hire of Goods', p. 491, that these cases are supportable only 'as examples of a peculiar rule of maritime law derived from the Law Merchant [which] provide no authority outside that area'. It has to be said that there is nothing in these cases themselves to suggest that the courts thought they were dealing with a principle special to maritime property, and indeed, except in so far as a matter is covered by the Merchant Shipping Acts, ships are treated in property law in the same way as any other goods. However, in the absence of more recent direct authority, the question of enforceability probably remains open.

17.4.5.4.   Other proprietary indicia

Nevertheless, there are other ways in which bailees are treated as having more than a personal right in respect of the bailed goods. Because the bailee has possession, bailees have the *locus standi* to bring actions for trespass and wrongful interference with goods. Also, a bailee has, in his own right, an insurable interest in the thing bailed, and is entitled to insure for the full value of the thing, not just for his own personal loss or to cover any personal liability he may owe to the bailor in the event of loss of the thing (*Hepburn* v. *A. Tomlinson (Hauliers) Ltd* [1966] AC 451, and see Palmer, *Bailments*, pp. 56 and 364–74). The same is not true of licensees of goods or agents holding goods on behalf of their principals – they can insure only to recover their own personal loss, or on behalf of their licensor/principal. As Lord Pearce explained in *Hepburn* v. *A. Tomlinson (Hauliers) Ltd* [1966] AC 451:

> So far as concerns an agent who has no interest and is effecting an insurance for others, however, his unilateral intention is of importance to this extent that, unless he intends to effect the insurance on behalf of his principal, he is simply wagering and there is nothing which an undisclosed principal can ratify.
>
> The bailee of goods, however, is in a very different position. He has a right to sue for conversion, holding in trust for the owner such of the damages as represent the owner's interest. He may likewise sue in negligence for the full value of the goods, though he would have had a good answer to an action by the bailor for the loss of the goods bailed (*The Winkfield* [1902] P 42, CA). It would seem irrational, therefore, if he could not also insure for their full value. Both those who have the legal title and those who have a right to possession have an insurable interest in the real or personal property in question. There seems, therefore, no reason in principle why they should not be entitled to insure for the whole value and recover it. They must, however (like plaintiffs in actions of trover or negligence), hold in trust for the other parties interested so much of the moneys recovered as is attributable to the other interests . . .
>
> In *Castellain* v. *Preston* (1883) 11 QBD 380 at 398, however, Bowen LJ, having referred to mortgagees and bailees and admitted their right to recover, made observations to the effect that no part owner could recover for more than the interest which he had intended to insure. Taken in their full meaning his words create some difficulty, but the judgment was not reserved and his remarks were *obiter*. His real point was that a part owner could not recover for himself (so as to put into his own pocket) more than the value of his interest; for if he intended to do that he would simply be wagering.
>
> A bailee or mortgagee, therefore (or others in analogous positions) has, by virtue of his position and his interest in the property, a right to insure for the whole of its value, holding in trust for the owner or mortgagor the amount attributable to their interest. To hold otherwise would be commercially inconvenient and would have no justification in common sense.

This provides additional support for the conclusion reached by Gerard McMeel in 'The Redundancy of Bailment' (see above) that bailment is proprietary, and reinforces the conclusion that (despite his arguments to the contrary) there are sufficient common characteristics in the different categories of bailment to make it an analytically useful concept.

18

Security interests

18.1. The nature and function of security

18.1.1. Nature of security

A security interest is a proprietary interest in an asset owned by someone else, which is held *only* as security for the payment of a debt or performance of an obligation, in the sense that, as soon as the debt is repaid or the obligation is performed, the security interest ends.

18.1.1.1. Terminology problems

As we see below, there are four main types of security interest in English law: the mortgage, the charge, the pledge or pawn, and the lien. These are four quite distinct categories and they have different characteristics. The terminology, however, is not always strictly applied. In particular, the terms 'mortgage' and 'charge' are sometimes used interchangeably, and both are sometimes used as generic terms referring to any type of security interest. To compound the confusion, the only type of legal security interest that can now be created over an interest in land – the 'charge by way of legal mortgage' – is a statutorily created hybrid of the first and second categories, borrowing characteristics from both.

Another terminological oddity is that the lay terms used to describe secured transactions give a wholly inaccurate description of the technical nature of the transaction. In lay terms, aspiring property owners 'get' a mortgage (a valuable commodity) from a bank or building society (which is in the business of 'offering' mortgages to borrowers), and the bank or building society may then allow the owners to 'keep' the mortgage when they move house. And, if there is a default in repayment, the bank or building society may then decide to 'repossess' the property – as if taking back its own.

Technically, what is happening is quite different. A security interest is a derivative interest carved out of the borrower's property interest (and so granted by the borrower to the lender, not the other way round) to secure repayment of the debt. The grant of the security interest does not diminish the value of the secured asset to the grantor: it just earmarks the secured asset for the repayment of that debt rather than any other debt owed by the borrower, as Mr Justice Millett pointed out in *Re M. C. Bacon Ltd* [1990] BCC 78. Nor of course does the security interest have any value to the borrower, other than that his ability to offer to grant it to the lender is a means of persuading the lender to lend him money. The security interest does have a value to the lender, but it is directly related to the amount of the outstanding loan: it is worth precisely the same as the outstanding indebtedness, and, as that decreases as the borrower repays instalments of capital, so too does the value of the mortgage to the lender. If there is a default in repayment, the lender can then enforce the security, which it usually does by selling the *borrower's* interest in the secured asset, free from the security, by using what is essentially an exception to the *nemo dat* rule, which gives it power to sell a greater interest in the asset than it itself holds.

18.1.1.2.   Legal and equitable rights to redeem

The borrower has a contractual right to have the security interest discharged by making repayment on the due date. This is known as the legal right to redeem. In addition, whatever form the security takes and notwithstanding anything to the contrary in the security documents, equity confers on the borrower an *equitable right to redeem* the asset (i.e. to have the security interest discharged by paying everything due) at any time *after* the legal date for repayment has passed, regardless of default, and extinguishable only on a sale by the mortgagee in exercise of its power of sale (or on foreclosure, but this is now obsolete). This is one aspect of the special protection that equity has traditionally given to mortgagors. We will come across other aspects later.

18.1.1.3.   Creation, attachment and perfection of security

A final terminological point. It is sometimes useful to distinguish three different stages in the creation of a security interest. The security interest is *created* at the point when a present right, enforceable against the grantor, is conferred on the grantee. It *attaches* to an asset as soon as a specific asset becomes subject to the interest, so that from that point the grantee has a proprietary interest in the secured asset. It is then *perfected* once any necessary steps have been taken to make it enforceable against third parties (for example, registration). All three events may well take place simultaneously, but they need not. If, for example, you are proposing to buy the fee simple interest in land financed by a mortgage loan and you execute the mortgage deed before you have completed the purchase, the mortgage is *created* when you execute the mortgage deed, it *attaches* to the fee simple interest when you subsequently acquire it, and it is *perfected* when the mortgagee registers the mortgage at the Land Registry.

18.1.2.   Function

Secured lending is extraordinarily prolific in this country, as we see below, and it is important to appreciate why this is so. Security offers a lender things that he cannot get by using the legal machinery provided for enforcement of debts which are unsecured. If I fail to repay an unsecured bank loan, the bank can sue for repayment, obtain a court order for repayment, and then (if it wants to choose this in preference to other available enforcement measures) get the court to make a charging order over any of my assets under the Charging Orders Act 1979. This will enable the asset to be sold, and the bank will be entitled to recoup the debt (plus interest and costs) out of the sale proceeds. As far as the bank is concerned, there are three snags in this procedure. First, even if I held more than enough assets to cover the debt at the time when I borrowed the money, I might have sold them all and spent the money before the bank is able to apply for a charging order. Secondly, even if I still have the assets, I might owe money to other lenders and the total value of my debts might exceed the total value of my assets. Other creditors might therefore get to the assets first, in which case the bank will get nothing, or I might go bankrupt, in which case all my unsecured assets will be sold and the proceeds (minus considerable costs) will be divided proportionately between the unsecured creditors. The bank, like all the other creditors, will inevitably receive less than full repayment, and will have to accept it as final settlement of the debt. Thirdly, I might have already mortgaged or charged all my assets to some other creditor, which would mean that any charging order the bank obtains over an asset will take priority after the pre-existing mortgage or charge over that asset. If the bank then requires the asset to be sold (as the charging order entitles it to do), the sale proceeds will be used first to pay off the whole of the debt secured by the pre-existing mortgage or charge over the asset (plus interest and costs) before anything is made available to the bank. The bank would have been better off if it had taken security, in a number of ways.

18.1.2.1.   Right of first recourse

First, security over an asset gives the security interest holder the right of first recourse to it. If there is default in repayment, the secured creditor can sell the asset and obtain repayment out of the proceeds of sale in priority to anyone else (except someone with a prior-ranking security interest over the same asset). Most importantly, this applies even if the debtor goes bankrupt. A secured creditor is largely unaffected by the bankruptcy or liquidation of its debtor: its power to sell the asset and recoup all its debt (including interest and costs) out of the sale proceeds is generally not restricted in any way. If there is a surplus left after it has done so, that goes into the general pool of assets to be divided among the unsecured creditors. So, in any bankruptcy or liquidation, unsecured creditors are paid just a fraction of what they are owed (almost invariable a tiny fraction) whereas secured creditors are paid in full (assuming the secured asset was worth more than the total indebtedness).

This is not only a good thing in itself, as far as the secured creditor is concerned. It also dramatically reduces the risk in lending. Provided the lender ensures that there is a sufficient margin between the value of the asset it accepts as security and the amount it lends, its return of its capital is more or less guaranteed.

18.1.2.2.   Attachment to the asset

Since security interests are property interests in the secured asset, they are attached to the asset, in the sense that the asset owner cannot sell the asset free from the security interest unless he either pays off the debt or obtains the lender's consent. If he does neither, the security interest will be fully enforceable against the buyer (subject to the enforceability rules discussed in Chapters 14 and 15 above). This does not make the buyer personally liable for the debt, but it does entitle the security interest holder to sell the asset and recoup the debt out of the proceeds, handing back to the buyer only whatever is left after that.

18.1.2.3.   Non-judicial enforcement

The security interest holder's primary remedy (although not the only one, as we see later) is to sell the secured asset, and in most cases it can do so without first obtaining a court order, or going through any other formal procedure. It does not even have to sell by auction: the sale will be an ordinary private sale. This ability to enforce security by a simple self-help process is uncommon in other jurisdictions. It has considerable attractions for lenders. It means that the lender does not have to satisfy anyone in advance that default has justified enforcement or that this is the most appropriate way of obtaining repayment, there is no public scrutiny of the conduct of the sale or the price obtained, and no time-consuming, costly court process to go through. For reasons considered later, it is not common for mortgagees of owner-occupied dwellings to sell without first obtaining a court order, but it is routinely done by lenders with security interests over all other types of asset.

18.1.2.4.   The hostage function

A secured lender's first concern is the same as that of an unsecured lender: to ensure that the borrower repays the loan in accordance with the terms of the loan agreement. Security acts as a hostage, providing an incentive for the borrower to comply with the loan agreement. If a lender takes security over an asset that the borrower values highly, fear of losing the asset will induce the borrower to go to greater lengths than it might otherwise have done to keep up repayments. When money is short, it will make these repayments before paying other debts, and it will hesitate before engaging in risky behaviour which might endanger its ability to repay. From this perspective, the best kind of asset to take security over (assuming you are the lender) is something that the debtor values as thing rather than as wealth, such as his small child, or a pound of his flesh, or his home. This helps to explain why lending money on the security of people's homes is such good business. Homes are in many ways the ideal hostage, because not only will the borrower give first priority to keeping up the mortgage repayments, but the secured asset has a more or less stable, predictable market value (unlike small children and pounds of flesh) so that the lender can be reasonably confident of recouping all the indebtedness if the borrower does default and it has to have recourse to the security.

18.1.2.5.   Signalling, monitoring and control

A debtor who offers a valued asset as security can be said to be signalling his confidence that he will be able to repay, thus lessening the need for the lender to engage in expensive checks on his creditworthiness. If the asset has a predictable market value which is greater than the proposed loan, the creditor has even less need to check creditworthiness. In other words, security can be said to operate as a signalling device, enabling lenders to identify reliably and cheaply which potential borrowers are creditworthy, or alternatively allowing them to dispense with costly credit-checking at the outset and monitoring of behaviour during the security. Arguments on these lines can be found in Scott, 'A Relational Theory of Secured Financing', Goode, 'Is the Law Too Favourable to Secured Creditors?' and Buckley, 'The Bankruptcy Priority Puzzle', pp. 1395–6.

On the other hand, security can also be used as a means of *enabling* the lender to monitor the behaviour of the borrower. The terms of a security interest over assets will usually require the borrower to maintain the value of the secured asset by keeping it in a good state of repair, to insure it and ensure that the insurance is maintained at a sufficient level, and to notify the lender of any event threatening the value of the secured asset or the ability of the borrower to repay. In this country, bank loans to businesses are usually secured by security interests taken over *all* the assets of the business. This not only gives the lender access to comprehensive information about the running of the business, but also gives the lender the opportunity to exercise a significant level of control over decision-making, as well as enabling the lender to take early action to safeguard its interests. In particular, it enables the lender to take over management and control of the business if it fears the borrower will default, by exercising the security interest holder's remedy of appointing a receiver of the secured assets (an ability now curtailed, but not removed altogether, by changes made to receivership by the Enterprise Act 2002). As Riz Mokal points out in 'The Floating Charge – A Eulogy', this ability to bring in outside management to an ailing business may benefit not only the secured creditor, but also the business itself and other creditors (always assuming it succeeds in rescuing the business or minimising the loss caused by its collapse).

18.1.3.   Efficiency

This brings us to the question of whether the prevalence of secured credit in this country is a good thing. There is considerable academic dispute about whether or not secured lending is efficient. Intuitively, it seems likely that it is, because it has been so pervasive in market economies for such a long time (see, for example, the argument to this effect in White, 'Efficiency Justifications for Personal Property Security', pp. 479–80). But efficient for whom? It seems fairly obvious that it is efficient for the secured creditor, in that the risk of not recovering the loan in full is decreased. This should result in lenders charging a lower rate of interest for secured loans, which suggests that secured credit is more advantageous for borrowers as well. However, while the risk of not being repaid in full is decreased for the secured creditor, it is correspondingly increased for all the unsecured creditors of the same debtor, because the secured assets are removed from the pool of assets out of which they can be repaid. So, at best, unsecured creditors will increase the rate of interest they charge the debtor by an amount corresponding to the discounted rate charged by the secured creditor, and secured credit then becomes merely a 'zero sum game'. Even in such a case, the outcome is likely to be inefficient rather than neutral because setting up security arrangements is costly, so the debtor's total credit bill (i.e. adding together the costs of both the secured and the unsecured credit) will be greater in a world where secured credit is permitted than it would be in a world where it is prohibited. At worst – and this is rather more in line with what actually happens in the real world – some of the unsecured creditors will be unable to respond to the granting of secured credit by raising their interest rates (because they are involuntary creditors, or are not in a position to negotiate or renegotiate the terms on which they extend credit). This benefits the debtor, but it does mean that the advantages to the debtor and the sophisticated and relatively affluent creditor are bought at the expense of the relatively poor and unsophisticated creditor. In other words, it may be the case that secured credit is pervasive, not because it is efficient overall but because it permits 'informed' creditors to capture wealth at the expense of 'uninformed' ones. These arguments are developed in more detail in Scott, 'A Relational Theory of Secured Financing', and in Schwartz, 'Security Interests and Bankruptcy Priorities'.

However, there are other benefits that secured lending brings. We have already noted that the monitoring and control functions that security enables the creditor to undertake can benefit everybody. Further, the overall costs of monitoring and regulating debtor behaviour may be reduced, as argued by Jackson and Kronman, 'Secured Financing and Priorities Among Creditors'; and see also White, 'Efficiency Justifications for Personal Property Security', and, more generally, Mokal, 'The Search for Someone to Save'. Whether these advantages outweigh the disadvantages remains a matter of debate.

18.1.4. Use of security

Statistics produced by the Council of Mortgage Lenders (CML) and the Office of the Deputy Prime Minister reveal that, in 2003, CML members (estimated to provide approximately 95 per cent of residential mortgage lending) held just under 11.5 million mortgages of UK dwellings, at a time when there were approximately 18 million owner-occupied dwellings in all in the UK. According to figures published by the Bank of England, total outstanding secured lending to individuals and housing associations at November 2003 was over £750 billion, and the CML reports that new loans totalling over £200 billion were made by its members in 2002 and secured by mortgages over dwellings. Mortgage debt secured on dwellings accounted for over 50 per cent of GDP in the UK in 2001, the fourth highest in

Europe (Denmark was top with 70 per cent of GDP and Italy bottom with 10 per cent: European Mortgage Federation).

During the eleven-year period from 1991 to 2002, enforcement of mortgages of dwellings ranged from a low of 11,970 (0.11 per cent of total mortgages) in 2002 to a high of 75,540 (0.77 per cent of total mortgages) in 1991.

Comparable statistics are not available for security interests over other assets, but the Department of Trade and Industry's annual report for 2002/2003 shows that between 150,000 and 250,000 new mortgages and charges have been granted by companies every year since 1998. Most businesses are largely reliant on bank finance, and all UK banks routinely require security over business assets as a condition of extending credit.

18.2. Forms of security

It is important to keep in mind that the grant of a security interest generally involves two distinct transactions. By the first transaction, D borrows money from C or incurs some other obligation to C. By the second transaction, O, the holder of a property interest in an asset, grants C a security interest over it in order to secure D's obligations under the first transaction. O and D may, but will not necessarily, be the same person: you can mortgage your house to the bank to secure your own indebtedness to the bank or, if you want, to secure someone else's indebtedness.

Security interests that are granted consensually in this way must take one of four forms, as noted above. The significance of the differences between these forms appears from *Re Cosslett (Contractors) Ltd* [1998] 2 WLR 131 (extracted at www.cambridge.org/propertylaw/). An outline of the salient points follows.

18.2.1. Property transfer securities: the mortgage

Any property interest in any kind of asset can be mortgaged – i.e. any legal or equitable interest in land, in goods, or in any kind of intangible property. In the case of a mortgage of anything other than a legal estate in land, O mortgages her property interest to C by *transferring it* to C, with a proviso that C will transfer it back to O when the obligation is discharged. Since the transfer of title is by way of security only (i.e. for C to hold as security for performance of the obligation, rather than for C's own beneficial use), O is regarded by equity as retaining a proprietary interest (an 'equity of redemption') in the mortgaged property. This is a *sui generis* property interest, which amounts to an acknowledgment by equity that the mortgagor remains the 'true' owner notwithstanding the transfer of her interest to the mortgagee.

In other words, in a mortgage the mortgagor transfers ownership of the asset (or the whole of her interest, if less than ownership) to the mortgagee, retaining only the equity of redemption. In the case of goods, since ownership carries with it the right to possession of the goods, it is the mortgagee and not the mortgagor who is entitled to possession of the asset throughout the period of the mortgage. These two factors combine to make the mortgage a most unsuitable form of security for goods, particularly from the mortgagor's point of view: she loses possession of the asset throughout the period of the mortgage, even if she does not make any default in repayment, and she has only an equitable interest in the asset which would not be enforceable against a good faith purchaser if the mortgagee were to sell the asset pretending it was his own. This creates problems, because none of the other forms of security is particularly suitable for goods either. The pawn tends to be used only for small, short-term domestic borrowings, as we see below, and the charge can only exist as an equitable interest, which leaves the chargee in a dangerously exposed position, with his interest not enforceable against a good faith purchaser if the chargor sells the goods without his consent.

Mortgages can be legal or equitable. A mortgage of a legal interest can be either legal or equitable depending on the formalities used (see Chapter 12 above). A mortgage of an equitable interest can only be equitable.

Since 1925, a legal mortgage of a legal estate in land (i.e. a fee simple absolute in possession or a legal lease) takes a special form, which we look at separately below.

18.2.2.   Possessory securities: pledge or pawn

O pledges or pawns property by retaining title to it but delivering *possession* to C by way of security, on the condition that possession will be redelivered when the obligation is discharged. Since a pledge or pawn necessarily involves a delivery of possession, the only kinds of property that can be pledged or pawned are chattels and some documentary intangibles (in theory probably land as well, but never in practice). Again, the fact that pawn involves the delivery of possession limits its usefulness for commercial borrowers, but pawnbroking remains a thriving institution among consumer borrowers, providing relatively small loans for short periods usually against the security of personal belongings.

18.2.3.   Hypothecations: the charge

A charge is the most sophisticated form of security. It has always been recognised in civil law systems but was never recognised by the common law. It was finally introduced into English law by equity, and as a consequence charges can only be equitable (leaving aside some statutory charges). A charge does not involve a transfer of ownership or a delivery of possession to C. Instead, what C gets is a *sui generis* proprietary interest in the charged property interest, which consists of a present right of first recourse to it in the event of a default in the performance of the obligation secured by the charge. So, from the moment the charge is created, the charged property is appropriated to, or earmarked for, the satisfaction of C's claim in priority to any other claim that anyone else might have in respect of it.

In many ways, the charge is the ideal form of security, since it gives the chargee only and precisely the rights it needs as against the security asset – i.e. a present right to have recourse to the asset only as and when there has been a default under the loan agreement and the chargee therefore wants to enforce the security. This is in marked contrast to the cumbersome common law mortgage, which gives the mortgagee the inappropriately extensive rights of ownership of the security from the outset long before the mortgagee needs or even wants them. The disadvantage in our system, however, is the purely equitable status of the charge, as noted above.

Any kind of property interest can be charged. A charge may be 'fixed' (attached to a specific asset) or 'floating' (floating over all assets of a specified description from time to time owned by O). When a specified event (e.g. default in repayment) occurs, a floating charge 'crystallises', i.e. it attaches as a fixed charge to every asset of that description which O then owns. Floating charges, like fixed charges, are equitable only, and they can only be created by companies: an individual cannot grant a floating charge over her assets. The juridical nature of the floating charge is controversial, as can be seen from *Agnew* v. *Inland Revenue Commissioner* [2001] UKPC 28, PC (extracted at www.cambridge.org/propertylaw/).

18.2.4. Liens

The term 'lien' covers a variety of different, very specialised types of security interest, but the essential idea of a lien is that C becomes entitled to *detain* property of O until O's obligation is fulfilled, as Lord Millett explains in *Re Cosslett*. Most liens are non-consensual (e.g. maritime liens, unpaid vendor's lien, repairer's lien, solicitor's lien) but they can be created by agreement.

18.2.5. Property retention securities

A sale of property by S to B may be structured in such a way that title or possession passes to B before the full purchase price is paid, but S retains a proprietary interest in the property to be sold pending full payment. The interest retained by S in such a transaction (e.g. under a hire-purchase or conditional sale agreement, or a retention of title clause) is in all essentials a security interest, but the courts have sometimes been sympathetic towards attempts to characterise it as something else (most notably, in *Aluminium Industrie Vaassen BV* v. *Romalpa Aluminium* [1976] 1 WLR 676, where the court accepted that the seller's nominal retention of title until paid in full did not amount to a charge created by the buyer; this led to the widespread adoption of such provisions in continuing supply contracts: see Goode, *Proprietary Rights and Insolvency in Sales Transactions*, pp. 84–110).

18.2.6. Charge by way of legal mortgage

This is now, in practice at least, the only way of creating a legal security interest over a fee simple or leasehold interest in land. In order to understand the way it functions it is, unfortunately, necessary to understand its historical origins.

Until 1925, the ordinary property-transfer mortgage noted in section 18.2.1 above was used to mortgage fee simples and leases in English law. However, in 1925 it was thought that this form of mortgage would not fit well into the land registration system introduced by the Land Registration Act 1925, because under such a mortgage the owner has only an equitable (and therefore unregistrable) interest, i.e. the equity of redemption. It was therefore decided to replace it with a new charge-like security interest, the charge by way of legal mortgage. However, it was feared that the immediate and compulsory replacement of the mortgage with this new type of security interest would be too radical a step for most lenders to take willingly. The mortgage by demise, a less radical modification of the property-transfer mortgage, was therefore also introduced at the same time, as an alternative to the charge by way of legal mortgage. It was anticipated that, as the advantages of the new charge by way of legal mortgage became apparent, use of the mortgage by demise would decline and it would eventually fall into disuse. This did indeed happen. It became obsolete (in about the 1960s or 1970s), and the Law Commission recommended its abolition in its report, *Transfer of Land: Land Mortgages* (Law Commission Report No. 204, 1991). This has not yet happened, but the Land Registration Act 2002 has now made it impossible to create a mortgage by demise over a registered title (see section 23(1) of the 2002 Act). Since a legal mortgage of a registrable estate is an event that triggers first registration of title, as we saw in Chapter 15, this means that in practice a mortgage by demise can no longer be created, even if anyone wanted to do so. However, its ghost lives on, because in the Law of Property Act 1925 the charge by way of legal mortgage is defined in terms of the mortgage by demise: section 87(1) provides that:

> Where a legal mortgage of land is created by a charge ... by way of legal mortgage, the mortgagee shall have the same *protection, powers and remedies* ... as if [the mortgage was a mortgage by demise].

Since nothing else is said in the 1925 Act about the nature of this new statutory creation, the charge by way of legal mortgage, or the rights, duties and obligations of the parties to it, this can only mean that they are the same as they would have been under a mortgage by demise, and indeed this is the approach that the courts have always adopted (see, for example, *Grand Junction Co. Ltd* v. *Bates* [1954] 2 QB 160, *Regent Oil Co. Ltd* v. *J. A. Gregory (Hatch End) Ltd* [1966] Ch 402, and *Thompson* v. *Salah* [1972] 1 All ER 530).

It therefore remains necessary to understand the mortgage by demise. The idea behind it was to modify the property-transfer mortgage only so far as necessary to give both mortgagor and mortgagee a legal registrable interest. Consequently, section 85(1) of the Law of Property Act 1925 provides that the mortgage by demise operates as a grant to the mortgagee of a legal lease of the land for a term of 3,000 years, but subject to 'cesser on redemption' (i.e. the term automatically terminates on repayment of the indebtedness). This leaves the mortgagor with a technically unwieldy bundle of rights consisting of a legal freehold reversion on a 3,000-year lease, plus an equity of redemption, plus an equitable right to redeem. These are, therefore, the rights that mortgagor and mortgagee have under a charge by way of legal mortgage. As the Law Commission pointed out in paragraphs 2.17–2.18 of *Transfer of Land: Land Mortgages* (Law Commission Report No. 204, 1991), this is deeply unsatisfactory since it leaves both parties with inappropriate rights:

INAPPROPRIATENESS OF FORM

2.17. The second root cause of the artificiality and complexity of mortgage law is that the methods used to create security interests in land give rise to inappropriate relationships between the parties. This is particularly apparent in the mortgage by demise ...

MORTGAGE BY DEMISE

2.18. The problem here is of central importance because it affects not only the mortgage by demise, but also the charge by way of legal mortgage which is treated by statute as if it were a mortgage by demise, and the equitable mortgage of a legal estate, which is treated in equity as if it were a legal mortgage, and hence a mortgage by demise. The problem is that it creates a relationship of landlord and tenant between the parties. There is nothing unusual about using the leasehold relationship as an investment device: institutional lenders are probably more likely to use leases rather than mortgages as a means of financing property development or investing in non-residential land. However, in the case of the mortgage by demise the leasehold relationship is the wrong way round: as tenant, the mortgagee has an inherent right to possession which would more appropriately lie with the mortgagor (subject to whatever restrictions may be necessary to protect and enforce the security). Similarly, it is necessary for the preservation of the security that the mortgagor should be under a duty to the mortgagee to keep the property repaired and insured, yet this is a duty more usually imposed by a landlord on a tenant, rather than by a tenant on a landlord. Even if reversed, the landlord–tenant relationship is fundamentally different from that created by a mortgage: investors under a lease-based arrangement buy outright a share in the property, and the value of the share fluctuates in direct proportion to the value of the retained property; mortgagee-investors, on the other hand, have an interest in the property only for the temporary purpose of safeguarding the repayment of a loan or performance of an obligation, and the value of the mortgagee's interest can never exceed the value of the obligation secured. Historically, the mortgage by demise was a useful device to bridge the gap between abolition of the mortgage by assignment and general acceptance of the legal charge. Now that it has fulfilled that purpose, it seems an unnecessary impoverishment of the system to blur the distinction between lease and mortgage by continuing to define one device in terms of the other.

In the charge by way of legal mortgage (and indeed the mortgage by demise), significant modifications are made by the Law of Property Act 1925 to the basic leasehold relationship created by the security. So, for example, the mortgagee is given a statutory power to sell the mortgagor's interest in the land free from the mortgage (section 101(1)(i): applies to all mortgages and charges made by deed) and the mortgagor is given a limited statutory power to grant leases (section 99: without such a power it would lack the capacity to do so). Also, as we see later, sometimes equity will modify the mortgagee's common law rights to make them exercisable only for the protection or enforcement of the security. And finally the parties may, and frequently do, exclude or vary both the common law rights and the statutory modifications of them by express provision in the mortgage documents.

Notes and Questions 18.1

Read *Re Cosslett (Contractors) Ltd* [1998] Ch 495; [1998] 2 WLR 131; [1997] 4 All ER 115, CA, and *Agnew* v. *Inland Revenue Commissioner* [2001] UKPC 28; [2001] 2 AC 710; [2001] 3 WLR 454, PC, either in full or as extracted at www.cambridge.org/propertylaw/, and consider the following:

1 Another aspect of the dispute which was the subject of the Court of Appeal decision in *Re Cosslett* was litigated in different proceedings on the same facts, and the House of Lords approved Millett LJ's analysis in *Re Cosslett*: see *Smith* v. *Bridgend County Borough Council* [2002] 1 AC 336; [2001] UKHL 58.

2 Explain why, according to Millett LJ in *Re Cosslett*, the agreement between Cosslett and the council did not transfer ownership of the plant to the council, and why it did not give rise to a mortgage, pledge, lien or fixed charge in favour of the council. Precisely which elements of the agreement gave rise to a charge in favour of the council?

3 Assume you own a valuable painting, and you want to offer it to your bank as security for a loan. Which type of security interest would be most appropriate? Which would be best from your point of view – a mortgage, a charge, a pawn or a lien? Which would you expect the bank to prefer?

4 Explain the difference between a fixed charge and a floating charge. According to Millett LJ in *Re Cosslett* and in *Agnew*, what are the determining characteristics of a floating charge?

5 Despite Millett LJ's analysis, the precise nature of many aspects of the floating charge remains controversial. In particular, there are conflicting analyses as to the nature of the interest the chargeholder (i.e. the lender) has in the assets before crystallisation. The question at issue is whether the chargeholder can be said to have a proprietary right in the assets before crystallisation. Nolan summarises the arguments in 'Property in a Fund', and concludes that it does, suggesting an analogy with a trust fund. The analogy is not wholly convincing, however. A trust fund is a fund held entirely for the benefit of the present and future beneficiaries, whereas assets subject to a floating charge are not held for the benefit of the chargee. It therefore makes sense to regard the chargee's right of recourse to the assets as inchoate before crystallisation, whereas it would be quite wrong to regard the interest of a beneficiary under a trust in that way.

6 It has been argued that a floating charge over all the assets of a company gives the chargeholder an unfair monopoly over the provision of credit to the company. Explain why, and consider the validity of the argument. Might this help explain why individuals cannot grant floating charges over their assets?

18.3.   Control over the terms of the relationship

18.3.1.   Equitable supervisory jurisdiction

There is a long-established equitable jurisdiction to strike out terms of a security interest which are inconsistent with its nature as a security interest. The jurisdiction applies to all types of security interest over any kind of property. The scope of the jurisdiction was settled in a series of major cases in the nineteenth and early twentieth centuries, in very different social and economic conditions, and there is some difficulty in applying the principles they established in present conditions.

Equity's historic intervention in mortgage and loan transactions was influenced by three principal factors. We have already noted the first: the excessive and inappropriate legal rights a mortgagee has always had in the mortgaged property because of the nature of common law security interests. The common law never devised a *sui generis* security interest, it merely utilised inappropriate property interests and relationships such as ownership, lease and bailment (for the pawn). This explains equity's creation of the equity of redemption (a development chronicled by Sugarman and Warrington in 'Telling Stories: Rights and Wrongs of the Equity of Redemption' (Extract 18.1 below); and see also Lord Parker's narration in *Kreglinger* v. *New Patagonia Meat & Cold Storage Co. Ltd* [1914] AC 25, extracted at www.cambridge.org/propertylaw/). It also explains equity's recognition of the charge as a security device.

The second factor was a deep-rooted distaste for the underlying bargain, usually a contract for the loan of money at interest. As Paddy Ireland relates in 'Company Law and the Myth of Shareholder Ownership' (Extract 18.2 below), usury was for a long time prohibited in this country, then prohibited unless licensed under the Moneylenders Acts, and, whether licensed or not, interest rates were regulated with a prescribed maximum rate. Lord Haldane and Lord Parker assess the significance of this point in *Kreglinger* in the passages extracted at www.cambridge.org/propertylaw/.

The third factor was that, at least at the beginning of the period of equitable intervention, mortgagors tended to be regarded as needing and deserving protection. It was partly a question of perceived inequality of bargaining power ('necessitous men are not free men'), but more because the weaker party was a landowner, as were most of the judiciary, whereas the stronger party was a moneylender or financier. In this early period of development most of the judiciary would have considered it a great social evil for a landed estate which had been in the same family for generations to fall into the hands of moneylenders through the enforcement of a mortgage, as Sugarman and Warrington note in Extract 18.1 below.

These second and third factors were particularly strong during equity's most active period of development, and during that time quite a high level of equitable intervention in mortgage transactions developed. But, by the mid to late nineteenth century, attitudes were changing. Provision of credit was beginning to be regarded as a social and economic good rather than as pernicious, and the judiciary's class identification with mortgagors had begun to break down. Mortgage relationships no longer all fitted into the traditional landowner/money-lender stereotype, and in any event judges began to be drawn from professional classes instead of from landed families (a development noted by Manchester, *A Modern Legal History of England and Wales 1750–1950*, p. 81), and were therefore as likely to identify with bankers and merchants as with landowners, if indeed it was any longer accurate to draw such a distinction. So, from the middle of the nineteenth century, the courts were increasingly uncomfortable with the equitable interventionist principles they had developed, and began to qualify the protection they provided. *Kreglinger* v. *New Patagonia Meat & Cold Storage Co. Ltd* [1914] AC 25 epitomises the turn away from protectionism, and the principles it establishes are essentially those still applicable today.

The problem is that the pattern of secured finance today is as far removed from that which was developing at the time when *Kreglinger* was decided, as the latter was from the pattern which existed when equity first started to intervene in mortgage transactions. Even within the limited field of land mortgages, there are at least three very different secured credit markets. We have already noted the routine financing of virtually all commercial sectors by secured credit, and the vast house-purchase and home-improvement loan markets. The latter in particular is remarkably low-risk, lucrative and highly competitive. On the other hand, there is also a significant market for high-risk last-resort secured lending of the type described by Dyson LJ in *Broadwick Financial Services Ltd* v. *Spencer* [2002] EWCA Civ 35 (extracted at www.cambridge.org/propertylaw/). The type and level of protection appropriate is quite different for each of these three sectors, and that provided by the *Kreglinger* principles is not particularly apt for any of them. Also, there is the complicating factor that the courts are wary of doing anything that would have an impact on the supply of credit, understandably unsure whether increasing or varying equitable protection principles will have unwelcome social and economic consequences.

18.3.2. The *Kreglinger* principles

The parties in *Kreglinger* emphatically did not fit the landowner/moneylender stereotype. The borrower was a manufacturer – meat preservers and canners, and renderers of animal products – and the lender was a woolbroker, i.e. an intermediary between sheepskin producers such as the borrower and manufacturers of wool/sheepskin products. The woolbroker lent the meat company £10,000 (not repayable for five years if no default, although the borrower could repay earlier if it wanted) at an interest rate of 6 per cent, and the meat company also granted the woolbroker a right of pre-emption on all its sheepskins for five years, the wool-broker to pay the 'best market price' for all sheepskins it chose to buy *and* to receive 1 per cent 'commission' on all those it did not buy and which the meat company sold elsewhere. To secure repayment, the meat company granted the woolbroker a floating charge over all its assets. The meat company repaid early, and then wanted to be freed from the right of pre-emption, claiming that it fettered its right to redeem (since if it redeemed within five years, it would not get back everything it mortgaged) and also that it gave the lender an improper collateral advantage in addition to repayment of its capital with interest. The House of Lords refused to intervene. Lord Haldane rationalised the principles on which equity would intervene in a mortgage transaction down to four. In his formulation (different formulations appear in the other judgments, a fertile source of dispute in later cases) the applicable principles are as follows:

1 Once a mortgage, always a mortgage. In other words, transactions which are in substance mortgages will be treated as such, even if they take some other form. So, for example, an apparent sale will be set aside if it took place only as security for an obligation, and that obligation has now been fulfilled, albeit too late.
2 Once the prohibition against usury was abolished in 1854, the parties to a mortgage are entitled to bargain for an additional advantage to be given to the lender *during* the mortgage (i.e. an advantage additional to repayment of capital plus interest) provided it is not unconscionable (variously expressed as 'imposed unfairly or oppressively' or as 'harsh and unconscionable', and see also Lord Parker at pp. 54–5 and 56 on this). This is just part of the general equitable jurisdiction to interfere in unconscionable bargains, not restricted to mortgages. This principle is, however, subject to the third principle, as follows.
3 Any term will be void in so far as it makes the mortgaged property 'irredeemable' – i.e. it removes, or fetters, the mortgagor's right to have the mortgaged asset back, free from any interest of, or obligation owed to, the mortgagee, by paying off everything due. The terms likely to have this effect are:
   a. a term which postpones the mortgagor's right to repay the loan, or perform the obligation, for an unduly long period;
   b. a term which confers on the mortgagee an advantage which continues *after* repayment, on the basis that this would deter the mortgagor from repaying (what is the point of repaying capital if you still have to go on, in effect, paying for the loan?), or alternatively that, having performed his obligation as agreed, the mortgagor ought to be able to get his asset back free from the mortgage;
   c. a term which gives the mortgagee an option to purchase the mortgaged property, or some interest in it which continues after repayment;
   d. a term which amounts to a penalty for early or late repayment.

In Lord Haldane's view, none of these principles was violated here. Principle 3(b), which seems a likely candidate, was inapplicable in his view because the sheepskin transaction was not a term of the mortgage at all but a separate transaction 'outside and clear of the mortgage', as Lord Parker put it (a difficult conclusion to accept, given that the security interest was a floating charge covering all the assets of the borrower, including its sheepskins). As later cases have demonstrated, it is easier to state this distinction than to apply it (see, for example, *Jones* v. *Morgan* [2001] EWCA Civ 995, and *Warnborough Ltd* v. *Garmite Ltd* [2003] EWCA Civ 1544, both concerning options to purchase the mortgaged property contained in commercial financing transactions, and the discussion by Alan Berg, 'Clogs on the Equity of Redemption – Or Chaining the Unruly Dog').

Lord Haldane's second principle is the one most frequently relied on by mortgagors complaining about high interest rates and other exorbitant payment terms. However, it has been established that this principle is applicable only where the terms complained of were *imposed* in a morally reprehensible manner (*Multiservice Bookbinding* v. *Marden* [1979] Ch 84). This has two consequences. First, however high the interest rate, and however harsh the repayment terms, the courts are most unlikely to interfere if the borrower was independently advised, or had other means of appreciating the financial significance of what it was doing. Secondly, it makes the principle inapplicable to excessive repayments arising out of the way in which the mortgagee exercises its right to vary the interest rate unilaterally. Variable interest rate mortgages are common in this country. Sometimes the mortgagee's right to vary the rate is contractually restricted in some way, so that, for example, the rate must remain within a specified range, or must follow variations in market rates. In other cases, however, there are no such restrictions. Lord Haldane's principles are of no use here, and it has been left to the common law to step in to make up the deficiencies in the equitable protection. In *Paragon Finance plc* v. *Staunton and Nash* [2002] 1 WLR 685, CA (extracted at www.cambridge.org/propertylaw/), the Court of Appeal held that, where the agreement allows the mortgagee to vary the interest rate at its absolute discretion, there is an implied term, first, that rates of interest will not be set dishonestly, for an improper purpose, capriciously or arbitrarily (*per* Dyson LJ at paragraph 36), and, secondly, that the lender will not exercise its discretion to vary the rate of interest in a way that no reasonable lender, acting reasonably, would do (paragraphs 41–2). It will be noted, however, that this was of no help to the borrowers in that case. Their interest rate, originally 2 per cent above the rate charged by the Halifax Bank, was increased to 5.14 per cent above the Halifax rate (so that they were paying 12.09 per cent when the Halifax was charging 6.95 per cent), but this was held not to be in breach of the implied term, for reasons apparent from the extract from Dyson LJ's judgment given at www.cambridge.org/propertylaw/.

18.3.3.   Statutory intervention

Largely as a result of the equitable jurisdiction's failure to adapt to the conditions of twentieth-century secured lending, some statutory regulation has been introduced, most notably by the Consumer Credit Act 1974. The Consumer Credit Act 1974 contains two sets of provisions relating to mortgages. The first set applies *only* to mortgages 'securing a regulated agreement' (in effect, only second mortgages securing loans not exceeding £25,000). These provisions impose detailed requirements about the form and content of the documentation, how and when documents are to be executed, and provision for printed warnings and cooling-off periods. These provisions are currently under review by the government.

The second set – the extortionate credit bargain provisions contained in sections 137–139 – apply to *all* mortgages where the borrower is an individual. There is no monetary limit. The scope of these provisions, and their limited effect in practice, is apparent from *Broadwick Financial Services Ltd* v. *Spencer* [2002] EWCA Civ 35 (extracted at www.cambridge.org/propertylaw/). In particular, it should be noted that they have been largely ineffective in controlling interest rates. The first reason for this is that it has been held that sections 137–139 share the defect of the equitable jurisdiction noted above: they do not cover the way in which lenders *operate* the terms of the agreement, notably by varying interest rates (see *Paragon Finance* again, in the passages cited in *Broadwick*). The second reason, however, is fundamental. The courts have taken the view that, in deciding whether an interest rate is 'extortionate', the appropriate comparable is the market rate charged *by that type of lender to that type of borrower*. Consequently, different sectors of the secured lending industry (including those at the shadier end of the spectrum) have been left free to set their own market rates. Only those who step out of line from their own market risk intervention under the 1974 Act.

The other source of statutory regulation is the Unfair Terms in Consumer Contracts Regulations 1999 (SI 1999 No. 2083), which apply to security interests, and which may prove to have some impact on standard form mortgage terms. They replace the 1994 Regulations of the same name (SI 1994 No. 3159), which implemented Council Directive 93/13/EEC on unfair terms in consumer contracts. It was not clear how far the 1994 Regulations applied to land transactions, but they certainly applied to the terms of loans provided by institutions to consumers. Changes made by the 1999 Regulations now make it clear that the Regulations apply to all aspects of land transactions between 'professionals' and consumers, including all standard form mortgages. For consideration of the scope of the Regulations, reference should be made to the House of Lords decision in *Director-General of Fair Trading* v. *First National Bank plc* [2001] UKHL 52.

Extract 18.1   David Sugarman and Ronnie Warrington, 'Telling Stories: Rights and Wrongs of the Equity of Redemption', in J. W. Harris (ed.), *Property Problems: From Genes to Pension Funds* (London: Kluwer, 1997)

I. THE RISE OF THE EQUITY OF REDEMPTION

1. Mortgages and the equity of redemption

Historically, a mortgage arose where an owner of property (usually land) required money and arranged to transfer the property to a lender as security in return for a loan. The loan agreement would generally provide for a reconveyance of the property to the borrower at a specific date on repayment of the money borrowed and the interest due. If the loan was not repaid, the property became forfeited to the lender. At common law, the date for repayment had to be strictly adhered to. Even one day's delay in tendering repayment could result in the borrower losing the entire property to the lender, though the amount of the loan was far less than the value of the land.

This interpretative stance was challenged by the courts of equity. Dating from at least the turn of the seventeenth century, the courts of equity determined that the strict date for repayment was somewhat irrelevant. Accordingly, the lender's claim to the property became subject: 'to a right called the equity of redemption, which arose from the court's consideration that the real object of the transaction was the creation of a security for the debt. This entitled the [borrower] to redeem (or recover the property), even though he had failed to repay by the appointed time.'

Time was not to be the essence of the agreement. Although the mortgagor's legal right to redeem the property was lost after the expiration of the time specified in the contract, in equity the mortgagor had an equitable right to redeem on payment within a reasonable period of the principal, interest and costs. A reasonable period could in some cases span many years. The rights of the mortgagor were further enhanced by the rules governing foreclosure.

The discretion to allow the borrower to get back property notwithstanding the contractual terms soon hardened into a right. In addition to this right (the fully fledged equity of redemption), the courts developed various analogous protections for borrowers. Partly under the umbrella of that seemingly tautological maxim of equity, 'once a mortgage always a mortgage', the courts also laid down that the borrower's right to get property back could not be rendered ineffective either by postponing the right for some unacceptable period or by making the right subject to some penalty, such as the borrower being deprived of some or all of the property mortgaged on exercising the right to redeem. What became known as a 'collateral advantage', that is, the lender asserting a claim to some or all of the borrower's property irrespective of repayment of the loan, was outlawed.

2. The establishment of the equity of redemption

It is generally agreed that the exact origin of the equity of redemption in its modern form is probably lost. A. W. B. Simpson suggested that the Chancery courts were prepared to relieve mortgagors from strict forfeiture conditions from the fifteenth century (Simpson, *An Introduction to the History of the Land Law* (1961), p. 227). But although there are examples to support this, these probably relate to what Simpson calls 'peculiarly scandalous cases'. The most common example of this would be where the mortgagee was repaid entirely from the rents and profits of the property and still refused to reconvey the property to the mortgagor. Richard Turner, the leading historian of the equity of redemption, concluded that the equity of redemption arose during the reign of Elizabeth I (Turner, *The Equity of Redemption* (1931)). While the court of Chancery did grant relief to mortgagors during this period, there are only two reported decisions where relief was given after a forfeiture. It was probably not until the start of the seventeenth century that courts began to grant relief to borrowers as a matter of course, without looking for the special circumstances that would have previously been necessary to activate equity's conscience. The courts gradually extended the list of circumstances that they regarded as causing the special hardship necessary for the court's protection. Thus, the jurisdiction to intervene which had originally operated only in exceptional circumstances became the rule; and the cases where no relief was granted became the exception. Despite the attempts of the

Commonwealth Parliament to limit the effectiveness of the right to redemption, and the effort of common lawyers to defeat the equity of redemption on the grounds that it was only a mere chose in action, that is, not a real property interest but merely a personal right recoverable by a suit at law, the mortgagor's claim to preferential treatment as against the mortgagee, irrespective of the terms of the contract, was established.

3. The jurisdiction consolidated

The courts quickly established that the mortgagor (the borrower) could not be prevented from redeeming, either before or after the contractual redemption date. Put simply, the date was fully effective against the lender, but rather less than effective against the borrower. Although later courts stressed that in certain circumstances the mortgagee may be prevented from redeeming early, the vital principle that a mortgagor cannot be prevented from seeking the return of the mortgaged property has been taken to be established in the seventeenth century by Lord Nottingham.

Lord Nottingham was instrumental in starting the shift of the equity of redemption from a 'thing' to an 'estate' in equity, that is, in conceptualising the equity of redemption as a kind of real property rather than as a kind of chattel property. Increasingly, mortgagors' claims were given precedence over other interests to which they had earlier been postponed: for example, mortgagors' claims came to take precedence even over a real property claim like the wife's right to dower. In *Attorney-General* v. *Pawlett* (1667), Lord Hale first characterised the equity of redemption as a title in equity. According to Lord Hale, a trust was contractual in nature, while the equity of redemption was proprietorial ...

Despite these legal developments, numerous lenders tried to circumvent the equitable protections. But time and again the courts stressed they would strike down the actual terms of a contract. Claims that the mortgage had subsisted for too long to permit a redemption were also rejected. Nor were the courts impressed when the mortgagee claimed to have suffered particular hardship or taken unusual risks. This justice was not an abstract principle. It turned upon the assumptions of those who were deciding what was or what was not 'just'. And, for most judges most of the time, justice in this context meant the restoration of landed property to the original owner.

As already suggested, Turner reduces much of his history of the equity of redemption to the 'personality' of the Chancellors. This allows him to move straight from Lord Nottingham, the father of the equity of redemption, to Lord Hardwicke, who became the most important figure in the story by 'consolidating' the work of Lord Nottingham. Lord Hardwicke's influential tenure as Lord Chancellor from 1736 to 1756 helped to settle equity as a system of general rules. If nothing else, Lord Hardwicke's claim to the central position in the story is assured by his famous decision in *Casborne* v. *Scarfe* (1735). While this case is by no means the first to define the equity of redemption as an estate, the importance of the equity of redemption as the equivalent of ownership limited through time is fundamental. It provided the legal foundation to underpin the 'fairness' of the courts' interference in contract. Not only was this just, it was technically correct. Although doubts lingered in the minds of some judges for a century or more as to the accuracy of characterising the equity of redemption as an estate, for practical purposes they were of no further significance. By 1822, Thomas Coventry could write as incontrovertible: 'An equity of redemption will follow the custom as to the legal estate.'

A similar transformation took place to the rules governing what were termed 'collateral advantages'. These rules policed any additional benefit that the mortgagee had extracted from the mortgagor, additional that is to the interest and the principal owed to the mortgagee. As with the rules relating to attempts to limit rights to redeem, anything that allowed the mortgagee the slightest opportunity of obtaining the mortgaged property itself was, by definition, oppressive or unjust.

When doubts were cast on these decisions by Lords Lindley, Romer, Jessel and others at the end of the nineteenth century, many reasons were given as to why the collateral advantage rules should not be followed. But, as we shall see, the crucial thing was that the late nineteenth-century courts no longer found these decisions 'just' or 'reasonable'. According to Lindley LJ, delivering judgment in 1898, to call a normal collateral agreement unconscionable, 'would shock any business man'. Perhaps it would, and in this area at least, so far as his Lordship was concerned, what did not shock a business man did not shock him.

In summary, the general effect of the rules governing the equity of redemption was to protect the owners of landed wealth as far as possible. The rules never purported to allow borrowers to escape from the actual debts they contracted, but the courts took it upon themselves to decide the limits beyond which lenders of money secured on landed estates could not go. In the mid-nineteenth century, the jurisdiction was seemingly incontrovertible. Even as late as 1912, Lord Halsbury spoke of 'this equitable doctrine which, I agree, is now part of the jurisprudence of this country'.

4. Little short of ideal

Why was this highly interventionist jurisdiction fair; and how was it justified? Judges and jurists tended to adopt two intersecting rationales for this special jurisdiction. First, one distinctive strand of equity's broad and highly discretionary jurisdiction in fraud concerned the protection of young heirs. In these cases it would be argued that landed heirs should be relieved from their bargains to borrow money, convey land, buy horses, jewellery, etc., because these bargains were unconscionable and fraudulent. They were fraudulent and unconscionable because the young heir concerned was in 'necessitous circumstances'. Because they felt impelled to undertake the sort of bargains that others would scorn, they were the obvious targets of what were characterised as 'unscrupulous moneylenders' or 'rogues' selling goods at a high price. It was co-extensive with these developments that equity developed and consolidated the equity of redemption. The doctrine was intended to protect the landowner from the money-hungry activity of commercial interests. The anomalous character of this protection for the 'necessitous' is evident when one considers the many other instances in which starker necessitousness did not postpone debts due.

Secondly, it was emphasised that the court's function was to ensure that ultimately land was returned to its 'rightful' (often meaning historical or traditional) owner. Even when the terms of the contract unequivocally pointed to an agreement to transfer the ownership of the land in exchange for money, goods or services, the courts were seemingly loath to accept it at face value.

As the story was told by Turner, the development of the equity of redemption was a minor miracle. Speaking of Lord Hardwicke's role in the development, he could hardly contain his enthusiasm. His Lordship had created a body of law that was 'fair', 'rational', and 'noble', 'a structure which soon became one of the most important features of English land law, having a far-reaching effect upon the internal economic position of the country'. Although Turner conceded that the end result was not quite up to the high standard of Roman law: 'The conceptions upon which the rules in application are based are sound in character and little short of the ideal.' He even allowed his enthusiasm to go so far as to suggest a comparison between the creation and development of the equity of redemption and the development of new symbols in mathematics making possible further advances into 'unknown realms of mathematical speculation'. Here was a doctrine that could indeed perform miracles.

Ironically, Turner completely failed to comprehend that this near perfect doctrine had been substantially recast by the House of Lords in *Kreglinger*, a case which he describes but whose significance escaped him. In this case, their Lordships sought to cut back the long-standing doctrine that all collateral advantages in favour of the mortgagee, that is, something granted to the mortgagee in addition to the return of the loan and interest, were invalid. These contracts were no longer viewed as automatically unfair and unconscionable. The result was that the equity of redemption had been significantly weakened. One conception of fairness (the fairness needed to protect and entrench the superior position of the landed oligarchy) had been largely supplanted by another conception of fairness (the fairness demanded by the financier) which appeared to demand the rigorous enforcement of the letter of contracts. Since Turner treated the development of the equity of redemption as intrinsically natural, desirable and superior, thereby abstracting the history of the doctrine from the context within which it was inscribed, he was unable to recognise that when circumstances changed the doctrine might no longer appear so natural and superior.

II. ANOTHER WAY OF SEEING: THE ECONOMIC, CULTURAL AND POLITICAL DIMENSIONS OF THE EQUITY OF REDEMPTION

1. England's patrician polity, the law of real property and myth-making

What were the particular circumstances that sustained the construction and expansion of the equity of redemption, and enabled the landed elite to exploit it? First and foremost was the fact that until the 1870s England was a 'patrician polity'. Until the 1870s, the landed establishment owned about four-fifths of the land in the British Isles. Their political, economic and cultural hegemony was exemplified by their pre-eminence in government, parliament, the law, the church, the civil service and the armed forces.

In Britain, land was sacred: it denoted status and citizenship. Most landowners were faced at some time or other with pressure to sell their land. Writing in 1827, Sir James Graham recognised the problems that heavy indebtedness caused many country gentlemen, and conceded that sale was a possibility:

But what agony of mind does that word convey? The snapping of a chain, linked perhaps by centuries, the destruction of the dearest attachments, the dissolution of the earliest friendships, the violation of the purest feelings of the heart.

This reluctance to sell was part of a larger ethos: namely, the landowners' desire to create and maintain a dynasty. As Edmund Burke put it, land ownership was: 'a partnership not only between those of the living, but between those who were living, those who were dead, and those who are to be born.' Most large landowning families schemed with varying degrees of success to ensure that the interests of future generations were secure. The legal system played a decisive role in these developments. As Maitland observed, 'our whole constitutional law seems at times to be but an appendix to the law of real property'.

The landed elite and the law were intensely bound together. From 1621 until 1844, the kingdom's supreme judges were not the professional lawyers of Kings Bench or Chancery but England's nobility assembled in parliament. The largest owners of property became the highest judges of the law of property. Even after 1844, England's most senior judges and law officers continued to be peers in part because the House of Lords remained the kingdom's supreme court of judicaters. The close relationship between the landed establishment and the law was reinforced by the fact that a significant proportion of the aristocracy took up the law in some form up to as late as the 1880s.

In myriad ways the law constituted and symbolised the elevated position of the landed establishment. Of major importance to the landed oligarchy was the fabrication of a system of equity alongside the common law from the fifteenth century onwards. The Court of Chancery was the great conduit of this equitable jurisdiction, a jurisdiction which tended to moderate the rigidities and formalism of the common law, particularly as it affected the landed. The close relationship between land and the law was further entwined with the privatisation of the process by which land ownership was transferred (conveyancing). In an elaborate process of judicial construction, the Statute of Uses of 1536 was interpreted so that conveyancing came to be undertaken by private contract, designed and overseen by lawyers, rather than involving the supervision of the courts. Nowhere was this dependence upon the legal profession more evident than in the extensive use that large land owning families made of the strict settlement, a legal device developed during the seventeenth century to forestall estate fragmentation.

The attitude that it was the landowners' natural privilege to take loans on security and then be relieved from the terms of the bargain, persisted until well into the nineteenth century. Lord Guildford borrowed money at 60 per cent when an expectant heir and then successfully claimed that the strict terms of the bond that he gave against the expectancy should not be upheld. The exchange between counsel for the lender and Lord Guildford shows his Lordship denying that he even understood the meaning of '60 per cent'. 'I did not know whether it high or low interest; I thought money-lenders always charged that amount' he said. Asked whether he thought the rate too high, he replied: 'I think they ought to let me have money at a lower interest; because they know perfectly well that I was certain to come into the property, and that I could pay them and I was quite right to borrow the money if I wanted it.'

To emphasise the significance of England's landed polity does not require that we marginalise the significance of commerce, and from the late eighteenth century to the Thatcher era, Britain's industrial and manufacturing economy. The significance of credit, and the relations of mutual dependence that it gave rise to helped to bind together landowners, bankers and shopkeepers. Indeed, the equity of redemption helped to foster increased consumption and the expansion of credit by convincing more landowners that the risk of losing their property by way of mortgage was minimal ...

5. The metamorphosis of the equity of redemption

As we have seen, there have always been some members of the judiciary who took issue with the doctrine of the equity of redemption even in its seventeenth and eighteenth-century heydays. These misgivings grow louder from about the middle of the nineteenth century. Those elements of resistance within the discourse itself were galvanised anew as a more middle class judiciary found themselves privileging a social group, the landed, who no longer seemed to need nor merit this privileging. The period from the late eighteenth to the late nineteenth century witnessed a 'shift in emphasis from property law to contract ... [The] equation of general principles of contract law with the free market economy led to an emphasis on the framework within which individuals bargained with each other.' Law was one of several discursive processes which helped to forge these new representations of the social world and personhood, determining who could speak and how. These narratives celebrated commerce, the crucial economic role played by the middle classes, the freedom of the market, self-help and a less aristocratic notion of property and personhood. Freedom of contract served to fuse the tradition of the ancient constitution to a new emphasis on business and the town as the expressions of a liberal sense of evolutionary progress and national advance. These narratives presented the middle classes as the real guardians of society.

The members of the judiciary closely involved with the equity of redemption at the end of the nineteenth century and the beginning of the twentieth century had lost their aristocratic bias and were strong advocates of the new contract orthodoxy. The mortgagor it argued was 'usually a grown-up man, with a very clear vision of his own interests, and quite able to take care of himself even without the solicitor who is generally found at his elbow'. Hence, presumably, there was no need for the classic equity of redemption. For these judges, their role was not to protect one species of property, land, but to protect contractual rights generally, that is, to protect forms of property including rights in land, but not privilege rights in land. If the courts were still to interfere with bargains freely made as the equity of redemption demanded, what would happen to sacred *laissez faire* doctrines? Faced with these two apparently conflicting positions, the courts decided, after some hesitation, that freedom of contract as they understood it meant more to them than anything else, including the classic form of the equity of redemption. From this perspective, the metamorphosis of the equity of redemption was part of a late exorcism of sixteenth, seventeenth and eighteenth-century notions of the place of land and the landed in English property holding and a manifestation of alternative conceptions of justice and Englishness.

The victory of freedom of contract over property had less to do with the intrinsic superiority of the arguments concerned than the circumstances in which they were expressed, which enabled certain groups to exploit them. From the Third Reform Act to the First World War, debates concerning citizenship intensified and progressive liberals sought to transcend the atomistic individualism of classic liberalism. In the eyes of old liberals like the constitutional lawyer, Albert Venn Dicey, the much-feared age of collectivism had arrived. From this perspective, the upholding of freedom of contract with respect to the equity of redemption, and by implication minimal state interference, was itself an attempt to entrench the individualism of classic liberalism in a period when it seemed increasingly under attack. Such, then, was the context within which the equity of redemption was reformulated by the House of Lords in 1914.

CONCLUSION

The belated metamorphosis of the equity of redemption, and therefore of the transformation of property, from older monopolistic forms of ownership grounded in the privileges of status to newer, contractual, individualistic and free-market forms of ownership, testifies to the tenacity of what some commentators have called the backward or feudal dimensions of modern English society. Yet, as with so much of English property law, its pre-modern form was deceptive and paradoxical. The tenacity of the equity of redemption demonstrates that in some areas of property relations commercial prosperity was parasitic upon the stability, strength and survival of the landed gentry. The mortgage, and the doctrine of the equity of redemption which accompanied it, facilitated both, on the one hand, the qualification, alienation and fragmentation of property, and, on the other hand, the concentration of landed wealth and more absolute and exclusive property rights. The rise and tenacity of the equity of redemption highlights some of the ways in which certain areas of property law privileged the rights of the landed for a longer time-span than is often assumed, yet, at the same time, fostered the extension of commercial contracts sustained by credit. From an economic perspective, the equity of redemption created a legal bulwark safeguarding land (and the landed) from the encroachments of capital, while helping to fashion the mortgage as a major vehicle for economic development. From a legal perspective, although the creation and development of the equity of redemption has been taken as exemplifying the law's increasing commitment to the notion of property as individual absolute dominion, it also illustrates the extent to which the law routinely fostered the qualification of property and restraints on alienation. Although the ideology of absolute private property denied those social and collaborative dimensions intrinsic to human endeavour, in practice the law continually threatened to undo the viability of one of the central tropes of eighteenth and nineteenth-century political discourse. In these ways it could be both feudal and modern.

Extract 18.2   Paddy Ireland, 'Company Law and the Myth of Shareholder Ownership' (1999) 62 *Modern Law Review* 32 at 34–7

USURY AND THE CONCEPT OF PARTNERSHIP

... Although the term usury eventually came widely to be used to describe any extortionate bargain, in its original sense it involved loaning money for interest. The usurer was thus an antiquated version of what Marx later called the money capitalist, the only significant difference between usurer's capital and interest-bearing or money capital lying not in their form (both entail a movement from M – M1) but in the social relations of production within which the money moves. Frowned upon in Greek and Roman times and completely prohibited in the Middle Ages, the taking of interest on loans was later permitted but rates of return regulated by statute, at which point usury came to be identified with the taking of excessive interest rather than with taking interest *per se*. To the modern mind, with its acceptance of the intrinsic productivity of money, this antipathy to 'investment', to money as capital, seems a rather anachronistic theological prejudice, a quaint, pre-modern, superstition. In this context, the survival of the usury laws into the nineteenth century appears rather odd; an example of law lagging behind economy. However, while the hostility to usury can be traced back to biblical sources and came to constitute one of the principal elements of canon law, it had social and political, as well as religious, underpinnings. These were influentially outlined by Aristotle and remain relevant today.

For Aristotle, exchange was central to the social intercourse which made community, the prerequisite of human happiness, possible. By providing a standard of commensurability for unlike things, money facilitated exchange and thereby made an important contribution to social bonding. Usury, Aristotle argued, undermined money's ability to perform these functions and subverted the fairness in exchange which was 'the salvation of states'. It was, he claimed, 'unnatural', for money was inherently unproductive. Lacking genitals – 'organs for generating any other such piece', as Bentham put it – money was sterile and barren; of all the ways of getting wealth, 'money produced out of money ... was the most contrary to nature'. The usurer made money without working for it, taking, in the form of interest, part of the product of the labour of others. Moreover, Aristotle argued, usury was also unnatural in the sense that the acquisition of money tended towards infinity and endless multiplication, encouraging greed for its own sake. One could, like Midas, have an abundance of money and yet still perish from hunger. For Aristotle, therefore, usury undermined justice in exchange, corrupted market relations and subverted the ethical roots of social, political and economic order. There were many later expressions of this view, among the most vivid, that found in *The Divine Comedy*, in which Dante located usurers, their faces charred beyond recognition by fiery rain, in the seventh circle of the Inferno at the very edge of the second division of hell, to reflect 'the degree to which [their] particular offense destroy[ed] communal life and the possibility of spiritual happiness'. In marked contrast to modern legal systems, Dante treated fraud more harshly than violence precisely because it eroded the trust and confidence without which community would disintegrate. The theory of usury which emerged in the Middle Ages was 'not, then, an isolated freak of casuistical ingenuity, but [a] subordinate element in a comprehensive system of social philosophy'.

The legal antipathy to usury can be traced back at least as far as Roman law. However, not only did Roman law permit usury as long as the interest charged was not excessive, it distinguished potentially usurious contracts of loan (*mutuum*) from other transactions in which payment for the use of money was considered legitimate, prominent among them the contract of partnership (*societas*). Over time, as trade expanded and money came increasingly to be borrowed as well as lent as capital (rather than to meet an immediate material need), the legitimacy of many forms of 'investment' was established through an expansion of the scope of concepts such as partnership and a corresponding narrowing of the concept of the (potentially usurious) loan. The result was the legal constitution of many inactive providers of money as 'partners' rather than 'lenders', essentially on the grounds that they put their capital at risk. The concept of partnership that emerged – the 'one great and universal form of licit investment in commerce throughout medieval Europe' – entered scholastic thought 'largely in the form given it by Roman law'. Despite their desire to prohibit usury, therefore, for most canonists and jurists 'there was a world of difference between usury, [profit obtained from] a contract of loan … and justifiable returns derived from partnerships, where there was a sharing of risk and venture of the capital'. Nevertheless, there was much disagreement (and confusion) among them as to the status of some contractual arrangements in which money was provided in return for a reward, particularly those in which the liability of investors to third parties was restricted. In 'analysing and systematising the law of usury for the first time', however, the canonists not only 'provided a rational foundation for the dramatic growth of commercial and financial life during the Middle Ages', they developed a very spacious theory of 'partnership' based around ideas of risk and ownership. It was encapsulated by Aquinas:

> He who commits his money to a merchant or craftsman by means of some kind of partnership does not transfer the ownership of his money to him but it remains his; so that at his risk the merchant trades, or the craftsman works with it; and therefore he can licitly seek part of the profit thence coming as from his own property.

According to this theory, if an investor of money shared the risk of a venture, the arrangement ceased to be a loan and became a partnership. As Patrick Atiyah points out, the concept of risk employed was rather odd for nobody who lends money is ever guaranteed to get it back. Under the theory, however, if, this inherent risk apart, the investor was promised his money back with an additional sum above that legally permitted, the transaction was a loan and potentially usurious. If, on the other hand, the return was neither guaranteed nor fixed in advance but depended on the success, or otherwise, of the venture, the investor was deemed a risk-taking partner. Usury thus entailed the idea of certain gain. As Aquinas emphasised, the issue of risk was itself bound up with the issue of ownership. In a loan arrangement, it was argued, the money lender transferred ownership of his money to the borrower, took a fixed and guaranteed return, and dispensed with the risk to his property; whereas in a partnership the provider of money retained ownership of his property and thus put it at risk. This not only justified his return, it made it possible to attribute it to the goods which the money had been used to buy, rather than to the sterile and barren money itself. In this way, over time, the usury laws contributed to the radical differentiation of two sorts of money investor: 'lenders' outside associations receiving interest; and 'partners' inside associations sharing profits.

The teaching of the canonists on usury was received in significant part into civil law, and in England, where 'any transaction which involved usury was clearly illegal in medieval common law', as late as the seventeenth century the legal conception of usury remained derivative of canon law. As the economic foundations of society changed, however, there gradually emerged more and more ways in which the usury laws could be circumvented and more and more methods of investment recognised as legitimate by both the religious and secular authorities, either by official declaration or by acquiescence. With this, the morality and legality of taking a return on money lent was increasingly accepted as long as only a moderate amount of interest and not *turpes usurae* had been charged. In a series of statutes passed in the sixteenth century, English law came effectively to permit the charging of interest of up to 10 per cent per annum; by 1713, however, this had fallen to 5 per cent, the level at which it remained for the rest of the century.

The result was that, during the eighteenth century, the formative period of the modern English law of partnerships, the usury laws, still 'feared and … far from obsolete', continued to influence the characterisation of different forms of 'investment' in English law. Thus, although the law of partnership 'presumed that each partner was an active trader in a joint concern [with] full power to act as agent of his fellow partners', in accordance with the 'risk' theory of partnership the legal status of inactive providers of money *vis-à-vis* third parties was determined by reference to the content of their financial return rather than by reference to their involvement (or otherwise) in the running of the concern. As Blackstone J explained in *Grace* v. *Smith*:

> the true criterion (when money is advanced to a trader) is to consider whether the profit or premium is certain and defined, or casual, indefinite, and depending on the accidents of the trade. In the former case it is a loan (whether usurious or not, is not material to the present question), in the latter a partnership.

Thus 'lenders' who received interest (a return 'certain and defined') were distinguished from 'partners' who received a share in profits (a return 'casual, indefinite and depending on the accidents of trade'), although both received the return on their capital in the same form – as a reward for the mere ownership of money.

Notes and Questions 18.2

Read *Kreglinger* v. *New Patagonia Meat & Cold Storage Co. Ltd* [1914] AC 25, *Paragon Finance plc* v. *Staunton and Nash* [2001] EWCA Civ 1466; [2002] 1 WLR 685; [2002] 2 All ER 248, CA, and *Broadwick Financial Services Ltd* v. *Spencer* [2002] EWCA Civ 35; [2002] 1 All ER (Comm) 446, either in full or as extracted at www.cambridge.org/propertylaw/, and consider the following:

1 Examine the reasons given by each of their Lordships in *Kreglinger* for concluding that the right of pre-emption was not a part of the mortgage transaction. How convincing are they?

2 In *Knightsbridge Estates Trust* v. *Byrne* [1939] 1 Ch 441, it was held, applying the *Kreglinger* principles, that, in a mortgage between commercial parties

bargaining at arm's length, a postponement of the right to redeem for fifty years was valid. Consider whether, in present market conditions, it would still be considered legitimate to lock a borrower into a loan agreement for such a period.

3 Consider whether, applying the *Kreglinger* principles, it is legitimate for mortgagees to charge an 'early redemption fee' to borrowers who wish to redeem early. Such charges are commonplace in modern mortgages: consider how they can be justified.

4 Is it legitimate, applying these principles, to include a provision in a mortgage that the interest rate will increase by a specified amount if there is default in repayment? If not, would it be legitimate to provide for an interest rate *reduction* on prompt payment?

5 It is argued that it is inappropriate for the courts to intervene where mortgages impose excessive interest rates, first because the remedy for a mortgagor in such a case is to remortgage elsewhere, i.e. move to a different lender, and secondly because control over interest rates is already exerted by the state, in that lenders such as these must be licensed by the Director-General of Fair Trading who will revoke the licence of any lender operating unfair lending practices. Examine the response Dyson LJ makes to these arguments in *Paragon* v. *Nash*. Is there anything else that could be said?

6 Robert Walker LJ expresses the view in *Broadwick* that sections 137–139 of the Consumer Credit Act 1974 'fail to achieve their purpose of protecting consumers, and especially "non-status" borrowers who are unable to obtain credit on more favourable terms from primary lenders'. Consider why this is the case. Is he right in saying that the 'legislative safeguards' he mentions in paragraph 89 will not always solve the problem? Compare this approach with that adopted by the Director-General of Fair Trading in his Guidelines for Lenders on Non-Status Lending (1997) (available from www.fisa.co.uk) referred to by Dyson LJ above.

18.4. Enforcement of security

18.4.1. Remedies

By far the most important remedy for any security interest holder is private sale. In the case of land mortgages, it is sometimes preceded by the mortgagee obtaining a court order for possession (nearly always if the property is residential and occupied). It is also possible for mortgagees (and, as we see later, mortgagors) to apply for a court order for sale under section 91 of the Law of Property Act 1925, but this is rarely done.

A significant alternative enforcement measure for non-residential mortgages is the appointment of a receiver, who is technically the agent of the *mortgagor* (section 109(2) of the Law of Property Act 1925) but whose function is to receive the income and/or to sell property in order to obtain repayment of the money owed to the mortgagee, as we see in *Downsview Nominees Ltd* v. *First City Corp. Ltd* [1993] 2 WLR 86, PC (extracted at www.cambridge.org/propertylaw/). The only other option – applicable only to mortgages, not to any other kind of security interest – is foreclosure, and this is no longer a practical proposition. It involves a court order extinguishing the mortgagor's interest in the mortgaged property, leaving the mortgagee as full legal and beneficial owner. This makes sense as a method of enforcing a property-transfer mortgage where the mortgagor's only interest is the equity of redemption, but even then it is capable of producing such startlingly unfair results that procedural safeguards had to be introduced which have complicated the procedure beyond the point at which it is usable, particularly as adapted to the enforcement of the mortgage by demise and the charge by way of legal mortgage. It is now obsolete, and has been for many years.

18.4.2. Possession

In land mortgages, the mortgagee is entitled to possession from the outset, as a matter of right, not just as a remedy. It is an inherent right, arising out of the mortgagee's status under the statutory charge by way of legal mortgage, which gives him all the rights he would have had if he held a 3,000-year lease as security. It is a right that the mortgagee does not need to exercise except for the purposes of protecting or enforcing the security, and indeed exercise of the right may well be confined to those circumstances by an express or implied term of the mortgage. In the absence of such a contractual restriction, however, the traditional view has always been that the mortgagee may take possession at any time and for any purpose and for any reason, and that equity will not intervene to restrict the exercise of the right.

Although this view has been reasserted repeatedly by the courts (for example, in, but certainly not confined to, *Four-Maids Ltd* v. *Dudley Marshall (Properties) Ltd* [1957] Ch 317, *Western Bank Ltd* v. *Schindler* [1976] 3 WLR 341, CA, and *Ropaigealach* v. *Barclays Bank plc* [1993] 3 WLR 17, CA), it is doubtful whether this principle would ever now be applied to allow a mortgagee to take possession in bad faith, or in circumstances where possession could not possibly be required for the protection or enforcement of the security. When a mortgagee applied to the court for possession in such circumstances in *Albany Home Loans Ltd* v. *Massey* [1997] 2 All ER 609 (extracted at www.cambridge.org/propertylaw/), it was refused, and the general statement of the scope of a mortgagee's rights and duties made by Nicholls LJ in *Palk* v. *Mortgages Services Funding plc* [1993] 2 WLR 415 (extracted at www.cambridge.org/propertylaw/) provides ample support for the decision. It is also worth noting that the Council of Mortgage Lenders, in its 1997 Statement of Practice, 'Handling of Arrears and Possessions' (Extract 18.3 below) confirmed that possession will be taken only as a last resort (paragraphs 13 and 16) and never in the circumstances given in paragraph 16.

In practice, of course, there is no reason why a mortgagee acting in good faith would want to take possession except for the purposes of protecting or enforcing the security. An institutional lender is unlikely to want to take possession for its own purposes, and fear of adverse publicity would probably deter it even if it did, at least if it was a lender operating in the competitive house-purchase home-loan sector.

There are also potential legal problems. If the premises are residential, there is a danger of committing a criminal offence under section 6 of the Criminal Law Act 1967 if the mortgagee takes possession of occupied premises without a court order (section 6 makes it an offence to use or threaten force to secure entry to residential premises if at the time there is someone present on the premises who objects to the entry and the entrant knows this). And, if the mortgagee decides to apply for a court order of possession, the court has jurisdiction to refuse it under section 36 of the Administration of Justice Act 1970 as amended if the premises are or include a dwelling-house: see *Western Bank Ltd* v. *Schindler* [1976] 3 WLR 341 and *Ropaigealach* v. *Barclays Bank plc* [1999] 3 WLR 17, CA, for the scope of the jurisdiction.

Also, no mortgagee would want to spend any appreciable time in possession because of the risk of incurring liabilities to the mortgagor. Mortgagees in possession are liable to keep the property in repair (see *Downsview Nominees Ltd* v. *First City Corp. Ltd* [1993] 2 WLR 86, PC) and also come under a duty to account to the mortgagor not only for any income or profits actually received from the property while in possession but also for whatever it could, but for its wilful default, have received. The classic authority on this duty to account is *White* v. *City of London Brewery Co.* (1889) LR 42 ChD 237, CA, although it has to be said that there is no modern authority on precisely what this would now involve. Also, if the premises are in active use as business premises and the business is viable, it might be difficult to avoid coming under a duty to carry on, or at least not sabotage, the business (see *AIB Finance Ltd* v. *Debtors* [1998] 2 All ER 929, where there was held to be no duty where the business had already collapsed by the time the mortgagee took possession). And, once a mortgagee does start to get involved in the management of the business, it then appears to come under a duty to do so 'with due diligence' (see *Medforth* v. *Blake* [1999] 3 All ER 97, CA, where a receiver was held to be in breach of duty to the mortgagor by failing to obtain a discount on pig feed; there seems no reason why the same should not apply to a mortgagee in possession).

18.4.3.　Sale

The reality is that, when a mortgagee does take possession, or applies to the court for a possession order, almost invariably it does so in order to obtain vacant possession with a view to selling the property under its power of sale.

18.4.3.1.　When the power arises

The mortgagee's statutory power of sale is conferred by section 101(1)(i) of the Law of Property Act 1925, and arises 'when the mortgage money has become due' (in other words, when any capital repayment is overdue). The statutory provision gives the mortgagee power to sell a greater interest than he himself has, i.e. the mortgagor's interest free from the mortgage and from any interest over which the mortgage takes priority. Consequently, any purported sale made by the mortgagee *before* the power has arisen will be ineffective because of the *nemo dat* rule: all that the purchaser can acquire is the mortgagee's own interest because that is all that the mortgagee has the capacity to convey.

18.4.3.2.   When the power becomes exercisable

Section 103 of the 1925 Act prohibits exercise of the power of sale unless and until one of the three conditions specified there has been satisfied. These are that there has been a default in payment of some part of the capital for three months after the mortgagee served notice demanding repayment, or that interest payable under the mortgage is two months in arrears, or that there has been a breach of some other provision in the mortgage. However, these restrictions are more apparent than real: even the most minor breach will suffice for the third condition to be satisfied, and in any event the terms of section 103 may be varied by express provision in the mortgage deed.

Even if the power of sale has not yet become exercisable, the sale will be effective to transfer title to the purchaser because, once the power has *arisen*, the mortgagee does have the capacity to transfer title. Section 104 also provides that a sale cannot be set aside on the ground that the power has not yet become exercisable, and that a purchaser need not concern itself to see whether it has or not. However, it has been held that section 103 cannot protect a purchaser buying with notice of any impropriety or irregularity in the sale (see *Lord Waring* v. *London and Manchester Assurance Co. Ltd* [1935] Ch 310 and the earlier cases considered there).

18.4.4.   Duties on enforcement

Up until the 1990s, the mortgagee's duty of care owed to the mortgagor in enforcing the security was formulated in negligence terms, i.e. a duty to take reasonable care in exercising its remedies. The classic statement of this appeared in *Cuckmere Brick* v. *Mutual Finance Ltd* [1971] Ch 949, where it was held that a mortgagee exercising the power of sale was under a duty to take reasonable care to obtain the market price for the property. One advantage of couching the duty in terms of negligence was that it made it clear that the duty was owed not only to the mortgagor but also, and to the same standard of care, to anyone reasonably foreseeably affected by the sale (for example, anyone holding a mortgage and charge taking priority after the mortgage, or a guarantor), and that a receiver appointed by a mortgagee owed the same duties as a mortgagee when enforcing the security.

However, in a series of cases culminating in the Privy Council decision in *Downsview Nominees Ltd* v. *First City Corp. Ltd* [1993] 2 WLR 86, PC, it was held that negligence is not an appropriate standard. The appropriate test, Lord Templeman said, is first, that in exercising its power of sale the mortgagee is under a duty to take reasonable care to obtain the market price (i.e. confirming the substance of the test in *Cuckmere Brick*), but, secondly, that, in exercising all its other rights, powers and remedies under the mortgage, the mortgagee's duty is only to act in good faith and 'for the sole purpose of securing repayments of the moneys owing under his mortgage'. For a consideration of what this might amount to in practice, see *Palk* v. *Mortgage Services Funding plc* [1993] 2 WLR 415 (extracted at www.cambridge.org/propertylaw/), where Sir Donald Nicholls VC argued that in addition a mortgagee has a duty to act fairly towards the mortgagor (a proposition that does not appear inconsistent with anything Lord Templeman says in *Downsview*). This is particularly striking when viewed in the context of the *Palk* case itself, where the court ordered a sale of the mortgaged property against the wishes of the mortgagee despite the fact that this would not raise anything like enough to repay all the indebtedness, because, although the mortgagee had sound commercial reasons for refusing to agree to a sale, the consequences of not selling would be disproportionately harsh on the borrower.

Finally, it is instructive to compare the standards of behaviour on enforcement expected by the courts with those the lending industry itself regards as good practice. In so far as these relate to residential mortgages, they were set out in the Council of Mortgage Lenders' Statement of Practice on the Handing of Arrears and Possessions (1997), extracted below. This Statement of Practice was withdrawn by the CML in October 2004, when residential mortgage lenders ceased to be self-regulated and instead became subject to regulation by the Financial Services Authority (see the Mortgage Conduct of Business Rules published by the Financial Services Authority and available on their website, www.fsa.gov.uk). The 1997 CML Statement of Practice can nevertheless still tell us something interesting about how reputable lenders consider they ought to behave.

Extract 18.3   Council of Mortgage Lenders, *Statement of Practice: Handling of Arrears and Possessions* (1997)

INTRODUCTION

1. This Statement provides an overview of how mortgage lenders currently deal with mortgage arrears and possession cases. The facts of each arrears and possession case are unique, and each case needs to be treated individually. Mortgage lenders adopt flexible procedures for the handling of arrears and possession cases which are aimed at assisting the borrower as far as possible in his or her particular circumstances. Individual practice will, of course, vary between lenders depending, in particular, on whether they operate on a centralised or decentralised basis. This Statement describes how lenders deal with mortgage arrears; the procedures adopted when handling possession cases; the subsequent sale of property in possession and finally the recovery of any outstanding debt. Individual circumstances might arise in which action outside those referred to in this Statement may need to be taken.

MORTGAGE ARREARS

General principles

2. The following general principles are relevant to the question of mortgage arrears:

(a) When a borrower falls into arrears, the problem should be handled sympathetically and positively by the lender. The lender's first step will be to try to contact the borrower to discuss the matter.

(b) As soon as financial difficulties arise, the borrower should let the lender know as soon as possible.

(c) Once contact has been established, a plan for dealing with the borrower's financial difficulties and clearing the arrears will be developed consistent with the interests of both the borrower and the lender.

(d) Possession of the property will be sought only as a last resort when attempts to reach alternative arrangements with borrowers have been unsuccessful. The borrower will remain liable for the full mortgage debt.

The handling of arrears: initial action taken by lenders

3. Mortgage lenders or their agents may use the following administrative procedures for dealing with arrears:

(a) The lender's first step will be to try to contact the borrower, for example, by letter or telephone.

(b) The lender may seek a meeting with the borrower to discuss the situation and examine ways to resolve the problems. Alternatively, this may be done via the telephone or letter.

(c) Once contact has been established, a plan for clearing the arrears will be developed consistent with the interests of both the borrower and the lender.

(d) If contact cannot be made with the borrower and payments continue to be missed, legal action to recover the arrears or take possession of the property may be necessary.

Alleviating arrears problems

4. Lenders have the following measures which they can use to help some borrowers in arrears difficulties:

(a) *Extend the term of the mortgage.* In the case of a repayment loan the term of the loan can be lengthened, although in most cases this does not make a significant difference to the monthly repayments.

(b) *Change the type of mortgage.* An investment backed mortgage may be changed to a repayment, or interest only, mortgage with a subsequent reduction in monthly outgoings. The borrower should also take appropriate professional advice.

(c) *Defer payment.* Payment of part of the interest may be deferred for a period. This may be particularly appropriate where there is a temporary shortfall of income (for example, because of an industrial dispute or a temporary illness), or where there has been a rapid increase in interest rates. Lenders may in certain circumstances be willing to accept, for a reasonable period of time, the most the borrower could reasonably afford if this is in the best interests of both the lender and the borrower. However, this is not a solution where, because of a permanent reduction in income, a borrower is unable to afford anywhere near the full mortgage repayments and there is little prospect of an improvement in the situation in the foreseeable future.

(d) *Capitalise interest.* Linked to (c) is the possibility of capitalising interest. This may be appropriate where arrears have built up but full monthly repayments can be resumed. The amount outstanding (capital sum and arrears of interest) may be rescheduled and repaid over the life of the loan. This might have an impact on the interest rate levied, whether a repayment vehicle will repay the loan in the case of an investment backed mortgage and eligibility for mortgage interest relief at source (MIRAS). Such an approach is unlikely to be adopted where the borrower has in the past failed to adhere to an alternative payment arrangement.

5. When agreeing alternative repayment arrangements, lenders will carry out an appraisal of a borrower's ability to meet the repayments. In some cases, the arrangements might be made for a specific period of time, after which an assessment is made as to whether the circumstances have changed to the extent that the arrangement can be varied.

6. In addition, lenders try to ensure that the borrower is aware of the availability of social security benefits which might apply such as income support to meet part of the mortgage interest repayments where a borrower is unemployed. Where the borrower has a multiple debt problem, the lender might suggest that the borrower contact a Citizens Advice Bureau or debt advice agency. At the borrower's request and with the borrower's consent, the lender will liaise wherever possible with a debt counselling organisation, for example, Citizens Advice Bureaux, money advice centres or the Consumer Credit Counselling Service.

7. In the vast majority of cases these approaches, together with the efforts of the borrower, are sufficient to prevent a minor arrears problem from becoming a major problem leading to possession. It is significant that, while many people fall into arrears for a short time, a much smaller proportion have large arrears and a very small proportion result in possession.

8. Where mortgage arrears have accrued on an account, lenders recognise the need for the account to be closely administered by staff with relevant expertise in dealing with borrowers experiencing repayment difficulties. Details of the mortgage account may be transferred to the lender's specialised mortgage arrears department, where the staff would liaise directly with the borrower. Alternatively, the account may be administered by the local branch, with overall monitoring by the lender's central arrears department. The borrower would be contacted to establish why the mortgage repayments were no longer being made, whether the borrower's circumstances had changed, for example, if the borrower was no longer employed, and if an alternative payment arrangement could be agreed. A record of the mortgage arrears may be held by a credit reference agency.

The levying of charges on accounts in arrear

9. In recent years, lenders have developed effective administrative and forbearance procedures to deal with cases where the borrower is unable to meet the mortgage

repayments in full. A great deal of time and resources has been devoted to ensuring that these procedures operate to assist defaulting borrowers remain in their homes. Taking into account the additional costs which might be incurred in administering accounts in arrear, lenders may levy a fee on the borrower's account to meet a proportion of these costs.

10. However, lenders also recognise the difficulties facing borrowers who are experiencing problems in meeting their mortgage repayments. If a fee is levied on an account, it usually represents the reasonable cost of the additional administration required. When fees are charged, these may be on either a monthly or quarterly basis. Alternatively, lenders may charge only where certain administrative procedures have been carried out, for example, a home visit by a money adviser (employed by the lender) or where legal proceedings have been initiated.

11. In practice, lenders advise borrowers of any fees which might be charged either prior to the fee being levied or, when the fee is in respect of services, prior to the services being provided. Lenders may also advise borrowers when they take out a mortgage that fees may be charged to the account if it falls into arrear. Information on any fees is usually incorporated in mortgage documentation or published tariffs.

12. In many cases, where borrowers are experiencing difficulties in meeting their mortgage repayments, an alternative payment arrangement may be reached between the lender and the borrower. If an alternative payment has been agreed, and is being adhered to by the borrower, lenders may either cease levying a fee on the account or continue to charge fees until the account has been brought up to date.

POSSESSION

Methods of obtaining possession

13. Possession of a property will be sought only as a last resort when all attempts to reach alternative arrangements with the borrower have been unsuccessful. A lender may obtain possession of a property in three ways:

(a) *By court order.* When pursuing possession proceedings through the courts, lenders must adhere to all the legal requirements and procedures to enforce their security, a number of which give considerable protection to the borrower. Proceedings may be suspended should the court consider that a borrower may be able, within a reasonable time period, to pay any sums due under the mortgage. The execution of the possession order may be postponed for a time to allow the borrower to secure alternative accommodation.

(b) *By voluntary agreement with the lender.* A borrower who has fallen into arrears and who has little prospect of repaying such arrears may reach an agreement with his lender to hand over the property to the lender without the need to obtain a court order. A borrower may also be asked to sign a voluntary possession declaration to confirm the agreement, which would make it clear that mortgage interest together with other charges will continue to accrue until the property is sold. A voluntary surrender may result in an earlier sale of the property than would be the case with court proceedings.

(c) *Surrender (or abandonment) by the borrower without notifying the lender.* In cases where a borrower has failed to discuss his mortgage arrears problems with the lender, or where suitable arrangements have not been reached between the lender and borrower, a borrower may simply vacate the property without advising the lender; often keys are sent to the lender, this being possibly the first intimation that the property has been surrendered. In such circumstances, the property would be sold by the lender. Again, the borrower is liable for the total debt including mortgage interest which accrues until the property is sold.

Irrespective of how the property is taken into possession, the borrower will remain liable for the outstanding debt including any accrued interest and charges between the date of possession and the date of sale.

In some cases, borrowers who have had their properties taken into possession may seek a mortgage on another property. Potential borrowers should not conceal the fact that they have defaulted on a previous loan. The subsequent lender will be aware of the previous mortgage either as a result of enquiries of the original lender or the CML Mortgage Possessions Register which lists borrowers who have had their properties taken into possession.

Administrative aspects

15. While lenders operate different administrative procedures to deal with possession cases, the following procedures are common:

(a) Should direct contact with the borrower not result in an arrangement (for example, an alternative payment arrangement) which would enable the borrower to remain in the property, then solicitors may be instructed to start possession proceedings. This is usually the only course of action available to the lender by that time.

(b) In some cases, further follow-up contact may continue to be made up until, and after, the court hearing, every effort being made to encourage the customer to discuss suitable repayment arrangements and avoid the need for possession.

(c) Instructions for a warrant to be issued for possession are implemented by the lender, after a full review of the borrower's file by a person fully aware of the facts, and a final letter or telephone call to the borrower.

(d) Before taking possession, a lender may liaise with the relevant local housing department. The borrower may also be advised to register on the local authority's list as soon as possible. Lenders recognise that it is important to give local authority housing departments as much notice as possible where borrowers and their families might need to be rehoused. However, this has to be balanced against the possibility that alternative arrangements might be reached between the lender and borrower which would enable the borrower to remain in the property. The timing of providing advice to housing departments will vary from case to case and lenders will only take this course of action with the consent of the borrower.

(e) On taking possession, the Court Officer may be accompanied by the lender's representative, after which the property will usually be put on the market as soon as possible to minimise the mortgage interest continuing to accrue on the account. A record of the possession may be held on the CML Possessions Register.

CML/GOVERNMENT STATEMENT ON ARREARS AND POSSESSION PROCEDURES

16. In December 1991, after detailed discussions with the government, the CML reaffirmed that it is the policy of lenders to take possession only as a last resort, and to handle arrears problems efficiently and sympathetically. A formal announcement was made by the Chancellor of the Exchequer in the House of Commons and at a CML Press Conference on 19 December 1991. The announcement referred to the fact that:

(a) Where borrowers have suffered a significant reduction in their income but are making a reasonable regular payment, lenders do not seek to take possession.

(b) In the knowledge that income support will in future be paid direct, lenders will not take possession in cases where mortgage interest payments are covered by income support.

17. From October 1995, income support has been paid by the Department of Social Security at a 'standard rate' of interest, which may be less than the interest rate charged by the lender. Borrowers will need to make up any shortfall in the mortgage repayment. Some lenders have decided not to participate in the direct payment scheme. In these cases, the borrower will be responsible for passing on the income support for mortgage interest payment to their lender.

SALE OF PROPERTIES IN POSSESSION

18. When selling properties which have been taken into possession lenders are under a duty to obtain the best price reasonably obtainable. A lender is not bound to postpone the sale in the hope of obtaining a better price at some future date; however, the lender should allow sufficient time to permit, for example, proper advertising so that the best price obtainable may be achieved. Mortgage lenders generally use the following administrative procedures for selling properties which have been taken into possession:

(a) *Administration.* The sale may be dealt with either via a lender's in-house department or through a separate property management company employed by the mortgage lender. Dedicated staff are responsible for co-ordinating the sale of properties in possession which will include reviewing the offers received from potential purchasers as well as monitoring the condition of these properties and their valuation.

(b) *Valuation.* A valuation of the property is obtained from either one or two qualified surveyors and another from the appointed estate agent. Prices are usually reviewed every three to four months and more often when the circumstances justify a revaluation.

(c) *Estate agents.* Properties are usually marketed through an estate agent in the immediate locality of the property being sold. Agents may advertise properties in the local press, with such advertisements being repeated as and when necessary. Mailshots and national advertising may also be carried out in some cases. In general, lenders do not market these properties as 'repossessed properties'; in many cases estate agents are specifically instructed not to do so.

(d) *Report on activity.* Estate agents are usually required to report on activity every four to six weeks if a property remains unsold. The estate agent will notify a mortgage lender of any offers received. Only when satisfied that the best price has been obtained, would the estate agent recommend this offer for acceptance. If the offer is substantially below the asking price, the agent must provide supporting evidence to suggest that this would be the best offer obtained. In practice, all offers are accepted or declined promptly. Where there are a number of very close offers on a property, a sealed bid procedure may be carried out whereby the person putting forward the best offer would be the successful purchaser.

(e) *Visits to the property*. The agent will usually visit the property on a regular basis and ensure that any repairs and maintenance to the property are carried out and that the property is secure. When properties are first put up for sale, mortgage lenders will usually arrange that essential repairs, cleaning and tidying of the garden are carried out. While the estate agent will take care of minor repairs which are identified on the regular visits, other repairs usually require the approval of the mortgage lender. Where this work is carried out, estate agents will be required to obtain competitive estimates. Prospective purchasers will normally be accompanied by the agent when viewing a property.

(f) *Auction*. Properties in possession may be sold via auction. These properties are reviewed relative to sales experience and the length of time on the market. There are occasions when properties may be sold by auction because either the auction is specifically targeted at the type of property in question, e.g. a period type of residence, or the property will generally appeal to the speculator market because of its condition. Such properties are referred to an appropriate auctioneer. A catalogue would be issued and the properties are available for viewing. A reserve price is usually based on information relating to the number of viewings and general level of interest. A reserve price is set several days before the auction following consultation with a surveyor on the valuation of the property.

Proceeds of sale

19. Following the sale of a property in possession, the proceeds of sale will be applied in the following way. First, the lender will use the funds to meet the costs incurred in selling the property and to repay the outstanding mortgage including interest. If there are subsequent loans secured against the property any surplus will also be applied to repay these loans prior to any amounts being paid to the borrower. If there are insufficient proceeds of sale to repay the mortgage, the borrower will remain liable to repay any outstanding debt.

Indemnity insurance

20. Mortgage indemnity is insurance which a lender may take out for its protection where a high percentage loan is made. This insurance policy covers the situation in which, at some future stage, the lender has to repossess the property and sell it and the lender suffers a loss. For example, if the property is sold for less than the amount of the borrower's outstanding mortgage (including accrued interest) the lender can claim on the mortgage indemnity to recover some of its loss. The basic security for the mortgage is the property. The mortgage indemnity, therefore, acts as a form of additional

security for the lender. It provides no protection to the borrower who gains no benefit, other than a high percentage loan advance than would otherwise have been granted.

21. In most cases, the mortgage indemnity will cover the lender only for part of its loss and, in addition, once an insurer has paid a mortgage indemnity claim, it gains the right of subrogation; this means that the insurer can reclaim from the borrower any money it has paid to the lender under the mortgage indemnity claim. Either the lender or its insurer may take legal action against the borrower to recover the shortfall if the borrower does not repay it voluntarily, although any action is taken in the name of the lender. In most cases, the lender contacts the borrower to recover the shortfall on behalf of itself and its insurer. This does not mean that the lender recovers the loss twice; any money paid by the insurer which is collected from the borrower is then passed back to the insurer.

Loss recovery procedures

22. Following the sale of a property, the borrower remains liable to repay any shortfall which might arise between the amount of the outstanding mortgage and the sale price obtained. When a borrower purchases a property with mortgage finance, the borrower enters into a personal covenant with the lender to repay the mortgage in full. When two or more borrowers purchase a property, the lender will treat them as jointly and severally liable for the entire amount borrowed, irrespective of how much each borrower actually contributed to the mortgage repayments on a monthly basis. The lender has 12 years (5 years in Scotland) in which to seek recovery of the shortfall via the courts. Direct recovery could extend beyond that point.

23. After the sale of a property, the borrower should keep their lender advised of forwarding addresses so that contact can made regarding the sale and repayment of any shortfall. The lender will notify the borrower either by letter or by telephone as soon as practicably possible of the amount of the shortfall. If the borrower has not provided a forwarding address, the lender will try to locate and make contact with the former borrower.

24. The lender and the borrower will generally agree a repayment arrangement taking into account the borrower's current income and expenditure. In the majority of cases, payment arrangements are made without the need for court proceedings; this enables both parties to review the arrangement as and when necessary should circumstances change. If the borrower is unwilling to enter into an acceptable voluntary arrangement, the lender may use other enforcement remedies via the courts to seek repayment. A record of the repayment arrangement might be held by a credit reference agency and the borrower will need to advise any future lender of the shortfall debt and repayment arrangement.

Notes and Questions 18.3

Read the above extract and also *Albany Home Loans Ltd* v. *Massey* [1997] 2 All ER 609, CA, *Downsview Nominees Ltd* v. *First City Corp. Ltd* [1993] AC 295; [1993] 2 WLR 86; [1993] 3 All ER 626, PC, and *Palk* v. *Mortgage Services Funding plc* [1993]

Ch 330; [1993] 2 WLR 415; [1993] 2 All ER 481, CA, either in full or as extracted at www.cambridge.org/propertylaw/. In the light of all these, consider the following:

1   Consider how far *Albany Home Loans Ltd* v. *Massey* is consistent with (a) *Four-Maids Ltd* v. *Dudley Marshall (Properties) Ltd* [1957] Ch 317, *Western Bank Ltd* v. *Schindler* [1976] 3 WLR 341, CA, and *Ropaigealach* v. *Barclays Bank plc* [1993] 3 WLR 17, CA, (b) the statements of principles established in *Downsview* and *Palk*, and (c) paragraphs 13 and 16 of the CML Statement of Practice.

2   Explain why a second mortgagee is entitled to buy up the first mortgage, by paying off everything due to the first mortgagee. Why would it want to do so?

3   Why does a first mortgagee and its receiver owe the same duty to the second mortgagee as it owes to the mortgagor?

4   According to the Privy Council in *Downsview*, what duties does a mortgagee owe to the mortgagor and others (a) when exercising the power of sale, and (b) when exercising any of its other rights and remedies under the mortgage? Why should there be two different levels of liability?

5   Can a mortgagee sell at whatever time it wants – for example, would it be in breach of duty if it sold within a few days of making the decision to sell, or sold at an auction held in the dead of night in the middle of the country without telling anyone? See *Predeth* v. *Castle Philips Finance Co. Ltd* [1986] 2 EGLR 144; (1986) 279 EG 1355, *American Express* v. *Hurley* [1985] 3 All ER 568, *Standard Chartered Bank Ltd* v. *Walker* [1982] 1 WLR 1410; [1982] 3 All ER 938, and *Palk* v. *Mortgage Services Funding plc* [1993] Ch 330; [1993] 2 WLR 415; [1993] 2 All ER 481.

6   If a receiver appointed by a mortgagee of freehold land subject to a lease negligently fails to exercise an option in the lease to increase the rent payable under the lease, would the receiver be in breach of duty? See *Knight* v. *Lawrence* [1991] BCC 411; [1993] BCLC 215; [1991] 01 EG 105, but note this case was decided before *Downsview*: would it have been decided differently if heard after *Downsview*? See *Medforth* v. *Blake*, noted in section 18.4.2 above.

7   It is said in *Downsview* that, if a mortgagee (or receiver) takes possession of business premises, it is not obliged to carry on the business of the mortgagee. How realistic is this: will it be in breach of its duty to take reasonable care to obtain the market value of business premises if it destroys any goodwill attaching to the premises by allowing a thriving business to collapse? See *AIB Finance* v. *Debtors*, particularly the judgment at first instance ([1997] 4 All ER 677), but also the opposite view on the point expressed *obiter* in the Court of Appeal ([1998] 2 All ER 929).

8   To what extent is the analysis of Nicholls VC in *Palk* inconsistent with what Lord Templeman says in *Downsview*? Are these differences in substance or just different ways of expressing the same thing?

9   The *dictum* of Lord Denning in *Quennell* v. *Maltby* was quoted in *Albany Home Loans Ltd* v. *Massey* as support for the court's decision in *Massey* not to grant a possession order against Mr Massey. Lord Denning said:

> A mortgagee will be restrained from getting possession except when it is sought bona fide and reasonably for the purpose of enforcing the security and then only subject to such conditions as the court thinks fit to impose.

In the light of the other cases discussed here, is this an accurate statement of the present law? If not, should it be adopted as a general principle of mortgage law?

Bibliography

Ackerman, Bruce, *Private Property and the Constitution* (New Haven and London: Yale University Press, 1977)

Alexander, Gregory S., *Commodity and Propriety: Competing Visions of Property in American Legal Thought 1776–1970* (Chicago: University of Chicago Press, 1997)

Anderson, Terry L., and Hill, P. J., 'The Evolution of Property Rights', in T. L. Anderson and F. S. McChesney (eds.), *Property Rights: Co-operation, Conflict, and Law* (Princeton: Princeton University Press, 2003), p. 135

Anderson, Terry L., and McChesney, Fred S., *Property Rights: Co-operation, Conflict, and Law* (Princeton: Princeton University Press, 2003)

Ausness, R., 'Water Rights, the Public Trust Doctrine and the Protection of Instream Uses' (1986) *University of Illinois Law Review* 407–37

Ballantine, H. W., 'Title by Adverse Possession' (1918) 32 *Harvard Law Review* 135

Barnsley, D. G., 'Co-owners' Rights to Occupy Trust Property' (1998) *Cambridge Law Journal* 123

Bartlett, Richard, 'Humpies Not Houses, or the Denial of Native Title: A Comparative Assessment of Australia's Museum Mentality' (2003) 10 *Australian Property Law Journal* 12

Barzel, Yoram, 'Optimal Timing of Innovations' (1968) 50 *Review of Economics and Statistics* 348

  Economic Analysis of Property Rights (2nd edn, Cambridge: Cambridge University Press, 1997)

Battersby, G., and Preston, A. D., 'The Concepts of "Property", "Title" and "Owner" Used in the Sale of Goods Act 1893' (1972) 35 *Modern Law Review* 268

Beaglehole, Earnest, *Property: A Study in Social Psychology* (London: Allen & Unwin, 1931)

Becker, Lawrence C., *Property Rights: Philosophic Foundations* (London: Routledge and Kegan Paul, 1977)

  'The Moral Basis of Property Rights', in J. Roland Pennock and John Chapman (eds.), *Nomos XXII: Property* (New York: New York University Press, 1980), Chapter 8

Bell, A. P., *Modern Law of Personal Property in England and Ireland* (London: Butterworths, 1989)

Bentham, Jeremy, *The Theory of Legislation, Principles of the Civil Code* (ed. C. K. Ogden, London: Kegan Paul & Co., 1931)

Berg, Alan, 'Clogs on the Equity of Redemption – Or Chaining the Unruly Dog' (2002) *Journal of Business Law* 335

Berle, Adolf A., and Means, Gardiner C., *The Modern Corporation and Private Property* (New York: Harcourt, Brace & World, 1932)

Birks, Peter, 'Five Keys to Land Law', in S. Bright and J. Dewar (eds.), *Land Law: Themes and Perspectives* (Oxford: Oxford University Press, 1998), Chapter 18

Blackstone, Sir William, *Commentaries on the Laws of England* (Chicago and London: Chicago University Press, 1979)

Brennan, Frank, *The Wik Debate: Its Impact on Aborigines, Pastoralists and Miners* (Sydney: New South Wales University Press, 1998)

Buckle, Stephen, *Natural Law and the Theory of Property: Grotius to Hume* (Oxford: Clarendon Press, 1991)

Buckley, F. H., 'The Bankruptcy Priority Puzzle' (1986) 72 *Virginia Law Review* 1393

Burn, E. H., *Cheshire and Burn's Modern Law of Real Property* (16th edn, London: Butterworths, 2000)

Byrne-Sutton, Quentin, 'The Goldberg Case: A Confirmation of the Difficulty in Acquiring Good Title to Valuable Stolen Cultural Objects' (1992) 1 *International Journal of Cultural Property* 151

Calabresi, Guido, and Melamed, A. Douglas, 'Property Rules, Liability Rules and Inalienability: One View of the Cathedral' (1972) 85 *Harvard Law Review* 1089

Carsberg, B. V., Page, M. J., Sindall, A. J., and Waring, L. D., *Small Company Financial Reporting* (Englewood Cliffs, NJ: Prentice Hall, 1986)

Chakravaty-Kaul, Minoti, *Common Lands and Customary Law: Institutional Change in North India Over The Past Two Centuries* (Oxford: Oxford University Press, 1996)

Cheffins, Brian, *Company Law: Theory, Structure and Operation* (Oxford: Clarendon Press, 1997)

Clarke, Alison, 'Property Law' (1996) 49 *Current Legal Problems* 97

'Ship Mortgages', in N. Palmer and E. McKendrick (eds.), *Interests in Goods* (2nd edn, London, Lloyd's of London Press, 1998)

'Use, Time and Entitlement' (2004) 57 *Current Legal Problems* 239

Coase, R. H., 'The Problem of Social Cost' (1960) 3 *Journal of Law and Economics* 1

Cohen, Felix S., 'Dialogue on Private Property' (1954) 9 *Rutgers Law Journal* 357

Coleman Jules L., and Kraus, Jody, 'Rethinking the Theory of Legal Rights' (1986) 95 *Yale Law Journal* 1335

Conveyancing and Land Law Committee of the Law Society, *Undue Influence – Solicitors' Duties Post-'Etridge'* (Guidance Note, May 2002)

Cooter, Robert D., 'Time, Property Rights, and the Common Law' (1986) 64 *Washington University Law Quarterly* 804

Cooter, Robert D., and Ulen, Thomas, *Law and Economics* (4th edn, Boston: Addison Wesley Longman, 2004)

Cotterrell, R., 'Some Sociological Aspects of the Controversy Around the Legal Validity of Private Purpose Trusts', in S. Goldstein (ed.), *Equity and Contemporary Legal Developments* (Jerusalem: H &M Sacher Institute, 1992)

Council of Mortgage Lenders, Handling of Arrears and Possessions (Statement of Practice, 1997)

Critchley, Patricia, 'Taking Formalities Seriously', in S. Bright and J. K. Dewar (eds.), *Land Law: Themes and Perspectives* (Oxford: Oxford University Press, 1998), Chapter 20

Cunningham, R. A., 'More on Adverse Possession: A Rejoinder to Professor Helmholz' (1986) 64 *Washington University Law Quarterly* 1167

Cunningham, R. A., Stoebuck, W. B., and Whitman, D. A., *The Law of Property* (3rd edn, St Paul, MN: West Group, 2000)

Dahlman, Carl, *The Open Field System and Beyond* (Cambridge: Cambridge University Press, 1980)

Dales, J. H., *Pollution Property and Prices: An Essay in Policy-Making and Economics* (Toronto: University of Toronto Press, 1968)

Dasgupta, P., and Stiglitz, J., 'Uncertainty, Industrial Structure, and the Speed of R&D' (1980) 11 *Bell. Journal of Economics* 1

De Alessi, Louis, 'Gains from Private Property', in T. L. Anderson and F. S. McChesney (eds.), *Property Rights: Co-operation, Conflict, and Law* (Princeton: Princeton University Press, 2003), Chapter 4

De Lacy, J., 'The Priority Rule of Dearle v. Hall Re-stated' (1999) *Conveyancer* 311

Deakin, S., Johnston, A., and Markesinis, B. S. (eds.), *Markesinis and Deakin's Tort Law* (5th edn, Oxford: Clarendon Press, 2003)

Demsetz, Harold, 'Towards a Theory of Property Rights' (1967) 57 *American Economic Review* 347

    'Ownership and the Externalities Problem', in T. L. Anderson and F. S. McChesney (eds.), *Property Rights: Co-operation, Conflict, and Law* (Princeton: Princeton University Press, 2003), Chapter 11

Department of the Environment, Transport and the Regions, *Good Practice Guide on Managing the Use of Common Land* (London: Department of the Environment, Transport and the Regions, June 1998)

Dharmapala, Dhammika, and Pitchford, Rohan, 'An Economic Analysis of "Riding to Hounds": Pierson v. Post Revisited' (2002) 18 *Journal of Law, Economics, and Organization* 39

Diamond, A. L., *A Review of Security Interests in Property* (London: HMSO, 1989)

Director-General of Fair Trading, *Guidelines for Lenders on Non-Status Lending* (London: Office of Fair Trading, 1997)

Dixon, Martin, 'Overreaching and the Trusts of Land and Appointment of Trustees Act 1996' (2000) *Conveyancer* 267

    'The Reform of Property Law and the Land Registration Act 2002: A Risk Assessment' (2003) *Conveyancer* 16

Dockray, Martin, 'Why Do We Need Adverse Possession?' (1985) *Conveyancer* 272

Dromgoole, Sarah, and Gaskell, Nicholas, 'Interests in Wrecks', in N. Palmer and E. McKendrick (eds.), *Interests in Goods* (2nd edn, London: Lloyd's of London Press, 1998) Chapter 7

Dunne, Paul, and Hughes, Alan, 'Age, Size, Growth and Survival: UK Companies in the 1980s' (1994) 42 *Journal of Industrial Economics* 115

Easterbrook F., and Fischel, D., *The Economic Structure of Corporate Law* (Cambridge, MA: Harvard University Press, 1991)

Ellickson, Robert C., 'Adverse Possession and Perpetuities Law: Two Dents in the Libertarian Model of Property Rights' (1986) 64 *Washington University Law Quarterly* 723

'A Hypothesis of Wealth-Maximising Norms: Evidence from the Whaling Industry' (1989) 5 *Journal of Law, Economics, and Organization* 83

'Property in Land' (1993) 102 *Yale Law Journal* 1315

Epstein, Richard A., 'Notice and Freedom of Contract in the Law of Servitudes' (1982) 55 *Southern California Law Review* 1353

'Past and Future: The Temporal Dimension in the Law of Property' (1986) 64 *Washington University Law Quarterly* 667

Etheleriadis, P., 'The Analysis of Property Rights' (1996) 16 *Oxford Journal of Legal Studies* 31

Farrand J. T. (ed.), *Wolstenholme and Cherry's Conveyancing Statutes*, vol. 1 (13th edn, London: Oyez Publishing Ltd, 1972)

Farrand, J. T., and Clarke, Alison (eds.), *Emmet and Farrand on Title* (19th edn, looseleaf, London: Sweet & Maxwell)

Feather J., 'Authors, Publishers and Politicians: The History of Copyright and the Book Trade' (1988) 12 *European Intellectual Property Review* 377

Fennell, Lee Anne, 'Common Interest Tragedies' (2004) 98 *Northwestern University Law Review* 907

Ferris, Graham, and Battersby, Graham, 'Overreaching and the Trusts of Land and Appointment of Trustees Act 1996 – A Reply to Mr Dixon' (2001) *Conveyancer* 221

'The Impact of the Trusts of Land and Appointment of Trustees Act 1996 on Purchasers of Registered Land' (1998) *Conveyancer* 168

'The General Principles of Overreaching and the Reforms of 1925' (2002) 118 *Law Quarterly Review* 270

Filmer, Sir Robert, *Patriarcha and Other Writings* (ed. Johann P. Sommerville, Cambridge: Cambridge University Press, 1991)

Flathman, Richard E., 'Impossibility of an Unqualified Disjustificatory Theory', in J. Roland Pennock and John Chapman (eds.), *Nomos XXII: Property* (New York: New York University Press, 1980), Chapter 3

Fleming, J., *The Law of Torts* (8th edn, London: Sweet & Maxwell, 1992)

Fox, David, 'Bona Fide Purchase and the Currency of Money' (1996) *Cambridge Law Journal* 547

Fuller, Lon, 'Form and Consideration' (1941) 41 *Columbia Law Review* 799

Furey, Nigel, 'Goods Leasing and Insolvency', in N. Palmer and E. McKendrick (eds.), *Interests in Goods* (2nd edn, London: Lloyd's of London Press, 1998), p. 787

Gallie, W. B., 'Essentially Contested Concepts' (1955–6) 56 *Proceedings of the Aristotelian Society* 167

Gardner, Simon, 'New Angles on Unincorporated Associations' (1992) *Conveyancer* 41

Gearty C., 'The Place of Private Nuisance in a Modern Law of Torts' (1989) *Cambridge Law Journal* 214

Golinveaux, J., 'What's in a Domain Name: Is "Cybersquatting" Trademark Dilution?' (1999) 33 *University of San Francisco Law Review* 641

Goode, R. M., 'Is the Law Too Favourable to Secured Creditors?' (1983–4) 8 *Canadian Business Law Journal* 53

   Proprietary Rights and Insolvency in Sales Transactions (2nd edn, London: Sweet & Maxwell and Centre for Commercial Law Studies, 1989)

   Commercial Law (2nd edn, London: Penguin Books, 1995)

Goodman, M., 'Adverse Possession of Land – Morality and Motive' (1970) 33 *Modern Law Review* 281

Gray, J. C., *The Nature and Sources of the Law* (ed. D. Campbell and P. Thomas, Aldershot: Dartmouth, 1996)

Gray, K., 'Property in Thin Air' (1991) *Cambridge Law Journal* 252

   Elements of Land Law (2nd edn, London: Butterworths, 1993)

   'Equitable Property' (1995) 48 *Current Legal Problems* 157

Gray, K., and Gray, S. F., *Elements of Land Law* (3rd edn, London: Butterworths, 2001)

   Elements of Land Law (4th edn, Oxford: Oxford University Press, 2005)

Grey, Thomas C., 'The Disintegration of Property', in J. Roland Pennock and John Chapman (eds.), *Nomos XXII: Property* (New York: New York University Press, 1980), Chapter 3

Grunebaum, James O., *Private Ownership* (London and New York: Routledge and Kegan Paul, 1987)

Hadden, Tom, *Company Law and Capitalism* (2nd edn, London: Weidenfeld & Nicolson, 1977)

Haddock, David, 'First Possession Versus Optimal Timing: Limiting the Dissipation of Economic Value' (1986) 64 *Washington University Law Quarterly* 775

Halstead, P., 'Human Property Rights' (2002) *Conveyancer* 513

Hanbury and Martin, *Modern Equity* (ed. J. E. Martin, 16th edn, London: Sweet & Maxwell, 2001)

Hardin, Garrett, 'The Tragedy of the Commons' (1968) 162 *Science* 1243

Hargreaves, A. D., 'Review of Modern Real Property' (1956) 19 *Modern Law Review* 14

   Introduction to the Principles of Land Law (4th edn, London: Sweet & Maxwell, 1963)

Harpum, Charles, 'Overreaching, Trustees' Powers and the Reform of the 1925 Legislation' (1990) *Cambridge Law Journal* 277

Harris, J. W., 'Ownership of Land in English Law', in N. MacCormick and P. Birks (eds.), *The Legal Mind* (Oxford: Clarendon Press, 1986)

Hayton, D. J., *Commentary and Cases on the Law of Trusts and Equitable Remedies* (11th edn, London: Sweet & Maxwell, 2001)

Hayton, D. J., and Marshall, O. R., *Cases and Commentary on the Law of Trusts* (9th edn, London: Sweet & Maxwell, 1991)

   Cases and Commentary on the Law of Trusts (10th edn, London: Sweet & Maxwell, 1996)

Hegel, G. W. F., *Philosophy of Right (1821)* (trans. with notes by T. M. Knox, Oxford: Oxford University Press, 1945)

Heller, Michael, 'The Tragedy of the Anticommons: Property in the Transition from Marx to Markets' (1998) 111 *Harvard Law Review* 621

Helmholz, R., 'Adverse Possession and Subjective Intent' (1983) 61 *Washington University Law Quarterly* 331

Hill, Jonathan, 'The Role of the Donee's Consent in the Law of Gift' (2001) 117 *Law Quarterly Review* 127

Hohfeld, Wesley Newcomb, 'Fundamental Legal Conceptions as Applied in Judicial Reasoning' (1913) 23 *Yale Law Journal* 16

Holdsworth, Sir William, *A History of English Law* (3rd edn, London: Methuen and Co. Ltd, 1923)

　Book Review (1933) 49 *Law Quarterly Review* 576

Honoré, A. M., 'Ownership', in A. M. Honoré, *Making Laws Bind* (Oxford: Clarendon Press, 1987)

Hudson, Anthony, 'Abandonment', in N. Palmer and E. McKendrick (eds.), *Interests in Goods* (2nd edn, London: Lloyd's of London Press, 1998), Chapter 23

Hume, David, *A Treatise of Human Nature* (ed. with notes by L. A. Selby-Bigge, Oxford: Clarendon Press, 1888)

International Federation of Surveyors, Statement on the Cadastre (International Federation of Surveyors, 1995)

Ireland, Paddy, 'Company Law and the Myth of Shareholder Ownership' (1999) 62 *Modern Law Review* 32

Jackson, T. H., and Kronman, A. T., 'Secured Financing and Priorities Among Creditors' (1979) 88 *Yale Law Journal* 1143

Kohler, Paul, 'The Whittling Away of Way' (1992) *Conveyancer* 354

　'Kentucky Fried Chicken' (1993) 2 *International Journal of Cultural Property* 133–45

Kohler, P., and Palmer, N., 'Information as Property', in N. Palmer and E. McKendrick (eds.), *Interests in Goods* (2nd edn, London: Lloyd's of London Press, 1998)

Kramer, Matthew H., *John Locke and the Origins of Private Property: Philosophical Explorations of Individualism, Community, and Equality* (Cambridge: Cambridge University Press, 1997)

Land Registry, *Annual Report and Accounts 2002–2003*

　Adverse Possession (Practice Guide No. 4, March 2003)

　Defining the Service: E-conveyancing (July 2004)

Law Commission, *Interim Report on Distress for Rent* (Law Commission Report No. 5, 1966)

　Transfer of Land: Appurtenant Rights (Law Commission Consultative Document No. 36, 1971)

　Transfer of Land: Land Registration (Second Paper) (Law Commission Consultative Document No. 37, 1971)

　Transfer of Land: The Law of Positive and Restrictive Covenants (Law Commission Report No. 127, 1984)

　Codification of the Law of Landlord and Tenant: Forfeiture of Tenancies (Law Commission Report No. 142, 1985)

　Distress for Rent (Law Commission Consultative Document No. 97, 1986)

　Deeds and Escrows (Law Commission Report No. 163, 1987)

　Third Report on Land Registration (Law Commission Report No. 158, 1987)

Landlord and Tenant Law: Privity of Contract and Estate (Law Commission Report No. 174, 1988)

Trusts of Land: Overreaching (Law Commission Consultative Document No. 106, 1988)

Transfer of Land: Overreaching: Beneficiaries in Occupation (Law Commission Report No. 188, 1989)

Transfer of Land: Trusts of Land (Law Commission Report No. 181, 1989)

Distress for Rent (Law Commission Report No. 194, 1991)

Transfer of Land: Land Mortgages (Law Commission Report No. 204, 1991)

Transfer of Land: Obsolete Restrictive Covenants (Law Commission Report No. 201, 1991)

Sale of Goods Forming Part of a Bulk (Law Commission Report No. 215, 1993)

Landlord and Tenant Law: Termination of Tenancies Bill (Law Commission Report No. 221, 1994)

Landlord and Tenant Law: Termination of Tenancies by Physical Re-entry: A Consultative Document (Law Commission Consultative Document, January 1998)

The Execution of Deeds and Documents by or on Behalf of Bodies Corporate (Law Commission Report No. 253, 1998)

The Rule Against Perpetuities and Excessive Accumulations (Law Commission Report No. 251, 1998)

Electronic Commerce: Formal Requirements in Commercial Transactions (Law Commission, December 2001)

Limitation of Actions (Law Commission Report No. 270, 2001)

Termination of Tenancies for Tenant Default (Law Commission Consultation Paper No. 174, 2004)

Law Commission and HM Land Registry, *Land Registration for the Twenty-First Century: A Consultative Document* (Law Commission Consultation Paper No. 252, 1998)

Land Registration for the Twenty-First Century: A Conveyancing Revolution (Law Commission Report No. 271, 2001)

Law Reform Committee, *The Acquisition of Easements and Profits by Prescription* (Law Reform Committee Fourteenth Report, Cmnd 3100, 1966)

Eighteenth Report on Conversion and Detinue (Cmnd 4774, 1971)

Law, John, 'Considerations sur le numeraire et le commerce', in E. Daire (ed.), *Economistes financiers du XVIIIe siecle* (Geneva: Slatkin Reprints, 1971)

Lawson, F. H., *The Rational Strength of English Law* (London: Stevens & Sons, 1951)

Remedies of English Law (2nd edn, London: Butterworths, 1980)

Lawson, F. H., and Rudden, B., *The Law of Property* (2nd edn, Oxford: Clarendon Press, 1982)

The Law of Property (3rd edn, Oxford: Clarendon Press, 2002)

Libecap, G. D., 'Contracting for Property Rights', in T. L. Anderson and F. S. McChesney (eds.), *Property Rights: Co-operation, Conflict, and Law* (Princeton: Princeton University Press, 2003), p. 150

Libling, David, 'The Concept of Property: Property in Intangibles' (1978) 94 *Law Quarterly Review* 103

Locke, John, 'On Property', in John Locke, *Second Treatise of Government* (1690)

Lokan, Andrew, 'From Recognition to Reconciliation: The Functions of Aboriginal Rights Law' (1999) 23 *Melbourne University Law Review* 65

Lucy, W. N. R., and Mitchell, C., 'Replacing Private Property: The Place for Stewardship' (1996) *Cambridge Law Journal* 566

Lueck, Dean, 'First Possession as the Basis of Property', in T. L. Anderson and F. S. McChesney (eds.), *Property Rights: Co-operation, Conflict, and Law* (Princeton: Princeton University Press, 2003), Chapter 8

Luther, Peter, 'William v. Hensman and the Uses of History' (1995) 15 *Legal Studies* 219

Macpherson, C. B., 'Capitalism and the Changing Concept of Property', in E. Kamenka and R. S. Neale (eds.), *Feudalism, Capitalism and Beyond* (London: Edward Arnold, 1975)

'Human Rights as Property Rights' (1977) 24 *Dissent* 72

Maitland, F. W., *Selected Essays* (ed. H. D. Hazeltine *et al.*, Cambridge: Cambridge University Press, 1936)

'The Beatitude of Seisin' (1888) 13 *Law Quarterly Review* 24

Manchester, A. H., *A Modern Legal History of England and Wales 1750–1950* (London: Butterworths, 1980)

Marx, Karl, and Engels, Frederick, *The Communist Manifesto* (ed. G. S. Jones, Penguin Classics, 1973)

Mason, J. K., and Laurie, G. T., 'Consent or Property? Dealing with the Body and Its Parts in the Shadow of Bristol and Alder Hey' (2001) 64 *Modern Law Review* 710

Matthews, Paul, 'A Problem in the Construction of Gifts to Unincorporated Associations' (1995) *Conveyancer* 302

McCay, B. J., 'The Making of an Environmental Doctrine', in K. Milton (ed.), *Environmentalism: The View from Anthropology* (London: Routledge, 1995)

McMeel, Gerard, 'The Redundancy of Bailment' (2003) *Lloyd's Maritime and Commercial Law Quarterly* 169

McNeil, K., *Common Law Aboriginal Title* (Oxford: Clarendon Press, 1989)

Megarry, R. M., and Wade, H. W. R., *The Law of Real Property* (5th edn, London: Stevens and Sons, 1984)

Melville, Herman, Moby-Dick (Everyman's Library, 1907)

Merrill, Thomas W., 'Property Rules, Liability Rules, and Adverse Possession' (1984–5) 79 *Northwestern University Law Review* 1122

'Time, Property Rights and the Common Law: Introduction' (1986) 64 *Washington University Law Quarterly* 661

(ed.), 'Symposium: Time, Property Rights, and the Common Law: Round Table Discussion' (1986) 64 *Washington University Law Quarterly* 793

Michelman, Frank, 'Ethics, Economics and the Law of Property', in J. Roland Pennock and J. Chapman (eds.), *Nomos XXIV: Ethics, Economics and the Law* (New York: New York University Press, 1982)

Mill, John Stuart, *Principles of Political Economy*, Book II (London: Penguin Classics, 1985)

Moffat, G., *Trusts Law: Texts and Materials* (3rd edn, London: Butterworths, 1999)

Mokal, Rizwaan Jameel, 'The Search for Someone to Save: A Defensive Case for the Priority of Secured Lending' (2002) 22 *Oxford Journal of Legal Studies* 687

'The Floating Charge – A Eulogy', in R. J. Mokal, *Corporate Insolvency Law – Theory and Application* (Oxford: Oxford University Press, 2005), Chapter 6

Mortensen, D. T., 'Property Rights and Efficiency in Mating, Racing and Related Games' (1982) 72 *American Economic Review* 968

Munzer, Stephen E., *A Theory of Property* (Cambridge: Cambridge University Press, 1990)

Neave, M. A., Rossiter, C. J., and Stone, M. A., *Sackville and Neave Property Law: Cases and Materials* (6th edn, Sydney: Butterworths, 1999)

Nolan, R. C., 'Property in a Fund' (2004) 120 *Law Quarterly Review* 108

Nozick, Robert, *Anarchy, State, and Utopia* (Oxford: Basil Blackwell, 1974)

Palmer, N. E., *Bailment* (2nd edn, London: Sweet & Maxwell, 1991)

Penner, J. E., 'The "Bundle of Rights" Picture of Property' (1996) 43 *UCLA Law Review* 711

Perillo, Joseph, 'The Statute of Frauds in the Light of the Functions and Dysfunctions of Form' (1974) 43 *Fordham Law Review* 39

Pigou, A. C., *The Economics of Welfare* (London: Macmillan, 1952)

Pollock, F., and Maitland, F. W., *The History of English Law* (2nd edn, Cambridge: Cambridge University Press, 1898)

Pollock, F., and Wright, R. S., *Possession in the Common Law* (Oxford: Clarendon Press, 1888)

Posner, Richard A., *Economic Analysis of Law* (6th edn, New York: Aspen Publishers, 2002)

Radin, Margaret Jane, 'Property and Personhood' (1982) 34 *Stanford Law Review* 957
    'Time, Possession, and Alienation' (1986) 64 *Washington University Law Quarterly* 739
    Reinterpreting Property (Chicago: University of Chicago Press, 1993)

Reich, Charles, 'The New Property' (1964) 73 *Yale Law Journal* 733
    'Individual Rights and Social Welfare: The Emerging Legal Issues' (1965) 74 *Yale Law Journal* 1245
    'Beyond the New Property: An Ecological View of Due Process' (1990–1) 56 *Brooklyn Law Review* 731

Rideout, Roger, 'The Limited Liability of Unincorporated Associations' (1996) 49 *Current Legal Problems* 187

Robbins, Lionel, *An Essay on the Nature and Significance of Economic Science* (London: Macmillan, 1935)

Rogers, W. V. H., *Winfield and Jolowicz on Tort* (16th edn, London: Sweet & Maxwell, 2002)

Rook, D., 'Property Law and the Human Rights Act 1998: A Review of the First Year' (2002) *Conveyancer* 316

Roper, R. B., *et al.*, *Ruoff and Roper on the Law and Practice of Registered with notes by Conveyancing* (2nd looseleaf edn, London: Sweet & Maxwell, 2003)

Rose, Carol M., 'Possession as the Origin of Property' (1985) 52 *University of Chicago Law Review* 73

Rousseau, Jean-Jacques, *A Discourse on the Origins of Inequality* (ed. R. D. Masters and C. Kelly, University Press of New England, 1992)

Royal Commission on Common Land, *Report of Royal Commission on Common Land 1955–1958* (Cmnd 462, London: HMSO)

Rudden, Bernard, 'Economic Theory v. Property Law: The "Numerus Clausus" Problem', in J. Eekelaar and J. Bell (eds.), *Oxford Essays in Jurisprudence: Third Series* (Oxford: Oxford University Press, 1987), p. 239

'Things as Thing and Things as Wealth' (1994) 14 *Oxford Journal of Legal Studies* 81

Ruoff, T. B. F., *An Englishman Looks at the Torrens System* (Sydney, Melbourne and Brisbane, 1957)

Ryan, Alan, *Property and Political Theory* (Oxford: Basil Blackwell, 1984)

Sackville, R., 'Property Rights and Social Security' (1978) 2 *University of New South Wales Law Journal* 246

'The Emerging Australian Law of Native Title: Some North American Comparisons' (2000) 74 *Australian Law Journal* 820

Sax, J. L., 'The Public Trust Doctrine in Natural Resources Law: Effective Judicial Intervention' (1969–70) 68 *Michigan Law Review* 471–566

Schwartz, A., 'Security Interests and Bankruptcy Priorities: A Review of Current Theories' (1981) 10 *Journal of Legal Studies* 1

Scott, R. E., 'A Relational Theory of Secured Financing' (1986) 86 *Columbia Law Review* 901

Seipp, D., 'The Concept of Property in the Early Common Law' (1994) 12 *Law and History Review* 29

Simpson, A. W. B., *A History of the Land Law* (2nd edn, Oxford: Clarendon Press, 1986)

Smith, Adam, *The Wealth of Nations* (London: Everyman's Library, 1991)

Sokol, Mary, 'Bentham and Blackstone on Incorporeal Hereditaments' (1994) 15 *Legal History* 287

Sreenivasan, Gopal, *The Limits of Lockean Rights in Property* (Oxford: Oxford University Press, 1995)

Stevenson, Glen G., *Common Property Economics: A General Theory and Land Use Applications* (Cambridge: Cambridge University Press, 1991)

Stillmann, Peter G., 'Property, Freedom and Individuality in Hegel's and Marx's Political Thought', in J. Roland Pennock and John Chapman (eds.), *Nomos XXII: Property* (New York: New York University Press, 1980), Chapter 6

Stone, Christopher, 'Should Trees Have Standing? – Towards Legal Rights for Natural Objects' (1972) 45 *Southern California Law Review* 450

Sugarman, David, and Warrington, Ronnie, 'Telling Stories: Rights and Wrongs of the Equity of Redemption', in J. W. Harris (ed.), *Property Problems: From Genes to Pension Funds* (London: Kluwer, 1997)

Swadling, W., 'The Proprietary Effect of a Hire of Goods', in N. Palmer and E. McKendrick (eds.), *Interests in Goods* (2nd edn, London, Lloyd's of London Press, 1998), p. 491

Tawney, R. H., 'Property and Creative Work', in R. H. Tawney, *The Acquisitive Society* (New York: Harcourt, Brace and Howe, 1920)

Tehan, Maureen, 'A Hope Disillusioned, an Opportunity Lost? Reflections on Common Law Native Title and Ten Years of the Native Title Act' (2003) 27 *Melbourne University Law Review* 523

Tettenborn, A., 'Covenants, Privity of Contract and the Purchaser of Personal Property' (1982) *Cambridge Law Journal* 82

Tully, James, *A Discourse on Property: John Locke and His Adversaries* (Cambridge: Cambridge University Press, 1980)

An Approach to Political Philosophy: Locke in Contexts (Cambridge: Cambridge University Press, 1993)

Turner, Richard W., *The Equity of Redemption* (Cambridge: Cambridge University Press, 1931)

Umbeck, J., 'A Theory of Contract Choice and the California Gold Rush' (1977) 20 *Journal of Law and Economics* 421

Waldron, Jeremy, *The Right to Private Property* (Oxford: Clarendon Press, 1988)

Weir, Tony, *A Casebook on Tort* (10th edn, London: Sweet & Maxwell, 2004)

Weiss, E. B., 'The Planetary Trust: Conservation and Intergenerational Equity' (1983–4) 11 *Ecology Law Quarterly* 495–581

Whalan, D. J., 'Title by Possession and the Land Transfer Act' (1963) 48 *New Zealand Law Journal* 524

Whelan, F. G., 'Property as Artifice: Hume and Blackstone', in J. Roland Pennock and John Chapman (eds.), *Nomos XXII: Property* (New York: New York University Press, 1980), Chapter 5

White, J. J., 'Efficiency Justifications for Personal Property Security' (1984) 37 *Vanderbilt Law Review* 473

Whiteman, J., 'Nuisance – The Environmental Tort?' (1998) 61 *Modern Law Review* 870

Wu, Tang Hang, 'The Right of Lateral Support of Buildings from the Adjoining Land' (2002) *Conveyancer* 237

Zerbe, 'Time, Property Rights, and the Common Law' (1986) 64 *Washington University Law Quarterly* 793

Index

18266139R10449

Printed in Great Britain
by Amazon